# PSYCHOLOGICAL DIMENSIONS OF ORGANIZATIONAL BEHAVIOR

# PSYCHOLOGICAL DIMENSIONS OF ORGANIZATIONAL BEHAVIOR

**Edited by**

## Barry M. Staw

University of California, Berkeley

Macmillan Publishing Company
**New York**

Collier Macmillan Canada
**Toronto**

Maxwell Macmillan International
**New York   Oxford   Singapore   Sydney**

Editor: C. E. Stewart, Jr.
Production Supervisor: Publication Services, Inc.
Production Manager: Aliza Greenblatt
Text Designer: Publication Services, Inc.
Cover Designer: Ken Fredette, Fredette/Sparango
Cover photograph: Marjory Dressler
Illustrations: Publication Services, Inc.

This book was set in Bembo Medium by Publication Services, Inc., and printed and bound by Book Press. The cover was printed by Lehigh Press.

Macmillan Publishing Company
866 Third Avenue, New York, New York 10022

Collier Macmillan Canada, Inc.
Suite 200, 1200 Eglinton Avenue, E.
Don Mills, Ontario, M3C, 3N1

Library of Congress Cataloging-in-Publication Data

Psychological dimensions of organizational behavior / edited by Barry M. Staw.
     p.    cm.
  ISBN 0-02-416150-0
  1. Organizational behavior.   2. Industrial psychology.   I. Staw, Barry M.
  HD58.7.P758 1991                                                    90-41493
  158.7–dc20                                                          CIP

Printing:   2 3 4 5 6 7 8      Year: 1 2 3 4 5 6 7 8 9

# PREFACE

Welcome to the fascinating world of organizational behavior. Here you will learn about the nature of people and how their behavior is influenced by others in organizations. You will study some basics of individual motivation, perception, and decision making, and see how these human tendencies are forged into organizational actions. You will read about how people are influenced by and in turn exert influence on their organizational environments. Finally, you will study what it takes to assume a leadership position and what leads to organizational innovation, along with some guidelines for designing a satisfying and effective organization.

This book is organized into seven major dimensions. In each, one or more "foundation" readings are presented in which basic knowledge from the behavioral sciences is reviewed. Then "applications" are presented from the literature of organizational behavior. The readings cover most of the major topics of the organizational behavior field and reflect the current state of our knowledge. Some chapters are research summaries; some are think pieces. All have been selected by the combined criteria of writing style and content. Thus, if a piece appears a bit dry, bear with it; it should contain enough content to be worth the effort. If a piece is especially interesting, enjoy the experience. When you finish this anthology you should not only understand more about how people think and behave, but have some new ideas about how such behavior can be pulled together to form a productive and healthy organization.

# CONTENTS

# INDIVIDUAL PERFORMANCE

Motivation is the first stop on your tour of human behavior. Here you will learn about some typical individual needs, desires, and valued outcomes—in other words, the things people strive to achieve and avoid in carrying out their behavior. In this section you will also read about the circumstances in which people try to rationalize their behavior; that is, when people strive so hard to appear competent that they end up doing silly or even stupid things. Finally, you will read an interview with B. F. Skinner in which behavior modification techniques are discussed. Behavior modification, in its purest form, makes little or no use of human needs in predicting behavior. Yet it has proved itself a powerful technology in changing behavior in a diversity of social settings.

After considering these foundations of human motivation, the anthology turns to applications of motivation theory in organizations. Expectancy theory, a derivative of both need and cognitive theories of behavior, will be covered first. Then goal setting, a widely validated approach to increas-ing performance, is outlined. The problem of misapplying rewards in an effort to change behavior is then considered so that one can more thoughtfully use reinforcement and expectancy theories in the organizational context. Finally, the motivating features of the job itself are examined, showing how job redesign can improve performance.

Keep one caveat in mind while reading about theories of human motivation. Don't become oversold on any particular approach to the exclusion of the others. People are complex and often motivated by a mulitplicity of forces. Even widely divergent theories often have more in common than they let on in their most argumentative forms. Therefore, think of each theory as a limited piece of the puzzle of human behavior and each technique as a possibly useful, though limited tool in changing behavior. The behavioral sciences can help us understand and predict behavior, much like the familiar weather forecast, yet they do not lead to absolutely precise predictions or guaranteed results.

# Foundations of Work Motivation

## 1.   DRIVES, NEEDS, AND OUTCOMES

Edward E. Lawler III

For centuries, psychologists and philosophers have tried to explain why some objects or outcomes seem to be desired by people while others are not. The concepts of instinct, drive, intrinsic motives, functional autonomy, derived motives, and many others have been used to explain this phenomenon. This chapter will review many of these concepts and present an integrated view of present knowledge about why certain outcomes are desirable or attractive to people.

An adequate explanation of why certain outcomes are desirable must deal with three separate but interrelated questions.

1. What is it about the nature of individuals that causes outcomes to become desirable to them?
2. What general classes or groups of outcomes do people find desirable or undesirable?
3. What factors influence the desirability of outcomes: that is, how does the desirability of outcomes change over time and why do individuals differ in the importance they attach to various outcomes?

Unless the second and third questions are answered, it is impossible to predict the kind of behavior choices a person will make. Although the answer to the first question is not needed in order to predict behavior, most theorists have found that answering it is a prerequisite to answering questions two and three. That is, these theorists have found it necessary to make assumptions about what causes outcomes to be important in the first place in order to make statements about the kinds of outcomes people value and the things that are likely to influence the attractiveness of outcomes.

Our first question has typically been answered by a set of assumptions about man's internal state. For example, some theorists have assumed that man has homeostatic drives, others have talked of instincts, while still others have talked of learned drives. The second question has been answered by the development of a number of need or outcome classification systems. Some of these systems assume only two classes of needs while others assume more than 20. The third question has been answered in many different ways. Maslow (1943), for example, has theorized that needs are arrayed in a hierarchy such that the lower-level needs have to be satisfied before the higher-level needs come into play. Other psychologists have stressed that learned associations can cause change in the attractiveness of outcomes.

Not every theory that has dealt with the attractiveness of outcomes has attempted to answer all of these questions. In fact, some theories have dealt essentially with only one of the questions. For example, in his discussion of the competence motive, White (1959) is concerned with establishing the existence of that motive. He does not present a general classification of motives, nor does he make statements about what influences the importance of other motives. As we discuss the various theories dealing with the attractiveness of outcomes, it is important to note which of the three questions are answered and which are ignored.

Let us now turn to a consideration of some of the more prominent theories.

## HISTORICAL APPROACHES

Prior to the 1940s three theoretical approaches to explaining why outcomes are valued dominated the thinking in psychology. The first two, instinct theory and hedonism, do not make scientifically testable predictions of what outcomes people will seek. The third, drive theory, represents an attempt to develop a theory that does make testable predictions.

### Instinct Theory

Charles Darwin was the first to call the attention of the scientific world to the possibility that much of human and animal behavior may be determined by instincts. He thought that many "intelligent" actions were inherited, and he provided a number of examples from his research on animals to support this view. William James, Sigmund Freud, and William McDougall developed the instinct doctrine as an important concept in their

psychological theories. Some theorists thought of instincts as mechanical and automatic rather than as conscious motivators of behavior, but McDougall, who developed the most exhaustive taxonomy of instincts, thought of them as purposive, inherited, goal-seeking tendencies.

McDougall (1908) wrote that "we may then define an instinct as an inherited or innate psycho-physical disposition that determines the possessor to perceive and pay attention to objects of a certain class, to experience an emotional excitement of a particular quality on perceiving such an object, and to act in regard to it in a particular manner, or at least to experience an impulse to such action" (p. 39). Thus, the "pugnacity instinct" was an instinct that manifested itself in fighting when the organism was exposed to appropriate stimuli. At first McDougall thought he could account for all behavior in terms of about a dozen instincts. However, as time progressed he added more and more instincts to his list so that by 1932 his list included 19 instincts. Other psychologists added more, so that by the 1920s the list of instincts totaled nearly 6,000, including the "instinct to avoid eating apples in one's own orchard" (Murray, 1964, p. 6).

In a sense, instinct theory died of its own weight. As more and more instincts were stated, psychologists began to question the explanatory usefulness of the approach. To say that an animal fights because of the instinct of pugnacity or that an individual takes a job because he has an instinct to work is merely to give a redundant description of the observed behavior that adds nothing to our understanding of why the behavior took place. The tendency of some psychologists to add a new instinct to explain each new behavior that was observed also weakened the theory. As instinct theory developed, it seemed to provide unsatisfactory answers to all of our questions. It said that heredity determined which goals or outcomes organisms would seek (which was incomplete and misleading) and that people's goals consisted of the objects they sought (a circular definition). Thus, instinct theory did not allow for the prediction of which outcomes would be sought; it allowed only for the *post hoc* explanation of why certain goals were sought. Instinct theory also failed to provide a useful classification of the type of outcomes people sought. The original list of instincts was too short and the later ones were so long that they proved useless.

## Hedonism

The origins of most contemporary conceptions of motivation can be traced to the principle of hedonism (Atkinson, 1964). In turn, hedonism can be traced to the original writings of the English utilitarians. The central assumption is that behavior is directed toward outcomes that provide pleasure and away from those that produce pain. In every situation people strive to obtain those goals or outcomes that provide the most pleasure. Despite its simplicity and popularity, the principle of hedonism fails to answer any of our three questions adequately. Nothing is said about why certain things give pleasure while others don't. There is no specification of the types of outcomes that are pleasurable or painful or even how these outcomes can be determined in advance for a particular individual. Any kind of behavior can be explained after the fact by postulating that particular outcomes were sources of either pain or pleasure. Finally, nothing is said about how the attractiveness of outcomes may be modified by experience or environmental circumstances. In short, the hedonistic assumption has no real empirical content leading to predictions of behavior and, thus, it is untestable.

Despite the fact that hedonism can be described as circular and lacking in content, its influence on psychology has been extensive. As one psychologist stated, "the study of motivation by psychologists has largely been directed toward filling in the missing empirical content in hedonism" (Vroom, 1964, p. 10). It is certainly true that almost all modern theories assume that people direct their behavior toward outcomes that they find pleasurable and away from those that they find unattractive. However, most modern theories do attempt to overcome the circularity of hedonism. They specify in advance how attractive specific outcomes will be to particular individuals

and they develop models that predict when the attractiveness of outcomes will change.

## Drive Theory

Drive theory developed partially as a reaction to instinct theory and hedonism. It is in the tradition of hedonism, but it is more closely tied to empirical events and therefore more testable. In 1918, R. S. Woodworth published a little book entitled *Dynamic Psychology* in which he advanced the view that psychologists should study what induces people to behave in particular ways. He referred to this inducement as drive, and the concept of drive soon replaced the concept of instinct in the psychologist's glossary of important terms. Later, the term "drive" took on a very precise meaning in the writings of C. L. Hull (1943). He assumed that all behavior is motivated by either primary or secondary drives. According to Hull, the primary drives were biologically based; they represented states of homeostatic imbalance. Hull's position was that:

*The major primary needs or drives are so ubiquitous that they require little more than to be mentioned. They include the need for foods of various sorts (hunger), the need for water (thirst), the need for air, the need to avoid tissue injury (pain), the need to maintain an optimal temperature, the need to defecate, the need to micturate, the need for rest (after protracted exertion), the need for sleep (after protracted wakefulness), and the need for activity (after protracted inaction). The drives concerned with the maintenance of the species are those which lead to sexual intercourse and the need represented by nest building and care of the young [pp. 59–60].*

In Hull's theory, outcomes become rewards when they are able to reduce primary drives and thereby reduce homeostatic imbalance and the tension that occurs when organisms are in a state of ecological deprivation. Thus, food is a reward to a hungry person and water is a reward to a thirsty person. Hull also stressed that drive strength can be increased by deprivation and reduced as needs become satisfied. Thus, the hungrier a person gets, the more he desires food; but as he eats food, he becomes less hungry and his desire diminishes. Although Hull assumed that all rewards and drives are ultimately based on the reduction of primary drives, he recognized that certain secondary drives and rewards could develop—or be "learned"—if in the past they were associated with food or other primary rewards. Thus, money is a secondary reward because it is often associated with food and other primary rewards. Social approval becomes a reward for children who are praised for eating well, or dressing themselves, and so on. According to Hull's view, most of the rewards used by work organizations would be considered secondary rewards.

Hull's theory represents a significant advance over the previous theories of motivation. It gives a clear-cut answer to the question of what objects or outcomes have value—that is, objects or outcomes that either reduce primary, biologically based drives or have been related to outcomes that do. It also provides a classification of drives that is still commonly used (it divides them into primary and secondary drives, and it specifies what the primary drives are). Finally, it says that deprivation increases drive strength, whereas obtaining the desired outcomes reduces drive strength. Thus, Hull's theory has answers to all three of our questions. But the real significance of Hull's theory rests in the fact that it is empirically testable. Since it specifies in detail the relationship between such measurable things as deprivation, drive, and learning, the theory can be tested, and it has spawned a large number of research studies.

At this point it is safe to say that these studies have found Hull's theory to be inadequate in a number of important respects. The most important shortcomings have to do with the ability of the theory to explain motivation that is not based on primary drives. Hull's basic point about organism's possessing certain primary drives that become stronger with deprivation and weaker with satisfaction still seems valid. What does not seem valid is his argument that all secondary motives are learned on the basis of primary physiological or homeostatic drives.

There is no solid evidence that drives can be learned on the basis of their association with pos-

itive drives such as hunger and thirst (Cravens and Renner, 1970). There is evidence that organisms will work for rewards that have been associated with the reduction of a primary drive if the primary drive is present. However, when the primary drive is not present, there seems to be no "acquired" drive to obtain the reward. For example, in the classic experiments of Wolfe (1936) and Cowles (1937), chimpanzees learned to associate tokens with the acquisition of food. Initially, the chimps learned to operate an apparatus that required lifting a weight to obtain grapes. They continued to operate it when the only visible reward was a token that had been associated with the grapes. However, they didn't seem to develop an acquired need for tokens, since they were willing to work to obtain the tokens only as long as they were hungry and the tokens led to something they desired—that is, food. Hence, it is difficult to see how Hull's explanation can help us understand why workers continue to work for more money even when their basic needs are satisfied.

More damaging to Hull's view than the evidence on the failure of animals to acquire learned drives is the great amount of evidence indicating that people and animals are attracted to many outcomes that do not seem to be directly related to primary needs. Rats will learn mazes in order to explore novel environments, monkeys will solve puzzles even though they receive no extrinsic rewards, and people will work simply in order to develop their skills and abilities and to increase their competence. These and many other phenomena cannot be explained easily by drive theory.

## CONTEMPORARY APPROACHES

Recently, many psychologists have rejected the emphasis of drive theory on primary drives and have argued that people have many needs. This argument has come particularly from those psychologists who are interested in studying human behavior. As we shall see, they have proposed a number of needs that do not seem to be directly related to homeostatic imbalance, organism survival, or species survival. This recent work on motivation has produced two somewhat different approaches.

Researchers in one group have focused on establishing the existence of one or two human motives that they consider to be particularly important. Thus, McClelland has focused on the achievement motive and White has focused on the competence motive. They have not tried to develop complex need, or motive, classification systems. In other words, they have not tried to answer our second question. They have contented themselves with trying to understand why one set or type of outcomes is attractive to people. Other researchers have tried to develop need, or motive, classification systems in an attempt to predict which kinds of outcomes will be attractive to people. Murray's (1938) list of needs and Maslow's (1943) statement of a need hierarchy are examples of this approach. But before we consider these classification systems, we need to look at some of the needs that have been proposed as necessary additions to the primary drives observed by Hull.

## The Affiliation Motive

A number of researchers have presented evidence to show that an affiliation motive exists. They have shown that social interaction is attractive to people and that it is particularly likely to occur under certain conditions. For example, Schachter (1959) has shown that people seek the companionship of others when they are anxious and confused about their motives. In Schachter's work, college students faced with the prospect of being shocked were given the opportunity to be with another person. The subjects under such anxiety were more likely to accept invitations to be with others than were subjects who were not under such anxiety. This result occurred even when the subjects were not permitted to talk to the person they were to be with. Other research suggests that people are likely to seek social interaction at times when they are doubting their self-esteem.

Harlow (1958) has presented some interesting evidence suggesting that the social motive may be innate. As part of his work with monkeys he raised some infant monkeys, providing them with two surrogate mothers in place of their natural mothers. One surrogate mother consisted of a cylinder of wire mesh with an opening in the center of the "breast" for a bottle. The other was similarly shaped but was covered with cotton terry cloth. In the experiment, baby monkeys were placed in cages containing the two "mothers." Half were fed from the cloth mother, the other half from the wire mother. According to drive theory, the monkeys who were fed by the wire mother should have become attached to the wire mother because it provided the drive reduction—that is, the milk. However, it did not work out that way. The monkeys who were fed on the wire mother spent most of their time clinging to the cloth mother. Thus, it appears that monkeys develop their attachment to their mothers based on contact comfort rather than on primary-drive reduction.

However, the important point for us about the research on the need for social contact is not whether this need is innate or acquired but that it exists in most adult human beings. It clearly is an important motivation—one that has a significant impact on behavior in organizations. Many organizations have discovered—to their sorrow—that jobs that do not provide opportunities for social contact have higher turnover and absenteeism rates because employees simply cannot stand the isolation. Frequently, unnecessary social isolation results from mechanical and architectural designs that do not consider employees' needs for social relationships.

## Need for Equity

People want to be treated fairly. They observe what happens to other people and if they receive either "too much" or "too little" in comparison to other people it makes them uncomfortable. For example, one study showed that dissatisfaction with promotion was highest in Army units where promotion rates were high. Why? Because the individuals who weren't promoted in these units felt unfairly treated. Adams (1963, 1965) has developed a theory that makes a number of interesting predictions about the effects of wage inequity on work output, work quality, and attitudes toward work. Although this theory is a general theory of social inequity, it has been tested largely with respect to the effects of wage inequity, and it has some interesting things to say about how equity may affect the attractiveness of rewards. Its predictions seem to be particularly relevant to understanding the effects of offering various sizes of pay increases and the effects of paying different wage rates.

Adams (1965) defines inequity as follows:

*Inequity exists for Person when he perceives that the ratio of his outcomes to inputs and the ratio of Other's outcomes to Other's inputs are unequal. This may happen either (a) when he and Other are in a direct exchange relationship or (b) when both are in an exchange relationship with a third party, and Person compares himself to Other [p. 280].*

Outcomes in the job situation include pay, fringe benefits, status, the intrinsic interest of the job, and so on. Inputs include how hard the person works, his education level, his general qualifications for the job, and so on. It must be remembered that what determines the equity of a particular input-outcome balance is the individual's perception of what he is giving and receiving; this cognition may or may not correspond to an observer's perception or to reality.

Equity theory states that the presence of inequity will motivate an individual to reduce inequity and that the strength of the motivation to reduce inequity varies directly with the perceived magnitude of the imbalance experienced between inputs and outcomes. Feelings of inequity can be produced in a variety of ways and in a variety of situations. Adams has studied inequity produced by overpayment. His research suggests that overpayment is less attractive to employees than equitable payment is. There is no evidence, for example, that when a person is paid on a piece rate and feels overpaid, he will reduce his productivity in order to reduce the amount of pay he

receives. The important thing for this discussion about the research on equity theory is that people tend to seek equity in their work activities, which can affect their job behavior.

## Activity and Exploration

Too little stimulation is very uncomfortable for humans. In one study, college students were employed at $20 a day to stay in a low stimulation environment (Bexton, Heron, & Scott, 1954). They were asked to remain for as many days as they could, lying on a cot in a lighted, partially sound-deadened room. They wore translucent goggles, gloves, and cardboard cuffs that minimized tactile stimulation. An air conditioner provided a noise that blocked out other sounds, and the students rested their heads on a U-shaped pillow. After a certain period—usually filled with sleeping—the subjects found this situation impossible to tolerate and asked to leave the experiment. Rarely did a subject endure it for as long as 2 days despite the fact that the pay was relatively high. Other studies have reported similar results, stressing that under these conditions people seem to develop a hunger for stimulation and action leading to such responses as touching the fingers together and twitching the muscles.

Research by Scott (1969) has shown that the results are very similar when people are given repetitive tasks to perform. They develop a negative attitude toward the task, and, as time goes on, they take more breaks and try in many ways to vary their behavior. As we shall see, this finding has direct implications for the design of jobs in organizations.

Other studies have shown that both people and animals seek out opportunities to experience novel situations. Butler (1953) has shown that monkeys will learn to push open a window for no reward other than being able to see what is going on in a room, and they will keep doing it. Butler has also shown that the strength of the drive for novel stimulation can be increased by deprivation. An experiment by Smock and Holt (1962) has shown that if children are given a chance to control what they see on a television screen, they will look at objects that offer complex stimuli rather than unconflicting, simple stimuli.

Many studies of rats have shown that they will learn certain behaviors in order to experience novel stimuli. In one experiment, rats preferred a goal box that contained objects to an empty goal box. Miles (1958) found that kittens would learn things when the reward was simply the opportunity to explore a room. There is much evidence that humans and animals will try to solve puzzles simply because of the stimulation provided by working on them. Harlow (1953) has shown that monkeys will persist in solving puzzles for many days. One monkey, who was presented with a square peg and a round hole, persisted for months in trying to get the two to fit together. (The monkey finally died of perforated ulcers.)

Several theorists have suggested that the results of both the stimulus-deprivation studies and the studies of novel-stimulus environments can be explained by considering how novelty affects stimulus attractiveness (Berlyne, 1967). According to activation theory, people become used to a certain level and pattern of stimulation from the environment. For some people this adaptation level may be a relatively low level of stimulation; for others it may be a rather high level. Regardless of where a person's level of adaptation is, however, psychologists hypothesize that deviation from it will have a strong impact on the person. Slight deviations will be experienced as pleasurable and rewarding while large deviations will be experienced as noxious and dissatisfying. Figure 1.1 illustrates this point graphically. According to this approach, the subjects in the stimulus-

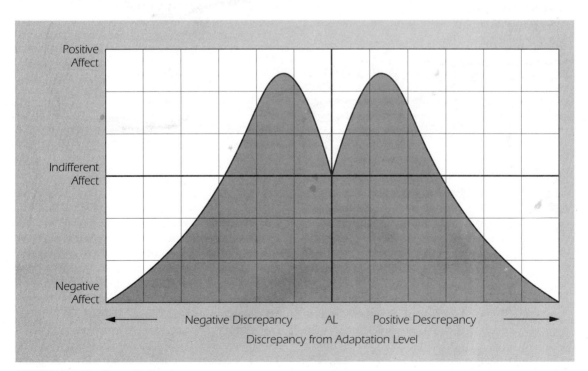

**FIGURE 1.1 The Butterfly Curve.**

From R. N. Haber, "Discrepancy from Adaptation Level as a Source of Affect." *Journal of Experimental Psychology,* 1958, 56, 370–75. Copyright 1958 by the American Psychological Association. Reproduced by permission.

deprivation experiment were uncomfortable because the situation fell too far below the adaptation level. The animals who wanted to explore new things were attracted to them because these new things represented stimulus situations that were somewhat above their adaptation levels. Presumably if the stimulus situations had been too far above their adaptation levels, the animals would have avoided them, and indeed there is evidence that both animals and people fear situations that are very unfamiliar to them.

One of the problems with activation theory is that it can be very difficult to measure in advance what a person's adaptation level is. Still, the theory and its related research provide some interesting evidence to support the point that not all drives or needs are either primary or learned on the basis of primary drives. It is hard to see how people's reactions to different levels of stimulation can be explained by reference to a drive that has been learned on the basis of a primary drive.

## Achievement

The achievement motive has been extensively studied by D. C. McClelland. It is defined by McClelland (1951, 1961) as a desire to perform in terms of a standard of excellence or as a desire to be successful in competitive situations. McClelland stresses that achievement motivation is present in most people but that the amount people have depends on a number of things, including how they were treated during childhood. One study has shown that high-need-achievement people tend to come from families where high demands were made for independence and performance at an early age. Their mothers evaluated their accomplishments favorably and rewarded them liberally.

McClelland measures the strength of people's achievement motive by scoring their responses to a series of pictures. The pictures are shown to individuals who are asked to write a five-minute story about what is going on in the picture. The stories are scored on the basis of how frequently achievement-oriented themes are mentioned (for example, "He will try his best to succeed"). The following is an example of a story showing a young boy in the foreground and a hazy representation of an operation in the background.

*A boy is dreaming of being a doctor. He can see himself in the future. He is hoping that he can make the grade. It is more or less a fantasy. The boy has seen many pictures of doctors in books, and it has inspired him.* He will try his best *and hopes to become the best doctor in the country. He can see himself as a very important doctor. He is performing a very dangerous operation. He can see himself victorious and is proud of it. He gets world renown for it. He will become the best doctor in the U.S. He will be an honest man, too. His name will go down in medical history as one of the* greatest men [Atkinson, 1958. p. 193].

McClelland's research has shown that under certain conditions achievement motivation can be an important motivator of good performance in work organizations. When achievement motivation is operating, good job performance becomes very attractive to people; as a result, the motivation to perform well is higher. Achievement motivation typically does not operate when people are performing routine or boring tasks where no competition is involved. However, when challenge and competition are involved, achievement motivation can stimulate good performance. A study by French (1955) clearly illustrates this point. In French's study, Officer Candidate School cadets performed a simple task under three different sets of instructions. Under the "relaxed" instructions the subjects were told that the experimenter was merely interested in determining what kinds of scores people make on the test. The "task-motivated" instructions said that the task was a measure of people's ability to deal rapidly with new materials. The "extrinsically motivated" instructions said that the best performers could leave while the others had to continue performing. Performance was highest under the "task-motivated" instructions and lowest under the "relaxed" instructions. Subjects with high need for achievement performed better on the "task-motivated" instructions but not under the two other kinds of instructions.

Other studies also support the view that people can be motivated simply by a drive to achieve. For example, Alper (1946) gave two groups of subjects a list of nonsense syllables to learn. Only one group was told it was an intelligence test. A test given 24 hours later showed that the "intelligence test" group remembered more of what they had learned. McClelland (1961) showed that successful people in competitive occupations tend to be universally high in achievement motivation. For example, he showed that successful managers from countries such as the United States, Italy, and India tend to be high in achievement motivation.

Overall, the research on achievement motivation suggests that such motivation is most likely to be present when moderately challenging tasks have to be performed (where about a 50–50 chance of success exists), in competitive situations, in situations where performance is perceived to depend upon some important or valued skill, and in situations where performance feedback is given. The research also suggests that people with a high need for achievement tend to seek out situations in which they can achieve, and they tend to find successful performance attractive once they are in these situations. These points have important implications for the design of jobs in organizations and for the kinds of people that are attracted to jobs in different types of work situations.

Judging from the research cited earlier on the effects of child rearing on the strength of need for achievement, it seems certain that achievement motivation is a partly learned drive. McClelland in fact argues that it is differentially present in certain cultures precisely because child-rearing practices differ. However, even though achievement motivation is a learned drive, it is hard to see how it could develop because of the primary drives. There may be some relationship here, since success often helps people to obtain primary rewards, such as food; but it is hard to see how the primary drive approach can explain the fact that early independence training leads to a strong need for achievement. Thus, even though achievement is a learned drive, it seems that it is only partially learned on the basis of primary drives.

## Competence

Robert W. White (1959) has argued for the existence of a competence motive. He uses competence to refer to an organism's capacity to interact effectively with its environment. In organisms capable of little learning, competence is considered to be innate; however, competence in man—that is, his fitness to interact with the environment—is slowly attained through prolonged feats of learning. The human learning that is needed to gain competence is characterized by high persistence and a strong goal orientation. Because of this dedication to learning, White argues that it is necessary to treat competence as having a motivation aspect that is separate from motivation derived from primary drives or instincts. He presents considerable evidence of organisms trying to cope with their environment seemingly for no other reason than that they want to master it. As White notes, there are repeated references in psychological literature

*...to the familiar series of learned skills which starts with sucking, grasping, and visual exploration and continues with crawling and walking, acts of focal attention and perception, memory, language and thinking, anticipation, the exploring of novel places and objects, effecting stimulus changes in the environment, manipulating and exploiting the surroundings, and achieving higher levels of motor and mental coordination.... Collectively they are sometimes referred to as mechanisms ... but on the whole we are not accustomed to cast a single name over the diverse feats whereby we learn to deal with the environment.... I now propose that we gather the various kinds of behavior just mentioned, all of which had to do with effective interaction with the environment, under the general heading of competence ... it is necessary to make competence a motivational concept; there is a competence motivation [1959, pp. 317–318].*

White argues that competence motivation is aroused when people are faced with somewhat new situations and wanes when a situation has been explored and mastered to the point at which it no longer presents a challenge.

There is an obvious similarity between White's view of when competence motivation is aroused and the activation theorists' view of how stimulus novelty affects motivation. Both argue for high motivation when somewhat novel situations are encountered. White's theory is also very closely related to the theory of achievement motivation, since both talk of man's need to perform adequately. In fact, White says that achievement may be one outcome of competence motivation. White's theory has some interesting implications for the design of jobs in organizations. It suggests that if presented with the right task people can be motivated to perform effectively without the use of extrinsic rewards such as pay and promotion. However, once the task is mastered, competence motivation will disappear. It is also interesting to note that White, like other recent theorists, argues that the competence motive is not based on any primary drive. Although he does not say exactly where it comes from, he does imply that man's desire to be competent is innate.

## Self-Actualization

In the last thirty years a number of psychologists have introduced concepts into their theories that have to do with people's need to grow and develop. Table 1.1 lists some of these theorists and their concepts. The work of Maslow has had by far the greatest impact on the thinking concerned with motivation in organizations. Maslow uses the term "self-actualization" to describe the need people have to grow and develop. According to him, it is the "desire for self-fulfillment, namely...the tendency [for a person] to become actualized in what he is potentially...the desire to become more and more of what one is, to become everything that one is capable of becoming ..." (1954, pp. 91–92). Maslow stresses that not all people function on the self-actualization level. He then goes on to describe the characteristics of people who are motivated by self-actualization. According to him, much of the self-actualizing person's behavior is motivated solely by the sheer enjoyment he obtains from using and developing his capacities. He does not necessarily behave in accordance with extrinsic goals or rewards. For him, the goal is simply to behave in a certain way or experience a certain feeling. Maslow makes the point like this:

*...we must construct a profoundly different psychology of motivation for self-actualizing people, e.g., expression motivation or growth motivation, rather than deficiency motivation. Perhaps it will be useful to make a distinction between living and preparing to live. Perhaps the concept of motivation should apply only to non-self-actualizers. Our subjects no longer strive in the ordinary sense, but rather develop. They attempt to*

**TABLE 1.1**
**List of Theorists Classified as Emphasizing Self-actualization, and the Term Each Uses**

Kurt Goldstein (1939): Self-actualization
Erich Fromm (1941): The productive orientation
Prescott Lecky (1945): The unified personality; self-consistency
Donald Snygg and Arthur Combs (1949): The preservation and enhancement of the phenomenal self
Karen Horney (1950): The real self and its realization
David Riesman (1950): The autonomous person
Carl Rogers (1951): Actualization, maintenance, and enhancement of the experiencing organism
Rollo May (1953): Existential being
Abraham Maslow (1954): Self-actualization
Gordon W. Allport (1955): Creative becoming

Adapted from Cofer, C. N., and Appley, M. H., *Motivation: Theory and Research.* Copyright ©1964 by John Wiley & Sons, Inc. Reprinted by permission.

*grow to perfection and to develop more and more fully in their own style. The motivation of ordinary men is a striving for the basic need gratifications that they lack. But self-actualizing people in fact lack none of these gratifications; and yet they have impulses. They work, they try, and they are ambitious, even though in an unusual sense. For them motivation is just character growth, character expression, maturation, and development; in a word self-actualization [p. 211].*\*

Thus, like White and others, Maslow is careful to say that all motivation is not tied to the primary drives. Maslow also stresses that people will work to obtain outcomes that are intrinsic, such as feelings of growth. He completely rejects the view that valued outcomes have to be related to such extrinsic rewards as food and water. Maslow probably goes further than any of the other theorists we have reviewed in stressing the differences between motivation based on primary drives and motivation that is independent of primary drives. He says that, unlike motivation based on primary drives, motivation based on growth needs does not decrease as the needs become satisfied. Quite to the contrary, Maslow argues that as people experience growth and self-actualization they simply want more. In his view, obtaining growth creates a desire for more growth, whereas obtaining food decreases one's desire for food.

Maslow argues that the concept of self-actualization can explain a significant amount of the motivation in organizations. He states that, particularly at the managerial level, many people are motivated by a desire to self-actualize. There is a considerable amount of evidence to support this point. In one study, managers rated the need for self-actualization as their most important need (Porter, 1964). In addition, most large organizations abound with training and development programs designed to help people develop their skills and abilities. Sometimes people do enter these programs in the hope of obtaining a

raise or promotion, but on other occasions they do it only because it contributes to their self-development. There is also evidence of people seeking more challenging jobs for no other reason than to develop themselves.

An interesting contrast to Maslow's work on self-actualization is provided by the work of existential psychologists such as Allport (1955) and Rogers (1961). They too talk of people being motivated by desires that are not related to obtaining rewards such as money and status. However, they give less emphasis to the development of skills and abilities and the achievement of goals than does Maslow, and they give more emphasis to new experiences as a way of learning about one's self. Rogers, for example, talks of people being motivated "to be that self which one truly is." He emphasizes self-discovery and the importance of being open to experience. Perhaps because they don't emphasize skill development and accomplishments as much as Maslow, the existential psychologists have not had much impact on the research of psychologists interested in work organizations. This is unfortunate, and it is important to remember that at times people may be motivated by nothing more than self-discovery and a desire to experience.

## Need-Classification Theories

Numerous lists and classifications of needs have been presented by psychologists. One of the most important is Henry A. Murray's (1938) list of "psychogenic" or "social" needs. This list, which contains more than 20 motives, was arrived at on the basis of the study of a number of "normal" people. Although Murray's list has been very influential in the field of psychology, it has not been applied very much to the study of motivation in organizations, probably because its length greatly reduces its usefulness. Like the early lists of instincts, it is so long that there is almost a separate

---

\* From *Motivation and Personality* (2nd ed.) by A. H. Maslow. Copyright © 1970 by Harper & Row, Publishers, Inc. Reprinted by permission of the publishers.

need for each behavior people demonstrate. A look at Table 1.2, which lists some of Murray's needs, may help the reader gain an impression of the nature of the problem. The issue is not whether Murray has identified separate kinds of behavior (he has) but whether these behaviors might not be better dealt with by a more parsimonious list of needs.

Maslow's hierarchical classification of needs has been by far the most widely used classification system in the study of motivation in organizations. Maslow differs from Murray in two important ways: first, his list is shorter; second, he argues that needs are arranged in a hierarchy.

Maslow's (1943, 1954, 1970) hierarchical model is composed of a five-level classification of human needs and a set of hypotheses about how the satisfaction of these needs affects their importance.

The five need categories are as follows:

1. *Physiological needs,* including the need for food, water, air, and so on.
2. *Safety needs,* or the need for security, stability, and the absence from pain, threat, or illness.
3. *Belongingness and love needs,* which include a need for affection, belongingness, love, and so on.
4. *Esteem needs,* including both a need for personal feelings of achievement or self-esteem and also a need for recognition or respect from others.
5. *The need for self-actualization,* a feeling of self-fulfillment or the realization of one's potential.

More important than the definition of these five need groups, however, is the *process* by which each class of needs becomes important or active. According to Maslow, the five need categories exist in a hierarchy of prepotency such that the lower or more basic needs are inherently more important (prepotent) than the higher or less basic needs. This means that before any of the higher-level needs will become important, a person's physiological needs must be satisfied. Once the physiological needs have been satisfied, however, their strength or importance decreases, and the next-higher-level need becomes the strongest motivator of behavior. This process of "increased satisfaction/decreased importance/ increased importance of the next higher need" repeats itself until the highest level of the hierarchy is reached. Maslow has proposed in later revisions of his theory (1968, 1970) that at the highest level of the hierarchy a reversal occurs in the satisfaction-importance relationship. He states that for self-actualization, increased satisfaction leads to *increased* need strength. "Gratification breeds increased rather than decreased motivation, heightened rather than lessened excitement" (1968, p. 30).

In short, individual behavior is motivated by an attempt to satisfy the need that is *most important* at that point in time. Further, the strength of any need is determined by its position in the hierarchy and by the degree to which it and all lower needs have been satisfied. Maslow's theory predicts a dynamic, step-by-step, casual process of human motivation in which behavior is governed by continuously changing (though predictable) set of "important" needs. An increase (change) in the satisfaction of the needs in one category *causes* the strength of these needs to decrease, which results in an increase in the importance of the needs at the next-higher level. Maslow does say that the hierarchy of needs is not a rigidly fixed order that is the same for all individuals. Especially in the case of needs in the middle of the hierarchy, the order varies somewhat from person to person. However, this view clearly states that physiological needs are the most prepotent and that self-actualization needs are usually the least.

Two other need-hierarchy theories have been stated. One is by Langer (1937)—predating Maslow's—and another by Alderfer (1969). Alderfer's (1972) theory is the best developed of these two theories. Alderfer argues for three levels of needs: existence, relatedness, and growth. Like Maslow, he argues that the satisfaction of a need influences its importance and the importance of higher-level needs. He agrees with Maslow's hypothesis that the satisfaction of growth needs makes them more important rather than less

**TABLE 1.2**
Murray's List of Needs

| Social Motive | Brief Definition |
|---|---|
| Abasement | To surrender. To comply and accept punishment. To apologize, confess, atone. Self-depreciation. Masochism. |
| Achievement | To overcome obstacles, to exercise power, to strive to do something difficult as well and as quickly as possible. |
| Affiliation | To form friendships and associations. To greet, join, and live with others. To cooperate and converse sociably others. To love. To join groups. |
| Aggression | To assault or injure an other. To murder. To belittle, harm, blame, accuse or maliciously ridicule a person. To punish severly. Sadism. |
| Autonomy | To resist influence or coercion. To defy an authority or seek freedom in a new place. To strive for independence. |
| Blamavoidance | To avoid blame, ostracism or punishment by inhibiting asocial or unconventional impulses. To be well-behaved and obey the law. |
| Counteraction | Proudly to refuse admission of defeat by restriving and retaliating. To select the hardest tasks. To defend one's honor in action. |
| Defendance | To defend oneself against blame or belittlement. To justify one's actions. To offer extenuations, explanations and excuses. To resist "probing." |
| Deference | To admire and willingly follow a superior allied other. To cooperate with a leader. To serve gladly. |
| Dominance | To influence or control others. To persuade, prohibit, dictate. To lead and direct. To restrain. To organize the behavior of a group. |
| Exhibition | To attract attention to one's person. To excite, amuse, stir, shock, thrill others. Self-dramatization. |
| Harmavoidance | To avoid pain, physical injury, illness and death. To escape from a dangerous situation. To take precautionary measures. |
| Infavoidance | To avoid failure, shame, humiliation, ridicule. To refrain from attempting to do something that is beyond one's powers. To conceal a disfigurement. |
| Nurturance | To nourish, aid or protect a helpless other. To express sympathy. To "mother" a child. |
| Order | To arrange, organize, put away objects. To be tidy and clean. To be scrupulously precise. |
| Play | To relax, amuse oneself, seek diversion and entertainment. To "have fun," to play games. To laugh, joke and be merry. To avoid serious tension. |
| Rejection | To snub, ignore or exclude an other. To remain aloof and indifferent. To be discriminating. |
| Sentience | To seek and enjoy sensuous impressions. |
| Sex | To form and further an erotic relationship. To have sexual intercourse. |
| Succorance | To seek aid, protection or sympathy. To cry for help. To plead for mercy. To adhere to an affectionate, nurturant parent. To be dependent. |
| Understanding | To analyze experience, to abstract, to discriminate among concepts, to define relations, to synthesize ideas. |

From H. A. Murray, *Explorations in Personality*, New York: Oxford, 1938.

important to people; however, he also hypothesizes that the lack of satisfaction of higher-order
needs can lead to lower-order needs becoming
more important to people. He then argues that
the importance of any need is influenced by the
satisfaction/frustration of the needs above and below it in the hierarchy. He also assumes that all
needs can be simultaneously active; thus, prepotency does not play as major a role in his theory
as it does in Maslow's.

From the point of view of the three questions
we asked at the beginning of the chapter, the hierarchical theories of Maslow and Alderfer provide
rather complete answers to the last two questions.
These theories make specific statements about
what outcomes people will value (outcomes that
satisfy whatever need or needs are active). They
also make specific predictions about what will influence the attractiveness of various outcomes—
for example, satisfaction of relevant needs including those lower on the hierarchy. They provide
less complete answers to our first question, since
they are not clear on why needs originate. They
do, however, imply that the lower-order needs are
innate and that the higher-order needs are present
in most people and will appear if not blocked
from appearing.

The hierarchical concept has received a great
deal of attention among those interested in organizations. This interest is undoubtedly because
the concept, if valid, provides a powerful tool for
predicting how the importance of various outcomes will change in response to certain actions
by organizations. It also can provide some important clues concerning what is likely to be important to employees. It suggests, for example,
that as people get promoted in organizations and
their lower-level needs become satisfied, they will
become concerned with self-actualization and
growth. It also suggests that if a person's job security is threatened, he will abandon all else in order
to protect it. Finally, it suggests that an organization can give an employee enough of the lower-
level rewards, such as security, but that it cannot
give him enough growth and development. Thus,
as employees receive more valued outcomes from
organizations, they will *want* more; although the

nature of what they want may change from things
that satisfy their lower-order needs to things that
satisfy their higher-order needs. As more than
one manager has noted, "we have given our employees good working conditions, high pay, and
a secure future. Now they want more interesting
jobs and a chance to make more decisions. Won't
they ever be satisfied?" Need hierarchy suggests
that they won't!

## AN APPROACH TO OUTCOME ATTRACTIVENESS

The approaches of Maslow, McClelland, and others are useful in thinking about motivation in organizations. They clearly indicate a number of
important points that need to be included in any
approach that tries to deal with the issue of why
certain outcomes are attractive to people. However, there are still many questions. The rest of
this chapter will be concerned with answering
these questions and with developing an approach
to explaining outcome attractiveness.

### Drives, Needs, Motives, or Just Outcomes?

All of the theorists discussed so far have assumed
that outcomes are attractive to a person because
of some drive, motive, or need the person has. On
the other hand, Vroom (1964) has taken a different approach. He does not use the terms drive,
need or motive in his theory. He simply says that
outcomes have value if they lead to other valued outcomes. Nothing is said about what causes
people to value those other outcomes nor about
what other outcomes are likely to be valued. Although it does solve the problem of trying to understand why individual outcomes are attractive,
a theory that deals with the problem as Vroom's
does sacrifices predictive power, in contrast to a
theory of needs that states in advance what outcomes are likely to be valued and what affects
their value.

A theory of needs can make some predictions—
such as when outcomes will be important and
what will be the effects of certain events—that

Vroom's theory cannot make. For example, if it is known that pay is important to an individual because it leads to prestige, Vroom's theory can only predict that, as prestige outcomes become less important, so will pay. On the other hand, a need theory such as Maslow's can make further predictions. It can predict what conditions will affect the importance of prestige outcomes—that is, satisfaction of esteem needs or lower-level needs—and can then predict what the effect of a number of factors, such as a promotion, will be on the importance of pay.

The issue of whether needs are innate or learned is an important one; but since we are dealing with adults whose need structures are already developed, it is not crucial for us. This issue is important for us only in the sense that it might provide information about how common it is for people to have a need. Innate needs should be present in a greater proportion of the society than learned needs. Of course, at this point no one seriously argues that any needs other than the basic ones are either purely learned or purely innate. Still, it does seem that the needs that are lower on Maslow's hierarchy are more innate and, therefore, more universally present than are those that are at the top of the hierarchy.

For our purposes a theory of needs does not have to specify why people have needs, since it can say something about the needs people have and the conditions under which certain needs operate without doing this. All it has to say is that certain outcomes can be grouped together because when one is sought the others are sought and when one is obtained the others are no longer sought. People often have several groups of such outcomes. The groups can be called "needs," and, if the same ones are sought by most people, then it is reasonable to speak of a "human need" for the group of outcomes. Perhaps it should be added that before a group of outcomes is called a need the outcomes should be sought as ends in themselves rather than as instruments for obtaining other outcomes. For example, food outcomes are sought as an end in themselves, and thus we speak of a *need* for food; a big office is not an end in itself, and thus cannot be called a need. Once

it is decided that people have needs, the question is "how many needs?".

## How Many Needs?

Interestingly, theorists defining different categories of human needs usually don't disagree over which specific outcomes are likely to be goals for people, but they do disagree on what kinds of needs lead to outcomes taking on goal characteristics. Psychologists have argued that people have from three to several hundred needs. Part of the reason for this variance rests in the way needs are defined. Originally, the criterion was simple; needs or drives were only said to exist when it could be established that a physiological basis could be found for the attractiveness of the outcomes sought by a person.

The recent research on higher-level needs has clearly shown this approach to be too restrictive. A suggested alternative is to use the term "need" to refer to clusters of outcomes that people seek as ends in themselves. This definition, however, does not solve the problem of how to determine what constitutes a valid cluster. Different foods provide a simple example of the problem. Various food objects can be grouped together in the sense that when a person wants one he often wants the others and when he gets enough of one he may lose interest in the others. Thus, we can say that people have a need for meat rather than saying that people have a need for roast beef or steak. By thinking in terms of outcome clusters such as the one just described, we move to a more general level and begin to group outcomes more parsimoniously. The question that arises now, however, is where to stop. That is, at what level of abstraction or generality should we stop grouping outcomes. Should we, for example, stop at the level of meat or put all food outcomes together and speak of a need for food, since food objects are somewhat similar in attractiveness as shown in Figure 1.2. The former is a tighter cluster in the sense that the attractiveness of different kinds of meat is probably more closely related than is the attractiveness of meat to the attractiveness of fruit. However, there are

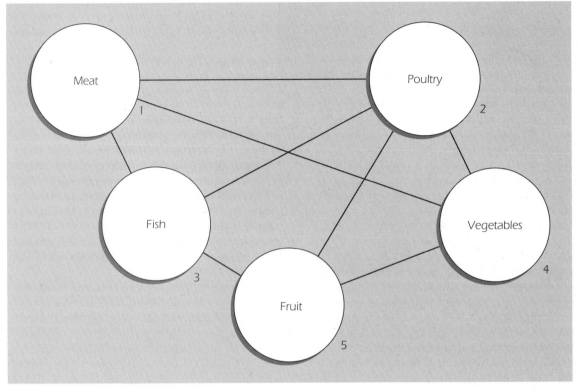

**FIGURE 1.2** An Outcome Cluster.

still tighter clusters (different kinds of steak), and thus there is no final answer to the question of how tight a cluster should be.

It is also possible to go to a higher level of abstraction and combine food outcomes with water and oxygen and call this combination an existence need (see Figure 1.3). This existence need includes all the outcomes that people need to sustain life. The criterion for grouping at this level is different from the criterion stated earlier (when one outcome is sought the other will be sought, and when one is obtained the attractiveness of the other is affected). The grouping in Figure 1.3 is based on the fact that all the outcomes have a common property: they are necessary for existence. Unlike the cluster shown in Figure 1.2, the attractiveness of one is not necessarily related to the other. Using this system, we would say that people desire food objects because of a

basic need to exist; whereas, if we operated at a lower level, we would say people desire food objects because of a need for nourishment. A somewhat similar grouping problem occurs with achievement, self-actualization, and competence. Although it is possible to say that these concepts each represent separate needs, they also overlap in many respects. They all focus on the attractiveness to people of dealing effectively with challenging problems. Thus, they can be grouped and labeled as "a need for competence and growth" or they can be treated separately.

Ultimately, the best approach to categorizing needs is that which allows the greatest prediction of behavior in organizations. Unfortunately, at the moment there is not enough research evidence to allow us to state conclusively which listing of needs leads to the greatest predictability. Because of this lack of evidence, the best

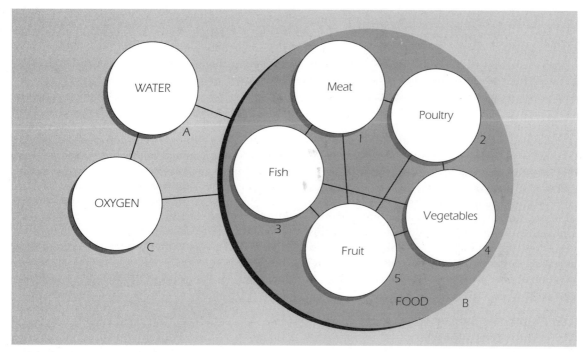

**FIGURE 1.3** An Existence-Need Cluster.

approach would seem to be grouping only those outcomes that have a strong empirical relationship to each other. By this condition we mean those outcomes that can be observed to have common degrees of attractiveness to people. Using this criterion and thinking in terms of organizations, the following needs can be identified:

1. A number of existence needs—primarily sex, hunger, thirst, and oxygen.
2. A security need.
3. A social need.
4. A need for esteem and reputation.
5. An autonomy or freedom need.
6. A need for competence and self-actualization.

## Is There a Need Hierarchy?

Now that we have identified a specific set of human needs, we must consider whether these needs should be arranged in a hierarchy. What does the evidence show about the existence of a need hierarchy?

There is strong evidence to support the view that unless existence needs are satisfied, none of the higher-order needs will come into play. There is also evidence that unless security needs are satisfied, people will not be concerned with higher-order needs. One report shows that subjects kept in a state of hunger think of little else than food (Keys, Brozek, Henschel, Mickelsen, & Taylor, 1950). Similar data is available in the literature on brainwashing and concentration camps (Lawler & Suttle, 1972).

There is, however, very little evidence to support the view that a hierarchy exists above the security level. Thus, it probably is not safe to assume more than a two-step hierarchy with existence and security needs at the lowest level and all the higher-order needs at the next level. This line of thinking leads to the prediction that unless these lower-order needs are satisfied, the others will not come into play. However, which higher-order needs come into play after the lower ones are satisfied and in what order they will come into play cannot be predicted. If anything, it seems that most people are simultaneously motivated by several of the same-level needs. On the other hand, people do not seem to be simultaneously motivated by needs from the two different levels. One person might, for example, be motivated by social and autonomy needs, while another might be motivated by hunger and thirst. Once a need appears, it does seem to persist until it is satisfied or the satisfaction of the lower-order needs is threatened. The one exception to this rule is the need for self-actualization and competence. Unlike the other needs, evidence shows that this need does not appear to be satiable and, thus, is not likely to cease to be important unless the satisfaction of one of the lower-level needs is threatened.

## Can Outcomes Satisfy More Than One Need?

There is a considerable amount of research evidence indicating that some outcomes are relevant to the satisfaction of more than one need. That is, when these outcomes are obtained they affect the attractiveness of more than one cluster of outcomes. A classic example is pay (Lawler, 1971). Pay appears to have the ability to satisfy not only existence needs but also security and esteem needs. For example, Lawler and Porter (1963) report that the more a manager is paid, the higher is his security- and esteem-need satisfaction. This statement means that when a person is trying to satisfy either security or esteem needs, pay will be important. It is not difficult to see why pay has the ability to satisfy a number of needs. Pay can be used to buy articles, such as food, that satisfy existence needs, and high pay also earns a certain amount of esteem and respect in our society.

## How Important Are Different Needs?

Literally hundreds of studies have tried to measure the importance of different needs and out-

comes to employees. Some idea of the importance of different needs can be obtained by looking at the data collected by Porter (1964), which appears in Figure 1.4. These data show that for over 1,900 managers sampled the higher-order needs are clearly the most important. Other data from the study show that the managers are most satisfied with the lower-order needs. Thus, it follows that these lower-order needs should be the least important. Whether this same concern with higher-order need satisfaction exists at the lower levels in organizations is not clear. The data presented in Figure 1.4 show that higher-order needs do seem to be somewhat less important to lower-level managers than to higher-level managers. Other data suggest that pay and certain lower-level needs are rated as more important by workers than by managers (Porter & Lawler, 1965). Dubin (1956), for example, argues that the work place is not a central part of the life of most industrial workers and that it is unwise to expect the workers to be concerned with fulfilling their higher-order needs within the context of their jobs.

Figure 1.5 shows the average ratings of the importance of job factors in a large number of studies (16 studies and 11,000 employees). Most of these studies were done on nonmanagerial employees. It shows job security and intrinsic job interest to be the most important factors to the employees. Lawler (1971) reviewed 43 studies in which pay was rated and found that its average rating was third. This is an interesting finding, but, like other findings that are based on employee ratings of how important various needs and job characteristics are, it must be interpreted very cautiously. These ratings are difficult for people to make and are strongly influenced by how the questions are worded. Thus, it is impossible to reach any strong conclusions about which job factors are the most important. Perhaps the most significant thing to remember from these studies is that employees rate a number of factors as very important. Some of these factors seem to be most strongly related to lower-order needs, while others are related to higher-order needs.

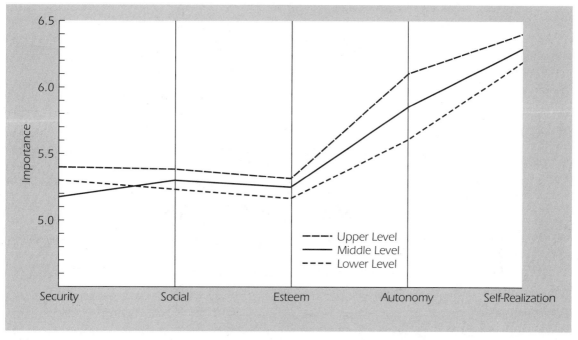

**FIGURE 1.4** Importance Attached to Five Needs by Managers from Three Organization Levels.

## Individual Differences in Need Strength

Large differences clearly exist in the goals and needs people have, and these differences must be considered when viewing individual motivation in organizations. For example, Lawler reports that in about ¼ of the cases he analyzed, pay was rated as first in importance, while in many other cases it was rated sixth or lower in importance. Because of these differences a pay system that will motivate one person is often seen as irrelevant by others. Porter's (1963) data show that managers at different organization levels differ in the degree to which they are motivated by higher-order needs. Other data show that managers are motivated by self-actualization, while others are motivated by autonomy. There is also evidence that some people seem to be fixated on such lower-order needs as security.

Many individual differences in need strength are understandable if we relate them to personal characteristics and situations. Hulin and Blood (1968), for example, point out that urban workers

have different values from those of rural workers. Urban workers seem to be more alienated from work and apparently are less concerned with fulfilling higher-order needs on the job. For an interesting example of the type of individual profile that can be drawn from the research on need strength, consider the profile of a person to whom money is likely to be very important (Lawler, 1971).

*The employee is a male, young (probably in his twenties); his personality is characterized by low self-assurance and high neuroticism; he comes from a small town or farm background; he belongs to few clubs and social groups, and he owns his own home and probably is a Republican and a Protestant [p. 51].*

In summary then, there are significant individual differences among employees in the importance of different needs and outcomes. These differences are not surprising; in fact, many are predictable from what has been said about how the importance of needs is affected by the

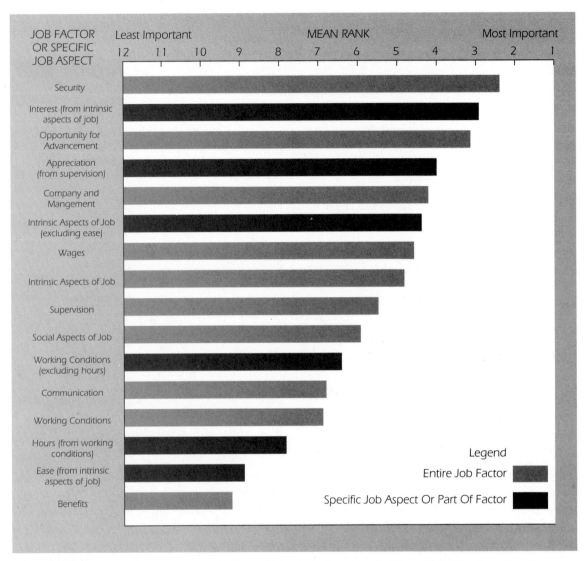

**FIGURE 1.5** Average Importance of Factors in Employee Attitudes (Compiled from 16 Studies, Including Over 11,000 Employees).

From Herzberg et al., *Job Attitudes: Review of Research and Opinion.* Copyright 1957 by the PSP Human Resource Development, Inc. Reprinted by permission.

satisfaction of needs and by certain child-rearing experience. There is also evidence that these individual differences are related in meaningful ways to a number of organizational factors, such as management level, and to personal characteris-

tics, such as age, sex, and education level. This point has some interesting implications for the management of organizations, since it means that it is possible to identify those people for whom a particular reward is likely to be important.

## How Changeable Is the Importance of Needs?

There is evidence to indicate that some things can and do influence the importance of needs. Still, the evidence suggests that organizations have relatively little influence over how important various outcomes will be to their members. The importance of needs is determined partly by hereditary factors and partly by childhood experiences—things over which organizations have no control. Organizations can influence only two of the factors that determine need importance: need satisfaction and need arousal. Satisfaction influences importance, and organizational practices strongly influence satisfaction. Achievement motivation can be aroused by certain tasks and situations, as can competence motivation. Since organizations do have partial control over the situation in which their employees work, they can create conditions that will arouse certain needs. However, these needs must be present in the individual in order to be aroused, and whether the needs are present is a function of many things beyond the control of the organization.

Probably the best opportunity organizations have to influence the needs of their employees is provided by the selection process. Since need importance is relatively fixed and it is possible to identify people who are high on particular needs, organizations can select people who have the kinds of need-strength patterns they want. This would seem to be a much better approach than trying to change people's needs once they join the organization. This point also has some interesting implications for managers who have to motivate employees. It suggests that rather than trying to change the needs of their subordinates, managers should concentrate on placing people in jobs where their need structure is appropriate. The motivation system that is used must fit the needs of the person or it will not work. If pay is not important to an employee, he or she will never be motivated by a pay-incentive system.

## Has There Been an Overall Change in the Relative Importance of Needs?

Many writers (for example, Roszak, 1969) have speculated that the strength of the various needs in the population has been changing over the past 60 years. They argue that only recently has a significant proportion of the population been concerned with needs such as self-actualization and autonomy. (And it is interesting to note that only recently have psychologists been concerned with needs such as self-actualization.) The concept of man as a self-actualizing organism is essentially a development of the 1960s.

Two reasons are generally advanced for the emergence of higher-order needs. First, there is the rising level of education in our society; approximately 40 percent of the high school graduates in the United States go to college. Second, the standard of living has constantly increased so that fewer and fewer people are concerned with satisfying their existence needs and, thus, can focus on satisfying their higher-order needs.

Unfortunately, there is very little evidence to either support or disprove the view that the strength of needs is changing. To test this view adequately we would have to compare need-strength data collected 60 years ago from a random population sample with data collected recently. Unfortunately, such data do not exist. There are, however, some data that can be said to support the view that higher-order needs have become more important. We've already seen that there is evidence to support a two-step hierarchy. If we accept the fact that the standard of living is higher, then, on the basis of a two-step hierarchy, this higher standard of living supports the view that higher-order needs probably are more important. In addition, Porter's (1962) data show that younger managers place greater importance on self-actualization than older managers do. This could, of course, be simply a function of age, but it could also be due to the higher education level of these younger managers and the fact that they never experienced a depression.

There is also some direct evidence that higher-educated people are more concerned with self-actualization. Finally, there is the fact that the idea of self-actualization has gained fairly wide attention in our society. It now seems "in" to talk about self-actualization; and, as we pointed out, the concept of "self-actualization" is now prominent in psychology. Although this evidence is only indirect, it does support the view that concern with self-actualization has increased recently. In summary, although there is little direct data to support the view, it probably is true that, in general, people are somewhat more concerned with satisfying higher-order needs than they used to be.

## SUMMARY AND CONCLUSIONS

The following statements summarize the major points that have been made so far about human needs.

1. Needs can be thought of as groups of outcomes that people seek.

2. Man's needs are arranged in a two-level hierarchy. At the lowest level are existence and security needs; at the other level are social, esteem, autonomy, and self-actualization needs.

3. The higher-level needs will appear only when the lower-level ones are satisfied.

4. All needs except self-actualization are satiable, and as needs become satisfied they decrease in importance.

5. A person can be motivated by more than one need at a given point in time and will continue to be motivated by a need until either it is satisfied or satisfaction of the lower-order needs is threatened.

Thus, we have answered two of the three questions asked at the beginning of the chapter. A classification system for needs has been developed, and statements have been made about what influences the importance of needs. No conclusions have been reached about why people develop needs or about whether needs are innate or learned because these questions don't seem to be answerable at this time.

## REFERENCES

Adams, J. S. Toward an understanding of inequity. *Journal of Abnormal Psychology,* 1963, **67,** 422–436.

Adams, J. S. Injustice in social exchange. In L. Berkowitz (Ed.), *Advances in experimental social psychology.* Vol. 2. New York: Academic Press, 1965.

Alderfer, C. P. An empirical test of a new theory of human needs. *Organizational Behavior and Human Performance.* 1969, **4,** 142–175.

Alderfer, C. P. *Existence, relatedness, and growth: Human needs in organizational settings.* New York: The Free Press, 1972.

Allport, G. W. *Becoming: Basic considerations for a psychology of personality.* New Haven: Yale University Press, 1955.

Alper, T. G. Task-orientation vs. ego-orientation in learning and retention. *American Journal of Psychology.* 1946, **38,** 224–238.

Atkinson, J. W. Towards experimental analysis of human motivation in terms of motives, expectancies, and incentives, In J. W. Atkinson (Ed.), *Motives in fantasy, action, and society.* Princeton, N.J.: Van Nostrand Reinhold, 1958.

Atkinson, J. W. *An introduction to motivation.* Princeton, N. J.: Van Nostrand Reinhold, 1964.

Berlyne, D. E. Arousal and reinforcement. In D. Levine (Ed.), *Nebraska symposium on motivation.* Lincoln: University of Nebraska Press, 1967.

Bexton, W. H., Heron, W., & Scott, T. H. Effects of decreased variation in the sensory environment. *Canadian Journal of Psychology.* 1954, **8,** 70–76.

Butler, R. A. Discrimination learning by rhesus monkeys to visual-exploration motivation. *Journal of Comparative and Physiological Psychology,* 1953, **46,** 95–98.

Cofer, C. N., & Appley, M. H. *Motivation: Theory and research.* New York: John Wiley & Sons, 1964.

Cowles, J. T. Food tokens as incentives for learning by chimpanzees. *Comparative Psychology Monograph,* 1937, **14** (No. 71).

Cravens, R. W., & Renner, K. E. Conditioned appetitive drive states: Empirical evidence and theoretical status. *Psychological Bulletin,* 1970, **73,** 212–220.

Dubin, R. Industrial workers' worlds: A study of the "central life interests" of industrial workers. *Social Problems,* 1956, **3,** 131–142.

French, E. G. Some characteristics of achievement motivation. *Journal of Experimental Psychology,* 1955, **50,** 232–236.

Fromm, E. *Escape from freedom.* New York: Rinehart & Winston, 1941.

Goldstein, K. *The organism.* New York: American Book, 1939.

Haber, R. N. Discrepancy from adaptation level as a source of affect. *Journal of Experimental Psychology,* 1958, **56,** 370–375.

Hall, C. S. & Lindzey, G. *Theories of personality.* New York: John Wiley & Sons, 1957.

Harlow, H. F. Mice, monkeys, men, and motives. *Psychological Review,* 1953, **60,** 23–32.

Harlow, H. F. The nature of love. *American Psychologist,* 1958, **13,** 673–685.

Herzberg, F., Mausner, B., Peterson, R. O., & Capwell, D. F. *Job attitudes: Review of research and opinion.* Pittsburgh: Psychological Service of Pittsburgh, 1957.

Horney, K. *Neurosis and human growth.* New York: W. W. Norton, 1950.

Hulin, C. L., & Blood, M. R. Job enlargement, individual differences, and worker responses. *Psychological Bulletin.* 1968 **69.** 41–55.

Hull, C. L. *Principles of Behavior.* New York: Appleton-Century-Crofts, 1943.

Keys, A., Brozek, J., Henschel, A., Mickelsen, O., & Taylor, H. *The biology of human starvation.* Minneapolis: University of Minnesota Press, 1950. 2 vols.

Langer, W. C. *Psychology and human living.* New York: Appleton-Century-Crofts, 1937.

Lawler, E. E. *Pay and organizational effectiveness: A psychological view.* New York: McGraw-Hill, 1971.

Lawler, E. E., & Porter, L. W. Perceptions regarding management compensation. *Industrial Relations,* 1963, **3,** 41–49.

Lawler, E. E., & Suttle, J. L. A causal correlational test of the need hierarchy concept. *Organizational Behavior and Human Performance,* 1972, **7,** 265–287.

Lecky, P. *Self-consistency: A theory of personality.* New York: Island Press, 1945.

McClelland, D. C. Measuring motivation in phantasy: The achievement motive. In H. Guetzkow (Ed.), *Groups, leadership, and men.* Pittsburgh: Carnegie Press, 1951.

McClelland, D. C. *The achieving society.* Princeton: Van Nostrand Reinhold, 1961.

McDougall, W. *An introduction to social psychology.* London: Methuen & Co., 1908.

Maslow, A. H. A theory of human motivation. *Psychological Review,* 1943, **50,** 370–396.

Maslow, A. H. *Motivation and personality.* New York: Harper & Row, 1954.

Maslow, A. H. *Toward a psychology of being.* (2nd ed.) Princeton, N. J.: Van Nostrand Reinhold, 1968.

Maslow, A. H. *Motivation and personality.* (2nd ed.) New York: Harper & Row, 1970.

May, R. *Man's search for himself.* New York: W. W. Norton, 1953.

Miles, R. C. Learning in kittens with manipulatory, exploratory, and food incentives. *Journal of Comparative and Physiological Psychology,* 1958, **51,** 39–42.

Murray, E. J. *Motivation and emotion.* Englewood Cliffs, N.J.: Prentice-Hall, 1964.

Murray, H. A. *Explorations in personality.* New York: Oxford University Press, 1938.

Porter, L. W. Job attitudes in management: I. Perceived deficiencies in need fulfillment as a function of job level. *Journal of Applied Psychology,* 1962, **46,** 375–384.

Porter, L. W. Job attitudes in management: II. Perceived importance of needs as a function of job level. *Journal of Applied Psychology,* 1963, **47,** 141–148.

Porter, L. W. *Organizational patterns of managerial job attitudes.* New York: American Foundation for Management Research, 1964.

Porter, L. W., & Lawler, E. E. Properties of organization structure in relation to job attitudes and job behavior. *Psychological Bulletin,* 1965, **64,** 23–51.

Riesman, D. *The lonely crowd.* New Haven: Yale University Press, 1950.

Rogers, C. R. *Client-centered therapy: Its current practice, implications and theory.* Boston: Houghton Mifflin, 1951.

Rogers, C. R. *On becoming a person.* Boston: Houghton Mifflin, 1961.

Roszak, Theodore. *The making of a counter culture.* Garden City, N.Y.: Doubleday, 1969.

Schachter, S. *The psychology of affiliation.* Stanford, Calif.: Stanford University Press, 1959.

Scott, W. E. The behavioral consequences of repetitive task design: Research and theory. In L. L. Cummings & W. E. Scott (Eds.), *Readings in organizational behavior and human performance.* Homewood, Ill.: Richard D. Irwin, 1969.

Smock, C. D., & Holt, B. G. Children's reactions to novelty: An experimental study of "curiosity motivation." *Child Development,* 1962, **33,** 631–642.

Snygg, D., & Combs, A. W. *Individual behavior.* New York: Harper & Row, 1949.

Vroom, V. H. *Work and motivation.* New York: John Wiley & Sons, 1964.

White, R. W. Motivation reconsidered: The concept of competence. *Psychological Review,* 1959, **66,** 297–333.

Wolfe, J. B. Effectiveness of token-rewards for chimpanzees. *Comparative Psychology Monograph,* 1936, **12,** 15.

Woodworth, R. S. *Dynamic psychology.* New York: Columbia University Press, 1918.

*Two conflicting beliefs in a single mind don't*
*cohabit comfortably. To defend his ego, man becomes*

## 2. THE RATIONALIZING ANIMAL

Elliot Aronson

Man likes to think of himself as a rational animal. However, it is more true that man is a *rationalizing* animal, that he attempts to appear reasonable to himself and to others. Albert Camus even said that man is a creature who spends his entire life in an attempt to convince himself that he is not absurd.

Some years ago a woman reported that she was receiving messages from outer space. Word came to her from the planet Clarion that her city would be destroyed by a great flood on December 21. Soon a considerable number of believers shared her deep commitment to the prophecy. Some of them quit their jobs and spent their savings freely in anticipation of the end.

On the evening of December 20, the prophet and her followers met to prepare for the event. They believed that flying saucers would pick them up, thereby sparing them from disaster. Midnight arrived, but no flying saucers. December 21 dawned, but no flood.

What happens when prophecy fails? Social psychologists Leon Festinger, Henry Riecken, and Stanley Schacther infiltrated the little band of believers to see how they would react. They predicted that persons who had expected the disaster, but awaited it alone in their homes, would simply lose faith in the prophecy. But those who awaited the outcome in a group, who had thus admitted their belief publicly, would come to believe even more strongly in the prophecy and turn into active proselytizers.

This is exactly what happened. At first the faithful felt despair and shame because all their predictions had been for nought. Then, after waiting nearly five hours for the saucers, the prophet had a new vision. The city had been spared, she said, because of the trust and faith of her devoted group. This revelation was elegant in its simplicity, and the believers accepted it enthusiastically. They now sought the press that they had previously avoided. They turned from believers into zealots.

## LIVING ON THE FAULT

In 1957 Leon Festinger proposed his theory of *cognitive dissonance,* which describes and predicts man's rationalizing behavior. Dissonance occurs whenever a person simultaneously holds two inconsistent cognitions (ideas, beliefs, opinions). For example, the belief that the world will end on a certain day is dissonant with the awareness, when the day breaks, that the world has not ended. Festinger maintained that this state of inconsistency is so uncomfortable that people strive to reduce the conflict in the easiest way possible. They will change one or both cognitions so that they will "fit together" better.

Consider what happens when a smoker is confronted with evidence that smoking causes cancer. He will become motivated to change either his attitudes about smoking or his behavior. And as anyone who has tried to quit knows, the former alternative is easier.

The smoker may decide that the studies are lousy. He may point to friends ("If Sam, Jack and Harry smoke, cigarettes can't be all that dangerous"). He may conclude that filters trap all the cancer-producing materials. Or he may argue that he would rather live a short and happy life with cigarettes than a long and miserable life without them.

The more a person is committed to a course of action, the more resistant he will be to information that threatens that course. Psychologists have reported that the couple who are least likely to believe the dangers of smoking are those who tried to quit—and failed. They have become more committed to smoking. Similarly, a person who builds a $100,000 house astride the San Andreas Fault will be less receptive to arguments about imminent earthquakes than would a person who is renting the house for a few months. The new homeowner is committed; he doesn't want to believe that he did an absurd thing.

When a person reduces his dissonance, he defends his ego, and keeps a positive self-image. But self-justification can reach startling extremes; people will ignore danger in order to avoid dissonance, even when that ignorance can cause their deaths. I mean that literally.

Suppose you are Jewish in a country occupied by Hitler's forces. What should you do? You could try to leave the country; you could try to pass as "Aryan"; you could do nothing and hope for the best. The first two choices are dangerous: if you are caught you will be executed. If you decide to sit tight, you will try to convince yourself that you made the best decision. You may reason that while Jews are indeed being treated unfairly, they are not being killed unless they break the law.

Now suppose that a respected man from your town announces that he has seen Jews being butchered mercilessly, including everyone who had recently been deported from your village. If you believe him, you might have a chance to escape. If you don't believe him, you and your family will be slaughtered.

Dissonance theory would predict that you will not listen to the witness, because to do so would be to admit that your judgment and decisions were wrong. You will dismiss his information as untrue, and decide that he was lying or hallucinating. Indeed, Eli Wiesel reported that this happened to the Jews in Sighet, a small town in Hungary, in 1944. Thus people are not passive receptacles for the deposit of information. The manner in which they view and distort the objective world in order to avoid and reduce dissonance is entirely predictable. But one cannot divide the world into rational people on one side and dissonance reducers on the other. While people vary in their ability to tolerate dissonance, we are all capable of rational or irrational behavior, depending on the circumstances—some of which follow.

## DISSONANCE BECAUSE OF EFFORT

Judson Mills and I found that if people go through a lot of trouble to gain admission to a group, and the group turns out to be dull and dreary, they will experience dissonance. It is a rare person who will accept this situation with an "Oh, pshaw. I worked hard for nothing. Too bad." One way to resolve the dissonance is to decide that the group is worth the effort it took to get admitted.

We told a number of college women that they would have to undergo an initiation to join a group that would discuss the psychology of sex. One third of them had severe initiation: they had to recite a list of obscene words and read some lurid sexual passages from novels in the presence of a male experimenter (in 1959, this really was a "severe" and embarrassing task). One third went through a mild initiation in which they read words that were sexual but not obscene (such as "virgin" and "petting"); and the last third had no initiation at all. Then all of the women listened to an extremely boring taped discussion of the group they had presumably joined. The women in the severe initiation group rated the discussion and its drab participants much more favorably than those in the other groups.

I am not asserting that people enjoy painful experiences, or that they enjoy things that are associated with painful experiences. If you got hit on the head by a brick on the way to a fraternity initiation, you would not like that group any better. But if you volunteered to get hit with a brick *in order to join* the fraternity, you definitely would like the group more than if you had been admitted without fuss.

After a decision—especially a difficult one that involves much time, money, or effort—people almost always experience dissonance. Awareness of defects in the preferred object is dissonance with having chosen it; awareness of positive aspects of the unchosen object is dissonance with having rejected it.

Accordingly, researchers have found that *before* making a decision, people seek as much information as possible about the alternatives. Afterwards, however, they seek reassurance that they did the right thing, and do so by seeking information in support of their choice or by simply changing the information that is already in their heads. In one of the earliest experiments on dissonance theory, Jack Brehm gave a group of women their choice between two appliances, such as a toaster or a blender, that they had previously rated for desirability. When the subjects reevaluated the appliances after choosing one of them, they increased their liking for the one they had chosen and downgraded their evaluation of the rejected appliance. Similarly, Danuta Ehrlich and her associates found that a person about to buy a new car does so carefully, reading all ads and accepting facts openly on advertisements more selectively, and he will tend to avoid ads for Volkswagens, Chevrolets, and so on.

## THE DECISION TO BEHAVE IMMORALLY

Your conscience, let us suppose, tells you that it is wrong to cheat, lie, steal, seduce your neigh-bor's husband or wife, or whatever. Let us suppose further that you are in a situation in which you are sorely tempted to ignore your conscience. If you give in to temptation, the cognition "I am a decent moral person" will be dissonant with the cognition "I have committed an immoral act." If you resist, the cognition "I want to get a good grade (have that money, seduce that person)" is dissonant with the cognition "I could have acted so as to get that grade, but I chose not to."

The easiest way to reduce dissonance in either case is to minimize the negative aspects of the action one has chosen, and to change one's attitude about its immorality. If Mr. C. decides to cheat, he will probably decide that cheating isn't really so bad. It hurts no one; everyone does it; it's part of human nature. If Mr. D. decides not to cheat, he will no doubt come to believe that cheating is a sin, and deserves severe punishment.

The point here is that the initial attitudes of these men is virtually the same. Moreover, their decisions could be a hair's breadth apart. But once the action is taken, their attitudes diverge sharply.

Judson Mills confirmed these speculations in an experiment with sixth-grade children. First he measured their attitudes toward cheating, and then put them in a competitive situation. He arranged the test so that it was impossible to win without cheating, and so it was easy for the children to cheat, thinking they would be unwatched. The next day, he asked the children again how they felt about cheating. Those who had cheated on the test had become more lenient in their attitudes; those who had resisted the temptation adopted harsher attitudes.

These data are provocative. They suggest that the most zealous crusaders are not those who are removed from the problem they oppose. I would hazard to say that the people who are most angry about "the sexual promiscuity of the young" are *not* those who have never dreamed of being promiscuous. On the contrary, they would be persons who had been seriously tempted by illicit sex, who came very close to giving in to their desires, but who finally resisted. People who almost live in glass houses are the ones who are most likely to throw stones.

## INSUFFICIENT JUSTIFICATION

If I offer George $20 to do a boring task, and offer Richard $1 to do the same thing, which one will decide that the assignment was mildly interesting? If I threaten one child with harsh punishment if he does something forbidden, and threaten another child with mild punishment, which one will transgress?

Dissonance theory predicts that when people find themselves doing something and they have neither been rewarded adequately for doing it nor threatened with dire consequences for not doing it, they will find *internal* reasons for their behavior.

Suppose you dislike Woodrow Wilson, and I want you to make a speech in his favor. The most efficient thing I can do is to pay you a lot of money for making the speech, or threaten to kill you if you don't. In either case, you will probably comply with my wish, but you won't change your attitude toward Wilson. If that were my goal, I would have to give you a *minimal* reward or threat. Then, in order not to appear absurd, you would have to seek additional reasons for your speech—this could lead you to find good things about Wilson and hence, to conclude that you really do like Wilson after all. Lying produces great attitude change only when the liar is undercompensated.

Festinger and J. Merrill Carlsmith asked college students to work on boring and repetitive tasks. Then the experimenters persuaded the students to lie about the work, to tell a fellow student that the task would be interesting and enjoyable. They offered half of their subjects $20 for telling the lie, and they offered the others only $1. Later they asked all subjects how much they had really liked the tasks.

The students who earned $20 for their lies rated the work as deadly dull, which it was. They experienced no dissonance: they lied, but they were well paid for that behavior. By contrast, students who got $1 decided that the tasks

were rather enjoyable. The dollar was apparently enough to get them to tell the lie, but not enough to keep them from feeling that lying for so paltry a sum was foolish. To reduce dissonance, they decided that they hadn't lied after all; the task was fun.

Similarly, Carlsmith and I found that mild threats are more effective than harsh threats in changing a child's attitude about a forbidden object, in this case a delightful toy. In the severe-threat condition, children refrained from playing with the toys and had a good reason for refraining—the very severity of the threat provided ample justification for not playing with the toy. In the mild-threat condition, however, the children refrained from playing with the toy but when they asked themselves, "How come I'm not playing with the toy?" they did not have a superabundant justification (because the threat was not terribly severe). Accordingly, they provided additional justification in the form of convincing themselves that the attractive toy was really not very attractive and that they didn't really want to play with it very much in the first place. Jonathan Freedman extended our findings and showed that severe threats do not have a lasting effect on a child's behavior. Mild threats, by contrast, can change behavior for many months.

Perhaps the most extraordinary example of insufficient justification occurred in India, where Jamuna Prasad analyzed the rumors that were circulated after a terrible earthquake in 1950. Prasad found that people in towns that were *not* in immediate danger were spreading rumors of impending doom from floods, cyclones, or unforeseeable calamities. Certainly the rumors could not help people feel more secure; why then perpetrate them? I believe that dissonance helps explain this phenomenon. The people were terribly frightened—after all, the neighboring villages had been destroyed—but they did not have ample excuse for their fear, since the earthquake had missed them. So they invented their own excuse; if a cyclone is on the way, it is reasonable to be afraid. Later, Durganand Sinha studied rumors in a town that had actually been destroyed. The people were scared, but they had good reason to be; they didn't need to seek additional justification for their terror. And their rumors showed no predictions of impending disaster and no serious exaggerations.

## THE DECISION TO BE CRUEL

The need for people to believe that they are kind and decent can lead them to say and do unkind and indecent things. After the National Guard killed four students at Kent State, several rumors quickly spread: the slain girls were pregnant, so their deaths spared their families from shame; the students were filthy and had lice on them. These rumors were totally untrue, but the townspeople were eager to believe them. Why? The local people were conservative, and infuriated at the radical behavior of some of the students. Many had hoped that the students would get their comeuppance. But death is an awfully severe penalty. The severity of this penalty outweighs and is dissonant with the "crimes" of the students. In these circumstances, any information that put the victims in a bad light reduces dissonance by implying, in effect, that it was good that the young people died. One high-school teacher even avowed that anyone with "long hair, dirty clothes, or [who goes] barefooted deserves to be shot."

Keith Davis and Edward Jones demonstrated the need to justify cruelty. They persuaded students to help them with an experiment, in the course of which the volunteers had to tell another student that he was a shallow, untrustworthy, and dull person. Volunteers managed to convince themselves that they didn't like the victim of their cruel analysis. They found him less attractive than they did before they had to criticize him.

Similarly, David Glass persuaded a group of subjects to deliver electric shocks to others. The subjects, again, decided that the victim must deserve the cruelty; they rated him as stupid, mean, etc. Then Glass went a step further. He found that a subject with high self-esteem was most likely to derogate the victim. This led Glass to conclude, ironically, that it is precisely because a person thinks he is nice that he decides that the person he has hurt is a rat. "Since nice guys like me don't go around hurting innocent people," Glass's subjects seemed to say, "you must have deserved it." But individuals who have *low* self-esteem do not feel the need to justify their behavior and derogate their victims; it is *consonant* for such persons to believe they have behaved badly. "Worthless people like me do unkind things."

Ellen Berscheid and her colleagues found another factor that limits the need to derogate one's victim: the victim's capacity to retaliate. If the person doing harm feels that the situation is balanced, that his victim will pay him back in coin, he has no need to justify his behavior. In Berscheid's experiment, which involved electric shocks, college students did not derogate or dislike the persons they shocked if they believed the victims could retaliate. Students who were led to believe that the victims would not be able to retaliate *did* derogate them. Her work suggests that soldiers may have a greater need to disparage civilian victims (because they can't retaliate) than military victims. Lt. William L. Calley, who considered the "gooks" at My Lai to be something less than human, would be a case in point.

## DISSONANCE AND THE SELF-CONCEPT

On the basis of recent experiments, I have reformulated Festinger's original theory in terms of the self concept. That is, dissonance is most powerful when self-esteem is threatened. Thus the important aspect of dissonance is not "I said one thing and I believe another," but "I have misled people—and I am a truthful, nice person." Conversely, the cognitions, "I believe the task is dull," and "I told someone the task was interesting," are not dissonant for a psychopathic liar.

David Mettee and I predicted in a recent experiment that persons who had low opinions of themselves would be more likely to cheat than persons with high self-esteem. We assumed that if an average person gets a temporary blow to his self-esteem (by being jilted, say, or not getting a promotion), he will temporarily feel stupid and worthless, and hence do any number of stupid and worthless things—cheat at cards, bungle an assignment, break a valuable vase.

Mettee and I temporarily changed 45 female students' self-esteem. We gave one third of them positive feedback about a personality test they had taken (we said that they were interesting, mature, deep, etc.); we gave one third negative feedback (we said that they were relatively immature, shallow, etc.); and one third of the students got no information at all. Then all the students went on to participate in what they thought was an unrelated experiment, in which they gambled in a competitive game of cards. We arranged the situation so that the students could cheat and thereby win a considerable sum of money, or not cheat, in which case they were sure to lose.

The results showed that the students who had received blows to their self-esteem cheated far more than those who had gotten positive feedback about themselves. It may well be that low self-esteem is a critical antecedent of criminal or cruel behavior.

The theory of cognitive dissonance has proved useful in generating research; it has uncovered a wide range of data. In formal terms, however, it is a very sloppy theory. Its very simplicity provides both its greatest strength and its most serious weakness. That is, while the theory has generated a great deal of data, it has not been easy to define the limits of the theoretical statements, to determine the specific predictions that can be made. All too often researchers have had to resort to the very unscientific rule of thumb, "If you want to be sure, ask Leon."

## LOGIC AND PSYCHOLOGIC

Part of the problem is that the theory does not deal with *logical* inconsistency, but *psychological* inconsistency. Festinger maintains that two cognitions are inconsistent if the opposite of one follows from the other. Strictly speaking, the information that smoking causes cancer does not make it illogical to smoke. But these cognitions produce dissonance because they do not make sense psychologically, assuming that the smoker does not want cancer.

One cannot always predict dissonance with accuracy. A man may admire Franklin Roosevelt enormously and discover that throughout his marriage FDR carried out a clandestine affair. If he places a high value on fidelity and he believes that great men are not exempt from this value, then he will experience dissonance. Then I can predict that he will either change his attitudes about Roosevelt or soften his attitudes about fidelity. But, he may believe that marital infidelity and political greatness are totally unrelated; if this were the case, he might simply shrug off these data without modifying his opinions either about Roosevelt or about fidelity.

Because of the sloppiness in the theory several commentators have criticized a great many of the findings first uncovered by dissonance theory. These criticisms have served a useful purpose. Often, they have goaded us to perform more precise research, which in turn has led to a clarification of some of the findings which, ironically enough, has eliminated the alternative explanations proposed by the critics themselves.

For example, Alphonse and Natalia Chapanis argued that the "severe initiation" experiment could have completely different causes. It might be that the young women were not embarrassed at having to read sexual words, but rather were aroused, and their arousal in turn led them to rate the dull discussion group as interesting. Or, to the contrary, the women in the severe-initiation condition could have felt much sexual anxiety, followed by relief that the discussion was so banal. They associated relief with the group, and so rated it favorably.

So Harold Gerard and Grover Mathewson replicated our experiment, using electric shocks in the initiation procedure. Our findings were supported—subjects who underwent severe shocks in order to join a discussion group rated that group more favorably than subjects who had undergone mild shocks. Moreover, Gerard and Mathewson went on to show that merely linking an electric shock with the group discussion (as in a simple conditioning experiment) did not produce greater liking for the group. The increase in liking for the group occurred only when subjects volunteered for the shock *in order to* gain membership in the group—just as dissonance theory would predict.

## ROUTES TO CONSONANCE

In the real world there is usually more than one way to squirm out of inconsistency. Laboratory experiments carefully control a person's alternatives, and the conclusions drawn may be misleading if applied to everyday situations. For example, suppose a prestigious university rejects a young Ph.D. for its one available teaching position. If she feels that she is a good scholar, she will experience dissonance. She can then decide that members of that department are narrow-minded and senile, sexist, and wouldn't recognize talent if it sat on their laps. Or she could decide that if they could reject someone as fine and intelligent as she, they must be extraordinarily brilliant. Both techniques will reduce dissonance, but not that they leave this woman with totally opposite opinions about professors at the university.

This is a serious conceptual problem. One solution is to specify the conditions under which a person will take one route to consonance over another. For example if a person struggles to reach a goal and fails, he may decide that the goal wasn't worth it (as Aesop's fox did) or that the effort was justified anyway (the fox got a lot of exercise in jumping for the grapes). My own research suggests that a person will take the first means when he has expended relatively little effort. But when he has put in a great deal of effort, dissonance will take the form of justifying the energy.

This line of work is encouraging. I do not think that it is very fruitful to demand to know what *the* mode of dissonance reduction is; it is more instructive to isolate the various modes that occur, and determine the optimum conditions for each.

## IGNORANCE OF ABSURDITY

No dissonance theorist takes issue with the fact that people frequently work to get rewards. In our experiments, however, small rewards tend to be associated with greater attraction and greater attitude change. Is the reverse ever true?

Jonathan Freedman told college students to work on a dull task after first telling them *(a)* their results would be of no use to him, since his experiment was basically over, or *(b)* their results would be of great value to him. Subjects in the first condition were in a state of dissonance, for they had unknowingly agreed to work on a boring chore that apparently had no purpose. They reduced their dissonance by deciding that the task was enjoyable.

Then Freedman ran the same experiment with one change. He waited until the subjects finished the task to tell them whether their work would be important. In this study he found incentive effects: students told that the task was valuable enjoyed it more than those who were told that their work was useless. In short, dissonance theory does not apply when an individual performs an action in good faith without having any way of knowing it was absurd. When we agree to participate in an experiment we naturally assume that it is for a purpose. If we are informed afterward that it *had* no purpose, how were we to have known? In this instance we like the task better if it had an important purpose. But if we agreed to perform it *knowing* that it had no purpose, we try to convince ourselves that it is an attractive task in order to avoid looking absurd.

## MAN CANNOT LIVE BY CONSONANCE ALONE

Dissonance reduction is only one of several motives, and other powerful drives can counteract it. If human beings had a pervasive, all-encompassing need to reduce all forms of dissonance, we would not grow, mature, or admit to our mistakes. We would sweep mistakes under the rug, or worse, turn the mistakes into virtues; in neither case would we profit from error.

But obviously people do learn from experience. They often do tolerate dissonance because the dissonant information has great utility. A person cannot ignore forever a leaky roof, even if that flaw is inconsistent with having spent a fortune in the house. As utility increases, individuals will come to prefer dissonance-arousing but useful information. But as dissonance increases, or when commitment is high, future utility and information tend to be ignored.

It is clear that people will go to extraordinary lengths to justify their actions. They will lie, cheat, live on the San Andreas Fault, accuse innocent bystanders of being vicious provocateurs, ignore information that might save their lives, and generally engage in all manner of absurd postures. Before we write off such behavior as bizarre, crazy, or evil, we would be wise to examine the situations that set up the need to reduce dissonance. Perhaps our awareness of the mechanism that makes us so often irrational will help turn Camus' observation on absurdity into a philosophic curiosity.

# 3.   CONVERSATION WITH B. F. SKINNER

William F. Dowling

B. F. Skinner is, in the opinion of his professional peers, the most influential psychologist in the country. He is already one of the best known among the general reading public. Certainly he is the most controversial psychologist. Whence the influence? Whence the celebrity? Whence the controversy?

Skinner is a behaviorist, which means that he seeks the explanations to human behavior not in the mind within but outside in those conditions in the environment that collectively determine behavior. His first fame came through the design of the "Skinner box," a controlled environment in which rats, pigeons, and eventually men underwent transformations in established patterns of behavior in response to changes in the environment.

Take one famous experiment with pigeons. Food was the reinforcer that moved the pigeon to behave in a particular way. Giving the food

"Conversation With B. F. Skinner" by William Dowling, Editor. Reprinted by permission of the publisher from *Organizational Dynamics,* Winter, 1973, copyright © 1973. American Management Associations, New York. All rights reserved.

to the pigeon when it made the desired response was the reinforcement. *Operant* is the term Skinner used to define the property upon which the reinforcement depended—in this case, the height to which the bird had to raise its head before it would be fed. The change in the frequency with which the head was lifted to this height Skinner called the process of operant conditioning.

All operants grow stronger through repetition— Rome wasn't built in a day—and some operants are inherently stronger than others because they produce consequences of greater importance in the life of the pigeon—or the life of the individual man. Pigeons and man alike behave not because of the consequences that are to follow their behavior but because of the consequences that have followed similar behavior in the past. In Skinner's terms, this is the law of effect or operant conditioning. Says Skinner, "Operant conditioning shapes behavior as a sculptor shapes a lump of clay. Although at some point the sculptor seems to have produced an entirely novel object, we can always follow the process back to the original undifferentiated lump."

Skinner's early reputation came from repeated demonstrations of the law of operant conditioning with pigeons and other animals. When he moved on to man—and his writings and researches have focused on human behavior for the past 25 years—he became both famous and controversial.

He held that man's behavior was every bit as controlled as the pigeons—the difference lay in the number and complexity of the determinants. Freedom was an illusion; when J. S. Mill asserted that "Liberty consists in doing what one desires," he merely begged the question by failing to look behind the desires themselves and asking what accounted for them. The distinction that makes sense to Skinner is not between freedom and control, but between feeling free and feeling controlled, between acting to avoid something—negative reinforcement—and acting to gain something—positive reinforcement. In the former case, the individual feels coerced and controlled. In the latter, he feels free.

Skinner goes beyond description to prescription. He isn't satisfied with enumerating the various controls that together make up the technology of behavior, but he goes on to specify the ways in which the technology available can be used to create a better world.

In fact, Skinner would argue that enlightened men of good will have a responsibility to employ the controls toward benevolent ends. As Skinner points out, the technology of behavior is ethically neutral; it is available on equal terms to villain and saint. "The industrialist may design a wage system," he maintains, "that maximizes his profits, or works for the good of his employees, or most effectively produces the goods a culture needs, with a minimal consumption of resources and minimal pollution." We also suspect that Skinner still adheres to the view he expressed in *Waldon Two* over twenty years ago: that the techniques are in the wrong hands, the end product of most manipulation being private profit or personal aggrandisement.

In other words, Skinner elevates the manipulation of behavior towards benevolent ends to the level of a civic responsibility, which raises the question whether or not it is fair and accurate to label Skinner a psycho-administrative fascist, to conclude with Stephen Spender that he advocates "fascism without tears."

The answer depends largely on how we define fascism. If we mean an ideology that exalts nation and race, then there is not a trace of it in Skinner. On the other hand, if we mean an ideology that asserts the positive value of economic and social regimentation, then there's a strong strain of fascism in Skinner's thinking.

The more interesting and significant question is, what goals does Skinner think the technology of behavior should be employed to reach? At two levels, the question is comparatively easy to answer. Skinner is for the maximum use of positive reinforcement and the minimal use of negative reinforcement that leaves the individual feeling controlled and coerced. And if we want Skinner's vision of the ideal society, we need only read *Walden Two*. If he's amended or altered his vision, we are unaware of it.

At the specific, pragmatic level it's much more difficult to answer the question. In general, Skinner's answer would be that benevolent ends are those that enhance the survival of the culture and of mankind. However, Skinner concedes that survival is a difficult value because it is hard to predict the conditions a culture must meet.

In reading a recent piece that Skinner wrote for *The New York Times,* the conditions that in his view enhance the survival of today's China are clear—he writes with obvious approval of the young Chinese who wear plain clothing, live in crowded quarters, eat simple diets, observe a rather puritanical sexual code, and work long hours for the greater glory of China—but it's impossible, at least based on what we have read of Skinner, to draw up an equivalent list of specific conditions for our own culture.

Given a sufficient threat to the culture we suspect that Skinner would justify the use of negative reinforcement and aversion therapy. Skinner might even approve of the drastic aversion therapy administered to Alex in the film "A Clockwork Orange" to make him good. Given the menace that the bad Alex presented, society realistically had only two choices: permanent incarceration or a drastic form of aversion therapy. This is only conjecture. We know that in the same *Times* article Skinner took issue with the reported statement of Anthony Burgess, author of the novel on which the film is based, that "What my parable tries to state is that it is preferable to have a world of violence undertaken in full awareness—of violence chosen as an act of will—than a world conditioned to be good or harmless." Dr. Skinner dissents—as would a good many other people, ourselves included.

To what extent does Skinner beg the question of the specific conditions that enhance our culture in 1972—the conditions that the technology of behavior should be employed to advance? The question is a difficult one to answer. As the conversation that follows makes plain, Skinner advocates some quite specific conditions in industry. The bigger social picture is not as clear nor are the mechanisms by which the destined changes will be arrived at.

Skinner consistently denies that the controlling he advocates will be done by a benevolent dictator or an equally benevolent behavioral engineer. When a bearded youth at a symposium at Yale on Skinner's ideas asked him "Who is going to program this whole thing?" Skinner replied that it was not a matter of someone pushing control buttons but of "the gradual improvement of the practices controlling the survival of the culture." At times the improvement in practices almost appears to be self-generated. Skinner asserts that "in certain respects operant reinforcement resembles the natural selection of evolutionary theory. Just as genetic characteristics which arise as mutations are selected or discarded by their consequences, so novel forms of behavior are selected and discarded through reinforcement."

These remarks on Skinner present a very partial and personal view of his ideas undertaken because our relatively brief conversation with Skinner gave us only enough time to probe the application of his ideas to business. For his general views we recommend his books, especially *Walden Two, Science and Human Behavior,* and the most recent, *Beyond Freedom and Dignity,* in which he restated them with unexampled grace, clarity, and passion. Not the least reason for Skinner's celebrity is his command of the written word; like Freud, he is a distinguished stylist as well as a profound and original thinker.

*Dowling.* You draw the analogy between operant condition and its role in cultural evolution and natural selection and its role in genetic evolution.

*Skinner.* Yes, and I think it's important, too, because selection is a very different kind of causality. Darwin's views came very late in the history of intellectual thought, and the way in which human behavior is shaped and maintained by its consequences has taken an even longer time to surface. That's what we've been studying in the laboratory for the past 40 years now, and we've discovered that when you arrange certain kinds of consequences, certain types of behavior are selected.

*Dowling.* You have come under a good deal of criticism on the grounds that operant conditioning destroys autonomous man and minimizes freedom. If I understand you correctly, your answer would be that the freedom that is being defended has been an illusion all along.

*Skinner.* The real distinction is between whether we are really free or whether we feel free. I want people to feel freer than they feel now. When you act to avoid punishment, or to avoid any kind of unpleasantness, you *have* to act and you don't feel free. But if you act in order to produce positive results—what we call positive reinforcements—then you feel free, and I'm all for that. I want to get away from punitive control, the kind of control that is used by governments with police and military forces, or that is exercised over students by teachers who threaten them with punishment if they don't study.

*Dowling.* Do you feel that punitive control is widely used in industry?

*Skinner.* There is more of it than you might think. Many people consider a weekly wage a positive reinforcement. You work and you get paid. But you don't work on Monday morning for something that is going to happen on Friday afternoon, when you get your paycheck. You work on Monday morning because there is a supervisor who can fire you if you don't work. You're actually working to avoid the loss of the standard of living maintained by that paycheck.

On the other hand, if you're on piece-work pay, you are positively reinforced for what you do, and you build up a very high tendency to respond—so much so that labor unions and other people who have the welfare of the worker at heart usually oppose that kind of incentive system. Salesmen are usually on both a salary and a percentage basis, because you can't send a supervisor out with every salesman to make sure that he works. He works for the additional commission, but it doesn't wear him out as a straight piece-work schedule does, because he has the salary to support him. Straight commissions work well but cause trouble. The commission system in brokerage firms, for example, often leads salesmen to exaggerate opportunities and pull other tricks that cause trouble for the firm.

*Dowling.* Witness that student in Philadelphia who opened accounts without any money and without even showing up in person. Let's talk a little more about punishment. I wonder if you could illustrate the various controls available to the manager as forms of punishment and what you feel are the alternatives to punishment.

*Skinner.* When a supervisor points out that a person has done something wrong, he is mildly punishing him. His comment is a threat in the direction of his being discharged or possibly laid off without pay. And when a supervisor thinks his job is to move around a plant and discover things being done wrong and to say "Watch that" or "You got into trouble with that the last time," he establishes an atmosphere that really doesn't benefit anyone. True, the worker may be less likely to do things wrong, but you can get the same effect if the supervisor simply discovers things being done right and says something like "Good, I see you're doing it the way that works the best." Supervision by positive reinforcement changes the whole atmosphere of the workspace and produces better results. A constantly critical posture on the part of the supervisor encourages bad morale, absenteeism, and job-changing. You get the work out, but at an exorbitant price. With positive reinforcement, you get at least the same amount of work, and the worker is more likely to show up every day and less likely to change jobs. In the long run, both the company and the worker are better off.

It does not cost the company anything to use praise rather than blame, but if the company then makes a great deal more money that way, the worker may seem to be getting gypped. However, the welfare of the worker depends on the welfare of the company, and if the company is smart enough to distribute some of the fruits of positive reinforcement in the form of higher wages and better fringe benefits, everybody gains from the supervisor's use of positive reinforcement.

*Dowling.* What about those occasions in which punishment is inevitable? Let's take a hypothetical case: The supervisor catches three of his workers shooting craps behind the machine when they should be working the machine. Under such circumstances, in which the imposition of punishment is really inevitable, is there one best way, one best method of applying it?

*Skinner.* I can't solve a problem like that sitting here in my office. I'd have to go into a given organization and see what's going on. I daresay there are times when you need some kind of punishment—docking pay, giving a verbal reprimand, threatening discharge, that kind of thing—but what you've just said is a clue to the kind of thing that would be better.

Why *are* the workers shooting craps? Look at the so-called contingencies of reinforcement. All gambling systems pay off on what is called a variable-ratio schedule of reinforcement. That's true of lotteries, roulette, poker, craps, one-armed bandits. They all pay off unpredictably, but in the long run on a certain schedule. Everyone would benefit if work could be organized so that it also pays off on that schedule. People would then work, and they would enjoy the excitement that goes with possessing a lottery ticket that may pay off at the end of the week. Management could solve some of its problems by adding a bit of a lottery to its incentive conditions. Suppose that every time a worker finished a job, he got a lottery ticket, and at the end of the week, there was a drawing. More jobs would be done, with greater pleasure.

Look at a room full of people playing bingo. They sit for hours, listening with extraordinary care to numbers being called out and placing counters on numbers with great precision. What would you give, as an industrialist, if your labor force worked that hard and that carefully! The bingo player works hard and carefully because of the schedule of payoff. It's a very poor one, because in the long run all players lose, but it commands an awesome amount of labor from people, with great precision and concentration.

Some industrial systems could be redesigned to have that same effect. And people would enjoy what they were doing as much as they enjoy playing bingo. Everybody would gain.

*Dowling.* Has it ever been tried in industry?

*Skinner.* I don't know, but I suspect it has. It has been tried in education very successfully, although it has not yet been widely adopted. But let's take an example of how you could use a lottery to solve the problem of absenteeism. With today's high wages, missing a day's wages doesn't much matter. But suppose you have something like a door prize every day. When you come to work, you get a ticket, and at the end of the day there's a drawing. Then a man will think twice before staying away. If absenteeism is a real problem, a reasonable prize per day might solve it.

*Dowling.* What's the relationship between the ratio or frequency of the reinforcement and the size of the reinforcement? And what effect do they have on productivity?

*Skinner.* The size of the reinforcement is, of course, important, but the schedule of reinforcement is more so. With a lower organism like a pigeon, we can get a fantastic amount of activity with very small amounts of reinforcement if we put it on an effective schedule. I've seen a pigeon peck a little disk on the wall ten thousand times in return for three seconds' access to pigeon feed, then go back and peck another ten thousand times. It is a long process but it's possible to build behavior up to the point at which more energy is expended than is received in the reinforcement.

*Dowling.* What analogy, if any, is there between the pigeon pecking ten thousand times and the worker in industry?

*Skinner.* I should hope there would be none. But there are many examples of so-called stretched schedules in everyday life. For example, people may be fond of fishing in a particular stream, but slowly they fish it out. The first time they catch the limit, the next time not quite so much, and finally they go back where they catch very little. They may seem foolish to those who have not had the same history.

*Dowling.* In talking about the effectiveness or the lack of effectiveness in the incentive systems, one of the reasons that a great many people have found that incentive systems have not paid off is that the incentive system came up against the informal group organization and against the competing and conflicting reinforcement provided by the group. You have said yourself that the group is an enormously powerful reinforcer, far more effective than any individual. Would you comment on the impact of informal organization and the informal group on the operation and the relative ineffectiveness of many incentive systems?

*Skinner.* One question to ask is whether the group is right about it. If people are working on a piece-rate basis and the group has set a quota, presumably the schedule is having an unwarranted or even a dangerous effect. That's one thing. And if a new person comes in and starts producing beyond the quota, he will be punished by the others. They are protecting their own interests by refusing to let the schedule work them too hard, and they could be right.

But if they are holding production down to a level at which the plant is being used inefficiently, you have to improve the contingencies. The workers will come round if you make it genuinely worth their while and provide a reasonable balance between what they're being paid and what it costs them in effort and fatigue. Piece-rate schedules as such may not do the job, if the group sets a quota and punishes anyone who exceeds it.

*Dowling.* When you say that what needs to be done in the case of a low producing group whose output is below what an objective observer would describe as reasonable is to improve the contingencies, what specifically do you have in mind?

*Skinner.* It is important to remember that an incentive system isn't the only factor to take into account. How pleasant work conditions are, how easy or awkward a job is, how good or bad tools are—many things of that sort make an enormous difference in what a worker will do for what he receives.

One problem of the production-line worker is that he seldom sees any of the ultimate consequences of his work. He puts on left front wheels day in and day out, and he may never see the finished car. There are also industries in which what is being made isn't worth making, and there is no good reinforcement if the worker is not producing something people need.

I can't take a specific problem of that sort and solve it without knowing all kinds of details. Suppose I were an engineer in the bridge-building business and you came to me and said, "I want to put a bridge across a certain river—tell me what to do." I couldn't tell you. I'd have to go and see the river, see what traffic the bridge is going to handle, what the nature of the terrain is, and so on. Just because I knew all about bridge building wouldn't mean that I could tell you what to do until I looked into things. Even if I knew all about incentive systems—which I don't—I couldn't solve a particular problem without looking at the situation.

*Dowling.* Are you familiar with William Whyte's piece in *Psychology Today?* I think he calls it "Persons, Pigeons, and Piece Rates."

*Skinner.* I believe I read it. I think he makes a point that some schedules don't work as anticipated, but that isn't quite true. They work as *I* anticipate, they're just not well applied. We have clearly demonstrated that schedules that work with pigeons work perfectly well with human beings. Other things are involved, however. If I were a pigeon, I could upset an experiment, so that things wouldn't seem to be working very well, but I should do so only if the circumstances induced me to do so. It's a question of knowing all the relevant facts and not simply of trying to solve a problem with one principle as if it existed in a vacuum.

*Dowling.* Whyte talks about the conflicting stimuli that operate frequently in an industrial situation. You've got, for example, a worker on incentives who is also encouraged by the suggestion system to submit ideas for improving work methods. In a sense, the suggestion system is a positive reinforcer—he will get an award if management accepts his improved work method. On the other hand, he knows that there's a chance that the incentive system will be changed because of his suggestion and that he will lose out. In addition, his buddies and peers will get no award, and they will also suffer from the incentive changes. Another example of conflicting stimuli would be the case of a man who knows that the rate is relatively loose and if he puts out he is going to make a very handsome week's pay this week, next week, and maybe the week after. On the other hand, he knows that when the other workers have behaved similarly the industrial engineering department has come in, restudied the job, and tightened the rates. I think we're talking about conflicting stimuli.

*Skinner.* I'm not sure that "conflicting stimuli" will explain it; these people are behaving exactly as would expect under these conditions. You don't expect an elevator operator to recommend an automatic elevator, and I'm not surprised when a man does not submit a suggestion that might cut him out of a job. You can't expect a man to make suggestions that will damage him in the long run, even though you give him a prize. What are described as "conflict situations" do not mean that there is anything wrong with operant conditioning. People are behaving exactly as they ought to in the cases Whyte described.

*Dowling.* In other words, it's an illustration of just how complex the variables frequently are. Speaking of variables, one phenomenon that has always fascinated me is rate busting. In a work group, under incentives, you might have maybe one or two out of thirty people who seem interested only in money; social approval or companionship mean absolutely nothing. How could you describe the rate buster in terms of operant conditioning?

*Skinner.* You put it very well: The rate buster is not controlled by his peers. Their censure or punishment are not important enough to keep him within the quota. The group doesn't control him, and therefore he's controlled by the schedule. The result doesn't violate any principle; it just shows the complexity of things.

*Dowling.* It would seem that there are considerable differences from individual to individual in the power of money to reinforce.

*Skinner.* Not necessarily. The opposing condition may be more powerful. If you offer me a given amount of money to do something dangerous, and I accept, it may mean that danger is not very aversive to me, or that money is very reinforcing. You cannot tell which.

*Dowling.* To get more to the general question of designing a compensation system, some people claim that if you want to improve performance and modify behavior, you should take whatever money is available and distribute almost all of it to the top performers—in other words, give them a really sizable reinforcer and more or less forget the rest.

*Skinner.* These are practical problems that I can't solve from here. But in general it is important that a person's pay should represent some reasonable fraction of what he contributes to the company. I remember a case in which salesmen were making calls in business offices. They could do two things: they could make appointments by phone, in which case they would see people pretty well up in the company but make few calls per day, or they could make door-to-door calls, in which case they would make many more calls but see people much further down. (Actually, they weren't making sales on the spot, just describing the service involved; the sales came through later.) From the point of view of the company, it was important that they saw the top people, because they were the people who actually bought the service, but the salesmen were paid in terms of the number of calls they made. An effective compensation system should reinforce the behavior that is worth the most to the company.

*Dowling.* Job enrichment is one of the great cries now. There is a feeling that youthful workers are less interested in money than their parents were, and more interested in a job where they can control many of the conditions under which they work. How would you relate job enrichment to your own psychology?

*Skinner.* I would not want to try to define "job enrichment." In interpreting what is happening with young people today, we have to take into account some very great changes that have occurred in the last generation. My father worked hard all his life because he was afraid of going to the poorhouse when he grew old. He wouldn't need to worry about that now; he would be on Social Security. People used to be afraid of losing their jobs; but now there is unemployment insurance. In other words, we have greatly reduced the significance of the money earned in a job. Diminish the significance of money, and other reinforcers obviously become important. What reinforcers do I mean? The work pace, schedules, how far you go in getting to work—these things become enormously more important. Forget about piped-in music. Look at the annoyances associated with the job and get rid of as many of them as you can. If, by moving the company into the suburbs, you can have your employees living close in, that's an important consideration.

Another question is whether what you're doing is worthwhile. People are much more alert to the ultimate value of things—for the culture and for the world—whether you're polluting the environment or using resources wastefully. Could you get any satisfaction from working in an industry that was making something that you regarded as worthless, or dangerous, or unnecessarily polluting?

*Dowling.* In the list of substitutes for money as reinforcers that you have just mentioned, you haven't given much recognition to controlling the conditions under which you work—if you want to put tags on it, to democratic or participative management. I gather you don't give them much of a role.

*Skinner.* The democratic principle lies in letting the worker tell you what he likes and doesn't like. He may not be the person to decide how to get rid of what he doesn't like or how to produce what he does like. Industry is a beautiful example of the failure of a control and counter-control to produce effective contingencies. A hundred years ago, someone said this in the *Scientific American:* "Management wants as much work for as little pay as possible and the workers want as much pay for as little work as possible." So what happens? They get together and do something called bargaining. Incentive conditions emerge as a result of a bargain. And it's often a bad bargain all around. The conditions are not really very efficient as far as management goes, and not very pleasant as far as labor goes. If most people are bored with their jobs, it's because the system is the product of a battle between opposing forces. Someone should design incentive systems with the dual objectives of getting things done and making work enjoyable.

*Dowling.* We recently did a survey for the first issue of *Organizational Dynamics,* in which we asked several hundred top managers what use they made of psychologists. The results were paradoxical: Top managers felt that there were many problems the psychologist could help them with, but there was very little inclination to use them. Only about 3 percent of the people surveyed had used psychologists and, even so, they used them sporadically on minute tasks. Which raises the question, what do you think psychology has contributed to industry, and what do you think it could contribute?

*Skinner.* I'm not a specialist in industrial psychology. I have only a casual acquaintance with the kinds of things done by Douglas McGregor and Abe Maslow. They do not strike me as being particularly effective. You can classify motives and still neglect contingencies of reinforcement, and the contingencies are the important things. Behavior modification is beginning to get into industry, and that may mean a change. Up to now it's been most effective in psychotherapy, in handling disturbed and retarded children, in the design of classroom management, and in programmed instruction. It is possible that we're going to see an entirely different kind of psychology in industry. Unfortunately, there are not yet many people who understand the principle. it is not something that can be taken over by the non-professional to use as a rule of thumb. It requires specific analysis and redesign of a situation. In the not-too-distant future, however, a new breed of industrial manager may be able to apply the principles of operant conditioning effectively.

# Motivating Individuals in Organizational Settings

## 4.   MOTIVATION: A DIAGNOSTIC APPROACH

David A. Nadler and Edward E. Lawler III

- What makes some people work hard while others do as little as possible?
- How can I, as a manager, influence the performance of people who work for me?
- Why do people turn over, show up late to work, and miss work entirely?

These important questions about employees' behavior can only be answered by managers who have a grasp of what motivates people. Specifically, a good understanding of motivation can serve as a valuable tool for *understanding* the causes of behavior in organizations, for *predicting* the effects of any managerial action, and for *directing* behavior so that organizational and individual goals can be achieved.

### EXISTING APPROACHES

During the past twenty years, managers have been bombarded with a number of different approaches to motivation. The terms associated with these approaches are well known—"human relations," "scientific management," "job enrichment," "need hierarchy," "self-actualization," etc. Each of these approaches has something to offer. On the other hand, each of these different approaches also has its problems in both theory and practice. Running through almost all of the approaches with which managers are familiar are a series of implicit but clearly erroneous assumptions.

*Assumption 1: All Employees Are Alike.* Different theories present different ways of looking at people, but each of them assumes that all employees are basically similar in their makeup: Employees all want economic gains, or all want a pleasant climate, or all aspire to be self-actualizing, etc.

*Assumption 2: All Situations Are Alike.* Most theories assume that all managerial situations are alike, and that the managerial course of action for motivation (for example, participation, job enlargement, etc.) is applicable in all situations.

*Assumption 3: One Best Way.* Out of the other two assumptions there emerges a basic principle that there is "one best way" to motivate employees.

When these "one best way" approaches are tried in the "correct" situation they will work. However, all of them are bound to fail in some situations. They are therefore not adequate managerial tools.

## A NEW APPROACH

During the past ten years, a great deal of research has been done on a new approach to looking at motivation. This approach, frequently called "expectancy theory," still needs further testing, refining, and extending. However, enough is known that many behavioral scientists have concluded that it represents the most comprehensive, valid, and useful approach to understanding motivation. Further, it is apparent that it is a very useful tool for understanding motivation in organizations.

The theory is based on a number of specific assumptions about the causes of behavior in organizations.

*Assumption 1: Behavior Is Determined by a Combination of Forces in the Individual and Forces in the Environment.* Neither the individual nor the environment alone determines behavior. Individuals come into organizations with certain "psychological baggage." They have past experiences and a developmental history which has given

them unique sets of needs, ways of looking at the world, and expectations about how organizations will treat them. These all influence how individuals respond to their work environment. The work environment provides structures (such as a pay system or a supervisor) which influence the behavior of people. Different environments tend to produce different behavior in similar people just as dissimilar people tend to behave differently in similar environments.

*Assumption 2: People Make Decisions About Their Own Behavior in Organizations.* While there are many constraints on the behavior of individuals in organizations, most of the behavior that is observed is the result of individuals' conscious decisions. These decisions usually fall into two categories. First, individuals make decisions about *membership behavior*—coming to work, staying at work, and in other ways being a member of the organization. Second, individuals make decisions about the amount of effort they will direct *towards performing their jobs.* This includes decisions about how hard to work, how much to produce, at what quality, etc.

*Assumption 3: Different People Have Different Types of Needs, Desires and Goals.* Individuals differ on what kinds of outcomes (or rewards) they desire. These differences are not random; they can be examined systematically by an understanding of the differences in the strength of individuals' needs.

*Assumption 4: People Make Decisions Among Alternative Plans of Behavior Based on Their Perceptions (Expectancies) of the Degree to Which a Given Behavior Will Lead to Desired Outcomes.* In simple terms, people tend to do those things which they see as leading to outcomes (which can also be called "rewards") they desire and avoid doing those things they see as leading to outcomes that are not desired.

In general, the approach used here views people as having their own needs and mental maps of what the world is like. They use these maps to make decisions about how they will behave, behaving in those ways which their mental maps indicate will lead to outcomes that will satisfy their needs. Therefore, they are inherently neither motivated nor unmotivated; motivation depends on the situation they are in, and how it fits their needs.

## THE THEORY

Based on these general assumptions, expectancy theory states a number of propositions about the process by which people make decisions about their own behavior in organizational settings. While the theory is complex at first view, it is in fact made of a series of fairly straightforward observations about behavior. (The theory is presented in more technical terms in Appendix A.) Three concepts serve as the key building blocks of the theory.

*Performance-Outcome Expectancy.* Every behavior has associated with it, in an individual's mind, certain outcomes (rewards or punishments). In other words, the individual believes or expects that if he or she behaves in a certain way, he or she will get certain things.

Examples of expectancies can easily be described. An individual may have an expectancy that if he produces ten units he will receive his normal hourly rate while if he produces fifteen units he will receive his hourly pay rate plus a bonus. Similarly an individual may believe that certain levels of performance will lead to approval or disapproval from members of her work group or from her supervisor. Each performance can be seen as leading to a number of different kinds of outcomes and outcomes can differ in their types.

*Valence.* Each outcome has a "valence" (value, worth, attractiveness) to a specific individual. Outcomes have different valences for different individuals. This comes about because valences result from individual needs and perceptions, which differ because they in turn reflect other factors in the individual's life.

For example, some individuals may value an opportunity for promotion or advancement because of their needs for achievement or power, while others may not want to be promoted and leave their current work group because of needs for affiliation with others. Similarly, a fringe benefit such as a pension plan may have great valence for an older worker but little valence for a young employee on his first job.

*Effort-Performance Expectancy.* Each behavior also has associated with it in the individual's mind a certain expectancy or probability of success. This expectancy represents the individual's perception of how hard it will be to achieve such behavior and the probability of his or her successful achievement of that behavior.

For example, you may have a strong expectancy that if you put forth effort, you can produce ten units an hour, but that you have only a fifty-fifty chance of producing fifteen units an hour if you try.

Putting these concepts together, it is possible to make a basic statement about motivation. In general, the motivation to attempt to behave in a certain way is greatest when:

a. The individual believes that the behavior will lead to outcomes (performance-outcome expectancy)

b. The individual believes that these outcomes have positive value for him or her (valence)

c. The individual believes that he or she is able to perform at the desired level (effort-performance expectancy)

Given a number of alternative levels of behavior (ten, fifteen, and twenty units of production per hour, for example) the individual will choose that level of performance which has the greatest motivational force associated with it, as indicated by the expectancies, outcomes, and valences.

In other words, when faced with choices about behavior, the individual goes through a process of considering questions such as, "Can I perform at that level if I try?" "If I perform at that level, what will happen?" "How do I feel about those things that will happen?" The individual then decides to behave in that way which seems to have the best chance of producing positive, desired outcomes.

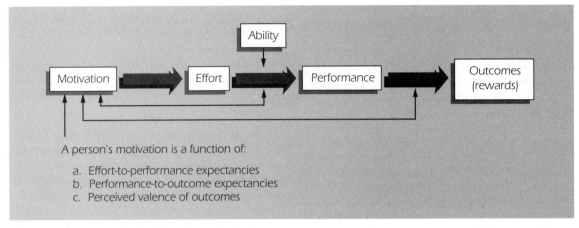

A person's motivation is a function of:

   a.  Effort-to-performance expectancies
   b.  Performance-to-outcome expectancies
   c.  Perceived valence of outcomes

**FIGURE 4.1** The Basic Motivation-Behavior Sequence.

## A General Model

On the basis of these concepts, it is possible to construct a general model of behavior in organizational settings (see Figure 4.1). Working from left to right in the model, motivation is seen as the force on the individual to expend effort. Motivation leads to an observed level of effort by the individual. Effort, alone, however, is not enough. Performance results from a combination of the effort that an individual puts forth *and* the level of ability which he or she has (reflecting skills, training, information, etc.) Effort thus combines with ability to produce a given level of performance. As a result of performance, the individual attains certain outcomes. The model indicates this relationship in a dotted line, reflecting the fact that sometimes people perform but do not get desired outcomes. As this process of performance-reward occurs, time after time, the actual events serve to provide information which influences the individual's perceptions (particularly expectancies) and thus influences motivation in the future.

Outcomes, or rewards, fall into two major categories. First, the individual obtains outcomes from the environment. When an individual performs at a given level he or she can receive positive or negative outcomes from supervisors, coworkers, the organization's rewards systems, or other sources. These environmental rewards are thus one source of outcomes for the individual. A second source of outcomes is the individual. These include outcomes which occur purely from the performance of the task itself (feelings of accomplishment, personal worth, achievement, etc.) In a sense, the individual gives these rewards to himself or herself. The environment cannot give them or take them away directly; it can only make them possible.

## Supporting Evidence

Over fifty studies have been done to test the validity of the expectancy-theory approach to predicting employee behavior.[1] Almost without exception, the studies have confirmed the predictions

---

[1] For reviews of the expectancy theory research see Mitchell, T. R. Expectancy models of job satisfaction, occupational preference and effort: A theoretical methodological, and empirical appraisal. *Psychological Bulletin,* 1974, 81, 1053–1077. For a more general discussion of expectancy theory and other approaches to motivation see Lawler, E. E. *Motivation in work organizations.* Belmont, Calif. Brooks/Cole, 1973.

of the theory. As the theory predicts, the best performers in organizations tend to see a strong relationship between performing their jobs well and receiving rewards they value. In addition they have clear performance goals and feel they can perform well. Similarly, studies using the expectancy theory to predict how people choose jobs also show that individuals tend to interview for and actually take those jobs which they feel will provide the rewards they value. One study, for example, was able to correctly predict for 80 percent of the people studied which of several jobs they would take.[2] Finally, the theory correctly predicts that beliefs about the outcomes associated with performance (expectancies) will be better predictors of performance than will feelings of job satisfaction since expectancies are the critical causes of performance and satisfaction is not.

## Questions About the Model

Although the results so far have been encouraging, they also indicate some problems with the model. These problems do not critically affect the managerial implications of the model, but they should be noted. The model is based on the assumption that individuals make very rational decisions after a thorough exploration of all the available alternatives and on weighing the possible outcomes of all these alternatives. When we talk to or observe individuals, however, we find that their decision processes are frequently less thorough. People often stop considering alternative behavior plans when they find one that is at least moderately satisfying, even though more rewarding plans remain to be examined.

People are also limited in the amount of information they can handle at one time, and therefore the model may indicate a process that is much more complex than the one that actually takes place. On the other hand, the model does provide enough information and is consistent enough with reality to present some clear implications for managers who are concerned with the question of how to motivate the people who work for them.

## Implications for Managers

The first set of implications is directed toward the individual manager who has a group of people working for him or her and is concerned with how to motivate good performance. Since behavior is a result of forces both in the person and in the environment, you as manager need to look at and diagnose both the person and the environment. Specifically, you need to do the following:

*Figure Out What Outcomes Each Employee Values.* As a first step, it is important to determine what kinds of outcomes or rewards have valence for your employees. For each employee you need to determine "what turns him or her on." There are various ways of finding this out, including (a) finding out employees' desires through some structured method of data collection, such as a questionnaire, (b) observing the employees' reactions to different situations or rewards, or (c) the fairly simple act of asking them what kinds of rewards they want, what kind of career goals they have, or "what's in it for them." It is important to stress here that it is very difficult to change what people want, but fairly easy to find out what they want. Thus, the skillful manager emphasizes diagnosis of needs, not changing the individuals themselves.

*Determine What Kinds of Behavior You Desire.* Managers frequently talk about "good performance" without really defining what good performance is. An important step in motivating is for you yourself to figure out what kinds of performance are required and what are adequate measures or indicators of performance (quantity, quality, etc.). There is also a need to be able to define those performances in fairly specific terms

---

[2] Lawler, E. E., Kuleck, W. J., Rhode, J. G., & Sorenson, J. E. Job choice and post-decision dissonance. *Organizational Behavior and Human Performance,* 1975, 13, 133–145.

so that observable and measurable behavior can be defined and subordinates can understand what is desired of them (e.g., produce ten products of a certain quality standard—rather than only produce at a high rate).

*Make Sure Desired Levels of Performance Are Reachable.* The model states that motivation is determined not only by the performance-to-outcome expectancy, but also by the effort-to-performance expectancy. The implication of this is that the levels of performance which are set as the points at which individuals receive desired outcomes must be reachable or attainable by these individuals. If the employees feel that the level of performance required to get a reward is higher than they can reasonably achieve, then their motivation to perform well will be relatively low.

*Link Desired Outcomes to Desired Performances.* The next step is to directly, clearly, and explicitly link those outcomes desired by employees to the specific performances desired by you. If your employee values external rewards, then the emphasis should be on the rewards systems concerned with promotion, pay, and approval. While the linking of these rewards can be initiated through your making statements to your employees, it is extremely important that employees see a clear example of the reward process working in a fairly short period of time if the motivating "expectancies" are to be created in the employees' minds. The linking must be done by some concrete public acts, in addition to statements of intent.

If your employee values internal rewards (e.g., achievement), then you should concentrate on changing the nature of the person's job, for he or she is likely to respond well to such things as increased autonomy, feedback, and challenge, because these things will lead to a situation where good job performance is inherently rewarding. The best way to check on the adequacy of the internal and external reward system is to ask people what their perceptions of the situation are. Remember it is the perceptions of people that determine their motivation, not reality. It doesn't matter for example whether you feel a subordi-

nate's pay is related to his or her motivation. Motivation will be present only if the subordinate sees the relationship. Many managers are misled about the behavior of their subordinates because they rely on their own perceptions of the situation and forget to find out what their subordinates feel. There is only one way to do this: ask. Questionnaires can be used here, as can personal interviews.

*Analyze the Total Situation for Conflicting Expectancies.* Having set up positive expectancies for employees, you then need to look at the entire situation to see if other factors (informal work groups, other managers, the organization's reward systems) have set up conflicting expectancies in the minds of the employees. Motivation will only be high when people see a number of rewards associated with good performance and few negative outcomes. Again, you can often gather this kind of information by asking your subordinates. If there are major conflicts, you need to make adjustments, either in your own performance and reward structure, or in the other sources of rewards or punishments in the environment.

*Make Sure Changes in Outcomes Are Large Enough.* In examining the motivational system, it is important to make sure that changes in outcomes or rewards are large enough to motivate significant behavior. Trivial rewards will result in trivial amounts of effort and thus trivial improvements in performance. Rewards must be large enough to motivate individuals to put forth the effort required to bring about significant changes in performance.

*Check the System for Its Equity.* The model is based on the idea that individuals are different and therefore different rewards will need to be used to motivate different individuals. On the other hand, for a motivational system to work it must be a fair one—one that has equity (not equality). Good performers should see that they get more desired rewards than do poor performers, and others in the system should see that also. Equity should not be confused with a system of equality where all are rewarded equally, with no regard to their performance. A system of equality is guaranteed to produce low motivation.

## Implications for Organizations

Expectancy theory has some clear messages for those who run large organizations. It suggests how organizational structures can be designed so that they increase rather than decrease levels of motivation of organization members. While there are many different implications, a few of the major ones are as follows:

*Implication 1: The Design of Pay and Reward Systems.* Organizations usually get what they reward, not what they want. This can be seen in many situations, and pay systems are a good example.[3] Frequently, organizations reward people for membership (through pay tied to seniority, for example) rather than for performance. Little wonder that what the organization gets is behavior oriented towards "safe," secure employment rather than effort directed at performing well. In addition, even where organizations do pay for performance as a motivational device, they frequently negate the motivational value of the system by keeping pay secret, therefore preventing people from observing the pay-to-performance relationship that would serve to create positive, clear, and strong performance-to-reward expectancies. The implication is that organizations should put more effort into rewarding people (through pay, promotion, better job opportunities, etc.) for the performances which are desired, and that to keep these rewards secret is clearly self-defeating. In addition, it underscores the importance of the frequently ignored performance evaluation or appraisal process and the need to evaluate people based on how they

perform clearly defined specific behaviors, rather than on how they score on ratings of general traits such as "honesty," "cleanliness," and other, similar terms which frequently appear as part of the performance appraisal form.

*Implication 2: The Design of Tasks, Jobs, and Roles.* One source of desired outcomes is the work itself. The expectancy-theory model supports much of the job enrichment literature, in saying that by designing jobs which enable people to get their needs fulfilled, organizations can bring about higher levels of motivation.[4] The major difference between the traditional approaches to job enlargement or enrichment and the expectancy-theory approach is the recognition by the expectancy theory that different people have different needs and, therefore, some people may not want enlarged or enriched jobs. Thus, while the design of tasks that have more autonomy, variety, feedback, meaningfulness, etc., will lead to higher motivation in some, the organization needs to build in the opportunity for individuals to make choices about the kind of work they will do so that not everyone is forced to experience job enrichment.

*Implication 3: The Importance of Group Structures.* Groups, both formal and informal, are powerful and potent sources of desired outcomes for individuals. Groups can provide or withhold acceptance, approval, affection, skill training, needed information, assistance, etc. They are a powerful force in the total motivational environment of individuals. Several implications emerge from the importance of groups. First, organizations should consider the structuring of at least a portion of rewards around group performance rather than individual performance. This is particularly important where group members have to cooperate

---

[3] For a detailed discussion of the implications of expectancy theory for pay and reward systems, see Lawler, E. E. *Pay and organizational effectiveness: A psychological view.* New York: McGraw-Hill, 1971.

[4] A good discussion of job design with an expectancy-theory perspective is in Hackman, J. R., Oldham, G. R., Janson, R., & Purdy, K. A new strategy for job enrichment. *California Management Review,* Summer, 1975, p. 57.

with each other to produce a group product or service, and where the individual's contribution is often hard to determine. Second, the organization needs to train managers to be aware of how groups can influence individual behavior and to be sensitive to the kinds of expectancies which informal groups set up and their conflict or consistency with the expectancies that the organization attempts to create.

*Implication 4: The Supervisor's Role.* The immediate supervisor has an important role in creating, monitoring, and maintaining the expectancies and reward structures which will lead to good performance. The supervisor's role in the motivation process becomes one of defining clear goals, setting clear reward expectancies, and providing the right rewards for different people (which could include both organizational rewards and personal rewards such as recognition, approval, or support from the supervisor). Thus, organizations need to provide supervisors with an awareness of the nature of motivation as well as the tools (control over organizational rewards, skill in administering those rewards) to create positive motivation.

*Implication 5: Measuring Motivation.* If things like expectancies, the nature of the job, supervisor-controlled outcomes, satisfaction, etc., are important in understanding how well people are being motivated, then organizations need to monitor employee perceptions along these lines. One relatively cheap and reliable method of doing this is through standardized employee questionnaires. A number of organizations already use such techniques, surveying employees' perceptions and attitudes at regular intervals (ranging from once a month to once every year-and-a-half) using either standardized surveys or surveys developed specifically for the organization. Such informa-

tion is useful both to the individual manager and to top management in assessing the state of human resources and the effectiveness of the organization's motivation systems.[5]

*Implication 6: Individualizing Organizations.* Expectancy theory leads to a final general implication about a possible future direction for the design of organizations. Because different people have different needs and therefore have different valences, effective motivation must come through the recognition that not all employees are alike and that organizations need to be flexible in order to accommodate individual differences. This implies the "building in" of choice for employees in many areas, such as reward systems, fringe benefits, job assignments, etc., where employees previously have had little say. A successful example of the building in of such choice can be seen in the experiments at TRW and the Educational Testing Service with "cafeteria fringe-benefits plans" which allow employees to choose the fringe benefits they want, rather than taking the expensive and often unwanted benefits which the company frequently provides to everyone.[6]

## SUMMARY

Expectancy theory provides a more complex model of man for managers to work with. At the same time, it is a model which holds promise for the more effective motivation of individuals and the more effective design of organizational systems. It implies, however, the need for more exacting and thorough diagnosis by the manager to determine (a) the relevant forces in the individual, and (b) the relevant forces in the environment, both of which combine to motivate different kinds of behavior. Following diagnosis, the

---

[5] The use of questionnaires for understanding and changing organizational behavior is discussed in Nadler, D. A. *Feedback and organizational development: Using data-based methods.* Reading, Mass.: Addison-Wesley, 1977.

[6] The whole issue of individualizing organizations is examined in Lawler, E. E. The individualized organization: Problems and promise. *California Management Review,* 1974, 17 (2), 31–39.

model implies a need to act—to develop a system of pay, promotion, job assignments, group structures, supervision, etc.—to bring about effective motivation by providing different outcomes for different individuals.

Performance of individuals is a critical issue in making organizations work effectively. If a manager is to influence work behavior and performance, he or she must have an understanding of motivation and the factors which influence an individual's motivation to come to work, to work hard, and to work well. While simple models offer easy answers, it is the more complex models which seem to offer more promise. Managers can use models (like expectancy theory) to understand the nature of behavior and build more effective organizations.

## APPENDIX A: THE EXPECTANCY THEORY MODEL IN MORE TECHNICAL TERMS

A person's motivation to exert effort towards a specific level of performance is based on his or her perceptions of associations between actions and outcomes. The critical perceptions which contribute to motivation are graphically presented in Figure 4.2. These perceptions can be defined as follows:

*a.* The effort-to-performance expectancy ($E \rightarrow P$): This refers to the person's subjective probability about the likelihood that he or she can perform at a given level, or that effort on his or her part will lead to successful performance. This term can be thought of as varying from 0 to 1. In

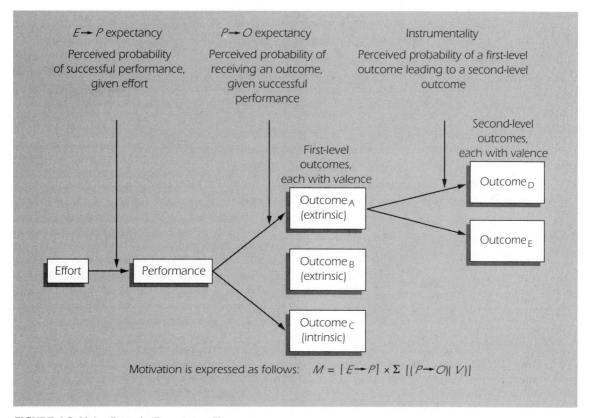

FIGURE 4.2 Major Terms in Expectancy Theory.

general, the less likely a person feels that he or she can perform at a given level, the less likely he or she will be to try to perform at that level. A person's $E \rightarrow P$ probabilities are also strongly influenced by each situation and by previous experience in that and similar situations.

*b.* The performance-to-outcomes expectancy ($P \rightarrow 0$) and valence (*V*): This refers to a combination of a number of beliefs about what the outcomes of successful performance will be and the value or attractiveness of these outcomes to the individual. Valence is considered to vary from +1 (very desirable) to −1 (very undesirable) and the performance-to-outcomes probabilities vary from +1 (performance sure to lead to outcome) to 0 (performance not related to outcome). In general, the more likely a person feels that performance will lead to valent outcomes, the more likely he or she will be to try to perform at the required level.

*c.* Instrumentality: As Figure 4.2 indicates, a single level of performance can be associated with a number of different outcomes, each having a certain degree of valence. Some outcomes are valent because they have direct value or attractiveness. Some outcomes, however, have valence because they are seen as leading to (or being "instrumental" for) the attainment of other "second level" outcomes which have direct value or attractiveness.

*d.* Intrinsic and extrinsic outcomes: Some outcomes are seen as occurring directly as a result of performing the task itself and are outcomes which the individual thus gives to himself (i.e., feelings of accomplishment, creativity, etc.). These are called "intrinsic" outcomes. Other outcomes that are associated with performance are provided or mediated by external factors (the organization, the supervisor, the work group, etc.). These outcomes are called "extrinsic" outcomes.

Along with the graphic representation of these terms presented in Figure 4.2, there is a simplified formula for combining these perceptions to arrive at a term expressing the relative level of motivation to exert effort towards performance at a given level. The formula expresses these relationships:

*a.* The person's motivation to perform is determined by the $P \rightarrow O$ expectancy multiplied by the valence (*V*) of the outcome. The valence of the first order outcome subsumes the instrumentalities and valences of second order outcomes. The relationship is multiplicative since there is no motivation to perform if either of the terms is zero.

*b.* Since a level of performance has multiple outcomes associated with it, the products of all probability-times-valence combinations are added together for all the outcomes that are seen as related to the specific performance.

*c.* This term (the summed $P \rightarrow O$ expectancies times valences) is then multiplied by the $E \rightarrow P$ expectancy. Again the multiplicative relationship indicates that if either term is zero, motivation is zero.

*d.* In summary, the strength of a person's motivation to perform effectively is influenced by (1) the person's belief that effort can be converted into performance, and (2) the net attractiveness of the events that are perceived to stem from good performance.

So far, all the terms have referred to the individual's perceptions which result in motivation and thus an intention to behave in a certain way. Figure 4.3 is a simplified representation of the total model, showing how these intentions get translated into actual behavior.[7] The model envisions the following sequence of events:

---

[7] For a more detailed statement of the model see Lawler, E. E. Job attitudes and employee motivation: Theory, research and practice. *Personnel Psychology,* 1970, 23, 223–237.

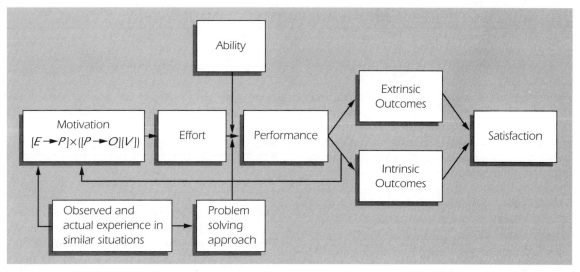

**FIGURE 4.3** Simplified Expectancy-Theory Model of Behavior.

*a.* First, the strength of a person's motivation to perform correctly is most directly reflected in his or her effort—how hard he or she works. This effort expenditure may or may not result in good performance, since at least two factors must be right if effort is to be converted into performance. First, the person must possess the necessary abilities in order to perform the job well. Unless both ability and effort are high, there cannot be good performance. A second factor is the person's perception of how his or her effort can best be converted into performance. It is assumed that this perception is learned by the individual on the basis of previous experience in similar situations. This "how to do it" perception can obviously vary widely in accuracy, and—where erroneous perceptions exist—performance is low even though effort or motivation may be high.

*b.* Second, when performance occurs, certain amounts of outcomes are obtained by the individual. Intrinsic outcomes, not being mediated by outside forces, tend to occur regularly as a result of performance, while extrinsic outcomes may or may not accrue to the individual (indicated by the wavy line of the model).

*c.* Third, as a result of the obtaining of outcomes and the perceptions of the relative value of the outcomes obtained, the individual has a positive or negative affective response (a level of satisfaction or dissatisfaction).

*d.* Fourth, the model indicates that events which occur influence future behavior by altering the $E \rightarrow P, P \rightarrow O$, and $V$ perceptions. This process is represented by the feedback loops running from actual behavior back to motivation.

# 5.   GOAL-SETTING—A MOTIVATIONAL TECHNIQUE THAT WORKS

Gary P. Latham and Edwin A. Locke

The problem of how to motivate employees has puzzled and frustrated managers for generations. One reason the problem has seemed difficult, if not mysterious, is that motivation ultimately comes from within the individual and therefore cannot be observed directly. Moreover, most managers are not in a position to change an employee's basic personality structure. The best they can do is try to use incentives to direct the energies of their employees toward organizational objectives.

Money is obviously the primary incentive, since without it few if any employees would come to work. But money alone is not always enough to motivate high performance. Other incentives, such as participation in decision making, job enrichment, behavior modification, and organizational development, have been tried with varying degrees of success. A large number of research studies have shown, however, that one very straightforward technique—goal setting—is probably not only more effective than alternative methods, but may be the major mechanism by which these other incentives affect motivation. For example, a recent experiment on job enrichment demonstrated that unless employees in enriched jobs set higher, more specific goals than do those with unenriched jobs, job enrichment has absolutely no effect on productivity. Even money has been found most effective as a motivator when the bonuses offered are made contingent on attaining specific objectives.

## THE GOAL-SETTING CONCEPT

The idea of assigning employees a specific amount of work to be accomplished—a specific task, a quota, a performance standard, an objective, or a deadline—is not new. The task concept, along with time and motion study and incentive pay, was the cornerstone of scientific management, founded by Frederick W. Taylor more than 70 years ago. He used his system to increase the productivity of blue-collar workers. About 20 years ago the idea of goal setting reappeared under a new name, management by objectives, but this technique was designed for managers.

In a 14-year program of research, we have found that goal setting does not necessarily have to be part of a wider management system to motivate performance effectively. It can be used as a technique in its own right.

### Laboratory and Field Research

Our research program began in the laboratory. In a series of experiments, individuals were assigned different types of goals on a variety of simple tasks—addition, brainstorming, assembling toys. Repeatedly it was found that those assigned hard goals performed better than did people assigned moderately difficult or easy goals. Furthermore, individuals who had specific, challenging goals outperformed those who were given such vague goals as to "do your best." Finally, we observed that pay and performance feedback led to improved performance only when these incentives led the individual to set higher goals.

While results were quite consistent in the laboratory, there was no proof that they could be applied to actual work settings. Fortunately, just as Locke published a summary of the laboratory studies in 1968, Latham began a separate series of experiments in the wood products industry that demonstrated the practical significance of these findings. The field studies did not start out as a validity test of a laboratory theory, but rather as a response to a practical problem.

In 1968, six sponsors of the American Pulpwood Association became concerned about increasing the productivity of independent loggers in the South. These loggers were entrepreneurs on whom the multimillion-dollar companies are largely dependent for their raw material. The problem was twofold. First, these entrepreneurs did not work for a single company; they worked for themselves. Thus they were free to (and often did) work two days one week, four days a second week, five half-days a third week, or whatever schedule they preferred. In short, these workers could be classified as marginal from the standpoint of their productivity and attendance, which were considered highly unsatisfactory by conventional company standards. Second, the major approach taken to alleviate this problem had been to develop equipment that would make the industry less dependent on this type of worker. A limitation of this approach was that many of the logging supervisors were unable to obtain the financing necessary to purchase a small tractor, let alone a rubber-tired skidder.

Consequently, we designed a survey that would help managers determine "what makes these people tick." The survey was conducted orally in the field with 292 logging supervisors. Complex statistical analyses of the data identified three basic types of supervisor. One type stayed on the job with their men, gave them instructions and explanations, provided them with training, read the trade magazines, and had little difficulty financing the equipment they needed. Still, the productivity of their units was at best mediocre.

The operation of the second group of supervisors was slightly less mechanized. These supervisors provided little training for their workforce. They simply drove their employees to the woods, gave them a specific production goal to attain for the day or week, left them alone in the woods unsupervised, and returned at night to take them home. Labor turnover was high and productivity was again average.

The operation of the third group of supervisors was relatively unmechanized. These leaders stayed on the job with their men, provided training, gave instructions and explanations, and in addition, set a specific production goal for the day or week. Not only was the crew's productivity high, but their injury rate was well below average.

Two conclusions were discussed with the managers of the companies sponsoring this study. First, mechanization alone will not increase the productivity of logging crews. Just as the average tax payer would probably commit more mathematical errors if he were to try to use a computer to complete his income tax return, the average logger misuses, and frequently abuses, the equipment he purchases (for example, drives a skidder with two flat tires, doesn't change the oil filter). This increases not only the logger's downtime, but also his costs which, in turn, can force him out of business. The second conclusion of the survey was that setting a specific production goal combined with supervisory presence to ensure goal commitment will bring about a significant increase in productivity.

These conclusions were greeted with the standard, but valid, cliché, "Statistics don't prove causation." And our comments regarding the value of machinery were especially irritating to these managers, many of whom had received degrees in engineering. So one of the companies decided to replicate the survey in order to check our findings.

The company's study placed each of 892 independent logging supervisors who sold wood to the company into one of three categories of supervisory styles our survey had identified—namely, (1) stays on the job but does not set specific production goals; (2) sets specific production goals but does not stay on the job; and (3) stays on the job and sets specific production goals. Once again, goal setting, in combination with the on-site presence of a supervisor, was shown to be the key to improved productivity.

## TESTING FOR THE HAWTHORNE EFFECT

Management may have been unfamiliar with different theories of motivation, but it was fully aware of one label—the Hawthorne effect. Managers in these wood products companies remained unconvinced that anything so simple as staying on the job with the men and setting a specific production goal could have an appreciable effect on productivity. They pointed out that the results simply reflected the positive effects any supervisor would have on the work unit after giving his crew attention. And they were unimpressed by the laboratory experiments we cited—experiments showing that individuals who have a specific goal solve more arithmetic problems or assemble more tinker toys than do people who are told to "do your best." Skepticism prevailed.

But the country's economic picture made it critical to continue the study of inexpensive techniques to improve employee motivation and productivity. We were granted permission to run one more project to test the effectiveness of goal setting.

Twenty independent logging crews who were all but identical in size, mechanization level, terrain on which they worked, productivity, and attendance were located. The logging supervisors of these crews were in the habit of staying on the job with their men, but they did not set production goals. Half the crews were randomly selected to receive training in goal setting; the remaining crews served as a control group.

The logging supervisors who were to set goals were told that we had found a way to increase productivity at no financial expense to anyone. We gave the ten supervisors in the training group production tables developed through time-and-motion studies by the company's en-

gineers. These tables made it possible to determine how much wood should be harvested in a given number of man hours. They were asked to use these tables as a guide in determining a specific production goal to assign their employees. In addition, each sawhand was given a tallymeter (counter) that he could wear on his belt. The sawhand was asked to punch the counter each time he felled a tree. Finally, permission was requested to measure the crew's performance on a weekly basis.

The ten supervisors in the control group—those who were not asked to set production goals—were told that the researchers were interested in learning the extent to which productivity is affected by absenteeism and injuries. They were urged to "do your best" to maximize the crew's productivity and attendance and to minimize injuries. It was explained that the data might be useful in finding ways to increase productivity at little or no cost to the wood harvester.

To control for the Hawthorne effect, we made an equal number of visits to the control group and the training group. Performance was measured for 12 weeks. During this time, the productivity of the goal-setting group was significantly higher than that of the control group. Moreover, absenteeism was significantly lower in the groups that set goals than in the groups who were simply urged to do their best. Injury and turnover rates were low in both groups.

Why should anything so simple and inexpensive as goal setting influence the work of these employees so significantly? Anecdotal evidence from conversations with both the loggers and the company foresters who visited them suggested several reasons.

Harvesting timber can be a monotonous, tiring job with little or no meaning for most workers. Introducing a goal that is difficult, but attainable, increases the challenge of the job. In addition, a specific goal makes it clear to the worker what it is he is expected to do. Goal feedback via the tallymeter and weekly recordkeeping provide the worker with a sense of achievement, recognition, and accomplishment. He can see how well he is doing now as against his past performance and, in some cases, how well he is doing in comparison with others. Thus the worker not only may expend greater effort, but may also devise better or more creative tactics for attaining the goal than those he previously used.

## NEW APPLICATIONS

Management was finally convinced that goal setting was an effective motivational technique for increasing the productivity of the independent woods worker in the South. The issue now raised by the management of another wood products company was whether the procedure could be used in the West with company logging operations in which the employees were unionized and paid by the hour. The previous study had involved employees on a piece-rate system, which was the practice in the South.

The immediate problem confronting this company involved the loading of logging trucks. If the trucks were underloaded, the company lost money. If the trucks were overloaded, however, the driver could be fined by the Highway Department and could ultimately lose his job. The drivers opted for underloading the trucks.

For three months management tried to solve this problem by urging the drivers to try harder to fill the truck to its legal net weight, and by developing weighing scales that could be attached to the truck. But this approach did not prove cost effective, because the scales continually broke down when subjected to the rough terrain on which the trucks traveled. Consequently, the drivers reverted to their former practice of underloading. For the three months in which the problem was under study the trucks were seldom loaded in excess of 58 to 63 percent of capacity.

At the end of the three-month period, the results of the previous goal-setting experiments were explained to the union. They were told three things—that the company would like to set a specific net weight goal for the drivers, that no monetary reward or fringe benefits other than verbal praise could be expected for improved performance, and that no one would be criticized for failing to attain the goal. Once again, the idea that simply setting a specific goal would solve a production problem seemed too incredible to be taken seriously by the union. However, they reached an agreement that a difficult, but attainable, goal of 94 percent of the truck's legal net weight would be assigned to the drivers, provided that no one could be reprimanded for failing to attain the goal. This latter point was emphasized to the company foremen in particular.

Within the first month, performance increased to 80 percent of the truck's net weight. After the second month, however, performance decreased to 70 percent. Interviews with the drivers indicated that they were testing management's statement that no punitive steps would be taken against them if their performance suddenly dropped. Fortunately for all concerned, no such steps were taken by the foremen, and performance exceeded 90 percent of the truck's capacity after the third month. Their performance has remained at this level to this day, seven years later.

The results over the nine-month period during which this study was conducted saved the company $250,000. This figure, determined by the company's accountants, is based on the cost of additional trucks that would have been required to deliver the same quantity of logs to the mill if goal setting had not been implemented. The dollars-saved figure is even higher when you factor in the cost of the additional diesel fuel that would have been consumed and the expenses incurred in recruiting and hiring the additional truck drivers.

Why could this procedure work without the union's demanding an increase in hourly wages? First, the drivers did not feel that they were really doing anything differently. This, of course, was not true. As a result of goal setting, the men began to record their truck weight in a pocket notebook, and they found themselves bragging about their accomplishments to their peers. Second, they viewed goal setting as a challenging game: "It was great to beat the other guy."

Competition was a crucial factor in bringing about goal acceptance and commitment in this study. However, we can reject the hypothesis that improved performance resulted solely from competition, because no special prizes or formal recognition programs were provided for those who came closest to, or exceeded, the goal. No effort was made by the company to single out one "winner." More important, the opportunity for competition among drivers had existed before goal setting was instituted; after all, each driver knew his own truck's weight, and the truck weight of each of the 36 other drivers every time he hauled wood into the yard. In short, competition affected productivity only in the sense that it led to the acceptance of, and commitment to, the goal. It was the setting of the goal itself and the working toward it that brought about increased performance and decreased costs.

## PARTICIPATIVE GOAL SETTING

The inevitable question always raised by management was raised here: "We know goal setting works. How can we make it work better?" Was there one best method for setting goals? Evidence for a "one best way" approach was cited by several managers, but it was finally concluded that different approaches would work best under different circumstances.

It was hypothesized that the woods workers in the South, who had little or no education, would work better with assigned goals, while the educated workers in the West would achieve higher productivity if they were allowed to help set the goals themselves. Why the focus on education? Many of the uneducated workers in the South could be classified as culturally disadvantaged. Such persons often lack self-confidence, have a poor sense of time, and are not very competitive. The cycle of skill mastery, which in turn guarantees skill levels high enough to prevent discouragement, doesn't apply to these employees. If, for example, these people were allowed to participate in goal setting, the goals might be too difficult or they might be too easy. On the other hand, participation for the educated worker was considered critical in effecting maximum goal ac-

ceptance. Since these conclusions appeared logical, management initially decided that no research was necessary. This decision led to hours of further discussion.

The same questions were raised again and again by the researchers. What if the logic were wrong? Can we afford to implement these decisions without evaluating them systematically? Would we implement decisions regarding a new approach to tree planting without first testing it? Do we care more about trees than we do about people? Finally, permission was granted to conduct an experiment.

Logging crews were randomly appointed to either participative goal setting, assigned (nonparticipative) goal setting, or a do-your-best condition. The results were startling. The uneducated crews, consisting primarily of black employees who participated in goal setting, set significantly higher goals and attained them more often than did those whose goals were assigned by their supervisor. Not surprisingly, their performance was higher. Crews with assigned goals performed no better than did those who were urged to do their best to improve their productivity. The performance of white, educationally advantaged workers was higher with assigned rather than participatively set goals, although the difference was not statistically significant. These results were precisely the opposite of what had been predicted.

Another study comparing participative and assigned goals was conducted with typists. The results supported findings obtained by researchers at General Electric years before. It did not matter so much *how* the goal was set. What mattered was *that* a goal was set. The study demonstrated that both assigned and participatively set goals led to substantial improvements in typing speed. The process by which these gains occurred, however, differed in the two groups.

In the participative group, employees insisted on setting very high goals regardless of whether they had attained their goal the previous week. Nevertheless, their productivity improved—an outcome consistent with the theory that high goals lead to high performance.

In the assigned-goal group, supervisors were highly supportive of employees. No criticism was given for failure to attain the goals. Instead, the supervisor lowered the goal after failure so that the employee would be certain to attain it. The goal was then raised gradually each week until the supervisor felt the employee was achieving his or her potential. The result? Feelings of accomplishment and achievement on the part of the worker and improved productivity for the company.

These basic findings were replicated in a subsequent study of engineers and scientists. Participative goal setting was superior to assigned goal setting only to the degree that it led to the setting of higher goals. Both participative and assigned-goal groups outperformed groups that were simply told to "do your best."

An additional experiment was conducted to validate the conclusion that participation in goal setting may be important only to the extent that it leads to the setting of difficult goals. It was performed in a laboratory setting in which the task was to brainstorm uses of wood. One group was asked to "do your best" to think of as many ideas as possible. A second group took part in deciding, with the experimenter, the specific number of ideas each person would generate. These goals were, in turn, assigned to individuals in a third group. In this way, goal difficulty was held constant between the assigned-goal and participative groups. Again, it was found that specific, difficult goals—whether assigned or set through participation—led to higher performance than did an abstract or generalized goal such as "do your best." And, when goal difficulty was held constant, there was no significant difference in the performance of those with assigned as compared with participatively set goals.

These results demonstrate that goal setting in industry works just as it does in the laboratory. Specific, challenging goals lead to better performance than do easy or vague goals, and feedback motivates higher performance only when it leads to the setting of higher goals.

It is important to note that participation is not only a motivational tool. When a manager has competent subordinates, participation is also a useful device for increasing the manager's knowledge and thereby improving decision quality. It can lead to better decisions through input from subordinates.

A representative sample of the results of field studies of goal setting conducted by Latham and others is shown in Table 5.1. Each of these ten studies compared the performance of employees given specific challenging goals with those given "do best" or no goals. Note that goal setting has been successful across a wide variety of jobs and industries. The effects of goal setting have been recorded for as long as seven years after the onset of the program, although the results of most studies have been followed up for only a few weeks or months. The median improvement in performance in the ten studies shown in Table 5.1 was 17 percent.

## A CRITICAL INCIDENTS SURVEY

To explore further the importance of goal setting in the work setting, Dr. Frank White conducted another study in two plants of a high-technology, multinational corporation on the East Coast. Seventy-one engineers, 50 managers, and 31 clerks were asked to describe a specific instance when they were especially productive and a specific instance when they were especially unproductive on their present jobs. Responses were classified according to a reliable coding scheme. Of primary interest here are the external events perceived by employees as being responsible for the high-productivity and low-productivity incidents. The results are shown in Table 5.2.

The first set of events—pursuing a specific goal, having a large amount of work, working under a deadline, or having an uninterrupted routine—accounted for more than half the high-productivity events. Similarly, the converse of these—goal blockage, having a small amount of work, lacking a deadline, and suffering work interruptions—accounted for nearly 60 percent of the low-productivity events. Note that the first set of four categories are all relevant to goal setting and the second set to a lack of goals or goal

**TABLE 5.1**
Representative Field Studies of Goal Setting

| Researcher(s) | Task | Duration of Study or of Significant Effects | Percent of Change in Performance★ |
|---|---|---|---|
| Blumenfeld and Leidy | Servicing soft drink coolers | Unspecified | +27 |
| Dockstader | Keypunching | 3 mos. | +27 |
| Ivancevich | Skilled technical jobs | 9 mos. | +15 |
| Ivancevich | Sales | 9 mos. | +24 |
| Kim and Hamner | Five telephone service jobs | 3 mos. | +13 |
| Latham and Baldes | Loading trucks | 9 mos.† | +26 |
| Latham and Yukl | Logging | 2 mos. | +18 |
| Latham and Yukl | Typing | 5 weeks | +11 |
| Migliore | Mass production | 2 years | +16 |
| Umstot, Bell, and Mitchell | Coding land parcels | 1–2 days‡ | +16 |

* Percentage changes were obtained by subtracting pre-goal-setting performance from post-goal-setting performance and dividing by pre-goal-setting performance. Different experimental groups were combined where appropriate. If a control group was available, the percentage figure represents the difference of the percentage changes between the experimental and control groups. If multiple performance measures were used, the median improvement on all measures was used. The authors would like to thank Dena Feren and Vicki McCaleb for performing these calculations.

† Performance remained high for seven years.

‡ Simulated organization.

**TABLE 5.2**
Events Perceived as Causing High and Low Productivity*

| Event | Percent of Times Event Caused | |
|---|---|---|
| | High Productivity | Low Productivity |
| Goal pursuit/Goal blockage | 17.1 | 23.0 |
| Large amount of work/Small amount of work | 12.5 | 19.0 |
| Deadline or schedule/No deadline | 15.1 | 3.3 |
| Smooth work routine/Interrupted routine | 5.9 | 14.5 |
| Intrinsic/Extrinsic factors | 50.6 | 59.8 |
| Interesting task/Uninteresting task | 17.1 | 11.2 |
| Increased responsibility/Decreased responsibility | 13.8 | 4.6 |
| Anticipated promotion/Promotion denied | 1.3 | 0.7 |
| Verbal recognition/Criticism | 4.6 | 2.6 |
| People/Company conditions | 36.8 | 19.1 |
| Pleasant personal relationships/Unpleasant personal relationships | 10.5 | 9.9 |
| Anticipated pay increase/Pay increase denied | 1.3 | 1.3 |
| Pleasant working conditions/Unpleasant working conditions | 0.7 | 0.7 |
| Other (miscellaneous) | — | 9.3 |

* $N = 152$ in this study by Frank White.

blockage. The goal category itself—that of pursuing an attainable goal or goal blockage—was the one most frequently used to describe high- and low-productivity incidents.

The next four categories, which are more pertinent to Frederick Herzberg's motivator-hygiene theory—task interest, responsibility, promotion, and recognition—are less important, accounting for 36.8 percent of the high-productivity incidents (the opposite of these four categories accounted for 19.1 percent of the lows). The remaining categories were even less important.

Employees were also asked to identify the responsible agent behind the events that had led to high and low productivity. In both cases, the employees themselves, their immediate supervisors, and the organization were the agents most frequently mentioned.

The concept of goal setting is a very simple one. Interestingly, however, we have gotten two contradictory types of reaction when the idea was introduced to managers. Some claimed it was so simple and self-evident that everyone, including themselves, already used it. This, we have found, is not true. Time after time we have gotten the following response from subordinates after goal setting was introduced: "This is the first time I knew what my supervisor expected of me on this job." Conversely, other managers have argued that the idea would not work, precisely *because* it is so simple (implying that something more radical and complex was needed). Again, results proved them wrong.

But these successes should not mislead managers into thinking that goal setting can be used without careful planning and forethought. Research and experience suggest that the best results are obtained when the following steps are followed:

*Setting the Goal.* The goal set should have two main characteristics. First, it should be specific rather than vague: "Increase sales by 10 percent" rather than "Try to improve sales." Whenever possible, there should be a time limit for goal accomplishment: "Cut costs by 3 percent in the next six months."

Second, the goal should be challenging yet reachable. If accepted, difficult goals lead to better performance than do easy goals. In contrast, if the goals are perceived as unreachable, employees will not accept them. Nor will employees get a sense of achievement from pursuing goals that are never attained. Employees with low self-confidence or ability should be given more easily attainable goals than those with high self-confidence and ability.

There are at least five possible sources of input, aside from the individual's self-confidence and ability, that can be used to determine the particular goal to set for a given individual.

The scientific management approach pioneered by Frederick W. Taylor uses time and motion study to determine a fair day's work. This is probably the most objective technique available, but it can be used only where the task is reasonably repetitive and standardized. Another drawback is that this method often leads to employee resistance, especially in cases where the new standard is substantially higher than previous performance and where rate changes are made frequently.

More readily accepted, although less scientific than time and motion study, are standards based on the average past performance of employees. This method was used successfully in some of our field studies. Most employees consider this approach fair but, naturally, in cases where past performance is far below capacity, beating that standard will be extremely easy.

Since goal setting is sometimes simply a matter of judgment, another technique we have used is to allow the goal to be set jointly by supervisor and subordinate. The participative approach may be less scientific than time and motion study, but it does lead to ready acceptance by both employee and immediate superior in addition to promoting role clarity.

External constraints often affect goal setting, especially among managers. For example, the goal to produce an item at a certain price may be dictated by the actions of competitors, and deadlines may be imposed externally in line with contract agreements. Legal regulations, such as attaining a certain reduction in pollution levels by a certain date, may affect goal setting as well. In these cases, setting the goal is not so much the problem as is figuring out a method of reaching it.

Finally, organizational goals set by the board of directors or upper management will influence the goals set by employees at lower levels. This is the essence of the MBO process.

Another issue that needs to be considered when setting goals is whether they should be designed for individuals or for groups. Rensis Likert and a number of other human relations experts argue for group goal setting on grounds that it promotes cooperation and team spirit. But one could argue that individual goals better promote individual responsibility and make it easier to appraise individual performance. The degree of task interdependence involved would also be a factor to consider.

*Obtaining Goal Commitment.* If goal setting is to work, then the manager must ensure that subordinates will accept and remain committed to the goals. Simple instruction backed by positive support and an absence of threats or intimidation were enough to ensure goal acceptance in most of our studies. Subordinates must perceive the goals as fair and reasonable and they must trust management, for if they perceive the goals as no more than a means of exploitation, they will be likely to reject the goals.

It may seem surprising that goal acceptance was achieved so readily in the field studies. Remember, however, that in all cases the employees were receiving wages or a salary (although these were not necessarily directly contingent on goal attainment). Pay in combination with the supervisor's benevolent authority and supportiveness were sufficient to bring about goal acceptance. Recent research indicates that whether goals are assigned or set participatively, supportiveness on the part of the immediate superior is critical. A supportive manager or supervisor does not use goals to threaten subordinates, but rather to clarify what is expected of them.

His or her role is that of a helper and goal facilitator.

As noted earlier, the employee gets a feeling of pride and satisfaction from the experience of reaching a challenging but fair performance goal. Success in reaching a goal also tends to reinforce acceptance of future goals. Once goal setting is introduced, informal competition frequently arises among the employees. This further reinforces commitment and may lead employees to raise the goals spontaneously. A word of caution here, however: We do not recommend setting up formal competition, as this may lead employees to place individual goals ahead of company goals. The emphasis should be on accomplishing the task, getting the job done, not "beating" the other person.

When employees resist assigned goals, they generally do so for one of two reasons. First, they may think they are incapable of reaching the goal because they lack confidence, ability, knowledge, and the like. Second, they may not see any personal benefit—either in terms of personal pride or in terms of external rewards like money, promotion, recognition—in reaching assigned goals.

There are various methods of overcoming employee resistance to goals. One possibility is more training designed to raise the employee's level of skill and self-confidence. Allowing the subordinate to participate in setting the goal—deciding on the goal level—is another method. This was found most effective among uneducated and minority group employees, perhaps because it gave them a feeling of control over their fate. Offering monetary bonuses or other rewards (recognition, time off) for reaching goals may also help.

The last two methods may be especially useful where there is a history of labor-management conflict and where employees have become accustomed to a lower level of effort than currently considered acceptable. Group incentives may also encourage goal acceptance, especially where there is a group goal, or when considerable cooperation is required.

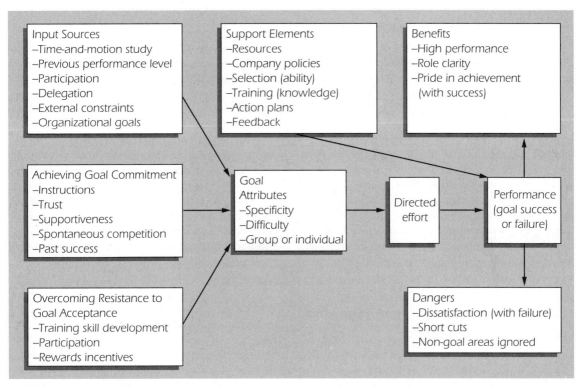

**FIGURE 5.1** Goal-Setting Model.

*Providing Support Elements.* A third step to take when introducing goal setting is to ensure the availability of necessary support elements. That is, the employee must be given adequate resources—money, equipment, time, help—as well as the freedom to utilize them in attaining goals, and company policies must not work to block goal attainment.

Before turning an employee loose with these resources, however, it's wise to do a quick check on whether conditions are optimum for reaching the goal set. First, the supervisor must make sure that the employee has sufficient ability and knowledge to be able to reach the goal. Motivation without knowledge is useless. This, of course, puts a premium on proper selection and training and requires that the supervisor know

the capabilities of subordinates when goals are assigned. Asking an employee to formulate an action plan for reaching the goal, as in MBO, is very useful, as it will indicate any knowledge deficiencies.

Second, the supervisor must ensure that the employee is provided with precise feedback so that he will know to what degree he's reaching or falling short of his goal and can thereupon adjust his level of effort or strategy accordingly. Recent research indicates that, while feedback is not a sufficient condition for improved performance, it is a necessary condition. A useful way to present periodic feedback is through the use of charts or graphs that plot performance over time.

Elements involved in taking the three steps described are shown in Figure 5.1, which illustrates in outline form our model of goal setting.

## CONCLUSION

We believe that goal setting is a simple, straightforward, and highly effective technique for motivating employee performance. It is a basic technique, a method on which most other methods depend for their motivational effectiveness. The currently popular technique of behavior modification, for example, is mainly goal setting plus feedback, dressed up in academic terminology.

However, goal setting is no panacea. It will not compensate for underpayment of employees or for poor management. Used incorrectly, goal setting may cause rather than solve problems. If, for example, the goals set are unfair, arbitrary, or unreachable, dissatisfaction and poor performance may result. If difficult goals are set without proper quality controls, quantity may be achieved at the expense of quality. If pressure for immediate results is exerted without regard to how they are attained, short-term improvement may occur at the expense of long-run profits. That is, such pressure often triggers the use of expedient and ultimately costly methods—such as dishonesty, high-pressure tactics, postponing of maintenance expenses, and so on—to attain immediate results. Furthermore, performance goals are more easily set in some areas than in others. It's all too easy, for example, to concentrate on setting readily measured production goals and ignore employee development goals. Like any other management tool, goal setting works only when combined with good managerial judgment.

## SELECTED BIBLIOGRAPHY

A summary of the early (mainly laboratory) research on goal setting may be found in E. A. Locke's "Toward a Theory of Task Motivation and Incentives" (*Organization Behavior and Human Performance,* May 1968). More recent reviews that include some of the early field studies are reported by G. P. Latham and G. A. Yukl's "Review of Research on the Application of Goal Setting in Organizations" (*Academy of Management Journal,* December 1975) and in R. M. Steers and L. W. Porter's "The Role of Task-Goal Attributes in Employee Performance" (*Psychological Bulletin,* July 1974).

An excellent historical discussion of management by objectives, including its relationship to goal-setting research, can be found in G. S. Odiorne's "MBO: A Backward Glance" (*Business Horizons,* October 1978).

A thorough review of the literature on participation, including the relationship of participation and goal setting, can be found in a chapter by E. A. Locke and D. M. Schweiger, "Participation in Decision-Making: One More Look," in B. M. Staw's edited work, *Research in Organizational Behavior* (Vol. 1, Greenwich, JAI Press, 1979). General Electric's famous research on the effect of participation in the appraisal interview is summarized in H. H. Meyer, E. Kay, and J. R. P. French, Jr.'s "Split Roles in Performance Appraisal" (*Harvard Business Review,* January-February 1965).

The relationship of goal setting to knowledge of results is discussed in E. A. Locke, N. Cartledge, and J. Koeppel's "Motivational Effects of Knowledge of Results: A Goal Setting Phenomenon?" (*Psychological Bulletin,* December 1968) and L. J. Becker's "Joint Effect of Feedback and Goal Setting on Performance: A Field Study of Residential Energy Conservation" (*Journal of Applied Psychology,* August 1978). Finally, the role of goal setting in virtually all theories of work motivation is documented in E. A. Locke's "The Ubiquity of the Technique of Goal Setting in Theories of and Approaches to Employee Motivation" (*Academy of Management Review,* July 1978).

# 6.   ON THE FOLLY OF REWARDING A, WHILE HOPING FOR B

Steven Kerr

Whether dealing with monkeys, rats, or human beings, it is hardly controversial to state that most organisms seek information concerning what activities are rewarded and then seek to do (or at least pretend to do) those things, often to the virtual exclusion of activities not rewarded. The extent to which this occurs of course will depend on the perceived attractiveness of the rewards offered, but neither operant nor expectancy theorists would quarrel with the essence of this notion.

Nevertheless, numerous examples exist of reward systems that are fouled up in that behaviors which are rewarded are those which the rewarder is trying to *discourage,* while the behavior he desires is not being rewarded at all.

In an effort to understand and explain this phenomenon, this paper presents examples from society, from organizations in general, and from profit-making firms in particular. Data from a manufacturing company and information from an insurance firm are examined to demonstrate the consequences of such reward systems for the organizations involved, and possible reasons why such reward systems continue to exist are considered.

## SOCIETAL EXAMPLES

### Politics

Official goals are "purposely vague and general and do not indicate...the host of decisions that must be made among alternative ways of achieving official goals and the priority of multiple goals..." (8, p. 66). They usually may be relied on to offend absolutely no one, and in this sense can be considered high-acceptance, low-quality goals. An example might be "build better schools." Operative goals are higher in quality but lower in acceptance, since they specify where the money will come from, what alternative goals will be ignored, etc.

The American citizenry supposedly wants its candidates for public office to set forth operative goals, making their proposed programs "perfectly clear," specifying sources and uses of funds, etc. However, since operative goals are lower in acceptance, and since aspirants to public office need acceptance (from at least 50.1 percent of the people), most politicians prefer to speak only of official goals, at least until after the election. They of course would agree to speak at the operative level if "punished" for not doing so. The electorate could do this by refusing to support candidates who do not speak at the operative level.

Instead, however, the American voter typically punishes (withholds support from) candidates who frankly discuss where the money will come from, rewards politicians who speak only of official goals, but hopes that candidates (despite the reward system) will discuss the issues operatively. It is academic whether it was moral for Nixon, for example, to refuse to discuss his 1968 "secret plan" to end the Vietnam war, his 1972 operative goals concerning the lifting of price controls, the reshuffling of his cabinet, etc. The point is that the reward system made such refusal rational.

It seems worth mentioning that no manuscript can adequately define what is "moral" and what

"On the Folly of Rewarding A, While Hoping for B" by Steven Kerr from *Academy of Management Journal*, 1975, 18, No. 4:769–83. Reprinted with permission.

is not. However, examination of costs and benefits, combined with knowledge of what motivates a particular individual, often will suffice to determine what for him is "rational."[1] If the reward system is so designed that it is irrational to be moral, this does not necessarily mean that immorality will result. But is this not asking for trouble?

## War

If some oversimplification may be permitted, let it be assumed that the primary goal of the organization (Pentagon, Luftwaffe, or whatever) is to win. Let it be assumed further that the primary goal of most individuals on the front lines is to get home alive. Then there appears to be an important conflict in goals—personally rational behavior by those at the bottom will endanger goal attainment by those at the top.

But not necessarily! It depends on how the reward system is set up. The Vietnam war was indeed a study of disobedience and rebellion, with terms such as "fragging" (killing one's own commanding officer) and "search and evade" becoming part of the military vocabulary. The difference in subordinates' acceptance of authority between World War II and Vietnam is reported to be considerable, and veterans of the Second World War often have been quoted as being outraged at the mutinous actions of many American soldiers in Vietnam.

Consider, however, some critical differences in the reward system in use during the two conflicts. What did the GI in World War II want? To go home. And when did he get to go home? When the war was won! If he disobeyed the orders to clean out the trenches and take the hills, the war would not be won and he would not go home. Furthermore, what were his chances of attaining his goal (getting home alive) if he obeyed the orders compared to his chances if he did not? What is being suggested is that the rational soldier in World War II, *whether patriotic or not,* probably found it expedient to obey.

Consider the reward system in use in Vietnam. What did the man at the bottom want? To go home. And when did he get to go home? When his tour of duty was over! This was the case *whether or not* the war was won. Furthermore, concerning the relative chance of getting home alive by obeying orders compared to the chance if they were disobeyed, it is worth noting that a mutineer in Vietnam was far more likely to be assigned rest and rehabilitation (on the assumption that fatigue was the cause) than he was to suffer any negative consequence.

In his description of the "zone of indifference," Barnard stated that "a person can and will accept a communication as authoritative only when . . . at the time of his decision, he believes it to be compatible with his personal interests as a whole" (1, p. 165). In light of the reward system used in Vietnam, would it not have been personally irrational for some orders to have been obeyed? Was not the military implementing a system which *rewarded* disobedience, while *hoping* that soldiers (despite the reward system) would obey orders?

## Medicine

Theoretically, a physician can make either of two types of error, and intuitively one seems as bad as the other. A doctor can pronounce a patient sick when he is actually well, thus causing him needless anxiety and expense, curtailment of enjoyable foods and activities, and even physical danger by subjecting him to needless medication and surgery. Alternately, a doctor can label a sick person well and thus avoid treating what may be a serious, even fatal ailment. It might be natural to

---

[1] In Simon's (10, pp. 76–77) terms, a decision is "subjectively rational" if it maximizes an individual's valued outcomes so far as his knowledge permits. A decision is "personally rational" if it is oriented toward the individual's goals.

conclude that physicians seek to minimize both types of error.

Such a conclusion would be wrong.[2] It is estimated that numerous Americans are presently afflicted with iatrogenic (physician *caused*) illnesses (9). This occurs when the doctor is approached by someone complaining of a few stray symptoms. The doctor classifies and organizes these symptoms, gives them a name, and obligingly tells the patient what further symptoms may be expected. This information often acts as a self-fulfilling prophecy, with the result that from that day on the patient for all practical purposes is sick.

Why does this happen? Why are physicians so reluctant to sustain a type 2 error (pronouncing a sick person well) that they will tolerate many type 1 errors? Again, a look at the reward system is needed. The punishments for a type 2 error are real: guilt, embarrassment, and the threat of lawsuit and scandal. On the other hand, a type 1 error (labeling a well person sick) "is sometimes seen as sound clinical practice, indicating a healthy conservative approach to medicine" (9, p. 69). Type 1 errors also are likely to generate increased income and a stream of steady customers who, being well in a limited physiological sense, will not embarrass the doctor by dying abruptly.

Fellow physicians and the general public therefore are really *rewarding* type 1 errors and at the same time *hoping* fervently that doctors will try not to make them.

## GENERAL ORGANIZATIONAL EXAMPLES

### Rehabilitation Centers and Orphanages

In terms of the prime beneficiary classification (2, p. 42) organizations such as these are supposed to exist for the "public-in-contact," that is, clients. The orphanage therefore theoretically is

interested in placing as many children as possible in good homes. However, often orphanages surround themselves with so many rules concerning adoption that it is nearly impossible to pry a child out of the place. Orphanages may deny adoption unless the applicants are a married couple, both of the same religion as the child, without history of emotional or vocational instability, with a specified minimum income and a private room for the child, etc.

If the primary goal is to place children in good homes, then the rules ought to constitute means toward that goal. Goal displacement results when these "means become ends-in-themselves that displace the original goals" (2, p. 229).

To some extent these rules are required by law. But the influence of the reward system on the orphanage's management should not be ignored. Consider, for example, that the:

1. Number of children enrolled often is the most important determinant of the size of the allocated budget.
2. Number of children under the director's care also will affect the size of his staff.
3. Total organizational size will determine largely the director's prestige at the annual conventions, in the community, etc.

Therefore, to the extent that staff size, total budget, and personal prestige are valued by the orphanage's executive personnel, it becomes rational for them to make it difficult for children to be adopted. After all, who wants to be the director of the smallest orphanage in the state?

If the reward system errs in the opposite direction, paying off only for placements, extensive goal displacement again is likely to result. A common example of vocational rehabilitation in many states, for example, consists of placing someone in a job for which he has little interest and few qualifications, for two months or so, and then "rehabilitating" him again in another

---

[2] In one study (4) of 14,867 films for signs of tuberculosis, 1,216 positive readings turned out to be clinically negative; only 24 negative readings proved clinically active, a ratio of 50 to 1.

position. Such behavior is quite consistent with the prevailing reward system, which pays off for the number of individuals placed in any position for 60 days or more. Rehabilitation counselors also confess to competing with one another to place relatively skilled clients, sometimes ignoring persons with few skills who would be harder to place. Extensively disabled clients find that counselors often prefer to work with those whose disabilities are less severe.[3]

## Universities

Society *hopes* that teachers will not neglect their teaching responsibilities but *rewards* them almost entirely for research and publications. This is most true at the large and prestigious universities. Clichés such as "good research and good teaching go together" notwithstanding, professors often find that they must choose between teaching and research oriented activities when allocating their time. Rewards for good teaching usually are limited to outstanding teacher awards, which are given to only a small percentage of good teachers and which usually bestow little money and fleeting prestige. Punishments for poor teaching also are rare.

Rewards for research and publications, on the other hand, and punishments for failure to accomplish these, are commonly administered by universities at which teachers are employed. Furthermore, publication oriented resumés usually will be well received at other universities, whereas teaching credentials, harder to document and quantify, are much less transferable. Consequently, it is rational for university teachers to concentrate on research, even if to the detriment of teaching and at the expense of their students.

By the same token, it is rational for students to act based upon the goal displacement which has occurred within universities concerning what they are rewarded for. If it is assumed that a primary goal of a university is to transfer knowledge from teacher to student, then grades become identifiable as a means toward that goal, serving as motivational, control, and feedback devices to expedite the knowledge transfer. Instead, however, the grades themselves have become much more important for entrance to graduate school, successful employment, tuition refunds, parental respect, etc., than the knowledge or lack of knowledge they are supposed to signify.

It therefore should come as no surprise that information has surfaced in recent years concerning fraternity files for examinations, term paper writing services, organized cheating at the service academies, and the like. Such activities constitute a personally rational response to a reward system which pays off for grades rather than knowledge.

## BUSINESS RELATED EXAMPLES

### Ecology

Assume that the president of XYZ Corporation is confronted with the following alternatives:

1. Spend $11 million for antipollution equipment to keep from poisoning fish in the river adjacent to the plant; or
2. Do nothing, in violation of the law, and assume a one-in-ten chance of being caught, with a resultant $1 million fine plus the necessity of buying the equipment.

Under this not unrealistic set of choices it requires no linear program to determine that XYZ Corporation can maximize its probabilities by flouting the law. Add the fact that XYZ's president is probably being rewarded (by creditors, stockholders, and other salient parts of his task environment) according to criteria totally unrelated to the number of fish poisoned, and his probable course of action becomes clear.

---

[3] Personal interviews conducted during 1972–1973.

## Evaluation of Training

It is axiomatic that those who care about a firm's well-being should insist that the organization get fair value for its expenditures. Yet it is commonly known that firms seldom bother to evaluate a new GRID, MBO, job enrichment program, or whatever, to see if the company is getting its money's worth. Why? Certainly it is not because people have not pointed out that this situation exists; numerous practitioner oriented articles are written each year to just this point.

The individuals (whether in personnel, manpower planning, or wherever) who normally would be responsible for conducting such evaluations are the same ones often charged with introducing the change effort in the first place. Having convinced top management to spend the money, they usually are quite animated afterwards in collecting arigorous vignettes and anecdotes about how successful the program was. The last thing many desire is a formal, systematic, and revealing evaluation. Although members of top management may actually *hope* for such systematic evaluation, their reward systems continue to *reward* ignorance in this area. And if the personnel department abdicates its responsibility, who is to step into the breach? The change agent himself? Hardly! He is likely to be too busy collecting anecdotal "evidence" of his own, for use with his next client.

## Miscellaneous

Many additional examples could be cited of systems which in fact are rewarding behaviors other than those supposedly desired by the rewarder. A few of these are described briefly below.

Most coaches disdain to discuss individual accomplishments, preferring to speak of teamwork, proper attitude, and a one-for-all spirit. Usually, however, rewards are distributed according to individual performance. The college basketball player who feeds his teammates instead of shooting will not compile impressive scoring statistics and is less likely to be drafted by the pros. The ballplayer who hits to right field to advance the runners will win neither the batting nor home run titles and will be offered smaller raises. It therefore is rational for players to think of themselves first and the team second.

In business organizations where rewards are dispensed for unit performance or for individual goals achieved without regard for overall effectiveness, similar attitudes often are observed. Under most Management by Objectives (MBO) systems, goals in areas where quantification is difficult often go unspecified. The organization therefore often is in a position where it *hopes* for employee effort in the areas of team building, interpersonal relations, creativity, etc., but it formally *rewards* none of these. In cases where promotions and raises are formally tied to MBO, the system itself contains a paradox in that it "asks employees to set challenging, risky goals, only to face smaller paychecks and possibly damaged careers if these goals are not accomplished" (5, p. 40).

It is *hoped* that administrators will pay attention to long-run costs and opportunities and will institute programs which will bear fruit later on. However, many organizational reward systems pay off for short-run sales and earnings only. Under such circumstances it is personally rational for officials to sacrifice long-term growth and profit (by selling off equipment and property, or by stifling research and development) for short-term advantages. This probably is most pertinent in the public sector, with the result that many public officials are unwilling to implement programs which will not show benefits by election time.

As a final, clear-cut example of a fouled-up reward system, consider the cost-plus contract or its next of kin, the allocation of next year's budget as a direct function of this year's expenditures. It probably is conceivable that those who award such budgets and contracts really hope for economy and prudence in spending. It is obvious, however, that adopting the proverb "to him who spends shall more be given," rewards not economy, but spending itself.

## TWO COMPANIES' EXPERIENCES

### A Manufacturing Organization

A Midwestern manufacturer of industrial goods had been troubled for some time by aspects of its organizational climate it believed dysfunctional. For research purposes, interviews were conducted with many employees, and a questionnaire was administered on a companywide basis, including plants and offices in several American and Canadian locations. The company strongly encouraged employee participation in the survey and made available time and space during the workday for completion of the instrument. All employees in attendance during the day of the survey completed the questionnaire. All instruments were collected directly by the researcher, who personally administered each session. Since no one employed by the firm handled the questionnaires, and since respondent names were not asked for, it seems likely that the pledge of anonymity given was believed.

A modified version of the Expect Approval scale (7) was included as part of the questionnaire. The instrument asked respondents to indicate the degree of approval or disapproval they could expect if they performed each of the described actions. A seven point Likert scale was used, with one indicating that the action would probably bring strong disapproval and seven signifying likely strong approval.

Although normative data for this scale from studies of other organizations are unavailable, it is possible to examine fruitfully the data obtained from this survey in several ways. First, it may be worth noting that the questionnaire data corresponded closely to information gathered through interviews. Furthermore, as can be seen from the results summarized in Table 6.1, sizable differences between various work units, and between employees at different job levels within the same work unit, were obtained. This suggests that response bias effects (social desirability in particular loomed as a potential concern) are not likely to be severe.

Most importantly, comparisons between scores obtained on the Expect Approval scale and a statement of problems which were the reason for the survey revealed that the same behaviors which managers in each division thought dysfunctional were those which lower-level employees claimed were rewarded. As compared to job levels 1 to 8 in Division B (see Table 6.1), those in Division A claimed a much higher acceptance by management of "conforming" activities. Between 31 and 37 percent of Division A employees at levels 1–8 stated that going along with the majority, agreeing with the boss, and staying on everyone's good side brought approval; only once (level 5–8 responses to one of the three items) did a majority suggest that such actions would generate disapproval.

Furthermore, responses from Division A workers at levels 1–4 indicate that behaviors geared toward risk avoidance were as likely to be rewarded as to be punished. Only at job levels 9 and above was it apparent that the reward system was positively reinforcing behaviors desired by top management. Overall, the same "tendencies toward conservatism and apple-polishing at the lower levels" which divisional management had complained about during the interviews were those claimed by subordinates to be the most rational course of action in light of the existing reward system. Management apparently was not getting the behaviors it was *hoping* for, but it certainly was getting the behaviors it was perceived by subordinates to be *rewarding*.

### An Insurance Firm

The Group Health Claims Division of a large eastern insurance company provides another rich illustration of a reward system which reinforces behaviors not desired by top management.

Attempting to measure and reward accuracy in paying surgical claims, the firm systematically keeps track of the number of returned checks and letters of complaint received from policyholders. However, underpayments are likely to provoke cries of outrage from the insured, while

**TABLE 6.1**
Summary of Two Divisions' Data Relevant to Conforming and Risk-Avoidance Behaviors
(extent to which subjects expect approval)

| Dimension | Item | Division and Sample | Total Responses | Percentage of Workers Responding | | |
|---|---|---|---|---|---|---|
| | | | | 1, 2, or 3 Disapproval | 4 | 5, 6, or 7 Approval |
| Risk avoidance | Making a risky decision based on the best information available at the time, but which turns out wrong | A, levels 1–4 (lowest) | 127 | 61 | 25 | 14 |
| | | A, levels 5–8 | 172 | 46 | 31 | 23 |
| | | A, levels 9 and above | 17 | 41 | 30 | 30 |
| | | B, levels 1–4 (lowest) | 31 | 58 | 26 | 16 |
| | | B, levels 5–8 | 19 | 42 | 42 | 16 |
| | | B, levels 9 and above | 10 | 50 | 20 | 30 |
| | Setting extremely high and challenging standards and goals and then narrowly failing to make them | A, levels 1–4 | 122 | 47 | 28 | 25 |
| | | A, levels 5–8 | 168 | 33 | 26 | 41 |
| | | A, levels 9+ | 17 | 24 | 6 | 70 |
| | | B, levels 1–4 | 31 | 48 | 23 | 29 |
| | | B, levels 5–8 | 18 | 17 | 33 | 50 |
| | | B, levels 9+ | 10 | 30 | 0 | 70 |
| | Setting goals which are extremely easy to make and then making them | A, levels 1–4 | 124 | 35 | 30 | 35 |
| | | A, levels 5–8 | 171 | 47 | 27 | 26 |
| | | A, levels 9+ | 17 | 70 | 24 | 6 |
| | | B, levels 1–4 | 31 | 58 | 26 | 16 |
| | | B, levels 5–8 | 19 | 63 | 16 | 21 |
| | | B, levels 9+ | 10 | 80 | 0 | 20 |
| Conformity | Being a "yes man" and always agreeing with the boss | A, levels 1–4 | 126 | 46 | 17 | 37 |
| | | A, levels 5–8 | 180 | 54 | 14 | 31 |
| | | A, levels 9+ | 17 | 88 | 12 | 0 |
| | | B, levels 1–4 | 32 | 53 | 28 | 19 |
| | | B, levels 5–8 | 19 | 68 | 21 | 11 |
| | | B, levels 9+ | 10 | 80 | 10 | 10 |
| | Always going along with the majority | A, levels 1–4 | 125 | 40 | 25 | 35 |
| | | A, levels 5–8 | 173 | 47 | 21 | 32 |
| | | A, levels 9+ | 17 | 70 | 12 | 18 |
| | | B, levels 1–4 | 31 | 61 | 23 | 16 |
| | | B, levels 5–8 | 19 | 68 | 11 | 21 |
| | | B, levels 9+ | 10 | 80 | 10 | 10 |
| | Being careful to stay on the good side of everyone, so that everyone agrees that you are a great guy | A, levels 1–4 | 124 | 45 | 18 | 37 |
| | | A, levels 5–8 | 173 | 45 | 22 | 33 |
| | | A, levels 9+ | 17 | 64 | 6 | 30 |
| | | B, levels 1–4 | 31 | 54 | 23 | 23 |
| | | B, levels 5–8 | 19 | 73 | 11 | 16 |
| | | B, levels 9+ | 10 | 80 | 10 | 10 |

overpayments often are accepted in courteous silence. Since it often is impossible to tell from the physician's statement which of two surgical procedures, with different allowable benefits, was performed, and since writing for clarifications will interfere with other standards used by the firm concerning "percentage of claims paid within two days of receipt," the new hire in more than one claims section is soon acquainted with the informal norm: "When in doubt, pay it out!"

The situation would be even worse were it not for the fact that other features of the firm's reward system tend to neutralize those described. For example, annual "merit" increases are given to all employees, in one of the following three amounts:

1. If the worker is "outstanding" (a select category, into which no more than two employees per section may be placed): 5 percent.
2. If the worker is "above average" (normally all workers not "outstanding" are so rated): 4 percent.
3. If the worker commits gross acts of negligence and irresponsibility for which he might be discharged in many other companies: 3 percent.

Now, since (a) the difference between the 5 percent theoretically attainable through hard work and the 4 percent attainable merely by living until the review date is small and (b) since insurance firms seldom dispense much of a salary increase in cash (rather, the worker's insurance benefits increase, causing him to be further overinsured), many employees are rather indifferent to the possibility of obtaining the extra one percent reward and therefore tend to ignore the norm concerning indiscriminate payments.

However, most employees are not indifferent to the rule which states that, should absences or latenesses total three or more in any six-month period, the entire 4 or 5 percent due at the next "merit" review must be forfeited. In this sense the firm may be described as hoping for performance, while rewarding attendance. What it gets, of course, is attendance. (If the absence-lateness rule appears to the reader to be stringent, it really

is not. The company counts "times" rather than "days" absent, and a ten-day absence therefore counts the same as one lasting two days. A worker in danger of accumulating a third absence within six months merely has to remain ill (away from work) during his second absence until his first absence is more than six months old. The limiting factor is that at some point his salary ceases, and his sickness benefits take over. This usually is sufficient to get the younger workers to return, but for those with 20 or more years' service, the company provides sickness benefits of 90 percent of normal salary, tax-free! Therefore....)

## CAUSES

Extremely diverse instances of systems which reward behavior A although the rewarder apparently hopes for behavior B have been given. These are useful to illustrate the breadth and magnitude of the phenomenon, but the diversity increases the difficulty of determining commonalities and establishing causes. However, four general factors may be pertinent to an explanation of why fouled up reward systems seem to be so prevalent.

### Fascination with an "Objective" Criterion

It has been mentioned elsewhere that:

*Most "objective" measures of productivity are objective only in that their subjective elements are (a) determined in advance, rather than coming into play at the time of the formal evaluation, and (b) well concealed on the rating instrument itself. Thus industrial firms seeking to devise objective rating systems first decide, in an arbitrary manner, what dimensions are to be rated, ... usually including some items having little to do with organizational effectiveness while excluding others that do. Only then does Personnel Division churn out official-looking documents on which all dimensions chosen to be rated are assigned point values, categories, or whatever (6, p. 92).*

Nonetheless, many individuals seek to establish simple, quantifiable standards against which to measure and reward performance. Such efforts may be successful in highly predictable areas within an organization but are likely to cause goal displacement when applied anywhere else. Overconcern with attendance and lateness in the insurance firm and with the number of people placed in the vocational rehabilitation division may have been largely responsible for the problems described in those organizations.

## Overemphasis on Highly Visible Behaviors

Difficulties often stem from the fact that some parts of the task are highly visible while other parts are not. For example, publications are easier to demonstrate than teaching, and scoring baskets and hitting home runs are more readily observable than feeding teammates and advancing base runners. Similarly, the adverse consequences of pronouncing a sick person well are more visible than those sustained by labeling a well person sick. Team-building and creativity are other examples of behaviors which may not be rewarded simply because they are hard to observe.

## Hypocrisy

In some of the instances described the rewarder may have been getting the desired behavior, notwithstanding claims that the behavior was not desired. This may be true, for example, of management's attitude toward apple-polishing in the manufacturing firm (a behavior which subordinates felt was rewarded, despite management's avowed dislike of the practice). This also may explain politicians' unwillingness to revise the penalties for disobedience of ecology laws, and the failure of top management to devise reward systems which would cause systematic evaluation of training and development programs.

## Emphasis on Morality or Equity Rather than Efficiency

Sometimes consideration of other factors prevents the establishment of a system which rewards behaviors desired by the rewarder. The felt obli-

gation of many Americans to vote for one candidate or another, for example, may impair their ability to withhold support from politicians who refuse to discuss the issues. Similarly, the concern for spreading the risks and costs of wartime military service may outweigh the advantage to be obtained by committing personnel to combat until the war is over.

It should be noted that only with respect to the first two causes are reward systems really paying off for other than desired behaviors. In the case of the third and fourth causes the system *is* rewarding behaviors desired by the rewarder, and the systems are fouled up only from the standpoints of those who believe the rewarder's public statements (cause 3), or those who seek to maximize efficiency rather than other outcomes (cause 4).

## CONCLUSIONS

Modern organization theory requires a recognition that the members of organizations and society possess divergent goals and motives. It therefore is unlikely that managers and their subordinates will seek the same outcomes. Three possible remedies for this potential problem are suggested.

### Selection

It is theoretically possible for organizations to employ only those individuals whose goals and motives are wholly consonant with those of management. In such cases the same behaviors judged by subordinates to be rational would be perceived by management as desirable. State-of-the-art reviews of selection techniques, however, provide scant grounds for hope that such an approach would be successful (for example, see 12).

### Training

Another theoretical alternative is for the organization to admit those employees whose goals are not consonant with those of management and then, through training, socialization, or whatever, alter employee goals to make them consonant. However, research on the effectiveness of such training programs, though limited, provides further grounds for pessimism (for example, see 3).

## Altering the Reward System

What would have been the result if:

1. Nixon had been assured by his advisors that he could not win reelection except by discussing the issues in detail?

2. Physicians' conduct was subjected to regular examination by review boards for type 1 errors (calling healthy people ill) and to penalties (fines, censure, etc.) for errors of either type?

3. The President of XYZ Corporation had to choose between *(a)* spending $11 million dollars for antipollution equipment, and *(b)* incurring a 50-50 chance of going to jail for five years?

Managers who complain that their workers are not motivated might do well to consider the possibility that they have installed reward systems which are paying off for behaviors other than those they are seeking. This, in part, is what happened in Vietnam, and this is what regularly frustrates societal efforts to bring about honest politicians, civic-minded managers, etc. This certainly is what happened in both the manufacturing and the insurance companies.

A first step for such managers might be to find out what behaviors currently are being rewarded. Perhaps an instrument similar to that used in the manufacturing firm could be useful for this purpose. Chances are excellent that these managers will be surprised by what they find—that their firms are not rewarding what they assume they are. In fact, such undesirable behavior by organi-

zational members as they have observed may be explained largely by the reward systems in use.

This is not to say that all organizational behavior is determined by formal rewards and punishments. Certainly it is true that in the absence of formal reinforcement some soldiers will be patriotic, some presidents will be ecology minded, and some orphanage directors will care about children. The point, however, is that in such cases the rewarder is not *causing* the behaviors desired but is only a fortunate bystander. For an organization to *act* upon its members, the formal reward system should positively reinforce desired behaviors, not constitute an obstacle to be overcome.

It might be wise to underscore the obvious fact that there is nothing really new in what has been said. In both theory and practice these matters have been mentioned before. Thus in many states Good Samaritan laws have been installed to protect doctors who stop to assist a stricken motorist. In states without such laws it is commonplace for doctors to refuse to stop, for fear of involvement in a subsequent lawsuit. In college basketball additional penalties have been instituted against players who foul their opponents deliberately. It has long been argued by Milton Friedman and others that penalties should be altered so as to make it irrational to disobey the ecology laws, and so on.

By altering the reward system the organization escapes the necessity of selecting only desirable people or of trying to alter undesirable ones. In Skinnerian terms (as described in 11, p. 704), "As for responsibility and goodness—as commonly defined—no one . . . would want or need them. They refer to a man's behaving well despite the absence of positive reinforcement that is obviously sufficient to explain it. Where such reinforcement exists, 'no one needs goodness.' "

## REFERENCE NOTES

1. Barnard, Chester I. *The functions of the executive.* Cambridge, Mass.: Harvard University Press, 1964.

2. Blau, Peter M., and Scott, W. Richard. *Formal organizations.* San Francisco: Chandler, 1962.

3. Fiedler, Fred E. Predicting the effects of leadership training and experience from the contingency model, *Journal of Applied Psychology*, 1972, 56:114–19.

4. Garland, L. H. Studies of the accuracy of diagnostic procedures, *American Journal Roentgenological, Radium Therapy Nuclear Medicine*, 1959, 82:25–38.

5. Kerr, Steven. Some modifications in MBO as an OD strategy, *Academy of Management Proceedings*, 1973:39–42.

6. Kerr, Steven. What price objectivity? *American Sociologist*, 1973, 8:92–93.

7. Litwin, G. H., and Stringer, R. A., Jr. *Motivation and organizational climate.* Boston: Harvard University Press, 1968.

8. Perrow, Charles. The analysis of goals in complex organizations, in A. Etzioni (ed.), *Readings on modern organizations.* Englewood Cliffs, N.J.: Prentice-Hall, 1969.

9. Scheff, Thomas J. Decision rules, types of error, and their consequences in medical diagnosis, in F. Massarik and P. Ratoosh (eds.), *Mathematical explorations in behavioral science.* Homewood, Ill.: Richard D. Irwin, Inc., 1965.

10. Simon, Herbert A. *Administrative Behavior.* New York: Free Press, 1957.

11. Swanson, G. E. Review symposium: Beyond freedom and dignity, *American Journal of Sociology*, 1972, 78:702–705.

12. Webster, E. *Decision making in the employment interview.* Montreal Industrial Relations Center, McGill University, 1964.

# 7.  A NEW STRATEGY FOR JOB ENRICHMENT

J. Richard Hackman, Greg Oldham, Robert Janson, and Kenneth Purdy

Practitioners of job enrichment have been living through a time of excitement, even euphoria. Their craft has moved from the psychology and management journals to the front page and the Sunday supplement. Job enrichment, which began with the pioneering work of Herzberg and his associates, originally was intended as a means to increase the motivation and satisfaction of people at work—and to improve productivity in the bargain.[1-5] Now it is being acclaimed in the popular press as a cure for problems ranging from inflation to drug abuse.

Much current writing about job enrichment is enthusiastic, sometimes even messianic, about what it can accomplish. But the hard questions of exactly what should be done to improve jobs, and how, tend to be glossed over. Lately, because the harder questions have not been dealt with adequately, critical winds have begun to blow. Job enrichment has been described as yet another "management fad," as "nothing new," even as a fraud. And reports of job-enrichment failures are beginning to appear in management and psychology journals.

This article attempts to redress the excesses that have characterized some of the recent writings about job enrichment. As the technique increases in popularity as a management tool, top managers inevitably will find themselves making decisions about its use. The intent of this paper is to help both managers and behavioral scientists become better able to make those decisions on a solid basis of fact and data.

Succinctly stated, we present here a new strategy for going about the redesign of work. The strategy is based on three years of collaborative work and cross-fertilization among the authors—two of whom are academic researchers and two of whom are active practitioners in job enrichment. Our approach is new, but it has been tested in many organizations. It draws on the contributions of both management practice and psychological theory, but it is firmly in the middle ground between them. It builds on and complements previous work by Herzberg and others, but provides for the first time a set of tools for *diagnosing* existing jobs—and a map for translating the diagnostic results into specific action steps for change.

What we have, then, is the following:

1. A theory that specifies when people will get personally "turned on" to their work. The theory shows what kinds of jobs are most likely to generate excitement and commitment about work, and what kinds of employees it works best for.

2. A set of action steps for job enrichment based on the theory, which prescribe in concrete terms what to do to make jobs more motivating for the people who do them.

3. Evidence that the theory holds water and that it can be used to bring about measurable—and sometimes dramatic—improvements in employee work behavior, in job satisfaction and in the financial performance of the organizational unit involved.

## THE THEORY BEHIND THE STRATEGY

### What Makes People Get Turned on to Their Work?

For workers who are really prospering in their jobs, work is likely to be a lot like play. Consider, for example, a golfer at a driving range, practicing to get rid of a hook. His activity is *meaningful* to him; he has chosen to do it because he gets a "kick" from testing his skills by playing the game. He knows that he alone is *responsible* for what happens when he hits the ball. And he has *knowledge of the results* within a few seconds.

Behavioral scientists have found that the three "psychological states" experienced by the golfer in the above example also are critical in determining a person's motivation and satisfaction on the job.

1. *Experienced meaningfulness:* The individual must perceive his work as worthwhile or important by some system of values he accepts.

2. *Experienced responsibility:* He must believe that he personally is accountable for the outcomes of his efforts.

3. *Knowledge of results:* He must be able to determine, on some fairly regular basis, whether or not the outcomes of his work are satisfactory.

When these three conditions are present, a person tends to feel very good about himself when he performs well. And those good feelings will prompt him to try to continue to do well—so he can continue to earn the positive feelings in the future. That is what is meant by "internal motivation"—being turned on to one's work because of the positive internal feelings that are generated by doing well, rather than being dependent on external factors (such as incentive pay or compliments from the boss) for the motivation to work effectively.

What if one of the three psychological states is missing? Motivation drops markedly. Suppose, for example, that our golfer has settled in at the driving range to practice for a couple of hours. Suddenly a fog drifts in over the range. He can no longer see if the ball starts to tail off to the left a hundred yards out. The satisfaction he got from hitting straight down the middle—and the moti-

vation to try to correct something whenever he didn't—are both gone. If the fog stays, it's likely that he soon will be packing up his clubs.

The relationship between the three psychological states and on-the-job outcomes is illustrated in Figure 7.1. When all three are high, then internal work motivation, job satisfaction, and work quality are high, and absenteeism and turnover are low.

## What Job Characteristics Make It Happen?

Recent research has identified five "core" characteristics of jobs that elicit the psychological states

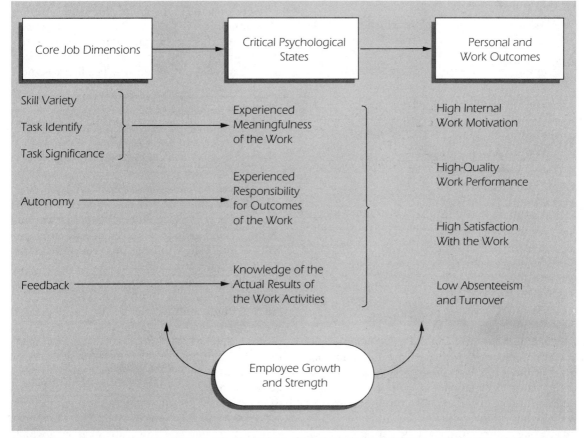

**FIGURE 7.1** Relationships Among Core Job Dimensions, Critical Psychological States, and On-the-Job Outcomes.

described above.[6-8] These five core job dimensions provide the key to objectively measuring jobs and to changing them so that they have high potential for motivating people who do them.

*Toward Meaningful Work.* Three of the five core dimensions contribute to a job's meaningfulness for the worker:

1. Skill variety—the degree to which a job requires the worker to perform activities that challenge his skills and abilities. When even a single skill is involved, there is at least a seed of potential meaningfulness. When several are involved, the job has the potential of appealing to more of the whole person, and also of avoiding the monotony of performing the same task repeatedly, no matter how much skill it may require.

2. Task identity—the degree to which the job requires completion of a "whole" and identifiable piece of work—doing a job from beginning to end with a visible outcome. For example, it is clearly more meaningful to an employee to build complete toasters than to attach electrical cord after electrical cord, especially if he never sees a completed toaster. (Note that the whole job, in this example, probably would involve greater skill variety as well as task identity.)

3. Task significance—the degree to which the job has a substantial and perceivable impact on the lives of other people, whether in the immediate organization or the world at large. The worker who tightens nuts on aircraft brake assemblies is more likely to perceive his work as significant than the worker who fills small boxes with paper clips—even though the skill levels involved may be comparable.

Each of these three job dimensions represents an important route to experienced meaningfulness. If the job is high in all three, the worker is quite likely to experience his job as very meaningful. It is not necessary, however, for a job to be very high in all three dimensions. If the job is low in any one of them, there will be a drop in overall experienced meaningfulness. But even when two dimensions are low the worker may find the job meaningful if the third is high enough.

*Toward Personal Responsibility.* A fourth core dimension leads a worker to experience increased responsibility in his job. This is *autonomy,* the degree to which the job gives the worker freedom, independence, and discretion in scheduling work and determining how he will carry it out. People in highly autonomous jobs know that they are personally responsible for successes and failures. To the extent that their autonomy is high, then, how the work goes will be felt to depend more on the individual's own efforts and initiatives—rather than on detailed instructions from the boss or from a manual of job procedures.

*Toward Knowledge of Results.* The fifth and last core dimension is *feedback.* This is the degree to which a worker, in carrying out the work activities required by the job, gets information about the effectiveness of his efforts. Feedback is most powerful when it comes directly from the work itself—for example, when a worker has the responsibility for gauging and otherwise checking a component he has just finished, and learns in the process that he has lowered his reject rate by meeting specifications more consistently.

*The Overall "Motivating Potential" of a Job.* Figure 7.1 shows how the five core dimensions combine to affect the psychological states that are critical in determining whether or not an employee will be internally motivated to work effectively. Indeed, when using an instrument to be described later, it is possible to compute a "motivating potential score" (MPS) for any job. The MPS provides a single summary index of the degree to which the objective characteristics of the job will prompt high internal work motivation. Following the theory outlined above, a job high in motivating potential must be high in at least one (and hopefully more) of the three dimensions that lead to experienced meaningfulness and high in both autonomy and feedback as well. The MPS provides a quantitative index of the degree to which this is in fact the case (see Appendix for detailed formula). As will be seen later, the MPS can be very useful in diagnosing jobs and in assessing the effectiveness of job-enrichment activities.

## Does the Theory Work for Everybody?

Unfortunately not. Not everyone is able to become internally motivated in his work, even when the motivating potential of a job is very high indeed.

Research has shown that the *psychological needs* of people are very important in determining who can (and who cannot) become internally motivated at work. Some people have strong needs for personal accomplishment, for learning and developing themselves beyond where they are now, for being stimulated and challenged, and so on. These people are high in "growth-need strength."

Figure 7.2 shows diagrammatically the proposition that individual growth needs have the power to moderate the relationship between the characteristics of jobs and work outcomes. Many workers with high growth needs will turn on eagerly when they have jobs that are high in the core dimensions. Workers whose growth needs are not so strong may respond less eagerly—or, at first, even balk at being "pushed" or "stretched" too far.

Psychologists who emphasize human potential argue that everyone has within him at least a spark of the need to grow and develop personally. Steadily accumulating evidence shows, however, that unless that spark is pretty strong, chances are it will get snuffed out by one's experiences in typical organizations. So, a person who has worked for twenty years in stultifying jobs may find it difficult or impossible to become internally motivated overnight when given the opportunity.

We should be cautious, however, about creating rigid categories of people based on their measured growth-need strength at any particular time. It is true that we can predict from these

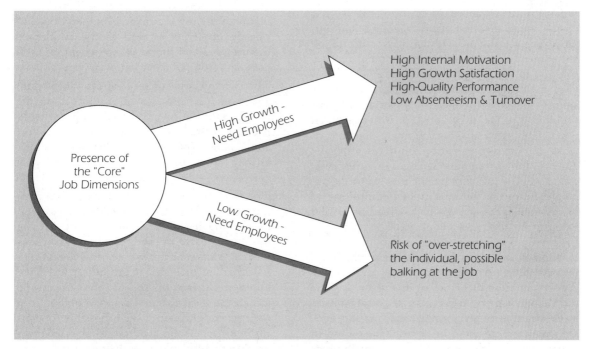

**FIGURE 7.2 The Moderating Effect of Employee Growth-Need Strength.**

measures who is likely to become internally motivated on a job and who will be less willing or able to do so. But what we do not know yet is whether or not the growth-need "spark" can be rekindled for those individuals who have had their growth needs dampened by years of growth-depressing experience in their organizations.

Since it is often the organization that is responsible for currently low levels of growth desires, we believe that the organization also should provide the individual with the chance to reverse that trend whenever possible, even if that means putting a person in a job where he may be "stretched" more than he wants to be. He can always move back later to the old job—and in the meantime the embers of his growth needs just might burst back into flame, to his surprise and pleasure, and for the good of the organization.

## FROM THEORY TO PRACTICE: A TECHNOLOGY FOR JOB ENRICHMENT

When job enrichment fails, it often fails because of inadequate *diagnosis* of the target job and employees' reactions to it. Often, for example, job enrichment is assumed by management to be a solution to "people problems" on the job and is implemented even though there has been no diagnostic activity to indicate that the root of the problem is in fact how the work is designed. At other times, some diagnosis is made—but it provides no concrete guidance about what specific aspects of the job require change. In either case, the success of job enrichment may wind up depending more on the quality of the intuition of the change agent—or his luck—than on a solid base of data about the people and the work.

In the paragraphs to follow, we outline a new technology for use in job enrichment which explicitly addresses the diagnostic as well as the action components of the change process. The technology has two parts: (1) a set of diagnostic tools that are useful in evaluating jobs and people's reactions to them prior to change—and in pinpointing exactly what aspects of specific jobs are most critical to a successful change attempt;

and (2) a set of "implementing concepts" that provide concrete guidance for action steps in job enrichment. The implementing concepts are tied directly to the diagnostic tools; the output of the diagnostic activity specifies which action steps are likely to have the most impact in a particular situation.

### The Diagnostic Tools

Central to the diagnostic procedure we propose is a package of instruments to be used by employees, supervisors, and outside observers in assessing the target job and employees' reactions to it.[9] These instruments gauge the following:

1. The objective characteristics of the jobs themselves, including both an overall indication of the "motivating potential" of the job as it exists (that is, the MPS score) and the score of the job on each of the five core dimensions described previously. Because knowing the strengths and weaknesses of the job is critical to any work-redesign effort, assessments of the job are made by supervisors and outside observers as well as the employees themselves—and the final assessment of a job uses data from all three sources.

2. The current levels of motivation, satisfaction, and work performance of employees on the job. In addition to satisfaction with the work itself, measures are taken of how people feel about other aspects of the work setting, such as pay, supervision, and relationships with coworkers.

3. The level of growth-need strength of the employees. As indicated earlier, employees who have strong growth needs are more likely to be more responsive to job enrichment than employees with weak growth needs. Therefore, it is important to know at the outset just what kinds of satisfactions the people who do the job are (and are not) motivated to obtain from their work. This will make it possible to identify which persons are best to start changes with and which may need help in adapting to the newly enriched job.

What then, might be the actual steps one would take in carrying out a job diagnosis using these tools? Although the approach to any particular diagnosis depends upon the specifics of the particular work situation involved, the sequence of questions listed below is fairly typical.

*Step 1. Are Motivation and Satisfaction Central to the Problem?* Sometimes organizations undertake job enrichment to improve the work motivation and satisfaction of employees when in fact the real problem with work performance lies elsewhere—for example, in a poorly designed production system, in an error-prone computer, and so on. The first step is to examine the scores of employees on the motivation and satisfaction portions of the diagnostic instrument. (The questionnaire taken by the employees is called the Job Diagnostic Survey and will be referred to hereafter as the JDS.) If motivation and satisfaction are problematic, the change agent would continue to Step 2; if not, he would look to other aspects of the work situation to identify the real problem.

*Step 2. Is the Job Low in Motivating Potential?* To answer this question, one would examine the motivating potential score of the target job and compare it to the MPS's of other jobs to determine whether or not *the job itself* is a probable cause of the motivational problems documented in Step 1. If the job turns out to be low on the MPS, one would continue to Step 3; if it scores high, attention should be given to other possible reasons for the motivational difficulties (such as the pay system, the nature of supervision, and so on).

*Step 3. What Specific Aspects of the Job Are Causing the Difficulty?* This step involves examining the job on each of the five core dimensions to pinpoint the specific strengths and weaknesses of the job as it is currently structured. It is useful at this stage to construct a "profile" of the target job, to make visually apparent where improvements need to be made. An illustrative profile for two jobs (one "good" job and one job needing improvement) is shown in Figure 7.3.

Job A is an engineering maintenance job and is high on all of the core dimensions; the MPS of this job is a very high 260. (MPS scores can range from 1 to about 350; an "average" score would be about 125.) Job enrichment would not be recommended for this job; if employees working on the job were unproductive and unhappy, the reasons are likely to have little to do with the nature or design of the work itself.

Job B, on the other hand, has many problems. This job involves the routine and repetitive processing of checks in the "back room" of a bank. The MPS is 30, which is quite low—and indeed, would be even lower if it were not for the moderately high task significance of the job. (Task significance is moderately high because the people are handling large amounts of other people's money, and therefore the quality of their efforts potentially has important consequences for their unseen clients.) The job provides the individuals with very little direct feedback about how effectively they are doing it; the employees have little autonomy in how they go about doing the job; and the job is moderately low in both skill variety and task identity.

For Job B, then, there is plenty of room for improvement—and many avenues to examine in planning job changes. For still other jobs, the avenues for change often turn out to be considerably more specific: for example, feedback and autonomy may be reasonably high, but one or more of the core dimensions that contribute to the experienced meaningfulness of the job (skill variety, task identity, and task significance) may be low. In such a case, attention would turn to ways to increase the standing of the job on these latter three dimensions.

*Step 4. How "Ready" Are the Employees for Change?* Once it has been documented that there is need for improvement in the job—and the particularly troublesome aspects of the job have been identified then it is time to begin to think about the specific action steps which will be taken to enrich the job. An important factor in such planning is the level of growth needs of the employees, since employees high on growth

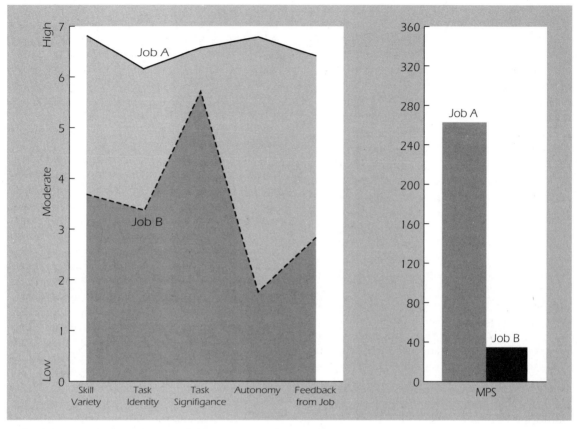

**FIGURE 7.3** The JDS Diagnostic Profile for a "Good" and a "Bad" Job.

needs usually respond more readily to job enrichment than do employees with little need for growth. The JDS provides a direct measure of the growth-need strength of the employees. This measure can be very helpful in planning how to introduce the changes to the people (for instance, cautiously versus dramatically), and in deciding who should be among the first group of employees to have their jobs changed.

In actual use of the diagnostic package, additional information is generated which supplements and expands the basic diagnostic questions outlined above. The point of the above discussion is merely to indicate the kinds of questions which we believe to be most important in diagnosing a job prior to changing it. We now turn to how the diagnostic conclusions are translated into specific job changes.

## The Implementing Concepts

Five "implementing concepts" for job enrichment are identified and discussed below.[10] Each one is a specific action step aimed at improving both the quality of the working experience for the individual and his work productivity. They are (1) forming natural work units; (2) combining tasks; (3) establishing client relationships; (4) vertical loading; (5) opening feedback channels.

The links between the implementing concepts and the core dimensions are shown in Figure 7.4—which illustrates our theory of job

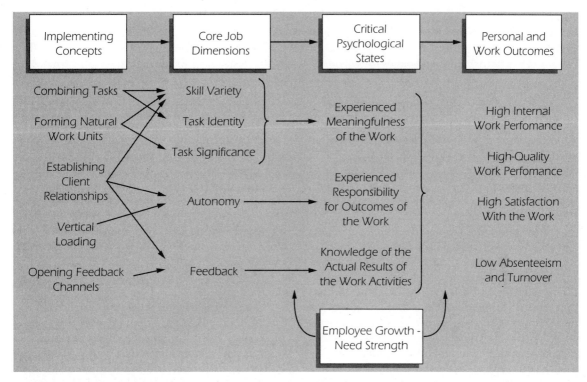

**FIGURE 7.4 The Full Model: How Use of the Implementing Concepts Can Lead to Positive Outcomes.**

enrichment, ranging from the concrete action steps through the core dimensions and the psychological states to the actual personal and work outcomes.

After completing the diagnosis of a job, a change agent would know which of the core dimensions were most in need of remedial attention. He could then turn to Figure 7.4 and select those implementing concepts that specifically deal with the most troublesome parts of the existing job. How this would take place in practice will be seen below.

*Forming Natural Work Units.* The notion of distributing work in some logical way may seem to be an obvious part of the design of any job. In many cases, however, the logic is one imposed by just about any consideration except job-holder satisfaction and motivation. Such considerations include technological dictates, level of worker

training or experience, "efficiency" as defined by industrial engineering, and current workload. In many cases the cluster of tasks a worker faces during a typical day or week is natural to anyone *but* the worker.

For example, suppose that a typing pool (consisting of one supervisor and ten typists) handles all work for one division of a company. Jobs are delivered in rough draft or dictated form to the supervisor, who distributes them as evenly as possible among the typists. In such circumstances the individual letters, reports, and other tasks performed by a given typist in one day or week are randomly assigned. There is no basis for identifying with the work or the person or department for whom it is performed, or for placing any personal value upon it.

The principle underlying natural units of work, by contrast, is "ownership"—a worker's sense of continuing responsibility for an identifiable body of work. Two steps are involved in creating natural work units. The first is to identify the basic work items. In the typing pool, for example, the items might be "pages to be typed." The second step is to group the items in natural categories. For example, each typist might be assigned continuing responsibility for all jobs requested by one or several specific departments. The assignments should be made, of course, in such a way that workloads are about equal in the long run. (For example, one typist might end up with all the work from one busy department, while another handles jobs from several smaller units.)

At this point we can begin to see specifically how the job-design principles relate to the core dimensions (cf. Figure 7.4). The ownership fostered by natural units of work can make the difference between a feeling that work is meaningful and rewarding and the feeling that it is irrelevant and boring. As the diagram shows, natural units of work are directly related to two of the core dimensions: task identity and task significance.

A typist whose work is assigned naturally rather than randomly—say, by departments—has a much greater chance of performing a whole job to completion. Instead of typing one section of a large report, the individual is likely to type the whole thing, with knowledge of exactly what the product of the work is (task identity). Furthermore, over time the typist will develop a growing sense of how the work affects coworkers in the department serviced (task significance).

*Combining Tasks.* The very existence of a pool made up entirely of persons whose sole function is typing reflects a fractionalization of jobs that has been a basic precept of "scientific management." Most obvious in assembly-line work, fractionalization has been applied to nonmanufacturing jobs as well. It is typically justified by efficiency, which is usually defined in terms of either low costs or some time-and-motion type of criteria.

It is hard to find fault with measuring efficiency ultimately in terms of cost-effectiveness. In doing so, however, a manager should be sure to consider *all* the costs involved. It is possible, for example, for highly fractionalized jobs to meet all the time-and-motion criteria of efficiency, but if the resulting job is so unrewarding that performing it day after day leads to high turnover, absenteeism, drugs and alcohol, and strikes, then productivity is really lower (and costs higher) than data on efficiency might indicate.

The principle of combining tasks, then, suggests that whenever possible existing and fractionalized tasks should be put together to form new and larger modules of work. At the Medfield, Massachusetts plant of Corning Glass Works the assembly of a laboratory hot plate has been redesigned along the lines suggested here. Each hot plate now is assembled from start to finish by one operator, instead of going through several separate operations that are performed by different people.

Some tasks, if combined into a meaningfully large module of work, would be more than an individual could do by himself. In such cases, it is often useful to consider assigning the new, larger task to a small *team* of workers—who are given great autonomy for its completion. At the Racine, Wisconsin plant of Emerson Electric, the assembly process for trash disposal appliances was restructured this way. Instead of a sequence of moving the appliance from station to station, the assembly now is done from start to finish by one team. Such teams include both men and women to permit switching off the heavier and more delicate aspects of the work. The team responsible is identified on the appliance. In case of customer complaints, the team often drafts the reply.

As a job-design principle, task combination, like natural units of work, expands the task identity of the job. For example, the hot-plate assembler can see and identify with a finished product ready for shipment, rather than a nearly invisible junction of solder. Moreover, the more tasks that are combined into a single worker's job, the greater the variety of skills he must call on in performing the job. So task combination also leads directly to greater skill variety—the third core dimension that contributes to the overall experienced meaningfulness of the work.

*Establishing Client Relationships.* One consequence of fractionalization is that the typical worker has little or no contact with (or even awareness of) the ultimate user of his product or service. By encouraging and enabling employees to establish direct relationships with the clients of their work, improvements often can be realized simultaneously on three of the core dimensions. Feedback increases because of additional opportunities for the individual to receive praise or criticism of his work outputs directly. Skill variety often increases because of the necessity to develop and exercise one's interpersonal skills in maintaining the client relationship. And autonomy can increase because the individual often is given personal responsibility for deciding how to manage his relationships with the clients of his work.

Creating client relationships is a three-step process. First, the client must be identified. Second, the most direct contact possible between the worker and the client must be established. Third, criteria must be set up by which the client can judge the quality of the product or service he receives. And whenever possible, the client should have a means of relaying his judgments directly back to the worker.

The contact between worker and client should be as great as possible and as frequent as necessary. Face-to-face contact is highly desirable, at least occasionally. Where that is impossible or impractical, telephone and mail can suffice. In any case, it is important that the performance criteria by which the worker will be rated by the client must be mutually understood and agreed upon.

*Vertical Loading.* Typically the split between the "doing" of a job and the "planning" and "controlling" of the work has evolved along with horizontal fractionalization. Its rationale, once again, has been "efficiency through specialization." And once again, the excess of specialization that has emerged has resulted in unexpected but significant costs in motivation, morale, and work quality. In vertical loading, the intent is to partially close the gap between the doing and the controlling parts of the job—and thereby reap some important motivational advantages.

Of all the job-design principles, vertical loading may be the single most crucial one. In some cases, where it has been impossible to implement any other changes, vertical loading alone has had significant motivational effects.

When a job is vertically loaded, responsibilities and controls that formerly were reserved for higher levels of management are added to the job. There are many ways to accomplish this:

1. Return to the job holder greater discretion in setting schedules, deciding on work methods, checking on quality, and advising or helping to train less experienced workers.

2. Grant additional authority. The objective should be to advance workers from a position of no authority or highly restricted authority to positions of reviewed, and eventually, near-total authority for their own work.

3. Time management. The job holder should have the greatest possible freedom to decide when to start and stop work, when to break, and how to assign priorities.

4. Troubleshooting and crisis decisions. Workers should be encouraged to seek problem solutions on their own, rather than calling immediately for the supervisor.

5. Financial controls. Some degree of knowledge and control over budgets and other financial aspects of a job can often be highly motivating. However, access to this information frequently tends to be restricted. Workers can benefit from knowing something about the costs of their jobs, the potential effect upon profit, and various financial and budgetary alternatives.

When a job is vertically loaded it will inevitably increase in *autonomy*. And as shown in Figure 7.4, this increase in objective personal control over the work will also lead to an increased feeling of personal responsibility for the work, and ultimately to higher internal work motivation.

*Opening Feedback Channels.* In virtually all jobs there are ways to open channels of feedback to individuals or teams to help them learn whether their performance is improving, deteriorating, or remaining at a constant level. While there are numerous channels through which information about performance can be provided, it generally is better for a worker to learn about his performance directly as he does his job—rather than from management on an occasional basis.

Job-provided feedback usually is more immediate and private than supervisor-supplied feedback, and it increases the worker's feelings of personal control over his work in the bargain. Moreover, it avoids many of the potentially disruptive interpersonal problems that can develop when the only way a worker has to find out how he is doing is through direct messages or subtle cues from the boss.

Exactly what should be done to open channels for job-provided feedback will vary from job to job and organization to organization. Yet in many cases the changes involve simply removing existing blocks that isolate the worker from naturally occurring data about performance—rather than generating entirely new feedback mechanisms. For example:

1. Establishing direct client relationships often removes blocks between the worker and natural external sources of data about his work.

2. Quality-control efforts in many organizations often eliminate a natural source of feedback. The quality check on a product or service is done by persons other than those responsible for the work. Feedback to the workers—if there is any—is belated and diluted. It often fosters a tendency to think of quality as "someone else's concern." By placing quality control close to the worker (perhaps even in his own hands), the quantity and quality of data about performance available to him can dramatically increase.

3. Tradition and established procedure in many organizations dictate that records about performance be kept by a supervisor and transmitted up (not down) in the organization hierarchy. Sometimes supervisors even check the work and correct any errors themselves. The worker who made the error never knows it occurred—and is denied the very information that could enhance both his internal work motivation and the technical adequacy of his performance. In many cases it is possible to provide standard summaries of performance records directly to the worker (as well as to his superior), thereby giving him personally and regularly the data he needs to improve his performance.

4. Computers and other automated operations sometimes can be used to provide the individual with data now blocked from him. Many clerical operations, for example, are now performed on computer consoles. These consoles often can be programmed to provide the clerk with immediate feedback in the form of a CRT display or a printout indicating that an error has been made. Some systems even have been programmed to provide the operator with a positive feedback message when a period of error-free performance has been sustained.

Many organizations simply have not recognized the importance of feedback as a motivator. Data on quality and other aspects of performance are viewed as being of interest only to management. Worse still, the *standards* for acceptable performance often are kept from workers as well. As a result, workers who would be interested in following the daily or weekly ups and downs of their performance, and in trying accordingly to improve, are deprived of the very guidelines they need to do so. They are like the golfer we mentioned earlier, whose efforts to correct his hook are stopped dead by fog over the driving range.

## THE STRATEGY IN ACTION: HOW WELL DOES IT WORK?

So far we have examined a basic theory of how people get turned on to their work; a set of core dimensions of jobs that create the conditions for such internal work motivation to develop on the job; and a set of five implementing concepts that are the action steps recommended to boost a job on the core dimensions and thereby increase employee motivation, satisfaction, and productivity.

The remaining question is straightforward and important: *Does it work?* In reality, that question is twofold. First, does the theory itself hold water, or are we barking up the wrong conceptual tree? And second, does the change strategy really lead to measurable differences when it is applied in an actual organizational setting?

This section summarizes the findings we have generated to date on these questions.

## Is the Job-Enrichment Theory Correct?

In general, the answer seems to be yes. The JDS instrument has been taken by more than 1,000 employees working on about 100 diverse jobs in more than a dozen organizations over the last two years. These data have been analyzed to test the basic motivational theory—and especially the impact of the core job dimensions on worker motivation, satisfaction, and behavior on the job. An illustrative overview of some of the findings is given below.[11]

1. People who work on jobs high on the core dimensions are more motivated and satisfied than are people who work on jobs that score low on the dimensions. Employees with jobs high on the core dimensions (MPS scores greater than 240) were compared to those who held unmotivating jobs (MPS scores less than 40). As shown in Figure 7.5, employees with high MPS jobs were higher on (a) the three psychological states, (b) internal work motivation, (c) general satisfaction, and (d) "growth" satisfaction.

2. Figure 7.6 shows that the same is true for measures of actual behavior at work—absenteeism and performance effectiveness—although less strongly so for the performance measure.

3. Responses to jobs high in motivating potential are more positive for people with weak needs for growth. In Figure 7.7 the linear relationship between the motivating potential of a job and employees' level of internal work motivation is shown, separately for people with high versus low growth needs as measured by the JDS. While both groups of employees

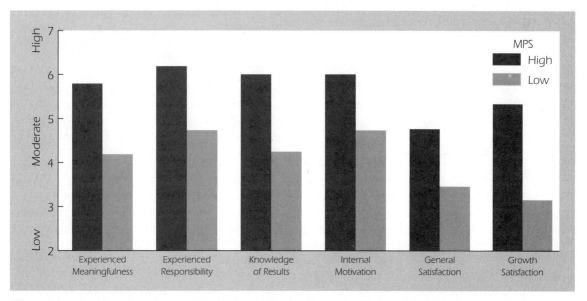

**FIGURE 7.5** Employee Reactions to Jobs High and Low in Motivating Potential for Two Banks and a Steel Firm.

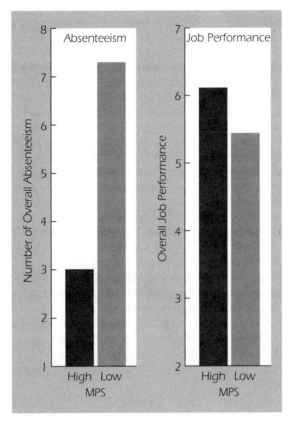

**FIGURE 7.6** Absenteeism and Job Performance for Employees with Jobs High and Low in Motivating Potential.

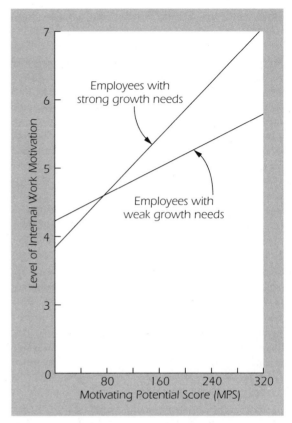

**FIGURE 7.7** Relationship Between the Motivating Potential of a Job and the Internal Work Motivation of Employees. (Shown Separately for Employees with Strong versus Weak Growth-Need Strength.)

show increases in internal motivation as MPS increases, the *rate* of increase is significantly greater for the group of employees who have strong needs for growth.

## How Does the Change Strategy Work in Practice?

The results summarized above suggest that both the theory and the diagnostic instrument work when used with real people in real organizations. In this section, we summarize a job-enrichment project conducted at The Travelers Insurance Companies, which illustrates how the change procedures themselves work in practice.

The Travelers project was designed with two

purposes in mind. One was to achieve improvements in morale, productivity, and other indicators of employee well-being. The other was to test the general effectiveness of the strategy for job enrichment we have summarized in this article.

The work group chosen was a keypunching operation. The group's function was to transfer information from printed or written documents onto punched cards for computer input. The work group consisted of ninety-eight keypunch operators and verifiers (both in the same job classification), plus seven assignment clerks. All reported to a supervisor who, in turn, reported to the assistant manager and manager of the data-input division.

The size of individual punching orders varied considerably, from a few cards to as many as 2,500. Some work came to the work group with a specified delivery date, while other orders were to be given routine service on a predetermined schedule.

Assignment clerks received the jobs from the user departments. After reviewing the work for obvious errors, omissions, and legibility problems, the assignment clerk parceled out the work in batches expected to take about one hour. If the clerk found the work not suitable for punching it went to the supervisor, who either returned the work to the user department or cleared up problems by phone. When work went to operators for punching, it was with the instruction, "Punch only what you see. Don't correct errors, no matter how obvious they look."

Because of the high cost of computer time, keypunched work was 100 percent verified—a task that consumed nearly as many man-hours as the punching itself. Then the cards went to the supervisor, who screened the jobs for due dates before sending them to the computer. Errors detected in verification were assigned to various operators at random to be corrected.

The computer output from the cards was sent to the originating department, accompanied by a printout of errors. Eventually the printout went back to the supervisor for final correction.

A great many phenomena indicated that the problems being experienced in the work group might be the result of poor motivation. As the only person performing supervisory functions of any kind, the supervisor spend most of his time responding to crisis situations, which recurred continually. He also had to deal almost daily with employees' salary grievances or other complaints. Employees frequently showed apathy or outright hostility toward their jobs.

Rates of work output, by accepted work-measurement standard, were inadequate. Error rates were high. Due dates and schedules frequently were missed. Absenteeism was higher than average, especially before and after weekends and holidays.

The single, rather unusual exception was turnover. It was lower than the companywide average for similar jobs. The company has attributed this fact to poor job market in the base period just before the product began, and to an older, relatively more settled work force—made up, incidentally, entirely of women.

*The Diagnosis.* Using some of the tools and techniques we have outlined, a consulting team from the Management Services Department and from Roy W. Walters & Associates concluded that the keypunch-operator's job exhibited the following serious weaknesses in terms of the core dimensions.

1. Skill variety: there was none. Only a single skill was involved—the ability to punch adequately the data on the batch of documents.

2. Task identity: virtually nonexistent. Batches were assembled to provide an even workload, but not whole identifiable jobs.

3. Task significance: not apparent. They keypunching operation was a necessary step in providing service to the company's customers. The individual operator was isolated by an assignment clerk and a supervisor from any knowledge of what the operation meant to the using department, let alone its meaning to the ultimate customer.

4. Autonomy: none. The operators had no freedom to arrange their daily tasks to meet schedules, to resolve problems with the using department, or even to correct, in punching, information that was obviously wrong.

5. Feedback: none. Once a batch was out of the operator's hands, she had no assured chance of seeing evidence of its quality or inadequacy.

*Design of the Experimental Trial.* Since the diagnosis indicated that the motivating potential of the job was extremely low, it was decided to attempt to improve the motivation and productivity of the work group through job enrichment. Moreover, it was possible to design an experimental test of the effects of the changes to be introduced: the results of the changes made in the target work group were to be compared with trends in a control work group of similar size and demographic makeup. Since the control group was located more than a mile away, there appeared to be little risk of communication between members of the two groups.

A base period was defined before the start of the experimental trial period, and appropriate data were gathered on the productivity, absenteeism, and work attitudes of members of both groups. Data also were available on turnover; but since turnover was already below average in the target group, prospective changes in this measure were deemed insignificant.

An educational session was conducted with supervisors, at which they were given the theory and implementing concepts and actually helped to design the job changes themselves. Out of this session came an active plan consisting of about twenty-five change items that would significantly affect the design of the target jobs.

*The Implementing Concepts and the Changes.* Because the job as it existed was rather uniformly low on the core job dimensions, all five of the implementing concepts were used in enriching it.

1. Natural units of work. The random batch assignment of work was replaced by assigning to each operator continuing responsibility for certain accounts—either particular departments or particular recurring jobs. Any work for those accounts now always goes to the same operator.

2. Task combination. Some planning and controlling functions were combined with the central task of keypunching. In this case, however, these additions can be more suitably discussed under the remaining three implementing concepts.

3. Client relationships. Each operator was given several channels of direct contact with clients. The operators, not their assignment clerks, now inspect their documents for correctness and legibility. When problems arise, the operator, not the supervisor, takes them up with the client.

4. Feedback. In addition to feedback from client contact, the operators were provided with a number of additional sources of data about their performance. The computer department now returns incorrect cards to the operators who punched them, and operators correct their own errors. Each operator also keeps her own file of copies of her errors. These can be reviewed to determine trends in error frequency and types of errors. Each operator receives weekly a computer printout of her errors and productivity, which is sent to her directly, rather than given to her by the supervisor.

5. Vertical loading. Besides consulting directly with clients about work questions, operators now have the authority to correct obvious coding errors on their own. Operators may set their own schedules and plan their daily work, as long as they meet schedules. Some competent operators have been given the option of not verifying their work and making their own program changes.

*Results of the Trial.* The results were dramatic. The number of operators declined from ninety-eight to sixty. This occurred partly through attrition and partly through transfer to other departments. Some of the operators were promoted to higher-paying jobs in departments whose cards they had been handling—something that had never occurred before. Some details of the results are given below.

1. Quantity of work. The control group, with no job changes made, showed an increase in productivity of 8.1 percent during the trial period. The experimental group showed an increase of 39.6 percent.

2. Error rates. To assess work quality, error rates were recorded for about forty operators in the experimental group. All were experienced, and all had been in their jobs before the job-enrichment program began. For two months before the study, these operators had a collective error rate of 1.53 percent. For two months toward the end of the study, the collective

error rate was 0.99 percent. By the end of the study the number of operators with poor performance had dropped from 11.1 percent to 5.5 percent.

3. Absenteeism. The experimental group registered a 24.1 percent decline in absences. The control group, by contrast, showed a 29 percent increase.

4. Attitudes toward the job. An attitude survey given at the start of the project showed that the two groups scored about average, and nearly identically, in nine different areas of work satisfaction. At the end of the project the survey was repeated. The control group showed an insignificant 0.5 percent improvement, while the experimental group's overall satisfaction score rose 16.5 percent.

5. Selective elimination of controls. Demonstrated improvements in operator proficiency permitted them to work with fewer controls. Travelers estimates that the reduction of controls had the same effect as adding seven operators—a saving even beyond the effects of improved productivity and lowered absenteeism.

6. Role of the supervisor. One of the most significant findings in the Travelers experiment was the effect of the changes on the supervisor's job, and thus on the rest of the organization. The operators took on many responsibilities that had been reserved at least to the unit leaders and sometimes to the supervisor. The unit leaders, in turn, assumed some of the day-to-day supervisory functions that had plagued the supervisor. Instead of spending his days supervising the behavior of subordinates and dealing with crises, he was able to devote time to developing feedback systems, setting up work modules and spearheading the enrichment effort—in other words, managing. It should be noted, however, that helping supervisors change their own work activities when their subordinates' jobs have been enriched is itself a challenging task. And if appropriate attention and help are not given to supervisors in such cases, they rapidly can become

disaffected—and a job-enrichment "backlash" can result.[12]

*Summary*  By applying work-measurement standards to the changes wrought by job enrichment—attitude and quality, absenteeism, and selective administration of controls—Travelers was able to estimate the total dollar impact of the project. Actual savings in salaries and machine rental charges during the first year totaled $64,305. Potential savings by further application of the changes were put at $91,937 annually. Thus, by almost any measure used—from the work attitudes of individual employees to dollar savings for the company as a whole—The Travelers test of the job-enrichment strategy proved a success.

## CONCLUSIONS

In this article we have presented a new strategy for the redesign of work in general and for job enrichment in particular. The approach has four main characteristics:

1. It is grounded in a basic psychological theory of what motivates people in their work.

2. It emphasizes that planning for job changes should be done on the basis of *data* about the jobs and the people who do them—and a set of diagnostic instruments is provided to collect such data.

3. It provides a set of specific implementing concepts to guide actual job changes, as well as a set of theory-based rules for selecting *which* action steps are likely to be most beneficial in a given situation.

4. The strategy is buttressed by a set of findings showing that the theory holds water, that the diagnostic procedures are practical and informative, and that the implementing concepts can lead to changes that are beneficial both to organizations and to the people who work in them.

We believe that job enrichment is moving beyond the stage where it can be considered "yet another management fad." Instead, it represents a potentially powerful strategy for change that can help organizations achieve their goals for higher quality work—and at the same time further the equally legitimate needs of contemporary employees for a more meaningful work experience. Yet there are pressing questions about job enrichment and its use that remain to be answered.

Prominent among these is the question of employee participation in planning an implementing work redesign. The diagnostic tools and implementing concepts we have presented are neither designed nor intended for use only by management. Rather, our belief is that the effectiveness of job enrichment is likely to be enhanced when the tasks of diagnosing and changing jobs are undertaken *collaboratively* by management and by the employees whose work will be affected.

Moreover, the effects of work redesign on the broader organization remain generally uncharted. Evidence now is accumulating that when jobs are changed, turbulence can appear in the surrounding organization—for example, in supervisory-subordinate relationships, in pay and benefit plans, and so on. Such turbulence can be viewed by management either as a problem with job enrichment, or as an opportunity for further and broader organizational development by teams of managers and employees. To the degree that management takes the latter view, we believe, the oft-espoused goal of achieving basic organizational change through the redesign of work may come increasingly within reach.

The diagnostic tools and implementing concepts we have presented are useful in deciding on and designing basic changes in the jobs themselves. They do not address the broader issues of who plans the changes, how they are carried out, and how they are followed up. The way these broader questions are dealt with, we believe, may determine whether job enrichment will grow up—or whether it will die an early and unfortunate death, like so many other fledgling behavioral-science approaches to organizational change.

## APPENDIX

For the algebraically inclined, the motivating Potential Score is computed as follows:

$$MPS = \left| \frac{\dfrac{Skill}{Variety} + \dfrac{Task}{Identity} + \dfrac{Task}{Significance}}{3} \right| \times Autonomy \times Feedback$$

It should be noted that in some cases the MPS score can be *too* high for positive job satisfaction and effective performance—in effect overstimulating the person who holds the job. This paper focuses on jobs which are toward the low end of the scale—and which potentially can be improved through job enrichment.

### Acknowledgments

The authors acknowledge with great appreciation the editorial assistance of John Hickey in the preparation of this paper, and the help of Kenneth Brousseau, Daniel Feldman, and Linda Frank in collecting the data that are summarized here. The research activities reported were supported in part by the Organizational Effectiveness Research Program of the Office of Naval Research, and the Manpower Administration of the U.S. Department of Labor, both through contracts to Yale University.

## NOTES

1. F. Herzberg, B. Mausner, and B. Snyderman, *The Motivation to Work* (New York: John Wiley & sons, 1959).

2. F. Herzberg, *Work and the Nature of Man* (Cleveland: World, 1966).

3. F. Herzberg, "One More Time: How Do You Motivate Employees?" *Harvard Business Review* (1968): 53–62.

4. W. J. Paul, Jr., K. B. Robertson, and F. Herzberg, "Job Enrichment Pays Off." *Harvard Business Review* (1969): 61–78.

5. R. N. Ford, *Motivation Through the Work Itself* (New York: American Management Association, 1969).

6. A. N. Turner and P. R. Lawrence, *Industrial Jobs and the Worker* (Cambridge, Mass.: Harvard Graduate School of Business Administration, 1965).

7. J. R. Hackman and E. E. Lawler, "Employee Reactions to Job Characteristics," *Journal of Applied Psychology Monograph* (1971): 259–86.

8. J. R. Hackman and G. R. Oldham, *Motivation Through the Design of Work: Test of a Theory*, Technical Report No. 6, Department of Administrative Sciences, Yale University, 1974.

9. J. R. Hackman and G. R. Oldham, "Development of the Job Diagnostic Survey," *Journal of Applied Psychology* (1975): 159–70.

10. R. W. Walters and Associates, *Job Enrichment for Results* (Cambridge, Mass.: Addison-Wesley, 1975).

11. Hackman and Oldham, "Development of the Job Diagnostic Survey."

12. E. E. Lawler III, J. R. Hackman, and S. Kaufman; "Effects of Job Redesign: A Field Experiment," *Journal of Applied Social Psychology* (1973): 49–62.

# PEOPLE'S EMOTIONS AND THEIR CONSEQUENCES

In this section you will read about the more emotional side of people. First an overview is presented that covers much of the recent psychological research on emotions or affect. Then the issue of job satisfaction is addressed. You will read about what leads to work satisfaction, how satisfaction and other emotions are expressed in the workplace, and whether satisfaction may come as much from the personality of the worker as from the work environment. Finally, you will examine two common consequences of work atitudes: absenteeism and turnover. What we know about the causes of absenteeism and how to reduce it are considered first. Then, a very popular theory of turnover is outlined. The section concludes with a controversial article on whether turnover from organizations can be too low as well as too high,

with some guidelines for determining the optimal level of exits from the firm.

Positive work attitudes and performance do not always go hand in hand. The satisfied worker is not always the top performer, and a substantial part of dissatisfaction may be due as much to the disposition of the worker as any objective features of the job. Still, these are not reasons to ignore either the nature of people or the emotional consequences of the workplace. Emotions can get expressed in many dysfunctional ways, ranging from conflict to absenteeism to poor mental and physical health. People spend much of their lives in organizational settings, so it obligates those in charge of companies to make the experience as positive and worthwhile as possible.

# Foundations of Affect

## 8.  AFFECT

Susan T. Fiske and Shelley E. Taylor

This section focuses on the consequences of affect for cognitions and cognitive processes. In particular, mood influences memory and judgment, and in general, emotions influence cognitive processes.

## MOOD EFFECTS ON MEMORY AND JUDGMENT

We have a friend who recently fell in love. He is delightful but difficult to be around for long. It is not that he continually talks about his newfound love, although she is a frequent topic of conversation. Rather, he has developed the disconcerting habit of finding everything uniformly wonderful. If your car breaks down, he extolls the virtues of walking. If it rains, he points out how much the city needs water. If someone insults you, he explains it as a temporary aberration. While it is nice to be around someone so cheerful, he is a little relentless. We also have a friend (in fact, several) who recently fell out of love—or more accurately, recently divorced. These people all tend to see the world through mud-colored glasses. Their cars never work right; it seems to rain selectively on them; and most people they encounter strike them as dreadful bores. Aware that their gloom darkens everything, they do struggle not to complain all the time, but their initial reactions to most situations are negative.

Research shows that people in good moods are more helpful, more open to conversations with strangers, like others more, and are more satisfied even with their cars and other possessions, compared with people in neutral moods (see M. S. Clark & Isen, 1982). Mood has been manipulated in a wide range of ways in this research, from receiving an unexpected gift to being congratulated on success at a task. For example, in one study, people in a shopping mall were given a free sample (a note pad or a nail clipper) by a female confederate. The experimenter then separately approached the people, who presumably were in a good mood, and gave them a seemingly unrelated consumer survey. People who had received a gift rated their cars and television sets more positively than people who did not (Isen, Shalker, Clark, & Karp, 1978).

The pervasive effects of mood on behavior and judgment seem to be caused by the availability of mood-congruent thoughts. That is, being in a good mood leads to positive associations in memory, and being in a bad mood tends to lead to negatively toned cognitions (Bartlett & Santrock, 1977; M. S. Clark & Waddell, 1983; Wright & Mischel, 1982). Researchers posit the basic process to be this: if similarly toned material tends to be linked in memory, then activating one positive or negative item automatically primes other positive or negative items. Figure 8.1 summarizes the effects of positive and negative moods.

Moods prime similarly toned material in memory, but the effect of negative mood is more variable than that of positive mood. This may be because they often operate in different ways. First, the priming process usually seems to operate automatically (M. S. Clark & Isen, 1982); that is, mood primes similarly toned material without one's awareness, effort, or intent. These features in part define an automatic process (W. Schneider & Shiffrin, 1977; Shiffrin & Schneider, 1977). However, priming can also be a controlled process. Controlled processes are deliberate, conscious strategies that require some effort. People in bad moods may be more likely to switch from automatic to controlled processes (M.S. Clark & Isen, 1982), in order to escape the bad mood. Consequently, people often take charge of their mind's propensity to jump from gloomy thought to gloomy thought. Controlled processes for short-circuiting negative associations include such old devices as counting your blessings, looking for the silver lining, and trying to remember your favorite things (S.E. Taylor, Lichtman, & Wood, in press). People in a bad mood also may pull themselves out of it by

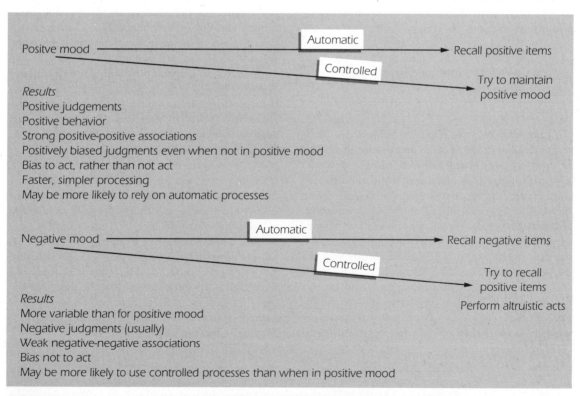

**FIGURE 8.1** Effects of positive and negative mood on cognition and cognitive processing.

being helpful to others (Cialdini & Kenrick, 1976; Kenrick, Baumann, & Cialdini, 1979), especially if the cost of helping is low (Weyant, 1978) and if helping would not destroy the good mood (Isen & Levin, 1972). Thus, although both good and bad moods can elicit controlled processes, negative moods seem more likely to do so.

The priming of negative associations differs from positive ones in another way, as a result of invoking controlled strategies. If people are more likely to resist automatic associations to negatively toned material, the negative-negative associations are likely to be weaker and fewer than the associations among positively toned material (M. S. Clark & Isen, 1982). These possibilities may help to account for the so-called Pollyanna effect (Matlin & Stang, 1978), the finding that positive material has a persistent advantage over negative material in information processing and judgments. People typically remember positive material more easily and make positively biased judgments. All other things being equal, most people seem to be moderately optimistic. The Pollyanna effect would stand to reason if positive material is linked to more things, and if therefore positive material is more accessible to memory than is negative. Since positive material is more likely to come to mind when one is making a judgment, presumably that would bias the judgment in a more positive direction.

Another distinction between positive and negative moods is that the former are more likely to facilitate many types of behavior. A good mood makes one think of all the good consequences of a given act, so one is more likely to follow through on the behavior. For example, when considering helping someone, people in a positive mood may think of their own pride in a good deed and of the other person's gratitude, rather than of the hassle involved. A bad mood, of course, makes one think of all the negative consequences of the act, which accentuates the costs of helping, making it less likely (M. S. Clark & Isen, 1982).

A final difference between the effects of positive and negative moods is a change in the decision processes likely to result from each. Mood affects the content of inferences, as we have seen,

and it may affect whether processing is automatic or controlled. Furthermore, mood affects one's style of decision making. That is, being in a good (as opposed to neutral) mood speeds processing of material relevant to the decision, facilitates the flow of ideas, makes things come to mind effortlessly, and simplifies the perceived complexity of the decision (Isen, Means, Patrick, & Nowicki, 1982; Masters, Barden, & Ford, 1979). For example, cheerful subjects were more likely to fall prey to the availability heuristic; that is, they were more likely to make frequency estimates by relying on ease of retrieval, rather than to use the normatively correct, more complex strategy in a frequency estimation task (Isen et al., 1982). Specifically, subjects were asked to estimate the proportion of famous people on a list in which the famous people actually were outnumbered; most subjects relied on the ease of retrieving names to estimate the proportions. That is, the famous names were easier to remember, so their frequency was overestimated. Happy subjects, however, were especially likely to base their estimates on fewer names and to make more mistakes in recall.

What does this research imply about the behavior of happy people? In general, happy subjects make faster decisions, based on less information, than do neutral controls. Sometimes happy subjects are more biased, as a result of overlooking important details, but sometimes they are more efficient, as a result of skipping redundant details. Happy subjects sometimes take more risks, as a result of being especially optimistic, and sometimes they take fewer risks, as a result of trying to maintain their current good mood. Although behavioral responses depend on the circumstances, happy subjects seem to behave more extremely than neutral subjects in any case (Isen et al., 1982). Figure 8.1 presents a summary of these lines of research.

## NETWORK MODELS OF THE EFFECTS OF MOOD ON MEMORY

Another research program studying the effects of mood on memory differs from the research we just discussed in three major ways: it uses different manipulations of mood, it focuses on constructing relatively more detailed process models, and it does not emphasize behavior as much as the social psychological research does. Bower's program of research (G. H. Bower, 1981; G. H. Bower & Cohen, 1982) has found that mood-congruent stimuli are more salient and better learned at encoding (cf. Nasby & Yando, 1982). For example, happy or sad subjects might read a story about a happy character and a sad character and then be asked with whom they identified. Or they might watch a videotape of themselves and another person, noting instances of positive and negative behavior. In both cases, subjects focus their attention on the character or the behaviors that are mood congruent (G. H. Bower & Cohen, 1982). Further, moods serve as retrieval cues; it is easier to remember things learned in a given mood when the same mood is reinstated at recall. Finally, moods influence judgments of friends, self, possessions, and the future (cf. M. Snyder & White, 1982).

The paradigm cognitive psychologist Bower uses differs from that of social psychologists Clark and Isen, in that Bower and his associates use hypnosis to induce moods. This distinction is important because they get similar results with a totally different method. Bower's method requires highly suggestible subjects, who are then hypnotized, and then instructed to replay an appropriately emotion-laden scene from their past. When the subjects have made themselves moderately happy or sad, they are asked to maintain the feeling as they undertake the experimental tasks. Other researcher's manipulations of mood include talking about happy or sad experiences (Bartlett, Burleson, & Santrock, 1982), reading emotionally evocative sentences (Teasdale & Fogarty, 1979), or manipulating people's facial expressions (Laird, Wagener, Halal, & Szegda, 1982). Moreover, the mood-congruent memory effect holds whether mood is positive or negative, as noted above, and whether the mood is high or low on physiological arousal (M.S. Clark, Milberg, & Ross, in press).

Across a wide range of manipulations and measures, emotionally consistent material is eas-

ier to recall than is inconsistent material. That is, material that matches one's mood at encoding or retrieval is easier to learn than material that does not. The theory created to account for these results posits that emotion is simply a retrieval cue like any other. This means that memories or events that come to mind at the same time as a given emotion are linked to that emotion, and hence (indirectly) to other emotion-congruent memories or events (see Figure 8.2). Mood-congruent learning may operate through subjects' elaborations; that is, elaborations create more links in memory for congruent material. Or it may operate because mood-congruent material is self-relevant, and the self is a rich source of retrieval cues. Or it may be that the intensity of emotional reactions creates stronger links to memory. In any case, if material relevant to a given mood all is linked in memory then reinstating that mood should help people remember that material. Greater memory for mood-congruent events seems to fit well into a network theory of memory (G. H. Bower, 1981; M.S. Clark & Isen, 1982).

Most network models would predict that memory is organized in clusters of conceptually related items. This implies that not only emotion but also conceptual similarity should determine the effects of mood on memory and judgment. However, research does not support the prediction that conceptual similarity enhances mood-priming effects (E.J. Johnson & Tversky, 1983). It turns out that reading a disturbing account of someone's gory death causes people to make more pessimistic predictions in *general*, about risks not even remotely related to the case history. This contradicts a simple network model of emotional memory, which would suggest affect generalization decreasing from more to less related items. To the extent that affect simply links similarly toned material, without regard for conceptual similarity, a network model may be an incomplete account.

To summarize, a number of studies demonstrate that people generally make mood-congruent judgments, remember mood-congruent material, and behave in mood-congruent ways. The effects are typically clearest for positive moods; negative

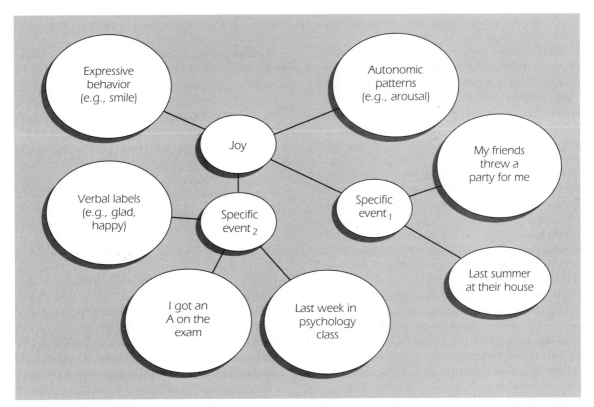

**FIGURE 8.2** A network model of emotion. (After G. H. Bower. 1981)

moods have more variable effects. The effects of mood on memory and judgment have been obtained under many research paradigms, with considerable consistency. Network models of memory have been proposed to account for these pervasive influences of affect on cognitions....

## THE ARGUMENT FOR AFFECT INDEPENDENT OF COGNITION

Despite the scientific and commonplace idea that we think about things in order to decide how we feel, there is a case for affect preceding cognition, rather than vice versa (Zajonc, 1980b). As an example, consider how you make major life decisions, such as where to go to college or who to pick for a long-term close relationship. At least one person talked about her decision process this way: "I kept thinking about what a good mate he would make. He is reliable, sensitive, caring, successful, and everything you could want. So why don't I love him?" Another person choosing between two jobs went through the exercise of listing all the pros and cons of each. But somehow it kept not coming out right. The one with more pros and fewer cons was not the one she wanted. A third person finally picked a college on the amazing ability of its student tour guide to walk backwards over curbs and cobblestones without tripping. How often do we make important decisions on the basis of rational cognitive analysis and how often on the basis of emotional preferences guided by no apparently relevant cognitive data? Affective processes may operate rather independently of cognitive processes, according to this view. The conceptual argument raised by Zajonc has generated a fair amount of theoretical controversy (Lazarus, 1982), so it is useful to understand his argument in some detail.

First, Zajonc suggests, affective reactions are primary. Evaluations are made and then justified; decisions are based on preference rather than computation. When one is picking a college, sometimes one's reasons simply do not add up rationally; one fundamentally knows one's preferred choice, but not necessarily the exact cognitive list that would justify it.

Second, affect is basic. Evaluation is a major and universal component of virtually all perception and meaning. Whether you visit the campus or talk to a student or read the brochure—that is, across a wide range of experiences—you are constantly having positive and negative reactions. It is difficult to understand something without evaluating it.

Third, affective reactions are inescapable. While you may or may not notice the details of the college buildings, you cannot easily avoid your feelings about the place. A growing sense of belonging there (or not) is more difficult to ignore than is the specific geography of the campus.

Fourth, affective judgments tend to be irrevocable, in contrast to cognitive judgments. One cannot be wrong about how one feels, but one can be wrong about what one believes: hence, affect is less vulnerable to persuasion than is cognition. Once having decided that you feel good (or bad) about a school, that feeling is more difficult to change than is your belief that it has a large library.

Fifth, affect implicates the self. While cognitive judgments rest on features inherent in the object, affective judgments describe our own reactions to the object. Your feelings about a college have to do with you yourself being a student in it. In contrast, your knowledge about the place (e.g., its reputation) can be independent of your own role in it.

Sixth, affective judgments are difficult to verbalize. Much emotional response is communicated nonverbally; words for affective reactions always seem to fall short of the experience. Chances are, you can talk more easily about the

college's features than you can about exactly how it makes you feel.

Seventh, affective reactions may not depend on cognition. The features that people use to discriminate a stimulus may not be the same features that people use to decide whether or not they like it. Totaling up the pros and cons of two choices, but deciding that the totals did not come out right, is a prime example of this. Since there is evidence on this point, we will come back to this surprising idea.

Finally, affective reactions may become separated from content. One sometimes can know how one feels about a person but cannot remember where and how the person was previously encountered. Think of the last time you passed someone vaguely familiar on the street. Chances are, you could more easily report how you felt about the person than how exactly you know each other. With regard to colleges, the point is that you may forget exactly which place had squash courts and which place had Chinese language classes, but you are unlikely to forget your feelings about the different places.

## MERE EXPOSURE RESEARCH

The last pair of arguments about the nature of affect formed the basis for a research program demonstrating that people can know how they feel about an object before they know how to recognize it. The opening bars of a classic old song on the radio may be enough to let most of us know whether or not this is a golden oldie we like, but many of us cannot identify it until hearing the words (and some of us not even then without the help of a resident expert). Several studies document precisely this phenomenon of feeling a warm familiar glow that is accompanied by a total lack of recognition. People grow to like an initially unobjectionable stimulus the more frequently it is encountered; this is called the *mere exposure effect* (Zajonc, 1968a).

In mere exposure studies, people see a series of nonsense words, Chinese characters, or yearbook photographs, either many times or few times. The more often people are exposed to the stimulus, the more they favor it. This effect has been thoroughly replicated across many specific circumstances. The relevant idea here is a golden oldies point: the mere exposure effect does not depend on being able to recognize the stimulus as familiar. In other words, people preferred frequent stimuli to nonfrequent stimuli, even when they could only recognize them both at levels approximating chance guessing.

One study showed that mere exposure to Japanese ideographs influenced affect, independent of recognition for them (Moreland & Zajonc, 1977). These particular results are controversial (Birnbaum & Mellers, 1979a, 1979b; Moreland & Zajonc, 1979); nevertheless, other research comes to the same conclusion using different paradigms. Liking for frequently heard tone sequences was found consistently, even though the tones were only recognized as familiar at approximately chance levels (W.R. Wilson, 1979). Further evidence came from a study using a dichotic listening task, in which one presents the tones in one ear but focuses subjects' attention on a literary passage presented to the other ear. Using this task, one can virtually eliminate recognition for the tone sequences, leaving affective reactions intact. Similar results have been obtained with stimuli more engaging than tone sequences and nonsense words, such as the photographs and interests of fellow students (Moreland & Zajonc, 1982). Thus it appears that affective processes more than cognitive ones underlie the mere exposure effect in person perception and attitude research.

## PERSON PERCEPTION AND ATTRIBUTION RESEARCH

A wide range of affective variables are independent of seemingly relevant cognitive variables. For example, evaluative impressions (one kind of affect) can be independent of memory for the details on which they were based (one kind of relevant cognition). Suppose you learn about a new acquaintance who buys groceries for an ailing elderly neighbor. This fact may influence whether you like him, and you may or may not remember his good deed, but the feeling and the memory can be separate (N.H. Anderson & Hubert, 1963; Dreben, Fiske, & Hastie, 1979; Riskey, 1979). Evaluations and recall can be uncorrelated for any given attribute. Similarly, people's affect-laden attributions can be independent of seemingly relevant memory (S. T. Fiske, Taylor, Etcoff, & Laufer, 1979). All this research is consistent with the idea that affect-laden judgments (evaluations, defensive attributions) are not dependent on recalled cognitions.

If affective judgments are not necessarily based on recalled cognitions, then it seems likely that affect is based on reactions to the stimulus at the time it is presented. That is, affect may occur directly upon encoding and categorizing a stimulus (S. T. Fiske, 1982). For example, your evaluation of your neighbor may occur at the time you meet him, based on your perception of his attributes, not afterward, based on your memory of his attributes. Person perception research supports this proposition. The importance of an attribute in an evaluation is not dependent on recall, as noted above, yet weight or importance is dependent on attention at the initial encounter. The longer people gaze at one of a person's attributes, the more weight the attribute carries in an overall evaluation of the person (S. T. Fiske, 1980).

There is an interesting implication of the idea that affect occurs at encoding and can be independent of memory-based cognitive processing. People sometimes may not consult their memories for past affective reactions to the same stimulus. For example, your neighbor may make you angry one day and pleased the next. If you do not remember and think about your past anger on the day he was pleasant to you, the two apparently conflicting emotional reactions you have to him may not be integrated. When people do not recall their previous affective reaction, there is no pressure to bring the separate affective responses into line with each other; it is perfectly reasonable to respond differently on different occasions. In this sense, affect is episodic (based on events) rather than semantic (based on overall consistency of meaning). People's cognitions about other people's traits, in contrast, seem to be more subject to semantic consistency pressures (Abelson *et al.*, 1982). Another manner in which affect and cognition can be relatively separate systems, then, comes from the independence of emotional reactions over time, which contrasts with the apparent dependence of more cognitive reactions over time.

To summarize, Zajonc has suggested that affective and cognitive processes can operate independently of each other. Moreover, affect can precede cognition, in his view. Mere exposure research supports this perspective by showing that liking a frequently seen stimulus is independent of remembering that one has seen it before. Person perception research supports a similar view by showing that affective reactions to others can be independent of memory for details about them. Affect may be based instead on the way the stimulus is encoded initially, rather than on memory....

## REFERENCES

Abelson, R., Kinder, D. R., Peters, M. D., & Fiske, S. T. Affective and semantic components in political person perception. *Journal of Personality and Social Psychology*, 1982, 42, 619–630.

Anderson, N. H., & Hubert, S. Effects of concommitant verbal recall on order effects in personality impression formation. *Journal of Verbal Learning and Verbal Behavior*, 1963, 2, 379–391.

Barlett, J. C., Burleson, G., & Santrock, J. W. Emotional mood and memory in young children. *Journal of Experimental Child Psychology*, 1982, 34, 59–76.

Barlett, J. C. & Santrock, J. W. Affect-dependent episodic memory in young children. *Child Development*, 1977, 50, 513–518.

Birnbaum, M. H., & Mellers, B. A. One-mediator model of exposure effects is still viable. *Journal of Personality and Social Psychology*, 1979, 37, 1090–1096.

Bower, G. H. Emotional modo and memory. *American Psychologist*, 1981, 36, 129–148.

Bower, G. H., & Cohen, P. R. Emotional influences in memory and thinking: Data and theory. In M. S. Clark & S. T. Fiske (Eds.), *Affect and cognition: The 17th Annual Carnegie Symposium on Cognition*. Hillsdale, N.J.: Erlbaum, 1982.

Cialdini, R. B., & Kenrick, D. T. Altruism as hedonism: A social development perspective on the relationship of negative mood state and helping. *Journal of Personality and Social Psychology*, 1976, 34, 907–914.

Clark, M. S., & Isen, A. M. Toward understanding the relationship between feeling states and social behavior. In a Hastorf & A. Isen (Eds.), *Cognitive social psychology*. New York: Elsevier North-Holland, 1982.

Clark, M. S., Milberg, S., & Ross, J. Arousal cues arousal-related material in memory: Implications for understanding effects of mood on memory. *Journal of Verbal Learning and Verbal Behavior*, in press.

Clark, M. S., & Waddell, B. A. Effects of moods on thoughts about helping, attraction and information acquisition. *Social Psychology Quarterly*, 1983, 46, 31–35.

Dreben, E. K., Fiske, S. T., & Hastie, R. The independence of item and evaluative information: Impression and recall order effects in behavior-based impression formation. *Journal of Personality and Social Psychology*, 1979, 37, 1758–1768.

Fiske, S. T. Attention and weight in person perception: The impact of negative and extreme behavior. *Journal of Personality and Social Psychology*, 1980, 38, 889–906.

Fiske, S. T. Schema-triggered affect: Applications to social perception. In M. S. Clark & S. T. Fiske (Eds.) Affect and Cognition: The 17th Annual Carnegie Symposium on Cognition. Hillsdale, N. J.: Erlbaum, 1981

Fiske, S. T., Taylor, S. E., Etcoff, N. L., & Laufer, J. K. Imaging, empathy, and causal attribution. *Journal of Experimental Social Psychology*, 1979, 15, 356–377.

Isen, A. M., & Levin, P. F. The effect of feeling good on helping: Cookies and kindness, *Journal of Personality and Social Psychology*, 1972, 21, 384–388.

Isen, A. M., Means, B., Patrick, R., & Nowicki, G. Some factors influencing decision-making strategy and risk taking. In M. S. Clark & S. T. Fiske (Eds.), *Affect and cognition: The 17th Annual Carnegie Symposium on Cognition*. Hillsdale, N. J.: Erlbaum, 1982.

Isen, A. M., Shalker, T. E., Clark, M. S., & Karp, L. Affect, accessibility of material in memory, and behavior: A cognitive loop? *Journal of Personality and Social Psychology*, 1978, 36, 1–12.

Johnson, E. J., & Tversky, A. Affect generalization and the perception of risk. *Journal of Personality and Social Psychology*, 1983, 45, 20–31.

Kenrick, D. T., Baumann, D. J., & Cialdini, R. B. A step in the socialization of altruism as hedonism: Effects of negative mood on children's generosity under public and private conditions. *Journal of Personality and Social Psychology*, 1979, 27, 747–755.

Laird, J. D., Wagener, J., Halal, M., & Szegda, M. Remembering what you feel: Effects of emotion on memory. *Journal of Personality and Social Psychology*, 1982, 42, 646–657.

Lazarus, R. S. Thoughts on the relations between emotion and cognition. *American Psychologist*, 1982, 37, 1019–1024.

Masters, J. C., Barden, R. D., & Ford, M. E. Affective states, expressive behavior, and learning in children. *Journal of Personality and Social Psychology*, 1979, 37, 380–390.

Matlin, M., & Stang, D. *The Pollyanna principle*. Cambridge, Mass.: Schenkma, 1978.

Moreland, R. L., & Zajonc, R. B. Is stimulus recognition a necessary condition for the occurrence of exposure effects? *Journal of Personality and Social Psychology*, 1977, 35, 191-199.

Moreland, R. L., & Zajonc, R. B. Exposure effects may not depend on stimulus recognition. *Journal of Personality and Social Psychology*, 1979, 37, 1085-1089.

Moreland, R. L., & Zajonc, R. B. Exposure effects in person perception: Familiarity, similarity, and attraction. *Journal of Experimental Social Psychology*, 1982, 18, 395–415.

Nasby, W., & Yando, R. Selective encoding and retrieval of affectively-valent information: Two cognitive consequences of mood. *Journal of Personality and Social Psychology*, 1982, 43, 1244–1253.

Schneider, W., & Shiffrin, R. M. Controlled and automatic human information processing: I. Detection, search, and attention. *Psychological Review*, 1977, 84, 1–66.

Shiffrin, R. M., & Schneider, W. Controlled and automatic human information processing: II. Perceptual learning, automatic attending, and general theory. *Psychological Review*, 1977, 84, 127–190.

Snyder, M., & White, P. Moods and memories: Elation, depression, and the remembering of events of one's life. *Journal of Personality*, 1982, 50, 149–167.

Taylor, S. E., Lichtman, R. R., & Wood, J. V. Attributions, beliefs about control, and adjustment to breast cancer. *Journal of Personality and Social Psychology*, in press.

Teasdale, J. D., & Fogarty, S. J. Differential effort of induced mood on retrieval of pleasant and unpleasant events from episodic memory. *Journal of Abnormal Psychology*, 1979, 88, 248–257.

Wilson, W. R. Feeling more than we can know: Exposure effects without learning. Journal of Personality and Social Psychology, 1979, 37, 811–821.

Wright, J., & Mischel, W. Influence of affect on cognitive social learning person variables. *Journal of Personality and Social Psychology*, 1982, 43, 901–914.

Zajonc, R. B. Attitudinal effects of mere exposure. *Journal of Personality and Social Psychology*, Monograph Supplement, 1986, 9, 1–27.

Zajonc, R. B. Feeling and thinking: Preferences need no inferences. *American Psychologist*, 1980, 35, 151–175.

# Job Satisfaction and Expression of Emotion in Organizations

## 9.  SATISFACTION AND BEHAVIOR

Edward E. Lawler III

...During the last 30 years, thousands of studies have been done on job satisfaction. Usually, these studies have not been theoretically oriented; instead, researchers have simply looked at the relationship between job satisfaction and factors such as age, education, job level, absenteeism rate, productivity, and so on. Originally, much of the research seemed to be stimulated by a desire to show that job satisfaction is important because it influences productivity. Underlying the earlier articles on job satisfaction was a strong conviction that "happy workers are productive workers." Recently, however, this theme has been disappearing, and many organizational psychologists seem to be studying job satisfaction simply because they are interested in finding its causes. This approach to studying job satisfaction is congruent with the increased prominence of humanistic psychology, which emphasizes human affective experience.

The recent interest in job satisfaction also ties in directly with the rising concern in many countries about the quality of life. There is an increasing acceptance of the view that material possessions and economic growth do not necessarily produce a high quality of life. Recognition is now being given to the importance of the kinds of affective reactions that people experience and to the fact that these are not always tied to economic or material accomplishments. Through the Department of Labor and the Department of Health, Education, and Welfare, the United States government has recently become active in trying to improve the affective quality of work life. Job satisfaction is one measure of the quality of life in organizations and is worth understanding and increasing even if it doesn't relate to performance. This reason for studying satisfaction is likely to be an increasingly prominent one as we begin to worry more about the effects working in organizations has on people and as our humanitarian concern for the kind of psychological experiences people have during their lives increases. What happens to people during the work day has profound effects both on the individual employee's life and on the society as a whole, and thus these events cannot be ignored if the quality of life in a society is to be high. As John Gardner has said.

*Of all the ways in which society serves the individual, few are more meaningful than to provide him with a decent job.... It isn't going to be a decent society for any of us until it is for all of us. If our sense of responsibility fails us, our sheer self-interest should come to the rescue. [1968, p. 25].*

As it turns out, satisfaction is related to absenteeism and turnover, both of which are very costly to organizations. Thus, there is a very "practical" economic reason for organizations to be concerned with job satisfaction, since it can influence organizational effectiveness. However, before any practical use can be made of the finding that job dissatisfaction causes absenteeism and turnover, we must understand what factors cause and influence job satisfaction. Organizations can influence job satisfaction and prevent absenteeism and turnover only if the organizations can pinpoint the factors causing and influencing these effective responses.

## THEORIES OF JOB SATISFACTION

Four approaches can be identified in the theoretical work on satisfaction. Fulfillment theory was the first approach to develop. Equity theory and discrepancy theory developed later, partially as reactions against the shortcomings of fulfillment theory. Two-factor theory, the fourth approach, represents an attempt to develop a completely new approach to thinking about satisfaction.

## Fulfillment Theory

Schaffer (1953) has argued that "job satisfaction will vary directly with the extent to which those needs of an individual which can be satisfied are actually satisfied" (p. 3). Vroom (1964) also sees job satisfaction in terms of the degree to which a job provides the person with positively valued outcomes. He equates satisfaction with valence and adds, "If we describe a person as satisfied with an object, we mean that the object has positive valence for him. However, satisfaction has a much more restricted usage. In common parlance, we refer to a person's satisfaction only with reference to objects which he possesses" (p. 100).* Researchers who have adopted the fulfillment approach measure people's satisfaction by simply asking how much of a given facet or outcome they are receiving. Thus, these researchers view satisfaction as depending on how much of a given outcome or group of outcomes a person receives.

Fulfillment theorists have considered how facet-satisfaction measures combine to determine overall satisfaction. The crucial issue is whether the facet-satisfaction measures should be weighted by their importance to the person when combined. We know that some job factors are more important than other job factors for each individual; therefore, the important factors need to be weighted more in determining the individual's total satisfaction. However, there is evidence that the individual's facet satisfaction scores reflect this emphasis already and thus do not need to be further weighted (Mobley & Locke, 1970).

A great deal of research shows that people's satisfaction is a function both of how much they receive and of how much they feel they should and/or want to receive (Locke, 1969). A foreman, for example, may be satisfied with a salary of $12,000, while a company president may be dissatisfied with a salary of $100,000, even though the president correctly perceives

---

* V. Vroom, *Work and Motivation.* Copyright ©1964 by John Wiley & Sons, Inc. This and all other quotes from the same source are reprinted by permission.

that he receives more than the foreman. The point is that people's reactions to what they receive are not simply a function of how much they receive; their reactions are strongly influenced by such individual-difference factors as what they want and what they feel they should receive. Individual-difference factors suggest that the fulfillment-theory approach to job satisfaction is not valid, since this approach fails to take into account differences in people's feelings about what outcomes they should receive.

Morse (1953) stated this point of view as follows:

*At first we thought that satisfaction would simply be a function of how much a person received from the situation or what we have called the amount of environmental return. It made sense to feel that those who were in more need-fulfilling environments would be more satisfied. But the amount of environmental return did not seem to be the only factor involved. Another factor obviously had to be included in order to predict satisfaction accurately. This variable was the strength of an individual's desires, or his level of aspiration in a particular area. If the environment provided little possibility for need satisfaction, those with the strongest desires, or highest aspirations, were the least happy [pp. 27–28].*

Discrepancy theory, which will be discussed next, represents an attempt to take into account the fact that people do differ in their desires.

## Discrepancy Theory

Recently many psychologists have argued for a discrepancy approach to thinking about satisfaction. They maintain that satisfaction is determined by the differences between the actual outcomes a person receives and some other outcome level. The theories differ widely in their definitions of this other outcome level. For some theories it is the outcome level the person feels should be received, and for other theories it is the outcome level the person expects to receive. All of the theoretical approaches argue that what is received should be compared with another outcome level, and when there is a difference—when received outcome is below the other outcome

level—dissatisfaction results. Thus, if a person expects or thinks he should receive a salary of $10,000 and he receives one of only $8,000, the prediction is that he will be dissatisfied with his pay. Further, the prediction is that he will be more dissatisfied than the person who receives a salary of $9,000 and expects or thinks he should receive a salary of $10,000.

Katzell (1964) and Locke (1968, 1969) have probably presented the two most completely developed discrepancy-theory approaches to satisfaction. According to Katzell, satisfaction = $1 - (|X - V|/V)$, where $X$ equals the actual amount of the outcome and $V$ equals the desired amount of the outcome. Like many discrepancy theorists, Katzell sees satisfaction as the difference between an actual amount and some desired amount; but, unlike most discrepancy theorists, he assumes that this difference should be divided by the desired amount of the outcome. If we use Katzell's formula, we are led to believe that the more a person wants of an outcome the less dissatisfied he will be with a given discrepancy. Katzell offers no evidence for this assumption, and it is hard to support logically. A discrepancy from what is desired would seem to be equally dissatisfying regardless of how much is desired. Katzell also speaks of "actual" discrepancies, while most discrepancy theorists talk of "perceived" discrepancies. Note also that by Katzell's formula, getting more than the desired amount should produce less satisfaction than getting the desired amount.

Locke (1969) has stated a discrepancy theory that differs from Katzell's in several ways. First, Locke emphasizes that the perceived discrepancy, not the actual discrepancy, is important. He also argues that satisfaction is determined by the simple difference between what the person wants and what he perceives he receives. The more his wants exceed what he receives, the greater his dissatisfaction. Locke says, "job satisfaction and dissatisfaction are a function of the perceived relationship between what one wants from one's job and what one perceives it is offering" (p. 316).

Porter (1961), in measuring satisfaction, asks people how much of a given outcome there should be for their job and how much of a given outcome there actually is; he considers the discrepancy between the two answers to be a measure of satisfaction. This particular discrepancy approach has been the most widely used. It differs from Locke's approach since it sees satisfaction as influenced not by how much a person wants but by how much he feels he should receive.

A few researchers have argued that satisfaction is determined by what a person expects to receive rather than by what he wants or feels he should receive. Thus, the literature on job satisfaction contains three different discrepancy approaches; the first looks at what people want, the second at what people feel they should receive, and the third at what people expect to receive. The last of these approaches has seldom been used and can be dismissed. As Locke (1969) points out, the expectation approach is hard to defend logically. Admittedly, getting what is not expected may lead to surprise, but it hardly need lead to dissatisfaction. What if, for example, it exceeds expectations? What if it exceeds expectations but still falls below what others are getting?

It is not obvious on logical grounds that either of the first two approaches can be rejected as meaningless. Both approaches seem to be addressing important but perhaps different affective reactions to a job. There clearly is a difference between asking people how much they want and how much they think they should receive. People do respond differently to those questions (Wanous & Lawler, 1972). In a sense, the two questions help us understand different aspects of a person's feelings toward his present situation. A person's satisfaction with the fairness of what he receives for his present job would seem to be more influenced by what he feels he should receive than by what he ultimately aspires to. The difference between what the person aspires to or wants and what he receives gives us an insight into his satisfaction with his present situation relative to his long-term aspired to, or desired, situation. These two discrepancy measures can and do yield different results. For example, a person can feel that his present pay is appropriate for his present job, and in this sense he can be satisfied;

however, he can feel that his present pay is much below what he wants, and in this sense he can be dissatisfied. In most cases, however, these two discrepancies probably are closely related and influence each other. Thus, the difference between the two discrepancies may not be as large or as important as some theorists have argued.

Like the fulfillment theorists, many discrepancy theorists argue that total job satisfaction is influenced by the sum of the discrepancies that are present for each job factor. Thus, a person's overall job satisfaction would be equal to his pay-satisfaction discrepancy plus his supervision-satisfaction discrepancy, and so on. It has been argued that in computing such a sum it is important to weight each of the discrepancies by the importance of that factor to the person, the argument being that important factors influence job satisfaction more strongly than unimportant ones. Locke (1969), however, argues that such a weighting is redundant, since the discrepancy score is a measure of importance in itself because large discrepancies tend to appear only for important items.

Most discrepancy theories allow for the possibility of a person saying he is receiving more outcomes than he should receive, or more outcomes than he wants to receive. However, the theories don't stress this point, which presents some problems for them. It is not clear how to equate dissatisfaction (or whatever this feeling might be called) due to over-reward with dissatisfaction due to under-reward. Are they produced in the same way? Do they have the same results? Do they both contribute to overall job dissatisfaction? These are some of the important questions that discrepancy theories have yet to answer. Equity theory, which will be discussed next, has dealt with some of these questions.

## Equity Theory

Equity theory is primarily a motivation theory, but it has some important things to say about the causes of satisfaction/dissatisfaction. Adams (1963, 1965) argues in his version of equity theory that satisfaction is determined by a person's perceived input-outcome balance in the following manner: the perceived equity of a person's rewards is determined by his input-outcome balance; this perceived equity, in turn, determines satisfaction. Satisfaction results when perceived equity exists, and dissatisfaction results when perceived inequity exists. Thus, satisfaction is determined by the perceived ratio of what a person receives from his job relative to what a person puts into his job. According to equity theory, either under-reward or over-reward can lead to dissatisfaction, although the feelings are somewhat different. The theory emphasizes that over-reward leads to feelings of guilt, while under-reward leads to feelings of unfair treatment.

Equity theory emphasizes the importance of other people's input-outcome balance in determining how a person will judge the equity of his own input-outcome balance. Equity theory argues that people evaluate the fairness of their own input-outcome balance by comparing it with their perception of input-outcome balance of their "comparison-other" (the person they compare with). This emphasis does not enter into either discrepancy theory or fulfillment theory as they are usually stated. Although there is an implied reference to "other" in the discussion of how people develop their feelings about what their outcomes should be, discrepancy theory does not explicitly state that this perception is based on perceptions of what other people contribute and receive. This difference points up a strength of equity theory relative to discrepancy theory. Equity theory rather clearly states how a person assesses his inputs and outcomes in order to develop his perception of the fairness of his input-outcome balance. Discrepancy theory, on the other hand, is vague about how people decide what their outcomes should be.

## Two-Factor Theory

Modern two-factor theory was originally developed in a book by Herzberg, Mausner, Peterson, and Capwell (1957), in which the authors stated that job factors could be classified according to whether the factors contribute primarily to satisfaction or to dissatisfaction. Two years later, Herzberg, Mausner, and Snyderman (1959) published the results of a research study, which they interpreted as supportive of the theory. Since 1959, much research has been directed toward testing two-factor theory. Two aspects of the theory are unique and account for the attention it has received. First, two-factor theory says that satisfaction and dissatisfaction do not exist on a continuum running from satisfaction through neutral to dissatisfaction. Two independent continua exist, one running from satisfied to neutral and another running from dissatisfied to neutral (see Figure 9.1). Second, the theory stresses that different job facets influence feelings of satisfaction and dissatisfaction. Figure 9.2 presents the results of a study by Herzberg et al., which show that factors such as achievement, recognition, work itself, and responsibility are mentioned in connection with satisfying experiences, while working conditions, interpersonal relations, supervision, and company policy are usually mentioned in connection with dissatisfying experiences. The figure shows the frequency with which each factor is mentioned in connection with high (satisfying) and low (dissatisfying) work experiences. As can be seen, achievement was present in over 40 percent of the satisfying experiences and less than 10 percent of the dissatisfying experiences.

Perhaps the most interesting aspect of Herzberg's theory is that at the same time a person can be very satisfied and very dissatisfied. Also the theory implies that factors such as better working conditions cannot increase or cause satisfaction, they can only affect the amount of dissatisfaction that is experienced. The only way satisfaction can be increased is by effecting

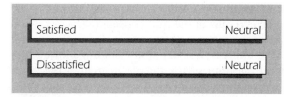

**FIGURE 9.1 Two-Factor Theory: Satisfaction Continua.**

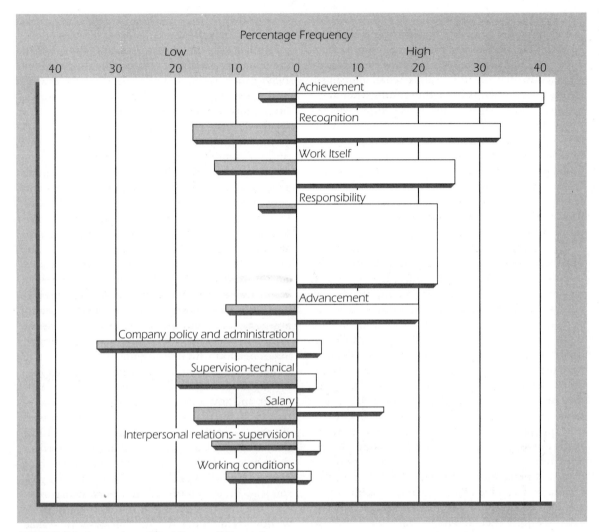

**FIGURE 9.2** Comparison of Satisfiers and Dissatisfiers.

Source: Adapted from Herzberg et al. *The Motivation to Work*, 2d ed. Copyright © 1959 by John Wiley & Sons, Inc. Reprinted by permission.

changes in those factors that are shown in Figure 9.2 as contributing primarily to satisfaction.

The results of the studies designed to test two-factor theory have not provided clear-cut support for the theory, nor have these studies allowed for total rejection of the theory. In many cases, the studies have only fueled the controversy that surrounds the theory. It is beyond the scope of this reading to review the research that has been done

on the theory. What we can do, however, is to consider some of the conclusions to which two-factor theory has led. Perhaps the most negative summary of the evidence is the account presented by Dunnette, Campbell, and Hakel (1967). According to them:

*It seems that the evidence is now sufficient to lay the two-factor theory to rest, and we hope that it may be buried peaceably. We believe that it is important that this be done so that researchers will address themselves to studying the full complexities of human motivation, rather than continuing to allow the direction of motivational research or actual administrative decisions to be dictated by the seductive simplicity of two-factor theory [p. 173].*

This opinion has been rejected by many researchers as too harsh and negative, and indeed research on the theory has continued since the publication of the Dunnette et al. study. Still, research on the theory has raised serious doubts about its validity. Even proponents of the theory admit that the same factors can cause both satisfaction and dissatisfaction and that a given factor can cause satisfaction in one group of people and dissatisfaction in another group of people. Other researchers have pointed out that results supporting the theory seem to be obtainable only when certain limited research methodologies are used.

The major unanswered question with respect to two-factor theory is whether satisfaction and dissatisfaction really are two separate dimensions. The evidence is not sufficient to establish that satisfaction and dissatisfaction are separate, making this the crucial unproven aspect of the theory. Neither the fact that some factors can contribute to both satisfaction and dissatisfaction nor the fact that, in some populations, factors contribute to satisfaction while, in other populations, these factors contribute to dissatisfaction is sufficient reason to reject the theory. Although these findings raise questions about the theory, they do not destroy its core concept, which is that satisfaction and dissatisfaction are, in fact, on different continua.

Significantly, while considerable research has tried to determine which factors contribute to satisfaction and dissatisfaction, little attention has been directed toward testing the motivation and performance implications of the theory. The study of Herzberg et al. (1959) did ask the subjects (engineers and accountants) to report how various job factors affected their performance. In agreement with the theory, the subjects reported that the presence of satisfiers boosted

performance, while the presence of dissatisfiers reduced performance. At best, the results of this study give weak evidence that these job factors influence performance as suggested by the theory. Only self-reports of performance were used, and in many cases the subjects were reporting on events that had happened some time prior to the date of the interviews. The evidence, although not at all conclusive, at least suggests the kinds of experiences that might lead to a strong motivation to perform effectively. Unfortunately, Herzberg et al. did not develop any theoretical concepts to explain why the job factors should affect performance. Their theory contains little explanation of why outcomes are attractive, and it fails to consider the importance of associative connections in determining which of a number of behaviors a person will choose to perform in order to obtain a desired outcome. Thus, it is not a theory of motivation; rather, it is a theory primarily concerned with explaining the determinants of job satisfaction and dissatisfaction.

## Equity Theory and/or Discrepancy Theory

Equity and theory and discrepancy theory are the two strongest theoretical explanations of satisfaction. Either theory could be used as a basis for thinking about the determinants of satisfaction. Fortunately it is not necessary to choose between the theories, since it is possible to build a satisfaction model that capitalizes on the strengths of each theory. In this reading, we will try to build such a model. In many ways, equity theory and discrepancy theory are quite similar. Both theories stress the importance of a person's perceived outcomes, along with the relationship of these outcomes to a second perception. In discrepancy theory, the second perception is what the outcomes should be or what the person wants the outcomes to be; in equity theory, the second perception is what a person's perceived inputs are in relation to other people's inputs and outcomes. Clearly, it could be argued that the two theories are talking about very similar concepts when they talk about perceived inputs and what the subject's feeling about what his outcomes should be. A person's perception of what his outcomes should be is partly determined by what he feels his inputs are. Thus, the "should be" phrase from discrepancy theory and the "perceived inputs relative to other people's inputs and outcomes" phrase from equity theory are very similar.

Equity theory and discrepancy theory do differ in that equity theory places explicit emphasis on the importance of social comparison, while discrepancy theory does not. This is a strength of equity theory because it helps to make explicit what influences a person's "should be" judgment. Finally, discrepancy theory talks in terms of a *difference*, while equity theory talks in terms of a *ratio*. For example, equity theory would predict that a person with 16 units of input and 4 units of outcome would feel the same as a person with 8 units of input and 2 units of outcome (same ratio, 1 to 4). Although discrepancy theory does not talk specifically in terms of inputs, if we consider input as one determinant of what outcomes should be, then discrepancy theory would not go along with equity theory. Discrepancy theory would argue that the person with 16 units of input will be more dissatisfied than the person with 8 units of input because the difference between his input and outcomes is greater. The two theories also suggest different types of relationships between dissatisfaction and feelings of what rewards should be. Discrepancy theory would predict a linear relationship such that, rewards being constant, increases in a person's perception of what his outcomes should be would be directly proportionate to increases in dissatisfaction. Equity theory, on the other hand, would predict a nonlinear relationship [satisfaction = (is getting/should be getting)] such that if a poor ratio exists, a further increase in "should be getting" will have little effect on satisfaction.

In building our "model of satisfaction," we will use the difference approach rather than the ratio approach. This choice is one of the few either/or choices that must be made between the two theories. It is not a particularly crucial choice from the point of view of measurement because methods of measurement in the field of psychology are not precise enough so that discrepancy theory and equity theory would yield very different results. Measurement scales with true zero points and equal distances between all points on the scale (for example, as in measuring weight and height) are required, and such scales are not used when attitudes are measured.

Once it has been decided to think of satisfaction in terms of a difference, the key question becomes what difference or differences should be considered. There is clear agreement that one element in the discrepancy should be what the person perceives that he actually receives. The second element could be one of two other perceptions: (1) what a person thinks he should receive, or (2) what a person wants to receive. As we've already seen, these two perceptions are closely related. However, there is a difference. Overall, it seems preferable to focus more on what a person feels he should receive than on what a person wants to receive.

If satisfaction is conceptualized as the difference between what one receives and what one wants, it is difficult to talk meaningfully about satisfaction with one's present job. Such an approach partially removes satisfaction from the context of the job and the situation. The question "How much do you want?" is an aspiration-level variable, which is not as closely related to the job situation as the question "How much should there be?" An answer to the first question is more a statement of personal goals than a statement of what is appropriate in a particular situation. Research data show that employees consistently give higher answers to the "how much do you want" question than to the "how much should there be" question (Wanous & Lawler, 1972); answers to the "should be" question seem to vary more with such organization factors as job level. Thus, in studying people's feelings about their jobs, it seems logical to focus on what employees feel they should receive from their jobs. This perception would seem to be strongly influenced by organization practices, and it would seem to be a perception that must be studied if we are to understand employees' affective reactions to their jobs and the behavioral responses these reactions produce.

## A MODEL OF FACET SATISFACTION

Figure 9.3 presents a model of the determinants of facet satisfaction. The model is intended to be applicable to understanding what determines a person's satisfaction with any facet of the job. The model assumes that the same psychological processes operate to determine satisfaction with job factors ranging from pay to supervision and satisfaction with the work itself. The model in Figure 9.3 is a discrepancy model in the sense that it shows satisfaction as the difference between *a*, what a person feels he should receive, *b*, what he perceives that he actually receives. The model indicates that when the person's perception of what his outcome level is and his perception of what

his outcome level should be are in agreement, the person will be satisfied. When a person perceives his outcome level as falling below what he feels it should be, he will be dissatisfied. However, when a person's perceived outcome level exceeds what he feels it should be, he will have feelings of guilt and inequity and perhaps some discomfort (Adams, 1965). Thus, for any job factor, the assumption is that satisfaction with the factor will be determined by the difference between how much of the factor there is and how much of the factor the person feels there should be.

Present outcome level is shown to be the key influence on a person's perception of what rewards he receives, but his perception is also shown to be influenced by his perception of what

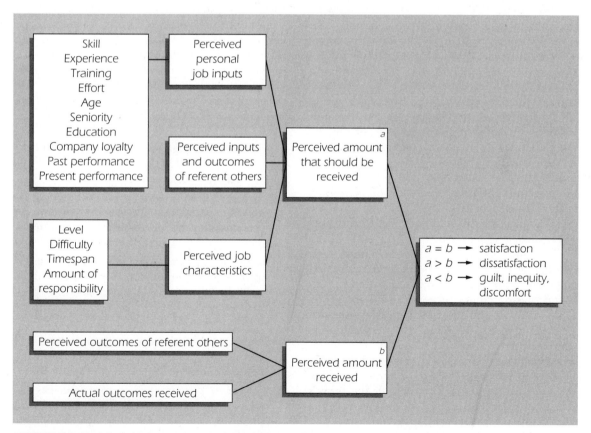

**FIGURE 9.3** Model of the Determinants of Satisfaction.

his "referent others" receive. The higher the outcome levels of his referent others, the lower his outcome level will appear. Thus, a person's psychological view of how much of a factor he receives is said to be influenced by more than just the objective amount of the factor. Because of this psychological influence, the same amount of reward often can be seen quite differently by two people; to one person it can be a large amount, while to another person it can be a small amount.

The model in Figure 9.3 also shows that a person's perception of what his reward level should be is influenced by a number of factors. Perhaps the most important influence is perceived job inputs. These inputs include all of the skills, abilities, and training a person brings to the job as well as the behavior he exhibits on the job. The greater he perceives his inputs to be, the higher will be his perception of what his outcomes should be. Because of this relationship, people with high job inputs must receive more rewards than people with low job inputs or they will be dissatisfied. The model also shows that a person's perception of what his outcomes should be is influenced by his perception of the job demands. The greater the demands made by the job, the more he will perceive he should receive. Job demands include such things as job difficulty, responsibilities, and organization level. If outcomes do not rise along with these factors, the clear prediction of the model is that the people who perceive they have the more difficult, higher-level jobs will be the most dissatisfied.

The model shows that a person's perception of what his outcomes should be is influenced by what the person perceives his comparison-other's inputs and outcomes to be. This aspect of the model is taken directly from equity theory and is included to stress the fact that people look at the inputs and outcomes of others in order to determine what their own outcome level should be. If a person's comparison-other's inputs are the same as the person's inputs but the other's outcomes are much higher, the person will feel that he should be receiving more outcomes and will be dissatisfied as a result.

The model allows for the possibility that people will feel that their outcomes exceed what they should be. The feelings produced by this condition are quite different from those produced by under-reward. Because of this difference, it does not make sense to refer to a person who feels over-rewarded as being dissatisfied. There is considerable evidence that very few people feel over-rewarded, and this fact can be explained by the model. Even when people are highly rewarded, the social-comparison aspect of satisfaction means that people can avoid feeling over-rewarded by looking around and finding someone to compare with who is doing equally well. Also, a person tends to value his own inputs much higher than they are valued by others (Lawler, 1967). Because of this discrepancy, a person's perception of what his outcomes should be is often not shared by those administering his rewards, and is often above what he actually receives. Finally, the person can easily increase his perception of his inputs and thereby justify a high reward level.

As a way of summarizing some of the implications of the model, let us briefly make some statements about who should be dissatisfied if the model is correct. Other things being equal:

1. People with high perceived inputs will be more dissatisfied with a given facet than people with low perceived inputs.

2. People who perceive their job to be demanding will be more dissatisfied with a given facet than people who perceive their jobs as undemanding.

3. People who perceive similar others as having a more favorable input-outcome balance will be more dissatisfied with a given facet than people who perceive their own balance as similar to or better than that of others.

4. People who receive a low outcome level will be more dissatisfied than those who receive a high outcome level.

5. The more outcomes a person perceives his comparison-other receives, the more dissatisfied he will be with his own outcomes.

This should be particularly true when the comparison-other is seen to hold a job that demands the same or fewer inputs.

## OVERALL JOB SATISFACTION

Most theories of job satisfaction argue that overall job satisfaction is determined by some combination of all facet-satisfaction feelings. This could be expressed in terms of the facet-satisfaction model in Figure 9.3 as a simple sum of, or average of, all $a - b$ discrepancies. Thus, overall job satisfaction is determined by the difference between all the things a person feels he should receive from his job and all the things he actually does receive.

A strong theoretical argument can be made for weighting the facet-satisfaction scores according to their importance. Some factors do make larger contributions to overall satisfaction than others. Pay satisfaction, satisfaction with the work itself, and satisfaction with supervision seem to have particularly strong influences on overall satisfaction for most people. Also, employees tend to rate these factors as important. Thus, there is a connection between how important employees say job factors are and how much job factors influence overall job satisfaction (Vroom, 1964). Conceptually, therefore, it seems worthwhile to think of the various job-facet-satisfaction scores as influencing total satisfaction in terms of their importance. One way to express this relationship is by defining overall job satisfaction as being equal to $\sum$ (facet satisfaction × facet importance). However, as stressed earlier, actually measuring importance and multiplying it by measured facet satisfaction often isn't necessary because the satisfaction scores themselves seem to take importance into account. (The most important items tend to be scored as either very satisfactory or very dissatisfactory; thus, these items have the most influence on any sum score.) Still, on a conceptual level, it is important to remember that facet-satisfaction scores do differentially contribute to the feeling of overall job satisfaction.

A number of studies have attempted to determine how many workers are actually satisfied with their jobs. Our model does not lead to any predictions in this area. The model simply gives the conditions that lead to people experiencing feelings of satisfaction or dissatisfaction. Not surprisingly, the studies that have been done do not agree on the percentage of dissatisfied workers. Some suggest figures as low as 13 percent, others give figures as high as 80 percent. The range generally reported is from 13 to 25 percent dissatisfied. Herzberg et al. (1957) summarized the findings of research studies conducted from 1946 through 1953. The figures in their report showed a yearly increase in the median percentage of job-satisfied persons (see Table 9.1). Figure 9.4 presents satisfaction-trend data for 1948 through 1971. These data also show an overall increase in the number of satisfied workers, which is interesting because of recent speculation that satisfaction is decreasing. However, due to many measurement problems, it is impossible to conclude that a real decline in number of dissatisfied workers has taken place.

The difficulty in obtaining meaningful conclusions from the data stems from the fact that different questions yield very different results. For example, a number of studies, instead of directly asking workers "How satisfied are you?," have asked "If you had it to do over again, would you pick the same job?" The latter question produces much higher dissatisfaction scores than

**TABLE 9.1**

Median Percentage of Job-Dissatisfied Persons Reported from 1946 to 1953

| Year | Median Percentage of Job Dissatisfied |
|------|--------------------------------------|
| 1953 | 13 |
| 1952 | 15 |
| 1951 | 18 |
| 1950 | 19 |
| 1949 | 19 |
| 1948 | 19 |
| 1946–1947 | 21 |

Source: From Herzberg et al., *Job Attitudes: Review of Research and Opinion*. Copyright 1957 by the Psychological Service of Pittsburgh. Reprinted by permission.

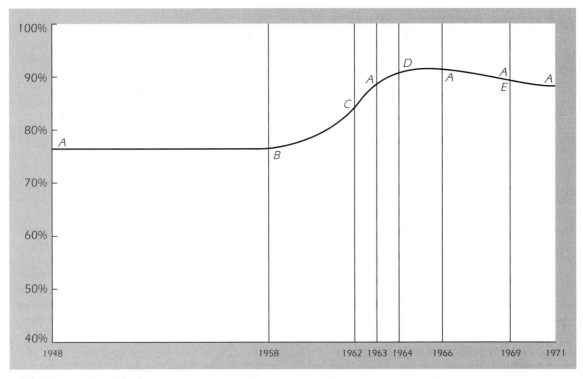

**FIGURE 9.4** *Percentage of "Satisfied" Workers, 1948–1971.*

Source: From Quinn, Staines, and McCullough, 1973.

Note: "Don't know" and "Uncertain" have been excluded from the base of the percentages. Sources: *A* = Gallup, or Gallup as reported by Roper; *B* = Survey Research Center (Michigan); *C* = NORC; *D* = Survey Research Center (Berkeley); *E* = 1969–1970 Survey of Working Conditions.

does the simple "how satisfied are you" question. One literature review showed that 54 percent of the workers tended to say that they were sufficiently dissatisfied with their jobs that they would not choose them again. On the other hand, the straight satisfaction question shows between 13 and 25 percent dissatisfied. However, even this figure is subject to wide variation depending on how the question is asked. When the question is asked in the simple form, "Are you satisfied, yes or no?," the number of satisfied responses is large. When the question is changed so that the employees can respond yes, no, or undecided — or satisfied, dissatisfied, or neutral — the number of satisfied responses drops.

Because of these methodological complexities, it is difficult to draw conclusions about the number of workers who are or are not satisfied with their jobs or with some facet of their jobs. This drawback does not mean, however, that meaningful research on satisfaction is impossible. On the contrary, interesting and important research has been and can be done on the determinants of job satisfaction. For example, the relationship between personal-input factors — such as education level, sex, and age and seniority — and job or facet satisfaction can be ascertained by simply comparing those people who report they are satisfied with those people who report they are dissatisfied and checking the results to see if the two groups differ in any systematic manner. The number of people reporting satisfaction is not crucial for this purpose. What is important is that we distinguish those people who tend to be more satisfied from those people who tend to be less satisfied. This distinction can be made with many of the better-known satisfaction-measuring instruments, such as the Job Description Index (Smith, Kendall, & Hulin, 1969) and Porter's (1961) need-satisfaction instrument.

A number of studies have tried to determine the amount of employee dissatisfaction that is associated with different job facets. Although these studies have yielded interesting results, some serious methodological problems are involved in this work. As with overall job satisfaction, factors such as type of measurement scale used and manner of wording questions seriously affect the number of people who express dissatisfaction with a given facet. For example, a question about pay satisfaction can be asked in a way that will cause few people to express dissatisfaction, while a question about security satisfaction can be asked in a way that will cause many people to express dissatisfaction. In this situation, comparing the number of people expressing security satisfaction with the number of people expressing pay dissatisfaction might produce very misleading conclusions. This problem is always present no matter how

carefully the various items are worded because it is impossible to balance the items so they are comparable for all factors.

Despite methodological problems, the data on relevant satisfaction levels with different job factors are interesting. These data show that the factors mentioned earlier as being most important—that is, pay, promotion, security, leadership, and the work itself—appear in these studies as the major sources of dissatisfaction. Porter (1961) designed items using Maslow's needs as a measure of satisfaction. With these items, he collected data from various managers. The results of his study (see Table 9.2) show that more managers express high-order-need dissatisfaction than express lower-order-need dissatisfaction. The results also show that a large number of managers are dissatisfied with their pay and with the communications in their organizations and that middle-level managers tend to be better satisfied in all areas than lower-level managers.

Porter's data also show that managers consider the areas of dissatisfaction to be the most important areas. It is not completely clear whether the dissatisfaction causes the importance or the importance causes the dissatisfaction. The research reviewed earlier suggests that the primary causal direction is from dissatisfaction to importance, although there undoubtedly is a two-way influence process operating. The important thing to

**TABLE 9.2**

Differences Between Management Levels in Percentage of Subjects Indicating Need-Fulfillment Deficiencies

| Questionnaire Items | % Bottom Management (N = 64) | % Middle Management (N = 75) | % Difference |
|---|---|---|---|
| Security needs | 42.2 | 26.7 | 15.5 |
| Social needs | 35.2 | 32.0 | 3.2 |
| Esteem needs | 55.2 | 35.6 | 19.6 |
| Autonomy needs | 60.2 | 47.7 | 12.5 |
| Self-actualization needs | 59.9 | 53.3 | 6.6 |
| Pay | 79.7 | 80.0 | 0.3 |
| Communications | 78.1 | 61.3 | 16.8 |

Source: Adapted from Porter, 1961

remember is that employees do report varying levels of satisfaction with different job factors, and the factors that have come out high on dissatisfaction have also been rated high on importance and have the strongest influence on overall job satisfaction.

A study by Grove and Kerr (1951) illustrates how strongly organizational conditions can affect factor satisfaction. Grove and Kerr measured employee satisfaction in two plants where normal work conditions prevailed and found that 88 percent of the workers were satisfied with their job security, which indicated that security was one of the least dissatisfying job factors for employees in these two plants. In another plant where layoffs had occurred, only 17 percent of the workers said they were satisfied with the job security, and job security was one of the most dissatisfying job factors for this plant's employees.

## DETERMINANTS OF SATISFACTION

The research on the determinants of satisfaction has looked primarily at two relationships: (1) the relationship between satisfaction and the characteristics of the job, and (2) the relationship between satisfaction and the characteristics of the person. Not surprisingly, the research shows that satisfaction is a function of both the person and the environment. These results are consistent with our approach to thinking about satisfaction, since our model (shown in Figure 9.3) indicates that personal factors influence what people feel they should receive and that job conditions influence both what people perceive they actually receive and what people perceive they should receive....

The evidence on the effects of personal-input factors on satisfaction is voluminous and will be only briefly reviewed. The research clearly shows that personal factors do affect job satisfaction, basically because they influence perceptions of what outcomes should be. As predicted by the satisfaction model in Figure 9.3, the higher a person's perceived personal inputs—that is, the greater his education, skill, and performance—

the more he feels he should receive. Thus, unless the high-input person receives more outcomes, he will be dissatisfied with his job and the rewards his job offers. Such straightforward relationships between inputs and satisfaction appear to exist for all personal-input factors except age and seniority. Evidence from the study of age and seniority suggests a curvilinear relationship (that is, high satisfaction among young and old workers, low satisfaction among middle-age workers) or even a relationship of increasing satisfaction with old age and tenure. The tendency of satisfaction to be high among older, long-term employees seems to be produced by the effects of selective turnover and the development of realistic expectations about what the job has to offer.

## CONSEQUENCES OF DISSATISFACTION

Originally much of the interest in job satisfaction stemmed from the belief that job satisfaction influenced job performance. Specifically, psychologists thought that high job satisfaction led to high job performance. This view has now been discredited and most psychologists feel that satisfaction influences absenteeism and turnover but not job performance. However, looking at the relationship among satisfaction, absenteeism, and turnover, let's review the work on satisfaction and performance.

### Job Performance

In the 1950s two major literature reviews showed that in most studies only a slight relationship had been found between satisfaction and performance. A later review by Vroom (1964) also showed that studies had not found a strong relationship between satisfaction and performance; in fact, most studies had found a very low positive relationship between the two. In other words, better performers did seem to be slightly more satisfied than poor performers. A considerable amount of recent work suggests that the slight existing relationship is probably due to better performance indirectly causing satisfaction rather

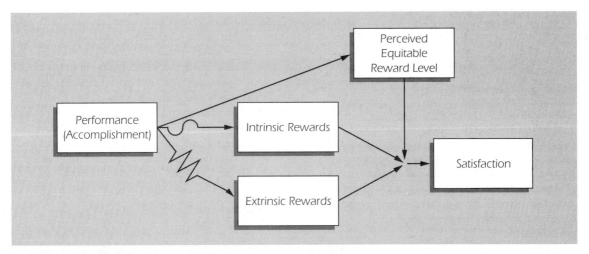

**FIGURE 9.5** Model of the Relationship of Performance to Satisfaction.

Source: From E. E. Lawler and L. W. Porter, "The Effect of Performance on Job Satisfaction," *Industrial Relations* 7 (1967): 20–28. Reprinted by permission of the publisher, Industrial Relations.

than the reverse. Lawler and Porter (1967) explained this "performance causes satisfaction" viewpoint as follows:

*If we assume that rewards cause satisfaction, and that in some cases performance produces rewards, then it is possible that the relationship found between satisfaction and performance comes about through the action of a third variable—rewards. Briefly stated, good performance may lead to rewards, which in turn lead to satisfaction; this formulation then would say that satisfaction, rather than causing performance, as was previously assumed, is caused by it.*

*[Figure 9.5] shows that performance leads to rewards, and it distinguishes between two kinds of rewards and their connection to performance. A wavy line between performance and extrinsic rewards indicates that such rewards are likely to be imperfectly related to performance. By extrinsic rewards is meant such organizationally controlled rewards as pay, promotion, status, and security—rewards that are often referred to as satisfying mainly lower-level needs. The connection is relatively weak because of the difficulty of tying ex-*

*trinsic rewards directly to performance. Even though an organization may have a policy of rewarding merit, performance is difficult to measure, and in dispensing rewards like pay, many other factors are frequently taken into consideration.*

*Quite the opposite is likely to be true for intrinsic rewards, however, since they are given to the individual by himself for good performance. Intrinsic or internally mediated rewards are subject to fewer disturbing influences and thus are likely to be more directly related to good performance. This connection is indicated in the model by a semi-wavy line. Probably the best example of an intrinsic reward is the feeling of having accomplished something worthwhile. For that matter any of the rewards that satisfy self-actualization needs or higher-order growth needs are good examples of intrinsic rewards [pp. 23-24].★*

Figure 9.5 shows that intrinsic and extrinsic rewards are not directly related to job satisfaction, since the relationship is moderated by perceived equitable rewards (what people think they should receive). The model in Figure 9.5 is similar to the

---

★ E. E. Lawler and L. W. Porter, "The Effect of Performance on Job Satisfaction," *Industrial Relations* 7 (1967) 20–28. Reprinted by permission of the publisher, *Industrial Relations*.

model in Figure 9.3, since both models show that satisfaction is a function of the amount of rewards a person receives and the amount of rewards he feels he should receive.

Because of the imperfect relationship between performance and rewards and the important effect of perceived equitable rewards, a low but positive relationship should exist between job satisfaction and job performance in most situations. However, in certain situations, a strong positive relationship may exist; while in other situations, a negative relationship may exist. A negative relationship would be expected where rewards are unrelated to performance or negatively related to performance.

To have the same level of satisfaction for good performers and poor performers, the good performers must receive more rewards than the poor performers. The reason for this, as stressed earlier, is that performance level influences the amount of rewards a person feels he should receive. Thus, when rewards are not based on performance — when poor performers receive equal rewards or a larger amount of rewards than good performers — the best performers will be the least satisfied, and a negative satisfaction-performance relationship will exist. If, on the other hand, the better performers are given significantly more rewards, a positive satisfaction-performance relationship should exist. If it is assumed that most organizations are partially successful in relating rewards to performance, it follows that most studies should find a low but positive relationship between satisfaction and performance. Lawler and Porter's (1967) study was among those that found this relationship; their study also found that, as predicted, intrinsic-need satisfaction was more closely related to performance than was extrinsic-need satisfaction.

In retrospect, it is hard to understand why the belief that high satisfaction causes high performance was so widely accepted. There is nothing in the literature on motivation that suggests this causal relationship. In fact, such a relationship is opposite to the concepts developed by both drive theory and expectancy theory. If anything, these two theories would seem to predict that high

satisfaction might reduce motivation because of a consequent reduction in the importance of various rewards that may have provided motivational force. Clearly, a more logical view is that performance is determined by people's efforts to obtain the goals and outcomes they desire, and satisfaction is determined by the outcomes people actually obtain. Yet for some reason, many people believed — and some people still do believe — that the "satisfaction causes performance" view is best.

## Turnover

The relationship between satisfaction and turnover has been studied often. In most studies, researchers have measured the job satisfaction among a number of employees and then waited to see which of the employees studied left during an ensuing time period (typically, a year). The satisfaction scores of the employees who left have then been compared with the remaining employees' scores. Although relationships between satisfaction scores and turnover have not always been very strong, the studies in this area have consistently shown that dissatisfied workers are more likely than satisfied workers to terminate employment; thus, satisfaction scores can predict turnover.

A study by Ross and Zander (1957) is a good example of the kind of research that has been done. Ross and Zander measured the job satisfaction of 2,680 female workers in a large company. Four months later, these researchers found that 169 of these employees had resigned; those who left were significantly more dissatisfied with the amount of recognition they received on their jobs, with the amount of achievement they experienced, and with the amount of autonomy they had.

Probably the major reason that turnover and satisfaction are not more strongly related is that turnover is very much influenced by the availability of other positions. Even if a person is very dissatisfied with his job, he is not likely to leave unless more attractive alternatives are available. This observation would suggest that in times of economic prosperity, turnover should be high, and a strong relationship should exist between turnover and satisfaction; but in times of economic hardship, turnover should be low, and little relationship should exist between turnover and satisfaction. There is research evidence to support the argument that voluntary turnover is much lower in periods of economic hardship. However, no study has compared the relationship between satisfaction and turnover under different economic conditions to see if it is stronger under full employment.

## Absenteeism

Like turnover, absenteeism has been found to be related to job satisfaction. If anything, the relationship between satisfaction and absenteeism seems to be stronger than the relationship between satisfaction and turnover. However, even in the case of absenteeism, the relationship is far from being isomorphic. Absenteeism is caused by a number of factors other than a person's voluntarily deciding not to come to work; illness, accidents, and so on can prevent someone who wants to come to work from actually coming to work. We would expect satisfaction to affect only voluntary absences; thus, satisfaction can never be strongly related to a measure of overall absence rate. Those studies that have separated voluntary absences from overall absences have, in fact, found that voluntary absence rates are much more closely related to satisfaction than are overall absence rates (Vroom, 1964). Of course, this outcome would be expected if satisfaction does influence people's willingness to come to work.

## Organization Effectiveness

The research evidence clearly shows that employees' decisions about whether they will go to work on any given day and whether they will quit are affected by their feelings of job satisfaction. All the literature reviews on the subject have reached this conclusion. The fact that present satisfaction influences future absenteeism and turnover clearly indicates that the causal direction is from

satisfaction to behavior. This conclusion is in marked contrast to our conclusion with respect to performance—that is, behavior causes satisfaction....

The research evidence on the determinants of satisfaction suggests that satisfaction is very much influenced by the actual rewards a person receives; of course, the organization has a considerable amount of control over these rewards. The research also shows that, although not all people will react to the same reward level in the same manner, reactions are predictable if something is known about how people perceive their inputs. The implication is that organizations can influence employees' satisfaction levels. Since it is possible to know how employees will react to different outcome levels, organizations can allocate outcomes in ways that will either cause job satisfaction or job dissatisfaction.

Absenteeism and turnover have a very direct influence on organizational effectiveness. Absenteeism is very costly because it interrupts scheduling, creates a need for over-staffing, increases fringe-benefit costs, and so on. Turnover is expensive because of the many costs incurred in recruiting and training replacement employees. For lower-level jobs, the cost of turnover is estimated at $2,000 a person; at the managerial level, the cost is at least five to ten times the monthly salary of the job involved. Because satisfaction is manageable and influences absenteeism and turnover, organizations can control absenteeism and turnover. Generally, by keeping satisfaction high and, specifically, by seeing that the best employees are the most satisfied, organizations can retain those employees they need the most. In effect, organizations can manage turnover so that, if it occurs, it will occur among employees the organization can most afford to lose. However, keeping the better performers more satisfied is not easy, since they must be rewarded very well...although identifying and rewarding the better performers is not always easy, the effort may have significant payoffs in terms of increased organizational effectiveness.

## REFERENCES

Adams, J. S. "Toward an Understanding of Inequity." *Journal of Abnormal Psychology* 67 (1963); 422–36.

Adams, J. S. "Injustice in Social Exchange," In *Advances in Experimental Social Psychology*, vol. 2, edited by L. Berkowitz. New York: Academic Press, 1965.

Dunnette, M. D; Campbell, J. P.; and Hakel, M. D. "Factors Contributing to Job Satisfaction and Job Dissatisfaction in Six Occupational Groups." *Organizational Behavior and Human Performance* 2 (1967): 143–74.

Gardner, J. W. *No Easy Victories*. New York: Harper & Row, 1968.

Grove, E. A., and Kerr, W. A. "Specific Evidence on Origin of Halo Effect in Measurement of Employee Morale." *Journal of Social Psychology* 34 (1951): 165–70.

Herzberg, F; Mausner; B.; Peterson, R. O; and Capwell. D. F. *Job Attitudes: Review of Research and Opinion*. Pittsburgh: Psychological Service of Pittsburgh. 1957.

Herzberg, F; Mausner, B., and Snyderman, B. *The Motivation to Work*, 2nd ed. New York; John Wiley & Sons, 1959.

Katzell, R. A. "Personal Values, Job Satisfaction, and Job Behavior." In *Man in a World of Work*, edited by H. Borow. Boston; Houghton Mifflin, 1964.

Lawler, E. E. "The Multitrait-Multirater Approach to Measuring Managerial Job Performance." *Journal of Applied Psychology* 51 (1967). 369–81.

Lawler, E E., and Porter, L. W. "The Effect of Performance on Job Satisfaction." *Industrial Relations* 7 (1967) 20–28.

Locke, E. A. "What Is Job Satisfaction?" Paper presented at the APA Convention, San Francisco, September 1968.

Locke, E. A. "What Is Job Satisfaction?" *Organizational Behavior and Human Performance* 4 (1969): 309–36.

Mobley, W H., and Locke, E A. "The Relationship of Value Importance to Satisfaction." *Organizational Behavior and Human Performance* 5 (1970): 463–83.

Morse, N. C. *Satisfactions in the White-Collar Job*. Ann Arbor: University of Michigan, Institute for Social Research, Survey Research Center, 1953.

Porter, L. W. "A Study of Perceived Need Satisfactions in Bottom and Middle Management Jobs." *Journal of Applied Psychology* 45 (1961): 1–10.

Ross, I. E., and Zander, A. F. "Need Satisfaction and Employee Turnover." *Personnel Psychology* 10 (1957): 327–38.

Schaffer, R. H. "Job Satisfaction as Related to Need Satisfaction in Work." *Psychological Monographs* 67 (1953): 14, whole no. 364.

Smith, P,; Kendall, L.; and Hulin, C. *The Measurement of Satisfaction in Work and Retirement*. Chicago: Rand McNally & Company, 1969.

Vroom, V. H. *Work and Motivation*. New York: John Wiley & Sons, 1964.

Wanous, J. P., and Lawler, E. E. "Measurement and Meaning of Job Satisfaction." *Journal of Applied Psychology* 56 (1972): 95–105.

# 10.  EXPRESSION OF EMOTION AS PART OF THE WORK ROLE

Anat Rafaeli and Robert I. Sutton

Research on feelings experienced and expressed by organizational members emphasizes emotions as indicators of well-being and happiness. Writings on job stress, for example, view affective responses primarily as dependent variables that change in response to objective or subjective threats to well-being (Kahn, 1981). Related writings convey that "burnout" is a syndrome of emotional exhaustion among workers in the helping professions (Maslach, 1978a). Perhaps the greatest attention to emotion as a dependent variable is found in the job satisfaction literature. Locke's (1976) widely cited review defines job satisfaction as "a pleasurable or positive emotional state resulting from the appraisal of one's job or job experiences" (p.1300).

Yet viewing emotion only as an intrapsychic outcome masks the complex role it plays in organizational life. In service organizations, for example, effectiveness is thought to hinge partly on the emotions expressed by employees (Czepiel, Solomon, & Surprenant, 1985). To illustrate, check-out clerks working at one chain of supermarkets are issued a handbook that commands:

YOU *are the company's most effective representative. Your customers judge the entire company by your actions. A cheerful "Good Morning" and "Good Evening" followed by courteous, attentive treatment, and a sincere "Thank you, please come again," will send them away with a friendly feeling and a desire to return. A friendly smile is a must.*

The feelings offered by this employee to customers are not indicators of well-being. Rather, smiling and acting "friendly" are part of the work role.

The display of friendliness and good cheer are expected in an array of service occupations including flight attendants, servants, and sales clerks. In contrast, bill collectors and bouncers are paid to convey hostility. Funeral directors express sadness. Other roles call for the suppression of emotion: "good" academic deans display neutrality, especially around budget time. Many roles call for variation in expressed emotions. For example, a case study of a team of surgical nurses (Denison & Sutton, in press) revealed that members were expected to present an emotionally flat demeanor in the operating room, to be warm when talking with patients and their families, and to encourage one another to express "true feelings" such as rage and disgust during breaks and informal meetings with other nurses.

Yet expectations about emotional expression have been largely ignored by organizational theorists who have adopted role theory. The widely cited work by Kahn and his colleagues (Kahn, Wolfe, Quinn, Snoek, & Rosenthal, 1964; Katz & Kahn, 1978) focused on sent and received role expectations that are excessive, ambiguous, or in conflict. The sources of expectations about emotional expressions and the effects of displayed feelings are not addressed explicitly in Kahn's work, or in the more general writings on role theory (Biddle, 1979). Goffman's (1969) work, however, addressed the causes and consequences of expressed emotions. His writings on strategic interaction focus on how people manipulate emotional expression to promote their own interests. But employees also display feelings to promote the interests of other role senders including clients and co-workers. This paper follows the spirit of Goffman's writings and considers work settings in which employees display emotions in order to fulfill role expectations.

Anat Rafaeli and Robert I. Sutton, "Expression of Emotion as Part of the Work Role" in *Academy of Management Review*, 1987, vol. 12, no. 1, p.p. 23-27. Reprinted by permission.

## CONCEPTUAL FRAMEWORK

The conceptual territory covered by the framework proposed here includes the sources of role expectations about emotional expression, the range of such emotional expressions, and the influence expressed feelings have on the organization and on the role occupant (see Figure 10.1). The underlying assumption is that many of the emotions conveyed by employees can be thought of as "control moves" (Goffman, 1969), which refer to "the intentional effort of an informant to produce expressions that he thinks will improve his situation if they are gleaned by the observer" (p. 12). It is further proposed that emotions expressed without the intention of influencing others can serve as control moves.

The attributes of expressed emotions are central to our framework. Developing a complete theory of emotion is a task that has intrigued and puzzled writers from a variety of disciplines. Such theories are sometimes the subject of entire books (Darwin, 1965; DeRivera, 1977; Hillman, 1961); identifying the full range of human emotion is beyond the scope of this paper. Nonetheless, a pair of imperfect dimensions is useful for developing theory about emotions conveyed as part of the job. First, emotions can be arrayed on a continuum ranging from positive, through neutral, to negative. Expression of positive affect includes smiling and enthusiasm. Negative affect includes frowning and disgust.

One limitation of this continuum is that some emotions are difficult to classify. Is the sadness expressed by a funeral director positive or

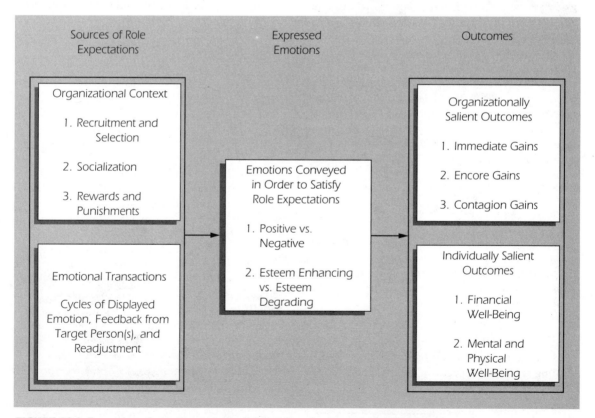

**FIGURE 10.1** Expression of emotion as part of the work role: A conceptual framework.

negative? Further, depending on which perspective is adopted, the same expressed emotion can be positive or negative. The friendly smile of, say a waitress, may be positive from the customer's point of view, but may be construed as artificial and thus negative by the waitress.

The second continuum is the extent that expressed emotions reinforce the target person's self-esteem. Some occupations require employees to support co-workers or clients (social workers, physicians, receptionists); others require employees to remain neutral (judges and referees); and some jobs require the role occupant to degrade the self-esteem of others (drill sergeants, poker players).

This second continuum is also imperfect; because of differences in cultural backgrounds and personality, it is difficult to predict the influence an expressed emotion will have on a person's self-esteem. Taken together, however, these continua indicate that for expressed emotions (or any other human communication) to convey meaning, the message must be encoded by a source and decoded by a receiver (Osgood, Suci, & Tannenbaum, 1957). The positive-negative continuum highlights feelings encoded by the role occupant; the esteem enhancing-degrading continuum accentuates expressed emotions decoded by the audience.

## SOURCES OF ROLE EXPECTATIONS

Two sources of role expectations are proposed that create, influence, and maintain the emotions expressed in organizational life: the *organizational context* and *emotional transactions*. The organizational context comprises formal and informal practices used by a larger organization to influence emotions displayed by members. Following Trist's (1977) distinction between contextual and transactional environments, the organizational context can be distinguished from emotional transactions. The organizational context includes selection, socialization, and reward systems; emotional transactions comprise the sequence of communication that occurs when an employee displays emotion, notes the reaction of a "target" person, and adjusts or maintains expressed feelings.

## Organizational Context

The present authors propose that three dimensions of the organizational context create and maintain expectations about emotional expression: recruitment and selection, socialization, and rewards and punishments. For the sake of simplicity, most of this discussion considers incumbents who are influenced by the context of a single organization. Nevertheless, in practice, a person may be affected by the selection, socialization, and reward systems of more than one organization. Some people are members of more than one organization. Boundary-spanners are influenced by the norms of outside organizations encountered in their work. Moreover, contexts encountered in prior organizational memberships (schools attended, previous jobs) may influence emotions that are expressed in current roles.

*Recruitment and selection.*    Organizations seek to employ people who can convey emotions deemed to be appropriate for the role. For example, a manual produced by McDonald's "Hamburger University" urges store managers "Your windowmen and outside order-takers must impress customers as being 'All-American' boys. They must display desirable traits such as sincerity, enthusiasm, confidence, and a sense of humor" (Boas & Chain, 1976, p.84). Newspaper ads solicit sales people who are "young-minded with a positive attitude," "personable," "aggressive," and "convincing." Also, Playboy bunnies were required to be charming as well as sexy (Steinem, 1983).

Although emotional expression is not discussed explicitly in the literature on job analysis, some job analysis techniques imply that displayed feelings are job requirements (McCormick, 1979). For example, the traits required to deal with other people such as diverting, serving, and persuading are included in the rating scales used by the United States Employment Service (U.S. Department of Labor, 1972).

Hypothesis testing studies on the recruitment and selection of incumbents on the basis of emotional skills are rare, but some research suggests that job prospects are brighter for interviewees who convey positive emotions and hide negative feelings. Forbes and Jackson (1980) reported that interviewees who smiled, maintained eye contact, and nodded their heads were most likely to be offered jobs. In contrast, rejected candidates in this study "were characterized by more avoidance gaze; eye wandering, more neutral facial expression, and less smiling" (p. 70). Similar findings were reported by Imada and Hakel (1977), as well as McGovern and Tinsley (1978).

Research is needed, however, on whether such decisions are intentional. Moreover, these studies do not distinguish between the emotions required to get a job and the emotions needed to do the job.

*Socialization.* Organizational socialization often includes learning norms, or "feeling rules" (Hochschild, 1979), about which emotions ought to be displayed and which ought to be hidden. Feeling rules can be learned in an organization other than the one in which a member practices his or her occupation. The "University of Santa Claus," for example, teaches Santas who will work in department stores to smile and be jolly "even when a kid who isn't quite potty trained has an accident" ("Rules for Santas," 1984). Similarly, law schools and medical schools teach professional norms, including norms about emotional expression.

Many organizations provide internal training about feeling rules. Walt Disney World uses classes, handbooks, and billboards to teach newcomers that they must convey positive and esteem-enhancing emotions to customers. A hand-book advises:

*First, we practice a friendly smile at all times with our guests and among ourselves. Second, we use friendly, courteous phrases. "May I help you."... "Thank you."... "Have a nice day."... "Enjoy the rest of your stay." and many others are all part of our daily working vocabulary (Walt Disney Productions, 1982, p. 6, emphasis in the original).*

In the Disney tradition, newcomers learn the sharp distinction between being "onstage" (where Disney patrons can go) and being "offstage" (where only employees are allowed). When onstage, employees must follow concise guidelines about which emotions can, and cannot, be expressed (Peters & Waterman, 1982; Tyler & Nathan, 1985). Newcomers hear in lectures at Disney University and read in handbooks (Walt Disney Productions, 1982, p. 2): "You were cast for a role, not hired for a job" and "Our audience is composed of *guests* not customers...and we as cast members are *hosts* and *hostesses*" (emphasis in original). Such metaphors teach and maintain an organizational culture that emphasizes the display of good cheer and the skilled utterance of social amenities, perhaps above all else.

Disney's approach may seem extreme, but socialization practices used by other service organizations place similar emphasis on the display of appropriate feelings. Examples include Mrs. Fields' Cookies (Richman, 1984), Delta Airlines (Hochschild, 1983), and McDonald's Hamburgers (Boas & Chain, 1976).

Some organizations even use operant conditioning to teach employees how to express appropriate emotions. Behavioral modification was used by Komaki, Blood, and Holder (1980) to teach employees in a fast food restaurant how to be friendly. Friendliness was operationalized as smiling at customers and exchanging polite remarks such as "Is this your first visit?"

Perhaps more powerful than formal socialization practices are lessons about emotional display learned through the informal organization. The stories told and actions taken by role models provide opportunities for social learning (Bandura, 1977). Bandura's work suggests that newcomers learn norms about emotional expression through both vicarious processes and imitation. The expression and control of emotions is frequently mentioned in the "war stories" that experienced street cops tell to rookie officers (Van Maanen, 1973, 1978). Storytelling provides an opportunity for vicarious learning about feeling rules; as role models tell stories, rookies imagine how *they* would have acted.

Social learning theory also suggests that newcomers learn about the display of emotion by observing and then imitating more experienced co-workers. By watching experienced physicians, for example, medical interns learn that mild compassion is the expected emotional posture and that there is a permissive attitude about physicians who express indifference toward patients (Daniels, 1960).

Explicit feedback from insiders and other newcomers is another means through which feeling rules are learned. A medical intern writes in the *Journal of The American Medical Association*:

*In my first months as a medical student, I was called a "softie" when I cried about patients; being a woman made it only worse. Classmates and physicians told me "You get too emotionally involved with patients. You will never be a 'good' doctor." (Bell, 1984, p. 2684).*

Employees not only learn which feelings should be expressed to clients or other outsiders; they also learn which feelings should be displayed in the presence of co-workers. The medical intern in the above example learned that fellow interns and teaching physicians did not want to see her cry.

The treatment of socialization presented here emphasizes the expression of emotion. Yet socialization in some roles entails learning how to suppress or disguise feelings—examples include judges, academic deans, and referees. Margaret Mead (1951) described a technique used by a communist party member to suppress his emotions:

*By smoking a heavy pipe, you are sure of yourself. Through the heaviness of the pipe, the lips become deformed and cannot react spontaneously (pp. 65–66).*

*Rewards and punishments.* Reward and solicitation processes overlap since learning a role includes encounters with the reward system. Yet it is useful to discuss these processes separately: Socialization teaches newcomers which emotions are expected, while rewards and punishments maintain (or alter) such behaviors.

As with socialization, rewards and punishments are supplied by both the formal and in-formal organization. Many organizations monitor employees to assure that displayed feelings are "correct." To illustrate, The University of Michigan's Survey Research Center monitors telephone interviewers (see Groves & Kahn, 1979; Survey Research Center, 1976). Feedback to interviewers includes comments about the quality of their emotion work. Interviewers are encouraged to say kind things when respondent's answers are "acceptable" (e.g., "Thanks" or "That's helpful"), and to withhold positive affect when the respondent's actions are unacceptable. Moreover, interviewers are forbidden to express certain emotions such as anger. Data gatherers who convey a "professional attitude of neutrality and acceptance" (Survey Research Center, 1976, p. 130) are more likely to receive pay increases; those who do not express required emotions are reprimanded.

Similarly, conversations with executives from a national chain of grocery stores reveal that "employee courtesy" is monitored by "mystery shoppers." Ratings provided by such shoppers are entered into the employee's personnel file. A recent study by another chain of stores indicated that, in over 2000 interactions between "mystery shoppers" and clerks, only 21 percent of the clerks smiled and only 25 percent greeted customers. These findings disappointed top executives. As a result, employee courtesy contests are being held in some regions. Clerks who are "caught" smiling, greeting customers, and expressing thanks may receive prizes including a new car.

## Emotional Transactions

An organization may use selection, socialization, and rewards to encourage the display of certain emotions. But the verbal and nonverbal cues sent by target persons also may influence the feelings conveyed by an employee. Thus, the organizational context can be distinguished from emotional transactions. Emotional transactions are a sequence of communication between sender and receiver. The organizational context has the strongest influence over feelings conveyed at the outset of an emotional transaction. Yet the emotions sent by an employee may be modified as the sequence of communication unfolds; the reactions of "receivers" or "targets" serve as feedback that can influence and constrain subsequent sent emotions.

Emotional transactions can be viewed as "double interacts" (Weick, 1979). According to Weick (1979, p. 115), the initial emotions sent by a focal employee (an "act") stimulate the target person to respond with implicit or explicit feedback about the continuation of the displayed emotion (an "interact"). The sender of emotion reacts to such feedback by readjustments including abandoning, revising, or maintaining the displayed emotion (completing a "double interact"). The sender and receiver of displayed emotion use one or more double interacts to reach agreement, or reduce equivocality (Weick, 1979), about which feelings should be conveyed and which should be hidden.

Clark and LaBeef (1982), for example, studied the tactics used by physicians, nurses, police officers, and clergy in delivering the news of a person's death. Their qualitative research suggests that "death tellers" first deliver the news of death to the friend or relative in a somber manner (an initial emotional "act"). Next, the reactions of people who receive the bad news can influence the "death tellers'" subsequent emotion work (an "interact"). Finally, the death teller continues, modifies, or abandons displayed emotions in response to such cues (a "double interact"). Reactions by friends or relatives to the sad news range from crying, to silence, to expressing anger and blame toward the death teller. The professionals studied by Clark and LaBeef made a similarly wide range of adjustments in the emotions they expressed. They sometimes hugged crying relatives and friends, or even cried along with them. In contrast, when family or friends became angry, death tellers tended to withdraw.

The cycles of displayed emotion, reaction, and readjustment may reinforce or weaken the effects of feeling rules as an emotional transaction unfolds. For example, Hochschild (1983) described a double interact in which a somewhat insulting customer encourages an unsmiling flight attendant to conform to organizational rules.

*On a 15-hour flight from Hong Kong to New York, a young businessman put his drink down, leans back, and takes in a flight attendant.... "Hey honey," he calls out, "give me a smile." (p. 35).*

Reactions by the targets of emotion also can encourage employees to abandon required emotional displays. Consider the advice offered by two restaurant reviewers (Unterman & Sesser, 1984) who are appalled by food servers who offer organizationally specified emotions:

*Nothing can put a damper on a meal quicker than having a waiter bug you with "Hi, my name's Bruce" and continuing with "Is everything satisfactory?" about twenty times. When you see that sort of behavior going on at other tables, bring out a good put-down line. We've found one that works: as soon as the waiter walks up, stick out your hand and say in as cheerful a voice you can manage, "Hi, my name's Dave and I'm your customer tonight." That's guaranteed to stop them speechless (p. vi).*

## OUTCOMES OF EXPRESSED EMOTIONS

### Organizationally Salient Outcomes

The expression of emotions by organizational members may, in the aggregate, have a positive or a negative influence on organizational performance. The present authors propose that emotion work can bring about immediate, encore, and contagion gains (or losses) for the organization (see Figure 10.1).

*Immediate gains.* Emotions can have an immediate impact on organizationally salient outcomes. Such effects are obvious in sales jobs. Rosci (1981) urged vendors to "Grin and Sell it" because "salespeople profit by combining the principles of body language with professional selling skills" (p. 106). Rosci described a training course that teaches salespeople to employ nonverbal signals such as "friendly, smiling, enthusiastic face, arms and hands that are relaxed and open" (p. 107) to enhance sales. The consultants who offer the course claim that 2,400 salespeople have taken the course and average sales for these people have increased by 41 percent.

Arthur and Caputo (1959) also illustrated how employees can use emotional expressions to garner immediate gains. Their book *Interrogation for Investigators* provides guidance for police officers who seek to gain confessions from criminals. They suggest using the "Silent Approach" on "The Cool Customer":

*Using this approach, you enter the interrogation room with a slight smile on your face, sit comfortably down in your chair, look him straight in the eye, and say absolutely nothing.... The senior author once sat for some 25 minutes without moving or taking his gaze from the suspect's face. The suspect, who was very loud before the interrogation, suddenly broke down and began to cry. Within 3 minutes he gave a full confession (pp. 75–76).*

To use Goffman's (1969) terminology, such police interrogation techniques are a rich example of "control moves" that influence the actions of others.

In contrast, Driscoll, Meyer, and Schanie (1973) described how other police officers used positive and esteem-enhancing emotions to garner immediate gains. They used presentations, films, roleplays, and feedback sessions to train six teams in the skills required for family crisis investigations. Much of the training focused on emotion work. The program was evaluated with telephone interviews and questionnaires completed by complaining citizens. The study compared 129 "domestic trouble" calls answered by trained officers to 292 calls answered by untrained officers. The trained officers were perceived to be more supportive of citizens and to have greater overall effectiveness at crisis intervention.

The link between emotion work and immediate gains does not always depend on formal training. Consider the following example:

*Bradshaw (1980) noticed that nuns who regularly solicit alms in Grand Central Terminal in New York customarily look rather glum. One day, however, Bradshaw saw one nun smiling brightly and "the activity at her basket seemed unusually brisk." Bradshaw subse-*

*quently disguised herself as a nun and positioned herself in the terminal. She spent the first day with a suitable glum visage and collected $143 . . . and the second day with a smile which resulted in a total contribution of $186 (described in Webb, Campbell, Schwartz, Sechrest, & Grove, 1981, p. 154).*

*Encore gains.* The emotions conveyed by role occupants also have long-term effects on the organization. Emotion work may lead to further gains either by repeat encounters with the same 'other' (i.e., encore gains), or through the comments that are passed by him or her to a third party (i.e., contagion gains).

Skilled emotion work can bring encore gains even when the organization's product is of questionable quality:

*This is hard for some restaurant reviewers to stomach, but there are some restaurants where it just doesn't seem to matter whether the food is good or not. While we may be sitting at a table with plates of barely tasted food everyone in the place seems to be having a great time. The North Beach Restaurant, almost a San Francisco institution, is a prime example.... The waiters, probably the best group we've ever seen in a large restaurant, don't hurt any. No matter how pressed they are, they're resolutely cheerful and always willing to explain and offer suggestions. However, this book is about food and not about atmosphere, and here the North Beach Restaurant strikes out (Unterman & Sesser, 1984, p. 118).*

Quantitative evidence for the influence of emotion work on encore gains was found in the police training intervention mentioned earlier (Driscoll, Meyer, & Schanie, 1973). The evaluation indicated that, in addition to greater immediate success at crisis intervention, families treated by trained police were more likely to ask for assistance the next time that they faced a crisis.

*Contagion gains.* The long-term effects of emotion work also transcend the reactions of the target person. The reputation of a sales clerk or a university administrator may spread through word of mouth. Advertising research suggests that word of mouth is among the most potent of communication sources. In a study of the effectiveness of a bank advertising campaign, for example, Anderson and Golden (1984) found that word of mouth communication (in comparison to other sources) was associated with the highest believability and increased likelihood of bank patronage.

## Individually Salient Outcomes

Expressed emotions also influence outcomes that are salient to the role occupant (see Figure 10.1). Here, the influence of emotion work on individual financial well-being and on mental and physical well-being are explored.

*Financial well-being.* The link between emotion work and financial well-being is explicit when employees depend on tips from customers. We have all noticed how friendly even the most incompetent food server can become as "tip time" approaches. And empirical research suggests that such friendliness is rewarded. Tidd and Lockard (1978), for example, described the "Monetary Significance of the Affiliative Smile." They examined the influence of a "maximal" versus a "minimal" smile on the tips received by a cocktail waitress who served 48 men and 48 women. The waitress:

*approached each individual with either a minimal smile (mouth corners noticably turned up but no teeth showing) or a maximal smile (mouth corners turned up to extensively expose the closed front on a "natural" appearing broad smile) (p. 344).*

Tidd and Lockard (1978) reported that the degree of smiling had no effect on the number of drinks ordered. But broad smiles yielded bigger tips. In the aggregate, the maximal smile brought $23.20, while the 48 victims of the minimal smile tipped a total of $9.40.

Emotion work also includes physical contact. Crusco and Wetzel (1984) described "The Midas Touch"—the positive effect of touching (by 2 waitresses) on tipping (by 114 diners). Customers who were not touched tipped an average of 12.2 percent. Customers who received a fleeting touch

on the palm tipped an average of 16.7 percent, while the diners given longer touches on a shoulder tipped an average tip of 14.4 percent.

Professional poker players use an array of emotion work techniques to influence opponents (Goffman, 1967). Hayano's (1982) participant-observation research on *poker faces* indicates that successful players are skilled at "stifling emotions when defeated, tired, or angry" (p. 89). Further, while the exchange of ritualistic insults may ease tension, Hayano contended:

*Insults may also have the intended or unintended effect of changing, destroying, or weakening opponents thereby making them more likely to commit errors or begin "steaming." ["Steaming" is the expression used by poker players to describe what happens when a poker player loses his or her temper.] Raking in the chips the winner tells the loser to "get a job" or threatens to send him and the other "poker bums" back to the freeway forever. These gabby methods of intimidation are highly effective in many instances, especially against players who are easily flustered (p.56).*

Hayano also reported that insults are used to convince "tight" players or "rocks" (i.e., financially conservative players) to bet their money more freely.

The influence of displayed emotions on financial well-being is sometimes more subtle. A pediatrician who does not express warmth and empathy may lose clients and a lawyer who is cold and abrupt may alienate juries, hence losing his or her share of the damages awarded.

*Mental and physical well-being.* Hochschild (1983) is perhaps most adamant about the negative impact of emotion work on psychological well-being. She compares the physical exploitation of a child laborer in the 19th century to the emotional exploitation of a female flight attendant in the 20th century. Hochschild argued that, while the hours of work and physical conditions for the flight attendant are superior to those of the child laborer, the flight attendant gives even more of herself to the organization than did the child laborer; the employer controls not only her physical activities, but also her feelings.

Hochschild's qualitative evidence from flight attendants at Delta Airlines leads her to argue that, in the short-term, the strain of emotional labor can cause a loss of emotional control:

*A young businessman said to a flight attendant, "Why aren't you smiling?" She put her tray back on the food cart, looked him in the eye, and said, "I'll tell you what. You smile first, then I'll smile." The businessman smiled at her. "Good," she replied. "Now freeze and hold that smile for fifteen hours." (Hochschild, 1983, p. 127).*

In the long-term, Hochschild contended, the constant pressure of emotional labor may lead to drug use, excessive drinking, headaches, absenteeism, and sexual dysfunction.

The display of expected emotion is not always detrimental to well-being. The financial gains described above for food servers and poker players likely evoke feelings of satisfaction and security. Moreover, despite Hochschild's emphasis on the damage caused by emotion work, flight attendants whom the present authors have spoken with take pride in their ability to cope with airborne emergencies by hiding their own fears and offering calm faces to passengers.

The display of normative emotions may also protect incumbents from ill-being. The professional socialization of physicians, for example, entails learning how to appear concerned, but not so concerned that it causes severe psychological distress (Daniels, 1960). Thus, the physicians' ability to distinguish between the emotions they feel and those they convey to others helps them to continue performing effectively.

Further, Zajonc (1985) argued that smiling brings about physiological changes that cause the experience of subjective well-being. In other words, smiling makes us feel happy. Zajonc reclaimed a theory first proposed by Wynbaum in 1906. In brief, Wynbaum pointed out that the face has over 80 muscles and that all changes in facial expression influence the flow of blood to the brain. Smiling and laughing entail contraction of the zygomatic muscle, which increases blood flow to the brain. Zajonc contended that "It is like taking an oxygen bath. The cells and tissues

receive an increased supply of oxygen, causing a feeling of exuberance" (p. 10). This creative argument suggests that employees who are expected to smile may benefit from feelings of elation and exuberance. We must learn more about this interesting hypothesis, but implications for the link between emotional labor and subjective well-being are intriguing.

## EXPERIENCED EMOTIONS, FEELING RULES, AND INTERNALIZED FEELING RULES

The framework presented here emphasizes emotional expression, not emotions as intrapsychic states. But the discussion of well-being suggests that the match between felt emotions and expectations about emotional display is a promising area for future research. Specifically, expressed feelings may match well or poorly with: (a) experienced feelings, especially "true" feelings about the target of emotional expression; (b) external feeling rules; and (c) internalized feeling rules. Building on Hochschild (1979, 1983) and Thoits (1985), the match between feelings expressed in the role and these three demands on expression can lead to: *emotional harmony, emotional dissonance,* or *emotional deviance.*

*Emotional harmony* occurs when expressed feelings are congruent with experienced emotions, feeling rules, and expectations the incumbent holds for himself or herself about emotional expression. To illustrate, Mary Kay Ash, the founder of Mary Kay Cosmetics, insists that her salespeople exude enthusiasm (Ash, 1984). They are expected to take a "Vow of Enthusiasm" and sing the lyrics to "I've got the Mary Kay Enthusiasm." Emotional harmony is experienced by a salesperson who expresses normative enthusiasm, feels enthusiastic, and expects himself or herself to act enthusiastic.

Emotional harmony is an indicator of good fit between person and environment. More specifically, according to person-environment fit theory (Caplan, 1983), an employee will be free from occupational stress to the extent there is congruence among the behavior expected by role senders, the behavior that an employee expects of himself or herself, and the employee's personal characteristics. Thoits (1985) made a stronger argument: she contended that freedom from mental illness depends, in part, on the belief that one is acting in concert with feeling norms. Both perspectives lead to the hypothesis that emotional harmony is associated with well-being.

*Emotional dissonance,* according to Hochschild (1983), occurs when expressed emotions satisfy feeling rules, but clash with inner feelings. The effects of emotional dissonance depend on the internalization of feeling rules. Some people display "fake" emotions, yet believe that such acting should *not* be part of the job; this is *faking in bad faith.* To illustrate, a check-out clerk who was interviewed resented acting friendly to customers because "pasting on a smile should not be part of the job." The present authors are unable to find quantitative research on such emotional dissonance. But this is an example of person-role conflict, or a clash between personal values and role requirements. Research indicates that person-role conflict is a clear threat to employee well-being (Caplan, Cobb, French, Harrison, & Pinneau, 1975; Kahn et al., 1964). Moreover, since people who fake in bad faith have not internalized feeling rules, they are likely to be poor employees because they may comply with feeling rules only when monitored closely.

In contrast, the effects of suppressing true feelings are less clear when feeling rules are internalized. Some people display "fake" normative emotions and believe that such expressions should be part of the job; this is *faking in good faith.* Hochschild (1983) argued that faking in good faith is a threat to well-being because it causes estrangement between felt and expressed emotions. She contended, for example, that poor mental health may be suffered by outwardly cheerful flight attendants who have internalized norms about acting friendly, and who hide their contempt for passengers.

Yet writings on the burnout syndrome (e.g., Maslach, 1978a, 1978b, 1982) identify settings in which faking in good faith can enhance well-being. Mashlach (1978a) argued that members of helping professions can cope with burnout by acting concerned about clients, but allowing themselves to feel emotionally detached. Perhaps these are competing hypotheses. Or perhaps faking in good faith decreases stress only when it helps an employee cope with emotions that are felt too deeply.

*Emotional deviance* occurs when expressed emotions clash with local norms. Emotional deviance is the opposite of emotional dissonance because the organization member expresses inner feelings and disregards feeling rules. Again, however, internalization of feeling rules may influence the effects of incongruence between felt and expressed emotions.

Employees who express inner feelings and who reject local feeling rules may be punished. A rude flight attendant is likely to be fired, as is a funeral director who displays good cheer. Or such employees may quit. One student quit working as a Mary Kay Cosmetics salesperson because she thought that the norms were silly and "I couldn't bring myself to act happy and enthusiastic enough."

However, more serious consequences may haunt employees who express inner feelings that clash with role expectations, but have internalized those expectations. One sign of the burnout syndrome is that a person is unable to express empathy and concern, even though he or she believes that expressing such feelings is part of the job (Maslach, 1978a, 1978b). Similarly, Thoits (1985) maintained that people who perceive themselves as consistently expressing deviant emotions may label themselves as mentally ill. Essential to Thoits' argument is that the emotional deviant has internalized feeling rules. Both perspectives suggest that such emotional deviants risk poor mental health because they want to control the expression of inner feelings, but are unable to do so. Research is needed on emotional deviance in organizations. Is it as damaging as Thoits implies? Or are there unrecognized advantages?

Emotional harmony, dissonance, and deviance are thought to influence behavior in all work roles. Nevertheless, the most valuable occupations for research are those in which the demands on emotional expression or experience are strongest. Occupations with strong external demands for emotional display discussed here include flight attendants, "performers" at Disney World, and bill collectors. Perhaps the most revealing occupations, however, are those in which the internal feelings evoked by the job clash with feeling rules. Examples include poker players, judges, and referees; performing these jobs requires tolerating, and even enjoying, emotional dissonance.

## TOWARD FUTURE RESEARCH

The perspective outlined here is intended to encourage and guide further research on emotions displayed as part of the job. Future research on the match between experienced and expressed emotions has been discussed. Subsequent work in this area may also benefit from consideration of three additional questions: How should expressed emotions be measured? How powerful are the effects of displayed emotions? How should emotion work be managed?

### How Should Expressed Emotions Be Measured?

The study of displayed feelings is fraught with methodological hazards. Distinguishing between varieties of expressed emotions will be essential for future research. But this task may prove impossible because scholars do not agree about how long the list of emotions should be, nor do they agree about the boundaries between types of emotions (Kemper, 1981).

Studies also may be hampered because questionnaires, interviews, and records data—the staples of organizational research—will be of limited use. Employee self-reports about displayed emotions are suspect and few organizations keep records about such behaviors. Structured observation, the most promising method, could be difficult because emotions are displayed through a complex combination of facial expression, body language, spoken words, and tone of voice. Thus, a comprehensive method would require elaborate coding schemes for all four of these modes of emotional expression.

Some evidence suggests that initial efforts at structured observation may benefit from focusing on facial expressions. Leathers and Emigh (1980) reported that laboratory subjects who examined photographs could reliably associate emotion labels with facial expressions. For example, happiness, sadness, and surprise were decoded with over 95 percent accuracy. These results imply that structured observation could be used to reliably decode the facial expressions of organizational members. But field research poses the additional problem of rating the variable behavior of live subjects rather than the constant stimuli provided by photographs. Perhaps this hazard could be overcome by using multiple raters and video tape.

### How Powerful Are the Effects of Displayed Emotions?

A causal link between emotional display and outcomes for organizations and individuals has been proposed. These links require further empirical support. Managers of retail stores, for example, assume that "friendly" employees produce profits. Is this a valid assumption? Or are sales only influenced by variables such as store location or prices? A field study could be conducted to test the hypothesis that organizational gains are greater in stores where employees act friendlier.

That emotional transactions between members of the same organization may influence organizational performance also was suggested. For example, members of the team that designed Apple's Macintosh computer only selected newcomers who displayed wild enthusiasm about the machine (Tyler & Nathan, 1985). They claimed that shared enthusiasm about the machine and each other was essential to the team's success. Research could be conducted to discover if effort and creativity is higher among product design teams in which members act more enthusiastic. Or perhaps a curvilinear relationship between enthusiasm and creativity should be hypothesized—teams in which members feel compelled to express constant enthusiasm may suffer from groupthink (Janis, 1982).

The relationship between expressed emotion and organizational outcomes may be influenced by a host of contingencies; two are offered as a start for future research. The first contingency is the extent to which attributes other than expressed emotions do not vary. For example, the prices of airline tickets were strictly controlled by the Civil Aeronautics Board before the Airline Deregulation Act was passed in 1978. Before deregulation, advertisements focused heavily on the quality of service because all airlines were required to charge identical prices. The 1978 Act enabled airlines to compete on the basis of ticket prices. It is hypothesized that the strength of relationship between employee courtesy and ticket sales has been weakened by deregulation since the prices of tickets are no longer held constant.

The second contingency is the extent to which employees experience role overload, particularly when employees have too many customers or clients. Customers of uncrowded stores and patrons of empty restaurants expect employees to act friendly and relaxed. In contrast, customers who have been waiting for a clerk in a store or a seat in a restaurant may care only about the speed of the service, and may become irritated by employees who take time for polite conversation with each customer.

## How Should Emotion Work Be Managed?

There is a dearth of literature about how management can best influence the emotions conveyed in organizational settings. The emerging literature on interactions between employees and customers addresses a range of issues including the structure of verbal exchanges (Stiles, 1985), control over employee behavior (Mills, 1985), and the psychology of waiting in lines (Maister, 1985). The management of emotional display is addressed indirectly in this literature, but little

research explores this subject explicitly. Hypotheses testing is rare, and to what extent emotion work can be managed is not even known.

If organizations seek to hire employees who can convey certain emotions, then more questions arise. Can the ability to display such emotions be predicted? If so, how? Previous research suggests that behavior in the employment interview does not generalize well to the work role (Arvey & Campion, 1982). Thus, emotions displayed in the interview may not be expressed on the job. Moreover, as argued earlier, the emotions that enable an interviewee to *get* a job may be different than the emotions needed to *do* the job. Can interviewers be trained to overcome these weaknesses of the selection interview? Or perhaps other tools can be developed to identify a candidate's emotional skills.

A related question is how to teach emotion work skills, or perhaps such skills cannot be taught. Classroom programs often are used to teach employees to display expected emotions (Hochschild, 1983; Tyler & Nathan, 1985). Transfer of such behaviors from the classroom to the job is unlikely (Goldstein, 1974), but the present authors are not aware of any evaluation reports. Komaki, Blood, and Holder (1980) reported that behavior modification techniques can be used to enhance emotion work, but additional evidence is needed.

## CONCLUSION

The proposed framework is best viewed as a point of departure for both theory testing and theory building. The discussion suggests testable hypotheses. But it also suggests that more inductive work is needed so that our theories can capture the complexities of emotional expression in organizational life. And such inductive work ought to include field research. As Sherlock Holmes put it, "The temptation to form premature theories upon insufficient data is the bane of our profession" (Barring-Gould, 1967; cited in Van Maanen, 1979, p. 539).

# REFERENCES

Anderson, W. T., & Golden, L. (1984) Bank promotion strategy. *Journal of Advertising Research*, 24(2), 53–65.

Arther, R. O., & Caputo, R. R. (1959) *Interrogation for investigators.* New York: William C. Copp and Associates.

Arvey, R. P., & Campoin, J. E. (1982) The employment interview: A summary and review of recent research. *Personnel Psychology*, 35, 281–322.

Ash, M. K. (1984) *Mary Kay on people management.* New York: Warner Books.

Bandura, A. (1977) *Social learning theory.* Englewood Cliffs, NJ: Prentice-Hall.

Bell, M. (1984) Teaching of the heart. *The Journal of the American Medical Association*, 252, 2684.

Biddle, B. J. (1979) *Role theory: Expectations, identities, and behaviors.* San Francisco: Academic Press.

Boas, M., & Chain, S. (1976) *Big Mac: The unauthorized story of McDonald's.* New York: Dutton.

Caplan, R. D. (1983) Person-environment fit: Past, present and future. In C. L. Cooper (Ed.), *Stress research: Issues for the eighties* (pp. 35–77). Ann Arbor, MI: Institute for Social Research.

Caplan, R. D., Cobb, S., French, J. R. P., Harrison, R. V., & Pinneau, S. R. (1975) *Job demands and worker health* (Report No. 75–160). Washington, DC: U.S. Department of Health, Education, & Welfare.

Clark, R. E., & LaBeef, E. E. (1982) Death telling: Managing the delivery of bad news. *Journal of Health and Social Behavior*, 23, 366-380.

Crusco, A. H., & Wetzel, C. G. (1984) The Midas touch: The effects of interpersonal touch on restaurant tipping. *Personality and Social Psychology Bulletin*, 10(4), 512–517.

Czepiel, J. A., Solomon, M. E., & Surprenant, C. F. (1985) *The service encounter.* Lexington, MA: Lexington Books.

Daniels, M. J. (1960) Affect and its control in the medical intern. *American Journal of Sociology*, 66, 259–267.

Darwin, C. (1965) *The expression of emotions in man and animals.* Chicago: University of Chicago Press.

Denison, D. R., & Sutton, R. I. (in press) Surgical nurses: Issues in the design of a loosely-bounded team. In J. R. Hackman (Ed.), *Groups that work.*

De Rivera, J. (1977) *A structural theory of emotions.* New York: International Universities Press.

Driscoll, J. M., Meyer, R. G., & Schanie, C. F. (1973) Training police in family crisis intervention. *Journal of Applied Behavioral Science*, 9, 62–82.

Forbes, R. J., & Jackson, P. R. (1980) Non-verbal behavior and the outcome of selection interviews. *Journal of Occupational Psychology*, 53, 65–72.

Goffman, E. (1959) *The presentation of self in everyday life.* New York: Doubleday Anchor.

Goffman, E (1967) *Interaction ritual.* New York: Doubleday Anchor.

Goffman, E. (1969) *Strategic interaction.* Philadelphia: University of Pennsylvania Press.

Goldstein, I. I. (1974) *Training: Program development and evaluation.* Monterey, CA: Brooks/Cole.

Groves, R., & Kahn, R. L. (1979) *Surveys by telephone: A national comparison with personal interviews.* New York: Academic Press.

Hayano, D. M. (1982) *Poker faces.* Berkeley: University of California Press.

Hillman, J. (1961) *Emotion.* Evanston, IL: Northwestern University Press.

Hochschild, A. (1979) Emotion work, feeling rules and social structure. *American Journal of Sociology,* 85, 551-575.

Hochschild, A. R. (1983) *The managed heart.* Berkeley: University of California Press.

Imada, A. S., & Hakel, M. D. (1977) Influence of nonverbal communication and rater proximity on impressions and decisions in simulated employment interviews. *Journal of Applied Psychology,* 62, 295–300.

Janis, I. L. (1982) *Groupthink.* Boston: Houghton Mifflin.

Kahn, R. L. (1981) *Work and health.* New York: Wiley.

Kahn, R. L., Wolfe, D. M., Quinn, R. P., Snoek, J. D., & Rosenthal, R. A. (1964) *Organizational stress: Studies in role conflict and ambiguity.* New York: Wiley.

Katz, D., & Kahn, R. L. (1978) *Social psychology of organizations* (2nd ed.). New York: Wiley.

Kemper, T. D. (1981) Social constructionist and positivist approaches to the sociology of emotions. *American Journal of Sociology,* 87, 336-362.

Komaki, J., Blood, M. R., & Holder, D. (1980) Fostering friendliness in a fast food franchise. *Journal of Organizational Behavior Management,* 2, 151–164.

Leathers, D. G., & Emigh, T. H. (1980) Decoding facial expressions: A new test with decoding norms. *Quarterly Journal of Speech,* 66, 418–436.

Locke, E. A. (1976) The nature and causes of job satisfaction. In M. D. Dunnette (Ed.), *Handbook of industrial and organizational psychology* (pp. 1297–1350). Chicago: Rand McNally.

Maister, D. H. (1985) The psychology of waiting in lines. In J.. A. Cziepiel, M. R. Solomon, & C. F. Surprenant (Eds.), *The service encounter* (pp. 113-123). Lexington, MA: Lexington Books.

Maslach, C. (1978a, Spring) How people cope. *Public Welfare,* 36, 56–58.

Maslach, C. (1978b) The client role in staff burnout. *Journal of Social Issues,* 34, 4.

Maslach, C. (1982) Understanding burnout: Definitional issues in analyzing a complex phenomenon. In W. S. Paine (Ed.), *Job stress and burnout* (pp. 111-124). Beverly Hills, CA: Sage.

McCormick, E. J. (1979) *Job analysis: Methods and applications.* New York: American Management Association.

McGovern, T. V., & Tinsley, H. E. (1978) Interviewer evaluations of interviewee nonverbal behavior. *Journal of Vocational Behavior,* 13, 163–171.

Mead, M. (1951) *Soviet attitudes toward authority.* New York: McGraw-Hill.

Mills, P. K. (1985) The control mechanisms of employees at the encounter of service organizations. In J. A. Cziepiel, M. R. Solomon, & C. F. Surprenant (Eds.), *The service encounter* (pp. 163–178). Lexington, MA: Lexington Books.

Osgood, C. E., Suci, G. J., & Tannenbaum, P. H. (1957) *The measurement of meaning.* Urbana: University of Illinois Press.

Peters, T. J., & Waterman, R. H., Jr. (1982) *In search of excellence.* New York: Harper & Row.

Richman, T., (1984, July) A tale of two companies. *Inc.,* pp. 38–43.

Rosci, F. (1981 June) Grin and sell it. *Successful Meetings,* 106–107.

Rules for Santas—Don't say "ho, ho, ho." (1984, November 15) *San Francisco Chronicle,* p. 3.

Steinem, G. (1983) *Outrageous acts and everyday rebellions.* New York: Holt, Rinehart and Winston.

Stiles, W. B. (1985) Measuring roles in service encounters: The verbal exchange structure. In J. A. Cziepiel, M. R. Solomon, & C. F. Surprenant (Eds.,), *The service encounter* (pp. 213–224). Lexington, MA: Lexington Books.

Survey Research Center (1976) *Interviewer's manual* (rev. ed.). Ann Arbor, MI: Institute for Social Research.

Thoits, P. A. (1985) Self-labeling processes in mental illness: The role of emotional deviance. *American Journal of Sociology, 91,* 221-247.

Tidd, K. L., & Lockard, J. S. (1978) Monetary significance of the affiliative smile. *Bulletin of the Psychonomic Society, 11,* 344–346.

Trist, E. (1977) Collaboration in work settings: A personal perspective. *Journal of Applied Behavioral Science, 13,* 268–278.

Tyler, S. (Producer), & Nathan,J., (Producer) (1985) *In search of excellence* [Film]. New York: Public Broadcast System.

Unterman, P., & Sesser, S. (1984) *Restaurants of San Francisco.* San Francisco: Chronicle Books.

U.S. Department of Labor, Manpower Administration (1972) *Handbook for analyzing jobs.* (Stock No. 2900-0131) Washington, DC: U. S. Government Printing Office.

Van Maanen, J. (1973) Observations on the making of policemen. *Human Organizations, 32,* 407–417.

Van Maanen, J. (1978) The asshole. In P. K. Manning & J. Van Maanen (Eds.), *Policing: A view from the streets* (pp. 231–238). Santa Monica, CA: Goodyear.

Van Maanen, J. (1979) The fact of fiction in organizational ethnography. *Administrative Science Quarterly, 24,* 539–550.

Walt Disney Productions (1982) *Your role in the Walt Disney World show.* Orlando, FL: Walt Disney Productions.

Webb, E. J., Campbell, D. T., Schwartz, D. S., Sechrest, L., & Grove, J. B. (1981) *Nonreactive measures in the social sciences.* Boston: Houghton Mifflin.

Weick, K. (1979) *The social psychology of organizing* (2nd ed.). Reading, MA: Addison-Wesley.

Zajonc, R. B. (1985, April 5) Emotion and facial efference: An ignored theory reclaimed. *Science,* pp. 15–21.

# 11.  ORGANIZATIONAL PSYCHOLOGY AND THE PURSUIT OF THE HAPPY/PRODUCTIVE WORKER

Barry M. Staw

What I am going to talk about in this article is an old and overworked topic, but one that remains very much a source of confusion and controversy. It is also a topic that continues to attract the attention of managers and academic researchers alike, frequently being the focus of both popular books and scholarly articles. The issue is how to manage an organization so that employees can be both happy and productive—-a situation where workers and managers are both satisfied with the outcomes.

The pursuit of the happy/productive worker could be viewed as as impossible dream from the Marxist perspective of inevitable worker–management conflict. Such a goal could also be seen as too simple or naive from the traditional industrial relations view of outcomes being a product of necessary bargaining and compromise. Yet, from the psychological perspective, the pursuit of the happy/productive worker has seemed a worthwhile though difficult endeavor, one that might be achieved if we greatly increase our knowledge of work attitudes and behavior. In this article, I will examine this psychological perspective and try to provide a realistic appraisal of where we now stand in the search for satisfaction and productivity in work settings.

## APPROACHES TO THE HAPPY/PRODUCTIVE WORKER

One of the earliest pursuits of the happy/productive worker involved the search for a relationship between satisfaction and productivity. The idea was that the world might be neatly divided into situations where workers are either happy and productive or unhappy and unproductive. If this were true, then it would be a simple matter to specify the differences between management styles present in the two sets of organizations and to come up with a list of prescriptions for improvement. Unfortunately, research has never supported such a clear relationship between individual satisfaction and productivity. For over thirty years, starting with Brayfield and Crockett's classic review of the job satisfaction-performance literature,[1] and again with Vroom's discussion of satisfaction-performance research,[2] organizational psychologists have had to contend with the fact that happiness and productivity may not necessarily go together. As a result, most organizational psychologists have come to accept the argument that satisfaction and performance may relate to two entirely different individual decisions—decisions to participate and to produce.[3]

Though psychologists have acknowledged the fact that satisfaction and performance are not tightly linked, this has not stopped them from pursuing the happy/productive worker. In fact, over the last thirty years, an enormous variety of theories have attempted to show how managers can reach the promised land of high satisfaction and productivity. The theories shown in Table 11.1 constitute only an abbreviated list of recent attempts to reach this positive state.

None of the theories in Table 11.1 have inherited the happy/productive worker hypothesis in the simple sense of believing that job satisfaction and performance generally co-vary in the world *as it now exists*. But, these models all make either indirect or direct assumptions that *it is possible*

Barry M. Staw, "Organizational Psychology and the Pursuit of the Happy/Productive Worker" in *California Management Review*, Vol. XXVIII, No.4, summer 1986. Copyright ©1986 by the Regents of the University of California. Reprinted with permission.

**TABLE 11.1**

Paths to the Happy/Productive Worker

| | |
|---|---|
| Worker Participation | The Pursuit of Excellence |
| Supportive Leadership | Socio-Technical Systems |
| 9–9 Systems | Organizational Commitment |
| Job Enrichment | High Performing Systems |
| Behavior Modification | Theory Z |
| Goal Setting | Strong Culture |

to achieve a world where both satisfaction and performance will be present. Some of the theories focus on ways to increase job satisfaction, with the implicit assumption that performance will necessarily follow; some strive to directly increase performance, with the assumption that satisfaction will result; and some note that satisfaction and performance will be a joint product of implementing certain changes in the organization.

Without going into the specifics of each of these routes to the happy/productive worker, I think it is fair to say that most of the theories in Table 11.1 have been oversold. Historically, they each burst on the scene with glowing and almost messianic predictions, with proponents tending to simplify the process of change, making it seem like a few easy tricks will guarantee benefits to workers and management alike. The problem, of course, is that as results have come in from both academic research and from wider practical application, the benefits no longer have appeared so strong nor widespread. Typically, the broader the application and the more well-documented the study (with experimental controls and measures of expected costs and benefits), the weaker have been the empirical results. Thus, in the end, both managers and researchers have often been left disillusioned, sceptical that any part of these theories are worth a damn and that behavioral science will ever make a contribution to management.

My goal with this article is to *lower our expectations*—to show why it is so difficult to make changes in both satisfaction and performance. My intention is not to paint such a pessimistic picture as to justify not making any changes at all, but to innoculate us against the frustrations of slow progress. My hope is to move us toward a

reasoned but sustainable pursuit of the happy/-productive worker—away from the alternating practice of fanfare and despair.

## CHANGING JOB ATTITUDES

Although organizational psychologists have accepted the notion that job satisfaction and performance do not necessarily co-vary, they have still considered job attitudes as something quite permeable or subject to change. This "blank slate" approach to job attitudes comes from prevailing psychological views of the individual, where the person is seen as a creature who constantly appraises the work situation, evaluates the merits of the context, and formulates an attitude based on these conditions. As the work situation changes, individuals are thought to be sensitive to the shifts adjusting their attitudes in a positive or negative direction. With such an approach to attitudes, it is easy to see why job satisfaction has been a common target of organizational change, and why attempts to redesign work have evolved as a principal mechanism for improving job satisfaction.

Currently, the major debate in the job design area concerns whether individuals are more sensitive to objective job conditions or social cues. In one camp are proponents of job redesign who propose that individuals are highly receptive to concrete efforts to improve working conditions. Hackman and Oldham, for example, argue that satisfaction can be increased by improving a job in terms of its variety (doing a wider number of things), identity (seeing how one's various tasks make a meaningful whole), responsibility (being in charge of one's own work and its quality), feedback (knowing when one has done a good job), and significance (the meaning or relative importance of one's contribution to the organization or society in general).[4] In the opposing camp are advocates of social information processing. These researchers argue that jobs are often ambiguous entities subject to multiple interpretations and perceptions.[5] Advocates of social information processing have noted that the positive or negative labeling of a task can greatly determine one's attitude toward the job, and that important determinants of this labeling are the opinions of co-workers who voice positive or negative views of the work. These researchers have shown that it may be as easy to persuade workers that their jobs are interesting by influencing the *perception* of a job as it is to make objective changes in the work role.

The debate between job design and social information processing has produced two recent shifts in the way we think about job attitudes. First, organizational psychology now places greater emphasis on the role of cognition and subjective evaluation in the way people respond to jobs. This is probably helpful, because even though we have generally measured job conditions with perceptual scales, we have tended to confuse these perceptions with objective job conditions. We need to be reminded that perceptions of job characteristics do not necessarily reflect reality, yet they can determine how we respond to that reality.

The second shift in thinking about job attitudes is a movement toward situationalism, stressing how even slight alterations in job context can influence one's perception of a job. It is now believed that people's job attitudes may be influenced not only by the objective properties of the work, but also by subtle cues given off by co-workers or supervisors that the job is dull or interesting. I think this new view is a mistake since it overstates the role of external influence in the determination of job attitudes. The reality may be that individuals are quite resistant to change efforts, with their attitudes coming more as a function of personal disposition than situational influence.

## THE CONSISTENCY OF JOB ATTITUDES

Robert Kahn recently observed that, although our standard of living and working conditions have improved dramatically since World War II, reports of satisfaction on national surveys have not changed dramatically.[6] This implies that job satisfaction might be something of a "sticky variable," one that is not easily changed by outside influence. Some research on the consistency of job attitudes leads to the same conclusion. Schneider and Dachler, for example, found very strong consistency in satisfaction scores over a 16-month longitudinal study (averaging .56 for managers and .58 for non-managers).[7] Pulakos and Schmitt also found that high school students' pre-employment expectations of satisfaction correlated significantly with ratings of their jobs several years later.[8] These findings, along with the fact that job satisfaction is generally intertwined with both life satisfaction and mental health, imply that there is some ongoing consistency in job attitudes, and that job satisfaction may be determined as much by dispositional properties of the individual as any changes in the situation.

A Berkeley colleague, Joseph Garbarino, has long captured this notion of a dispositional source of job attitudes with a humorous remark, "I always told my children at a young age that their most important decision in life would be whether they wanted to be happy or not; everything else is malleable enough to fit the answer to this question." What Garbarino implies is that job attitudes are fairly constant, and when reality changes for either the better or worse, we can easily distort that reality to fit our underlying disposition. Thus, individuals may think a great deal about the nature of their jobs, but satisfaction can result as much from the unique way a person views the world around him as from any social influence or objective job characteristics. That is, individuals predisposed to be happy may interpret their jobs in a much different way than those with more negative predispositions.

## The Attitudinal Consistency Study

Recently, I have been involved with two studies attempting to test for dispositional sources of job attitudes. In the first study, Jerry Ross and I reanalyzed data from the National Longitudinal Survey, a study conducted by labor economists at Ohio State.[9] We used this survey to look at the stability of job attitudes over time and job situations. The survey's measures of attitudes were not very extensive but did provide one of the few available sources of data on objective job changes.

The National Longitudinal Survey data revealed an interesting pattern of results. We found that job satisfaction was fairly consistent over time, with significant relationships among job attitudes over three- and five-year time intervals. We also found that job satisfaction showed consistency *even when people changed jobs*. This later finding is especially important, since it directly contradicts the prevailing assumptions of job attitude research.

Most job design experiments and organizational interventions that strive to improve job attitudes change a small aspect of work, but look for major changes in job satisfaction. However, the National Longitudinal Survey data showed that when people changed their place of work (which would naturally include one's supervisor, working conditions, and procedures), there was still significant consistency in attitudes. One could, of course, argue that people leave one terrible job for another, and this is why such consistency in job attitude arises. Therefore, we checked for consistency across occupational changes. The National Longitudinal Survey showed consistency not only across occupational changes, but also when people changed *both* their employers and their occupations. This evidence of consistency tells us that people may not be as malleable as we would like to think they are, and that there may be some underlying tendency toward equilibrium in job attitudes. If you are dissatisfied in one job context, you are also likely to be dissatisfied in another (perhaps better) environment.

## The Dispositional Study

The consistency data from the National Longitudinal Survey, while interesting, do not tell us what it is that may underlie a tendency to be satisfied or dissatisfied on the job. Therefore, Nancy Bell (a doctoral student at the Berkeley Business School), John Clausen (a developmental sociologist at Berkeley), and I undertook a study to find some of the dispositional sources of job satisfaction.[10] We sought to relate early personality characteristics to job attitudes later in life, using a very unusual longitudinal data source.

There are three longitudinal personality projects that have been running for over fifty years at Berkeley (the Berkeley Growth Study, the Oakland Growth Study, and the Guidance Study), and they have since been combined into what is now called the Intergenerational Study. Usually when psychologists speak of longitudinal studies, they mean data collected from one or two year intervals. These data span over 50 years. Usually, when psychologists refer to personality ratings, they mean self-reports derived from the administration of various questionnaires. Much of the Intergenerational Study data are clinical ratings derived from questionnaires, observation, and interview materials evaluated by a different set of raters for each period of the individual's life. Thus, these data are of unusual quality for psychological research.

Basically what we did with data from the Intergenerational Study was to construct an affective disposition scale that measured a very general positive-negative orientation of people. We then related this scale to measures of job attitudes at different periods in people's lives. The ratings used for our affective disposition scale included items such as "cheerful," "satisfied with self," and "irritable" (reverse coded), and we correlated this scale with measures of job and career satisfaction. The results were very provocative. We found that affective dispositions, from as early as the junior-high-school years, significantly predicted job attitudes during middle and late adulthood (ages 40–60). The magnitude of correlations was not enormous (in the .3 to .4

range). But, these results are about as strong as we usually see between two attitudes measured on the same questionnaire by the same person at the same time—yet, these data cut across different raters and over fifty years in time.

What are we to conclude from this personality research as well as our reanalyses of the National Longitudinal Survey? I think we can safely conclude that there is a fair amount of consistency in job attitudes and that there may be dispositional as well as situational sources of job satisfaction. Thus, it is possible that social information processing theorists have been on the right track in viewing jobs as ambiguous entities that necessitate interpretation by individuals. But, it is also likely that the interpretation of jobs (whether they are perceived as positive or negative) can come as much from internal, dispositional causes (e.g., happiness or depression) as external sources. Consequently, efforts to improve job satisfaction via changes in job conditions will need to contend with stable personal dispositions toward work— forces that may favor consistency or equilibrium in the way people view the world around them.

## THE INTRANSIGENCE OF JOB PERFORMANCE

Although we have not conducted research on the consistency of performance or its resistance to change, I think there are some parallels between the problems of changing attitudes and performance. Just as job attitudes may be constrained by individual dispositions, there are many elements of both the individual and work situation that can make improvements in job performance difficult.[11]

Most of the prevailing theories of work performance are concerned with individual motivation. They prescribe various techniques intended to stimulate, reinforce, or lure people into working harder. Most of these theories have little to say about the individual's limits of task ability, predisposition for working hard, or the general energy or activity level of the person. Somewhat naively, our theories have maintained that performance

is under the complete control of the individual. Even through there are major individual differences affecting the quantity or quality of work produced, we have assumed that *if the employee really wants to perform better, his or her performance will naturally go up.*

There already exist some rather strong data that refute these implicit assumptions about performance. A number of studies[12] have shown that mental and physical abilities can be reliable predictors of job performance, and it is likely that other dispositions (e.g., personality characteristics) will eventually be found to be associated with effective performance of certain work roles. Thus, influencing work effort may not be enough to cause wide swings in performance, unless job performance is somewhat independent of ability (e.g., in a low skill job). Many work roles may be so dependent on ability (such as those of a professional athlete, musician, inventor) that increases in effort may simply not cause large changes in the end product.

In addition to ability, there may also be other individual factors that contribute to the consistency of performance. People who work hard in one situation are likely to be the ones who exert high effort in a second situation. If, for example, the person's energy level (including need for sleep) is relatively constant over time, we should not expect wide changes in available effort. And, if personality dimensions such as dependability and self-confidence can predict one's achievement level over the lifecourse,[13] then a similar set of personal attributes may well constitute limitations to possible improvements in performance. Already, assessment centers have capitalized on this notion by using personality measures to predict performance in many corporate settings.

Performance may not be restricted just because of the individual's level of ability and effort, however. Jobs may *themselves* be designed so that performance is not under the control of the individual, regardless of ability or effort. Certainly we are aware of the fact that an assembly line worker's output is more a product of the speed of the line than any personal preference. In administrative jobs too, what one does may be constrained by the work cycle or technical procedures. There may be many people with interlocking tasks so that an increase in the performance of one employee doesn't mean much if several tasks must be completed sequentially or simultaneously in order to improve productivity. Problems also arise in situations where doing one's job better may not be predicted upon a burst of energy or desire, but upon increases in materials, financial support, power, and resources. As noted by Kanter, the administrator must often negotiate, hoard, and form coalitions to get anything done on the job, since there are lots of actors vying for the attention and resources of the organization.[14] Thus, the nature of the organization, combined with the abilities and efforts of individuals to maneuver in the organization, may serve to constrain changes in individual performance.

## ASSESSING THE DAMAGE

So far I have taken a somewhat dark or pessimistic view of the search for the happy/productive worker. I have noted that in terms of satisfaction and performance, it may not be easy to create perfect systems because both happiness and performance are constrained variables, affected by forces not easily altered by our most popular interventions and prescriptions for change. Should organizational psychologists therefore close up shop and go home? Should we move to a more descriptive study of behavior as opposed to searching for improvements in work attitudes and performance?

I think such conclusions are overly pessimistic. We need to interpret the stickiness of job attitudes and performance not as an invitation to complacency or defeat, but as a realistic assessment that it will take very strong treatments to move these entrenched variables. Guzzo, Jackson, and Katzell have recently made a similar point after a statistical examination (called *meta-analysis*) of organizational interventions designed to improve productivity.[15] They noted that the most effective changes are often *multiple treatments*, where several things are changed at once in a given organization. Thus, instead of idealistic and optimistic promises, we may literally need to throw the kitchen sink at the problem.

The problem of course is that we have more than one kitchen sink! As noted earlier, nearly every theory of organizational behavior has been devoted to predicting and potentially improving job attitudes and performance. And, simply aggregating these treatments is not likely to have the desired result, since many of these recommendations consist of conflicting prescriptions for change. Therefore, it would be wiser to look for compatible *systems* of variables that can possibly be manipulated in concert. Let us briefly consider three systems commonly used in organizational change efforts and then draw some conclusions about their alternative uses.

## THREE SYSTEMS OF ORGANIZATIONAL CHANGE

### The Individually-Oriented System

The first alternative is to build a strong individually-oriented system, based on the kind of traditional good management that organizational psychologists have been advocating for years. This system would emphasize a number of venerable features of Western business organizations such as:

- Tying extrinsic rewards (such as pay) to performance.
- Setting realistic and challenging goals.
- Evaluating employee performance accurately and providing feedback on performance
- Promoting on the basis of skill and performance rather than personal characteristics, power, or connections.
- Building the skill level of the workforce through training and development.
- Enlarging and enriching jobs through increases in responsibility, variety, and significance.

All of the above techniques associated with the individually-oriented system are designed to promote both satisfaction and productivity. The major principle underlying each of these features is to structure the work and/or reward system so that high performance is either intrinsically or extrinsically rewarding to the individual, thus creating a situation where high performance contributes to job satisfaction.

In practice, there can be numerous bugs in using an individually-oriented system to achieve satisfaction and performance. For example, just saying that rewards should be based on performance is easier than knowing what the proper relationship should be or whether there should be discontinuities at the high or low end of that relationship. Should we, for instance, lavish rewards on the few highest performers, deprive the lowest performers, or establish a constant linkage between pay and performance? In terms of goal-setting, should goals be set by management, workers, or joint decision making, and what should the proper baseline be for measuring improvements? In terms of job design, what is the proper combination of positive social cues and actual job enrichment that will improve motivation and satisfaction?

These questions are important and need to be answered in order to "fine-tune" or fully understand an individually-oriented system. Yet, even without answers to these questions, we already know that a well-run organization using an individually-oriented system *can* be effective. The problem is we usually don't implement such a system, either completely or very well, in most organizations. Instead, we often compare poorly managed corporations using individually-oriented systems (e.g., those with rigid bureaucratic structures) with more effectively run firms using another motivational system (e.g., Japanese organizations), concluding that the individual model is wrong. The truth may be that the individual model may be just as correct as other approaches, but we simply don't implement it as well.

## The Group-Oriented System

Individually-oriented systems are obviously not the only way to go. We can also have a group-oriented system, where satisfaction and performance are derived from group participation. In fact, much of organizational life could be designed around groups, if we wanted to capitalize fully on the power of groups to influence work attitudes and behavior.[16] The basic idea would be to make group participation so important that groups would be capable of controlling both satisfaction and performance. Some of the most common techniques would be:

- Organizing work around intact groups.
- Having groups charged with selection, training, and rewarding of members.
- Using groups to enforce strong norms for behavior, with group involvement in off-the-job as well as on-the-job behavior.
- Distributing resources on a group rather than individual basis.
- Allowing and perhaps even promoting intergroup rivalry so as to build within-group solidarity.

Group-oriented systems may be difficult for people at the top to control, but they can be very powerful and involving. We know from military research that soldiers can fight long and hard, not out of special patriotism, but from devotion and loyalty to their units. We know that participation in various high-tech project groups can be immensely involving, both in terms of one's attitudes and performance. We also know that people will serve long and hard hours to help build or preserve organizational divisions or departments, perhaps more out of loyalty and altruism than self-interest. Thus, because individuals will work to achieve group praise and adoration, a group-oriented system, effectively managed, can potentially contribute to high job performance and satisfaction.

## The Organizationally-Oriented System

A third way of organizing work might be an organizationally-oriented system, using the principles of Ouchi's Theory Z and Lawler's recommendations for developing high-performing systems.[17] The basic goal would be to arrange working conditions so that individuals gain satisfaction from contributing to the entire organization's welfare. If individuals were to identify closely with the organization as a whole, then organizational performance would be intrinsically rewarding to the individual. On a less altruistic basis, individuals might also gain extrinsic rewards from association with a high-performing organization, since successful organizations may provide greater personal opportunities in terms of salary and promotion. Common features of an organizationally-oriented system would be:

- Socialization into the organization as a whole to foster identification with the entire business and not just a particular subunit.

- Job rotation around the company so that loyalty is not limited to one subunit.

- Long training period with the development of skills that are specific to the company and not transferable to other firms in the industry or profession, thus committing people to the employing organization.

- Long-term or protected employment to gain organizational loyalty, with concern for survival and welfare of the firm.

- Decentralized operations, with few departments or subunits to compete for the allegiance of members.

- Few status distinctions between employees so that dissension and separatism are not fostered.

- Economic education and sharing of organizational information about products, financial condition, and strategies of the firm.

- Tying individual rewards (at all levels in the firm) to organizational performance through various forms of profit sharing, stock options, and bonuses.

The Japanese have obviously been the major proponents of organizationally-oriented systems, although some of the features listed here (such as profit sharing) are very American in origin. The odd thing is that Americans have consistently followed an organizationally-oriented system for middle and upper management and for members of professional organizations such as law and accounting firms. For these high-level employees, loyalty may be as valued as immediate performance, with the firm expecting the individual to defend the organization, even if there does not seem to be any obvious self-interest involved. Such loyalty is rarely demanded or expected from the lower levels of traditional Western organizations.

## EVALUATING THE THREE SYSTEMS

I started this article by noting that it may be very difficult to change job performance and satisfaction. Then I noted that recognition of this difficulty should not resign us to the present situation, but spur us to stronger and more systemic actions—in a sense, throwing more variables at the problem. As a result, I have tried to characterize three syndromes of actions that might be effective routes toward the happy/productive worker.

One could build a logical case for the use of any of the three motivational systems. Each has the potential for arousing individuals, steering their behavior in desired ways, and building satisfaction as a consequence of high performance. Individually-oriented systems work by tapping the desires and goals of individuals and by taking advantage of our cultural affinity for independence. Group-oriented systems work by taking advantage of our more social selves, using group pressures and loyalty as the means of enforcing desired behavior and dispensing praise for accomplishments. Finally, organizationally-oriented systems function by building intense attraction to the goals of an institution, where individual pleasure is derived from serving the collective welfare.

If we have three logical and defensible routes toward achieving the happy/productive worker, which is the best path? The answer to this question will obviously depend on how the question is phrased. If "best" means appropriate from a cultural point of view, we will get one answer. As Americans, although we respect organizational loyalty, we often become suspicious of near total institutions where behavior is closely monitored and strongly policed—places like the company town and religious cult. If we define "best" as meaning the highest level of current performance, we might get a different answer, since many of the Japanese-run plants are now outperforming the American variety. Still, if we phrase the question in terms of *potential* effectiveness, we may get a third answer. Cross-cultural comparisons, as I mentioned, often pit poorly managed individually-oriented systems (especially those with non-contingent rewards and a bureaucratic promotion system) against more smoothly running group or organizationally-oriented systems. Thus, we really do not know which system, managed to its potential, will lead to the greatest performance.

## Mixing the Systems

If we accept the fact that individual, group, and organizationally-oriented systems may each do *something* right, would it be possible to take advantage of all three? That is, can we either combine all three systems into some suprasystem or attempt to build a hybrid system by using the best features of each?

I have trepidations about combining the three approaches. Instead of a stronger treatment, we may end up with either a conflicted or confused environment. Because the individually-oriented system tends to foster competition among individual employees, it would not, for example, be easily merged with group-oriented systems that promote intragroup solidarity. Likewise, organizationally-oriented systems that emphasize how people can serve a common goal may not blend well with group-oriented systems that foster intergroup rivalry. Finally, the use of either a group- or organizationally-oriented reward system may diminish individual motivation, since it becomes more difficult for the person to associate his behavior with collective accomplishments and outcomes. Thus, by mixing the motivational approaches, we may end up with a watered-down treatment that does not fulfill the potential of *any* of the three systems.

In deciding which system to use, we need to face squarely the costs as well as benefits of the three approaches. For example, firms considering an individually-oriented system should assess not only the gains associated with increases in individual motivation, but also potential losses in collaboration that might result from interpersonal competition. Similarly, companies thinking of using a group-oriented system need to study the trade-offs of intergroup competition that can be a byproduct of increased intragroup solidarity. And, before thinking than an organizationally-oriented system will solve all the firm's problems, one needs to know whether motivation to achieve collective goals can be heightened to the point where it outweighs potential losses in motivation toward personal and group interests. These trade-offs are not trivial. they trigger considerations of human resource policy as well as more general philosophical issues of what the organization wants to be. They also involve technical problems for which current organizational research has few solutions, since scholars have tended to study treatments in isolation rather than the effect of larger systems of variables.

So far, all we can be sure of is that task structure plays a key role in formulating the proper motivational strategy. As an example, consider the following cases: a sales organization can be divided into discrete territories (where total performance is largely the sum of individual efforts), a research organization where several product groups are charged with making new developments (where aggregate performance is close to the sum of group efforts), and a high-technology company where success and failure is due to total collaboration and collective effort. In each of these three cases, the choice of the proper motivational system will be determined by whether one views individual, group, or collective effort as the most important element. Such a choice is also determined by the degree to which one is willing to sacrifice (or trade-off) a degree of performance from other elements of the system, be they the behavior of individuals, groups, or the collective whole. Thus, the major point is that each motivational system has its relative strengths and weaknesses—that despite the claims of many of our theories of management, there is no simple or conflict-free road to the happy/productive worker.

## CONCLUSION

Although this article started by noting that the search for the happy/productive worker has been a rather quixotic venture, I have tried to end the discussion with some guarded optimism. By using individual, group, and organizational systems, I have shown how it is *at least possible* to create changes than can overwhelm the forces for stability in both job attitudes and performance. None of these three approaches are a panacea that will solve all of an organization's problems, and no doubt some very hard choices must be made between them. Yet, caution need not preclude action. Therefore, rather than the usual academic's plea for further research or the consultant's claim for bountiful results, we need actions that are flexible enough to allow for mistakes and adjustments along the way.

## REFERENCES

1. A. H. Brayfield and W. H. Crockett, "Employee Attitudes and Employee Performance," *Psychological Bulletin*, 51 (1955):396–424.

2. Victor H. Vroom, *Work and Motivation* (New York, NY: Wiley, 1969).

3. James G. March and Herbert A. Simon, *Organizations* (New York, NY: Wiley, 1958).

4. Richard J. Hackman and Greg R. Oldham, *Work Redesign* (Reading, MA: Addison-Wesley, 1980).

5. E.g., Gerald R. Salancik and Jeffrey Pfeffer, "A Social Information Processing Approach to Job Attitudes and Task Design" *Administrative Science Quarterly*, 23 (1978):224–253.

6. Robert Kahn,(1985).

7. Benjamin Schneider and Peter Dachler, "A Note on the Stability of the Job Description Index," *Journal of Applied Psychology*, 63 (1978):650–653.

8. Elaine D. Pulakos and Neil Schmitt,"A Longitudinal Study of a Valance Model Approach for the Prediction of Job Satisfaction of New Employees,"*Journal of Applied Psychology,* 68 (1983):307–312.

9. Barry M. Staw and Jerry Ross, "Stability in the Midst of Change: A Dispositional Approach to Job Attitudes,"*Journal of Applied Psychology*, 70 (1985):469–480.

10. Barry M. Staw, Nancy E. Bell, and John A. Clausen,"The Dispositional Approach to Job Attitudes: A Lifetime Longitudinal Test,"*Administrative Science Quarterly* (March 1986).

11. See, Lawrence H. Peters, Edward J. O'Connor, andJoe R. Eulberg, "Situational Constraints: Sources, Consequences, and Future Considerations," in Kendreth M. Rowland and Gerald R. Ferris, eds., *Research in Personnel and Human Resources Management*, Vol. 3 (Greenwich, CT: JAI Press, 1985).

12. For a review, see Marvin D. Dunnette, "Aptitudes, Abilities, and Skills" in Marvin D. Dunnette, ed.,*Handbook of Industrial and Organizational Psychology* (Chicago, IL: Rand McNally, 1976).

13. As found by John Clausen, personal communications, 1986.

14. Rosabeth M. Kanter, *The Change Masters* (New York, NY: Simon& Schuster, 1983).

15. Richard A. Guzzo, Susan E. Jackson, and Raymond A. Katzell,"Meta-analysis Analysis," in Barry M. Staw and Larry L. Cummings, eds., *Research in Organizational Behavior*, Volume 9 (Greenwich, CT: JAI Press, 1987).

16. See, Harold J. Leavitt, "Suppose We Took Groups Seriously," in E. L. Cass and F. G. Zimmer, eds., *Man and Work in Society* New York, NY: Van Nostrand, 1975).

17. William Ouchi, *Theory Z: How American Business Can Meet the Japanese Challenge* (Reading, MA: Addison-Wesley, 1981); Edward E. Lawler, III, "Increasing Worker Involvement to Enhance Organizational Effectiveness," in Paul Goodman, ed., *Change in Organizations* (San Francisco, CA: Jossey-Bass, 1982).

# Absenteeism and Turnover

## 12. MAJOR INFLUENCES ON EMPLOYEE ATTENDANCE: A PROCESS MODEL*

Richard M. Steers and Susan R. Rhodes

Each year, it is estimated that over 400 million work days are lost in the United States due to employee absenteeism, or about 5.1 days lost per employee (Yolles, Carone, & Krinsky, 1975). In many industries, daily blue-collar absenteeism runs as high as 10% to 20% of the workforce (Lawler, 1971). A recent study by Mirvis and Lawler (1977) estimates the cost of absenteeism among non-managerial personnel to be about $66 per day per employee; this estimate includes both direct salary and fringe benefit costs, as well as costs associated with temporary replacement and estimated loss of profit. While such figures are admittedly crude, combining the estimated total days lost with the costs associated with absenteeism yields an estimated annual cost of absenteeism in the U.S. of $26.4 billion! Even taking the more conservative minimum wage rate yields

an estimated annual cost of $8.5 billion. Clearly, the phenomenon of employee absenteeism is an important area for empirical research and management concern....

A review of existing research indicates that investigators of employee absenteeism have typically examined bivariate correlations between a set of variables and subsequent absenteeism (Muchinsky, 1977; Nicholson, Brown, & Chadwick-Jones, 1976; Porter & Steers, 1973; Vroom, 1964). Little in the way of comprehensive theory-building can be found, with the possible exception of Gibson (1966). Moreover, two basic (and questionable) assumptions permeate the work that has been done to date. First, the current literature largely assumes that job dissatisfaction represents the primary cause of absenteeism. Unfortunately, however, existing

*Support for this paper was provided by funds supplied under ONR Contract No. N00014-76-C-0164, NR 170-812.

"Major Influence and Employee Attendance: A Process Model" by Richard M. Steers and Susan R. Rhodes from *Journal of Applied Psychology*, 1978. 63, 391–407. Copyright ©1978 by the American Psychological Association. Reprinted by permission of the publisher and Richard M. Steers.

research consistently finds only weak support for this hypothesis. Locke (1976), for example, points out that the magnitude of the correlation between dissatisfaction and absenteeism is generally quite low, seldom surpassing $r = .40$ and typically much lower. Moreover, Nicholson et al. (1976), in their review of 29 such studies, concluded that "at best it seems that job satisfaction and absence from work are tenuously related" (p. 734). Nicholson et al. also observed that the strength of this relationship deteriorates as one moves from group-based studies to individually-based studies. Similar weak findings have been reported earlier (Porter & Steers, 1973; Vroom, 1964). Implicit in these modest findings is the probable existence of additional variables (both personal and organizational) which may serve to moderate or enhance the satisfaction-attendance relationship.

The second major problem to be found in much of the current work on absenteeism is the implicit assumption that employees are generally free to choose whether or not to come to work. As noted by Herman (1973) and others, such is often not the case. In a variety of studies, important situational constraints were found which influenced the attitude-behavior relationship (Herman, 1973; Ilgen & Hollenback, 1977; Morgan & Herman, 1976; Smith, 1977). Hence, there appear to be a variety of situational constraints (e.g., poor health, family responsibilities, transportation problems) that can interfere with free choice in an attendance decision. Thus, a comprehensive model of attendance must include not only job attitudes and other influences on attendance motivation but also situational constraints that inhibit a strong motivation-behavior relationship.

In view of the multitude of narrowly-focused studies of absenteeism but the dearth of conceptual frameworks for integrating these findings, it appears useful to attempt to identify the major sets of variables that influence attendance behavior and to suggest how such variables fit together into a general model of employee attendance. Toward this end, a model of employee attendance is presented here. This model incorporates

both voluntary and involuntary absenteeism and is based on a review of 104 studies of absenteeism (see Rhodes & Steers, Note 4)....

## THE CONCEPTUAL MODEL

The model proposed here attempts to examine in a systematic and comprehensive fashion the various influences on employee attendance behavior. Briefly stated, it is suggested that an employee's attendance is largely a function of two important variables: (1) an employee's motivation to attend; and (2) an employee's ability to attend. Both of these factors are included in the schematic diagram presented in Figure 12.1 and each will be discussed separately as it relates to existing research. First, we shall examine the proposed antecedents of attendance motivation.

### Job Situation, Satisfaction, and Attendance Motivation

A fundamental premise of the model suggested here is that an employee's motivation to come to work represents the primary influence on actual attendance, assuming one has the ability to attend (Herman, 1973; Locke, 1968). Given this, questions must be raised concerning the major influences on attendance motivation. Available evidence indicates that such motivation is determined largely by a combination of: (1) an employee's effective responses to the job situation; and (2) various internal and external pressures to attend (Vroom, 1964; Hackman & Lawler, 1971; Locke, 1976; Porter & Lawler, 1968). In this section, we will examine the relationship between an employee's satisfaction with the job situation and attendance motivation. The second major influence on attendance motivation, pressures to attend, will be dealt with subsequently.

Other things being equal, when an employee enjoys the work environment and the tasks that characterize his or her job situation, we would expect that employee to have a strong desire

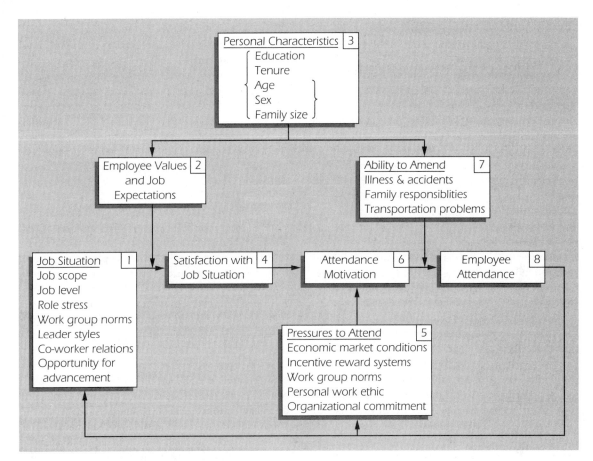

**FIGURE 12.1** A Model of Employee Attendance.

to come to work (Hackmanto & Lawler, 1971; Lundquist, 1958; Newman, 1974; Porter & Steers, 1973; Vroom, 1964). Under such circumstances, the work experience would be a pleasurable one. In view of this relationship, our first question concerns the manner in which the job situation affects one's attendance motivation. The job situation (box 1 in Figure 12.1), as conceived here, consists of those variables that characterize the nature of the job and the surrounding work environment. Included in the job situation are such variables as: (1) job scope; (2) job level; (3) role stress; (4) work group size; (5) leader style; (6) co-worker relations; and (7) opportunities for advancement. In essence, available evidence suggests that variables such as these strongly in-

fluence one's level of satisfaction which, in turn, influences attendance motivation. . . .

## The Role of Employee Values and Job Expectations

Considerable evidence suggests that the relationship between job situation variables and subsequent satisfaction and attendance motivation is not a direct one (Locke, 1976). Instead, a major influence on the extent to which employees experience satisfaction with the job situation is the values and expectations they have concerning the job (box 2). It has been noted previously that people come to work with differing values and job expectations; that is, they value different features in a job and expect these features to be present to a certain degree in order to maintain membership (Locke, 1976; Porter & Steers, 1973).

To a large extent these values and expectations are influenced by the personal characteristics and backgrounds of the employees (box 3). For example, employees with higher educational levels (e.g., a college degree) may value and expect greater (or at least different) rewards from an organization than those with less education (e.g., a private office, a secretary, a higher salary, greater freedom of action). Support for this contention can be found in Hedges (1973). Moreover, older and more tenured employees often value and expect certain perquisites because of their seniority (Baumgartel & Sobol, 1959; Cooper & Payne, 1965; Nicholson et al., 1976; Nicholson, Brown, & Chadwick-Jones; 1977, Hill & Trist, 1955; Martin, 1971).

Whatever the values and expectations that individuals bring to the job situation, it is important that these factors be largely met for the individual to be satisfied. In this regard, Smith (1972) found that realistic job previews created realistic job expectations among employees and led to a significant decline in absenteeism. Somewhat relatedly, Stockford (1944) found that absenteeism was higher among a sample of industrial workers whose previous training was not seen as relevant for their current positions than among a sample whose training was more closely aligned with the realities of the job situations (see also: Weaver & Holmes, 1972). Hence, based on the limited evidence that is available, it would appear that the extent to which an employee's values and expectations are met does influence the desirability of going to work.

## Pressures to Attend

While satisfaction with the job situation thus apparently represents a major influence on attendance motivation, the relationship is indeed not a perfect one. Other factors can be identified which serve to enhance attendance motivation, probably in an additive fashion (Garrison & Muchinsky, 1977; Ilgen & Hollenback, 1977;

Nicholson et al., 1976). These variables are collectively termed here "pressures to attend" and represent the second major influence on the desire to come to work. These pressures may be economic, social, or personal in nature and are represented in Figure 12.1 by box 5. Specifically, at least five major pressures can be identified: (1) economic and market conditions; (2) incentive/reward system; (3) work group norms; (4) personal work ethic; and (5) organizational commitment.

*Economic and Market Conditions.* The general state of the economy and the job market place constraints on one's ability to change jobs. Consequently, in times of high unemployment, there may be increased pressure to maintain a good attendance record for fear of losing one's job. Evidence suggests that there is a close inverse relationship between changes in unemployment levels within a given geographical region and subsequent absence rates (Behrend, Note 1; Crowther, 1957). Moreover, as the threat of layoff becomes even greater (e.g., when an employee's own employer begins layoffs), there is an even stronger decrease in absenteeism (Behrend, Note 1).

However, when an employee knows that *he* or *she* is to be laid off (as opposed to a knowledge that layoffs are taking place in general), the situation is somewhat different. Specifically, Owens (1966) found that railway repair employees in a depressed industry who had been given notice of layoff because of shop closure had significantly higher absence rates prior to layoffs than a comparable group of employees who were not to be laid off. Owens suggests that, in addition to being a reflection of manifest anxiety, the increased absenteeism allowed employees time to find new positions. On the other hand, Hershey (1972) found no significant differences in absence rates between employees who were scheduled for layoffs and employees not so scheduled. Hershey argued that the subjects in his study were much in demand in the labor market and generally felt assured of finding suitable jobs. (Improved unemployment compensation in recent years may also have been a factor in minimizing absenteeism among those to be laid off.)

Hence, economic and market factors may be largely related to attendance motivation and subsequent attendance through their effects on one's ability to change jobs. When *general* economic conditions are deteriorating, employees may be less likely to be absent for fear of reprisal. However, when the *individual* employee is to be laid off, absence rates are apparently influenced by one's perceptions of his or her ability to find alternate employment. Where such alternatives are readily available, no effect of impending layoff on absenteeism is noted; when such alternatives are not readily available, absence rates can be expected to increase as employees seek other employment.

*Incentive/Reward System.* A primary factor capable of influencing attendance motivation is the nature of the incentive or reward system used by an organization. Several aspects of the reward system have been found to influence attendance behavior.

When perceptual measures of pay and pay satisfaction are used, mixed results are found between such measures and absenteeism. Specifically, three studies among various work samples found an inverse relationship between pay satisfaction or perceived pay equity and absenteeism (Patchen, 1960; Dittrich & Carrell, 1976; Smith, 1977), while six other studies did not find such a relationship (Hackman & Lawler, 1971; Newman, 1974; Nicholson et al., 1976; Lundquist, 1958; Garrison & Muchinsky, 1977; Nicholson et al., 1977). Three other studies found mixed results (Waters & Roach, 1971, 1973; Metzner & Mann, 1953). In short, it is difficult to draw any firm conclusions about pay and absenteeism from these perceptual measures.

In contrast, when actual wage rates or incentive systems have been studied, the results are somewhat more definitive. Lundquist (1958), Fried et al. (1972), Beatty and Beatty (1975), and Bernardin (1977) all found a direct inverse relationship between wage rate and absenteeism. The Bernardin study is particularly useful here because several potentially spurious variables (e.g., age, tenure) were partialled out of the analysis and because the results were cross-validated. Moreover, the Lundquist study employed multiple absence measures with similar results. Other studies cited in Yolles et al. (1975) point to the same conclusion. However, studies by Fried et al. (1972) and Weaver and Holmes (1972), both using the less rigorous "total days absent" measure of absenteeism, did not support this relationship. In view of the objective nature of actual wage rates as opposed to perceptual measures, it would appear that greater confidence can be placed in them than in the perceptual studies mentioned above. Hence we would expect increases in salary or wage rates to represent one source of pressure to attend, even where the employee did not like the task requirements of the job itself.

Several factors must be kept in mind when considering the role of incentives or reward systems in attendance motivation. First, the rewards offered by the organization must be seen as being both attainable and tied directly to attendance. As Lawler (1971) points out, many organizations create reward systems that at least up to a point reward *non*attendance. For instance, the practice of providing 12 days "sick leave" which employees lose if they fail to use only encourages people to be "sick" 12 days a year (see also: Morgan & Herman, 1976). In this regard, Garrison and Muchinsky (1977) found a negative relationship between job satisfaction and absenteeism for employees absent without pay but no such relationship for employees absent with pay. Hence there must be an expectancy on the part of the employee that attendance (and not absenteeism) will lead to desirable rewards. Moreover, the employees must value the rewards available. If an employee would prefer a three-day weekend to having additional pay, there is little reason to expect that employee to be motivated to attend. On the other hand, an employee with a strong financial need (perhaps because of a large family) would be expected to attend if attendance was financially rewarded.

Oftentimes, a major portion of an employee's income is derived from overtime work.

Consequently, the effects of such overtime on absenteeism is important to note. Two studies found that the availability of overtime work among both male and female employees was *positively* related to absenteeism (Gowler, 1969; Martin, 1971), while two other studies found no such relationship (Buck & Shimmin, 1959; Flannagan, 1974). One could argue here that the availability of overtime with premium pay can lead to an incentive system that rewards absenteeism, not attendance. That is, if an employee is absent during regular working hours (and possibly compensated for this by sick leave), he or she can then work overtime later in the week to make up for the production lost earlier due to absenteeism. Clearly, such a reward system would operate differently than it was intended to. However, in view of the fact that all four relevant studies used either weak absence measures or unduly small samples, the influence of overtime availability on absenteeism must remain in the realm of conjecture pending further study.

Several attempts have been made to examine experimentally the effects of incentive or reward systems in work organizations. In one such study, Lawler and Hackman (1969; Scheflen, Lawler, & Hackman, 1971) experimentally introduced a bonus incentive plan to reward group attendance among a sample of part-time blue-collar employees. Two important findings emerged. First, the employees working under the bonus plan were found to have better attendance records than those not working under the plan. Moreover, the group that was allowed to participate in developing the bonus plan had higher attendance rates than the other experimental group that was given the bonus plan without an opportunity to participate in its design. (See also: Glaser, 1976). Hence, both the adoption of a bonus incentive system to reward attendance and employee participation in the development of such a system appear to represent important influences on subsequent attendance.

A few studies have examined the role of punitive sanctions by management in controlling absenteeism. Results have been mixed. Two studies found that the use of stringent reporting and control procedures (e.g., keeping detailed attendance records, requiring medical verifications for reported illnesses, strict disciplinary measures) was related to lower absence rates (Baum & Youngblood, 1975; Seatter, 1961), while one found no such relationship (Rosen & Turner, 1971). Moreover, Buzzard and Liddell (Note 2) and Nicholson (1976) found that such controls did not influence average attendance rates, but did lead to fewer but longer absences. Such contradictory results concerning the use of punitive sanctions suggests that more effective results may be achieved through more positive reward systems than through punishment.

One such positive approach is the use of a lottery reward system, where daily attendance qualifies employees for an opportunity to win some prize or bonus. This approach is closely tied to the behavior modification approach to employee motivation (Hamner & Hamner, 1976). Four studies report such lotteries can represent a successful vehicle for reducing absenteeism (Nord, 1970; Tjersland, 1972; Pedalino & Gamboa, 1974; Johnson & Wallin, Note 3). However, in view of the very small magnitude of the rewards available for good attendance, it is possible here that results were caused more by the "Hawthorne effect" than the lottery itself. As Locke (1977) points out, in at least one of the lottery experiments (Pedalino & Gamboa, 1974), absenteeism in the experimental group declined even before anyone in the group had been, or could have been, reinforced. In addition, more conventional behavior modification techniques for reducing absenteeism, reviewed in Hamner and Hamner (1976), show only moderate results over short periods of time.

Finally, other approaches to incentives and rewards relate to modifying the traditional work week. For instance, Golembiewski et al. (1974) and Robison (Note 5) both reported a moderate decline in absenteeism following the introduction of "flexitime," where hours worked can be altered somewhat to meet employee needs. Moreover, while Nord and Costigan (1973) found favorable results implementing a four-day (4–40) work week, Ivancevich (1974) did not. Since both of these studies used similar samples, it is difficult to draw meaningful conclusions about the utility of such programs for reducing absenteeism.

*Work Group Norms.* Pressure for or against attendance can also emerge from one's colleagues in the form of work group norms. The potency of such norms is clearly established (Cartwright & Zander, 1968; Shaw, 1976). Where the norms of the group emphasize the importance of good attendance for the benefit of the group, increased attendance would be expected (Gibson, 1966). Recent findings by Ilgen and Hollenback (1977) support such a conclusion. This relationship would be expected to be particularly strong in groups with a high degree of work group cohesiveness (Whyte, 1969). In his job attractiveness model of employee motivation, Lawler (1971) points out that members of highly cohesive groups view coming to work to help one's co-workers as highly desirable; hence, job attendance is more attractive than absenteeism. In this regard, several uncontrolled field experiments have been carried out (summarized by Glaser, 1976) which found that the creation of "autonomous work groups" consistently led to increased work group cohesiveness and reduced absenteeism. It should be remembered, however, that work group norms can also have a detrimental impact on attendance where they support periodic absenteeism and punish perfect attendance.

*Personal Work Ethic.* A further influence on attendance motivation is the personal value system that individuals have (Rokeach, 1973). Recent research on the "work ethic" has shown considerable variation across employees in the extent to which they feel morally obligated to work. In particular, several investigations have noted a direct relationship between a strong work ethic and the propensity to come to work (Goodale, 1973; Ilgen & Hollenback, 1977; Feldman, 1974; Searls et al., 1974). While more study is clearly in order here, it would appear that one major pressure to attend is the belief by individuals that work activity is an important aspect of life, almost irrespective of the nature of the job itself.

*Organizational Commitment.* Finally, somewhat related to the notion of a personal work ethic is the concept of organizational commitment (Porter, Steers, Mowday, & Boulian, 1974). Commitment represents an agreement on the part of the employees with the goals and objectives of an organization and a willingness to work towards those goals. In short, if an employee firmly believes in what an organization is trying to achieve, he or she should be more motivated to attend and contribute toward those objectives. This motivation may exist even if the employee does not enjoy the actual tasks required by the job (e.g., a nurse's aide who may not like certain distasteful aspects of the job but who feels he or she is contributing to worthwhile public health goals). Support for this proposition can be found in Steers (1977) and Smith (1977), where commitment and attendance were found to be related for two separate samples of employees. On the other hand, where an employee's primary commitments lie elsewhere (e.g., to a hobby, family, home, or sports), less internal pressure would be exerted on the employee to attend (Morgan & Herman, 1976). This notion of competing commitments is an important one often overlooked in research on absenteeism.

## Ability to Attend

A major weakness inherent in much of the current research on absenteeism is the failure to account for (and partial out) involuntary absenteeism in the study of voluntary absenteeism. This failure has led to many contradictions in the research literature that may be explained by measurement error alone. [In fact, in a comparison of five absenteeism measures, Nicholson and Goodge (1976) found an average intercorrelation of $r = .24$ between measures, certainly not an encouraging coefficient.] Thus, if we are serious about studying absenteeism, a clear distinction must be made between voluntary and involuntary attendance behavior and both must necessarily be accounted for in model-building efforts.

Even if a person wants to come to work and has a high attendance motivation, there are many instances where such attendance is not possible; that is, where the individual does not have behavioral discretion or choice (Herman, 1973). At least three such unavoidable limitations on attendance behavior can be identified: (1) illness and accidents; (2) family responsibilities; and (3) transportation problems (box 7).

*Illness and Accidents.* Poor health or injury clearly represents a primary cause of absenteeism (Hedges, 1973; Hill & Trist, 1955). Both illness and accidents are often associated with increased age (Baumgartel & Sobol, 1959; de la Mare & Sergean, 1961; Cooper & Payne, 1965; Martin, 1971). This influence of personal characteristics on ability to attend is shown in box 3 of Figure 12.1. Included in this category of health-related absences would also be problems of alcoholism and drug abuse as they inhibit attendance behavior. [See Yolles et al. (1975) for a review of the literature on health-related reasons for absenteeism.]

*Family Responsibilities.* The second constraint on attendance is often overlooked: namely, family responsibilities. As with health, this limitation as it relates to attendance is largely determined by the personal characteristics of the individual (sex, age, family size). In general, women as a group are absent more frequently than men (Covner, 1950; Hedges, 1973; Kerr et al., 1951; Kilbridge, 1961; Isambert-Jamati, 1962; Flanagan, 1974; Yolles et al., 1975). This finding is apparently linked, not only to the different types of jobs women typically hold compared to men, but also to the traditional family responsibilities assigned to women (that is, it is generally the wife or mother who cares for sick children). Support for this assumption comes from Naylor and Vincent (1959), Noland (1945), and Beatty and Beatty (1975). Hence, we would expect female absenteeism to increase with family size (Ilgen & Hollenback, 1977; Nicholson & Goodge, 1976; Isambert-Jamati, 1962).

It is interesting to note, however, that the available evidence suggests that the absenteeism rate for women declines throughout their work career (possibly because the family responsibilities associated with young children declines). For males, on the other hand, unavoidable absenteeism apparently increases with age (presumably because of health reasons), while avoidable absenteeism does not (Nicholson et al., 1977; Martin, 1971; Yolles et al., 1975). In any case, gender and family responsibilities do appear to place constraints on attendance behavior for some employees.

*Transportation Problems.* Finally, some evidence suggests that difficulty in getting to work can at times influence actual attendance. This difficulty may take the form of travel distance from work (Isambert-Jamati, 1962; Martin, 1971; Stockford, 1944), travel time to and from work (Knox, 1961), or weather conditions that impede traffic (Smith, 1977). Exceptions to this trend have been noted by Hill (1967) and Nicholson and Goodge (1976), who found no relationship between either travel distance or availability of public transportation and absence. In general, however, increased difficulty of getting to work due to transportation problems does seem to represent one possible impediment to attendance behavior for some employees, even when the individual is motivated to attend.

## Cyclical Nature of Model

Finally, as noted in Figure 12.1, the model as presented is a process model. That is, the act of attendance or absenteeism often influences the subsequent job situation and subsequent pressures to attend in a cyclical fashion. For example, a superior attendance record is often used in organizations as one indicator of noteworthy job performance and readiness for promotion. Conversely, a high rate of absenteeism may adversely affect an employee's relationship with his or her supervisor and co-workers and result in changes in leadership style and co-worker relations. Also, widespread absenteeism may cause changes in company incentive/reward systems, including absence control policies. Other outcomes could be mentioned. The point here is that the model, as suggested, is a dynamic one, with employee attendance or absenteeism often leading to changes in the job situation which, in turn, influence subsequent attendance motivation.

## CONCLUSION AND DISCUSSION

Our review of the research literature on employee absenteeism reveals a multiplicity of influences on the decision and ability to come to work. These influences emerge both from the individuals themselves (e.g., personal work ethic, demographic factors) and from the work environment (e.g., the job situation, incentive/reward systems, work group norms). Moreover, some of these influences are largely under the control of the employees (e.g., organizational commitment), while others are clearly beyond their control (e.g., health).

We have attempted to integrate the available evidence into a systematic conceptual model of attendance behavior. In essence, it is suggested that the nature of the job situation interacts with employee values and expectations to determine satisfaction with the job situation (Locke, 1976; Porter & Steers, 1973). This satisfaction combines in an additive fashion with various pressures to attend to determine an employee's level of attendance motivation. Moreover, it is noted that the relationship between attendance motivation and actual attendance is influenced by one's ability to attend, a situational constraint (Herman, 1973; Smith, 1977). Finally, the model notes that feedback from the results of actual attendance behavior can often influence subsequent perceptions of the job situation, pressures to attend, and attendance motivation. Hence, the cyclical nature of the model should not be overlooked.

The importance of the various factors in the model would be expected to vary somewhat across employees. That is, certain factors may facilitate attendance for some employees but not for others. For instance, one employee may be intrinsically motivated to attend because of a challenging job; this individual may not feel any strong external pressures to attend because he or she likes the job itself. Another employee, however, may have a distasteful job (and not be intrinsically motivated) and yet may come to work because of other pressures (e.g., financial need). Both employees would attend, but for somewhat different reasons.

This interaction suggests a substitutability of influences up to a point for some variables. For instance, managers concerned with reducing absenteeism on monotonous jobs may change the incentive/reward system (that is, increase the attendance-reward contingencies) as a substitute for an unenriched work environment. In fact, it has been noted elsewhere that most successful applications of behavior modification (a manipulation of behavior-reward contingencies) have been carried out among employees holding unenriched jobs (Steers & Spencer, 1977). Support for this substitutability principle can be found in Ilgen and Hollenback (1977), who found some evidence that various factors influence attendance in an additive fashion, not a multiplicative one. Thus, the strength of attendance motivation would be expected to increase as more and more major influences, or pressures, emerged.

In addition, differences can be found in the manner in which the various influences on attendance affect such behavior. That is, a few of the major variables are apparently fairly *directly* related to desire to attend (if not actual attendance). For instance, highly satisfied employees would probably want strongly to attend, while highly dissatisfied employees would probably want strongly not to attend. On the other hand, certain other factors appear to serve a *gatekeeper* function and do not covary directly with attendance. The most prominent gatekeeper variable is one's health. While sick employees typically do not come to work, it does not necessarily follow that healthy employees will attend. Instead, other factors (e.g., attendance motivation) serve to influence a healthy person's attendance behavior.

In conclusion, the proposed model of employee attendance identifies several major categories of factors that have been shown to influence attendance behavior. Moreover, the model specifies, or hypothesizes, how these various factors fit together to influence the decision to come to work. Throughout, the model emphasizes the psychological processes underlying attendance behavior and in this sense is felt to be superior to the traditional bivariate correlational studies that proliferate on the topic. It remains the task of future research to extend our knowledge on this important topic and to clarify further the nature of the relationships among variables as they jointly influence an employee's desire and intent to come to work. It is hoped that the model presented here represents one useful step toward a better understanding of this process.

## REFERENCE NOTES*

1.  Behrend, H. Absence under full employment. Monograph A3, University of Birmingham Studies in Economics and Society, 1951.

2.  Buzzard, R. B., & Liddell, F. D. K. Coal miners' attendance at work. NCB Medical Service, Medical Research Memorandum No. 3, 1958.

3.  Johnson, R. D., & Wallin, J. A. Employee attendance: An operant conditioning intervention in a field setting. Paper presented at American Psychological Association annual meeting, Washington, D.C., 1976.

4.  Rhodes, S. R., & Steers, R. M. Summary tables of studies of employee absenteeism. Technical Report No. 13, University of Oregon, 1977. This report is available from the second author at the Graduate School of Management, University of Oregon, Eugene, OR 97403.

5.  Robison, D. Alternate work patterns: Changing approaches to work scheduling. Report of a conference sponsored by National Center for Productivity and Quality of Working Life and the Work in America Institute, Inc., June 2, 1976, Plaza Hotel, New York.

## REFERENCES

Baum, J. F., & Youngblood, S. A. Impact of an organizational control policy on absenteeism, performance, and satisfaction. *Journal of Applied Psychology,* 1975, **60,** 688–694.

Baumgartel, H., & Sobol, R. Background and organizational factors in absenteeism. *Personnel Psychology,* 1959, **12,** 431–443.

Beatty. R. W., & Beatty, J. R. Longitudinal study of absenteeism of hard-core unemployed. *Psychological Reports,* 1975, **36,** 395–406.

Bernardin, H. J. The relationship of personality variables to organizational withdrawal. *Personnel Psychology,* 1977, **30,** 17–27.

Buck, L., & Shimmin, S. Overtime and financial responsibility. *Occupational Psychology,* 1959, **33,** 137–148.

Cartwright, D., & Zander, A. *Group dynamics.* New York: Harper & Row, 1968.

*Reference Notes and References have been abridged.

Cooper, R., & Payne, R. Age and absence: A longitudinal study in three firms. *Occupational Psychology*, 1965, **39**, 31–43.

Covner, B. J. Management factors affecting absenteeism. *Harvard Business Review*, 1950, **28**, 42–48.

Crowther, J. Absence and turnover in the divisions of one company—1950–55. *Occupational Psychology*, 1957, **31**, 256–270.

de la Mare, G., & Sergean, R. Two methods of studying changes in absence with age. *Occupational Psychology*, 1961, **35**, 245–252.

Dittrich, J. E., & Carrel, M. R. Dimensions of organizational fairness as predictors of job satisfaction, absence and turnover. *Academy of Management Proceedings '76*. Thirty-Sixth Annual Meeting of the Academy of Management, Kansas City, Missouri, August 11–14, 1976.

Feldman, J. Race, economic class, and the intention to work: Some normative and attitudinal correlates. *Journal of Applied Psychology*, 1974, **59**, 179–186.

Flanagan, R. J., Strauss, G., & Ulman, L. Worker discontent and work place behavior. *Industrial Relations*, 1974, **13**, 101–123.

Fried, J., Wertman, M., & Davis, M. Man-machine interaction and absenteeism. *Journal of Applied Psychology*, 1972, **56**, 428–429.

Garrison, K. R., & Muchinsky, R. M. Attitudinal and biographical predictors of incidental absenteeism. *Journal of Vocational Behavior*, 1977, **10**, 221–230.

Gibson, J. O. Toward a conceptualization of absence behavior of personnel in organizations. *Administrative Science Quarterly*, 1966, **11**, 107–133.

Glaser, E. M. *Productivity gains through worklife improvement*, New York: The Psychological Corporation, 1976.

Golembiewski, R. T., Hilles, R., & Kagno, M. S. A longitudinal study of flex-time effects: Some consequences of an OD structural intervention. *Journal of Applied Behavioral Science*, 1974, **10**, 503–532.

Goodale, J. G. Effects of personal background and training on work values of the hard-core unemployed. *Journal of Applied Psychology*, 1973, **57**, 1–9.

Gowler, D. Determinants of the supply of labour to the firm. *Journal of Management Studies*, 1969, **6**, 73–95.

Hackman, J. R., & Lawler, E. E., III. Employee reactions to job characteristics. *Journal of Applied Psychology Monograph*, 1971, **55**, 259–286.

Hamner, W. C., & Hamner, E. P. Behavior modification on the bottom line. *Organizational Dynamics*, 1976, 4(4), 2–21.

Hedges, J. N. Absence from work—A look at some national data. *Monthly Labor Review*, 1973, **96**, 24–31.

Herman, J. B. Are situational contingencies limiting job attitude-job performance relationships? *Organizational Behavior and Human Performance*, 1973, **10**, 208–224.

Hershey, R. Effects of anticipated job loss on employee behavior. *Journal of Applied Psychology*, 1972, **56**, 273–274.

Hill, J. M., & Trist, E. L. Changes in accidents and other absences with length of service. *Human Relations*, 1955, **8**, 121–152.

Ilgen, D. R., & Hollenback, J. H. The role of job satisfaction in absence behavior. *Organizational Behavior and Human Performance,* 1977, **19**, 148–161.

Isambert-Jamati, V. Absenteeism among women workers in industry. *International Labour Review,* 1962, **85**, 248–261.

Ivancevich, J. M. Effects of the shorter workweek on selected satisfaction and performance measures. *Journal of Applied Psychology,* 1974, **59**, 717–721.

Kerr, W., Koppelmeier, G., & Sullivan, J. Absenteeism turnover and morale in a metals fabrication factory. *Occupational Psychology,* 1951, **25**, 50–55.

Kilbridge, M. Turnover, absence, and transfer rates as indicators of employee dissatisfaction with repetitive work. *Industrial and Labor Relations Review,* 1961, **15**, 21–32.

Knox, J. B. Absenteeism and turnover in an Argentine factory. *American Sociological Review,* 1961, **26**, 424–428.

Lawler, E. E., III. *Pay and organizational effectiveness.* New York: McGraw-Hill, 1971.

Lawler, E. E., III, & Hackman, J. R. Impact of employee participation in the development of pay incentive plans: A field experiment. *Journal of Applied Psychology,* 1969, **53**, 467–471.

Locke, E. A. Toward a theory of task motivation and incentives. *Organizational Behavior and Human Performance,* 1968, **3**, 157–189.

Locke, E. A. The nature and causes of job satisfaction. In M. D. Dunnette (Ed.), *Handbook of industrial and organizational psychology.* Chicago: Rand McNally, 1976, pp. 1297–1349.

Locke, E. A. The myths of behavior mod in organizations. *Academy of Management Review,* 1977, **2**, 543–553.

Lundquist, A. Absenteeism and job turnover as a consequence of unfavorable job adjustment. *Acta Sociologica,* 1958, **3**, 119–131.

Martin, J. Some aspects of absence in a light engineering factory. *Occupational Psychology,* 1971, **45**, 77–91.

Metzner, H., & Mann, F. Employee attitudes and absences. *Personnel Psychology,* 1953, **6**, 467–485.

Mirvis, P. H., & Lawler, E. E., III. Measuring the financial impact of employee attitudes. *Journal of Applied Psychology,* 1977, **62**, 1–8.

Morgan, L. G., & Herman, J. B. Perceived consequences of absenteeism. *Journal of Applied Psychology,* 1976, **61**, 738–742.

Muchinsky, P. M. Employee absenteeism: A review of the literature. *Journal of Vocational Behavior,* 1977, **10**, 316–340.

Naylor, J. E., & Vincent, N. L. Predicting female absenteeism. *Personnel Psychology,* 1959, **12**, 81–84.

Newman, J. E. Predicting absenteeism and turnover. *Journal of Applied Psychology,* 1974, **59**, 610–615.

Nicholson, N. Management sanctions and absence control. *Human Relations,* 1976, **29**, 139–151.

Nicholson, N., Brown, C. A., & Chadwick-Jones, J. K. Absence from work and job satisfaction. *Journal of Applied Psychology,* 1976, **61**, 728–737.

Nicholson, N., Brown, C.A., & Chadwick-Jones, J. K. Absence from work and personal characteristics. *Journal of Applied Psychology,* 1977, **62,** 319–327.

Nicholson, N., & Goodge, P. M. The influence of social, organizational and biographical factors on female absence. *Journal of Management Studies,* 1976, **13,** 234–254.

Nicholson, N., Wall, T., & Lischeron, J. The predictability of absence and propensity to leave from employee's job satisfaction and attitudes toward influence in decision-making. *Human Relations,* 1977, **30,** 499–514.

Noland, E. W. Attitudes and industrial absenteeism: A statistical appraisal. *American Sociological Review,* 1945, **10,** 503–510.

Nord, W. Improving attendance through rewards. *Personnel Administration,* November 1970, 37–41.

Nord, W. R., & Costigan, R. Worker adjustment to the four-day week: A longitudinal study. *Journal of Applied Psychology,* 1973, **58,** 660–661.

Owens, A. C. Sick leave among railwaymen threatened by redundancy: A pilot study. *Occupational Psychology,* 1966, **40,** 43–52.

Patchen, M. Absence and employee feelings about fair treatment. *Personnel Psychology,* 1960, **13,** 349–360.

Pedalino, E., & Gamboa, V. V. Behavior modification and absenteeism: Intervention in one industrial setting. *Journal of Applied Psychology,* 1974, **59,** 694–698.

Porter, L. W., & Lawler, E. E. *Managerial attitudes and performance.* Homewood, Ill,: Irwin, 1968.

Porter, L. W., & Steers, R. M. Organizational, work, and personal factors in employee turnover and absenteeism. *Psychological Bulletin,* 1973, **80,** 151–176.

Porter, L. W., Steers, R. M., Mowday, R. T., & Boulian, P. V. Organizational commitment, job satisfaction, and turnover among psychiatric technicians. *Journal of Applied Psychology,* 1974, **59,** 603–609.

Rokeach, M. *The nature of human values.* New York: The Free Press, 1973.

Rosen, H., & Turner, J. Effectiveness of two orientation approaches in hard-core unemployed turnover and absenteeism. *Journal of Applied Psychology,* 1971, **55,** 296–301.

Scheflen, K. C., Lawler, E. E., III, & Hackman, J. R. Long-term impact of employee participation in the development of pay incentive plans: A field experiment revisited. *Journal of Applied Psychology,* 1971, **55,** 182–186.

Searls, D. J. Braucht, G. N., & Miskimins, R. W. Work values and the chronically unemployed. *Journal of Applied Psychology,* 1974, **59,** 93–95.

Seatter, W. C. More effective control of absenteeism. *Personnel,* 1961, **38,** 16–29.

Shaw, M. E. *Group dynamics.* New York: McGraw-Hill, 1976.

Smith, A. L. Oldsmobile absenteeism/turnover control program. *GM Personnel Development Bulletin,* February 1972.

Smith, F. J. Work attitudes as predictors of specific day attendance. *Journal of Applied Psychology,* 1977, **62,** 16–19.

Steers, R. M. Antecedents and outcomes of organizational commitment. *Administrative Science Quarterly,* 1977, **22,** 46–56.

Steers, R. M., & Spencer, D. G. The role of achievement motivation in job design. *Journal of Applied Psychology,* 1977, **4**, 472–479.

Stockford, L. O. Chronic absenteeism and good attendance. *Personnel Journal,* 1944, **23**, 202–207.

Tjersland, T. *Changing worker behavior.* New York: Manpower Laboratory, American Telephone and Telegraph, December 1972.

Vroom, V. *Work and motivation.* New York: Wiley, 1964.

Waters, L. K., & Roach, D. Relationship between job attitudes and two forms of withdrawal from the work situation. *Journal of Applied Psychology,* 1971, **55**, 92–94.

Waters, L. K., & Roach D. Job attitudes as predictors of termination and absenteeism: Consistency over time and across organizations. *Journal of Applied Psychology,* 1973, **57**, 341–342.

Weaver, C. N., & Holmes, S. L. On the use of sick leave by female employees. *Personnel Administration and Public Personnel Review,* 1972, **1**(2), 46–50.

Whyte, W. F. *Organizational behavior.* Homewood, Ill.: Irwin, 1969.

Yolles, S. F., Carone, P. A., & Krinsky, L. W. *Absenteeism in industry.* Springfield, Ill.: Charles C. Thomas, 1975.

# 13.  INTERMEDIATE LINKAGES IN THE RELATIONSHIP BETWEEN JOB SATISFACTION AND EMPLOYEE TURNOVER

William H. Mobley

Reviews of the literature on the relationship between employee turnover and job satisfaction have reported a consistent negative relationship (Brayfield & Crockett, 1955; Locke, 1975; Porter & Steers, 1973; Vroom, 1964). Locke (1976) noted that while the reported correlations have been consistent and significant, they have not been especially high (usually less than .40). It is probable that other variables mediate the re-lationship between job satisfaction and the act of quitting. Based on their extensive review, Porter and Steers (1973) concluded the following:

*Much more emphasis should be placed in the future on the psychology of the withdrawal process. . . . Our understanding of the manner in which the actual decision is made is far from complete [p. 173].*

The present paper suggests several of the possible intermediate steps in the withdrawal decision process (specifically, the decision to quit a job). Porter and Steers (1973) suggested that expressed "intention to leave" may represent the next logical step after experienced dissatisfaction in the withdrawal process. The withdrawal decision process presented here suggests that thinking of quitting is the next logical step after experienced dissatisfaction and that "intention to leave," following several other steps, may be the last step prior to actual quitting.

A schematic representation of the withdrawal decision process is presented in Figure 13.1. Block A represents the process of evaluating one's existing job, while Block B represents the resultant emotional state of some degree of satisfaction-dissatisfaction. A number of models have been proposed for the process inherent in Blocks A and B—for example, the value-percept discrepancy model (Locke, 1969, 1976), an instrumentality-valence model (Vroom, 1964), a met-expectations model (Porter & Steers, 1973), and a contribution/inducement ratio (March & Simon, 1958). Comparative studies that test the relative efficacy of these and other alternative models of satisfaction continue to be needed.

Most studies of turnover examine the direct relationship between job satisfaction and turnover. The model presented in Figure 13.1 suggests a number of possible mediating steps between dissatisfaction and actual quitting. Block C suggests that one of the consequences of dissatisfaction is to stimulate thoughts of quitting. Although not of primary interest here, it is recognized that other forms of withdrawal less extreme than quitting (e.g., absenteeism, passive job behavior) are possible consequences of dissatisfaction (see e.g., Brayfield & Crockett, 1955; Kraut, 1975).

Block D suggests that the next step in the withdrawal decision process is an evaluation of the expected utility of search and of the cost of quitting. The evaluation of the expected utility of search would include an estimate of the chances of finding an alternative to working in the present job, some evaluation of the desirability of possible alternatives, and the costs of search

(e.g., travel, lost work time, etc.). The evaluation of the cost of quitting would include such considerations as loss of seniority, loss of vested benefits, and the like. This block incorporates March and Simon's (1958) perceived ease of movement concept.

If the costs of quitting are high and/or the expected utility of search is low, the individual may reevaluate the existing job (resulting in a change in job satisfaction), reduce thinking of quitting, and/or engage in other forms of withdrawal behavior. Research is still needed on the determinants of alternative forms of withdrawal behavior and on how the expression of withdrawal behavior changes as a function of time and of changes in or reevaluation of the environment.

If there is some perceived chance of finding an alternative and if the costs are not prohibitive, the next step, Block E, would be behavioral intention to search for an alternative(s). As noted by Arrow (b) in Figure 13.1, non-job-related factors may also elicit an intention to search (e.g., transfer of spouse, health problem, etc.). The intention to search is followed by an actual search (Block F). If no alternatives are found, the individual may continue to search, reevaluate the expected utility of search, reevaluate the existing job, simply accept the current state of affairs, decrease thoughts of quitting, and/or engage in other forms of withdrawal behavior (e.g., absenteeism, passive job behavior).

If alternatives are available, including (in some cases) withdrawal from the labor market, an evaluation of alternatives is initiated (Block G). This evaluation process would be hypothesized to be similar to the evaluation process in Block A. However, specific job factors the individual considers in evaluating the present job and alternatives may differ. (See Hellriegel & White, 1973; and Kraut, 1975, for a discussion of this point.) Independent of the preceding steps, unsolicited or highly visible alternatives may stimulate this evaluation process.

The evaluation of alternatives is followed by a comparison of the present job to alternative(s) (Block H). If the comparison favors the alternative, it will stimulate a behavioral intention

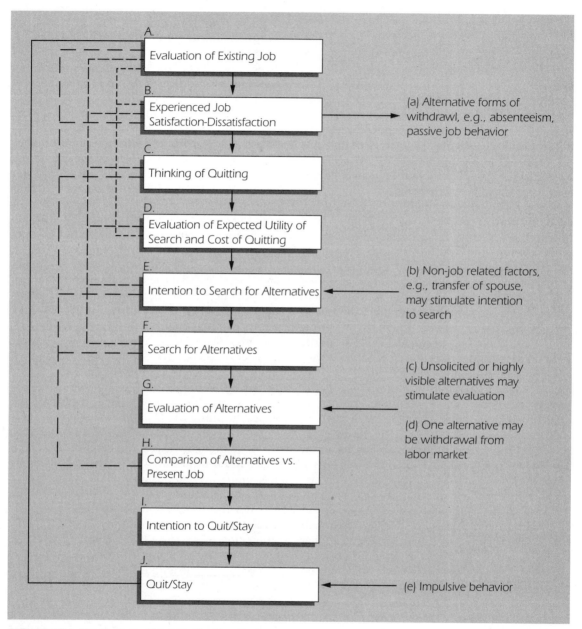

**FIGURE 13.1 The Employee Turnover Decision Process.**

to quit (Block I), followed by actual withdrawal (Block J). If the comparison favors the present job, the individual may continue to search, reevaluate the expected utility of search, reevaluate the existing job, simply accept the current state of affairs, decrease thoughts of quitting, and/or engage in other forms of withdrawal behavior.

Finally, Arrow (e) gives recognition to the fact that for some individuals, the decision to quit may be an impulsive act involving few, if any, of the preceding steps in this model. The relative incidence and the individual and situational determinants of an impulsive versus a subjectively rational decision process presents yet another area of needed research.

The model being described is heuristic rather than descriptive. There may well be individual differences in the number and sequence of steps in the withdrawal decision process, in the degree to which the process is conscious, and as noted earlier, in the degree to which the act of quitting is impulsive rather than based on a subjectively rational decision process. One value of such an heuristic model is to guide thinking and empirical research toward a valid descriptive model that can account for such individual differences.

There is a lack of research evaluating all or even most of the possible steps in the withdrawal decision process. There have been a few studies that have tested one or two of the intermediate linkages proposed in the present note. Mobley (Note 1) found high negative correlations between satisfaction and frequency of thinking of quitting (Blocks B and C). Atkinson and Lefferts (1972), who dealt with the association between Blocks C and J, found that the frequency with which people thought about quitting their job was significantly related to actual termination. Kraut (1975), looking at the associations among Blocks B, I, and J, found significant correlations between expressed intention to stay and subsequent employee participation. These correlations were much stronger than relationships between expressed satisfaction

and continued participation. Finally, Armknecht and Early's (1972) review is relevant to the relationships between Blocks D and/or F and Block J. They concluded that voluntary terminations are closely related to economic conditions.

Each of these studies fails to look at a complete withdrawal decision process. Such research would appear to be sorely needed. Several researchable questions that follow from the withdrawal decision process described in the present note were mentioned earlier. Additional questions include the following. Do individuals evaluate the expected utility of search? If so, what are the determinants and consequences of this evaluation? What are the consequences and determinants of behavior in the face of an unsuccessful search? In such cases, do individuals persist in search, reevaluate their existing jobs, reevaluate the cost of search, or engage in other forms of withdrawal? Is the process and/or content for evaluating alternative jobs the same as for evaluating the present job? Does satisfaction with the present job change as a function of the availability or evaluation of alternatives?

Attention to these sorts of questions rather than a continued replication of the direct relationship between job satisfaction and turnover would appear to be warranted. Particularly useful would be the longitudinal analysis of the variables and linkages suggested by the model. Such research would be responsive to Porter and Steers' (1973) conclusion that more emphasis should be placed on the psychology of the withdrawal decision process.

## REFERENCE NOTE

1. Mobley, W. H. *Job satisfaction and thinking of quitting* (Tech. Rep. 75-3). Columbia: University of South Carolina, College of Business Administration, Management and Organizational Research Center, 1975.

## REFERENCES

Armknecht, P. A., & Early, J. F. Quits in manufacturing: A study of their causes. *Monthly Labor Review*, 1972, **11**, 31–37.

Atkinson, T. J., & Lefferts, E. A. The prediction of turnover using Herzberg's job satisfaction technique. *Personnel Psychology,* 1972, **25,** 53–64.

Brayfield, A. H., & Crockett, W. H. Employee attitudes and employee performance. *Psychological Bulletin,* 1955, **52,** 396–424.

Hellriegel, D., & White, G. E. Turnover of professionals in public accounting: A comparative analysis. *Personnel Psychology,* 1973, **26,** 239–249.

Kraut, A. I. Predicting turnover of employees from measured job attitudes. *Organizational Behavior and Human Performance,* 1975, **13,** 233–243.

Locke, E. A. What is job satisfaction? *Organizational Behavior and Human Performance,* 1969, **4,** 309–336.

Locke, E. A. Personnel attitudes and motivation. *Annual Review of Psychology,* 1975, **26,** 457–480.

Locke, E. A. The nature and consequences of job satisfaction. In M. D. Dunnette (Ed.), *Handbook of industrial and organizational psychology.* Chicago: Rand-McNally, 1976.

March J. G., & Simon, H. A. *Organizations.* New York: Wiley, 1958.

Porter, L. W., & Steers, R. M. Organizational, work, and personal factors in employee turnover and absenteeism. *Psychological Bulletin,* 1973, **80,** 151–176.

Vroom, V. H. *Work and motivation.* New York: Wiley, 1964.

## 14. THE CONSEQUENCES OF TURNOVER

Barry M. Staw

### INTRODUCTION

The study of turnover has been a major interest of organizational psychologists for more than half a century. As Steers and Mowday (1980) have noted, over 1,000 separate studies on the subject can now be identified and at least 13 review articles have appeared in the literature over the last 25 years. The prime focus of all this empirical research has been to elaborate the antecedents of turnover, while theoretical efforts have largely been directed toward integrating the mass of findings into a model of turnover behavior (e.g., March & Simon, 1958; Price, 1977, Mobley et al, 1979; Steers & Mowday, 1980). This paper will neither review the turnover literature nor construct a new model to explain why individuals leave organizations.

The focus of the present paper will be upon the consequences rather than the antecedents of turnover. It is this author's contention that the yield of additional studies on the determinants of turnover will be rather low given the volume of existing empirical data and the detailed theoretical models already available. The chief goal of this paper, therefore, will be to make the case for a redirection of turnover research, illustrating the reasons for this change and showing the possible shape of new research.

## The Assumptions of Previous Turnover Research

Most of the existing empirical literature relates demographic, psychological, and economic data to instances of turnover, turnover being treated as a voluntary decision on the part of individuals to leave an organization. Because the goal of this research has been to predict or explain as much variance as possible in turnover rates for various jobs, occupations and organizational types, the implicit assumption underlying the effort has been that turnover is an important organizational problem—something which is costly to the organization and something which should be reduced. This assumption, as we will argue, is extremely suspect since turnover may bring positive as well as negative consequences to an organization.

The strength and endurance of the assumption that turnover is a negative consequence for organizations is understandable given three factors. First, turnover almost always involves some costs for the organization (e.g. recruitment, selection, training) and these costs may be more salient to administrators than any benefits which may result from a change in personnel. Second, because practicing organizational psychologists are generally charged with recruitment, selection, and training responsibilities within organizations, and since, as Pugh (1966) has noted, researchers in organizational psychology have tended to focus upon problems practitioners perceive as important, the negative side of turnover has been emphasized. From the perspective of a personnel department, turnover creates operating expenses for the organization and a major way for this department to contribute to the organization would seem to be a reduction in turnover expenses. Third, research in organizational psychol-

ogy has tended to focus on lower-level employees in organizations such as the behavior of blue-collar workers and their immediate supervisors. Research on turnover has been no exception, relatively few studies having been conducted on the turnover of managerial or professional personnel. Although there has existed a small literature on executive succession within sociology (which has interestingly *not* assumed turnover to be detrimental to the organization), there has been almost no interface between the succession and turnover literatures. As we will outline later in this paper, negative consequences may be more likely for turnover of lower-level employees than for managerial personnel. Thus, both practitioners' and researchers' assumptions about the nature of turnover may have been reaffirmed simply by the direction of their own inquiries.

In this paper we will outline several benefits as well as costs of turnover in organizations. What makes the task of understanding turnover difficult is the possibility of multiple and conflicting outcomes. In addition, it is likely that these outcomes are each conditioned by several moderating variables adding further complexity to the picture. Therefore, rather than simply listing and discussing potential benefits as well as costs for turnover, we will attempt to specify the conditions under which the benefits are likely to be greatest, the costs lowest, and vice versa. Because there is so little research on the consequences of turnover, our current analysis will necessarily be preliminary. But, before we can redirect empirical literature and build new predictive statements there is a need for systematic hypothesis formulation and speculation.

## THE COSTS OF TURNOVER

We will outline here some costs of turnover, most of which are well known and rather straightforward. We will, however, specify some moderating variables which may act to increase or decrease these costs for the organization. Thus, attention should be drawn to circumstances which can minimize or maximize the expense of turnover so that its role in organizational functioning can be more fully understood.

## Selection and Recruitment Costs

The most obvious consequence of turnover is the energy and expense of finding replacement personnel. When someone leaves an organization others must be recruited, screened through some selection mechanism, and finally hired. If large numbers of people leave an organization on a regular basis, the organization will most likely have adapted to this consequence by retaining full-time specialists in recruitment and selection, thereby increasing its administrative intensity (Kasarda, 1973). In fact, for organizations who hold members for only a relatively short and specified period (e.g., the military, universities, social clubs), the search for potential members and their selection becomes a very major function of the organization. However, if turnover is low or occurs on an irregular basis, organizational staff are usually assigned to recruitment duties on a temporary basis and this function may be subcontracted to another more specialized organization (e.g., personnel consultants, executive search agencies). Because large amounts of selection and recruitment generally lead organizations to institutionalize these functions, there may be certain economies of scale for these activities. Nonetheless, recruitment and selection can involve substantial costs to the organization, and these costs can be moderated by several additional variables.

One obvious moderator of the cost of turnover is the tightness of the labor market facing the organization for the particular position to be filled. In an extremely tight market the only place qualified candidates may be found is in competing organizations or in related occupational positions (e.g., someone with similar training but practicing an alternative specialty). Sometimes, it may even be necessary to isolate potential hires while they are still in training. The market for faculty with doctorates in accounting is so tight in American universities, for example, that doctoral students are frequently contacted by potential employers very early in their educational programs. In contrast to these efforts, recruitment in

a strong labour market may require nothing more than an appropriately written advertisement in order to secure hundreds of qualified applicants (advertisements for humanities faculty in American universities would be a clear example).

A second moderator of the cost of turnover is the level of complexity of the job to be filled. At high levels, potential candidates are difficult to isolate and agree upon by organizational members. It is not uncommon, for example, that the search for an executive will stretch out over a year's time due to both the uncertainty of the criteria being attached to the choice as well as the difficulty of reaching consensus on any particular candidate. Low-level positions, on the other hand, may have much clearer criteria against which to measure candidates, making both recruitment and selection a relatively routine process.

A third moderator of selection and recruitment costs is whether inside or outside succession is followed by the organization. If existing organizational personnel can be promoted or reassigned to the departed person's position, recruitment and selection costs may be drastically reduced. In fact, one person's departure from a high-level position may cause a chain of welcome promotions within the organization, necessitating the hiring of only one additional person at the bottom of the hierarchy.

## Training and Development Costs

Even when organizational members can be easily recruited and selected for an organization it may be months before the new employee can perform at the level of the departed member of the organization. If the role is complex the new member may need a long period of training; if the role is unprogrammed and the procedures as well as objectives undefined the individual may require time to build his or her own role in the organization (Graen, 1976). Thus, training costs can involve the direct expenses of formalized instruction programs, the costs of having other employees informally help the new organizational member, as well as the time period in which role performance is below that of the veteran employee. The moderators of training and development costs are nearly the same variables as those considered for selection and recruitment expenses. The level and complexity of the job will clearly affect the amount of training or time necessary to reach an effective level of performance. Succession of an insider versus the hiring of an outsider also will likely moderate training and development costs. Thus, on low-level jobs or inside promotions to higher level positions, training and development costs will be relatively lower than under other conditions.

## Operational Disruption

Aside from the recruitment, selection, training and development costs associated with turnover, the loss of large numbers of personnel or key members of the organization will sometimes prove costly in terms of general disruption. When people leave it may affect the ability of others to produce their work because of interdependence of work roles within the organization. If a key person leaves the whole system may break down if the organization is both highly interdependent and specialized. As a result, many organizations have backup personnel for key roles, and if a large number of roles are essential for functioning, employees may be trained in a multiplicity of skills. At the extreme, when members of a team are both necessary to the functioning of a mission and at the same time vulnerable to loss, each member may be trained to carry out the most essential tasks of the entire work unit.

The chief moderator of whether turnover causes an operational disruption is the centrality of the particular role to the organization's functioning. In general, the higher the level of the position to be filled the greater is the potential for disruption. Yet, there are some exceptions to this general rule. The loss of a key production manager or even a specialized equipment repair person (Crozier, 1964) may cause greater disruption to the organization than changing executive officers. Across all positions, the predictability of turnover will also be important (Price, 1977). Some organizations expect large amounts of turnover for lower-

level employees and have routinized the replacement of much of the organization. For higher-level positions, indication of impending departure greatly reduces risks of disruption since procedures can often be implemented to bypass the particular position in the organization or to fill it temporarily while a replacement is found.

## Demoralization of Organizational Membership

Having people leave an organization may involve costs beyond replacement and operational disruption. Because people typically leave one organization for an alternative organization, turnover may undermine the attitudes of those remaining. Those remaining in the organization may see their own fates as less desirable (left behind) and they may question their own motivation for staying. In essence, turnover provides salient cues about the organization and a role model for others. Thus, turnover may by itself trigger additional turnover by prompting a deterioration in attitudes toward the organization and making salient alternative memberships.

Like the other potential costs of turnover there may be several moderators of an effect of turnover on the demoralization of membership. As Steers and Mowday (1980) have noted, the perceived reason for leaving is one key moderator. If members are perceived to leave for nonorganizational reasons such as family problems, location, or economic conditions it will produce less of a demoralization effect than if turnover is perceived to result from the nature of the work, pay, or supervision. Likewise, if those who leave are members of a cohesive work group or possess high social status among the organizational membership, turnover will likely lead to greater demoralization. Finally, if the organization considers as one of its goals the maintenance of a stable membership (e.g., a voluntary organization such as a religious or social group), turnover will be a more severe blow than if the organization trains people who frequently follow multi-organizational careers (Hall, 1977). Many professional organizations, for example, employ individuals whose careers involve a sequence of organizational memberships. In such cases, departure to another high-prestige organization may actually bolster the attitudes of the membership, assuring them that commitment to the present organization is instrumental to their own long-term career goals.

## Summary of Potential Negative Consequences

Most people who have served on a search committee or have been employed in an organization during a turnover transition will testify that turnover presents certain costs to the organization. The cost of recruitment, selection, and training are salient to the organization, and are often quantified for the replacement of lower-level personnel. For the turnover of higher officials attention is generally focused upon possible disruption and demoralization effects.

We have identified several moderating variables which can serve to minimize these adverse effects of turnover. As we have noted, turnover will be least costly for persons in lower-level positions, in plentiful labor markets, in noninterdependent roles, from noncohesive work groups, who leave for nonwork reasons, provide advance indication of departure, and who are replaced by persons from inside the organization. Thus, the statement that turnover is costly for organizations should really be translated to an inquiry into the extent to which turnover will prove burdensome for the organization. Only in this way will one be able to evaluate the tradeoffs between the potential costs and benefits of turnover.

## POSITIVE CONSEQUENCES

The potential positive consequences of turnover have received very little attention in organizational psychology. The benefits of turnover are somewhat less obvious than the costs in that they may be less quantifiable and less attainable in the near-term. Yet, the positive aspects of turnover may contribute to the long-run viability of the organization.

As a rather crude way of demonstrating the potential positive consequences of turnover, one might examine some descriptive data on job tenure published by the U.S. Bureau of Labor Statistics. Table 14.1 compares job tenure among several major industries in the U.S. economy. One can see from this table that job tenure in the railroad industry (19.6 years) is more than three times that in durable goods manufacturing (5.7) and nondurable goods manufacturing (5.3), while over seven times that of wholesale and retail trade (2.6). Job tenure is also relatively higher in the U.S. Postal Service (10.3) than in private industrial jobs. Because the U.S. railroad industry and postal systems are reputed to be among the most inefficient units of the American economy, these data are at least suggestive of the fact that turnover may be too low rather than too high for many organizations and industries.

## Increased Performance

Because turnover by its very nature leads to training and development costs, it is often implicitly assumed that there is some standard level of performance that most individuals reach after an initial time period or passage through a learning curve. This traditional perspective leads one to assume that performance of a new employee will be initially low and, only after experience, will reach the level of the preceding employee. The obvious drawback to this perspective is that insufficient attention is paid to potential gains in performance following turnover. The new arrival may be more highly motivated than the old employee and may possess greater abilities and training. As an example, consider the effective work life of employees in high-stress roles such as air traffic controllers, in roles demanding of physical endurance such as mining and construction, or in roles requiring changing technical skills such as electronics engineering. These jobs would more likely contain a performance curve that is shaped as an inverted $U$ rather than the traditional $J$ shape (see Figure 14.1). In addition, consider many public service jobs such as social work, nursing, and police work in which the psychological demands of the job are relatively high. In these jobs new

**TABLE 14.1**
Median Years on the Job for Male Workers in Selected Industries

| Industry | Median Years on Job |
|---|---|
| Railroads and railway express | 19.6 |
| Agriculture | 11.5 |
| Postal service | 10.3 |
| Federal public administration | 7.6 |
| Automobile manufacturing | 7.0 |
| Chemical and allied products manufacturing | 6.8 |
| Mining | 6.4 |
| Electrical machinery manufacturing | 5.7 |
| Communications | 5.2 |
| Instrument manufacturing | 5.1 |
| Food and kindred products manufacturing | 5.1 |
| Finance, insurance, and real estate | 4.0 |
| Rubber and plastics manufacturing | 4.0 |
| Medical and other health services | 2.8 |
| Construction | 2.7 |
| Wholesale and retail trade | 2.6 |
| Entertainment and recreation services | 1.9 |
| All durable good manufacturing | 5.7 |
| All nondurable goods manufacturing | 5.3 |

Source: Bureau of Labor Statistics, 1975: A-13.

employees tend to be more idealistic and motivated to serve public needs immediately upon being hired and over each subsequent year tend either to conform more to a bureaucratic role (Blau & Scott, 1962; Van Maanen, 1975) or are subject to a psychological 'burn-out' in which employees distance themselves from the client being served (Maslach, 1978).

We would argue that most jobs have an inverted $U$ performance curve simply because performance is generally a joint function of skills and effort. While experience may contribute positively to job skills and knowledge, effort or motivation may be at its highest when the individual first arrives in the organization. The new employee may be characterized as optimistic, energetic, but also naive. In contrast, the long-term employee must be wise, but also cynical and sluggish. These hypothesized relationships between

skills, effort and experience are outlined in Figure 14.2 and, as shown, can provide the basis for the inverted $U$ performance curve. It should be noted, however, than any alteration of these underlying relationships would also change the resultant curve. There no doubt can be roles in which effort remains high over times as well as roles in which skills deteriorate with each passing year.

Greater effort should be placed into identifying jobs in which physical or psychological demand are patterned so that performance peaks early in employment and subsequently declines. In such cases, the average tenure of organizational members should be kept low in order to increase average individual performance. Thus, research should be placed into studying the relationship between individual job tenure and performance so that the *appropriate* rate of turnover

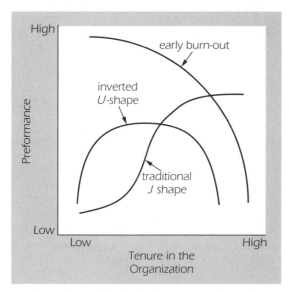

**FIGURE 14.1** Hypothetical Performance Curves.

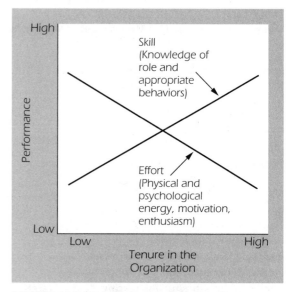

**FIGURE 14.2 Hypothesized Relationship Between Motivation, Skill, and Years Experience.**

could be identified. For some jobs tenure may have a positive-linear relation to performance and some a negative-linear relation, yet for most jobs tenure and performance will be nonlinearly related as either a narrowly or widely inverted *U*.

While research on the relation between job tenure and performance should be encouraged for the individual level or analysis, some research should also be directed at the effects of the *distribution* of tenure within organizations. As Pfeffer (1979) has noted, organizations and work units may differ in performance because their age and tenure distributions differ. Pfeffer argues for the study of "organizational demography" and we would support such an effort since there may not be a simple parallel between relationships at the individual and collective levels (Staw & Oldham, 1978). On the surface, one might think that a particular curve obtained for the individual tenure-performance relationship would also apply to the work group. In practice, however, tenure may not affect work groups in the same way as individuals since group functions may be dispersed among the membership (Bales, 1958; Bavelas, 1960). Within a work group some members may fulfill the knowledge function (actually serving as the unit's memory for experiences,

shortcuts and traditions) while others may serve an an energizing function (generating enthusiasm or providing perseverance on the most difficult tasks). Therefore, a mixture of younger and older members may lead to more effective group functioning than uniformity at any level of experience.

Wells and Pelz (1966) in a study of 83 research and development work groups found a curvilinear effect of average job tenure on scientific contribution, peaking at four to five years of "group age." Because the average of individual tenure in research groups was used to calculate "group age," it is not possible to discern from this finding whether an aggregate level of turnover or a particular distribution of tenure is related to group performance. However, organizations often display a preference for a mixture of new and experienced members. Sport teams, for example, frequently opt for a blend of veteran and rookie players. Likewise, academic departments in universities frequently employ a range of faculty at different ranks and levels of experience. It is interesting to note that, with recent budgeting cutbacks in American universities, the average age and tenure of faculty has increased dramatically. University administrators have subsequently argued that this change in tenure distribution will adversely affect scholarly output of academic departments, although no systematic research has yet examined this issue.

Implicit in our discussion of potential benefits of turnover is the assumption that organizational membership can be renewed before it reaches the downward sloping part of the performance curve. Given this reasoning, the benefits of turnover will obviously depend on the nature of the task and whether it requires physical or psychological strengths which are depletable resources. The benefits of turnover also depend on who "turns over": if it is the older, long-tenured employees or the newcomers to the organization. Turnover rates do not as a statistic provide such information. However, our argument for the benefits of turnover obviously assumes a normal progression of employees through the organization rather than a continual recirculation of newcomers into the system.

The issue of who "turns over" has also been addressed in some early work by Lawler (1971) in which he argued that organizational resources should be allocated on a highly contingent basis. One logical consequence of contingent pay schemes would be differential satisfaction and turnover according to performance. For example, the organization that pays its high and low performers widely differing amounts is more likely to retain its highly desired employees and lose its less desired ones. Conversely, an organization that allocates resources equally is most likely to lose its highly valued personnel, assuming they are also valued by other organizations and possess greater external opportunities. Thus, an organization with resources allocated on a highly contingent basis implicitly encourages turnover on the assumption that new employees are likely to be an improvement over departing ones. So far, there has been no research on the relationship between pay contingency and turnover nor between such turnover and subsequent unit performance. However, we do know that most employees currently perceive outcomes at their employing organizations not to be contingent on their performance (Lawler, 1973). We also know from at least three empirical studies (Allison, 1974; Bassett, 1967; Office of State Merit Systems, 1968)

that leavers tend to be above average performers in the organization (Price, 1977). Therefore, one reason organizations may attempt to lower their rates of turnover is to retain their most valued employees; with contingent reward systems the exact opposite behavior would be logical on the part of organizations.

## Reduction of Entrenched Conflict

Sometimes one of the precipitating causes of turnover is conflict. This conflict could be hierarchical such as that between workers and a supervisor, department heads and a higher executive, or between a vice president and the chief executive. The conflict could also be lateral such as between workers on the shop floor, members of organizational staff, or coequal executive officers. In any of these cases, turnover may result from conflicts which are not easily resolved and in which one side decides to leave the organization rather than continue to fight.

Much literature has been devoted to techniques and strategies of conflict resolution and much organizational energy is often devoted to the smoothing of conflict, arbitration of differences, or working through differences via various intervention strategies. One assumption of the conflict literature (be it based on game theory, labor relations, or organization development concepts) is that the participants in the conflict are rather permanent members of the organization. A second assumption is that conflict can and should be mediated, arbitrated, resolved, or "worked through" in order for the organization to function effectively. In practice, however, many conflicts, be they personal or task oriented, are not easily resolved and stem from differences in fundamental values or core beliefs. In such cases it may be functional for turnover to become the ultimate "resolver" of conflict. In government and business organizations, for example, it is quite frequent for one party to seek the ouster of another, to make life so difficult as to "drive the other out." Turnover is thus the ultimate safety valve for organizational strife, given the fact that the conflicting parties have alternatives to which to go.

As a general statement, the more firmly held are beliefs and the more difficult they are to disconfirm, the greater will be the probability of unresolved strife. In political and religious organizations, for example, conflict among the organization's membership is likely to persist and detract from collective solidarity and purpose. Conflict in these organizations is usually resolved only by the departure of a minority, perhaps setting up its own autonomous organization or splinter group. In a study of turnover of academic department heads (Salancik, Staw, & Pondy, in press) the paradigm development of academic fields was related to the turnover of department heads. In fields with low paradigm development there is little consensus on core beliefs and it is difficult to validate one position over another. Therefore conflicts may have persisted longer in the departments with low rather than high paradigm development and resulted in more administrative turnover. Turnover, in many of these cases, may not have been a cost to the organization, but instead may have helped to resolve deep-seated conflicts among organizational membership.

## Increased Mobility and Morale

Earlier we had noted that turnover might have a demoralization effect on the organization since members might inpute certain motives for people leaving. In order to seek a balanced approach we should note that turnover could also have a positive effect on membership attitudes. If undsirable supervisors or coworkers leave the organization, this event might obviously cheer some members (Guest, 1962). However, even if well liked and/or productive people exit the organization, the turnover might still open positions in an otherwise impenetrable hierarchy. An organization with little turnover may have nowhere to promote highly competent employees with upward mobility strivings unless the organization is expanding rapidly by acquisition or internal growth. But, since economic growth has slackened in many industries, turnover in middle- and high-level positions may be the only way upwardly mobile employees can be encouraged to stay with an otherwise stable organization. Thus, turnover may be the primary determinant of promotion

opportunities, contributing to a positive relation between turnover and organizational morale.

## Innovation and Adaptation

An important consequence of turnover is the opportunity it provides for the organization to adapt to its environment. One means of adaptation is through strategic decision making (Chandler, 1962; Child, 1972; Miles & Snow, 1978), and along with strategic changes generally comes some reallocation of organizational resources. But resources cannot often be simply increased to accommodate new activities and purposes; they must be shifted from one department to another or from an outmoded function to a newly established endeavor. Generally a major aspect of a shift in resources is a shift of positions and personnel, and this may involve the shrinkage of one organizational unit to allow for the growth of another. Thus, turnover is a very major means by which reorientation of the organization occurs. If the shift in purpose or activity is small in comparison to the size of the organization, older units will be allowed to skrink by attrition while resources are funnelled to newer units. But, if a shift is massive, resignations may be forced or conditions of employment made difficult enough to encourage additional voluntary turnover. In either case, turnover may be integral to organizational adaptation, and the role of turnover would be especially important when resources are not easily procured from the environment.

In addition to turnover's use in conscious or strategic adaptation of the organization to its environment, turnover may also be useful from a nonpurposive, evolutionary perspective (Aldrich, 1979; Hannon & Freeman, 1977; Weick, 1979). Although most organizations attempt to select new organizational members which match the profile of previously successful members, selection procedures (including interviews, personality inventories, and application blanks) are notoriously ineffective as screening devices (Porter, Lawler, & Hackman, 1975). This "ineffectiveness" of recruiting and selection may, however, constitute one of the most beneficial consequences of turnover. Turnover and the resulting inflow of new organizational members may be the primary source of variety (Campbell, 1965) within organizations. Almost every other process within organizations promotes homogeneity. Rules, normative sanctions, filtering of information, as well as the exposure to a common set of experiences breed similarity in point of view and knowledge. Also, participation in previous decisions fosters commitment to policies even if they may be outmoded or inappropriate (Staw, 1976; Fox & Staw, 1979). These sources of homogeneity and stability may be costly when radical changes in the environment require new values, viewpoints, and knowledge bases. An organization can therefore use turnover as a constant source of input from the environment to help keep organizational beliefs and information congruent with outside changes. Because variety increases chances for survival (Campbell, 1965; Weick, 1979), turnover can be an important source of organizational adaptation, even though this adaptation may be nonconscious and nonstrategic from the policy maker's perspective.

The effect of turnover on organizational adaptation may vary greatly with the level at which it occurs. With increased level in an organizational hierarchy typically comes increased influence over the actions of others and more central functions of the organization. Also associated with increasing levels in an organizational hierarchy is an increase in decision making and uncertainty absorption. Thus, changes in top management can be followed by major changes in organizational policy, while turnover on lower-level jobs which are highly formalized or machine-paced is unlikely to provide much change to the organization.

The reason for adaptive change being associated with the hierarchical level of turnover is due to the differing discretionary component of various organizational roles and the role occupant's influence on others. However, the *potential* for innovation does exist on all organizational levels with many valuable improvements coming from middle and lower levels of the organization. For example, it is often the case that formal procedures must be bypassed, revised, and machinery altered in order for organizational members

to fulfill their roles satisfactorily. Unfortunately, many of these "innovations" are not officially sanctioned by upper levels and do not diffuse freely throughout the organization. Therefore, the major impact of new employees at low or intermediate levels of the organization may be their indirect effect upon the work of longer tenured and higher-level professionals (Price, 1977). More influential members of the organization may be subtly influenced by the ideas or approaches of the new employee, but ownership of any innovations may not necessarily be credited to the new arrival.

A second moderator of the effect of turnover upon organizational adaptation is whether there is a policy of inside or outside succession. While inside succession may have a beneficial effect on organizational morale it negates much of the potential adaptation value of turnover (Carlson, 1962). The new role occupant, up from the ranks, is likely to have similar background, experiences, and policy commitments to the departed member. The outside replacement, in contrast, is more likely to bring new perspectives and information to the organization, and if the new person has had reinforcing experiences elsewhere, he or she is less likely to conform to the new organization than the inside successor. Thus, turnover at high levels in the organization, accompanied by replacement with an experienced and successful outsider, may maximize the adaptive consequences of turnover.

Finally, whether turnover and any subsequent adaptation are useful for the organization depends upon the rate of change encountered by the organization. Organizations in an unchanging environment do not need diversity and could well find it more efficient to specialize by fitting its membership precisely to the current demands of its environment. However, organizations with higher rates of change and which experience unexpected developments in markets, social or political factors, may be well served by a higher level of turnover and the diversity it provides.

## Summarizing the Positive Consequences

We have outlined several positive consequences of turnover and have shown how each could be moderated by other variables. Turnover can increase organizational performance, but this effect depends on the role performance curve and the contingency of the organization's reward system. In addition, turnover could increase performance simply because the labor market has improved over time, allowing the organization to recruit increasingly better members. As we have noted, turnover may also reduce conflict in the organization, but this result depends on the ideological nature of the organization and whether core beliefs or values are involved in the conflict. We also noted that turnover may benefit organizational mobility to the extent that there is little organizational growth and policies of inside succession are followed. Finally, we noted that turnover may lead to organizational innovation and adaptation, but this result may, in turn, be moderated by the hierarchical level at which turnover occurs and whether inside or outside succession is followed.

## ASSESSING THE CONSEQUENCES OF TURNOVER

A large number of moderators were specified in the discussion of potential consequences of turnover and each of these is outlined in Figure 14.3. Once elaborated, it is evident that turnover is an extremely complex process, having an effect on multiple aspects of organizational functioning and with each of these effects themselves moderated by other contextual variables.

By examining Figure 14.3 it also becomes clear that some moderating variables may control the effect of turnover upon several different outcomes. For example, the higher turnover occurs in the organizational hierarchy the greater will be the costs of recruitment, selection, and training and also greater will be the potential for operational disruption. However, turnover at high levels in the organization is also associated with greater possibilities for innovation and adaptation. Likewise, inside succession following turnover eases the cost of recruitment and training and may have a positive effect on organizational morale, yet at the same time it may not produce as much innovation and adaptation as would outside

succession. Thus, some moderators may affect both the costs and benefits of turnover.

Hypothetically, an administrator could use Figure 14.3 as a checklist for examining the consequences of turnover. By examining and categorizing the organization's current situation on each moderator variable it would be possible to assess the magnitude of various costs and benefits of turnover. Such an assessment would of course be highly speculative since there has not been systematic research supporting each of the linkages in Figure 14.3. Such an assessment would also be largely qualitative since quantitative measures will likely exist only for estimating some of the more routine costs of turnover.

The outcome variables listed in Figure 14.3 reflect consequences that extend over several aspects of organizational functioning. Many of these outcomes (e.g., recruitment and selection costs) would normally be considered as direct costs by managers while other outcomes (e.g., reduction in conflict and increased innovation) might be considered as rather indirect means toward other more tangible goals (i.e., increased sales or profit). However, viewed from a systems perspective (Katz & Kahn, 1978), there is no substantive reason for treating routine turnover expenses differently from other outcomes. It is only because accounting systems are currently devised to account for expense items in one measure of organizational well being (profit) that selection and training costs appear most quantifiable. In terms of organizational functioning, it is not yet clear whether expenses which are directly accountable are more or less useful than other indices in measuring the effectiveness of an organization (cf. Steers, 1977). Certainly, in principle, scales could be constructed to measure each of these outcome variables on an ongoing basis.

Some sort of scale conversion is necessary for any judgment of the consequences of turnover. We must, for example, be able to tell whether an operational disruption is trivial or severe, and be able to compare the utility/disutility for this outcome with that for varying the potential for innovation. Obviously, this task entails the same problems and pitfalls as any examination of organizational effectiveness (cf. Goodman &

INDEPENDENT VARIABLE        MODERATING VARIABLES                                    OUTCOMES VARIABLE

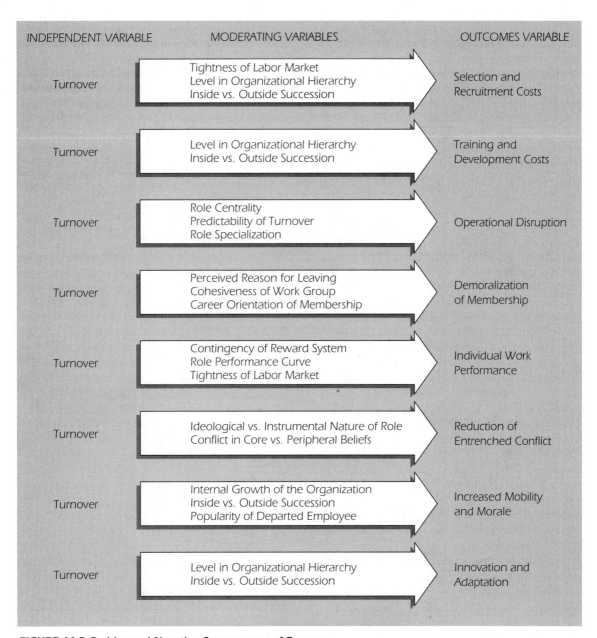

FIGURE 14.3 Positive and Negative Consequences of Turnover.

Pennings, 1977). That is, each of the outcome variables listed in Figure 14.3 may be weighted differently by different constituents comprising the organization (Hall, 1977). Also, members of the same constituent group (e.g., management) may view the importance of various outcome variables differently, depending upon their own organizational roles. Immediate expenditures for recruitment or possible disruptions in production may appear important to a department manager trying to keep within budget and meet sales quotas, while interunit relations and innovations may be more heavily weighted by top levels of the organization. Thus, the perceived utility of each consequence of turnover may be conditioned by whatever administrator's lay theories of organizational effectiveness happen to be. The consequences of turnover will likely be moderated by administrators' conceptions of overall organizational welfare, its relevant indicators, and casual mappings (Abelson, 1976; Weick, 1979) about how each variable is believed to affect others within the system.

Given our currently primitive knowledge of organizational effectiveness, we are not yet ready to place any sort of objective weightings upon the various consequences of turnover. Some higher-order variables or "meta-moderators" of the utility of turnover do seem fairly straightforward, however, and have been implicit in our discussion throughout this paper. First, we have assumed that innovation is important for the organization because of the need to adapt to a changing environment. Thus, one moderator of the utility of innovation is the rate of change with which an organization must cope. Second, the current level of performance by the organization (e.g., sales, profitability, resource procurement) may determine how acceptable or desirable drastic change would be. When things are desperately bad, even random variations may improve the situation. Finally, turnover of the role occupant must be capable of effecting some change in organizational actions or interpersonal relations. A role which is inconsequential, routinized, or devoid of influence can rarely lead to organizational change with or without turnover.

## Research on Managerial Succession

At present, the only stream of research on the consequences of turnover focuses on managerial succession. For example, early research by Grusky (1963) found that the turnover of baseball managers was related to team performance. Subsequent work, however, showed that turnover of baseball managers may primarily be a scapegoating phenomenon and may not be associated with improved performance (Gamson & Scotch, 1964). It could be that the baseball manager never does have much effect upon team performance because, as Weiss (1979) has argued, the game is not a highly interactive task which requires substantial coordination skills. It may also be that more drastic change is needed (e.g., turnover of player personnel) for outcome variables to change.

Research by Lieberson and O'Connor (1972) examined the effect of mangerial succession upon the financial performance of large corporations. They found that turnover of top executives did significantly relate to financial performance of firms but the magnitude of the effect varied greatly by industry. Likewise, Salancik and Pfeffer (1977) found some effect of mayors upon city budget allocations, but the magnitude of the effect also differed widely by the characteristics of the city. The apparent moderator of turnover effects in both the Lieberson and O'Connor (1972) and Salancik and Pfeffer (1977) studies was the extent of external constraints facing the chief executive. When a corporate president faced many external market constraints and government regulations he/she was constrained in strategic options. Likewise, the mayor who faced highly organized political forces and interest groups within a city was greatly restrained in possible actions. In each case there are substantial forces with which leaders had to contend, and these forces accounted for more variance in organizational outcomes than the effects of leadership changes.

As evidenced in research on managerial succession, turnover of top executives does not guarantee organizational improvement or adaptation to the environment. Yet, a change in leadership sometimes accompanies and even signifies a radical change in direction for an organization. As Pfeffer and Salancik (1977) noted in the case of hospitals, newly appointed administrators are more likely to possess skills in areas which are problematic for the organization than long-tenured executives. Thus, turnover among administrators can constitute a means by which the organization realigns itself with a changing environment. Turnover can also constitute a critical symbolic act that change is expected, positively sanctioned or to be initiated by the organization. Managerial shake-ups following financial adversity and cabinet realignments following political setbacks are obvious examples of the symbolic significance of turnover at high levels of an organization. It remains for future research to discover whether turnover's effect is more symbolic than substantive or whether the symbolic changes are what enable substantive changes to occur.

## RESTORING THE BALANCE

Although we cannot now predict which of the consequences of turnover *should* be more important for a particular organization at a particular point in time, this does not negate the argument that turnover is probably treated inappropriately by many organizations. Our argument is based simply on the information salience of positive and negative consequences of turnover rather than any normative arguments for a reweighting of outcome criteria.

At present, negative consequences of turnover usually attract much more attention than positive outcomes. Certainly, conventional accounting systems only report realized expenses and do not account for nonmonetary gains. Also, any disruption in operations is likely to cause difficulty for line administrators charged with day to day management. Finally, possible demoralization effects will affect the immediate climate with which an administrator works, making leadership both more necessary and difficult to carry out. In sum, there are several major sources of adverse consequences for a line manager facing high turnover rates, and these consequences may directly affect the nature of the administrator's job within an immediate time horizon.

In contrast to the negative effects of turnover, most of the positive consequences affect the organization as a collectivity rather than a specific administrator's job. In addition, performance improvements resulting from turnover may depend on the abilities or efforts of a successor being superior in some respect to the departed employee. Positive consequences are thus further along in a causal chain than negative consequences,

and may be weakened or confused with exogenous factors. An energetic and innovative manager may, for example, replace an outmoded administrator, yet the innovative actions of the new person may not be accepted by the organization or they may be blocked by environmental constraints (e.g., regulations, actions of competitors). In such a situation, the benefits of turnover will be masked while the expenses of turnover would still be quite evident as they are stored in the short-term accounting system of the organization.

### Tasks for Future Research

As we have noted, research on turnover currently concentrates on the antecedents rather than the consequences of turnover. Although turnover is a very old research topic almost nothing is therefore known about most of the questions we have addressed in this paper. The following research tasks would thus seem most relevant for future analysis.

1. We need to identify each of the consequences of turnover in longitudinal and quasi-experimental designs. Organizations experiencing increases in turnover should be identified and compared to control organizations both before and after turnover has changed. This list of variables and moderators in Figure 14.3 needs to be tested empirically so as to move beyond the speculation stage.

2. We need to research the relationship between the level of turnover and effectiveness indicators for various types of organizations, subunits, and organizational roles. It is important to know what the turnover rates are for organizations which are successful in particular industries or facing particular types of constraints. As noted in Table 14.1, there do exist differences in turnover across industries, but we do not yet know how turnover relates to performance within industries or suborganizational environments. In a sense, the outcome variables listed in Figure 14.3 could be viewed as intermediate variables which are in turn related to end-result variables such as sales, profit, won-loss record, resources procured,

etc. Thus, any relationship found between the level of turnover and effectiveness measures would subsume the more specific and intermediate linkages.

3. We need to know more about the attributions and lay theories of administrators in regard to turnover. As Abelson (1976) has noted, people may possess scripts or scenarios of what kind of events are associated with increases in turnover. Turnover sets off a whole series of uncertainties that the administrator may find aversive. Because adverse consequences of turnover must generally be faced personally by the administrator while positive consequences are far off in time and organizational space (they may only affect one's successor!) negative scenarios may be most salient within the organization.

The three research tasks we have outlined are all designed to provide a descriptive base for understanding the consequences of turnover. The first point raises the need for research on the effects of turnover upon various aspects of organizational functioning (e.g., monetary expenses, morale, conflict, innovation). The second point stresses the need for relating turnover to more global measures of organizational effectiveness. Hypothetically, global measures of profitability, survival, won-loss record, and the like should encompass the impact of the more specific outcome variables in Figure 14.3. However, it may be beneficial to study the effects of turnover on intermediate outcomes at the same time as we study turnover's effect on more global measures of effectiveness. Placing intermediate outcomes into a system which relates to more global outcomes probably should await further developments in a theory of organizational effectiveness. Finally, as a third area of research, we have proposed descriptive analyses of how turnover currently is viewed by organizational administrators. If we understand more fully why administrators react to turnover the way they presently do (see Steers & Mowday, 1980) it may be easier to change these behaviors in the future.

In summary, what we have done by proposing an intensive study of turnover's consequences is to convert a rather normative field of study into one of descriptive inquiry. Because previous research has treated turnover as a simple negative consequence, turnover studies have been labeled as extremely applied research. However, when the utility of turnover is questioned, the study of turnover must stand on its own as more basic research into an important organizational phenomenon. In this way, turnover research has the potential to illuminate central aspects of organizational functioning and may accomplish this with a rather unified and delimited focus.

## REFERENCES

Abelson, R. P. (1976). "Script processing in attitude formation and decision making," In: Carroll, J. S. and Payne, J. W. (Eds), *Cognition and Social Behavior*, Lawrence Erlbaum Publishers, Hillsdale, New Jersey.

Aldrich, H. (1979). *Environments and Organizations*, Prentice-Hall, Englewood Cliffs, New Jersey.

Allison, P. D. (1974). "Inter-organizational mobility of academic scientists," 69th annual meeting of American Sociological Association, Montreal, Canada.

Bales, R. F. (1958). "Task roles and social roles in problem-solving groups," In: Maccoby, E. E., Newcomb, T. M. and Hartley, K. L. (Eds), *Readings in Social Psychology*, Holt, New York, pp. 437–446.

Bassett, G. (1967). *A Study of Factors Associated with Turnover of Exempt Personnel*. Personnel and Industrial Relations Services, General Electric.

Bavelas, A. (1960). "Leadership: man and function," *Administrative Science Quarterly*, **4**, 491–498.

Blau, P. M. and Scott, W. R. (1962). *Formal Organizations.* Chandler Publishing Co., San Francisco, California.

Campbell, D. T. (1965). "Variation and selection retention in socio-cultural evolution," In: Barringer, H. R., Blanksten, G. I. and Mack, R. (Eds), *Social Change in Developing Areas,* Schenkman, Cambridge, Massachusetts.

Carlson, R. O. (1962). *Executive Succession and Organizational Change.* Midwest Administration Center, University of Chicago, Chicago, Illinois.

Chandler, A. D. (1962). *Strategy and Structure,* Doubleday, Garden City, New York.

Child, J. (1972). "Organizational structure, environment, and performance—the role of strategic choice," *Sociology,* **6,** 1–22.

Crozier, M. (1964). *The Bureaucratic Phenomenon,* University of Chicago Press, Chicago, Illinois.

Fox, F. V. and Staw, B. M. (1979). "The trapped administrator: effects of job insecurity and policy resistance upon commitment to a course of action," *Administrative Science Quarterly,* **24,** 449–471.

Gamson, W. A. and Scotch, N. (1964). "Scapegoating in baseball," *American Journal of Sociology,* **70,** 69–76.

Goodman, P. S. and Pennings, J. M. (1977). *New Perspectives on Organizational Effectiveness.* Jossey-Bass, San Francisco.

Graen, G. (1976). "Role-making processes within complex organizations," In: Dunnette, M. D. (Ed), *Handbook of Industrial and Organizational Psychology,* Rand-McNally, Chicago.

Grusky, O. (1963). "Managerial succession and organizational effectiveness," *American Journal of Sociology,* **69,** 21–31.

Guest, R. H. (1962). "Managerial succession in complex organization," *American Journal of Sociology,* Free Press, New York.

Hall, D. T. (1976). *Careers in Organizations,* Goodyear Publishing, Santa Monica, California.

Hall, R. H. (1977). *Organizations: Structure and Process* (2nd ed.), Prentice-Hall, Englewood Cliffs, New Jersey.

Hannon, M. and Freeman, J. (1977). "The population ecology of organizations," *American Journal of Sociology,* **82,** 929–964.

Kasarda, J. O. (1973). "Efforts of personnel turnover, employee qualifications, and professional staff ratios on administrative intensity and overhead," *Sociological Quarterly,* **14,** 350–358.

Katz, D. and Kahn, R. (1978). *The Social Psychology of Organizations* (2nd ed.), Wiley, New York.

Lawler, E. E. (1971). *Pay and Organizational Effectiveness: A Psychological View,* McGraw-Hill, New York.

Lawler, E. E. (1973). *Motivation in Work Organizations,* Brooks-Cole, Monterey, California.

Lieberson, S. and O'Connor, J. F. (1972). "Leadership and organizational performance: a study of large corporations," *American Sociological Review,* **37,** 117–130.

March, J. G. and Simon, H. (1958). *Organizations,* Wiley, New York.

Maslach, C. (1978). "Client role in staff burn-out," *Journal of Social Issues,* **34,** 111–124.

Miles, R. E. and Snow, C. C. (1978). *Organizational Strategy, Structure, and Process,* McGraw-Hill, New York.

Mobley, W. H., Griffeth, R. W., Hand, H. H. and Meglino, B. M. (1979). "Review and conceptual analysis of the employee turnover process," *Psychological Bulletin,* **86,** 493–522.

Office of State Merit Systems (1968). "Analysis of appointments, separations, promotions," U.S. Department of Health, Education, and Welfare, Washington, D.C.

Pfeffer, J. (1979). "Some consequences of organizational demography: potential impacts of an aging work force on formal organizations," Paper prepared for the Committee on Aging, National Research Council, National Science Foundation, Washington, D.C.

Pfeffer, J. and Salancik, G. R. (1977). "Organizational context and the characteristics and tenure of hospital administrators," *Academy of Management Journal,* **20,** 74–88.

Porter, L. W., Lawler, E. E. and Hackman, J. R. (1975). *Behavior in Organizations,* McGraw-Hill, New York.

Price, J. L. (1977). *The Study of Turnover,* Iowa State University Press, Ames, Iowa.

Pugh, D. S. (1966). "Modern organization theory: a psychological and sociological study," *Psychological Bulletin,* **66,** 235–251.

Salancik, G. R. and Pfeffer, J. (1977). "Constraints on administrator discretion: the limited influence of mayors on city budgets," *Urban Affairs Quarterly,* **12,** 475–498.

Salancik, G. R., Staw, B. M. and Pondy, L. R. (1980). "Administrative turnover as a response to unmanaged organizational interdependence," *Academy of Management Journal,* pp. 422–437.

Staw, B. M. (1976). "Knee-deep in the big muddy: a study of escalating commitment to a chosen course of action," *Organizational Behavior and Human Performance,* **16,** 27–44.

Staw, B. M. and Oldham, G. R. (1978). "Reconsidering our dependent variables: a critique and empirical study," *Academy of Management Journal,* **21,** 539–559.

Steers, R. M. (1977). *Organizational Effectiveness: A Behavioral View.* Goodyear Publishing Co., Santa Monica, California.

Steers, R. M. and Mowday, R. T. (1980). "Employee turnover and post-decision accommodation process," In: Cummings, L. L. and Staw, B. M. (Eds), *Research in Organizational Behavior,* JAI Press, Greenwich, Connecticut.

U.S. Department of Labor (1975). *Job Tenure of Workers: 1973,* Special Labor Report No. 172, Washington, D.C.

Van Maanen, J. (1975). "Police socialization: a longitudinal examination of job attitudes in an urban police department," *Administrative Science Quarterly,* **20,** 207–228.

Weick, K. (1972). *The Social Psychology of Organizing* (2nd ed.), Addison-Wesley, Reading, Massachusetts.

Weiss, R. M. (1979). "Managerial succession and organizational effectiveness: beyond the baseball diamond," Paper presented at 1979 meeting of Academy of Management.

Wells, W. P. and Pelz, D. C. (1966). "Groups," In: Pelz, D. C. and Andrews, F. M. (Eds), *Scientists in Organizations: Productive Climates for Research and Development,* Wiley, New York.

# SOCIAL AND SELF PERCEPTION

Now that you have studied many of the motives behind people's behavior and some of the patterns of their emotional expression, it is time to delve more deeply into the cognitive side of life. In this section you will learn about the quirks of perception. First will be a chapter on the errors and biases people introduce when they perceive other people. Then you will learn about some of the ways people delude themselves in order to maintain a positive self-image. As this book turns to perceptual issues in the workplace, a chapter will cover some of the strange things that can happen when people are paid to perform an interesting task—they may actually start to like it less! The perceptual nature of tasks and how social information affects one's attitude toward the work is treated next. You will learn how task attitudes are influenced by the perceptions of others and the positive or negative labeling of work. Finally, you

will read how vivid, qualitative data can be more powerful than numbers—that is, how organizational stories can promote widespread beliefs in organizations, which may or may not be beneficial to the corporation.

In studying these articles on individual perception you will be struck by the many errors people make as well as the biases they hold. However, do not be deluded into thinking that people are totally inept in perceiving other people and judging the characteristics of their work enviroments. Objective reality does count, although it is not the only factor in determining people's opinions about others, themselves, or the workplace. Thus, knowledge about the perceptual process—its general tendencies and inherent shortcomings—is a necessary but not sufficient aspect of understanding behavior in organizations.

# Foundations of Perception

## 15.  PERCEIVING PERSONS

Sharon S. Brehm and Saul M. Kassin

On October 19, 1987, the stock market crashed, resulting in the unprecedented loss of an estimated $500 billion. As nervous investors wondered whether they should buy or sell, Wall Street analysts were embroiled in debate: Was the market on the verge of collapse, or was the decline due to rumors and false public perceptions? In short, was the problem one of economics, or of social psychology?

During the winter of 1988, when Soviet leader Mikhail Gorbachev visited the White House for the first time, it was easy to get swept up in the drama of such a significant historical event. And yet, as the hammer-and-sickle flag hung within view of the Reagan White House, some Americans were doubtful: Is Gorbachev for real, or are his overtures a ploy? Is he extending the olive branch because he really wants peace, or because he is trying to lull the West into a false sense of security?

Three months after Gorbachev's visit, spring was in the air as the Kansas Jayhawks basketball team—not even ranked among the top twenty college teams—came out of nowhere to win the NCAA Championship. As KU students took to the streets in celebration, sports fans all around the country wondered: Is the team really that good, or did they just luck out?

Whatever the year, and whatever the topic—business, politics, sports, or personal events closer to home—we are all active and interested participants in **social perception**, the processes by which people come to understand one another. This chapter is divided into four major components. First, we look at the "raw data" of social perception—other persons, situations, and behavior. Second, we examine how perceivers explain and analyze the behavior of others. Third, we consider how people integrate their various explanations into a clear and coherent picture of other persons. Fourth, we discuss the subtle ways in which our impressions can create a distorted picture of reality, and even a self-fulfilling prophecy. As you read this chapter, you will notice that the various processes are considered from a perceiver's vantage point. Keep in mind, however, that in the events of everyday life, you are both a *perceiver* and the *target* of others' perceptions....

## ATTRIBUTION: FROM THE ELEMENTS TO DISPOSITIONS

In interacting with others, it is useful to know how they feel and when they can be trusted. But to understand people well enough to predict their future behavior, we also need to try to identify their **dispositions**—that is, relatively stable characteristics of a person such as personality traits, attitudes, and abilities. Since we cannot actually see dispositions, we can only infer them from what a person says and does. In this section, we look at the processes that lead us to make these inferences.

### Attribution Theory: The Logic of Social Perception

Do you ever think about the influence you have on other people? What about the influence of genetic factors, childhood experiences, and social forces? Do you wonder why some people succeed, while others fail? Some of us are more concerned than others about explaining the events of human behavior. Among college students, for example, psychology majors seem more curious about such matters than do natural science majors (Fletcher et al., 1986). Although there are individual differences, most people tend to be inquisitive about events that are negative or unexpected (Hastie, 1984; Weiner, 1985). When something *unexpected* occurs, perceivers want to know why (Pyszczynski & Greenberg, 1981; Wong & Weiner, 1981). In a study of 200 corporations, it was found that their annual reports to shareholders contained a large number of casual explanations when business was either better or worse than expected (Bettman & Weitz, 1983). *Negative* events such as illness, conflict, and failure also lead people to search for causes. For example, husbands and wives think more about what caused their partners to behave in negative ways than they do about what caused positive behavior (Holtzworth-Munroe & Jacobson, 1985).

To make sense of our social world, we try to understand the causes of our own and other people's behavior. But what kinds of explanations do we make, and how do we go about making them? In his book, *The Psychology of Interpersonal Relations*, Fritz Heider (1958) took the first step toward answering these questions. To Heider, we are all scientists of a sort. Motivated to understand people well enough to manage our social environment, we observe, analyze, and explain their behavior. The explanations we come up with are called attributions; the theory to describe the process is called **attribution theory**. The questions raised in the beginning of this chapter—about the stock market, Gorbachev, and the Kansas Jayhawks—are all questions of attribution.

Although there are many possible explanations for the events of human behavior, Heider found it useful to group them into two major categories: personal and situational. When an investor loses money in the stock market, he or she can be blamed for making unsound decisions (a **personal** or *internal* attribution), or the loss can be attributed to unforeseeable changes in the marketplace (a **situational** or *external* attribution). When a world leader makes concessions at the negotiating table, that leader can be credited with a lasting, personal disposition toward peace, or the concessions can be attributed to external pressures. And when a team wins a coveted championship, the victory can be attributed to that team's outstanding ability, or to luck. For the attribution theorist, the task is not to determine the *true* causes of these events, but to discern people's *perceptions* of the causes. In the coming pages, three major attribution theories are described.

### *Jones's Correspondent Inference Theory*

According to Edward Jones and Keith Davis (1965), each of us tries to understand other people by analyzing their behavior. Jones and Davis's **correspondent inference theory** predicts that people try to *infer* from an action whether it *corresponds* to an enduring personal characteristic of the actor. Is the person who commits an act of aggression a beast? Is the person who donates money to charity an altruist? To answer these kinds of questions, people generally make inferences based on three factors.

The first factor is a person's degree of *choice*. Behaviors that are freely chosen are more informative than behaviors that are coerced. In one study, for example, subjects read a speech, presumably written by a college student, that either favored or opposed Fidel Castro, the communist leader of Cuba. Some subjects were told that the student had freely chosen his or her position, while others were told that the student was assigned to take that position by a professor. When asked to estimate the student's true attitude, subjects were more likely to assume that there was a correspondence between the student's essay (behavior) and attitude (disposition) when the student had a choice than when he or she was assigned to the role (Jones & Harris, 1967; see Figure 15.1). Keep this study in mind. It supports correspondent inference theory but, as we will see, it also demonstrates one of the most tenacious biases of social perception.

The second factor that leads people to make dispositional inferences is the *expectedness* of behavior. As we suggested earlier in the chapter, actions that depart from the norm tell us more about a person than actions that are typical, part of a social role, or otherwise expected under the circumstances (Jones et al., 1961). Thus, people think they know more about the personality of a student who wears three-piece suits to class or of a citizen who openly refuses to pay taxes than about a student who wears blue jeans to class or a citizen who files tax returns on April 15th.

Third, people consider the intended *effects* or consequences of someone's behavior. Acts that produce many desirable outcomes do not reveal a person's specific motives as clearly as acts that produce only a single desirable outcome (Newtson, 1974). For example, we are likely to be uncertain about why a person stays on a job that is enjoyable, high paying, and in an attractive location—three desirable outcomes, each sufficient to explain the behavior. In contrast, we feel more certain about why a person stays on a job that is tedious and low paying, but is in an attractive location—only one desirable outcome.

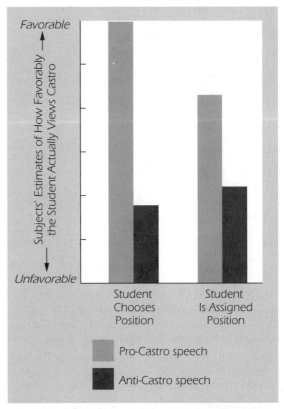

**FIGURE 15.1** What Does This Speechwriter Really Believe? As predicted by correspondent inference theory, subjects who read a student's speech (behavior) were more likely to assume that it reflected the student's true attitude (disposition) when the position taken was freely chosen (left) rather than assigned (right). But also note the evidence for a fundamental attribution error...: even subjects who thought the student was assigned a position inferred his or her attitude from the speech [Data from Jones & Harris, 1967]

### Kelley's Covariation Theory

Correspondent inference theory describes how people try to determine someone's personal characteristics from a slice of behavioral evidence. However, behavior can be attributed not only to personal factors but to situational factors as well. How is the distinction made? In graduate school, prospective social psychologists are beaten over the head with the message that the causes of human behavior can only be derived by conducting *experiments.* That is, one has to make more than a single observation and compare behavior in two or more settings in which everything stays the same except for the independent variables. Harold Kelley (1967) agrees with Heider that people are much like scientists in this regard. They may not observe others in a laboratory, but they too make comparisons and think in terms of experiments. According to Kelley, people make attributions by using the **covariation principle**. This principle states that for something to be the cause of a behavior, it must be present when the behavior occurs and absent when it does not. Three kinds of covariation information are particularly useful for people: consensus, distinctiveness, and consistency.

To illustrate these concepts, imagine you are standing on a street corner one hot evening minding your own business, when all of a sudden a stranger bursts out of an air-conditioned movie theater and blurts out, "Great flick!" Looking up, you don't recognize the movie title, so you wonder what to make of this candid recommendation. Was the behavior (the rave review) caused by something about the person (the stranger), the stimulus (the film), or the circumstances (the air-conditioned theater)? Possibly interested in spending a night at the movies, how would you proceed to explain what happened? What kinds of information would you seek?

Thinking like a scientist, you might collect **consensus information** to determine what happens when the person is different but the stimulus remains the same. In other words, how do *other persons* feel about this film? If others also rave about the film, the stranger's behavior is high in consensus and can be attributed to the stimulus. If others are critical of the film, the behavior is low in consensus and can be attributed to the person. Still thinking like a scientist, you might seek **distinctiveness information** to determine what happens when the person remains the same but the stimulus is different. How does *this person* feel about *other films*? If the stranger is critical of other films, the behavior is high in distinctiveness and can be attributed to the stimulus. If the stranger does rave about other films, however, the behav-

ior is low in distinctiveness and can be attributed to the person.

Finally, you might seek **consistency information** to determine what happens to the behavior at another time when the person and the stimulus both remain the same. How does *this person* feel about *this film* on *other occasions*? If the stranger raves about the film on video as well as in the theater, the behavior is high in consistency. If the stranger does not always enjoy the film, the behavior is low in consistency. According to Kelley, behavior that is high in consistency is attributed to the person when consensus and distinctiveness are also high, and to the stimulus when they are low. Behavior that is low in consistency, however, is attributed to transient circumstances, such as the temperature of the movie theater. Kelley's theory and the predictions it makes are represented in Figure 15.2.

At this point, you may be wondering whether people really make attributions as Kelley proposes. Research suggests they do. In a study by Douglas Hazlewood and James Olson (1986), subjects watched an interview with a female student. Actually, they saw a carefully staged exchange during which an interviewer asked the woman about her relationships with men. The woman flatly refused to answer the question, exclaiming that her private sex life was none of the interviewer's business and that "the people in this study sure get their kicks in strange ways." Subjects then received a pattern of information that—according to Kelley's theory—should lead them to make either a personal attribution for the woman's behavior (she is rude) or a stimulus attribution (the question is inappropriate). What effect did the information have? Rather than ask directly, the experimenter introduced subjects to the woman in question so they could conduct their own interview.

As if subjects had read Kelley's covariation theory, those who thought the woman's previous reaction was low in consensus and distinctiveness (other interviewees had not refused to answer the question; this woman refused to answer many other questions) seated themselves at a further distance from her, asked fewer questions, and

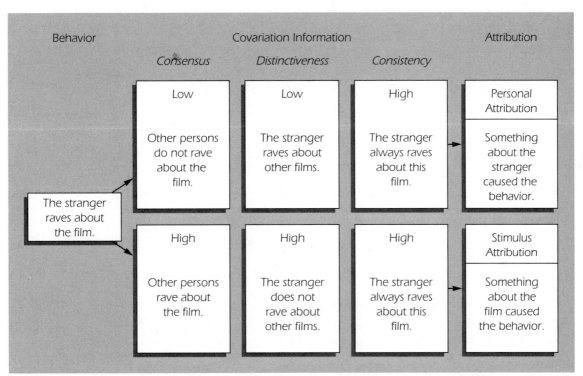

| Behavior | Covariation Information | | | Attribution |
|---|---|---|---|---|
| | *Consensus* | *Distinctiveness* | *Consistency* | |
| | Low | Low | High | Personal Attribution |
| The stranger raves about the film. | Other persons do not rave about the film. | The stranger raves about other films. | The stranger always raves about this film. | Something about the stranger caused the behavior. |
| | High | High | High | Stimulus Attribution |
| | Other persons rave about the film. | The stranger does not rave about other films. | The stranger always raves about this film. | Something about the film caused the behavior. |

**FIGURE 15.2** Kelley's Covariation Theory of Attribution. For behaviors that are high in consistency, Kelley predicts that people make personal attributions under conditions of low consensus and low distinctiveness (top row), and stimulus attributions under conditions of high consensus and high distinctiveness (bottom row). Behaviors that are low in consistency (not shown) are attributed to passing circumstances. [Based on Kelley, 1967.]

smiled less often than those who thought her behavior was high in consensus and distinctiveness (other interviewees had also refused to answer the question; this woman did not refuse to answer other questions). Subjects thus used attributions to guide their own behavior. In a good deal of other research as well; subjects who are asked to make attributions for various events employ the logic of Kelley's theory (Hewstone & Jaspars, 1987; McArthur, 1972).

### Weiner's Three-Dimensional Taxonomy

Kelley's theory tells us what kinds of information elicit personal or stimulus attributions in general. But there are many different kinds of attributions within these two categories. To describe the possibilities, Bernard

Weiner (1986) proposed a three-dimensional taxonomy of attributions for success and failure. According to Weiner, people can attribute outcomes to factors that are not only (1) *internal* (personal) or *external* (situational), but (2) *stable* or *unstable*, and (3) *controllable* or *uncontrollable*. Whether we are trying to explain a sports victory or defeat (McAuley & Gross, 1983), an exam grade (Vallerand & Richer, 1988), the failure of a consumer product (Folkes, 1984), unemployment (Schaufelt, 1988), or loneliness (Michela et al., 1982), our explanations often fall within the eight possible attributions produced by combining these three dimensions (see Figure 15.3).

Think, for example, about the attributions that can be made when a college basketball team wins the NCAA Championship. One might attribute its success to the players' ability, the amount of

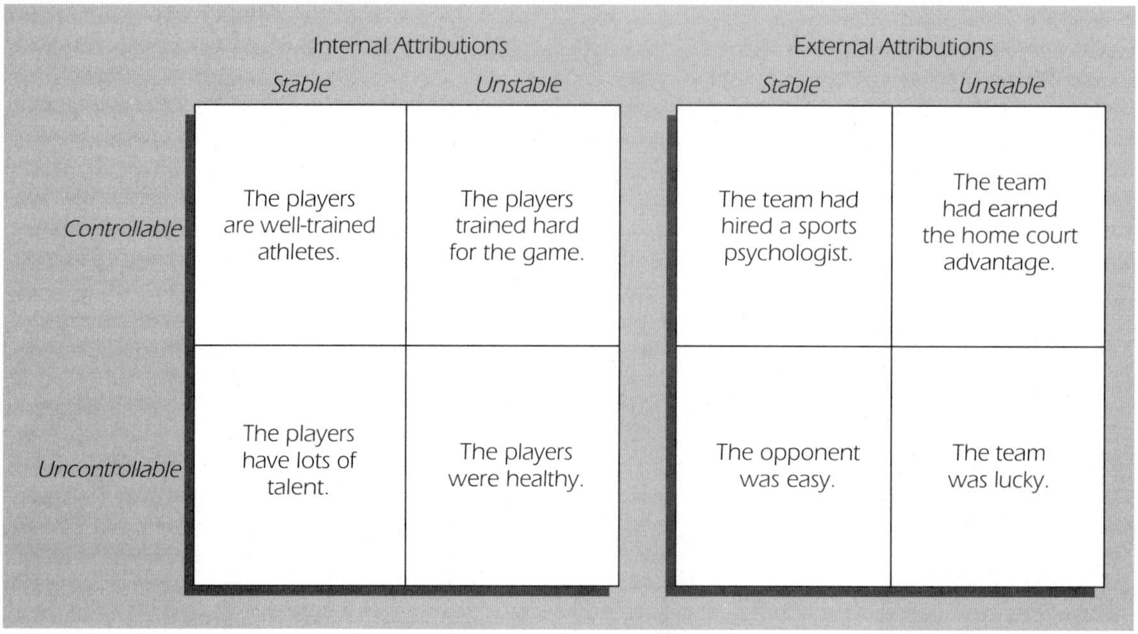

| | Internal Attributions | | External Attributions | |
|---|---|---|---|---|
| | *Stable* | *Unstable* | *Stable* | *Unstable* |
| *Controllable* | The players are well-trained athletes. | The players trained hard for the game. | The team had hired a sports psychologist. | The team had earned the home court advantage. |
| *Uncontrollable* | The players have lots of talent. | The players were healthy. | The opponent was easy. | The team was lucky. |

**FIGURE 15.3** Weiner's Three-Dimensional Taxonomy of Attributions. What kinds of attributions do you typically make for victory and defeat? According to Weiner, people attribute success and failure to factors that are (1) *internal* or *external*, (2) *stable* or *unstable*, and (3) *controllable* or *uncontrollable*. By combining these three dimensions, eight types of attributions are possible. Do the examples shown sound familiar?

effort they exerted during the tournament, or the fact that all the key players were healthy. Since ability, effort, and physical well-being are factors that reside within the person (or team), they are considered internal attributions. But ability is an enduring factor, while effort and health are unstable factors that tend to fluctuate over time. And although effort and health are both unstable attributions, they also have different implications. Effort is a factor that can be controlled, while physical health often cannot. External attributions — an easy schedule, the home court advantage, assistance from a sports psychologist, or sheer luck — can be distinguished in the same manner.

Weiner's taxonomy is consistent with intuition. When subjects are asked to explain various positive and negative outcomes — their own or someone else's — their attributions often fit nicely into Weiner's categories (J. P. Meyer, 1980; Russell, 1982). Also, different kinds of attributions can have important motivational and emotional consequences when people explain their own performance. We all feel better about ourselves and others after victory than after defeat, but the attributions we make for these outcomes can be just as important as the outcomes themselves.

According to Weiner (1986), the internal or external locus of an attribution influences the *esteem-related emotions* that accompany performance (Weiner et al., 1979). People feel more pride after success, and also more shame after failure, when they attribute those outcomes to internal factors (ability or effort) than to external factors (task characteristics or luck). In contrast, it is the stability of an attribution that determines *future expectations*. When people attribute success or failure to factors that do not change from one moment to the next — whether internal (ability) or external (task factors) — they raise and lower their hopes according to performance. When people attribute the same outcomes to unstable factors (effort or luck), however, their hopes about future performance remain relatively intact (Weiner et al., 1976). Finally, the controllability of an attribution arouses what Weiner calls *social emotions*, emotions directed at others. When people attribute negative outcomes to factors within another person's control (a lack of effort), they become angry. When they attribute these same outcomes to uncontrollable factors (a lack of ability), however, they react with pity (Weiner et al., 1982).

## Attribution Biases: The "Bloopers" of Social Perception

After the major theories of attribution were first proposed, they were represented by such complicated flow charts, cubes, formulas, and diagrams that many social psychologists began to wonder: Do people really analyze behavior as one might expect of computers? Do social perceivers have the time, the motivation, or the cognitive capacity for such elaborate, mindful processes?

Sometimes yes, sometimes no. As social perceivers, we may be limited in our ability to process all relevant information, or we may lack the kinds of training needed to fully employ the logic of attribution theory (Allen et al., 1987; Fong et al., 1986; Kassin, 1981). More importantly, we often just don't make an effort to think carefully about our attributions. With so much to explain and not enough time in the day, people take short cuts, hope for the best, and get on with life (Kahneman et al., 1982; Nisbett & Ross, 1980; Taylor & Fiske, 1978). The problem is, with speed comes bias, and perhaps even a loss of accuracy. In this section, we examine the consequences of these short cuts, or what could be called the bloopers of social perception.

### The Fundamental Attribution Error

By the time you complete this textbook, you will have learned what is perhaps the fundamental lesson of social psychology; that people are influenced in profound ways by the *situational* context of behavior. This point is not as obvious as it may seem. Parents are very often shocked

when they learn that their most mischievous child—the family monster—is a perfect angel in school. Likewise, students are surprised when they realize that their favorite professor—so eloquent in the lecture hall—stumbles and mutters in less formal surroundings. These examples illustrate an extremely well-documented feature of social perception. When people explain the behavior of others, they underestimate the impact of situations and overestimate the role of personal factors. Because this bias is so pervasive, and often so misleading, it is called the **fundamental attribution error** (Ross, 1977)...

### The Actor-Observer Effect

We may be prone to commit the fundamental attribution error when we explain the behavior of others, but do we exhibit the same bias in explaining our own behavior? Before reading further, look at the questionnaire in Table 15.1. First, complete it for yourself by indicating for each of the twenty items whether you have a certain trait or its opposite, or whether your behavior depends on the situation. Next, pick a friend and describe that friend on the same items. When you're done, count up the number of times you described yourself and your friend by selecting a trait rather than the situation option. Is there a difference? Based on the research, we would predict that you checked off the situation option more for yourself and the trait option more for your friend (Nisbett et al., 1973). When Lewis Goldberg (1978) administered 2,800 English trait adjectives to 14 groups, each consisting of 100 subjects, he found that 85 percent of his subjects checked off more traits for other persons than for themselves.

The tendency to make personal attributions for the behavior of others and situational attributions for our own behavior is called the **actor-observer effect** (Jones & Nisbett, 1972; Monson & Snyder, 1977; Watson, 1982). The actor-observer effect has been widely demonstrated. In a study patterned after the events of Watergate, college students were approached with a request to commit an actual burglary. Whether they agreed or refused, subjects attributed their decisions

**TABLE 15.1**
Trait Attribution Questionnaire

Complete this questionnaire for yourself by checking either the first trait, the second trait, or the "depends on the situation" option for each of the twenty items. Then use the same questionnaire to describe a friend. Finally, count up the total number of traits in columns A *and* B that you checked off for yourself. Do the same for the Friend. Notice any difference? [From Nisbett et al., 1973].

| | A | | | | B | | | | C | | |
|---|---|---|---|---|---|---|---|---|---|---|---|
| | Self | Friend | | | Self | Friend | | | Self | Friend | |
| 1. | ___ | ___ | Serious | ___ | ___ | Easygoing | ___ | ___ | Depends on the situation |
| 2. | ___ | ___ | Subjective | ___ | ___ | Analytic | ___ | ___ | Depends on the situation |
| 3. | ___ | ___ | Future-oriented | ___ | ___ | Present-oriented | ___ | ___ | Depends on the situation |
| 4. | ___ | ___ | Energetic | ___ | ___ | Relaxed | ___ | ___ | Depends on the situation |
| 5. | ___ | ___ | Unassuming | ___ | ___ | Self-asserting | ___ | ___ | Depends on the situation |
| 6. | ___ | ___ | Lenient | ___ | ___ | Firm | ___ | ___ | Depends on the situation |
| 7. | ___ | ___ | Reserved | ___ | ___ | Emotionally expressive | ___ | ___ | Depends on the situation |
| 8. | ___ | ___ | Dignified | ___ | ___ | Casual | ___ | ___ | Depends on the situation |
| 9. | ___ | ___ | Realistic | ___ | ___ | Idealistic | ___ | ___ | Depends on the situation |
| 10. | ___ | ___ | Intense | ___ | ___ | Calm | ___ | ___ | Depends on the situation |
| 11. | ___ | ___ | Skeptical | ___ | ___ | Trusting | ___ | ___ | Depends on the situation |
| 12. | ___ | ___ | Quiet | ___ | ___ | Talkative | ___ | ___ | Depends on the situation |
| 13. | ___ | ___ | Cultivated | ___ | ___ | Natural | ___ | ___ | Depends on the situation |
| 14. | ___ | ___ | Sensitive | ___ | ___ | Tough-minded | ___ | ___ | Depends on the situation |
| 15. | ___ | ___ | Self-sufficient | ___ | ___ | Sociable | ___ | ___ | Depends on the situation |
| 16. | ___ | ___ | Steady | ___ | ___ | Flexible | ___ | ___ | Depends on the situation |
| 17. | ___ | ___ | Dominant | ___ | ___ | Deferential | ___ | ___ | Depends on the situation |
| 18. | ___ | ___ | Cautious | ___ | ___ | Bold | ___ | ___ | Depends on the situation |
| 19. | ___ | ___ | Uninhibited | ___ | ___ | Self-controlled | ___ | ___ | Depends on the situation |
| 20. | ___ | ___ | Conscientious | ___ | ___ | Happy-go-lucky | ___ | ___ | Depends on the situation |

to compelling factors within the situation. However, observers who read about what the subjects decided, attributed these decisions to aspects of the subjects' character (West et al., 1975a). Similarly, when sixty prison inmates were asked to explain why they had committed their offenses, and their counselors were asked the same, the counselors cited enduring personal characteristics, while the prisoners referred to transient situational factors (Saulnier & Perlman, 1981). Even in letters to "Ann Landers" and "Dear Abby," those seeking advice explained other people's actions in more dispositional terms than they did their own (Schoeneman & Rubanowitz, 1985).

Two factors are particularly important in producing the differences between actors and observers. First, people have more varied *information* about themselves than about others—enough to know that their own behavior often changes from one situation to the next (Eisen, 1979; Hansen & Lowe, 1976). Second, perceptual salience again comes into play. As observers, our attention is focused on people whose behavior we are trying to explain. As actors, however, the situation commands our attention. Absorbed in conversation, we gaze at our partner; playing tennis, we keep a close eye on the ball; taking an exam, we stare at the questions. Could the difference in visual perspective produce the actor-observer effect? Michael Storms (1973) found that it can. When pairs of subjects engaged in face-to-face conversation in front of pairs of observers, actors—as usual—viewed their own behavior in situational terms, while observers made personal attributions. But here's the clincher. The conversations were recorded by different cameras placed in the positions of actors and observers. After each session, Storms had everyone review their conversation on videotape, and for half the subjects he reversed their original perspective. The manipulation worked like magic. When actors watched themselves from the observers' points of view, they made more personal attributions for their own behavior; when observers watched through the actors' eyes, they made more situational attributions. Reversing the subjects' natural perspectives also reversed the actor-observer effect.

## Distortions of Consensus

Attribution theories claim that to draw inferences about an individual, people compare behavior to social *norms*. Actions assumed to be atypical, or low in consensus, should elicit personal attributions; actions that are typical, or high in consensus, should be attributed more to the situation (Jones & Davis, 1965; Kelley, 1967). The theory is logical and follows intuition: And yet, when people make attributions, they often fail to make adequate use of normative information (Borgida & Brekke, 1981; Kassin, 1979). There are two problems, as we are about to see; the false-consensus effect and the base-rate fallacy.

A few years ago, one of the authors of this textbook conducted a government-sponsored study of federal judges. After reading about cases in which plaintiffs sued defendants, 292 judges made hypothetical decisions and predicted how their colleagues would have voted. Although opinions varied widely, the judges exhibited astonishing nearsightedness. They consistently (and often erroneously) believed that their peers would make the same decisions they had made. Those who ruled *for* the plaintiff estimated that 63 percent of other judges would favor the plaintiff as well; judges who ruled *against* the plaintiff estimated that only 15 percent of their peers would favor the plaintiff (Kassin, 1985). This result illustrates the **false-consensus effect**—the tendency for people to overestimate the consensus that exists for their own opinions, attributes, and behaviors (Ross et al., 1977b).

The false-consensus effect is pervasive. Whether subjects are asked to predict how others feel about drugs, abortion, Dan Rather, the defense budget, Jane Fonda, or Campbell's Soup, their estimates predictably exaggerate the percentage of others who agree with their views (Mullen et al., 1985; Nisbett & Kunda, 1985). Why? There are at least two reasons: one cognitive, the other motivational. First, there is the cognitive problem of *selective exposure*. People's assumptions about consensus are based on a distorted sample of observations, because people tend to associate with others who are similar to them in important ways (Deutsch, 1989; Sherman et al., 1983). Second, there is the influence of *self-serving motivation*. We overestimate the consensus of our own behavior in order to reassure ourselves that what we do is normal, correct, and appropriate (Sherman et al., 1984). According to Gary Marks and Norman Miller (1987), selective exposure, self-serving motivation, and other factors combine to produce the false-consensus bias.

There's yet another problem. Even when social perceivers are provided with social norms that are accurate, they often neglect to use the information. Isn't it odd, for example, that so many people buy lottery tickets, despite the very low odds, or that so many people are afraid of flying, when the chances of dying in an automobile accident are much greater? These behaviors illustrate the **base-rate fallacy**, that people are relatively insensitive to consensus information presented in the form of base rates, or numerical probabilities (Bar-Hillel, 1980; ;Kahneman & Tversky, 1973). Instead, we are moved by graphic anecdotes—the sight of a million-dollar lottery winner rejoicing on TV, or photographs of bodies being pulled from the wreckage of a plane crash.

Every day, we are besieged by both kinds of information. We hear about the unemployment rate, and we watch interviews with job seekers; we read about the casualty rates of violence, and we witness the agony of parents who have lost a child. And yet, although logic says that information derived from many people's experiences is more informative than a single anecdote, social perceivers march to a different drummer (Hamill et al., 1980; Rook, 1987b). In one experiment, for example, college students were asked to fill out a tentative course schedule for future semesters. To assist their decisions, some subjects heard firsthand comments from two or three more experienced students about various courses. Others read the results of comprehensive, numerical course evaluations reflecting the opinions of a large number of students. Defying logic, subjects' plans were swayed more by the personal recommendations than by the dry population base rates (Borgida & Nisbett, 1977). As long as the personal information emanates from a source that is cred-

ible (Hinsz et al., 1988), it seems that one anecdote is worth a thousand numbers.

## Motivational Biases

In *The Devil in the Shape of a Woman*, Carol Karlsen (1987) reports that many women accused of witchcraft in colonial New England were branded not because they were witches, but because they had shown signs of independence, were too smart, too attractive, or had too much money for their own good. Rather than accept these qualities as natural, the women's accusers—often jealous peers, neighbors, or rejected lovers—made attributions to the devil.

When people explain their own behavior, they often do so in a self-serving manner, taking the credit for success but not the blame for failure ...When it comes to others, we are not similarly motivated. Jealousy can lead us to deny others the credit they deserve; other defensive motives can lead us to blame others for their misfortunes. Consider, for example, the following experiment. Subjects thought they were taking part in an emotion-perception study. One subject, actually a confederate, was selected by lottery to take a memory test while the others looked on. Each time a mistake was made on the test, the confederate was jolted by a painful electric shock. (Actually, there was no shock; subjects watched a videotape staged by the confederate.) Since they knew that only the luck of the draw had kept them off the "hot seat," you would expect subjects to react with understanding, sympathy, and compassion. Instead, however, they belittled the hapless confederate, viewing her as relatively unlikable (Lerner & Simmons, 1966). But why?

Melvin Lerner (1980) proposes that the human tendency to disparage victims can be explained by the **belief in a just world**. According to Lerner, people need to view the world as a just place in which we "get what we deserve" and "deserve what we get." To believe in a just world is to believe that hard work and a clean life always pay off, and that laziness and a sinful life are always punished. To believe otherwise, people would have to concede that they too are vulnerable to the twists and turns of fate. So how do people defend themselves from this realization? If people cannot assist or compensate the victims of misfortune, they turn on them. Thus, it is commonly assumed that poor people are lazy (Furnham & Gunter, 1984), that theft victims are careless (Tyler & Devinitz, 1981), that battered wives provoke their abusive husbands (Summers & Feldman, 1984), and that sick people don't take care of themselves (Gruman & Sloan, 1983).

The tendency to disparage victims may seem like just another symptom of the fundamental attribution error, too much focus on the person and not enough on the situation. When the conditions that influence this tendency are considered, however, there seems to be more to it than that. Studies of **defensive attribution** indicate that accident victims are held more responsible for their fate when the consequences of the accident are severe rather than mild (Walster, 1966), when the victim is in a situation similar to the perceiver's (Burger, 1981, Shaver, 1970), and when the perceiver is emotionally aroused by the event (Thornton et al., 1986). In other words, the more personally threatened people feel by an apparent injustice, the greater their need to protect themselves from the implication that the same thing could happen to *them*. One means of defending their shaken belief in a just world is to psychologically distance themselves from the victim through disparagement. Fortunately, there are other means of coping as well. People need not resort to derogation when they are able to restore justice by helping the victim (Lerner & Simmons, 1966) or when they are encouraged to empathize with the victim (Aderman et al., 1974)....

## CONFIRMATION BIAS: FROM IMPRESSIONS TO REALITY

*"Please your majesty," said the knave, "I didn't write it and they can't prove I did; there's no name signed at the end." "If you didn't sign it," said the King, "that only makes the matter worse. You must have meant some mischief, or else you'd have signed your name like an honest man."*

This exchange, taken from Lewis Carroll's *Alice's Adventures in Wonderland,* illustrates the power of existing impressions. It is striking but often true: once people make up their minds about something—even if based on incomplete information—they become more and more unlikely to change their minds when later confronted with the evidence. Political leaders refuse to withdraw their support for government programs that do not work, and scientists may stubbornly defend their theories in the face of conflicting research data. These instances are easy to explain. Politicians and scientists have a personal investment in their points of view; pride, reputation, and funding may be at stake. But what about people who more innocently fail to revise their opinions, to their own detriment? What about the baseball manager who clings to strategies that are ineffective, or the trial lawyer who repeatedly selects juries according to false stereotypes? Why are such people often so slow to face the facts? As we will see, people are subject to various types of **confirmation bias**: the tendency to *seek, interpret, and create* information in ways that verify existing beliefs.

### Confirmatory Hypothesis Testing

Social perceivers are not just passive recipients of information. Like detectives, we can ask questions and actively search for clues. But do we seek information objectively, or are we inclined to confirm the suspicions we already hold? Mark Snyder and William Swann, Jr. (1978a) addressed this question by asking pairs of subjects—strangers to one another—to participate in an interview. Within each pair, one subject was asked to interview the other. But first, that subject was falsely led to believe that the person to be interviewed was either introverted or extroverted (actually, subjects were assigned on a random basis to these conditions) and was then told to select his or her questions from a prepared list. Those who thought they were talking to an introvert chose to ask mostly introvert-oriented questions ("Have you ever felt left out of some social group?"), while those who thought they were talking to an extrovert asked extrovert-oriented questions ("How do you liven things up at a party?"). Expecting a certain kind of person, subjects unwittingly sought evidence that confirmed their expectations. In fact, by asking loaded questions, the interviewers actually gathered support for their beliefs. When neutral observers listened to the tapes, they too were left with the mistaken impression that the interviewees really were as introverted and extroverted as the interviewers had assumed they were.

When you think about it, this last part of the study is profound but not really surprising. Imagine yourself on the receiving end of an interview. Asked about what you do to liven up parties, you would probably talk about organizing group games, playing dance music, and telling jokes. On the other hand, if you were asked about difficult social situations, you might talk about being nervous before oral presentations or what it feels like to be the new kid on the block. In other words, simply by answering the questions that are asked, you provide evidence confirming the interviewer's beliefs. Thus, perceivers set in motion a vicious cycle: thinking someone has a certain trait, they engage in a one-sided search for information and, in doing so, they create a reality that ultimately supports their beliefs (Snyder, 1984).

Are people so blinded by their own beliefs that they can't manage an objective search for evidence? It depends on the situation. In the circumstances matching those devised by Snyder and Swann (1978a), people consistently engage in a biased, confirmatory search for information. Even experienced psychotherapists—yes, professionals trained in diagnosis—may select questions to confirm their initial beliefs (Dallas & Baron, 1985). But different circumstances can produce different results. When subjects doubt their initial beliefs and worry about the accuracy of their impressions (Kruglanski & Mayseless, 1988), when they prepare their own interview questions (Trope et al., 1984), or when the available nonconfirmatory questions are better than the confirmatory questions (Skov & Sherman, 1986: Trope & Bassock, 1983), then a more neutral search for information is pursued.

## Perseverance of Beliefs

Imagine you are looking at a slide that is completely out of focus. Gradually, it is focused enough so that a blurred image becomes visible. At this point, the experimenter wants to know if you can recognize the picture. Your likely response is interesting. Subjects have more trouble making an accurate identification if they watch the gradual focusing procedure than if they simply view the final, blurry image. Apparently, in the mechanics of the perceptual process, people form early impressions that later interfere with their ability to "see straight" once presented with improved evidence (Bruner & Potter, 1964). In this section, we will see that social perception is subject to this same kind of interference. Indeed, it is one reason why first impressions so often stick after we are forced to confront nonsupportive information or information that discredits our existing beliefs.

Consider what happens when a person is led to expect something that does not materialize. In one study, subjects were asked to evaluate the academic potential of a nine-year-old white girl named Hannah. One group was led to believe Hannah came from an upper-middle-class environment in which both parents were well-educated professionals (high expectations). A second group thought she was from a run-down urban neighborhood and that both her parents were poorly educated blue-collar workers (low expectations). As one might predict, subjects in the first group were slightly more optimistic in their ratings of Hannah's potential than were those in the second group. In each of these groups, however, half the subjects watched a videotape of Hannah taking a short achievement test. Her performance on the tape seemed about average. She correctly answered some difficult questions but missed others that were relatively easy. Even though all subjects saw the same tape, the poor Hannah now received much lower ratings of ability than the affluent Hannah (see Figure 15.4). Presenting an identical body of mixed evidence did not *extinguish* the biasing effects of beliefs, it *fueled* it (Darley & Gross, 1983).

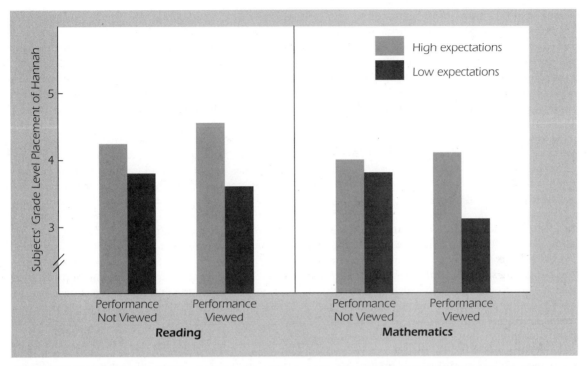

**FIGURE 15.4 Mixed Evidence: Does It Extinguish or Fuel our First Impressions?** In this study, subjects evaluated the scholastic potential of an elementary school girl. Without viewing her test performance, subjects with high expectations rated her slightly higher than those with lower expectations. However, among subjects who watched the girl take a test, with about average performance, those with initially high expectations rated her much more favorably than those with initially low expectations. Rather than extinguish the first-impression bias, the behavioral evidence provided by test performance actually fueled it. [Data from Darley & Gross, 1983.]

Events that are ambiguous enough to support contrasting interpretations are like inkblots: in them, perceivers see what they expect to see. But what about information that plainly disconfirms a person's beliefs? What happens to our first impressions under those circumstances? Craig Anderson and his colleagues (1980) addressed this question by supplying subjects with false information. After the subjects had had enough time to think about the information, they were told that it was untrue. In one experiment, half the subjects read two case studies suggesting that individuals who take risks make better firefighters than do those who are cautious. The other half read cases suggesting the opposite conclusion. Next, subjects were asked to come up with a theory for the suggested correlation. The possibili-

ties are easy to imagine: "He who hesitates is lost" supports risk taking, while "You have to look before you leap" supports caution. Finally, subjects were led to believe the experiment was over and were told that the information they had received was fictitious, manufactured for the sake of the experiment. But is was too late; subjects did not abandon their firefighter theories. Instead they exhibited **belief perseverance**—the tendency to stick to initial beliefs even after they have been discredited. Apparently, it's far easier to get people to build a theory than to convince them to tear it down. Even social psychologists may be slow to change their theories in light of inconsistent research data (Greenwald et al., 1986).

Why do beliefs often outline the evidence on which they are supposed to be based? The main reason seems to be that when we conjure up explanations that make sense, those explanations take on a life of their own. Indeed, once people form an opinion, that opinion is strengthened by merely *thinking* about the topic—even without articulating the reasons for the opinion (Tesser, 1978). Of course, therein lies the solution. By asking people to think about and explain why an *alternative* theory might be true, belief perseverance can be reduced or eliminated (Anderson & Sechler, 1986).

## Self-Fulfilling Prophecies

In 1948, sociologist Robert Merton told a story about Cartwright Millingville, president of the Last National Bank during the depression. Although the bank was solvent, a rumor began to spread that it was floundering. Within hours, hundreds of depositors were lined up to withdraw their savings before no money was left to withdraw. The rumor was false, but the bank eventually failed. Using stories such as this, Merton proposed what seemed like an outrageous hypothesis: that a perceiver's expectation can actually lead to its own fulfillment, a **self-fulfilling prophecy**.

Merton's hypothesis lay dormant within psychology until Robert Rosenthal and Lenore Jacobson (1968) published the results of a study entitled *Pygmalion in the Classroom*. Noticing that teachers have higher expectations for better students, they wondered whether teacher expectations actually *influenced* student performance. To address the question, they told teachers in a San Francisco elementary school that certain pupils were on the verge of an intellectual growth spurt. Although the results of an IQ test were cited, in fact the pupils were randomly selected. Eight months later, Rosenthal and Jacobson administered real tests, and found that the "late bloomers"—but not children assigned to a control group—improved their IQ scores by as much as 30 points. They were also evaluated more favorably by their classroom teachers.

When the Pygmalion study was published, it was greeted with chagrin. If positive teacher expectations can increase student performance, can negative expectations have the reverse ef-

fect? And what about the social implications? Could it be that wealthy children are destined for success and disadvantaged children doomed to failure because educators hold different expectations for them? Many researchers were critical of the study and skeptical about the generality of the results. Unfortunately, however, the Pygmalion effect is for real. Teachers form expectations early in the school year based on a student's background, reputation, physical appearance, initial performance, and standardized-test scores. Teachers then alter their behavior toward the student accordingly. If expectations are high rather than low, students receive more attention, emotional support, challenging assignments, and favorable feedback (Cooper & Good, 1983). All in all, teacher expectations have significantly influenced student academic performance in 36 percent of the 400 experiments designed to test the hypothesis (Rosenthal, 1985). In fact, student expectations of a teacher can have similar effects. When two high school classes were led to believe that their new English teacher was highly regarded, they became noticeably more attentive in class and achieved higher final grades as a result (Jamieson et al., 1987).

How does the Pygmalion effect work? How do social perceivers transform their expectations into reality? The research on teacher expectations indicates that it is helpful to view the self-fulfilling prophecy as a three-step process (see Figure 15.5).

First, the perceiver forms an impression of the target person. The impression may be based on initial interactions with the target or on hearsay. Second, the perceiver behaves in a manner that is consistent with that first impression. Third, the target unwittingly adjusts his or her behavior according to the perceiver's actions. Whether inside or outside the classroom, the effect is quite powerful (Darley & Fazio, 1980; Harris & Rosenthal, 1985; Jussim, 1986; Miller & Turnbull, 1986).

As discussed earlier, Snyder and Swann's work offers convincing evidence for this circular chain of events (Snyder, 1984). Recall the experiment discussed earlier, in which interviewers created introverted and extroverted self-reports by asking leading questions (Snyder & Swann, 1978a). In a similar study, subjects who were led to

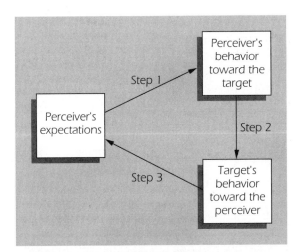

**FIGURE 15.5** Self-Fulfilling Prophecy as a Three-Step Process. How does the self-fulfilling prophecy work? How do people transform their expectations into reality? (1) The process begins with a perceiver's expectations of a target person; (2) the perceiver then behaves in a manner consistent with those expectations; and (3) the target unwittingly adjusts his or her behavior according to the perceiver's actions.

believe that their opponent in a laboratory game was hostile behaved more competitively themselves. Before too long, their fears came true; opponents reciprocated by behaving in a hostile manner (Snyder & Swann, 1978b). Gordon Allport (1960) once said that when nations expect to go to war, they go to war. One nation communicates its expectations to the enemy; fearing a military build-up, the enemy increases its defense spending. Before long, initial expectations are confirmed. The rest is, quite literally, history.

Now, let's straighten out this picture of human nature. It would be a sad commentary, indeed, if each of us could be so easily molded by other's extroverted, competitive or cooperative, warm or cold. The effects are well established, but thankfully, there are limits. By viewing the interper-

sonal expectancy effect as a three-step process, it is possible to identify two links in the chain that can be broken to prevent the vicious, self-fulfilling cycle.

Consider the first step, the link between a perceiver's expectations and behavior toward the target. In many studies, perceivers interact with the target on only a casual basis. But when perceivers are highly motivated to seek the truth (as when they need to consider the target as a possible teammate), they may probe for accurate information and, in so doing, fail to confirm their expectations (Darley et al., 1988). Forewarned that someone is unfriendly, people may even go out of their way to be nice in an effort to *dis*confirm an unwelcome expectation (Ickes et al., 1982).

Next consider the second step, the relationship between a perceiver's behavior and the target's response. In much of the research, as in much of life, target persons are unaware of others' false impressions. It is unlikely, for example, that Rosenthal and Jacobson's "late bloomers" knew of their teachers' high expectations, or that Snyder and Swann's "introverts" and "extroverts" knew of their interviewers' misconceptions. But what if they did? How would you react if *you* found yourself cast in a particular light? When it happened to subjects in one study, they managed to overcome the interpersonal expectancy effect by behaving in ways that led perceivers to abandon their initial expectations (Hilton & Darley, 1985). This result is most likely to occur when perceiver expectations clash with target persons' expectations of themselves. Thus, when targets with extroverted self-concepts were interviewed by perceivers who thought they were introverted (and vice versa), what changed as a result of the interaction were the perceivers' beliefs—not the targets' behavior (Swann & Ely, 1984). It is important to keep in mind that the persons we perceive have their own prophecies to fulfill...

## REFERENCES

Aderman, D., Brehm, S. S., & Katz, B. (1974). Empathic observation of an innocent victim: The just world revisited. *Journal of Personality and Social Psychology*, 29, 342–347.

Allen, J. L., Walker, L. D., Schroeder, D. A., & Johnson, D. E. (1987). Attributions and attribution-behavior relations: The effect of level of cognitive development. *Journal of Personality and Social Psychology*, 52, 1099–1109.

Allport, G. W. (1960). *Personality and social encounter*. Boston: Beacon Press.

Anderson, C. A., & Sechler, E. S. (1986). Effects of explanation and counterexplanation on the development and use of social theories. *Journal of Personality and Social Psychology*, 50, 24–34.

Anderson, N. H., & Hubert, S. (1963). Effects of concomitant verbal recall on order effects in personality impression formation. *Journal of Verbal Learning and Verbal Behavior*, 2, 379–391.

Asch, S. E., & Zukier, H. (1984), Thinking about persons. *Journal of Personality and Social Psychology*, 46, 1230–1240.

Bar-Hillel, M. (1980). The base-rate fallacy in probability judgments. *Acta Psychologica*, 44, 211-213.

Belmore, S. M. (1987). Determinants of attention during impression formation. *Journal of Experimental Psychology: Learning, Memory, and Cognition*, 13, 480–489.

Benassi, M. A. (1982). Effects of order of presentation, primacy, and physical attractiveness on attributions of ability. *Journal of Personality and Social Psychology*, 43, 48–58.

Bettman, J. R., & Weitz, B. A. (1983). Attributions in the boardroom: Causal reasoning in corporate annual reports. *Administrative Science Quarterly*, 28, 165–183.

Borgida, E., & Brekke, N. (1981). The base-rate fallacy in attribution and prediction. In J. H. Harvey, W. J. Ickes, & R. F. Kidd (Eds.), *New directions in attribution research* (Vol. 3, pp. 66–95). Hillsdale, NJ: Erlbaum.

Borgida, E., & Nisbett, R. E. (1977). The differential impact of abstract vs. concrete information on decisions. *Journal of Applied Social Psychology*, 7, 258–271.

Bruner, J. S., & Potter, M. C. (1964). Interference in visual recognition. *Science*, 144, 424–425.

Burger, J. M. (1981). Motivational biases in the attribution of responsibility for an accident: A meta-analysis of the defensive-attribution hypothesis. *Psychological Bulletin*, 90, 496–512.

Burnstein, E., & Schul, Y. (1982). The information basis of social judgments: The operations in forming an impression of another person. *Journal of Experimental Social Psychology*, 18, 217–234.

Cooper, H., & Good, T. (1983). *Pygmalion grows up: Studies in the expectation communication process*. New York: Longman.

Dallas, M. E., & Baron, R. S. (1985). Do psychotherapists use a confirmatory strategy during interviewing? *Journal of Social and Clinical Psychology*, 3, 106–122.

Darley, J. M., & Gross, P. H. (1983). A hypothesis-confirming bias in labeling effects. *Journal of Personality and Social Psychology*, 44, 20–33.

Darley, J. M., Fleming, J. H., Hilton, J. L., & Swann, W. B., Jr. (1988). Dispelling negative expectancies: The impact of interaction goals and target characteristics on the expectancy confirmation process. *Journal of Experimental Social Psychology*, 24, 19–36.

Deutsch, F. M. (1989). The false consensus effect: Is the self-justification hypothesis justified? *Basic and Applied Social Psychology*, 10, 83–90.

Eisen, S. V. (1970). Actor-observer differences in information inference and causal attribution. *Journal of Personality and Social Psychology*, 37, 261–272.

Fletcher, G. J. O., Danilovics, P., Fernandez, G., Peterson, D., & Reeder, G. D. (1986). Attributional complexity: An individual differences measure. *Journal of Personality and Social Psychology*, 51, 875–884.

Folkes, V. S., (1984). Consumer reactions to product failure: An attributional approach. *Journal of Consumer Research*, 10, 398–409.

Fong, G. T., Krantz, D. H., & Nisbett, R. E. (1986). The effects of statistical training on thinking about everyday problems. *Cognitive Psychology*, 18, 253–292.

Furnham, A., & Gunter, B. (1984). Just world beliefs and attitudes towards the poor. *British Journal of Social Psychology*, 23, 265–269.

Goldberg, L. R. (1978). Differential attribution of trait-descriptive terms to oneself as compared to well-liked, neutral, and disliked others: A psychometric analysis. *Journal of Personality and Social Psychology*, 36, 1012–1028.

Greenwald, A. G., Pratkanis, A. R., Leippe, M. R., & Baumgardner, M. H. (1986). Under what conditions does theory obstruct research progress? *Psychological Review*, 93, 216–229.

Gruman, J. C., & Sloan, R. P. (1983). Disease as justice: Perceptions of the victims of physical illness. *Basic and Applied Social Psychology*, 4, 39–46.

Hamill, R., Wilson, T. D., & Nisbett, R. E. (1980). Insensitivity to sample bias: Generalizing from atypical cases. *Journal of Personality and Social Psychology*, 39, 578–589.

Hamilton, D. L., & Zanna, M. P. (1974). Context effects in impression formation: Changes in connotative meaning. *Journal of Personality and Social Psychology*, 29, 649–654.

Hansen, R. D., & Lowe, C. A. (1976). Distinctiveness and consensus: The influence of behavioral information on actors' and observers' attributions. *Journal of Personality and Social Psychology*, 34, 425–434.

Harris, M. J., & Rosenthal, R. (1985). Mediation of interpersonal expectancy effects. *Psychological Bulletin*, 97, 363–386.

Hastie, R. (1984). Causes and effects of causal attribution. *Journal of Personality and Social Psychology*, 46, 44–56.

Hazlewood, J. D., & Olson, J. M. (1986). Covariation information, causal questioning, and interpersonal behavior. *Journal of Experimental Social Psychology*, 22, 276–291.

Heider, F. (1985). *The psychology of interpersonal relations.* New York: Wiley.

Hewstone, M., & Jaspars, J. (1987). Covariation and causal attribution: A logical model of the intuitive analysis of variance. *Journal of Personality and Social Psychology*, 53, 663–672.

Hilton, J. L., & Darley, J. M. (1985). Constructing other persons: A limit on the effect. *Journal of Experimental Social Psychology*, 21, 1–18.

Hinsz, V. B., Tindale, R. S., Nagao, D. H., Davis, J. H., & Robertson, B. A. (1988). The influence of the accuracy of individuating information on the use of base rate information in probability judgment. *Journal of Experimental Social Psychology*, 24, 127–145.

Holtzworth-Munroe, A., & Jacobson, N. S. (1985). Causal attributions of marital couples: When do they search for causes? What do they conclude when they do? *Journal of Personality and Social Psychology*, 48, 1398–1412.

Ickes, W. J., Patterson, M., Rajecki, D. W., & Tanford, S. (1982). Behavioral and cognitive consequences of reciprocal versus compensatory responses to preinteraction expectancies. *Social Cognitive*, 1, 160–190.

Jamieson, D. W., Lydon, J. E., Stewart, G., & Zanna, M. P. (1987). *Journal of Educational Psychology*, 79, 461–466.

Jones, E. E., & Davis, K. E. (1965). A theory of correspondent inferences: From acts to dispositions. In L. Berkowitz (Ed.), *Advances in experimental social psychology* (Vol. 2, pp. 219–266). New York: Academic Press.

Jones, E. E., Davis, K. E., & Gergen, K. (1961). Role playing variations and their informational value for person perception. *Journal of Abnormal and Social Psychology*, 63, 302–310.

Jones, E. E., & Harris, V. A. (1967). The attribution of attitudes. *Journal of Experimental Social Psychology*, 3, 1–24.

Jones, E. E., & Nisbett, R. E. (1972). The actor and the observer: Divergent perceptions of causality. In E. E. Jones et al. (Eds.), *Attribution: Perceiving the causes of behavior* (pp. 79–94). Morristown, NJ: General Learning Press.

Jussim, L. (1986). Self-fulfilling prophecies: A theoretical and integrative view. *Psychological Review*, 93, 429–445.

Kahneman, D., Slovic, P., & Tversky, A. (Eds.) (1982). *Judgement under uncertainty: Heuristics and biases.* New York: Cambridge University Press.

Kahneman, D., & Tversky, A. (1973). On the psychology of prediction. *Psychological Review*, 80, 237–251.

Karlsen, C. F. (1987). *The devil in the shape of a woman.* New York: Norton.

Kassin, S. M. (1979). Consensus information, prediction, and causal attribution: A review of the literature and issues. *Journal of Personality and Social Psychology*, 37, 1966–1981.

Kassin, S. M. (1981). From laychild to "layman": Developmental causal attribution. In S. Brehm, S. Kassin, & F. Gibbons (Eds.), *Developmental social psychology: Theory and research* (pp. 169–190). New York: Oxford University Press.

Kassin, S. M. (1985). *An empirical study of Rule 11 sanctions.* Washington, DC: The Federal Judicial Center.

Kelly, H. H. (1967). Attribution theory in social psychology. In D. Levine (Ed.), *Nebraska Symposium on Motivation* (Vol. 15, pp. 192–241). Lincoln, NE: University of Nebraska Press.

Kruglanski, A. W., & Freund, T. (1983). The freezing and unfreezing of lay-inferences: Effects of impressional primacy, ethnic stereotyping, and numerical anchoring. *Journal of Experimental Social Psychology*, 19, 448–468.

Kruglanski, A. W., & Mayseless, O. (1989). Contextual effects in hypothesis testing: The role of competing alternatives and epistemic motivations. *Social Cognition*, 6, 1–20.

Lerner, M. J. (1980). *The belief in a just world: A fundamental delusion.* New York: Plenum.

Lerner, M. J., & Simmons, C. H. (1966). Observers' reaction to the "innocent victim": Compassion or rejection? *Journal of Personality and Social Psychology*, 4, 203–210.

Marks, G., & Miller, N. (1987). Ten years of research on the false-consensus effect: An empirical and theoretical review. *Psychological Bulletin*, 102, 72–90.

McArthur, L. A. (1972). The how and what of why: Some determinants and consequences of causal attribution. *Journal of Personality and Social Psychology*, 22, 171–193.

McAuley, E., & Gross, J. G. (1983). Perceptions of causality in sport: An application of the causal dimension scale. *Journal of Sport Psychology*, 5, 72–76.

Meyer, J. P. & Mulherin, A. (1980). From attribution to helping: An analysis of the mediating effects of affect and expectancy. *Journal of Personality and Social Psychology*, 39, 201–210.

Michela, J. L., Peplau, L. A. & Weeks, D. G. (1982). Perceived dimensions of attributions for loneliness. *Journal of Personality and Social Psychology*, 43, 929–936.

Miller, D. T., & Turnbull, W. (1986). Expectancies and interpersonal processes. *Annual Review of Psychology*, 37, 233–256.

Monson, T. C., & Snyder, M. (1977). Actors, observers, and the attribution process: Toward a reconceptualization. *Journal of Experimental Social Psychology*, 13, 89–111.

Mullen, B., Atkins, J. L. Champion, D. S., Edwards, C., Hardy, D., Story, J. E., & Vanderklok, M. (1985). The false consensus effect: A meta-analysis of 115 hypothesis tests. *Journal of Experimental Social Psychology*, 21, 262–283.

Newston, D. (1974). Dispositional inference from effects of actions: Effects chosen and effects foregone. *Journal of Experimental Social Psychology*, 10, 487–496.

Nisbett, R. E., Caputo, C., Legant, P., & Maracek, J. (1973). Behavior as seen by the actor and as seen by the observer. *Journal of Personality and Social Psychology*, 27, 154–164.

Nisbett, R. E., & Kunda, Z. (1985). Perception of social distributions. *Journal of Personality and Social Psychology*, 48, 297–311.

Nisbett, R. E., & Ross, l. (1980). *Human inference: Strategies and the shortcomings of social judgment.* Englewood Cliffs, NJ: Prentice-Hall.

Peabody, D. (1984). Personality dimensions through trait inferences. *Journal of Personality and Social Psychology*, 46, 384–403.

Pyszczynski, T. A., & Greenberg, J. (1981). Role of disconfirmed expectancies in the instigation of attributional processing. *Journal of Personality and Social Psychology*, 40, 31–38.

Rook, K. S. (1987). Effects of case history versus abstract information on health attitudes and behaviors. *Journal of Applied Social Psychology*, 17, 533–553.

Rosenthal, R. (1985). From unconscious experimenter bias to teacher expectancy effects. In J. B. Dusek, V. C. Hall, & W. J. Meyer (Eds.), *Teacher expectancies* (pp. 37–65). Hillsdale, NJ: Erlbaum.

Rosenthal, R., & Jacobson, L. (1968). *Pygmalion in the classroom: Teacher expectation and pupils' intellectual development.* New York: Holt, Rinehart & Winston.

Ross, L. (1977). The intuitive psychologist and his shortcomings: Distortions in the attribution process. In L. Berkowitz (Ed.), *Advances in experimental social psychology* (Vol. 10). New York: Academic Press.

Ross, L., Greene, D., & House, P. (1977). The false consensus phenomenon: An attributional bias in self-perception and social-perception processes. *Journal of Experimental Social Psychology*, 13, 279–301.

Russell, D. (1982). The causal dimension scale: A measure of how individuals perceive causes. *Journal of Personality and Social Psychology*, 42, 1137–1145.

Saulnier, D., & Perlman, D. (1981). The actor-observer bias is alive and well in prison: A sequel to Wells. *Personality and Social Psychology Bulletin, 7*, 559–564.

Schaufeli, W. B., (1988). Perceiving the causes of unemployment: An evaluation of the causal dimension scale in a real-life situation. *Journal of Personality and Social Psychology, 54*, 347–356.

Schoeneman, J. J., & Rubanowitz, D. E. (1985). Attributions in the advice columns: Actors and observers, causes and reasons. *Personality and Social Psychology Bulletin, 11*, 315–325.

Shaver, K. G. (1970). Defensive attribution: Effects of severity and relevance on the responsibility assigned for an accident. *Journal of Personality and Social Psychology, 14*, 101–113.

Sherman, S. J., Presson, C., & Chassin, L. (1984). Mechanisms underlying the false consensus effect: The special role of threats to the self. *Personality and Social Psychology Bulletin, 10*, 127–138.

Sherman, S. J., Presson, C., Chassin, l., Corty, E., & Olschavshy, R. (1983). The false consensus effect in estimates of smoking prevalence: Underlying mechanisms. *Personality and Social Psychology Bulletin, 9*, 197–207.

Silka, L. (1989). *Intuitive judgments of change.* New York. Springer-Verlag.

Skov, R. B., & Sherman, S. J. (1986). Information-gathering processes: Diagnosticity, hypothesis confirmatory strategies, and perceived hypothesis confirmation. *Journal of Experimental Social Psychology, 22*, 93–121.

Snyder, M. (1984). When beliefs create reality. In L. Berkowitz (Ed.), *Advances in experimental social psychology* (Vol. 18, pp. 247–305). New York: Academic Press.

Snyder, M., & Swann, W. B., Jr. (1978a). Behavioral confirmation in social interaction: From social perception to social reality. *Journal of Personality and Social Psychology, 36*, 1202–1212.

Snyder, M., & Swann, w. B., Jr. (1978b). Hypothesis testing processes in social interaction. *Journal of Experimental Social Psychology, 14*, 148–12.

Storms, M. D. (1973). Videotape and the attribution process: Reversing actors' and observers' points of view. *Journal of Personality and Social Psychology, 27*, 165–175.

Summers, G., & Feldman, J. S. (1984). Blaming the victim versus blaming the perpetrator: An attributional analysis of spouse abuse. *Journal of Social and Clinical Psychology, 2*, 339–347.

Swann, W. B., Jr., & Ely, R. J. (1984). A battle of wills: Self-verification versus behavioral confirmation. *Journal of Personality and Social Psychology, 46*, 1287–1302.

Taylor, S. E., & Fiske, S. T. (1978). Salience, attention, and attribution: Top of the head phenomena. In L. Berkowitz (Ed.), *Advances in experimental social psychology* (Vol. 11, pp. 249–288). New York: Academic Press.

Tesser, A. (1978). Self-generated attitude change. In L. Berkowitz (Ed.), *Advances in experimental social psychology* (Vol. 11, pp. 288–338). New York: Academic Press.

Tetlock, P. E. (1983). Accountability and the perseverance of first impressions. *Social Psychology Quarterly, 46*, 285–292.

Thornton, B., Hogate, L., Moirs, K., Pinette, M., & Presby, W. (1986). Physiological evidence for an arousal-based motivational bias in the defensive attribution of responsibility. *Journal of Experimental Social Psychology, 22*, 148–162.

Trope, Y., & Bassock, M. (1983). Information gathering strategies in hypothesis testing. *Journal of Experimental Social Psychology*, 19, 560–576.

Tyler, T. R., & Devinitz, V. (1981). Self-serving bias in the attribution of responsibility: Cognitive versus motivational explanations. *Journal of Experimental Social Psychology*, 17, 408–416.

Vallerand, R. J., & Richer, F. (1988). On the use of the causal dimension scale in a field setting: A test with confirmatory factor analysis in success and failure situations. *Journal of Personality and Social Psychology*, 54, 704–712.

Walster, E. (1966). Assignment of responsibility for important events. *Journal of Personality and Social Psychology*, 3, 73–79.

Watkins, M. J., & Peynircioglu, Z. F. (1984). Determining perceived meaning during impression formation: Another look at the meaning change hypothesis. *Journal of Personality and Social Psychology*, 46, 1005–1016.

Watson, D. (1982). The actor and the observer: How are their perceptions of causality divergent? *Psychological Bulletin*, 92, 682–700.

Weiner, B. (1986). *An attributional theory of emotion and motivation*. New York: Springer-Verlag.

Weiner, B. (1985). "Spontaneous" causal thinking. *Psychological Bulletin*, 97, 74–84.

Weiner, B., Graham, S., & Chandler, C. C. (182). Pity, anger, and guilt: An attributional analysis. *Personality and Social Psychology Bulletin*, 8, 226–232.

Weiner, B., Nierenberg, R., & Goldstein, M. (1976). Social learning (locus of control) versus attributional (causal stability) interpretations of expectancy for success. *Journal of Personality*, 44, 52–68.

Weiner, B., Russell, D., & Lerman, D. (1979). The cognition-emotion process in achievement-related contexts. *Journal of Personality and Social Psychology*, 37, 1211–1220.

West, S. G., Gunn, S. P. & Chernicky, P. (1975). Ubiquitous Watergate: An attributional analysis. *Journal of Personality and Social Psychology*, 32, 55–65.

Wong, P. T. P., & Weiner, B. (1981). When people ask "why" questions, and the heuristics of attributional search. *Journal of Personality and Social Psychology*, 40, 650–663.

Wyer, R. S. (1974). Changes in meaning and halo effects in personality impression formation. *Journal of Personality and Social Psychology*, 29, 829–835.

# 16.   ESCAPE FROM REALITY: ILLUSIONS IN EVERYDAY LIFE

Shelley E. Taylor

## INTRODUCTION

One of the first things an infant learns is that the self is a separate person. Upon seeing his reflection, the very young baby will pat his image and pat himself in return, knowing that what he is seeing is himself. Much of early knowledge involves distinguishing what is the self from other important people in the environment, especially the mother and father. As a consequence, the self helps to organize thinking around its attributes and its relationships to the social world.[1] Mental health experts suggest that the process by which this differentiation of self occurs should involve the capacity to perceive the self realistically, that is, to acknowledge faithfully both one's strengths and one's weaknesses. This is not, in fact, how the process evolves.

Before the exigencies of the world impinge upon the child's self-concept, the child is his or her own hero. With few exceptions, most children think very well of themselves. They believe they are capable at many tasks and abilities, including those they have never tried. They see themselves as popular. Most kindergartners and first-graders say they are at or near the top of the class. They have great expectations for their future success. Moreover, these grandiose assessments are quite unresponsive to negative feedback, at least until approximately age seven. Children see themselves as successful on most tasks, even ones on which they failed. They seem quite cheerfully oblivious to feedback from others that they have not performed as well as they think they have.[2] An architect friend recounts the time he took his five-year-old daughter to work with him. As he finalized some building plans at his drafting

table, the child scrupulously mimicked the behavior at a nearby desk. Amused passersby came over to see what the child had accomplished, and one kindly friend remarked, "Someday you'll be an even better architect than your daddy." The child looked up in surprise and responded, "But I already am," and went back to work.

Why do children have such unrealistically positive assessments of their abilities that, moreover, appear to be so unresponsive to feedback? Psychologist Deborah Stipek argues, in part, that children do not necessarily view failure as failure. To a child, the fact that a goal has not been attained does not mean that something bad has occurred or that the experience has any implications for the future. Eventually children learn to judge their performance as a success or failure, but in very young children these concepts have little meaning. Children have fairly short memories and may actually forget how they have done. Children also see ability and effort as very much the same thing, and so they see any activity in pursuit of a goal, whether successful or unsuccessful, as progress. As one child noted, "If you study, it helps the brain and you get smarter."[3] Young children do not differentiate very well between what they wish could be true and what they think is true, and thus they show wishful thinking in their estimations of their abilities.[4]

The view of oneself as a hero who possesses all the qualities necessary to succeed in a world filled with opportunities fades somewhat in late childhood, but it is nonetheless present in adults as well as children. Although mental health experts regard the well-adjusted person as being aware and accepting of negative as well as positive aspects of the self, in fact, most adults hold very positive views of themselves. When asked to describe themselves, most people mention many positive qualities and few, if any, negative ones.[5] Even when people acknowledge that they have faults, they tend to downplay those weaknesses as unimportant or dismiss them as inconsequential.[6]

For those who are mathematically inclined, the world is awash with arithmetic problems waiting to be solved. For those with little talent in that direction, the tasks are best left undone or delegated to a spouse or an accountant. People regard activities that do not hold their interest as less important than things that interest them. To a football fan, football is an important part of life. To those uninterested in football, it is a slow-moving, bizarre contest between surreal giants who could surely think of better ways to spend their time. When people recognize their lack of talent in a particular area, they are likely to see it as a common fault shared by others. Favored abilities, in contrast, are typically regarded as rare and distinctive signs of unusual talent.[7] The child who can hop on one foot is convinced no one else can do it quite as well, while this same child would insistently argue that all her friends eat cereal with their fingers, too. Thus, far from being balanced between positive and negative conceptions, the image that most people hold of themselves is heavily weighted in a positive direction.[8]

But are those self-perceptions actually unrealistic? Is the positive self-image an illusion or a reality? An imbalance in self-perceptions does not in and of itself mean that people's self-perceptions are biased. Most people commit positive actions most of the time, and consequently people's favorable attributes and actions considerably outweigh their negative ones. There is, however, some evidence that adult's positive self-perceptions are unrealistic. Most people, for example, see themselves as better than others and as above average on most of their qualities. When asked to describe themselves and other people, most people provide more positive descriptions of themselves than they do of friends. This tendency to see the self as better than others occurs across a wide variety of tasks and abilities.[9] Because it is logically impossible for most people to be better than everyone else, the positive view

that most people have of themselves appears to be, at least to some degree, illusory in nature. Most people even believe that they drive better than others. For example, in one survey, 90 percent of automobile drivers considered themselves better than average drivers. Indeed, these beliefs sometimes show an unresponsiveness to feedback that reminds one of the very young child. When people whose driving had involved them in accidents serious enough to involve hospitalization were interviewed about their driving skills and compared with drivers who had not had accident histories, the two groups gave almost identical descriptions of their driving abilities. Irrespective of their accident records, people judged themselves to be more skillful than average, and this was true even when the drivers involved in accidents had been responsible for them.[10]

The evaluations people offer of themselves are also typically more favorable than judgments made by others about them.[11] For example, when people's descriptions are contrasted with the descriptions of them offered by their friends or acquaintances, the self-descriptions tend to be more positive. Typically, we see ourselves in more flattering terms than we are seen by others. The perception of self that most people hold, then, is not as well balanced as traditional theories of mental health suggest. Rather than being attentive to both the favorable and unfavorable aspects of the self, most people appear to be very cognizant of their strengths and assets and considerably less aware of their weaknesses and faults. Our self-aggrandizing perceptions may result in part from biases in how we remember ourselves and our past actions.

## The Self As Personal Historian

Our minds are constructed not only to sift through and digest the information available to us in the present, but to store and make sense of all the information that has been part of the past. In a sense each person acts as a personal historian, recording the events of which he or she has been a part. Rather than acting as a dispassionate recorder of events as they transpire, the self appears to actively fabricate and revise personal history. Moreover, this task is accomplished in a way that makes the self an important, central, and positive figure in that history.

In his landmark essay, "The Totalitarian Ego," psychologist Anthony Greenwald argues that "the past is remembered as if it were a drama in which the self is the leading player."[12] In some ways, this fact is a necessity of memory. One can remember only events in which one participated because, by definition, events from which one was absent cannot be remembered, only heard about. Moreover, memory must be limited by our own perceptions of what transpired. We cannot remember other people's interpretations of situations, only our own. We can experience only our own sensations and emotional reactions to situations and not other people's. Since memory is often enriched by the recall of particular feelings or sensations, these details will, of necessity, be egocentric, that is, centered around the self. In recalling a dinner party of the night before, I may remember that I had slightly too much to drink, told an off-color story about a colleague that might best have been censored, and was otherwise fairly outgoing and a little funnier than usual. Were I to share these perceptions with another who had been a guest at the party, they would no doubt bear little resemblance to his recollections. He might dimly remember my off-color story, have no awareness that I had slightly too much to drink, nor be particularly cognizant of the fact that I was entertaining. Rather, his own recollection of the party might involve wondering whether people noticed that he was feeling low and whether they would properly attribute this to problems in his marriage. He might remember several of the stories told, but not necessarily who told which one. He might recall wondering at ten o'clock if the party would ever end, and the relief he felt when at eleven fifteen people finally pushed their chairs away from the table to say good night. The comparison of these experiences suggests that we were at different dinner parties, which indeed is exactly what happened in certain respects. In the absence of any active reconstruction or distortion, memory is egocentric, organized entirely around the experiences of the person constructing the memory.

But memory is egocentric in more impor-tant ways as well. Our memories of situations not only bear the traces of egocentric sensations and perspectives, but are also actively organized around our own interests and concerns. Each of us has qualities that we consider to be character-istic of ourselves. One person may think of him-self as witty, musical, and hopelessly lacking in athletic ability. Another person may regard her-self as kind, overweight, and intelligent. Psychol-ogists call these enduring beliefs that people have about themselves *self-schemas*.[13] Self-schemas are important because they guide the selection and interpretation of information in social situations. The man who thinks of himself as musical will almost certainly remember that a Mozart clar-inet concerto played in the background during the dinner party, whereas someone who does not consider himself to be musical might not even be aware that music was playing. The person who thinks of himself as witty is likely to interpret his barbed remark toward another dinner guest as humorous, whereas a person for whom kind-ness is an important dimension may interpret the same behavior as rude and unkind. The woman who thinks of herself as overweight will almost certainly remember the entire menu, what she ate and what she didn't eat, and the approximate caloric value of each food item.

Self-schemas, then, impose an additional se-lectivity on the information that people construe from situations and later remember about them. In recalling information that fits self-schemas, those self-schemas are inadvertently reinforced by memory. For example, each situation that a witty person interprets as an example of his own witty banter provides him with additional evi-dence that he is witty. If he construes three or four remarks that he made as examples of his wit, then his self-perception as a witty person is strength-ened by each of these events. Other guests at the party, however, may remember only one or two of the remarks, considering neither especially funny. Self-schemas, then, enable us to take in the infor-mation that fits our prior conceptions of what we are like and what interests us and simultaneously helps cement those self-impressions.

Psychologists generally interpret the effects of self-schemas on memory to mean that memory is organized efficiently in a limited number of categories. That is, given that no one can take in all of the available information in a situation, self-schemas provide guidelines for which information should be noticed, thought about, and put away in memory. The fact that these organizing categories are related to the self is in some respects an accident of the fact that the self is taking in the information. If one takes a functional perspective for a moment, however, it is clear that the egocentric organization of information can be very useful. People make a rough cut on information as "relevant to me" or "not relevant to me." Next they interpret exactly how the information is relevant. When that information is later stored egocentrically in memory, it can be applied in extremely useful ways. For example, a woman for whom kindness is important not only uses kindness as a way of sorting people into the categories of kind and unkind, she may also use the information as a basis for her own future social interactions. Having determined that the witty man is unkind, she would be very likely to avoid him in future situations, a highly adaptive maneuver from her standpoint. Clearly, the egocentric organization of memory is useful from an economic standpoint, that is, in reducing information to a manageable load.[14] But beyond this, it may be very adaptive in helping people to construct their future activities.[15]

Most of us think well of ourselves on most attributes, so self-schemas are more likely to be positive than negative. This recognition leads to the realization that memory for past events will likely be recalled in a positive manner, one that reflects well on the self. This logical inference yields a third way in which memory is biased, namely toward positive construals of one's own attributes and roles in events gone by.[16] Indeed, the capacity of memory to recast events in a positive light almost immediately after they have transpired is almost astonishing. People who have just performed poorly on a task such as doing mathematics problems can be asked to recall their performance a scant twenty minutes later, and even in the short interval they misremember their performance as better than it actually was. Within a few days or weeks, the event may be forgotten altogether. If I rush a student in and out of my office in a few minutes, knowing that he has not had a chance to discuss his research with me fully, I may feel guilty shortly thereafter, but will likely have put the event totally out of mind within days. If I later learn that he has told other students that I am too busy to provide useful advice, I might be hurt and amazed by this betrayal, totally forgetting that I once believed it to hold a kernel of truth.

When people are asked to recall their personal qualities, they typically come up with more positive than negative information. Positive information about one's own personality is easily recalled and efficiently processed, whereas negative information about one's personality is poorly processed and difficult to recall.[17] There are, of course, qualifications to this general rule. Most of us know that in making our qualities known to another person, to brag endlessly of our talents without any assessment of our weaknesses would make us appear conceited. In order to achieve the positive picture we wish to construct for others, sometimes we may admit to certain faults. However, even the faults or weaknesses may be carefully chosen to round out a warm, human portrait, rather than one that is balanced between the positive and negative.[18] A woman may be more likely to admit to others that she is hopeless at math than to confess that she sometimes cheats on her husband. Thus, while our characterizations of ourselves to others may incorporate a certain socially desirable modesty, the portraits that we actually believe, when we are given freedom to voice them, are dramatically more positive than reality can sustain. As writer Carlos Fuentes so acutely noted, "Desire will send you back into memory...for memory is desire satisfied."[19]

Greenwald's characterization of these memory processes as totalitarian is apt. Unlike the academic historian, who is expected to adhere closely to the facts and insert a personal evaluation only in the interpretation, the personal historian takes unbridled license with the facts themselves, rearranging and distorting them and omitting aspects of history altogether in an effort to create and maintain a positive image of the self.

We control the present by using our own interests and attributes as ways of selecting and organizing available information, and then we store it in memory in ways that are both highly positive and consistent with our existing impressions of ourselves. We use the present to construct a benign portrait of the past with ourselves as central actors. In so doing, we pave the way for a similar future.

## The Self as Causal Actor

Taking in and recalling information are not the only cognitive tasks that people must perform. Active interpretation of the present is also required. Perceptions of what caused events to happen are among the most important beliefs that people hold about social situations. Here, too, the self is self-serving. A consistent and ubiquitous research finding is that people take credit for good things that happen and deny responsibility for the bad things that happen.[20] This self-serving bias, as it has been called, shows up in a broad array of situations. For example, on the tennis court, after you have soundly beaten an opponent, rarely do you hear the gratifying, "Gee, you're much better than I am, aren't you?" Usually you hear that it was a bad day, your opponent's serve was off, he is still working on his backhand, or the light was in his eyes. On the other hand, when you have just been badly beaten, the smug look and condescending "bad luck" from the opponent are particularly grating because you know that he does not believe it was bad luck for a moment; he simply thinks he is better. Positive outcomes or actions tend to be attributed to one's own personal qualities, whereas negative outcomes are regarded as the result of bad luck or factors beyond one's control.

The following examples from the *San Francisco Chronicle* of drivers' explanations of their accidents to the police reveal how reluctantly people assume blame for negative events.

*As I approached an intersection, a sign suddenly appeared in a place where a stop sign had never appeared before. I was unable to stop in time to avoid an accident.*

*The telephone pole was approaching. I was attempting to swerve out of its way when it struck my front end.*[21]

And commenting on students' evaluations of final exams, Greenwald notes:

*I have repeatedly found a strong correlation between obtained grade and the belief that the exam was a proper measure. Students who do well are willing to accept credit for success; those who do poorly, however, are unwilling to accept responsibility for failure, instead seeing the exam (or the instructor) as being insensitive to their abilities.*[22]

How do people maintain the perception that they cause good things to happen but bear less responsibility for bad outcomes? Is this simply some sleight of mind analogous to the magician's sleight of hand? Or can it be understood as an adaptive cognitive process? Perhaps when people try to understand why an event occurred, they confuse their intentions with their actions.[23] Usually we intend to cause good things and not bad things. When those good things do occur, the tendency to see ourselves as having brought them about may be quite justifiable, given that we did indeed mean to bring the outcome about. However, when our actions produce bad outcomes, we may look for circumstantial explanations precisely because no adverse outcomes were intended. The man who backs out of his driveway and hits a small child may blame the automobile manufacturers for having rear-view mirrors that fail to pick up low objects. Alternatively, he may blame the child's parents for not having trained the child to stay out of the street. He is unlikely to blame himself, because he never intended to hit the child. Whether the confusion of intention and causality underlies the tendency to attribute good outcomes to oneself to a greater degree than bad outcomes remains to be seen. The interpretational bias itself, however, is well established and constitutes yet another way in which the mind actively fosters a positive view of the self.

Self-serving biases in the perception of the causes of events are strengthened by the fact that people typically exaggerate how much of a role they have in any task, particularly one with a good outcome.[24] To take a simple example, when two people have written a book together and are asked to estimate how much of the book they are personally responsible for, the estimates added together will typically exceed 100 percent. The same feature characterizes more mundane tasks. Asked to estimate how much of a contribution they make to housework, adding together husbands' and wives' estimates of their own efforts produces a total that greatly exceeds 100 percent.[25] Even the lore surrounding Nobel Prize winners is filled with such accounts.

*In 1923, two Canadians, Banting and Macleod, were awarded the Nobel Prize for their discovery of insulin. Upon receiving the prize, Banting contended that Macleod, who was head of the laboratory, had been more of a hindrance than a help. On the other hand, Macleod managed to omit Banting's name in speeches describing the research leading up to discovery of insulin.[26]*

What leads people to overestimate their role in jointly undertaken ventures? Egocentric memory appears once again to be the culprit. We notice our own contributions to a joint task because we are mentally and physically present when making our own contributions. When the other person is contributing his or her share to the joint task, we may not be physically present to observe it or we may be distracted from noticing the other person's effort. When asked to recall who contributed what to the task, it will subsequently be easier to recall one's own contributions, having attended to them better in the first place, than to recall the other person's.[27]

There will also likely be interpretational biases in what constitutes a contribution.[28] A recent tiff between two authors of a book centered on the fact that while one wrote his share of the chapters rather quickly, the other put a great deal more time into preparing his chapters. Because the first writer was more experienced, his chapters needed few revisions; but the second author's chapters required several drafts and received comments from the first author. The first author perceived that he had borne the lion's share of the effort, by both being responsible for his own chapters and critiquing those of his collaborator. The collaborator, in contrast, felt that he had done the most, because his work had taken three times as long

as the first author's. Who is right? Clearly it depends on one's perspective, and one can make a case for either position.

The tendency to take more than one's share of credit for a joint outcome would appear to be a maladaptive bias, inasmuch as it creates so many opportunities for misunderstandings. However, the bias may have benefits as well as potential liabilities. By perceiving one's share of a joint product to be larger than it is, people may feel more responsible for the outcome and work harder to make it a positive one. Moreover, the process of contributing to the activity may instill a sense of commitment to the project and to one's collaborators that may undermine, at least temporarily, any feelings of having done more than one's share. The bias, too, may be more one of memory than of active construction during the time that the tasks are being performed. Often, when two people have jointly achieved greatness, the falling out over who was most responsible for the product occurs after the outcome has been achieved, not while the task is going on. Commitment and a sense of responsibility may carry the joint product through completion, but egocentric memory may distort later reconstructions of what actually took place.[29]

At this point, it is useful to take stock and reassess whether normal human self-perception is characterized by realism or not. The evidence from numerous research investigations with both children and adults clearly indicates that people's assessments of their own capabilities are ego-enhancing rather than realistic. The fact that this bias is so clearly prevalent in the normal human mind is surprising. Psychologists have typically interpreted blatant ego enhancement as the resort of weak and insecure people attempting to bolster fragile self-esteem. Weak egos are thought to need narcissism to survive.[30] Alternatively, ego defensiveness has been viewed as a handy refuge for all of us during weak or threatening moments.[31] In this view, we may need the occasional self-serving interpretation to recover from a blow to self-esteem, but not otherwise. The picture furnished by the evidence, however, is quite different and suggests that ego enhancement characterizes most perception most of the time. This fact, in itself, does not make self-enhancement adaptive, but it does make it normal. As such, this picture is in opposition to the portrait of normal functioning painted by many theories of mental health.

## THE NEED FOR CONTROL

In 1971, psychologist B. F. Skinner published a book, *Beyond Freedom and Dignity*, that sparked heated debate. Among other points, Skinner argued that freedom and individual will are illusions because behavior is under the control of positive and negative reinforcements provided by the environment. The uproar created by this argument is testimony to the attachment people have to their perceptions of freedom, personal choice, and control. Indeed, Skinner may have gone too far. While there is certainly a basis for contending that freedom, control, and personal will are constructions that people impose on events rather than factors inherent in events themselves, what people construe about their behavior is of great importance. Interpretations enable people to make sense of their experience; moreover, they can have important personal consequences. As psychologist Herbert Lefcourt notes:

*To believe that one's freedom is a false myth and that one should submit to wiser or better controls contains the assumption that beliefs or illusions have no immediate consequences. . . . This assumption is specious. Illusions have consequences and . . . the loss of the illusion of freedom may have untoward consequences for the way men live.*[32]

Since the days of Aristotle and Plato, philosophers have argued that a sense of personal control is vital to human functioning. Psychologists from many theoretical viewpoints, including social psychologist Fritz Heider, developmental psychologist Robert White, learning theorist Albert Bandura, and psychoanalytic theorists Alfred Adler and Sandor Fenichel, have maintained that the self-concept cannot mature without a sense of personal control.

## The Child's Need For Control

The desire to control and manipulate the world is evident from a remarkably early age. Within weeks after birth, an infant actively explores the environment, responding to a new stimulus, such as a brightly colored rattle, with rapt attention and babbling. Soon, however, when the rattle has been fully explored, the infant shows little response when the rattle is again dangled before her, but may react with the same excitement to a new checkerboard that she has not previously seen. The infant, then, is primed to master new experiences.[33] At first, psychologists observing this behavior tried to identify what reinforcements it might bring for the child. Were the parents more likely to feed or comfort the child when he or she explored and manipulated the environment? What rewards did curiosity evoke that maintained this behavior? Soon it became evident that the child pursued these exploratory activities for their own sake. Exploration and the ability to bring about change in the environment are their own rewards.[34]

As a result of these observations, psychologists believe that even newborn infants have an intrinsic need to understand and manage the environment.[35] Even the youngest children seem to do what is good for them to bring about their own effective learning. They seek out tasks and sources of stimulation that lead to the development of new skills. Children seem to derive pleasure from engaging in this mastery-oriented behavior, and when a child has accomplished some task—that is, when mastery is attained—he or she seems to experience joy and satisfactions. Both pleasure in the activity itself and enjoyment of the sense of mastery promote similar activities in the future.

So evident is this drive toward mastery that psychologists believe the need to master the environment, or at least its basic elements, is wired in via a mastery-motivation system that instigates, maintains, and reinforces activities that lead to the development of new skills. White refers to this as competence motivation, arguing that the process of learning about the environment and gaining mastery over it is actually intrinsic to the child's development and will occur of its own accord unless disrupted by a biological malfunction or an impoverished environment.[36] Daniel Berlyne refers to a curiosity motivation by which the child constantly seeks more and varied objects to manipulate and explore.[37]

Some of the child's exploratory activities involve stretching already evident skills to try something new. For example, the infant who is able to reach and grasp a stationary toy may be stimulated more by a new toy that is moving than by another stationary toy. The moving toy forces her to extend her abilities to track the toy with her eyes and grasp it as it comes into reach. Children seek and produce novel activity and stimulus variability. Moderately new environments that include objects the child has not seen before are far more interesting and stimulating than either radically different environments or environments full of familiar objects.

The child's mastery needs, then, have a certain orderly progression to them that is responsive both to the demands of tasks and to the limits of existing skills.[38] Any parent attempting unrealistically to throw a birthday party for a one-year-old will stumble upon this fact. As each gift is unwrapped, the child reacts not to the contents but to the wrappings, balling up the paper to make a wonderful crumpling noise and waving the brightly colored ribbons overhead. The empty box makes a perfect hat and is far more valued a toy than the train that came in it, which may not be admired and played with for another six or eight months. Children learn and perform new tasks that are just beyond their range of competence. The young child does not try to drive a car. He depresses the accelerator repeatedly. The adolescent, ready for such a challenge, rolls the car down the driveway at night and practices driving while his parents sleep. The very young child's early cooking efforts extend to baking cookies by stirring in the flour and eating too many chocolate bits. The adolescent can cook an entire meal, assuming she can be induced to do so. Mastery skills are used in a discriminating fashion, moving a step or two ahead of the child's current abilities.

By learning to master their own environments, children alter their parents' behaviors dramatically. Parents quickly learn that if they want the infant to reward them with enthusiastic sounds, the best way to achieve this goal is to gradually introduce more and varied novel experiences. Even infants are able to enlist the cooperation of the social environment to their own mastery needs.[39]

The desire to master the environment, then, appears to be a basic drive, perhaps even a fundamental need of the human organism. By learning that he or she can have an impact on the environment, the child acquires the valuable skills, crucial for adult functioning, that enable him or her to actively intervene in the world so as to bring about desired outcomes. The implicit assumption that underlies a functional interpretation of the need to master is that such early experiences provide the child with a realistic sense of self-efficacy, that is, a realization of those things that can be actively changed and controlled in order to realize personal goals. In fact, however, the sense of control that young children develop appears to be exaggerated rather than tempered by realism.

As young children are learning *how* to control the environment, so too are they learning *that* they can control it. Early in development, children gain the sense that they can make things happen.[40] This, too, may be intrinsic to the child's nature, for it can easily be observed in extreme and dramatic form in the young child. In his conversations with children, the esteemed developmental psychologist Jean Piaget discovered that children believe not only that they can master what goes on in the immediate environment but that they control the movements of the sun, moon, and stars as well.[41] The child's sense of omnipotence is so strong that when family crises arise, such as a sibling's illness or parents' divorce, young children may react very strongly, in part because they believe they brought the tragic events about.[42]

The child's sense of omnipotence extends to schoolwork and other learning tasks. When asked to guess how well they will do on tasks, young children usually substantially overestimate their performance because they believe they can master the tasks easily. Psychologist Carol Dweck and her associates argue that a mastery orientation toward tasks develops and coheres quite early in life.[43] Mastery-oriented children approach new tasks with the question, "How can this best be accomplished and what should I do to solve it correctly?" When they run into trouble on a difficult task, these mastery-oriented children talk to themselves, trying to figure out what is wrong with their performance and developing strategies to change it so they will be more effective. Often they encourage themselves, letting themselves know that they can do the task correctly.

The competence drive that one sees in the infant and young child is remarkably simple, but extraordinary in its effects. On the one hand, it requires no plan or intention. Yet it enables the child to fashion his or her environment in an increasingly complex way, enlisting the cooperation and talents of several powerful adults in the process, and to derive great pleasure and satisfaction from the results, while simultaneously building essential intellectual skills.

Over time, the child's sense of personal control diminishes somewhat, becoming responsive to realistic limits on talents and the limitations inherent in difficult tasks.[44] Despite this movement toward realism, adults not only continue to have a need and desire to control the environment, but also maintain an exaggerated faith in their ability to do so.

## The Adult's Need For Control

Most adults believe the world to be inherently controllable. They have faith that a combination of personal effort and advanced technology can solve most of the world's problems. To the extent that we have been unsuccessful in controlling natural forces or, for that matter, the economic, social, and political dilemmas we have ourselves created, we perceive it to be through lack of effort, not ability, that the problems have remained unsolved. We believe that people succeed through their own efforts, and this leads us to impute effort to those who are highly successful and laziness to those who are not.[45] Even

if evidence is all around us suggesting that events are less orderly and systematic than we think they are, rarely do we develop a full appreciation of this fact. The failure to recognize the role of random, unsystematic forces in many aspects of life may come, in part, from our need to see the world as a systematic and orderly place. As Ernest Becker noted in his Pulitzer Prize-winning book, *The Denial of Death,* through the imposition of logic and order on the world we spare ourselves the constant realization of the random terror of death.

One source of faith in personal control is that the environment often cooperates in maintaining it. People are typically quite cognizant of the effects of their own actions on the environment, but are considerably less so regarding the effects of the environment on their own actions. We underestimate the degree to which our behavior is determined by social and physical forces that not only are uncontrollable but often escape awareness altogether.[46] One of my colleagues believes, only half in jest, that he can will a parking place in any lot in which he needs to find one. The reason he holds this belief is that apparently most lots into which he drives have one or two spaces left. Until recently, it had escaped his attention that building projects must create an appropriate number of parking spaces. Thus, while he no doubt overestimates the number of times he gets the last spot, it is also the case that getting one of the last spots is a highly probably event, given the small miracle of city planning.

Another source of the belief in control is that people confuse what they want to have happen with what they can actually bring about, and if the desired event occurs, they conclude that they controlled it.[47] I once observed this in a young boy who had been hospitalized for diabetes. Although not confined to bed, he remained in the hospital for observation because his blood sugar level changed erratically and required monitoring. The hospital environment was dull for this youngster, and he soon took to riding the elevators to provide himself with some semblance of stimulation. Deciding that he would become the elevator operator, he positioned himself in front of the control panel, making it impossible for others to press any but the floor numbers. At each floor, the boy would push the "Door Open" button; when the passenger had departed, the boy would push the "Door Close" button. The door obediently opened and shut. The regular passengers tolerated this unusual behavior because they could see that the boy needed to believe that something, however small, was under his personal control. No one had the heart to tell him, and he never figured out on his own, that the elevator was controlled entirely automatically, and that his button presses had no effect whatsoever on its operation. Because the door repeatedly opened and shut when he wanted it to, he mistakenly assumed that his behavior was actually bringing it about.

The process of evaluating whether or not an event is controllable is an example of a broader fallacy of reasoning, namely the search for examples that confirm prior beliefs.[48] To see how this logical fallacy operates, consider the popular belief that people can cure themselves of serious illnesses through positive thinking. Many people believe that illness results primarily from stressful events and that those who are able to maintain a positive attitude can exert control over their bodily processes and drive illness away. What kind of evidence leads people to hold such a belief? Examples of the mental control of illness are readily available. Norman Cousin's book, *Anatomy of an Illness*, describes in warm and humorous detail the methods the author used to treat himself for a disease that is usually fatal. Magazines contain stories of people who have apparently healed themselves of advanced malignancies through positive thinking. Cultural mythology abounds with examples of shamans who cured their sick neighbors through a variety of useless but dramatic ceremonies. These positive examples make compelling reading, but the logical error lies in precisely this point: they are all positive instances.

Suppose one wanted to determine scientifically whether people are able to cure their diseases through positive attitudes. What would one need to know? Most people immediately recognize the need to find examples of people who tried to cure their diseases through positive thinking and were successful. If pushed, one might come up with the observation that it would be useful to find out how many people tried to cure their diseases through positive thinking and failed. What most people miss is that an accurate sense of whether people can cure their illnesses depends on at least two more types of information: the number of people who did not try to cure their incurable illnesses and survived nonetheless, and the number of people who did not make an effort to cure their illnesses and died. In other words, to establish that people can survive a serious illness if they have effectively tried to control it, one needs all four types of information.

Unfortunately, the world of disease is full of people who have tried valiantly to cure themselves of their illnesses and have ultimately failed. Those who have worked extensively with the chronically ill also know that many people survive years longer than expected without having made any effort in their own behalf at all. These people are often just as bewildered as their physicians, family, and friends to find themselves alive some five or ten years after their initial diagnosis, when everyone expected them to die within months.

In short, it is logically incorrect to conclude that people can control their illnesses simply because one can readily find apparent examples. When one is forced to survey all of the evidence—instead of just the positive cases that are so compelling—judgments of control are considerably more muted, and enthusiasm for the initial belief is somewhat diminished.

This is not to say that people are unable to improve their health by maintaining a positive attitude. The jury is still out on this issue. Rather, the point is that people "see" their beliefs confirmed in incomplete evidence that leads them prematurely to desired conclusions. They fail to see that evidence they have ignored is also relevant. Decision theorists despair of ever getting people to avoid this error. Moreover, on this bias, the average person is in good company. The error is virtually irresistible, not only to the general public but to high-level decision makers in government and industry as well. The analysis of numerous policy decisions, such as the disastrous Bay of Pigs invasion in 1961, has implicated as the basis of the failure the tendency to incorporate primarily positive information and to ignore negative information.[49]

## The Illusion of Control

As the previous analysis suggests, people not only believe that the world is inherently controllable, they believe that their own ability to personally control events around them is exceptional. Psychologist Ellen Langer argues that most people succumb to an illusion of control, in which they believe they can affect events more than is actually the case. To demonstrate this point, Langer chose gambling.[50]

Gambling is a clear case in which the relative importance of personal control and chance are often confused. Sociologist Erving Goffman, who once took a job as a croupier in Las Vegas, noted that dealers who experienced runs of bad luck, leading the house to lose heavily, ran the risk of losing their jobs, even though the reason for the run of bad luck was ostensibly chance.[51] Experienced dice players engaged in a variety of behaviors suggesting a belief that they could control what numbers the dice turned up. They threw the dice softly if they wanted low numbers to come up and hard if they were trying to get high numbers. Moreover, they believed that effort and concentration were important and often would not roll the dice unless there was silence and they had a few seconds to concentrate on the number they wanted to get.[52] These kinds of behaviors make perfect sense if a game involves skill. They do not make much sense when the outcome is controlled by chance.

Most of us are not heavy gamblers. In an intriguing set of studies, however, Langer was able to demonstrate that virtually all people are subject to the same illusions of control as veteran gamblers. Beginning with the recognition that people often fail to distinguish between controllable and uncontrollable events, she argued that one reason for this fact is that the cues people use to differentiate situations of luck and skill are often confused. In skill situations, there is a causal link between one's own behavior and likely outcomes. By choosing materials appropriate for a problem, deciding what responses to make, familiarizing oneself with those materials and responses, spending time thinking about the tasks, coming up with strategies that might be used, and exerting effort, people increase their likelihood of succeeding on a skill-based task.[53] On tasks determined by chance, such behaviors have no effect at all.

Langer showed that by introducing skill-related cues into a chance situation, people came to behave as if the situations were under their personal control and not a result of luck at all. Among her observations were the following: If a person had to bet against a suave, confident opponent, he bet less money than if the opponent appeared to be meek and ineffective. When people were able to choose their own lottery card, as opposed to having it chosen for them, they were less likely to turn it in for a new lottery card that offered them a better chance of winning, simply because they felt it was now *their* card and they wanted to hold onto it. The longer a person held on to a lottery card and presumably had time to think about the likelihood of winning and what he would do with all the money, the less likely he was to turn the lottery card in for a ticket in a drawing with better odds. Langer was able to show that perfectly normal people engaged in a wide variety of superstitious and nonsensical behaviors in chance situations, when cues suggesting skill had been subtly introduced.[54]

The significance of Langer's research extends far beyond its curious but rather minor implications regarding gambling. Any situation in which a person confronts options, develops strategies, and devotes thought to a problem is vulnerable to an illusion of control. For several months, I have been plagued with a problem that until recently proved to be intractable, namely the fact that my dogs eat the pansies growing in the backyard. A variety of disciplinary actions as well as the application of foul-smelling but harmless chemicals to the flower beds have proven unsuccessful in keeping them from these meals. Now, however, I have mastered the situation, by planning to plant pansies only in the beds around the front door. In the backyard I will plant marigolds, which are not nearly as appealing to dogs. The successful solution to this problem bolsters my confidence that I am able to handle stressful events. One can legitimately ask, of course, who actually has control in this situation, me or the dogs? While in my weaker moments I acknowledge that one can probably make the stronger case for the dogs, most of the time this does not dampen my self-congratulations at having successfully mastered the problem by choosing an effective solution. The fact that this "choice" was fully constrained by the situation and was the only option remaining, other than eliminating the dogs, is conveniently forgotten.

The illusion of control has powerful effects on the human psyche. Psychologists have demonstrated that people can tolerate extreme distress if they believe they have the ability to control the source of that distress.[55] The following study conducted with college students makes this point. The students were brought into the laboratory for a study of reactions to electric shock. Half of the students were told that once the shock began, they could terminate it simply by pressing a button in front of them. The other half of the students were not given a button to press to terminate the shock. All the students were then exposed to a series of uncomfortable but harmless electric shocks. The shocks were rigged so that both groups of students received exactly the same amount of shock. Despite this fact, those able to terminate the event by pressing the button themselves experienced less psychological distress, fewer symptoms of physiological arousal, and less physical discomfort.[56] This study and ones like it have been carried out many times with different stressful events and, in every known case, those who can exert control over the stressful event experience less distress and arousal than those who cannot. In fact, those able to control the event often show no more psychological distress or physiological arousal than people receiving no aversive experience at all.[57] Clearly it is not the adverse event itself that leads people to feel physically aroused and psychologically distressed, but rather the perception that it cannot be controlled.

Why do we perceive as controllable things that either are not controllable or are much less so

than we think they are? We understand control. We know what it means to seek a goal, to develop methods for obtaining it, and then to employ those methods until the goal is obtained. There is an order, logic, and process to control. There is no order or logic to randomness. Perhaps as well we need to see events as controllable and this is why our minds are predisposed to focus in selectively on instances that support our preconceptions. Perhaps it is the false belief in control that makes people persist in pursuing their goals. Would a novelist undertaking her first work want to contemplate other writers who were catapulted into success by their first works, or would she want to focus instead on the far larger group of writers whose first novels never even attracted a publisher? Clearly, the answer is the former. Our need to see things as inherently controllable may well be adaptive, and our tendency to focus on positive cases of the relationships we expect and so badly wish to see may have value, even as it distorts perceptions.

## UNREALISTIC OPTIMISM ABOUT THE FUTURE

Most people are oriented toward the future. When asked to describe what occupies their thoughts, people typically mention issues of immediate or future concern.[58] Moreover, optimism pervades thinking about the future. We seem to be optimistic by nature, some of us more than others, but most more than reality can support.[59] Each year, survey researchers query the American public about their current lives and what they think their lives will be like in five years. Most surveys find people reporting that the present is better than the past and that the future will be even better. More than 95 percent of people questioned in these surveys typically believe that the economic picture will be good for everyone and that their personal economic future will be even better than that of others. People are characteristically hopeful and confident that things will improve.[60] Although this warm and generous vision is extended to all people, it is most clearly evident in visions of one's own future. Students asked to envision what their future lives would be like said they were more likely to graduate at the top of the class, get a good job, have a high starting salary, like their first job, receive an award for work, get written up in the paper, and give birth to a gifted child than their classmates. Moreover, they considered themselves far less likely than their classmates to have a drinking problem, to be fired from a job, to get divorced after a few years of marriage, to become depressed, or to have a heart attack or contract cancer.[61]

Unrealistic optimism is not confined to the idealistic young. Older adults also underestimate the likelihood that they will encounter a large number of negative, but unhappily common, events such as having an automobile accident, being a crime victim, having job problems, contracting major diseases, or becoming depressed. Unrealistic optimism appears to be unaffected by age, education, sex, or occupational prestige. The old and young, the well- and the poorly-educated, men and women, and people in all areas of life show unrealistic optimism in their assessments of the future.[62]

When asked to predict the future, most people predict what they would like to see happen, rather than what is objectively likely. Whether it be in a volleyball game, on a driving test, or on a report prepared for one's boss, most people believe that they will do well in the future. People expect to improve their performance over time, and moreover, this optimism typically increases with the importance of the task.[63] People are more unrealistically optimistic about the prospects for their future jobs than about their gardens, for example. People are even unrealistically optimistic about events that are completely determined by chance, such as whether they will win the lottery and whether the weather will be good for a picnic. People seem to be saying, in effect, "The future will be great, especially for me."

One of the more charming optimistic biases that people share is the belief that they can accomplish more in a given period of time than is humanly possible. This bias persists in the face of innumerable contradictions. Perhaps the most poignant example of this unrealistic optimism is

the daily to-do list. Each day, the well-organized person makes a list of the tasks to be accomplished and then sets out to get them done. Then the exigencies of the day begin to intrude: phone calls, minor setbacks, a miscalculation of how long a task will take, or a small emergency. The list that began the day crisp and white is now in tatters, with additions, cross-outs and, most significantly, half its items left undone. Yet at the end of the day, the list maker cheerfully makes up another overly optimistic list for the next day, or if much was left undone, simply crosses out the day at the top of the list and writes in the next day. This all-too-familiar pattern is remarkable not only because a to-do list typically includes far more than any person could reasonably expect to accomplish in a given time period, but also because the pattern persists day after day, completely unresponsive to the repeated feedback that it is unrealistic.[64]

Like the overly positive view of the self and the illusion of control, unrealistic optimism develops very early in life. When children are asked how well they will do on a future task, their expectations are typically very high, higher than is realistic. Moreover, unrealistically optimistic assessments of future performance are not very responsive to feedback, such as actual performance, grades in class, comments from teachers, or reactions of parents. By about age seven or eight, children begin to be aware of the meaning of negative feedback. They become more responsive to what their teachers and parents tell them. They also know what objective tests are, and so they are able to use both objective information and feedback from others to evaluate whether or not they have done a good job.[65] In some respects, this intruding realism is a sad aspect of growing older. Stipek notes:

*It is perhaps unfortunate that children's naive optimism declines so soon after they enter school. To some degree the development of more realistic expectations is unavoidable and even desirable. However ... if children were only given tasks on which they could succeed with some effort, continually high expectations for success and the adaptive behaviors that are associated with high expectations might be maintained throughout the school years. Rather than lamenting children's unrealistic judgments about their competencies, perhaps we should try harder to design educational environments that maintain their optimism and eagerness.*[66]

But is unrealistic optimism adaptive? Just as ego-enhancing biases have been regarded as defenses against threats to self-esteem, unrealistic optimism has been thought of as a defensive reaction, a distortion of reality designed to reduce anxiety.[67] Consider the following opinions:

*Optimism ...is a mania for maintaining that all is going well when things are going badly. (Voltaire)*

*Optimism, not religion, is the opiate of the people. (Lionel Tiger)*

*The place where optimism most flourishes is in the lunatic asylum. (Havelock Ellis)*

Two arguments have been made against unrealistic optimism. The first is that optimism about the future is an irrational defense against reality that enables people to ward off the anxiety of threatening events without successfully coming to terms with it. The second is related to the first in maintaining that unrealistic optimism keeps people from perceiving the objective risks of external threats and preparing for them.[68] Several points argue against the appropriateness of these concerns. If unrealistic optimism were merely a defense against anxiety, one would expect that more serious and threatening events would elicit more unrealistic optimism than minor risks. In fact, the evidence does not support this position. The degree of threat posed by a risk is unrelated to the amount of unrealistic optimism people have about their lack of susceptibility to the problem.[69]

Moreover, unrealistic optimism about the future is highly and appropriately responsive to objective qualities of events, including their frequency and whether or not a person has any past experience with that event. People are less unrealistically optimistic about their chances of experiencing common events like divorce or chronic illness than they are about less frequent events, such as being the victim of a flood or fire. Past experience with a threatening event can eliminate unrealistic optimism altogether. Children of divorced parents, for example, regard their own

chances of getting divorced as higher than people whose parents were not divorced. People are also more unrealistically optimistic about future events over which they have some control than they are about those that are uncontrollable. For example, although people estimate their chances of winning a lottery to be higher than is objectively likely, they recognize that winning a large amount of money in a lottery is far less likely than having a satisfying job, an event over which they presumably have more direct control. And finally, unrealistic optimism is responsive to information. When people receive objective evidence about the likelihood of risks, they change their estimates accordingly.[70] These qualities most clearly distinguish illusion from delusion. Delusions are false beliefs that persist despite the facts. Illusions accommodate them, though perhaps reluctantly.

Unrealistic optimism, then, is not a Panglossian whitewash that paints all positive events as equally and commonly likely and all negative events as equally and uncommonly unlikely. Rather, unrealistic optimism shows a patterning that corresponds quite well to the objective likelihood of events, to relevant personal experiences with events, and to the degree to which one can actively contribute to bringing events about. Positive events are simply regarded as somewhat more likely and negative events as somewhat less likely to occur than is actually the case.

What accounts for unrealistic optimism? Optimism seems to be intimately bound up with other illusions of life, especially the belief in personal control.[71] Most people think they can control future events more than is actually the case, and consequently they may underestimate their vulnerability to random events. A driver may perceive the chance of an automobile accident to be low because she believes she is a better than average driver who can avoid such problems. She may conveniently forget the joy-riding teenager or the drunk driver who may cause an accident. People think they can avoid health problems by getting enough sleep or eating well, forgetting that hereditary factors, chance encounters with viruses, or environmental threats of which they may be ignorant can override even the most careful program of health habits. An active homosexual man in the 1970s might have given some thought to the possibility of contracting gonorrhea, but could he possibly have anticipated the horror of AIDS? Could the people attending the American Legion convention in Philadelphia in 1976 have guessed that the air in their hotel held a deadly contaminant, producing what we now call Legionnaires' disease? When people think of the future, they think of events they would like to see happen and the ones they believe they can bring about, rather than the chance events that may disrupt goals and plans.

Reflection suggests that the failure to consider the role of chance is not as surprising as first might appear. What exactly would constitute an effective recognition of chance? Should one begin driving each day with the image of a truck out of control bearing down on one's car? Should one regard every social situation as a potential opportunity for viruses to spread? Should every walk along city streets be considered a potential encounter with a mugger or rapist? While people certainly need to incorporate a certain amount of caution and defensiveness into their daily behavior, to do so by envisioning these potentially tragic but random events is hardly appropriate. Because chance and random factors are precisely that, their importance cannot be assessed in any reasonable way for any given situation. Therefore, people quite properly do not have chance at the forefront of consciousness when they assess their risks.

The belief in personal control may also account for why people see their personal likelihood of experiencing positive events as higher and negative events as lower than those of other people. When people focus on their own behaviors that might enable them to achieve desirable outcomes or avoid bad ones, they may forget that other people have just as many resources in their own lives.[72] People misjudge their risk that negative events can befall them because they have clear-cut stereotypes of the kinds of people who typically succumb to these events.[73] People who foolishly wander down dark streets at night are people who get mugged. Passive, repressed people who do not express their feelings get cancer. With these stereotypes in mind, we are able to comfort ourselves that adverse events will not befall us. The fact that each of us is engaging in this process—that is, imagining how he or she can avoid negative events—appears to escape attention altogether.

Unrealistic optimism may result from more than simple stereotypes about the kinds of people on whom bad outcomes descend. Psychologist Ziva Kunda suggests that people actively construct theories of why positive and negative events occur; in so doing they draw on their own attributes in order to defend against the possibility that the negative events might befall them and to enhance the perceived likelihood that the positive events will happen to them. For example, upon learning that the divorce rate for first marriages is 50 percent, most people predict that they will not be in that 50 percent, but rather will remain married to their spouse throughout their lifetime. They convince themselves that this is the case, Kunda has shown, by highlighting their personal attributes that might be associated with a stable marriage and downplaying the significance of or actively refuting information that might suggest a vulnerability to divorce. Thus, for example, one might point to one's parents' fifty-year marriage, the close family life that existed in one's early childhood, and the fact that one's high school relationship lasted a full four years as evidence to predict a stable marriage. The fact that one's husband has already been divorced once—a factor that predicts a second divorce— might be reinterpreted not only as not leading to divorce in one's own case, but as a protective factor ("He knows he does not want this marriage to fail like the last one, and so he's working especially hard to keep our relationship strong"). The ability to draw seemingly rational relationships between our own assets and good events and to argue away associations between our own attributes and negative events helps to maintain unrealistic optimism.[74]

## The Illusion of Progress

The ability to sustain an optimistic view of the future may also come in part from the ability to misconstrue events as progress. There is a well-established bias indicating that people see themselves as having improved even when no actual progress has been made.[75] We all know that people seek out the company of others who are likely to give them positive feedback. It is only reasonable that we should want as friends people who like and value us. There is a corresponding, less obvious tendency to like others whose evaluations of us improve over time. The initially hard to get girlfriend or boyfriend may, for example, be more highly valued than an old faithful partner who was responsive all along. When people's impressions improve over time, rather than staying at a positive level, it simultaneously enhances several other positive beliefs: it encourages a feeling of personal impact, the idea that one can positively affect other people's evaluations. In so doing, it encourages feelings of interpersonal control, the belief that one can bring out in people the kinds of evaluations and judgments of the self that one would like to achieve. And it creates a future as optimistic as the one mentally constructed because just as one fantasizes that progress will occur, progress appears to be made.[76]

This tendency to construct the future so that it will be better than the past is not limited to social interaction. In an intriguing study, Michael Conway and Michael Ross invited college students who were having difficulty studying to enroll in a program designed to show them how to improve their study skills and achieve higher grades.[77] Half of the students who applied to the program were accepted immediately and the other half were put on a waiting list. The first group of students then went through a three-week study skills program. As it happens, most study skills programs are actually quite ineffective in imparting new skills and raising grades,[78] and such was the case with the study skills program initiated by Conway and Ross. The students who took the program did not differ in final grades or study skills from students who had not participated in the program.

Nonetheless, students in the program perceived that they had improved dramatically. They reported better study skills, and they expected better final exam grades. They also distorted retrospectively how bad their study skills had been before going into the program. Moreover, even after final grades had been calculated, the students overestimated their grades for the term. Thus, by revising what they had initially had, the students were able to achieve, at least mentally, what they wanted, namely improvement in their study skills and grades. Failure ("I failed the test") can be reinterpreted as progress ("but I got practice that will help on this kind of test next time"). Through such distortions, several positive biases may be enhanced. One sees oneself in a positive light and as efficacious, and one simultaneously reconstructs the past and future so as to achieve an illusion of progress.

## The Effects of Outcomes on Optimism

People are optimistic about the future most of the time, but when something good happens to them, they become even more so.[79] Doing well at work, for example, leads a person to believe that his children will improve their grades in school and that he will win the weekend tennis tournament. Moreover, a good event acts as a generalized opportunity signal, increasing the belief in the likelihood of all kinds of positive events. Happy events are seen as portents of yet more happy things to come. Similarly, when a bad event happens, it increases the perception that other bad events may lie ahead.[80] Getting sick, being burglarized, or failing a test all move beliefs in the direction of pessimism. Even a transitory mood can yield these same effects.[81] on a day when a person feels good for no particular reason, optimism is higher. Likewise, on a day when a person is low for no particular reason, pessimism may set in. The negative event or mood seems to act as a danger signal. Moreover, this danger signal appears to be a general one, in that it sometimes increases the perception that any bad event may follow, even ones having little or nothing to do with the negative event that has already transpired. If a person fails her driving test, she might logically fear that she may do so again, but why should her fear of developing cancer increase? Why should a burglary increase a sense of vulnerability to diabetes? Similarly, why should receiving a raise at work lead to the belief that one can improve one's marriage?

Perhaps when something good happens, it re-inforces a person's belief that he or she is an effective, competent person who can make things happen. Since people exaggerate their ability to control events, even those that are determined by chance, any positive outcome may make people think that they can produce other positive outcomes. Similarly, a negative event, such as getting sick, may undermine a person's sense of control and competence by pointing out that one can get in harm's way without much effort. As the person attempts to make sense of the negative event, he or she may become aware of vulnerability in general, increasing the sense that he or she can fall victim to other negative events. Sociologist Kai Erikson describes this feeling from the standpoint of natural disasters:

*One of the bargains men make with one another in order to maintain their sanity is to share an illusion that they are safe, even when the physical evidence in the world around them does not seem to warrant that conclusion. The survivors of a disaster, of course, are prone to overestimate the perils of their situation, if only to compensate for the fact that they underestimated those perils once before; but what is worse, far worse, is that they sometimes live in a state of almost constant apprehension because they have lost the human capacity to screen out the signs of danger out of their line of vision.*[82]

The generalized danger signal created by negative events lasts only as long as the negative event or bad mood exists. Once these unpleasant experiences pass, unrealistic optimism returns. An obvious and therefore tempting interpretation is that the generalized danger signal has a certain survival value. When the organism is in a weakened state, physically or psychologically, the generalized perception of danger may keep it appropriately timid, modest, and relatively inactive in order that it not overextend its reduced resources. Once the problem passes and physical and psychological resources are replenished, the organism is once again able to assert itself in the world. At this point, unrealistic optimism may return to diminish the sense of threat. Similarly, the generalized opportunity signal created by optimism may lead people to investigate opportunities that they might not otherwise pursue and to pay little heed to information that would suggest more caution. Optimism may, then, be a significant factor in personal progress.[83]

## Illusions of the Mind

What we see in the normal human mind does not correspond very well to the predominant view of mental health. Instead of an awareness and acceptance of both the positive and the negative elements of their personalities, most people show a keen awareness of their positive qualities and attributes, an extreme estimation of their ability to master the environment, and a positive assessment of the future. Not only are these assessments positive, they appear to be unrealistically so. It is not just that people believe they are good, but that they think they are better than reality can sustain. Judgments of mastery greatly exceed the actual ability to control many events. Views of the future are so rosy that they would make Pollyanna blush.

Should we say simply that most people are optimists at heart? Are these so-called illusions of everyday life merely a reflection of some underlying optimistic stance, a tendency to look on the good side of things? While there is surely an optimistic core to self-aggrandizing beliefs about the self, the world, and the future, these illusions also differ in important ways from optimism. One difference is that illusions critically concern the self. While most people are optimistic, the illusions they demonstrate habitually in their thought patterns concern their own attributes, their beliefs in personal mastery, and concerns about their own futures, rather than a positive view of the world more generally. Another difference is that as a general term, *optimism* refers simply to the expectation that things will turn out well, without any consideration of how those beneficial outcomes will be achieved. The illusion of control, a vital part of people's beliefs about their own attributes, is a personal statement about how postive outcomes will be achieved, not merely by wishing and hoping that they will happen, but by making them happen through one's own capabilities. Finally, ...it is the specific content of illusions, namely beliefs about the self, one's mastery, and the future, that promote psychological adjustment, not simply the underlying optimism reflected in those illusions.

I have repeatedly referred to these beliefs as illusions, and a word must be said about the selection of this term. In some respects, *illusion* is an unfortunate choice, for it evokes images of a conjuror flirting with the border between reality and fantasy. Moreover, when applied to human thought, it suggests a naive blind spot or weakness. Yet *illusion* is appropriate. The terms *error* and *bias*, which one might employ instead, suggest short-term accidental mistakes and distortions, respectively, that might be caused by some careless oversight or other temporary negligence. The term *illusion*, in contrast, reflects a broader and more enduring pattern of beliefs.

*Illusion is a perception that represents what is perceived in a way different from the way it is in reality. An illusion is a false mental image or conception which may be a misinterpretation of a real appearance or may be something imagined. It may be pleasing, harmless or even useful.*[84]

In this sense, then, illusion captures the essence of these phenomena. People hold mild and benignly positive illusions about themselves, the world, and the future. Moreover, they are linked in mutually reinforcing and thematically consistent ways. While illusion does not characterize everyone's thinking about all issues regarding the self, the world, and the future, these illusions are common, widespread, and easily documented.

The fact that positive illusions are so dramatic in early childhood and lessen over time is especially intriguing. It suggests that they are natural, intrinsic to the cognitive system, and become worn down and tamed through the feedback that life provides. What we see in adults is not a carefully cultivated and crafted positive glow that is provided by years of experience with the adaptiveness of viewing things in a positive light. Rather, we see instead the residual inflated view of oneself and the future that exists in extreme and almost magical form in very young children.

The illusions that adults hold about their attributes, their capacity for control, and the beneficent future are, in fact, quite mild, nowhere near the dillusional distortions that one frequently observes in mental patients, for example. As a consequence, it is tempting to dismiss them as ultimately inconsequential, amusing peccadillos that put a pleasant twist on incoming information without many consequences for important matters. Indeed, one argument for the adaptiveness of positive illusions maintains that these biases are evident primarily when information is inconsequential and not when the stakes are higher. According to this argument, people may hold falsely positive judgments about themselves on unimportant matters that may buffer them in more serious and consequential circumstances when they are forced to become more realistic. In fact, the evidence tends to suggest the opposite conclusion: people's positive distortions often increase, not decrease, as matters become more important and consequential.[85] The more ego-enhancing a situation is, the more likely it is to evoke positive, self-serving interpretations. When outcomes are important, self-enhancing causal attributions are more likely. Positive illusions, then, are pervasive and not confined to the unimportant matters of life.

The fact that positive illusions exist in normal thought raises the larger question of why they exist and whether they serve any useful purpose. Are they simply a surprising and rather charming aspect of human thought, or are they actually adaptive? Trying to understand their prevalence leads one prematurely to suggest why they might be functional, the implicit assumption being that, like other organs, the mind does not evolve in ways that are inherently injurious to its own functioning. Yet these suggestions of adaptiveness have been speculative only, and the next task is to determine whether this is indeed the case.

## NOTES

1. Stipek, 1984; Harter, 1981; Greenwald, 1980.

2. See Stipek, 1984; Stipek and MacIver, in press; Harter, 1981, for reviews.

3. Harari and Covington, 1981, p. 25.

4. Stipek, 1984.

5. Alicke, 1985; Brown, 1986; Campbell, 1986; Larwood and Whittaker, 1977; see also Shrauger and Kelly, in press.

6. Campbell, 1986; Marks, 1984; Harackiewicz, Sansone, and Manderlink, 1985; Lewicki, 1984.

7. Campbell, 1986; Marks, 1984.

8. See Greenwald, 1980; Taylor and Brown, 1988, for reviews. One might argue that overly positive self-descriptions reflect public posturing rather than privately held beliefs. Several factors, however, argue against the plausibility of a strict self-presentational interpretation of this phenomenon. For example, Greenwald and Breckler (1985) reviewed evidence indicating that (a) self-evaluations are at least as favorable under private conditions as they are under public conditions; (b) favorable self-evaluations occur even when strong constraints to be honest are present; (c) favorable self-referent judgments are made very rapidly, suggesting that people are not engaging in deliberate (time-consuming) fabrication; and (d) self-enhancing judgments are acted on. For these as well as other reasons, a consensus is emerging at the theoretical level that individuals offer flattering self-evaluations not merely as a means of managing a public impression of competency but also as a means of managing impressions of themselves for themselves (see Schlenker, 1980; Tesser and Moore, 1986; Tetlock and Manstead, 1985).

9. Brown, 1986; Lewinsohn, Mischel, Chaplin, and Barton, 1980; Forsyth and Schlenker, 1977; Green and Gross, 1979; Mirels, 1980; Schlenker and Miller, 1977; Brown, 1985; Campbell, 1986; Rosenberg, 1979; Sachs, 1982.

10. Svenson, 1981.

11. E.g., Lewinsohn et al., 1980; see Shrauger 1975, 1982, for a review.

12. Greenwald, 1980, p. 64.

13. Markus, 1977.

14. Greenwald, 1980.

15. Markus, 1977.

16. Greenwald, 1980.

17. Kuiper and Derry, 1982; Kuiper and MacDonald, 1982; Kuiper, Olinger, MacDonald, and Shaw, 1985.

18. Schlenker, 1980; Snyder and Wicklund, 1981.

19. Fuentes, 1964, p. 58.

20. See Bradley, 1978; Miller and Ross, 1975; Ross and Fletcher, 1985; Zuckerman, 1979, for reviews.

21. *San Francisco Sunday Examiner and Chronicle.* April 22, 1979, cited in Greenwald, 1980.

22. Greenwald, 1980, p. 605.

23. Miller and Ross, 1975.

24. Ross, 1981; Ross and Sicoly, 1979.

25. Thompson and Kelley, 1981.

26. Harris, 1946, recounted in Ross, 1981.

27. Ross, 1981; Thompson and Kelley, 1981; Ross and Sicoly, 1979.

28. Thompson and Kelley, 1981.

29. See Ross, 1981.

30. Erikson, 1950; Alper, 1952; Sherif and Cantril, 1947.

31. Miller and Ross, 1975; Snyder, Stephan, and Rosenfield, 1978.

32. Lefcourt, 1973, p. 417.

33. White, 1959.

34. Berlyne, 1960; Fowler, 1965; White, 1959.

35. Donaldson, 1978; Harter 1981; White, 1959.

36. White, 1959.

37. Berlyne, 1960.

38. Piaget, 1954; White, 1959.

39. White, 1959.

40. Diener and Dweck, 1978, 1980; Weisz, 1986.

41. Piaget, 1954.

42. E.g., Lindsay and McCarthy, 1974.

43. Diener and Dweck, 1978, 1980.

44. Stipek, 1984.

45. Ryan, 1971.

46. Jones and Davis, 1965; Jones and Harris, 1967.

47. Miller and Ross, 1975.

48. Crocker, 1981; Smedslund, 1963; Ward and Jenkins, 1965; Arkes and Harkness, 1980; Bower, Black, and Turner, 1979; Franks and Bransford, 1971; Owens, Bower, and Black, 1979; Harris, Teske, and Ginns, 1975; Jennings, Amabile, and Ross, 1982.

49. Janis, 1982.

50. Langer, 1975; Langer and Roth, 1975.

51. Goffman, 1967.

52. Henslin, 1967.

53. Langer, 1975; Langer and Roth, 1975; see also Gilovich, 1983.

54. Langer, 1975.

55. See Thompson, 1981; Averill, 1973; Miller, 1979, for reviews.

56. Geer, Davison, and Gatchel, 1970; Geer and Maisel, 1972.

57. Laudenslager, Ryan, Drugan, Hyson, and Maier, 1983; Hanson, Larson, and Snowden, 1976.

58. Gonzales and Zimbardo, 1985. In this study, 57 percent of the people interviewed said that they thought primarily about the present and the future, and another 33 percent were oriented primarily toward the future. Only 1 percent spent most of their time thinking about the past.

59. Tiger, 1979.

60. Free and Cantril, 1968; Brickman, Coates, and Janoff-Bulman, 1978.

61. Markus and Nurius, 1986; Weinstein, 1980, 1982, 1984; see Perloff, 1983, for a review.

62. Crandall, Solomon, and Kelleway, 1955; Irwin, 1944, 1953; Marks, 1951; Robertson, 1977; Perloff and Fetzer, 1986; Weinstein, 1980; Kuiper, MacDonald, and Derry, 1983.

63. Frank, 1953; Pruitt and Hoge, 1965.

64. Hayes-Roth and Hayes-Roth, 1979.

65. Stipek, 1984; Marks, 1951; Irwin, 1953.

66. Stipek, 1984, p. 53.

67. Kirscht, Haefner, Kegeles, and Rosenstock, 1966; Lund, 1975.

68. Weinstein, 1980, 1982.

69. Weinstein, 1980, 1982.

70. Weinstein, 1980, 1982, 1984.

71. Seligman, 1975; Tiger, 1979.

72. Weinstein and Lachendro, 1982.

73. Kunda, 1987.

74. Kunda, 1987.

75. Conway and Ross, 1984.

76. Aronson and Linder, 1965.

77. Conway and Ross, 1984.

78. Gibbs, 1981.

79. Johnson and Tversky, 1983.

80. Kulik and Mahler, 1987.

81. See Clark and Isen, 1982.

82. Erikson, 1976, p. 234.

83. See Tiger, 1979, for a discussion of these issues.

84. *Random House Dictionary, the English Language*, ed. J. Stein, New York: Random House, p. 662.

85. E.g., Nicholls, 1975; Miller, 1976; Snyder et al., 1978; see Greenwald, 1980, for a review and discussion of this issue.

# REFERENCES

Alicke, M. D. (1985). Global self-evaluation as determined by the desirability and uncontrollability of trait adjectives. *Journal of Personality and Social Psychology, 49,* 1621–1630.

Alper, T. G. (1952). The interrupted task method in studies of selective recall: A re-evaluation of some recent experiments. *Psychological Review, 59,* 71–88.

Arkes, R. M., & Harkness, A. R. (1980). Effect of making a diagnosis on subsequent recognition of symptoms. *Journal of Experimental Psychology: Human Learning and Memory, 6,* 568–575.

Aronson, E., & Linder, D. (1965). Gain and loss of esteem as determinants of interpersonal attractiveness. *Journal of Experimental Social Psychology, 1,* 156–172.

Averill, J. R. (1973). Personal control over aversive stimuli and its relationship to stress. *Psychological Bulletin, 80,* 286–303.

Berlyne, D. C. (1960). *Conflict, arousal, and curiosity.* New York: McGraw-Hill.

Bower, G. H., Black, J. B., & Turner, T. J. (1979). Scripts in memory for text. *Cognitive Psychology, 11,* 177–220.

Bradley, G. W. (1978). Self-serving biases in the attribution process: A reexamination of the fact or fiction question. *Journal of Personality and Social Psychology, 36,* 56–71.

Brickman, P., Coates, D., & Janoff-Bulman, R. (1978). Lottery winners and accident victims: Is happiness relative? *Journal of Personality and Social Psychology, 35,* 917–927.

Brown, J. D. (1985). *Self-esteem and unrealistic optimism about the future.* Unpublished data, University of California, Los Angeles.

Brown, J. D. (1986). Evaluations of self and others: Self-enhancement biases in social judgments. *Social Cognition, 4,* 353–376.

Campbell, J. D. (1986). Similarity and uniqueness: The effects of attribute type, relevance, and individual differences in self-esteem and depression. *Journal of Personality and Social Psychology, 50,* 281–294.

Clark, M. S., & Isen, A. M. (1982). Toward understanding the relationship between feeling states and social behavior. In A. H. Hastorf & A. M. Isen (Eds.), *Cognitive social psychology* (pp. 73–108). New York: Elsevier.

Conway, M., & Ross, M. (1984). Getting what you want by revising what you had. *Journal of Personality and Social Psychology, 47,* 738–748.

Crandall, V. J., Solomon, D., & Kelleway, R. (1955). Expectancy statements and decision times as functions of objective probabilities and reinforcement values. *Journal of Personality, 24,* 192–203.

Crocker, J. (1981). Judgment of covariation by social perceivers. *Psychological Bulletin, 90,* 272–292.

Diener, C. I., & Dweck, C. S. (1978). An analysis of learned helplessness: Continuous changes in performance, strategy, and achievement cognitions following failure. *Journal of Personality and Social Psychology, 36,* 451–462.

Diener, C. I., & Dweck, C. S. (1980). An analysis of learned helplessness: 2. The processing of success. *Journal of Personality and Social Psychology, 39,* 940–952.

Donaldson, M. (1978) *Children's minds.* New York: Norton.

Erikson, E. H. (1950). *Childhood and society* (2nd ed.). New York: Norton.

Erikson, K. T. (1976). *Everything in its path: Destruction of community in the Buffalo Creek flood.* New York: Simon & Schuster.

Forsyth, D. R., & Schlenker., B. R. (1977). Attributing the causes of group performance: Effects of performance quality, task importance, and future testing. *Journal of Personality, 45*, 220–236.

Fowler, H. (1965). *Curiosity and exploratory behavior.* New York: Macmillan.

Frank, J. D. (1953). Some psychological determinants of the level of aspiration. *American Journal of Psychology, 47*, 285–293.

Franks, J. J., & Bransford, J. D. (1971). Abstraction of visual patterns. *Journal of Experimental Social Psychology, 90*, 65–74.

Free, L. A., & Cantril, H. (1968). *The political beliefs of Americans: A study of public opinion.* New York: Clarion.

Fuentes, C. (1964). *The death of Artemio Cruz.* New York: Farrar Straus Giroux.

Geer, J. H., Davison, G. C., & Gatchel, R. I. (1970). Reduction of stress in humans through nonveridical perceived control of aversive stimulation. *Journal of Personality and Social Psychology, 16*, 731–738.

Geer, J. H., & Maisel, E. (1972). Evaluating the effects of the prediction–control confound. *Journal of Personality and Social Psychology, 23*, 314–319.

Gibbs, G. (1981). *Teaching students to learn.* Milton Keynes, England: Open University Press.

Gilovich, T. (1983). Biased evaluation and persistence in gambling. *Journal of Personality and Social Psychology, 44*, 1110–1126.

Goffman, E. (1967). *Interaction ritual.* Newport Beach, CA: Westcliff.

Gonzales, A., & Zimbardo, P. G. (1985, March). Time in perspective. *Psychology Today*, pp. 21–26.

Green, S. K., & Gross, A. E. (1979). Self-serving biases in implicit evaluations. *Personality and Social Psychology Bulletin, 5*, 214–217.

Greenwald, A. G. (1980). The totalitarian ego: Fabrication and revision of personal history. *American Psychologist, 35*, 603–618.

Greenwald, A. G., & Breckler, S. J. (1985). To whom is the self presented? In B. Schlenker (Ed.), *The self and social life* (pp. 126–145). New York: McGraw-Hill.

Hanson, J. D., Larson, M. C. & Snowden, C. T. (1976). The effects of control over high intensity noise on plasma control in rhesus monkeys. *Behavioral Biology, 16*, 333–334.

Harackiewicz, J. M., Sansone, C., & Manderlink, G. (1985). Competence, achievement orientation, and intrinsic motivation: A process analysis. *Journal of Personality and Social Psychology, 48*, 493–508.

Harari, O., & Covington, M. (1981). Reactions to achievement from a teacher and student perspective: A developmental analysis. *American Educational Research Journal, 18*, 15–28.

Harris, R. J., Teske, R. R., & Ginns, M. J. (1975). Memory for pragmatic implications from courtroom testimony. *Bulletin of the Psychonomic Society, 6*, 494–496.

Harris, S. (1946). *Banting's miracle: The story of the discovery of insulin.* Toronto: J. M. Dent & Sons.

Harter, S. (1981). A model of intrinsic mastery motivation in children: Intrinsic differences and developmental change. In W. A. Collins (Ed.), *Minnesota Symposium on Child Psychology* (Vol. 14, pp. 215–255). Hillsdale, NJ: Erlbaum.

Hayes-Roth, B., & Hayes-Roth, F. (1979). A cognitive model of planning. *Cognitive Science, 3*, 275–310.

Henslin, J. M. (1967). Craps and magic. *American Journal of Sociology, 73*, 316–330.

Irwin, F. W. (1944). The realism of expectations. *Psychological Review, 51*, 120–126.

Irwin, F. W. (1953). Stated expectations as functions of probability and desirability of outcomes. *Journal of Personality, 21*, 329–335.

Janis, I. L. (1982). *Groupthink: Psychological studies of policy decisions and fiascoes* (2nd ed.). Boston: Houghton Mifflin.

Jennings, D., Amabile, T. M., & Ross, L. (1982). Informal covariation assessment: Data-based versus theory-based judgments. In A. Tversky, D. Kahneman, & P. Slovic (Eds.), *Judgment under uncertainty: Heuristics and biases* (pp. 211–230). New York: Cambridge University Press.

Johnson, J. E., & Tversky, A. (1983). Affect generalization and the perception of risk. *Journal of Personality and Social Psychology, 45*, 20–31.

Jones, E. E., & Davis, K. E. (1965). From acts to dispositions: The attribution process in person perception. In L. Berkowitz (Ed.), *Advances in experimental social psychology* (Vol. 2, pp. 219–266). New York: Academic Press.

Jones, E. E., & Harris, V. A. (1967). The attribution of attitudes. *Journal of Experimental Social Psychology, 3*, 1–24.

Kirscht, J. P., Haefner, D. P., Kegeles, F. S., & Rosenstock, I. M. (1966). A national study of health beliefs. *Journal of Health and Human Behavior, 7*, 248-254.

Kuiper, N. A., & Derry, P. A. (1982). Depressed and nondepressed content self-reference in mild depression. *Journal of Personality, 50*, 67–79.

Kuiper, N. A., & MacDonald, M. R. (1982). Self and other perception in mild depressives. *Social Cognition, 1*, 233–239.

Kuiper, N. A., MacDonald, M. R., & Derry, P. A. (1983). Parameters of a depressive self-schema. In J. Suls & A. G. Greenwald (Eds.), *Psychological perspectives on the self* (Vol. 2, pp. 191–217). Hillsdale, NJ: Erlbaum.

Kuiper, N. A., Olinger, L. J., MacDonald, M. R., & Shaw, B. F. (1985). Self-schema processing of depressed and nondepressed content: The effects of vulnerability on depression. *Social Cognition, 3*, 77-93.

Kulik, J. A., & Mahler, I. M. (1987). Health status, perceptions of risk, and prevention interest for health and nonhealth problems. *Health Psychology, 6*, 15–28.

Kunda, Z. (1987). Motivated inference: Self-serving generation and evaluation of causal theories. *Journal of Personality and Social Psychology, 53*, 636–647.

Langer, E. J. (1975). The illusion of control. *Journal of Personality and Social Psychology, 32*, 311–328.

Langer, E. J., & Roth, J. (1975). Heads I win, tails it's chance: The illusion of control as a function of the sequence of outcomes in a purely chance task. *Journal of Personality and Social Psychology, 32*, 951–955.

Larwood, L., & Whittaker, W. (1977). Managerial myopia: Self-serving biases in organizational planning. *Journal of Applied Psychology, 62*, 194–198.

Laudenslager, M. C., Ryan, S. M., Drugan, R. C., Hyson, R. L., & Maier, S. F. (1983). Coping and immunosuppression: Inescapable but not escapable shock suppresses lymphocyte proliferation. *Science, 231*, 568–570.

Lefcourt, H. M. (1973, May). The function of the illusions of control and freedom. *American Psychologist*, pp. 417–425.

Lewicki, P. (1984). Self-schema and social information processing. *Journal of Personality and Social Psychology, 48*, 463–574.

Lewinsohn, P. M., Mischel, W., Chaplin, W., & Barton, R. (1980). Social competence and depression: The role of illusory self-perceptions. *Journal of Abnormal Psychology, 89*, 203–212.

Lindsay, M., & McCarthy, D. (1974). Caring for the brothers and sisters of a dying child. In T. Burton (Ed.), *Care of the child facing death* (pp. 189–206). Boston, MA: Routledge & Kegan Paul.

Lund, F. H. (1975). The psychology of belief: A study of its emotional and volitional determinants. *Journal of Abnormal and Social Psychology, 20*, 63–81.

Marks, G. (1984). Thinking one's abilities are unique and one's opinions are common. *Personality and Social Psychological Bulletin, 10*, 203–208.

Marks, R. W. (1951). The effect of probability, desirability, and "privilege" on the stated expectations of children. *Journal of Personality, 19*, 332–351.

Markus, H. (1977). Self-schemata and processing information about the self. *Journal of Personality and Social Psychology, 35*, 63-78.

Markus, H., & Nurius, P. (1986). Possible selves. *American Psychologist, 41*, 954–969.

Miller, D. T. (1976). Ego involvement and attributions for success and failure. *Journal of Personality and Social Psychology, 34*, 901–906.

Miller, D. T., & Ross, M. (1975). Self-serving biases in attribution of causality: Fact or fiction? *Psychological Bulletin, 82*, 213–225.

Miller, S. M. (1979). Controllability and human stress: Method, evidence and theory. *Behaviour Research and Therapy, 17*, 287-304.

Mirels, H. L. (1980). The avowal of responsibility for good and bad outcomes: The effects of generalized self-serving biases. *Personality and Social Psychology Bulletin, 6*, 299–306.

Nicholls, J. G. (1975). Causal attributions and other achievement-related cognitions: Effects of task outcome, attainment value, and sex. *Journal of Personality and Social Psychology, 31*, 379–389.

Owens, J., Bower, G. H., & Black, J. B. (1979). The "soap-opera" effect in story recall. *Memory and Cognition, 7*, 185–191.

Perloff, L. S. (1983). Perceptions of vulnerability to victimization. *Journal of Social Issues, 39*, 41–61.

Perloff, L. S., & Fetzer, B. K. (1986). Self-other judgments and perceived vulnerability to victimization. *Journal of Personality and Social Psychology, 50*, 502–510.

Piaget, J. (1954). *The construction of reality in the child*. New York: Basic Books.

Pruitt, D. G., & Hoge, R. D. (1965). Strength of the relationship between the value of an event and its subjective probability as a function of method of measurement. *Journal of Experimental Psychology, 5*, 483–489.

Robertson, L. S. (1977). Car crashes: Perceived vulnerability and willingness to pay for crash protection. *Journal of Community Health, 3*, 136–141.

Rosenberg, M. (1979). *Conceiving the self.* New York: Basic Books.

Ross, L. (1981). The "intuitive scientist" formulation and its developmental implications. In J. H. Flavell & L. Ross (Eds.), *Social cognitive development: Frontiers and possible futures* (pp. 1–42). Cambridge: Cambridge University Press.

Ross, M., & Fletcher, G. J. O. (1985). Attribution and social perception. In G. Lindzey & A. Aronson (Eds.). *The handbook of social psychology* (3rd ed., pp. 73–122). Reading, MA: Addison-Wesley.

Ross, M., & Sicoly, F. (1979). Egocentric biases in availability and attribution. *Journal of Personality and Social Psychology, 37*, 322–337.

Ryan, W. (1971). *Blaming the victim.* New York: Vintage Books.

Sachs, P. R. (1982). Avoidance of diagnostic information in self-evaluation of ability. *Personality and Social Psychology Bulletin, 8*, 242–246.

Schlenker, B. R. (1980). *Impression management.* Monterey, CA: Brooks/Cole.

Schlenker, B. R., & Miller, R. S. (1977). Egocentrism in groups: Self-serving biases or logical information processing? *Journal of Personality and Social Psychology, 35*, 755–764.

Seligman, M. E. P. (1975). *Helplessness: On depression, development and death.* San Francisco: Freeman.

Sherif, M., & Cantril, H. (1947). *The psychology of ego-involvements.* New York: Wiley.

Shrauger, J. S. (1975). Responses to evaluation as a function of initial self-perception. *Psychological Bulletin, 82*, 581–596.

Shrauger, J. S. (1982). Selection and processing of self-evaluative information: Experimental evidence and clinical implications. In G. Weary & H. L. Mirels (Eds.), *Integrations of clinical and social psychology* (pp. 128–153). New York: Oxford University Press.

Shrauger, J. S., & Kelley, R. J. (in press). Global self-evaluation and changes in self description as a function of information. *Journal of Personality.*

Smedslund, J. (1963). The concept of correlation in adults. *Scandinavian Journal of Psychology, 4*, 165–173.

Snyder, M. L., Stephan, W. G., & Rosenfield, C. (1978). Attributional egotism. In J. H. Harvey, W. J. Ickes, & R. F. Kidd (Eds.), *New directions in attribution research* (Vol. 2, pp. 91–117). Hillsdale, NJ: Erlbaum.

Snyder, M. L., & Wicklund, R. A. (1981). Attribute ambiguity. In J. H. Harvey, W. Ickes, & R. F. Kidd (Eds.), *New directions in attribution research* (Vol. 3, pp. 197–221). Hillsdale, NJ: Erlbaum.

Stipek, D. J. (1984). Young children's performance expectations: Logical analysis or wishful thinking? In I. Nicholls (Ed.), *Advances in motivation and achievement* (Vol. 3, pp. 33–56). Greenwich, CT: JAI Press.

Stipek, D., & MacIver, D. (in press). Developmental change in children's assessment of intellectual competence. *Child Development.*

Svenson, O. (1981). Are we all less risky and more skillful than our fellow drivers? *Acta Psychologica, 47*, 143–148.

Taylor, S. E., & Brown, J. (1988). Illusion and well-being: A social psychological perspective on mental health. *Psychological Bulletin, 103*, 193–210.

Tesser, A., & Moore, J. (1986). On the convergence of public and private aspects of self. In R. F. Baumeister (Ed.), *Public self and private life* (pp. 99–116). New York: Springer.

Tetlock, P. E., & Manstead, A. S. R. (1985). Impression management versus intrapsychic explanations in social psychology: A useful dichotomy? *Psychological Review, 92*, 59–77.

Thompson, S. C. (1981). Will it hurt less if I can control it? A complex answer to a simple question. *Psychological Bulletin, 90*, 89–101.

Thompson, S. C., & Kelley, J. J. (1981). Judgments of responsibility for activities in close relationships. *Journal of Personality and Social Psychology, 41*, 469–477.

Tiger, L. (1979). *Optimism: The biology of hope.* New York: Simon & Schuster.

Ward, W. D., & Jenkins, H. M. (1965). The display of information and the judgment of contingency. *Canadian Journal of Psychology, 19*, 231–241.

Weinstein, N. D. (1980). Unrealistic optimism about future life events. *Journal of Personality and Social Psychology, 39*, 806–820.

Weinstein, N. D. (1982). Unrealistic optimism about susceptibility to health problems. *Journal of Behavioral Medicine, 5*, 441–460.

Weinstein, N. D. (1984). Why it won't happen to me: Perceptions of risk factors and susceptibility. *Health Psychology, 3*, 431–457.

Weinstein, N. D., & Lachendro, E. (1982). Egocentrism as a source of unrealistic optimism. *Personality and Social Psychology Bulletin, 8*, 195–200.

Weisz, J. R. (1986). Understanding the developing understanding of control. In M. Perlmutter (Ed.), *Minnesota symposia on child psychology: Vol. 18. Cognitive perspectives on children's social and behavioral development* (pp. 219–285). Hillsdale, NJ: Erlbaum.

White, R. W. (1959). Motivation reconsidered: The concept of competence. *Psychological Review, 66*, 297–335.

Zuckerman, M. (1979). Attribution of success and failure revisited, or: The motivational bias is alive and well in attribution theory. *Journal of Personality, 47*, 245–287.

# Effects of Perception on Organizational Behavior

## 17.   THE SELF-PERCEPTION OF MOTIVATION[1]

Barry M. Staw

Within the area of interpersonal perception, it has been noted (Heider, 1958) that an individual may infer the causes of another's actions to be a function of personal and environmental force:

Action = f (personal force + environmental force)

This is quite close to saying that individuals attempt to determine whether another person is intrinsically motivated to perform an activity (action due to personal force), or extrinsically motivated (action due to environmental force), or both. The extent to which an individual will infer intrinsic motivation on the part of another is predicted to be affected by the clarity and strength of external forces within the situation (Jones & Davis, 1965; Jones & Nisbett, 1971; Kelley 1967). When there are strong forces bearing on the individual to perform an activity, there is little reason to assume that a behavior is self-determined, whereas a high level of intrinsic motivation might be inferred if environmental force is minimal. Several studies dealing with interpersonal perception have supported this general conclusion (Jones, Davis, & Gergen, 1961; Jones & Harris, 1967; Strickland, 1958; Thibaut & Riecken, 1955).

Bem (1967a, b) extrapolated this interpersonal theory of causal attribution to the study of self-perception or how one views his *own* behavior within a social context. Bem hypothesized that the extent to which external pressures are sufficiently strong to account for one's behavior will determine the likelihood that a person will attribute his own actions to internal causes. Thus if a person acts under strong external rewards or punishments, he is likely to assume that his behavior is under external control. However, if extrinsic contingencies are not strong or salient, the individual is likely to assume that his behavior is due to his own interest in the activity or that his behavior is intrinsically motivated. De Charms has made a similar point in his discussion of individual's perception of personal causation (1968, p. 328):

*As a first approximation, we propose that whenever a person experiences himself to be the locus of causality for his own behavior (to be an Origin), he will consider himself to be intrinsically motivated. Conversely, when a person perceives the locus of causality for his behavior to be external to himself (that he is a Pawn), he will consider himself to be extrinsically motivated.*

De Charms emphasized that the individual may attempt psychologically to label his actions on the basis of whether or not he has been instrumental in affecting his own behavior; that is, whether his behavior has been intrinsically or extrinsically motivated.

## THE CASE FOR A NEGATIVE RELATIONSHIP BETWEEN INTRINSIC AND EXTRINSIC MOTIVATION

The self-perception approach to intrinsic and extrinsic motivation leads to the conclusion that there may be a negative interrelationship between these two motivational factors. The basis for this prediction stems from the assumption that individuals may work backward from their own actions in inferring sources of causation (Bem, 1967a, b; 1972). For example, if external pressures on an individual are so high that they would ordinarily cause him to perform a given task regardless of the internal characteristics of the activity, then the individual might logically infer that he is extrinsically motivated. In contrast, if external reward contingencies are extremely low or non-salient, the individual might then infer that his behavior is intrinsically motivated. What is important is the fact that a person, in performing an activity, may *seek out* the probable cause of his own actions. Since behavior has no doubt been caused by something, it makes pragmatic, if not scientific, sense for the person to conclude that

the cause is personal (intrinsic) rather than extrinsic if he can find no external reasons for his actions.

Two particular situations provide robust tests of the self-perception prediction. One is a situation in which there is insufficient justification for a person's actions, a situation in which the intrinsic rewards for an activity are very low (e.g., a dull task) and there are no compensating extrinsic rewards (e.g., monetary payment, verbal praise). Although rationally, one ordinarily tries to avoid these situations, there are occasions when one is faced with the difficult question of "why did I do that?" The self-perception theory predicts that in situations of insufficient justification, the individual may cognitively reevaluate the intrinsic characteristics of an activity in order to justify or explain his own behavior. For example, if the individual performed a dull task for no external reward, he may "explain" his behavior by thinking that the task was not really so bad after all.

Sometimes a person may also be fortunate enough to be in a situation in which his behavior is oversufficiently justified. For example, a person may be asked to perform an interesting task and at the same time be lavishly paid for his efforts. In such situations, the self-perception theory predicts that the individual may actually reevaluate the activity in a downward direction. Since the external reward would be sufficient to motivate behavior by itself, the individual may mistakenly infer that he was extrinsically motivated to perform the activity. He may conclude that since he was forced to perform the task by an external reward, the task probably was not terribly satisfying in and of itself.

Figure 17.1 graphically depicts the situations of insufficient and overly sufficient justification. From the figure, we can see that the conceptual framework supporting self-perception theory raises several interesting issues. First, it appears from this analysis that there are only two fully stable attributions of behavior: (1) the perception of extrinsically motivated behavior in which the internal rewards associated with performing an activity are low while external rewards are high; and (2) the perception of

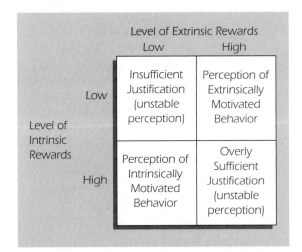

**FIGURE 17.1** A Conceptual of Self-Perception Theory.

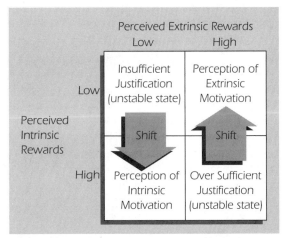

**FIGURE 17.2** A Schematic Analysis of the Self-Perception of Intrinsic and Extrinsic Motivation.

intrinsically motivated behavior in which the task is inherently rewarding but external rewards are low. Furthermore, it appears that situations of insufficient justification (where intrinsic and extrinsic rewards are both low) and oversufficient justification (where intrinsic and extrinsic rewards are both high) involve unstable attribution states. As shown in Figure 17.2, individuals apparently resolve this attributional instability by altering their perceptions of intrinsic rewards associated with the task.

An interesting question posed by the self-perception analysis is why individuals are predicted to resolve an unstable attribution state by cognitively reevaluating a task in terms of its intrinsic rewards rather than changing their perceptions of extrinsic factors. The answer to this question may lie in the relative clarity of extrinsic as compared with intrinsic rewards, and the individual's relative ability to distort the two aspects of the situation. Within many settings (and especially within laboratory experiments) extrinsic rewards are generally quite salient and specific, whereas an individual must judge the intrinsic nature of a task for himself. Any shifts in the perception of intrinsic and extrinsic rewards may therefore be more likely to occur in the intrinsic factor. As shown in Figure 17.2 it is these

predicted shifts in perceived intrinsic rewards that may theoretically underlie a negative relationship between intrinsic and extrinsic motivation.

## Empirical Evidence: Insufficient Justification

Several studies have shown that when an individual is induced to commit an unpleasant act for little or no external justification, he may subsequently conclude that the act was not so unpleasant after all. Actually, the first scientific attempt to account for this phenomenon was the theory of cognitive dissonance (Festinger, 1957). It was predicted by dissonance theorists (Aronson, 1966; Festinger, 1957) that, since performing an unpleasant act for little or no reward would be an inconsistent (and seemingly irrational) thing to do, an individual might subsequently change his attitude toward the action in order to reduce the inconsistency or to appear rational. Bem's self-perception theory yields the same predictions but does not require one to posit that there is a motivating state such as dissonance reduction or self-rationalization. To Bem, since the individual examines his own behavior in light of the forces around him, he is simply more likely to come to the conclusion that his actions were intrinsically satisfying if they were performed under minimal external force.

In general, two types of experiments have been designed to assess the consequences of insufficient justification. One type of design has involved the performance of a dull task with varied levels of reward (Brehm & Cohen, 1962; Freedman, 1963; Weick, 1964; Weick & Penner, 1965). A second and more popular design has involved some form of counterattitudinal advocacy, either in terms of lying to a fellow subject about the nature of an experiment or writing an essay against one's position on an important issue (Carlsmith, Collins, & Helmreich, 1966; Festinger & Carlsmith, 1959; Linder, Cooper, & Jones, 1967). Fundamentally, the two types of designs are not vastly different. Both require subjects to perform an intrinsically dissatisfying act under varied levels of external inducement, and both predict that, in the low payment condition, the subject will change his attitude toward the activity (i.e., think more favorably of the task or begin to believe the position advocated).

The most well-known experiment designed to test the insufficient justification paradigm was conducted by Festinger and Carlsmith (1959). Subjects participated in a repetitive and dull task (putting spools on trays and turning pegs) and were asked to tell other waiting subjects that the experiment was enjoyable, interesting, and exciting. Half the experimental subjects were paid $1, and half were paid $20 for the counterattitudinal advocacy (and to be "on call" in the future), while control subjects were not paid and did not perform the counterattitudinal act. As predicted, the smaller the reward used to induce subjects to perform the counterattitudinal act, the greater the positive change in their attitudes toward the task. Although the interpretation of the results of this study have been actively debated (e.g., between dissonance and self-perception theorists) the basic findings have been replicated by a number of different researchers. It should be noted, however, that several mediating variables have also been isolated as being necessary for the attainment of this dissonance or self-perception effect: free choice (Linder, Cooper, & Jones, 1967),

commitment or irrevocability of behavior (Brehm & Cohen, 1962), and substantial adverse consequences (Calder, Ross, & Insko, 1973; Collins & Hoyt, 1972).

Recently, a strong test of the insufficient justification paradigm was also conducted outside the laboratory (Staw, 1974a). A natural field experiment was made possible by the fact that many young men had joined an organization (Army ROTC) in order to avoid being drafted, *and* these same young men subsequently received information (a draft lottery number) that changed the value of this organizational reward. Of particular relevance was the fact that those who joined ROTC did so not because of their intrinsic interest in the activities involved (e.g., drills, classes, and summer camp), but because they anticipated a substantial extrinsic reward (draft avoidance). As a result, those who received draft numbers that exempted them from military service subsequently faced a situation of low extrinsic as well as intrinsic rewards, a situation of insufficient justification. In contrast, persons who received draft numbers that made them vulnerable to military call-up found their participation in ROTC perfectly justified—they were still successfully avoiding the draft by remaining in the organization. To test the insufficient justification effect, both the attitudes and the performance of ROTC cadets were analyzed by draft number before and after the national draft lottery. The results showed that those in the insufficient justification situation enhanced their perception of ROTC and even performed somewhat better in ROTC courses after the lottery. It should be recognized, however, that this task enhancement occurred only under circumstances very similar to those previously found necessary for the dissonance or self-perception effect (i.e., high commitment, free choice, and adverse consequences).

## Empirical Evidence: Overly Sufficient Justification

There have been several empirical studies designed to test the self-perception prediction within the context of overly sufficient justification.

Generally, a situation in which an extrinsic reward is added to an intrinsically rewarding task has been experimentally contrived for this purpose. Following self-perception theory, it is predicted that an increase in external justification will cause individuals to lose confidence in their intrinsic interest in the experimental task. Since dissonance theory cannot make this prediction (it is neither irrational nor inconsistent to perform an activity for too many rewards), the literature on overly sufficient justification provides the most important data on the self-perception prediction. For this reason, we will examine the experimental evidence in some detail.

In an experiment specifically designed to test the effect of overly sufficient justification on intrinsic motivation, Deci (1971) enlisted a number of college students to participate in a problem-solving study. All the students were asked to work on a series of intrinsically interesting puzzles for three experimental sessions. After the first session, however, half of the students (the experimental group) were told that they would also be given an extrinsic reward (money) for correctly solving the second set of puzzles, while the other students (the control group) were not told anything about the reward. In the third session, neither the experimental nor the control subjects were rewarded. This design is schematically outlined below:

**Basic Design of Deci (1971) Study**

|  | Time 1 | Time 2 | Time 3 |
|---|---|---|---|
| Experimental group | No payment | Payment | No payment |
| Control group | No payment | No payment | No payment |

Deci had hypothesized that the payment of money in the second experimental session might decrease subjects' intrinsic motivation to perform the task. That is, the introduction of an external force (money) might cause participants to alter their self-perception about why they are working on the puzzles. Instead of being intrinsically motivated to solve the interesting puz-

zles, they might find themselves working primarily to get the money provided by the experimenter. Thus Deci's goal in conducting the study was to compare the changes in subjects' intrinsic motivation from the first to third sessions for both the experimental and control groups. If the self-perception hypothesis was correct, the intrinsic motivation of the previously paid experimental subjects would decrease in the third session, whereas the intrinsic motivation of the unpaid controls should remain unchanged.

As a measure of intrinsic motivation, Deci used the amount of free time participants spent on the puzzle task. To obtain this measure, the experimenter left the room during each session, supposedly to feed some data into the computer. As the experimenter left the room, he told the subjects they could do anything they wanted with their free time. In addition to the puzzles, current issues of *Time, The New Yorker,* and *Playboy* were placed near the subjects. However, while the first experimenter was out of the laboratory, a second experimenter, unknown to the subjects, observed their behavior through a one-way mirror. It was reasoned that if the subject worked on the puzzles during this free time period, he must be intrinsically motivated to perform the task. As shown in Table 17.1, the amount of free time spent on the task decreased for those who were previously paid to perform the activity, while there was a slight increase for the unpaid controls. Although the

**TABLE 17.1**

**Mean Number of Seconds Spent Working on the Puzzles during the Free Time Periods**

| Group | Time 1 | Time 2 | Time 3 | Time 3 − Time 1 |
|---|---|---|---|---|
| Experimental ($n = 12$) | 248.2 | 313.9 | 198.5 | −49.7 |
| Control ($n = 12$) | 213.9 | 202.7 | 241.8 | 27.9 |

Source: E.L. Deci, "The Effects of Externally Mediated Rewards on Intrinsic Motivation," *Journal of Personality and Social Psychology* 18 (1971) 105–15. Copyright 1971 by the American Psychological Association. Reprinted by permission.

difference between the experimental and control groups was only marginally significant, the results are suggestive of the fact that an overly sufficient extrinsic reward may decrease one's intrinsic motivation to perform a task.

Lepper, Greene, and Nisbett (1973) also conducted a study that tested the self-perception prediction in a situation of overly sufficient justification. Their study involved having nursery school children perform an interesting activity (playing with Magic Markers) with and without the expectation of an additional extrinsic reward. Some children were induced to draw pictures with the markers by promising them a Good Player Award consisting of a big gold star, a bright red ribbon, and a place to print their name. Our children either performed the activity without any reward or were told about the reward only after completing the activity. Children who participated in these three experimental conditions (expected reward, no reward, unexpected reward) were then covertly observed during the following week in a free-play period. As in the Deci (1971) study, the amount of time children spent on the activity when they could do other interesting things (i.e., playing with other toys) was taken to be an indicator of intrinsic motivation.

The findings of the Lepper, Greene, and Nisbett study showed that the introduction of an extrinsic reward for performing an already interesting activity caused a significant decrease in intrinsic motivation. Children who played with Magic Markers with the expectation of receiving the external reward did not spend as much subsequent free time on the activity as did the children who were not given a reward or those who were unexpectedly offered the reward. Moreover, the rated quality of drawings made by children with the markers was significantly poorer in the expected-reward group than either the no-reward or unexpected-reward groups.

The results of the Lepper et al. study help to increase our confidence in the findings of the earlier Deci experiment. Not only are the earlier findings replicated with a different task and subject population, but an important methodological problem is minimized. By reexamining Table 17.1, we can see that the second time period in the Deci experiment was the period in which payment was expected by subjects for solving the puzzles. However, we can also see that in time 2 there was a whopping increase in the free time subjects spent on the puzzles. Deci explained this increase as an attempt by subjects to practice puzzle solving to increase their chances of earning money. However, what Deci did not discuss is the possibility that the subsequent decrease in time 3 was due not to the prior administration of rewards but to the effect of satiation or fatigue. One contribution of the Lepper et al. study is that its results are not easily explained by this alternative. In the Lepper et al. experiment, there was over one week's time between the session in which an extrinsic reward was administered and the final observation period.

Although both the Deci and Lepper et al. studies support the notion that the expectation of an extrinsic reward may decrease intrinsic interest in an activity, there is still one important source of ambiguity in both these studies. You may have noticed that the decrease in intrinsic motivation follows not only the prior administration of an extrinsic reward, but also the withdrawal of this reward. For example, in the Deci study, subjects were not paid in the third experimental session in which the decrease in intrinsic motivation was reported. Likewise, subjects were not rewarded when the final observation of intrinsic motivation was taken by Lepper, Greene, and Nisbett. It is therefore difficult to determine whether the decrease in intrinsic interest is due to a change in the self-perception of motivation following the application of an extrinsic reward or merely to frustration following the removal of the reward. An experiment by Kruglanski, Freedman, and Zeevi (1971) helps to resolve this ambiguity.

Kruglanski et al. induced a number of teenagers to volunteer for some creativity and memory tasks. To manipulate extrinsic rewards, the experimenters told half the participants that because they had volunteered for the study, they would be taken on an interesting tour of the psychology laboratory; the other participants were not offered this extrinsic reward. The results showed that teenagers offered the reward were less satisfied with the experimental tasks and were less likely to volunteer for future experiments of a similar nature than were teenagers who were not offered the extrinsic reward. In addition, the extrinsically rewarded group did not perform as well on the experimental task (in terms of recall, creativity, and the Zeigarnik effect) as the nonrewarded group. These findings are similar to those of Deci (1971) and Lepper et al. (1973), but they cannot be as easily explained by a frustration effect. Since in the Kruglanski et al. study the reward was never withdrawn for the experimental group, the differences between the experimental (reward) and control (no reward) conditions are better explained by a change in self-perception than by a frustration effect.

The designs of the three overly sufficient justification studies described above have varying strengths and weaknesses (Calder & Staw, 1975a), but taken together, their results can be interpreted as supporting the notion that extrinsic rewards added to an already interesting task can decrease intrinsic motivation. This effect, if true, has important ramifications for educational, industrial, and other work settings. There are many situations in which people are offered extrinsic rewards (grades, money, special privileges) for accomplishing a task which may already be intrinsically interesting. The self-perception effect means that, by offering external rewards, we may sometimes be sacrificing an important source of task motivation and not necessarily increasing either the satisfaction or the performance of the participant. Obviously, because the practical implications of the self-perception effect are large, we should proceed with caution. Thus, in addition to scrutinizing the validity of the findings themselves (as we have done above), we should also attempt to determine the exact conditions under which they might be expected to hold.

Earlier, Deci (1971, 1972) had hypothesized that only rewards contingent on a high level of task performance are likely to have an adverse effect on intrinsic motivation. He had reasoned that a reward contingent upon specific behavioral demands is most likely to cause an individual to infer that his behavior is extrinsically rather than intrinsically motivated and that a decrease in intrinsic motivation may result from this change in self-perception. Although this assumption seems reasonable, there is not a great deal of empirical support for it. Certainly in the Kruglanski et al. and Lepper et al. studies all that was necessary to cause a decrease in intrinsic motivation was for rewards to be contingent upon the completion of an activity. In each of these studies what seemed to be important was the cognition that one was performing an activity in order to get an extrinsic reward rather than a prescribed goal for a particular level of output. Thus as long as it is salient, a reward contingency based upon the completion of an activity may decrease intrinsic motivation just like a reward contingency based on the quality or quantity of performance.

Ross (1975) recently conducted two experiments that dealt specifically with the effect of the salience of rewards on changes in intrinsic motivation. In one study, children were asked to play a musical instrument (drums) for either no reward, a nonsalient reward, or a salient reward. The results showed that intrinsic motivation, as measured by the amount of time spent on the drums versus other activities in a free play situation, was lowest for the salient reward condition. Similar results were found in a second study in which some children were asked to think either of the reward (marshmallows) while playing a musical instrument, think of an extraneous object (snow), or not think of anything in particular. The data for this second study showed that intrinsic motivation was lowest when children consciously thought about the reward while performing the task.

In addition to the salience of an external reward, there has been empirical research on one other factor mediating the self-perception effect, the existing norms of the task situation. In examining the prior research using situations of overly sufficient justification, Staw, Calder, and Hess (1976) reasoned that there is one common element which stands out. Always, the extrinsic reward appears to be administered in a situation in which persons are not normally paid or otherwise reimbursed for their actions. For example, students are not normally paid for laboratory participation, but the Deci (1971) and Kruglanski et al. (1971) subjects were. Likewise, nursery school children are not normally enticed by special recognition or rewards to play with an interesting new toy, but both the Lepper et al. (1973) and Ross (1975) subjects were. Thus Staw, Calder, and Hess (1976) manipulated norms for payment as well as the actual payment of money for performing an interesting task. They found an interaction of norms and payment such that the introduction of an extrinsic reward decreased intrinsic interest in a task only when there existed a situational norm for no payment. From these data and the findings of the Ross study, it thus appears that an extrinsic reward must be both salient and situationally inappropriate for there to be a reduction in intrinsic interest.

## Reassessing the Self-Perception Effect

At present there is growing empirical support for the notion that intrinsic and extrinsic motivation *can* be negatively interrelated. The effect of extrinsic rewards on intrinsic motivation has been replicated by several researchers using different classes of subjects (males, females, children, college students) and different activities (puzzles, toys), and the basic results appear to be internally valid. As we have seen, however, the effect of extrinsic rewards is predicated on certain necessary conditions (e.g., situational norms and reward salience), as is often the case with psychological findings subjected to close examination.

To date, the primary data supporting the self-perception prediction have come from situations of insufficient and overly sufficient justification. Empirical findings have shown that individuals may cognitively reevaluate intrinsic rewards in an upward direction when their behavior is insufficiently justified and in a downward direction when there is overly sufficient justification. In general, it can be said that the data of these two situations are consistent with the self-perception hypothesis. Still, theoretically, it is not immediately clear why previous research has been restricted to these two particular contexts. No

doubt it is easier to show an increase in intrinsic motivation when intrinsic interest is initially low (as under insufficient justification) or a decrease when intrinsic interest is initially high (as under overly sufficient justification). Nevertheless, the theory should support a negative interrelationship of intrinsic and extrinsic factors at *all levels*, since it makes the rather general prediction that the greater the extrinsic rewards, the less likely is the individual to infer that he is intrinsically motivated.

One recent empirical study has tested the self-perception hypothesis by manipulating *both* intrinsic and extrinsic motivation. Calder and Staw (1975b) experimentally manipulated both the intrinsic characteristics of a task as well as extrinsic rewards in an attempt to examine the interrelationship of these two factors at more than one level. In the study male college students were asked to solve one of two sets of puzzles identical in all respects except the potential for intrinsic interest. One set of puzzles contained an assortment of pictures highly rated by students (chiefly from *Life* magazine but including several *Playboy* centerfolds); another set of puzzles was blank and rated more neutrally. To manipulate extrinsic rewards, half the subjects were promised $1 for their 20 minutes of labor (and the dollar was placed prominently in view), while for half of the subjects, money was neither mentioned nor displayed. After completing the task, subjects were asked to fill out a questionnaire on their reactions to the puzzle-solving activity. The two primary dependent variables included in the questionnaire were a measure of task satisfaction and a measure of subjects' willingness to volunteer for additional puzzle-solving exercises. The latter consisted of a sign-up sheet on which subjects could indicate the amount of time they would be willing to spend (without pay or additional course credit) in future experiments of a similar nature.

The results of the Calder and Staw experiment showed a significant interaction between task and payment on subjects' satisfaction with the activity and a marginally significant interaction on subjects' willingness to volunteer for additional work without extrinsic reward. These data provided empirical support for the self-perception effect in a situation of overly sufficient justification, but not under other conditions. Specifically, when the task was initially interesting (i.e., using the picture puzzle activity), the introduction of money caused a reduction of task satisfaction and volunteering. However, when the task was initially more neutral (i.e., using the blank puzzle activity), the introduction of money increased satisfaction and subjects' intentions to volunteer for additional work. Thus if we consider Calder and Staw's dependent measures as indicators of intrinsic interest, the first finding is in accord with the self-perception hypothesis, while the latter result is similar to what one might predict from a reinforcement theory. The implications of these data, together with previous findings, are graphically depicted in Figure 17.3.

As shown in the figure, self-perception effects have been found *only* at the extremes of insufficient and overly sufficient justification. Thus it may be prudent to withhold judgment on the general hypothesis that there is a uniformly negative relationship between intrinsic and extrinsic motivation. Perhaps we should no longer broadly posit that the greater external rewards and pressures, the weaker the perception of intrinsic interest in an activity; and the lower external pressures,

the stronger intrinsic interest. Certainly, under conditions other than insufficient and overly sufficient justification, reinforcement effects of extrinsic rewards on intrinsic task satisfaction have readily been found (Cherrington, 1973; Cherrington, Reitz, & Scott, 1971; Greene, 1974).

At present it appears that only in situations of insufficient or overly sufficient reward will there be attributional instability of such magnitude that shifts will occur in the perception of intrinsic rewards. We might therefore speculate that either no attributional instability is evoked in other situations or it is just not strong enough to overcome a countervailing force. This writer would place his confidence in the latter theoretical position. It seems likely that both self-perception *and* reinforcement mechanisms hold true, but that their relative influence over an individual's task attitudes and behavior varies according to the situational context. For example, only in situations with insufficient or overly sufficient justification will the need to resolve attributional instability probably be strong enough for external rewards to produce a decrease in intrinsic motivation. In other situations we might reasonably expect a more positive relationship between intrinsic and extrinsic factors, as predicted by reinforcement theory.

Although this new view of the interrelationship between intrinsic and extrinsic motivation remains speculative, it does seem reasonable in light of recent theoretical and empirical work. Figure 17.4 graphically elaborates this model and shows how the level of intrinsic and extrinsic motivation may depend on the characteristics of the situation. In the figure, secondary reinforcement is depicted to be a general force for producing a positive relationship between intrinsic and extrinsic motivation. However, under situations of insufficient and oversufficient justification, self-perception (and dissonance) effects are shown to provide a second but still potentially effective determinant of a negative interrelationship between intrinsic and extrinsic motivation. Figure 17.4 shows the joint operation of these two theoretical mechanisms and illustrates their ultimate effect on individuals' satisfaction, persistence, and performance on a task.

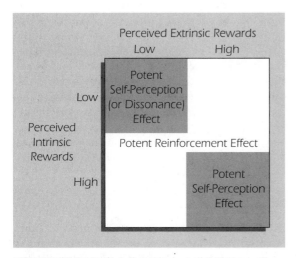

**FIGURE 17.3 The Relative Potency of Self-Perception and Reinforcement Mechanisms.**

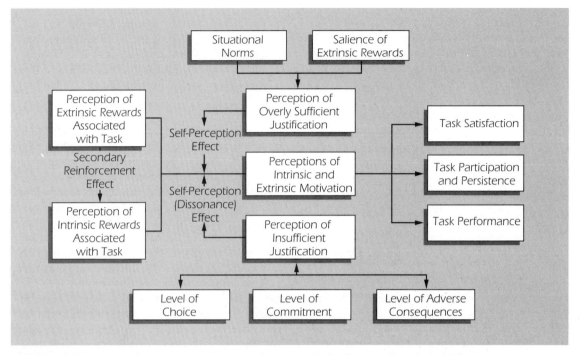

**FIGURE 17.4** The Interrelationship of Intrinsic and Extrinsic Motivation as a Function of Situational Characteristics.

## IMPLICATIONS OF INTRINSIC AND EXTRINSIC MOTIVATION

In this discussion we have noted that the administration of both intrinsic and extrinsic rewards can have important effects on a person's task attitudes and behavior. Individually, extrinsic rewards may direct and control a person's activity on a task and provide an important source of satisfaction. By themselves, intrinsic rewards can also motivate task-related behavior and bring gratification to the individual. As we have seen, however, the joint effect of intrinsic and extrinsic rewards may be quite complex. Not only may intrinsic and extrinsic factors not be additive in their overall effect on motivation and satisfaction, but the interaction of intrinsic and extrinsic factors may under some conditions be positive and under other conditions be negative. As illustrated in Figures 17.3 and 17.4, a potent reinforcement effect will often cause intrinsic and extrinsic motivation to be positively interrelated, although on occasion a self-perception mechanism may be so powerful as to create a negative relationship between these two factors.

The reinforcement predictions of Figures 17.3 and 17.4 are consistent with our common sense. In practice, extrinsic rewards are relied upon heavily to induce desired behaviors, and most allocators of rewards (administrators, teachers, parents) operate on the theory that extrinsic rewards will positively affect an individual's intrinsic interest in a task. We should therefore concentrate on those situations in which our common sense may be in error—those situations in which there may in fact be a negative relationship between intrinsic and extrinsic motivation.

### Motivation in Educational Organizations

One of the situations in which intrinsic and extrinsic motivation may be negatively interrelated is our schools. As Lepper and Green (1975) have noted, many educational tasks are inherently interesting to students and would probably be performed without any external force. However, when grades and other extrinsic inducements are added to the activity, we may, via overly sufficient justification, be converting an interesting activity into work. That is, by inducing students to perform educational tasks with strong extrinsic rewards or by applying external force, we may be converting learning activities into behaviors that will not be performed in the future without some additional outside pressure or extrinsic force.

Within the educational context, a negative relationship between intrinsic and extrinsic motivation poses a serious dilemma for teachers who allocate external rewards. For example, there is no doubt that grades, gold stars, and other such incentives can alter the direction and vigor of specific "in school" behaviors (e.g., getting students to complete assigned exercises by a particular date). But because of their effect on intrinsic motivation, extrinsic rewards may also weaken a student's general interest in learning tasks and decrease voluntary learning behavior that extends beyond the school setting. In essence, then, the extrinsic forces that work so well at motivating and controlling specific task behaviors may actually cause the extinction of these same behaviors within situations devoid of external reinforcers. This is an important consideration for educational organizations, since most of an individual's learning activity will no doubt occur outside the highly regulated and reinforced setting of the classroom.[2]

In order to maintain students' intrinsic motivation in learning activities it is recommended that the use of extrinsic rewards be carefully controlled. As a practical measure, it is recommended that when a learning task is inherently interesting (and would probably be performed without any external force) all external pressures on the individual be minimized. Only when a task is so uninteresting that individuals would not ordinarily perform it should extrinsic rewards be applied. In addition, it is suggested that the student role be both enlarged and enriched to increase rather

directly the level of intrinsic motivation. The significance of learning tasks, responsibility for results, feedback, and variety in student activities are all areas of possible improvement.

## Motivation in Work Organizations

Voluntary work organizations are very much like educational organizations; their members are often intrinsically motivated to perform certain tasks and extrinsic rewards are generally not necessary to induce the performance of many desired behaviors. Moreover, if for some reason extrinsic rewards were to be offered to voluntary workers for performing their services we would expect to find, as in the educational setting, a decrease in intrinsic motivation. As in the educational context, we would expect an external reward to decrease self-motivated (or voluntary) behavior in settings free from external reinforcement, although the specific behaviors which are reinforced might be increased. As a concrete example, let us imagine a political candidate who decides to "motivate" his volunteer campaign workers by paying them for distributing flyers to prospective voters. In this situation, we might expect that the administration of an extrinsic reward will increase the number of flyers distributed. However, the political workers' subsequent interest in performing other campaign activities *without pay* may subsequently be diminished. Similarly, the volunteer hospital worker who becomes salaried may no longer have the same intrinsic interest in his work. Although the newly professionalized worker may exert a good deal of effort on the job and be relatively satisfied with it, his satisfaction may stem from extrinsic rather than intrinsic sources of reward.

Let us now turn to the implications of intrinsic and extrinsic motivation for nonvoluntary work organizations. Deci (1972), in reviewing his research on intrinsic motivation, cautioned strongly against the use of contingent monetary rewards within industrial organizations. He maintained that paying people contingently upon the performance of specific tasks may reduce intrinsic motivation for these activities, and he recommended noncontingent reinforcers in their stead. As we have seen, however, a decrease in intrinsic motivation does not always occur following the administration of extrinsic rewards; certain necessary conditions must be present before there is a negative relationship between intrinsic and extrinsic motivation. Generally, industrial work settings do not meet these necessary conditions.

First, within industrial organizations, a large number of jobs are not inherently interesting enough to foster high intrinsic motivation. Persons would not ordinarily perform many of the tasks of the industrial world (e.g., assembly line work) without extrinsic inducements, and this initial lack of intrinsic interest will probably preclude the effect of overly sufficient justification. Second, even when an industrial job is inherently interesting, there exists a powerful norm for extrinsic payment. Not only do workers specifically join and contribute their labor in exchange for particular inducements, but the instrumental relationship between task behavior and extrinsic rewards is supported by both social and legal standards. Thus the industrial work situation is quite unlike that of either a voluntary organization or an educational system. In the latter cases, participants may be initially interested in performing certain tasks without external force, and the addition of overly sufficient rewards may convey information that the task is not intrinsically interesting. Within industrial organizations, on the other hand, extrinsic reinforcement is the norm, and tasks may often be perceived to be even more interesting when they lead to greater extrinsic rewards.

The very basic distinction between nonvoluntary work situations and other task settings (e.g., schools and voluntary organizations) is that, without extrinsic rewards, nonvoluntary organizations would be largely without participants. The important question for industrial work settings is therefore not one of payment versus nonpayment, but of the recommended degree of contingency between reward and performance. On the basis of current evidence, it would seem prudent to suggest that, within industrial organizations, rewards continue to be made contingent upon behavior. This could be accomplished through performance evaluation, profit sharing, or piece-rate incentive schemes. In addition, intrinsic motivation should be increased directly via the planned alteration of specific job characteristics (e.g., by increasing task variety, complexity, social interaction, task identity, significance, responsibility for results, and knowledge of results).

## A FINAL COMMENT

Although the study of the interaction of intrinsic and extrinsic motivation is a relatively young area within psychology, it has been the intent of this paper to outline a theoretical model and provide some practical suggestions based upon the research evidence available to date. As we have seen, the effects of intrinsic and extrinsic motivation are not always simple, and several moderating variables must often be taken into account before specific predictions can be made. Thus in addition to providing "answers" to theoretical and practical problems, this paper may illustrate the complexities involved in drawing conclusions from a limited body of research data. The main caution for the reader is to regard these theoretical propositions and practical recommendations as working statements subject to the influence of future empirical evidence.

## NOTES

1. The author wishes to express his gratitude to Bobby J. Calder and Greg R. Oldham for their critical reading of the manuscript, and to the Center for Advanced Study at the University of Illinois for the resources and facilities necessary to complete this work.

2. It is interesting to note that Kazdin and Bootzin (1972) have made a quite similar point in their recent review of research on token economies. They noted that while operant conditioning procedures have been quite effective in altering focal behaviors within a controlled setting, seldom have changes been found to generalize to natural, nonreinforcing environments.

## REFERENCES

Aronson, E. "The Psychology of Insufficient Justification: An Analysis of Some Conflicting Data." In *Cognitive Consistency: Motivational Antecedents and Behavior Consequences*, edited by S. Feldman. Academic Press, 1966.

Bem, D. J. "Self-perception: An Alternative Interpretation of Cognitive Dissonance Phenomena." *Psychological Review* 74 (1967): 183–200. (a)

————."Self-perception: The Dependent Variable of Human Performance." *Organizational Behavior and Human Performance* 2 (1967): 105–21. (b)

————."Self-perception Theory." In *Advances in Experimental Social Psychology*, vol. 6, edited by L. Berkowitz. New York: Academic Press, 1972.

Brehm, J. W., and Cohen, A. R. *Explorations in Cognitive Dissonance*. New York: Wiley, 1962.

Calder, B. J., Ross, M.; and Insko, C. A. "Attitude Change and Attitude Attribution: Effects of Incentive, Choice, and Consequences." *Journal of Personality and Social Psychology* 25 (1973): 84–100.

————, and Staw, B. M. "The Interaction of Intrinsic and Extrinsic Motivation: Some Methodological Notes." *Journal of Personality and Social Psychology* 31 (1975): 76–80. (a)

————, and Staw, B. M. "Self-perception of Intrinsic and Extrinsic Motivation." *Journal of Personality and Social Psychology* 31 (1975): 599–605. (b)

Carlsmith, J. M.; Collins, B.E.; and Helmreich, R. L. "Studies in Forced Compliance: The Effect of Pressure for Compliance on Attitude Change Produced by Face-to-Face Role Playing and Anonymous Essay Writing." *Journal of Personality and Social Psychology* 4 (1966): 1–13.

Cherrington, D. J. "The Effects of a Central Incentive—Motivational State on Measures of Job Satisfaction." *Organizational Behavior and Human Performance* 10 (1973): 27–89.

————, Reitz, H. J.; and Scott, W. E. "Effects of Reward and Contingent Reinforcement on Satisfaction and Task Performance." *Journal of Applied Psychology* 55 (1971): 531–36.

Collins, B. E., and Hoyt, M. F. "Personal Responsibility-for-Consequences: An Integration and Extension of the Forced Compliance Literature." *Journal of Experimental Social Psychology* 8 (1972): 558–94.

de Charms, R. *Personal Causation: The Internal Affective Determinants of Behavior*. New York: Academic Press, 1968.

Deci, E. L. "The Effects of Externally Mediated Rewards on Intrinsic Motivation." *Journal of Personality and Social Psychology* 18 (1971): 105–15.

————. "The Effects of Contingent and Noncontingent Rewards and Controls on Intrinsic Motivation." *Organizational Behavior and Human Performance* 8 (1972): 217–29.

Festinger, L. *A Theory of Cognitive Dissonance*. Palo Alto: Stanford University Press, 1957.

———, and Carlsmith, J. M. "Cognitive Consequences of Forced Compliance." *Journal of Abnormal and Social Psychology* 58 (1959): 203–10.

Freedman, J. L. "Attitudinal Effects of Inadequate Justification," *Journal of Personality* 31 (1963): 371–85.

Greene, C. N. "Causal Connections Among Manager's Merit Pay, Job Satisfaction, and Performance." *Journal of Applied Psychology* 58 (1974): 95–100.

Heider, F. *The Psychology of Interpersonal Relations*. New York: Wiley, 1958.

Jones, E. E., and Davis, K. E. "From Acts to Dispositions: The Attribution Process in Person Perception." In *Advances in Experimental Psychology*, vol. 2, edited by L. Berkowitz. New York: Academic Press, 1965.

———; Davis, K. E., and Gergen, K. E.; "Role Playing Variations and Their Informational Value for Person Perception." *Journal of Abnormal and Social Psychology* 63 (1961): 302–10.

———, and Harris, V. A. "The Attribution of Attitudes." *Journal of Experimental Social Psychology* 3 (1967): 1–24.

———, and Nisbett, R. E. *The Actor and the Observer: Divergent Perceptions of the Causes of Behavior*. New York: General Learning Press, 1971.

Kazdin, A. E., and Bootzen, R. R. " The Token Economy: An Evaluative Review." *Journal of Applied Behavior Analysis* 5 (1972): 343–72.

Kelley, H. H. "Attribution Theory in Social Psychology." In *Nebraska Symposium on Motivation*, vol. 15, edited by D. Levine. University of Nebraska Press, 1967.

Kruglanski, A. W.; Freedman, I.; and Zeevi, G. "The Effects of Extrinsic Incentives on Some Qualitative Aspects of Task Performance." *Journal of Personality* 39 (1971): 606–17.

Lepper, M. R., and Greene, D. "Turning Play into Work: Effects of Adult Surveillance and Extrinsic Rewards on Children's Intrinsic Motivation." *Journal of Personality and Social Psychology*, in press.

———; Greene, D.; and Nisbett, R. E. "Undermining Children's Intrinsic Interest with Extrinsic Rewards: A Test of the 'Overjustification' Hypothesis." *Journal of Personality and Social Psychology* 28 (1973): 129–37.

Linder, D. E.; Cooper, J.; and Jones, E. E. "Decision Freedom as a Determinant of the Role of Incentive Magnitude in Attitude Change." *Journal of Personality and Social Psychology* 6 (1967): 245–54.

Ross, M. "Salience of Reward and Intrinsic Motivation." *Journal of Personality and Social Psychology* 32 (1975): 245–254.

Staw, B. M. "Attitudinal and Behavioral Consequences of Changing a Major Organizational Reward: A Natural Field Experiment." *Journal of Personality and Social Psychology* 6 (1974): 742–51. (a)

———. "Notes Toward a Theory of Intrinsic and Extrinsic Motivation." Paper presented at Eastern Psychological Association, 1974. (b)

———; Calder, B. J.; and Hess, R. "Intrinsic Motivation and Norms About Payment." Working paper, Northwestern University, 1975.

Strickland, L. H. "Surveillance and Trust." *Journal of Personality* 26 (1958): 200–215.

Thibaut, J. W., and Riecken, H. W. "Some Determinants and Consequences of the Perception of Social Causality." *Journal of Personality* 24 (1955): 113–33.

Weick, K. E. "Reduction of Cognitive Dissonance Through Task Enhancement and Effort Expenditure." *Journal of Abnormal and Social Psychology* 68 (1964): 533–39.

————, and Penner, D. D. "Justification and Productivity." Unpublished manuscript, University of Minnesota, 1965.

# 18.  THE POWER OF SOCIAL INFORMATION IN THE WORKPLACE

Joe G. Thomas and Ricky W. Griffin

After meeting with his district sales managers for the first time, John Rogers, the newly hired vice-president of marketing, reflected on the particularly puzzling conversations he had had with two of them—Bill Adams and Dick Woods. Both men had very similar backgrounds and experiences: They had been classmates at a prestigious eastern university and had started employment with the company immediately after college. They had been successful sales representatives and had been promoted to regional sales manager positions after approximately four years with the company. Although they managed different sales areas, both areas appeared equally attractive.

The puzzling part of the conversations with Adams and Woods was their inconsistent views of the organization and their future roles in it. Woods had been particularly positive about the work environment, describing the company as "fair" and the work as "challenging, exciting, and worthwhile." He had praised the company for its excellent reputation with its employees and customers, saying "It's really nice to have a job where you are helping people, where what you do really

makes a difference!" Adams, on the other hand, had complained that the company was "ripping off" everybody and that the work was "a real bore." "The customers do not appreciate the quality of service they receive. The employees constantly complain about hours and working conditions. You just cannot keep them happy," he had said. Since both managers were working for the same company and in the same capacity—and had so much in common—how could they see things so differently?

Most people have been in situations similar to the one experienced by John Rogers—situations in which, from an objective viewpoint, everything seems the same yet the people involved see things quite differently. Even though managers recognize that people's perceptions differ, they tend to assume that all employees evaluate and react to their jobs similarly. That kind of attitude is reflected in the following comment, made by a client in an executive development program: "The job is the same for everybody. There are job descriptions for each job. The employees do exactly what is stated in the job description. We are careful to stick to the job descriptions and not let anyone do more for fear of having problems with the union and EEOC."

The common thread between the experiences of John Rogers and the client in the executive development program is the assumption that employees respond only to the "objective" job. In reality, employees respond to their jobs as they perceive them. Moreover, their perceptions are influenced, at least to some degree, by information they receive from others. Yet much of management research and practice is based on the assumption that managers and employees respond strictly to an objective job.

In their article "A Social Information Processing Approach to Job Attitudes and Task Design" (*Administrative Science Quarterly*, June 1978), Gerald Salancik and Jeffrey Pfeffer reopened the question as to the extent of objectivity in evaluating work settings. Their theoretical framework, depicted in a simplified form in Figure 18.1, has served as a springboard for various research studies examining employees' reactions to social information. This line of research, commonly referred to as "social information processing," argues that people adopt attitudes, behaviors, and beliefs in light of social information provided by others.

In his book *Organizations and Organization Theory* (Pitman, 1982), Pfeffer notes that "whether one characterizes jobs using dimensions such as variety, autonomy, feedback, and skill required or dimensions such as pay, effort required, and physical surroundings is in part under the control of a social environment in which some dimensions become talked about and other dimensions are ignored and thus are not salient." In one early experiment examining the influence of information from the social environment ("Informational Influence as a Determinant of Perceived Task Characteristics and Job Satisfaction," *Journal of Applied Psychology*, February 1979), Charles O'Reilly and David Caldwell showed that informational cues have a greater impact on reported task characteristics than do the objective task dimensions. In a later study of public health nurses in which objective jobs were identical ("Perceptual Measures of Task Characteristics: The Biasing Effects of Differing Frames of Reference and Job Attitudes," *Academy of Management Journal*, March 1980), Charles O'Reilly, G. N. Parlette, and J. R. Bloom reported that the perception of task characteristics is influenced by family and professional orientations. In a more recent study of nurses ("Sources of Social Information: A Longitudinal Analysis," *Human Relations*, September 1986), Joe G. Thomas found that information sources perceived as most relevant varied for different aspects of jobs. For example, family members were perceived as important in helping nurses see the significance of their work, but co-workers were

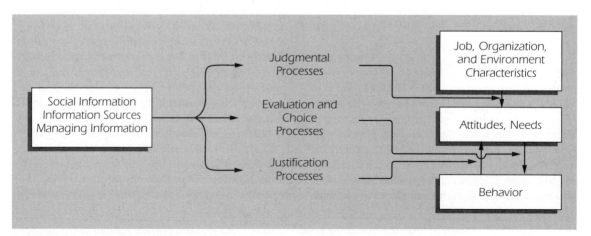

**FIGURE 18.1** Strategic Influence Processes

perceived as most important in helping nurses develop new job skills.

Social information refers to comments, observations, and similar cues provided by people whose view of the job an employee considers relevant. It may be provided by people directly associated with the job, such as co-workers, supervisors, and customers, or it may be provided by people not employed by the company, such as family members and friends. Although not all aspects of a job are likely to be influenced by cues from others (a hot work environment will be hot despite what anyone tells a worker), it seems realistic to assume that most of an employee's perceptions of job characteristics are subject to influence from information provided by others with whom the employee has contact.

## IMPACT OF SOCIAL INFORMATION

Social information can influence an employee's view of the job in several different ways, as shown in Figure 18.1. Social information causes some characteristics of the job to be judged important, and attitudes about these salient characteristics are formed. Once attitudes are formed, social cues offer suggestions in evaluating and choosing appropriate behaviors. Finally, social cues influence the explanations or rationales offered for behavior. To understand and use social information, a manager must first recognize the probable impact of such information on employees and identify sources of information considered relevant.

## IDENTIFICATION OF ORGANIZATION AND JOB CHARACTERISTICS

Jobs have many different facets. They allow varying degrees of autonomy, feedback, and job significance. They aid (or inhibit) employees in developing new skills and preparing for advancement. They are performed in a variety of settings, differing in terms of work conditions (such as temperature and noise level), work schedules (such as starting times, break schedules, and time clocks), rewards, and quality of supervision. Organizations differ in terms of attitudes, policies, and treatment of workers. All of these characteristics may influence an employee's feelings about his or her job. However, not all of them are viewed as equally important in each organization.

## IMPORTANCE OF CHARACTERISTICS

Social information helps employees identify which characteristics of the job and the organization are considered important by other people. If the temperature in a work area or the requirement of clocking in and out is frequently discussed, those characteristics of the job setting receive increased attention from workers. Frequent discussion of such characteristics increases their perceived importance, and they become more salient.

Rarely discussed job characteristics are less likely to be considered important by job incumbents, although the same job characteristics may be considered essential in another organization. Relatively high noise levels or bureaucratic travel-reimbursement policies, for example, may be major sources of employee concern in one organization, while employees of another organization may dismiss those job characteristics as just a fact of organizational life.

Mining accidents provide an example of job characteristics that may be perceived quite differently by people, depending on their situation. Someone outside the industry may be astonished at a miner's ability to go to work with little apparent fear shortly after a disastrous mining accident at a neighboring mine. Miners *want to believe* information provided by the company and co-workers that there is little probability of an accident happening to them. They perceive occasional industrial accidents as an undesirable but largely unavoidable part of the job. To people outside the industry, however, the danger seems unbelievably high. The different assessments of the danger are at least partly the result of different evaluations of the information provided about the risks of an accident.

## EVALUATION OF JOB CHARACTERISTICS

Other people's information about a job reveals their perceptions of the job to employees. All organizations develop cultures that are transmitted to workers. Organizations differ, for example, in terms of the importance attached to customer satisfaction and quality versus quantity of output, employee and subunit autonomy, administrative structures, and attitudes toward risk and diversification. Rituals, stories, symbols, and language are all used to inform employees about the organization and individual jobs.

Military training provides recruits the information they need to evaluate military jobs. That information, much like the information provided to miners, may initially be perceived as inconsistent with the information held by the general public. However, as boot camp continues, the recruits generally become more accepting of authority, place greater importance on military values, and become willing to sacrifice their lives for the good of others. Rituals (such as basic training and mock battles), stories of both successful and unsuccessful missions, symbols (such as the U.S. flag and military heroes), as well as language (such as code words and slang) are used to influence the recruits' perceptions of the organization and their place in it. In effect, social information leads to a reevaluation of the basic meaning of life and its importance to the individual. Orientation programs for new employees are designed to accomplish similar ends, although the change in attitudes may be less marked.

People outside the organization also provide information that is used to evaluate job and organization characteristics. Statements such as "You guys sure have to work some odd hours" or "Isn't that work boring!" provide information about what the speaker considers important as well as the speaker's evaluation of the work situation. A family member who constantly reminds a miner about the dangers of the job will likely increase the attention the miner gives to safety and may force the miner to reassess the risks of the occupation.

## JUSTIFICATION OF WORKERS' PERCEPTIONS

Employees who have perceptions of their jobs or behavior that is inconsistent with the social information they receive may attempt to convince the information source of the inaccuracy of the information. Alternately, employees may justify (or rationalize) away the differences, or they may decide to adjust their perceptions to be consistent with the information they receive.

Employees frequently change their perception of a situation to conform with the perception of information sources. In what has become known as the "Asch light experiment," subjects were asked to judge the lengths of lines of light. Less than 1% of the subjects misjudged line length when working individually. However, when co-workers (actually confederates in the experiment) provided incorrect judgments, more than one-third of the subjects gave an incorrect answer consistent with the incorrect answer provided by their co-workers. (See "Studies of Independence and Conformity: A Minority of One Against a Unanimous Majority" by Solomon E. Asch in *Psychological Monographs* No. 9 1956). If people are willing to change their perceptions of objective phenomena such as the length of a line, they probably are even more likely to change their views of the less objective elements of jobs.

## SOURCES OF INFORMATION

Employees can receive information from a wide variety of sources, ranging from bathroom graffiti to the evening news. However, the most likely sources of social information are the people employees come into contact with regularly—co-workers, supervisors, friends, family members and, in some cases, customers or clients.

## Co-workers

Generally, co-workers are important sources of information for an employee. They not only spend several hours per day with the employee but also are most likely to be familiar with the employee's work. Co-workers' knowledge of a job makes their views of job characteristics, the importance of specific characteristics, and the evaluation of those characteristics particularly credible. Furthermore, the day-to-day contact with co-workers allows frequent discussion of workplace phenomena and thereby reinforces the perceptions co-workers have of a particular job.

To illustrate the latter point, let's return to the story of John Rogers. As John became better acquainted with his new employer and with Adams and Woods, he began to agree with Adams that the work environment was less than ideal. Adams had complained that his job was boring and that he felt unappreciated—relatively mild criticisms compared with the views held by most of the salesforce. Adams and many other employees perceived the company as a place to obtain work experience and a "livable" salary until something better came along. His co-workers explained to John that other companies in the industry offered better benefits, more autonomy, and greater opportunities for advancement. As most employees agreed, promotion out of their adequately paid but dead-end jobs should be a primary career goal.

## Supervisors

In many instances, supervisors are also a source of information. They can have a dual impact on worker's job perceptions. Obviously, a supervisor is a representative of higher levels of management and as such has an opportunity to present the organization's view of the job and the characteristics of the job considered important by the organization. For employees seeking rapid upward mobility and other "company" employees, the organization's view of the workplace as presented by the supervisor may be accepted with minimal questioning.

In addition to being "management's representative," a supervisor may function in the capacity of a friend or co-worker. Employees and their supervisors may work as peers to solve particular problems. Similarly, they may interact on an informal basis during breaks, lunch, social functions, and so forth. The supervisor is in a position to comment on various elements of an employee's job during these informal times and may indirectly influence the employee's job perception.

Woods, who had given John a positive view of the job during their conversation, was not particularly influenced by the information provided by his co-workers. Woods had been a personal friend of his division manager before being hired. The division manager continually provided Woods with information from upper management that advancement was almost automatic for employees who remained loyal to the company. Loyalty, seniority, and good performance were the keys to advancement. The division manager had convinced Woods that, although promotions were not as rapid as at other organizations, job pressures were less and job security was better. Woods did not consider himself to be a fast-track employee and preferred the relative safety and low pressure he associated with his current employer.

## Friends and Family

Friends and family members provide a perspective on an employee's work situation that is often quite different from the perspective provided by supervisors and co-workers. Friends and family members who are not employed by the company are less subject to its influence and the influence of its employees. Thus they often are in a position to provide a different, and probably more objective, assessment of what a worker should experience on a job. New employees may attach greater validity to information provided by someone from outside the organization, believing that person to be less biased than a co-worker, especially if the person has the added credibility of being a trusted friend or family member. Alternately, some people may discount evaluations made by family members as being uninformed or naive.

Family members and friends also are in a position to provide an external reference point. For example, they can inform a worker about jobs at other organizations. Discussing such jobs allows the employee to compare his or her job with situations elsewhere to determine the relative importance of various job characteristics and the relative merit of the company.

Further, family members and friends often are an especially powerful source of support for new employees and employees who are having problems at work. Discussions with people outside the company allow employees to vent their feelings about their jobs. Family members and friends also provide support for the employee's self-image. They help an employee understand the rationale for particular characteristics of the job. Particularly for new employees, this kind of rationalizing is part of the process whereby a person's perception of what is important is modified to more closely parallel the information provided by others.

In the original example, Woods' family members provided additional information, causing him to be satisfied with the company's slow rate of promotion. John learned that Woods was from a family of blue-collar workers. Woods had been the first family member to earn a college degree and to advance to a management position. Relative to other members of the family, Woods was doing quite well and was earning more than any of them. Besides, a quick promotion would almost certainly mean a transfer from the area, an alternative he did not really want to consider. Therefore, Woods was content to remain in his position and wait for a promotion that did not require a move.

## Customers or Clients

In some cases, customers or clients provide workers with job-related information. Especially for employees of service companies, customers provide an evaluation of the company and its prod-ucts. Such evaluations may not pertain to a specific job, but customers' assessments of the organization become part of its culture. Companies whose products are poorly received by customers are likely to have different expectations for their employees. Pressures to reduce costs, improve product quality, and/or increase quantity of output are usually greater at companies that are performing poorly. On the other hand, contacts with customers and customer treatment may be important considerations for an organization. These customer contacts, for example, often distinguish a self-service discount store from a store providing full service.

Employees may perceive the importance of their work differently if the product is well accepted. Extremely poor customer relations may threaten the survival of the company and increase the attention employees focus on job security. Employees are more likely to feel that their job is secure and that they have career opportunities when a company has good customer relations.

In organizations that encourage full service and personal contact with customers, the customer is likely considered an important source of job-related information. Both the employee and the employer are encouraged to be attentive to the needs and reactions of customers. Organizations with cultures attaching less significance to customer contact and satisfaction would likewise be expected to attribute less validity to information provided by customers. At those organizations, the line "This would not be a bad place to work if it were not for the customers" is too often said with sincerity by employees.

## GUIDELINES FOR USING AND MANAGING SOCIAL INFORMATION

Managers often discuss the influence that groups have on the behavior of workers. Yet in planning interactions with employees, managers tend to overlook the social influence on employee behavior. Employee experience is an important factor affecting the ability of social information to influence behavior. Managers should also be sensitive to the impact of different information sources on employee behavior and attitudes. Moreover, they should use caution in attributing the results of various job measures to the "true, objective" job rather than to cues provided by others about the job.

## Employee Experience

The length of time an employee has been in a particular position will likely influence the employee's susceptibility to information about the job. Employees who are new to the job, either newly hired workers or those transferred or promoted into a new position, are likely to be more receptive to social information than are employees who have greater seniority in the position. Especially when an employee is new to the job and the organization, a considerable amount of time is spent listening to many employees' views about the company's operations.

The variety of information sources used by an employee decreases with his or her experience in the job, although reliance on a few selected sources may increase. The number of sources used decreases since much of the information provided from some sources is learned quickly. Thus those sources no longer contribute information of significant value to the employee. Other people, however, evolve as credible sources of worthwhile information. The latter will exert increased influence as employees gain work experience.

## INFORMATION SOURCE USAGE

There are a vast number of potential sources of job-related information. As discussed above, family members, friends, customers, co-workers, and supervisors often are highly valued sources of information.

During crisis periods of employment, family members and friends can be especially useful sources of information for an employee by helping the employee retain self-confidence. Family members and friends can encourage a new employee to keep trying and promise support if the new job does not work out.

Although there is very little that managers can do to control information obtained from family members and friends, they need to be aware that information from such sources restricts the range of strategies available for responding to employees. Managers also must realize that employees are aware of the things other companies are doing. Depending on their information sources, some employees may know more about other organizations than their supervisors know.

Customers and clients provide information about the value of a company's products relative to a competitor's products. Their evaluations may give employees insight into the probable success (or failure) of the company's product line. Frequent negative criticism of a company's product, for example, tells an employee that the product is inferior in some respect. Continued criticism may cause the employee to question the quality of the product, the quality of the company, and the probability of stable long-term employment. Ultimately, such negative information may provide the incentive for an employee to leave the organization.

As with feedback from the family members and friends, companies have little opportunity to insulate employees from feedback from customers. Instead, they must be sensitive to the feedback employees are receiving. Discussing with employees the information they receive enables management to explain steps the company is taking to correct problems and to assure employees of the company's integrity and stability. It also gives management the opportunity to learn about major developments at other organizations.

Managers may be able to influence the initial image new employees have of the organization by selecting the co-workers to whom they are exposed. Assigning a new employee to a work group supportive of management will likely produce a more favorable initial attitude toward the company than assigning the worker to a more negative work group. However, assignment of coworkers is obviously a temporary control measure. Eventually, the new employee will be exposed to negative views of the company. If the criticisms seem more credible than the positive information provided by the first co-workers, management may be perceived as manipulative. Thus control of co-worker information must be used with discretion.

The social information over which management has the greatest control is information provided by supervisors. Managers often overlook the influence supervisors have on their employees. For many employees, the immediate supervisor *is* the organization. A supervisor's negative attitude about the company or its management can be transmitted to employees, who in turn develop a negative attitude. Employees often know little about top management. Frequent critical remarks by a supervisor, even if the remarks are made in jest, may support negative information from other sources and cause employees to develop critical views of top management as well as the organization.

In his article "Objective and Social Sources of Information in Task Redesign: A Field Experiment" (*Administrative Science Quarterly*, June 1983), Ricky W. Griffin reported that managers could change employees' perceptions of the job and organization *without* changing the job. One group of managers was trained to provide positive social or informational cues to employees. The employees' perceptions of task characteristics such as task variety, autonomy, feedback, and friendship opportunities differed significantly from the perceptions of the control group whose managers had no training in providing positive social or informational cues.

### Objective Job Versus Social Information

Managers must be cautious when interpreting data gathered from employees through surveys and interviews. In taking steps to change jobs in response to data collected from employees, managers must be careful to distinguish between responses stemming from the "objective" job and from social information. If the responses are the result of the objective job, changing the objective job likely will change employees' perceptions and attitudes. However, if the responses are the result of information from the social context in which the job is being performed, changing the job will likely have minimal impact on employees' perceptions of and attitudes about the job as long as the social information provided about the job remains unchanged.

### SUMMARY

Jobs and the characteristics associated with them rarely are totally objective. Employees' reactions to their jobs are influenced by information provided by co-workers, supervisors, family members, friends, and perhaps customers or clients. New employees are especially likely to use information from external sources to shape their perceptions of the job and the company. Long-term employees also respond to information provided by others. However, they tend to be more selective about their information sources than are new employees.

Recent research suggests that for some aspects of work, social information about the job may be more important to understanding how employees view the job than is the actual "objective" job. Managers frequently overlook the impact that information from various sources may have on employees' perceptions. In fact, changing the job may have little effect on employees' feelings about the job if information provided by others remains unchanged.

### SELECTED BIBLIOGRAPHY

The sources of citations in this article are, in order: Gerald R. Salancik and Jeffrey Pfeffer's "A Social Information Processing Approach to Job Attitudes and Task Design" (*Administrative Science Quarterly*, June 1978); Jeffrey Pfeffer's *Organizations and*

*Organization Theory* (Pitman, 1982); Charles O'Reilly and David Caldwell's "Informational Influence as a Determinant of Perceived Task Characteristics and Job Satisfaction" (*Journal of Applied Psychology*, February 1979);Charles O'Reilly, G. N. Parlette, and J. R. Bloom's "Perceptual Measures of Task Characteristics: The Biasing Effects of Differing Frames of Reference and Job Attitudes" (*Academy of Management Journal*, March 1980); Joe G. Thomas' "Sources of Social Information: A Longitudinal Analysis" (*Human Relations*, September 1986); Solomon. E. Asch's "Studies of Independence and Conformity: A Minority of One Against a Unanimous Majority" (*Psychological Monographs*, No. 9 1956); Ricky W. Griffin's "Objective and Social Sources of Information in Task Redesign: A Field Experiment" (*Administrative Science Quarterly*, June 1983).

The previous citations are intended to provide some insight into the social information processing literature. More extensive reviews of the literature can be found in Gary J. Blau and Ralph Katerburg's "Toward Enhancing Research with the Social Information Processing Approach to Job Design," (*Academy of Management Review*, October 1982); Joe G. Thomas and Ricky W. Griffin's "The Social Information Processing Model of Task Design: A Review of the Literature" (*Academy of Management Review*, October 1983); and Ricky W. Griffin, Thomas S. Bateman, Sandy J. Wayne, and Thomas C. Head's "Objective and Social Factors as Determinants of Task Perceptions and Responses: An Integrated Perspective and Empirical Investigation" (*Academy of Management Journal*, September 1987).

As is shown in Figure 18.1, the environment in which an employee and organization operate is also subject to social influence. Questions of whether organizations respond to "real" or "constructed" environments is gaining acceptance in the literature on strategic planning. Insight into the social influence processes at a macro-level can be found in Gregory G. Dess and Nancy Origer's "Environment, Structure, and Consensus in Strategy Formulation: A Conceptual Integration" (*Academy of Management Review*, April 1987); Jane Dutton and Susan Jackson's "Categorizing Strategic Issues: Links to Organizational Action" (*Academy of Management Review*, January 1987); Don Hambrick and Phyllis Mason's "Upper Echelons: The Organization as a Reflection of Its Top Managers" (*Academy of Management Review*, April 1984).

The importance attached to developing a clear mission and the ability to focus an organization's energies on the external, on service, on quality, on people, on informality, and on wanting to be "the best" at something has been effectively presented by Tom Peters and Robert H. Waterman in their book *In Search of Excellence: Lessons from America's Best-Run Companies* (Harper & Row, 1982). According to Peters and Waterman, part of the function of top management is to clarify to employees what the company views as important. The argument, as developed by Linda Smircich and Charles Stubbart in "Strategic Management in an Enacted World" (*Academy of Management Review*, October 1985), is essentially that a company's strategy becomes a reflection of the concerns of top management; it is a reflection of the issues management considers important.

The position that the receptiveness of employees to social cues varies with work experience draws from research on socialization. Two of the most cited books on socialization, John Wanous' *Organizational Entry* (Addison-Wesley, 1980) and Edgar Schein's *Career Dynamics* (Addison-Wesley, 1978), support the view that information source usage becomes more selective and limited as employees become more oriented to their jobs. This view is also supported in Joe G. Thomas' "Sources of Social Information: A Longitudinal Analysis" (*Human Relations*, September 1986).

# 19. ORGANIZATIONAL STORIES: MORE VIVID AND PERSUASIVE THAN QUANTITATIVE DATA

Joanne Martin and Melanie E. Powers

Many organizations have become adept at symbolic means of communicating information about their philosophy of management, the culture of their organization, and the humanistic rationale for their policies. Symbolic forms of management include the creation of rituals of initiation and transition, the evolution of shared jargon and special metaphors, and—the focus of this chapter—the telling of organizational sagas, myths, legends, and stories.

## COLLECTING HEADS, TAMING WILD DUCKS, AND J.F.K.

One organization that has become known for its attention to symbolic forms of management is I.B.M. Under the guidance of its founder, T. J. Watson, Sr., I.B.M. developed a distinctive culture, a well-articulated philosophy of management, and a strong demand for conformity (cf. Belden & Belden, 1962; Foy, 1975; Malik, 1975). For example the famous I.B.M. dress code required male employees to wear dark suits, crisp white shirts, and narrow black ties. The organizational culture included rules concerning sexual relations between employees (not advisable), the use of coarse language or alcohol during working hours (don't ), and the way to make a speech (list key points using simple words on a flip chart). T. J. Watson, Sr. reinforced these forms of organizational control with numerous rituals and ceremonies. For example, until the company became too large, employees lived temporarily in tents on company grounds during the annual picnic.

There they sang company songs and listened to speeches given with evangelical fervor.

When T. J. Watson, Jr., took over the leadership of I.B.M. from his father, he wanted to improve the functioning of the corporation and leave his personal mark on its distinctive philosophy of management and culture. One means to these ends was to change the rhetoric, and perhaps the reality, of the corporation's demands for conformity. T. J. Watson, Jr., stated this objective directly in his speeches at company functions: "I just wish somebody would stick his head in my office and say (to me) 'you're wrong.' I would really like to hear that. I don't want yes-men around me" (Malik, 1975, p. 210).

Watson, Jr., justified his encouragement of dissent by citing *The Organization Man*: "When an organization tries to get too close to its people and makes a lot of the team idea, the individual gets swallowed up, loses his identity, and becomes a carbon copy of his fellow employees" (Watson, Jr., 1963, pp. 24–25). He claimed that the company already had in its ranks a number of employees who would dare express dissent:

*[Our company] has more than 125,000 employees. A substantial number of them, many of whom I could pick out by name, are highly individualistic men and women. They value their intellectual freedom and I question whether they would surrender it at any price. Admittedly, they may like their jobs and the security and salaries that go along with them. But I know of few who would not put on their hats and slam the door if they felt the organization had intruded so heavily on them they no longer owned themselves. (Watson, Jr., 1963, pp. 25–26)*

Such abstract, direct statements of this change in the demand for the conformity were dismissed as corporate propaganda by many employees: "[Watson, Jr.] says to us to stick our heads into his office and say 'you are wrong'; you should see the collection of heads that he has" (Malik, 1975, p. 210).

Watson, Jr., seemed to recognize the difficulty of convincing I.B.M. employees that this change in policy was truthful, and not corporate propaganda. He repeatedly supplemented abstract, direct statements, such as that quoted above, with stories illustrating his point. His favorite story concerned wild ducks:

*The moral is drawn from a story by the Danish philosopher, Soren Kierkegaard. He told of a man on the coast of Zealand who liked to watch the wild ducks fly south in great flocks each fall. Out of charity, he took to putting feed for them in a nearby pond. After a while some of the ducks no longer bothered to fly south; they wintered in Denmark on what he fed them.*

*In time they flew less and less. When the wild ducks returned, the others would circle up to greet them but then head back to their feeding grounds on the pond. After three or four years they grew so lazy and fat that they found difficulty in flying at all.*

*Kierkegaard drew his point—you can make wild ducks tame, but you can never make tame ducks wild again. One might also add that the duck who is tamed will never go anywhere anymore.*

*We are convinced that any business needs its wild ducks. And in I.B.M. we try not to tame them. (Watson, Jr., 1963, pp. 27–28)*

This metaphorical story also failed to convince many employees. Indeed, some researchers (cf. Ott, 1979) expressed skepticism about it. One employee put his reaction succinctly: "Even wild ducks fly in formation" (Malik, 1975, p. 210). Watson, Jr., had another story he told which made a similar point. The main characters in this story were I.B.M. employees.

*Early in 1961, in talking to our sales force, I attempted to size up the then new Kennedy Administration as I saw it. It was not a political talk. I urged no views on them. It was an optimistic assessment, nothing more.*

*But at the close of the meeting, a number of salesmen came up front. They would listen to what I had to say about business, they said, but they didn't want to hear about the new Administration in a company meeting.*

*On my return to New York, I found a few letters in the same vein. Lay off, they seemed to say, you're stepping on our toes in something that's none of your business.*

*At first I was a bit annoyed at having been misunderstood. But when I thought about it, I was pleased, for they had made it quite clear they wore no man's collar and they weren't at all hesitant to tell me so. From what I have read of organization men, that is not the way they are supposed to act. (Watson, Jr., 1963, p. 26)*

This last story was more credible than his other statements which encouraged dissent. Even self-appointed critics of I.B.M. do not usually doubt the truthfulness of this particular story (cf. Malik, 1975), although they may continue to be skeptical of the company's actual tolerance of dissent.

This skepticism is not misplaced. Even in public statements, Watson, Jr., betrayed his unchanged desire for conformity:

*It's going to be a prodigious job for every one of us to make all of them look and act and have the same basic philosophies in their business lives and their community lives that all of us have... I wish I could put it in a page or two and hand it out and say "Give this to every new employee," who will then automatically start to look and act and think as we do. (Belden & Belden, 1962, p. 249)*

In this I.B.M. example, Watson, Jr.'s policy change was more rhetoric than reality. Of all the various forms of communicating this purported policy change, the story about organizational employees seemed to arouse the least skepticism. Thus, it was most likely to generate commitment to the policy. Direct statements of the policy in abstract language were apparently less effective.

If organizational stories are a particularly effective means of generating commitment, they are a potentially powerful management tool. From a management point of view, it would be useful to know whether in fact an organizational story is a more effective way to generate commitment than other forms of communicating information. It would also be useful to know the conditions under which an organizational story would lose its impact.

From an employee's point of view, different issues are salient. An employee needs to know whether to believe a given statement is true or whether to dismiss it as corporate propaganda. It is also useful for an employee to know if a particular form of communication, such as a story, is likely to be particularly persuasive. If so, the employee can be wary when information is communicated in this form. These concerns of top management and lower-level employees suggest that symbolic forms of management, such as organizational stories, are an important topic for researchers to investigate.

## ORGANIZATIONAL STORIES, MYTHS, LEGENDS, AND SAGAS

Some organizational research indicates that the persuasive power of the story in the I.B.M. example is representative of other organizational settings. This research focuses on organizational stories, myths, sagas, and legends (e.g., Clark, 1970; Meyer & Rowan, 1978; Selznick, 1957). Wilkins and Martin (1979) define an organizational story as an anecdote about an event sequence, apparently drawn from an accurate version of an organization's history. The main characters are organizational participants, usually employees rather than clients.

This research on organizational stories has relied predominantly on qualitative methods (e.g., Clark, 1970; Selznick, 1957). Researchers have found examples of organizational stories in the transcripts of open-ended interviews and in archival material, such as memoranda, brochures, letters, and records of speeches given by company executives.

This organizational research speculates that organizational stories may serve many of the same functions that anthropologists have found

myths to serve in tribal societies (e.g., Cohen, 1969; Malinowski, 1948): organizational stories legitimate the power relations within the organization; they rationalize existing practices, traditions, and rituals; and they articulate through examplars the philosophy of management and the policies which make the organization distinctive. In short, this research suggests the proposition that there is an association between stories and organizational commitment. The next section of this chapter examines this proposition in detail.

## STORIES AND COMMITMENT

Alan Wilkins (1978) tested this proposition using a mixture of qualitative and quantitative methods. He obtained transcripts of organizational stories through interviews with employees of two companies, and measured levels of employee commitment with a survey instrument. In the organization in which commitment was stronger, a larger number of stories were told, and their content was more favorable to the organization. Thus Wilkins' research found an association between organizational stories and commitment.

The organizational research discussed above, including Wilkins' work, raises two interesting questions. The first concerns causality. Does the telling of organizational stories increase employee commitment to the organization? Or, is the direction of causality reversed, so that committed employees are more likely to tell favorable stories? Another possibility is that there may not be a causal relationship at all between stories and commitment. The second question concerns the relative impact of stories on commitment, compared to other methods of communicating information about management philosophy or policy. Such other means of communicating information might include abstract policy statements, such as corporate objectives, or a table of statistical data. Are stories a more effective means of generating commitment than these other forms of information? The types of research designs and methodologies used in the organizational research discussed above raised these questions, but did not attempt to provide answers to them (Clark, 1970; Meyer & Rowan, 1978; Selznick, 1957; Wilkins, 1978).

We decided to seek answers to these two questions by using experimental laboratory methods. This methodology is well suited to address these questions. In an experiment it is possible to manipulate the form of information presented to subjects. Potentially confounding variables such as tenure can be controlled by the design of the experimental context and by random assignment of subjects to conditions. Hence a well-designed experiment can provide a context for testing questions of causality and for measuring the comparative strength of various means of communicating information.

We designed experiments to test two propositions based on the organizational research discussed above. We proposed, first, that supporting a management philosophy statement with an organizational story would increase the subjects' commitment to that philosophy. Second, we proposed that stories would produce more commitment than other forms of information.

As considered in more detail elsewhere (Martin, in press), a body of experimental social cognition research is relevant to these propositions. This cognitive research begins with a premise concerning sample size which is familiar to all students of statistical inference: a judgment based on multiple observations should be more reliable than a judgment based on a single observation. Furthermore, if data based on multiple observations is supplemented by an additional observation, then that additional data point should be treated merely as one of the set of observations.

This premise concerning sample size raises some issues about the impact of an organizational story. A story—indeed, any case example—is based on a single observation. Therefore, if the sample size premise is followed, a story should have much less impact than would data based on multiple observations.

Considerable cognitive research suggests that people do not behave in a manner consistent with the sample size premise (Borgida & Nisbett, 1977; McArthur, 1972, 1976; Nisbett & Borgida, 1975; Nisbett & Ross, 1980; Tversky & Kahneman, 1973). Typically in this research, some subjects were randomly selected to receive distributional data about the behavior of a number of other people (consensus information) or the characteristics of a sample (base-rate information). The remaining subjects received the distributional information, plus additional information about a single case example. The dependent variables usually required subjects to make rational cognitive judgments about relatively academic tasks.

The engineers and lawyers problem is representative of these experimental tasks (Kahneman & Tversky, 1973). Subjects were given base-rate data about the percentages of engineers and lawyers in a given sample. Some of the subjects were also given personally descriptive information about a single individual. Subjects were then asked to estimate the probability that this individual was an engineer.

In accord with the sample size premise, subjects exposed only to the distributional data based their cognitive judgments on that data. Subjects exposed both to the distributional data and to the case example, however, weighted the case example much more heavily in their judgments than they should have, had they behaved in accord with sample size considerations.

More recently, researchers have attempted to find the limits of this phenomenon. Some recent research has found that for tasks such as this, the impact of distributional data was equal to or greater than the impact of a single case example (Azjen, 1977; Feldman, Higgins, Karlovac, & Ruble, 1976; Hansen & Donoghue, 1977; Manis, Dovalina, Avis, & Cardoze, 1980; Wells & Harvey, 1977). Even in these studies, though, case examples are usually given weight beyond that dictated by the sample size premise. To summarize, social cognition research provides an experimental paradigm for examining the two hypotheses discussed above. It also provides additional support for the second of the two propositions to be tested: a case example, such as an organizational story, may have strong impact on judgments, stronger than that predicted by sample size considerations alone.

These conclusions, however, assume that the cognitive research results are generalizable to organizational contexts. This assumption may not be warranted, for two reasons. First, the experimental tasks used in the cognitive research require subjects to make rational, usually statistical, judgments. Subjects' knowledge of statistical principles may be sufficient to produce a correct solution to the problem. In organizational contexts, judgments are usually more complex and subjective. Second, the source of the distributional and case example information appears to be objective in the cognitive research. Subjects would have little reason to doubt the truthfulness of this information. In organizational contexts, though, the credibility of the source of information is often questionable. Organizational representatives have been known to distort information about their organizations.

Both of these limitations of the cognitive research suggest the importance of exploring ideas drawn from the cognitive research in contexts which are organizationally relevant. In such contexts, experimental tasks would require complex and subjective solutions, not derivable from statistical principles. The source of the information, whether it is based on single or multiple observations, would be of potentially questionable credibility.

We conducted two experiments with these organizationally relevant characteristics. In each experiment we gave all subjects a statement of an organizational policy, phrased in abstract language. Some subjects also received additional information presented in the form of data (based on multiple observations); others received additional information in the form of an organizational story (based on a single observation). Still others received both the data and the story. Because of the complexity of the information, we were able to incorporate into our questionnaire a broader range of dependent variables than were used in the cognitive research. We included the usual cognitive dependent variables plus accuracy of recall and attitudinal dependent variables such as belief in and commitment to the policy statement. Our two experiments are described below.

# SELLING CALIFORNIA WINE WITH A STORY

In the first experiment (Martin & Powers, 1979) M.B.A. students were recruited as subjects for a study of the effectiveness of an advertisement for a winery. An abstract policy statement (an advertisement) was read by all subjects. According to this statement, the new Joseph Beaumont Winery used many of the same excellent winemaking techniques as used in the famed Chablis region of France, thus producing California wine as fine as French chablis.

The text of the advertisement contained this policy statement plus some supplemental information. The supplemental information detailed the winemaking procedures used by the Joseph Beaumont winery. Subjects were randomly assigned to receive this information in one of three forms: a story, a table of statistics, or a combination of story plus statistics. Like many organizational stories, the story concerned the founder of a business:

*Joseph Beaumont's father spent most of his life growing grapes in Chablis, the famous winemaking area of France. After World War II, Joe's father came to the United States, to live in the Napa area of California. The gravelly soil and cool climate there reminded him of the stony fields and cool nights in Chablis. All the time Joe was growing up, his father would tell him how the wonderful, flinty, dry wines of Chablis were made. Before his father died, Joe promised him that someday he would make a California wine using the traditional winemaking techniques of Chablis.*

*For ten years, Joe worked at some of the most famous vineyards in the Napa Valley, putting all his savings into a winery and vineyard, which he named Beaumont. Although money was sometimes scarce, Joe has struggled for the last two years to duplicate the old, but unfortunately expensive, methods of winemaking of Chablis. His Pinot Chardonnay vines were too new; they didn't supply all the grapes he needed and he was forced to buy some inferior grape varieties. He wanted to use glass-lined tanks, like those in Chablis, but could only afford 7 of the 10 he needed, so he had to use a few of the steel tanks usually used in California. In spite of these difficulties, Joe made no other compromises.*

*He ordered special Limosin oak barrels, from the same suppliers used by Chablis winemakers. He filtered his wine using natural methods — egg whites rather than the chemical filters favored by other California wineries. As Joe tasted his first vintage wine he thought, "My father would have been proud of this wine."*

In the statistics condition, subjects were given a table summarizing information comparing the winemaking procedures (such as the types of grapes and oak barrels) used at the Joseph Beaumont Winery, at other California wineries, and in Chablis, France. In the story condition, subjects received the story, but no statistical data. In the combination condition, subjects received both the story and the table of statistics. After reading this material, subjects answered a questionnaire about the advertisement which contained the dependent measures of willingness to predict that the organization would behave in accord with the abstract policy statement; willingness to believe the policy statement; ability to recognize its content accurately; and willingness to consider the advertisement a persuasive marketing technique.

Our hypothesis, labeled *the story hypothesis*, predicted the same pattern of results for each of these classes of dependent variables: the story should have the greatest impact, followed by the combination condition, and then the statistics condition. An alternate hypothesis, labeled the *data hypothesis*, predicted the opposite pattern of results: statistics > combination > story.

In contrast to subjects in the other two conditions, subjects who read only the story were slightly more likely to predict that the winery would continue to use the winemaking procedures from France. These subjects were significantly more likely to believe that the advertisement was truthful, to believe that the Beaumont winery actually had used the French winemaking procedures, and to distort their memory of the policy statement, in a direction favorable to the winery. In summary, in accord with the story hypothesis, the story generally had stronger impact than the combination of story plus statistics; and the combination had more impact than did the statistics by themselves.

Interestingly, the subjects were apparently unaware of the strong impact of the story. In accord with the data hypothesis, subjects in the statistics condition rated the advertisement they had read as somewhat more persuasive than did subjects who had read both the story and the statistics. Furthermore, subjects in the statistics condition rated the advertisement as considerably more persuasive than did subjects in the other conditions. Thus the subjects did not realize how powerfully the story had affected their responses. It created a "true believer" reaction even in these quantitatively well-trained M.B.A. students.

## GENERATING COMMITMENT TO A POLICY STATEMENT WITH A STORY

In the first experiment the supplemental information supported the policy statement. In this second study (Martin & Powers, 1980), the supplemental information either supported or disconfirmed the policy statement. As in the first study, three forms of that information were used: a story, a table of statistics, or a combination of story plus statistics. Thus in this second study two independent variables were manipulated, creating a two-by-three factorial design.

The M.B.A. subjects all read a policy statement. This policy, based on an actual company policy studied by Wilkins (1978), stated that the company would avoid mass layoffs in times of economic difficulty by asking employees to take a temporary 10% cut in pay. In the story condition, the subjects read about a single employee, Phil Locke. The product which was produced by Phil's division was going to have to be discontinued. According to the story, Phil was worried:

*Phil had a wife and two kids. Add to that the usual mortgage payments, car payments, insurance premiums, taxes — you know, he was overextended financially. Well, all that was pretty unsettling for Phil. He's one of those Yankee conservatives who thinks borrowing money is immoral.*

*Phil knew he was really banking on Electrotec's layoff policy. In fact, that policy was one reason why he had come to Electrotec in the first place. Still, he knew he shouldn't depend totally on the company to protect his career and his family's welfare. He began to look at sales jobs at other firms in the area—just in case. The problem was that none of these jobs fit his training and interests as well as the job he already had, and the market was getting worse.*

*Phil was in the cafeteria when his secretary came after him with the news that his boss wanted to see him right away.*

*Phil broke out in a cold sweat as he walked into his boss's office. His boss didn't say much, just something like, "I'm sorry, Phil. I just got the news we've all been dreading; the inertial navigation products are going to be dropped from our line. You and I have been together for a long time, and I will miss you, but . . . "*

Two endings for this story were prepared. Subjects in the policy supporting conditions read that:

*. . . you'll still have a job with Electrotec. I even think we'll be able to set one up for you in one of the other military hardware divisions. Of course, this means a temporary 10% cut in pay." Not fired! Phil said later he felt as if he had been given a reprieve from a death sentence.*

Subjects in the disconfirming conditions read a different ending to the story: "' . . . I have to let you go' Fired! Phil said later he felt as if he had been given the death sentence."

In the statistics conditions subjects were given numerical data concerning the frequencies of turnover (voluntary and involuntary) and paycuts, both before and after the products were discontinued. In the supporting conditions, the turnover data indicated that no mass layoffs had occurred and that most employees had taken a 10% cut in pay after the product was discontinued. In the disconfirming conditions, the frequency of turnover implied that a mass layoff had occurred and that pay cuts were rare. In the combination conditions subjects received either the supporting story plus the supporting statistics or the disconfirming story plus the disconfirming statistics.

When the information supported the policy statement, subjects in the story condition, in contrast to subjects in the combination and statistics

conditions, were more likely to predict that mass layoffs would be avoided, to believe the policy statement was truthful, and to require a larger salary increase before they would quit for a comparable job at another company. The opposite pattern of effects was found when the information disconfirmed the policy condition. The disconfirming story had an impact equal to or less than the impact of the disconfirming statistics or the combination of disconfirming story plus disconfirming statistics.

In summary, when subjects were given information which supported a policy statement and were then asked to make predictions, to assess their belief in the truthfulness of the policy, or to indicate their commitment to the organization, the supporting story had a stronger impact than the other forms of communication. The power of a story however, is not limitless. When the information disconfirmed the policy statement, the story never had a stronger impact, and frequently had a significantly weaker impact, than the disconfirming statistics and the disconfirming combination of story plus statistics.

## CONCLUSIONS

In this final section of the chapter, the theoretical contributions of these experimental results are discussed. The practical implications for organizational employees are outlined and several ethical concerns are raised.

The results of these two studies can be summarized in terms of the two questions raised by the organizational research. First, stories caused commitment. Second, stories caused more commitment than other means of communicating information, such as statistics.

In addition to addressing questions raised by the organizational research, these two experiments extend the results of the cognitive research. A wider range of dependent variables was considered. Whereas previous cognitive research had used dependent measures concerning cognitive judgments, these two experiments also measured belief in the truthfulness of information and commitment to the values underlying the information. The two experiments demonstrated that case examples, such as organizational stories, have strong impact on these attitudes as well as on cognitions.

The second experiment also produced a finding which was not anticipated by previous organizational or cognitive research. It demonstrated a boundary condition or limit to the powerful impact of case examples such as stories. When the content of the information disconfirmed, rather than supported, the policy statement, the story lost its power. Disconfirming statistics had an impact on attitudes and cognitions that was equal to, sometimes even greater than, a disconfirming story. Subjects apparently dismissed the disconfirming story as the single exception to the general rule. The results of the second experiment suggest that if a story is to have strong impact, it must be congruent with prior knowledge.

The results of these two experiments have some clear practical implications. Frequently managers wish to communicate information about a policy change or their philosophy of management. Obviously, they want their messages to be memorable and believable, so that employees will be committed to these ideas. The studies discussed above indicate that the most effective tactic would be to support their points with an organizational story, rather than with statistical information.

Watson, Jr., of I.B.M. was using this tactic when he told the stories about the wild ducks or about the negative reaction to his speech supporting John F. Kennedy. Unfortunately, Watson ran afoul of the boundary condition discovered in the second experiment. He told stories which disconfirmed the employees' prior knowledge about the I.B.M. emphasis on conformity. Consequently, these disconfirming stories were dismissed, by many employees, as corporate propaganda.

The I.B.M. example raises some ethical issues. Employees need to be wary of the potentially powerful impact that a seemingly innocuous story can have. Management, indeed anyone, could use the power of a story to manipulate beliefs about a policy and to generate commitment to an organization when the information is, in fact, corporate propaganda. As this caveat indicates, symbolic forms of management, such as the telling of organizational stories, are powerful and potentially dangerous tools.

## REFERENCES

Azjen, I. Intuitive theories of events and the effects of base-rate information on prediction. *Journal of Personality and Social Psychology*, 1977, thirty-five, 303–314.

Belden, T. G., & Belden, M. R. *The lengthening shadow: The life of Thomas J. Watson.* Boston: Little, Brown, Borgida, E., & Nisbett, R. E. The differential impact of abstract vs. concrete information on decisions. *Journal of Applied Social Psychology*, 1977, seven, 258–271.

Clark, B. *The distinctive college: Antioch, Reed and Swarthmore.* Chicago: Aldine, 1970.

Cohen, P. S. Theories of myth. *Man*, 1969, four, 337–353.

Feldman, N. S., Higins, E. T., Karlovac, M., & Ruble, D. N. Use of consensus information in causal attributions as a function of temporal presentation and availability of direct information. *Journal of Personality and Social Psychology*, 1976, thirty-four, 694–698.

Foy, N. *The sun never sets on IBM.* New York: William Morrow & Company, Inc., 1975.

Hansen, R. D., & Donoghue, J. The power of consensus: Information derived from one's and others' behavior. *Journal of Personality and Social Psychology*, 1977, thirty-five, 294–302.

Kahneman, D., & Tversky, A. On the psychology of prediction. *Psychological Review*, 1973, eighty, 237–251.

Malik, R. *And tomorrow... the world? Inside IBM*. London: Millington HD, 1975.

Malinowski, B. Myth in primitive psychology. In *Magic, science, and religion, and other essays*. Boston: Beach Press, 1948.

Manis, M., Dovalina, I., Avis, N., & Cardoze, S. Base rates can affect individual predictions. *Journal of Personality and Social Psychology*, 1980, thirty-eight, 231–248.

Martin, J. Stories and scripts in organizational settings. In A. Hastprf and A. Isen (Eds.), *Cognitive Social Psychology*. New York: Elsevier-North Holland, Inc., In Press.

Martin, J., & Powers, M. E. *If case examples provide no proof, why under-utilize statistical information?* Paper presented at the meetings of the American Psychological Association, New York, September 1979.

Martin, J., & Powers, M. E. *Skepticism and the true believer: The effects of case and/or base rate information on belief and commitment.* Paper presented at the meeting of the Western Psychological Association, Honolulu, May 1980.

McArthur, L. Z. The how and what of why: Some determinants and consequences of causal attribution. *Journal of Personality and Social Psychology*, 1972. twenty-two, 171–193.

McArthur, L. Z. The lesser influence of consensus than distinctiveness information on causal attributions: A test of the person-thing hypothesis. *Journal of Personality and Social Psychology*, 1976, thirty-three, 733–742.

Meyer, J. W., & Rowan, B. Institutionalized organizations: Formal structure as myth and ceremony. In M. M. Meyer & Associates, *Environment and organizations: Theoretical and empirical perspectives*. San Francisco: Jossey-Bass, Inc., 1978, 78–109.

Nisbett, R. E., & Borgida, E. Attribution and the psychology of prediction. *Journal of Personality and Social Psychology*, 1975, thirty-two, 932–943.

Nisbett, R. E., & Ross, L. *Human inference: Strategies and shortcomings of social judgment*. Englewood Cliffs, N.J.: Prentice-Hall, Inc., 1980.

Ott, R. *Are wild ducks really wild: Symbolism and behavior in the corporate environment*. Paper presented at the meeting of the Northeastern Anthropological Association, March 1979.

Selznick, P. *Leadership and administration*. Evanston, Ill: Row, Peterson, 1957.

Tversky, A., & Kahneman, D. Availability: A heuristic for judging frequency and probability. *Cognitive Psychology*, 1973, five, 207–232.

Watson, Jr., T. J. *A business and its beliefs: The ideas that helped build IBM*. New York: McGraw-Hill Book Company, Inc., 1963.

Wells, G. L., & Harvey, J. H. Do people use consensus information in making causal attributions? *Journal of Personality and Social Psychology*, 1977, thirty-five 279–293.

Wilkins, A. *Organizational stories as an expression of management philosophy: Implications for social control in organizations*. Unpublished doctoral dissertation, Stanford University, 1978.

Wilkins, A., & Martin, J. *Organizational legends* (Research Paper No. 521). Graduate School of Business, Stanford University, 1979.

# SOCIAL INFLUENCE

This section of the book deals with the broad topic of social influence. First you will read about the fundamentals of imitation, conformity, and compliance. Then you will study socialization into organizations. The intricacies of how organizations bring people into the firm, build individual commitment, and shape behavior into a common culture will be discussed from several points of view. You will learn about development of shared beliefs, the pivotal role of the founder in creating an organization's culture, and cross-cultural differences in organizational culture. By the time you finish this section you should therefore have a good picture of how people influence each other in social settings and how organizations can play either a positive or negative role in this shaping.

Next you will turn to a section on diversity and interaction. First is a chapter on the role of women and minorities in management, considering the special hurdles and hazards these parties face in climbing the corporate ladder and exerting influence in organizations. From the topic of women and minorities, the discussion is broadened to the consequences of having a diversity of people in organizations, along with the problems of managing such differences. Finally, the issue of attraction between men and women is addressed. Now that the gender composition of the workforce is becoming equalized, so is the opportunity for more intimate relationships to arise in the organization. Ways of resolving the isssues of attraction, diversity, as well as prejudice against minorities and women are each addressed in this section.

Social power and leadership are considered next. First a chapter is presented which shows how one can exert influence in an organization without formal authority—that is, how to persuade, negotiate, exchange, and cajole others to get things done in a corporation. Then, there is a no-holds-barred look at who attains power and how those in power hold on to their privileges. From this background you will then move to the rather elusive topic of leadership. Four perspectives on leadership are represented here: the path-goal model in which a leader is one who motivates subordinates by helping them achieve their goals; the group participation model in which effective leadership involves the right mix of decision making for each situation; the descriptive model in which leadership is what managers actually do when they work in organizations; and the notion of charismatic leadership in which special characterisitcs or behaviors of the leader are necessary to transform groups and organizations to new states.

Throughout this section you will learn about the strength of the social environment—how other people, groups, and organizations can influence and shape your behavior. Power may thus conjure up manipulative and sinister connotations. Yet, one must keep in mind that knowledge of social influence is important, not only as an instrument of change but as a way to protect oneself against the forces of constancy. If you are going to make an impact on the organization and help lead it in new directions, then the use of power and various forms of social influence are essential to your organizational life.

# Foundations of Social Influence

## 20.  IMITATION, CONFORMITY, AND COMPLIANCE

Leonard Berkowitz

## IMITATION AND MODELING

In some instances an individual follows another's actions in the absence of any social pressures. The other person sets an example which is copied in one way or another. Psychologists usually speak of *imitation* when the observer duplicates what he or she sees fairly closely, but they talk about *modeling* when the examplar's influence is somewhat broader and the observer's action isn't an exact replica of the model's behavior (Bandura, 1969, 1970). Since it is a more extensive concept than imitation, modeling refers to a wider range of processes. The conditions that produce imitation don't necessarily operate in every case of modeling.

Albert Bandura (1969, 1970) at Stanford University is perhaps the leading theorist in this area; he has discussed three kinds of modeling effects: response stimulation (which he terms "response facilitation"), observational learning, and the lowering of inhibitions. We'll follow his analysis with some modifications.

## Response Stimulation

*Reflexive Imitation.* Researchers tell us that several species of animals have a "monkey see, monkey do" tendency, in which one animal sometimes copies the behavior of another almost reflexively (Tolman, 1968). Human infants imitate the facial expressions of nearby adults in this involuntary manner, and even grown-ups may show this simple copying, as when one person's yawn causes a contagion of yawning throughout a group. Most important, this relatively primitive imitation doesn't involve the transmission of information from the model to the observer. The model's action doesn't explicitly tell the observer, "Do what I do if you want to get a reward." The imitation is largely involuntary and can thus be viewed as an instance of our Theme I, involuntary responses to external events.

I occasionally exhibit this kind of reaction on fall Sunday afternoons when I look at football on TV. Watching a particular player closely, not having any distracting thoughts, and not being engaged in any competing activities, I sometimes

---

dart and lunge along with him as he moves. This reflexive copying of another may not have been learned, although learning can add to and complicate the reaction.

A team of investigators at the University of Texas may have observed such a blend of learned reactions and stimulus-elicited copying as they recorded the behavior of pedestrians at a traffic light (Lefkowitz, Blake, & Mouton, 1955).

*At the appropriate time, right after the traffic signal at a busy street corner commanded the pedestrians to "wait," a 31-year-old man (the experimenters' accomplice) disregarded the red light and walked across the street. On some occasions his clothing (business suit, shirt and tie, and highly polished shoes) indicated he had a relatively high social status, whereas at other times he wore soiled and patched work clothes, suggesting that he had a lower status. The violator's apparent social level affected the extent to which the other pedestrians crossed the street with him. As is typical in this kind of situation, the traffic light violator's action probably stimulated some onlookers to move. He started crossing and some other pedestrians automatically did the same thing. But the stimulation effect was greater when the violator seemed to have a high social status. (While only 1 percent of the pedestrians crossed against the traffic when the accomplice hadn't violated the signal, 4 percent of the onlookers disregarded the light when the illegally acting model had low status, and 14 percent crossed when he was well-dressed.) The onlookers may have paid greater attention to the high-status than to the low-status model. Whatever the explanation, in this study one person's movement prompted others to start forward also. . . .*

*The Contagion of Violence.* News stories reporting violent crimes can [also] have [an] imitative effect. The widespread publicity produces a contagion of violence as other persons are stimulated to carry out similar actions. In the late nineteenth century the French sociologist Gabriel Tarde described what he called "suggesto-imitative-assaults." Coining what used to be a well-known phrase, he wrote that epidemics of crime "follow the line of the telegraph." That is, news of a spectacular crime in one community suggests the idea to other people, leading to imitative crimes.

According to Tarde (1912), the brutal Jack the Ripper murders in London inspired a series of female mutilation cases in other sections of England. Police officials in the United States have offered similar observations. The Chicago Police Department reported, for example, that Richard Speck's murder of eight nurses in Chicago in July 1966 and Charles Whitman's shooting of 45 people from the University of Texas Tower the next month were followed by an unusually sharp increase in homicides in Chicago (*Look Magazine*, September 19, 1967). Also, that fall an 18-year-old high school senior shot four women and a child in an Arizona beauty parlor. He told police afterwards that he had gotten the idea for a mass killing from the news stories of the Speck and Whitman crimes.

Other illustrations of the contagion of violence can also be cited if we classify suicides as violence. Evidence (Phillips, 1974) indicates that suicides increase immediately after a suicide story has been publicized in the newspapers. And the greater the publicity devoted to a suicide story, the greater is the subsequent rise in the suicide rate. When movie actress Marilyn Monroe committed suicide, there was a 12-percent increase in the suicides in the United States and a 10-percent rise in England and Wales in the next month. The ideas and feelings evoked in susceptible people when they see these news stories need not produce only a close imitation; they may end their own lives by any available means. In a careful statistical analysis, Phillips (1978) has demonstrated that widely publicized murder-suicides tend to be followed by a significant increase in private and business airplane crashes. The greater the publicity given to any murder-suicide, the more crashes occurred. Some people with suicidal tendencies are apparently stirred to action by news stories of suicides, so that they may use the opportunity of an airplane flight to kill themselves, even if they take other persons' lives as well. . . . You may recall the television movie *The Doomsday Flight.* . . . The film portrays an attempt to extort money from an airline by threatening to blow up a passenger plane in flight. The showing of this movie in the United States and abroad provoked a rash of hoax telephone calls warning about bombs aboard airlines, and some flights had to be re-called or canceled. Indeed, this happened so regularly each time the film was telecast that the Federal Aviation Administration asked television stations not to air it. Similarly, airplane hijackings have shown a contagion effect (see Figure 20.1). Besides giving some people ideas they may otherwise not have had (an involuntary reaction), the story provides information: It tells them how they can get money (or some other goal) and just what they have to do to reach this goal.

A good deal of what we know and much of what we do has been acquired through observational learning. We have learned how to get to some locations in our community, play certain games, put on some items of clothing, and carry out at least part of our jobs by watching other persons engage in similar activities. Adults serve as models for children and deliberately or inadvertently teach them how to behave in various

situations. Parental actions often speak louder than words. Parents frequently exhort their sons and daughters to work hard, although they themselves seem bent on having an easy time; to be honest, although they themselves try to cheat whenever possible; and to be helpful and considerate toward others, although they themselves are often selfish and inconsiderate. Needless to say, youngsters who see adult hypocrisy frequently copy what their parents do and not what they say (Bryan, 1970).

The influence any model will have depends on several considerations. Observers don't automatically learn every detail of the lesson before them. If the learning is to last, the watchers have to *attend* to the model's action and then *rehearse* what they see. Onlookers won't watch the model carefully, however, if they aren't interested in the activity or if the model isn't attractive or prestigious enough to command their attention. Moreover, observers will probably remember the witnessed action better if they describe or repeat the lesson to themselves as they watch (Bandura, Grusec, & Menlove, 1966; Jeffery, 1976).

*Qualities of Influential Models.* The models' characteristics often affect the extent to which their actions are copied, partly by influencing what the observers learn (Bandura, 1969). Especially important is the models' control over the observers' goals (Bandura, Ross, & Ross, 1963; Grusec, 1971; Mischel & Grusec, 1966). If the observers realize that the model can determine whether they will get what they want or whether they'll be punished, they are more likely to look closely at what the model does and to think about his activity, implicitly practicing it, as he performs.

Investigations of the effects of the model's power illustrate how laboratory experiments can throw light on child development. Social scientists have long been interested in *identification*, the process by which a child adopts someone else's qualities and ways of acting.

Bandura et al. (1963) studied identification experimentally by establishing three-person groups composed of two adults and a child to represent the nuclear family—a "father," "mother,"

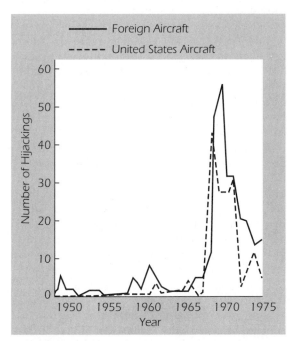

**FIGURE 20.1** The Number of Airplane Hijackings in the United States and Abroad Between 1947 and 1972.

and "child." Researchers' accomplices filled the parental roles, whereas the subject—a nursery-school-aged boy or girl—played the part of the offspring. It was quickly apparent that one of the adults—sometimes the man and sometimes the woman—was the powerful member of the "family" and determined who could play with the attractive toys in the room. As the power in the family, this adult dispensed the rewards. The powerful adult rewarded the subject allowing the rewarded individual to have the attractive toys in some cases and the other adult in other cases. After these conditions had been established, the two adults exhibited distinctively different behaviors while working on another task, and the child was given an opportunity to copy them. Defining "identification" for their purposes as imitation, the psychologists recorded the number of times each child imitated either adult's actions. As Table 20.1 shows, the children were most likely to copy the powerful adult rather than the less powerful one (the sex of the model didn't have any significant effect). Furthermore, the subjects tended to imitate even a powerful model who had been somewhat frustrating to them.

In Bandura et al.'s study (1963) the subjects carried out the novel behaviors they learned, but this is not always the case. People usually don't

**TABLE 20.1**

Mean Number of Imitative Responses Shown by Children in Reaction to Model's Power and Extent to Which the Model Had Rewarded the Subject

| | Object of Imitation | |
|---|---|---|
| Reward Conditions | Powerful Model | Less Powerful Model |
| When other adult is rewarded | 26.88 | 13.60 |
| When the subject is rewarded | 27.46 | 22.38 |

Adapted from Ross A. Bandura and S. A. Ross, "A comparative test of the status envy, social power, and secondary reinforcement theories of identificatory learning." *Journal of Abnormal Social Psychology, 67,* 1963. pp. 527–34. Copyright 1963 by the American Psychological Association. Reprinted by permission of the author.

display the lesson taught to them unless they are also motivated to act. By seeing a violent model we can learn how to be aggressive and even that violence is appropriate behavior in some situations, but we can still restrain ourselves if we think aggression will be punished in the particular setting (Bandura, 1965). Aggressive models can teach others that aggression is sometimes desirable and can even evoke aggressive inclinations (as indicated earlier), but this readiness to carry out the witnessed behavior may not be translated into open action if the observers are strongly inhibited or have good reason to believe that they won't benefit by acting this way or (in the absence of an incentive) if they aren't sufficiently excited as they watch the model's behavior.

The observer's similarity to the model is another important factor affecting the likelihood of imitation. Both children and adults have a greater tendency to copy the actions of someone who is similar to them than of someone who is greatly different (Bandura, 1969). It's easy to see why this should occur. As we watch someone similar to us behave, we're apt to infer that what happens to this individual will also happen to us. We're less likely to make this assumption if we're very different from the person we're observing. If the similar model is rewarded, or at least isn't punished, we're inclined to think our behavior will have the same outcome, and we accordingly imitate the model's behavior.

Bandura (1969) suggested that the most important kind of similarity is *similarity in previous reinforcements.* Let me explain what this concept means. As children grow up, they find that they get the same kind of benefits that certain other persons obtain when they exhibit a given kind of behavior. Susan learns that she and other young girls receive approval when they act like grown-up women in some ways; all of these persons (Susan, other young girls, grown-up women) are thus similarly reinforced for displaying certain actions. This similarity in reinforcement contingencies heightens the chances of imitation, so that Susan will be particularly likely to copy other females. Bussey and Perry (1976) verified this reasoning in an experiment with Australian schoolchildren. When the young boys and girls watched an adult make a series of choices, they were more imitative of the adult in their later choices if they had previously experienced the same reinforcement contingencies as the adult model. That is, when the children saw that both they and the adult had been given the same rewards for doing the same things, they tended to copy the adult's behavior afterwards.

*Seeing Others Be Brave.* Observational learning of the kind described here can have very powerful effects. As a consequence of the experiences (and reinforcements) we share with others in the course of growing up, we can be profoundly influenced by the things we see happen to other persons. We may react emotionally to the painful treatment someone else receives (Berger, 1962) or get over some of our fears by watching other persons act fearlessly. In one experiment (Bandura, Blanchard, & Ritter, 1969) adults who were very afraid of snakes watched a series of models handle snakes. Where many of the adults hadn't been able to even look at the reptiles, after only two hours of exposure to the fearless models, over 90 percent of the subjects could allow a snake to crawl freely over their hands, neck and arms. Seeing someone else be brave can lessen our own fear.

This effect isn't necessarily a matter of putting up a brave front. Let's say that Daphne Wardle is so frightened of electric shocks that she is upset by even the possibility of a mild electrical tingle on her hands. Now imagine that Daphne sees another woman receive a series of electric shocks of increasing intensity and not show any signs of discomfort. Soon afterwards, when it's Daphne's turn to be shocked, she may be able to take a fairly high level of electric shocks herself, higher than otherwise would have been the case. It's not that Daphne is only trying to look just as good as the other woman and is gritting her teeth in order to withstand the pain. If she is typical of the subjects in two experiments reported by Kenneth Craig (Craig & Neidermeyer, 1974; Craig & Prkachin, 1978), the model's fearless response to the shocks could actually make Daphne

experience less pain. The information transmitted by the model's behavior can influence the way that observers interpret their own sensations. To a great extent, our feeling of pain is the result of our interpretations of physical sensations; and these interpretations can be shaped by external events, including the actions of others.

## Raising and Lowering Restraints

In addition to stimulating certain responses within us and teaching us something, a model's behavior or its outcome may also affect our attitude toward the kind of conduct we see. As we look at the model and note what happens to her, we get some idea of the likely consequences should we behave the same way. We're not particularly inclined to copy the model's aggressiveness, at least for a while, if we see her punished for being violent; we may be more willing to emulate her if we see that her conduct pays off (Bandura, 1965).

Our moral judgments can also be temporarily influenced by the events we watch. This has been demonstrated repeatedly in research on movie violence, in my own laboratory (Berkowitz & Geen, 1967; Berkowitz & Rawlings, 1963), elsewhere (Hoyt, 1970; Meyer, 1972), and in experiments with juvenile delinquents as well as with college men (Berkowitz, Parke, Leyens, & West, 1974). All of these studies found that angry subjects became more willing to attack the person who had provoked them earlier if they had just seen a movie "bad guy" get the beating he supposedly deserved, than if they had watched "less justified" aggression in which a sympathetic movie character received unwarranted punishment. The events on the screen apparently colored the subjects' judgment of the propriety of their own aggression. "Good" aggression in the film—a scoundrel supposedly getting what was coming to him— meant that they could hurt the scoundrel in their own lives.

Hollywood movies often portray such "good" aggression. As the hero triumphs over the villains, he frequently beats them up, giving them their just desserts. All this is often emotionally satisfying for the audience—justice has been served, an eye has been given for an eye, equity has been attained, bad people have gotten their deserved punishment. But the "warranted" violence on the screen may also induce angry people in the audience to think (for a short while) that their own aggression is also warranted.

## CONFORMITY: YIELDING TO OTHERS

In most of the above instances an individual imitated the actions of others with relatively little thought or, in other cases, with little questioning. The person wasn't under any social pressure and copied others' behavior quite freely. This type of modeling influence should be differentiated from *conformity*, which social psychologists usually define as yielding to group pressure of some sort. When people conform, they change their behavior or beliefs, moving from an earlier way of acting or thinking toward the position advocated by those around them "as a result of real or imagined group pressure" (Kiesler & Kiesler, 1969). Patricia Hearst's conduct right after she joined the Symbionese Liberation Army may be viewed as conformity. Because of the psychological power the terrorists had over her she may have felt some pressure to conform to her captors' views.

This definition refers to a *change* in behavior or belief, which means that people aren't necessarily conforming when they go along with or act in the same way as others. They could be following a social rule or convention which they accept just because they have grown up in a particular society. When Americans answer the telephone, they usually say "Hello" or give their name, because this is what one does in this type of situation. People can also be conventional in their tastes in home furnishings or clothing. Their choices reflect what they are accustomed to or what they are used to wearing. They haven't given up other tastes or other modes of conduct in response to real or implied pressures.

## The Benefits of Conformity

We are especially likely to accede to social pressures when we think it is to our benefit to do so. On these occasions we follow the old political dictum, "If you want to get along, go along." We realize there's something to be gained by conforming to other persons' views and something to be lost if we are different. This is a very commonplace observation, but it's still impressive how widespread is the tendency to conform in order to avoid social costs.

*The Asch Experiments.* One of the classic demonstrations of people yielding to others can be found in Solomon Asch's research (1958) on conformity, which started in the early 1950s.

Seven male undergraduates listened to the experimenter explain that they were participating in a study of the judgment of perceptual relations. On each trial in the series, the men were told, they would be shown four lines—a standard line and three others of varying lengths. Their task was simply to say which of the latter three lines was the same length as the standard. The experiment began with each subject expressing his judgments aloud. Then, on the third trial, something unexpected happened. To his surprise, subject 6 heard one person after another report that the standard's best match was with line A— which actually appeared somewhat longer than the standard—even though he clearly saw that line C was the closest in length. What should he say when his turn came? The other men were unanimously contradicting the evidence provided by his own senses.

Not realizing that the other undergraduates were the experimenter's confederates and had been instructed to express wrong judgments on certain trials, subject 6 was faced perhaps for the first time in his life with a situation in which he had to decide whether to go along with the group's unanimous judgment or report what his eyes told him was correct. Even though he knew the judgment was incorrect, the typical subject 6 in this study went along with the group on about

4 of the 12 trials in which the majority gave a wrong answer.

This is a graphic case of conformity. The subjects in these experiments seemed to be well aware of the correct answer, yet about one-third of them surrendered to the erroneous majority by voicing the wrong answer. Was it possible that a good portion of those who went along with the majority actually believed that the majority was right? When Asch interviewed his subjects afterwards, many of the conformists claimed that they had thought the majority opinion was probably correct. Since all of the others were in agreement, these subjects said, they suspected something was wrong with their own eyesight. Now, is this the case? Did many of the conformists actually believe the majority judgment was probably right?

An interesting answer to this question is given in a later variation of the Asch experiments. A few years after Asch published the first report of his research, Deutsch and Gerard (1955) repeated the study with some modifications. Most important for our purposes, they established one condition in which subjects could express their estimates anonymously, so that no one else in the group supposedly knew who gave what judgment. This anonymity greatly reduced conformity to the incorrect majority to well below the incidence observed by Asch. Many of the conformists in Asch's initial studies apparently tried to justify their yielding by claiming that they thought the majority was right. They had evidently known the majority was wrong, but went along anyway. Even though the others in the room were strangers whom they might not see again, the yielders publicly conformed to the erroneous majority judgment in order to avoid seeming different.

*Types of Conformity.* In the words of some social psychologists (Kiesler & Kiesler, 1969), Asch's subjects exhibited *compliance* in going along with the others without a true (or private) acceptance of the group's opinions. If the stimulus had been much more ambiguous, so that these subjects hadn't been so certain of what was right, many more of them would have acceded to the group's judgments and would have believed that the majority was probably correct. Deutsch and Gerard used two now well-known concepts to refer to these different kinds of social influence. Adapting their terminology, we would say that the compliance shown by Asch's conformists arose through *normative social influence*; these persons conformed to the others' view because they thought that it would be to their benefit. Other people's opinions are truly accepted, however, when there is *informational social influence*, and other's views are taken "as evidence about reality."

*Independence Versus Rebelliousness.* So far we've been talking about distinctions in cases of going along with others. Are there any differentiations we should make when an individual doesn't follow the others around her? In a variation of the Asch procedure (Milgram, 1961), Norwegian and French university students were led to think that other students occasionally differed with them in judging the duration of sounds. The Norwegians were more inclined than the French to yield to the wrong opinions of their peers. But what were the French students doing when they didn't conform? Were they truly independent in the sense of being indifferent to the majority judgment, or did they notice the majority view and decide to rebel against it? We can't tell which reaction occurred in this situation. Truly *independent* people know what others expect of them, but don't use these expectations as a guide for their own behavior; they are indifferent to them. *Rebelliousness*—or what some social psychologists call *anticonformity*—exists when the individual reacts against the group's expectations and moves away from the actions or beliefs it advocates (Hollander & Willis, 1967).

Perhaps we can apply this distinction between independence and rebelliousness to the social scene of the mid-1960s to early 1970s. Although some young men and women prided themselves on their independence, they weren't indifferent to society's rules and conventions, but only rebelled against them. They were self-conscious rebels rather than being quietly and self-confidently independent.

## Factors Influencing Compliance

*Deviation May Be Dangerous.* Compliance basically arises because we realize that we are likely to be punished in some way if we don't conform. The other people around us are apt to hurt us, psychologically or at times even physically, if we depart from their norms, their standards defining what is proper behavior. For example, throughout much of the 1960s long-haired youths were often subjected to scorn and even harassment because many people assumed that the youths rejected other social norms and values besides those concerned with appearance and dress. Workers in industry frequently apply sanctions against others in their group who deviate from the work norms they've informally agreed on (Homans, 1961). I recently heard that a young and still eager janitor at my university had been punched, harried, and generally mistreated by other janitors in his section who thought he worked too hard and did too much.

Even if the majority is in no real danger as a result of the nonconformist's failure to adhere to its standards, such resistance to the group norm can be disturbing. The deviation may cast doubt on the majority's cherished attitudes and values; seeing the "odd man out" cling to his discrepant views, the majority may begin to wonder if their own beliefs are right (Moscovici & Faucheux, 1972). Young married couples with babies who hear their friends insist that they won't have any children may question the wisdom of their own decision to raise a family. Then too, as some writers have pointed out (Kiesler, 1973), people holding the predominant position often regard the norm violator as disturbingly unpredictable. The deviant may be doing something unexpected when she insists on her unusual views, and this unpredictability can be bothersome.

Most of us are aware of these possibilities. We know that we may be punished by being rejected or by not being liked or worse, and we're inclined to comply with others' expectations, especially if these people can give us something we desire.

*The Person's Goals.* An individual will follow the views of the people around her, even when she doesn't agree with them, if she thinks that compliance will bring her something she wants. On the other hand, if she's basically interested in determining what is the right belief or in defending her own opinion, she may not yield to others' pressure on her to change. She's much more apt to submit if she is concerned with gaining their approval or keeping their goodwill.

Thibaut and Strickland (1956) have demonstrated how a person's goals can affect his reaction to group pressures. Male students at the University of North Carolina were assembled in small groups and required to make complex judgments of physical stimuli. Each subject was induced to become somewhat committed to his initial opinion (by telling him he would have to justify his answers later). Then the experimenter led him to think that the other group members unanimously disagreed with him. At this point the student received written messages, ostensibly from his partners, which put either high, moderate, or low pressure on him to alter his judgment. Crosscutting this variation, half of the subjects were made to be concerned about the task and about getting the best answer to the problem, while the others were led to be more interested in their social relationships.

The proportion of subjects in each condition who conformed to group pressure is shown in Figure 20.2. Look first at the responses of those who were primarily interested in getting the best answer to the problem. Being somewhat committed to their own ideas, the more pressure the other persons placed on them, the more likely these subjects were to hold on to their initial beliefs. The subjects who were problem oriented evidently experienced reactance ... and resented the pressure on them to change; they were apt to cling doggedly to their own views. However, the students who were concerned with their social relationships showed a very different pattern. The greater the pressure the other group members imposed on them, the more likely they were to yield and go along with them.

Many Americans appear to be equally concerned with their social relationships. When we meet someone new, we usually want to get along

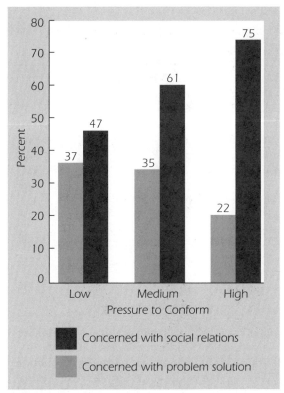

**FIGURE 20.2** Percentage of Subjects Yielding to a Fictitious Majority Under Different Degrees of Group Pressure.

with her or even be liked by her. If we aren't strongly committed to a particular attitudinal position, we may be inclined to accede to her opinions, at least overtly, in order to win her acceptance, especially if we know we'll meet again in the future (Lears, et al., 1972).

Many of us especially desire to be accepted after we find that we've expressed deviant views on some issue. Knowing that people are usually suspicious of those who are "different," we may become anxious at learning we've just voiced a minority opinion. If we have another opportunity to state our beliefs (on another issue) right afterwards, we may take care to go along with someone else in order to avoid being frowned on as an oddball (Darley, Moriarty, Darley, & Berscheid, 1974).

*The Others' Attractiveness.* While many of us seek the approval of strangers, we are even more intent on keeping the goodwill of those who are attractive to us. We like being with them and would be hurt if they rejected us. The more we care for people, the more apt we are to go along with their views if we know how they want us to act and if they can see what we do (Berkowitz, 1954). Unless we're very sure of these people, we don't want to risk offending them by conspicuously departing from their standards.

There may be personality differences in this regard, however. In connection with the Thibaut and Strickland study, we saw that conformity is heightened when a person is interested in social relationships with others rather than in getting the best answer. Some individuals are preoccupied with having others like them, while other persons mainly want to find out what's right. The former are more inclined to yield to the majority's opinions (McDavid, 1959) and are probably also particularly responsive to the views of people they find attractive. By contrast, people who usually focus on learning the correct solution tend to go along with unattractive people as readily as with those they find attractive (Wilson, 1960).

## Social Status and Compliance

Much of what we have been discussing can be translated into power terms. When we learn that other people are important to us because they can either provide us with the rewards we greatly desire or punish us in ways we especially fear (for example, by rejecting us), we come under their control to a considerable extent. They have some power over us. Attractive people have power over us because they control something we want—their approval. An individual's status in a group often determines how much power the other group members have over him and how much influence he can exert over them.

*Low Status.* We are in a very precarious position if we have low status in our group, aren't well accepted by the others, or are afraid that we may be completely excluded. Clinging to our precious foothold in the group—maybe even hoping we can better our position—we walk the straight and narrow, not daring to deviate openly from the group's standards. We may not even like the other group members because they don't seem to care for us, so that we don't truly adopt their point of view (Dittes & Kelley, 1956). However, such surface compliance comes about when the low-status individual is interested in maintaining or even improving her standing in the group. If we've given up on the others, we won't bother to hide our real opinions and will show our noncompliance (Harvey & Consalvi, 1960).

*High Status.* The high-status group member is in a much more fortunate position, especially if his rank is unlikely to change. His status gives him the security to express disagreement if he differs from the majority at any time. Norma Feshbach (1967) assembled four-man groups of fraternity members, seeing that two of the members were among the most popular people in the fraternity (high status) and the other two were relatively unpopular (low status). Moreover, the high- and low-status members had the task of deciding which card of the two presented to them on each trial contained the greater number of dots. Even though incorrect estimates would hurt their group and possibly cost their fraternity a $25 prize, the low-status members were generally reluctant to disagree with the high-status members' incorrect judgments. When each person was misled into thinking that his partners were unanimously wrong, the high-status fraternity members were much more willing to deviate from this view than were their less popular counterparts.

There are most likely two interrelated reasons for the high-status fraternity members' feeling that they could safely stand apart from their group. One has to do with differences in power. The highly popular people were undoubtedly aware that their partners needed their approval more than they required these others' goodwill. Then too, groups may actually permit high-status members greater freedom to deviate from the majority position. These persons are often given "idiosyncrasy credit," as Hollander (1958) put it, and allowed to be oddballs.

I suspect that high-status members who occupy a formally designated position symbolizing the group's ideals, such as the president of the United States or the king of England, don't have an idiosyncrasy credit in matters that are important to the group. Indeed, they probably have less freedom to deviate from approved standards in these areas than the average group member. Edward VIII couldn't marry a divorced woman and remain king; and Princess Margaret was discouraged from marrying a divorced man, even though a British commoner could do so without suffering ostracism. The group may hold fairly stringent expectations for certain high-status members on important matters at least, and would be quite annoyed if the high-status people violated these expectations (Wahrman, 1970).

## Compliance with Authority

In January 1942 a group of top-level civil servants in the Nazi government met in a suburb of Berlin to coordinate efforts to the Final Solution, Hitler's plan to exterminate the Jews of Europe. Adolf Eichmann, head of the Jewish Office in the German Secret Police, or Gestapo, was impressed by the meeting. Here he was chatting and drinking with high governmental officials, despite his humble background.

*There was another reason that made the day ... unforgettable for Eichmann. Although he had been doing his best right along to help with the Final Solution, he had still harbored some doubts about "such a bloody solution through violence," and these doubts had now been dispelled. "Here now ... the most prominent people had spoken. ..." Not only Hitler ... not just the S.S. or the Party, but the elite of the good old Civil Service were vying and fighting with each other for the honor of taking the lead in these bloody matters. "At that moment, I sensed a kind of Pontius Pilate feeling, for I felt free of all guilt." Who was he to judge? (Arendt, 1963, p. 101).*

Eichmann was reassured and led to believe that the plan must be all right, since all these important people agreed on it. As he told the court during his trial in Jerusalem in 1961, his conscience was soothed because "he could see no one, no one at all, who actually was against the Final Solution" (quoted in Arendt, 1963, p. 103). Moreover, even if he had any misgivings in the coming months and years, as millions of Jewish men, women, and children were slaughtered, he could always tell himself that "This was the way things were, this was the new law of the land, based on the Fuhrer's order; whatever he did he did, as far as he could see, as a law-abiding citizen. He did his duty, as he told the [Jerusalem] court over and over again; he not only obeyed orders, he also obeyed the law" (Arendt, 1963, p. 120).

"Following orders" is a defense that the German generals were to repeat again and again after World War II: "I wasn't really responsible for the deaths of those thousands of civilians ruthlessly shot by my soldiers; I was a soldier myself, obeying a superior's orders" (see, for example, Shirer, 1960, p. 380). The Germans aren't the only ones who have tried to excuse or explain their actions in such terms. In every country "good soldiers" have said that if they hurt someone in the performance of their duties, they were absolved of blame because they were only following orders or obeying the law. Hannah Arendt, the author of the book on Eichmann just cited, has maintained that this pattern of behavior is now all too prevalent in our society. Western history, she believes, has produced a type of official who, "for the sake of his pension, his life insurance, the security of his wife and children [is] prepared to do literally anything" (Arendt, 1978). He follows his superiors' orders, partly because he believes they have the right to tell him what to do, but also because he believes compliance is to his benefit.

In some ways, such compliance is part of an age-old problem: the relation of the individual to the authority systems of society, or the conflict between personal freedom and the requirements of the social order. Long before the rise of Nazi Germany, the Greek philosopher Plato asked whether a person is obliged to obey an unjust law. Plato's teacher Socrates had thought there were only a few limited alternatives to

obedience to the state and had accepted his society's right to condemn him to death.

*The Right to Give Orders.* We have now observed that people have sometimes given other persons the right to tell them what to do in some domains of life. In my view, this permission may be an automatic, relatively unthinking, response (Theme I) to persons who carry the symbols of legitimate authority.

The social order is a network of interlocking roles and statuses in which some positions have authority over other roles. Thus, judges can impose fines, parents can legitimately tell children what to do in some situations, teachers can influence their students' activities in the classroom, and employers can properly direct their workers. These expectations hold for subordinates as well as for those exerting power, so that on at least some occasions, most of us think we ought to obey those having recognized authority over us.

*Research on Reactions to Legitimate Authority.* A well-known research program conducted by Stanley Milgram (1963), now of the City University of New York, demonstrates how many United States citizens have learned to follow the dictates of those in authority.

Milgram's male subjects, recruited by newspaper ads, had a much more diverse background than is customary in psychological experiments. They were blue-collar workers, salesmen, businessmen, and professionals between 20 and 50 years of age. Each man thought he was a "teacher" in a learning experiment who had the job of punishing another subject (actually the investigator's accomplice) each time that person made a mistake on the learning task. The teacher was to administer electric shocks as the punishment, increasing the shock intensity regularly as the mistakes continued. The "mistakes" were prearranged so that each subject was required to raise the shock intensity 30 times, supposedly in 15-volt steps, going from 15 to 450 volts, with the last electric switch bearing the sign, "Danger, Severe Shock." If the subject seemed reluctant to proceed with this assignment and was slow to go on to the next shock switch, the watching experimenter instructed him to continue, even though the confederate learner in the next room occasionally pounded the wall and cried out in pain. No one was really shocked, but almost every subject thought he was hurting the person next door (although he had been reassured that there would be "no permanent tissue damage").

All of the subjects complied with the experimenter's orders until they reached the 300-volt level (switch 20), the point at which the learner next door began pounding the wall. Either then or at the next switch, 22 percent refused to continue despite the experimenter's insistence. A few more went a little bit further and then refused to go on. But only a minority resisted the authority of the experimenter; 65 percent obeyed the instructions and steadily increased the punishment they inflicted up to the maximum, and supposedly dangerous, level. They believed they were hurting someone badly, yet they did what they were told.

Other experiments have since determined how our willingness to inflict pain in response to the dictates of authority is affected by various situational conditions. For example, Milgram (1965) found that the investigator's commands became less effective as the victim's suffering was made clearer. While only 35 percent of the subjects refused to follow the experimenter's orders at some point in the procedure when the victim was next door, about 60 percent defied the authority's instructions before they reached the maximum intensity if the victim was in the same room, and 70 percent refused to go all the way if they had to forcibly hold the victim's hand on the shock-plate as the shocks were administered. Evidently, it became more difficult for the subjects to hurt someone in compliance with orders when they could readily see the consequences of their acquiescence (also see Tilker, 1970). They couldn't keep punishing the victim severely unless they had a strong respect for the authority or, possibly, a low regard for the victim.

Another factor is also at work here. Notice that subjects showed the greatest resistance to authority when they had to hold the victim down. These men couldn't pass the buck; they couldn't tell themselves that they were passively following orders because they actively contributed to the injury done to the other person. So they had to take some of the blame if they continued. Not wanting to feel personal responsibility for the pain they inflicted, they defied their instructions. Two other experiments—one in West Germany (Mantell, 1971) and the other in the United States (Tilker, 1970)—have shown that many people are reluctant to hurt others if they have to take personal responsibility for their actions. Thus, in the West German study (Mantell, 1971), only 7 percent of the "teachers" gave the maximum shocks when they were told it was up to them to decide whether and how much the "learner" was to be punished. By contrast, in the baseline condition (exactly the same as Milgram's original condition) 85 percent of the subjects administered the maximum punishment.

We can easily translate the research on obedience to authority into terms applicable to our own country. Suppose you were an American soldier in Vietnam in the late 1960s. On patrol in possibly dangerous territory, your platoon enters a small village. Everyone is on edge, even scared. Then your commanding officer orders the platoon to shoot any Vietnamese on sight. What would you do? Would you obey orders?

*Unthinking Reactions to Legitimate Authority.* Authorities are obeyed to a very substantial extent because we have learned to give them the right to tell us what to do in certain situations. Much of the time we don't have to be forced to comply. Indeed, coercion is unlikely to hold an organization together for long. If the group is to be stable, its members must submit voluntarily to those in command (Weber, 1947). As the eminent sociologist Robert Nisbet (1970) observed, "For most persons, most of the time, in most places, the authorities they obey are perceived as legitimate authorities. Obedience is willed, or at least not checked, in light of this legitimacy" (p. 140). As one testimonial to the power of legitimacy, the West German version of Milgram's study (Mantell, 1971) demonstrated a drop in subjects' compliance with the experimenter's instructions when his legitimacy was undermined. The subjects accorded him less right to control their actions when they didn't think his job was to tell them what to do.

Since the authority's legitimacy is so important, any comprehensive analysis of compliance requires a greater understanding of the sources of legitimacy than we now possess. Why are some people empowered with the right to influence others, and—an especially intriguing question nowadays—why do previously accepted authorities sometimes come under attack so that their areas of influence shrink?

Probably more than any other factor, *collective approval*—the agreement of the group members—legitimates the patterns of dominance and subordination in the group (Blau, 1964). In our society, collective approval usually becomes explicit when someone is elected to the authority role. What we often see, then, is that election justifies the adoption of power. We may strongly oppose a politician's candidacy in an election campaign, but if she is elected we usually accept her right to exert the authority of the office. By the same token, when a person in a small work group starts telling the other group members what to do, these people are more apt to feel that he has a right to prescribe behavior for them if he has been elected to the supervisory position than if he has simply usurped this job. And in the former case, group members are also more inclined to adopt the leader's prescriptions as their own beliefs (French & Raven, 1959; Raven & French, 1958); the election has legitimated his influence attempts.

The great sociological theorist Max Weber (1947) has also pointed out that legitimacy is frequently derived from rational considerations. Modern societies tend to regard authorities as legitimate if they operate in a reasonable manner. Thus, the authorities exercise their control on the basis of their knowledge rather than because they have been born into the right family or group. Evan and Zelditch (1961) used this conception in a laboratory analog of a bureaucratic organization. In this experiment college students worked under the guidance of an appointed supervisor, who they were led to believe knew either more, the same, or less about the job than they did. Supervisors should be more expert than their subordinates, and their appointment isn't reasonable (or legitimate) if they know less. In keeping with Weber's view, the students were more disobedient to the supervisor's commands, particularly in hard-to-see ways, if his knowledge was supposedly inferior to theirs. His position was apparently not totally legitimate if it had an illogical basis.

*Some Concluding Thoughts.* Authority is not a simple matter, and there is no easy way to eliminate the wrongs committed in authority's name. As long as society continues, some people will violate the trust we place in them or abuse the power given them or hurt other persons if they think their job requires this. But we can't do away with all authority. Even the leading theorists of the anarchist movement thought that some authority was necessary and indispensable (Nisbet, 1970, p. 141). Every social order must have a regulatory system (hopefully one that is humane and just), an agreed-upon conception of what is legitimate authority, and a widespread willingness to comply with the rules laid down in the appropriate, "proper" manner—or else brute force will control how people interact. Maybe, as some writers have suggested and as the founders of the American Republic recognized, it is best to have institutionalized checks and balances in which countervailing authorities press against each other. "Whether authority is in fact limited or total depends upon norms of freedom and authority . . . and also . . . upon the degree to which that authority is checked, limited, challenged, and countervailed by other authorities in the social order" (Nisbet, 1970, p. 135).

## TRUE ACCEPTANCE OF OTHERS' STANDARDS

### Social Consensus and Informational Influence

*Authoritative Opinions.* Most of us not only comply with the dictates of authority, but frequently think that the attitudes or practices advocated by government officials are correct. Throughout the Johnson and Nixon administrations, millions of Americans approved of the Vietnam war because this was the President's policy. Since the government had undertaken to fight this war, many citizens believed that it must be the right thing to do. Similarly, when English university students were told that laws defined certain behaviors as legal (or illegal), their judgments of the moral propriety of these actions were correspondingly affected to a slight but significant degree (Berkowitz & Walker, 1967). Actions certified by legal authority gained in moral rightness, whereas conduct condemned by the laws was regarded more morally improper than it had been before.

*Consensus and the Social Definition of Reality.* There are a number of reasons why legitimate authority can validate particular opinions or actions. One possibility has to do with the social consensus implicitly supporting the authority. We're generally aware that duly constituted government ultimately rests upon the approval of the governed. Thus, a law is implicitly right or correct to the extent that it is backed by a widespread social consensus. The obvious defiance of the no-liquor laws of the Prohibition era probably further weakened their effectiveness; people who once thought Prohibition was a good idea no longer backed this policy when they saw that many of their peers disapproved of it.

Adolf Eichmann's belief that the Final Solution was a proper course of action is also a testimony to the power of social consensus. His doubts about "such a bloody solution through violence" were largely obliterated by the agreement of the top-level officials meeting to implement the plan. Not one person disagreed with the proposal, he said, so he thought it must be all right.

In all of these instances the group consensus defined the validity, the correctness, perhaps even the "truth," of the issue. We can look at this in terms of Theme III and say that the agreement among the people in the situation affected any one person's interpretation of the ambigu-

ous stimulation (that is, the nature of the information received). As some social psychologists have stated, the consensus provided a social definition of reality. Social agreement creates reality in many different walks of life and even, to some extent, in the Asch experiment and its later variations. Earlier in this chapter I mentioned the variation of Asch's experiment in which the subjects were permitted to express their views anonymously (Deutsch & Gerard, 1955). Although this procedure reduced the amount of compliance to the erroneous majority opinion, as I reported, a small number of subjects still yielded to the majority view. These few were apparently so lacking in self-confidence that they doubted their own senses in the face of others' unanimity. Questioning themselves, they thought the others might be right since everyone else had the same judgment.

*The Sherif Experiment.* A classic experiment carried out by Muzafer Sherif (1936) in the mid-1930s illustrates how agreement among the members of a group can define reality. In contrast to the Asch study, where the subject could easily see what was right, the situation was much more ambiguous in Sherif's experiment.

In this investigation, the subject sat in a completely darkened room along with two other college students, looking at a point of light waving back and forth in the distance. The walls were not visible, nor were there any other physical frames of reference for subjects to use in their task of judging how far the light moved as it followed its erratic course in the darkness. Because the stimulus was so ambiguous, the three people didn't "see" it in exactly the same way at first. After a while, however, their estimates converged. They developed a common perception, a shared way of viewing the light. In the next phase of the experiment the subject was alone in the darkened room, and he again had to say how far the light moved. As he stared at the faint glow, he wondered if the light was acting in the same way as before. Yes it was, he decided. It appeared to be moving just as much as it had in the group session.

Unknown to the subject, however, the light actually was physically stationary at all times and only *seemed* to be moving, an illusion called the "autokinetic effect." The ambiguous stimulus was defined in a certain way by the group, and the subjects then carried the group's definition with them when they were alone. This earlier experience in the group taught them how to view the stimulus.

*Social Support May Break Consensus.* We can also see the effects of consensus when we look at what happens when the group's unanimity is broken. In Asch's original research the subjects were less likely to yield to the erroneous majority when there was another dissident in the room than when they were alone against the group. Destroying the group's unanimity increased the student's resistance to the pressures of the majority. There are several reasons for this finding. For example, the naive subject may have been less afraid of being ostracized or laughed at if someone else also refused to go along with the group. In addition, the other deviant (who gave his judgments before subject 6 did) might have weakened the group's credibility—the majority opinion seemed less right—and also heightened the individual's confidence in his own belief.

An experiment by Allen and Levine (1969) at the University of Wisconsin shows how the group's credibility is lessened when the members are no longer unanimous.

Using a modification of the Asch procedure devised by Crutchfield, the psychologists placed five people in separate booths. Each subject was told he would be the fifth person in the group to express his answer to the presented problem and that signal lights in his cubicle would let him know how each of the others had responded.... Unknown to the subjects, these lights were actually controlled by the experimenter, who gave each student prearranged information about his partners' views.

The first three persons answering were always in agreement, and on the 18 critical trials they expressed highly unusual judgments (as determined by prior testing with college students) that were different from the subjects' own opinions. The fourth member's answers varied with the experi-

mental condition. In the social support condition his responses were in complete accord with the subjects' judgments (which had been ascertained previously), while in the extreme dissent condition his answers were even more incorrect than those stated by the erroneous majority. Finally, in the no-support condition the fourth person always went along with the majority. Thus, there were two conditions in which the group consensus was lowered; but only in the first of these treatments, the social support group, did the deviant agree with the subject's own views.

The subjects were given three types of problems—visual (as in the original Asch experiment), information, and opinion. Allen and Levine found that the weakened group consensus in both the social support and extreme dissent conditions significantly reduced the level of conformity to the incorrect majority on the visual and information items, and substantially decreased the yielding to the majority on the opinion items (see Figure 20.3). However, on the opinion items there was less conformity in the social support than in the extreme dissent treatment.

As Allen and Levine (1969) suggest, most people probably expect complete agreement on factual matters such as the visual and information problems. Should the consensus be less complete, the group is regarded as a defective judge of reality and can be disregarded. In other words, on objective problems it doesn't matter whether others agree with us or if they have another judgment; as long as the group is not unanimous, its credibility is suspect. On more subjective issues, such as opinions, we're not surprised if there's less than perfect agreement. In this case we usually think that the greater the consensus, the greater the probability that the others may be right. But if someone sides with us on such ambiguous issues, we're more confident of our own judgments (Allen & Levine, 1971). Social agreement defines reality primarily in subjective matters for which we know there is no single, unquestioned truth.

Another study indicates that the time at which its consensus is broken can be very important in

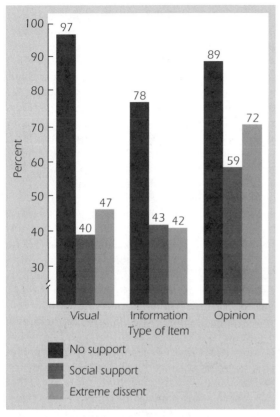

**FIGURE 20.3** Mean Conformity to Majority as a Function of Type of Item and Type of Support.

## Influence of the Minority on the Majority

Until now we've focused on the effects of the group on the individual. Two French social psychologists, Moscovici and Faucheux (1972), have pointed out, however, that such a one-sided emphasis neglects the considerable impact that a few determined persons sometimes have on the larger group. Every now and then a small band has triumphed over the many, convincing a once scornful majority to accept ideas it had previously rejected. History has been made by such innovators as Copernicus in astronomy, Luther in religion, and Freud in psychology. If social psychology is to say anything about social innovations, it must consider the minority's influence as well as the majority's power.

Moscovici and his associates (Moscovici & Faucheux, 1972; Moscovici & Nemeth, 1974) have argued that a persistent few can change the prevailing group norms by maintaining their own deviant views consistently, coherently, and forcefully. The minority's continuous and determined pressure raises doubts where certainty existed before. The others begin to wonder if the majority consensus does indeed define what is true or correct, and they open their minds to the ideas they repudiated earlier. Thus, in keeping with our present information-processing theme (Theme III), a determined minority can influence the majority by shaping the majority's understanding. Other investigators have obtained some evidence consistent with this reasoning (see Nemeth & Wachtler, 1974).

*Reasonably Self-confident.* According to this later research, dedicated dissidents are particularly likely to be convincing when they express their minority views with confidence and with reason. Let's suppose that Daphne Wardle is involved in an argument with the other women in her dormitory and finds herself holding a minority position. Where most of the residents favor one policy, Daphne and one or two others prefer a very different proposal. How can Daphne convince the majority? Well, an experiment by a Swiss psychologist (Mugny, 1975) tells us she should appear firm, but not dogmatic. In this study a

determining the amount of power the majority will have over the individual. According to Morris and Miller (1975), we are less likely to go along with a majority holding a very different view if someone else expresses a judgment close to our own ideas before we hear the people in the majority. Then, when it's our turn to offer an opinion, we're more likely to hold on to our own judgment. The other person's initial statement corroborates our own first thoughts, strengthening our confidence in our own views, so that we can withstand the majority's divergent judgment. More strongly convinced of the rightness of our initial opinion because of the support provided by the other person, we don't believe the majority has correctly defined what is real and true. . . .

group member's minority opinion was less likely to be accepted by the others if he seemed to be rigidly dogmatic rather than reasonably firm. The people in the majority were more inclined to go along with the deviant when he acknowledged that their views were reasonable while arguing for his position.... If we want to convince other persons, we're often better off if we don't flatly repudiate their beliefs in a head-on confrontation. But the minority has to seem self-confident; individuals who appear very sure of themselves are especially likely to be influential (Spitzer & Davis, 1978). Charlan Nemeth and her colleagues (Nemeth, Swedlund, & Kanki, 1974; Nemeth & Wachtler, 1974) have demonstrated that dissidents can waver occasionally and still be convincing, as long as their variations don't create an impression of uncertainty. Thus, Daphne Wardle doesn't have to be rigidly consistent if she states her views with confidence.

As I said before, this self-assurance makes the people in the majority question the correctness of their own beliefs and causes them to wonder if the minority isn't right after all. But the minority's persuasiveness is also helped by anything else that adds credence to its position, such as someone's past history of success and even the size of the minority.

*Minority Size and the Perceived Correctness of the Minority.* Consider the matter of the minority's size. Would Daphne Wardle be better off in her efforts to convince the majority in her dormitory if she had only a few people on her side or if she had lots of adherents?

Nemeth pointed out that we can expect two different things to happen as the minority gets larger (Nemeth, Wachtler, & Endicott, 1977). For one thing, the majority may assume that the dissidents are less self-confident as their numbers grow. Think of this in attribution theory terms. If a single person holds out as the lone dissenter against the pressure of the majority, we tend to assume this individual must be quite self-confident. The majority thus attributes the deviation to an internal factor, the person's self-assurance. However, the discounting principle may come into

play as the minority gets larger.... We tend to rule out internal factors as a possible cause of someone's behavior if we can reasonably attribute the action to external circumstances (Kelley, 1972, 1973). This means observers will be less likely to believe that any one deviant is self-confident, the more dissidents there are. The majority assigns the minority's stance to an external factor (the support the dissidents provide each other) and not to internal self-confidence. On the other hand, as Nemeth also noted, increased numbers may also enhance the perceived correctness of the minority position, as when social consensus defines reality in ambiguous matters. The more people there are who share a given opinion, up to some maximum number, the more likely it is that we will think they are probably right (Asch, 1958). Putting all of these findings together, we would expect an increasing minority to be regarded as (1) somewhat less self-confident, but (2) more correct.

Nemeth et al. (1977) examined the effect of the minority's size upon its persuasiveness as a function of the two components of perceived self-confidence and correctness. Undergraduate women were assembled in groups of six naive subjects together with a certain number of investigators' confederates. Some groups had only one confederate, other groups had two, and some other groups had either three or four confederates. All of the people in the group had to express judgments about the colors of stimuli that were shown to them, but where the naive subjects in the majority were quite sure these stimuli were blue, the confederates adopted the minority position and persisted in labeling the stimuli "blue-green."

The subjects' ratings of the minority at the end of the session are summarized in Table 20.2. As you can see, the larger the size of the minority, the more correct (competent), but less self-confident, they were thought to be. In this study at least, the minority's perceived correctness was generally more important than their self-assurance in determining their persuasiveness. In general, even though the majority rejected the dissident viewpoint most of the time (the

**TABLE 20.2**
Reactions of Majority Members to Those in Minority

| | Minority Size | | | |
|---|---|---|---|---|
| | 1 | 2 | 3 | 4 |
| Number of times minority judgment was adopted* | 1.35 | 1.31 | 2.25† | 1.88 |
| Perceived confidence of minority‡ | 5.67 | 5.22 | 5.29 | 5.13 |
| Perceived competence of minority‡ | 3.78 | 4.28 | 4.42 | 4.52 |

*In the control condition containing no confederates, no subject ever gave the response persistently voiced by the confederates.

† This mean is significantly greater than the mean in the one-confederate condition.

‡ There were siginifcant linear trends for these two measures so that we can say there was a regular decrease in the minority's assumed confidence and a regular increase in their perceived competence.

Data from Nemeth et al. (1977).

stimulus was much too clear-cut), the naive subjects were somewhat more accepting of the minority judgment, the more people there were in the minority. Despite this finding, other evidence indicates that both the perceived self-confidence and the perceived correctness of the minority contributed to the minority's influence. When the researchers formed a composite index based on the subjects' ratings of both of these qualities, this combination was a better predictor of the minority's influence than either characteristic alone.

If we can generalize from this particular experiment, Daphne would be well advised to seek additional adherents to her cause. The other women might think Daphne and her supporters weren't especially self-confident, but the dissident arguments might appear more valid as the minority grew.

*Breaking the Majority's Consensus.* Just as the dissidents' consensus can affect the onlookers' estimate of how correct their own opinions are, so can agreement among the majority influence its members' confidence in their own viewpoint.

This point has implications for how the minority may go about convincing the majority. What happens, we may ask, if some people desert the majority cause and take up the minority opinion? Kiesler and Pallak's study (1975) indicates that those in the minority should "chip away" at a susceptible member of the majority in order to get her over to their side. The people who remain in the majority aren't going to like the "switcher," according to Kiesler and Pallak, and may even regard her as a renegade, but the switch tends to make the majority lose confidence. "Maybe there's a good reason why that person joined the other side," they think. As their doubts mount, they can be more easily persuaded by the persistent minority.

My impression is that this type of process was at work in the United States during the Vietnam War. As the war continued, quite a few people who initially supported the United States government's policy in Asia began to side with the antiwar protestors. The former supporters' desertion of the majority cause undoubtedly contributed to the majority's growing doubts about the wisdom of continuing the struggle.

## SELF-PERCEPTION IN COMPLIANCE

### Low Balling the Customer

Joe Arbuthnot received a substantial amount of money as a birthday present and decided to buy a new car. Determined to be a smart customer, he told a salesperson at one of the largest automobile dealerships in the city that he would only buy a new car from that firm if he received a good deal on his present vehicle as a trade-in. The salesperson assured Joe he would get the best trade-in value in town, and Joe chose the new model he wanted. But when Joe sat down to sign the necessary papers for the purchase, the salesperson told Joe that the manager would have to approve the amount offered for Joe's old car. In a little while the salesperson returned and said the manager had rejected the trade-in price. The manager was supposed to have said that the firm wouldn't make enough money on the sale if he paid that much for Joe's old car. If Joe wanted the new automobile he had selected, he would have to spend several hundred dollars more than he had thought just a few minutes earlier.

Joe's experience wasn't unique. He was the victim of "low balling," a reprehensible but widespread practice used by many salespeople, especially in the automobile industry (*Consumer Reports,* May 1974, p. 368). The idea is to get the customer committed to the purchase on the basis of a very favorable deal and then eliminate some of the favorable features after the customer is "hooked." Joe had made his decision after being told he would have to pay only a certain amount of money for the new car. However, once Joe "bit" and was psychologically committed to the purchase, the salesperson informed him that he would have to spend more. ¡This manipulative technique is frequently effective.

I think we can see why low balling works if we look at it in connection . . . with the self in social behavior. A customer who agrees to make the purchase does two things: (1) He *activates* his intentions. . . . It's not enough just to expect or intend to do something. We also have to think *actively* of carrying out that behavior if the intention is to be translated into action (Leventhal, Singer, & Jones, 1965). Thus, the customer's decision to buy the product could start him moving psychologically toward that goal. (2) As Cialdini, Cacioppo, Bassett, and Miller (1978) have suggested, the decision makes the customer feel *personally committed* to the purchase. From our present point of view, we can say his failure to carry through might then reflect negatively on his self-image. "I agreed to do this and I should be consistent," he may tell himself.

Cialdini et al. (1978) have reported three experiments which testify to the effectiveness of the low-balling technique. These investigations were carried out in naturalistic and artificial settings. We'll discuss their last study, which provides a good example of low balling. Male and female undergraduates serving in the study to gain extra class credit were told that the research required them to take one of two different personality tests, and they were provided with a brief description of the tests. In two conditions (both analogs of the low-balling procedure) the students were informed that they would receive twice as much credit if they worked on one test (call it test A) rather than on the other. And one of these groups was also told the choice was up to the subjects. Needless to say, when the people in this group made their selection right after this, they overwhelmingly preferred test A. The subjects in the second condition had no choice and were instructed to work on test A. After the students in these two conditions had rated their impressions of the personality tests, the experimenter supposedly noticed that he had made a mistake and said he wouldn't be able to award the extra credit for test A. Then, whether or not they had been told the choice was up to them, all of the people in these conditions were instructed that they were free to work on either of the two tests. In a third, control condition the experimenter didn't say anything about extra credit for test A. Here too, the subjects were asked which test they wanted to take after they read the description of the tests.

The findings indicated the students typically wanted to carry through with the commitment they had voluntarily undertaken, even when the extra inducement used to win this commitment was withdrawn. Sixty-one percent of the subjects in the choice condition still agreed to do test A, as compared to only 42 percent of those in the no-choice group and 31 percent in the control condition.

Most of the students in the choice group evidently wanted to be consistent. They had freely agreed to carry out the given activity (they thought), and they went through with it. Their self-image would suffer if they changed their mind. Of course, many more subjects would have refused to honor this commitment if they believed they had been tricked into making their decision. In real life, people can stop such manipulation if they realize the salesperson's initial offer may simply be a trick to get them hooked on the line before the attractive inducement is withdrawn.

## The Foot in the Door

Low balling is quite similar to another procedure used by salespeople and others. In this second technique the would-be influencer makes a small and fairly reasonable request in order to get a foot in the door. When the unknowing individual complies, the influencer then brings the real major request forward.

Two well-known field experiments by Jonathan Freedman and Scott Fraser (1966) illustrate how effective this procedure can be. In one of these investigations the experimenters started out with a small request. They asked housewives to install a small sign on their lawns urging motorists to drive carefully. Several weeks later, when other interviewers contacted the women and asked them to put up a monstrous sign with the same message, three-quarters of them complied. By contrast, fewer than one-fifth of another group of women who hadn't received the first request agreed to install the large, ugly sign. The researchers had increased their persuasiveness by getting subjects to do them a small favor (the foot in the door) and then asking for a much more substantial favor. This phenomenon isn't limited to cases in which the first and second requests are very similar, such as in putting up signs. Other findings indicate that the tendency to comply can generalize to quite different situations. Freedman and Fraser first asked another group of housewives to sign a petition in favor of keeping their state beautiful. Even though this initial request was different in both form (petition) and topic (state beauty), almost half of the women later agreed to put up the big, ugly safe-driving sign—as against less than one-fifth of the control group.

The foot-in-the-door technique can also be understood in terms of...the role of self-concept in social behavior. Freedman and Fraser suggest that when the women complied with the first request they thought of themselves as people who acted responsibly. They were people who did good things such as supporting highway safety or state beautification. When the interviewers came along with the second request, they essentially reminded the women of this self-conception and thus motivated them to live up to this image of themselves.

The issues need not be as socially desirable as those used by Freedman and Fraser for this technique to work. As long as we can induce people to think of themselves in a certain way, we theoretically should be able to have them try to live up to this self-conception. After Snyder and Cunningham (1975) led some of their subjects to view themselves as people who agreed to reasonable requests, these subjects were inclined to go along with even larger requests of the same nature. The researchers telephoned a sample of Minneapolis residents, soliciting their participation in a telephone survey for a public service organization. Some were asked if they would answer eight questions in this survey (small request), whereas others were requested to answer a long series of 50 questions. Two days later all of these persons were called back and a moderate favor was solicited for a different organization: Would they answer 30 questions? In comparison with control subjects, for whom no request was made, those who had complied to the previous small request were much more likely to agree (52 percent saying yes). The persons who had been asked to do the much more substantial favor, on the other hand, were much less inclined to comply (22 percent acquiescing). As you can see, as a result of going along with the first small request, the former subjects apparently thought of themselves as the kind of people who would do a reasonable favor for others; and they later acted in keeping with this self-concept, even though the second requester was supposedly someone else.

The findings also tell us something else. The initial request has to be small enough so that the first favor is granted, but not so small that the right kind of self-concept isn't established. If we ask people to do something trivial, they may well agree without viewing themselves as good persons; the action is just too easy. Seligman, Bush, and Kirsch (1976) showed this in a study similar to that of Snyder and Cunningham. Bush and Kirsch's telephone callers first asked for favors of various magnitudes, ranging from very easy to more difficult. Those who complied with the easiest requests weren't inclined to grant the second, more substantial favor two days later. When people grant the first favor, the compliance has to be significant enough that they think of themselves as having done something special.

This research reveals how people can be manipulated through their self-concepts. We often urge those we know to be true to themselves, as if they will become more independent if they live up to their image of themselves. The paradox is that a would-be influencer can alter people's self-concepts (at least temporarily and to some degree), so that people are exploited as they try to adhere to their self-concepts. The persuasion operates through people's desire to be true to themselves.

## REFERENCES

Allen, V. L., and Levine, J. M. Consensus and conformity. *Journal of Experimental Psychology*, 1969, *5*, 389–399.

Allen, V. L., and Levine, J. M. Social support and conformity. The role of independent assessment of reality. *Journal of Experimental Social Psychology*, 1971, 7, 48–58.

Arendt, H. *Eichmann in Jerusalem*. New York: Viking, 1963.

Asch, S. E. Effects of group pressures upon modification and distortion of judgments. In E. E. Maccoby, T. M. Newcomb, and E. L. Hartley (Eds.), *Readings in social psychology*, New York: Holt, Rinehart and Winston, 1958, 174–183.

Bandura, A. Vicarious processes: A case of no-trial learning. In L. Berkowitz (Ed.), *Advances in experimental social psychology*, Vol. 2, New York: Academic Press, 1965.

Bandura, A. *Principles of behavior modification*. New York: Holt, Rinehart and Winston, 1969.

Bandura, A. *Theories of modeling*. New York: Atherton Press, 1970.

Bandura, A., Blanchard, B., and Ritter, B. Relative efficacy of desensitization and modeling approaches for inducing behavioral, affective, and attitudinal changes. *Journal of Personality and Social Psychology*, 1969, *13*, 173–199.

Bandura, A., Grusec, J. E., and Menlove, F. L. Observational learning as a function of symbolization and incentive set. *Child Development*, 1966, *37*, 499–506.

Bandura, A., Ross, D., and Ross, S. A. A comparative test of the status envy, social power, and secondary reinforcement theories of identificatory learning. *Journal of Abnormal Social Psychology*, 1963, *67*, 527–534.

Berger, S. M. Conditioning through vicarious instigation. *Psychological Review*, 1962, *69*, 450–466.

Berkowitz L. Group standards, cohesiveness and productivity. *Human Relations*, 1954, 7, 509–519.

Berkowitz L. Some determinants of impulsive aggression: The role of mediated associations with reinforcements for aggression. *Psychological Review*, 1974, *81*, 165–176.

Berkowitz L., and Geen, R. G. Stimulus qualities of the target of aggression: A further study. *Journal of Personality and Social Psychology*, 1967, *5*, 364–368.

Berkowitz L., Parke, R. D., Leyens, J-P., and West, S. G. Reactions of juvenile delinquents to "justified" and "less justified" movie violence. *Journal of Research in Crime and Delinquency*, 1974, *11*, 16–24.

Berkowitz L., and Rawlings, E. Effects of film violence on inhibitions against subsequent aggression. *Journal of Abnormal and Social Psychology*, 1963, *66*, 405–412.

Berkowitz L., and Walker, N. Laws and moral judgments. *Sociometry*, 1967, *30*, 410–422.

Blau, P. M. *Exchange and power in social life*. New York: Wiley, 1964.

Bryan, J. H. Children's reactions to helpers: Their money isn't where their mouths are. In J. Macaulay and L. Berkowitz (Eds.), *Altruism and helping behavior*. New York: Academic Press, 1970, 61–73.

Bussey, K., and Perry, D. G. Sharing reinforcement contingencies with a model: A social-learning analysis of similarity effects in imitation research. *Journal of Personality and Social Psychology*, 1976, *34*, 1168–1176.

Cialdini, R. B., Cacioppo, J. T., Bassett, R., and Miller, J. A. Low-ball procedure for producing compliance: Commitment then cost. *Journal of Personality and Social Psychology*, 1978, *36*, 463–476.

Craig, K. D., and Neidermeyer, H. Autonomic correlates of pain thresholds influenced by social modeling. *Journal of Personality and Social Psychology*, 1974, *29*, 246–252.

Craig, K. D., and Prkachin, K. M. Social modeling influences on sensory decision theory and psychophysiological indexes of pain. *Journal of Personality and Social Psychology*, 1978, *36*, 805–815.

Darley, J. M., Moriarty, T., Darley, S., and Berscheid, E. Increased conformity to a fellow deviant as a function of prior deviation. *Journal of Experimental Social Psychology*, 1974, *10*, 211–223.

Deutsch, M., and Gerard, H. B. A study of normative and informational social influences upon individual judgment. *Journal of Abnormal and Social Psychology*, 1955, *51*, 629–636.

Dittes, J. E., and Kelley, H. H. Effects of different conditions of acceptance upon conformity to group norms. *Journal of Abnormal and Social Psychology*, 1956, *53*, 100–107.

Evan, W., and Zelditch, M., Jr. A laboratory experiment on bureaucratic authority. *American Sociological Review*, 1961, *26*, 883–893.

Feshbach, N. D. Nonconformity to experimentally induced group norms of high-status versus low-status members. *Journal of Personality and Social Psychology*. 1967, *6*, 55–63.

Freedman, J. L., and Fraser, S. C. Compliance without pressure: The foot-in-the-door technique. *Journal of Personality and Social Psychology*, 1966, *4*, 195–202.

French, J. R. P., Jr., and Raven, B. The bases of social power. In D. Cartwright (Ed.), *Studies in social power*, Ann Arbor, Mich.: Institute for Social Research, 1959.

Grusec, J. E. Power and the internalization of self-denial. *Child Development*, 1971, *42*, 93–105.

Harvey, O. J., and Consalvi, C. Status and conformity to pressures in informal groups. *Journal of Abnormal and Social Psychology*, 1960, *60*, 182–187.

Hollander, E. P. Conformity, status and idiosyncrasy credit. *Psychological Review*, 1958, *65*, 117–127.

Hollander, E. P., and Willis, R. H. Some current issues in the psychology of conformity and nonconformity. *Psychological Bulletin*, 1967, *68*, 62–76.

Homans, G. C. *Social behavior: Its elementary forms*. New York: Harcourt, Brace Jovanovich, 1961.

Hoyt, J. L. Effect of media violence "justification" on aggression. *Journal of Broadcasting*, 1970, *16*, 455–464.

Jeffery, R. W. The influence of symbolic and motor rehearsal on observational learning. *Journal of Research in Personality*, 1976, *10*, 116–127.

Kelley, H. H. *Causal schemata and the attribution process*. Morristown, N.J.: General Learning Press, 1972.

Kelley, H. H. The process of causal attribution. *American Psychologist*, 1973, *28*, 107–128.

Kiesler, C. A., and Kiesler, S. B. *Conformity*, Reading, Mass.: Addison-Wesley, 1969.

Kiesler, C. A., and Pallak, M. S. Minority influence: The effect of majority reactionaries and defectors, and minority and majority compromisers, upon majority opinion and attraction. *European Journal of Social Psychology*, 1975, *5*, 237–256.

Kiesler, S. B. Preference for predictability or unpredictability as a mediator of reactions to norm violations. *Journal of Personality and Social Psychology*, 1973, *27*, 354–359.

Lefkowitz, M., Blake, R. R., and Mouton, J. S. Status factors in pedestrian violation of traffic signals. *Journal of Abnormal and Social Psychology*, 1955, *51*, 704–706.

Leventhal, H., Singer, R., and Jones, S. Effects of fear and specificity of recommendations upon attitudes and behavior. *Journal of Personality and Social Psychology*, 1965, *2*, 20–29.

Mann, J., Berkowitz, L., Sidman, J., Starr, S., and West, S. Satiation of the transient stimulating effects of erotic films. *Journal of Personality and Social Psychology*, 1974, *30*, 729–735.

Mann, J., Sidman, J., and Starr, S. Effects of erotic films on the sexual behavior of married couples. In *Technical report of the Commission on Obscenity and Pornography, Vol. 8*, Washington, D.C.: U.S. Government Printing Office, 1971, 170–254.

Mantell, D. M. The potential for violence in Germany. *Journal of Social Issues*, 1971, *27*, 101–112.

McDavid, J. W. Personality and situational determinants of conformity. *Journal of Abnormal and Social Psychology*, 1959, *58*, 241–246.

Meyer, T. P. Effects of viewing justified and unjustified real film violence on aggressive behavior. *Journal of Personality and Social Psychology*, 1972, *23*, 21–29.

Milgram, S. Nationality and conformity. *Scientific American*, 1961, *205*, 45–51.

Milgram, S. Behavioral study of obedience. *Journal of Abnormal and Social Psychology*, 1963, *67*, 371–378.

Milgram, S. Some conditions of obedience and disobedience to authority. *Human Relations*, 1965, *18*, 57–75.

Mischel, W., and Grusec, J. Determinants of the rehearsal and transmission of natural and aversive behaviors. *Journal of Personality and Social Psychology*, 1966, *3*, 197–203.

Morris, W. N., and Miller, R. S. The effects of consensus-breaking and consensus-preempting partners on reduction of conformity. *Journal of Experimental Social Psychology*, 1975, *11*, 215–223.

Moscovici, S., and Faucheux, C. Social influence, conformity bias, and the study of active minorities. In L. Berkowitz (Ed.), *Advances in experimental social psychology, Vol. 6*, New York: Academic Press, 1972, 149–202.

Moscovici, S. and Nemeth, C. Social influence. II. Minority influence. In C. Nemeth (Ed.), *Social psychology: Classic and contemporary integrations*, Chicago: Rand McNally, 1974.

Mugny, G. Negotiations, image of the other and the process of minority influence. *European Journal of Social Psychology*, 1975, *5*, 209–228.

Nemeth, C., Swedlund, M, and Kanki, B. Patterning of the minority's responses and their influence on the majority. *European Journal of Social Psychology*, 1974, *4*, 53–64.

Nemeth, C., and Wachtler, J. Creating the perceptions of consistency and confidence: A necessary condition for minority influence. *Sociometry*, 1974, *37*, 529–540.

Nemeth, C., Wachtler, J., and Endicott, J. Increasing the size of the minority: Some gains and some losses. *European Journal of Social Psychology*, 1977, *7*(1), 15–27.

Nisbet, R. A. *The social bond*. New York: Knopf, 1970.

Phillips, D. P. The influence of suggestion on suicide: Substantive and theoretical implications of the Werther effect. *American Sociological Review*, 1974, *39*, 340–354.

Phillips, D. P. Airplane accident fatalities increase after newspaper stories about murder and suicide. *Science*, 1978, *201*, 748–750.

Raven, B. H., and French, J. R. P., Jr. Legitimate power, coercive power, and observability in social influence. *Sociometry*, 1958, *21*, 83–97.

Seligman, C., Bush, M., and Kirsch, K. Relationship between compliance in the foot-in-the-door paradigm and size of the first request. *Journal of Personality and Social Psychology*, 1976, *33*, 517–520.

Sherif, M. *The psychology of social norms*. New York: Harper & Row, 1936.

Shirer, W. L. *The rise and fall of the Third Reich*. New York: Simon and Schuster, 1960.

Snyder, M., and Cunningham, M. R. To comply or not comply: Testing the self-perception explanation of the "foot-in-the-door" phenomenon. *Journal of Personality and Social Psychology*, 1975, *31*, 64–67.

Spitzer, C. E., and Davis, J. H. Mutual social influence in dynamic groups. *Social Psychology*, 1978, *41*, 24–33.

Tarde, G. *Penal philosophy*. Boston: Little, Brown, 1912.

Thibaut, J. W., and Strickland, L. H. Psychological set and social conformity. *Journal of Personality*, 1956, *25*, 115–129.

Tilker, H. A. Socially responsible behavior as a function of observer responsibility and victim feedback. *Journal of Personality and Social Psychology*, 1970, *14*, 95–100.

Tolman, C. W. The role of the companion in social facilitation of animal behavior. In E. C. Simmel, R. A. Hoppe, and G. A. Milton (Eds.), *Social facilitation and imitative behavior*, Boston: Allyn and Bacon, 1968, 33–54.

Wahrman, R. High status, deviance and sanctions. *Sociometry*, 1970, *33*, 485–504.

Weber, M. *The theory of social and economic organization*. New York: Oxford University Press, 1947.

Wilson, R. S. Personality patterns, source attractiveness, and conformity. *Journal of Personality*, 1960, *28*, 186–199.

# PART B

# Socialization and Organizational Culture

## 21. CORPORATIONS, CULTURE, AND COMMITMENT: MOTIVATION AND SOCIAL CONTROL IN ORGANIZATIONS

Charles O'Reilly

Corporate culture is receiving much attention in the business press. A recent article in *Fortune* describes how the CEO at Black & Decker "transformed an entire corporate *culture*, replacing a complacent manufacturing mentality with an almost manic, market-driven way of doing things."[1] Similarly, the success of Food Lion (a $3 billion food-market chain that has grown at an annual rate of 37% over the past 20 years with annual returns on equity of 24%) is attributed to a culture which emphasizes "hard work, simplicity, and frugality."[2] Other well-known firms such as 3M, Johnson & Johnson, Apple, and Kimberly-Clark have been routinely praised for their innovative cultures.[3] Even the success of Japanese firms in the U.S. has been partly attributed to their ability to change the traditional culture developed under American managers. Peters and Waterman report how a U.S. television manufacturing plant, under Japanese management, reduced its defect rate from 140 to 6, its com-

plaint rate from 70% to 7%, and the turnover rate among employees from 30% to 1%, all due to a changed management philosophy and culture.[4]

Even more dramatic is the turnaround at the New United Motors Manufacturing Incorporated (NUMMI) plant in Fremont, California. When General Motors closed this facility in 1982, it was one of the worst plants in the GM assembly division with an 18 percent daily absenteeism rate and a long history of conflict in its labor relations. The plant reopened as a joint venture between Toyota and GM in 1983. Over 85 percent of the original labor force was rehired, and workers are still represented by the UAW. Although the technology used is vintage 1970s and the plant is not as automated as many others within GM and Toyota, productivity is almost double what GM gets in other facilities. In 1987, it took an estimated 20.8 hours to produce a car at NUMMI versus 40.7 in other GM plants and 18.0 at Toyota. Quality of the NUMMI automobiles is the highest in

Charles O' Reilly, "Corporations, Culture and Commitment: Motivation and Social Control in Organizations" from *California Management Review*, Summer 1989, Vol. 31, No. 4 pp. 9–25.

the GM system, based on both internal audits and owner surveys, and absenteeism is at 2 percent compared to 8 percent at other GM facilities. What accounts for this remarkable success? According to one account, "At the system's core is a *culture* in which the assembly line workers maintain their machines, ensure the quality of their work, and improve the production process."[5]

But a culture is not always a positive force. It has also been implicated when firms run into difficulties. The CEO of financially troubled Computerland, William Tauscher, has attempted to restructure the firm, noting that "a low-cost culture is a must."[6] Henry Wendt, CEO of SmithKline Beckman, has attributed his firm's current difficulties to complacency. "We've been victims of our own success....I want to create a new culture."[7] Corporate culture has also been implicated in problems faced by Sears, Caterpillar, Bank of America, Polaroid, General Motors, and others. Even difficulties in mergers and acquisitions are sometimes attributed to cultural conflicts which make integration of separate units difficult. Failure to merge two cultures can lead to debilitating conflict, a loss of talent, and an inability to reap the benefits of synergy.

But what is really meant when one refers to a firm's "culture"? Do all organizations have them? Are they always important? Even if we can identify cultures, do we know enough about how they work to manage them? Four major questions need to be answered:

- What is culture?
- From a manager's perspective, when is culture important?
- What is the process through which cultures are developed and maintained?
- How can cultures be managed?

## WHAT IS CULTURE?

If culture is to be analyzed and managed, it is important that we be clear about what is meant by the term. Failure to clearly specify what "culture"

is can result in confusion, misunderstanding, and conflict about its basic function and importance.

## Culture as Control

Clearly, little would get done by or in organizations if some control systems were not in place to direct and coordinate activities. In fact, organizations are often seen to be efficient and effective solely because control systems operate.[8]

But what is a "control system"? A generic definition might be that a control system is "the knowledge that someone who knows and cares is paying close attention to what we do and can tell us when deviations are occurring?" Although broad, this definition encompasses traditional formal control systems ranging from planning and budgeting systems to performance appraisals. According to this definition, control systems work when those who are monitored are aware that someone who matters, such as a boss or staff department, is paying attention and is likely to care when things aren't going according to plan.

Several years ago a large toy manufacturer installed, at considerable expense, a management-by-objectives (MBO) performance appraisal system. After a year or so, top management became aware that the system was working well in one part of the organization but not another. They conducted an investigation and discovered the reason for the failure. In the part of the organization where MBO was working well, senior management was enthusiastic and committed. They saw real benefits and conveyed their belief up and down the chain of command. In the part of the organization where the system had failed, senior management saw MBO as another bureaucratic exercise to be endured. Subordinate managers quickly learned to complete the paperwork but ignore the purpose. The lesson here was that a control system, no matter how carefully designed, works only when those being monitored believe that people who matter care about the results and are paying close attention. When Jan Carlzon became head of SAS Airline, he was concerned about the poor on-time record. To correct this, he personally requested a daily accounting of the on-time status of all flights. In the space of two years, SAS on-time record went from 83% to 97%.[9]

In designing formal control systems, we typically attempt to measure either outcomes or behaviors. For example, in hospitals it makes no sense to evaluate the nursing staff on whether patients get well. Instead, control systems rely on assessing behaviors. Are specified medical procedures followed? Are checks made at appropriate times? In other settings, behavior may not be observable. Whenever possible, we then attempt to measure outcomes. Sales people, for instance, are usually measured on their productivity, since the nature of their job often precludes any effective monitoring of their behavior. In other situations, control systems can be designed that monitor both behaviors and outcomes. For example, for some retail sales jobs both behaviors (how the customer is addressed, how quickly the order is taken, whether the sales floor is kept stocked) and outcomes (sales volume) can be measured.

However, it is often the case that neither behavior nor outcomes can be adequately monitored.[10] These are the activities that are non-routine and unpredictable, situations that require initiative, flexibility, and innovation. These can be dealt with only by developing social control systems in which common agreements exist among people about what constitutes appropriate attitudes and behavior.

Culture may be thought of as a potential social control system. Unlike formal control systems that typically assess outcomes or behaviors only intermittently, social control systems can be much more finely tuned. When we care about those with whom we work and have a common set of expectations, we are "under control" whenever we are in their presence. If we want to be accepted, we try to live up to their expectations. In this sense, social control systems can operate more extensively than most formal systems. Interestingly, our response to being monitored by formal and social control systems may also differ. With formal systems people often have a sense of external constraint which is binding and un-

satisfying. With social controls, we often feel as though we have great autonomy, even though paradoxically we are conforming much more.

Thus, from a management perspective, culture in the form of shared expectations may be thought of as a social control system. Howard Schwartz and Stan Davis offer a practical definition of culture as "a pattern of beliefs and expectations shared by the organization's members. These beliefs and expectations produce norms that powerfully shape the behavior of individuals and groups."[11]

## Culture as Normative Order

What Schwartz and Davis are referring to as culture are the central norms that may characterize an organization. Norms are expectations about what are appropriate or inappropriate attitudes and behaviors. They are socially created standards that help us interpret and evaluate events. Although their content may vary, they exist in all societies and, while often unnoticed, they are pervasive. For instance, in our society we have rather explicit norms about eye-contact. We may get uncomfortable when these are violated. Consider what happens when someone doesn't look at you while speaking or who continues to look without pause. In organizations we often find peripheral or unimportant norms around issues such as dress or forms of address. In the old railroads, for example, hats were a must for all managers, while everyone addressed each other with a formal "mister."

More important norms often exist around issues such as quality, performance, flexibility, or how to deal with conflict. In many organizations, it is impolite to disagree publicly with others. Instead, much behind-the-scenes interaction takes place to anticipate or resolve disputes. In other organizations, there may be norms that legitimate and encourage the public airing of disputes. Intel Corporation has an explicit policy of "constructive confrontation" that encourages employees to deal with disagreements in an immediate and direct manner.

In this view, the central values and styles that characterize a firm, perhaps not even written down, can form the basis for the development of norms that attach approval or disapproval to holding certain attitudes or beliefs and to acting in certain ways. For instance, the fundamental value of aggressiveness or competition may, if widely held and supported, be expressed as a norm that encourages organizational participants to stress winning competition. Pepsico encourages competition and punishes failure to compete.[12] Service is a pivotal norm at IBM; innovation is recognized as central at 3M. It is through norms—the expectations shared by group members and the approval or disapproval attached to these expectations—that culture is developed and maintained.

However, there is an important difference between the guiding beliefs or vision held by top management and the daily beliefs or norms held by those at lower levels in the unit or organization. The former reflect top managements' beliefs about how things ought to be. The latter define how things actually are. Simply because top management is in agreement about how they would like the organization to function is no guarantee that these beliefs will be held by others. One CEO spoke at some length about the glowing corporate philosophy that he believed in and felt characterized his firm's culture. After spending some time talking to mid-level managers in the organization, a very different picture emerged. A central norm shared by many of these managers was "Good people don't stay here." It is a common occurrence to find a noble sounding statement of corporate values framed on the wall and a very different and cynical interpretation of this creed held by people who have been around long enough to realize what is really important.

Moreover, norms can vary on two dimensions: the intensity or amount of approval/disapproval attached to an expectation; and the crystallization or degree of consensus or consistency with which a norm is shared. For instance, when analyzing an organization's culture it may be that for certain values there can be wide consensus but no intensity. Everyone understands what top management values, but there is no strong approval or disapproval attached to these beliefs

or behaviors. Or, a given norm, such as innovation, can be positively valued in one group (e.g., marketing or R& D) and negatively valued in another (manufacturing or personnel). There is intensity but no crystallization.

It is only when there exist both intensity and consensus that strong cultures exist. This is why it is difficult to develop or change culture. Organizational members must come to know and share a common set of expectations. These must, in turn, be consistently valued and reinforced across divisions and management levels.[13] Only when this is done will there be both intensity and consensus. Similarly, a failure to share the central norms or to consistently reinforce them may lead to vacuous norms, conflicting interpretations, or to microcultures that exist only within subunits.

To have a strong culture, an organization does not have to have very many strongly held values. Only a few core values characterize strong culture firms such as Mars, Marriott, Hewlett-Packard, and Walmart. What is critical is that these beliefs be widely shared and strongly held; that is, people throughout the organization must be willing to tell one another when a core belief is not being lived up to.

## The Role of Culture in Promoting Innovation

How is it that firms such as Intel, Hewlett-Packard, Cray Research, 3M, and Johnson & Johnson successfully develop both new products and new ways of doing things? How can culture help or hinder this process? The answer lies in those norms that, if they were widely shared and strongly held by members of the organization, would actively promote the generation of new ideas and would help in the implementation of new approaches.

What are these norms? This question was put to over 500 managers in firms as diverse as pharmaceuticals, consumer products, computers and semiconductors, and manufacturing. Table 21.1 contains a list of the norms that were most frequently cited. Several things are notable about this list. First, regardless of the industry or

**TABLE 21.1**
**Norms That Promote Innovation**

| A. Norms to Promote Creativity | B. Norms to Promote Implementation |
|---|---|
| 1) Risk Taking | 1) Common Goals |
| • freedom to try things and fail | • sense of pride in the organization |
| • acceptance of mistakes | • teamwork |
| • allow discussion of "dumb" ideas | • willingness to share the credit |
| • no punishments for failure | • flexibility in jobs, budgets, functional areas |
| • challenge the status quo | • sense of ownership |
| • forget the past | • eliminate mixed messages |
| • willingness *not* to focus on the short term | • manage interdependencies |
| • expectation that innovation is part of your job | • shared visions and a common direction |
| • positive attitudes about change | • build consensus |
| • drive to improve | • mutual respect and trust |
|  | • concern for the whole organization |
| 2) Rewards for Change |  |
| • ideas are valued | 2) Autonomy |
| • respect for beginning ideas | • decision-making responsibility at lower levels |
| • build into the structure: | • decentralized procedures |
|   • budgets   • opportunities | • freedom to act |
|   • resources   • tools | • expectation of action |
|   • time   • promotions | • belief that *you* can have an impact |
| • top management attention and support | • delegation |
| • celebration of accomplishments | • quick, flexible decision making |
| • suggestions are implemented | • minimize the bureaucracy |
| • encouragement |  |
|  | 3) Belief in Action |
| 3) Openness | • don't be obsessed with precision |
| • open communication and share information | • emphasis on results |
| • listen better | • meet your commitments |
| • open access | • anxiety about timeliness |
| • bright people, strong egos | • value getting things done |
| • scanning, broad thinking | • hard work is expected and appreciated |
| • force exposure outside the company | • empower people |
| • move people around | • emphasis on quality |
| • encourage lateral thinking | • eagerness to get things done |
| • adopt the customer's perspective | • cut through the bureaucracy |
| • accept criticism |  |
| • don't be too sensitive |  |
| • continuous training |  |
| • intellectual honesty |  |
| • expect and accept conflict |  |
| • willingness to consult others |  |

technology, managers identified virtually the same sets of norms as important. While the progress of innovation varies widely across efforts to discover new drugs, improve oil exploration, build new electronic devices, or develop a new toilet bowl cleaner, the norms that facilitate these efforts are remarkably consistent. Second, these norms all function to facilitate the process of introducing new ways of doing things and to help people implement them. For example, when people share the expectation that it is not only permissible but also desirable to challenge the status quo, the likelihood of innovation is increased.

At Cray Research, a prime example of a firm whose success depends on its ability to innovate, creativity and diversity are seen as virtues. Similarly, at Intel Corporation, a company whose strategy has long been to be a first-mover and innovator, all employees are told to expect conflict and to deal with it directly. To resolve conflicts, employees are trained in a process called "constructive confrontation," which helps them deal with the conflict in productive rather than destructive ways. At Johnson & Johnson a similar belief is referred to as "creative conflict."

To appreciate how critical the norms shown in Table 21.1 can be to innovation, envision an organization that is characterized by norms the opposite of those listed. Imagine an organization where failure is punished severely, where no recognition or rewards are provided for those doing things differently, where the past is venerated and only ideas generated internally are considered worthwhile, where "dumb" ideas are ridiculed and people are never encouraged to take risks, and where there is no drive to change or improve things. In this environment, one would be amazed to see any change. Contrast this with an organization such as 3M in which a basic financial goal is to have 25 percent of annual sales come from products developed over the last five years. Allen Jacobsen, 3M's CEO, says, "People ask me how do you get people to be innovative. It's simple. You give them responsibility for their own destinies and encourage them to take risks."[14] The secret to 3M's success isn't in Mr. Jacobsen's words but in the norms that form

3M's culture. These norms are widely shared and strongly held because management up and down the line provides the resources and encouragement to sustain them. It is the expectations held by people throughout the company, not just in R&D, that makes 3M and similar firms so innovative.

There is nothing magical or elusive about corporate culture. One has only to be clear about the specific attitudes and behaviors that are desired, and then to identify the norms or expectations that promote or impede them.

## WHY CULTURE IS IMPORTANT

There are two reasons why a strong culture is valuable:

- the fit of culture and strategy, and
- the increased commitment by employees to the firm.

Both these factors provide a competitive edge, giving a strong culture firm an advantage over its competitors.[15]

### Strategy and Corporate Culture

Every firm has, implicitly or explicitly, a competitive strategy which dictates how it attempts to position itself with respect to its competitors. Once established, a firm's strategy dictates a set of critical tasks or objectives that must be accomplished through a congruence among the elements of people, structure, and culture. For example, a decision to compete on innovation rather than price requires an appropriate formal structure and control system which then indicates the types of people required to accomplish the objectives and to fit the structure. The choice of a strategy also has significant implications for the informal organization or culture; that is, the norms of the organization must help execute the strategy.

An illustration of the importance of fit between strategy, people, structure, and culture can be seen in the history of the three major Silicon Valley firms that manufacture integrated circuits. Although operating in the same product market, Intel, National Semiconductor, and Advanced Micro Devices have each pursued a different strategy that is reflected in their people, structures, and cultures. National Semiconductor has chosen to compete largely as a low-cost manufacturer. To do this, it emphasizes strict cost control, a functional organizational structure, and a culture emphasizing numbers, a lack of frills, and a certain ruthlessness that has earned its people the sobriquet of "animals of the valley." Intel, however, has chosen to compete on product innovation. It has a looser formal organization with a culture valuing collegial interaction and the development of new technologies and products. Advanced Micro Devices has chosen a marketing strategy offering very high quality products, often as second source. Its strength has been in its marketing, and its culture reflects the value placed on selling, service, and quality.

For a strategy to be successfully implemented, it requires an appropriate culture. When firms change strategies, and often structures, they sometimes fail because the underlying shared values do not support the new approach. For example, a large, integrated electronics firm with a very strong culture based on technical excellence decided to enter the word processing market. Although they already made equipment that could easily be used as a basis for a word processor, the culture that made them successful in the design and manufacture of satellites and other sophisticated equipment ultimately sabotaged their efforts to design a word processor. The firm's engineers had a strong ethic of "getting it right" and would not release the machine. The window of opportunity for entry into the market passed, leaving the firm with a $40 million write-off of their investment. The point is both simple and important. As firms grow and strategies change, the culture or social control system also needs to be realigned to reflect the new direction.

## Culture and Commitment

Culture is critical in developing and maintaining levels of intensity and dedication among employees that often characterizes successful firms. This strong attachment is particularly valuable when the employees have knowledge that is instrumental to the success of the organization or when very high levels of motivation are required. When IBM bought ROLM, the critical resource was not the existing product line but the design and engineering expertise of ROLM's staff. A failure to gain the commitment of employees during mergers and acquisitions can diminish or destroy the value of the venture. In contrast, a highly dedicated work-force represents a significant competitive advantage. Under turbulent or changing conditions, relying on employees who wait to be told exactly what to do can be a liability.

How, then, do strong culture organizations develop intensity and commitment? A 20-year veteran of IBM was quoted in a *Wall Street Journal* article as saying, "I don't know what a cult is and what it is those bleary-eyed kids selling poppies really do, but I'm probably that deeply committed to the IBM company."[16] To understand this process, we need to consider what commitment is and how it is developed. By understanding the underlying psychology of commitment, we can then think about how to design systems to develop such an attachment among employees.

### Organizational Commitment

What is meant by the term "organizational commitment"? It is typically conceived of as an individual's psychological bond to the organization, including a sense of job involvement, loyalty, and a belief in the values of the organization. There are three processes or stages of commitment: *compliance, identification,* and *internalization.*[17] In the first stage, *compliance,* a person accepts the influence of others mainly to obtain something from others, such as pay. The second stage is *identification* in which the individual accepts influence in order to maintain a satisfying, self-defining relationship. People feel pride in belonging to the firm. The final stage of commitment is *internalization* in which the individual finds the values of the organization to be intrinsically rewarding and congruent with personal values.

Conceiving of commitment as developing in this manner allows us to understand how a variety of organizations—ranging from cults to strong culture corporations—generate commitment among their members. In fact, these organizations can be categorized based on the type of commitment displayed by their members. Cults and religious organizations, for example, typically have members who have internalized the values of the organization and who become "deployable agents," or individuals who can be relied upon to go forth and proselytize.[18] Japanese organizations, Theory Z, and strong culture firms are characterized by members who have a strong identification with the organization. These employees identify with the firm because it stands for something they value. In typical corporations, members comply with directions but may have little involvement with the firm beyond self-interest; that is, there is no commitment with the firm beyond that of a fair exchange of effort for money and, perhaps, status.

## HOW CULTURE IS DEVELOPED

How do people become committed to organization? Why, for example, would someone choose to join a cult? How do firms such as NUMMI get the incredible levels of productivity from their employees (as one team member said, "I like the new system so much it scares me. I'm scared because it took me 18 years to realize that I blew it at GM. Now we have a chance to do things a different way.")? The answer to this puzzle is simultaneously simple and nonobvious. As Jerry Salancik has noted, "commitment is too easy," yet it relies on an understanding of human motivation that is counter-intuitive.[19]

### Constructing Social Realities

Most discussions of motivation assume a stable set of individual needs and values.[20] These are seen as shaping expectations, goals, and attitudes. In turn, these are presumed to guide behavior and people's responses to situations. In Maslow's the-

ory, for instance, people are assumed to have a hierarchy of needs.[21] The managerial consequence of this view can be seen in our theories of job design in which jobs are supposed to be designed to take advantage of the desire of people to grow and self-actualize.[22] But are such theories correct? The empirical evidence is weak at best.[23] In spite of numerous efforts to demonstrate the effect of needs and personality, there is little support for the power of individual differences to predict behavior.

Consider the results of two experiments. In the first, Christian seminary students were approached and given one of two requests. Both asked them to extemporaneously address a visiting class in a discussion of the parable of the Good Samaritan. They were told to walk over to a classroom building to do this. In one condition they were informed that the class was already there and that they should hurry. In the other condition they were told that the class would arrive in several minutes. As they walked to the classroom, all subjects passed an old man (the "victim") dressed in shabby clothes and in obvious need of help. The experimenters were interested in what proportion of Christian seminarians thinking of the Good Samaritan would stop and help this person. Surprisingly, in the condition in which the subjects were told to hurry, only 30 percent paid any attention. Think about this. Seventy percent of a group of individuals with religious values who were training to be ministers failed to stop. Ninety-five percent of those who were not in a hurry stopped to help.

In another experiment, researchers observed when students using a campus restroom washed their hands. They discovered that when another person was visible in the restroom, 90 percent washed their hands. When no other person was visible, less than 20 percent did so.

What explains these and other findings? What often seems to account for behavior are the expectations of others. As individuals, we are very susceptible to the informational and normative influence of others. We pay attention to the actions of others and learn from them. "In actuality, virtually all learning phenomena resulting from direct experience occur on a vicarious basis by observing other people's behavior and its consequences for them." We watch others and form expectations about how and when we should act.[24]

Yet, we are not sensitive to how much of our world is really a social construction-one that rests on shared agreements. We often tend to underestimate the degree to which situations and the expectations of others can constrain and shape behavior. Strong situations—ones in which there are very clear incentives and expectations about what constitutes appropriate attitudes and behavior—can be very powerful. When we care what others think, the power of these norms or social expectations can be heightened.

## Mechanisms for Developing Culture

How can cultures be developed and managed in organizations? All organizations—from cults to strong culture corporations—draw on the same underlying psychology and create situations characterized by strong norms that focus people's attention, provide clear guidance about what is important, and provide for group reinforcement of appropriate attitudes and behavior. Four common mechanisms are used to accomplish this. What varies across these organizations is not what is done but only the degree to which these mechanisms are used.

### Participation

The first mechanism that is critical in developing or changing a culture are systems that provide for participation. These systems encourage people to be involved and send signals to the individual that he or she is valued. These may range from formal efforts such as quality circles and advisory boards to less formal efforts such as suggestion systems and opportunities to meet with top managers and informal social gatherings. What is important about these processes is that people are encouraged to make incremental choices and develop a sense of responsibility for their actions. In some cases, such as work design, the specific choices made may be less important for future

success than the fact that people had the chance to make them.

From a psychological perspective, choice is often associated with commitment. When we choose of our own volition to do something, we often feel responsible.[25] When the choice is volitional, explicit, public, and irrevocable, the commitment is even more binding.[26] For instance, direct sales companies have learned that by getting the customer to fill out the order sheet, they can cut cancellations dramatically. A large number of psychological experiments have convincingly shown that participation can lead to both commitment and enjoyment, even when people are induced to engage in physically and emotionally stressful activities such as eating earthworms and becoming bone marrow donors.[27]

How do organizations use participation? Marc Galanter has documented how members of the Unification Church use processes of incremental commitment to recruit cult members.[28] Individuals are invited to dinner, convinced to spend the weekend for a seminar, and in some cases, induced to remain permanently with their new found "friends." Interestingly, there is no evidence that people who join cults under these circumstances are suffering from any psychopathology. Religious organizations often use elaborate systems of incremental choice and participation leading to greater and greater involvement. Japanese-managed automobile companies in the U.S. also have elaborate systems of selection and orientation that rely heavily on these approaches, as do American "strong culture" firms.

### Management as Symbolic Action

The second mechanism commonly seen in strong culture organizations is that of clear, visible actions on the part of management in support of the cultural values.[29] In organizations, participants typically want to know what is important. One way we gain this information is to carefully watch and listen to those above us. We look for consistent patterns. When top management not only says that something is important but also consistently behaves in ways that support the message, we begin to believe what is said. When the CEO of Xerox, David Kearns, began his quest for improved quality, there was some initial uncertainty about whether he meant it. Over time, as the message was repeated again and again, and as resources continued to be devoted to the quality effort, norms developed setting expectations about the role and importance of quality throughout the corporation.[30]

An important function of management is to provide interpretations of events for the organization's members. Without a shared meaning, confusion and conflict can result. Managers need to be sensitive to how their actions are viewed. Interpreting (or reinterpreting) history, telling stories, the use of vivid language, spending time, and being seen as visible in support of certain positions are all potential ways of shaping the organization's culture. This does not mean that managers need to be charismatic. However, managers need to engage in acts of "mundane symbolism." By this they can insure that important issues get suitable amounts of time, that questions are continually asked about important topics, and that the subject gets on the agenda and it is followed up.

The appropriate use of symbols and ceremonies is also important. When Jerry Sanders, CEO of Advanced Micro Devices, decided to shift the firm's strategy toward innovation, he not only made substantive changes in budget, positions, and organizational structure, he also used a symbol. As a part of the many talks he had with employees describing the need to change, Sanders would also describe how important it was to invest in areas that others could not easily duplicate—such as investing in proprietary products. He would describe how a poor farmer would always need a cash crop at the end of the year if he was to survive. But if he began to prosper, a smart farmer would begin to plant crops that others might not be able to afford—crops, for example, that took more than a year to come to fruition; crops like asparagus. The notion of asparagus became a visible and important symbol for change within AMD, even to the point where managers begin referring to revenues from

new proprietary products as "being measured on asparagus."

Symbols are not a substitute for substance, and ceremonies cannot replace content. Rather, many of the substantive changes that occur in organizations, such as promotions or reorganizations have multiple meanings and interpretations. Over time, people may lose a clear sense for what the superordinate goals are and why their jobs are important. In strong culture organizations, managers frequently and consistently send signals helping to renew these understandings. They do this by continually calling attention to what is important, in word and in action.

### Information from Others

While clear messages from management are an important determinant of a culture, so too are consistent messages from coworkers. If control comes from the knowledge that someone who matters is paying attention, then the degree to which we care about our coworkers also gives them a certain control over us. Years ago, several researchers conducted an experiment in which subjects were placed in a room to complete a questionnaire. While they were doing this, smoke began to flow from an air vent. While 75% of the subjects who were alone responded by notifying the experimenter of a possible fire, only 38% did so when in the company of two other subjects. When these other two were confederates of the experimenter and deliberately said nothing, only 10% of the subjects responded. One conclusion from this and other similar experiments is that we often take our cue from others when we are uncertain what to do.

In organizations, during periods of crisis or when people are new to the situation, they often look to others for explanations of what to do and how to interpret events. Strong cultures are typically characterized by consensus about three questions. In these settings there are often attempts made to insure a consistency of understanding and to minimize any us-them attitudes between parts of the organization. For instance, strong culture firms often pride themselves on the equality of treatment of all employees. At Mars, all employees punch a time clock and no one has a private secretary. At Gore-Tex, WalMart, Disney, and others there are no employees or managers, only associates, team members, and hosts. At NUMMI, Honda, and Nissan there are no private dining rooms for managers and both managers and workers often wear uniforms. In the Rajneesh Commune, everyone wore clothes with the color magenta.

The goal here is to create a strong social construction of reality by minimizing contradictory interpretations. In cults, this is often done by isolating the members from family and friends. Some religious organizations do this by encouraging extensive involvement in a variety of church activities and meetings. Japanese firms expect after work socializing. At NUMMI, for instance, each work team is given a semiannual budget to be spent only on team-sponsored activities where the entire team participates. In corporations, 60 hour work weeks can also isolate people from competing interpretations. Some electronics firms in Silicon Valley have provided employee T-shirts with slogans such as "Working 80 hours a week and loving it." With this commitment of time, workers may be as isolated as if they had joined a cult.

### Comprehensive Reward Systems

A final mechanism for promoting and shaping culture is the reward system, but not simply monetary rewards. Rather, these systems focus on rewards such as recognition and approval which can be given more frequently than money. These rewards also focus on the intrinsic aspects of the job and a sense of belonging to the organization. Recognition by your boss or coworkers for doing the right thing can be more potent in shaping behavior than an annual bonus. In the words of a popular management book, the trick is to catch someone doing something right and to reward it on the spot. While tokens such as scrolls or badges can be meaningless, under the right circumstances they can also be highly valued.

It is easy to desire one type of behavior while rewarding another. Often management professes a concern for quality while systematically rewarding only those who meet their goals, regardless of the quality. Innovation may be espoused but even the slightest failure is punished. At its simplest, people usually do what they are rewarded for and don't do what they're punished for. If this is true and to be taken seriously, then a simple analysis of what gets management's attention should give us a sense for what the culture supports. Who gets promoted? At 3M, one important aspect of success is to be associated with a new product introduction. If innovation is espoused, but doing things by-the-book is what is rewarded, it doesn't take a psychologist to figure out what the firm actually values. In fact, if there are inconsistencies between what top management says and what is actually rewarded, the likely outcome will be confusion and cynicism.

## MANAGING CULTURE

Each of these can affect the development of a shared set of expectations. As shown in Figure 21.1, the process begins with words and actions on the part of the group's leaders. Even if no explicit statements are made, subordinates will attempt to infer a pattern. If management is credible and communicates consistently, members of the group may begin to develop consistent expectations about what is important. When this consensus is also rewarded, clear norms can then emerge.

Whether or not these norms constitute a desirable culture depends on the critical tasks to be accomplished and whether the formal control system provides sufficient leverage to attain these. If culture *is* important, four steps can help a manager understand how to manage it.

- Identify the strategic objectives of the unit. Once identified, specify the short-term objectives and critical actions that need to be accomplished if the strategic objectives are to be accomplished.

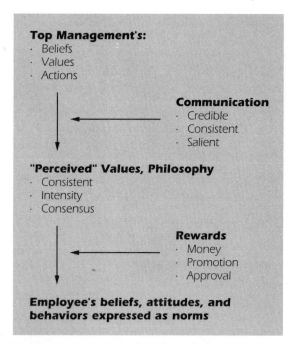

**Top Management's:**
· Beliefs
· Values
· Actions

**Communication**
· Credible
· Consistent
· Salient

**"Perceived" Values, Philosophy**
· Consistent
· Intensity
· Consensus

**Rewards**
· Money
· Promotion
· Approval

**Employee's beliefs, attitudes, and behaviors expressed as norms**

**FIGURE 21.1** Employee's beliefs, attitudes, and behaviors expressed as norms.

- Analyze the existing values and norms that characterize the organization. This can be done by focusing on what people in the unit feel is expected of them by their peers and bosses and what is actually rewarded. What does it take to get ahead? What stories are routinely told? Who are the people who exemplify the group? Look for norms that are widely shared and strongly felt.

- Once these are identified, look for norms that may hinder the accomplishment of critical tasks; norms that would help but are not currently present; and conflicts between what is needed and what is currently rewarded.

- Once these are identified, programs can be designed to begin to shape or develop the desired norms. These can draw upon the psychological mechanisms discussed previously.

The logic here is straightforward and links culture to those activities critical for the implementation of strategy and for generating widespread understanding and commitment among the organization's members. Obviously, these actions take time and management resources to accomplish. However, to ignore them is to ignore a social control system that may already be operating in the organization. The issue is whether this system is helping or hindering. Managers need to be sensitive to what the central organizational norms are and how they can affect them. To not be sensitive to these issues is to ignore the advice of a CEO who said, "We will either be a victim or a successful result of our culture."

## REFERENCES

1. *Fortune*, January 2, 1989.

2. *Fortune*, August 15, 1988.

3. *Fortune*, June 6, 1988.

4. T. Peters and R. H. Waterman, *In Search of Excellence: Lessons From America's Best-Run Companies* (New York, NY: Harper & Row, 1982), p. 32.

5. *Fortune*, January 30, 1989.

6. *Business Week*, October 10, 1988.

7. *Business Week*, October 10, 1988.

8. A. Wilkins and W. Ouchi, "Efficient Cultures: Exploring the Relationship between Culture and Organizational Performance." *Administrative Science Quarterly*, 28 (1983): 468–481: O. Williamson, *Markets and Hierarchies* (New York, NY: The Free Press, 1975).

9. J. Carlzon, *Moments of Truth* (Cambridge, MA: Ballinger, 1987).

10. S. Dornbusch and W. R. Scott, *Evaluation and the Exercise of Authority* (San Francisco, CA: Jossey-Bass, 1975).

11. H. Schwartz and S. Davis, "Matching Corporate Culture and Business Strategy," *Organizational Dynamics* (1981), pp. 30–48.

12. *Fortune*, April 10, 1989.

13. D. Feldman, "The Development and Enforcement of Group Norms," *Academy of Management Review*, 9 (1984): 47–53.

14. Fortune, June 6, 1988.

15. For example, see S. Davis, *Managing Corporate Culture* (Cambridge, MA: Ballinger, 1984); T. Deal and A. Kennedy, *Corporate Cultures* (Reading, MA: Addison-Wesley, 1982); Peters and Waterman, op. cit.

16. *Wall Street Journal*, April 7, 1986.

17. C. O'Reilly and J. Chatman, "Organizational Commitment and Psychological Attachment: The Effects of Compliance, Identification and Internalization on Prosocial Behavior," *Journal of Applied Psychology*, 71 (1986): 492–499.

18. W. Appel, *Cults in America* (New York, NY: Holt, Rinehart and Winston, 1983); D. Gerstel, *Paradise Incorporated: Synanon* (San Francisco, CA: Presidio Press, 1982).

19. G. Salancik, "Commitment Is Too Easy!" *Organizational Dynamics* (Summer 1977), pp. 62–80.

20. For example, see F. Herzberg, B. Mausner, and B. Snyderman, *The Motivation to Work* (New York, NY: John Wiley, 1959); A. Maslow, *Motivation and Personality* (New York, NY: Harper & Row, 1970).

21. Maslow, op. cit.

22. For example, see J. R. Hackman and G. Oldham, *Work Redesign* (Reading, MA: Addison-Wesley, 1980).

23. For example, see G. Salancik and J. Pfeffer, "A Social Information Processing Approach to Job Attitudes and Task Design," *Administrative Science Quarterly*, 23 (1978): 224–253.

24. For example, see S. Milgram, *Obedience to Authority* (New York, NY: Harper & Row, 1969); A. Bandura, *Social Learning Theory* (Englewood Cliffs, NJ: Prentice-Hall, 1977).

25. Salancik, op. cit.

27. For example, see I. Janis and L. Mann, *Decision Making: A Psychological Analysis of Conflict, Choice, and Commitment* (New York, NY: Free Press, 1977).

28. M. Galanter, "Psychological Induction into the Large Group: Findings from a Modern Religious Sect." *American Journal of Psychiatry*, 137 (1980): 1574–1579.

29. J. Pfeffer, "Management as Symbolic Action: The Creation and Maintenance of Organizational Paradigms," in L. Cummings and B. Staw, eds., *Research in Organizational Behavior*, Volume 3 (Greenwich, CT: JAI Press, 1981).

30. G. Jacobsen and J. Hillkirk, *Xerox: American Samurai* (New York, NY: Collier Books, 1986).

# 22. COMMITMENT AND THE CONTROL OF ORGANIZATIONAL BEHAVIOR AND BELIEF

Gerald R. Salancik

Most articles on organizational commitment extol the virtues of commitment. In them, you will find that the committed employee is the happy employee, the success of the organization is a matter of its members sacrificing their time and effort, and commitment to the values of the organization gives meaning to a person's life. In them commitment enhances productivity, assures quality in the final product, and guarantees the flow of adaptive innovation. In them, you will find, in short, a lot of nonsense mixed with a lot of common sense. But from them your understanding of commitment may not be enhanced....

The view of commitment we present in this paper is one which is grounded in behavior and the implications of behavior in one situation for behavior in another. The view derives primarily from the model of commitment developed by Kiesler (1971), with intellectual roots going back to Festinger (1957, 1964) and Lewin (1947). We borrow considerably from Keisler's work, and deviate in significant ways. As a working definition, "commitment is the binding of the individual to behavioral acts" (Kiesler & Sakumura, 1966). The important words are "binding" and "acts."

To act is to commit oneself. A person may talk about how important it is to keep the population growth rate down, but to be sterilized is to give eloquent, unshakeable force to the statement. An adulterer may proclaim unrelenting devotion to a lover, but to give up children, home, and joint bank accounts is to put meaning into the procla-

mation. Thus, at a minimum, a concept of commitment implies that behavior, or action, be a central focus.

## DETERMINANTS OF COMMITMENT

While action is a necessary ingredient in commitment, all behaviors are not equally committing. There are degrees of commitment. A statement of a belief or attitude is a less committing action than the signing of a petition in favor of the belief, which in turn is less committing than actively advocating the belief to a hostile or skeptical audience.

The degree of commitment derives from the extent to which a person's behaviors are binding. Four characteristics of behavioral acts make them binding, and hence determine the extent of commitment: explicitness; revocability; volition; and publicity. The first is the *explicitness* or deniability of the act, and concerns the extent to which an action can be said to have taken place. Two contributors to explicitness are the observability of the act and the unequivocality of the act. Some acts are not observable and we may know them only by inference from assumed consequences. You leave a dollar bill on a checkout counter, turn away for a moment, then find it missing. The consequence is obvious, but do you know if the customer next to you took it or if it was carried away by a draft from the open door? Acts themselves can be equivocal, forgotten, or otherwise intractable. A person who says, "I sometimes think..." is behaving more equivocally than one who says, "I think...."

A second characteristic of behavior affecting commitment is the *revocability* or reversibility of the action. Some actions are like trials. We try them out, see how they fit with us, and if they don't suit us we change our minds and do something else. Few actions are really irreversible. Even a vasectomy can be undone. Promises can be made and broken. Jobs can be quit. Marriages can be dissolved; engagements, broken. Contracts can be torn up. On the other hand, some actions are permanent and having occurred, they cannot be undone. They are committing. Slapping someone in the face can be excused, forgiven, forgotten or reciprocated, but it cannot be taken back. Consumption of food or drink may be regretted but not reversed. Pulling the trigger of a loaded gun pointed at a friend commits all to its gross reality.

The explicitness and irrevocability of an act link action to an indelible reality. *Volition*, a third characteristic of committing behaviors, links action to the individual. This is one of the more difficult characteristics of human action to define precisely, and is frequently associated with such concepts as freedom and personal responsibility. What makes definition difficult is that all human action is both free and constrained, being done under one's own volition and in response to contingencies. Even the most seemingly free and personal action can be perceived as constrained. Artists and writers, such as Dostoevski and George Bernard Shaw, describe their acts of creation as the result of compulsions and external forces. And even the most seemingly constrained acts can be considered free. A person with a gun to his head ultimately is free to choose, whether to comply or accept the consequences of noncompliance. The perception of volition, moreover, can vary with the consequences that follow acts. A manager who takes a decision which turns out to be a disaster for his firm may make every effort to divest himself of responsibility. And one can observe in the annual reports of most corpo-

rations the following simple relationship. When sales increase from the previous year, the annual report points out how management's ingenious investments and development programs are paying off; when, the next year, sales decrease, an astounding downturn in the economy is lugubriously noted.

Despite difficulties in developing a precise concept of volition, volition wields powerful influences on the attitudes and behaviors of people, at least in Western culture. Some major characteristics found to relate to the degree of perceived volition of action are: (1) choice; (2) the presence of external demands for action; (3) the presence of extrinsic bases for action; and (4) the presence of other contributors to action. Thus a person who works hard in order to make a lot of money is not perceived as having as much volition as a person who works hard for nothing. A person who works hard because his superior stands over him constantly is not perceived as having as much volition as one who does as much on his own. With regard to choice, a person who buys a Ford because that is the only car available for sale is not perceived as having as much volition as one who passes over a hundred other models to make the same purchase....

A fourth characteristic of action affecting commitment is the *publicity* or publicness of the act. This characteristic links the action into a social context. While all action and behavior is by definition observable, publicity refers to the extent to which others know of the action and the kinds of persons who know of it. Some audiences are unimportant to us, as are their observations of our behavior. One of the simplest ways to commit yourself to a course of action is to go around telling all your friends that you are definitely going to do something. You will find yourself bound by your own statements. The same commitment will not develop from proclamations to strangers you meet on trains. The publicity of one's action places the action in a social context which is more or less binding and, as we shall describe, contributes to directing the effect of those behaviors on subsequent behaviors....

## COMMITMENT TO ORGANIZATIONS

A careless interpretation of the consistency assumption might lead one to infer that having chosen to join an organization or to do a job, individuals will be willing to stay with it and be quite satisfied. After all, one implication of taking a job is that the person likes it. Choice, however, is not enough. The choice itself must be committing. The person must be bound to this choice....

### Sacrifice and Initiation Rites

Some organizations prefer not to leave a member's commitment to the happenstance of his own decision process. Corporations frequently publicize the decisions of their new managers. The *Wall Street Journal* is crammed with advertisements by companies announcing that a particular individual has joined their firm, an act giving instant status to the manager's new role. Friends and past associates call in their congratulations and set into motion a climate of expectation that he is part of that firm. In recent years, insurance companies have been taking full spreads in such magazines as *Time* and *Newsweek* to publish the pictures of their sales personnel. Western Electric has done the same with television scans of their employees working on the job. For a few hundred dollars, an individual is identified with the organization. Next-door neighbors rush to ask, "Say, is this you?" One implication of the advertisement to both the employee and his friends is that the company really cares about its employees, and as a consequence it becomes more and more difficult to complain about it to friends. Harvard Business School uses a particularly effective method of maintaining long-term commitment from its graduates. Entering MBAs are immediately assigned to a group of classmates. This class does everything together from then on. They live in the same dormitories, hear the same lectures, and take the same exams. Virtually everything is scheduled for the class as a whole. Within each class, individuals are identified by namecards so that everyone knows the name of everyone else

and is referred to by name in classroom discussions. Twenty years later, when the individuals have long departed the ivy-draped halls, the social network created there continues to operate. One of the things it is used for is to drum donations to the "B School," as it is fondly called.

In addition to advertising a person's commitment, some organizations take pains to make sure the individual is aware he has made a decision. Like the experiments with a well-constructed social psychological choice manipulation, the new employer commits the beginner: "Now, we want to be sure you're taking this job because you want to. We know you've given up a lot to come here and we're grateful. You left your home, your old friends. It must have been very difficult for you. And the salary we're offering, while more than you were making, is never enough to compensate for that."

The idea of giving up something to join the organization is one exploited in many ways. A common form is the initiation rites which still persist in college fraternities and sororities, fraternal clubs like the Masons or Elks, prisons, military organizations, revolutionary cadres, communal living experiments, police academies and religious organizations, orders and cults. An important part of the initiation process is the forcing of a sacrifice, in which members are asked to give up something as a price of membership (Karter, 1968). College fraternities require pledges to do hours of push-ups, to take verbal abuse, to have their privileges restricted, to accept subservient roles; in the end, those who endure love it. The effect is obvious. The individual in order to give meaning to his sacrifices is left to conclude they were made because of his devotion to the organization, a conclusion made more likely by his public pledge to enter the organization out of his own choosing. Other organizations have less colorful forms of sacrifice. Exclusive country clubs require their new members to make large initial donations in addition to yearly fees. The donations themselves provide for no services, and members pay for almost all services. But having given up an initial thousand, or a few thousand dollars, members feel a certain compulsion to spend $3.00 for a martini at the club's bar rather than half that at a public lounge.

## Investments and Tenure

Many organizations do not exploit the idea of sacrifice as a price of membership. Instead they emphasize the instrumental or exchange bases for participation. Members are hired rather than invited into the organization. Commitment under such circumstances will obviously be more difficult.

Studies on commitment to organizations that emphasize the instrumental bases for membership—work organizations—have consistently found two factors as most reliably related to commitment. The two factors are position in the organization and tenure with the organization. Study after study on the issue comes down to: People with good jobs are willing to stay in them, and, the longer a person has been with an organization, the more he wants to stay. Unfortunately, most of the studies were done in such ways that it is difficult, and in many cases impossible, to interpret the meaning of the findings.

The relationship of tenure to organizational commitment is predictable from the model of commitment presented in this chapter and has been discussed in a related manner. Howard Becker (1960) suggested that individuals build up commitment over time through certain "side-bets" they make in the organization. One obvious form of accumulation investments in an organization is the build-up of pension benefits and credits over the course of a lifetime. Until recently, such employee benefits, often called the "golden padlock," were not transferable from one organization to another. If an individual terminated in one organization he lost some of his future wealth or security and had to begin accumulating it again in another organization. The costs of leaving the organization thus increase the longer one's involvement and one becomes more and more likely to continue where one is.

Regardless of financial investments, mobility also declines with tenure in an organization. As time goes by, one becomes less employable. And one's expertise becomes increasingly specific to one's current organization. Some organizations purposely manipulate the costs of leaving for some individuals. Universities will promote some of their assistant professors at rapid rates, making it more costly for other organizations to entice them away. Some business organizations will give young managers attractive positions unusual for their age, knowing it would be difficult for them to obtain equivalent offers elsewhere and also knowing it is cheaper to buy their commitment at an early age than it would be when they become industry hot-shots....

## WORK ENVIRONMENTS AND ORGANIZATIONAL COMMITMENT

Thus far we have discussed commitment to the organization as the result of the constraints on an individual's ability to leave the organization, and the extent to which the individual himself has made a definite and committing choice. In reading this over, one gets the feeling that commitment to an organization is an entrapment: an individual is either cut off from other alternatives because no one else wants him or because his own situation doesn't allow him to change it. Thus, individuals rarely make job changes involving moves when their children are entrenched in a school. In all, it is a rather negative view of commitment. You are committed because the facts of your life have bound you.

What about more positive features? Do people become committed to their jobs because they are attracted to them and find then enjoyable? The research on this issue is unimpressive. Much is based on termination interviews which find that workers who quit say they quit because they didn't like the job or the pay. Having taken so decisive a step, it would be rather amusing to find them saying that they loved the job. Studies attempting to predict employee turnover or absenteeism from prior reports of job satisfaction have been notoriously unsuccessful from a practical point of view; that is, the studies report statistically reliable relationships of so low a magnitude that they predict little about behavior. Even superior measurement techniques do poorly (Newman, 1974).

The typical relationship found between job attitudes and turnover or absenteeism is clouded by other factors. We have already discussed that one of these factors is the tenure of the employee. Job satisfaction increases with age and tenure, as does commitment to the organization (see Grupp & Richards, 1975; Organ & Greene, 1974; Gow, Clark, & Dossett, 1974 for illustrative studies). Where investigators have bothered to make the necessary causal analyses, they have found that the change is a "real" one and not simply a function of changes in position, jobs, or salary (Stagner, 1975). As a person becomes more able to cope with the negative and positive features of his job....

## Commitment and Job Features

Despite the rather unpredictable relationship between job attitudes, absenteeism, turmoil, and turnover, the model of commitment presented here does suggest that certain features of a person's job situation will affect his commitment. In general, any characteristic of a person's job situation which reduces his felt responsibility will reduce his commitment. As for the relationship between commitment and satisfaction, our own view is that enjoyment is more likely to follow commitment than the reverse.

Many characteristics of job situations can affect a person's perception of responsibility. Some positions simply carry more responsibility, and persons in higher positions tend to be more committed. Similarly, some jobs offer more discretion and self-determination to their occupants, and it has been found that employees in autonomous positions generally have more favorable attitudes than those with little freedom to decide how to do their jobs (Hackman & Lawler, 1971; Hackman & Oldham, 1974).

In addition to the job and the freedom it permits, the manner by which the job is supervised or monitored can affect perceptions of responsibility. The supervisor who stands over a subordinate provides an excuse for the subordinate's behavior. When unpleasant aspects of the job become apparent, rather than coping with them, and finding some joy in the job, the subordinate can attribute his endurance to the supervisor's tenacious pressure. Lepper and Greene (1975) found that surveillance deteriorates interest in a task. Zanna (1970) found that when students are led to believe they worked very hard for a nasty supervisor, they enjoyed the task more than when they worked very hard for a nice supervisor. When they work for a nice person they attribute their effort to their liking for him, not the job. This would be an unrealistic attribution to a nasty boss, so they like the job more.

If a supervisor merely stands by without taking an active part in determining the subordinate's behavior, his presence may serve to reinforce the subordinate's felt responsibility. Maguire and Ouchi (1975) found that close output supervision improves employee satisfaction but that close behavioral supervision does not. Monitoring and providing an individual with feedback about his work performance can increase a person's felt responsibility. The person, knowing his outcomes and knowing his outcomes are known by others, may become more aware that the outcomes are his responsibility. Hackman and Oldham (1974) found worker's perception of responsibility was in part a function of feedback about their performance. While the precise effects of various supervisory conditions on commitment have not been well studied, we would expect that high output monitoring coupled with low behavioral control would lead to the greatest felt responsibility on the part of the worker. Whether or not these conditions will lead to greater satisfaction, would depend on whether or not the worker can handle the task. Maguire and Ouchi (1975) found more satisfaction among monitored workers who could do their jobs without depending on others (i.e., low interdependence), than those who could not.

Commitment also derives from the relation of an employee's job to those of others in the organization. Some jobs are rather isolated and can be done independently of other jobs in the organization. It has been found that jobs which are not integrated with the work activities of others tend to be associated with less favorable attitudes (Sheperd, 1973). Gow, Clark and Dossett (1974), for instance, find that telephone operators who quit tend to be those who are not integrated into the work group. Work integration can affect commitment by the fact that integrated jobs are likely to be associated with salient demands from others in the organization. If a person has a job which affects the work of others in the organization, it is likely that those others will communicate their expectations for performance of that job. Such expectations can be committing in that the other people implicitly or explicitly hold the person accountable for what he does. Earlier we mentioned that when individuals did not know what was expected of them they tended to be less committed to the organization. One reason an individual will not know what is expected is because no one is telling him. In general, we would expect that anything which contributes to creating definite expectations for a person's behavior would enhance his felt responsibility, and hence commitment. Integration may be one such contributor.

Perhaps the most pervasive condition of a job which affects commitment is its instrumentality, the fact that work is a means to some other end. While all jobs in industrial and commercial organizations are done in exchange for salary, there are perhaps great variations in the extent to which the instrumental basis for the work is salient or not. In general, we would expect that when the instrumental basis for work is salient it will reduce a person's felt responsibility. The attribution, "I am doing this job only for the money," should inhibit commitment. A similar point was raised by Ingham (1970), who analyzed absenteeism and turnover in light engineering firms in Bradford, England. Observing that larger organizations had more absenteeism (but lower turnover), he argued that workers were attracted to large firms because of the higher pay offered, but that this instrumental orientation led to little personal involvement with the organization....

There is far too little empirical work on the nature of commitment to jobs, and how features of the work situation lead to or detract from feelings of personal responsibility for work. Much more detailed accountings of the particulars of job situations need to be made.

## REFERENCES

Becker, H. S. Notes on the concept of commitment. *American Journal of Sociology*, 1960, 66, 32–40.

Festinger, L. *A theory of cognitive dissonance.* Stanford, Calif.: Stanford University Press, 1957.

Festinger, *Conflict, decision, and dissonance.* Stanford, Calif.: Stanford University Press, 1964.

Gow, J. S. Clark, A. W., & Dossett, G. S. A path analysis of variables influencing labour turnover. *Human Relations.* 1974, 27, 703–19.

Hackman, J. R., & Lawler, E. E. Employee reactions to job characteristics. *Journal of Applied Psychology*, 1971, 55, 259–86.

Hackman, J. R., & Oldham, G. R. Motivation through the design of work: Test of a theory. Technical Report no. 6, Administrative Sciences, Yale University, 1974.

Ingham, G. K. *Size of industrial organizations and worker behavior.* Cambridge: Cambridge University Press, 1970.

Kanter, R. M. Commitment and social organizations. *American Sociological Review.* 1968.

Kiesler, C. A. *The psychology of commitment: Experiments linking behavior to belief.* New York: Academic Press, 1971.

Kiesler, C. A. Sakumura, J. A test of a model for commitment. *Journal of Personality Social Psychology*, 1966,3 349–53.

Lepper, M. R., Greene, D., & Nisbett, R. E. Undermining children's intrinsic interest with extrinsic rewards: A test of the "overjustifiaction" hypothsis. *Journal of Personality and Social Psychology*, 1973, 28, 129–37.

Lewin, K. Gruop decision and social change. In T. M. Newcomb and E.L. Hartley (Eds.), *Readings in social psychology*. New York: Holt, Reinhart & Winston, 1947, pp. 330–44.

Maguire, M. A., & Ouchi, W. Organizational control and work satisfaction. Research Paper no. 278, Graduate School of Business, Stanford University, 1975.

Newman, J. E. Predicting absenteeism and turnover: A field comparison of Fishbein's model and traditional job attitude measures. *Journal of Applied Psychology*, 1975, 17, 69–78.

Organ, D. W., & Greene, N. The perceived purposefulness of of job behavior: Antecedents and consequences . *Academy of Management Journal*, 1974, 17,69–78.

Stagner, R. Boredom on the assembly line: Age and personality variables. *Industrial Gerontology*, 1975, 21, 23–44.

Zanna, M. P. Attitude inference in a low choice setting. Ph. D. dissertation, Yale University, 1970.

# 23. THE ROLE OF THE FOUNDER IN CREATING ORGANIZATIONAL CULTURE

Edgar H. Schein

How do the entrepreneur/founders of organizations create organizational cultures? And how can such cultures be analyzed? These questions are central to this article. First I will examine what organizational culture is, how the founder creates and embeds cultural elements, why it is likely that first-generation companies develop distinctive cultures, and what the implications are in making the transition from founders or owning families to "professional" managers.

The level of confusion over the term *organizational culture* requires some definitions of terms at the outset. An organizational culture depends for its existence on a definable organization, in the sense of a number of people interacting with each other for the purpose of accomplishing some goal in their defined environment. An organization's founder simultaneously creates such a group and, by force of his or her personality, begins to shape the group's culture. But that new group's culture does not develop until it has overcome various crises of growth and survival, and has worked out solutions for coping with its external problems of adaptation and its internal problems of creating a workable set of relationship rules.

Organizational culture, then, is the pattern of basic assumptions that a given group has invented, discovered, or developed in learning to cope with its problems of external adaptation and internal integration—a pattern of assumptions that has worked well enough to be considered valid and, therefore, to be taught to new members as the correct way to perceive, think, and feel in relation to those problems.

In terms of external survival problems, for example, I have heard these kinds of assumptions in first-generation companies:

*The way to decide on what products we will build is to see whether we ourselves like the product; if we like it, our customers will like it.*

*The only way to build a successful business is to invest no more than 5 percent of your own money in it.*

*The customer is the key to our success, so we must be totally dedicated to total customer service.*

In terms of problems of internal integration the following examples apply:

*Ideas can come from anywhere in this organization, so we must maintain a climate of total openness.*

*The only way to manage a growing business is to supervise every detail on a daily basis.*

*The only way to manage a growing business is to hire good people, give them clear responsibility, tell them how they will be measured, and then leave them alone.*

Several points should be noted about the definition and the examples. First, culture is not the overt behavior or visible artifacts one might observe on a visit to the company. It is not even the philosophy or value system that the founder may articulate or write down in various "charters." Rather, it is the assumptions that underlie the values and determine not only behavior patterns, but also such visible artifacts as architecture, office layout, dress codes, and so on. This distinction is important because founders bring many of these assumptions with them when the organization begins; their problem is how to articulate, teach, embed, and in other ways get their own assumptions across and working in the system.

Founders often start with a theory of how to succeed; they have a cultural paradigm in their heads, based on their experience in the culture in which they grew up. In the case of a founding *group*, the theory and paradigm arise from the way that group reaches consensus on their assumptions about how to view things. Here, the evolution of the culture is a multi-stage process reflecting the several stages of group formation. The ultimate organizational culture will always reflect the complex interaction between (1) the assumptions and theories that founders bring to the group initially and (2) what the group learns subsequently from its own experiences.

## WHAT IS ORGANIZATIONAL CULTURE ABOUT?

Any new group has the problem of developing shared assumptions about the nature of the world in which it exists, how to survive in it, and how to manage and integrate internal relationships so that it can operate effectively and make life livable and comfortable for its members. These external and internal problems can be categorized as shown in Table 23.1.

The external and internal problems are always intertwined and acting simultaneously. A group cannot solve its external survival problem without being integrated to some degree to

**TABLE 23.1**
External and internal problems

Problems of External Adaptation and Survival

1. Developing consensus on the *primary task, core mission, or manifest and latent functions of the group*—for example, strategy.
2. Consensus on *goals*, such being the concrete reflection of the core mission.
3. Developing consensus on the *means to be used* in accomplishing the goals—for example, division of labor, organization structure, reward system, and so forth.
4. Developing consensus on the *criteria to be used in measuring how well the group is doing against its goals and targets*—for example, information and control systems.
5. Developing consensus on *remedial or repair strategies* as needed when the group is not accomplishing its goals.

Problems of Internal Integration

1. *Common language and conceptual categories.* If members cannot communicate with and understand each other, a group is impossible by definition.
2. Consensus on *group boundaries and criteria for inclusion and exclusion.* One of the most important areas of culture is the shared consensus on who is in, who is out, and by what criteria one determines membership.
3. Consensus on *criteria for the allocation of power and status.* Every organization must work out its pecking order and its rules for how one gets, maintains, and loses power. This area of consensus is crucial in helping members manage their own feelings of aggression.
4. Consensus on *criteria for intimacy, friendship, and love.* Every organization must work out its own rules of the game for peer relationships, for relationships between the sexes, and for the manner in which openness and intimacy are to be handled in the context of managing the organization's tasks.
5. Consensus on *criteria for allocation of rewards and punishments.* Every group must know what its heroic and sinful behaviors are: what gets rewarded with property, status, and power; and what gets punished through the withdrawal of rewards and, ultimately, excommunication.
6. Consensus on *ideology and "religion."* Every organization, like every society, faces unexplainable events that must be meaning so that members can respond to them and avoid the anxiety of dealing with the unexplainable and uncontrollable.

permit concerted action, and it cannot integrate itself without some successful task accomplishment vis-à-vis its survival problem or primary task.

The model of organizational culture that then emerges is one of shared solutions to problems which work well enough to begin to be taken for granted—to the point where they drop out of awareness, become unconscious assumptions, and are taught to new members as a reality and as the correct way to view things. If one wants to identify the elements of a given culture, one can

go down the list of issues and ask how the group views itself in relation to each of them: What does it see to be its core mission, its goals, the way to accomplish those goals, the measurement systems and procedures it uses, the way it remedies actions, its particular jargon and meaning system, the authority system, peer system, reward system, and ideology? One will find, when one does this, that there is in most cultures a deeper level of assumptions which ties together the various solutions to the various problems, and this deeper level deals with more ultimate questions. The real

**TABLE 23.2**
**Basic Underlying Assumptions around which Paradigms Form**

1. *The organization's relationship to its environment.* Reflecting even more basic assumptions about the relationship of humanity to nature, one can assess whether the key members of the organization view the relationship as one of dominance, submission, harmonizing, finding an appropriate niche, and so on.

2. *The nature of reality and truth.* Here are the linguistic and behavioral rules that define what is real and what is not, what is a "fact," how truth is ultimately to be determined, and whether truth is "revealed" or "discovered"; basic concepts of time as linear or cyclical, monochronic or polychronic; basic concepts such as space as limited or infinite and property as communal or individual; and so forth.

3. *The nature of human nature.* What does it mean to be "human," and what attributes are considered intrinsic or ultimate? Is human nature good, evil, or neutral? Are human beings perfectible or not? Which is better, Theory X or Theory Y?

4. *The nature of human activity.* What is the "right" thing for human beings to do, on the basis of the above presumptions about reality, the environment, and human nature; to be active, passive, self-developmental, fatalistic, or what? What is work and what is play?

5. *The nature of human relationships.* What is considered to be the "right" way for people to relate to each other, to distribute power and love? Is life cooperative or competitive; individualistic, group collaborative, or communal; based on traditional lineal authority, law, or charisma, or what?

---

cultural essence, then, is what members of the organization assume about the issues shown in Table 23.2.

In a fairly "mature" culture—that is, in a group that has a long and rich history—one will find that these assumptions are patterned and interrelated into a "cultural paradigm" that is the key to understanding how members of the group view the world. In an organization that is in the process of formation, the paradigm is more likely to be found only in the founder's head, but it is important to try to decipher it in order to understand the biases or directions in which the founder "pushes" or "pulls" the organization.

## HOW DO ORGANIZATIONAL CULTURES BEGIN?

### The role of the founder

Groups and organizations do not form accidentally or spontaneously. They are usually created because someone takes a leadership role in seeing how the concerted action of a number of people

could accomplish something that would be impossible through individual action alone. In the case of social movements or new religions, we have prophets, messiahs, and other kinds of charismatic leaders. Political groups or movements are started by leaders who sell new visions and new solutions. Firms are created by entrepreneurs who have a vision of how a concerted effort could create a new product or service in the marketplace. The process of culture formation in the organization begins with the founding of the group. How does this happen?

In any given firm the history will be somewhat different, but the essential steps are functionally equivalent:

1. A single person (founder) has an idea for a new enterprise.

2. A founding group is created on the basis of initial consensus that the idea is a good one: workable and worth running some risks for.

3. The founding group begins to act in concert to create the organization by raising funds, obtaining patents, incorporating, and so forth.

4. Others are brought into the group according to what the founder or founding group considers necessary, and the group begins to function, developing its own history.

In this process the founder will have a major impact on how the group solves its external survival and internal integration problem. Because the founder had the original idea, he or she will typically have biases on how to get the idea fulfilled—biases based on previous cultural experiences and personality traits. In my observation, entrepreneurs are very strong-minded about what to do and how to do it. Typically they already have strong assumptions about the nature of the world, the role their organization will play in that world, the nature of human nature, truth, relationships, time, and space.

## Three examples

*Founder A,* who built a large chain of supermarkets and department stores, was the dominant ideological force in the company until he died in his seventies. He assumed that his organization could be dominant in the market and that his primary mission was to supply his customers with a quality, reliable product. When A was operating only a corner store with his wife, he built customer relations through a credit policy that displayed trust in the customer, and he always took products back if the customer was not satisfied. Further, he assumed that stores had to be attractive and spotless, and that the only way to ensure this was by close personal supervision. He would frequently show up at all his stores to check into small details. Since he assumed that only close supervision would teach subordinates the right skills, he expected all his store managers to be very visible and very much on top of their jobs.

A's theory about how to grow and win against his competition was to be innovative, so he encouraged his managers to try new approaches, to bring in consulting help, to engage in extensive training, and to feel free to experiment with new technologies. His view of truth and reality was to find it wherever one could and, therefore, to be open to one's environment and never take it for granted that had all the answers. If new things worked, A encouraged their adoption.

Measuring results and fixing problems was, for A, an intensely personal matter. In addition to using traditional business measures, he went to the stores and, if he saw things not to his liking, immediately insisted that they be corrected. He trusted managers who operated on the basis of similar kinds of assumptions and clearly had favorites to whom he delegated more.

Authority in this organization remained very centralized; the ultimate source of power, the voting shares of stock, remained entirely in the family. A was interested in developing good managers throughout the organization, but he never assumed that sharing ownership through some kind of stock option plan would help in that process. In fact, he did not even share ownership with several key "lieutenants" who had been with the company through most of its life but were not in the family. They were well paid, but received no stock. As a result, peer relationships were officially defined as competitive. A liked managers to compete for slots and felt free to get rid of "losers."

A also introduced into the firm a number of family members who received favored treatment in the form of good developmental jobs that would test them for ultimate management potential. As the firm diversified, family members were made division heads even though they often had relatively little general management experience. Thus peer relationships were highly politicized. One had to know how to stay in favor, how to deal with family members, and how to maintain trust with nonfamily peers in the highly competitive environment.

A wanted open communication and high trust levels, but his own assumptions about the role of the family, the effect of ownership, and the correct way to manage were, to some degree, in conflict with each other, leading many of the members of the organization to deal with the conflicting signals by banding together to form a kind of counter-culture within the founding culture. They were more loyal to each other than to the company.

Without going into further detail, I want to note several points about the "formation" of this organization and its emerging culture. By definition, something can become part of the culture only if it works. A's theory and assumptions about how things "should be" worked, since his company grew and prospered. He personally received a great deal of reinforcement for his own assumptions, which undoubtedly gave him increased confidence that he had a correct view of the world. Throughout his lifetime he steadfastly adhered to the principles with which he started, and did everything in his power to get others to accept them as well. At the same time, however, A had to share concepts and assumptions with a great many other people. So as his company grew and learned from its own experience, A's assumptions gradually had to be modified, or A had to withdraw from certain areas of running the business. For example, in their diversification efforts, the management bought several production units that would permit backward integration in a number of areas—but, because they recognized that they knew little about running factories, they brought in fairly strong, autonomous managers and left them alone.

A also had to learn that his assumption did not always lead to clear signals. He thought he was adequately rewarding his best young general managers, but could not see that for some of them the political climate, the absence of stock options, and the arbitrary rewarding of family members made their own career progress too uncertain. Consequently, some of his best people left the company—a phenomenon that left A perplexed but unwilling to change his own assumptions in this area. As the company matured, many of these conflicts remained and many subcultures formed around groups of younger managers who were functionally or geographically insulated from the founder.

*Founder B* built a chain of financial service organizations using sophisticated financial analysis techniques in an urban area where insurance companies, mutual funds, and banks were only beginning to use these techniques. He was the conceptualizer and the salesman in putting together the ideas for these new organizations, but he put only a small percentage of the money up himself, working from a theory that if he could not convince investors that there was a market, then the idea was not sound. His initial assumption was that he did not know enough about the market to gamble with his own money—an assumption based on experience, according to a story he told about the one enterprise in which he had failed miserably. With this enterprise, he had trusted his own judgment on what customers would want, only to be proven totally wrong the hard way.

B did not want to invest himself heavily in his organizations, either financially or personally. Once he had put together a package, he tried to find people whom he trusted to administer it. There were usually people who, like himself, were fairly open in their approach to business and not too hung up on previous assumptions about how things should be done. One can infer that B's assumptions about concrete goals, the means to be used to achieve them, measurement criteria, and repair strategies were pragmatic: Have a clear concept of the mission, test it by selling it to investors, bring in good people who understand what the mission is, and then leave them alone to implement and run the organization, using only ultimate financial performance as a criterion.

B's assumptions about how to integrate a group were, in a sense, irrelevant since he did not inject himself very much into any of his enterprises. To determine the cultures of those enterprises, one had to study the managers put into key positions by B—matters that varied dramatically from one enterprise to the next. This short example illustrates that there is nothing automatic about an entrepreneur's process of inserting personal vision or style into his or her organization. The process depends very much on whether and how much that person wants to impose himself or herself.

*Founder C*, like A, was a much more dominant personality with a clear idea of how things should be. He and four others founded a manufacturing concern several years ago, one based on the founder's product idea along with a strong intuition that the market was ready for such a product. In this case, the founding group got together because they shared a concept of the core mission, but they found after a few years that the different members held very different assumptions about how to build an organization. These differences were sufficient to split the group apart and leave C in control of the young, rapidly growing company.

C held strong assumptions about the nature of the world—how one discovers truth and solves problems—and they were reflected in his management style. He believed that good ideas could come from any source; in particular, he believed that he himself was not wise enough to know what was true and right, but that if he heard an intelligent group of people debate an idea and examine it from all sides, he could judge accurately whether it was sound or not. He also knew that he could solve problems best in a group where many ideas were batted around and where there was a high level of mutual confrontation around those ideas. Ideas came from individuals, but the testing of ideas had to be done in a group.

C also believed very strongly that even if he knew what the correct course of action was, unless the parties whose support was critical to implementation were completely sold on the idea, they would either misunderstand or unwittingly sabotage the idea. Therefore, on any important decision, C insisted on wide debate, many group meetings, and selling the idea down and laterally in the organization; only when it appeared that everyone understood and was committed would he agree to going ahead. C felt so strongly about this that he often held up important decisions even when he personally was already convinced of the course of action to take. He said that he did not want to be out there leading all by himself if he could not count on support from the troops; he cited past cases in which, thinking he had group support, he made a decision and, when it failed, found his key subordinates claiming that he had been alone in the decision. These experiences, he said, taught him to ensure commitment before going ahead on anything, even if doing so was time-consuming and frustrating.

While C's assumptions about how to make decisions led to a very group-oriented organization, his theory about how to manage led to a strong individuation process. C was convinced that the only way to manage was to give clear and simple individual responsibility and then to measure the person strictly on those responsibilities. Groups could help make decisions and obtain commitment, but they could not under any circumstance be responsible or accountable. So once a decision was made, it had to be carried out by individuals. If the decision was complex, involving a reorganization of functions, C always insisted that the new organization had to be clear and simple enough to permit the assignment of individual accountabilities.

C believed completely in a proactive model of man and in man's capacity to master nature; hence he expected of his subordinates that they would always be on top of their jobs. If a budget had been negotiated for a year, and if after three months the subordinate recognized that he would overrun the budget, C insisted that the subordinate make a clear decision either to find a way to stay within the budget or to renegotiate a larger budget. It was not acceptable to allow the overrun to occur without informing others and renegotiating, and it was not acceptable to be ignorant of the likelihood that there would be an overrun. The correct way to behave was always to know what was happening, always to be responsible for what was happening, and always to feel free to renegotiate previous agreements if they no longer made sense. C believed completely in open communications and the ability of people to reach reasonable decisions and compromises if they confronted their problems, figured out what they wanted to do, were willing to marshal arguments for their solution, and scrupulously honored any commitments they made.

On the interpersonal level, C assumed "constructive intent" on the part of all members of the organization, a kind of rational loyalty to organizational goals and to shared commitments. This did not prevent people from competitively trying to get ahead—but playing politics, hiding information, blaming others, or failing to cooperate on agreed-upon plans were defined as sins. However, C's assumptions about the nature of truth and the need for every individual to keep thinking out what he or she thought was the correct thing to do in any given situation led to frequent interpersonal tension. In other words, the rule of honoring commitments and following through on consensually reached decision was superseded by the rule of doing only what you believed sincerely to be the best thing to do in any given situation. Ideally, there would be time to challenge the original decision and renegotiate, but in practice time pressure was such that the subordinate, in doing what was believed to be best, often had to be insubordinate. Thus people in the organization frequently complained that decisions did not "stick," yet had to acknowledge that the reason they did not stick was that the assumption that one had to do the correct thing was even more important. Subordinates learned that insubordination was much less likely to be punished than doing something that the person knew to be wrong or stupid.

C clearly believed in the necessity of organization and hierarchy, but he did not trust the authority of position nearly so much as the authority of reason. Hence bosses were granted authority only to the extent that they could sell their decisions; as indicated above, insubordination was not only tolerated, but actively rewarded if it led to better outcomes. One could infer from watching this organization that it thrived on intelligent, assertive, individualistic people—and, indeed, the hiring policies reflected this bias.

So, over the years, the organization C headed had a tendency to hire and keep the people who fit into the kind of management system I am describing. And those people who fit the founder's assumptions found themselves feeling increasingly like family members in that strong bonds of mutual support grew up among them, with C functioning symbolically as a kind of benign but demanding father figure. These familial feelings were very important, though quite implicit, because they gave subordinates a feeling of security

that was needed to challenge each other and C when a course of action did not make sense.

The architecture and office layout in C's company reflected his assumptions about problem solving and human relationships. He insisted on open office landscaping; minimum status differentiation in terms of office size, location, and furnishings (in fact, people were free to decorate their offices any way they liked); open cafeterias instead of executive dining rooms; informal dress codes; first-come, first-serve systems for getting parking spaces; many conference rooms with attached kitchens to facilitate meetings and to keep people interacting with each other instead of going off for meals; and so forth.

In summary, C represents a case of an entrepreneur with a clear set of assumptions about how things should be, both in terms of the formal business arrangements and in terms of internal relationships in the organization—and these assumptions still reflect themselves clearly in the organization some years later.

Let us turn next to the question of how a strong founder goes about embedding his assumptions in the organization.

## HOW ARE CULTURAL ELEMENTS EMBEDDED?

The basic process of embedding a cultural element—a given belief or assumption—is a "teaching" process, but not necessarily an explicit one. The basic model of cultural formation, it will be remembered, is that someone must propose a solution to a problem the group faces. Only if the group shares the perception that the solution is working will that element be adopted, and only if it continues to work will it come to be taken for granted and taught to newcomers. It goes without saying, therefore, that only elements that solve group problems will survive, but the previous issue of "embedding" is how a founder or leader gets the group to do things in a certain way in the first place, so that the question of whether it will work can be settled. In other words, embedding a cultural element in this context means only that the founder/leader has ways of getting the group to try out certain responses. There is no guarantee that those responses will, in fact, succeed in solving the group's ultimate problem. How do founder/leaders do this? I will describe a number of mechanisms ranging from very explicit teaching to very implicit messages of which even the founder may be unaware. These mechanisms are shown in Table 23.3.

As the above case examples tried to show, the initial thrust of the messages sent is very much a function of the personality of the founder; some founders deliberately choose to build an organization that reflects their own personal biases while others create the basic organization but then turn it over to subordinates as soon as it has a life of its own. In both cases, the process of culture formation is complicated by the possibility that the founder is "conflicted," in the sense of having in his or her own personality several mutually contradictory assumptions.

The commonest case is probably that of the founder who states a philosophy of delegation but who retains tight control by feeling free to intervene, even in the smallest and most trivial decisions, as A did. Because the owner is granted the "right" to run his or her own company, subordinates will tolerate this kind of contradictory behavior and the organization's culture will develop complex assumptions about how one runs the organization "in spite of" or "around" the founder.

**TABLE 23.3**

**How is Culture Embedded and Transmitted?**

Each of the mechanisms listed below is used by founders and and key leaders to embed a value or assumption they hold, though the message may be very implicit in the sense that the leader is not aware of sending it. Leaders also may be conflicted, which leads to conflicting messages. A given mechanism may convey the message very explicitly, ambiguously, or totally implicitly. The mechanisms are listed below from more or less explicit to more or less implicit ones.

1. *Formal statements of organizational philosophy, charters, creeds, materials used for recruitment and selection, and socialization.*
2. *Design of physical spaces, facades, buildings.*
3. *Deliberate role modeling, teaching, and coaching by leaders.*
4. *Explicit reward and status system, promotion criteria.*
5. *Stories, legends, myths, and parables about key people and events.*
6. *What leaders pay attention to, measure, and control.*
7. *Leader reactions to critical incidents and organizational crises* (times when organizational survival is threatened, norms are unclear or challenged, insubordination occurs, threatening or meaningless events occur, and so forth).
8. *How the organization is designed and structured.* (The design of work, who reports to whom, degree or decentralization, functional or other criteria for differentiation, and mechanisms used for integration carry implicit messages of what leaders assume and value.)
9. *Organizational systems and procedures.* (The types of information, control, and decision support systems in terms of categories of information, and when and how performance appraisal and other review processes are conducted carry implicit messages of what leaders assume and value.)
10. *Criteria used for recruitment, selection, promotion, leveling off, retirement, and "excommunication" of people.* (The implicit and possibly unconscious criteria that leaders use to determine who "fits" and who doesn't "fit" membership roles and key slots in the organization).

If the founder's conflicts are severe to the point of interfering with the running of the organization, buffering layers of management may be built in or, in the extreme, the board of directors may have to find a way to move the founder out altogether.

The mechanisms listed in Table 23.3 are not equally potent in practice, but they can reinforce each other to make the total message more potent than individual components. In my observation the most important or potent messages are role modeling by leaders (item3), what leaders pay attention to (item 6), and leader reactions to critical events (item 7). Only if we observe these leader actions can we begin to decipher how members of the organization "learned" the right and proper things to do, and what model of reality they were to adopt.

To give a few examples, A demonstrated his need to be involved in everything at a detailed level by frequent visits to stores and detailed inspections of what was going on in them. When he went on vacation, he called the office every single day at a set time and wanted to know in great detail what was going on. This behavior persisted into his period of semi-retirement, when he would still call *daily* from his retirement home, where he spent three winter months.

A's loyalty to his family was quite evident: He ignored bad business results if a family member was responsible, yet punished a non-family member involved in such results. If the family member was seriously damaging the business, A put a competent manager in under him, but did not always give that manager credit for subsequent good results. If things continued to go badly, A would finally remove the family member, but always with elaborate rationalizations to protect the family image. If challenged on this kind of blind loyalty, A would assert that owners had certain rights that could not be challenged. Insubordination from a family member was tolerated and excused, but the same kind of insubordination from a non-family member was severely punished.

In complete contrast, B tried to find competent general managers and turn a business over to them as quickly as he could. He involved himself only if he absolutely had to in order to save the business, and he pulled out of businesses as soon as they were stable and successful. B separated his family life completely from his business and had no assumptions about the rights of a family in a business. He wanted a good financial return so that he could make his family economically secure, but he seemed not to want his family involved in the businesses.

C, like B, was not interested in building the business on behalf of the family; his preoccupation with making sound decisions overrode all other concerns. Hence C set out to find the right kinds of managers and then "trained" them through the manner in which he reacted to situations. If managers displayed ignorance or lack of control of an area for which they were responsible, C would get publicly angry at them and accuse them of incompetence. If managers overran a budget or had too much inventory and did not inform C when this was first noticed, they would be publicly chided, whatever the reason was for the condition. If the manager tried to defend the situation by noting that it developed because of actions in another part of the same company, actions which C and others had agreed to, C would point out strongly that the manager should have brought that issue up much earlier and forced a rethinking or renegotiation right away. Thus C made it clear through his reactions that poor ultimate results could be excused, but not being on top of one's situation could never be excused.

C taught subordinates his theory about building commitment to a decision by systematically refusing to go along with something until he felt the commitment was there, and by punishing managers who acted impulsively or prematurely in areas where the support of others was critical. He thus set up a very complex situation for his subordinates by demanding on the one hand a strong individualistic orientation (embodied in official company creeds and public relations literature) and, on the other, strong rules of consensus and mutual commitment (embodied in organizational stories, the organization's design, and many of its systems and procedures).

The above examples highlighted the differences among the three founders to show the biases and unique features of the culture in their respective companies, but there were some common elements as well that need to be mentioned. All three founders assumed that the success of their business(es) hinged on meeting customer needs: their most severe outbursts at subordinates occurred when they learned that a customer had not been well treated. All of the official message highlighted customer concern, and the reward and control systems focused heavily on such concerns. In the case of A, customer needs were even put ahead of the needs of the family; one way a family member could really get into trouble was to mess up a customer relationship.

All three founders, obsessed with product quality, had a hard time seeing how some of their own managerial demands could undermine quality by forcing compromises. This point is important because in all the official messages, commitment to customers and product quality were uniformly emphasized—making one assume that this value was a clear priority. It was only when one looked at the inner workings of A's and C's organizations that one could see that other assumptions which they held created internal conflicts that were difficult to overcome—conflicts that introduced new cultural themes into the organizations.

In C's organization, for example, there was simultaneously a concern for customers and an arrogance toward customers. Many of the engineers involved in the original product designs had been successful in estimating what customers would really want—a success leading to their assumption that they understood customers well enough to continue to make product designs without having to pay too much attention to what sales and marketing were trying to tell them. C officially supported marketing as a concept, but his underlying assumption was similar to that of his engineers, that he really understood what his customers wanted; this led to a systematic ignoring of some inputs from sales and marketing.

As the company's operating environment changed, old assumptions about the company's

role in that environment were no longer working. But neither C nor many of his original group had a paradigm that was clearly workable in the new situation, so a period of painful conflict and new learning arose. More and more customers and marketing people began to complain, yet some parts of the organization literally could not hear or deal with these complaints because of their belief in the superiority of their products and their own previous assumptions that they knew what customers wanted.

In summary, the mechanisms shown in Table 23.3 represent *all* of the possible ways in which founder messages get communicated and embedded, but they vary in potency. Indeed, they may often be found to conflict with each other—either because the founder is internally conflicted or because the environment is forcing changes in the original paradigm that lead different parts of the organization to have different assumptions about how to view things. Such conflicts often result because new, strong managers who are not part of the founding group begin to impose their own assumptions and theories. Let us look next at how these people may differ and the implications of such differences.

## FOUNDER/OWNERS VS. "PROFESSIONAL MANAGERS"

Distinctive characteristics or "biases" introduced by the founder's assumptions are found in first-generation firms that are still heavily influenced by founders and in companies that continue to be run by family members. As noted above, such biases give the first-generation firm its distinctive character, and such biases are usually highly valued by first-generation employees because they are associated with the success of the enterprise. As the organization grows, as family members or non-family managers begin to introduce new assumptions, as environmental changes force new responses from the organization, the original assumptions begin to be strained. Employees begin to express concern that some of their "key" values will be lost or that the characteristics that made the company an exciting place to work are gradually disappearing.

Clear distinctions begin to be drawn between the founding family and the "professional" managers who begin to be brought into key positions. Such "professional" managers are usually identified as non-family and as non-owners and, therefore, as less "invested" in the company. Often they have been specifically educated to be managers rather than experts in whatever is the company's particular product or market. They are perceived, by virtue of these facts, as being less loyal to the original values and assumptions that guided the company, and as being more concerned with short-run financial performance. They are typically welcomed for bringing in much needed organizational and functional skills, but they are often mistrusted because they are not loyal to the founding assumptions.

Though these perceptions have strong stereotypic components, it's possible to see that much of the stereotype is firmly based in reality if one examines a number of first-generation and family-owned companies. Founders and owners do have distinctive characteristics that derive partly from their personalities and partly from their structural position as owners. It is important to understand these characteristics if one is to explain how strongly held many of the values and assumptions of first-generation or family-owned companies are. Table 23.4 examines the "stereotype" by polarizing the founder/owner and "professional" manager along a number of motivational, analytical, interpersonal, and structural dimensions.

The main thrust of the differences noted is that the founder/owner is seen as being more self-oriented, more willing to take risks and pursue non-economic objectives and, by virtue of being the founder/owner, more *able* to take risks and to pursue such objectives. Founder/owners, are more often intuitive and holistic in their thinking, and they are able to take a long-range point of view because they are building their own identities through their enterprises. They are often more particularistic in their orientation, a characteristic that results in the building of more of

a community in the early organizational stages. That is, the initial founding group and the first generation of employees will know each other well and will operate more on personal acquaintance and trust than on formal principles, job descriptions, and rules.

The environment will often be more political than bureaucratic, and founder-value biases will be staunchly defended because they will form the basis for the group's initial identity. New members who don't fit this set of assumptions and values are likely to leave because they will be uncomfortable, or they will be ejected because their failure to confirm accepted patterns is seen as disruptive.

Founder/owners, by virtue of their position and personality, also tend to fulfill some *unique functions* in the early history of their organizations:

1. *Containing and absorbing anxiety and risk.* Because they are positionally more secure and personally more confident, owners more than managers absorb and contain the anxieties and risks that are inherent in creating, developing, and enlarging an organization. Thus in time of stress, owners play a special role in reassuring the organization that it will survive. They are the stakeholders; hence they do have the ultimate risk.

2. *Embedding non-economic assumptions and values.* Because of their willingness to absorb risk and their position as primary stakeholders, founder/owners are in a position to insist on doing things which may not be optimally efficient from a short-run point of view, but which reflect their own values and biases on how to build an effective organization and/or how to maximize the benefits to themselves and their families. Thus founder/owners often start with humanistic and social concerns that become reflected in organizational structure and process. Even when "participation," or "no layoffs," or other personnel practices such as putting marginally competent family members into key slots are "inefficient," owners can insist that this is the only way to run the business and make that decision stick in ways that professional managers cannot.

**TABLE 23.4**

**How Do Founder/Owners Differ from Professional Managers?**

| Motivation and Emotional Orientation | |
|---|---|
| *Entrepreneurs/founders/owners are...* | *Professional managers are...* |
| Oriented toward creating, building. | Oriented toward consolidating, surviving, growing. |
| Achievement-oriented. | Power- and influence-oriented. |
| Self-oriented, worried about own image; needs for "glory" high | Organization-oriented, worried about company image. |
| Jealous of own prerogatives, need for autonomy high. | Interested in developing the organization and subordinates. |
| Loyal to own company, "local". | Loyal to profession of management, "cosmopolitan". |
| Willing and able to take moderate risks on own authority. | Able to take risks, but more cautious and in need of support. |

| Analytical Orientation | |
|---|---|
| Primarily intuitive, trusting of own intuitions. | Primarily analytical, more cautious about intuitions. |
| Long-range time horizon. | Short-range time horizon. |
| Holistic; able to see total picture, patterns. | Specific; able to see details and their consequences. |

| Interpersonal Orientation | |
|---|---|
| "Particularistic," in the sense of seeing individuals as individuals. | "Universalistic," in the sense of seeing individuals as members of categories like employees, customers, suppliers, and so on. |
| Personal, political, involved. | Impersonal, rational, uninvolved. |
| Centralist, autocratic. | Participative, delegation-oriented. |
| Family ties count. | Family ties are irrelevant. |
| Emotional, impatient, easily bored. | Unemotional, patient, persistent. |

| Structural/Positional Differences | |
|---|---|
| Have the privileges and risks of ownership. | Have minimal ownership; hence fewer privileges and risks. |
| Have secure position by virtue of ownership. | Have less secure position, must constantly prove themselves. |
| Are generally highly visible and get close attention. | Are often invisible and do not get much attention. |
| Have the support of family members in the business. | Function alone or with the support of non-family members. |
| Have the obligation of dealing with family members and deciding on the priorities family issues should have relative to company issues. | Do not have to worry about family issues at all, which are by definition irrelevant. |
| Have weak bosses, Boards that are under their own control. | Have strong bosses, Boards that are not under their own control. |

3. *Stimulating innovation.* Because of their personal orientation and their secure position, owners are uniquely willing and able to try new innovations that are risky, often with no more than an intuition that things will improve. Because managers must document, justify, and plan much more carefully, they have less freedom to innovate.

As the organization ages and the founder becomes less of a personal force, there is a trend away from this community feeling toward more of a rational, bureaucratic type of organization dominated by general managers who may care less about the original assumptions and values, and who are not in a position to fulfill the unique functions mentioned above. This trend is often feared and lamented by first- and second-generation employees. If the founder introduces his or her own family into the organization, and if the family assumptions and values perpetuate those of the founder, the original community feeling may be successfully perpetuated. The original culture may then survive. But at some point there will be a complete transition to general management, and at that point it is not clear whether the founding assumptions survive, are metamorphosed into a new hybrid, or are displaced entirely by other assumptions more congruent with what general managers as an occupational group bring with them.

4. *Originating evolution through hybridization.* The founder is able to impose his or her assumptions on the first-generation employees, but these employees will, as they move up in the organization and become experienced managers, develop a range of new assumptions based on their own experience. These new assumptions will be congruent with some of the core assumptions of the original cultural paradigm, but will add new elements learned from experience. Some of these new elements or new assumptions will solve problems better than the original ones because external and internal problems will have changed as the organization matured and grew. The founder often recognizes that these new assumptions are better solutions, and will delegate increasing amounts of authority to those

managers who are the best "hybrids": those who maintain key old assumptions yet add relevant new ones.

The best example of such hybrid evolution comes from a company that was founded by a very free-wheeling, intuitive, pragmatic entrepreneur: "D" who, like C in the example above, believed strongly in individual creativity, a high degree of decentralization, high autonomy for each organizational unit, high internal competition for resources, and self-control mechanisms rather than tight, centralized organizational controls. As this company grew and prospered, coordinating so many autonomous units became increasingly difficult, and the frustration that resulted from internal competition made it increasingly expensive to maintain this form of organization.

Some managers in this company, notably those coming out of manufacturing, had always operated in a more disciplined, centralized manner—without, however, disagreeing with core assumptions about the need to maximize individual autonomy. But they had learned that in order to do certain kinds of manufacturing tasks, one had to impose some discipline and tight controls. As the price of autonomy and decentralization increased, D began to look increasingly to these manufacturing managers as potential occupants of key general management positions. Whether he was conscious of it or not, what he needed was senior general managers who still believed in the old system but who had, in addition, a new set of assumptions about how to run things that were more in line with what the organization now needed. Some of the first-generation managers were quite nervous at seeing what they considered to be their "hardnosed" colleagues groomed as heirs apparent. Yet they were relieved that these potential successors were part of the original group rather than complete outsiders.

From a theoretical standpoint, evolution through hybrids is probably the only model of culture change that can work, because the original culture is based so heavily on community assumptions and values. Outsiders coming into such a community with new assumptions are likely to find the culture too strong to budge, so they either give up in frustration or find themselves ejected by the organization as being too foreign in orientation. What makes this scenario especially likely is the fact that the *distinctive* parts of the founding culture are often based on biases that are not economically justifiable in the short run.

As noted earlier, founders are especially likely to introduce humanistic, social service, and other non-economic assumptions into their paradigm of how an organization should look, and the general manager who is introduced from the outside often finds these assumptions to be the very thing that he or she wants to change in the attempt to "rationalize" the organization and make it more efficient. Indeed, that is often the reason the outsider is brought in. But if the current owners do not recognize the positive functions their culture plays, they run the risk of throwing out the baby with the bath water or, if the culture is strong, wasting their time because the outsider will not be able to change things anyway.

The ultimate dilemma for the first-generation organization with a strong founder-generated culture is how to make the transition to subsequent generations in such a manner that the organization remains adaptive to its changing external environment without destroying cultural elements that have given it its uniqueness, and that have made life fulfilling in the internal environment. Such a transition cannot be made effectively if the succession problem is seen only in power or political terms. The thrust of this analysis is that the *culture* must be analyzed and understood, and that the founder/owners must have sufficient insight into their own culture to make an intelligent transition process possible.

## ACKNOWLEDGMENTS AND SELECTED BIBLIOGRAPHY

The research on which this paper is based was partly sponsored by the Project on the Family Firm, Sloan School of Management, M.I.T., and by the Office of Naval Research, Organizational Effectiveness Research Programs, under Contract No. N00014–80–C–0905, NR 170–911.

The ideas explored here have been especially influenced by my colleague Richard Beckhard and by the various entrepreneurs with whom I have worked for many years in a consulting relationship. Their observations of themselves and their colleagues have proved to be an invaluable source of ideas and insights.

Earlier work along these lines has been incorporated, into my book *Career Dynamics* (Addison-Wesley, 1978). Further explication of the ideas of an organizational culture can be found in Andrew M. Pettigrew's article "On Studying Organizational Cultures" (*Administrative Science Quarterly*, December 1979), Meryl Louis's article "A Cultural Perspective on Organizations" (*Human Systems Management*, 1981, 2, 246–258), and in H. Schwartz and S. M. Davis's "Matching Corporate Culture and Business Strategy" (*Organizational Dynamics*, Summer 1981).

The specific model of culture that I use was first published in my article "Does Japanese Management Style Have a Message for American Managers?" (*Sloan Management Review*, Fall 1981) and is currently being elaborated into a book on organizational culture.

# 24.  EMPLOYEE WORK ATTITUDES AND MANAGEMENT PRACTICE IN THE U.S. AND JAPAN: EVIDENCE FROM A LARGE COMPARATIVE SURVEY

James R. Lincoln

What do we really know about the work motivation of the Japanese and the role of Japanese management practice in shaping it? How deeply rooted in the culture of Japan and the psyches of the Japanese people is the legendary commitment and discipline of the Japanese labor force? How important are Japanese work patterns and the internal management of the Japanese firm for explaining the Japanese economic miracle, as compared with the macro forces of state guidance, *keiretsu* enterprise groupings, corporate strategy, and low-cost capital? If Japanese management practice does provide part of the explanation for the cooperation and productivity of the Japanese, does it only work with Japanese employees? That is to say, how transportable is Japanese management style: do overseas Japanese firms produce similar results with foreign workers? Do American and European firms that organize in "Japanese" fashion achieve the labor discipline, cooperation, and commitment that seem to characterize Japan?

Attempts to answer these and similar questions have filled the pages of the business press as well as scholarly journals in the nearly 8 years since the publication of *Theory Z* and *The Art of Japanese Management* marked the onset of the Japanese management boom.[1] The quality of these accounts has ranged widely. Too many are ill-informed and opportunistic efforts to capitalize on the explosive demand for information on Japan and Japanese business. Others are thoughtful, incisive discussions by expert journalists, scholars, and consultants able to bring to bear on the issue rich experience from studying,

living, and working in Japan. Notably absent until quite recently is much prominent commentary by the Japanese themselves, who, to a surprising extent, have followed the lead and absorbed the claims of Western observers of the Japanese management scene.[2]

Even the recent expert testimony of writers like Abegglen, Dore, and Vogel on Japanese organization and its lessons for the West is based much more on long personal experience, intuitive understanding, and generally "soft" journalistic research.[3] What does quantitative social science have to say about the contrasts in work motivation and worker productivity between Japan and the U.S.? Though the United States arguably has the world's largest, best-funded, and technically most sophisticated behavioral science community, surprisingly little of this research expertise has been aimed at a problem of critical contemporary importance to Americans: the nature, scope, and origins of the Japanese labor productivity advantage in manufacturing.

This article reviews a large survey research investigation of 106 factories in the U.S. (central Indiana) and Japan (Kanagawa Prefecture) and 8,302 of their employees. Between 1981 and 1983, my colleagues and I interviewed factory executives about the management style and organization of the plant and distributed questionnaires to representative samples of employees. To the best of our knowledge, the resulting data set is the largest and most detailed body of survey information on American and Japanese factory workers and their employing organizations.

James R. Lincoln, "Employee Work Attitudes and Management Practice in the U.S. and Japan: Evidence from a Large Comparative Survey" from *California Management Review*, Fall 1989, vol. 32, No. 1, pp. 89–106.

# ARE WORK ATTITUDES DIFFERENT IN JAPAN AND THE U.S.?

## The Japanese Are Less Satisfied...

A twofold question motivated our research: how do the work attitudes of Japanese manufacturing employees differ between Japan and the U.S.; and do those differences depend on the management and organization of the factory? Let's take the question of work attitudes first. We sought to measure through questionnaire items two attitude dimensions: job satisfaction and commitment to the company. Many would expect Japanese workers to score higher than Americans on both. The long hours, low absenteeism and turnover, the productivity and esprit de corps, the careers spent within a single company, the reluctance even to take time off for vacation—these are all well-documented patterns of Japanese worker behavior. Surely they suggest that job satisfaction and commitment to a particular company are extraordinarily high in Japan.

As Table 24.1 shows, however, what we initially found was quite different. If our survey data are to be believed, it appears that commitment to the company is essentially the same in our American and Japanese employee samples. The specific questionnaire items in the six-item factor-weighted scale likewise either show no difference or the Americans appear to give the "more committed" response. Is the much-touted loyalty of the Japanese employee, then, a myth? Does the stability and discipline of Japanese labor have no basis in the attitudes and values of Japanese workers? These results seemed so at odds with expectations and the impressions of previous scholars that we were quite taken aback.

On the other hand, Table 24.1 *does* show large country differences in the job satisfaction items, but the direction is *contrary* to expectations. American employees seem much more satisfied with their jobs than do the Japanese. We were not, in fact, surprised by this finding. Every prior survey contrasting Japanese and Western work attitudes has likewise found work satisfaction to be lowest among the Japanese.[4]

How are we to interpret these results? Any first-year MBA student knows that high job satisfaction does not spell high work motivation.[5] As Ronald Dore suggests, low job satisfaction in Japan may imply a restless striving for perfection, an ongoing quest for fulfillment of lofty work values and company goals.[6] By the same token, American observers have cautioned that the high percentages of the U.S. workforce routinely reporting satisfaction with their jobs may be more cause for concern than complacency.[7] It may signal low expectations and aspirations, a willingness to settle for meager job rewards, and a preoccupation with leisure-time pursuits.[8]

Another possibility, of course, is that the Japan-U.S. differences in work attitudes we found are due, not to real cultural contrasts in work motives and values, but to measurement biases.[9] Many would argue that a distinctly American impulse is to put the best face on things, to be upbeat and cheerful, to appear in control and successful even when uncertainty is high and the future looks bleak. The Japanese, it appears, bias their assessments in the opposite direction. From the Japanese mother who turns aside praise of her child's piano playing with: *"ie, mada heta desu!"* (no, it is still bad) to the Japanese politicians who, despite Japan's booming economy, persist in protesting the country's weak and dependent posture in world affairs—the Japanese seem to color their evaluations of nearly everything with a large dose of pessimism, humility, and understatement.

## ...But More Committed

In order to better understand the country differences in our sample's work attitudes, we estimated a statistical simultaneous equations model which assumed that satisfaction and commitment are each caused by the other (and by other variables as well). The results showed that commitment to the company is strongly determined by job satisfaction but the reverse relation is weak to nonexistent.[10] Moreover, with the causal reciprocity thus statistically controlled, we found satisfaction still lower in Japan but commitment to the company proved substantially higher. Our initial impression of no commitment difference, it appeared, was due to our earlier failure to adjust for the very large gap in reported job satisfaction. The resulting picture of Japanese work attitudes as combining low job satisfaction and high organizational commitment is not inconsistent with what some theories hold to be a state of strong work motivation. We thus took this evidence as support for our hypothesis that the

**TABLE 24.1**
Descriptive Statistics for Measures of Organizational Commitment and Job Satisfaction

|  | U.S. Mean (SD) | Japan Mean (SD) |
| --- | --- | --- |
| **Organizational Commitment Scale**[a] (alpha = .75,U.S.;.79,Japan) | 2.13(.469) | 2.04(.503)[b] |
| "I am willing to work harder than I have to in order to help this company succeed." (1 = strongly disagree, 5 = strongly agree) | 3.91(.895) | 3.44(.983)[b] |
| "I would take any job in order to continue working for this company."(same codes) | 3.12(1.14) | 3.07(1.13) |
| "My values and the values of this company are quite similar." | 3.15(1.06) | 2.68(.949)[b] |
| "I am proud to work for this company." (same codes) | 3.70(.943) | 3.51(1.02)[b] |
| "I would turn down another job for more pay in order to stay with this company."(same codes) | 2.71(1.17) | 2.68(1.08) |
| "I feel very little loyalty to this company." (1 = strongly agree, 5 = strongly disagree) | 3.45(1.13) | 3.40(1.03) |
| **Job Satisfaction Scale** (alpha = .78, U.S.; .65, Japan) | 1.54(.449) | .962(.350)[b] |
| "All in all, how satisfied would you say you are with your job?" (0 = not at all, 4 = very) | 2.95(1.12) | 2.12(1.06)[b] |
| "If a good friend of yours told you that he or she was interested in working at a job like yours at this company, what would you say?" (0 = would advise against it, 1 = would have second thoughts, 2 = would recommend it) | 1.52(.690) | .909(.673)[b] |
| "Knowing what you know now, if you had to decide all over again whether to take the job you now have, what would you decide?" (0 = would not take job again, 1 = would have some second thoughts, 2 = would take job again) | 1.61(.630) | .837(.776)[b] |
| "How much does your job measure up to the kind of job you wanted when you first took it?"(0 = not what I wanted, 1 = somewhat, 2 = what I wanted) | 1.20(.662) | .427(.591)[b] |

[a] **Factor-weighted composite of commitment (satisfaction) items. "Alpha" is Cronbach's measure of internal consistency reliability.**

[b] **Difference in means between countries significant at p<.001.**

discipline of the Japanese work force does have some basis in the work attitudes of Japanese employees.

## WORK ATTITUDES AND JAPANESE-STYLE ORGANIZATION

What then about the other questions we raised—particularly the extent to which management and organization have something to do with Japan-U.S. differences in work attitudes? Much has been written on the distinctiveness of Japanese management and its power to motivate work effort and loyalty among employees. While our survey could not address all the ways the Japanese firm is thought to be successful at mobilizing its human assets, we were nonetheless able to examine several such hypotheses.

### Seniority Systems Breed Workforce Commitment

First, consider the age and seniority of the worker. The pervasive age and seniority-grading (*nenko*) of Japanese organizations is a much discussed and documented phenomenon.[11] Once maligned as arational and feudalistic, more and more economic and organizational theory has come to recognize the inner logic to seniority systems, particularly in work settings where skills are hard to measure and are peculiar to the firm.[12] Moreover, part of the motivational logic to an employment system that couples permanent employment with seniority compensation is that it builds loyalty and identification with the company's goals. With time spent in the organization individuals accumulate investments and incur opportunity costs. To realize a fair return on these investments they must stick with the company and work to maximize its success. Moreover, the psychological phenomenon of cognitive dissonance—the need to seek congruence or equilibrium between one's acts and one's cognitions—leads people to justify to themselves their past organizational investments by embracing the company's values and goals as their own.

Our survey found, as previous studies had, that age and seniority are strong predictors of company commitment and job satisfaction. Moreover, we found pervasive evidence that these and other work attitudes were more age-dependent in Japan. Part of the reason, it appears, is that rewards and opportunities are more likely to be explicitly tied to age and seniority than in the American workplace. Another reason has less to do with age or seniority per se than with differences among generations. Given Japan's rapid postwar social change, older Japanese are apt to have the scarcity-and-production-mentality typical of populations in the early stages of economic development. Younger Japanese are much more likely to share American-style values of leisure, consumption, and affluence. The latter fact evokes endless fretting by Japanese elders over the erosion of traditional values and its dire implications for Japan's future productivity and economic growth.

### Strong Social Bonds Foster Positive Work Attitudes

One of the very distinctive features of Japanese work organization is the cohesiveness of work groups and the strong social bonds that develop between superiors and subordinates.[13] Our survey findings underscore these patterns. The Japanese employees in our sample reported an average of more than two close friends on the job, while the Americans' averaged fewer than one. Moreover, the much-noted Japanese practice of *tsukiai* (work group socializing over food and drink) appears in our finding that Japanese employees were far more likely than Americans to get together after hours with workmates and supervisors. Our study found that employees enmeshed in such networks of coworker relationships, whether Japanese or American, had more positive attitudes toward the company and the job. The clear implication is that a rise in the cohesion of the U.S. workplace to the level typical of Japanese firms would help to narrow the U.S. "commitment gap" with Japan.

There is still the question of whether work group cohesion in the Japanese company is an outcome of rational management efforts at job and organizational design. The alternative interpretation is that Japanese people are simply culturally inclined to cluster into tight-knit cliques.[14] The cultural explanation has many advocates, and certainly a strong case can be made that Japanese values motivate people to bind themselves to groups. On the other side is all the evidence that the Japanese workplace is organized in ways that seem consciously aimed at fostering enterprise community.

## AUTHORITY AND STATUS HIERARCHIES

### Are Japanese Hierarchies "Flat?"

A number of observers have pointed to the shape of the management pyramid in Japanese companies as an example of organizational architecture whose logic is that of fostering commitment to the firm. While American executives and consultants commonly allude (often as a rationale for middle-management reductions at home) to the lean and flat hierarchies of Japanese firms,[15] most scholars generally agree that finely graded hierarchies and narrow spans of control are typical of Japanese organization.[16]

Japanese companies are on the average smaller, more specialized to particular industries, and less likely to use the decentralized, multidivisional structures typical of large, diversified U.S. firms.[17] These traits imply smaller corporate staffs and economies in the deployment of middle-level functional managers. But within a particular plant or business unit, one tends to find levels proliferating, as well as status rankings (based largely on seniority) which bear little direct relation to decision making and responsibility.

Does the shape of Japanese managerial hierarchies play a role in promoting workforce discipline, integration, and commitment? A number of thoughtful observers believe that they do. A finely layered management pyramid implies opportunities for steady progression up long career paths, a critical factor in motivation

when employees expect to spend their working lives within a single firm. Status differentiation also works to avert the polarization and alienation, common in U.S. and British manufacturing, when a rigid class division is drawn between homogeneous "management" and "labor" groups. Japanese hierarchies incorporate many small steps which break up this homogeneity and serve as career ladders. Yet the inequality in status and reward between peak management and production rank-and-file is typically much smaller than in comparably-sized U.S. firms.[18] To many observers, this kind of structure figures importantly in the company-wide community and commitment for which the Japanese company is renowned.

Our survey of 51 Japanese factories and 55 American plants showed the Japanese organizations, despite their smaller mean size (461 vs. 571 employees), averaging 5.5 management levels compared with 4.9 for the American plants. The samples did not differ in average first-line supervisor's span of control, but we did find some evidence in the Japanese plants of more organizational subunits for the same number of employees; a pattern indicative of smaller spans of control.

### Do Flat Hierarchies Produce Positive Work Attitudes?

Japanese plants may have taller hierarchies, but *in both countries* plants with more levels proved to have less committed and satisfied employees.[19] This was the only instance where an organizational design feature typical of U.S. manufacturing appeared to have the motivational advantage. And even here there were some indications that the Japanese approach had merit. We found clear and consistent evidence across a large number of indicators that work attitudes, behaviors, and relations were far less determined by the employee's status position than in the U.S. As we argued above, this is part of the motivational logic of a finely graded hierarchy—to blur the boundaries and reduce the distance between echelons and hence the potential for conflict.

## Do Narrow Spans of Control Mean Domineering Supervisors?

Another highly distinctive feature of Japanese authority hierarchies is the nature of supervision and the quality of the superior-subordinate relationship. Rather than bosses exercising direct authority and issuing commands to subordinate employees, Japanese supervisors seem to function as counselor and confidante to their work groups, building communication and cohesion with a minimum of direct, authoritarian control.[20] In sharp contrast to American workers who generally favor an arm's-length, strictly business, low-intensity relationship with their supervisors, workforce surveys in Japan regularly turn up evidence that Japanese employees prefer a paternalistic, diffuse, and personal supervisory style.[21]

Our study revealed a number of differences in Japanese and U.S. patterns of supervision.[22] The Japanese were much more likely to get together socially with supervisors outside of work. This, of course, is part of *tsukiai*, the Japanese practice of after hours socializing with workgroups. The Japanese were also much less likely than the American respondents to report that their supervisors: "*let them alone unless they asked for help.*"[23] Moreover, such contact with supervisors raised the morale of the Japanese employees but lowered that of the Americans. Finally, we found clear evidence in the American sample that narrow supervisory spans of control reduced commitment and satisfaction. This was not the case in Japan. It appears that narrow spans in the American workplace have a connotation, absent in Japan, of "close and domineering supervision."

These findings paint a consistent picture: frequent supervisor-subordinate interactions have a positive quality in Japanese work settings which is missing in the U.S. While American manufacturing employees keep their distance from supervisors, Japanese employees seek such contact and through it develop stronger bonds to the work group and the organization as a whole.

## DECISION-MAKING STRUCTURES

### Japanese Organizations Are Centralized But Participatory...

Japanese decision-making styles are commonly characterized as participatory, consensus-seeking, and "bottom-up."[24] At the management level, they involve less formal delegation of authority to individual managers and more informal networking (*nemawashi*) to draw people into the decision process. The ironic result is that the formal structure of Japanese decision making appears quite centralized. High-level executives bear at least symbolic responsibility for many decisions which, in U.S. firms, are typically delegated.[25]

The *ringi* system exemplifies this pattern. A middle-level manager drafts a document proposing a course of action (*ringi-sho*). It then circulates up through the hierarchy, acquiring the "chops" (personal stamps) of other managers symbolizing their participation in the decision and willingness to commit to it.

At the shop- or office-floor level, participation operates through small group activities such as quality circles, production teams, and high-responsibility systems that hold workers accountable for quality, minor maintenance, and clean-up in the conduct of their tasks.[26]

We measured decision making in our Japanese and U.S. plants in three ways. First, we used a modification of the standard Aston scale of centralization.[27] For each of 37 standard decision-items, the chief executive of the plant was asked to report the hierarchical level where: the formal authority for the decision was located; and where, in practice, the decision was usually made. Averaged over the 37 decisions, we found strong evidence that, compared with U.S. plants, authority was more centralized in the Japanese plants but there was also more *de facto* participation by lower ranks.

Secondly, in the Japanese plants, we measured the prevalence of *ringi* by asking whether, for each of 37 decisions, the *ringi* system was used. Averaged across the 51 Japanese plants, our informants reported that the *ringi* method was applied to approximately one-third of this set of decisions.

Finally, we measured quality circle participation from our questionnaire survey of employees. We found that 81% of the Japanese plants had quality circle programs in which 94% percent of the employees of those plants participated; 62% of the U.S. plants had circles and 44% of their employees were members.

Our survey results are thus consistent with the impressions of more casual observers: Japanese organizations centralize authority but decentralize participation in decision. The *ringi* system is used to a substantial degree in decision making in Japanese factories. And quality circle participation is close to universal in Japanese plants, though it is reasonably widespread in American plants as well.[28]

## ...A Pattern Which Produces Positive Work Attitudes in Both Countries

The question then becomes: do Japanese decision-making practices help shape the work attitudes of Japanese employees? As with work group cohesion, the motivational payoff to participation has been a central theme in management theory, at least since the Hawthorne studies. We found *in both countries* that organizations which in Japanese fashion coupled formal centralization with de facto participation had more committed and satisfied employees.

Why? This outcome fits the general proposition that Japanese-style management works in the U.S. as well as in Japan. But it is not obvious why this particular configuration should have greater motivational value than one in which formal and *de facto* authority are aligned and both decentralized. Our reasoning is that formal decentralization (as the Aston scale measures it) taps delegation of specialized decision-making roles to lower management positions. First- and second-line supervisors in American manufacturing commonly enjoy a good deal of power over narrow jurisdictional areas. Yet that kind of delegation opens up few opportunities for participation either by the rank-and-file *or* by supervisors in other areas.

When formal authority stays high in the organization but widespread participation occurs, the power of lower management is reduced and decision making becomes the diffuse, participatory kind typical of Japanese organization, not the individualistic, compartmentalized delegation found in American firms. Clark has argued that Japanese middle managers are delegated so little formal authority that they have no choice but to negotiate with their employees in order to get things done.[29] In his view, the networking and consensus-seeking found in Japanese organizations are a direct response to their centralized authority structures.

## Ringi and Quality Circles Also Produce Positive Work Attitudes

What about the specific participatory practices of *ringi* and quality circles? Do they also foster job satisfaction and commitment to a company? Our data suggest that they do. In the sample of Japanese plants, we found a statistically significant positive association between a plant's use of the *ringi* system and the employee's commitment to the firm. This was a noteworthy finding, for the majority of our employee sample were rank-and-file people who would not ordinarily be involved in the *ringi* process. The use of *ringi* is probably symptomatic of a generally participatory decision-making climate which has motivational value for workers and managers alike.

There are good reasons to suppose that quality circle programs are quite different in the U.S. and Japan. Owing in large part to the centralized over-sight of the Japan Union of Scientists and Engineers, quality circle programs in Japanese industry generally comprise a much more uniform set of practices than in the United States. They require a high level of technical training on the part of production workers and a substantial commitment of resources on the part of the firm. American quality circle programs, with much less centralized guidance form professional and managerial bodies, are generally a hodgepodge. Few such programs exhibit the rigor and structure of Japanese practice.

Yet quality circle participation proved to be positively associated with job satisfaction and organizational commitment in both the U.S. and Japan. Moreover, the effect was stronger in the U.S. sample. The reason may in part lie in the later inception of American quality circles which give them a novelty value that has worn off the more established Japanese programs. Recent observers of Japanese quality circle programs have commented on growing problems of maintaining worker interest and motivation.[30]

In summary, our evidence, with rather remarkable consistency, suggests that Japanese-style decision-making arrangements (quality circles, *ringi*, centralized authority combined with dispersed participation) have positive effects on the work attitudes of Japanese and American employees alike. The fact that such arrangements are much more prevalent in Japanese industry suggest a partial explanation for the Japanese edge in labor discipline and commitment.

## COMPANY-SPONSORED EMPLOYEE SERVICES

Yet another distinctive feature of the Japanese employment system is the large bundle of services, programs, and social activities that Japanese firms sponsor and provide for their employees. Such services figure significantly in the traditional portrait of Japanese "paternalism" in industry.[31] The array of programs, activities, classes, ceremonies, peptalks, calisthenics, songs, and other practices that Japanese firms employ in the quest of building community and commitment among the workforce is downright dizzying.[32]

How effective are such programs as motivational devices? Would more ceremonies, company picnics, sports teams, newsletters, and the like create a stronger bond between the U.S. manufacturing worker and the firm? Or, as many Western observers seem to think, are individualistic British and American workers likely to be contemptuous of overt management gestures at creating a

happy corporate family?[33] Once again, a case can be made that employee services in Japan are a reflection, not a cause, of Japanese work values and attitudes. Cultural and historical forces have bred within companies an inclusive enterprise community one sign of which is a profusion of company-planned activities and services.

Still, there are some indications in the historical record that Japanese employers set upon welfarism (along with permanent employment and other labor practices) as a rational instrument for curbing labor militancy and creating, in a time of labor shortage, a more docile and dependent workforce.[34] Its timing coincided with the era of "welfare capitalism" in the United States (the 1920s), which large firms ushered in for similar purposes of managing an unruly labor force and appeasing the growing ranks of muckrakers and progressivist reformers. Why welfarism seemed to "stick" in Japan but faded in the U.S., at least until the postwar period, may be due to several forces: the milder impact on Japan of the Great Depression (which in the U.S. led many firms to jettison expensive welfare programs); the heightened stress on industrial discipline produced by militarist and imperialist policies; and, for cultural reasons, the greater receptivity of Japanese workers to corporate paternalism and the principle of an enterprise family.[35]

### Employee Services Are More Abundant in Japan...

Our strategy for measuring the level of welfare, social, and ceremonial activity was a relatively simple one. We inquired of our informants in each plant whether a list of nine company-sponsored activities/services were present. The list included: outside training, in-house training, an employee newsletter, company ceremonies, company-sponsored sports and recreation programs, new employee orientation programs, an employee handbook, regular plant-wide information-sharing/"pep-talk" sessions, and a morning calisthenics program.

Our hypothesis was that such programs are more prevalent in Japanese firms. That proved to be the case for most of them, specifically: in-house training (by a small margin), formal ceremonies (present in all Japanese plants), sports and recreational activities, formal orientation programs, peptalks, and morning exercise sessions (nonexistent in the U.S. plants we studied). On the other hand, the American plants were more likely to encourage and support enrollment in high school and college coursework (by a large margin) and (by a small one) to provide employees with a company handbook. We found no difference between Japanese and U.S. plants in the likelihood of publishing a company newspaper. The indices proposed by summing these items had acceptable internal consistency reliability levels of .60 in the Japanese sample and .62 in the U.S. sample, indicating that these services tended to cluster in the same firms.

## ... But Raise Commitment and Satisfaction in Both Countries

When we estimated the effect of the services index on employee commitment to the company and satisfaction with the job, we found almost identical positive associations in the two countries. Individualistic or not, the Americans in our sample appeared to react every bit as favorably as the Japanese to company-sponsored employee-oriented services. Once again the lesson seems clear: were such services in American industry to rise to the level typical of Japanese manufacturers, we should witness a corresponding shrinkage in the Japan-U.S. commitment gap.

## ENTERPRISE UNIONS

Finally we consider the structure of unions and their implication for employee work attitudes. A legacy of the postwar Occupation reforms, Japanese unions are organized on a per-enterprise basis, concentrated in the largest firms, and combined into weak federations at higher levels.[36] They organize all regular (blue- and white-collar) employees, up to second-line supervision. Much debate has centered on whether

Japanese enterprise unions are truly independent labor organizations in the Western sense. Some writers see them as highly dependent upon and easily coopted by the company, avoiding confrontations to advance their members' interests and working to build commitment to the firm. Hanami expresses this view well:

*There exists a climate of collusion ... between the employers and the union representing the majority of employees ... Basically the relationship is one of patronage and dependence, though the unions frequently put on an outward show of radical militancy in their utterances and behavior. [Moreover] the president of an enterprise union is in effect the company's senior executive in charge of labor relations.[37]*

Yet other observers argue that, despite the constraints posed by dependence on a single firm, Japanese unions bargain hard on wage and benefit issues and have effectively coordinated their militancy in the annual Spring offensives (*shunto*) which present groups of employers with a set of unified wage demands.[38] A study by Koshiro concludes that union militancy has been an important factor behind rising aggregate wage levels in the postwar Japanese economy.[39]

## U.S. Unions Foster Negative Work Attitudes, Japanese Unions Do Not

What, however, about the impact of unionism on employee work attitudes? Much survey research shows that U.S. union members report *lower* job satisfaction than do nonunion employees.[40] This pattern seems consistent with the goals of American union strategy: to aggregate grievances, foster an adversarial industrial relations climate, and drive a wedge between the worker and the firm.

Yet unionized workers are less likely to quit their jobs than nonunion employees.[41] One interpretation is that "true" dissatisfaction is probably no higher among union members but that the union politicizes the employment relation and encourages workers to inflate and publicize their grievances. In the nonunion workplace, by contrast, workers have no such vehicle for airing dissatisfactions and therefore act on them by simply terminating their relationship with the firm. This view, grounded in Albert Hirschman's "exit-voice-loyalty" model,[42] is also supported by evidence that grievance rates are higher in union shops even when objective working conditions are no worse.[43]

We would not anticipate finding similar union effects on the work attitudes of Japanese unionists. Indeed, a reasonable argument can be made for the opposite prediction: that enterprise unions build support for and loyalty to the company—that they are, in effect, one more Japanese management device for building motivation and commitment.

Our data do not show that. We find no statistically significant effect of union membership on job satisfaction, although we do find a slight tendency for company commitment to be lower in union plants. Thus, it does not appear that Japanese unions are in some sense instruments of a proactive policy of building discipline and dedication in the workforce. On the other hand, what we find in the U.S. still poses a decisive contrast with the Japan case. Consistent with other research, our survey produced strong and clear evidence that unions in U.S. factories give rise to sharply more negative employee work attitudes. Holding constant a large number of variables pertaining to the pay, status, job, skills, and gender of the worker, plus the size, age, and technology of the plant, company commitment and job satisfaction in our Indiana sample were markedly lower among the unionized plants.

The implications appear to be as follows. Japanese unions are not the agents of management that some critics hold them to be. But neither do they present the challenge to harmonious labor-management relations or high workforce morale that U.S. unions historically have posed. Since enterprise-specific unions are generally absent from the U.S. economy, we have no evidence on how they might perform in an American setting.

Some circumstantial evidence from the New United Motors Manufacturing, Inc. (NUMMI) plant in Fremont, California (the Toyota-GM joint venture), suggests, however, that U.S. workers may react very well to Japanese-style collective bargaining.[44] The union at NUMMI is a local of the United Auto Workers, but it made a number of concessions to the company in the area of work rules and job classifications. In turn, the company provides the union with space in the plant, shares information extensively, and enlists the cooperation of the union in enforcing policy with respect to absenteeism, quality, safety, and other issues. Though a small dissident movement has been formed, the level of labor-management cooperation and the productivity and discipline of the workforce at NUMMI has few parallels in the American auto industry. The special relationship between the company and the UAW local, reminiscent of the interdependence between enterprise unions and firms in Japan, is clearly part of the reason.

## DISCUSSION

What conclusions can be drawn from our survey evidence on Japanese and U.S. work attitudes and the role of plant organization and management practice in shaping them? First, though a preliminary reading of the data sends mixed signals, the Japanese employee's combination of high commitment coupled with low satisfaction is in line with the hypothesis of a highly motivated Japanese workforce. Second, we found quite consistent evidence that "Japanese-style" management and employment methods, whether practiced by Japanese or U.S. plants, produce very similar gains in employee work attitudes (see the summary of findings in Table 24.2). These include cohesive work groups, quality circles, participatory (but not delegated) decision making, and company-sponsored services. The fact that such practices are more widely deployed in Japanese than in U.S. industry does suggest they may provide part (though we would hardly argue all) of the reason for the Japan-U.S. "commitment gap" in manufacturing.

Other management and employment practices we examined are not directly comparable across countries and our results cannot therefore be interpreted in this way. They nonetheless testify that tangible differences in Japanese and U.S.

**TABLE 24.2**

Do "Japanese"-Style Management Practices Produce Company Commitment and Job Satisfaction in Japan and in the U.S.?

| "Japanese" Management/ Employment Practice | Impact on Work Attitudes |
|---|---|
| long-term employment and age/ seniority grading | positive in both countries[a] |
| cohesive work groups | positive in both countries |
| dense supervision; close supervisor-subordinate contact | positive in Japan; negative in U.S. |
| "tall," finely-layered hierarchies | negative in both countries; but contributes to management-labor consensus in Japan |
| formal centralization/de facto decentralization of decision–making | positive in both countries |
| *ringi* system | positive in Japan[b] |
| quality circle participation | positive in both countries |
| welfare services | positive in both countries |
| unions (enterprise-specific in Japan; industry/occupation–specific in the U.S.) | weak negative to null in Japan; strongly negative in U.S. |

[a] In the sense that psychological attachment to the firm is found in both countries to rise with age and seniority.

[b] No comparable measure from the U.S. survey.

management translate into competitive advantages for Japanese firms in the area of employee motivation and cooperative industrial relations. In both countries, rising age and seniority engender increasingly positive work attitudes. As career employment and seniority promotion and compensation are more central to Japanese than U.S. employment practice, Japanese companies are better able to capitalize on these motivational returns. The Japanese system of enterprise unions offers collective bargaining in an atmosphere of mutual dependence and cooperation, and, in sharp contrast to U.S. unions, does little to foster tension between the worker and the firm.

Our findings seem to contradict the argument that Japanese management styles are only effective with employees who hold Japanese-type work values. The credibility of this view, which has much face validity, is also undercut by the apparent success of Japanese manufacturing firms in managing their U.S. operations and their American employees. Japanese management is no panacea, and mindless attempts to copy from the Japanese are doubtless doomed to failure. Still, our study strongly suggests that Japanese management practices are in part responsible for the work motivation of Japanese employees and that similar practices in the American workplace yield similar returns. Careful attempts on the part of U.S. managers to move in the direction of Japanese organizational design and human resource management may well yield some long-run competitive payoffs for American manufacturing.

## REFERENCES

1. William G. Ouchi, *Theory Z: How American Business Can Meet the Japanese Challenge* (Reading, MA: Addison-Wesley, 1981); Richard Tanner Pascale and Anthony G. Athos, *The Art of Japanese Management: Applications for American Managers* (New York, NY: Simon and Schuster, 1981).

2. But see, Masahiko Aoki, "Risk Sharing in the Corporate Group," in Masahiko Aoki, ed., *The Economic Analysis of the Japanese firm* (Amsterdam: North-Holland, 1984), pp. 259–264; Taishiro Shirai, ed., *Contemporary Industrial Relations in Japan* (Madison, WI: University of Wisconsin Press, 1983).

3. James C. Abegglen and George Stalk, Jr., *Kaisha: The Japanese Corporation* (New York, NY: Basic Books, 1985); Ronald Dore, *Flexible Rigidities* (Stanford, CA: Stanford University Press, 1987); Ronald Dore. *Taking Japan Seriously* (Stanford, CA: Stanford University Press, 1987); Ezra F. Vogel, *Comeback* (New York, NY: Simon and Schuster, 1985).

4. See the review in James R. Lincoln and Kerry McBride, "Japanese Industrial Organization in Comparative Perspective," *Annual Review of Sociology*, 13(1987): 289–312.

5. See, for example, Charles Perrow, *Complex Organizations: A Critical Essay*, 3rd edition (Glenview, IL: Scott, Foresman, 1986).

6. Ronald Dore, *British Factory, Japanese Factory: The Origins of Diversity in Industrial Relations* (Berkeley, CA: University of California Press, 1973).

7. Robert Blauner, "Work Satisfaction and Industrial Trends in Modern Society," in Walter Galenson and Seymour Martin Lipset, eds., *Labor and Trade Unionism* (New York, NY: John Wiley, 1960), pp. 339–360; HEW Report, *Work in America* (Cambridge, MA: MIT Press, 1973).

8. John H. Goldthorpe, David Lockwood, F. Bechhofer, and J. Platt, *The Affluent Worker: Industrial Attitudes and Behavior* (London: Cambridge University Press, 1968).

9. Dore, 1973, op. cit.

10. James R. Lincoln and Arne L. Kalleberg, "Work Organization and Workforce Commitment: A Study of Plants and Employees in the U.S. and Japan," *American Sociological Review*, 50 (1985): 738-760; James R. Lincoln and Arne L. Kalleberg, *Culture, Control, and Commitment: A Study of Work Organization and Work Attitudes in the U.S. and Japan* (Cambridge: Cambridge University Press, 1989).

11. Kazuo Koike, "Internal Labor Markets: Workers in Large Firms," in Taishiro Shirai, ed., op. cit., pp. 29–62.

12. Edward Lazear, "Why Is There Mandatory Retirement?" *Journal of Political Economy*, 87(1979): 1261–1284.

13. Robert E. Cole, "Permanent Employment in Japan: Facts and Fantasies," *Industrial and Labor Relations Review*, 26 (1972): 612–630; Thomas P. Rohlen, *For Harmony and Strength* (Berkeley, CA: University of California Press, 1974).

14. See, for example, Chie Nakane, *Japanese Society* (Berkeley, CA: University of California Press, 1970).

15. Thomas J. Peters and Robert H. Waterman, Jr., *In Search of Excellence: Lessons from America's Best-Run Companies* (New York, NY: Harper and Row, 1982).

16. Michael Y. Yoshino, *Japan's Managerial System: Tradition and Innovation* (Cambridge, MA: MIT Press, 1968); Dore, 1973, op. cit.; Richard Tanner Pascale, "Zen and the Art of Management," *Harvard Business Review*, 56 (1978): 153–162.

17. Rodney C. Clark, *The Japanese Company* (New Haven, CT: Yale, 1979).

18. Abegglen and Stalk, op. cit.

19. Lincoln and Kalleberg, 1985, op. cit.

20. Dore, 1973, op. cit.; Cole, 1972, op. cit.

21. Robert M. Marsh and Hiroshi Mannari, *Modernization and the Japanese Factory* (Princeton, NJ: Princeton University Press, 1977); Arthur M. Whitehill and Shinichi Takezawa, *The Other Worker: A Comparative Study of Industrial Relations in the U.S. and Japan* (Honolulu, HI: East-West Center Press, 1968).

22. Lincoln and Kalleberg, 1989, op. cit., Chapter 4.

23. Pascale and Athos, op. cit., p. 183.

24. Ouchi, op. cit.

25. Ezra F. Vogel, *Modern Japanese Organization and Decision-Making* (Berkeley, CA: University of California Press, 1975); Yoshino, op. cit.

26. Robert E. Cole, *Work, Mobility, and Participation* (Berkeley, CA: University of California Press, 1979).

27. D. S. Pugh, D. J. Hickson, C. R. Hinings, and C. Turner, "Dimensions of Organization Structure," *Administrative Science Quarterly*, 13 (1968): 65–91; James R. Lincoln, Mitsuyo Hanada, and Kerry McBride, "Organizational Structures in Japanese and U.S. Manufacturing," *Administrative Science Quarterly*, 31 (1986): 338–364.

28. Robert E. Cole, *Strategies for Learning: Small Group Activities in American, Japanese, and Swedish Industry* (Berkeley, CA: University of California Press, 1989).

29. Clark, op. cit.

30. Kunio Odaka, "The Japanese Style of Workers' Self-Management: From the Voluntary to the Autonomous Group," in Velnko Rus, Akihiro Ishikawa, and Thomas Woodhouse, eds., *Employment and Participation* (Tokyo: Chuo University Press, 1982), p. 323.

31. John W. Bennett and Iwao Ishino, *Paternalism in the Japanese Economy* (Minneapolis, MN: University of Minnesota Press, 1963).

32. See, for example, Dore, 1973, op. cit.; Rohlen, op. cit.; Marsh and Mannari, op. cit.

33. See, for example, Goldthorpe et al., op. cit.

34. Cole, 1979, op. cit.

35. Yoshino, op. cit.

36. H. Kawada, "Workers and Their Organizations," in Bernard Karsh and Solomon B. Levine, eds., *Workers and Employers in Japan* (Tokyo: University of Tokyo Press), pp. 217–268; Shirai, op. cit.

37. Tadashi Hanami, *Labor Relations in Japan Today* (Tokyo: Kodansha International Ltd., 1979), p. 56.

38. Jean Bounine-Cabale, Ronald Dore, and Kari Tapiola, "Flexibility in Japanese Labor Markets," Report of the OECD Team, 1988.

39. Kazutoshi Koshiro, "The Quality of Life in Japanese Factories," in Taishiro Shirai, ed., *Contemporary Industrial Relations in Japan* (1983), pp. 63–88.

40. Richard B. Freeman and James L. Medoff, *What Do Unions Do?* (New York, NY: Basic Books, 1984), Chapter 9.

41. Ibid., p. 139.

42. Albert O. Hirschman, *Exit, Voice, and Loyalty* (Cambridge, MA: Harvard University Press, 1970).

43. Freeman and Medoff, op. cit., p. 139.

44. Clair Brown and Michael Reich, "When Does Union-Management Cooperation Work: A Look at NUMMI and GM-Van Nuys," in Daniel J. B. Mitchell and Jane Wildhorn, eds., *Can California Be Competitive and Caring?* (Los Angeles, CA: Institute of Industrial Relations, University of California, 1989), pp. 115–147.

# Diversity and Interaction

## 25. WOMEN AND MINORITIES IN MANAGEMENT

*Ann M. Morrison and Mary Ann Von Glinow*

Management and executive positions, along with professional and technical jobs, are among the fastest growing occupations between 1984 and 1995 (U.S. Department of Labor, 1987). However, these occupations include jobs not traditionally held by women and minorities, who comprise the new work force. Therefore, one challenge for American organizations is to assimilate a more diverse labor force into high–status, high–skill management roles.

In this article we examine the current status of women and minorities in management, including some recent changes. We present theoretical models from psychology and other social sciences, supported by recent data, to explain the progress and the barriers experienced by women and minorities. Finally, we explore potential remedies for the problems that endure, including programs and practices currently being applied in U.S. organizations as well as research directions that may increase our understanding of relevant issues.

We discuss White women and a wide range of minority groups, including Blacks, Hispanics, and Asians, but relevant research varies considerably in its coverage of various groups. The literature on White women is substantial, evidenced in part by the number of literature reviews done (nine reviews within the last 10 years were cited by Dipboye in 1987). In contrast, the research base on other minorities in management is quite small and is dominated by studies of Black men. Even employment statistics are difficult to uncover for minority groups in management (Cox & Nkomo, 1987; Larwood, Szwajkowski, & Rose, 1988a; Leinster, 1988; Thomas & Alderfer, 1989). Reviews of research on White women are cited instead of individual studies whenever possible, and our focus is on U.S. studies published since 1980.

### CURRENT DATA ON THE STATUS OF WOMEN AND MINORITIES IN MANAGEMENT

According to an Equal Employment Opportunity Commission (EEOC) report (cited by Bradsher, 1988), the number of women, Blacks, and Hispanics in management has quadrupled since 1970, and the number of Asians has increased eightfold. However, the rate of upward movement of women and minority managers provides "clear evidence of nothing less than the abiding racism and sexism of the corporation" (Bradsher, 1988, p. 1).

There is considerable evidence that White women and people of color encounter a "glass ceiling" in management. The glass ceiling is a concept popularized in the 1980s to describe a barrier so subtle that it is transparent, yet so strong that it prevents women and minorities from moving up in the management hierarchy. "Today, women fill merely a third of all management positions (up from 19% in 1972), but most are stuck in jobs with little authority and relatively low pay" (Hymowitz & Schellhardt, 1986, p. 1D). A Korn/Ferry International (1982) survey reported that only 2% of 1,362 senior executives were women. A study of the Fortune 500, the Fortune Service 500, and the 190 largest health care organizations in the United States (Von Glinow & Krzyczkowska-Mercer, 1988) similarly found that only 3.6% of board directorships and 1.7% of corporate officerships in the Fortune 500 were held by women; the Fortune Service 500 and the health industry indicated that 4.4% of board members were women and that 3.8% and 8.5% of their corporate officers, respectively, were women.

Women do not fare any better in management in government or educational institutions. The U.S. government reported only 8.6% women in Senior Executive Service levels (U.S. Office of Personnel Management, 1989), with most female employees clustered in low-paying, non-prestigious GS 5–10 levels (U.S. Department of Labor, 1986). In education, Sandler's 1986 report shows that "on the average, colleges and universities nationwide employ 1.1 senior women (dean and above) per institution" (p. 14).

With regard to the racial composition of management ranks, the statistics show less progress than for women. Only one Black heads a Fortune 1000 company (Leinster, 1988). In the senior ranks, studies by Korn/Ferry International (reported by Jones, 1986) show little change. Of 1,708 senior executives surveyed in 1979, 3 were Black, 2 were Asian, and 2 were Hispanic; only 8 were women, all of them White. In 1985, the list showed 4 Blacks, 6 Asians, 3 Hispanics, and 29 women. In Jones's (1986) words, "I think it's fair to say that this is almost no progress at all" (p. 84).

Some evidence also exists of a glass ceiling for Asians (Lan, 1988). In 1988, only 2.2% of California's Career Executive Assignment positions were held by Asians despite larger representation at the journey and midmanagement levels "that could be considered as qualifying developmental experience for these assignments" (Lan, 1988, p. 11).

With regard to management, one of the few surveys on minorities in business shows that in 1986 in 400 of the Fortune 1000 companies, less that 9% of all managers were minorities, including Blacks, Hispanics, and Asians. A 1986 Equal Employment Opportunity Commission survey (cited by Leavitt, 1988) shows that from 1974 to 1984, the percentage of Black women officials and managers grew at 0.7% of the total, to 1.7%. Malveaux and Wallace (1987), Nkomo (1988), and others claimed that minority women are doubly disadvantaged in terms of upward mobility. They also noted that research on certain minority women, particularly Asians and American Indians, has essentially slipped through the cracks.

Those women and minorities who have advanced into management often find reward differentials. There is evidence that at higher occupational levels, women are less satisfied with their pay than are men (Varca, Shaffer, & McCauley, 1983). One study of 2,600 employees found substantial wage differences between men and women in managerial levels (Drazin & Auster, 1987); another reported that "women at the vice presidential levels and above earn 42% less than their male peers" (Nelton & Berney, 1987, p. 17). Earnings of Black men in management come closer to those of White men (Ploski & Williams, 1983).

The exodus of women and Blacks from corporate America is a disturbing trend sometimes attributed to differential treatment in management (Ellis, 1988; James, 1988; Leinster, 1988; Taylor, 1986). Women started their own businesses at six times the rate that men did between 1974 and 1984 (Leavitt, 1988). Of the 100 leading corporate women identified by a *Business Week* survey in 1976, nearly one third had left their corporate jobs for other pursuits 10 years later (DeGeorge, 1987).

A study by Morrison, White, Van Velsor, and the Center for Creative Leadership (1987) concluded that obstacles related to the glass ceiling will impede women's progress toward top management for the next several decades. Others concur, citing little hope for women or minorities in the near future. Dipboye (1987) claimed that even though female managers are progressing faster than their counterparts of decades ago, they still fail in terms of their rate of progress when compared with White males. *Business Week* recently concluded that "except for the true stars, the first generation of Black managers is destined to top out in middle levels" ("Progress Report," 1984, p. 105).

## THEORETICAL PERSPECTIVES

A number of theories have been offered as to why sexual and racial differences exist within management. These theories tend to fall into three general groups. First are theories that assume that differences handicap women and minorities; these theories postulate that deficiencies in underrepresented groups are largely responsible for their differential treatment in management. Second are theories that cite discrimination by the majority population as the major cause of inequities. Here, bias and stereotyping on the part of White men in power are held to account for the slow progress of women and minorities. Third are theories that pinpoint structural, systemic discrimination as the root cause of differential treatment rather than actions or characteristics of individuals. These theories claim that widespread policies and practices in the social system perpetuate discriminatory treatment of women and people of color.

### Theories Postulating Differences

Riger and Galligan (1980) noted that psychological researchers have emphasized person-centered variables to explain women's low job status.

Women's traits, behaviors, attitudes, and socialization are said to make them inappropriate or deficient as managers because of such factors as their alleged fear of success or their unwillingness to take risks. Riger and Galligan noted that investigations of sex differences have yielded mixed results overall but that current field studies have generally refuted this explanation.

Data disputing both sex and race deficiencies come from the AT&T Assessment Center reports (Howard & Bray, 1988), which showed that female and male managers were more similar than different on personality and motivation factors as well as abilities. Race differences were greater than sex differences, but among the high-potential managers assessed, the relative weaknesses among Blacks in intellectual ability were compensated for by superior performance in interpersonal skills and stability of performance. There is considerable other evidence that women and men in management roles have similar aspirations, values, and other personality traits as well as job-related skills and behaviors (Dipboye, 1987; Dobbins & Platz, 1986; Harlan & Weiss, 1981; Liden, 1985; Morrison et al., 1987; Noe, 1988b; Powell, 1988; Riger & Galligan, 1980; Ritchie & Moses, 1983; White, Crino, & DeSanctis, 1981). Donnell and Hall's (1980) unusually large field study of nearly 2,000 matched pairs of female and male managers led them to conclude that "the disproportionately low numbers of women in management can no longer be explained away by the contention that women practice a different brand of management from that practiced by men" (p. 76).

The human capital theory attempts to explain continued sex- and race-related differences in management by suggesting that individuals are rewarded in their current jobs for their past investment in education and job training (Blau & Ferber, 1987). Workers may choose to accept a wage or to invest in acquiring new skills and experiences to qualify for higher-paying jobs. Blau and Ferber (1987) contended that if this explanation is correct, then women should choose the occupational setting they prefer and invest accordingly in their own human capital. Any policy changes that may be called for to correct differential treatment should be directed to the educational process rather than the employment setting because no differences other than those in human capital are seen as operating.

The human capital explanation assumes that investment pays off equally for all groups, but recent studies suggest that investment yields higher returns for White men than for women and minorities. Education level has not fully accounted for discrepancies in level or pay in recent studies of sex and race differences in management (Cabezas, Shinagawa, & Kawaguchi, 1989; Larwood et al., 1988a; Madden, 1985). Results of a survey of Asian Americans in professional and managerial positions indicate that education and work experience yield low returns in promotion or advancement (Cabezas, Tam, Lowe, Wong, & Turner, in press). Thus, person-centered theory cannot adequately explain differential treatment in management; other factors must also be considered.

## Discrimination Explanations

The second group of theories targets bias on the part of the dominant group as the cause of differential treatment. The labor market discrimination explanation is an economic theory that assumes that relevant stakeholders—employers, customers, employees, and so forth—have discriminatory tastes even when women or minorities are perfect economic substitutes for White men in the workplace (Becker, 1957). Blau and Ferber (1987) pointed out that employers with discriminatory tastes hire women only at a wage discount large enough to compensate for the loss of utility or level of discomfort associated with employing them.

The rational bias explanation is a psychological theory that suggests that discrimination is influenced by contextual circumstances in which sexual or racial bias results in career rewards or punishment (Larwood, Gutek, & Gattiker, 1984; Larwood et al., 1988a; Larwood, Szwajkowski, & Rose, 1988b). In this case, a manager's decision to discriminate is based on whether such discrimination will be viewed positively or negatively by relevant stakeholders and on the possibility of re-

ceiving rewards for discriminating. Rational bias illustrates why discrimination can continue to occur despite substantial regulations against it (Larwood et al., 1988a, 1988b).

Discrimination by the dominant group was also addressed by Wells and Jennings (1983), who argued that Black individuals are not rewarded on the basis of their performance. Organizations that espouse and even mandate racial equality are also characterized by a psychological mind-set of entitlement on the part of the dominant Whites. Blacks' access to resources is limited, Wells and Jennings claimed, and Blacks are systematically excluded from advancement except for a few who are allowed in "threshold" or acceptable positions.

Discrimination occurs in part because of the belief by White men that women and people of color are less suited for management than White men. Comparing actual performance in managerial jobs is difficult, but there is growing concern that differential treatment of women and Blacks is not related to performance alone. Some studies suggest that deficiencies are presumed even when no differences exist because stereotypes based on historical roles persist (Davis & Watson, 1982; Dubno, 1985; Larwood et al., 1984; Leinster, 1988; Powell, 1988; Stevens, 1984; Thomas & Alderfer, 1989). The "good manager" is still described as masculine, rather than androgynous, despite the growing number of female managers (Powell & Butterfield, 1989). Ambiguity or lack of specific information about an individual contributes to bias against women and minorities because judgments are based on negative stereotypes of the group as a whole (Heilman & Martell, 1986; Nieva & Gutek, 1981; Noe, 1988b; Powell, 1988). For example, pay differentials for women may be related more to the salary allocation process than to performance evaluation because salary decisions are made by people less familiar with female managers than are their immediate supervisors (who conduct their performance appraisals), and so bias is more likely (Drazin & Auster, 1987; Freedman & Phillips, 1988). The stereotypes are so strong that contrary data are sometimes ignored in managerial selection and other managerial decisions (Freedman &

Phillips, 1988; Heilman & Martell, 1986; Ilgen & Youtz, 1986). This research suggests that individuals, consciously or not, contribute to differential treatment of women and minorities in management.

## Systemic Barriers

The third set of theories highlights structural discrimination. Intergroup theory (Alderfer, 1986; Thomas & Alderfer, 1989) suggests that two types of groups exist in organizations—identity groups (based on race, ethnicity, family, gender, or age) and organization groups (based on common work tasks, work experiences, and position in the hierarchy). Tension results because organization group membership changes, whereas identity group membership does not. When the pattern of group relations within an organization mirrors the pattern in society as a whole, such as when Whites predominate in high-status positions and Blacks are concentrated in low-status jobs, then evaluations of Blacks (or members of other low-status groups) are likely to be distorted by prejudice or anxiety as racist assumptions go unquestioned in the organization (Thomas & Alderfer, 1989).

Intergroup theory has elements in common with the dual labor market concept in economics. Dual labor market theory was proposed as an alternative explanation to the human capital theory of the 1960s when education and training of inner-city minority workers did not reduce their unemployment rate as much as was anticipated by policymakers at the time (Thurow, 1969). The dual labor market consists of a set of better, or primary, jobs and a set of worse, or secondary, jobs, with little mobility between the two. Groups most frequently associated with the secondary labor market (including women and minorities) are largely confined there, and discrimination is often justified as economic efficiency (Larwood & Gattiker, 1987; Osajima, 1988). Within management, the secondary jobs may be not only those at lower levels but also those in staff (vs. line) functions, wherein women and minorities are found in disproportionate numbers. Staff positions typically are out of the mainstream of the business and do

not lead to top management posts (Jones, 1986; Larwood & Gattiker, 1987; Powell, 1988).

In the field of psychology, structural barriers are included as part of the situation-centered perspective (Riger & Galligan, 1980) and the organization structure perspective (Fagenson, 1988a; Kanter, 1977), which emphasize that women's lack of opportunity and power in organizations and the sex ratio of groups within organizations explain women's lack of managerial success. For example, Kanter's classic research pointed out that if a management cadre is at least 85% men, then the women in the group are "tokens" who very visibly represent women as a category whether they want to or not. These tokens' performances are hindered because of the pressure to which their visibility subjects them and because members of the dominant group exaggerate differences according to stereotypes they believe about women. Because people of color also become tokens in management ranks, the same dynamics may affect them (Ilgen & Youtz, 1986). Women, however, also face sexual harassment, which may be a result of skewed sex ratios favoring men (Gutek, 1985).

The dominance of White men in management poses another structural problem for underrepresented groups. Minorities struggle with fitting into two distinct cultural worlds, a concept called *biculturalism* that has been documented in studies of Black Americans (Thomas & Alderfer, 1989). Bell's (1988) research on bicultural conflict among Black women shows that those from cultures other than that of the dominant work group must choose how to manage the stress of moving physically, cognitively, and emotionally between the two cultural systems. For women of all races, responsibility for home, family, and social activities still accompanies a demanding management job, adding other major sources of pressure (Dipboye, 1987; Morrison et al., 1987; Powell, 1988).

The impact of structural factors is shown by researchers such as Irons and Moore (1985) in their study of the banking industry. They identified the three most significant problems faced by Blacks: (a) not knowing what is going on in the organization or not being in the network (rated as the most serious problem by 75% of survey respondents), (b) racism, and (c) inability to get a mentor. Irons and Moore pointed out that these results concur with those of Fernandez (1981) in showing a strong perception that minorities are excluded from informal work groups. In a study of Asian Americans in professional and management jobs, similar barriers to upward mobility were most often cited: a corporate culture alien to some Asian Americans, management insensitivity, and a lack of networks, mentors, and role models (Cabezas et al., in press). Other research has shown that many female and Black managers feel excluded from informal relationships with their White male colleagues (Rogan, 1984; Rosen, Templeton, & Kichline, 1981; Thomas & Alderfer, 1989).

Mentors and sponsors represent key relationships attributed to career success and, although research results are inconclusive as to whether women and minorities find fewer mentors than do White men, there is some indication that mentor relationships are harder to manage and provide a narrower range of benefits for women and minorities (Dickens & Dickens, 1982; Fagenson, 1988b; Fitt & Newton, 1981; Ford & Wells, 1985; Gooden, 1980; Herbert, 1986; Hunt & Michael, 1983; Kram, 1985; Noe, 1988b; Thomas & Alderfer, 1989). For example, cross-race relationships take longer to initiate, are more likely to end in an unfriendly fashion, and provide less psychosocial support than same-race relationships (Bearden, 1984; Thomas, 1986). Cross-sex mentor relationships are subjected to sexual innuendo, and Black women face taboos across both sex and race (Feinstein, 1987; Kram, 1985; Thomas, 1986). Women and minorities may need more mentors or sponsors than do their White male counterparts—White male superiors in their own area and same-sex or same-race mentors in other areas of the organization who increase their comfort (Thomas & Alderfer, 1989).

Major career development theories do not consider race as a factor, yet evidence from recent studies of Black managers suggests that Black identity development may slow or alter the career development process and affect Blacks' willingness to accept White mentors (Thomas & Alderfer, 1989). Larwood and Gattiker (1987) studied the career development of 215 employees in 17 firms and postulated a dual development model because career patterns differ between women and men as a result of widespread discrimination, competing demands outside work, and other structural barriers. Greenhaus, Parasuraman, and Wormley (1988) studied the career success of 828 managers in three companies. They found differences by sex and race, with Black women having more negative experiences than any other group. To the extent that organizational structures and practices follow models based solely on how White men develop, women and minorities are disadvantaged.

It is possible that elements of all three theoretical approaches described are significantly related to the lack of upward mobility in management for women and minorities. According to some, the interaction of situational factors (in the organization and in society at large) with person-centered characteristics (related to sex and race) accounts for differential treatment (Fagenson, 1988a; Fagenson & Horowitz, 1985; Ilgen & Youtz, 1986; Riger & Galligan, 1980). For example, without opportunities to take challenging assignments, minority managers may fall behind their White cohorts in terms of knowledge and skill development, or they may internalize negative evaluations and stereotypes to the point where they limit themselves and turn down future opportunities for fear they will not succeed (Ilgen & Youtz, 1986). Tests of the interaction between gender and job factors lend some support to this combined approach (Fagenson & Horowitz, 1985; Mainiero, 1986; Yammarino & Dubinsky, 1988) and suggest that remedies and continued research should be directed at all three sets of theories presented here.

## REMEDIAL ACTIONS

In 1977, Kanter recommended that adjustments be made in the workplace to better accommodate women. She rejected the notion that women bear sole responsibility for equal opportunity in business. It is no longer uncommon to hear similar sentiment regarding both women and minorities

(Larwood et al., 1984, 1988a), although actual implementation of adjustments remains an unmet goal for many organizations.

Some organizations may be able to make adjustments more effectively than others depending on the current status of the diversity in their management. A team at Procter & Gamble recommended that firms go beyond two generations of affirmative action into true "multicultural management" (Merenivitch & Reigle, 1979). Most firms tend to be in what they describe as the first generation of affirmative action, characterized by a focus on numbers that stimulates superficial and crisis-oriented actions, racial or sexual hostility, lack of trust, and a widespread presumption that women and minorities are less capable. Compliance with government regulations is the main goal. Some organizations have evolved to a second generation, where they meet most numerical goals and attempt to provide the necessary critical mass for support and role models. Their concern over retaining high-performing women and minorities means implementing accountability for effectively managing these groups.

Merenivitch and Reigle (1979) proposed that in multicultural organizations, the culture recognizes and appreciates diversity, resources and influence are distributed without regard to race or sex, and policies and practices are responsive to all employees' needs. In effect, the multicultural organization deliberately capitalizes on its diversity. As organizations evolve, different techniques for halting discrimination may be advocated depending on which phase the organization is in.

A variety of techniques are being used to reduce differential treatment and to bring diversity into organizations' cultures. Some techniques appear to be targeted toward the human capital issue, some toward discriminatory treatment, and some toward the structural and contextual barriers. Some techniques cover aspects of more than one theory. Education and training, for example, can be important steps for an organization. Some organizations, such as DuPont and GTE, provide additional classroom-training opportunities to women once they are hired, but the trend is to avoid segregating women or minorities so they are not seen as needing special help to become

equally qualified. Many companies, such as IBM and Hewlett-Packard, provide no training at the corporate level for women per se, expecting that the training programs already being offered apply to all equally (Lee, 1986).

A recent development in training is the variety of programs geared to help managers work together within a diverse workforce and reduce discrimination. The value of programs on managing diversity is that issues are brought out into the open, allowing people to discuss their beliefs. One problem this addresses is that women and minorities who have felt pressure to remain silent on issues of sexism and racism now can confront the system rather than have doubts raised about their loyalty or be seen as "too ambitious" ("Blacks in Management," 1983; Jones, 1986; Lee, 1986; Morrison et al., 1987; Rosener, 1986). Eastman Kodak offers such a program to top division managers, and other firms run them for mixed groups, ensuring that at least one third to one half of the underrepresented groups participate in each program. DuPont began running its "Men and Women Working Together" program specifically for managers of saleswomen, but it has since opened it to various employee groups. A spinoff is a program for women only (Lee, 1986).

Despite these attempts to avoid treating women as different, demand for women-only programs is still strong. Because companies have made varying degrees of progress in attacking discrimination, and because some women and minorities rebel against attending segregated programs, the flexibility of organizations in providing different types of training is commendable. Limited research suggests that training may be most useful not in skill-building, but in areas such as career and self-awareness, mentoring, and leadership development (Dipboye, 1987; Lee, 1986; Staley, 1984; White et al., 1981).

Because women and minorities face special situations as tokens, they may need to perfect certain competencies such as conflict resolution. Researchers who have studied Black managers conclude that special skills and, therefore, specialized training may be needed by Blacks. If Blacks do not resolve conflicts that involve themselves or their area, they are likely to be blamed for the conflict (Dickens & Dickens, 1982). Blacks need to be skilled at managing racism and at managing their own rage over the racism they encounter (Cox & Nkomo, 1986; Dickens & Dickens, 1982; Simpson, 1981; Thomas & Alderfer, 1989). Thus, some skill-building programs, as well as awareness and assessment programs, may be appropriate to help women and minorities compete and cope in management.

Some research suggests that bias is most effectively decreased not only by education but also by exposure to and experience with members of the opposite sex and other races (Noe, 1988b; Powell, 1988). Working alongside a woman or a minority group member may be the key to quelling the discriminatory tastes of White men.

Incentives may also be needed to help overcome rational bias and other discrimination that legislation has failed to address and to reduce the effects of tokenism. Some organizations such as Corning Glass Works and Gannett are giving equal employment opportunity accountability to line managers, using bonuses as an incentive. Minority recruitment at Gannett, for example, is monitored by a committee of its publishers and factored into managers' bonus payouts (Roberts, 1988, Schmidt, 1988).

Other organizations use task forces to mandate and even implement changes. The Equitable Financial Company has been using the Women's Business Resource Group to identify and solve women's issues that emerge from the corporation's annual employee survey. According to Nelton and Berney (1987), this task force has been responsible for redesigning the job posting system as well as implementing flextime for working parents and toughening the company stand on sexual harassment. Task forces used in this way — to actually define the problem as well as create the cure — are more unusual than those aimed at problems already targeted, such as those on combining family and career. The task forces most highly praised seem to share several characteristics: direct access to the office of the president, influential members, and the resources required to try out new solutions (Lee, 1986; Nelton & Berney, 1987).

Career management is another key technique for eliminating the glass ceiling for women and people of color. Some research (McCall, Lombardo, & Morrison, 1988; Morrison et al., 1987) has suggested that challenging, successfully completed assignments are important to executives' development. Yet some assignments cited most frequently by the male executives studied were rarely cited by female executives. The indicators are that these assignments are less available to women, including start-ups, troubleshooting, and international experience (Morrison, 1988). The same kind of restrictions on minority managers may also block their advancement. One unusual task force has taken on the challenge of increasing the mobility of women and minorities between "secondary" jobs and primary jobs. Mobil's Committee of Executives targets high-potential women and minorities and places them in key line jobs (Nelton & Berney, 1987).

Senior managers can help move women and minorities out of secondary or threshold management posts by giving them opportunities to take such challenging assignments in the mainstream of the organization and to reinforce their authority in those assignments. A recent study revealed that "only one woman in five found the professional impact of gender to be primarily negative abroad" (Jelinek & Adler, 1988, p. 16). However, confronting superiors' resistance to get the assignment abroad was a major hurdle. Once a woman began the job, her senior male colleagues, particularly from the head office, became important in redirecting early client conversations away from her male colleagues and toward the woman herself to establish smooth, ongoing work relationships (Jelinek & Adler, 1988).

Career development functions such as these are often attributed to mentors; yet, as we noted, women and minorities face special problems with mentoring relationships. Some companies such as Ortho Pharmaceutical Corporation (Zintz, 1988) have tried formally assigning mentors to promising women and minorities, sometimes also including White male protégés in the program as well. However, there is little evidence that assigning mentors is effective (Feinstein, 1987; Noe, 1988a; Zey, 1985). One suggested alternative (or complement) to a formal mentor program is to provide training on how to be a mentor and how to be mentored (Dickens & Dickens, 1982; Feinstein, 1987; Willbur, 1987). Not only may this approach help build awareness of the barriers involved, but it may also allow the element of choice to continue in relationships initiated both by women and minorities seeking a mentor and by more senior managers who want to help.

Support groups may also help. Security Pacific National Bank created a program called Black Officers Support System (BOSS) to help recruit Blacks and reduce their turnover (Irons & Moore, 1985). The Executive Leadership Council in Washington, DC, consists of about 50 Black line managers from major industries who recruit and hire minorities (Leinster, 1988). These groups, along with the many internal women's networks and community groups for women and minorities, may help by providing career guidance and psychological support in managing biculturalism and other tensions.

Despite the existence of these various remedies, the glass ceiling continues to frustrate ambitious women and minorities. Although employers' attitudes appear to be changing, the lack of results can be partly attributed to the lack of employers committed to equal opportunity. A 1983 survey of nearly 800 business opinion leaders (reported by Jones, 1986) showed that of 25 possible human resource priorities, the issue of affirmative action for minorities and women ranked 23rd. Some efforts to attack discrimination in organizations have no doubt been piecemeal, and some may even have been harmful. When women believed they were hired only to meet EEOC guidelines, there was a negative effect on their self-image and development (Heilman, Simon, & Repper, 1987).

Poor results may also be attributed to confusion over which remedies affect which symptoms or causes of differential treatment. As Dipboye (1987) pointed out, few attempts have been made to evaluate training programs, as evidenced by the sparsity of evaluation studies in the literature.

## RESEARCH NEEDED

Evaluating potential remedies to sex- and race-based differential treatment in management is no small task. One difficulty is that the organizational context is so complicated that factors external to specific remedies may affect the outcome more than the remedies themselves. Interventions that can and should be made in critical organizational practices such as recruitment and selection, evaluation, career development, and promotion may be greatly influenced by what Merlin Pope called "contextual prejudices," or exclusionary mechanisms that subtly keep women and minorities on the outside (Jaffe, 1985; Lee, 1986; Morrison et al., 1987; Nelton, 1988; Noe, 1988b; Powell, 1988; Sandler, 1986). A major challenge for researchers is to assess specific techniques, taking into account the effects of organizational culture and other contextual factors. Research across organizations to assess techniques would provide useful data that would allow executives to select those techniques shown to be more effective under circumstances matching those in their own organizations. Better links between specific techniques and theoretical constructs such as those reviewed here are also needed.

Many more fundamental research issues are apparent by the questions that remain. These include unraveling the effects of race, sex, and age in studies by separating female subjects by age and race, separating Blacks by sex and age, and so on. Another needed step is separating one minority group from another rather than grouping them as "minorities"; data on Hispanics and Asians are particularly needed. Assumptions are made about how White women experience the same or different treatment as men or women of color, but little research addresses this issue. Studies that separate the various groups would provide useful comparison data, particularly with regard to the impact of various remedial actions within organizations. Further theoretical refinement is also needed so that theories based on one group (such as White men) are not erroneously generalized to all others. Career development is one such area in which models developed on White males' career experiences may be inappropriately applied to women or minorities (Thomas & Alderfer, 1989).

The number of promising research areas is indicated by the number of questions this review has raised. We especially encourage research in organizations using actual managers and multiple methods so that the results reflect realistic situations. However, it is important that research be done on a variety of theoretical and applied issues.

Research is needed to answer questions about whether actual or perceived differences are keeping women and minorities below a glass ceiling in management and the extent to which the structures and systems or organizations contribute to limited upward mobility. With the demographic changes already taking place in the U.S. labor force, restricting the pool of potential organizational leaders to White men only is foolhardy. Achieving diversity in management requires action. Continued research will help ensure that effective action is taken.

## REFERENCES

Alderfer, C. P. (1986). An intergroup perspective on group dynamics. In J. Lorsch (Ed.), *Handbook of organizational behavior* (pp. 190–222). Englewood Cliffs, NJ: Prentice-Hall.

Bearden, K. W. (1984). *Women proteges' perception of the mentoring process.* Unpublished doctoral dissertation, University of Louisville.

Becker, G. (1957). *The economics of discrimination.* Chicago: University of Chicago Press.

Bell, E. L. (1988). *The bicultural life experience of career oriented black women.* Unpublished manuscript.

Blacks in management: No progress. (1983, January). *Management World,* p. 24.

Blau, F. D., & Ferber, M. A. (1987). Occupations and earnings of women workers. In K. S. Koziara, M. H. Moskow, & L. D. Tanner (Eds.), *Working women: Past, present, future* (pp. 37–68). Washington, DC: BNA Books.

Bradsher, K. (1988, March 17). Women gain numbers, respect in board rooms. *The Los Angeles Times,* pp. l, 6.

Cabezas, A., Shinagawa, L. H., & Kawaguchi, G. (1989). Income and status differences between White and minority Americans: A persistent inequality. In S. Chan (Ed.), *Persistent inequality in the United States.* Lewiston, NY: Edwin Mellen Press.

Cabezas, A., Tam, T. M., Lowe, B. M., Wong, A., & Turner, K. (in press). Empirical study of barriers to upward mobility of Asian Americans in the San Francisco Bay area. In G. Nomura, R. Endo, R. Leong, & S. Sumida (Eds.), *Frontiers of Asian American studies.* Pullman: Washington State University Press.

Cox, T., Jr., & Nkomo, S. (1986). Differential performance appraisal criteria: A field study of black and white managers. *Group and Organization Studies. 11,* 101–119.

Cox, T., Jr., & Nkomo, S. (1987). *Race as a variable in OB/HRM research: A review and analysis of the literature.* Paper presented at the Symposium on Black Career Research, Drexel University, Philadelphia, PA.

Davis, G., & Watson, G. (1982). *Black life in corporate America.* Garden City, NY: Anchor Press/Doubleday.

DeGeorge, G. (1987, June 22). Where are they now? Business Week's leading corporate women of 1976. *Business Week,* pp. 76–77.

Dickens, F., Jr., & Dickens, J. B. (1982). *The black manager: Making it in the corporate world.* New York: Amacom.

Dipboye, R. L. (1987). Problems and progress of women in management. In K. S. Koziara, M. H. Moskow, & L. D. Tanner (Eds.), *Working women: Past, present, future* (pp. 118–153). Washington, DC: BNA Books.

Dobbins, G. H., & Platz, S. J. (1986). Sex differences in leadership: How real are they? *Academy of Management Review, 11,* 118-127.

Donnell, S. M., & Hall, J. (1980, Spring). Men and women as managers: A significant case of no significant difference. *Organizational Dynamics, 8,* 60–76.

Drazin, R., & Auster, E. R. (1987, Summer). Wage differences between men and women: Performance appraisal ratings vs. salary allocation as the locus of bias. *Human Resource Management, 26,* 157–168.

Dubno, P. (1985). Attitudes toward women executives: A longitudinal approach. *Academy of Management Journal, 28,* 235–239.

Ellis, J. (1988, March 14). The black middle class. *Business Week,* pp. 62–70.

Fagenson, E. A. (1988a). *At the heart of women in management research: Theoretical and methodological approaches and their biases.* Paper presented at the Women in Management (WIM) Conference, Halifax, Nova Scotia.

Fagenson, E. A. (1988b). The power of a mentor. *Group & Organization Studies, 13,* 182–194.

Fagenson, E. A., & Horowitz, S. V. (1985). On moving up: A rest of the person-centered, organization-centered and interactionist perspectives. *Academy of Management Proceedings,* 345–348.

Feinstein, S. (1987, November 10). Women and minority workers in business find a mentor can be a rare commodity. *The Wall Street Journal,* p. 39.

Fernandez, J. P. (1981). *Racism and sexism in corporate life.* Lexington, MA: Lexington Books.

Fitt, L. W., & Newton, D. A. (1981, March–April). When the mentor is a man and the protege a woman. *Harvard Business Review,* pp. 56–60.

Ford, D., & Wells, L., Jr. (1985). Upward mobility factors among black public administrators. *Centerboard: Journal of the Center for Human Relations Studies, 3*(1), 38–48.

Freedman, S. M., & Phillips, J. S. (1988). The changing nature of research on women at work. *Journal of Management, 14,* 231–251.

Gooden, W. (1980). *The adult development of black men.* Unpublished doctoral dissertation, Yale University.

Greenhaus, J. H., Parasuraman, S., & Wormley, W. M. (1988, August). *Organizational experiences and career success of black and white managers.* Paper presented at the Annual Meeting of the Academy of Management, Anaheim, CA.

Gutek, B. A. (1985). *Sex and the workplace.* San Francisco: Jossey-Bass.

Harlan, A., & Weiss, C. (1981, September). *Moving up: Women in managerial careers* (Working Paper No. 86). Wellesley, MA: Wellesley College, Center for Research on Women.

Heilman, M. E., & Martell, R. F. (1986). Exposure to successful women: Antidote to sex discrimination in applicant screening decisions? *Organizational Behavior and Human Decision Processes, 37,* 376–390.

Heilman, M. E., Simon, M. C., & Repper, D. P. (1987). Intentionally favored, unintentionally harmed? Impact of sex-based preferential selection on self-perceptions and self-evaluations. *Journal of Applied Psychology, 72,* 62–68.

Herbert, J. I. (1986). *The adult development of black male entrepreneurs.* Unpublished doctoral dissertation, Yale University.

Howard, A., & Bray, D. W. (1988) *Managerial lives in transition.* New York: Guilford.

Hunt, D. M., & Michael, C. (1983, July). Mentorship: A career training and development tool. *Academy of Management Review, 8,* 475–486.

Hymowitz, C., & Schellhardt, T. D. (1986, March 24). The glass ceiling. *The Wall Street Journal,* pp. 1D, 4D–5D.

Ilgen, D. R., & Youtz, M. A. (1986). Factors affecting the evaluation and development of minorities in organizations. *Personnel and Human Resources Management, 4,* 307–337.

Irons, E. D., & Moore, G. W. (1985). *Black managers: The case of the banking industry.* New York: Praeger.

Jaffe, B. (1985, September). A forced fit. *Training and Development Journal, 39*(9), 82–83.

James, F. E. (1988, June 7). More blacks quitting white-run firms: Many cite bias, desire to help minority firms. *The Wall Street Journal,* p. 37.

Jelinek, M., & Adler, N. J. (1988, February). Women: World-class managers for global competition. *Executive, II,* 11–19.

Jones, E. W., Jr. (1986, May–June). Black managers: The dream deferred. *Harvard Business Review,* pp. 84–93.

Kanter R., (1977). *Men and women of the corporation.* New York: Basic Books.

Korn/Ferry International. (1982). *Profile of women senior executives.* New York: Author.

Kram, K. E. (1985). *Mentoring at work.* Glenview, IL: Scott, Foresman.

Lan, D. (1988, September 7). *Information hearing on Asian, Filipino, Pacific Islander (AFPI) demographics and employment.* Memo presented to the California State Personnel Board.

Larwood, L., & Gattiker, U. E. (1987). A comparison of the career paths used by successful women and men. In B. A. Gutek & L. Larwood (Eds.), *Women's career development* (pp. 129–156). Newbury Park, CA: Sage.

Larwood, L., Gutek, B., & Gattiker, U. E. (1984). Perspectives on institutional discrimination and resistance to change. *Group and Organization Studies, 9,* 333–352.

Larwood, L., Szwajkowski, E., & Rose, S. (1988a). Sex and race discrimination resulting from manager-client relationships: Applying the rational bias theory of managerial discrimination. *Sex Roles, 18,* 9–29.

Larwood, L., Szwajkowski, E., & Rose, S. (1988b). When discrimination makes "sense"—The rational bias theory of discrimination. In B. A. Gutek, A. H., Stromberg, & L. Larwood (Eds.), *Women and work.* Beverly Hills, CA: Sage.

Leavitt, J. A. (1988). *Women in administration and management: An information sourcebook.* New York: Oryx Press.

Lee, C. (1986, December). Training for women: Where do we go from here? *Training,* pp. 26–40.

Leinster, C. (1988, January 18). Black executives: How they're doing. *Fortune,* pp. 109–120.

Liden, R. C. (1985). Female perceptions of female and male managerial behavior. *Sex Roles, 12,* 421–433.

Madden, J. F. (1985). The persistence of pay differentials: The economics of sex discrimination. In L. Larwood, A. H. Stromberg, & B. A. Gutek (Eds.), *Women and work: An annual review.* (Vol. l, pp. 76–114). Beverly Hills, CA: Sage.

Mainiero, L. A. (1986). Coping with powerlessness: The relationship of gender and job dependency to empowerment-strategy usage. *Administrative Science Quarterly, 31,* 633–653.

Malveaux, J., & Wallace, P. (1987). Minority women in the work-place. In K. S. Koziara, M. H. Moskow, & L. D. Tanner (Eds.), *Working women: Past, present, future* (pp. 265–298). Washington, DC: BNA Books.

McCall, M. W., Jr. Lombardo, M. M., & Morrison, A. M. (1988). *The lessons of experience.* Lexington, MA: Lexington Books.

Merenivitch, J., & Reigle, D. (1979, January). *Toward a multicultural organization.* (Available from The Proctor & Gamble Company, Personnel Development Department, Cincinnati, OH.)

Morrison, A. M. (1988, May). *Comparing the career paths of men and women.* Paper presented at The Conference Board's conference on *Women in the corporation: The value added.* New York.

Morrison, A. M., White, R. P., Van Velsor, E., & the Center for Creative Leadership (1987). *Breaking the glass ceiling: Can women reach the top of America's largest corporations?* Reading, MA: Addison Wesley.

Nelton, S. (1988, July). Meet your new work force. *Nation's Business,* pp. 14–21.

Nelton, S., & Berney, K. (1987, May). Women: The second wave. *Nation's Business,* pp. 18–27.

Nieva, V. F., & Gutek, B. A. (1981). *Women and work: A psychological perspective.* New York: Praeger.

Nkomo, S. M. (1988). Race and sex: The forgotten case of the black female manager. In S. Rose & L. Larwood (Eds.), *Women's careers: Pathways and pitfalls.* New York: Praeger.

Noe, R. A. (1988a). An investigation of the determinants of successful assigned mentoring relationships. *Personnel Psychology, 41,* 457–479.

Noe, R. A. (1988b). Women and mentoring: A review and research agenda. *Academy of Management Review, 13,* 65–78.

Osajima, K. (1988). Asian Americans as the model minority: An analysis of the popular press image in the 1960s and 1980s. In G. Y. Okihiro, S. Hune, A. A. Hansen, & J. M. Liu (Eds.), *Reflections on shattered windows: Promises and prospects for Asian American studies.* Pullman: Washington State University Press.

Ploski, H. A., & Williams, J. (1983). *The Negro almanac: A reference work on the Afro-American.* New York: Wiley.

Powell, G. N. (1988). *Women and men in management.* Newbury Park, CA: Sage.

Powell, G. N., & Butterfield, D. A. (1989). The "good manager": Did androgyny fare better in the 1980's? *Group and Organization Studies, 14*(2), 216–233.

Progress report on the Black executive: The top spots are still elusive. (1984). *Business Week,* pp. 104–105.

Riger, S., & Galligan, P. (1980). An exploration of competing paradigms. *American Psychologist, 35,* 902–910.

Ritchie, R. J., & Moses, J. L. (1983, May). Assessment center correlates of women's advancement into middle management: A 7-year longitudinal analysis. *Journal of Applied Psychology, 68,* 227–231.

Roberts, J. L. (1988, May 11). Gannett surpasses other newspaper firms in the hiring and promotion of minorities. *The Wall Street Journal,* p. 25.

Rogan, H. (1984, October 26). Young executive women advance farther, faster than predecessors. *The Wall Street Journal,* p. 31.

Rosen, B., Templeton, N. C., & Kichline, K. (1981, December). First few years on the job: Women in management. *Business Horizons, 24,* 26–29.

Rosener, J. B. (1986, December 7). Coping with sexual static. *The New York Times Magazine,* pp. 89, 120–121.

Sandler, B. R. (1986, October). *The campus climate revisited: Chilly for women faculty, administrators, and graduate students.* Washington, DC: The Project on the Status and Education of Women, Association of American Colleges.

Schmidt, P. (1988, October 16). Women and minorities: Is industry ready? *The New York Times,* pp. 25, 27.

Simpson, J. C. (1981, January). The woman boss. *Black Enterprise,* pp. 20–25.

Staley, C. C. (1984, September). Managerial women in mixed groups: Implications of recent research. *Groups and Organization Studies, 9,* 316–332.

Stevens, G. E. (1984, June). Attitudes toward blacks in management are changing. *Personnel Administrator,* pp. 163–171.

Taylor, A., III. (1986). Why women managers are bailing out. *Fortune,* pp. 16–23.

Thomas, D. A. (1986). *An intra-organizational analysis of black and white patterns of sponsorship and the dynamics of cross-racial mentoring.* Unpublished doctoral dissertation, Yale University.

Thomas, D. A., & Alderfer, C. P. (1989). The influence of race on career dynamics: Theory and research on minority career experiences. In M. Arthur, D. Hall, & B. Lawrence (Eds.), *Handbook of career theory.* Cambridge, England: Cambridge University Press.

Thurow, L. (1969). *Poverty and discrimination.* Washington, DC: The Brookings Institute.

U.S. Department of Labor. (1986). *Meeting the challenges of the 1980's..* Washington, DC: Women's Bureau, U.S. Department of Labor.

U.S. Department of Labor. (1987, May). *Work force 2000.* Washington, DC: Employment and Training Administration, U.S. Department of Labor.

U.S. Office of Personnel Management (1989). *Report on minority group and sex by pay plan and appointing authority* (EPMD Report No. 40, March 31, 1989). Washington, DC: U.S. Office of Personnel Management.

Varca, P., Shaffer, G. S., & McCauley, C. D. (1983, June). Sex differences in job satisfaction revisited. *Academy of Management Journal, 26,* 348–353.

Von Glinow, M. A., & Krzyczkowska-Mercer, A. (1988, Summer). Women in corporate America: A caste of thousands. *New management, 6,* pp. 36–42.

Wells, L., & Jennings, C. L. (1983). Black career advances and white reactions: Remnants of Herrenvolk democracy and the scandalous paradox. In D. Vails-Webber & W. N. Potts (Eds.), *Sunrise seminars* (pp. 41–47). Arlington, VA: NTL Institute.

White, M. C., Crino, M. D., & DeSanctis, G. L. (1981). A critical review of female performance, performance training and organizational initiatives designed to aid women in the work-role environment. *Personnel Psychology, 34,* 227–248.

Willbur, J. (1987, November). Does mentoring breed success? *Training and Development Journal,* pp. 38–41.

Yammarino, F. J., & Dubinsky, A. J. (1988). Employee responses: Gender- or job-related differences? *Journal of Vocational Behavior, 32,* 366–383.

Zintz, A. C. (1988, May). *Succession planning, career tracks and mentoring.* Paper presented at The Conference Board, Inc.'s conference on "Women in the Corporation: The Value Added," New York.

Zey, M. (1985, February). Mentor programs: Making the right moves. *Personnel Journal,* pp. 53–57.

# 26. ORGANIZATIONAL DEMOGRAPHY: IMPLICATIONS FOR MANAGEMENT

Jeffrey Pfeffer

"IEEE to Ask Gov't to Investigate Lockheed 'Selective Hiring' Policy" was the headline in the September 10, 1984 issue of *Electronic Engineering Times.* Apparently, the news organization had obtained a copy of the July edition of an internal company newsletter in which hiring of engineers between 30 and 45 in the spacecraft engineering area was advocated "to flatten the current bimodal distribution of 40–60-year-olds and 25–30-year-olds, with a gap in the middle." The newsletter cited the need for a more even distribution of workforce experience and education. Beyond the legalities of whether or not hiring on the basis of age is permissible, the situation described in the article is one that is all too familiar in business and other organizations. In the present instance, Lockheed, which has a high proportion of people who spend most of their career with the company, had undergone a period of downturn in the late 1960s and early 1970s, doing little new hiring and losing some engineers to better opportunities elsewhere. Now, in the late 1970s and early 1980s, with renewed expansion, a younger cohort of engineers was being rapidly added. What the company now faced was an older senior management that would begin to retire and a younger, inexperienced group not quite ready to take their place. Thus, there was the need to hire engineers of moderate age and experience to smooth the distribution and provide an orderly transition of management. Of course, this policy would threaten the younger engineers who had been recruited with the promise of rapid promotion and even the older engineers who could foresee pressures for early retirement to make room for the middle group. The article quoted a Lockheed spokesman trying to address both of these issues: "There are going to be more opportunities for younger engineers, but that doesn't mean that there are going to be less opportunities for older employees."

The type of problems represented in the Lockheed situation arise because organizations, until confronted with some kind of crisis, are often fairly insensitive to managing the demography of their workforce (by which I mean simply its composition in terms of age and length of service, as well as its educational and other compositional characteristics). Only when there are crises of succession—conflict between cohorts that differ vastly in age or time in the organization, or other visible manifestations of problems that are caused by demographic issues—is attention paid to this important factor, and then, often only briefly.

Why is there such myopia about this fundamental aspect of organizations? Organizations are full of people. It often seems only natural and appropriate to analyze and manage organizations using individuals as the units of analysis.[1] Moreover, the emphasis on the individual fits prevailing social values and customs; thus, organization theorists have tried to comprehend organizations in terms of the needs, values, attitudes, cognitions, expectancies, and characteristics of individuals.[2] Managers have often followed this lead and have implemented programs of work redesign, leadership training, and other programs focused primarily on changing the psychology of the individuals in place. This emphasis in both theory and practice on individual-level intrapsychic processes has had at least two deleterious effects. First, it has encouraged organization theorists and managers alike to go into the lay psychology business. However, changing attitudes, beliefs, or perceptions as a way of changing behavior is both difficult and occasionally ineffective. Predicating management practice on what goes on inside people's heads means that one must be able to measure intrapsychic processes—not an easy task.

Moreover, management research and practice, in its almost exclusive emphasis on the individual, has lost sight of that fact that organizations are fundamentally relational entities. People in organizations interact with one another, both in formal and informal structures. There are several ways of thinking about organizations which explicitly encompass their relational properties, including measuring and paying attention to networks of interaction directly. Another such perspective involves analyzing the demography of the organizations.

## WHAT IS ORGANIZATIONAL DEMOGRAPHY?

Most, if not all, surveys include questions on the backgrounds of the respondents, such as their age and time in the organization. Similarly, most organizational personnel information systems contain basic demographic information such as date of hire (and, by inference, time in the organization), age, and sex. The demography of an organization is nothing more than describing it in terms of the distribution on these various dimensions. Organizational demography is based on the data gathered on individuals, but is, in fact, a collective or unit-level property.

Demographic factors are important in understanding and managing organizations because similarity is one of the most important bases of interpersonal attraction,[3] and demographic features such as age, race, and sex both help to determine similarity and also signal that those who share these features are more likely to be similar. People who share experiences and attitudes are more likely to like each other because they will understand each other better, and because liking someone who is similar is self-reinforcing as it ratifies one's own qualities. People in an organization who have gone through a financial crisis or business downturn together will feel closer to each other for having shared the experience, just as employees at People Express who were present during the hectic start-up days have developed a common bond and attraction for each other through that shared experience. Also, attitudinal similarity promotes interpersonal attraction, as we tend to like those who think like we do and have similar beliefs.

Figure 26.1 presents a model of how demographic similarity, particularly along the dimension of time of entry, promotes the development of cohorts and integration and cohesion within such cohorts. When people enter an organization, they begin immediately to develop networks of relations both in order to solve problems of task interdependence and to provide social support and friendship. People who have been in the organization longer will have already developed extensive communication networks and will therefore have less time or capacity to interact with the new entrants. Thus, other things being equal, the new entrants are likely to interact more with other newer employees who are also just getting to know the place and who have more opportunity to develop relationships with them. Similarity in time of entry and in other dimensions such as age and education will lead to increased communication frequency. Communication frequency both tends to increase similarity in values and perspective and is enhanced further by similarity in attitudes and beliefs. All these factors produce greater integration and cohesion among the group that has entered at the same time. In this way, cohorts based on date of entry into the organization

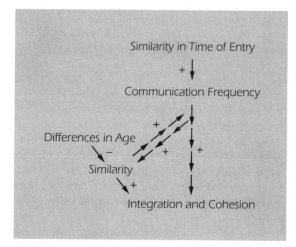

**FIGURE 26.1**

tend to develop. One can observe this effect most strongly in time-of-entry-graded organizations such as law firms, accounting firms, consulting firms, and university faculties, where status and rank are very much based on time of entry and persons tend to enter at one time during the year.

Because similarity is such an important property defining social relations, the most useful measures of organizational demography are those that assess the extent to which a group of persons is heterogeneous or homogeneous. There are a number of measures that have been developed to measure inequality or diversity in social groups, including the Gini index,[4] measures based on the concept of entropy,[5] and other measures of heterogeneity.[6] A review of these measures by Allison suggested that one of the simplest, the coefficient of variation, is one of the best measures of inequality (or its converse, homogeneity) in a group.[7] The coefficient of variation is simply the standard deviation, divided by the mean value of the variable in question. A second useful measure is the proportion of people in an organization or organizational unit of a certain type.

## THE EFFECTS OF DEMOGRAPHY

Demography is measurable; it captures relations among individuals but is a property of the social aggregate and is important in affecting similarity and social relations. It is this latter point, its effect on social relations and behavior, that makes demography important for understanding many things which occur in organizations. Following is a brief review of some of the major research findings on the effects of demography on social systems.

## The Effects of Proportions

There is growing recognition that interaction patterns among individuals are determined, at least in part, by the structural features of the interaction, among the most prominent of which is the relative proportion of persons of different types. On a societal level, Marcia Guttentag and Paul Secord have examined, both historically and across countries, the relative numbers of men and women of marriageable ages.[8] They argue that whether there are relatively more men than women (so that women have more dyadic power) or women than men (so that men have dyadic power) helps to account both over time and across cultures for variations in practices such as the bride providing a dowry or the man paying the father of the bride for the privilege of marrying her, the treatment of women in literature and music, practices of monogamy, and labor force participation and fertility of women.

Perhaps better known to organizational analysts is Rosabeth Kanter's arguments on the effects of occupying a token status.[9] Kanter argued that people occupying token status, such as women in managerial ranks in many organizations, received more attention because of their distinctiveness and that this visibility heightened performance pressures. Also, because of their difference from the majority, tokens caused an increased awareness of boundaries and faced pressures to conform to social expectations or stereotypes about women. Women in token status, in situations in which there were few or no other women, confronted problems in interacting with their co-workers and in receiving credit and attention as individuals rather than as representatives of some group. Kanter's study reported

that women in token status experience more turnover and failure.

Two subsequent studies have attempted to further explore the effect of proportions, both examining the proportion of women in particular settings. In one study,[10] two law schools were compared, one in which women constituted about a third of the student body, and the other in which they constituted about one fifth. The women law students tended to pick more traditionally "female" law specialties, participated less in class, and performed more poorly in the school in which they were a small minority. In a study of government agencies with different proportions of women, Charles Bonjean and his colleagues found less direct support for Kanter's predictions.[11] They noted that to the extent minority group members began to become more numerous, their threat to those in power, the majority, grew. The effect of larger numbers as a threat might thus overcome some of the advantages of diminished uniqueness and visibility for any single individual.

## The Effects of Cohort Size

In addition to their composition, the size of cohorts also can affect the organization as well as members of the cohort. A cohort is simply a group of people who have entered a social system at a given time. Cohorts are defined in terms of age in societies and in terms of date of entry in most organizational settings. Some organizations even speak of entering groups in terms of classes of cohorts—e.g., in law firms there are first-year associates, second-years, and so forth. Similarly, in other professional organizations in which advancement to partnership or other senior status is the result of a review conducted at a specified time after entry—as in promotion in universities and partnership decisions in accounting and managerial consulting firms—there are clear date-of-entry cohorts and gradings.

Again, the effect of cohort size was investigated first at the societal level. In a provocative work on the effect of cohort size on career prospects and other outcomes, Richard Easterlin argued that in the presence of relatively stable economic growth in the U.S., the variation in cohort size caused by radical changes in fertility behavior during the Great Depression and particularly World War II had consequences for the economic prospects of children born during the baby boom or baby bust years.[12] Children born into large cohorts, Easterlin argued, would have more competition for jobs and positions throughout their lives and would therefore achieve relatively less economic success. He further argued that this reduced economic success would manifest itself in diminished fertility in that cohort as well as greater marital instability.

Paul Maxim has investigated the effect of cohort size on juvenile delinquency.[13] Since criminal behavior is age-related, it is fairly well established that the larger the relative size of a youthful cohort, the higher will be the overall crime rate. However, there is also an argument that larger cohorts will tend to exhibit a higher crime rate than small cohorts of the same youthful age. This is because society has a relatively more difficult time in assimilating a larger cohort, since there are comparatively fewer resources and people to accomplish the socialization compared to the number of persons to be socialized. In particular, a large juvenile cohort strains society's attempts to socialize these youths and also facilitates the development of a unique youth subculture. Using data from Ontario, Canada, Maxim found support for the argument that larger youth cohorts would have higher crime rates than smaller ones.

Shelby Stewman has investigated the effects of cohort sizes on promotion chances in formal organizations, finding a similar pattern of results in terms of economic advancement.[14] Stewman observed that if one was a member of a comparatively small cohort, not only were one's own promotion chances better, but every promotion out of the cohort left even fewer subsequent competitors to be selected. It therefore seems clear that cohort sizes and the patterns of recruitment that produce either larger or smaller cohorts are important factors affecting mobility prospects and consequences of mobility, such as motivation and career-plateauing issues.

## Demography and Turnover

The study of the effects of demography on either societies or organizations is really still in its infancy, but the most studied topic to date has been the effect of demography on organizational turnover. The fundamental set of ideas underlying most of this research includes the following:

- turnover is produced, at least in part, by conflict and disagreement within the organization, as well as by a lack of social integration into the social structure;
- similarity and cohesion are both facilitated by demographic similarity, and particularly, by date-of-entry similarity;
- therefore, to the extent that organizations or units or groups are demographically heterogeneous, particularly in terms of the date of entry, there will be more turnover.

The effect of demography on turnover was investigated first in a sample of academic departments on two University of California campuses.[15] The argument was that turnover should be greater to the extent there were cleavages or gaps between the dates of entry of persons into the organization and to the extent that the organizational length-of-service distribution was lumpy rather than smooth. Turnover would be less, the argument went, if there were persons of more continuous time of entry into the organization, so that distinct cleavages among cohorts would not be present.

In this study, other factors that might affect the amount of turnover (such as department size, the level of resources available to the unit, and the extent to which the department operated in a field with a well-developed scientific paradigm so that there was consensus and uniformity on academic issues) were controlled. Both the size of the older cohort and the number of gaps of five to eight years among adjacent members in the department produced significant effects on turnover (which was classified into six types: assistant, associate, and full professor resignations, full professor early retirements, assistant professor non-renewal of contracts, and a summary measure of turnover including the five preceding types).

A subsequent study examined turnover in top management groups in a sample of 31 U.S. corporations.[16] It measured demography in a more refined way, using distance from other members of the group by either age or date of entry. Controlling for the firm's financial performance and other factors, evidence was again found indicating that demography could predict both the amount of turnover at the corporation level of analysis and who turned over at the individual level of analysis. At the top-management group level, it was the more heterogeneous groups (with larger coefficients of variation of distance) that experienced more turnover; at the individual level, it was the most distant or least similar individuals who tended to leave the group.

Another study examined turnover among nurses in U.S. hospitals.[17] Using the Gini index and the index of diversity as measures of demography, this study found that the more heterogeneous the nurse population in terms of date of entry, the greater the turnover—even after controlling for other factors such as wage levels, the local unemployment rate, and collective bargaining status. These three studies taken together seem to offer fairly strong support for the idea that demographic factors are important in accounting for variation in turnover rates across organizational units.

## Demographic Effects of Innovation and Performance

Not only do these turnover effects suggest that demography can be used to help forecast manpower accession requirements and to predict and control turnover, but they may also have some positive consequences for performance, particularly in research and development settings, that can be managed and planned for. Barry Staw was among the first to recognize that turnover, though often associated with costs and ineffectiveness (as in the phrase, "the turnover problem"), was also potentially associated with some positive outcomes as well.[18] In particular, Staw suggested that there were two effects of a long time in the job—one involved increasing skill and familiarity in doing the job, which should positively affect performance; and the second involved diminished interest and motivation because of the loss of novelty and stimulation over time, which should negatively affect performance. The combination of these two effects, Staw reasoned, should produce an inverted U-shaped relationship in which performance should rise for a while (as length of service increased) and then decline (as the diminished motivation and creativity associated from long exposure to the same task overcame the effects of increased proficiency).

This inverted U-shaped effect has been observed when research and development group performance has been plotted against group age, by which is meant the average length of time that members in the group have been on the particular project. Ralph Katz observed that groups with either very young or very old average amount of time on the project performed less well than groups of intermediate age.[19] Katz further went on to show that this was because both intra- and inter-project communication decreased in groups that had been together longer. Groups that were very new had to work out communication and interaction patterns and learn the task, making them somewhat less effective. Groups that had been together on the project a long time routinized behavior to such an extent that communication, and presumably learning and exposure to new ideas, diminished. It was groups intermediate in age that performed most effectively.

## SOME IMPLICATIONS FOR MANAGERIAL PRACTICE

The most fundamental implication of the research on the effects of demography on organizations is that we need to pay attention to this variable as both a cause of behavior and as something to be attended to in thinking about growth patterns, accessions, and other aspects of manpower planning. Human resource planning is important to both anticipate demographic issues before they arise and to manage the demography of the firm and its consequences. A sensitivity to demographic effects can help provide a context to understand organizational behavior. More fundamentally, examining the demographic structure of organizations can assist in the human resource planning function.

There are other, more specific implications. Following are a few representative examples to illustrate how a sensitivity to demographic concerns can help managers in their day-to-day work.

## Choosing Assistants

Most managers occasionally find themselves in the position of choosing people to assist them. Deans choose associate deans, chief executive officers may have occasion to choose the top executive officers who report to them, the managing partner in a professional firm may choose or otherwise influence the selection of a managing committee which assists in the governance task, and presidents choose their cabinet officers and assistants. In each instance, the natural tendency will be to pick people from one's cohort. For example, to fill six key administrative positions, the new Dean of the Harvard Business School chose people who, for the most part, he knew well. Four of them had entered the business school within three years of the time he did. It is not surprising that he would pick from his own cohort. After all, if our arguments about interaction are correct, these are the people he has interacted with most and thus knows best, has the most confidence in, and with whom he is likely to agree and think alike. One would always want to have, as assistants, people on the same wavelength, whom one can trust, whom one understands implicitly, and whom one is socially integrated with. Such a tendency is observed in many other situations. Indeed, ties formed during school or during the first years on the job are well known for producing contacts that lead to subsequent positions and promotions.

Weighed against the advantages of choosing from within one's cohort may be the possible disadvantages of isolating the administrative structure from other important elements in the organization. Indeed, when I have observed deans or other administrators having some difficulty because of a lack of confidence in the rest of the organization, it is often the case that they have assembled an administrative cadre that leaves them well integrated into one cohort in the organization but isolated from others. If there are distinct cleavages and cohort groups within an organization, particularly one that is professional and tends to be administered on a more collegial and participative basis, it becomes important to choose assistants who represent the various cohorts present in the organization. In this way, these cohorts both feel and are represented in policy-making circles. They become more integrated into the governance structure and are less likely to cause trouble as a united and isolated opposition.

## Bringing People In

Since communication is dependent on time of entry and whom one enters with, it is more difficult to bring in people one at a time. To bring in people as a group gives each the opportunity of building links with others for purposes of both task accomplishment and social support. Bringing in people one at a time makes it more likely that they will not effectively get into the social structure, will suffer decreased performance, and will be more likely to leave.

As an example of a company which acts on this insight, consider the Harris Corporation. Harris hires a large number of new engineers and faces the task of getting these new hires rapidly integrated into the firm and up to speed. They use college affiliations as a way of helping this social integration process. For instance, if you are a graduate from Georgia Tech, the company helps you meet and socialize with other Georgia Tech graduates. By helping people find others who share common backgrounds, the corporation seeks to smooth and hasten their integration into the firm.

Many academic departments implicitly recognize the importance of cohorts in the decisions to admit graduate students and to hire faculty. Particularly in the case of student admissions to doctoral programs, concern is often expressed that persons be brought in as part of a small group rather than as lone individuals. The prediction would be that students admitted as part of a group would have a more successful experience in the program than those who have to make their way alone through the often stressful graduate education experience. Also, some departments often try to hire assistant professors in pairs or groups, to make integration into the school easier and to provide ready access to collegial support of all kinds.

Anecdotal evidence suggests that senior executives brought in from outside the organization by themselves are likely to leave and to perform less effectively. The problems of bringing in executive talent from the outside have often been attributed to lack of knowledge of the particular business. Kotter's research on effective general managers indicates that one of their defining characteristics is an extensive network of personal ties and contacts.[20] Executives brought in from outside not only lack that network but, if they are brought by themselves into pre-existing groups, are unlikely to easily break into the existing social structure.

If people cannot be added in groups, then sensitivity to the demographic issues involved can lead the organization to take actions to ease the transition and to provide other mechanisms that will facilitate the interaction and social structural development. In the case of chief executive officers, the problem is most often solved by the individuals bringing in others from their previous organization to help them run their new business.[21] However, there are other mechanisms for facilitating integration into the new social structure which can possibly substitute for wholesale replacement of people.

## Movement, Rotation, and Development of Personnel

The analysis of interaction and communication behavior as a function of time together has implications for both the development of individuals and the enhancement of organizational performance. In the latter instance, Katz[22] and others strongly suggest that the composition of research and development and other groups from whom innovation is expected should be managed to keep average group age in an intermediate range. Programs of systematic job rotation can possibly help to ensure that both individual and group performance remains more in the high point of the inverted U-shaped curve rather than at either end. Indeed, several companies are trying programs along this line to try to ensure that employees develop requisite experience but do not become stale by being kept in the same place too long. What the work on demography suggests is that focusing such programs on the individual is not sufficient. It is the composition of groups and relationships among individuals that are critical variables to keep in mind.

Many corporations have experimented with so called "fast-track" programs. Such programs are often started in recognition of the need to try to attract and, particularly, retain very promising high-potential managers or other employees. Such programs typically involve an extra measure of exposure to different aspects or divisions of the business on a faster time schedule and more rapid promotion up the organizational ladder. Not all of these programs have met with unqualified success, and the concept of demography can help us understand some of the issues involved. On the one hand, the special attention and enhanced mobility experience and future prospects are clearly motivating, particularly to those in the program obtaining these rewards. However, even the "chosen few" may face some problems as a result of this experience. By being moved frequently, communication networks and personal relationships that might normally form are disrupted. As persons move up the organizational hierarchy rapidly, they are more and more in contact with and dependent upon people from different cohorts and with different experiences. Thus, the fast-track employee becomes a token, or a person in a minority status in some respects, with all the pressures this entails. Moreover, because the individual has moved more rapidly than many of his or her peers, the natural linkages to those who entered at around the same time are severed and the individual can find himself in a position of comparative isolation in the social structure in which he or she must operate.

One foreign country's military service experienced just such a result from its fast-track program. Persons promoted rapidly seemed highly satisfied; but once at the rank of major, many of them left, and those who remained often expressed dissatisfaction and had various kinds of performance problems. One explanation is that by moving these few individuals up rapidly, they were separated from their peers with whom they had entered the service. At the rank of major, the interdependence required by the duties of the job increased significantly, requiring more lateral communication and getting things done through relationships. Yet, the individuals who were rapidly promoted were now working with people from a different cohort in terms of both time of entry and age. They were in a token status and, moreover, had few social or communication ties to these people. The job environment was difficult, which may help explain what happened to them in terms of turnover and job performance.

This is not to imply that everyone should necessarily be advanced at the same rate or that promotion or mobility should not be used as reward. Rather, the implication is that by paying attention to the potentially disruptive and costly aspects of such programs, some of the costs might be avoided. For instance, instead of focusing only on the individual and individual movement, it might be possible to move and place people in pairs or small groups—which, while still based on ability, are consistent with their time of entry into the organization, age, or other relevant demographic factors. Cohorts remind us of the essentially relational or group aspects of organizations. Many personnel development and rotation policies are keyed to the individual, neglecting ideas of relationships and thereby causing unnecessary problems for both the individuals and the organizations.

As a simple example, when the so-called whiz kids left the military after the Second World War, they went *as a group* to the Ford Motor Corporation. Consider what might have happened to that group, including McNamara and Arjay Miller, had they gone off to a number of different organizations. They would not have been able to take advantage of their experience in working together; and isolated in separate companies, they might have occupied more of a token or minority status, with all the costs that entails. Their success at Ford was probably a function not only of their singular talents but also of the fact that they entered and moved in the organization as a group.

## Change

Concepts such as demography and cohorts help us to understand that change in organizations is often, if not predominantly, generational.[23] In other words, change occurs through changes in who is in the organization. Of course, this idea is inconsistent with the belief of many who write in the organizational change literature and who seem to believe that individuals are relatively malleable, at least if the correct change technology is employed. However, studies of both organizations and societies seem to suggest that change through generational replacement, or the replacement of one cohort by another, is at least as important and fundamental as change accomplished by the transformation of those already in place.[24]

Such change may not be inevitable or accomplished without friction. Joseph Gusfield has written an interesting analysis of the Women's Christian Temperance Union.[25] The WCTU was originally populated with persons who saw alcohol as a moral issue and who adopted tactics such as legislation aimed at prohibition and other programs founded on morality and religion. Subsequently, younger and newer persons saw alcohol more as a social or medical problem and advocated a set of activities more consistent with that view. The older persons, who were in control of the WCTU, were able to resist the newer viewpoint and maintain their control over the organization and its view of alcohol. Unfortunately for the WCTU, this failure of generational change led to a decline in the organization's membership and influence.

In general, it seems clear that when organizations change directions or strategy, they do so most often through a change in personnel. Indeed, matching the demographics and human resources to organizational strategy and operational requirements is a growing topic in the human resource management literature.[26] Academic disciplines change as new ideas get absorbed in graduate schools and then brought into the field by young faculty. Consulting, legal, and accounting practices change, in part, as new techniques and knowledge are developed and transmitted to the newer practitioners of the field. This generational change in disciplines is most evident in engineering, where technical obsolescence is a recognized problem and has led to a premium being placed on the hiring of the newest graduates with the newest and most current knowledge.

If change is generational, accomplished in important respects through the replacement of one cohort by another, then there are several implications. First, change takes time; unless outside forces intervene, a process of generational change is likely to be lengthy. Second, when cohorts do turn over, as in the political leadership in the People's Republic of China and the Soviet Union, it is important to consider which of the succeeding cohorts to bring in. It is possible, as in the case of the WCTU, to find people in the newer cohorts who carry the identical ideas of those being replaced. At the time of turnover among governing cohorts, such a choice as to who and what point of view or orientation will be brought into power becomes critical, for it imprints the organization and its future operations. This analysis suggests that change is carried in cohorts, not in single individuals.

## CONCLUSION

Ideas of organizational demography can be useful in sensitizing both managers of organizations as well as organizational researchers and analysts to some fundamental ways of thinking about social structures and in some more specific implications for analysis, prediction, and action. In particular, demographic concepts help orient us to the essentially relational nature of organizations. As

Harold Leavitt pointed out a while ago, because of the individualistic values of the society, we tend to think of things in individualistic terms.[27] Thus, we manage careers of individuals; concern ourselves with individual attitudes, needs, and demographic characteristics; and concern ourselves with finding the best individuals and rewarding them individually. The difficulty with this approach is its neglect of the interdependence and relationships that are the essential, indeed defining, characteristic of organizations. For instance, to predict performance or turnover on the basis of an individual's sex is not likely to be productive, though knowing what the sex composition is of the organization or work unit does enable one to make some predictions about performance pressure and social integration. Similarly, tenure in the organization helps to explain turnover, but not as much as when the composition of the whole organization in terms of tenure is considered. The time a person has worked on a research and development team tells us less about the performance of the team than does the average time team members have worked on the particular project together. This shift in focus away from individual to compositional and relational elements is an important feature of demographic analyses.

A second, equally important feature is the shift in orientation toward measurable properties of social units rather than the attention most often paid to intrapsychic processes and psychological constructs. Particularly from the perspective of prediction and management, there is much to be gained from focusing on observable and more manipulable elements of social structure. Thus, one can manage research and development teams to control group age, concern oneself with the demographic composition of top management teams or academic departments to mitigate conflict and facilitate integration, and plan accessions and choose staff to link governance structures across cohorts and other demographic groups. While sensitive to underlying psychological processes of integration, cohesion, and communication, the demographic ideas do not require measurement or management of these variables directly.

Finally, by focusing on cohorts and other salient demographic entities, this perspective helps us bring into focus the importance of generations, generational change, and the relative permanence of social structural arrangements. This is not to suggest that change within persons is impossible, but only that generational or cohort change is another important mechanism by which transformations of organizations occur. Indeed, the literature on organizational change has probably been overly optimistic about the possibility of individual malleability. The concepts of demography suggest how and why permanence becomes institutionalized as well as how change comes about.

Organizational demography is certainly not the only, or perhaps even the most, important concept necessary to analyze and manage organizations. Yet, because of some of the subtle but important shifts in focus it facilitates, it does offer some new insights and some new tools for analyzing formal organizations.

## REFERENCES

1. Charles Perrow, *Organizational Analysis: A Sociological View* (Belmont, CA: Wadsworth, 1970), pp. 3–5.

2. See, for example, Gerald R. Salancik and Jeffrey Pfeffer, "An Examination of Need-Satisfaction Models of Job Attitudes," *Administrative Science Quarterly*, 22 (September 1977): 427–456 for a review of much more of this literature.

3. Ellen Berscheid and Elaine Walster, *Interpersonal Attraction* (Reading, MA: Addison-Wesley, 1969).

4. Joseph L. Gastwirth, "The Estimation of the Lorenz curve and the Gini Index," *Review of Economics and Statistics*, 54 (1972): 306–316.

5. Henry Theil, *Economics and Information Theory* (Chicago, IL: Rand McNally, 1967).

6. Peter M. Blau, *Inequality and Heterogeneity* (New York, NY: Free Press, 1977).

7. Paul D. Allison, "Measures of Inequality," *American Sociological Review*, 43 (December 1978): 865–880.

8. Marcia Guttentag and Paul F. Secord, *Too Many Women? The Sex Ratio Question* (Beverly Hills, CA: Sage Publications, 1983).

9. Rosabeth Moss Kanter, *Men and Women of the Corporation* (New York, NY: Basic Books, 1977), Ch. 8.

10. Eva Spangler, Marsha A. Gordon, and Ronald M. Pipkin, "Token Women: An Empirical Test of Kanter's Hypothesis," *American Journal of Sociology*, 85 (1978): 160–170.

11. Scott J. South, Charles M. Bonjean, William T. Markham, and Judy Corder, "Social Structure and Intergroup Interaction: Men and Women of the Federal Bureaucracy," *American Sociological Review*, 47 (October 1982): 587–599.

12. Richard A. Easterlin, *Birth and Fortune: The Impact of Numbers on Personal Welfare* (New York, NY: Basic Books, 1980).

13. Paul S. Maxim, "Cohort Size and Juvenile Delinquency: A Test of the Easterlin Hypothesis," *Social Forces*, 63 (March 1985): 661–681.

14. Shelby Stewman and Suresh L. Konda, "Careers and Organizational Labor Markets: Demographic Models of Organizational Behavior," *American Journal of Sociology*, 88 (January 1983): 637–685.

15. Bruce McCain, Charles A. O'Reilly, and Jeffrey Pfeffer, "The Effects of Departmental Demography on Turnover: The Case of a University," *Academy of Management Journal*, 26 (1983): 626–641.

16. W. Gary Wagner, Jeffrey Pfeffer, and Charles A. O'Reilly, "Organizational Demography and Turnover in Top-Management Groups," *Administrative Science Quarterly*, 29 (March 1984): 74–92.

17. Jeffrey Pfeffer and Charles O'Reilly, "Hospital Demography and Turnover Among Nurses," unpublished ms., Palo Alto, CA: Graduate School of Business, Stanford University.

18. Barry M. Staw, "The Consequences of Turnover," *Journal of Occupational Behavior*, 1 (1980): 253–273.

19. Ralph Katz, "Project Communication and Performance: An Investigation Into the Effects of Group Longevity," *Administrative Science Quarterly*, 27 (1982): 81–104.

20. John P. Kotter, *The General Managers* (New York, NY: Free Press, 1982).

21. This is illustrated in Lee Iacocca's description of what he did when he took over the Chrysler corporation, in Lee Iacocca, *Iacocca: An Autobiography* (New York, NY: Bantam Books, 1984).

22. Ralph Katz, op. cit.

23. Theodore L. Reed, "Organizational Change in the American Foreign Service, 1925–1965: The Utility of Cohort Analysis," *American Sociological Review*, 43 (1978): 404–421.

24. Norman B. Ryder, "The Cohort as a Concept in the Study of Social Change," *American Sociological Review*, 30 (1966): 843–861.

25. Joseph R. Gusfield, "The Problem of Generations in an Organizational Structure," *Social Forces*, 35 (1957): 322–330.

26. Andrew D. Szilagyi, Jr., and David M. Schweiger, "Matching Managers to Strategies: A Review and Suggested Framework," *Academy of Management Review*, 9 (1984): 626–637.

27. Harold J. Leavitt, "Suppose We Took Groups Seriously ...," in Euguene L. Cass and Frederick G. Zimmer, eds., *Man and Work in Society* (New York, NY: Van Nostrand Reinhold Company, 1975).

# 27. MANAGING ATTRACTION AND INTIMACY AT WORK

Marcy Crary

In recent years the number of women in management and professional positions has increased, so men and women are working together more frequently than ever before. As a result, we now have a relatively new and unstudied phenomenon in organizations: attraction and intimacy at work.

A large part of the writing to date on this topic has dealt with the "office romance," the ways in which managers can deal with these romances, and the problems these relationships create for others in the organization. However, little attention has been devoted to the two people actually involved in a relationship (whether sexual, nonsexual, or assumed by others to be sexual) and to understanding what it is like to be attracted to a co-worker of the opposite sex. There has been little discussion of the ways in which people deal with these feelings and the intense emotional responses that frequently can accompany them.

The label of "office romance" often trivializes the range and complexity of the issues faced by people in a close relationship at work. Outsiders' views of the attraction between two people typically oversimplify the experiences those individuals may be struggling with. These views may also be distorted by the viewer's projection of his or her own concerns into the situation.

Whether one is the person who feels attracted, the one who is the object of attraction, or the manager who is faced with the situation, all three individuals can profit from a better understanding of attractions and close relationships between men and women in organizations. Furthermore, this understanding should emerge from the perspective of the individual involved.

The observations in this article are drawn from the author's research on individuals' experiences of attraction and closeness in the workplace. This work has involved conversations with professional men and women whose workplaces include financial services companies, consulting groups, mental health clinics, state agencies, hospitals, and universities. These people have primarily been individuals in their thirties or forties, married or single, in either the early or the middle stages of their careers. The issues covered include (1) what "intimacy" at work means to different people, (2) what it is like to feel attracted to someone at work, (3) the choice between closeness and distance in female-male work relationships, and (4) the tensions and dilemmas of being in an "intimate" relationship at work (see Table 27.1). The final section of this article discusses the broader implications of these data for people and their organizations.

## DIFFERENT MEANINGS OF ATTRACTION AND INTIMACY AT WORK

Part of the complexity of male-female relationships in the workplace is that individuals may experience the phenomena of attraction and intimacy in very different ways. (The discussions in this article can apply to same-gender work relationships in which there is a conscious component of sexuality present. There are obviously further complexities in peoples' experiences with homosexual relationships, given the organizational and cultural taboos against homosexuality.) Being "attracted" to or feeling "intimate" with a member of the opposite sex at work can have a variety of meanings. Attraction is not always based on physical attractiveness; it can be based upon any number of factors, including one's

Marcy Crary, "Managing Attraction and Intimacy at Work" from *Organizational Dynamics*, Spring 1987.

**TABLE 27.1**
Questionnaire on Attraction and Intimacy at Work

Think of a time when you felt attracted to someone of the opposite sex at work. . .

What did you do with these feelings?
a. I ignored them, hoping they would go away.
b. I talked about them with someone else.
c. I talked about them with the person to whom I was attracted.

How did you behave with the person?
a. I avoided him/her.
b. I continued to work with him/her, but I stayed distant emotionally.
c. I tried to get to know him/her better personally.
d. I sought out more opportunities to work with him/her.

Think of a close relationship you have with a colleague of the opposite sex. . .

How would youy define/describe the closeness of the relationship?
a. Purely professional.
b. Emotional.
c. Spiritual.
d. Sexual.
e. None of the above.
f. Some of the above.
g. All of the above.
h. Other.

What tensions or dilemmas have you had about this relationship at work?
a. I felt vulnerable around him/her.
b. I worried about what other people would be thinking.
c. I worried about what would happen if something/someone came between us.
d. It was hard to balance work and personal time.
e. All of the above.
f. Some of the above.

What effect did the relationship have upon your work?
a. I felt more productive.
b. It interfered with my work.
c. It had no impact on my work.

The questions reflect a sampling of the issues encountered by people who are attracted to or have close relationships with work colleagues of the opposite sex. Deciding how to manage one's own feelings and behavior in these situations is not often easy, and the norms of most workplaces do not make it any easier.

attraction to the other's competence, power, values and beliefs, and so forth.

Similarly, "intimacy" at work can refer to relationships that are close but not necessarily sexual. If people's experiences are to be guides in our thinking about male-female relationships at work, intimacy and sexuality need to be treated as separate dimensions of such relationships.

What then do people mean by "intimacy" at work? The individuals who were interviewed gave a wide range of comments:

*It's being able to exchange honest, straightforward, constructive feedback on our work.*

*We have very creative, free exchanges of ideas about the things we are working on.*

*I can share any or all of the 'backstage' thoughts and feelings that come up for me in this place or in my life outside work.*

*I have the feeling that she is always looking out for me, always ready to help me out or make suggestions.*

Some people describe intimate work relationships that are or have been sexual, but the experience of intimacy at work is not as automatically associated with sexuality as one might think.

In brief, the experience of "intimacy" at work varies from person to person, and ranges in the depth of self shared, the degree to which it involves the task at hand, and the extent to which a sexual relationship is involved. These variations undoubtedly reflect the differences in the needs and interests that people bring to cross-gender relationships at work, the nature of their work and the degree of interaction it requires, their position in the organization, and the organization's norms about closeness at work.

## DEALING WITH ATTRACTIONS AT WORK

Individuals have different ways of managing their feelings of attraction and closeness to the opposite sex; the interview data bear this out. Some of the aspects involved are the degree of awareness of the attraction, feelings about attraction, and problems with expressing attraction.

### The Degree of Awareness of One's Attractions

There are significant differences in people's ability to observe and talk about their experiences of attraction (often the first stage in the development of a close relationship). Some people seem very aware of their feelings when they are drawn to another person. For example, one woman who was interviewed about her experiences of attraction was able to describe 11 different steps in her typical attraction experience (see Table 27.2). Her response shows a strong familiarity with the experience of attraction to others in her work setting, as well as an unusual ability to describe her own experience in the process. Most people find

it difficult to step back and make such observations about their own experiences. The people who have a greater awareness of these feelings are probably also more skilled in discussing and managing their feelings of attraction.

### Feelings About Attraction: Positive or Negative?

Feeling attracted to a member of the opposite sex at work can be very stimulating and productive for some people. However, attraction is also associated with a range of negative feelings. A number of people talked about feeling intensely distracted by their feelings of attraction, to the point where they were unable to attend to their work. In some cases such a feeling leads to uncertainty, confusion, and frustrations. For example, one woman said, "For me, attraction equals tension. I don't know what he is thinking or feeling—it makes me feel *really* insecure. I hope I look okay, I can't be casual with him or around him. I'm on eggshells!"

One male professor described the difficulties he experienced when he felt attracted to one of his students:

*I had a young woman in two of my classes this semester who was strikingly beautiful and, I thought, quite sexy. I found I noticed her more than others in the classroom. As a result, I also felt more uptight when I was around her. In some way I felt disempowered by her, or maybe it was that I was empowering her. It felt like our relationship was cluttered by my sexual fantasies. Some of my uptightness was in response to my assumption that I was not equally attractive to her. Plus, I assumed she could see my interest in her given how strongly I felt attracted to her. My vulnerability in this situation is that if she knows I'm attracted to her, she can somehow use that against me.*

Attraction can also be associated with fear, or even with resentment or anger. Obvious difficulties can arise when a person feels attraction but also resents these very feelings (and the person who evokes them) because of the internal tensions they generate. One organizational consultant who was interviewed said, "If you show me some avoidance or punitive behavior between a

**TABLE 27.2**
One Woman's Description of the Process of "Getting Attracted" to Someone in the Workplace.

1. I'm first attracted to the person-as-a-person—noticing his intelligence, the way he talks, etc. I'll find myself noticing something about his physical appearance (clothes, jewelry, hair) in the midst of a conversation.

2. Apart from his physical self, I may find myself remembering or ruminating over some personal data about him. I find myself thinking about something that is interesting about him, something that has piqued my curiosity.

3. The person may appear in my dreams. (This is an indication to me that I'm using him psychically, as a symbol of something in myself; he is becoming a source of my own growth.)

4. At this point I start really to pay attention to him. I'm interested in him on a psychic level, interested in him as a person; I want to relate to him apart from the work context. I've moved into a more active process at this point.

5. I begin to ask him questions about himself, watching how he is with other people, perhaps getting into conversations with friends at work about who's cute or not and thinking of him. This kind of talk with others helps to crystallize my feelings, making me aware of my own internal "ranking" of this person. The opinion of others also affects my interest in the other, perhaps magnifying my attraction.

6. I am consciously paying attention to his clothing, watching how he moves, perhaps giggling at his jokes more. I notice what I like about his personality and his abilities.

7. I'll initiate more conversations with him. At meetings that he attends, I find myself stretching the "inclusion stage," the initial warm-up time in the meeting, by asking questions about his weekend, seeking more personal data.

8. At this point, if I'm really interested in him, I may covertly pass on information about my availablility by not mentioning that I was with another person when I went to the movie over the weekend. I notice whom he mentions and whom he doesn't mention in his discussions of his weekend.

9. I move into a more personal state. I seek contact with him outside the workplace, or we might celebrate a work event by going somewhere outside the workplace.

10. Another signal of the intensifying of the relationship is his frequent appearance in my dreams. I may also be physically turned on by something he tells me about himself.

11. At this point, I'm usually clear that I want to develop a friendship with this person. I may or may not seek a sexual relationship with him. I can nurse such attractions and not act on them, but just enjoy them as they unfold.

man and a woman in a workplace that needs to be addressed or resolved—and that is not tied to some specific incident—my bet is that they have some attraction to each other that they can't deal with." His observation was confirmed by other comments by a number of the people interviewed. Feelings of attraction can, ironically, be a reason for distancing oneself from a colleague at work.

## Problems with Expressing One's Attraction

Many people struggle with the question of whether to discuss an attraction with the other person. The difficulty with *not* discussing the attraction is that one can end up with pent-up energy, which can in turn lead to a preoccupation with the attraction and sometimes even to counterproductive behavior. (Some people seek the aid of a close but neutral party to help them sort out their feelings and gain some perspective on their attraction—particularly when the costs of directly expressing that attraction to the person seem too high.)

Often, people are afraid that discussing the attraction will propel them into acting on it, thus causing them to lose control of the situation. They worry that revealing their feelings will galvanize the relationship with the other person, making the situation even more difficult to manage because they then have the other person's feelings to deal with as well as their own.

There are also fears that their intentions will be misunderstood by the other individual. One woman consultant said:

*I chose to tell him that I was attracted to him but that for a number of reasons I was not going to act on it. This was in response to his telling me that he found me very attractive. Well, it turned out that in telling him I was attracted to him I had made the situation much worse. He continued to pursue the issue, so much so that it almost felt like sexual harassment. I then chose to back off from working with him because he was making it so difficult.*

This woman went on to talk about how painful she found the issue of managing attraction. All of her experiences to date had been very difficult, and none of them had had happy endings. She now feels scared when she feels attracted to a man at work.

The decision of whether to express one's attraction to the other person can have ramifications far beyond the literal act of self-expression. There are often other "publics" to keep in mind. The complexity of this decision making can be seen in one man's description of the process he goes through before deciding whether to be open about his feelings.

*I may have the feeling of "Wow, that person excites me." Depending on the environment, I am cautious about acting on the excitement. . . . If there is enough energy so that the attraction is not just fleeting, and I think about it beyond our last face-to-face contact . . . I start wondering if I should make the statement publicly or privately to her. The more I feel at risk, the more likely I am to make the statement publicly. It gives it less power, diffuses it.*

*The risk here is that if I make the statement to a woman who is part of a minority in the organization, she may feel undermined. If you make a public statement that demonstrates affection or intimacy, it can be undermining because it may be seen as turfstaking, a signal of ownership, thus decreasing her power and influence among men in the room. My own risk is that if we don't have enough of a relationship to support my*

*statement, she may misconstrue it and use it against me. By making the statement publicly, I make sure that there are other versions of it available.*

For this man, managing the internal tension is closely linked to his concerns about the interpersonal, group, and organizational "fallout" concerning the expression of his attraction. He was particularly aware of the political implications of his behavior and had many different ways of managing his feelings in relation to others' needs and behaviors. For others, less skilled in managing their own attractions, however, the question of how, when, where, and if to express their attraction becomes an emotional maze. The effective resolution of the "attraction question" between two people can make a noticeable contribution to the development of a more productive work relationship. However, the way to achieve this resolution is not always readily apparent to those involved.

## THE CHOICE OF "GETTING CLOSER" VS. "KEEPING ONE'S DISTANCE"

Whether there is initial attraction or not, and whether this attraction is sexual or not, people differ in terms of the amount of distance they consider appropriate in their relationships with the opposite sex at work. Degrees of closeness versus distance in work relationships can generally be seen in (1) the amount and quality of self-disclosure shared with the other person, (2) the kinds of shared activities and interactions on and off the job, and (3) the extent to which these interactions are solely work-role related. But how and why individuals choose to shape the distance between themselves and their colleagues of the opposite sex varies a great deal from person to person.

Crane, one of the bank managers interviewed, was a strong believer in the "keep your distance" orientation. He described his own attitudes and behaviors toward women in his work setting as follows:

*I can see nothing more damaging than getting involved with someone at work. I don't do it, ever. It can demoralize staff and add complications to your personal life.*

*I have no attractions. I keep myself as tightly controlled as I possibly can. My eyes don't rove.*

*It's a litigious society. Others' perceptions rule. I'd rather err on the side of being fearful of others' perceptions than be overly supportive to my women subordinates.*

To Crane, keeping distance between himself and other employees at work meant, among other things, never discussing his personal life with anyone. He took pride in the fact that his boss did not know where he lived. For a number of different reasons, Crane also felt it particularly appropriate to keep women apart from his personal self at work. While he might have lunch or play squash with a male colleague, he would avoid such situations with women colleagues. He characterized women in their twenties and thirties as "seething with emotion"—emotions that in turn might affect him. He expressed a preference for working with older women whose emotions had "cooled off with age" and were therefore more stable to work with. By choosing to keep a distance between himself and his female colleagues, he hoped to preclude the dangers of attractions at work.

Ben provides a sharp contrast to Crane's orientation toward women at work. Ben, a psychologist, described his relationships with women with whom he has worked in this way:

*In every job I've had, I have always been attracted to one woman in a "monogamous," sexually tinged, intense, emotionally seductive relationship. We usually show a lot of physical attention and give a lot of emotional support to each other.*

The intimacy Ben developed in a number of his cross-gender work relationships was very functional to the work he did. These pairings provided an important emotional and political base of operations within the highly charged situations in which he worked. Ben indicated that none of these relationships were physically sexual ones; the "monogamy" he refers to evolved from his tendency to pair with one woman in the organization with whom he could share emotional, professional, and organizational secrets. (Their pairing was often thought to be sexual by others, given the frequency with which they met and the intensity of their emotional connectedness.)

These two cases provide very different examples of how people resolve the dilemma of whether to be close to fellow workers or to keep them at a distance. Most people's work relationships with the opposite sex are variations on the patterns found in the experiences of these two men.

People seem to have different reasons for seeking closeness or keeping distance in these relationships. These differences may partly stem from different levels of the need for intimacy. In his book *Power, Intimacy and the Life Story* (Dorsey Press, 1985), D.P. McAdams found that "individuals high on intimacy motivation have been shown to spend more time thinking about relationships with others, to engage in more conversations with others, and to experience more positive effects when interacting with others than individuals scoring low on intimacy motivation."

Issues of power and/or sexuality are also likely to influence peoples' orientations toward closeness or distance at work. For some, having power may enable them to create close relationships and not have to worry about the ramifications; for others, having power may lead them to avoid closeness with work colleagues. On the other hand, people may seek distance to avoid dealing with issues of sexuality. As one woman put it,

*I find it difficult to deal with intimacy and professionalism together because I link intimacy and sexuality. I can't separate the two. I am more likely to choose distance in most situations because of this.*

For whatever reasons, each of us makes choices about this fundamental question—to be close or to be distant—whether we are conscious of it or not.

## BEING IN AN INTIMATE RELATIONSHIP AT WORK

Many of the close relationships described by the individuals interviewed were obviously of enormous importance to them—whether it be to their personal, social, professional, or physical well-being. Descriptions of the positive side of these relationships include the following:

*I delight in our ability to think together; we have "sophisticated" communication between us. We shoot meta-level analyses of what is going on in the work situation back and forth at each other in meetings. We're both good at systems thinking.*

*When I'm with him I feel centered, fully alive, more resourceful. I feel more generous to the world. I am the "better half" of myself.*

*When we work together I feel effective, centered— almost like I'm "tripping out" on myself and on him.*

At the same time many of the professionals interviewed were explicit about the personal difficulties they experience when they are in an "intimate" relationship (whether sexual or nonsexual) with another person at work. Four different categories of problems can be isolated in these people's experiences: (1) the tension of balancing intimacy with work, (2) the feeling of increased vulnerability both inside and outside the relationship, (3) dealing with outsiders' views and feelings about the relationship, and (4) dealing with ongoing changes in the definition of the relationship.

## Balancing Intimacy and Work with the Same Person

Most of us have been socialized into thinking of intimacy and work as two separate compartments in our lives; intimacy takes place at home and work takes place at our place of employment. But for many people the realities of day-to-day experiences at work belie these rational arrangements of our worlds. Working closely together can create a sense of intimacy between people, or the creation of intimate relationships may be essential to performing the task itself. One woman's success as a consultant depended on establishing good relationships with the line managers she worked with; she saw these close connections as essential to the quality of their mutual effort, stating that "our intimacy makes for a better business relationship."

But the combination of intimacy and work is not an easy blend for many people; it presents significant emotional challenges. Romantic relationships at work require balancing the roles of boyfriend/girlfriend with one's organizational responsibilities. For some, the conflicting demands are too much, while for others the challenge is stimulating.

Allen, who worked in a financial services firm, talked about a romantic relationship he developed with one of his female co-workers. Having his girlfriend in his work group became problematic over time:

*She walks into my office unannounced, and I don't have the time to be with her. When I'm in the office I'm always very short with people—and I was with her on a number of occasions as well. I also felt that I couldn't comfortably talk about what we were going to do that night. This was interfering with my performance at work. I felt I should spend time with her and I couldn't; she didn't like that.*

For Allen, the experience of having a girlfriend in his workplace felt too complicated and jeopardized the quality of his work. He expressed a strong preference, after having had this experience, for keeping his personal and professional lives separate. Putting them together created too many emotional and psychological stresses for him. According to his theory, keeping them separate would allow him to express his "work self" at work and his intimate self at home. These two selves seemed incompatible in a single setting.

A contrasting example came from David, who stated that he had little difficulty in having a romantic relationship in his company. He talked about his decision to start up a sexual relationship with a younger woman in his own company. Both of them kept this secret. His initial attraction to the woman had in fact distracted him from work, but once he developed an intimate, sexual relationship with her, he reported little difficulty in keeping his attention on his work. (However, he did not rule out possible difficulties in the future if others found out about the relationship.)

Part of the relative ease he experienced, in contrast to Allen, may have come from his position as president of the company and his years of experience on the job. His external power and established expertise may have minimized the internal anxieties that are usually associated with such a relationship at work.

The tensions of people caught in the dilemmas of balancing an intimate relationship with a working relationship may stem partly from their difficulties in sorting out their own needs as they relate to the other person. The difficulties seemed particularly great when people's work attitudes and behaviors were significantly different from the kinds of attitudes and behaviors they exhibited when they were with that other person. In effect, the work self collided with the intimate self. Putting their two different "selves" together in the same physical space was dysfunctional for them, for the relationship, and in some cases for the organization. There are other people, however, for whom the intimate and work selves are in less intense conflict; for these individuals, managing intimacy at work may be less difficult.

## Increased Vulnerability Within and Outside of the Relationship

Maintaining a close relationship at work makes some people feel more vulnerable both to the other person involved and to others in the work environment. Things shared within the relationship can be misused by that other person. This kind of vulnerability may be illustrated by an incident involving one man's interaction with a female employee to whom he had felt quite close. They shared a common outlook on many different issues, worked very well together, and shared a lot of personal feelings. One day he walked past her as she was talking with some of his other employees. As he passed by, she remarked, "You look like a sad little boy." Although he kept walking and did not respond, a number of strong feelings welled up in him. He said, "She was exactly right. She cut me to the quick with her remark. I was surprised; I didn't know I was so accessible to others. I felt really exposed." He felt she had misused knowledge she had gained through their friendship to embarrass him in front of his other employees. She had made a public observation about what he felt was a private part of

himself. This was double vulnerability, both inside and outside of the relationship.

## Dealing with Outsiders' Views of the Relationship

An increased vulnerability to outsiders' attitudes often accompanies an intimate relationship at work. Everyone is aware of the taboo against sexual intimacy at work; indeed, many people have their own rules about not having a sexual relationship with colleagues or clients. But an obvious closeness to a colleague of the opposite sex invites outsiders to make their own interpretations about the nature of the relationship. They will usually suspect that the relationship is sexual, whether or not this is actually true.

Some of the women interviewed talked about their fears of being disempowered by outsiders' perceptions (or misperceptions) of their closeness to a male colleague or client. They feared the classic accusation that associates a woman's rise in an organization with her sexual activity rather than with her competence. As a result these women have learned to be very discreet in managing their close relationships, whether these relationships are sexual or not. They also feel that they must always be aware of how others perceive their relationships. One single female consultant stated that she wished she were married, if only to be rid of other people's constant assumptions that her relationships with male clients were sexual. (Interestingly enough, very few of the people interviewed mentioned concerns about their being unfair or unobjective as a result of their close relationships. Ironically, these are the concerns expressed most often by outsiders.)

## Dealing with Changes in the Relationship

The development and maintenance of any close relationship involves various changes in the relationship over time. The degrees of involvement in, commitment to, and dependence on the relationship are significant dimensions that are subject to change. Many of the difficulties reported by people in close relationships at work involve coping with the ongoing issues raised by such changes. Because these relationships develop in a work setting, the changes in them are apt to have organizational as well as personal implications.

In ongoing intimate relationships, many women and men struggle with the issue of sexual involvement. When there is a lack of reciprocal interest in exploring such involvement, it can be very difficult for one of the pair to respond to this issue and not hurt the other's feelings, the quality of the relationship, or the quality of their work together.

One woman commented, "If you pay attention to men at certain levels emotionally and develop a close relationship, they often sexualize it. I have to be careful about this." Her statement was based on the experience she had had with a male manager in her organization who was her boss's peer. They had built a relationship based on their conversations about company management styles and a variety of outside interests that they shared. She had sometimes gone to his office to chat with him. Finally one day he told her that if they wanted to have a personal relationship they should have it outside work, or people might talk. She knew that this statement was also an invitation. She was surprised by his comment because she had never wanted to develop a personal relationship with him outside the company. She cut down on the amount of contact they had in order to keep their relationship on a more professional basis. As a result of this experience, she became more careful of her interactions with men in the work environment.

A male manager reported a similar experience in which his female boss thought he wanted to begin a more personal and potentially sexual relationship. He did not share her needs and interests, and he had to communicate this to her very delicately in order to maintain both their professional relationship and his career.

Another difficulty with work relationships is the question of how deeply the intimacy should be carried into the individuals' projects. One woman reported an incident in which she worked closely with a man she was employing as a consultant on her art project. They had been working intensely together for a number of months and had achieved a special intimacy from their similar spiritual and aesthetic orientations. They were agonizing over a particularly difficult decision when the man drew back and said, "Well, it's your project, you decide." At that moment, the woman felt confronted with the deep division between their respective personal investments in the project. The limits to their intimacy were exposed to her in a very abrupt, raw fashion.

Subtle shifts in interest and investment in a relationship may seem relatively unimportant to outsiders. For the people in the relationship, however, these changes can have a substantial impact.

## CONCLUSION

The data presented in this paper have implications not only for individual employees, but for the organizations in which they work as well.

### Issues for Employees

Figure 27.1 lists some common questions a person may have as he or she deals with the issues of attraction and intimacy at work. How one deals with these questions will have an obvious impact on the kinds of experiences a person will encounter. Negative and positive responses lead one in different directions.

For example, people who always respond negatively to the question will probably not experience the problems that arise from attempting to get closer to another person. Being unaware of one's feelings, having negative reactions to one's feeling of attraction, and avoiding the person to whom one is attracted can distance one from the emotional complexity of managing closeness in a work relationship. To these people, such distance from one's feelings and from colleagues of the opposite sex seems safer. In remaining distant, one avoids potential misunderstandings that may lead to charges of sexual harassment or other volatile outcomes. But there are potential costs to the choice of distance from one's feelings and one's colleagues. These costs are highlighted in

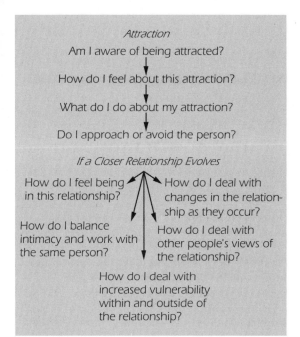

*Attraction*

Am I aware of being attracted?

How do I feel about this attraction?

What do I do about my attraction?

Do I approach or avoid the person?

*If a Closer Relationship Evolves*

How do I feel being in this relationship?

How do I deal with changes in the relationship as they occur?

How do I balance intimacy and work with the same person?

How do I deal with other people's views of the relationship?

How do I deal with increased vulnerability within and outside of the relationship?

**FIGURE 27.1** Attraction and Intimacy Questions for the Employee

a 1981 *Wall Street Journal* article that quoted a female manager for AT&T who was 29 years old and single:

*I build an iron fence around myself for twelve hours a day. That isn't really me, but I feel it's a responsibility I have to take as a woman, to make clear I'm not available. I'm sociable; lunch or a drink after work is fine because it's work related. But if I find myself attracted to a colleague, I just don't allow it to go anywhere, and I don't let myself get into a situation with that person in which it might be hard to control my feelings.*

Though no more detail is given about this woman and her life apart from her career, one must wonder about the potential costs of her choice of behavior: (1) Might she be keeping herself from forming interpersonal friendships that could contribute to her own personal development? (2) Might she be keeping herself from opportunities to form close relationships with male colleagues, connections that might help to advance her career? (3) Might she be keeping herself from experiencing and expressing her own emo-

tional needs? Several women interviewed mentioned their experience of feeling neutered in their workplace. This may work insofar as suppressing one's sexuality is one way of resolving the problem of attractions at work—but again, at what cost?

Choosing closeness in a cross-gender work relationship, however, leads a person into a challenging set of personal and interpersonal issues. One must manage a more complex set of needs and concerns in relation to both one's self and the other person. One risks feelings of increased vulnerability; one must manage outsiders' interpretations of the relationship; one has to meet the changing needs and concerns of both people involved. But if the result of one's efforts is a good working relationship with a colleague of the opposite sex, one has a precious commodity.

## Issues for Organizations

What is the significance of employee attraction and intimacy for organizations and their managers? Experiences in these areas involve strong feelings; for better or for worse, these feelings affect people's behavior and performance on the job. Because there is such variation in the way people deal with these issues, managers need a better understanding of how people experience these situations and how their behavior is affected by them. Managers also need to become more aware of their own attitudes on these issues.

Managers themselves face a number of risks in assuming that all people's experiences are similar, or in not understanding how those involved in the situation actually feel. If they don't understand differences between people, or if they have a simplistic or negative view of intimacy at work, they will often react negatively to such intimate relationships, including some in which intimacy could be very productive both for the involved individuals and the organization.

These negative reactions can also make managers avoid relationships in which they themselves anticipate "intimacy problems." In this case, these people may miss out on the potential growth that develops out of working through complex issues with close colleagues. Moreover, the organization risks losing the potential synergy and creativity that these relationships may bring to the work environment.

Organizations as a whole need to develop constructive standards about close male-female relationships. As Edgar H. Schein has pointed out in his article "Coming to a New Awareness of Organizational Culture" (*Sloan Management Review*, Winter 1984), one of the major issues of internal integration within an organization's culture is the problem of intimacy, friendship, and love. Organizations need to develop a consensus regarding closeness among their members. But if the consensus-building process (and the rules that result from it) are to be effective as a cultural "solution" for the organization, they must include the perceptions, thoughts, and feelings of that organization's members. Managers cannot merely legislate "solutions" to attraction and intimacy by making rules that prohibit romantic involvements. Such formal rules and sanctions only drive emotions underground, thus preventing people from dealing more constructively with the issues involved.

A consensus-building process requires open conversation and active participation. Companies can make it easier for people to learn about and manage issues of attraction and intimacy at work by making conversations about these issues easier. Internal training programs can make em-

ployees more sensitive to differences in people's experiences in these areas, as well as to the tensions and dilemmas associated with close male-female relationships at work. Skill-building sessions can help people assess the costs and benefits of their own ways of managing these issues (both for themselves and for others in the organization), and they can teach people alternative strategies. Role models of close, effective male-female relationships in management can have an obvious impact on people's hopes and fears concerning attraction and intimacy at work. With a more open climate in which to approach these issues, men and women should be freer to create high-quality working relationships that contribute to both their personal and professional development. Organizations will be rewarded in turn with the energy and creativity these relationships may contribute to the resolution of organizational problems.

## ACKNOWLEDGMENT

I would like to thank Fernando Bartolomé, Tim Hall, Meryl Louis, Carolyn Lukensmeyer, Asya Pazy, Duncan Spelman, and Peter Vaill for their feedback on earlier versions of this paper. I am especially indebted to the people who were willing to talk with me about their own experiences with attraction and intimacy at work.

## SELECTED BIBLIOGRAPHY

Issues of attraction and intimacy at work must be understood in terms of the development of working relationships. For an excellent overview of the literature on this subject, see John J. Gabarro's chapter on "The Development of Working Relationships" in *The Handbook of Organizational Behavior*, edited by Jay W. Lorsch (Prentice-Hall, 1986). Kathy E. Kram's *Mentoring at Work* (Scott Foresman, 1985) provides a very thorough discussion of the complexities of close working relationships.

A knowledge of the role of intimacy in adult development contributes a very different perspective to the issues of intimacy at work. Capacities for understanding and managing intimacy can be linked to stages of adult development. Robert Kegan describes different stages in the evolution of one's understanding of the self and one's relations to others in *The Evolving Self* (Harvard University Press, 1982). *Communication, Intimacy, and Close Relationships* (Academic Press, 1984), edited by Valerian J.

Derlega, presents a rich compilation of theories and research on intimate relationships. The chapter by Dan McAdams, "Human Motives and Personal Relationships," explores the roles of power and intimacy in close relationships.

For a discussion of intimacy and its relation to organizational culture, see Edgar H. Schein's article, "Coming to a New Awareness of Organizational Culture" (*Sloan Management Review*, Winter 1984).

An excellent general reference for issues relating to sexuality in the workplace is *Sexuality in Organizations*, edited by Dale A. Neugarten and Jay M. Shafritz (Moore, 1980). This book addresses the overall complexity of managing attraction in hierarchical structures. Of particular interest are the articles "The Executive Man and Woman: The Issue of Sexuality" by David L. Bradford, Alice G. Sargent, and Melinda Sprague, and "Coping with Cupid: The Formation, Impact and Management of Romantic Relationships in Organizations" by Robert E. Quinn. Bradford et al. examine how the issues of sexuality *per se* influence male-female working relationships. Quinn's article presents his research on the effects of office affairs on superiors', co-workers', and other employees' attitudes and behaviors. A more recent treatment of sexual politics at work is Robert E. Quinn and Patricia L. Lees' article "Attraction and Harassment: Dynamics of Sexual Politics in the Workplace" (*Organizational Dynamics*, Autumn 1984).

A number of interesting articles have been written on managing attraction in the workplace. An article by Lynn R. Cohen, "Minimizing Communication Breakdowns Between Male and Female Managers" (*Personnel Administrator*, 1982) offers an explanation of nonverbal cues that create sexual tension in the office. James G. Clawson and Kathy E. Kram examine the dilemmas of intimacy versus distance in male-female developmental work relationships in their article "Managing Cross-Gender Mentoring" (*Business Horizons*, May/June 1984). In the *Harvard Business Review* (September/October 1983), Eliza G. C. Collins examines the impact of love relationships between top executives in a company and explores the options of dealing with them in ways to maintain organizational stability. In the article "Sexual Relationships at Work: Attraction, Transference, Coercion or Strategy" (*Personnel Administrator*, March 1982), Natasha Josefowitz describes the stages of attraction and the different reasons why people have sexual relationships at work. In the article "Managing Sexual Attraction in the Workplace" (*Personnel Administrator*, August 1983), Kaleel Jamison makes suggestions about what the manager can do to deal with incidents of sexual attraction in his or her company. Duncan Spelman, Marcy Crary, Kathy Kram, and James Clawson discuss the range of forces within the individual, work group, and organization that influence the development and management of attractions at work in their chapter "Sexual Attractions at Work: Managing the Heart" in *Not As Far As You Think* (Lexington Books, 1986), edited by Lynda L. Moore.

For a fascinating discussion of managing emotional expression on the job and its effects on the individual, see Arlene R. Hochschild's *The Managed Heart* (University of California Press, 1983).

# Power and Influence

## 28.   INFLUENCE WITHOUT AUTHORITY: THE USE OF ALLIANCES, RECIPROCITY, AND EXCHANGE TO ACCOMPLISH WORK

Allan R. Cohen and David L. Bradford

Bill Heatton is the director of research at a $250 million division of a large West Coast company. The division manufactures exotic telecommunications components and has many technical advancements to its credit. During the past several years, however, the division's performance has been spotty at best; multimillion dollar losses have been experienced in some years despite many efforts to make the division more profitable. Several large contracts have resulted in major financial losses, and in each instance the various parts of the division blamed the others for the problems. Listen to Bill's frustration as he talks about his efforts to influence Ted, a colleague who is marketing director, and Roland, the program manager who reports to Ted.

*Another program is about to come through. Roland is a nice guy, but he knows nothing and never will. He was responsible for our last big loss, and now he's in charge of this one. I've tried to convince Ted, his boss, to get Roland off the program, but I get nowhere. Although Ted doesn't argue that Roland is capable, he doesn't*

*act to find someone else. Instead, he comes to me with worries about my area.*

*I decided to respond by changing my staffing plan, assigning to Roland's program the people they wanted. I had to override my staff's best judgment about who should be assigned. Yet I'm not getting needed progress reports from Roland, and he's never available for planning. I get little argument from him, but there's no action to correct the problem. That's bad because I'm responding but not getting any response.*

*There's no way to resolve this. If they disagree, that's it. I could go to a tit-for-tat strategy, saying that if they don't do what I want, we'll get even with them next time. But I don't know how to do that without hurting the organization, which would feel worse than getting even!*

*Ted, Roland's boss, is so much better than his predecessor that I hate to ask that he be removed. We could go together to our boss, the general manager, but I'm very reluctant to do that. You've failed in a matrix organization if you have to go to your boss. I have to try hard because I'd look bad if I had to throw it in his lap.*

Allan R. Cohen and David L. Bradford,"Influence Without Authority: the Use of Alliances, Reciprocity, and Exchange to Accomplish Work" from *Organizational Dynamics,* Winter 1989.

*Meanwhile, I'm being forceful, but I'm afraid it's in a destructive way. I don't want to wait until the program has failed to be told it was all my fault.*

Bill is clearly angry and frustrated, leading him to behave in ways that he does not feel good about. Like other managers who very much want to influence an uncooperative co-worker whom they cannot control, Bill has begun to think of the intransigent employee as the enemy. Bill's anger is narrowing his sense of what is possible; he fantasizes revenge but is too dedicated to the organization to actually harm it. He is genuinely stuck.

Organizational members who want to make things happen often find themselves in this position. Irrespective of whether they are staff or line employees, professionals or managers, they find it increasingly necessary to influence colleagues and superiors. These critical others control needed resources, possess required information, set priorities on important activities, and have to agree and cooperate if plans are to be implemented. They cannot be ordered around because they are under another area's control and can legitimately say no because they have many other valid priorities. They respond only when they choose to. Despite the clear need and appropriateness of what is being asked for (certainly as seen by the person who is making the request), compliance may not be forthcoming.

All of this places a large burden on organizational members, who are expected not only to take initiatives but also to respond intelligently to requests made of them by others. Judgment is needed to sort out the value of the many requests made of anyone who has valuable resources to contribute. As Robert Kaplan argued in his article "Trade Routes: The Manager's Network of Relationships" (*Organizational Dynamics,* Spring 1984), managers must now develop the organizational equivalent of "trade routes" to get things done. Informal networks of mutual influence are needed. In her book *The Change Masters* (Simon & Schuster, 1983) Rosabeth Moss Kanter showed that developing and implementing all kinds of innovations requires coalitions to be built to shape and support new ways of doing business.

A key current problem, then, is finding ways to develop mutual influence without the formal authority to command. A peer cannot "order" a colleague to change priorities, modify an approach, or implement a grand new idea. A staff member cannot "command" his or her supervisor to back a proposal, fight top management for greater resources, or allow more autonomy. Even Bill Heatton, in dealing with Roland (who was a level below him in the hierarchy but in another department), could not dictate that Roland provide the progress reports that Bill so desperately wanted.

## EXCHANGE AND THE LAW OF RECIPROCITY

The way influence is acquired without formal authority is through the "law of reciprocity"— the almost universal belief that people should be paid back for what they do, that one good (or bad) deed deserves another. This belief is held by people in primitive and not-so-primitive societies all around the world, and it serves as the grease that allows the organizational wheels to turn smoothly. Because people expect that their actions will be paid back in one form or another, influence is possible.

In the case of Bill Heatton, his inability to get what he wanted from Roland and Ted stemmed from his failure to understand fully how reciprocity works in organizations. He therefore was unable to set up mutually beneficial exchanges. Bill believed that he had gone out of his way to help the marketing department by changing his staffing patterns, and he expected Roland to reciprocate by providing regular progress reports. When Roland failed to provide the reports, Bill believed that Ted was obligated to remove Roland from the project. When Ted did not respond, Bill became angry and wanted to retaliate. Thus Bill recognized the appropriateness of exchange in making organizations work. However, he did not understand how exchange operates.

Before exploring in detail how exchange can work in dealing with colleagues and superiors, it is important to recognize that reciprocity is the basic principle behind all organizational transactions. For example, the basic employment contract is an exchange ("an honest day's work for an honest day's pay"). Even work that is above and beyond what is formally required involves exchange. The person who helps out may not necessarily get (or expect) immediate payment for the extra effort requested, but some eventual compensation is expected.

Think of the likely irritation an employee would feel if his or her boss asked him or her to work through several weekends, never so much as said thanks, and then claimed credit for the extra work. The employee might not say anything the first time this happened, expecting or hoping that the boss would make it up somehow. However, if the effort were never acknowledged in any way, the employee, like most people, would feel that something important had been violated.

The expectation of reciprocal exchanges occurs between an employee and his or her supervisor, among peers, with higher-level managers in other parts of the organization, or all of the above. The exchange can be of tangible goods, such as a budget increase, new equipment, or more personnel; of tangible services, such as a faster response time, more information, or public support; or of sentiments, such as gratitude, admiration, or praise. Whatever form exchanges take, unless they are roughly equivalent over time, hard feelings will result.

Exchanges enable people to handle the give-and-take of working together without strong feelings of injustice arising. They are especially important during periods of rapid change because the number of requests that go far beyond the routine tends to escalate. In those situations, exchanges become less predictable, more free-floating and spontaneous. Nevertheless, people still expect that somehow or other, sooner or later, they will be (roughly) equally compensated for the acts they do above and beyond those that are covered by the formal exchange agreements in their job. Consequently, some kind of "currency" equivalent needs to be worked out, im-

plicitly if not explicitly, to keep the parties in the exchange feeling fairly treated.

## CURRENCIES: THE SOURCE OF INFLUENCE

If the basis of organizational influence depends on mutually satisfactory exchanges, then people are influential only insofar as they can offer something that others need. Thus power comes from the ability to meet others' needs.

A useful way to think of how the process of exchange actually works in organizations is to use the metaphor of "currencies." This metaphor provides a powerful way to conceptualize what is important to the influencer and the person to be influenced. Just as many types of currencies are traded in the world financial market, many types are "traded" in organizational life. Too often people think only of money or promotion and status. Those "currencies," however, usually are available only to a manager in dealing with his or her employees. Peers who want to influence colleagues or employees who want to influence their supervisors often feel helpless. They need to recognize that many types of payments exist, broadening the range of what can be exchanged.

Some major currencies that are commonly valued and traded in organizations are listed in Table 28.1. Although not exhaustive, the list makes evident that a person does not have to be at the top of an organization or have hands on the formal levers of power to command multiple resources that other may value.

Part of the usefulness of currencies comes from their flexibility. For example, there are many ways to express gratitude and to give assistance. A manager who most values the currency of appreciation could be paid through verbal thanks, praise, a public statement at a meeting, informal comments to his peers, and/or a note to her boss. However, the same note of thanks seen by one person as a sign of appreciation may be seen by another person as an attempt to brownnose or by a third person as a cheap way to try to repay extensive favors and service. Thus currencies have

**TABLE 28.1**
Commonly Traded Organizational Currencies

*Inspiration-Related Currencies*

| | |
|---|---|
| Vision | Being involved in a task that has larger significance for the unit, organization, customers, or society. |
| Excellence | Having a chance to do important things really well. |
| Moral/Ethical Correctness | Doing what is "right" by a higher standard than efficiency. |

*Task-Related Currencies*

| | |
|---|---|
| Resources | Lending or giving money, budget increases, personnel, space, and so forth. |
| Assistance | Helping with existing projects or undertaking unwanted tasks. |
| Cooperation | Giving task support, providing quicker response time, approving a project, or aiding implementation. |
| Information | Providing organizational as well as technical knowledge. |

*Position-Related Currencies*

| | |
|---|---|
| Advancement | Giving a task or assignment that can aid in promotion. |
| Recognition | Acknowledging effort, accomplishment, or abilities. |
| Visibility | Providing chance to be known by higher-ups or significant others in the organization. |
| Reputation | Enhancing the way a person is seen. |
| Importance/Insiderness | Offering a sense of importance, of "belonging." |
| Network/Contacts | Providing opportunities for linking with others. |

*Relationship-Related Currencies*

| | |
|---|---|
| Acceptance/Inclusion | Providing closeness and friendship. |
| Personal Support | Giving personal and emotional backing. |
| Understanding | Listening to others' concerns and issues. |

*Personal-Related Currencies*

| | |
|---|---|
| Self-Concept | Affirming one's values, self-esteem, and identity. |
| Challenge/Learning | Sharing tasks that increase skills and abilities. |
| Ownership/Involvement | Letting others have ownership and influence. |
| Gratitude | Expressing appreciation or indebtedness. |

value not in some abstract sense but as defined by the receiver.

Although we have stressed the interactive nature of exchange, "payments" do not always have to be made by the other person. They can be self-generated to fit beliefs about being virtuous, benevolent, or committed to the organization's welfare. Someone may respond to another person's request because it reinforces cherished values, a sense of identity, or feelings of self-worth. The exchange is interpersonally stimulated be-

cause the one who wants influence has set up conditions that allow this kind of self-payment to occur by asking for cooperation to accomplish organizational goals. However, the person who responds because "it is the right thing to do" and who feels good about being the "kind of person who does not act out of narrow self-interest" is printing currency (virtue) that is self-satisfying.

Of course, the five categories of currencies listed in Table 28.1 are not mutually exclusive. When the demand from the other person is high, people are likely to pay in several currencies across several categories. They may, for example stress the organizational value of their request, promise to return the favor at a later time, imply that it will increase the other's prestige in the organization, and express their appreciation.

## ESTABLISHING EXCHANGE RATES

What does it take to pay back in a currency that the other party in an exchange will perceive as equivalent? In impersonal markets, because everything is translated into a common monetary currency, it generally is easy to say what a fair payment is. Does a ton of steel equal a case of golfclubs? By translating both into dollar equivalents, a satisfactory deal can be worked out.

In interpersonal exchanges, however, the process becomes a bit more complicated. Just how does someone repay another person's willingness to help finish a report? Is a simple thank-you enough? Does it also require the recipient to say something nice about the helper to his or her boss? Whose standard of fairness should be used? What if one person's idea of fair repayment is very different from the other's?

Because of the natural differences in the way two parties can interpret the same activity, establishing exchanges that both parties will perceive as equitable can be problematic. Thus it is critical to understand what is important to the person to be influenced. Without a clear understanding of what that person experiences and values, it will be extremely difficult for anyone to thread a path through the minefield of creating mutually satisfactory exchanges.

Fortunately, the calibration of equivalent exchanges in the interpersonal and organizational worlds is facilitated by the fact that approximations will do in most cases. Occasionally, organizational members know exactly what they want in return for favors or help, but more often they will settle for very rough equivalents (providing that there is reasonable goodwill).

## THE PROCESS OF EXCHANGE

To make the exchange process effective, the influencer needs to (1) think about the person to be influenced as a potential ally, not an adversary; (2) know the world of the potential ally, including the pressures as well as the person's needs and goals; (3) be aware of key goals and available resources that may be valued by the potential ally; and (4) understand the exchange transaction itself so that win-win outcomes are achieved. Each of these factors is discussed below.

### Potential Ally, Not Adversary.

A key to influence is thinking of the other person as a potential ally. Just as many contemporary organizations have discovered the importance of creating strategic alliances with suppliers and customers, employees who want influence within the organization need to create internal allies. Even though each party in an alliance continues to have freedom to pursue its own interests, the goal is to find areas of mutual benefit and develop trusting, sustainable relationships. Similarly, each person whose cooperation is needed inside the organization is a potential ally. Each still has self-interests to pursue, but those self-interests do not preclude searching for and building areas of mutual benefit.

Seeing other organizational members as potential allies decreases the chance that adversarial relationships will develop—an all-too-frequent result (as in the case of Bill Heatton) when the eager influencer does not quickly get the assistance or cooperation needed. Assuming that even a difficult person is a potential ally makes it easier to understand that person's world and thereby discover what that person values and needs.

### The Potential Ally's World

We have stressed the importance of knowing the world of the potential ally. Without awareness of what the ally needs (what currencies are valued), attempts to influence that person can only be haphazard. Although this conclusion may seem self-evident, it is remarkable how often people attempt to influence without adequate information about what is important to the potential ally. Instead, they are driven by their own definition of "what should be" and "what is right" when they should be seeing the world from the other person's perspective.

For example, Bill Heatton never thought about the costs to Ted of removing Roland from the project. Did Ted believe he could coach Roland to perform better on this project? Did Ted even agree that Roland had done a poor job on the previous project, or did Ted think Roland had been hampered by other departments' shortcomings? Bill just did not know.

Several factors can keep the influencer from seeing the potential ally clearly. As with Bill Heatton, the frustration of meeting resistance from a potential ally can get in the way of really understanding the other person's world. The desire to influence is so strong that only the need for cooperation is visible to the influencer. As a result of not being understood, the potential ally digs in, making the influencer repeat an inappropriate strategy or back off in frustration.

When a potential ally's behavior is not understandable ("Why won't Roland send the needed progress report?"), the influencer tends to stereotype that person. If early attempts to influence do not work, the influencer is tempted to write the person off as negative, stubborn, selfish, or "just another bean counter/whiz kid/sales-type" or whatever pejorative label is used in that organizational culture to dismiss those organizational members who are different.

Although some stereotypes may have a grain of truth, they generally conceal more than they reveal. The actuary who understands that judgment, not just numbers, is needed to make decisions disappears as an individual when the stereotype of "impersonal, detached number machine" is the filter through which he or she is seen. Once the stereotype is applied, the frustrated influencer is no longer likely to see what currencies that particular potential ally actually values.

Sometimes, the lack of clear understanding about a potential ally stems from the influencer's failure to appreciate the organizational forces acting on the potential ally. To a great extent, a person's behavior is a result of the situation in which that person works (and not just his or her personality). Potential allies are embedded in an organizational culture that shapes their interests and responses. For example, one of the key determinants of anyone's behavior is likely to be the way the person's performance is measured and rewarded. In many instances, what is mistaken for personal orneriness is merely the result of the person's doing something that will be seen as good performance in his or her function.

The salesperson who is furious because the plant manager resists changing priorities for a rush order may not realize that part of the plant manager's bonus depends on holding unit costs down—a task made easier with long production runs. The plant manager's resistance does not necessarily reflect his or her inability to be flexible or lack of concern about pleasing customers or about the company's overall success.

Other organizational forces that can affect the potential ally's behavior include the daily time demands on that person's position; the amount of contact the person has with customers, suppliers, and other outsiders, the organization's information flow (or lack of it); the style of the potential ally's boss; the belief and assumptions held by that person's co-workers; and so forth. Although some of these factors cannot be changed by the influencer, understanding them can be useful in figuring out how to frame and time requests. It also helps the influencer resist the temptation to stereotype the noncooperator.

## Self-Awareness of the Influencer

Unfortunately, people desiring influence are not always aware of precisely what they want. Often their requests contain a cluster of needs (a certain product, arranged in a certain way, delivered at a specified time). They fail to think through which aspects are more important and which can be jettisoned if necessary. Did Bill Heatton want Roland removed, or did he want the project effectively managed? Did he want overt concessions from Ted, or did he want better progress reports?

Further, there is a tendency to confuse and intermingle the desired end goal with the means of accomplishing it, leading to too many battles over the wrong things. In *The Change Masters,* Kanter reported that successful influencers in organizations were those who never lost sight of the ultimate objective but were willing to be flexible about means.

Sometimes influencers underestimate the range of currencies available for use. They may assume, for example, that just because they are low in the organization they have nothing that others want. Employees who want to influence their boss are especially likely not to realize all of the supervisor's needs that they can fulfill. They become so caught up with their feelings of powerlessness that they fail to see the many ways they can generate valuable currencies.

In other instances, influencers fail to be aware of their preferred style of interaction and its fit with the potential ally's preferred style. Everyone has a way of relating to others to get work done. However, like the fish who is unaware of the water, many people are oblivious of their own style of interaction or see it as the only way to be. Yet interaction style can cause problems with potential allies who are different.

For example, does the influencer tend to socialize first and work later? If so, that style of interaction will distress a potential ally who likes to dig right in to solve the problem at hand and only afterward chat about sports, family, or office politics. Does the potential ally want to be approached with answers, not problems? If so, a tendency to start influence attempts with open-ended, exploratory problem solving can lead to rejection despite good intentions.

## Nature of the Exchange Transaction

Many of the problems that occur in the actual exchange negotiation have their roots in the failure to deal adequately with the first three factors outlined above. Failure to treat other people as potential allies, to understand a potential ally's world, and to be self-aware are all factors that interfere with successful exchange. In addition, some special problems commonly arise when both parties are in the process of working out a mutually satisfactory exchange agreement.

*Not knowing how to use reciprocity.* Using reciprocity requires stating needs clearly without "crying wolf," being aware of the needs of an ally without being manipulative, and seeking mutual gain rather than playing "winner takes all." One trap that Bill Heatton fell into was not being able to "close on the exchange." That is, he assumed that if he acted in good faith and did his part, others would automatically reciprocate. Part of his failure was not understanding the other party's world; another part was not being able to negotiate cleanly with Ted about what each of them wanted. It is not even clear that Ted realized Bill was altering his organization as per Ted's requests, that Ted got what he wanted, or that Ted knew Bill intended an exchange of responses.

*Preferring to be right rather than effective.* This problem is especially endemic to professionals of all kinds. Because of their dedication to the "truth" (as their profession defines it), they stubbornly stick to their one right way when trying to line up potential allies instead of thinking about what will work given the audience and conditions. Organizational members with strong technical backgrounds often chorus the equivalent of "I'll be damned if I'm going to sell out and become a phony salesman, trying to get by on a shoe-shine and smile." The failure to accommodate to the potential ally's needs and desires often kills otherwise sound ideas.

*Overusing what has been successful.* When people find that a certain approach is effective in many situations, they often begin to use it in places where it does not fit. By overusing the approach, they block more appropriate methods. Just as a weight lifter becomes muscle-bound from overdeveloping particular muscles at the expense of others, people who have been reasonably successful at influencing other people can diminish that ability by overusing the same technique.

For example, John Brucker, the human resources director at a medium-size company, often cultivated support for new programs by taking people out to fancy restaurants for an evening of fine food and wine. He genuinely derived pleasure from entertaining, but at the same time he created subtle obligations. One time, a new program he wanted to introduce required the agreement of William Adams, head of engineering. Adams, an old-timer, perceived Brucker's proposal as an unnecessary frill, mainly because he did not perceive the real benefits to the overall organization. Brucker responded to Adam's negative comments as he always did in such cases—by becoming more friendly and insisting that they get together for dinner soon. After several of these invitations, Adams became furious. Insulted by what he considered to be Brucker's attempts to buy him off, he fought even harder to kill the proposal. Not only did the program die, but Brucker lost all possibility of influencing Adams in the future. Adams saw Brucker's attempts at socializing as a sleazy and crude way of trying to soften him up. For his part, Brucker was totally puzzled by Adams's frostiness and assumed that he was against all progress. He never realized that Adams had a deep sense of integrity and a real commitment to the good of the organization. Thus Brucker lost his opportunity to sell a program that, ironically, Adams would have found valuable had it been implemented.

As the case above illustrates, a broad repertoire of influence approaches is needed in modern organizations. Johnny-one-notes soon fall flat.

## THE ROLE OF RELATIONSHIPS

All of the preceding discussion needs to be conditioned by one important variable: the nature of the relationship between both parties. The greater the extent to which the influencer has

worked with the potential ally and created trust, the easier the exchange process will be. Each party will know the other's desired currencies and situational pressures, and each will have developed a mutually productive interaction style. With trust, less energy will be spent on figuring out the intentions of the ally, and there will be less suspicion about when and how the payback will occur.

A poor relationship (based on previous interactions, on the reputation each party has in the organization, and/or on stereotypes and animosities between the functions or departments that each party represents) will impede an otherwise easy exchange. Distrust of the goodwill, veracity, or reliability of the influencer can lead to the demand for "no credit; cash up front," which constrains the flexibility of both parties.

The nature of the interaction during the influencer process also affects the nature of the relationship between the influencer and the other party. The way that John Brucker attempted to relate to William Adams not only did not work but also irreparably damaged any future exchanges between them.

Few transactions within organizations are one-time deals. (Who knows when the other person may be needed again or even who may be working for him or her in the future?) Thus in most exchange situations two outcomes matter: success in achieving task goals and success in improving the relationship so that the next interaction will be even more productive. Too often, people who want to be influential focus only on the task and act as if there is no tomorrow. Although both task accomplishment and an improved relationship cannot always be realized at the same time, on some occasions the latter can be more important than the former. Winning the battle but losing the war is an expensive outcome.

## INCONVERTIBLE CURRENCIES

We have spelled out ways organizational members operate to gain influence for achieving organizational goals. By effectively using exchange, organizational members can achieve their goals and at the same time help others achieve theirs. Exchange permits organizational members to be assertive without being antagonistic by keeping mutual benefit a central outcome.

In many cases, organizational members fail to acquire desired influence because they do not use all of their potential power. However, they sometimes fail because not all situations are amenable to even the best efforts at influencing. Not everything can be translated into compatible currencies. If there are fundamental differences in what is valued by two parties, it may not be possible to find common ground, as illustrated in the example below.

The founder and chairman of a high-technology company and the president he had hired five years previously were constantly displeased with one another. The president was committed to creating maximum shareholder value, the currency he valued most as a result of his M.B.A. training, his position, and his temperament. Accordingly, he had concluded that the company was in a perfect position to cash in by squeezing expenses to maximize profits and going public. He could see that the company's product line of exotic components was within a few years of saturating its market and would require massive, risky investment to move to sophisticated end-user products.

The president could not influence the chairman to adopt this direction, however, because the chairman valued a totally different currency, the fun of technological challenge. An independently wealthy man, the chairman had no interest in realizing the $10 million or so he would get if the company maximized profits by cutting research and selling out. He wanted a place to test his intuitive, creative research hunches, not a source of income.

Thus the president's and chairman's currencies were not convertible into one another at an acceptable exchange rate. After they explored various possibilities but failed to find common ground, they mutually agreed that the president should leave—on good terms and only after a more compatible replacement could be found. Although this example acknowledges that influence through alliance, currency conversion, and exchange is not always possible, it is hard to be certain that any situation is hopeless until the person desiring influence has fully applied all of the diagnostic and interpersonal skills we have described.

Influence is enhanced by using the model of strategic alliances to engage in mutually beneficial exchanges with potential allies. Even though it is not always possible to be successful, the chances of achieving success can be greatly increased. In a period of rapid competitive, technological, regulative, and consumer change, individuals and their organizations need all the help they can get.

## SELECTED BIBLIOGRAPHY

Some of the classic work on exchange as a process of influence was done by Peter Blau. His book *The Dynamics of Bureaucracy* (University of Chicago Press, 1963) was a landmark study of how tax assessors traded gratitude for expert assistance. When exchange is added to notions about the universality of reciprocity, as outlined by Alvin Gouldner in his pioneering article "The Norm of Reciprocity: A Preliminary Statement" (*American Sociological Review,* 25, 1960), a powerful way of thinking about influence is created.

David Berlew picked up on these ideas and wrote an interesting piece addressed to people who want more influence: "What You Can Do When Persuasion Doesn't Work" (*NTL Connection*, 1986). He discussed three types of exchange that can be used by those attempting to get things done.

The case for managers needing to build alliances in order to accomplish work was made by Robert Kaplan in his article "Trade Routes: The Manager's Network of Relationships" (*Organization Dynamics,* 1984). John Kotter found in his study of successful general managers (*The General Managers,* Free Press, 1982) that they had wide networks of contacts in their organizations, which helped them find the right person(s) when trying to make things happen. Rosabeth Moss Kanter's *The Change Masters* (Simon & Schuster, 1983) is the best examination of the ways organization members go about achieving major innovations through alliances. It shows the steps that innovative members go through, including the many ways they use influence to build coalitions and overcome resistance. We have built on her work by looking with a microscope at the mechanisms behind the processes she describes.

Other researchers have explored influence processes from many angles. David Kipnis and his collaborators found that they can categorize influence styles along seven dimensions. In "Patterns of Managerial Influence: Shotgun Managers, Tacticians, and Bystanders" (*Organizational Dynamics,* 1984), they identify the problem of managers who lack organizational power (and by implication what to do about it) and therefore give up attempting to influence. John Kotter addressed ways of increasing influence in *Power in Management: How to Understand, Acquire and Use It,* (AMACOM, 1979). He shows the advantages and disadvantages of different methods.

Our own book *Managing for Excellence: The Guide to High Performance in Contemporary Organizations* (John Wiley & Sons, 1984) addresses influence downward by arguing that shared responsibility is needed with subordinates in order to get the best from them and that treating them as full partners in the unit's management is necessary even though formal authority rests with the manager. We also show that mutual influence is needed to allow both parties to use their full strength. These ideas translate directly into lessons for influence when formal authority is lacking.

Finally, the literature of negotiations has many applications for using exchange for influence. Although there are popular books on negotiating that overlook important issues of trust when relationships are ongoing within the same organization, there is much to be learned from applying negotiating insights. Roger Fisher's and William Ury's book *Getting to Yes* (Houghton Mifflin, 1981) is helpful on ways to approach someone to look for common interests despite having differing specific objectives. An excellent overview of the issues involved in any kind of negotiation can be found in Roy Lewicki and Joseph Litterer's test *Negotiation* (R.D. Irwin, 1985). Their discussion of exchange and equity is particularly relevant to influence as we have described it. In addition, Roy Lewicki's comments on an earlier draft of this article were particularly helpful, and we are grateful for his wisdom and generosity.

# 29. WHO GETS POWER—AND HOW THEY HOLD ON TO IT: A STRATEGIC-CONTINGENCY MODEL OF POWER

Gerald R. Salancik and Jeffrey Pfeffer

Power is held by many people to be a dirty word or, as Warren Bennis has said, "It is the organization's last dirty secret."

This article will argue that traditional "political" power, far from being a dirty business, is, in its most naked form, one of the few mechanisms available for aligning an organization with its own reality. However, institutionalized forms of power—what we prefer to call the cleaner forms of power: authority, legitimization, centralized control, regulations, and the more modern "management information systems"—tend to buffer the organization from reality and obscure the demands of its environment. Most great states and institutions declined, not because they played politics, but because they failed to accommodate to the political realities they faced. Political processes, rather than being mechanisms for unfair and unjust allocations and appointments, tend toward the realistic resolution of conflicts among interests. And power, while it eludes definition, is easy enough to recognize by its consequences—the ability of those who possess power to bring about the outcomes they desire.

The model of power we advance is an elaboration of what has been called strategic-contingency theory, a view that sees power as something that accrues to organizational subunits (individuals, departments) that cope with critical organizational problems. Power is used by subunits, indeed, used by all who have it, to enhance their own survival through control of scarce critical resources, through the placement of allies in key positions, and through the definition of organizational problems and policies. Because of the processes by which power develops and is used, organizations become both more aligned and more misaligned with their environments. This contradiction is the most interesting aspect of organizational power and one that makes administration one of the most precarious of occupations.

## WHAT IS ORGANIZATIONAL POWER

You can walk into most organizations and ask without fear of being misunderstood, "Which are the powerful groups of people in this organization?" Although many organizational informants may be *unwilling* to tell you, it is unlikely they will be *unable* to tell you. Most people do not require explicit definitions to know what power is.

Power is simply the ability to get things done the way one wants them to be done. For a manager who wants an increased budget to launch a project that he thinks is important, his power is measured by his ability to get that budget. For an executive vice president who wants to be chairman, his power is evidenced by his advancement toward his goal.

People in organizations not only know what you are talking about when you ask who is influential but they are likely to agree with one another to an amazing extent. Recently, we had

---

a chance to observe this in a regional office of an insurance company. The office had 21 department managers; we asked 10 of these managers to rank all 21 according to the influence each one had in the organization. Despite the fact that ranking 21 things is a difficult task, the managers sat down and began arranging the names of their colleagues and themselves in a column. Only one person bothered to ask, "What do you mean by influence?" When told "power," he responded, "Oh," and went on. We compared the rankings of all ten managers and found virtually no disagreement among them in the managers ranked among the top five or the bottom five. Differences in the rankings came from department heads claiming more influence for themselves than their colleagues attributed to them.

Such agreement on those who have influence, and those who do not, was not unique to this insurance company. So far we have studied over 20 very different organizations—universities, research firms, factories, banks, retailers, to name a few. In each one we found individuals able to rate themselves and their peers on a scale of influence or power. We have done this both for specific decisions and for general impact on organizational policies. Their agreement was unusually high, which suggests that distributions of influence exist well enough in everyone's mind to be referred to with ease—and we assume with accuracy.

## WHERE DOES ORGANIZATIONAL POWER COME FROM?

Earlier we stated that power helps organizations become aligned with their realities. This hopeful prospect follows from what we have dubbed the strategic-contingencies theory of organizational power. Briefly, those subunits most able to cope with the organization's critical problems and uncertainties acquire power. In its simplest form, the strategic-contingencies theory implies that when an organization faces a number of lawsuits that threaten its existence the legal department will gain power and influence over organizational decisions. Somehow other organizational interest groups will recognize its critical importance and confer upon it a status and power never before enjoyed. This influence may extend beyond handling legal matters and into decisions about product design, advertising production, and so on. Such extensions undoubtedly would be accompanied by appropriate, or acceptable, verbal justifications. In time, the head of the legal department may become the head of the corporation, just as in times past the vice president for marketing had become the president when market shares were a worrisome problem and, before him, the chief engineer, who had made the production line run as smooth as silk.

Stated in this way, the strategic-contingencies theory of power paints an appealing picture of power. To the extent that power is determined by the critical uncertainties and problems facing the organization and, in turn, influences decisions in the organization, the organization is aligned with the realities it faces. In short, power facilitates the organization's adaptation to its environment—or its problems.

We can cite many illustrations of how influence derives from a subunit's ability to deal with critical contingencies. Michael Crozier described a French cigarette factory in which the maintenance engineers had a considerable say in the plant-wide operation. After some probing he discovered that the group possessed the solution to one of the major problems faced by the company, that of trouble-shooting the elaborate, expensive, and irascible automated machines that kept breaking down and dumbfounding everyone else. It was the one problem that the plant manager could in no way control.

The production workers, while troublesome from time to time, created no insurmountable problems; the manager could reasonably predict their absenteeism or replace them when necessary. Production scheduling was something he could deal with since, by watching inventories and sales, the demand for cigarettes was known long in advance. Changes in demand could be accommodated by slowing down or speeding up the line. Supplies of tobacco and paper were also easily dealt with through stockpiles and advance orders.

The one thing that management could neither control nor accommodate to, however, was the seemingly happenstance breakdowns. And the foremen couldn't instruct the workers what to do when emergencies developed since the maintenance department kept its records or problems and solutions locked up in a cabinet or in its members' heads. The breakdowns were, in truth, a critical source of uncertainty for the organization, and the maintenance engineers were the only ones who could cope with the problem.

The engineers' strategic role in coping with breakdowns afforded them a considerable say on plant decisions. Schedules and production quotas were set in consultation with them. And the plant manager, while formally their boss, accepted their decisions about personnel in their operation. His submission was to his credit, for without their cooperation he would have had an even more difficult time in running the plant.

## Ignoring Critical Consequences

In this cigarette factory, sharing influence with the maintenance workers reflected the plant manager's awareness of the critical contingencies. However, when organizational members are not aware of the critical contingencies they face and do not share influence accordingly, the failure to do so can create havoc. In one case, an insurance company's regional office was having problems with the performance of one of its departments, the coding department. From the outside, the department looked like a disaster area. The clerks who worked in it were somewhat dissatisfied; their supervisor paid little attention to them, and they resented the hard work. Several other departments were critical of this manager, claiming that she was inconsistent in meeting deadlines. The person most critical was the claims manager. He resented having to wait for work that was handled by her department, claiming that it held up his claims adjusters. Having heard the rumors about dissatisfaction among her subordinates, he attributed the situation to poor su-

pervision. He was second in command in the office and therefore took up the issue with her immediate boss, the head of administrative services. They consulted with the personnel manager, and the three of them concluded that the manager needed leadership training to improve her relations with her subordinates. The coding manager objected, saying it was a waste of time, but agreed to go along with the training and also agreed to give more priority to the claims department's work. Within a week after the training, the results showed that her workers were happier but that the performance of her department had decreased, save for the people serving the claims department.

About this time, we began, quite independently, a study of influence in this organization. We asked the administrative services director to draw up flow charts of how the work of one department moved onto the next department. In the course of the interview, we noticed that the coding department began or interceded in the work flow of most of the other departments and casually mentioned to him, "The coding manager must be very influential." He said "No, not really. Why would you think so?" Before we could reply, he recounted the story of her leadership training and the fact that things were worse. We then told him that it seemed obvious that the coding department would be influential from the fact that all the other departments depended on it. It was also clear why productivity had fallen. The coding manager took the training seriously and began spending more time raising her workers' spirits than she did worrying about the problems of all the departments that depended on her. Giving priority to the claims area only exaggerated the problem, for their work was getting done at the expense of the work of the other departments. Eventually the company hired a few more clerks to relieve the pressure in the coding department and performance returned to a more satisfactory level.

Originally we got involved with this insurance company to examine how the influence of each manager evolved from his or her department's handling of critical organizational contingencies.

we reasoned that one of the most important contingencies faced by all profit-making organizations was that of generating income. Thus we expected managers would be influential to the extent to which they contributed to this function. Such was the case. The underwriting managers, who wrote the policies that committed the premiums, were the most influential; the claims managers, who kept a lid on the funds flowing out, were a close second. Least influential were the managers of functions unrelated to revenue, such as mailroom and payroll managers. And contrary to what the administrative services manager believed, the third most powerful department head (out of 21) was the woman in charge of the coding function, which consisted of rating, recording, and keeping track of the codes of all policy applications and contracts. Her peers attributed more influence to her than could have been inferred from her place on the organization chart. And it was not surprising, since they all depended on her department. The coding department's records, their accuracy, and the speed with which they could be retrieved, affected virtually every other operating department in the insurance office. The underwriters depended on them in getting the contracts straight; the typing department depended on them in preparing the formal contract document; the claims department depended on them in adjusting claims; and accounting depended on them for billing. Unfortunately, the "bosses" were not aware of these dependences, for unlike the cigarette factory, there were no massive breakdowns that made them obvious, while the coding manager, who was a hardworking but quiet person, did little to announce her importance.

The cases of this plant and office illustrate nicely a basic point about the source of power in organizations. The basis for power in an organization derives from the ability of a person or subunit to take or not take actions that are desired by others. The coding manager was seen as influential by those who depended on her department, but not by the people at the top. The engineers were influential because of their role in keeping the plant operating. The two cases differ in these

respects: The coding supervisor's source of power was not as widely recognized as that of the maintenance engineers, and she did not use her source of power to influence decisions; the maintenance engineers did. Whether power is used to influence anything is a separate issue. We should not confuse this issue with the fact that power derives from a social situation in which one person has a capacity to do something and another person does not but wants it done.

## POWER SHARING IN ORGANIZATIONS

Power is shared in organizations; and it is shared out of necessity more than out of concern for principles of organizational development or participatory democracy. Power is shared because no one person controls all the desired activities in the organization. While the factory owner may hire people to operate his noisy machines, once hired they have some control over the use of the machinery. And thus they have power over him in the same way he has power over them. Who has more power over whom is a mooter point than that of recognizing the inherent nature of organizing as a sharing of power.

Let's expand on the concept that power derives from the activities desired in an organization. A major way of managing influence in organizations is through the designation of activities. In a bank we studied, we saw this principle in action. This bank was planning to install a computer system for routine credit evaluation. The bank, rather progressive-minded, was concerned that the change would have adverse effects on employees and therefore surveyed their attitudes.

The principal opposition to the new system came, interestingly, not from the employees who performed the routine credit checks, some of whom would be relocated because of the change, but from the manager of the credit department. His reason was quite simple. The manager's primary function was to give official approval to the applications, catch any employee mistakes before giving approval, and arbitrate any difficulties the clerks had in deciding what to do. As a consequence of his role, others in the organization, including his superiors, subordinates, and colleagues, attributed considerable importance to him. He, in turn, for example, could point to the low proportion of credit approvals, compared with other financial institutions, that resulted in bad debts. Now, to his mind, a wretched machine threatened to transfer his role to a computer programmer, a man who knew nothing of finance and who, in addition, had ten years less seniority. The credit manager eventually quit for a position at a smaller firm with lower pay, but one in which he would have more influence than his redefined job would have left him with.

Because power derives from activities rather than individuals, an individual's or subgroup's power is never absolute and derives ultimately from the context of the situation. The amount of power an individual has at any one time depends, not only on the activities he or she controls, but also on the existence of other persons or means by which the activities can be achieved and on those who determine what ends are desired and, hence, on what activities are desired and critical for the organization. One's own power always depends on other people for these two reasons. Other people, or groups or organizations, can determine the definition of what is a critical contingency for the organization and can also undercut the uniqueness of the individual's personal contribution to the critical contingencies of the organization.

Perhaps one can best appreciate how situationally dependent power is by examining how it is distributed. In most societies, power organizes around scarce and critical resources. In the United States, a person doesn't become powerful because he or she can drive a car. There are simply too many others who can drive with equal facility. In certain villages in Mexico, on the other hand, a person with a car is accredited with enormous social status and plays a key role in the community. In addition to scarcity, power is also limited by the need for one's capacities in a social system. While a racer's ability to drive a car around a 90° turn at 80 mph may be sparsely distributed in a society, it is not likely to lend the

driver much power in the society. The ability simply does not play a central role in the activities of the society.

The fact that power revolves around scarce and critical activities, of course, makes the control and organization of those activities a major battleground in struggles for power. Even relatively abundant or trivial resources can become the bases for power if one can organize and control their allocation and the definition of what is critical. Many occupational and professional groups attempt to do just this in modern economies. Lawyers organize themselves into associations, regulate the entrance requirements for novitiates, and then get laws passed specifying situations that require the services of an attorney. Workers had little power in the conduct of industrial affairs until they organized themselves into closed and controlled systems. In recent years, women and blacks have tried to define themselves as important and critical to the social system, using law to reify their status.

In organizations there are obviously opportunities for defining certain activities as more critical than others. Indeed, the growth of managerial thinking to include defining organizational objectives and goals has done much to foster these opportunities. One sure way to liquidate the power of groups in the organization is to define the need for their services out of existence. David Halberstam presents a description of how just such a thing happened to the group of correspondents that evolved around Edward R. Murrow, the brilliant journalist, interviewer, and war correspondent of CBS News. A close friend of CBS chairman and controlling stockholder William S. Paley, Murrow, and the news department he directed, were endowed with freedom to do what they felt was right. He used it to create some of the best documentaries and commentaries ever seen on television. Unfortunately, television became too large, too powerful, and too suspect in the eyes of the federal government that licensed it. It thus became, or at least the top executives believed it had become, too dangerous to have in-depth, probing commentary on the news. Crisp, dry, uneditorializing headliners were considered safer. Murrow was out and Walter Cronkite was in.

The power to define what is critical in an organization is no small power. Moreover, it is the key to understanding why organizations are either aligned with their environments or misaligned. If an organization defines certain activities as critical when in fact they are not critical, given the flow of resources coming into the organization, it is not likely to survive, at least in its present form.

Most organizations manage to evolve a distribution of power and influence that is aligned with the critical realities they face in the environment. The environment, in turn, includes both the internal environment, the shifting situational contexts in which particular decisions are made, and the external environment that it can hope to influence but is unlikely to control.

## THE CRITICAL CONTINGENCIES

The critical contingencies facing most organizations derive from the environmental context within which they operate. This determines the available needed resources and thus determines the problems to be dealt with. That power organizes around handling these problems suggests an important mechanism by which organizations keep in turn with their external environments. The strategic-contingencies model implies that subunits that contribute to the critical resources of the organization will gain influence in the organization. Their influence presumably is then used to bend the organization's activities to the contingencies that determine its resources. This idea may strike one as obvious. But its obviousness in no way diminishes its importance. Indeed, despite its obviousness, it escapes the notice of many organizational analysts and managers, who all too frequently think of the organization in terms of a descending pyramid, in which all the departments in one tier hold equal power and status. This presumption denies the reality that departments differ in the contributions they are believed to make to the overall organization's resources, as well as to the fact that some are more equal than others.

Because of the importance of this idea to organizational effectiveness, we decided to examine it carefully in a large midwestern university. A university offers an excellent site for studying power. It is composed of departments with nominally equal power and is administered by a central executive structure much like other bureaucracies. However, at the same time it is a situation in which the departments have clearly defined identities and face diverse external environments. Each department has its own bodies of knowledge, its own institutions, its own sources of prestige and resources. Because the departments operate in different external environments, they are likely to contribute differentially to the resources of the overall organization. Thus a physics department with close ties to NASA may contribute substantially to the funds of the university; and a history department with a renowned historian in residence may contribute to the intellectual credibility or prestige of the whole university. Such variations permit one to examine how these various contributions lead to obtaining power within the university.

We analyzed the influence of 29 university departments throughout an 18-month period in their history. Our chief interest was to determine whether departments that brought more critical resources to the university would be more powerful than departments that contributed fewer or less critical resources.

To identify the critical resources each department contributed, the heads of all departments were interviewed about the importance of seven different resources to the university's success. The seven included undergraduate students (the factor determining size of the state allocations by the university), national prestige, administrative expertise, and so on. The most critical resource was found to be contract and grant monies received by a department's faculty for research or consulting services. At this university, contract and grants contributed somewhat less than 50 percent of the overall budget, with the remainder primarily coming from state appropriations. The importance attributed to contract and grant monies, and the rather minor importance of undergraduate students, was not surprising for this particular university. The university was a major center for graduate education; many of its departments ranked in the top ten of their respective fields. Grant and contract monies were the primary source of discretionary funding available for maintaining these programs of graduate education, and hence for maintaining the university's prestige. The prestige of the university itself was critical both in recruiting able students and attracting top-notch faculty.

From university records it was determined what relative contributions each of the 29 departments made to the various needs of the university (national prestige, outside grants, teaching). Thus, for instance, one department may have contributed to the university by teaching 7 percent of the instructional units, bringing in 2 percent of the outside contracts and grants, and having a national ranking of 20. Another department, on the other hand, may have taught one percent of the instructional units, contributed 12 percent to the grants, and be ranked the third best department in its field within the country.

The question was: Do these different contributions determine the relative power of the departments within the university? Power was measured in several ways; but regardless of how measured, the answer was "Yes." Those three resources together accounted for about 70 percent of the variance in subunit power in the university.

But the most important predictor of departmental power was the department's contribution to the contracts and grants of the university. Sixty percent of the variance in power was due to this one factor, suggesting that the power of departments derived primarily from the dollars they provided for graduate education, the activity believed to be the most important for the organization.

## THE IMPACT OF ORGANIZATIONAL POWER ON DECISION MAKING

The measure of power we used in studying this university was an analysis of the responses of the department heads we interviewed. While such perceptions of power might be of interest in their own right, they contribute little to our understanding of how the distribution of power might serve to align an organization with its critical realities. For this we must look to how power actually influences the decisions and policies of organizations.

While it is perhaps not absolutely valid, we can generally gauge the relative importance of a department of an organization by the size of the budget allocated to it relative to other departments. Clearly it is of importance to the administrators of those departments whether they are squeezed in a budget crunch or are given more funds to strike out after new opportunities. And it should also be clear that when those decisions are made and one department can go ahead and try new approaches while another must cut back on the old, then the deployment of the resources of the organization in meeting its problems is most directly affected.

Thus our study of the university led us to ask the following question: Does power lead to influence in the organization? To answer this question, we found it useful first to ask another one, namely: Why should department heads try to influence organization decisions to favor their own departments to the exclusion of other departments? While this second question may seem a bit naive to anyone who has witnessed the political realities of organizations, we posed it in a context of research on organizations that sees power as an illegitimate threat to the neater rational authority of modern bureaucracies. In this context, decisions are not believed to be made because of the dirty business of politics but because of the overall goals and purposes of the organization. In a university, one reasonable basis for decision making is the teaching workload of departments and the demands that follow from that workload. We would expect, therefore, that departments with heavy student demands for courses would be able to obtain funds for teaching. Another reasonable basis for decision making is quality. We would expect, for that reason, that departments with esteemed reputations would be able to obtain funds both because their quality suggests they might use such funds effectively and because such funds would allow them to maintain their quality. A rational model of bureaucracy intimates, then, that the organizational decisions taken would favor those who perform the stated purposes of the organization—teaching undergraduates and training professional and scientific talent—well.

The problem with rational models of decision making, however, is that what is rational to one person may strike another as irrational. For most departments, resources are a question of survival. While teaching undergraduates may seem to be a major goal for some members of the university, developing knowledge may seem so to others; and to still others, advising governments and other institutions about policies may seem to be the crucial business. Everyone has his own idea of the proper priorities in a just world. Thus goals rather than being clearly defined and universally agreed upon are blurred and contested throughout the organization. If such is the case, then the decisions taken on behalf of the organization as a whole are likely to reflect the goals of those who prevail in political contests, namely, those with power in the organization.

Will organizational decisions always reflect the distribution of power in the organization? Probably not. Using power for influence requires a certain expenditure of effort, time, and resources. Prudent and judicious persons are not likely to use their power needlessly or wastefully. And it is likely that power will be used to influence organizational decisions primarily under circumstances that both require and favor its use. We have examined three conditions that are likely to effect the use of power in organizations: scarcity, criticality, and uncertainty. The first suggests that subunits will try to exert influence when the resources of the organization are scarce. If there is an abundance of resources, then a particular department or a particular individual has little need to attempt influence. With little effort, he can get all he wants anyway.

The second condition, criticality, suggests that a subunit will attempt to influence decisions to obtain resources that are critical to its own sur-

vival and activities. Criticality implies that one would not waste effort, or risk being labeled obstinate, by fighting over trivial decisions affecting one's operations.

An office manager would probably balk less about a threatened cutback in copying machine usage than about a reduction in typing staff. An advertising department head would probably worry less about losing his lettering artist than his illustrator. Criticality is difficult to define because what is critical depends on people's beliefs about what is critical. Such beliefs may or may not be based on experience and knowledge and may or may not be agreed upon by all. Scarcity, for instance, may itself affect conceptions of criticality. When slack resources drop off, cutbacks have to be made—those "hard decisions, " as congressmen and resplendent administrators like to call them. Managers then find themselves scrapping projects they once held dear.

The third condition that we believe affects the use of power is uncertainty: When individuals do not agree about what the organization should do or how to do it, power and other social processes will affect decisions. The reason for this is simply that, if there are no clear-cut criteria available for resolving conflict of interest, then the only means for resolution is some form of social process, including power, status, social ties, or some arbitrary process like flipping a coin or drawing straws. Under conditions of uncertainty, the powerful manager can argue his case on any grounds and usually win it. Since there is no real consensus, other contestants are not likely to develop counterarguments or amass sufficient opposition. Moreover, because of his power and their need for access to the resources he controls, they are more likely to defer to his arguments.

Although the evidence is slight, we have found that power will influence the allocations of scarce and critical resources. In the analysis of power in the university, for instance, one of the most critical resources needed by departments is the general budget. First granted by the state legislature, the general budget is later allocated to individual departments by the university administration in response to requests from the department heads. Our analysis of the factors that contribute to a department getting more or less of this budget indicated that subunit power was the major predictor, overriding such factors as student demand for courses, national reputations of departments, or even the size of a department's faculty. Moreover, other research has shown that when the general budget has been cut back or held below previous uninflated levels, leading to monies becoming more scarce, budget allocations mirror departmental powers even more closely.

Student enrollment and faculty size, of course, do themselves relate to budget allocations, as we would expect since they determine a department's need for resources, or at least offer visible testimony of needs. But departments are not always able to get what they need by the mere fact of needing them. In one analysis it was found that high-power departments were able to obtain budget without regard to their teaching loads and, in some cases, actually in inverse relation to their teaching loads. In contrast, low-power departments could get increases in budget only when they could justify the increases by a recent growth in teaching load, and then only when it was far in excess of norms for other departments.

General budget is only one form of resource that is allocated to departments. There are others such as special grants for student fellowships or faculty research. These are critical to departments because they affect the ability to attract other resources, such as outstanding faculty or students. We examined how power influenced the allocations of four resources department heads had described as critical and scarce.

When the four resources were arrayed from the most to the least critical and scarce, we found that departmental power best predicated the allocations of the most critical and scarce resources. In other words, the analysis of how power influences organizational allocations leads to this conclusion: Those subunits most likely to survive in times of strife are those that are more critical to the organization. Their importance to the organization gives them power to influence resource allocations that enhance their own survival.

## HOW EXTERNAL ENVIRONMENT IMPACTS EXECUTIVE SELECTION

Power not only influences the survival of key groups in an organization, it also influences the selection of individuals to key leadership positions, and by such a process further aligns the organization with its environmental context.

We can illustrate this with a recent study of the selection and tenure of chief administrators in 57 hospitals in Illinois. We assumed that since the critical problems facing the organization would enhance the power of certain groups at the expense of others, then the leaders to emerge should be those most relevant to the context of the hospitals. To assess this we asked each chief administrator about his professional background and how long he had been in office. The replies were then related to the hospitals' funding, ownership, and competitive conditions for patients and staff.

One aspect of a hospital's context is the source of its budget. Some hospitals, for instance, are run much like other businesses. They sell bed space, patient care, and treatment services. They charge fees sufficient both to cover their costs and to provide capital for expansion. The main source of both their operating and capital funds is patient billings. Increasingly, patient billings are paid for, not by patients, but by private insurance companies. Insurers like Blue Cross dominate and represent a potent interest group outside a hospital's control but critical to its income. The insurance companies, in order to limit their own costs, attempt to hold down the fees allowable to hospitals, which they do effectively from their positions on state rate boards. The squeeze on hospitals that results from fees increasing slowly while costs climb rapidly more and more demands the talents of cost accountants or people trained in the technical expertise of hospital administration.

By contrast, other hospitals operate more like social service institutions, either as government healthcare units (Bellevue Hospital in New York City and Cook County Hospital in Chicago, for example) or as charitable institutions. These hospitals obtain a large proportion of their operating and capital funds, not from privately insured patients, but from government subsidies or private donations. Such institutions rather than requiring the talents of a technically efficient administrator are likely to require the savvy of someone who is well integrated into the social and political power structure of the community.

Not surprisingly, the characteristics of administrators predictably reflect the funding context of the hospitals with which they are associated. Those hospitals with larger proportions of their budget obtained from private insurance companies were most likely to have administrators with backgrounds in accounting and least likely to have administrators whose professions were business or medicine. In contrast, those hospitals with larger proportions of their budget derived from private donations and local governments were most likely to have administrators with business or professional backgrounds and least likely to have accountants. The same held for formal training in hospital management. Professional hospital administrators could easily be found in hospitals drawing their incomes from private insurance and rarely in hospitals dependent on donations or legislative appropriations.

As with the selection of administrators, the context of organizations has also been found to affect the removal of executives. The environment, as a source of organizational problems, can make it more or less difficult for executives to demonstrate their value to the organization. In the hospitals we studied, long-term administrators came from hospitals with few problems. They enjoyed amicable and stable relations with their local business and social communities and suffered little competition for funding and staff. The small city hospital director who attended civic and Elks meetings while running the only hospital within a 100-mile radius, for example, had little difficulty holding on to his job. Turnover was highest in hospitals with the most problems, a phenomenon similar to that observed in a study of industrial organizations in which turnover was highest among executives in industries with competitive environments and unstable market conditions. The interesting thing is that instability characterized the industries rather than the individual firms in them. The troublesome conditions in the individual firms were attributed, or rather misattributed, to the executives themselves.

It takes more than problems, however, to terminate a manager's leadership. The problems themselves must be relevant and critical. This is clear from the way in which an administrator's tenure is affected by the status of the hospital's operating budget. Naively we might assume that all administrators would need to show a surplus. Not necessarily so. Again, we must distinguish between those hospitals that depend on private donations for funds and those that do not. Whether an endowed budget shows a surplus or deficit is less important than the hospital's relations with benefactors. On the other hand, with a budget dependent on patient billing, a surplus is almost essential; monies for new equipment or expansion must be drawn from it, and without them quality care becomes more difficult and patients scarcer. An administrator's tenure reflected just these considerations. For those hospitals dependent upon private donations, the length of an administrator's term depended not at all on the status of the operating budget but was fairly predictable from the hospital's relations with the business community. On the other hand, in hospitals dependent on the operating budget for capital financing, the greater the deficit the shorter was the tenure of the hospital's principal administrators.

## CHANGING CONTINGENCIES AND ERODING POWER BASES

The critical contingencies facing the organization may change. When they do, it is reasonable to expect that the power of individuals and subgroups will change in turn. At times the shift can be swift and shattering, as it was recently for powerholders in New York City. A few years ago it was believed that David Rockefeller was one of the ten most powerful people in the city, as tallied by *New York* magazine, which annually sniffs out power for the delectation of its readers. But that was before it was revealed that the city was in financial trouble, before Rockefeller's Chase Manhattan Bank lost some of its own financial luster, and before brother Nelson lost some of his political influence in Washington. Obviously David Rockefeller was no longer as well positioned to help bail the city out. Another loser was an attorney with considerable personal connections to the political and religious leaders of the city. His talents were no longer in much demand. The persons with more influence were the bankers and union pension fund executors who fed money to the city; community leaders who represent blacks and Spanish-Americans, in contrast, witnessed the erosion of their power bases.

One implication of the idea that power shifts with changes in organizational environments is that the dominant coalition will tend to be that group that is most appropriate for the organization's environment, as also will the leaders of an organization. One can observe this historically in the top executives of industrial firms in the United States. Up until the early 1950s, many top corporations were headed by former production line managers or engineers who gained prominence because of their abilities to cope with the problems of production. Their success, however, only spelled their demise. As production became routinized and mechanized, the problem of most firms became one of selling all those goods they so efficiently produced. Marketing executives were more frequently found in corporate boardrooms. Success outdid itself again, for keeping markets and production steady and stable requires the kind of control that can only come from acquiring competitors and suppliers or the invention of more and more appealing products—ventures that typically require enormous amounts of capital. During the 1960s, financial executives assumed the seats of power. And they, too, will give way to others. Edging over the horizon are legal experts, as regulation and antitrust suits are becoming more and more frequent in the 1970s, suits that had their be-

ginnings in the success of the expansion generated by prior executives. The more distant future, which is likely to be dominated by multinational corporations, may see former secretaries of state and their minions increasingly serving as corporate figureheads.

## THE NONADAPTIVE CONSEQUENCES OF ADAPTATION

From what we have said thus far about power aligning the organization with its own realities, an intelligent person might react with a resounding ho-hum, for it all seems to obvious: Those with the ability to get the job done are given the job to do.

However, there are two aspects of power that make it more useful for understanding organization and their effectiveness. First, the "job" to be done has a way of expanding itself until it becomes less and less clear what the job is. Napoleon begun by doing a job for France in the war with Austria and ended up Emperor, convincing many that only he could keep the peace. Hitler began by promising an end to Germany's troubling postwar depression and ended up convincing more people than is comfortable to remember that he was destined to be the savior of the world. In short, power is a capacity for influence that extends far beyond the original bases that created it. Second, power tends to take on institutionalized forms that enable it to endure well beyond its usefulness to an organization.

There is an important contradiction in what we have observed about organizational power. On the one hand we have said that power derives from the contingencies facing an organization and that when those contingencies change so do the bases for power. On the other hand we have asserted that subunits will tend to use their power to influence organizational decisions in their own favor, particularly when their own survival is threatened by the scarcity of critical resources. The first statement implies that an organization will tend to be aligned with its environment since power will tend to bring to key positions those with capabilities relevant to the context. The second implies that those in power will not give up their positions so easily; they will pursue policies that guarantee their continued domination. In short, change and stability operate through the same mechanism, and as a result, the organization will never be completely in phase with its environment or its needs.

The study of hospital administrators illustrates how leadership can be out of phase with reality. We argued that privately funded hospitals needed trained technical administrators more so than did hospitals funded by donations. The need as we perceived it was matched in most hospitals, but by no means in all. Some organizations did not conform with our predictions. These deviations imply that some administrators were able to maintain their positions independent of their suitability for those positions. By dividing administrators into those with long and short terms of office, one finds that the characteristics of longer-termed administrators were virtually unrelated to the hospital's content. The shorter-termed chiefs on the other hand had characteristics more appropriate for the hospital's problems. For a hospital to have a recently appointed head implies that the previous administrator had been unable to endure by institutionalizing himself.

One obvious feature of hospitals that allowed some administrators to enjoy a long tenure was a hospital's ownership. Administrators were less entrenched when their hospitals were affiliated with and depended upon larger organizations, such as governments or churches. Private hospitals offered more secure positions for administrators. Like private corporations, they tend to have more diffused ownership, leaving the administrator unopposed as he institutionalizes his reign. Thus he endures, sometimes at the expense of the performance of the organization. Other research has demonstrated that corporations with diffuse ownership have poorer earnings than those in which the control of the manager is checked by a dominant shareholder. Firms that overload their boardrooms with more insiders than are appropriate for their context have also been found to be less profitable.

A word of caution is required about our judgment of "appropriateness." When we argue some capabilities are more appropriate for one context than another, we do so from the perspective of an outsider and on the basis of reasonable assumptions as to the problems the organization will face and the capabilities they will need. The fact that we have been able to predict the distribution of influence and the characteristics of leaders suggests that our reasoning is not incorrect. However, we do not think that all organizations follow the same pattern. The fact that we have not been able to predict outcomes with 100 percent accuracy indicates they do not.

## MISTAKING CRITICAL CONTINGENCIES

One thing that allows subunits to retain their power is their ability to name their functions as critical to the organization when they may not be. Consider again our discussion of power in the university. One might wonder why the most critical tasks were defined as graduate education and scholarly research, the effect of which was to lend power to those who brought in grants and contracts. Why not something else? The reason is that the more powerful departments argued for those criteria and won their case, partly because they were more powerful.

In another analysis of this university, we found that all departments advocate self-serving criteria for budget allocation. Thus a department with large undergraduate enrollments argued that enrollments should determine budget allocations, a department with a strong national reputation saw prestige as the most reasonable basis for distributing funds, and so on. We further found that advocating such self-serving criteria actually benefited a department's budget allotments but, also, it paid off more for departments that were already powerful.

Organizational needs are consistent with a current distribution of power also because of a human tendency to categorize problems in familiar ways. An accountant sees problems with organizational performances as cost accountancy problems or inventory flow problems. A sales manager sees them as problems with markets, promotional strategies, or just unaggressive salespeople. But what is the truth? Since it does not automatically announce itself, it is likely that those with prior credibility, or those with power, will be favored as the enlightened. This bias, while not intentionally self-serving, further concentrates power among those who already possess it, independent of changes in the organization's content.

## INSTITUTIONALIZING POWER

A third reason for expecting organizational contingencies to be defined in familiar ways is that the current holders of power can structure the organization in ways that institutionalize themselves. By institutionalization we mean the establishment of relatively permanent structures and policies that favor the influence of a particular subunit. While in power, dominant coalition has the ability to institute constitutions, rules, procedures, and information systems that limit the potential power of others while continuing their own.

The key to institutionalizing power always is to create a device that legitimates one's own authority and diminishes the legitimacy of others. When the "Divine Right of Kings" was envisioned centuries ago it was to provide an unquestionable foundation for the supremacy of royal authority. There is generally a need to root the exercise of authority in some higher power. Modern leaders are no less affected by this need. Richard Nixon, with the aid of John Dean, reified the concept of executive privilege, which meant in effect that what the President wished not to be discussed need not be discussed.

In its simpler form, institutionalization is achieved by designating positions or roles for organizational activities. The creation of a new post legitimizes a function and forces organization members to orient to it. By designating how this new post relates to older, more established posts, moreover, one can structure an organization to enhance the importance of the function

in the organization. Equally, one can diminish the importance of traditional functions. This is what happened in the end with the insurance company we mentioned that was having trouble with its coding department. As the situation unfolded, the claims director continued to feel dissatisfied about the dependency of his functions on the coding manager. Thus he instituted a reorganization that resulted in two coding departments. In so doing, of course, he placed activities that affected his department under his direct control, presumably to make the operation more effective. Similarly, consumer-product firms enhance the power of marketing by setting up a coordinating role to interface production and marketing functions and then appoint a marketing manager to fill the role.

The structures created by dominant powers sooner or later become fixed and unquestioned features of the organization. Eventually, this can be devastating: It is said that the battle of Jena in 1806 was lost by Frederick the Great, who died in 1786. Though the great Prussian leader had no direct hand in the disaster, his imprint on the army was so thorough, so embedded in its skeletal underpinnings, that the organization was inappropriate for others to lead in different times.

Another important source of institutionalized power lies in the ability to structure information systems. Setting up committees to investigate particular organizational issues and having them report only to particular individuals or groups facilitates their awareness of problems by members of those groups while limiting the awareness of problems by the members of other groups. Obviously, those who have information are in a better position to interpret the problems of an organization, regardless of how realistically they may, in fact, do so.

Still another way to institutionalize power is to distribute rewards and resources. The dominant group may quiet competing interest groups with small favors and rewards. The credit for this artful form of co-optation belongs to Louis XIV. To avoid usurpation of his power by the nobles of France and the Fronde that had so troubled his father's reign, he built the palace at Versailles to occupy them with hunting and gossip. Awed, the courtiers basked in the reflected glories of the "Sun King" and the overwhelming setting he had created for his court.

At this point, we have not systematically studied the institutionalization of power. But we suspect it is an important condition that mediates between the environment of the organization and the capabilities of the organization for dealing with that environment. The more institutionalized power is within an organization, the more likely an organization will be out of phase with the realities it faces. President Richard Nixon's structuring of his White House is one of the better documented illustrations. If we go back to newspaper and magazine descriptions of how he organized his office from the beginning in 1968, most of what occurred subsequently follows almost as an afterthought. Decisions flowed through virtually only the small White House staff; rewards, small presidential favors of recognition, and perquisites were distributed by this staff to the loyal; and information from the outside world—the press, Congress, the people on the streets—was filtered by the staff and passed along only if initialed "bh." Thus it was not surprising that when Nixon met war protestors in the early dawn, the only thing he could think to talk about was the latest football game, so insulated had he become from their grief and anger.

One of the more interesting implications of institutionalized power is that executive turnover among the executives who have structured the organization is likely to be a rare event that occurs only under the most pressing crisis. If a dominant coalition is able to structure the organization and interpret the meaning of ambiguous events like declining sales and profits or lawsuits, then the "real" problems to emerge will easily be incorporated into traditional molds of thinking and acting. If opposition is designed out of the organization, the interpretations will go unquestioned. Conditions will remain stable until a crisis develops, so overwhelming and visible that even the most adroit rhetorician would be silenced.

## IMPLICATIONS FOR THE MANAGEMENT OF POWER IN ORGANIZATIONS

While we could derive numerous implications from this discussion of power, our selection would have to depend largely on whether one wanted to increase one's power, decrease the power of others, or merely maintain one's position. More important, the real implications depend on the particulars of an organizational situation. To understand power in an organization one must begin by looking outside it—into the environment—for those groups that mediate the organization's outcomes but are not themselves within its control.

Instead of ending with homilies, we will end with a reversal of where we began. Power, rather than being the dirty business it is often made out to be, is probably one of the few mechanisms for reality testing in organizations. And the cleaner forms of power, the institutional forms, rather than having the virtues they are often credited with, can lead the organization to become out of touch. The real trick to managing power in organizations is to ensure somehow that leaders cannot be unaware of the realities of their environments and cannot avoid changing to deal with those realities. That, however, would be like designing the "self-liquidating organization," an unlikely event since anyone capable of designing such an instrument would be obviously in control of the liquidations.

Management would do well to devote more attention to determining the critical contingencies of their environments. For if you conclude, as we do, that the environment sets most of the structure influencing organizational outcomes and problems, and that power derives from the organization's activities that deal with those contingencies, then it is the environment that needs managing, not power. The first step is to construct an accurate model of the environment, a process that is quite difficult for most organizations. We have recently started a project to aid administrators in systematically understanding their environments. From this experience, we have learned that the most critical blockage to perceiving an organization's reality accurately is a failure to incorporate those with the relevant expertise into the process. Most organizations have the requisite experts on hand but they are positioned so that they can be comfortably ignored.

One conclusion you can, and probably should, derive from our discussion is that power—because of the way it develops and the way it is used—will always result in the organization suboptimizing its performance. However, to this grim absolute, we add a comforting caveat: If any criteria other than power were the basis for determining an organization's decisions, the results would be even worse.

## SELECTED BIBLIOGRAPHY

The literature on power is at once both voluminous and frequently empty of content. Some is philosophical musing about the concept of power, while other writing contains popularized palliatives for acquiring and exercising influence. Machiavelli's *The Prince,* if read carefully, remains the single best prescriptive treatment of power and its use. Most social scientists have approached power descriptively, attempting to understand how it is acquired, how it is used, and what its effects are. Mayer Zald's edited collection *Power in Organizations* (Vanderbilt University Press, 1970) is one of the more useful sets of thoughts about power from a sociological perspective, while James Tedeschi's edited book, *The Social Influence Processes* (Aldine-Atherton, 1972) represents the social psychological approach to understanding power and influence. The strategic contingencies's approach, with its emphasis on the importance of uncertainty for understanding power in organizations, is described by David Hickson and his colleagues in "A Strategic Contingencies Theory of Intraorganizational Power" (*Administrative Science Quarterly,* December 1971, pp. 216–29).

Unfortunately, while many have written about power theoretically, there have been few empirical examinations of power and its use. Most of the work has taken the form of case studies. Michel Crozier's *The Bureaucratic Phenomenon* (University of Chicago Press, 1964) is important because it describes a group's source of power as control over critical activities and illustrates how power is not strictly derived from hierarchical position. J. Victor Baldridge's *Power and Conflict in the University* (John Wiley & Sons, 1971) and Andrew Pettigrew's study of computer purchase decisions in one English firm (*Politics of Organizational Decision Making,* Tavistock, 1973) both present insights into the acquisition and use of power in specific instances. Our work has been more empirical and comparative, testing more explicitly the ideas presented in this article. The study of university decision making is reported in articles in the June 1974, pp. 135–51, and December 1974, pp. 453–73, issues of the *Administrative Science Quarterly,* the insurance firm study in J. G. Hunt and L. L. Larson's collection, *Leadership Frontiers* (Kent State University Press, 1975), and the study of hospital administrator succession appeared in 1977 in the *Academy of Management Journal.*

# P  A  R  T      E

# Organizational Leadership

## 30.  PATH-GOAL THEORY OF LEADERSHIP

Robert J. House and Terence R. Mitchell

An integrated body of conjecture by students of leadership, referred to as the "Path-Goal Theory of Leadership," is currently emerging. According to this theory, leaders are effective because of their impact on subordinates' motivation, ability to perform effectively, and satisfactions. The theory is called Path-Goal because its major concern is how the leader influences the subordinates' perceptions of their work goals, personal goals, and paths to goal attainment. The theory suggests that a leader's behavior is motivating or satisfying to the degree that the behavior increases subordinate goal attainment and clarifies the paths to these goals.

## HISTORICAL FOUNDATIONS

The path-goal approach has its roots in a more general motivational theory called expectancy theory.[1] Briefly, expectancy theory states that an individual's attitudes (e.g., satisfaction with supervision or job satisfaction) or behavior (e.g., leader behavior or job effort) can be predicted from: (1) the degree to which the job, or behavior, is seen as leading to various outcomes (expectancy) and (2) the evaluation of these outcomes (valences). Thus, people are satisfied with their job if they think it leads to things that are

---

Robert J. House and Terence R. Mitchell, "Path-Goal Theory of Leadership" from *Journal of Contemporary Business*, University of Washington, Autumn 1974, 3, no. 4, pp. 81–97. Reprinted with permission from the publisher.

[1] T. R. Mitchell, "Expectancy Model of Job Satisfaction, Occupational Preference and Effort: A Theoretical, Methodological and Empirical Appraisal," *Psychological Bulletin* (1974).

highly valued, and they work hard if they believe that effort leads to things that are highly valued. This type of theoretical rationale can be used to predict a variety of phenomena related to leadership, such as why leaders behave the way they do, or how leader behavior influences subordinate motivation.[2]

This latter approach is the primary concern of this article. The implication for leadership is that subordinates are motivated by leader behavior to the extent that this behavior influences expectancies, e.g., goal paths and valences, e.g., goal attractiveness.

Several writers have advanced specific hypotheses concerning how the leader affects the paths and the goals of subordinates.[3] These writers focused on two issues: (1) how the leader affects subordinates' expectations that effort will lead to effective performance and valued rewards, and (2) how this expectation affects motivation to work hard and perform well.

While the state of theorizing about leadership in terms of subordinates' paths and goals is in its infancy, we believe it is promising for two reasons. First, it suggests effects of leader behavior that have not yet been investigated but which appear to be fruitful areas of inquiry. And, second, it suggests with some precision the situational factors on which the effects of leader behavior are contingent.

The initial theoretical work by Evans asserts that leaders will be effective by making rewards available to subordinates and by making these rewards contingent on the subordinate's accomplishment of specific goals.[4] Evans argued that one of the strategic functions of the leader is to clarify for subordinates the kind of behavior that leads to goal accomplishment and valued rewards. This function might be referred to as path clarification. Evans also argued that the leader increases the rewards available to subordinates by being supportive toward subordinates, i.e., by being concerned about their status, welfare, and comfort. Leader supportiveness is in itself a reward that the leader has at his or her disposal, and the judicious use of this reward increases the motivation of subordinates.

Evans studied the relationship between the behavior of leaders and the subordinates' expectations that effort leads to rewards and also studied the resulting impact on ratings of the subordinates' performance. He found that when subordinates viewed leaders as being supportive (considerate of their needs) and when these superiors provided directions and guidance to the subordinates there was a positive relationship between leader behavior and subordinates' performance ratings.

However, leader behavior was only related to subordinates' performance when the leader's be-

---

[2] D. M. Nebeker and T. R. Mitchell, "Leader Behavior: An Expectancy Theory Approach," *Organization Behavior and Human Performance*, 11(1974): 355–67.

[3] M. G. Evans, "The Effects of Supervisory Behavior on the Path-Goal Relationship," *Organization Behavior and Human Performance*, 55(1970): 277–98; T. H. Hammer and H. T. Dachler, "The Process of Supervision in the Context of Motivation Theory," Research Report no. 3 (University of Maryland, 1973); F. Dansereau, Jr., J. Cashman, and G. Graen, "Instrumentality Theory and Equity Theory as Complementary Approaches in Predicting the Relationship of Leadership and Turnover among Managers," *Organization Behavior and Human Performance*, 10(1973): 184–200; R. J. House, "A Path-Goal Theory of Leader o Effectiveness," *Administrative Science Quarterly*, 16, 3(September 1971): 321–38; T. R. Mitchell, "Motivation and Participation: An Integration," *Academy of Management Journal*, 16, 4(1973): 160–79; G. Graen, F. Dansereau, Jr., and T. Minami, "Dysfunctional Leadership Styles," *Organization Behavior and Human Performance*, 7(1972): 216–36; G. Graen, F. Dansereau, Jr. and T. Minami, "An Empirical Test of the Man-in-the-Middle Hypothesis among Executives in a Hierarchical Organization Employing a Unit Analysis," *Organization Behavior and Human Performance*, 8(1972): 262–85; R. J. House and G. Dessler, "The Path-Goal Theory of Leadership: Some Post Hoc and a Priori Tests," to appear in J. G. Hunt, ed., *Contingency Approaches to Leadership* (Carbondale, Ill: Southern Illinois University Press, 1974).

[4] M. G. Evans, "Effects of Supervisory Behavior"; M. G. Evans, "Extensions of a Path-Goal Theory of Motivation," *Journal of Applied Psychology*, 59(1974): 172–78.

havior also was related to the subordinates' expectations that their effort would result in desired rewards. Thus, Evans's findings suggest that the major impact of a leader on the performance of subordinates is clarifying the path to desired rewards and making such rewards contingent on effective performance.

Stimulated by this line of reasoning, House, and House and Dessler advanced a more complex theory of the effects of leader behavior on the motivation of subordinates.[5] The theory intends to explain the effects of four specific kinds of leader behavior on the following three subordinate attitudes or expectations: (1) the satisfaction of subordinates, (2) the subordinates' acceptance of the leader and (3) the expectations of subordinates that effort will result in effective performance and that effective performance is the path to rewards. The four kinds of leader behavior included in the theory are: (1) directive leadership, (2) supportive leadership, (3) participative leadership and (4) achievement-oriented leadership. Directive leadership is characterized by a leader who lets subordinates know what is expected of them, gives specific guidance as to what should be done and how it should be done, makes his or her part in the group understood, schedules work to be done, maintains definite standards of performance and asks that group members follow standard rules and regulations. Supportive leadership is characterized by a friendly and approachable leader who shows concern for the status, well-being and needs of subordinates. Such a leader does little things to make the work more pleasant, treats members as equals, and is friendly and approachable. Participative leadership is characterized by a leader who consults with subordinates, solicits their suggestions, and takes these suggestions seriously into consideration before making a decision. An achievement-oriented leader sets challenging goals, expects subordinates to perform at their highest level, continuously seeks improvement in performance *and* shows a high degree of confidence that the subordinates will assume responsibility, put forth effort, and accomplish challenging goals. This kind of leader constantly emphasizes excellence in performance and simultaneously displays confidence that subordinates will meet high standards of excellence.

A number of studies suggest that these different leadership styles can be shown by the same leader in various situations.[6] For example, a leader may show directiveness toward subordinates in some instances and be participative or supportive in other instances.[7] Thus, the traditional method of characterizing a leader as either highly participative and supportive *or* highly directive is invalid; rather, it can be concluded that leaders vary in the particular fashion employed for supervising their subordinates. Also, the theory, in its present stage, is a tentative explanation of the effects of leader behavior—it is incomplete because it does not explain other kinds of leader behavior and does not explain the effects of the leader on factors other than subordinate acceptance, satisfaction, and expectations. However, the theory is stated so that additional variables may be included in it as new knowledge is made available.

## PATH-GOAL THEORY

### General Propositions

The first proposition of path-goal theory is that leader behavior is acceptable and satisfying to

---

[5] R. J. House, "A Path-Goal Theory"; R. J. House and G. Dessler, "Path-Goal Theory of Leadership."

[6] R. J. House and G. Dessler, "Path-Goal Theory of Leadership"; R. M. Stogdill, *Managers, Employees, Organization* (Ohio State University, Bureau of Business Research, 1965); R. J. House, A. Valency, and R. Van der Krabben, "Some Tests and Extensions of the Path-Goal Theory of Leadership" (in preparation).

[7] W. A. Hill and D. Hughes, "Variations in Leader Behavior as a Function of Task Type." *Organization Behavior and Human Performance*, 11, 1(1974): 83–96.

subordinates to the extent that the subordinates see such behavior as either an immediate source of satisfaction or as instrumental to future satisfaction.

The second proposition of this theory is that the leader's behavior will be motivational, i.e., increase effort, to the extent that (1) such behavior makes satisfaction of subordinates' needs contingent on effective performance and (2) such behavior complements the environment of subordinates by providing the coaching, guidance, support, and rewards necessary for effective performance.

These two propositions suggest that the leader's strategic functions are to enhance subordinates' motivation to perform, satisfaction with the job, and acceptance of the leader. From previous research on expectancy theory of motivation, it can be inferred that the strategic functions of the leader consist of: (1) recognizing and/or arousing subordinates' needs for outcomes over which the leader has some control, (2) increasing personal payoffs to subordinates for work-goal attainment, (3) making the path to those payoffs easier to travel by coaching and direction, (4) helping subordinates clarify expectancies, (5) reducing frustrating barriers and (6) increasing the opportunities for personal satisfaction contingent on effective performance.

Stated less formally, the motivational functions of the leader consist of increasing the number and kinds of personal payoffs to subordinates for work-goal attainment and making paths to these payoffs easier to travel by clarifying the paths, reducing road blocks and pitfalls, and increasing the opportunities for personal satisfaction en route.

## Contingency Factors

Two classes of situational variables are asserted to be contingency factors. A contingency factor is a variable which moderates the relationship between two other variables such as leader behavior and subordinate satisfaction. For example, we might suggest that the degree of structure in the task moderates the relationship between leaders'

directive behavior and subordinates' job satisfaction. Figure 30.1 shows how such a relationship might look. Thus, subordinates are satisfied with directive behavior in an unstructured task and are satisfied with nondirective behavior in a structured task. Therefore, we say that the relationship between leader directiveness and subordinate satisfaction is contingent upon the structure of the task.

The two contingency variables are (*a*) personal characteristics of the subordinates and (*b*) the environmental pressures and demands with which subordinates must cope in order to accomplish the work goals and to satisfy their needs. While other situational factors also may operate to determine the effects of leader behavior, they are not presently known.

With respect to the first class of contingency factors, the characteristics of subordinates, path-goal theory asserts that leader behavior will be acceptable to subordinates to the extent that the subordinates see such behavior as either an immediate source of satisfaction or as instrumental to future satisfaction. Subordinates' characteristics are hypothesized to determine this percep-

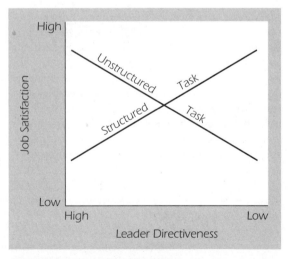

**FIGURE 30.1** Hypothetical Relationship Between Directive Leadership and Subordinate Satisfaction with Task Structure as a Contingency Factor.

tion partially. For example, Runyon[8] and Mitchell[9] show that the subordinate's score on a measure called Locus of Control moderates the relationship between participative leadership style and subordinate satisfaction. The Locus-of-Control measure reflects the degree to which an individual sees the environment as systematically responding to his or her behavior. People who believe that what happens to them occurs because of their behavior are called internals; people who believe that what happens to them occurs because of luck or chance are called externals. Mitchell's findings suggest that internals are more satisfied with a participative leadership style and externals are more satisfied with a directive style.

A second characteristic of subordinates on which the effects of leader behavior are contingent is subordinates' perception of their own ability with respect to their assigned tasks. The higher the degree of perceived ability relative to task demands, the less the subordinate will view leader directiveness and coaching behavior as acceptable. Where the subordinate's perceived ability is high, such behavior is likely to have little positive effect on the motivation of the subordinate and to be perceived as excessively close control. Thus, the acceptability of the leader's behavior is determined in part by the characteristics of the subordinates.

The second aspect of the situation, the environment of the subordinate, consists of those factors that are not within the control of the subordinate but which are important to need satisfaction or to ability to perform effectively. The theory asserts that effects of the leader's behavior on the psychological states of subordinates are contingent on other parts of the subordinates' environment that are relevant to subordinate motivation. Three broad classifications of contingency factors in the environment are:

The subordinates' tasks.

The formal authority system of the organization.

The primary work group.

Assessment of the environmental conditions makes it possible to predict the kind and amount of influence that specific leader behaviors will have on the motivation of subordinates. Any of the three environmental factors could act upon the subordinate in any of three ways: first, to serve as stimuli that motivate and direct the subordinate to perform necessary task operations; second, to constrain variability in behavior. Constraints may help the subordinate by clarifying expectancies that effort leads to rewards or by preventing the subordinate from experiencing conflict and confusion. Constraints also may be counterproductive to the extent that they restrict initiative or prevent increases in effort from being associated positively with rewards. Third, environmental factors may serve as rewards for achieving desired performance, e.g., it is possible for the subordinate to receive the necessary cues to do the job and the needed rewards for satisfaction from sources other than the leader, e.g., co-workers in the primary work group. Thus, the effect of the leader on subordinates' motivation will be a function of how deficient the environment is with respect to motivational stimuli, constraints, or rewards.

With respect to the environment, path-goal theory asserts that when goals and paths to desired goals are apparent because of the routine nature of the task, clear group norms or objective controls of the formal authority systems, attempts by the leader to clarify paths and goals will be both redundant and seen by subordinates as imposing unnecessary, close control. Although such control may increase performance by pre-

[8] K. E. Runyon, "Some Interactions between Personality Variables and Management Styles," *Journal of Applied Psychology*, 57, 3(1973): 288–94; T. R. Mitchell, C. R. Smyser, and S. E. Weed, "Locus of Control: Supervision and Work Satisfaction," *Academy of Management Journal*, 18, 3(1975): 623–31.

[9] T. R. Mitchell, "Locus of Control."

venting soldiering or malingering, it also will result in decreased satisfaction (see Figure 30.1).
Also with respect to the work environment, the
theory asserts that the more dissatisfying the task,
the more the subordinates will resent leader behavior directed at increasing productivity or enforcing compliance to organizational rules and
procedures.

Finally, with respect to environmental variables the theory states that leader behavior will
be motivational to the extent that it helps subordinates cope with environmental uncertainties,
threats from others or sources of frustration. Such
leader behavior is predicted to increase subordinates' satisfaction with the job context and to be
motivational to the extent that it increases the
subordinates' expectations that their effort will
lead to valued rewards.

These propositions and specification of situational contingencies provide a heuristic framework on which to base future research. Hopefully,
this will lead to a more fully developed, explicitly
formal theory of leadership.

Figure 30.2 presents a summary of the theory.
It is hoped that these propositions, while admittedly tentative, will provide managers with some
insights concerning the effects of their own leader
behavior and that of others.

## EMPIRICAL SUPPORT

The theory has been tested in a limited number
of studies which have generated considerable empirical support for our ideas and also suggest areas in which the theory requires revision. A brief
review of these studies follows.

### Leader Directiveness

Leader directiveness has a positive correlation
with satisfaction and expectancies of subordinates who are engaged in ambiguous tasks and
has a negative correlation with satisfaction and
expectancies of subordinates engaged in clear
tasks. These findings were predicted by the theory and have been replicated in seven organizations. They suggest that when task demands are
ambiguous or when the organization procedures,
rules, and policies are not clear a leader behaving in a directive manner complements the tasks
and the organization by providing the necessary
guidance and psychological structure for subordinates.[10] However, when task demands are clear
to subordinates, leader directiveness is seen more
as a hindrance.

However, other studies have failed to confirm these findings.[11] A study by Dessler[12] sug-

---

[10] R. J. House, "A Path-Goal Theory"; R. J. House and G. Dessler, "Path-Goal Theory of Leadership"; A. D. Szalagyi and H. P. Sims, "An Exploration of the Path-Goal Theory of Leadership
in a Health Care Environment," *Academy of Management Journal* (in press); J. D. Dermer, "Supervisory Behavior and Budget Motivation" (Cambridge, Mass: unpublished, MIT, Sloan School of
Management, 1974); R. W. Smetana, "The Relationship between Managerial Behavior and Subordinate Attitudes and Motivation: A Contribution to a Behaviorial Theory of Leadership" (Ph.D.
dissertation, Wayne State University, 1974).

[11] S. E. Weed, T. R. Mitchell, and C. R. Smyser, "A Test of House's Path-Goal Theory of Leadership
in an Organizational Setting" (paper presented at Western Psychological Assn., 1974); J. D. Dermer
and J. P. Siegel, "A Test of Path-Goal Theory: Disconfirming Evidence and a Critique" (unpublished,
University of Toronto, Faculty of Management Studies, 1973); R.S. Schuler, "A Path-Goal Theory
of Leadership: An Empirical Investigation" (Ph.D. dissertation, Michigan State University, 1973); H.
K. Downey, J. E. Sheridan, and J. W. Slocum, Jr., "Analysis of Relationships among Leader Behavior,
Subordinate Job Performance and Satisfaction: A Path-Goal Approach" (unpublished mimeograph,
1974); J. E. Stinson and T. W. Johnson, "The Path-Goal Theory of Leadership: A Partial Test and
Suggested Refinement," *Proceedings* (Kent, Ohio: 7the Annual Conference of the Midwest Academy
of Management, April 1974): 18–36.

[12] G. Dessler, "An Investigation of the Path-Goal Theory of Leadership" (Ph.D. dissertation, City
University of New York, Bernard M. Baruch College, 1973).

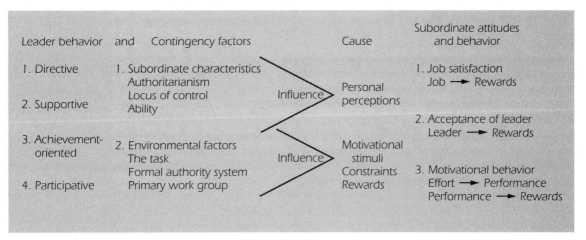

**FIGURE 30.2** Summary of Path-Goal Relationships.

gests a resolution to these conflicting findings—he found that for subordinates at the lower organizational levels of a manufacturing firm who were doing routine, repetitive, unambiguous tasks, directive leadership was preferred by closed-minded, dogmatic, authoritarian subordinates and nondirective leadership was preferred by nonauthoritarian, open-minded subordinates. However, for subordinates at higher organizational levels doing nonroutine, ambiguous tasks, directive leadership was preferred for both authoritarian and nonauthoritarian subordinates. Thus, Dessler found that two contingency factors appear to operate simultaneously: subordinate task ambiguity and degree of subordinate authoritarianism. When measured in combination, the findings are as predicted by the theory; however, when the subordinate's personality is not taken into account, task ambiguity does not al-

ways operate as a contingency variable as predicted by the theory. House, Burill, and Dessler recently found a similar interaction between subordinate authoritarianism and task ambiguity in a second manufacturing firm, thus adding confidence in Dessler's original findings.[13]

## Supportive Leadership

The theory hypothesizes that supportive leadership will have its most positive effect on subordinate satisfaction for subordinates who work on stressful, frustrating, or dissatisfying tasks. This hypothesis has been tested in 10 samples of employees,[14] and in only one of these studies was the hypothesis disconfirmed.[15] Despite some inconsistency in research on supportive leadership, the evidence is sufficiently positive to suggest that managers should be alert to the critical need

---

[13] R. J. House, D. Burrill, and G. Dessler, "Tests and Extensions of Path-Goal Theory of Leadership, I" (unpublished, in process).

[14] R. J. House, "A Path-Goal Theory"; R. J. House and G. Dessler, "Path-Goal Theory of Leadership"; A. D. Szalagyi and H. P. Sims, "Exploration of Path-Goal"; J. E. Stinson and T. W. Johnson, *Proceedings*; R. S. Schuler, "Path-Goal: Investigation"; H. K. Downey, J. E. Sheridan, and J. W. Slocum, Jr., "Analysis of Relationships"; S. E. Weed, T. R. Mitchell, and C. R. Smyser, "Test of House's Path-Goal."

[15] A. D. Szalagyi and H. P. Sims, " Exploration of Path-Goal."

for supportive leadership under conditions where tasks are dissatisfying, frustrating, or stressful to subordinates.

## Achievement-oriented Leadership

The theory hypothesizes that achievement-oriented leadership will cause subordinates to strive for higher standards of performance and to have more confidence in the ability to meet challenging goals. A recent study by House, Valency, and Van der Krabben provides a partial test of this hypothesis among white-collar employees in service organizations. [16] For subordinates performing ambiguous, nonrepetitive tasks, they found a positive relationship between the amount of achievement orientation of the leader and subordinates' expectancy that their effort would result in effective performance. Stated less technically, for subordinates performing ambiguous, nonrepetitive tasks, the higher the achievement orientation of the leader, the more the subordinates were confident that their efforts would pay off in effective performance. For subordinates performing moderately unambiguous, repetitive tasks, there was no significant relationship between achievement-oriented leadership and subordinate expectancies that their effort would lead to effective performance. This finding held in four separate organizations.

Two plausible interpretations may be used to explain these data. First, people who select ambiguous, nonrepetitive tasks may be different in personality from those who select a repetitive job and may, therefore, be more responsive to an achievement-oriented leader. A second explanation is that achievement orientation only affects expectancies in ambiguous situations because there is more flexibility and autonomy in such tasks. Therefore, subordinates in such tasks are more likely to be able to change in response to such leadership style. Neither of the above

interpretations have been tested to date; however, additional research is currently under way to investigate these relationships.

## Participative Leadership

In theorizing about the effects of participative leadership, it is necessary to ask about the specific characteristics of both the subordinates and their situation that would cause participative leadership to be viewed as satisfying and instrumental to effective performance.

Mitchell recently described at least four ways in which a participative leadership style would impact on subordinate attitudes and behavior as predicted by expectancy theory. [17] First, a participative climate should increase the clarity of organizational contingencies. Through participation in decision making, subordinates should learn what leads to what. From a path-goal viewpoint participation would lead to greater clarity of the paths to various goals. A second impact of participation would be that subordinates, hopefully, should select goals they highly value. If one participates in decisions about various goals, it makes sense that this individual would select goals he or she wants. Thus, participation would increase the correspondence between organization and subordinate goals. Third, we can see how participation would increase the control the individual has over what happens on the job. If our motivation is higher (based on the preceding two points), then having greater autonomy and ability to carry out our intentions should lead to increased effect and performance. Finally, under a participative system, pressure towards high performance should come from sources other than the leader or the organization. More specifically, when people participate in the decision process, they become more ego-involved; the decisions made are in some part their own. Also, their peers know what is expected and the social pressure has a greater impact. Thus, motivation to per-

---

[16] R. J. House, A. Valency, and R. Van der Krabben, "Tests and Extensions of Path-Goal Theory of Leadership, II" (unpublished, in process).

[17] T. R. Mitchell, "Motivation and Participation."

form well stems from internal and social factors as well as formal external ones.

A number of investigations prior to the above formulation supported the idea that participation appears to be helpful,[18] and Mitchell presents a number of recent studies that support the above four points.[19] However, it is also true that we would expect the relationship between a participative style and subordinate behavior to be moderated by both the personality characteristics of the subordinate and the situational demands. Studies by Tannenbaum and Allport and Vroom have shown that subordinates who prefer autonomy and self-control respond more positively to participative leadership in terms of both satisfaction and performance than subordinates who do not have such preferences.[20] Also, the studies mentioned by Runyon[21] and Mitchell[22] showed that subordinates who were external in orientation were less satisfied with a participative style of leadership than were internal subordinates.

House also has reviewed these studies in an attempt to explain the ways in which the situation or environment moderates the relationship between participation and subordinate attitudes and behavior.[23] His analysis suggests that where participative leadership is positively related to satisfaction, regardless of the predispositions of subordinates, the tasks of the subjects appear to be ambiguous and ego-involving. In the studies in which the subjects' personalities or predisposi-

tions moderate the effect of participative leadership, the tasks of the subjects are inferred to be highly routine and/or nonego-involving.

House reasoned from this analysis that the task may have an overriding effect on the relationship between leader participation and subordinate responses and that individual predispositions or personality characteristics of subordinates may have an effect only under some tasks. It was assumed that when task demands are ambiguous subordinates will have a need to reduce the ambiguity. Further, it was assumed that when task demands are ambiguous participative problem solving between the leader and the subordinate will result in more effective decisions than when the task demands are unambiguous. Finally, it was assumed that when the subordinates are ego-involved in their tasks they are more likely to want to have a say in the decisions that affect them. Given these assumptions, the following hypotheses were formulated to account for the conflicting findings reviewed above:

When subjects are highly ego-involved in a decision or a task and the decision or task demands are ambiguous, participative leadership will have a positive effect on the satisfaction and motivation of the subordinate, *regardless* of the subordinate's predisposition toward self-control, authoritarianism, or need for independence.

When subordinates are not ego-involved in their tasks and when task demands are clear, sub-

[18] H. Tosi, "A Reexamination of Personality as a Determinant of the Effects of Participation," *Personnel Psychology*, 23(1970): 91–99; J. Sadler "Leadership Style, Confidence in Management and Job Satisfaction," *Journal of Applied Behavioral Sciences*, 6(1970); 3–19; K. N. Wexley, J. P. Singh, and J. A. Yukl, "Subculture Personality as a Moderator of the Effects of Participation in Three Types of Appraisal Interviews," *Journal of Applied Psychology*, 83, 1(1973): 54–59.

[19] T. R. Mitchell, "Motivation and Participation."

[20] A. S. Tannenbaum and F. H. Allport, "Personality Structure and Group Structure: An Interpretive Study of Their Relationship through an Event-Structure Hypothesis," *Journal of Abnormal and Social Psychology*, 53(1956): 272–80; V. H. Vroom, "Some Personality Determinants of the Effects of Participation," *Journal of Abnormal and Social Psychology*, 59(1959): 322–27.

[21] K. E. Runyon, "Some Interactions between Personality Variables and Management Styles," *Journal of Applied Psychology*, 57, 3(1973): 288–94.

[22] T. R. Mitchell, C. R. Smyser, and S. E. Weed, "Locus of Control."

[23] R. J. House, "Notes on the Path-Goal Theory of Leadership," (University of Toronto, Faculty of Management Studies, May 1974).

ordinates who are not authoritarian and who have high needs for independence and self-control will respond favorably to leader participation and their opposite personality types will respond less favorably.

These hypotheses were derived on the basis of path-goal theorizing, i.e., the rationale guiding the analysis of prior studies was that both task characteristics and characteristics of subordinates interact to determine the effect of a specific kind of leader behavior on the satisfaction, expectancies, and performance of subordinates. To date, one major investigation has supported some of these predictions[24] in which personality variables, amount of participative leadership, task ambiguity, and job satisfaction were assessed for 324 employees of an industrial manufacturing organization. As expected, in nonrepetitive, ego-involving tasks, employees (regardless of their personality) were more satisfied under a participative style than a nonparticipative style. However, in repetitive tasks which were less ego-involving, the amount of authoritarianism of subordinates moderated the relationship between leadership style and satisfaction. Specifically, low authoritarian subordinates were *more satisfied* under a participative style. These findings are exactly as the theory would predict; thus, it has promise in reconciling a set of confusing and contradictory findings with respect to participative leadership.

## SUMMARY AND CONCLUSIONS

We have attempted to describe what we believe is a useful theoretical framework for understanding the effect of leadership behavior on subordinate satisfaction and motivation. Most theorists today have moved away from the simplistic notions that all effective leaders have a certain set of personality traits or that the situation completely determines performance. Some researchers have presented rather complex attempts at matching certain types of leaders with certain types of situations....But, we believe that a path-goal approach goes one step further. It not only suggests what type of style may be most effective in a given situation—it also attempts to explain *why* it is most effective.

We are optimistic about the future outlook of leadership research. With the guidance of path-goal theorizing, future research is expected to unravel many confusing puzzles about the reasons for and effects of leader behavior that have, heretofore, not been solved. However, we add a word of caution: the theory, and the research on it, are relatively new to the literature of organizational behavior. Consequently path-goal theory is offered more as a tool for directing research and stimulating insight than as a proven guide for managerial action.

---

[24] R. S. Schuler, "Leader Participation, Task Structure, and Subordinate Authoritarianism" (unpublished mimeograph, Cleveland State University, 1974).

# 31.   LEADERSHIP REVISITED

Victor H. Vroom

## RESEARCH ON LEADERSHIP TRAITS

Early research on the question of leadership had roots in the psychology of individual differences and in the personality theory of that time. The prevailing theory held that differences among people could be understood in terms of their traits—consistencies in behavior exhibited over situations. Each person could be usefully described on such dimensions as honesty-dishonesty, introversion-extroversion or masculine-feminine. In extrapolating this kind of theory to the study of leadership, it seemed natural to assume that there was such a thing as a trait of leadership, i.e., it was something that people possessed in different amounts. If such differences existed, they must be measurable in some way. As a consequence, psychologists set out, armed with a wide variety of psychological tests, to measure differences between leaders and followers. A large number of studies were conducted including comparisons of bishops with clergymen, sales managers with salesmen and railway presidents with station agents. Since occupancy of a leadership position may not be a valid reflection of the degree of leadership, other investigators pursued a different tack by looking at the relationship between personal traits of leaders and criteria for their effectiveness in carrying out their positions.

If this search for the measurable components of this universal trait of leadership had been effective, the implications for society would have been considerable. The resulting technology would have been of countless value in selecting leaders for all of our social institutions and would have eliminated errors inevitably found in the subjective assessments which typically guide this process. But the search was largely unsuccessful and the dream of its byproduct—a general technology of leader selection—was unrealized. The results, which have been summarized elsewhere (Bass, 1960; Gibb, 1969; Stogdill, 1948) cast considerable doubt on the usefulness of the concept of leadership as a personality trait. They do not imply that individual differences have nothing to do with leadership, but rather that their significance must be evaluated in relation to the situation.

Written more than 25 years ago, Stogdill's conclusions seem equally applicable today:

*The pattern of personal characteristics of the leader must bear some relevant relationship to the characteristics, activities and goals of the followers. . . . It becomes clear that an adequate analysis of leadership involves not only a study of leaders, but also of situations. (1948, pp. 64–65)*

The study of leadership based on personality traits had been launched on an oversimplified premise. But as Stogdill's conclusions were being written, social scientists at Ohio State University and at the University of Michigan were preparing to launch another and quite different attack on the problem of leadership. In these ventures, the focus was not on personal traits but on leader behavior and leadership style. Effective and ineffective leaders may not be distinguishable by a battery of psychological tests but may be distinguished by their characteristic behavior patterns in their work roles.

## RESEARCH ON EFFECTIVE
## LEADERSHIP METHODS

The focus on behavior of the leader rather than his personal traits was consistent with Lewin's classic dictum that behavior is a function of both person and environment (Lewin, 1951) and of growing recognition that the concept of trait provided little room for environmental or situational influences on behavior. Such a focus also envisioned a greater degree of consistency in behavior across situations than has been empirically demonstrated (Hartshorne & May, 1928; Mischel, 1968; Vroom & Yetton, 1973).

If particular patterns of behavior or leadership styles were found which consistently distinguished leaders of effective and ineffective work groups, the payoff to organizations and to society would have been considerable, but of a different nature than work based on the trait approach. Such results would have less obvious implications for leader selection but would have significant import for leader development and training. Knowledge of the behavior patterns which characterize effective leaders would provide a rational basis for the design of educational programs in an attempt to instill these patterns in actual or potential leaders.

Space does not permit a detailed account of the Ohio State and Michigan research or of its offshoots in other institutions. It is fair to say, however, that the success of this line of inquiry in developing empirically based generalizations about effective leadership styles is a matter of some controversy. There are some who see in the results a consistent pattern sufficient to constitute the basis of technologies of organization design or leader development. Likert (1967), reviewing the program of research at Michigan, finds support for what he calls System 4, a participative group-based conception of management. Similarly, Blake and Moulton (1964), with their conceptual roots in the Ohio State research program, argue that the effective leader exhibits concern for both production and employees (their 9-9 style) and have constructed a viable technol-

ogy of management and organization development based on that premise.

On the other hand, other social scientists including the present writer (Korman, 1966; Sales, 1966; Vroom, 1964) have reviewed the evidence resulting from these studies and commented lamentably on the variability in results and the difficulty in making from them any definitive statements about effective leader behavior without knowledge of the situation in which the behavior has been exhibited.

At first glance, these would appear to be two directly opposing interpretations of the same results, but that would probably be too strong a conclusion. The advocates of general leadership principles have stated these principles in such a way that they are difficult to refute by empirical evidence and at the same time provide considerable latitude for individual interpretation. To say that a leader should manage in such a way that personnel at all levels feel real responsibility for the attainment of the organization's goals (Likert, 1967) or alternatively that he should exhibit concern for both production and his employees (Blake and Mouton, 1964) are at best general blueprints for action rather than specific blueprints indicating how these objectives should be achieved. The need for adapting these principles to the demands of the situation is recognized by most social scientists. For example, Likert writes:

*Supervision is . . . always a relative process. To be effective and to communicate as intended, a leader must always adapt his behavior to take into account the expectations, values, and interpersonal skills of those with whom he is interacting. . . . There can be no specific rules of supervision which will work well in all situations. Broad principles can be applied in the process of supervision and furnish valuable guides to behavior. These principles, however, must be applied always in a manner that takes fully into account the characteristics of the specific situation and of the people involved. (1961, p. 95)*

To this writer, the search for effective methods of supervision management and leadership has come close to foundering on the same rocks as the trait approach. It too has failed to deal explicitly with differences in situational requirements for leadership. If the behavioral sciences are to make a truly viable contribution to the management of the contemporary organization, they must progress beyond an advocacy of power equalization with appropriate caveats about the need for consideration of situational differences and attempt to come to grips with the complexities of the leadership process.

## INVESTIGATION ON LEADERSHIP STYLES

These convictions, whether right or wrong, provided the basis for a new approach to the investigation of leadership style—its determinants and consequences—launched about six years ago by the author and Phillip Yetton, then a graduate student at Carnegie Mellon University. We set ourselves two goals: (1) to formulate a normative or prescriptive model of leader behavior which incorporated situational characteristics in an explicit manner and which was consistent with existing empirical evidence concerning the consequences of alternative approaches; and (2) to launch an empirical attack on the determinants of leader behavior which would reveal the factors both within the person and in the situation which influence leaders to behave in various ways.

In retrospect, these goals were ambitious ones and the reader will have to judge for himself the extent to which either has been achieved. We attempted to make the task more managable by focusing on one dimension of leader behavior—the degree to which the leader encourages the participation of his subordinates in decision-making. This dimension was chosen both because it was at the core of most prescriptive approaches to leadership and because a substantial amount of research had been conducted on it.

The first step was to review that evidence in detail. No attempt will be made here to repeat that review. (The reader interested in this question may consult Lowin, 1968; Vroom, 1964; or Wood, 1974.) Instead, we will restrict our attention to a summary of the major conclusions which appeared justifiable by the evidence.

1. Involvement of subordinates in "group decision making" is costly in terms of time. Autocratic decision-making processes are typically faster (and thus of potential value in emergency or crisis situations) and invariably require less investment in man-hours of the group in the process of decision-making than methods which provide greater opportunities for participation by subordinates, particularly those decision processes which require consensus by the group.

2. Participation by subordinates in decision making creates greater acceptance of decisions which in turn is reflected in better implementation. There is a wide range of circumstances under which "people support what they helped to build." Increasing the opportunity for subordinates to have a significant voice in decisions which affect them results in greater acceptance and commitment to the decisions, which will in turn be reflected in more effective and reliable implementation of the decision.

3. The effects of increased participation by subordinates in decision making on the quality or rationality of decisions tend to be positive, although the effects are likely to depend on several identifiable factors. Extensive research has been conducted on group and individual problem solving. Group decisions tend to be higher in quality when the relevant information is widely distributed among group members, when the problem is unstructured, and when there exists a mutual interest or common goal among group members.

4. Involvement of subordinates in decision making leads to growth and development of subordinates. This consequence of participation has been least researched and its assertion here is based primarily on theoretical rather than empirical grounds. It is different from the three previous factors (time, acceptance, and quality of decision) in its long-term nature.

From this general research foundation a normative model was constructed. The model utilized five decision processes which vary in the amount of opportunity afforded subordinates to

**TABLE 31.1**
**Types of Management Decision Styles**

| | |
|---|---|
| AI | You solve the problem or make the decision yourself using information available to you at that time. |
| AII | You obtain necessary information from subordinate(s) and then decide on a solution to the problem yourself. You may or may not tell subordinates what the problem is in getting the information from them. The role played by your subordinates in making the decision is clearly one of providing necessary information to you, rather that generating or evaluating alternative solutions. |
| CI | You share the problem with relevant subordinates individually, getting their ideas and suggestions without bringing them together as a group. Then you make the decision which may or may not reflect your subordinates' influence. |
| CII | You share the problem with your subordinates as a group, collectively obtaining their ideas and suggestions. Then, *you* make the decision which may or may not reflect your subordinates' influence. |
| GII | You share the problem with your subordinates as a group. Together you generate and evaluate alternatives and attempt to reach agreement (consensus) on a solution. Your role is much like that of a chairman. You do not try to influence the group to adopt "your" solution and are willing to accept and implement any solution which has the support of the entire group. |

participate in decision making. These processes are shown in Table 31.1.

The model to be described is a contingency model. It rests on the assumption that no one decision-making process is best under all circumstances, and that its effectiveness is dependent upon identifiable properties of the situation. However, it is different from other contingency models in the fact that the situational characteristics are attributes of the particular problem or decision rather than more general role characteristics. To distinguish this type of situational variable from others we have designated them as problem attributes. These attributes are the building blocks of the model and represent the means of diagnosing the nature of the problem or decision at hand so as to determine the optimal decision process.

The most recent form of the model is shown in Figure 31.1. It is expressed here in the form of a decision tree. The problem attributes are arranged along the top and are shown here in the form of yes-no questions. To use the model to determine the decision process, one starts at the left-hand side of the diagram and asks the question pertaining to attribute *A*. The answer (yes or no) will determine the path taken. When a second box is encountered, the question pertaining to that attribute is asked and the process contin-

ued until a terminal node is reached. At that node one will find a number (indicating problem type) and a feasible set of decision processes.

For some problem types only one decision process is shown; for others there are two, three, four or even all five processes. The particular decision processes shown are those that remain after a set of seven rules has been applied. The rules function to protect both the quality and the acceptance by eliminating methods that have a substantial likelihood of jeopardizing either of these two components of an effective decision. The interested reader should consult Vroom and Yetton (1973) for a detailed statement, in both verbal and mathematical form, of these rules.

If more than one alternative remains in the feasible set, there are a number of bases for choosing among them. One of them is time. The methods are arranged in ascending order of the time in man-hours which they require. Accordingly, a time minimizing model (which we have termed Model A) would select that alternative that is farthest to the left within the feasible set. An alternative to minimizing time is maximizing development of subordinates. This model (which we have termed Model B) would select that decision process which is farthest to the right within the feasible set.

While we have attempted to phrase the questions pertaining to the problem attributes in

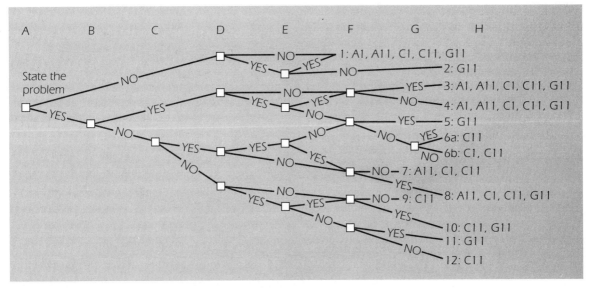

**FIGURE 31.1** Decision-Process Flow Chart for Group Problems.

**A** Is there a quality requirement such that one solution is likely to be more rational than another?
**B** Do I have sufficient info to make a high-quality decision?
**C** Is the problem structured?
**D** Is acceptance of decision by subordinates critical to effective implementation?
**E** If I were to make the decision myself, is it reasonably certain that it would be accepted by my subordinates?
**F** Do subordinates share the organizational goals to be attained in solving this problem?
**G** Is conflict among subordinates likely in preferred solutions? (This question is relative to individual problems.)
**H** Do subordinates have sufficient info to make a high-quality decision?

as meaningful a fashion as possible, the reader should keep in mind that they are really surrogates for more detailed specifications of the underlying variables. The reader interested in more information on the meaning of the attributes, the threshold for yes-no judgments or their rationale for inclusion in the model should consult Vroom and Yetton (1973). Illustrations of the model application to concrete cases can be found in Vroom (1973); Vroom and Yetton (1973); and Vroom and Jago (1974).

The model shown in Figure 31.1 is intended to apply to a domain of managerial decision making which Maier, Solem, and Maier (1957) refer to as group problems, i.e., problems which have potential effects on all or a substantial subset of the manager's subordinates. Recently, we have become interested in extending the model to "individual problems," i.e., those affecting only one subordinate. For these decisions, the first three decision processes shown in Table 31.1 represent

potentially reasonable alternatives, but there are at least two other viable alternatives not yet represented. One of these we have called GI, which is a form of group decision involving only a single subordinate. (A GI manager shares the problem with the subordinate and together they analyze the problem and arrive at a mutually satisfactory solution.) The other, which we have designated as DI, consists of delegating the problem or decision to the subordinate.

Many of the considerations used in building the model for group problems—such as problem attributes and rules—could easily be adapted to the domain of individual problems. There remained, however, one major structural difference. For group problems, there was at tradeoff between the short-run consideration of time efficiency (which favored autocratic methods) and longer-range considerations involving subordinate development (which favored participative

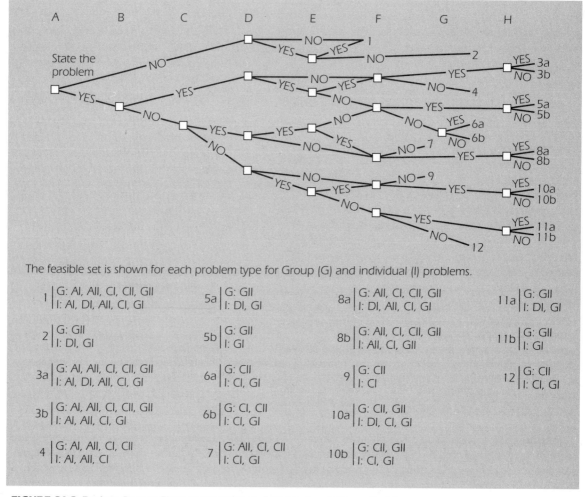

The feasible set is shown for each problem type for Group (G) and individual (I) problems.

1 | G: AI, AII, CI, CII, GII
  | I: AI, DI, AII, CI, GI

5a | G: GII
   | I: DI, GI

8a | G: AII, CI, CII, GII
   | I: DI, AII, CI, GI

11a | G: GII
    | I: DI, GI

2 | G: GII
  | I: DI, GI

5b | G: GII
   | I: GI

8b | G: AII, CI, CII, GII
   | I: AII, CI, GII

11b | G: GII
    | I: GI

3a | G: AI, AII, CI, CII, GII
   | I: AI, DI, AII, CI, GI

6a | G: CII
   | I: CI, GI

9 | G: CII
  | I: CI

12 | G: CII
   | I: CI, GI

3b | G: AI, AII, CI, CII, GII
   | I: AI, AII, CI, GI

6b | G: CI, CII
   | I: CI, GI

10a | G: CII, GII
    | I: DI, CI, GI

4 | G: AI, AII, CI, CII
  | I: AI, AII, CI

7 | G: AII, CI, CII
  | I: CI, GI

10b | G: CII, GII
    | I: CI, GI

**FIGURE 31.2** Decison-Process Flow Chart for Both Individual and Group Problems.

*A* Is there a quality requirement such that one solution is likely to be more rational than another?
*B* Do I have sufficient info to make a high-quality decision?
*C* Is the problem structured?
*D* Is acceptance of decision by subordinates critical to effective implementation?
*E* If I were to make the decision by myself, is it reasonably certain that it would be accepted by subordinates?
*F* Do subordinates share the organizational goals to be attained in solving this problem?
*G* Is conflict among subordinates likely in perferred solutions? (This question is irrevelant to individual problems.)
*H* Do subordinates have sufficient info to make a high-quality decision?

methods). The reader will recall that Model A and Model B represented two extreme modes of resolution of that tradeoff. For individual problems, the differences in time requirements of the five processes (AI, AH, CI, GI, DI) are not nearly as large and the alternative which provides the greatest amount of subordinate influence or participation, DI, can hardly be argued to be least time efficient. This difference in the correlation between time efficiency and participation for individual and group problems required an adjustment in the location of DI in the ordering of alternatives in terms of time. Model A and Model B retain their original meaning from the earlier model, but they are no longer polar opposites.

Figure 31.2 contains a model also expressed as a decision tree which purports to guide choices among decision processes for both individual and group problems. The only differences lies in the specifications of two feasible sets (one for group and one for individual problems) for each problem type.

Is the model in its present form an adequate guide to practice? Would managers make fewer errors in their choices of decision processes if they were to base them on the model? We would be less than honest if we said we knew the answers to such questions. Most managers who have had sufficient training in the use of the model to be able to use it reliably report that it is a highly useful guide, although there are occasionally considerations not presently contained in the model—such as geographical dispersion of subordinates—which prevents implementation of its recommendations. Some research has been conducted in an attempt to establish the validity of the model (see Vroom & Yetton, 1973: 182–84), but the results, while promising, are not conclusive. Perhaps the most convincing argument for the development of models of this kind is that they can serve as a guide for research that can identify their weaknesses and that superior models can later be developed.

The reader will note that flexibility in leader behavior is one of the requirements of use of the model. To use it effectively, the leader must adapt his approach to the situation. But how flexible are leaders in the approaches they use? Do they naturally try and vary their approach with the situation? Is it possible to develop such flexibility through training? These questions were but a few of those which guided the next phase of our inquiry into how leaders do in fact behave and into the factors both within the leader himself and in the situations with which he deals which cause him to share decision-making power with his subordinates.

Two different research methods have been used in an attempt to answer questions such as these. The first investigation utilized a method

that can be referred to as "recalled problems." Over 500 managers from 11 different countries representing a variety of firms were asked to provide a written description of a problem that they had recently had to solve. These varied in length from one paragraph to several pages and covered virtually every facet of managerial decision making. For each case, the manager was asked to indicate which of the decision processes shown in Table 31.1 he used to solve the problem. Finally, each manager was asked to answer the questions corresponding to the problem attributes used in the normative model with his own case in mind.

These data made it possible to determine the frequency with which the managers' decision process was similar to that of the normative model and the factors in their description of the situation which were associated with the use of each decision process. This investigation provided results which were interesting but also led to the development of a second more powerful method for investigating the same questions. This method, which will be termed "standardized problems," used some of the actual cases written by the managers in the construction of a standardized set of cases, each of which depicts a manager faced with a problem to solve or decision to make. In each case, a leader would be asked to assume the role of the manager faced with the situation described and to indicate which decision process he would use if faced with that situation.

Several such sets of cases have been developed. In early research, each set consisted of thirty cases, but more recently longer sets of forty-eight and fifty-four cases have been used. Composition of each set of standardized cases was in accordance with multifactorial experimental design. Cases varied in terms of each of the eight problem attributes used in the normative model, and variation in each attribute was independent of each other attribute. This feature permits the assessment of the effects of each of the problem attributes on the decision processes used by a given manager.

The cases themselves spanned a wide range of managerial problems including production scheduling, quality control, portfolio management, personnel allocation, and research and development project selection. To date, several thousand managers in the United States and abroad have been studied using this approach.

## RESULTS AND CONCLUSIONS

To summarize everything learned in the course of this research is well beyond the scope of this reading, but it is possible to discuss some of the highlights. Since the results obtained from the two research methods—recalled and standardized problems—are consistent, the major results can be presented independent of the method used.

Perhaps the most striking finding is the weakening of the widespread view that participativeness is a general trait that individual managers exhibit in different amounts. To be sure, there were differences among managers in their general tendencies to utilize participative methods as opposed to autocratic ones. On the standardized problems, these differences accounted for about 10 percent of the total variance in the decision processes observed. Furthermore, those managers who tended to use more participative methods such as CH and GH with group problems also tended to use more participative methods like delegation for dealing with individual problems.

However, these differences in behavior between managers were small in comparison with differences within managers. On the standardized problems, no manager has indicated that he would use the same decision process on all problems or decisions, and most use all methods under some circumstances. Taking managers' reports of their behavior in concrete situations, it is clear that they are striving to be flexible in their approaches to different situations.

Some of this variance in behavior within managers can be attributed to widely shared tendencies to respond to some situations by sharing power and others by retaining it. It makes more sense to talk about participative and autocratic situations than it does to talk about participative and autocratic managers. In fact, on the standardized problems, the variance in behavior across problems or cases is from three to five times as large as the variance across managers.

What are the characteristics of an autocratic as opposed to a participative situation? An answer to this question would constitute a partial descriptive model of this aspect of the decision-making process and has been the goal of much of the research conducted. From observations of behavior on both recalled problems and on standardized problems, it is clear that the decision making process employed by a typical manager is influenced by a large number of factors, many of which also show up in the normative model. Following are several conclusions substantiated by the results on both recalled and standardized problems.

Managers use decision processes providing less opportunity for participation (1) when they possess all the necessary information rather when they lack some of the needed information; (2) when the problem they face is well-structured rather than unstructured; (3) when their subordinates' acceptance of the decision is not critical for the effective implementation of the decision or when the prior probability of acceptance of an autocratic decision is high; and (4) when the personal goals of their subordinates are not congruent with the goals of the organization as manifested in the problem.

These findings concern relatively common or widely shared ways of dealing with organizational problems. The results also strongly suggest that managers have ways of "tailoring" their decision process to the situation that distinguish one manager from another. Theoretically, these can be thought of as differences among managers in decision rules that they employ about when to encourage participation.

Consider, for example, two managers who have identical distributions of the use of the five decision processes shown in Table 31.1 on a set of thirty cases. In a sense, they are equally participative (or autocratic). However, the situations in which they permit or encourage participation in decision making on the part of their subordinates may be very different. One may restrict the participation of his subordinates to decisions without a quality requirement, whereas the other may restrict their participation to problems with a quality requirement. The former would be more inclined to use participative decision processes (like

GII) on such decisions as what color the walls should be painted or when the company picnic should be held. The latter would be more likely to encourage participation in decision making on decisions that have a clear and demonstrable impact on the organization's success in achieving its external goals.

Use of the standardized problem set permits the assessment of such differences in decision rules that govern choices among decision-making processes. Since the cases are selected in accordance with an experimental design, they can indicate differences in the behavior of managers attributable not only to the existence of a quality requirement in the problem but also in the effects of acceptance requirements, conflict, information requirements, and the like.

The research using both recalled and standardized problems has also permitted the examination of similarities and differences between the behavior of the normative model and the behavior of a typical manager. Such an analysis reveals, at the very least, what behavioral changes could be expected if managers began using the normative model as the basis for choosing their decision-making processes.

A typical manager says he would (or did) use exactly the same decision process as that shown in Figure 31.1 in about 40 percent of the group problems. In two-thirds of the situations, his behavior is consistent with the feasible set of methods proposed in the model. However, in the remaining one-third of the situations, his behavior violates at least one of the seven rules underlying the model. Results show significantly higher agreement with the normative model for individual problems than for group problems.

The rules designed to protect the acceptance or commitment of the decision have substantially higher probabilities of being violated than do the rules designed to protect the quality or rationality of the decision. Assuming for the moment that these two sets of rules have equal validity, these findings strongly suggest that the decisions made by typical managers are more likely to prove ineffective due to deficiencies of acceptance by subordinates than due to deficiencies in decision quality.

Another striking difference between the behavior of the model and of the typical manager lies in the fact that the former shows far greater variance with the situation. If a typical manager voluntarily used the model as the basis for choosing his methods of making decisions, he would become both more autocratic and more participative. He would employ autocratic methods more frequently in situations in which his subordinates were unaffected by the decision and participative methods more frequently when his subordinates' cooperation and support were critical and/or their information and expertise were required.

It should be noted that the typical manager to whom we have been referring is merely a statistical average of the several thousand who have been studied over the last three or four years. There is a great deal of variation around that average. As evidenced by their behavior on standardized problems, some managers are already behaving in a manner that is highly consistent with the model, while others' behavior is clearly at variance with it.

The research program that has been summarized was conducted in order to shed new light on the causes and consequences of decision-making processes used by leaders in formal organizations. In the course of research, it was realized that the data collection procedures, with appropriate additions and modifications, might also serve a useful function in leadership development. From this realization evolved an important byproduct of the research activities—a new approach to leadership training based on the concepts in the normative model and the empirical methods of the descriptive research.

A detailed description of this training program and of initial attempts to evaluate its effectiveness may be found in Vroom and Yetton (1973, chap. 8). It is based on the premise that one of the critical skills required of all leaders is the ability to adapt their behavior to the demands of the situation and that a component of this skill involves selecting the appropriate decision-making process for each problem or decision they confront. The purpose of the program is not to "train" managers to use the model in their everyday decision-making activities. Instead the model serves as a device for encouraging managers to examine their leadership styles and for coming to a conscious realization of their own, often implicit, choices among decision processes, including their similarity and dissimilarity with the model. By helping managers to become aware of their present behavior and of alternatives to it, the training provides a basis for rethinking their leadership style to be more consistent with goals and objectives. Succinctly, the training is intended to transform habits into choices rather than to program a leader with a particular method of making choices.

A fundamental part of the program in its present form is the use of a set of standardized cases previously described in connection with the decision process he would employ if he were the leader described in the case. His responses to the entire set of cases are processed by computer, which generates a highly detailed analysis of his leadership style. The responses for all participants in a single course are typically processed simultaneously, permitting the calculation of differences between the person and others in the same program.

In its latest form, a single computer printout for a person consists of seven 15" by 11" pages, each filled with graphs and tables highlighting different features of his behavior. Understanding the results requires a detailed knowledge of the concepts underlying the model, something already developed in one of the previous phases of the training program. The printout is accompanied by a manual that aids in explaining the results and provides suggested steps to be followed in extracting the full meaning from the printout.

Following are a few of the questions that the printout answers:

1. How autocratic or participative am I in my dealings with subordinates in the program?

2. What decision processes do I use more or less frequently than the average?

3. How close does my behavior come to that of the model? How frequently does my behavior agree with the feasible set? What evidence is there that my leadership style reflects the pressure of time as opposed to a concern with the development of my subordinates? How do I compare in these respects with other participants in the program?

4. What rules do I violate most frequently and least frequently? On what cases did I violate these rules? Does my leadership style reflect more concern with getting decisions that are high in quality or with getting decisions that are accepted?

When a typical manager receives his printout, he immediately goes to work trying to understand what it tells him about himself. After most of the major results have been understood, he goes back to the set of cases to reread those on which he has violated rules. Typically, managers show an interest in discussing and comparing their results with others in the program. Gatherings of four to six people comparing their results and their interpretations of them, often for several hours at a stretch, were such a common feature that they have recently been institutionalized as part of the procedure.

It should be emphasized that this method of providing feedback on their leadership style is just one part of the total training experience which encompasses over thirty hours over a period of three successive days. To date, no long-term evaluations of its effectiveness have been undertaken, but initial results appear quite promising.

## SUMMARY

How far has the understanding of leadership progressed in the 50 years since the Hawthorne Studies? The picture that has been painted in this reading is one of false starts stemming from oversimplified conceptions of the process. An encouraging sign, however, is the increased interest in contingency theories or models incorporating both leader and situational variables. In this reading I have spent much time describing one kind of contingency model; Professor Fiedler, who accompanies me on this panel, has developed another form of contingency model.

These two models share a number of qualities, but are different in several important aspects. I believe that Professor Fiedler sees much greater consistency and less flexibility in leader behavior than is required by the normative model or exhibited in manager's statements of how they would behave on the problem set. I suspect that we also have substantially different views on the potential for modification of leadership style through training and development.

Both of these are fascinating and important questions, and I for one would enjoy exploring them during our later discussion. But there is one prediction about which I feel quite confident. Fifty years from now, both contingency models will be found wanting in detail if not in substance. If either Professor Fiedler or I am remembered at that time, it will be for the same reason that we meet to commemorate the Hawthorne Studies this week—the kinds of questions we posed rather than the specific answers we provided.

## REFERENCES

Bass, B. M. *Leadership, Psychology and Organizational Behavior*. New York: Harper, 1960.

Blake, R., and Mouton, J. *The Managerial Grid*. Houston: Gulf, 1964.

Gibb, C. A. "Leadership," in *Handbook of Social Psychology*, edited by G. Lindzey and E. Aronson, vol. 4. Reading, Mass.: Addison-Wesley, 1969.

Hartshorne, H., and MAY, M. A. *Studies in Deceit*. New York: Macmillan, 1928.

Korman, A. K. " 'Consideration,' 'Initiating Structure,' and Organizational Criteria— A Review," *Personnel Psychology* 19 (1966).

Lewin, K. *Field Theory in Social Science*, edited by D. Cartwright. New York: Harper, 1951.

Likert, R. *New Patterns of Management*. New York: McGraw-Hill, 1961.

_____.*The Human Organization*. New York: McGraw-Hill, 1967.

Lowin, A. "Participative Decision-Making: A Model, Literature Critique, and Prescriptions for Research." *Organizational Behavior and Human Performance* 3(1968).

Mischel, W. *Personality and Assessment*. New York: Wiley, 1968.

Maier, N. R. F., Solem, A. R., and Maier, A. A. *Supervisory and Executive Development: A Manual for Role Playing*. New York: Wiley, 1954.

Sales, S. M. "Supervisory Style and Productivity: Review and Theory." *Personnel Psychology* 19(1966).

Stogdill, R. M. "Personal Factors Associated with Leadership: A Survey of the Literature." *Journal of Psychology* 25(1948).

Vroom, V. H. *Work and Motivation*. New York: Wiley, 1964.

_____. "A New Look at Managerial Decision-Making." *Organizational Dynamics* 1(1973).

_____, and Jago, A. G. "Decision-Making as a Social Process: Normative and Descriptive Models of Leader Behavior." *Decision Science*, 1974.

_____, and Yetton, P. W. "A Normative Model of Leadership Styles." In *Readings in Managerial Psychology*, edited by H. J. Leavitt and L. Pondy, 2d ed. Chicago: University of Chicago Press, 1973.

Wood, M. J. "Power Relationships and Group Decision Making in Organizations." *Psychological Bulletin*, 1974.

# 32. THE MANAGER'S JOB: FOLKLORE AND FACT

*Henry Mintzberg*

If you ask a manager what he does, he will most likely tell you that he plans, organizes, coordinates, and controls. Then watch what he does. Don't be surprised if you can't relate what you see to these four words.

When he is called and told that one of his factories has just burned down, and he advises the caller to see whether temporary arrangements can be made to supply customers through a foreign subsidiary, is he planning, organizing, coordinating, or controlling? How about when he presents a gold watch to a retiring employee? Or when he attends a conference to meet people in the trade? Or on returning from that conference, when he tells one of his employees about an interesting product idea he picked up there?

The fact is that these four words, which have dominated management vocabulary since the French industrialist Henri Fayol first introduced them in 1916, tell us little about what managers actually do. At best, they indicate some vague objectives managers have when they work.

The field of management, so devoted to progress and change, has for more than half a century not seriously addressed *the* basic question: What do managers do? Without a proper answer, how can we teach management? How can we design planning or information systems for managers? How can we improve the practice of management at all?

Our ignorance of the nature of managerial work shows up in various ways in the modern organization—in the boast by the successful manager that he never spent a single day in a management training program; in the turnover of corporate planners who never quite understood what it was the manager wanted; in the computer consoles gathering dust in the back room because the managers never used the fancy on-line MIS some analyst thought they needed. Perhaps most important, our ignorance shows up in the inability of our large public organizations to come to grips with some of their most serious policy problems.

Somehow, in the rush to automate production, to use management science in the functional areas of marketing and finance, and to apply the skills of the behavioral scientist to the problem of worker motivation, the manager—that person in charge of the organization or one of its subunits—has been forgotten.

My intention in this article is simple: to break the reader away from Fayol's words and introduce him to a more supportable, and what I believe to be a more useful, description of managerial work. This description derives from my review and synthesis of the available research on how various managers have spent their time.

In some studies, managers were observed intensively ("shadowed" is the term some of them used); in a number of others, they kept detailed diaries of their activities; in a few studies, their records were analyzed. All kinds of managers were studied—foremen, factory supervisors, staff managers, field sales managers, hospital administrators, presidents of companies and nations, and even street gang leaders. These "managers" worked in the United States, Canada, Sweden, and Great Britain. [A brief review of the major studies that I found most useful in developing this description, including my own study of five American chief executive officers, is informative.]

A synthesis of these findings paints an interesting picture, one as different from Fayol's classical view as a cubist abstract is from a Renaissance painting. In a sense, this picture will be obvious to anyone who has ever spent a day in a manager's office, either in front of the desk or behind it. Yet, at the same time, this picture may turn out to be revolutionary, in that it throws into doubt so much of the folklore that we have accepted about the manager's work.

I first discuss some of this folklore and contrast it with some of the discoveries of systematic research—the hard facts about how managers spend their time. Then I synthesize these research findings in a description of ten roles that seem to describe the essential content of all managers' jobs. In a concluding section, I discuss a number of implications of this synthesis for those trying to achieve more effective management, both in classrooms and in the business world.

## SOME FOLKLORE AND FACTS ABOUT MANAGERIAL WORK

There are four myths about the manager's job that do not bear up under careful scrutiny of the facts.

### 1

*Folklore. The manager is a reflective, systematic planner.* The evidence on this issue is overwhelming, but not a shred of it supports this statement.

*Fact. Study after study has shown that managers work at an unrelenting pace, that their activities are characterized by brevity, variety, and discontinuity, and that* *they are strongly oriented to action and dislike reflective activities.* Consider this evidence:

- Half the activities engaged in by the five chief executives of my study lasted less than nine minutes, and only 10% exceeded one hour.[1] A study of 56 U.S. foremen found that they average 583 activities per eight-hour shift, an average of 1 every 48 seconds.[2] The work pace for both chief executives and foremen was unrelenting. The chief executives met a steady stream of callers and mail from the moment they arrived in the morning until they left in the evening. Coffee breaks and lunches were inevitably work related, and ever-present subordinates seemed to unsurp any free moment.

- A diary study of 160 British middle and top managers found that they worked for a half hour or more without interruption only about once every two days.[3]

- Of the verbal contacts of the chief executives in my study, 93% were arranged on an ad hoc basis. Only 1% of the executives' time was spent in open-ended observational tours. Only 1 out of 368 verbal contacts was unrelated to a specific issue and could be called general planning. Another researcher finds that "in *not one single case* did a manager report the obtaining of important external information from a general conversation or other undirected personal communication."[4]

- No study has found important patterns in the way managers schedule their time. They seem to jump from issue to issue, continually responding to the needs of the moment.

Is this the planner that the classical view describes? Hardly. How, then, can we explain this

---

[1] All the data from my study can be found in Henry Mintzberg, *The Nature of Managerial Work* (New York: Harper & Row, 1973).

[2] Robert H. Guest, "Of Time and the Foreman," *Personnel*, May 1956, p. 478.

[3] Rosemary Stewart, *Managers and Their Jobs* (London: Macmillan, 1967); see also Sune Carlson, *Executive Behavior* (Stockholm: Strombergs, 1951), the first of the diary studies.

[4] Francis J. Aguilar, *Scanning the Business Environment* (New York: Macmillan, 1967), p. 102.

behavior? The manager is simply responding to the pressures of his job. I found that my chief executives terminated many of their own activities, often leaving meetings before the end, and interrupted their desk work to call in subordinates. One president not only placed his desk so that he could look down a long hallway but also left his door open when he was alone—an invitation for subordinates to come in an interrupt him.

Clearly, these managers wanted to encourage the flow of current information. But more significantly, they seemed to be conditioned by their own work loads. They appreciated the opportunity cost of their own time, and they were continually aware of their ever-present obligations—mail to be answered, callers to attend to, and so on. It seems that no matter what he is doing, the manager is plagued by the possibilities of what he might do and what he must do.

When the manager must plan, he seems to do so implicitly in the context of daily actions, not in some abstract process reserved for two weeks in the organization's mountain retreat. The plans of the chief executives I studied seemed to exist only in their heads—as flexible, but often specific, intentions. The traditional literature notwithstanding, the job of managing does not breed reflective planners; the manager is a real-time responder to stimuli, an individual who is conditioned by his job to prefer live to delayed action.

## 2

*Folklore. The effective manager has no regular duties to perform.* Managers are constantly being told to spend more time planning and delegating, and less time seeing customers and engaging in negotiations. These are not, after all, the true tasks of the manager. To use the popular analogy, the good manager, like the good conductor, carefully orchestrates everything in advance, then sits back to enjoy the fruits of his labor, responding occasionally to an unforeseeable exception.

But here again the pleasant abstraction just does not seem to hold up. We had better take a closer look at those activities managers feel compelled to engage in before we arbitrarily define them away.

*Fact. In addition to handling exceptions, managerial work involves performing a number of regular duties, including ritual and ceremony, negotiations, and processing of soft information that links the organization with its environment.* Consider some evidence from the research studies:

- A study of the work of the presidents of small companies found that they engaged in routine activities because their companies could not afford staff specialists and were so thin on operating personnel that a single absence often required the president to substitute.[5]

- One study of field sales managers and another of chief executives suggest that it is a natural part of both jobs to see important customers, assuming the managers wish to keep those customers.[6]

- Someone, only half in jest, once described the manager as that person who sees visitors so that everyone else can get his work done. In my study, I found that certain ceremonial duties—meeting visiting dignitaries, giving out gold watches, presiding at Christmas dinners—were an intrinsic part of the chief executive's job.

- Studies of managers' information flow suggest that managers play a key role in securing "soft" external information (much of it available only to them because of their status) and in passing it along to their subordinates.

---

[5] Unpublished study by Irving Choran, reported in Mintzberg, *The Nature of Managerial Work.*

[6] Robert T. Davis, *Performance and Development of Field Sales Managers* (Boston: Division of Research, Harvard Business School, 1957); George H. Copeman, *The Role of the Managing Director* (London: Business Publications, 1963).

**3**

*Folklore. The senior manager needs aggregated information, which a formal management information system best provides.* Not too long ago, the words *total information system* were everywhere in the management literature. In keeping with the classical view of the manager as that individual perched on the apex of a regulated, hierarchical system, the literature's manager was to receive all his important information from a giant, comprehensive MIS.

But lately, as it has become increasingly evident that these giant MIS systems are not working—that managers are simply not using them—the enthusiasm has waned. A look at how managers actually process information makes the reason quite clear. Managers have five media at their command—documents, telephone calls, scheduled and unscheduled meetings, and observational tours.

*Fact. Managers strongly favor the verbal media—namely, telephone calls and meetings.* The evidence comes from every single study of managerial work. Consider the following:

- In two British studies, managers spent an average of 66% and 80% of their time in verbal (oral) communication.[7] In my study of five American chief executives, the figure was 78%.

- These five chief executives treated mail processing as a burden to be dispensed with. One came in Saturday morning to process 142 pieces of mail in just over three hours, to "get rid of all the stuff." This same manager looked at the first piece of "hard" mail he had received all week, a standard cost report, and put it aside with the comment, "I never look at this."

- These same five chief executives responded immediately to 2 of the 40 routine reports they received during the five weeks of my study and to four items in the 104 periodicals. They skimmed most of these periodicals in seconds, almost ritualistically. In all, these chief executives of good-sized organizations initiated on their own—that is, not in response to something else—a grand total of 25 pieces of mail during the 25 days I observed them.

An analysis of the mail the executives received reveals an interesting picture—only 13% was of specific and immediate use. So now we have another piece in the puzzle: not much of the mail provides live, current information—the action of a competitor, mood of a government legislator, or the rating of last night's television show. Yet this is the information that drove the managers, interrupting their meetings and rescheduling their workdays.

Consider another interesting finding. Managers seem to cherish "soft" information, especially gossip, hearsay, and speculation. Why? The reason is its timeliness; today's gossip may be tomorrow's fact. The manager who is not accessible for the telephone call informing him that his biggest customer was seen golfing with his main competitor may read about a dramatic drop in sales in the next quarterly report. But then it's too late.

To assess the value of historical, aggregated, "hard" MIS information, consider two of the manager's prime uses for his information—to identify problems and opportunities[8] and to build his own mental models of the things around him (e.g., how his organization's budget system works, how his customers buy his product, how changes in the economy affect his organization,

---

[7] Stewart, *Managers and Their Jobs*; Tom Burns, "The Directions of Activity and Communication in a Departmental Executive Group," *Human Relations* 7, no. 1(1954): 73.

[8] H. Edward Wrapp, "Good Managers Don't Make Policy Decisions," *Harvard Business Review,* September–October 1967, p. 91; Wrapp refers to this as spotting opportunities and relationships in the stream of operating problems and decisions; in his article Wrapp raises a number of excellent points related to this analysis.

and so on). Every bit of evidence suggests that the manager identifies decision situations and builds models not with the aggregated abstractions an MIS provides, but with specific tidbits of data.

Consider the words of Richard Neustadt, who studied the information-collecting habits of Presidents Roosevelt, Truman, and Eisenhower:

*It is not information of a general sort that helps a President see personal stakes; not summaries, not surveys, not the bland amalgams. Rather . . . it is the odds and ends of tangible detail that pieced together in his mind illuminate the underside of issues put before him. To help himself he must reach out as widely as he can for every scrap of fact, opinion, gossip, bearing on his interests and relationships as President. He must become his own director of his own central intelligence.*[9]

The manager's emphasis on the verbal media raises two important points:

First, verbal information is stored in the brains of people. Only when people write this information down can it be stored in files of the organization—whether in metal cabinets or on magnetic tape—and managers apparently do not write down much of what they hear. Thus the strategic data bank of the organization is not in the memory of its computers but in the minds of its managers.

Second, the manger's extensive use of verbal media helps to explain why he is reluctant to delegate tasks. When we note that most of the manager's important information comes in verbal form and is stored in his head, we can well appreciate his reluctance. It is not as if he can hand a dossier over to someone; he must take the time to "dump memory"—to tell that someone all he knows about the subject. But this could take so long that the manager may find it easier to do the task himself. Thus the manager is damned by his own information system to a "dilemma of delegation"—to do too much himself or to delegate to his subordinates with inadequate briefing.

**4**

*Folklore. Management is, or at least is quickly becoming, a science and a profession.* By almost any definitions of *science* and *profession*, this statement is false. Brief observation of any manager will quickly lay to rest the notion that managers practice a science. A science involves the enaction of systematic, analytically determined procedures or programs. If we do not even know what procedures managers use, how can we prescribe them by scientific analysis? And how can we call management a profession if we cannot specify what managers are to learn? For after all, a profession involves "knowledge of some department of learning or science" (Random House Dictionary).[10]

*Fact. The managers' programs—to schedule time, process information, make decisions, and so on—remain locked deep inside their brains.* Thus, to describe these programs, we rely on word like *judgment* and *intuition*, seldom stopping to realize that they are merely labels for our ignorance.

I was struck during my study by the fact that the executives I was observing—all very competent by any standard—are fundamentally indistinguishable from their counterparts of a hundred years ago (or a thousand years ago, for that matter). The information they need differs, but they seek it in the same way—by word of mouth. Their decisions concern modern technology, but the procedures they use to make them are the same as the procedures of the nineteenth-century manager. Even the computer, so important for the specialized work of the organization, has apparently had no influence on the work procedures of general managers. In fact, the manager is a kind of loop, with increasingly heavy work pressures but no aid forthcoming from management science.

Considering the facts about managerial work, we can see that the manager's job is enormously complicated and difficult. The manager is over-

---

[9] Richard E. Neustadt, *Presidential Power* (New York John Wiley, 1960). pp. 153–154; italics added.

[10] For a more thorough, though rather different, discussion of this issue, see Kenneth R. Andrews, "Toward Professionalism in Business Management," *HBR* March–April 1969. p. 49

burdened with obligations; yet he cannot easily delegate his tasks. As a result, he is driven to overwork and is forced to do many tasks superficially. Brevity, fragmentation and verbal communication characterize his work. Yet these are the very characteristics of managerial work that have impeded scientific attempts to improve it. As a result, the management scientist has concentrated his efforts on the specialized functions of the organizations, where he could more easily analyze the procedures and quantify the relevant information.[11]

But the pressures of the manager's job are becoming worse. Where before he needed only to respond to owners and directors, now he finds that subordinates with democratic norms continually reduce his freedom to issue unexplained orders, and a growing number of outside influences (consumer groups, government agencies, and so on) expect his attention. And the manager has had nowhere to turn for help. The first step in providing the manager with some help is to find out what his job really is.

## BACK TO A BASIC DESCRIPTION OF MANAGERIAL WORK

Now let us try to put some of the pieces of this puzzle together. Earlier, I defined the manager as that person in charge of an organization or one of its subunits. Besides chief executive officers, this definition would include vice presidents, bishops, foremen, hockey coaches, and prime ministers. Can all of these people have anything in common? Indeed they can. For an important starting point, all are vested with formal authority over an organizational unit. From formal authority comes status, which leads to various interpersonal relations, and from these comes access to information. Information, in turn, enables the manager to make decisions and strategies for his unit.

The manager's job can be described in terms of various "roles," or organized sets of behaviors identified with a position. My description, shown in Figure 32.1, comprises ten roles. As we shall see, formal authority gives rise to the three interpersonal roles, which in turn give rise to the three informational roles; these two sets of roles enable the manager to play the four decisional roles.

### Interpersonal Roles

Three of the manager's roles arise directly from his formal authority and involve basic interpersonal relationships.

1. First is the *figurehead* role. By virtue of his position as head of an organizational unit, every manager must perform some duties of a ceremonial nature. The president greets the touring dignitaries, the foreman attends the wedding of a lathe operator, and the sales manager takes an important customer to lunch.

The chief executives of my study spent 12% of their contact time on ceremonial duties; 17% of their incoming mail dealt with acknowledgments and requests related to their status. For example, a letter to a company president requested free merchandise for a crippled schoolchild; diplomas were put on the desk of the school superintendent for his signature.

Duties that involve interpersonal roles may sometimes be routine, involving little serious communication and no important decision making. Nevertheless, they are important to the smooth functioning of an organization and cannot be ignored by the manager.

2. Because he is in charge of an organizational unit, the manager is responsible for the work of the people of that unit. His actions in this regard constitute the *leader* role. Some of these actions involve leadership directly—for example, in most organizations the manager is normally responsible for hiring and training his own staff.

---

[11] C. Jackson Grayson, Jr., in "Management Science and Business Practice" *HBR* July–August 1973, p. 41, explains in similar terms why as chairman of the Price Commission, he did not use those very techniques that he himself promoted in his earlier career as a management scientist.

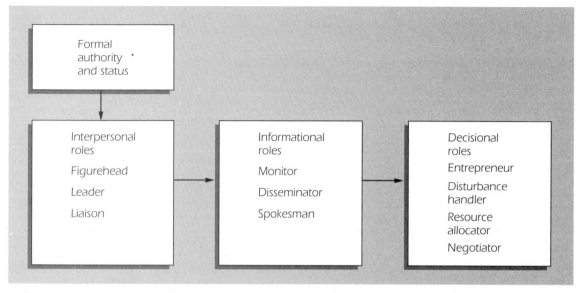

**FIGURE 32.1** The Manager's Roles.

In addition, there is the indirect exercise of the leader role. Every manager must motivate and encourage his employees, somehow reconciling their individual needs with the goals of the organization. In virtually every contact the manager has with his employees, subordinates seeking leadership clues probe his actions. "Does he approve?" "How would he like the report to turn out?" "Is he more interested in market share than high profits?"

The influence of the manager is most clearly seen in the leader role. Formal authority vests him with great potential power; leadership determines in large part how much of it he will realize.

3. The literature of management has always recognized the leader role, particularly those aspects of it related to motivation. In comparison, until recently it has hardly mentioned the *liaison* role, in which the manager makes contacts outside his vertical chain of command. This is remarkable in light of the finding of virtually every study of managerial work that managers spend as much time with peers and other people outside their units as they do with their own subordinates — and, surprisingly, very little time with their own superiors.

In Rosemary Stewart's diary study, the 160 British middle and top managers spent 47% of their time with peers, 41% of their time with people outside their unit, and only 12% of their time with their superiors. For Robert H. Guest's study of U.S. foremen, the figures were 44%, 46% and 10%. The chief executives of my study averaged 44% of their contact time with people outside their organizations, 48% with subordinates, and 7% with directors and trustees.

The contacts the five CEOs made were with an incredibly wide range of people: subordinates; clients, business associates, and suppliers; and peers — managers of similar organizations, government and trade organization officials, fellow directors on outside boards, and independents with no relevant organizational affiliations. The chief executives' time with and mail from these groups is shown in Figure 32.2. Guest's study of foremen shows, likewise, that their contacts were numerous and wide ranging, seldom involving fewer than 25 individuals, and often more than 50.

As we shall see shortly, the manager cultivates such contacts largely to find information. In effect, the liaison role is devoted to building up

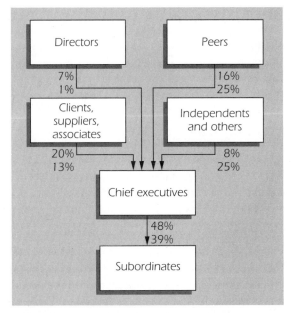

**FIGURE 32.2 The Chief Executives' Contacts.**

Note: The top figure indicates the proportion of total contact time spent with each group and the bottom figure, the proportin of mail irom each group.

the manager's own external information system—informal, private, verbal, but, nevertheless, effective.

## Informational Roles

By virtue of his interpersonal contacts, both with his subordinates and with his network of contacts, the manager emerges as the nerve center of his organizational unit. He may not know everything, but he typically knows more than any member of his staff.

Studies have shown this relationship to hold for all managers, from street gang leaders to U.S. presidents. In *The Human Group*, George C. Homans explains how, because they were at the center of the information flow in their own gangs and were also in close touch with other gang leaders, street gang leaders were better informed than any of their followers.[12] And Richard Neustadt describes the following account from his study of Franklin D. Roosevelt:

*The essence of Roosevelt's technique for information-gathering was competition. "He would call you in,"* one of his aides once told me, *"and he'd ask you to get the story on some complicated business, and you'd come back after a couple of days of hard labor and present the juicy morsel you'd uncovered under a stone somewhere, and* then *you'd find out he knew all about it, along with something else you didn't know. Where he got this information from he wouldn't mention, usually, but after he had done this to you once or twice you got damn careful about your information."*[13]

We can see where Roosevelt "got this information" when we consider the relationship between the interpersonal and informational roles. As leader, the manager has formal and easy access to every member of his staff. Hence, as noted earlier, he tends to know more about his own unit than anyone else does. In addition, his liaison contacts expose the manager to external information to which his subordinates often lack access. Many of these contacts are with other managers of equal status, who are themselves nerve centers in their own organization. In this way, the manager develops a powerful data base of information.

The processing of information is a key part of the manager's job. In my study, the chief executives spent 40% of their contact time on activities devoted exclusively to the transmission of information; 70% of their incoming mail was purely informational (as opposed to requests for action). The manager does not leave meetings or hang up the telephone in order to get back to work. In large part, communication *is* his work.

12 George C. Homans, *The Human Group* (New York: Harcourt, Brace & World, 1950), based on the study by William F. Whyte entitled *Street Corner Society*, rev. ed. (Chicago: University of Chicago Press, 1955).

13 Neustadt, *Presidential Power*, p. 157.

Three roles describe these informational aspects of managerial work.

1. As *monitor*, the manager perpetually scans his environment for information, interrogates his liaison contacts and his subordinates, and receives unsolicited information, much of it as a result of the network of personal contacts he has developed. Remember that a good part of the information the manager collects in his monitor role arrives in verbal form, often as gossip, hearsay, and speculation. By virtue of his contacts, the manager has a natural advantage in collecting this soft information for his organization.

2. He must share and distribute much of this information. Information he gleans from outside personal contacts may be needed within his organization. In his *disseminator* role, the manager passes some of his privileged information directly to his subordinates, who would otherwise have no access to it. When his subordinates lack easy contact with one another, the manager will sometimes pass information from one to another.

3. In his *spokesman* role, the manager sends some of his information to people outside his unit—a president makes a speech to lobby for an organization cause, or a foreman suggests a product modification to a supplier. In addition, as part of his role as spokesman, every manager must inform and satisfy the influential people who control his organizational unit. For the foreman, this may simply involve keeping the plant manager informed about the flow of work through the shop.

The president of a large corporation, however, may spend a great amount of his time dealing with a host of influences. Directors and shareholders must be advised about financial performance; consumer groups must be assured that the organization is fulfilling its social responsibilities; and government officials must be satisfied that the organization is abiding by the law.

## Decisional Roles

Information is not, of course, an end in itself; it is the basic input to decision making. One thing is clear in the study of managerial work: the manager plays the major role in his unit's decision-making system. As its formal authority, only he can commit the unit to important new courses of action; and as its nerve center, only he has full and current information to make the set of decisions that determines the unit's strategy. Four roles describe the manager as decision-maker.

1. As *entrepreneur*, the manager seeks to improve his unit, to adapt it to changing conditions in the environment. In his monitor role, the president is constantly on the lookout for new ideas. When a good one appears, he initiates a development project that he may supervise himself or delegate to an employee (perhaps with the stipulation that he must approve the final proposal).

There are two interesting features about these development projects at the chief executive level.

First, these projects do not involve single decisions or even unified clusters of decisions. Rather, they emerge as a series of small decisions and actions sequenced over time. Apparently, the chief executive prolongs each project so that he can fit it bit by bit into his busy, disjointed schedule and so that he can gradually come to comprehend the issue, if it is a complex one.

Second, the chief executives I studied supervised as many as 50 of these projects at the same time. Some projects entailed new products or processes; others involved public relations campaigns, improvement of the cash position, reorganization of a weak department, resolution of a morale problem in a foreign division, integration of computer operations, various acquisitions at different stages of development, and so on.

The chief executive appears to maintain a kind of inventory of the development projects that he himself supervises—projects that are at various stages of development, some active and some in limbo. Like a juggler, he keeps a number of projects in the air; periodically, one comes down, is given a new burst of energy, and is sent back into orbit. At various intervals, he puts new projects on-stream and discards old ones.

2. While the entrepreneur role describes the manager as the voluntary initiator of change, the *disturbance handler* role depicts the manager involuntarily responding to pressures. Here change is

beyond the manager's control. He must act because the pressures of the situation are too severe to be ignored: strike looms, a major customer has gone bankrupt, or a supplier reneges on his contract.

It has been fashionable, I noted earlier, to compare the manager to an orchestra conductor, just as Peter F. Drucker wrote in *The Practice of Management:*

*The manager has the task of creating a true whole that is larger than the sum of its parts, a productive entity that turns out more than the sum of the resources put into it. One analogy is the conductor of a symphony orchestra, through whose effort, vision and leadership individual instrumental parts that are so much noise by themselves become the living whole of music. But the conductor has the composer's score: he is only interpreter. The manager is both composer and conductor.*[14]

Now consider the words of Leonard R. Sayles, who has carried out systematic research on the manager's job:

*[The manager] is like a symphony orchestra conductor, endeavouring to maintain a melodious performance in which the contributions of the various instruments are coordinated and sequenced, patterned and paced, while the orchestra members are having various personal difficulties, stage hands are moving music stands, alternating excessive heat and cold are creating audience and instrument problems, and the sponsor of the concert is insisting on irrational changes in the program.*[15]

In effect, every manager must spend a good part of his time responding to high-pressure disturbances. No organization can be so well run, so standardized, that it has considered every contingency in the uncertain environment in advance. Disturbances arise not only because poor managers ignore situations until they reach crisis proportions, but also because good managers cannot possibly anticipate all the consequences of the actions they take.

3. The third decisional role is that of *resource allocator.* To the manager falls the responsibility of deciding who will get what in his organizational unit. Perhaps the most important resource the manager allocates is his own time. Access to the manager constitutes exposure to the unit's nerve center and decision-maker. The manager is also charged with designing his unit's structure, that pattern of formal relationships that determines how work is to be divided and coordinated.

Also, in his role as resource allocator, the manager authorizes the important decisions of his unit before they are implemented. By retaining this power, the manager can ensure that decisions are interrelated; all must pass through a single brain. To fragment this power is to encourage discontinuous decision making and a disjointed strategy.

There are a number of interesting features about the manager's authorizing others' decisions. First, despite the widespread use of capital budgeting procedures—a means of authorizing various capital expenditures at one time—executives in my study made a great many authorization decisions on an ad hoc basis. Apparently, many projects cannot wait or simply do not have the quantifiable costs and benefits that capital budgeting requires.

Second, I found that the chief executives faced incredibly complex choices. They had to consider the impact of each decision on other decisions and on the organization's strategy. They had to ensure that the decision would be acceptable to those who influence the organization, as well as ensure that resources would not be overextended. They had to understand the various costs and benefits as well as the feasibility of the proposal. They also had to consider questions of timing. All this was necessary for the simple approval of someone else's proposal. At the same time, however, delay could lose time, while quick approval could be ill considered and quick rejection

---

[14]  Peter F. Drucker, *The Practice of Management* (New York: Harper & Row, 1954). pp. 431–432.

[15]  Leonard R. Sales, *Managerial Behavior* (New York: McGraw-Hill, 1964). p. 162.

might discourage the subordinate who had spent months developing a pet project.

One common solution to approving projects is to pick the man instead of the proposal. That is, the manager authorizes those projects presented to him by people whose judgment he trusts. But he cannot always use this simple dodge.

4. The final decisional role is that of *negotiator*. Studies of managerial work at all levels indicate that managers spend considerable time in negotiations; the president of the football team is called in to work out a contract with the holdout superstar; the corporation president leads his company's contingent to negotiate a new strike issue; the foreman argues a grievance problem to its conclusion with the shop steward. As Leonard Sayles puts it, negotiations are a "way of life" for the sophisticated manager.

These negotiations are duties of the manager's job; perhaps routine, they are not to be shirked. They are an integral part of his job, for only he has the authority to commit organizational resources in "real time," and only he has the nerve center information that important negotiations require.

## The Integrated Job

It should be clear by now that the ten roles I have been describing are not easily separable. In the terminology of the psychologist, they form a gestalt, an integrated whole. No role can be pulled out of the framework and the job he left intact. For example, a manager without liaison contacts lacks external information. As a result, he can neither disseminate the information his employees need nor make decisions that adequately reflect external conditions. (In fact, this is a problem for the new person in a managerial position, since he cannot make effective decisions until he has built up his network of contacts.)

Here lies a clue to the problems of team management.[16] Two or three people cannot share a single managerial position unless they can act as one entity. This means that they cannot divide up the ten roles unless they can very carefully reintegrate them. The real difficulty lies with the informational roles. Unless there can be full sharing of managerial information—and, as I pointed out earlier, it is primarily verbal—team management breaks down. A single managerial job cannot be arbitrarily split, for example, into internal and external roles, for information from both sources must be brought to bear on the same decisions.

To say that the ten roles form a gestalt is not to say that all managers give equal attention to each role. In fact, I found in my review of the various research studies that

. . . *sales managers seem to spend relatively more of their time in the interpersonal roles, presumably a reflection of the extrovert nature of the marketing activity;*

. . . *production managers give relatively more attention to the decisional roles, presumably a reflection of their concern with efficient work flow;*

. . . *staff managers spend the most time in the informational roles, since they are experts who manage departments that advise other parts of the organization.*

Nevertheless, in all cases the interpersonal, informational, and decisional roles remain inseparable.

## TOWARD MORE EFFECTIVE MANAGEMENT

What are the messages for management in this description? I believe, first and foremost, that this description of managerial work should prove more important to managers than any prescription they might derive from it. That is to say, *the manager's effectiveness is significantly influenced by his insight into his own work.* His performance depends

---

[16] See Richard C. Hodgson, Daniel J. Levinson, and Abraham Zaleznik, *The Executive Role Constellation* (Boston: Division on Research, Harvard Business School, 1965), for a discussion of the sharing of roles.

on how well he understands and responds to the pressures and dilemmas of the job. Thus managers who can be introspective about their work are likely to be effective at their jobs....

Let us take a look at three specific areas of concern. For the most part, the managerial logjams—the dilemma of delegation, the data base centralized in one brain, the problems of working with the management scientist—evolve around the verbal nature of the manager's information. There are great dangers in centralizing the organization's data bank in the minds of its managers. When they leave, they take their memory with them. And when subordinates are out of convenient verbal reach of the manager, they are at an informational disadvantage.

# 1

*The manager is challenged to find systematic ways to share his privileged information.* A regular debriefing session with key subordinates, a weekly memory dump on the dictating machine, the maintaining of a diary of important information for limited circulation, or other similar methods may ease the logjam of work considerably. Time spent disseminating this information will be more than regained when decisions must be made. Of course, some will raise the question of confidentiality. But managers would do well to weigh the risks of exposing privileged information against having subordinates who can make effective decisions.

If there is a single theme that runs through this article, it is that the pressures of his job drive the manager to be superficial in his actions—to overload himself with work, encourage interruption, respond quickly to every stimulus, seek the tangible and avoid the abstract, make decisions in small increments, and do everything abruptly.

# 2

*Here again, the manager is challenged to deal consciously with the pressures of superficiality by giving serious attention to the issues that require it, by stepping back from his tangible bits of information in order to see a broad picture, and by making use of analytical inputs.* Although effective managers have to be adept at responding quickly to numerous and varying problems, the danger in managerial work is that they will respond to every issue equally (and that means abruptly) and that they will never work the tangible bits and pieces of informational input into a comprehensive picture of their world.

As I noted earlier, the manager uses these bits of information to build models of his world. But the manager can also avail himself of the models of the specialists. Economists describe the functioning of markets, operations researchers simulate financial flow processes; and behavioral scientists explain the needs and goals of people. The best of these models can be searched out and learned.

In dealing with complex issues, the senior manager has much to gain from a close relationship with the management scientists of his own organization. They have something important that he lacks—time to probe complex issues. An effective working relationship hinges on the resolution of what a colleague and I have called "the planning dilemma."[17] Managers have the information and the authority; analysts have the time and the technology. A successful working relationship between the two will be effected when the manager learns to share his information and the analyst learns to adapt to the manager's need. For the analyst, adaptation means worrying less about the elegance of the method and more about its speed and flexibility.

It seems to me that analysts can help the top manager especially to schedule his time, feed in analytical information, monitor projects under his supervision, develop models to aid in making choices, design contingency plans for disturbances that can be anticipated, and conduct "quick-and-dirty" analysis for those that cannot. But there can be no cooperation if the

---

[17] James S. Hekimian and Henry Mintzberg, "The Planning Dilemma," *The Management Review*, May 1968, p.4.

analysts are out of the mainstream of the manager's information flow.

# 3

*The manager is challenged to gain control of his own time by turning obligations to his advantage and by turning those things he wishes to do into obligations.* The chief executives of my study initiated only 32% of their own contacts (and another 5% by mutual agreement). And yet to a considerable extent they seemed to control their time. There were two key factors that enabled them to do so.

First, the manager has to spend so much time discharging obligations that if he were to view them as just that, he would leave no mark on his organization. The unsuccessful manager blames failure on the obligations; the effective manager turns his obligations to his own advantage. A speech is a chance to lobby for a cause; a meeting is a chance to reorganize a weak department; a visit to an important customer is a chance to extract trade information.

Second, the manager frees some of his time to do those things that he—perhaps no one else—thinks important by turning them into obligations. Free time is made, not found, in the manager's job; it is forced into the schedule. Hoping to leave some time open for contemplation or general planning is tantamount to hoping that the pressures of the job will go away. The manager who wants to innovate initiates a project and obligates others to report back to him; the manager who needs certain environmental information establishes channels that will automatically keep him informed; the manager who has to tour facilities commits himself publicly.

## The Educator's Job

Finally, a word about the training of managers. Our management schools have done an admirable job of training the organization's specialists—management scientists, marketing researchers, accountants, and organizational development specialists. But for the most part they have not trained managers.[18]

Management schools will begin the serious training of managers when skill training takes a serious place next to cognitive learning. Cognitive learning is detached and informational, like reading a book or listening to a lecture. No doubt much important cognitive material must be assimilated by the manager-to-be. But cognitive learning no more makes a manager than it does a swimmer. The latter will drown the first time he jumps into the water if his coach never takes him out of the lecture hall, gets him wet, and gives him feedback on his performance.

In other words, we are taught a skill through practice plus feedback, whether in a real or a simulated situation. Our management schools need to identify the skills managers use, select students who show potential in these skills, put the students into situations where these skills can be practiced, and then give them systematic feedback on their performance.

My description of managerial work suggests a number of important managerial skills—developing peer relationships, carrying out negotiations, motivating subordinates, resolving conflicts, establishing information networks and subsequently disseminating information, making decisions in conditions of extreme ambiguity, and allocating resources. Above all, the manager needs to be introspective about his work so that he may continue to learn on the job.

Many of the manager's skills can, in fact, be practiced, using techniques that range from role playing to videotaping real meetings. And our management schools can enhance the entrepreneurial skills by designing programs that encourage sensible risk taking and innovation.

---

[18] See J. Sterling Livingston, "Myth of the Well-Educated Manager," *HBR* January–February 1971, p. 79.

No job is more vital to our society than that of the manager. It is the manager who determines whether our social institutions serve us well or whether they squander our talents and resources. It is time to strip away the folklore about managerial work, and time to study it realistically so that we can begin the difficult task of making significant improvements in its performance.

# 33. CHARISMATIC AND NONCHARISMATIC LEADERS: DIFFERENCES IN BEHAVIOR AND EFFECTIVENESS

Robert J. House, James Woycke, and Eugene M. Fodor

Research on leadership in the 1960s and early 1970s was predominantly concerned with identifying leader behaviors that had a significant impact on follower attitudes, behavior, and performance. During this period, a major portion of this research was conceived within a transactional or exchange framework of leader/follower relationships. Research in the late 1970s and 1980s, however, included not only tests and extensions of transactional theories but also an emphasis on a new class of theories referred to as charismatic or transformational theories of leadership.

In this chapter, we contrast transactional and charismatic or transformational theories of leadership. We then briefly review prior research and evidence on charismatic and transformational theory. This evidence is primarily concerned with determining the kinds of leader behavior that contribute to charismatic or transformational leader effectiveness. Our review demonstrates that there is a substantial convergence of findings that provides a rather clear picture of the behavior involved in effective charismatic and transformational leadership. Finally, we present a study designed to test predictions of theories concerning the effects and behavior of charismatic compared with noncharismatic United States presidents.

## THEORIES OF LEADER BEHAVIOR

### Transactional Theories

This class of leadership theories is founded on the idea that leader/follower relationships are based on a series of exchanges or implicit bargains be-

Robert J. House, James Woycke, and Eugene M. Fodor, "Charismatic and Noncharismatic Leaders: Differences in Behavior and Effectiveness" from *Charismatic Leadership*, edited by Jay A. Conger, Rabinda N. Kanugo & Associates, Jossey-Bass Publishers, 1988.

tween leaders and followers (Evans, 1970; Hollander, 1964; House, 1971; House & Mitchell, 1974; Graen & Cashman, 1975; Graen & Scandura, 1987). The general notion that runs through this class of theories is that when the job and the environment of the follower fail to provide the necessary motivation, direction, and satisfaction, the leader, through his or her behavior, will be effective by compensating for the deficiencies.

The leader provides for subordinates "that which is missing" but which is required for them to perform effectively and achieve their goals. In this manner, the leader compensates for, or overcomes, obstacles and deficiencies in the followers' environment. What is missing is determined by the environment, the task, and the competence and motivation of followers. It is the role of the leader to complement that which "is missing" to enhance followers' motivation, satisfaction, and performance. It is also the role of the leader to enhance follower competence through coaching and support and by making available to followers opportunities for growth and development in the form of challenging tasks and opportunities to work under conditions of autonomy.

Two such transactional theories have been subjected to rather extensive testing: the Path-Goal Theory of Leadership (Evans, 1970; House, 1971; House & Mitchell, 1974) and the Vertical Dyadic Theory of Role Making (Graen & Cashman, 1975; Graen & Scandura, 1987). Both have received considerable empirical support (see Indvik, 1986, regarding the path-goal theory and Graen & Scandura, 1987, regarding the vertical dyadic theory).

These theories call attention to the importance of situational factors that moderate the effects of a leader's behavior. They also call attention to dyadic relationships between superiors and subordinates and suggest that these relationships need to be measured along with more aggregate measures (such as group members' average perceptions of the leader) in order to predict the effects of leader behavior on individuals. In general, these compensatory theories emphasize the need for managers to diagnose what is missing and take action to facilitate followers' performance. Transactional theories have been suc-

cessful in predicting variance in subordinate satisfaction, turnover, motivation, role ambiguity, and performance, as these variables normally vary.

## Charismatic or Transformational Theories

In contrast to transactional theories, charismatic or transformational theories of leadership predict performance beyond expectations—that is, where substantial and voluntary efforts over and above the call of duty are made by followers. Further, these theories predict emotional attachment to the leader on the part of the followers, as well as emotional and motivational arousal of the followers as a consequence of the leader's behavior.

In contrast to transactional theories, which focus on the effects of leader behaviors on follower cognitions, motivation, and performance, charismatic or transformational leadership theories take as their dependent variables followers' emotional responses to work-related stimuli, as well as their values, self-esteem, trust and confidence in the leader, and motivation to perform above and beyond the call of duty. Further, in contrast to transactional leadership theories that describe leaders in terms of task-and person-oriented behavior, these newer theories describe leaders in terms of articulating and focusing a vision and mission; creating and maintaining a positive image in the minds of followers, peers, and superiors; exhibiting a high degree of confidence in themselves and their beliefs; setting challenging goals for followers; providing a personal example for followers to emulate; showing confidence in and respect for followers; behaving in a manner that reinforces the vision and mission of the leader; and possessing a high degree of liguitic ability and nonverbal expressiveness. Theoretical perspectives of this kind have been advanced by Berlew (1974), House (1977), Burns (1978), Bennis and Nanus (1985), and Bass (1985) and by other authors.... All of these perspectives describe charismatic or transformational leaders as individuals who provide for their followers a vision of the future that promises a better and more meaningful way of life.

The difference between transactional theories and transformational or charismatic theories of leadership behavior lies in the components of the subordinate's motivation that are affected by the leader's behavior and in the specific behaviors of the leader that affect components of the subordinate's motivation. Transactional leaders have their primary effects on follower cognitions and abilities. Charismatic leaders have their major effects on the emotions and self-esteem of followers—the affective motivational variables rather than the cognitive variables.

To put the position succinctly, despite some danger of oversimplification, transactional theories describe actions of leaders that result in work behavior becoming more instrumental in followers reaching their *existing* goals while at the same time contributing to the goals of the organization. In contrast, charismatic or transformational theories address the actions of leaders that result in subordinates *changing* their values, goals, needs, and aspirations. This is somewhat of an oversimplification, since certain charismatic leader behaviors may also have instrumental effects. While [others] review many of the empirical studies of charismatic leadership, we will briefly report on studies that have not been described in detail and that directly link the effects of charismatic and transformational leader behavior to specific follower outcomes, such as motivation and productivity.

Smith (1982), for example, found that thirty leaders who had reputations for being charismatic had significantly different effects on followers than did thirty effective but noncharismatic leaders. Followers of reputed charismatic leaders were found to be more self-assured, experienced more meaningfulness in their work, reported more back-up from their leaders, reported working longer hours, reported higher trust in their leaders, saw their leaders as more dynamic, and had higher performance ratings than did the followers of the noncharismatic but effective leaders.

Using the followers' questionnaire responses, Smith conducted and cross-validated a discriminant function analysis. This analysis classified followers into two groups. Eighty-one percent of the followers who reported to charismatic leaders were clustered together and 66.7 percent of the followers of the noncharismatic leaders were clustered together, yielding an overall hit rate of 80 percent (p $= < .0009$).

Additional support for this class of theories is provided by a laboratory experiment conducted by Howell and Frost (forthcoming) and by a field study of four military samples conducted by Yukl and Van Fleet (1982). Howell and Frost compared the effects of charismatic leader behavior on followers with the effects of directive and considerate leader behavior under experimentally induced high- and low-productivity norm conditions. The findings showed that charismatic leader behavior, as specified by prior theory (House, 1977), had a stronger and more positive influence on the performance, satisfaction, and adjustment of followers than did directive and considerate leader behavior.

A multiple analysis of variance in follower role conflict, role ambiguity, satisfaction, and adjustment to the leader demonstrated that the leader behavior treatment accounted for 96 percent of the variance in these dependent variables. It is most interesting that only the charismatic leader behavior was able to overcome the negative effects of the low-productivity norm condition. Those working under charismatic leaders had higher general satisfaction, higher specific task satisfaction, and less role conflict than did individuals working under structuring or considerate leaders. Under the latter two conditions, the negative effects of the low-productivity norm treatment persisted.

Another empirical study relevant to charismatic theory is presented by Yukl and Van Fleet (1982). These authors found in four separate military samples that "inspirational leadership" was significantly related to leader effectiveness and high levels of follower motivation. These findings held under combat, noncombat, and simulated combat conditions. Thus, studies of charismatic (or inspirational) leaders demonstrated that the behaviors specified by prior theory (House, 1977) rather consistently have the effects predicted by that theory.

A second theory of the same genre is the transformational leadership theory advanced by James MacGregor Burns (1978). According to Burns, transformational leadership occurs "when one or more persons *engage* with others in such a way that leaders and followers raise one another to higher levels of motivation and morality" (p. 20). Accordingly, transformational leaders address themselves to followers' "wants, needs, and other motivations, as well as their own and, thus, they serve as an *independent force in changing the make-up of followers' motive base through gratifying their motives*" (p. 20).

...Bass and his associates have conducted a substantial amount of research testing hypotheses derived from Burns's theory of transformational leadership. These studies have yielded an impressive set of empirical findings. Specifically, leaders who are rated by subordinates to be transformational as compared with other leaders have been found to:

- receive high performance ratings from superiors (Bass, 1985; Hater & Bass, forthcoming)

- be rated more frequently by superiors as top performers (Hater & Bass, 1986)

- be rated more frequently by superiors as having potential for advancement (Avolio & Bass, 1985) or as having excellent ability to manage (Hater and Bass, forthcoming)

- be classified more frequently by independent experts as transformational leaders (Bass, 1985)

- be more frequently classified as "great or world-class leaders" by biographers and historians (Bass, 1985)

- have higher-performing teams in a management simulation exercise (Avolio, Waldman, & Einstein, forthcoming)

- take greater strategic risks in the same management simulation (Avolio & Bass, 1985)

- have subordinates who report greater satisfaction and more or "extra" work effort (Bass, 1985; Hater & Bass, forthcoming; Pereira, 1987) and greater organizational and unit effectiveness (Pereira, 1987)

- have subordinates who also demonstrate transformational leader behaviors (Bass, Waldman, Avolio, & Bebb, 1987)

- have higher-performing work groups (Hater and Bass, forthcoming)

These findings are impressive because the correlations between transformational leader behavior, followers' performance, and satisfaction are significantly higher under transformational leaders than under transactional leaders, because the correlations between transformational leader behaviors and ratings by followers and superiors are consistently above .5 and often as high as .7, and because they have been corroborated in India as well as in the United States (Pereira, 1987).

These findings indicate that leaders who engage in the theoretical charismatic or transformational leader behaviors do indeed produce the predicted charismatic effects and are viewed as more effective leaders by their superiors and followers than are transactional leaders. Further, the correlations between charismatic leader behavior and follower satisfaction and performance are consistently high compared with prior field studies' findings concerning other leader behavior.

The theories and supporting evidence presented in this section inform us of the kinds of behaviors that differentiate charismatic from noncharismatic leaders. Specifically, as stated previously, charismatic leaders articulate a mission or vision in ideological terms, demonstrate a high degree of self-confidence and a high degree of involvement in the mission, set a personal example for followers to emulate, create and maintain a positive image in the minds of followers, peers, and superiors, communicate high performance expectations to follower and confidence in followers' ability to meet such expectations, behave in a manner that reinforces the vision and the mission of the leader, show individualized consideration toward followers, and provide intellectual stimulation to followers. While laboratory and field evidence supports these conclusions, there have been no studies to date designed to test charismatic or transformational theories with respect to political leaders responsible for the management of government organizations. In the following section, we describe such a study and its implications for management practice.

# A STUDY OF UNITED STATES PRESIDENTS

The study reported here was designed to test the following hypotheses: (1) The biographies of cabinet members reporting to charismatic United States presidents include more incidents of positive affective relations with the presidents and more positive affective reactions to their positions than do those of cabinet members reporting to noncharismatic United States presidents. (2) The biographies of cabinet members reporting to charismatic United States presidents include more incidents of charismatic behaviors on the part of the presidents than do biographies of noncharismatic presidents.

## Method

### Classification of Presidents

Nine well-reputed political historians, each with broad expertise in American history, received a questionnaire asking them to classify American presidents as charismatic, noncharismatic, neither charismatic nor noncharismatic, or uncertain (no opinion), using the following guideline: "Charisma is defined as the ability to exercise diffuse and intensive influence over the normative or ideological orientations of others (Etzioni, 1961). As a result, we can identify charismatic leaders by their effects on their followers such that followers of charismatic leaders: (a) have a high degree of loyalty, commitment, and devotion to the leader; (b) identify with the leader and the mission of the leader; (c) emulate his or her values, goals, and behavior; (d) see the leader as a source of inspiration; (e) derive a sense of high self-esteem from their relationship with the leader and his or her mission; and (f) have an exceptionally high degree of trust in the leader and the correctness of his or her beliefs." The historians were asked to classify the leaders with respect to their relationship to cabinet members rather than their relationship to United States voters, because our primary interest in this study was organizational leadership rather than mass or political leadership. Presidents who had served less than two full years in office were not included in the sample.

Seven presidents met the criterion for classification as charismatic leaders; that is, at least eight of the nine historians agreed that these presidents should so be designated. Six presidents met the criterion (eight or more historians agreeing) to qualify as noncharismatic leaders. The historians rated as charismatic Jefferson, Jackson, Lincoln, Theodore Roosevelt, Franklin Roosevelt, Kennedy, and Reagan. They classified as noncharismatic Coolidge, Harding, Arthur, Buchanan, Pierce, and Tyler.

In addition to the charismatic and noncharismatic presidents referred to above, three additional presidents were included in this study. These were Truman, Cleveland, and Polk, who declined renomination and died shortly after leaving office. Eight of the political historians agreed that these three presidents were neither charismatic nor noncharismatic. However, all three are consistently rated in pools of political historians as either "great" or "near great" (Murray & Blessing, 1983). These three presidents provide a comparison group of effective but noncharismatic presidents. Thus, the final sample includes seven charismatic presidents, six noncharismatic presidents, and three presidents who are viewed by political historians as great or near great but who were rated neither charismatic nor noncharismatic. We refer to these three groups as effective charismatics, effective noncharismatics, and ineffective noncharismatics in the remainder of this chapter. We assign these normative labels on the basis of historians' ratings of presidential greatness plus the fact that six of the seven charismatic presidents were reelected, whereas none of the noncharismatic presidents was reelected. The one charismatic president who was not elected to a second term was Kennedy, who was assassinated in his first term.

### Biographical Data

In the next part of the study, the biographies of two or more cabinet members reporting to each president were content analyzed to determine whether there was evidence that (1) charismatic presidents engaged more frequently in behaviors that theoretically differentiate charismatic from noncharismatic leaders, and (2) charismatic presidents had a significantly more positive effect on their cabinet members than did noncharismatic presidents. The content analysis was applied to descriptions of the cabinet members' experiences in the first term of the presidents' administrations only, because no noncharismatic president served more than one term (defined as more than two years of any normal four-year term). President Reagan was not included in this analysis because there were no biographies of his cabinet members written at the time of the study.

To measure the effects of presidents on follower affective states, passages of the biographies of cabinet members that described interactions between the presidents and the cabinet members were coded. These interactions were coded as indicating positive effects of the presidents on the affective states of the secretaries if there was evidence of positive attitudes toward the president, willingness to accept his mission, enthusiasm for the mission, and generally positive attitudes concerning the cabinet member's role in the administration.

To measure the behavior of the presidents, passages were coded that indicated the presidents' expression of self-confidence, high performance expectations of followers, confidence in followers' abilities and performance, strong ideological goals, and individualized consideration for followers.

The use of scholarly biographies for this purpose is a well-accepted practice in social science studies (see Bass, Avolio, & Goodheim, 1987; Bass & Farrow, 1977; Simonton, 1986; Winter, 1987; Woodward, 1974). Cabinet secretaries are well-suited to reflect charismatic effects, because often they have not been associated with the president, they may be unknown to him, and they may have been chosen for party-political reasons (some were rival contenders for the presidential nomination). The best recent one-volume scholarly biography of each cabinet secretary was selected on the basis of references in *The Harvard Guide to American History* (Freidel, 1974) and the *Biographical Directory of the United States Executive Branch, 1774–1977* (Sobel, 1977). Biographies published since 1977 were identified in the

University of Toronto library and confirmed on the basis of reviews in the *American Historical Review* and the *Journal of American History*. All cabinet secretaries (except postmasters general) about whom a scholarly biography or monograph had been written were included in the study. Further, we specifically included secretaries of state from each administration.

Only multivolume biographies were available for cabinet secretaries Caleb Cushing, Henry A. Wallace, and Robert Kennedy. In these cases, we used either the volume dealing with the first term or, when the first-term material spanned more than more than one volume, the complete index. Three secretaries—Thomas F. Bayard, Frank B. Kellogg, and Henry C. Wallace—were represented by scholarly monographs. Two secretaries—Frederick T. Frelinghuysen and Philander C. Knox—were represented by doctoral dissertations.

Biographies were scanned for relevant passages containing substantive remarks (author statements or direct quotations) pertaining to the relationship between the president and the secretary. Mundane or routine remarks were excluded. Passages were selected by scanning the chapter or chapters dealing with the relationship during the first term, provided that such material did not exceed fifty pages. If the chapter or chapters dealing with the first term exceeded fifty pages, we used the index to identify passages. If a relationship was illustrated by fewer than three extracts from any one source, that material was dropped. If more than fifteen extracts were obtained, the number was randomly reduced to fifteen. This selective process is a conservative one in that it increases the number of passages for those low on the criterion variables and reduces the number for those high on the criterion variables.

All passages in the indexes of the biographies referring to the president were transcribed onto index cards. Using House's (1977) theory as a guide, descriptions of each behavior and each effect thought to describe charisma were developed. A set of leadership passages separate from those to be used in the study was developed so that the operationalization of the behaviors and effects could be clarified. Two independent indi-

**TABLE 33.1**
Number of Biographies Analyzed and Passages Coded.

|  | Effective Charismatics | Effective Noncharismatics | Ineffective Noncharismatics |
|---|---|---|---|
| Number of biographies | 19 | 9 | 12 |
| Number of passages describing affective states | 180 | 50 | 59 |
| Number of passages | 139 | 56 | 46 |

viduals coded these practice passages, discussed their ratings, and then clarified the descriptions where necessary. Four iterations of rating and discussion were completed before it was felt that there was an unambiguous operationalization of each behavior and each effect. The final coding of these practice passages became the key on which the subjects were trained.

### Recruitment: Testing and Training of Coders

Undergraduate students were recruited and given a reading test to ensure that their reading comprehension was adequate for the material they would have to read. Students were trained on either behaviors or effects and were randomly assigned to each. Using the precoded practice material and the descriptions of the behaviors and effects, the students were trained so that they understood and were able to code the passages accurately. The students who were trained to code behaviors were 73 to 88 percent accurate. The students trained to code effects were 78 to 83 percent accurate. (Accuracy means they agreed with the key.) Students' accuracy was checked af-

ter every seventy-five experimental passages they coded, and the same level of accuracy was found to be maintained.

Table 33.1 presents the number of biographies and passages for each classification of leader. The behavior of the presidents and the affective responses of the cabinet members described in these passages were coded separately by two coders, one who coded behaviors and one who coded effects. The identities of the cabinet members were disguised so that the coders could not determine the names of the cabinet members to which the passages applied. Further, the coders were unaware of the hypotheses of the study.

## Results

### Biographical Analyses

Table 33.2 presents the results of the biographical content analysis concerning affective responses of cabinet members. This table reports the mean number of passages describing positive effects of the leaders per biography, per leader. The difference between effective charismatics and effective

**TABLE 33.2**
Analysis of Variance Comparing Mean Frequency of Affective Responses Reported per Cabinet Member Biography.

|  | Effective Charismatics ($N = 6$) | Effective Noncharismatics ($N = 3$) | Ineffective Noncharismatics ($N = 6$) |
|---|---|---|---|
| Mean | 9.01 | 5.56 | 4.42 |
| S.D. | 3.47 | 3.40 | 2.60 |

Note: $F$ for effective charismatics versus noncharismatics = 6.77, $p < .04$.

noncharismatics was significant at the .04 level ($F = 6.77$). These passages reflect positive attitudes toward the president, trust in and obedience to the president, willingness to accept the president's mission, enthusiasm for the mission, and generally positive statements concerning the cabinet member's role in the administration.

These findings are significant for two reasons. First, they serve as a check on the validity of the classification procedure. They confirm that those presidents classified as charismatic by historians are also described by biographers as having charismatic effects on cabinet members. Thus, the findings provide an independent check on the procedure used to classify charismatic and noncharismatic leaders. Second, these findings further confirm the theoretical definition of charismatic leaders as leaders who have significant effects on the affective state of their followers, thus providing support for hypothesis one.

Table 33.3 presents the results of the biographical content analysis concerning the frequency of charismatic behaviors by the presidents reported in the biographies.

A test of the difference between the behaviors of effective charismatics and ineffective noncharismatics demonstrated a significant difference in the mean charismatic behaviors per biography for these two groups ($F = 7.42$; $p < .04$), thus providing support for hypothesis two. The specific behaviors that differentiate effective charismatics from ineffective noncharismatics are the leaders' display of self-confidence, high performance expectations of followers, confidence in followers' abilities and performance, strong ideological goals, and individualized consideration for followers.

## Relationship to Previously Published Data

In addition to the test of the hypotheses reported above, we can also relate our presidential classifications to data published in the political science literature. There have been several surveys of political historians concerning presidential greatness. The results of the more prominent surveys are displayed in Table 33.4. In four of these surveys, the respondents were asked to indicate, for each United States president, whether he or she viewed the president as great, near great, average, below average, or a failure. These ratings provide us with expert (political historian) opinions concerning presidential greatness. In these surveys, Lincoln, Franklin D. Roosevelt, and Jefferson were consistently rated as great. Jackson and Theodore Roosevelt were rated as great in two of these surveys and near great in the remaining two. While not rated as charismatic in our poll of political historians, Washington and Wilson also were consistently rated as great or near great in the polls of political historians.

The members of the effective noncharismatic group were consistently rated as near great, with the exception of the survey by Porter, reported in Murray and Blessing (1983), in which Cleveland was rated as average. The members of the noncharismatic sample were consistently rated as average or below. None of these presidents was rated as great or near great.

These findings suggest a strong relationship between charismatic leadership and presidential greatness. Further, considering another aspect of presidential performance, five of the six charismatic leaders were reelected. The one exception, Kennedy, was assassinated. In contrast, ineffective noncharismatic leaders consistently were not

**TABLE 33.3**

Analysis of Variance Comparing Mean Frequency of Charismatic Leader Reported per Cabinet Member Biography.

|  | Effective Charismatics | Effective Noncharismatics | Ineffective Noncharismatics |
| --- | --- | --- | --- |
| Mean | 7.54 | 6.22 | 3.06 |
| S.D. | 2.99 | 6.73 | 2.76 |

Note: $F$ for effective charismatics versus noncharismatics $= 7.42$, $p < .04$.

**TABLE 33.4**
Ratings of Presidential Performance in Five Surveys of Political Scientists.

| Porter 1981 (N = 41) | Schlesinger 1962 (N = 75) | Schlesinger 1948 (N = 55) | Murray-Blessing 1982 (N = 846) | Mode | Mean | Chicago Tribune 1982 (N = 49) |
|---|---|---|---|---|---|---|
| Lincoln* | Lincoln* | Lincoln* | Lincoln* | 1 | 1.13 | Lincoln* |
| Washington* | Washington | Washington | F. Roosevelt* | 1 | 1.22 | Washington* |
| F. Roosevelt* | F. Roosevelt* | F. Roosevelt* | Washington | 1 | 1.27 | F. Roosevelt* |
| Jefferson* | Wilson | Wilson | Jefferson* | 1 | 1.70 | T. Roosevelt* |
| T. Roosevelt* | Jefferson* | Jefferson* | T. Roosevelt | 2 | 1.93 | Jefferson* |
| Wilson | Jackson* | Jackson* | Wilson | 2 | 2.07 | Wilson |
| Jackson* | T. Roosevelt* | T. Roosevelt* | Jackson* | 2 | 2.32 | Jackson* |
| Truman** | Polk** | Cleveland** | Truman** | 2 | 2.45 | Truman** |
| Polk** | Truman** | J. Adams | J. Adams | 3 | 2.85 | Eisenhower |
| J. Adams | J. Adams | Polk** | L. Johnson | 3 | 2.87 | Polk** |
| L. Johnson | Cleveland** | J.Q. Adams | Eisenhower | 3 | 2.99 | McKinley |
| Eisenhower | Madison | Monroe | Polk** | 3 | 3.06 | L. Johnson |
| Madison | J.Q. Adams | Hayes | Kennedy* | 3 | 3.13 | Cleveland** |
| Kennedy | Hayes | Madison | Madison | 3 | 3.30 | Kennedy* |
| Cleveland** | McKinley | Van Buren | Monroe | 3 | 3.35 | J. Adams } tie |
| McKinley | Taft | Taft | J.Q. Adams | 3 | 3.42 | Monroe |
| Monroe | Van Buren | Arthur*** | Cleveland** | 3 | 3.43 | Madison |
| J.Q. Adams | Monroe | McKinley | McKinley | 4 | 3.78 | Van Buren |
| Van Buren | Hoover | A. Johnson | Taft | 4 | 3.87 | J.Q. Adams |
| Hayes | B. Harrison | Hoover | Van Buren | 4 | 3.97 | Taft |
| Taft | Arthur*** | B. Harrison | Hoover | 4 | 4.03 | Hoover |
| Hoover | Eisenhower | Tyler*** | Hayes | 4 | 4.05 | Hayes |
| Carter | A. Johnson | Coolidge*** | Arthur*** | 4 | 4.24 | Ford |
| Arthur*** | Taylor | Fillmore | Ford | 4 | 4.32 | Arthur*** |
| B. Harrison | Tyler*** | Taylor*** | Carter | 4 | 4.36 | B. Harrison |
| Ford | Fillmore | Buchanan*** | B. Harrison | 4 | 4.40 | Taylor |
| Taylor | Coolidge*** | Pierce*** | Taylor | 5 | 4.45 | Carter |
| Tyler*** | Pierce*** | Grant | Tyler*** | 5 | 4.61 | Tyler*** |
| Fillmore | Buchanan*** | Harding*** | Fillmore | 5 | 4.64 | Coolidge*** |
| Coolidge*** | Grant | | Coolidge*** | 5 | 4.65 | A. Johnson |
| A. Johnson | Harding*** | | Pierce*** | 5 | 4.95 | Fillmore |
| Grant | | | A. Johnson | 6 | 5.10 | Grant |
| Pierce*** | | | Buchanan | 6 | 5.15 | Pierce*** |
| Nixon*** | | | Nixon | 6 | 5.18 | Buchanan*** |
| Buchanan*** | | | Grant | 6 | 5.25 | Nixon |
| Harding*** | | | Harding*** | 6 | 5.56 | Harding*** |

Category groupings (shown as rotated side-labels in the original):

- **Porter 1981:** Great (Lincoln–T. Roosevelt); Near great (Wilson–J. Adams); Average (L. Johnson–Ford); Below average (Taylor–Pierce); Failure (Nixon–Harding).
- **Schlesinger 1962:** Great (Lincoln–Jefferson); Near great (Jackson–Cleveland); Average (Madison–Fillmore); Below average (Coolidge–Harding); Failure.
- **Schlesinger 1948:** Great (Lincoln–Jackson); Near great (T. Roosevelt–Polk); Average (J.Q. Adams–B. Harrison); Below Average (Tyler–Buchanan); Failure (Pierce–Harding).
- **Murray-Blessing 1982:** Great (Lincoln–Jefferson); Near great (T. Roosevelt–Truman); Above average (J. Adams–Cleveland); Average (McKinley–B. Harrison); Below average (Taylor–Pierce); Failure (A. Johnson–Harding).
- **Chicago Tribune 1982:** Ten Best (Lincoln–Polk); Ten Worst (Carter–Harding).

\* Effective charismatic
\*\* Effective noncharismatic
\*\*\* Ineffective noncharismatic

nominated by their parties for reelection, except for Harding, who died in office, and Coolidge, who declined to seek renomination.

It is possible to relate our classifications of presidents to political historians' opinions concerning several performance criteria of the presidency. Table 33.5 recasts data reported by Maranell (1970) into our classifications of presidents. These data are based on a poll of 846 political historians. From this table it is clear that charismatic presidents are rated as significantly higher than noncharismatics on general prestige, strength of action, presidential activeness, flexibility, accomplishment of their administrations, and the amount of information about the president available to respondents. Thus, it is clear that United States political historians are in substantial agreement with respect to their opinions concerning presidential performance.

These data show that charismatic presidents are given the majority of attention in the literature, as demonstrated by responses of political historians, which indicates that more information is available about the charismatic presidents than about the noncharismatic presidents. This finding is further confirmed by our own finding that more biographies were available describing cabinet members of charismatic United States presidents than noncharismatic presidents.

These findings suggest a possible bias in the political historians' classification of presidents as charismatic or noncharismatic. It is likely that our expert classifiers are influenced by the results of prior polls concerning presidential greatness and by the fact that those presidents classified as charismatic were reelected or assassinated. If this is true, we may have a confounding of our independent variable—classification of presidents as charismatic or not—with ratings of presidential achievements. This could be due to a misattribution problem in which the attribution of charisma is made on the basis of the same data used to assess presidential performance. Further, it can be argued that all three sources of information (biographers, political historians who classified the presidents in the present study, and political historians polled in prior studies) may be generally informed by the same literature and therefore may all indirectly reflect a common source bias.

This explanation, while undoubtedly true to some extent, is considerably weakened by two observations. The first observation concerns the presidential classifications. Washington and Wilson were consistently rated as great in all four polls of political historians and as above great in the Maranell poll. However, these presidents were not classified as charismatic in the present study. Further, a large number of presidents were rated as below average or as failures but were not classified as noncharismatic in the present study. Thus, presidential greatness or failure alone does not account for the political historians' attribution of charisma. Second, the charismatic presidents were described by biographers as engag-

**TABLE 33.5**
Ratings of Presidents by Political Historians.

|  | Charismatic | Neutral | Noncharismatic |
|---|---|---|---|
| General prestige | 1.30[a] | 0.50 | −1.22 |
| Strength of action | 1.39 | 0.60 | −0.90 |
| Presidental activeness | 1.34 | 0.68 | −0.95 |
| Flexibility | 1.23 | 0.13 | 0.21 |
| Accomplishment of their administrations | 1.30 | 0.58 | −0.91 |
| Respondent's amount of information | 1.25 | 0.35 | −0.92 |

[a] **Index of number of standard deviations above or below the mean of all presidents.**

**Source: Maranell, 1970.**

ing in more charismatic behaviors than the noncharismatic presidents. Since such behavior was *not* used as a criterion for presidential classification, the behavioral data can reasonably be regarded as independent of the classification process and thus can shed additional light on the nature of the charismatic phenomenon.

## ORGANIZATIONAL IMPLICATIONS

The above findings have several implications for organizational theory and practice.

### Commitment to Organizational Goals

The first implication concerns the effect of charismatic leader behavior on follower commitment to the mission of the leader or the organization. The findings of Smith (1982), Bass and his associates as reviewed earlier in this chapter, and Howell and Frost (forthcoming), as well as the present study, all demonstrate that a high level of organizational commitment on the part of followers is associated with charismatic behavior of leaders. Thus, this kind of leader behavior provides a strong link between organizational goals and member commitment to such goals.

### Early Detection of Charismatic Potential

The entire pattern of affective and behavioral data in the present study, as well as biographical ratings of presidential greatness and Maranell's (1970) findings with respect to attributes of presidential administrations, suggests a clear picture of charismatic leadership in the United States presidential office. Charismatic United States presidents are extremely active, assertive, and energetic, as are other charismatic leaders studied in prior investigation. Further, their effects on the affective states of followers suggest that charismatic leaders are socially sensitive to the needs of their followers. These findings suggest that it is likely that individuals who have charismatic potential can be identified through psychological testing and observation of behavior in simulations, such as management games and assessment center exercises. Recall that Avolio and Bass

(1985) found such leaders to behave differently from other leaders in a management game and that their teams performed more effectively than did teams led by noncharismatic leaders.

What should we make of these findings and speculations? We believe that at this time there is sufficient knowledge concerning leader personality to warrant the development and testing of selection procedures for identifying charismatic leadership potential. Clearly, selection validation studies are called for.

### Conditions Requiring Charismatic Leadership

The findings from this and prior studies also suggest the conditions under which charismatic leadership is most likely to be required and effective. Our findings suggest that effective charismatic presidents were active, energetic, assertive, and socially sensitive individuals. Further recall that the cabinet members of charismatic presidents have expressed a high degree of commitment to the leader and his mission and a high degree of positive affect toward the leader and toward their position in his cabinet.

We speculate from these findings that charismatic leadership is required, or at least is more appropriate, in situations that require a combination of highly involved and active leadership plus emotional commitment and extraordinary effort by both leader and followers in pursuit of ideological goals. We speculate that situations that require these attributes are thus situations that require charismatic leadership. Under conditions requiring routine but reliable performance in the pursuit of pragmatic goals, charismatic leadership is not likely required and may even be dysfunctional.

### Managerial Training and Development

The findings from prior studies have implications for managerial training, for role modeling and coaching by superiors, and for career counseling and planning. Bass, Waldman, Avolio, and Bebb (1987) demonstrated a role modeling effect of charismatic leaders. Specifically, followers of charismatic leaders were found to engage in behavior similar to that of their leaders. Evidence also suggests, although presently still somewhat tenuously, that charismatic leader behavior can be learned through training. Major evidence for the efficacy of charismatic training is Howell and Frost's (forthcoming) laboratory study of the effects of leader behavior. These researchers found that they were able to train selected individuals to engage in charismatic behavior as well as other kinds of leader behaviors.

If the Howell and Frost finding that charismatic leader behavior is trainable in a laboratory situation is found in future research to be generalizable to field settings, we would recommend such training efforts to develop such behavior. Clearly, a field test of the efficacy of charismatic leadership training in field settings is called for.

We would caution the reader, however, to expect the effects of such training to be conditional on the personality, ideological or goal commitment, and interpersonal skills of trainees. We would expect such training to be most effective for individuals who have shown a strong commitment to organizational goals, have demonstrated a high degree of involvement in their work, have high needs for achievement and power, and possess skills of linguistic and nonverbal expressiveness. Further, we would expect such training to be more effective under conditions requiring involved and active leadership, high levels of follower commitment, and follower effort beyond the call of duty.

## CONCLUSION

Our study of United States presidents is intended to further our understanding of the elusive phenomenon referred to as charismatic or transformational leadership. We believe that we have shown in our review of prior theory and research evidence, in our review of political historians' opinion polls, and in our research on presidential biographical and motivation data that: (1) Reputed charismatic leaders have the affects hypothesized in theories of charismatic and transformational leadership. These affects distinguish charismatic from noncharismatic leaders. (2) Reported charismatic leaders engage in behaviors hypothesized in theories of charismatic and transformational leadership. These behaviors distinguish charismatic from noncharismatic leaders. These conclusions appear to be generalizable, at least in the North American culture, since they have been demonstrated in field, laboratory, and historical studies.

The above conclusions are derived from studies conducted in the Western world plus one study conducted in India. It will be interesting to follow the development of theory and research in this domain. We hope that cross-cultural research will inform us of the generalizability of these findings beyond the Western world and of the applicability of charismatic and transformational theory to leadership in complex organizations.

## REFERENCES

Avolio, B. J., and Bass, B. M. "Charisma and Beyond." Paper presented at the Academy of Management, San Diego, Aug. 1985.

Avolio, B. J., Waldman, D. A., and Einstein, W. O. "Transformational Leadership in a Management Game Simulation." *Group and Organized Studies*, forthcoming.

Bass, B. M. *Leadership and Performance Beyond Expectations*. New York: Free Press, 1985.

Bass, B. M. Avolio, B. J., and Goodheim, L. "Biography and the Assessment of Transformational Leadership at the World-Class Level." *Journal of Management*, 1987, *13* (1), 7–20.

Bass, B. M., and Farrow, D. L. "Quantitative Analysis of Biographies of Political Figures." *Journal of Psychology*, 1977, *97*, 281–296.

Bass, B. M., Waldman, D. A., Avolio, B. J., and Bebb, M. "Transformational Leadership and the Falling Dominoes Effect." *Group and Organization Studies*, 1987, *12* (1), 73–87.

Bennis, W., and Nanus, B. *Leaders: The Strategies for Taking Charge.* New York: Harper & Row, 1985.

Berlew, D. E. "Leadership and Organizational Excitement." *California Management Review*, 1974, *17* (2), 21–30.

Burns, J. M. *Leadership.* New York: Harper & Row, 1978.

Etzioni, A. *A Comparative Analysis of Complex Organizations.* New York: Free Press, 1961.

Evans, M. G. "The Effects of Supervisory Behavior on the Path-Goal Relationship." *Organizational Behavior and Human Performance*, 1970, *5*, 277–298.

Freidel, F. (ed.). *The Harvard Guide to American History.* Cambridge, Mass: Harvard University Press, 1974.

Graen, G., and Cashman, J. F. "A Role-Making Model of Leadership in Formal Organizations: A Developmental Approach." In J. G. Hunt and L. L. Larson (eds.), *Leadership Frontiers.* Kent, Ohio: Kent State University Press, 1975.

Graen, G. B., and Scandura, T. A. "Toward a Psychology of Dyadic Organizing." In L. L. Cummings and B. M. Staw (eds.), *Research in Organizational Behavior.* Greenwich, Conn.: JAI Press, 1987.

Hater, J. J., and Bass, B. M. "Superiors' Evaluations and Subordinates' Perceptions of Transformational and Transactional Leadership." *Journal of Applied Psychology*, forthcoming.

Hollander, E. P. *Leaders, Groups, and Influence.* New York: Oxford University Press, 1964.

House, R. J. "Path-Goal Theory of Leader Effectiveness." *Administrative Science Quarterly*, 1971, *16*, 321–338.

House, R. J., "A 1976 Theory of Charismatic Leadership." In J. G. Hunt and L. L. Larson (eds.), *Leadership: The Cutting Edge.* Carbondale: Southern Illinois University Press, 1977.

House, R. J., and Mitchell, T. R. "Path-Goal Theory of Leadership." *Journal of Contemporary Business*, 1974, *5*, 81–94.

Howell, J. M., and Frost, P. "A Laboratory Study of Charismatic Leadership." *Organizational Behavior and Human Decision Processes*, forthcoming.

Indvik, J. "Path-Goal Theory of Leadership: A Meta-Analysis." *Proceedings*, Academy of Management, Chicago, 1986.

Maranell, G. M. "The Evaluation of Presidents: An Extension of the Schlesinger Polls." *Journal of American History*, 1970, *57*, 104–113.

Murray, R. K., and Blessing, T. H. "The Presidential Performance Study: A Progress Report." *Journal of American History*, 1983, *70*, 535–555.

Pereira, D. F. "Factors Associated with Transformational Leadership in an Indian Engineering Firm." Unpublished paper, Lawson & Toubro Ltd., Bombay, India, 1987.

Simonton, D. K. "Presidential Personality: Biographical Use of the Group Adjective Checklist." *Journal of Personality and Social Psychology*, 1986, *51*, 149–160.

Smith, B. J. "An Initial Test of a Theory of Charismatic Leadership Based on the Responses of Subordinates." Unpublished doctoral dissertation, University of Toronto, 1982.

Sobel, R. (ed.). *Biographical Directory of the United States Executive Branch, 1774–1977.* Westport, Conn.: Greenwood Press, 1977.

Winter, D. G. *The Power Motive.* New York: Free Press, 1973.

Winter, D. G. "Leader Appeal, Leader Performance, and the Motives Profile of Leaders and Followers: A Study of American Presidents and Elections." *Journal of Personality and Social Psychology*, 1987, *52* (1), 196–202.

Woodward, C. V. *Responses of the Presidents to Charges of Misconduct.* New York: Dell, 1974.

Yukl, G. A. *Leadership in Organizations.* Englewood Cliffs, N.J.: Prentice-Hall, 1981.

Yukl, G. A., and Van fleet, D. D. "Cross Situational Multi-method Research on Military Leader Effectiveness." *Organizational Behavior and Human Performance*, 1982, *30*, 87–108.

# DECISION MAKING

You are now ready to learn about the foibles of decision making. To start things off, a series of exercises are presented which will graphically demonstrate some of the decision biases we are all subject to. People use heuristics, or shortcuts, to process information and make decisions, but with these heuristics come biases and errors. Problems with decision making do not stop with individuals, however. The limited information processing capacity of people gets reflected in the way both groups and organizations make decisions. The tendency of organizations to become locked into losing courses of action is, for example, a systems-level bias you will read about. Another is excess risk taking by groups, where policy-making groups may make damaging decisions because of a number of shortcomings in the group process. Finally, some positive ways of implementing group decision making are discussed. The advantages of quality circles, currently one of the most popular means of involving workers in decisions, are noted in the final selection of this section.

In reading about decision making, you may be surprised at the number of systematic errors individuals make, and the problems both groups and organizations face in choosing correct courses of action. Knowing these biases is useful, since they can be counteracted. Individuals who are aware of their limitations can take more care in processing information and formulating solutions. By the same token, both groups and organizations can build-in some structural mechanisms to improve decision making. Therefore, as you read these selections, try to think about possible ways to correct or compensate for the biases that almost naturally creep into decision making. Also, keep in mind that, even with all our limitations, we did manage to get to the moon! Our decision making thus may be flawed but it is not totally deficient; our organizations may be inefficient yet they do still accomplish many of their goals. Consequently, the readings in this section can help us both appreciate our capabilities and understand how we may improve upon our performance.

# Foundations of Decision Processes

## 34. BIASES

Max H. Bazerman

This chapter is written to provide you with the opportunity to audit your own decision making and identify the biases that affect you. A number of problems are presented that allow you to examine your problem solving and learn how your judgments compare to the judgments of others. The quiz items are then used to illustrate 13 predictable biases to which managers are prone, and that frequently lead to judgments that systematically deviate from rationality.

To start out, consider the following two problems:

**Problem 1:** The following 10 corporations were ranked by *Fortune* magazine to be among the 500 largest United States–based firms according to sales volume for 1987:

*Group A:* Gillette, Coca-Cola Enterprises, Lever Brothers, Apple Computers, Hershey Foods

*Group B:* Coastal, Weyerhaeuser, Northrup, CPC International, Champion International

Which group of five organizations listed (A or B) had the larger total sales volume?

**Problem 2:** (Adapted from Kahneman & Tversky, 1973) The best student in my introductory MBA class this past semester writes poetry and is rather shy and small in stature. What was the student's undergraduate major:

(A) Chinese studies or
(B) Psychology?

What are your answers? If you answered *A* for each of the two problems, you may gain comfort in knowing that the majority of respondents choose *A*. If you answered *B*, you are part of the minority. In this case, however, the minority represents the correct response. All corporations in group B were ranked in the Fortune 100, while none of the corporations in group A had sales as large. In fact, the total sales for group B was more than double the total sales for group A. In the second problem, the student was actually a psychology major, but more important, selecting psychology as the student's major represents a more rational response given the limited information.

Problem 1 illustrates the availability heuristic.... In this problem, group A contains consumer firms, while group B consists of industrial firms and holding companies. Most of us

---

are more familiar with consumer firms than conglomerates and can more easily generate information in our minds about their size. If we were aware of our bias resulting from the availability heuristic, we would recognize our differential exposure to this information and adjust, or at least question, our judgments accordingly.

Problem 2 illustrates the representativeness heuristic. The reader who responds "Chinese studies" has probably overlooked relevant *base-rate* information—namely, the likely ratio of Chinese studies majors to psychology majors within the MBA student population. When asked to reconsider the problem in this context, most people change their response to "psychology" in view of the relative scarcity of Chinese studies majors seeking MBAs. This example emphasizes that logical base-rate reasoning is often overwhelmed by qualitative judgments drawn from available descriptive information.

The purpose of problems 1 and 2 is to demonstrate how easily faulty conclusions are drawn when we overrely on cognitive heuristics. In the remainder of this chapter, additional problems are presented to further increase your awareness of the impact of heuristics on your decisions and to help you develop an appreciation for the systematic errors that emanate from overdependence on them. The goal of the chapter is to help you "unfreeze" your decision-making patterns and realize how easily heuristics become biases when improperly applied. By working on numerous problems that demonstrate the failures of these heuristics, you will become more aware of the biases in your decision making. By learning to spot these biases, you can improve the quality of your decisions.

Before reading further, please take a few minutes to respond to the problems outlined in Table 34.1. They will be used to illustrate the 13 decision biases presented in the remainder of this chapter.

**TABLE 34.1**
Chapter Problems

---

*Respond to the following 11 problems before reading the chapter.*

**Problem 3:** Which is riskier:
  **a.** driving a car on a 400-mile trip?
  **b.** flying on a 400-mile commercial airline flight?

**Problem 4:** Are there more words in the English language
  **a.** that start with an *r*?
  **b.** for which *r* is the third letter?

**Problem 5:** Mark is finishing his MBA at a prestigious university. He is very interested in the arts and at one time considered a career as a musician. Is Mark more likely to take a job
  **a.** in the management of the arts?
  **b.** with a management consulting firm?

**Problem 6:** In 1986, two research groups sampled consumers on the driving performance of the Dodge Colt versus the Plymouth Champ in a blind road test; that is, the consumers did not know when they were driving the Colt or the Champ. As you may know, these cars were identical; only the marketing varied.

One research group (A) sampled 66 consumers each day for 60 days (a large number of days to control for weather and other variables), while the other research group (B) sampled 22 consumers each day for 50 days. Which consumer group observed more days in which 60 percent or more of the consumers tested preferred the Dodge Colt:
  **a.** Group A?
  **b.** Group B?

---

*(continued)*

**TABLE 34.1 (cont.)**
Chapter Problems

**Problem 7:** You are about to hire a new central-region sales director for the fifth time this year. You predict that the next director should work out reasonably well, since the last four were "lemons," and the odds favor hiring at least one good sales director in five tries. This thinking is
   a. Correct.
   b. Incorrect.

**Problem 8:** You are the sales forecaster for a department store chain with nine locations. The chain depends on you for quality projections of future sales in order to make decisions on staffing, advertising, information system developments, purchasing, renovation, and the like. All stores are similar in size and merchandise selection. The main difference in their sales occurs because of location and random fluctuations. Sales for 1989 were as follows:

| Store | 1989 | 1991 |
|---|---|---|
| 1 | $12,000,000 | $_____ |
| 2 | 11,500,000 | _____ |
| 3 | 11,000,000 | _____ |
| 4 | 10,500,000 | _____ |
| 5 | 10,000,000 | _____ |
| 6 | 9,500,000 | _____ |
| 7 | 9,000,000 | _____ |
| 8 | 8,500,000 | _____ |
| 9 | 8,000,000 | _____ |
| TOTAL | $ 90,000,000 | $ 99,000,000 |

Your economic forecasting service has convinced you that the best estimate of total sales increases between 1989 and 1991 is 10 percent (to $ 99,000,000). Your task is to predict 1991 sales for each store. Since your manager believes strongly in the economic forecasting service, it is imperative that your total sales equal $ 99,000,000.

**Problem 9:** Linda is 31 years old, single, outspoken, and very bright. She majored in philosophy. As a student, she was deeply concerned with issues of discrimination and social justice, and she participated in antinuclear demonstrations.

Rank order the following eight descriptions in terms of the probability (likelihood) that they describe Linda.

____   a. Linda is a teacher in an elementary school.
____   b. Linda works in a bookstore and takes yoga classes.
____   c. Linda is active in the feminist movement.
____   d. Linda is a psychiatric social worker.
____   e. Linda is a member of the League of Women Voters.
____   f. Linda is a bank teller.
____   g. Linda is an insurance salesperson.
____   h. Linda is a bank teller who is active in the feminist movement.

**Problem 10:** A newly hired engineer for a computer firm in the Boston metropolitan area has four years of experience and good all-around qualifications. When asked to estimate the starting salary for this employee, my secretary (knowing very little about the profession or the industry) guessed an annual salary of $ 23,000. What is your estimate?

$_____per year.

(continued)

**TABLE 34.1 (cont.)**

**Chapter Problems**

**Problem 11:** Which of the following appears most likely?
Which appears second most likely?
  **a.** Drawing a red marble from a bag containing 50 percent red marbles and 50 percent white marbles.
  **b.** Drawing a red marble seven times in succession, with replacement (a selected marble is put back in the bag before the next marble is selected), from a bag containing 90 percent red marbles and 10 percent white marbles.
  **c.** Drawing at least one red marble in seven tries, with replacement, from a bag containing 10 percent red marbles and 90 percent white marbles.

**Problem 12:** Listed below are 10 uncertain quantities. Do no look up any information on these items. For each, write down your best estimate of the quantity. Next, put a lower and upper bound around your estimate, such that you are 98 percent confident that your range surrounds the actual quantity.

———   **a.** Mobil Oil's sales in 1987
———   **b.** IBM's assets in 1987
———   **c.** Chrysler's profit in 1987
———   **d.** The number of U.S. industrial firms in 1987 with sales greater than those of Conslidated Papers.
———   **e.** The U.S. gross national product in 1945
———   **f.** The amount of taxes collect by the U.S. Internal Revenue Service in 1970
———   **g.** The length (in feet) of the Chesapeake Bay Bridge–Tunnel
———   **h.** The area (in square miles) of Brazil
———   **i.** The size of the black population of San Francisco in 1970
———   **j.** The dollar value of Canadian exports of lumber in 1977

**Problem 13:** (Adapted from Einhorn & Hogarth, 1978) It is claimed that when a particular analyst predicts a rise in the market, the market always rises. You are to check this claim. Examine the information available about the following four events (cards):

| Card 1 | Card 2 | Card 3 | Card 4 |
|---|---|---|---|
| Prediction: | Prediction: | Outcome: | Outcome: |
| Favorable report | Unfavorable report | Risk in the market | Fall in the market |

You currently see the predictions (cards 1 and 2) *or* outcomes associated with four events. You are seeing one side of a card. On the other side of cards 1 and 2 is the actual outcome, while on the other side of cards 3 and 4 is the prediction that the analyst made. Evidence about the claim is potentially available by turning over the card(s). Which cards would you turn over for the evidence that you need to check the analyst's claim? (Circle the appropriate cards.)

## BIASES EMANATING FROM THE AVAILABILITY HEURISTIC

### Bias 1—Ease of Recall (based upon vividness and recency)

**Problem 3:** Which is riskier:

**a.** driving a car on a 400-mile trip?

**b.** flying on a 400-mile commercial airline flight?

Many people respond that flying in a commercial airliner is far riskier than driving a car. The media's tendency to sensationalize airplane crashes contributes to this perception. In actuality, the safety record for flying is far better than that for driving. Thus, this example demonstrates that a particularly *vivid* event will systematically influence the probability assigned to that type of event by an individual in the future. This bias occurs because vivid events are more easily remembered and consequently are more available when making judgments.

Consider another example. A buyer of women's wear for a leading department store is assessing her purchasing needs in footwear. To fill the demand for casual shoes, she needs to choose between a proven best-selling brand of running shoes and a newer line of boating shoes. The buyer recalls having seen a number of friends wearing boating shoes at a recent party and concludes that demand for boating shoes is increasing. She decides to order more boating shoes and reduce her order of the historically popular running shoes.

In making this choice, the buyer has biased her ordering decision based upon limited data and the ease with which it came to mind. The buyer judged the demand for boating shoes by the availability of her recollection of a recent party. Under the influence of this bias, she will be consistently less likely to buy popular shoes worn by other groups with whom she tends not to socialize—even though aggregate demand for these alternative styles may be higher.

Tversky and Kahneman (1974) argue that when an individual judges the frequency of an event by the *availability* of its instances, an event whose instances are more easily recalled will appear more numerous than an event of equal frequency whose instances are less easily recalled. They cite evidence of this bias in a lab study in which individuals were read lists of names of well-known personalities of both sexes and asked to determine whether the lists contained the names of more men or women. Different lists were presented to two groups. One group received lists bearing the names of women who were relatively more famous than the listed men, but included more men's names overall. The other group received lists received lists bearing the names of men who were relatively more famous than the listed women, but included more women's names overall. In each case, the subjects incorrectly guessed that the sex that had the more famous personalities was the more numerous.

Many examples of this bias can be observed in the decisions made by managers in the workplace. The following came from the experience of one of my MBA students: As a purchasing agent, he had to select one of several possible suppliers. He chose the firm whose name was the most familiar to him. He later found out that the salience of the name resulted from recent adverse publicity concerning the firm's extortion of funds from client companies!

Managers conducting performance appraisals often fall victim to the availability heuristic. Working from memory, the vivid instances relating to an employee that are more easily recalled from memory (either pro or con) will appear more numerous and will therefore be weighted more heavily in the performance appraisal. Managers also give more weight to performance during the three months prior to the evaluation than to the previous nine months of the evaluation period.

Many consumers are annoyed by repeated exposure to the same advertising message and often wonder why the advertiser doesn't give more useful information, without repeating it so many times. After all, we are smart enough to understand it the first time! Unfortunately, both the frequency and the vividness of the message have been shown to affect our purchasing. This bombardment of repeated, uninformative messages makes the product more easily recalled from memory and is often the best way to get us to buy a product (Alba & Marmorstein, 1987).

Because of our susceptibility to vividness and recency, Kahneman and Tversky suggest that we are particularly prone to overestimating unlikely events. For instance, if we actually witness a burning house, the impact on our assessment of the probability of such accidents is probably greater than the impact of reading about a fire in the local newspaper. The direct observation of such an event makes it more salient to us. Similarly, Slovic and Fischhoff (1977) discuss the implications of the misuse of the availability heuristic on the perceived risks of nuclear power. They point out that any discussion of the potential hazards, regardless of likelihood, will increase the memorability of those hazards and increase their perceived risks.

The stock market provides some telling examples of the tendency to overreact to vivid and recent information in this way. After the April 1986 nuclear accident at Chernobyl in the Soviet Union, U.S. investors sold their nuclear stocks, which caused a dramatic fall in prices. Yet the real safety of the nuclear systems did not change dramatically as a result of the Chernobyl accident. Similarly, the stock of Union Carbide fell 30 percent within three weeks of the December 1984 tragedy at its chemical plant in Bhopal, India. Few investors stopped to realize that Union Carbide might reach an acceptable out-of-court settlement. It was more salient to imagine Union Carbide being hit with a devastating financial penalty. More rational investors who bought the stock at its low point turned a hefty profit—even before the stock moved up higher on an unsuccessful takeover bid (Curran, 1987).

## Bias 2—Retrievability (Based Upon Memory Structures)

**Problem 4:** Are there more words in the English language
a. that start with an *r*?
b. for which *r* is the third letter?

If you responded "start with an *r*," you have joined the majority. Unfortunately, this is again the incorrect answer. Kahneman and Tversky (1973) explain that people typically solve this problem by first recalling words that begin with *r* (like *ran*) and words that have an *r* as the third letter (like *bar*). The relative difficulty of generating words in each of these two categories is then assessed. If we think of our mind as being organized like a dictionary, it is easier to find lots of words that start with an *r*. The dictionary, and our minds, are less efficient at finding words that follow a rule that is inconsistent with the organizing structure—like words that have an *r* as the third letter. Thus, words that start with a particular letter are more available from memory, even though most consonants are more common in the third position than in the first.

Just as our tendency to alphabetize affects our vocabulary-search behavior, organizational modes affect information-search behavior within our work lives. We structure organizations to provide order, but this same structure can lead to confusion if the presumed order is not exactly as suggested. For example, many organizations have a management information systems (MIS) division that has generalized expertise in computer applications. Assume that you are a manager in a product division and need computer expertise. If that expertise exists within MIS, the organizational hierarchy will lead you to the correct resource. If they lack the expertise in a specific application, but it exists elsewhere in the organization, the hierarchy is likely to bias the effectiveness of your search. I am not arguing for the overthrow of organizational hierarchies; I am merely identifying the dysfunctional role of hierarchies in potentially biasing search behavior. If we are aware of the potential bias, we need not be affected by this limitation.

Retail store location is influenced by the way in which consumers search their minds when seeking a particular commodity. Why are multiple gas stations at the same intersection? Why do "upscale" retailers want to be in the same mall? Why are the best bookstores in a city often all located within a couple blocks of each other? An important reason for this pattern is that consumers learn the "location" for a particular type of product or store and organize their minds accordingly. To maximize traffic, the retailer needs to be in the location that consumers associate with this type of product or store.

## Bias 3—Presumed Associations

People frequently fall victim to the availability bias in their assessment of the likelihood of two events occurring together. For example, consider the following questions: Is marijuana use related to delinquency? Are couples who get married under the age of 25 more likely to have bigger families? How would you respond if asked these questions? In assessing the marijuana question, most people typically remember several delinquent marijuana users and assume a correlation or not based upon the availability of this mental data. However, proper analysis would include recalling four groups of observations: marijuana users who are delinquents, marijuana users who are not delinquents, delinquents who do not use marijuana, and nondelinquents who do not use marijuana. The same analysis applies to the marriage question. Proper analysis would include four groups: couples who married young and have large families, couples who married young and have small families, couples who married older and have large families, and couples who married older and have small families. Indeed, there are always at least four separate situations to be considered in assessing the association between two dichotomous events, but our everyday decision making commonly ignores this scientifically valid fact.

Chapman and Chapman (1967) have noted that when we have the probability of two instances in our minds, we usually assign an inappropriately high probability that the two events will co-occur again. Thus, if we know a lot of marijuana users who are delinquents, we assume that marijuana use is related to delinquency. Similarly, if we know of a lot of couples who married young and have had large families, we assume that this trend is more prevalent than it may actually be. In testing for this bias, Chapman and Chapman provided subjects with information about hypothetical psychiatric patients. The information included a written clinical diagnosis of the "patient" and a drawing of a person made by the "patient." The subjects were asked to estimate the frequency with which each diagnosis (for example, suspiciousness or paranoia) was accompanied by various facial and body features in the drawings (for example, peculiar eyes). Throughout the study, subjects markedly overestimated the frequency of pairs commonly associated together by social lore. For example, diagnoses of suspiciousness were overwhelmingly associated with peculiar eyes. In addition, Chapman and Chapman found that conclusions, such as those just noted, were extremely resistant to change, even in the face of contradictory information. Furthermore, the overwhelming impact of this bias toward presumed associations prevented the subjects from detecting other relationships that were, in fact, present.

*Summary*. A lifetime of experience has led us to believe that, in general, more frequent events are recalled in our minds more easily than less frequent ones, and likely events are easier to recall than unlikely events. In response to this learning, we have developed the availability heuristic for estimating the likelihood of events. In many instances, this simplifying heuristic leads to accurate, efficient judgments. However, as these first three biases (ease or recall, retrievability, and presumed associations) indicate, the misuse of the availability heuristic can lead to systematic errors in managerial judgment. We too easily assume that our available recollections are truly representative of some larger pool of occurrences that exist outside our range of experience.

## BIASES EMANATING FROM THE REPRESENTATIVENESS HEURISTIC

### Bias 4—Insensitivity to Base Rates

> **Problem 5:** Mark is finishing his MBA at a prestigious university. He is very interested in the arts and at one time considered a career as a musician. Is Mark more likely to take a job
> a. in the management of the arts?
> b. with a management consulting firm?

How did you decide on your answer? How do most people make this assessment? How *should* people make this assessment? Using the representativeness heuristic... most people approach this problem by analyzing the degree to which Mark is representative of their image of individuals who take jobs in each of the two areas. Consequently, they usually conclude "in the management of the arts." However, as we discussed in the first part of this chapter, this response overlooks relevant base-rate information. Reconsider the problem in light of the fact that a much larger number of MBAs take jobs in management consulting than in the management of the arts—relevant information that should enter into any reasonable prediction of Mark's career path. With this base-rate data, it is only reasonable to predict "management consulting."

Judgmental biases of this type frequently occur when individuals cognitively ask the wrong question. If you answered "in the management of the arts," you were probably thinking in terms of the question "How likely is it that a person working in the management of the arts would fit Mark's description?" However, the problem necessitates the question "How likely is it that someone fitting Mark's description will choose arts management?" By itself, the representativeness heuristic incorrectly leads to a similar answer to both questions, since this heuristic leads individuals to compare the resemblance of the personal description and the career path. However, when base-rate data is considered, it is irrelevant to the first question listed, but it is crucial to a reasonable prediction on the second question. While a large percentage of individuals in arts management may fit Mark's description, there are undoubtedly a larger absolute number of management consultants fitting Mark's description because of the relative preponderance of MBAs in management consulting.

An interesting finding of the research done by Kahneman and Tversky (1972, 1973) is that subjects do use base-rate data correctly when no other information is provided. For example, in the absence of a personal description of Mark in problem 5, people will choose "management consulting" based on the past frequency of this career path for MBAs. Thus, people understand the relevance of base-rate information, but tend to disregard this data when descriptive data is also available.

### Bias 5—Insensitivity to Sample Size

> **Problem 6:** In 1986, two research groups sampled consumers on the driving performance of the Dodge Colt versus the Plymouth Champ in a blind road test; that is, the consumers did not know when they were driving the Colt or the Champ. As you may know, these cars were identical; only the marketing varied.
> One research group (A) sampled 66 consumers each day for 60 days (a large number of days to control for weather and other variables), while the other research group (B) sampled 22 consumers each day for 50 days. Which consumer group observed more days in which 60 percent or more of the consumers tested preferred the Dodge Colt:
> a. group A?
> b. group B?

Most individuals expect research group A to provide more 60-percent days for the Dodge Colt, because of the larger number of sample days—in other words, there are 60 chances compared to 50. In contrast, simple statistics tells us that it is much more likely to observe more 60-percent days on daily samples of 22 than on daily samples of 66, and the correct answer is group B. This is because a large sample is far less likely to stray from the expected 50-percent preference split between the Dodge Colt and Plymouth Champ—since the cars are identical. (The interested reader can verify this fact with the use of an introductory statistics book.)

While the importance of sample size is fundamental in statistics, Kahneman and Tversky (1974) note that it "is evidently not part of people's repertoire of intuitions" (p. 1126). Why is this? When responding to problems dealing with sampling, people often use the representativeness heuristic. In their minds, they ask the question, Which group is likely to have more days in which the results are skewed to 60 percent for the Dodge Colt instead of the expected 50 percent? From there, the representative heuristic leads them to focus on the number of days as the pertinent variable for comparison. They then conclude that the group covering the greater number of total days will experience the greater number of total deviations. However, this analogy ignores the issue of sample size—which is critical to an accurate assessment of the problem.

Tversky and Kahneman (1974) first discovered this bias toward ignoring the role of sample size, even when these data were emphasized in the formation of the problem, in testing the following research problem:

*A certain town is served by two hospitals. In the larger hospital about 45 babies are born each day, and in the smaller hospital about 15 babies are born each day. As you know, about 50 percent of all babies are boys. However, the exact percentage varies from day to day. Sometimes it may be higher than 50 percent, sometimes lower.*

*For a period of one year, each hospital recorded the days on which more than 60 percent of the babies born were boys. Which hospital do you think recorded more such days?*

*The larger hospital? (21)*
*The smaller hospital? (21)*

*About the same? (53)*
*(that is, within 5 percent of each other)*

The values in parentheses represent the number of individuals who chose each answer. As explained earlier, sampling theory tells us that the expected number of days on which more than 60 percent of the babies are boys is much greater in the small hospital, since a large sample is less likely to stray from the mean. However, most subjects judged the probability to be the same in each hospital, effectively ignoring sample size.

Consider the implications of this bias in advertising, where people trained in market research understand the need for a sizable sample, but employ this bias to the advantage of their clients. "Four out of five dentists surveyed recommend sugarless gum for their patients who chew gum." There is no mention of the number of dentists involved in the survey and the fact that without these data, the results of the survey are meaningless. If only 5 or 15 dentists were surveyed, the size of the sample would not be generalizable to the overall population of dentists.

## Bias 6—Misconceptions of Chance

**Problem 7:** You are about to hire a new central-region sales director for the fifth time this year. You predict that the next director should work out reasonably well, since the last four were "lemons," and the odds favor hiring at least one good sales director in five tries. This thinking is
a. correct.
b. incorrect.

Most people are comfortable with the foregoing logic, or at least have been guilty of using similar logic in the past. However, the performance of the first four sales directors will not directly affect the performance of the fifth sales director, and the logic in problem 7 is incorrect. Most individuals frequently rely upon their intuition and the representativeness heuristic and incorrectly conclude that a poor performance is unlikely because the probability of getting five "lemons" in a row is extremely low. Unfortunately, this logic ignores the fact that we have already witnessed four "lemons" (an unlikely occurrence), and the performance of the fifth sales director is independent of that of the first four.

This question parallels Kahneman and Tversky's (1972) work in which they show that people expect that a sequence of random events will "look" random. They present evidence of this bias in their finding that subjects routinely judged the sequence of coin flips H-T-H-T-T-H to be more likely than H-H-H-T-T-T, which does not "appear" random, and more likely than the sequence H-H-H-H-T-H, which does not represent the equal likelihood of heads and tails. Simple statistics, of course, tell us that each of these sequences is equally likely because of the independence of multiple random events.

Problem 7 moves beyond dealing with random events in recognizing our inappropriate tendency to assume that random *and* nonrandom events will "balance out." Will the fifth sales director work out well? Maybe. You might spend more time and money on selection, and the randomness of the hiring process may favor you this time. But your earlier failures in hiring sales directors will not directly affect the performance of the new sales director.

The logic concerning misconceptions of chance provides a process explanation of the gambler's fallacy. After holding bad cards on ten hands of poker, the poker player believes that he is due for a good hand. After winning $1,000 in the Pennsylvania State Lottery, a woman changes her regular number—because after all, how likely is it that the same number will come up twice? Tversky and Kahneman (1974) note that "Chance is commonly viewed as a self-correcting process in which a deviation in one direction induces a deviation in the opposite direction to restore the equilibrium. In fact, deviations are not corrected as a chance process unfolds, they are merely diluted."

In each of the preceding examples, individuals expected probabilities to even out. In some situations, our minds misconceptualize chance in exactly the opposite way. In sports (basketball specifically), we often think of a particular player as having a "hot hand" or "being on a good streak." If your favorite player has hit his last four shots, is the probability of his making his next shot higher, lower, or the same as the probability of his making a shot without the preceding four hits? Most sports fans, sports commentators, and players believe that the answer is "higher." In fact, there are many biological, emotional, and physical reasons that this answer could be correct. However, it is wrong! Gilovich, Vallone, and Tversky (1985) did an extensive analysis of the shooting of Philadelphia 76ers and Boston Celtics and found that immediately prior shot performance did not change the likelihood of success on the upcoming shot. Out of all of the findings in this book, this is the effect that my managerial students have had the hardest time believing. The reason is that we can all remember sequences of five hits in a row: streaks are part of our conception of chance in athletic competition. However, our minds do not categorize a string of "four in a row" as being a situation in which "he missed his fifth shot." As a result, we have a misconception of connectedness, when, in fact, chance (or the player's normal probability of success) is really in effect.

The belief in the hot hand is especially interesting because of its implication for how players play the game. Passing the ball to the player who is "hot" is commonly endorsed as a good strategy. It can also be expected that the opposing team will concentrate on guarding the hot player. Another player, who is less "hot" but is equally skilled, may have a better chance of scoring. Thus the belief in the "hot hand" is not just erroneous, but could also be costly if you play professional basketball.

Tversky and Kahneman's (1971) work shows that misconceptions of chance are not limited to gamblers, sportsfans, or laypersons. Research psychologists also fall victim to the "law of small numbers." They believe that sample events should be far more representative of the population from which they were drawn than simple statistics would dictate. The researchers put too much faith in the results of initial samples and grossly overestimate the replicability of empirical findings. This suggests that the representativeness heuristic may be so well institutionalized in our decision processes that even scientific training and its emphasis on the proper use of statistics may not effectively eliminate its biasing influence.

## Bias 7—Regression to the Mean

**Problem 8:** You are the sales forecaster for a department store chain with nine locations. The chain depends on you for quality projections of future sales in order to make decisions on staffing, advertising, information system developments, purchasing, renovation, and the like. All stores are similar in size and merchandise selection. The main difference in their sales occurs because of location and random fluctuations. Sales for 1989 were as follows:

| Store | 1989 | 1991 |
|---|---|---|
| 1 | $ 12,000,000 | $_____ |
| 2 | 11,500,000 | _____ |
| 3 | 11,000,000 | _____ |
| 4 | 10,500,000 | _____ |
| 5 | 10,000,000 | _____ |
| 6 | 9,500,000 | _____ |
| 7 | 9,000,000 | _____ |
| 8 | 8,500,000 | _____ |
| 9 | 8,000,000 | _____ |
| TOTAL | $ 90,000,000 | $ 99,000,000 |

Your economic forecasting service has convinced you that the best estimate of total sales increases between 1989 and 1991 is 10 percent (to $99,000,000). Your task is to predict 1991 sales for each store. Since your manager believes strongly in the economic forecasting service, it is imperative that your total sales are equal to $99,000,000.

Think about the processes used to answer this problem. Consider the following logical pattern of thought: "The overall increase in sales

is predicted to be 10 percent ($99,000,000 − $90,000,000/$90,000,000). Lacking any other specific information on the stores, it makes sense to simply add 10 percent to each 1989 sales figure to predict 1991 sales. This means that I predict sales of $13,2000,000 for store 1, sales of $12,650,000 for store 2, and so on." This logic, in fact, is the most common approach in responding to this item. Unfortunately, this logic is faulty.

Why was the logic presented faulty? Statistical analysis would dictate that we first assess the predicted relationship between 1989 and 1991 sales. This relationship, formally known as a **correlation**, can vary from total independence (that is, 1989 sales do not predict 1991 sales) to perfect correlation (1989 sales are a perfect predictor of 1991 sales). In the former case, the lack of a relationship between 1989 and 1991 sales would mean that 1989 sales would provide absolutely no information about 1991 sales, and your best estimates of 1991 sales would be equal to total sales divided by the number of stores ($99,000,000 divided by 9 equals $11,000,000). However, in the latter case of perfect predictability between 1989 and 1991 sales, our initial logic of simply extrapolating from 1989 performance by adding 10 percent to each store's performance would be completely accurate. Obviously, 1989 sales are most likely to be *partially predictive* of 1991 sales—falling somewhere between independence and perfect correlation. Thus, the best prediction for store 1 should lie between $11,000,000 and $13,200,000 depending upon how predictive you think 1989 sales will be of 1991 sales. The key point is that in virtually all such predictions, you should expect the naive $13,200,000 estimate to regress toward the overall mean($11,000,000).

In a study of sales forecasting, Cox and Summers (1987) examined the judgments of professional retail buyers. They examined the sales data from 2 department stores for 6 different apparel styles for a total of 12 different sales forecasts over a 2-week period. They found that sales between the 2 weeks regressed to the mean. However, the judgment of all 31 buyers from 5 different department stores failed to reflect the tendency for regression to the mean. As a result, Cox and Summers argued that a sales-forecasting model that considered regression to the mean could outperform the judgments of all 31 professional buyers.

Many effects regress to the mean. Brilliant students frequently have less successful siblings. Short parents tend to have taller children. Great rookies have mediocre second years (the "sophomore jinx"). Firms that have outstanding profits one year tend to have lesser performances the next year. In each case, individuals are often surprised when made aware of these predictable patterns of regression to the mean.

Why is the regression-to-the mean concept, while statistically valid, counterintuitive? Kahneman and Tversky (1973) suggest that the representativeness heuristic accounts for this systematic bias in judgment. They argue that individuals typically assume that future outcomes (for example, 1991 sales) will be maximally representative of past outcomes (1989 sales). Thus, we tend to naively develop predictions that are based upon the assumption of perfect correlation with past data.

In some unusual situations, individuals do intuitively expect a regression-to-the-mean effect. In 1980, when George Brett batted .384, most people did not expect him to hit .384 the following year. When Wilt Chamberlain scored 100 points in a single game, most people did not expect him to score 100 points in his next game. When a historically 3.0 student got a 4.0 one semester, her friends did not expect a repeat performance the following semester. When a real estate agent sold five houses in one month (an abnormally high performance), his co-agents did not expect similar performance in the following month. Why is regression to the mean more intuitive in these cases? Because the performance is so extreme that we know it cannot last. Thus, under very unusual circumstances, we expect performance to regress. However, we generally do not recognize the regression effect in less extreme cases.

Consider Kahneman and Tversky's (1973) classic example in which the misconceptions surrounding regression led to overestimation of the effectiveness of punishment and the underestima-tion of the power of reward. Here, in a discussion about flight training, experienced instructors noted that praise for an exceptionally smooth landing was typically followed by a poorer landing on the next try, while harsh criticism after a rough landing was usually followed by an improvement on the next try. The instructors concluded that verbal rewards were detrimental to learning, while verbal punishments were beneficial. Obviously, the tendency of performance to regress to the mean can account for the results; verbal feedback may have had absolutely no effect. However, to the extent that the instructors were prone to biased decision making, they were prone to reach the false conclusion that punishment is more effective than positive reinforcement in shaping behavior.

How do managers respond when they do not acknowledge the regression principle? Consider an employee with very high performance in one performance period. He (and his boss) may inappropriately expect similar performance in the next period. What happens when his performance regresses toward the mean? He (and his boss) begin to make excuses for not meeting expectations. Obviously, they are likely to develop false explanations and may inappropriately plan their future efforts.

## Bias 8—The Conjunction Fallacy

**Problem 9:** Linda is 31 years old, single, outspoken, and very bright. She majored in philosophy. As a student, she was deeply concerned with issues of discrimination and social justice, and she participated in antinuclear demonstrations.

Rank order the following eight descriptions in terms of the probability (likelihood) that they describe Linda:

—**a.** Linda is a teacher in an elementary school.

—**b.** Linda works in a bookstore and takes yoga classes.

—**c.** Linda is active in the feminist movement.

—**d.** Linda is a psychiatric social worker.

—**e.** Linda is a member of the League of Women Voters.
—**f.** Linda is a bank teller.
—**g.** Linda is an insurance salesperson.
—**h.** Linda is a bank teller who is active in the feminist movement.

Examine your rank orderings of descriptions C, F, and H. Most people rank order C as more likely than H and H as more likely than F. The reason for this ordering is that C-H-F is the order of the degree to which the descriptions are *representative* of the short profile of Linda. The description of Linda was constructed by Tversky and Kahneman to be representative of an active feminist and unrepresentative of a bank teller. Recall from the representativeness heuristic that people make judgments according to the degree to which a specific description corresponds to a broader category within their minds. Linda's description is more representative of a feminist than of a feminist bank teller, and is more representative of a feminist bank teller than of a bank teller. Thus, the representativeness heuristic accurately predicts that most individuals will rank order the items C-H-F.

Although the representativeness heuristic accurately predicts how individuals will respond, it also leads to another common, systematic distortion of human judgment—the **conjunction fallacy** (Tversky & Kahneman, 1983). This is illustrated by a reexamination of the potential descriptions of Linda. One of the simplest and most fundamental qualitative laws of probability is that a subset (for example, being a bank teller and a feminist) cannot be more likely than a larger set that completely includes the subset (e.g., being a bank teller). Statistically speaking, the broad set "Linda is a bank teller" must be rated at least as likely, if not more so, than the description "Linda is a bank teller and a feminist." After all, there is some chance (although it is small) that Linda is a bank teller but not a feminist. Based upon this logic, a rational assessment of the likelihoods of Linda being depicted by the eight descriptions must include a more likely rank for F than H.

While simple statistics can demonstrate that a conjunction (a combination of two or more descriptors) cannot be more probable than any one of its descriptors, the conjunction fallacy predicts and demonstrates that a conjunction will be judged more probable than a single component descriptor when the conjunction appears more representative than the component descriptor. Intuitively, thinking of Linda as a feminist bank teller "feels" more correct than thinking of her as only a bank teller.

The conjunction fallacy can also operate based on greater *availability* of the conjunction than one of the unique descriptors (Yates & Carlson, 1986). That is, if the conjunction creates more intuitive matches with vivid events, acts, or people than a component of the conjunction, the conjunction is likely to be perceived falsely as more probable than the component. For example, Tversky and Kahneman (1983) found experts (in July 1982) to evaluate the probability of

*a complete suspension of diplomatic relations between the USA and the Soviet Union, sometime in 1983*

as less likely than the probability of

*a Russian invasion of Poland, and a complete suspension of diplomatic relations between the USA and the Soviet Union, some time in 1983.*

As earlier demonstrated, suspension is necessarily more likely than *invasion and suspension*. However, a Russian invasion followed by a diplomatic crisis provides a more intuitively viable story than simply a diplomatic crisis. Similarly, in the domain of natural disasters, Kahneman and Tversky's subjects rated

*a massive flood somewhere in North America in 1989, in which 1,000 people drown*

as less likely than the probability of

*an earthquake in California sometime in 1989, causing a flood in which more than 1,000 people drown.*

It is obvious that the latter possibility is a subset of the former, and many other events could cause the flood in North America.

Tversky and Kahneman (1983) have shown that the conjunction fallacy is likely to lead to deviations from rationality in the judgments of sporting events, criminal behavior, international relations, and medical judgments. Our obvious concern with biased decision making resulting from the conjunction fallacy is that if we make systematic deviations from rationality in the prediction of future outcomes, we will be less prepared for dealing with future events.

*Summary.* This discussion concludes our examination of the five biases (insensitivity to base rates, insensitivity to sample size, misconceptions of chance, regression to the mean, and the conjunction fallacy) that emanate from the use of the representativeness heuristic. Experience has taught us that the likelihood of a specific occurrence *is* related to the likelihood of a group of occurrences that that specific occurrence represents. Unfortunately, we tend to overuse this information in making decisions. The five biases we have just explored illustrate the systematic irrationalities that can occur in our judgments when we are not aware of this overreliance.

## BIASES EMANATING
## FROM ANCHORING AND ADJUSTMENT

### Bias 9—Insufficient Anchor Adjustment

> Problem 10: A newly hired engineer for a computer firm in the Boston metropolitan area has four years of experience and good all-around qualifications. When asked to estimate the starting salary for this employee, my secretary (knowing very little about the profession or the industry) guessed an annual salary of $23,000. What is your estimate?
>
> $_____ per year.

Was your answer affected by my secretary's response? Most people do not think that my secretary's response affected their response. However, individuals *are* affected by the fairly irrelevant information contained in my secretary's estimate. Reconsider how you would have responded if my secretary had estimated $80,000. On

average, individuals give higher salary estimates to the problem when the secretary's estimate is stated as $80,000 than when it is stated as $23,000. Why? Studies have found that people develop estimates by starting from an initial anchor, based upon whatever information is provided, and adjusting from there to yield a final answer. Slovic and Lichtenstein (1971) have provided conclusive evidence that adjustments away from anchors are usually not sufficient to negate the effects of the anchor. In all cases, answers are biased toward the initial anchor, even if it is irrelevant. Different starting points yield different answers. Tversky and Kahneman (1973) named this phenomenon **anchoring and adjustment**.

Tversky and Kahneman (1974) provide systematic, empirical evidence of the anchoring effect. For example, in one study, subjects were asked to estimate the percentage of African countries in the United Nations. For each subject, a *random* number (obtained by an observed spin of a roulette wheel) was given as a starting point. From there, subjects were asked to state whether the actual value of the quantity was higher or lower than this random value and then develop their best estimate for the actual quantity. It was found that the *arbitrary* values from the roulette wheel had a substantial impact on estimates. For example, for groups that received 10 countries and 65 countries as starting points, the median estimates were 25 and 45, respectively. Thus, even though the subjects were aware that the anchor was random and unrelated to the judgment task, the anchor had a dramatic effect on their judgment. Interestingly, paying subjects differentially based upon accuracy did not reduce the magnitude of the anchoring effect.

Salary negotiations represent a very common context for observing anchoring in the managerial world. For example, pay increases often come in the form of a percentage increase. A firm may have an average increase of 8 percent, with increases for specific employees varying from 3 percent to 13 percent. While society has led us to accept such systems as equitable, I believe that such a system falls victim to anchoring and leads to substantial inequities. What happens if an employee has been *substantially* underpaid to begin with? The pay system described does not rectify past inequities, since a pay increase of 11 percent will probably leave that employee still underpaid. Conversely, the system would work in the employee's favor had she been overpaid. It is common for an employer to ask job applicants their current salaries. Why? Employers are searching for a value from which they can anchor an adjustment. If the employee is worth far more than his current salary, the anchoring and adjustment hypothesis predicts that the firm will make an offer below the employee's true value. Does this figure provide fully accurate information about the true worth of the employee? I think not. Thus, the use of such compensation systems accepts past inequities as an anchor and makes inadequate adjustments from that point. Further, these findings suggest that in deciding what offer to make to a potential employee, any anchor that creeps into the discussion is likely to have an inappropriate effect on the eventual offer, even if the anchor is "ignored" as being ridiculous.

There are numerous examples of the anchoring-and-adjustment phenomenon in everyday life.

- In education, children are tracked by a school system that may categorize them into a certain level of performance at an early age. For example, a child who is anchored in the *C* group may meet expectations of mediocre performance. Conversely, a child of similar abilities anchored in the *A* track may strive to meet expectations, which will keep him in the *A* track.

- We have all fallen victim to the first-impression syndrome when meeting someone for the first time. We often place so much emphasis on first impressions that we do not adjust our opinion appropriately at a later date.

- Prior to 1973–1974, the speed limit on most interstate highways was 65 miles per hour (mph), with a normal cruising speed in the left-hand lane of 70 to 75 mph. This did not seem to be an extraordinarily unsafe speed to most people. After 1974, the speed limit was reduced to 55 mph. Most people changed their judgments to view a speed of 70 to 75 mph as

extremely unsafe—"something only crazy kids would do." Today, the reinstitution of the 65 mph limit on nonurban highways has rejustified the safety of the 70 to 75 mph speed.

In a fascinating study of anchoring and adjustment in the real estate market, Northcraft and Neale (1987) surveyed an association of real estate brokers, who indicated that they believed that they could assess the value of properties to within 5 percent of their true or appraised value. Further, they were unanimous in stating that they did not factor the listing price of the property into their personal estimate of its "true" value. Northcraft and Neale then asked four groups of professional real estate brokers and undergraduate students to estimate the value of a real house. Both brokers and students were randomly assigned to one of four experimental groups. In each group, all participants were given a 10-page packet of information about the house that was being sold. The packet included not only background on the house, but also considerable information about prices and characteristics of other houses in the area that had recently been sold. The only difference in the information given to the four groups was the listing price for the house, which was selected to be +11 percent, +4 percent, −4 percent, and −11 percent of the actual appraised value of the property. After reading the material, all participants toured the house, as well as the surrounding neighborhood. Participants were then asked for their estimate of the house's price. The final results suggested that *both* brokers and students were *significantly* affected by the listing price (the anchor) in determining the value. While the students readily admitted the role that the listing price played in their decision-making process, the brokers flatly denied their use of the listing price as an anchor for their evaluations of the property—despite the evidence to the contrary. This study provides convincing data to indicate that even experts are susceptible to the anchoring bias. Furthermore, experts are less likely to realize their use of this bias in making decisions.

Joyce and Biddle (1981) have also provided empirical support for the anchoring-and-adjustment effect on practicing auditors of Big Eight accounting firms. Specifically, subjects in one condition were asked the following:

*It is well known that many cases of management fraud go undetected even when competent annual audits are performed. The reason, of course, is that Generally Accepted Auditing Standards are not designed specifically to detect executive-level management fraud. We are interested in obtaining an estimate from practicing auditors of the prevalence of executive-level management fraud as a first step in ascertaining the scope of the problem.*

1. Based on your audit experience, is the incidence of significant executive-level management fraud more than 10 in each 1,000 firms (that is, 1 percent) audited by Big Eight accounting firms?

   **a.** Yes, more than 10 in each 1,000 Big Eight clients have significant executive-level management fraud.

   **b.** No, fewer than 10 in each 1,000 Big Eight clients have significant executive-level management fraud.

2. What is your estimate of the number Big Eight clients per 1,000 that have significant executive-level management fraud? (Fill in the blank below with the appropriate number.)
   _____ in each 1,000 Big Eight clients have significant executive-level management fraud.

The second condition differed only in that subjects were asked whether the fraud incidence was more or less than 200 in each 1,000 audited, rather than 10 in 1,000. Subjects in the former condition estimated a fraud incidence of 16.52 per 1,000 on average, compared with an estimated fraud incidence of 43.11 per 1,000 in the second condition! Here, even professional auditors fell victim to anchoring and adjustment.

The tendency to make insufficient adjustments is a direct result of the anchoring-and-adjustment heuristic.... Interestingly, Nisbett and Ross (1980) present an argument that suggests that the anchoring-and-adjustment bias itself dictates that it will be very difficult to get *you* to

change your decision-making strategies as a result of reading this book. They argue that each of the heuristics that we identify are currently serving as your cognitive anchors and are central to your current judgment processes. Thus, any cognitive strategy that I suggest must be presented and understood in a manner that will force you to break your existing cognitive anchors. Based on the evidence in this section, this should be a difficult challenge—but one that is important enough to be worth the effort!

## Bias 10—Conjunctive and Disjunctive Events Bias

**Problem 11:** Which of the following appears most likely? Which appears second most likely?
**a.** Drawing a red marble from a bag containing 50 percent red marbles and 50 percent white marbles.
**b.** Drawing a red marble seven times in succession, with replacement (a selected marble is put back in the bag before the next marble is selected), from a bag containing 90 percent red marbles and 10 percent white marbles.
**c.** Drawing at least one red marble in seven tries, with replacement, from a bag containing 10 percent red marbles and 90 percent white marbles.

The most common answer in ordering the preferences is B-A-C. Interestingly, the correct order of likelihood is C (52 percent), A (50 percent), B (48 percent)—the exact opposite of the most common intuitive pattern! This result illustrates a general bias to overestimate the probability of conjunctive events—events that must occur in conjunction with one another (Bar-Hillel, 1973)—and to underestimate the probability of disjunctive events—events that occur independently (Tversky & Kahneman, 1974). Thus, when multiple events all need to occur (problem B), we overestimate the true likelihood, while if only one of many events needs to occur (problem C), we underestimate the true likelihood.

Kahneman and Tversky (1974) explain these effects in terms of the anchoring-and-adjustment heuristic. They argue that the probability of any one event occurring (for example, drawing one red marble) provides a natural anchor for the judgment of the total probability. Since adjustment from an anchor is typically insufficient, the perceived likelihood of choice B stays inappropriately close to 90 percent, while the perceived probability of choice C stays inappropriately close to 10 percent.

How is each of these biases manifested in an applied context? The overestimation of conjunctive events is a powerful explanation of the timing problems in projects that require multistage planning. Individuals, businesses, and governments frequently fall victim to the conjunction-events bias in terms of timing and budgets. Public works projects seldom finish on time or on budget. New product ventures frequently take longer than expected.

Consider the following:

■ You are planning a construction project that consists of five distinct components. Your schedule is tight, and every component must be on time in order to meet a contractual deadline. Will you meet this deadline?

■ You are managing a consulting project that consists of six teams, each of which is analyzing a different alternative. The alternatives cannot be compared until all teams complete their portion. Will you meet the deadline?

■ After three years of study, doctoral students typically dramatically overestimate the likelihood of completing their dissertations within a year. At this stage, they typically can tell you how long each remaining component will take. Why do they not finish in one year?

The underestimation of disjunctive events explains our surprise when an unlikely event occurs. As Tversky and Kahneman (1974) argue, "A complex system, such as a nuclear reactor or the human body, will malfunction if any of its essential components fails. Even when the likelihood of failure in each component is slight, the probabil-

ity of an overall failure can be high if many components are involved." In *Normal Accidents*, Perrow (1984) argues against the safety of technologies like nuclear reactors and DNA research. He fears that society significantly underestimates the likelihood of system failure because of our judgmental failure to realize the multitude of things that can go wrong in these incredibly complex and interactive systems.

The understanding of our underestimation of disjunctive events also has its positive side. Consider the following:

*It's Monday evening (10:00 P.M.). You get a phone call telling you that you must be at the Chicago office by 9:30 A.M. the next morning. You call all five airlines that have flights that get into Chicago by 9:00 A.M. Each has one flight, and all the flights are booked. When you ask the probability of getting on each of the flights if you show up at the airport in the morning, you are disappointed to hear probabilities of 30 percent, 25 percent, 15 percent, 20 percent, and 25 percent. Consequently, you do not expect to get to Chicago in time.*

In this case, the disjunctive bias leads you to expect the worst. In fact, if the probabilities given by the airlines are unbiased and independent there is a 73 percent chance of getting on one of the flights (assuming that you can arrange to be at the right ticket counter at the right time)!

## Bias 11—Overconfidence

**Problem 12:** Listed below are 10 uncertain quantities. Do not look up any information on these items. For each, write down your best estimate of the quantity. Next, put a lower and upper bound around your estimate, such that you are 98 percent confident that your range surrounds the actual quantity.

___a. Mobil Oil's sales in 1987
___b. IBM's assets in 1987
___c. Chrysler's profit in 1987
___d. The number of U.S. industrial firms in 1987 with sales greater than those of Consolidated Papers
___e. The U.S. gross national product in 1945

__f. The amount of taxes collected by the U.S. Internal Revenue Service in 1970

__g. The length (in feet) of the Chesapeake Bay Bridge-Tunnel

__h. The area (in square miles) of Brazil

__i. The size of the black population of San Francisco in 1970

__j. The dollar value of Canadian exports of lumber in 1977

How many of your 10 ranges will actually surround the true quantities? If you set your ranges so that you were 98 percent confident, you should expect to correctly bound approximately 9.8 or 9 to 10 of the 10 quantities. Let's look at the correct answers: (a) $51,223,000,000; (b) $63,688,000,000; (c) $1,289,700,000; (d) 381; (e) $212,300,000,000; (f) $195,722,096,497; (g) 93,203; (h) 3,286,470; (i) 96,078; (j)$2,386,282,000.

How many of your ranges actually surrounded the true quantities? If you surround 9–10, we can conclude that you were appropriately confident in your estimation ability. Most people only surround between 3 (30 percent) and 7 (70 percent), despite claiming a 98 percent confidence that each of the ranges will surround the true value. Why? Most of us are *overconfident* in our estimation abilities and do not acknowledge the actual uncertainty that exists.

In Alpert and Raiffa's (1969) initial demonstration of overconfidence based upon 1,000 observations (100 subjects on 10 items), 42.6 percent of quantities fell outside 90% confidence ranges. Since then, overconfidence has been identified as a common judgmental pattern and demonstrated in a wide variety of settings. For example, Fischhoff, Slovic, and Lichtenstein (1977) found that subjects who assigned odds of 1,000:1 of being correct were correct only 81 to 88 percent of the time. For odds of 1,000,000:1, their answers were correct only 90 to 96 percent of the time! Hazard and Peterson (1973) identified overconfidence among members of the armed forces, while Cambridge and Shreckengost (1980) found extreme overconfidence in CIA agents.

The most well-established finding in the overconfidence literature is the tendency of people to be most overconfident of the correctness of their answers when asked to respond to questions of moderate to extreme difficulty (Fischhoff, Slovic, & Lichtenstein, 1977; Koriat, Lichtenstein, & Fischhoff, 1980; Lichtenstein & Fischhoff, 1977, 1980). That is, as subjects' knowledge of a question decreases, they do not correspondingly decrease their level of confidence (Nickerson & McGoldrick, 1965; Pitz, 1974). However, subjects typically demonstrate no overconfidence, and often some underconfidence, to questions with which they are familiar. Thus we should be most alert to overconfidence in areas outside of our expertise.

There is a large degree of controversy over the explanations of why overconfidence exists (see Lichtenstein, Fischhoff, & Phillips [1982] for an extensive discussion). Tversky and Kahneman (1974) explain overconfidence in terms of anchoring. Specifically, they argue that when individuals are asked to set a confidence range around an answer, their initial estimate serves as an anchor which biases their estimation of confidence intervals in both directions. As explained earlier, adjustments from an anchor are usually insufficient, resulting in an overly narrow confidence band.

In their review of the overconfidence literature, Lichtenstein, Fischhoff, and Phillips (1982) suggest two viable strategies for eliminating overconfidence. First, they have found that giving people feedback about their overconfidence *based on their judgments* has been moderately successful at reducing this bias. Second, Koriat, Lichtenstein, and Fischhoff (1980) found that asking people to explain why their answers might be wrong (or far off the mark) can decrease overconfidence by getting subjects to see contradictions in their judgment.

Why should you be concerned about overconfidence? After all, it has probably given you the courage in the past to attempt endeavors that have stretched your abilities. However, consider the following:

■ You are a medical doctor and are considering performing a difficult operation. The patient's family needs to know the likelihood of his surviving the operation. You respond "95 percent." Are you guilty of malpractice if you tend to be overconfident in your projections of survival?

■ You work for the Nuclear Regulatory Commission and are 99.9 percent confident that a reactor will not leak. Can we trust your confidence? If not, can we run the enormous risks of overconfidence in this domain?

■ Your firm has been threatened with a multimillion dollar law suit. If you lose, your firm is out of business. You are 98 percent confident that the firm will not lose in court. Is this degree of certainty sufficient for you to recommend rejecting an out-of-court settlement? Based on what you know now, are you still comfortable with your 98 percent estimate?

■ You have developed a market plan for a new product. You are so confident in your plan that you have not developed any contingencies for early market failure. The plan of attack falls apart. Will your overconfidence wipe out any hope of expediting changes in the marketing strategy?

In each of these examples, we have introduced serious problems that can result from the tendency to be overconfident. Thus, while confidence in your abilities is necessary for achievement in life, and perhaps to inspire confidence in others, you may want to monitor your overconfidence to achieve more effective professional decision making.

*Summary.* The need for an initial anchor weighs strongly in our decision-making processes when we try to estimate likelihoods (such as the probability of on-time project completion) or establish values (like what salary to offer). Experience has taught us that starting from somewhere is easier than starting from nowhere in determining such figures. However, as the last three biases (insufficient anchor adjustment, conjunctive and disjunctive events bias, and overconfidence) show, we frequently overrely on these anchors and seldom question their validity or appropriateness in

a particular situation. As with the other heuristics, we frequently fail even to realize that this heuristic is impacting our judgments.

## TWO MORE GENERAL BIASES

### Bias 12—The Confirmation Trap

**Problem 13:** (Adapted from Einhorn and Hogarth, 1978)

It is claimed that when a particular analyst predicts a rise in the market, the market always rises. You are to check this claim. Examine the information available about the following four events (cards):

Card 1
Prediction:

Favorable report

Card 2
Prediction:

Unfavorable report

Card 3
Outcome:

Risk in the market

Card 4
Outcome:

Fall in the market

You currently see the predictions (cards 1 and 2) *or* outcomes (cards 3 and 4) associated with four events. You are seeing one side of a card. On the other side of cards 1 and 2 is the actual outcome, while on the other side of cards 3 and 4 is the prediction that the analyst made. Evidence about the claim is potentially available by turning over the card(s). Which cards would you turn over for the evidence that you need to check the analyst's claim? (Circle the appropriate cards.)

Consider the two most common responses: (1) "Card 1 (only)—that is the only card that I know has a favorable report and thus allows me to see whether a favorable report is actually followed by a rise in the market" and (2) "Cards 1 and 3—card 1 serves as a direct test, while card 3 allows me to see whether they made a favorable report when I know the market rose." Logical? Most people think that at least one of these two common responses is logical. However, both strategies demonstrate the tendency to search for confirming, rather than disconfirming, evidence. Einhorn and Hogarth (1978) argue that 1 and 4 is the correct answer to this quiz item. Why? Consider the following logic:

*Card 1 allows me to test the claim that a rise in the market will add confirming evidence, while a fall in the market will fully disconfirm the claim, since the claim is that the market will always rise following a favorable report. Card 2 has no relevant information, since the claim does not address unfavorable reports by the analyst. While card 3 can add confirming evidence to card 1, it provides no unique information, since it cannot disconfirm the claim. That is, if an unfavorable report was made on card 3, then the event is not addressed by the claim. Finally, card 4 is critical. If it says "favorable report" on the other side, the claim is disconfirmed.*

If you chose cards 1 and 3, you may have obtained a wealth of confirmatory information and were likely to inappropriately accept the claim. Only by including card 4 is there potential for disconfirmation of the hypothesis. Why do very few subjects select card 4? *Most of us seek confirmatory evidence and exclude the search for disconfirming information from our decision process.* However, it is typically not possible to know something to be true without checking for possible disconfirmation.

The initial demonstration of our tendency to ignore disconfirming information was provided in a series of projects by Wason (1960, 1968a, 1968b). In the first study, Wason (1960) presented subjects with the three-number sequence 2-4-6. The subject's task was to discover the numeric rule to which the three numbers conformed. To determine the rule, subjects were allowed to gen-

erate other sets of three numbers that the experimenter would classify as either conforming or not conforming to the rule. At any point, subjects could stop when they thought that they had discovered the rule. How would you approach this problem?

Wason's rule was "any three ascending numbers"—a solution which required the accumulation of disconfirming, rather than confirming, evidence. For example, if you thought the rule included "the difference between the first two numbers equaling the difference between the last two numbers" (a common expectation), you must try sequences that do *not* conform to this rule to find the actual rule. Trying the sequences 1-2-3, 10-15-20, 122-126-130, and so on, will only lead you into the confirmation trap. In Wason's (1960) experiment, only 6 out of 29 subjects found the correct rule the first time that they thought they knew the answer. Wason concluded that obtaining the correct solution necessitates "a willingness to attempt to falsify hypotheses, and thus to test those intuitive ideas which so often carry the feeling of certitude" (p. 139).

This result was also observed by Einhorn and Hogarth (1978) with a sample of 23 statisticians. When that group responded to a problem very similar to problem 13, eleven asked for card 1; one asked for card 1 or 3; one asked for any one card; two asked for card 1 or 4; three asked for card 4 alone; and only five trained statisticians asked for cards 1 and 4. Thus, this group tended to realize the worthlessness of card 3 but failed to realize the importance of card 4. This leads to the conclusion that the tendency to exclude disconfirming information in the search process is not eliminated by the formal scientific training that is expected of statisticians.

It is easy to observe the confirmation trap in your decision-making processes. You make a tentative decision (to buy a new car, to hire a particular employee, to start research and development on a new product line). Do you search for data that support your decision before making the final commitment? Most of us do. However, the existence of the confirmation trap implies that the search for challenging, or disconfirming, evidence will provide the most useful insights. For example, in confirming your decision to hire a particular employee, it is probably easy to find supporting positive information on the individual, but in fact the key issue may be the degree to which negative information on this individual, as well as positive information on another potential applicant, also exists.

## Bias 13—Hindsight

Consider the following scenarios:

- You are an avid football fan, and you are watching a critical game in which your team is behind 35–31. With three seconds left, and the ball on the opponent's three-yard line, the quarterback *unsuccessfully* calls a pass play into the corner of the endzone. You immediately respond, "I knew that he shouldn't have called that play."

- You are riding in an unfamiliar area, and your spouse is driving. You approach an unmarked fork in the road, and your spouse decides to go to the right. Four miles and fifteen minutes later, it is clear that you are lost. You blurt out, "I knew that you should have turned left at the fork."

- A manager who works for you hired a new supervisor last year. You were well aware of the choices he had at the time and allowed him to choose the new employee on his own. You have just received production data on every supervisor. The data on the new supervisor are terrible. You call in the manager and claim, "There was plenty of evidence that he (the supervisor) was not the man for the job."

- As director of marketing in a consumer-goods organization, you have just presented the results of an extensive six-month study on current consumer preferences for the products manufactured by your organization. After the conclusion of your presentation, a senior vice-president responds, "I don't know why we spent so much time and money to collect these data. I could have told you what the results were going to be."

Do you recognize yourself? Do you recognize someone else? Each scenario is representative of a phenomenon that has been named "the Monday morning quarterback syndrome" (Fischhoff, 1975b), "the knew-it-all-along effect" (Wood, 1978), "creeping determinism" (Fischhoff, 1975a, 1975b, 1980), and "the hindsight bias" (Fischhoff, 1975a, 1975b). This body of research demonstrates that people are typically not very good at recalling or reconstructing the way an uncertain situation appeared to them *before* finding out the results of the decision. What play would have you called? Did you *really* know that your spouse should have turned left? Was there *really* evidence that the selected supervisor was not the man for the job? Could the senior vice-president *really* have predicted the results of the survey? Perhaps our intuition is sometimes accurate, but we tend to overestimate what we knew and distort our beliefs about what we knew beforehand based upon what we later found out. The phenomenon occurs when people look back on the judgment of others, as well as of themselves.

Fischhoff has provided substantial evidence of the prevalence of the hindsight effect (1975a, 1975b, 1977; Fischhoff & Beyth, 1975; Slovic & Fischhoff, 1977). For example, Fischhoff (1975a) examined the differences between hindsight and foresight in the context of judging historical events and clinical instances. In one study, subjects were divided into five groups and asked to read a passage about the war between the British and Gurka forces in 1814. One group was not told the result of the war. The remaining four groups of subjects were told either that (1) the British won; (2) the Gurkas won; (3) a military stalemate was reached with no peace settlement; or (4) a military stalemate was reached with a peace settlement. Obviously, only one group was told the truthful outcome—(1) in this case. Each subject was then asked what his or her subjective assessments of the probability of each of the outcomes would have been without the benefit of knowing the reported outcome. Based upon this and other varied examples, the strong, consistent finding was that knowledge of an outcome increases an individual's belief about the degree to which he or she would have predicted that outcome without the benefit of that knowledge.

A number of explanations of the hindsight effect have been offered. One of the most pervasive is to explain hindsight in terms of the heuristics discussed in this book (Tversky & Kahneman, 1974). Anchoring may contribute to this bias when individuals interpret their prior subjective judgments of probabilities of an event's occurring in reference to the anchor of knowing whether or not that outcome actually occurred. Since adjustments to anchors are known to be inadequate, hindsight knowledge can be expected to bias perceptions of what one thinks one knew in foresight. Further, to the extent that the various pieces of data on the event vary in terms of their support for the actual outcome, evidence that is consistent with the known outcome may become cognitively more salient and thus more *available* in memory (Slovic & Fischhoff, 1977). This will lead an individual to justify a claimed foresight in view of "the facts provided." Finally, the relevance of a particular piece of data may later be judged important to the extent to which it is *representative* of the final observed outcome.

Claiming that what has happened was predictable based on foresight knowledge puts us in a position of using hindsight to criticize another's foresight judgment. In the short run, hindsight has a number of advantages. In particular, it is very flattering to believe that your judgment is far better than it actually is! However, hindsight reduces our ability to learn from the past and to evaluate objectively the decisions of ourselves and others. Leading researchers in performance evaluation (cf. Feldman, 1981) and decision theory (cf. Einhorn & Hogarth, 1981) have argued that, where possible, individuals should be rewarded based on the process and logic of their decisions, not on the results. A decision maker who makes a high-quality decision that does not work out should be rewarded, not punished. The rationale for this argument is that the results are affected by a variety of factors outside the direct control of the decision maker. However, to the extent that we rely on results and the hindsight corresponding to them, we will inappropriately evaluate the logic used by the decision maker in terms of the outcomes that occurred, not the methods that were employed.

## INTEGRATION AND COMMENTARY

Heuristics, or rules of thumb, are the cognitive tools we use to simplify decision making. The preceding pages have described 13 of the most common biases that result when we overrely on these judgmental heuristics. These biases are summarized in Table 34.2, along with their asso-

**TABLE 34.2**
**Summary of 13 Biases**

| Bias | Description |
| --- | --- |
| Biases Emanating from the Availability Heuristic | |
| 1. Ease of recall | Individuals judge events that are more easily recalled from memory, based upon vividness or recency, to be more numerous than events of equal frequency whose instances are less easily recalled. |
| 2. Retrievability | Individuals are biased in their assessments of the frequency of events based upon how their memory structures affect the search process. |
| 3. Presumed associations | Individuals tend to overestimate the probability of two events co-occurring based upon the number of similar associations that are easily recalled, whether from experience or social influence. |

*(continued)*

**TABLE 34.2 (cont.)**
**Summary of 13 Biases**

| | |
|---|---|
| **Biases Emanating from the Representativeness Heuristic** | |
| 4. Insensitivity to base rates | Individuals tend to ignore base rates in assessing the likelihood of events when any other descriptive information is provided— even if it is irrelevant. |
| 5. Insensitivity to sample size | Individuals frequently fail to appreciate the role of sample size in assessing the reliability of sample information. |
| 6. Misconceptions of chance | Individuals expect that a sequence of data generated by a random process will look "random," even when the sequence is too short for those expectations to be statistically valid. |
| 7. Regression to the mean | Individuals tend to ignore the fact that extreme events tend to regress to the mean on subsequent trials. |
| 8. The conjunction fallacy | Individuals falsely judge that conjunctions (two events co-occuring) are more probable than a global set of occurrences of which the conjunction is a subset. |
| **Biases Emanating from Anchoring and Adjustment** | |
| 9. Insufficient anchor adjustment | Individuals make estimates for values based upon an initial value (derived from past events, random assignment, or whatever information is available) and typically make insufficient adjustments from that anchor when establishing a final value. |
| 10. Conjunctive and disjunctive events bias | Individuals exhibit a bias toward overestimating the probability of conjunctive events and underestimating the probability of disjunctive events. |
| 11. Overconfidence | Individuals tend to be overconfident of the infallibility of their judgments when answering moderately to extremely difficult questions. |
| **Two More General Biases** | |
| 12. The confirmation trap | Individuals tend to seek confirmatory information for what they think is true and neglect the search for disconfirmatory evidence. |
| 13. Hindsight | After find out whether or not an event occurred, individuals tend to overestimate the degree to which they would have predicted the correct outcome. |

ciated heuristics. Again, it should be emphasized that more than one heuristic can be operating on our decision-making processes at any one time. We have attempted to identify only the dominant heuristic affecting each bias. In the last two biases, their effects are so broad that it is difficult to even determine a dominant heuristic.

While the use of quiz items has emphasized the biases that our heuristics create, it should be stressed that, overall, the use of these heuristics results in far more adequate than inadequate decisions. Our minds adopt these heuristics because, on average, any loss in quality of decisions is outweighed by the time saved. However, we ar-

gue against blanket acceptance of heuristics based upon this logic. First, as we have demonstrated in this chapter, there are many instances in which the loss in the quality of decisions far outweighs the time saved by the use of the heuristics. Second, the foregoing logic suggests that we have voluntarily accepted tradeoffs associated with the use of heuristics. But in reality, we have not: Most of us are unaware of their existence and their ongoing impact upon our decision making. The difficulty with heuristics is that we typically do not recognize that we are using them, and we consequently fail to distinguish between situations in which their use is more and less appropriate.

## REFERENCES

Alba, J. W., and Marmorstein, H. (1987). The effects of frequency knowledge on consumer decision making. *Journal of Consumer Research* 14, 14–25.

Alpert, M., and Raiffa, H. (1969). A progress report on the training of probability assessors. Unpublished manuscript.

Bar-Hillel, M. (1973). On the subjective probability of compound events. *Organizational Behavior and Human Performance* 9, 396–406.

Cambridge, R. M., and Shreckengost, R. C. (1980). Are you sure? The subjective probability assessment test. Unpublished manuscript. Langley, VA: Office of Training, Central Intelligence Agency.

Chapman, L. J., and Chapman, J. P. (1967). Genesis of popular but erroneous diagnostic observations. *Journal of Abnormal Psychology* 72, 193–204.

Cox, A. D., and Summers, J. O. (1987). Heuristics and biases in the intuitive projection of retail sales. *Journal of Marketing Research* 24, 290–297.

Curran, J. J. (1987). Why investors make the wrong choices. *Fortune, 1987 Investor's Guide*.

Einhorn, H. J., and HOGARTH, R. M. (1987). Confidence in Judgment: Persistence in the illusion of validity. *Psychological Review* 85, 395–416.

Einhorn, H. J., and Hogarth, R. M. (1981). Behavioral decision theory: Processes of judgment and choice. *Annual Review of Psychology* 32, 53–88.

Feldman, J. M. (1981). Beyond attribution theory: Cognitive processes in performance appraisal. *Journal of Applied Psychology* 66, 127–148.

Fischhoff, B. (1975a). Hindsight = foresight: The effect of outcome knowledge on judgment under uncertainty. *Journal of Experimental Psychology: Human Perception and Performance* 1, 228–299.

Fischhoff, B. (1975b). Hindsight: Thinking backward. *Psychology Today* 8, 71–76.

Fischhoff, B. (1977). Cognitive liabilities and product liability. *Journal of Products Liability* 1, 207–220.

Fischhoff, B. (1980). For those condemned to study the past: Reflections on historical judgment. In R. A. Shweder and D. W. Fiske (Eds.). *New directions for methodology of behavior science: Fallible judgement in behavioral research.* San Francisco: Jossey-Bass.

Fischhoff, B., and Beyth, R. (1975). "I knew it would happen":—Remembered probabilities of once-future things. *Organizational Behavior and Human Performance* 13, 1–16.

Fischhoff, B., Slovic, P., and Lichtenstein, S. (1977). Knowing with certainty: The appropriateness of extreme confidence. *Journal of Experimental Psychology: Human Perception and Performance* 3, 552–564.

Gillovich, T., Vallone, R., and Tversky, A. (1985). The hot hand in basketball: On the misperception of random sequences. *Cognitive Psychology* 17, 295–314.

Hazard, T. H., and Peterson, C. R. (1973). Odds versus probabilities for categorical events (Technical report. 73-2). McLean, VA: Decisions and Designs, Inc.

Joyce, E. J., and Biddle, G. C. (1981). Anchoring and adjustment in probabilistic inference in auditing. *Journal of Accounting Research* 19, 120–145.

Kahneman, D., and Tversky, A. (1972). Subjective probability: A judgment of representativeness. *Cognitive Psychology* 3, 430–454.

Kahneman, D., and Tversky, A. (1973). On the psychology of prediction. *Psychological Review* 80, 237–251.

Koriat, A., Lichtenstein, S., and Fischhoff, B. (1980). Reasons for confidence. *Journal of Experimental Psychology: Human Learning and Memory* 6, 107–118.

Lichtenstein, S. and Fischhoff, B. (1977). Do those who know more also know more about how much they know? The calibration of probability judgments. *Organizational Behavior and Human Performance* 20, 159–183.

Lichtenstein,, S., and Fischhoff, B. (1980). Training for calibration. *Organizational Behavior and Human Performance* 26, 149–171.

Lichtenstein, S., Fischhoff, B., and Phillips, L. D. (1982). Calibration of probabilities: State of the art to 1980. In D. Kahneman, P. Slovic, and A. Tversky (Eds.), *Judgment under uncertainty: Heuristics and biases.* New York: Cambridge University Press.

Nickerson, R. S., and McGoldrick, C. C. (1985). Confidence ratings and level of performance on a judgmental task. *Perceptual and Motor Skills* 20, 311–316.

Nisbett, R., and Ross, L. (1980). *Human inference: Strategies and shortcomings of social judgment.* Englewood Cliffs, NJ: Prentice-Hall.

Northcraft, G. B., and NEALE, M. A. (1987). Experts, amateurs and real estate: An anchoring-and-adjustment perspective on property pricing decisions. *Organizational Behavior and Human Decision Processes* 39, 84–97.

Perrow, C. (1984). *Normal accidents.* New York: Basic Books.

Pitz, G. F. (1974). Subjective probability distributions for imperfectly known quantities. In L. W. Gregg (Ed.), *Knowledge and cognition* (pp. 29–41). New York: Wiley.

Slovic, P., and Fischhoff, B. (1977). On the psychology of experimental surprises. *Journal of Experimental Psychology: Human Perception and Performance* 3, 544–551.

Slovic, P., and Lichtenstein, S. (1971). Comparison of Bayesian and regression approaches in the study of information processing in judgment. *Organizational Behavior and Human Performance* 6, 649–744.

Slovic, P., Lichtenstein, S., and Fischhoff, B. (1979). Images of disaster: Perception and acceptance of risks from nuclear power. In G. Goodman and W. Rowe (Eds.), *Energy risk management*. London: Academic Press.

Tversky, A., and Kahneman, D. (1971). The belief in the "law of numbers." *Psychological Bulletin* 76, 105–110.

Tversky, A., and Kahneman, D. (1973). Availability: A heuristic for judging frequency and probability. *Cognitive Psychology* 5, 207–232.

Tversky, A., and Kahneman, D. (1974). Judgment under uncertainty: Heuristics and biases. *Science* 185, 1124–1131.

Tversky, A., and Kahneman, D. (1983). Extensional versus intuitive reasoning: The conjunction fallacy in probability judgment. *Psychological Review* 90, 293–315.

Wason, P. C. (1960). On the failure to eliminate the hypotheses in a conceptual task. *Quarterly Journal of Experimental Psychology* 12, 129–140.

Wason, P. C. (1968a). Reason about a rule. *Quarterly Journal of Experimental Psychology* 20, 273–283.

Wason, P. C. (1986b). On the failure to eliminate hypothesis ... A second look. In P. C. Wason and P. N. Johnson-Laird (Eds.), *Thinking and reasoning*. Harmandsworth: Penguin.

Wood, G. (1978). The knew-it-all-along effect. *Journal of Experimental Psychology: Human Perception and Performance* 4, 345–353.

# Individual Decisions in Organizations

## 35.  DECISION-MAKING STRATEGIES

Irving L. Janis and Leon Mann

When people are required to choose among alternative courses of action, what types of search, deliberation, and selection procedure do they typically use—that is, what decision-making strategy do they adopt?[1] Unfortunately, this question has so far received relatively little attention in behavioral science research. Most of the pertinent observations of decision-making strategies consist of case studies, impressionistic surveys, and anecdotes reported by scholars in administrative science and related fields that deal with organizational policy making. Administrative scientists have much more to say than social psychologists, both in their descriptions and in their theory, about when and why a decision maker uses one type of strategy rather than another. Although originally formulated in terms of organizational policy making by managers or bureaucrats, the concepts of specialists in organizational behavior embody relevant universal psychological assumptions about human beings as imper-

fect decision makers. Accordingly, we shall examine the answers they give concerning how "administrative man" typically carries out the tasks of decision making. The answers provide essential background material that we shall draw upon in developing a conflict theory concerning the causes and consequences of defective information processing—a theory we believe to be equally applicable to personal decisions (pertaining to marriage, career, health, life style, and all sorts of personal matters) and to executive decisions in an organizational context.

## OPTIMIZING AND THE PERILS OF SUBOPTIMIZING

Specialists in organizational decision making describe the optimizing strategy as having the goal of selecting the course of action with the highest payoff. Such a strategy requires estimating the comparative value of every viable alternative in terms of expected benefits and costs (see Young, 1966, pp. 138–47). But, as Herbert Simon (1976) has pointed out, human beings rarely adopt this decision-making approach: people simply do not have "the wits to maximize" (p. xxviii). Part of the problem is that determining all the potentially favorable and unfavorable consequences of all the feasible courses of action would require the decision maker to process so much information that impossible demands would be made on his resources and mental capabilities. In his attempts to obtain the degree of knowledge needed to anticipate alternative outcomes, the decision maker is likely to be overwhelmed by "information inundation, which can be quite as debilitating as information scarcity" (Miller & Starr, 1967, p. 62). Moreover, so many relevant variables may have to be taken into account that they cannot all be kept in mind at the same time. The number of crucially relevant categories usually far exceeds $7 \pm 2$, the limits of man's capacity for processing information in immediate memory (see Miller, 1956). Handicapped by the shortcomings of the human mind, the decision maker's attention, asserts Simon, "shifts from one value to another with consequent shifts in preference" (p. 83).

It is very costly in time, effort, and money to collect and examine the huge masses of information required when one uses an optimizing strategy to arrive at a decision. Furthermore, decision makers are often under severe pressure of time, which precludes careful search and appraisal. Managers in large companies, for example, seldom have time to engage in long-range planning because they are constantly occupied with current crises requiring emergency "fire fighting." The manager is likely to be "so busy solving immediate problems that he cannot effectively apply their solutions on a long-run recurrent basis; so busy manning the fire hose that he cannot devise a fire prevention program" (Young, p. 146).

As a result of personal limitations and various external constraints, a decision maker who does

the best he can to use an optimizing strategy is still prone to such gross miscalculations that he ends up with an unsatisfactory *suboptimizing* solution, one that maximizes some of the utilities he expected to gain at the expense of losing other utilities. Miller and Starr (1967) cite the example of an executive who chooses a new job that is optimal in terms of his main professional objectives but requires so much overtime and travel that he has little time available for family life. "This may have such adverse effects that the executive will find that his optimization in terms of one objective has produced an overall result which is much less than optimal in terms of all his objectives" (p. 48).

The perils of suboptimization abound in large organizations, where different units and different types of personnel have incompatible objectives. A hospital administrator may decide to hire a sizable number of paramedical aides to relieve overburdened nurses of nonprofessional chores and to provide additional services to the patients, such as writing letters for those who are incapacitated and separated from their families. But the additional personnel may unexpectedly overcrowd the hospital cafeteria, the rest rooms, the parking lot, and all the other employees' facilities to the point where the physicians, nurses, and orderlies become dissatisfied with the deteriorization in their working conditions and demand that new facilities be built. The decisions made by policy makers in large organizations are, according to Young, "usually of a suboptimal nature, and only rarely can we assume that an ideal or unimprovable solution has been achieved" (p. 144). It needs to be emphasized, however, that a suboptimal policy is not necessarily unsatisfactory, even though it fails to attain all the policy maker's objectives; it may be a marked improvement over the former policy and constitute a step toward an optimizing solution.

Evidence from various social science disciplines indicates that, besides man's severe limitations as a processor of information, other recurrent conditions also militate against the use of an optimizing approach, even though it might often seem to be the ideal strategy for making decisions (Brim et al., 1962; Etzioni, 1968; Johnson, 1974;

Katona, 1953; Miller & Starr, 1967; Simmons et al., 1973; Steinbrunner, 1974; Taylor, 1965; Vroom & Yetton, 1973).

*Contemporary developments in economics have emphasized the lack of realism of the assumption that individuals act so as to maximize their utility. There has not been an attack on the proposition that individuals should act so as to achieve a maximization of their utility. Rather, there has been sufficient evidence and supporting reasons to show that they do not act in this way. Among the reasons suggested have been the following: the inability of the individual to duplicate the rather recondite mathematics which economists have used to solve the problem of maximization of utility; the existence of other values (the higher values originally excluded by [Adam] Smith) which though not readily quantifiable, do cause divergences from the maximization of utility in the marketplace; the effect of habit; the influence of social emulation; the effect of social institutions.*

*. . . The work of psychologists would certainly tend to confirm the assertion that human beings have a variety of diverse motivations which do not lend themselves to maximization of utility—at least so long as utility is defined in terms of the satisfactions resulting from marketplace phenomena. . . . Similarly, sociologists have accumulated considerable evidence to demonstrate the enormous influence of social institutions, habit, and tradition on the choices and decisions made by individuals. The effect of these psychological and sociological factors leads individuals to make decisions and to take actions without recourse to maximization of utility in the classical economic sense. Alternatively phrased, it can be said that these factors cause people to act irrationally—but it should be noted that this is simply a matter of definition, rationality having been defined as maximization of economic utility [Miller & Starr, 1967, pp. 24–25].*

Even in decisions made by business firms, where the overriding value would seem to be to make the greatest amount of profit, decision makers often do not orient themselves toward finding the course of action that will maximize profits and other tangible net gains. Without careful search and appraisal, corporation executives often make judgments about a multiplicity of conflicting objectives, including "good will,"

"growth potential," "acceptability within the organization," and other intangible gains that are difficult to measure in any way (see Johnson, 1974).

In a study of corporate decision making, Stagner (1969) found that many policy-making business executives, rather than focusing primarily on maximizing profit, were guided by numerous values pertaining to the future welfare of the organization. To examine high-level decision-making practices, Stagner mailed a questionnaire to 500 vice-presidential-level executives belonging to 125 of America's largest and most successful corporations, as selected by *Fortune* magazine. Returns were received from about 50 percent of the executives. The data revealed that in many firms cost and marginal-profit estimates are not carefully made. In fact, a substantial number of executives (28 percent) indicated that only "rough estimates" were made of such variables; 65 percent of them reported that judgments about the company's public image often outweigh profit considerations; and 50 percent reported that considerable weight in making business decisions is attached to company tradition and past policies.[2]

Stagner points out that corporate decisions are not always made in terms of the long-range welfare of the organization, because some powerful executives are inclined to favor the objectives of their own division over those of the firm. Decisions by the manager of a unit are likely to be made with an eye toward local group loyalties and one-upmanship in the competitive struggle for power and influence among rival units, if not for personal advancement. According to numerous other observers, even when a policy maker is thinking in terms of the organization as a whole, he usually gives the devils of bureaucratic politics their due (Allison, 1971; Halperin, 1974; Lindblom, 1965; Johnson, 1974; Vroom & Yetton, 1973). Indeed, an executive risks failure if he overlooks the obligation to work out a policy that will be approved by higher executives or legal authorities within the organization and accepted by the managers who will be required to administer it. Then, too, he must try to avoid stirring up employee opposition, which could lead to disastrous slowdowns or a strike. Aside from the most obvious forms of employee resistance, there are other, subtle costs of implementing decisions that require the workers in a plant to change their work routines, to learn new operations, or to regroup into unaccustomed units; all such decisions result in some measure of lowered productivity.

Similarly, when an individual makes a vital decision bearing on his career, marriage, or health, or on any other aspect of his personal welfare, he does not think only about the major utilitarian goals to be attained. He also takes account of a multiplicity of intangible considerations bearing on the probable effects of the chosen and unchosen courses of action on relatives and friends. Anticipated feelings of high or low self-esteem with regard to living up to his own personal standards of conduct also affect his preferences for one alternative rather than another....

Miller and Starr (1967) emphasize that there is no sound way to combine all the considerations involved in decision making into a single, objective utility measure, even though the decision maker might be capable of giving honest ratings of the subjective utility value of every consideration that enters into his choice.

*The utility an individual gains from a commodity or a service can be measured to some degree by observable market phenomena (e.g., how much of the commodity he will buy at different prices). But there is no convenient measuring unit for the utility of an intangible such as dignity. Therefore, even if these other factors can be theoretically expressed in terms of [subjective] utility, the difficulties involved in measuring the utilities prevent the theory [of maximization of utilities] from satisfactorily explaining observed behavior and decisions [pp. 25–26].*

Many behavioral scientists regard the optimizing strategy as an excellent *normative* (or *prescriptive*) model—that is, a set of standards the decision maker *should* strive to attain when making vital decisions (to avoid miscalculations, wishful thinking, and vulnerability to subsequent disillusionment). Some, however, like Miller and Starr, question whether optimizing would very often prove to be the optimal strategy in view of its high costs and the usual constraints on the decision maker's resources; they strongly oppose prescriptive recommendations that might inadvertently encourage decision makers to strive blindly for optimizing solutions, regardless of the circumstances. Even more objections have been raised against the assumption that the optimizing strategy provides an accurate *descriptive* model of how people actually *do* make decisions. The numerous critiques we have just summarized pose a major problem for the psychology of decision making; if optimizing is *not* the dominant strategy actually used by most decision makers most of the time, then what is?

## SATISFICING

The most influential hypothesis concerning the way administrative man arrives at a new policy has been formulated by Herbert Simon (1976). The decision maker, according to Simon, *satisfices*, rather than maximizes; that is, he looks for a course of action that is "good enough," that meets a minimal set of requirements. Businessmen, for example, often decide to invest in a new enterprise if they expect it to return a "satisfactory profit," without bothering to compare it with all the alternative investments open to them. Sometimes more than one criterion is used, but always it is a question of whether the given choice will yield a "good enough" outcome. An executive looking for a new job, for example, is likely to settle for the first one to come along that meets his minimal requirements—satisfactory pay, good chance for advancement, adequate working conditions, and location within commuting distance of his home. The satisficing strategy involves more superficial search for information and less cognitive work than maximizing. All that the person has to do is consider alternative courses of action sequentially until one that "will do" is found.

Simon argues convincingly that the satisficing approach fits the limited information-processing capabilities of human beings. The world is peopled by creatures of "bounded or limited rationality," he says, and these creatures constantly resort to gross simplifications when dealing with complex decision problems. Man's limited ability to foresee future consequences and to obtain information about the variety of available alternatives inclines him to settle for a barely "acceptable" course of action that is "better than the way things are now." He is not inclined to collect information about all the complicated factors that might affect the outcome of his choice, to estimate probabilities, or to work out preference orderings for many different alternatives. He is content to rely on "a drastically simplified model of the buzzing, blooming confusion that constitutes the real world" (Simon, 1976, p. xxix).

According to Johnson (1974), executives often feel so uncertain about the outcome of what seems to be the best choice that they forego it in order to play safe: they gravitate toward a more conventional, "second-best" choice that will cause little immediate disturbance or disapproval because it will be seen as "acceptable" by superiors and peers who will review the decision and by subordinates who will implement it. Cyert and March (1963) suggest that the more uncertainty there is about a long-term outcome, the greater the tendency to make a policy decision on the basis of its short-term acceptability within the organization.

Organizational theorists assume that individuals use a satisficing strategy in personal decisions as well as organizational decisions (Etzioni, 1968; Miller & Starr, 1967; Simon, 1976; Young, 1966). As Etzioni puts it, "Simon's important distinction between optimizing and 'satisficing'... is ...independent of any socio-political system. It applies as much to a consumer in a supermarket as to the President of the United States" (p. 253). Whenever the consumer, the president, or anyone else is looking only for a choice that offers some degree of *improvement* over the present state of affairs, his survey, analysis, and evaluation are usually limited to just two alternatives—a new course of action that has been brought to his attention and the old one he has been pursuing. If neither meets his minimal requirements, he continues to look for other alternatives until he finds one that does. Consequently, the use of

a satisficing strategy does not preclude contemplating a fairly large number of alternatives, but they are examined *sequentially*, with no attempt to work out a comparative balance sheet of pros and cons.

The simplest variant of the satisficing strategy takes the form of relying upon a single formula as the sole decision rule, which comes down to using only one criterion for a tolerable choice. Paradoxically, this crude approach often characterizes the decision-making behavior of people who are facing major personal decisions that will affect their future health or welfare. Men and women in serious trouble are likely to consult whichever physician or lawyer is recommended by a trusted friend and then to accept whatever course of action the adviser recommends, without spending the money and effort required to get a second opinion. The sole decision rule in such cases is often simply "Tell a qualified expert about your problem and do whatever he says— that will be good enough." Simple decision rules are also prevalent in consumer behavior. Studies of consumer purchases indicate that people in shops and supermarkets sometimes buy on impulse, without any advance planning or deliberation (Engel, Kollat, & Blackwell, 1968; Hansen, 1972). The person notices something attractive that he would like to have, and, if the price is within the range he regards as "reasonable," he immediately decides to buy it. A similar decision rule may come into play when a customer impulsively decides to appropriate an attractive piece of merchandise if he sees that no one in the store is looking.

## Quasi-satisficing

Some people use a simple moral precept as the sole rule when making a decision to help someone in trouble. Schwartz (1970), in his account of the psychological basis of altruism, describes this approach as "moral decision making." Once the person realizes that someone requires aid and that there is some obvious way help can be given, he promptly takes action without deliberating about alternatives. This use of a simple decision rule is similar to a satisficing approach in all respects except one: the helper does not share the full-fledged satisficer's belief that his choice is *minimally* satisfactory. Instead of regarding his action as merely "good enough," the moral decision maker is convinced that it is the *best*, that no other course would be morally justifiable. Later on we shall examine well-documented examples of moral decision making observed when a member of the family of a patient suffering from kidney disease is asked to donate his own kidney to save the relative's life.

When a decision maker does not accept responsibility for dealing with another person's problem, he is not likely to use a moral precept as his decision rule. The more responsibility he feels, the greater the likelihood that he will follow a simple normative prescription of offering help when someone needs it. To some extent, the findings from experiments on altruism by Bickman (1971, 1972), Latané and Darley (1970), Piliavin, Rodin, and Piliavin (1969, 1975), and others illustrate this relationship between perceived responsibility and a normative approach. The evidence indicates that a person is especially likely to help a stranger if he perceives that he is the only one available to give help. Not everyone, however, adheres to a simple normative rule when he perceives himself as responsible; some people weigh carefully the costs and benefits of giving aid to a needy person. The more frequently a person has told others he is committed to the moral norm that one should selflessly give aid to others when they need it, the greater the likelihood that he will subsequently use that norm as the basis for his decision to intervene.

When a person uses a simple normative precept as his sole decision rule, he usually feels it would be immoral for him to deliberate about any other options open to him. There is a moral-imperative quality to the norm that makes him resist violating it. When this normative decision rule is used, anticipated self-disapproval and social disapproval take precedence over any utilitarian considerations that might be implicated by the decision.

It is apparent from the examples just cited that personal choices based on a quasi-satisficing

strategy that relies on a simple decision rule can result in either socially desirable or socially undesirable actions. The same can be said about domestic and foreign-policy decisions made by government leaders. Alexander George (1974) calls attention to the proclivity of national policy makers to rely on a simple formula rather than to attempt to master cognitively complex problems by means of careful search and analysis and weighing of alternatives. One type of decision rule frequently resorted to in a bureaucracy consists of using a simple criterion of "consensus," which requires only the single piece of information that could, in effect, be supplied by an opinion poll of the most powerful persons in the organization: thus, any policy is good enough to be adopted if the majority of influential people want it and will support it. Other simple decision rules sometimes used by policy makers consist of relying on, as a guide for action, a general ideological principle—e.g., "No appeasement of the enemy!"—or an operational code—e.g., the best tactic for dealing with an ultimatum from an enemy is to respond promptly with a more drastic ultimatum—(see George, 1974; Leites, 1953; Lindblom, 1965).

When making a major policy decision for which well-known historical precedents immediately come to mind, many national political leaders, according to historian Ernest May (1973) and political scientist Robert Jervis (1975), follow the simple decision rule "Do what we did last time if it worked and the opposite if it didn't."

*Policy-makers ordinarily use history badly. When resorting to an analogy, they tend to seize upon the first that comes to mind. They do not search more widely. Nor do they pause to analyze the case, test its fitness, or even ask in what ways it might be misleading. Seeing a trend running toward the present, they tend to assume that it will continue into the future, not stopping to consider what produced it or why a linear projection might prove to be mistaken [May 1973, p. xi].*

There is always a grave danger, as George (1974) points out, that relying on a simple decision rule will lead to a premature choice that overlooks nonobvious negative consequences. Some of those consequences might be averted if the decision were delayed until more thorough deliberation and evaluation were carried out after obtaining information from available intelligence resources.

## What Are the Variables?

Although it is not explicitly stated in the descriptive accounts of satisficing and quasi-satisficing by Simon, Jervis, May, George, and others, these strategies differ from optimizing in more than one important dimension. We find that at least four different variables are involved.[3]

1. *Number of requirements to be met*: One characteristic feature of the satisficing strategy is that the testing rule used to determine whether or not to adopt a new course of action specifies a *small amount of requirements* that must be met, sometimes only one (e.g., that a personal choice should be acceptable to one's spouse or that a policy choice should be acceptable to the majority of a policy-making group). The decision maker ignores many other values and spheres of interest that he realizes might also be implicated by his decision. In contrast, when the decision maker is using an optimizing strategy he takes account of a large number of requirements or objectives, with the intention of selecting the course of action that achieves the greatest possible satisfaction of the entire set of requirements. This is perhaps the most obvious characteristic that distinguishes satisficing from optimizing.

2. *Number of alternatives generated.* A decision maker using a satisficing strategy sequentially tests each alternative that comes to his attention; if the first one happens to be minimally satisfactory, he terminates his search. Since he makes little effort to canvass the full range of possible courses of action by searching his memory or by seeking suggestions from advisers, the decision maker is likely to generate *relatively few alternatives*. If he uses an optimizing strategy, on the other hand, the decision maker makes a thorough search and attempts to generate as *many* good alternatives as he can.

3. *Ordering and retesting of alternatives.* When using a satisficing strategy, the decision maker typi-

cally tests the alternatives only once and in a haphazard order, as one after another happens to come to his attention, until he finds one that meets his minimum requirements. When using an optimizing strategy, however, he selects the best alternatives and reexamines them repeatedly, ordering them in pairs or in some other way so as to make comparative judgments.

4. *Type of testing model used.* When testing to see if an alternative meets a given requirement, the satisficing decision maker typically limits his inquiry to seeing whether it falls above or below a *minimal cutoff point*. If there is more than one requirement, he treats each cutoff point in the same way, as equally important. In contrast to this simple, unweighted threshold model, the model used in the optimizing strategy is typically a weighted additive model, which requires the decision maker to arrive at an evaluation that takes account of the *magnitudes* of all the pros and cons with due regard for the relative importance of each objective. This gives him the opportunity to consider possible "tradeoffs" from gaining very high values in some important requirements in exchange for tolerating relatively low values on less important ones.

When a person's procedures fall at the low end of the continuum on all four variables, his decision-making strategy would be unambiguously classified as satisficing; when at the upper end of the continuum on all four variables, his strategy would be unambiguously classified as optimizing. But what if a person's pattern on the four variables is not consistent? Obviously, we can expect to find instances of quasi-satisficing or mixed strategies, where satisficing tendencies predominate on one or two variables but optimizing tendencies predominate on the others.

Even when someone warrants high ratings on all four variables, he might still fail to maximize all possible values, and hence fall far short of a genuinely optimizing strategy. Moreover, an unskilled or unwary decision maker with good intentions might obtain high ratings but nevertheless make gross miscalculations through ignorance, bias, overconcern about the foreseeable immediate consequences, or rigid belief in "the too-ready assumption that actions which have in the past led to the desired outcome will continue to do so" (Merton, 1936, p. 901). High ratings on the four variables might, therefore, be regarded as necessary, but not sufficient, conditions for optimizing.

Not unexpectedly, the four variables overlap to some extent with the seven criteria for vigilant information processing.... Anyone who uses a relatively pure satisficing strategy, as defined by the four variables, would obtain low scores on at least four of the seven variables that define vigilant information processing: he would fail to canvass a wide range of alternatives (criterion no. 1), to take account of the full range of short-term objectives and long-term values to be fulfilled by the choice (criterion no. 2), to weigh all he knows about the costs and risks of each alternative (criterion no. 3), and to reexamine the positive and negative consequences of all known alternatives (criterion no. 6). But the use of a satisficing strategy does not preclude meeting some of the criteria for vigilant information processing. Even within the confines of a pure satisficing strategy, a decision maker can still carry out an intensive search for relevant information, conscientiously assimilate information, and make provisions for implementation along with detailed contingency plans. Furthermore, it is possible for someone to meet all seven requirements for vigilant information processing and yet not obtain a high score on one or two of the variables that enter into the optimizing strategy, so that he would be classified as using a "quasi-optimizing" strategy. Taking account of the limitations of a "pure" optimizing strategy discussed earlier, we expect that for purposes of predicting gross miscalculations in decision making and subsequent postdecisional regret, the seven variables specified as the criteria for vigilant information processing will prove to be more valuable than the set of four variables differentiating between satisficing and optimizing.

## Elimination by Aspects

Instead of a single decision rule in a satisficing or quasi-satisficing strategy, a set of decision rules,

involving perhaps up to half a dozen considerations, is sometimes used. Still, the decision maker does not engage in anything like the amount of cognitive work that would be required if he were to evaluate and weigh the alternatives using an optimizing strategy. One such multiple-rule variant, designated as the *"elimination-by-aspects"* approach, has been described by Tversky (1972). It consists essentially of a combination of simple decision rules, which can be applied to select rapidly from a number of salient alternatives, one that meets a set of minimal requirements. Tversky illustrates this type of quasi-satisficing strategy by citing a television commercial screened in San Francisco. An announcer says:

*There are more than two dozen companies in the San Francisco area which offer training in computer programing. [He puts some two dozen eggs and one walnut on the table to represent the alternatives.] Let us examine the facts. How many of these schools have on-line computer facilities for training? [He removes several eggs.] How many of these schools have placement services that would help you find a job? [He removes some more eggs.] How many of these schools are approved for veterans' benefits? [This continues until the walnut alone remains. The announcer cracks the nutshell, revealing the name of the advertised company.] This is all you need to know, in a nutshell.*

When the elimination-by-aspects approach is used, decision making becomes essentially a sequential narrowing-down process, similar to the logic employed in the popular game Twenty Questions. Starting ordinarily with the most valued requirement, all salient alternatives that do not contain the selected aspect are eliminated, and the process continues for each requirement in turn until a single expedient remains. For example, in contemplating the purchase of a new car, the first aspect selected might be a $4,500 price limit; all cars more expensive than $4,500 are then excluded from further consideration. A second aspect might be high mileage per gallon; at this stage, all cars are eliminated that do not have this feature. Yet another aspect, say power steering, is examined for the remaining alternatives, and all cars not meeting this criterion are crossed off the "mental list." The process continues until all cars but one are eliminated.

Of course, the decision maker may run out of aspects before he arrives at a single remaining expedient; he will then have to introduce another decision rule in order to narrow his choice. Or he may run out of alternatives before he exhausts his list of minimal requirements. From a normative standpoint, however, a much more serious flaw of this complex form of satisficing lies in its failure to ensure that the alternatives retained are, in fact, superior to those eliminated. For example, in the alternative arrived at in the television commercial, the use of placement services as a criterion for elimination might lead to the rejection of programs whose overall quality far exceeds that of the advertised one despite the fact that they do not offer that particular service. Similarly, in the choice of a car, the use of power steering as a criterion for elimination could lead to rejection of vehicles otherwise far superior to the vehicle purchased. Part of the problem is that minor criteria may creep in early in the sequence or may survive to determine the final choice. Perhaps this drawback could be corrected in a way that would transform the elimination-by-aspects approach into a quasi-optimizing strategy by introducing procedures that reflect the decision maker's judgments about the differential weights to be assigned to various aspects. Even without any such refinement, however, this approach appears to be one of the most sophisticated and psychologically realistic of the quasi-satisficing strategies and might result in fewer miscalculations than the simpler variants that rely exclusively on a single decision rule (Abelson, 1976).

Some social science theorists would describe reliance on a single decision rule as less "rational" than the elimination-by-aspects approach, and all variants of satisficing as less "rational" than optimizing. But terms like *less rational, nonrational,* and *irrational* carry invidious connotations ("stupid," "crazy") that often do not correspond at all to the evaluations that would be made by objective observers. Indeed it could be argued that in certain circumstances it is not rational to waste time and effort in maximizing; even when the relevant information is available, a very simple form of satisficing sometimes may be the most sensible orientation, especially for many minor issues. For example, consumer research organizations have recommended that when purchasing aspirin at a registered pharmacy, one should follow the simple rule of selecting whichever brand is cheapest (because all brands must meet rigorous U.S. government specifications and, despite advertising claims to the contrary, there are no significant differences among them). As Miller and Starr (1967, p. 51) point out, "It is always questionable whether the optimum procedure is to search for *the* optimum value." Accordingly, we avoid characterizing the satisficing strategy or any other decision-making strategy in terms of "rationality" or "irrationality." We do not intend to bypass the important issue of determining the conditions under which one or another decision-making procedure will have unfavorable consequences for the decision maker; but we shall attempt to relate specific types of conditions to specific types of unfavorable consequences without using overinclusive, misleading labels like *irrational.*

## Incrementalism and Muddling Through

Organizational theorists recognize that despite its shortcomings, a satisficing strategy can result in slow progress toward an optimal course of action. Miller and Starr (1967), for example, speak about *incremental improvements* that sometimes come about as a result of a succession of satisficing policy choices, each small change presumably having been selected as "good enough" because it was seen as better than leaving the old policy unchanged. "Over time," Miller and Starr assert "both individuals and groups may be better off to move in incremental steps of reasonable size toward the perceived and bounded optimum than in giant strides based on long-range perceptions of where the ultimate optimal exists" (p. 51).

Charles E. Lindblom (1959, 1963, 1965) has given a detailed account of the incrementalist approach in an analysis of "the art of muddling through." When a problem arises requiring a change in policy, according to Lindblom, policy makers in government or large organizations generally consider a very narrow range of policy alternatives that differ to only a small degree from the existing policy. By sticking close to this familiar path of policymaking, the incrementalist shows his preference for the sin of "omission" over the sin of "confusion" (Lindblom, 1965, p. 146).

Incremental decision making is geared to alleviating concrete shortcomings in a present policy—putting out fires—rather than selecting the superior course of action. Since no effort is made to specify major goals and to find the best means for attaining them, "ends are chosen that are appropriate to available or nearly available means" (Hirschman and Lindblom, 1962, p. 215). The incremental approach allows executives to simplify the search and appraisal stages of decision making by carrying out successive comparisons with respect to policy alternatives that differ only slightly from the existing policy. Slovic (1971) postulates, on the basis of his experiments on the cognitive limitations displayed in gambling situations, that decision makers find the incremental approach attractive because it enables them to avoid difficult cognitive tasks: "Examination of business decision making and governmental policy making suggests that, whenever possible, decision makers avoid uncertainty and the necessity of weighting and combining information or trading-off conflicting values."

Often decision makers have no real awareness of trying to arrive at a new policy; rather, there is a never-ending series of attacks on each new problem as it arises. As policy makers take one small step after another to gradually change the existing policy, the satisficing criterion itself may change, depending on what is going wrong with the existing policy.[4] If there are strong objections to the policy on the part of other bureaucrats who have to implement it, the policy makers may find a satisficing solution that involves making a compromise in accord with the realities of bureaucratic politics. Incremental changes are often made primarily to keep other politically powerful groups in the hierarchy sufficiently satisfied so that they will stop complaining and will not obstruct the new trend (Halperin, 1974).

Braybrooke and Lindblom (1963) regard muddling-through incrementalism as the typical decision-making process of groups in pluralistic societies. Since the term *muddling through* evokes images of incompetence and aimlessness, it is tempting to conclude that it could be the preferred technique only of lazy or third-rate minds. But Braybrooke and Lindblom view it as the method by which societal decision-making bodies, acting as coalitions of interest groups, can effectively make cumulative decisions and arrive at workable compromises. Whenever power is distributed among a variety of influential executive leaders, political parties, legislative factions, and interest groups, one center of power can rarely impose its preferences on another and policies are likely to be the outcome of give and take among numerous partisans. The constraints of bureaucratic politics, with its shifting compromises and coalitions, constitute a major reason for the disjointed and incremental nature of the policies that gradually evolve.

Lindblom and his associates argue that incremental decisions based largely on the criterion of consensus, rather than on the actual values implicated by the issue, may avoid some of the social evils of undemocratic, centralized decision making. But other social scientists point out that incrementalism based largely on keeping fellow power holders reasonably contented cannot be expected to do very much about the vital needs of underprivileged people and politically weak groups (see Etzioni, 1968, pp. 272–73; Dror, 1969, pp. 167–69.)[5] Moreover, there is no guarantee that in the atomic age our government leaders will always somehow muddle through successfully as they "stagger through history like a drunk putting one disjointed incremental foot after another" (Boulding, 1964, p. 931). On the one hand, incremental policy formation based on a succession of satisficing choices can have functional value for decision makers who want to avoid the risks of drastic societal changes that "may easily lead," as Popper (1963, p. 158) says, "to an intolerable increase in human suffering." But on the other hand, there is the danger that it can prove to be a zigzag passage to unanticipated disaster.

Relatively little is to be found in the social psychological literature about muddling through on personal decisions. Probably the same type of incremental change, based on a simple satisficing strategy, is adopted whenever a person is ignorant of the fundamental issues at stake or when he wishes to avoid investing a great deal of time and energy in wrestling with a problem that appears, at the time, insoluble. Important life decisions are sometimes incremental in nature, the end product of a series of small decisions that progressively commit the person to one particular course of action. A stepwise increase in commitment can end up locking the person into a career or marriage without his ever having made a definite decision about it. . . .

Many individuals do not make a deliberate occupational choice but in haphazard, trial-and-error fashion leave their job whenever something that seems somewhat better comes along. Ginzberg et al. (1951) suggest that incremental steps may determine the career choices made by a sizable number of people even in skilled occupations. A man or woman starts off getting a certain type of job training and then finds it more and more difficult to switch to another type of career. The person anticipates social disapproval for "wasting" his training, which tends to increase with each increment of training or advancement. And, of course, he is also deterred from changing by his own sense of prior investment of time, effort, and money in the direction he has already moved.

Matza (1964) indicates that the careers of lawbreakers are often arrived at in the same stepwise, drifting fashion, without any single stage at which the offenders decide they are going to pursue a life of crime. Rather, they start with minor offenses, get into more and more trouble with the police, and proceed slowly to enlarge their repertoire of criminal acts until they reach the point where they are regularly committing serious crimes. Each successive crime in the series appears to be not very much worse than the preceding one, and in this stepwise fashion the person proceeds to move from minor delinquency to major crime.

A similar stepwise process has been reported for the decision to marry. Waller (1938, p. 259) noted that during the early decades of the twentieth century the process of mating unfolded gradually, in a series of steps whereby the person became increasingly committed in his own eyes and in those of others to the decision to marry. Each step involved the use of a few simple criteria, with no effort to weigh alternatives.

These observational reports about incremental decision making on such vital personal choices as marriage and career, although not sufficiently detailed to enable us to draw definitive conclusions about decision-making processes, suggest that the succession of small decisions may often be based on a satisficing or quasi-satisficing strategy, just as in the case of the incremental policy-making decisions described by administrative scientists.

## MIXED SCANNING

Etzioni (1967) has outlined a conglomerate strategy called mixed scanning, which he sees as a synthesis of the stringent rationalism of optimizing and the "muddling," slipshod approach of extreme incrementalism, displayed by bureaucrats who use consensus as their only satisficing criterion. The mixed-scanning strategy has two main components: (1) some of the features of the optimizing strategy combined with essential features of the elimination-by-aspects approach are used for fundamental policy decisions that set basic directions; and (2) an incremental process (based on simple forms of satisficing) is followed for the minor or "bit" decisions that ensue after the basic policy direction is set, resulting in gradual revisions and sometimes preparing the way for a new fundamental decision. Etzioni argues that this mixture of substrategies fits the needs of democratic governments and organizations. In noncrisis periods, it is easier to obtain a consensus on "increments similar to the existing policies than to gain support for a new policy" (p. 294). But in times of serious trouble, a crisis stimulates intensive search for a better policy and serves "to build consensus for major changes of direction which are overdue (e.g., governmental guidance of economic stability, the welfare state, desegregation)" (p. 294).

Etzioni uses the term *scanning* to refer to the search, collection, processing, evaluation, and weighing of information in the process of making a choice—i.e., the main cognitive activities that enter into the orientation we call vigilant information processing. The intensiveness of scanning can vary over a wide range, from very superficial to extremely intensive, depending on how much "coverage" the decision maker strives for when he surveys the relevant fields of information, how much detail he "takes in," and how completely he "explores alternative steps." Each time he faces a dilemma that requires choosing a new course of action, he has to make a deliberate prior judgment about how much of his resources of time, energy, and money he is willing to allocate to search and appraisal activities.

Etzioni's description of the mixed-scanning strategy includes a set of rules for allocating resources to scanning whenever a policy maker faces the type of crisis that leads him to realize that earlier policy lines ought to be reviewed and perhaps changed.

*Put into a program-like language, the [mixed-scanning] strategy roughly reads:*

*a.* On strategic occasions . . . *(i) list all relevant alternatives that come to mind, that the staff raises, and that advisers advocate (including alternatives not usually considered feasible).*

*(ii) Examine briefly the alternatives under (i). . . . and reject those that reveal a "crippling objection." These include: (a) utilitarian objections to alternatives which require means that are not available, (b) normative objections to alternatives which violate the basic values of the decision-makers, and (c) political objections to alternatives which violate the basic values or interests of other actors whose support seems essential for making the decision and/or implementing it.*

*(iii) For all alternatives not rejected under (ii), repeat (ii) in greater though not in full detail. . . .*

*(iv) For those alternatives remaining after (iii), repeat (ii) in still fuller detail. . . . Continue until only one alternative is left. . . .*

*b.* Before implementation *[in order to prepare for subsequent "incrementing"] (i) when possible, fragment the implementation into several sequential steps. . . .*

*(ii) When possible, divide the commitment to implement into several serial steps. . . .*

*(iii) When possible, divide the commitment of assets into several serial steps and maintain a strategic reserve. . . .*

*(iv) Arrange implementation in such a way that, if possible, costly and less reversible decisions will appear later in the process than those which are more reversible and less costly.*

*(v) Provide a time schedule for the additional collection and processing of information. . . .*

*c.* Review while implementing. *(i) Scan on a semi-encompassing level after the first sub-set of increments is implemented. If they "work," continue to scan on a semi-encompassing level after longer intervals and in full, over-all review, still less frequently.*

*(ii) Scan more encompassingly whenever a series of increments, although each one seems a step in the right direction, results in deeper difficulties.*

*(iii) Be sure to scan at set intervals in full, over-all review even if everything seems all right. . . .*

*d.* Formulate a rule for the allocation of assets and time among the various levels of scanning. . . . [pp. 286–88]

The only testing rule specified for fundamental decisions in the above program is one that would be rated as satisficing on one of the primary variables that defines the satisficing strategy—namely, rejecting every alternative that has a "crippling" objection, which is tantamount to using a minimal cutoff point. But instead of a quasi-satisficing approach, a quasi-optimizing approach could be used when dealing with those alternatives that survive the initial rejection test: each time the surviving alternatives are reexamined, the testing rule might be changed in the optimizing direction by raising the minimum standard (from "crippling" objections to more minor objections) or by introducing a comparative type of testing for selecting the least objectionable alternative. Etzioni no doubt assumes that the standards are raised each time the surviving alternatives are retested, since if the definition of *crippling* were to remain constant there would be little point in reexamining the alternatives, except to catch and correct blatant errors made the first time. In any case, if we assume that the proposed upgrading of the testing rule is introduced into Etzioni's program for making fundamental decisions, the program would directly or indirectly embody the seven criteria we have specified for a vigilant information-processing orientation. Four of the criteria are explicitly mentioned (no. 1—thorough canvassing of alternatives; no. 2—taking account of the full range of objectives and values to be fulfilled; no. 4—intensive search for new information; no. 7—detailed provisions for implementation, with contingency plans). Moreover, in order to carry out all the quasi-optimizing steps conscientiously, the decision maker would be required by the program to meet the other three criteria as well (no. 3—careful weighing of consequences of each alternative; no. 5—thorough assimilation of new information; no. 6—reexamination of consequences before making a final choice).

Although intended for policy makers, the same program, with minor modifications, could be applied to an individual's work-task decisions and to personal decisions involving career, marriage, health, or financial security. (Only a few slight changes in wording would be necessary—e.g., in step a (i), for personal decisions, *the staff* would be replaced by *family and friends*.)

The program for mixed scanning is presented by Etzioni primarily as a normative or prescriptive model, specifying what decision makers *should* do. The mixed-scanning strategy obviously has the virtue of adaptive flexibility at different stages of decision making, with a quasi-optimizing approach being used only while selecting the trunk of a new decision tree and a satisficing approach being used after the new fundamental policy has been chosen, as one moves

out along the branches. Etzioni expects that decision makers will improve their effectiveness in attaining their actual goals if they follow his recommendations to differentiate "fundamental" from "bit" decisions and carry out the intensive scanning procedures he prescribes for the fundamental ones.

Etzioni suggests further that the mixed-scanning strategy may be an accurate descriptive model of what governmental policy makers *actually* do. He offers no systematic evidence, however, to support this hypothesis, although he mentions a few case studies that seem to fit the model. He challenges the overgeneralizations that have been drawn from the finding that the United States Congress generally makes only marginal (incremental) changes in the annual budget for federal agencies, raising or lowering the amounts allocated by just a slight percentage from the amounts allocated the preceding year (Fenno, 1966). He points out that congressmen occasionally make a fundamental decision to increase drastically the percentage of the gross national product to be devoted to the federal budget, as they did at the outbreak of the Korean War in 1950. The U.S. defense budget jumped from 5.0 percent of the GNP in 1950 to 10.3 percent in 1951; thereafter it fluctuated between 9.0 and 11.3 percent during the next decade, reflecting incremental decisions. Etzioni cites a similar jump in the budget for the national space agency in 1958, when Congress agreed to support a new program for space exploration, which was followed by incremental changes during the subsequent years. In these instances, what appears to be a series of incremental decisions turns out to be an extension of a fundamental, nonincremental policy decision. Whether the fundamental decision in each instance was made in the way described by Etzioni's program, however, requires further evidence—which Etzioni does not examine—concerning the procedures used by the decision makers in arriving at a new policy. It remains an open, empirical question whether any sizable population or subpopulation of decision makers does, in fact, proceed along the lines specified in Etzioni's description of the mixed-scanning strategy.

## THE DECISION MAKER'S REPERTOIRE

Implicit in Etzioni's account is the assumption that every decision maker has in his repertoire all the component substrategies and orientations we have described in the preceding sections. Adopting a given strategy at one stage of the decision-making sequence does not preclude use of another strategy at a later stage, particularly if the earlier one proves ineffective in resolving the conflict. For some people, the work of making a decision involves switching from low-cost, low-energy substrategies to more costly, effortful ones as they realize they are unable to settle the decisional conflict.

We expect that when different strategies or substrategies are used, different information-processing orientations in the decision maker's repertoire come to the fore. When he is trying to optimize, as we have seen, the decision maker consistently behaves like an intelligent realist, pursuing maximum satisfaction or utility with single-minded attention. He uses his mental capacities to a remarkable degree while searching for all viable alternatives and trying to understand all their possible consequences.

When operating as a "mixed scanner," the decision maker solves the problem of his limited capacity to process information by classifying decisions as either fundamental or minor. He conserves his time and energy by scanning intensively only those choices that are the most important or most troublesome, treating all other choices much more superficially.

When satisficing, on the other hand, the decision maker deals with fundamental decisions in the same way as minor ones; he relies on one or a few rock-bottom principles that enable him to reduce a complex decisional problem into a matter of judging what will do and what won't do, which requires much less time and effort for search and appraisal. When in response to a profound challenge the decision maker functions as an incrementalist muddler, he resorts to the simplest form of satisficing, making only slight adjustments in an obsolete policy after doing little more than checking on the agreement of other interested parties. This crude form of satisficing is more likely than other strategies to lead to gross failures to meet the criteria for vigilant information processing. For vital decisions, the most damaging consequences are to be expected when the preliminary appraisal of the challenge is itself based on such a low level of vigilance that the person fails to realize the importance of the objectives and values at stake. But a muddling strategy might be adaptive in a stable environment, where few fundamental challenges to existing policies are encountered.

According to a general assumption, ... we expect that irrespective of the strategy adopted—i.e., whether the decision maker strives to optimize, settles for satisficing, or tries to follow a mixed strategy—the likelihood of miscalculation and postdecisional regret increases as a function of the degree to which he fails to engage in vigilant information processing (as defined by the seven criteria) during the period preceding commitment. Hence, according to this assumption, when attempting to predict the consequences of a satisficing strategy—or any other strategy—one needs to inquire into the degree to which the decision maker meets the seven criteria.

If we make the additional assumption that practically all the various strategies and substrategies we have discussed are in the repertoire of every decision maker, we find ourselves confronting a new set of research questions that need to be answered in order to develop an adequate descriptive theory of decision making. The old question, which has been addressed by many social scientists, was "Which strategy is the one most decision makers use most of the time?" The answer is still being debated, because no consistent evidence has as yet emerged. But the analysis presented in this chapter inclines us to be dubious about ever finding a general answer that will hold across all types of major and minor decisions, and in all circumstances. After all, being extremely

careful to meet the criteria for vigilant information processing would be almost as inappropriate for a trivial or routine decision among substi-
tutable alternatives as superficial satisficing would
be for a major decision. In *Up the Organization*,
Robert Townsend, the former chairman of the
board of the Avis Corporation, gives some conventional wisdom, well known to business executives who have managed to survive at the
top, about how to approach different kinds of
decisions:

*There are two kinds of decisions: those that are expen-
sive to change and those that are not.*

*A decision to build the Edsel or Mustang (or locate
your new factory in Orlando or Yakima) shouldn't be
made hastily; nor without plenty of inputs from operating people and specialists.*

*But the common or garden-variety decision—like
when to have the cafeteria open for lunch or what brand
of pencil to buy—should be made fast. No point in taking three weeks to make a decision that can be made
in three seconds—and corrected inexpensively later if
wrong. The whole organization may be out of business*
*while you oscillate between baby-blue or buffalo-brown
coffee cups [Townsend, 1970, p. 45)].*

We suspect that in addition to using a simple satisficing approach to relatively unimportant decisions and an optimizing approach to the most important ones, many executives use some form of
mixed strategy when dealing with decisions in the
intermediate range that fall between the two extremes Townsend is talking about. The important
point, however, is that people cannot be expected
to use the same strategy for all types of decisions.

Instead of the old question, then, about which
strategy is most prevalent, a new set of questions
must be confronted: Under what conditions are
people most likely to adopt a nonvigilant, satisficing strategy as opposed to a more vigilant
one? Under what conditions are people most motivated to devote the resources of time, energy,
and money necessary to seek an optimizing solution? What intervention procedures are available
to remedy careless, superficial, or impulsive approaches to decision making when vital consequences are at stake?...

## NOTES

1. In applying the term *strategy* for basic types of search and choice procedures—
optimizing, satisficing, mixed scanning, etc.—we are following the terminology of
George (1974), Etzioni (1968), and other social scientists who have made recent contributions to the analysis of decision-making processes. We do not use the term
*strategy* in the technical meaning it has in game theory.

2. There are, of course, obvious weaknesses in questionnaire research on corporate
decision making. Reliance on reports from a self-selected sample of vice-presidents
can be a risky venture, since industrial executives are likely to be untrained observers
with a strong inclination to bias their responses.

   To test the inter-observer reliability of his data, Stagner computed correlation
coefficients for the responses provided by pairs of executives responding from the
same firm. The level of correlation for pairs of executives describing the decision-
making process for their firm was statistically significant ($r = +.46, N = 52$). While
this level of agreement is encouraging, the amount of disagreement it implies suggests that, within firms, executives are not uniform in their observations of decision
making. Moreover, no estimate can be made of the extent to which the correlation
is inflated by the shared goals of so-called good public relations among the pairs
of executives who decided to return the questionnaires. Nevertheless, some of the
specific findings are not in accord with the usual myths and ideologies promoted
by large corporations, which suggests that the executives in his sample were at least
somewhat candid.

3. We are indebted to Robert Sternberg (private communication) for suggesting that the two main types of strategy described in the administrative sciences literature, optimizing and satisficing, are conglomerates of a number of different variables that should be specified.

4. Incrementalism, as described by Lindblom, is treated by most social scientists as a separate strategy, coordinate with the satisficing strategy. But it is apparent that it is a variant of the satisficing strategy once one recognizes that the content of the minimal requirements or the minimal cutoff points may change from one incremental decision to the next.

5. Dror's critique of the "science of muddling through" emphasizes that giving priority to the value of minimizing risks by continuing in the same direction may be appropriate in an unchanging social environment, but becomes inappropriate when conditions arise that require a fundamental change.

Unless three closely interrelated conditions are concurrently met, incremental change by "successive limited comparison" is not an adequate method for policy making. *These three essential conditions are*: (1) *the results of present policies must be in the main satisfactory (to the policy makers and the social strata on which they depend), so that marginal changes are sufficient for achieving an acceptable rate of improvement in policy-results*; (2) *there must be a high degree of continuity in the nature of the problems*; (3) *there must be a high degree of continuity in the available means for dealing with problems.*

When the results of past policies are undesirable, it is often preferable to take the risks involved in radical new departures. For instance, in newly developing states aspiring to accelerated socio-economic development, the policies followed by the former colonial policy makers clearly do not constitute an acceptable basis to be followed with only incremental change (Dror, 1969, pp. 167–168].

## REFERENCES

Abelson, R. P. Script processing in attitude formation and decision making. In J. S. Carroll and J. W. Payne (Eds.), *Cognition and social behavior*. New York: Lawrence Erlbaum Associates, 1976.

Allison, G. T. *Essence of decision: Explaining the Cuban missile crisis*. Boston: Little, Brown, and Co., 1971.

Barber, J. D. *The presidential character: Predicting performance in the White House*. Englewood Cliffs, N.J.: Prentice-Hall, 1972.

Bickman, L. The effect of another bystander's ability to help on bystander intervention in an emergency. *Journal of Experimental Social Psychology*, 1971. 7, 367–79.

Bickman, L. Social influence and diffusion of responsibility in an emergency. *Journal of Experimental Social Psychology*. 1972, 8, 438–45.

Boulding, K. Review of *A strategy of decision*. American Sociological Review, 1964, 29, 931.

Braybrooke, D., and C. E. Lindblom, *A strategy of decision*. New York: Free Press, 1963.

Brim, O. G., D. C. Glass, D. E. Lavin, and N. Goodman. *Personality and decision processes*. Stanford, Calif.: Stanford University Press, 1962.

Cyert, R. M., and J. G. March. *A behavioral theory of the firm*. Englewood Cliffs, N.J.: Prentice-Hall, 1963.

Dror, Y. Muddling through—science or inertia? In A. Etzioni (Ed.), *Readings on modern organization*. Englewood Cliffs, N.J.: Prentice-Hall, 1969.

Elms, A. C. *Social psychology and social relevance*. Boston: Little, Brown, 1972.

Elms, A. C. *Personality and politics*. New York: Harcourt Brace Jovanovich, 1976.

Engel, J. F., D. J. Kollat, and R. D. Blackwell. *Consumer behavior*. New York: Holt, Rinehart and Winston, 1968.

Etzioni, A. Mixed scanning: A third approach to decision making. *Public Administration Review*, 1967, *27*, 385–92.

Etzioni, A. *The active society*. New York: Free Press, 1968.

Fenno, R. F. *The power of the purse: Appropriations politics in Congress*. Boston: Little, Brown, 1966.

George, A. Adaptation to stress in political decision making. The individual, small group, and organizational contexts. In G. V. Coelho, D. A. Hamburg, and J. E. Adams (Eds.), *Coping and adaptation*. New York: Basic Books, 1974.

Ginzberg, E., S. W. Ginsburg, S. Axelrad, and J. L. Herma. *Occupational choice*. New York: Columbia University Press, 1951.

Halperin, M. H. *Bureaucratic politics and foreign policy*. Washington, D. C.: Brookings Institution, 1974.

Hansen, F. *Consumer choice behavior*. New York: Free Press, 1972.

Hirschman, A. O., and C. E. Lindblom. Economic development, research and development, policy making: Some converging views. *Behavioral Sciences*, 1962, *7*, 211–22.

Jervis, R. *Perception and misperception in international relations*. Princeton, N.J.: Princeton University Press, 1975.

Johnson, R. J. Conflict avoidance though acceptable decisions. *Human Relations*, 1974, *27*, 71–82.

Katona, G. Rational behavior and economic behavior. *Psychological Review*, 1953, *60*, 307–18.

Latane, B., and J. M. Darley. Social determinants of bystander intervention in emergencies. In J. Macauley and L. Berkowitz (Eds.), *Altruism and helping behavior*. New York: Academic Press, 1970.

Leites, N. *A study of Bolshevism*. New York: Free Press, 1953.

Lindblom, C. E. The science of muddling through. *Public Administration Review*, 1959, *19*, 79–99.

Lindblom, C. E. *The intelligence of democracy*. New York: Free Press, 1965.

Matza, D. *Delinquency and drift*. New York: Wiley, 1964.

May, E. R. *Lessons of the past*. New York: Oxford University Press, 1973.

Merton, R. K. The unanticipated consequences of purposive social action. *American Sociological Review*, 1936, *1*, 894–904.

Miller, D. W., and M. K. Starr. *The structure of human decisions*. Englewood Cliffs, N.J.: Prentice-Hall, 1967.

Miller, G. A. The magical number seven, plus or minus two. *Psychological Review*, 1956, *63*, 81–97.

Piliavin, I. M., J. A. Piliavin, and J. Rodin. Costs, diffusion, and the stigmatized victim. *Journal of Personality and Social Psychology*, 1975, *32*, 429–38.

Piliavin, I. M., J. Rodin, and J. A. Piliavin. Good Samaritanism: An underground phenomenon? *Journal of Personality and Social Psychology*, 1969, *12*, 289–99.

Popper, K. R. *The open society and its enemies.* Vol. 1. Princeton, N.J.: Princeton University Press, 1963.

Schwartz, S. Moral decision making and behavior. In J. Macauley and L. Berkowitz (Eds.), *Altruism and helping behavior.* New York: Academic Press, 1970.

Simmons, R. G., S. D. Klein, and K. Thornton. The family member's decision to be a kidney transplant donor. *Journal of Comparative Family Studies*, 1973, *4*, 88–115.

Simon, H. A. *Administrative behavior: A study of decision-making processes in administrative organization.* 2nd ed., New York: Macmillan, 1957, 3rd Ed., New York: Free Press, 1976.

Slovic, P. Limitations of the mind of man: Implications for decision making nuclear age. *Oregon Research Institute Bulletin*, 1971, *11*, 41–49.

Stagner, R. Corporate decision making: An empirical study. *Journal of Applied Psychology*, 1969, *53*, 1–13.

Steinbruner, J. D. *The cybernetic theory of decision.* Princeton, N.J.: Princeton University Press, 1974.

Taylor, D. W. Decision making and problem solving. In J. March (Ed.), *Handbook of organizations.* Chicago: Rand McNally, 1965.

Townsend, R. *Up the organization: How to stop the corporation from stifling people and strangling profits.* New York: Knopf, 1970.

Tversky, A. Elimination by aspects: A theory of choice. *Psychological Review*, 1972, *79*, 281–99.

Vroom, V. H., and P. W. Yetton. *Leadership and decision making.* Pittsburgh: University of Pittsburgh Press, 1973.

Waller, W. W. *The family: A dynamic interpretation.* New York: Cordon Co., 1938.

Young, S. *Management: A systems analysis.* Glenview, Ill.: Scott, Foresman, 1966.

# 36.  UNDERSTANDING BEHAVIOR IN ESCALATION SITUATIONS

Barry M. Staw and Jerry Ross

At an early stage of the Vietnam War, George Ball, then Undersecretary of State, wrote the following memo to Lyndon Johnson, warning him about the likely consequences of making further commitments of men and material:

*The decision you face now is crucial. Once large numbers of U.S. troops are committed to direct combat, they will begin to take heavy casualties in a war they are ill-equipped to fight in a noncooperative if not downright hostile countryside. Once we suffer large casualties, we will have started a well-nigh irreversible process. Our involvement will be so great that we cannot—without national humiliation—stop short of achieving our complete objectives. Of the two possibilities I think humiliation will be more likely than the achievement of our objectives—even after we have paid terrible costs [1 July 1965 (1), p. 450].*

George Ball's remarks were not only prophetic about the U.S. experience in Vietnam. They also pointed to the more general problem of coping with what are now called "escalation situations." These are situations in which losses have resulted from an original course of action, but where there is the possibility of turning the situation around by investing further time, money, or effort.

The frequency of escalation situations can be depicted by everyday examples. When an individual has a declining investment, a faltering career, or even a troubled marriage, there is often the difficult choice between putting greater effort into the present line of behavior versus seeking a new alternative. At the organizational level, similar dilemmas occur. Laboratories must make difficult decisions about whether to continue with or withdraw from disappointing research and development (R&D) projects; banks must decide how to manage their involvement in nonper-

forming loans; and industrial firms often need to determine whether to abandon a questionable venture versus investing further resources. In each of these situations it is frequently observed that individuals as well as organizations can become locked in to the existing course of action, throwing good money or effort after bad. This "decision pathology" has been variously labeled the escalation of commitment (2), the psychology of entrapment (3), the sunk cost effect (4), and the too-much-invested-to-quit syndrome (5). We will review the state of research on this problem and then provide a summary theoretical model along with some guidelines for future research.

## CLASSES OF ESCALATION DETERMINANTS

Much of the early work on the escalation problem focused on psychological factors that lead decision-makers to engage in seemingly irrational acts—that is, behavior not explained by either objective circumstances or standard economic decision-making (5–7). In response, some researchers have stressed that escalation does involve rational decision-making, because individuals do attend to the economic realities of escalation situations once they are made salient or clear to the person (8). Alternatively, others have found (9) that escalation behavior can be depicted as a rational calculus, but this requires going beyond the narrow economics of the situation to include many psychological and social costs of withdrawal, such as the personal and public embarrassment of admitting failure.

Debates over the rationality of behavior in escalation or any other situation are not likely to be

Barry M. Staw and Jerry Ross, "Understanding Behavior in Escalation Situations" from *Science*, Vol 246, October 1986, pp. 216–220.

settled soon. In fact, these arguments may detract attention away from the central phenomenon of interest, which is the tendency of individuals and organizations to persist in failing courses of action. To understand this tendency, one must account for a variety of forces, both behavioral and economic. We will therefore summarize research on four classes of determinants: those associated with objective characteristics of the project as well as psychological, social, and organizational variables.

## PROJECT DETERMINANTS

Project variables are the most obvious determinants of persistence in a course of action. Research has shown, for example, that commitment is affected by whether a setback is judged to be due to a permanent or temporary problem (10); by whether further investment is likely to be efficacious (11); by how large a goal or payoff may result from continued investment (7); by future expenditures or costs necessary to achieve a project's payoff (12); and by the number of times previous commitments have failed to yield returns (13).

A few project variables are less obvious causes of persistence. Endeavors such as R&D and construction projects often foster commitment because there is a long delay between expenditures and economic benefits. In these cases, shortfalls in revenue or outcomes may not be monitored closely or cause alarm, since losses are (at least initially) expected to occur. In other cases, projects may continue, in part, because they have little salvage value and involve substantial closing costs if terminated in midstream (8). For example, the World's Fair Expo 86 reached the point late in its construction in which continuation was expected to produce large losses, but even larger losses would have been sustained if the project had been aborted before its formal opening (14). In a few cases, projects can become so large that they literally trap the sponsoring organization into continuing the course of action. The Long Island Lighting Company's construction of the Shoreham Nuclear Power Plant is an example of such a no-win situation, in which persistence was seen as costly, yet withdrawal was (until very recently) viewed as bringing even worse economic consequences to the organization (15).

## PSYCHOLOGICAL DETERMINANTS

In addition to the objective properties of a project, several psychological variables can also influence persistence in losing courses of action. Probably the simplest of these determinants are information processing errors on the part of decision-makers.

Although accounting and economics texts routinely state that investments should only be made when marginal (future) revenues exceed marginal costs (16), people may not actually behave this way. Consider the responses of college students to the following two questions posed by Arkes and Blumer (4):

Question 3A. *As the president of an airline company, you have invested 10 million dollars of the company's money into a research project. The purpose was to build a plane that would not be detected by conventional radar, in other words, a radar-blank plane. When the project is 90% completed, another firm begins marketing a plane that cannot be detected by radar. Also, it is apparent that their plane is much faster and far more economical than the plane your company is building. The question is: should you invest the last 10% of the research funds to finish your radar-blank plane? Yes, 41; No, 7.*

Question 3B. *As president of an airline company, you have received a suggestion from one of your employees. The suggestion is to use the last 1 million dollars of your research funds to develop a plane that would not be detected by conventional radar, in other words, a radar-blank plane. However, another firm has just begun marketing a plane that cannot be detected by radar. Also, it is apparent that their plane is much faster and far more economical than the plane your company could build. The question is: should you invest the last million dollars of your research funds to build the radar-blank plane proposed by your employee? Yes, 10; No, 50.*

These data clearly indicate that sunk costs (those previously expended but not supposed to affect investment decisions) are not sunk psychologically. They continue to influence subsequent investment decisions.

Not only do escalation situations involve sunk costs in terms of money, time, and effort; they also are framed as losing situations in which new investments hold the promise of turning one's fortunes around. Unfortunately, this is exactly the context in which Kahneman and Tversky (17) and others (18) found individuals to be risk-seeking. People take more risks on investment decisions framed in a negative manner (for example, to recover losses or prevent injuries) than when the same decision is positively framed (to achieve gains).

The miscalculation of sunk costs and negative framing can be characterized as rather "cool" information processing errors, as heuristics (however faulty) called on by individuals to solve escalation problems. Escalation situations can also involve "warmer," more motivated cognitions, however. Self-justification biases (19) have been singled out as a major motivational cause of persistence.

In one of the earliest escalation experiments, Staw (6) hypothesized that people may commit more resources to a losing cause so as to justify or rationalize their previous behavior. He suggested that being personally responsible for losses is an important factor in becoming locked in to a course of action. This hypothesis was first tested in an experimental simulation with business school students. All subjects played the role of a corporate financial officer in allocating R&D funds to the operating divisions of a hypothetical company. Half the subjects allocated R&D funds to one of the divisions, were given feedback on their decisions, and then were asked to make a second allocation of R&D funds. The other half of the subjects did not make the initial investment decision themselves, but were told that it was made by another financial officer of the firm. Feedback was manipulated so that half the subjects received positive results on their initial decisions, while half received negative results.

Data from Staw's study showed that subjects allocated significantly more money to failing than to successful divisions. It was also found that

more money was invested in the chosen division when the participants, rather than another financial officer, were responsible for the earlier funding decision. These results suggest that individuals responsible for previous losses may try to justify (or save) their earlier decisions by committing additional resources to them. Also, because both high- and low-responsibility subjects faced a negative financial scenario (one with previous losses), it can be argued that justification motives may affect commitment above and beyond any sunk cost or framing effects. Several experiments have replicated this self-justification finding with similar responsibility manipulations (20).

Closely related to the self-justification explanation of persistence are the findings of other motivated biases. Cognitive studies show that people slant data in the direction of their pre-existing beliefs and discredit information that conflicts with their opinions (21). Parallel effects in the escalation area have demonstrated that decision-makers responsible for a failing course of action tend to make greatest use of positive and exonerating information (22). Thus, it appears that justification motives may not only affect decisions to save a risky course of action, but may also affect the accuracy of data on which such decisions are made.

In addition to efforts to justify behavior, some passive self-inference processes may also affect individuals in escalation situations. Salancik (23) and Kiesler (24) have posited that individuals are likely to become especially bound or committed to a prior behavior when (i) the individual's acts are explicit or unambiguous, (ii) the behavior is irrevocable or not easily undone, (iii) the behavior has been entered into freely or has involved a high degree of volition, (iv) the act has importance for the individual, (v) the act is public or is visible to others, and (vi) the act has been performed a number of times. These six self-inference conditions assume that individuals draw inferences about their own behavior and the context in which it occurs. Though self-inference theories are less motivational than those that use self-justification concepts (no needs for rationalization are implied), the two approaches overlap almost entirely in their empirical predictions (25).

## SOCIAL DETERMINANTS

Although most of the research on escalation has dealt with psychological or project variables, escalation situations are often more complicated social phenomena. For example, administrators may persist in a course of action, not just because they do not want to admit a mistake to themselves, but because they hesitate to expose their errors to others. Fox and Staw (26) tested this notion of external justification in a role-playing experiment. They found that subjects holding administrative roles with low job security and lack of support by management allocated the greatest resources to a losing course of action. Conceptually similar results were reported by Brockner, Rubin, and Lang (12). They found persistence to be highest under a large audience, high social-anxiety condition and interpreted these results as a face-saving effect. Additional evidence of face-saving can also be found in the bargaining literature (27), in which it is common to find an escalation of hostilities as both parties refuse to back down from earlier positions. For example, using Shubik's (28) dollar auction game, Tegar (5) found that competitive bidding was influenced first by a simple desire to make money, then as a way to recoup prior losses, and finally, as a means to defeat the other party.

The external binding of people to behavior may also be important in escalation situations. Just as it is possible for individuals to form personal beliefs through a self-inference process (23, 24), observers tend to infer motivation and personal characteristics to actors after observing their behavior (29). Thus, people's social identity may become externally bound by their actions with respect to a project. Though no research has specifically tested this idea, one would expect decision-makers to be most closely identified with a project when their advocacy of it has been public, explicit, perceived to be high in volition, and repeated. At the extreme, a project may start to carry the name of its sponsor (for example, "Reaganomics" or "Thatcherism"), increasing the binding of the person to the behavior,

thus making withdrawal from the course of action much more difficult.

Although face-saving and external binding can both be viewed as social factors that increase decision-makers' costs of withdrawal, research has also isolated some social rewards for persistence. Staw and Ross (30) had business students study the behavior of managers in a failing situation. Managers were described as either persisting in a losing course of action or switching to another alternative. The descriptions read by subjects also noted that managers' persistence or experimentation led either to further negative results or ultimate success. As predicted, managers were rated highest when they were persistent and successful. Most interestingly, the data also showed a significant interaction of persistence and outcome. This interaction can be interpreted as a "hero effect"—special praise and adoration for managers who "stick to their guns" in the face of opposition and seemingly bleak odds (31).

## ORGANIZATIONAL DETERMINANTS

Since many of the most costly escalation situations involve the persistence of an entire organization (rather than an isolated individual) to a losing course of action, it is important to consider some organizational determinants of persistence. Unfortunately, few organization-level studies have yet been conducted. Therefore, we are forced to rely more on relevant theory than concrete data in outlining likely organizational determinants of escalation.

Probably the simplest organizational determinant is institutional inertia. Just as there is less than full consistency between individual attitudes and behavior (32), there is also a very loose coupling between organizational goals and action (33). Organizations have imperfect sensory systems, making them relatively impervious to changes in their environments. And, because of breakdowns in internal communication and difficulties in mobilizing their constituents, organizations are slow to respond. Thus, even when the need for change is recognized, it may not occur. Moreover, if actions require altering long-standing policies, violating rules, or discarding accepted procedures, movement is not likely to happen at all, even though (to an outsider) it may seem obviously useful.

Organizations attempting to withdraw from a losing course of action must also contend with political forces. Not only those who are directly involved with a project will resist its dismantling, but so too will units interdependent or politically aligned with the venture. This can become a special problem when projects are important or central enough to have political support on governing bodies and budget committees charged with their fate. As Pfeffer and Salancik (*34*) have shown in their research on organizational decision-making, organizational actions may turn as much on politics as on any objective economic criteria.

At times, a project's support can go beyond politics. The project may be tied so integrally to the values and purposes of an organization that it becomes institutionalized (*35*), making withdrawal almost an "unthinkable" proposition. Two examples illustrate the problem. The first is Lockheed's L1011 Tri-Star Jet program. Although most outside analysts found the plane unlikely to earn a profit, Lockheed persisted in the venture for more than a decade, accumulating enormous losses (*36*). The issue was not ending the project, per se, but in having to reinterpret the company's role in commercial aviation. For Lockheed to drop the L1011 meant having to change its identity from a pioneer in commercial aircraft to that of simply a defense contractor. Pan American Airlines recently faced a similar institutional issue. More than most airlines, Pan Am suffered major losses after deregulation of the industry. However, as losses accumulated, it successively sold off most of its nonairlines assets. First, the Pan Am building was sold to meet debt obligations. Then, as losses continued to mount, the Intercontinental Hotel chain was sold. Finally, Pan Am was forced to sell its valuable Pacific routes to United Airlines. Withdrawing from the real estate

and hotel business was probably an easier decision for this organization than ending the more institutionalized airline operations, irrespective of the economics involved.

## THE DYNAMICS OF ESCALATION

This review of escalation research has been more illustrative than exhaustive. Yet, it is evident from even this brief summary that studies of escalation behavior have focused primarily on psychological determinants, with social and organizational variables only recently receiving attention. Unfortunately, this difference in research emphasis has had less to do with the relevance of particular determinants of escalation than with the difficulty of operationalizing concepts and conducting empirical studies at more macroscopic levels. Because many of the most disastrous escalation situations involve larger social entities such as governmental and business organizations, further macro-level studies of escalation are therefore needed.

As we have noted, escalation situations are also a forum for a variety of forces, both behavioral and economic. Consequently, an important question for future research is how these various forces combine to affect behavior in escalation contexts. Already some research suggests that escalation behavior may not only be multi-determined, but also temporally dependent. That is, escalation situations may change character over time, such that different determinants of persistence and withdrawal become dominant at separate stages in an escalation cycle. A preliminary model of how the influence of several key variables may unfold over time, based on two field studies of naturally occurring escalation situations (*14, 15*), is shown in Figure 36.1.

The first phase of escalation is dominated by the economics of a project, with the decision to begin a course of action made largely on the basis of the anticipation of economic benefits. However, when questionable or negative results are received (at Phase 2), the decision to persist is based not just on project economics, but also on psychological and social determinants.

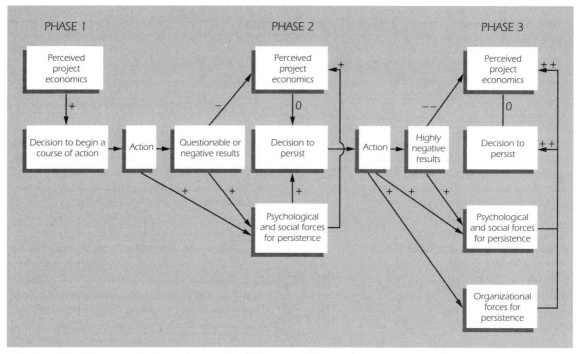

**FIGURE 36.1** A three-stage model of the escalation process. The +, −, and 0 show positive, negative, and neutral influences, respectively.

Assuming that psychological and social forces are strong enough to outweigh (or bias) any negative economic forecasts, further investment or persistence in the project is likely. If this additional investment does not turn the situation around and further negative results are received (at Stage 3), withdrawal tendencies may be heightened. Unfortunately, at this advanced stage in the escalation cycle any withdrawal tendencies (due to negative project economics) may be counterbalanced and biased by organizational forces for persistence. Thus, as economic outcomes worsen over time, it is possible for projects to be maintained by the accumulation of psychological, social, and organizational forces, each adding some weight to the decision to persist in a course of action.

At this time, the idea of distinct stages of escalation remains more of a heuristic for understanding the process of persistence than an empirically tested theory. Yet, two in-depth field studies—an analysis of British Columbia's decision to hold Expo 86 (*14*) and an examination of Long Island Lighting's commitment to the Shoreham nuclear power plant (*15*)—have provided support for a temporally based model. In each situation, economic variables were salient early on and psychological and social variables became important after negative consequences started to accumulate, whereas organizational determinants were manifested rather late in the escalation cycle. Of course, whether these time dependencies are always abrupt enough to constitute distinct stages, or whether in other contexts a more gradual shifting of influence occurs, is still an open question.

No doubt an important step in validating a temporal model of escalation will be the isolation of critical incidents setting off or preconditioning particular determinants of persistence. If these preconditions are found to follow a predictable sequence (that is, arising early or late in the escalation cycle) across a variety of contexts, then a strong case can be made for a temporal model.

In searching for the preconditions of escalation, we would argue that escalation situations typically involve the following sequence of events. First, in launching a new product or project, individual "project champions" will not only work hard to promote the venture but in so doing will probably sow the seeds for subsequent commitment (for example, via self-inference effects). Once questionable or adverse results are received, a negative perceptual frame and sunk costs may then become associated with the project. At this time, those who have had an active hand in developing the project will likely suffer personal embarrassment (or even loss of employment) with the failing situation, leading to self-justification and face-saving effects. And, once the losses associated with the project are fully recognized throughout the organization, external binding of the proponents to the project (for example, "that's Jim's baby") is likely to make withdrawal even more costly to the individuals involved. Finally, assuming that the project does survive several rounds of negative feedback, then more global, organizational processes may start to manifest themselves. Political support may arise as individual careers and whole departments become dependent on the project. And, if the project lasts long enough, withdrawal can become extremely costly not only in terms of the economics involved, but also in terms of the identity of the firm itself.

As elaborated here, the sequence of critical incidents in escalation situations may tend to move from the individual, to the interpersonal environment, and then to the larger organization. We believe this is a natural evolution as project originators (or champions) try to defend a losing course of action, first by themselves (via risk-taking and information biasing) and then by the mobilization of resources involving the larger organization. Additional research on the development of escalation situations is obviously needed to verify these temporal dynamics.

## ESCALATION AS A MULTIDETERMINED EVENT

Since several sources of commitment can be triggered by losing courses of action, one might conclude that persistence is an overdetermined variable, an almost inevitable consequence of escalation situations. A contrary view is that escalation is created by a series of small-impact variables, each insufficient by itself to cause one to remain in a losing situation. For example, if economic losses are large and they occur early in a project's life cycle, withdrawal may well be the dominant response. However, if losses do not appear until later in the process (after several behavioral effects have been initiated), then persistence could be the typical response. Thus, the speed and severity of negative economic data could be a crucial element in how relative forces unfold in escalation situations. Though not an explicit test of this hypothesis, an experiment by Golz (37) has shown how sensitive investment decisions are to the pattern of negative consequences. A slow and irregular decline may not only make a line of behavior difficult to extinguish (in the reinforcement theory sense), but may also allow the forces for persistence to grow over time. Adding support to this "unfolding argument" is a study by Brockner and Rubin (3), in which they found that negative economic data prompted withdrawal when it was introduced early in an escalation situation, but had little influence when introduced after the decision to commit resources had already been made.

## CONCLUSION

As shown by our temporal model, escalation situations contain a confluence of forces—some pulling toward withdrawal and others pushing toward persistence—with their relative strengths varying over time. This dynamic view of escalation is consistent with the contextualist perspective (38) in which social reality is seen as dependent on the situation in which it occurs. Contextualist reasoning supports the continued pursuit of case studies on the dynamics of escalation situations and supports efforts to add realism to experimental tests. Greater efforts are needed to capture experimentally the life-span of escalation episodes so that the relative influence of contributing variables can be tracked over time. Only with such temporally based studies, from both the laboratory and the field, are the dynamics of escalation situations likely to be fully understood.

## REFERENCES AND NOTES

1. The New York Times (based on the investigative reporting of Neil Sheehan), *The Pentagon Papers* (Bantam Books, New York, 1971).

2. B. M. Staw, *Acad. Manage. Rev. 6*, 577 (1981).

3. J. Brockner and J. Z. Rubin, *Entrapment in Escalating Conflicts* (Springer-Verlag, New York, 1985).

4. H. R. Arkes and C. Blumer, *Organ. Behav. Hum. Decis. Processes* **35**, 124 (1985).

5. A. Tegar. *Too Much Invested To Quit* (Pergamon Press, New York, 1980).

6. For example, B. M. Staw, *Organ. Behav. Hum. Performance* **16**, 27 (1976).

7. J. Z. Rubin and J. Brockner, *J. Pers. Soc. Psychol.* **31**, 1054 (1975).

8. For example, G. B. Northcraft and G. Wolf. *Acad. Manage. Rev.* **9**, 225 (1984).

9. B. M. Staw and J. Ross, in *Research in Organizational Behavior*, L. L. Cummings and B. M. Staw, Eds. (JAI Press, Greenwich, CT, 1987), vol. 9, pp. 39–78.

10. L. Leatherwood and E. Conlon, "The impact of prospectively relevant information and setbacks in persistence in a project following setback" (working paper 85-1, College of Business Administration, University of Iowa, 1985).

11. B. M. Staw and F. V. Fox, *Hum. Relat.* 30, 431 (1977); T. Bateman, "Resource allocation after success and failure: The roles of attributions of powerful others and probabilities of future success" (Department of Management, Texas A&M, College Station, TX 91983).

12. J. Brockner, J. Z. Rubin, E. Lang, *J. Exp. Soc. Psychol.* **17**, 68 (1981).

13. B. E. McCain, *J. Appl. Psychol.* **71**, 280 (1986).

14. J. Ross and B. Staw, *Adm. Sci. Q.* **31**, 224 (1986).

15. _____, "Escalation and the Long Island Lighting Company: The case of the Shoreham Nuclear Power Plant" (Working paper, Institute Européen d'Administration des Affaires, Fontainebleau, France, 1989).

16. P. A. Samuelson, *Economics* (McGraw-Hill, New York, 1988); C. T. Horngren, *Cost Accounting: A Managerial Emphasis* (Prentice-Hall, Englewood Cliffs, NJ, 1982).

17. D. Kahneman and A. Tversky, *Econometrica* 47, 263 (1979); D. Kahneman and A. Tversky, *Science* **211**, 453 (1981).

18. M. A. Davis and P. Bobko, *Organ. Behav. Hum. Decis. Processes* **37**, 121 (1986).

19. E. Aronson, *The Social Animal* (Freeman, San Francisco, 1984); L. Festinger, *Theory of Cognitive Dissonance* (Stanford Univ. Press, Stanford, CA, 1970).

20. M. H. Bazerman, R. I. Beekum, F. D. Schoorman, *J. Appl. Psychol.* **67**, 873 (1982); M. H. Bazerman *et al., Organ. Behav. Hum. Performance* **33**, *141* (1984); D. F. Caldwell and C. A. O'Reilly, *Acad. Manage. J.* **25**, 121 (1982).

21. T. Gilovich, *J. Pers. Soc. Psychol.* **44**, 1110 (1983); C. Lord, L. Ross, M. R. Lepper, *ibid.* **37**, 2098 (1979).

22. E. J. Conlon and J. M. Parks, *J. Appl. Psychol.* **72**, 344 (1987).

23. G. R. Salancik, in *New Directions in Organizational Behavior*, B. M. Staw and G. R. Salancik, Eds. (Krieger, Malabar, FL, 1977).

24. C. A. Kiesler, *The Psychology of Commitment* (Academic Press, New York, 1971).

25. P. E. Tetlock and A. Levi, *J. Exp. Soc. Psychol.* **18**, 68 (1982).

26. F. V. Fox and B. M. Staw, *Adm. Sci. Q.* **24**, 449 (1979).

27. H. Raiffa, *The Art and Science of Negotiation* (Harvard Univ. Press, Cambridge, MA 1982).

28. M. Shubik, *J. Conflict Resolut.* **15**, 109 (1971).

29. E. E. Jones and K. E. Davis, in *Advances in Experimental Social Psychology*, L. Berkowitz, Ed. (Academic Press, New York, 1965), vol. 2.

30. B. M. Staw and J. Ross, *J. Appl. Psychol.* **65**, 249 (1980).

31. M. G. Evans and J. W. Medcof, *Can. J. Adm. Sci.* **1**, 383 (1984).

32. M. P. Zanna and R. H. Fazio, in *Consistency in Social Behavior*, M. P. Zanna, E. T. Higgins, C. P. Herman, Eds. (Erlbaum, Hillsdale, NJ, 1982).

33. J. G. March and J. P. Olson, *Ambiguity and Choice in Organizations* (Universitetsforlaget, Bergen, Norway, 1976).

34. J. Pfeffer and G. R. Salancik, *Adm. Sci. Q.* **19**, 135 (1974); G. R. Salancik and J. Pfeffer, *ibid.*, p. 453.

35. P. S. Goodman, M. Bazerman, E. Conlon, in *Research in Organizational Behavior*, B. M. Staw and L. L. Cummings, Eds. (JAI Press, Greenwich, CT, 1980), vol. 2, pp. 215–246; L. G. Zucker in *Research in the Sociology of Organizations*, S. Bacharach, Ed. (JAI Press, Greenwich, CT, 1983).

36. U. E. Reinhardt, *J. Finance* **28**, 821 (1973).

37. S. M. Golz, "A learning-based analysis of escalation of commitment, sunk cost, and entrapment," paper presented at American Psychological Association meeting, Atlanta, GA, August 1988.

38. W. J. McGuire, in *Advances in Experimental Social Psychology*, L. Berkowitz, Ed. (Academic Press, New York, 1984).

39. Supported by the Institute of Industrial Relations, University of California, Berkeley.

# Group Process and Decision Making

## 37.   SUPPOSE WE TOOK GROUPS SERIOUSLY...

Harold J. Leavitt

## INTRODUCTION

This chapter is mostly a fantasy, but not a utopian fantasy. As the title suggests, it tries to spin out some of the things that might happen if we really took small groups seriously; if, that is, we really used groups, rather than individuals, as the basic building blocks for an organization.

This seems an appropriate forum for such a fantasy. It was fifty years ago, at Hawthorne, that the informal face-to-face work group was discovered. Since then groups have been studied inside and out; they have been experimented with, observed, built, and taken apart. Small groups have become the major tool of the applied behavioral scientist. Organizational development methods are group methods. Almost all of what is called participative management is essentially based on group techniques.

So the idea of using groups as organizational mechanisms is by no means new or fantastic. The fantasy comes in proposing to start with groups,

not add them in; to design organizations from scratch around small groups, rather than around individuals.

But right from the start, talk like that appears to violate a deep and important value, individualism. But, this fantasy will not really turn out to be anti-individualistic in the end.

The rest of this chapter will briefly address the following questions: (1) Is it fair to say that groups have not been taken very seriously in organizational design? (2) Why are groups even worth thinking about as organizational building materials? What are the characteristics of groups that might make them interesting enough to be worth serious attention? (3) What would it mean "to take groups seriously?" Just what kinds of things would have to be done differently? (4) What compensatory changes would probably be needed in other aspects of the organization, to have groups as the basic unit? And finally, (5) is the idea of designing the organization around small face-to-face groups a very radical idea, or is it just an extension of a direction in which we are already going?

From *Man and Work in Society*, edited by E. L. Cass and F. G. Zimmer. Copyright©1975 by Western Electric Company, Inc. Reprinted with permission of AT&T.

## HAVEN'T GROUPS BEEN TAKEN SERIOUSLY ENOUGH ALREADY?

The argument that groups have not been taken "seriously" doesn't seem a hard one to make. The contemporary ideas about groups didn't really come along until the 30s and 40s. By that time a logical, rationalistic tradition for the construction of organizations already existed. That tradition was very heavily based on the notion that the individual was the construction unit. The logic moved from the projected task backward. Determine the task, the goal, then find an appropriate structure and technology, and last of all fit individual human beings into predefined man-sized pieces of the action. That was, for instance, what industrial psychology was all about during its development between the two world wars. It was concerned almost entirely with individual differences and worked in the service of structuralists, fitting square human pegs to predesigned square holes. The role of the psychologist was thus ancillary to the role of the designers of the whole organization. It was a backup, supportive role that followed more than it led design.

It was not just the logic of classical organizational theory that concentrated on the individual. The whole entrepreneurial tradition of American society supported it. Individuals, at least male individuals, were taught achievement motivation. They were taught to seek individual evaluation, to compete, to see the world, organizational or otherwise, as a place in which to strive for individual accomplishment and satisfaction.

In those respects the classical design of organizations was consonant with the then existent cultural landscape. Individualized organizational structures blended with the environment of individualism. All the accessories fell into place: individual incentive schemes for hourly workers, individual merit rating and assessment schemes, tests for selection of individuals.

The unique characteristic of the organization was that it was not simply a racetrack within which individuals could compete, but a system in which somehow the competitive behavior of individuals could be coordinated, harnessed and controlled in the interest of the common tasks. Of course one residual of all that was a continuing tension between individual and organization, with the organization seeking to control and coordinate the individual's activities at the same time that it tried to motivate him, while the competitive individual insisted on reaching well beyond the constraints imposed upon him by the organization. One product of this tension became the informal organization discovered here at Western; typically an informal coalition designed to fight the system.

Then it was discovered that groups could be exploited for what management saw as positive purposes, *toward* productivity instead of away from it. There followed the era of experimentation with small face-to-face groups. We learned to patch them on to existing organizations as bandaids to relieve tensions between individual and organization. We promoted coordination through group methods. We leaned that groups were useful to discipline and control recalcitrant individuals.

Groups were fitted onto organizations. The group skills of individual members improved so that they could coordinate their efforts more effectively, control deviants more effectively and gain more commitment from subordinate individuals. But groups were seen primarily as tools to be tacked on and utilized in the preexisting individualized organizational system. With a few notable exceptions, like Renis Likert (1961), most did not design organizations around groups. On the contrary, as some of the ideas about small groups began to be tacked onto existing organizational models, they generated new tensions and conflicts of their own. Managers complained not only that groups were slow, but that they diffused responsibility, vitiated the power of the hierarchy because they were too "democratic and created small in-groups empires which were very hard for others to penetrate." There was the period, for example, of the great gap between T-group training (which had to be conducted on "cultural islands") and the organization back home. The T-groups therefore talked a lot about the "reentry problem," which meant in part the problem of movement from a new culture (the T-group culture) designed around groups back into the organizational culture designed around individuals.

But of course groups didn't die despite their difficulties. How could they die? They had always been there, though not always in the service of the organization. They turned out to be useful, indeed necessary, though often unrecognized tools. For organizations were growing, and professionalizing, and the need for better coordination grew even as the humanistic expectations of individuals also grew. So "acknowledged" groups (as distinct from "natural," informal groups) became fairly firmly attached even to conservative organizations, but largely as compensating addenda very often reluctantly backed into by organizational managers.

Groups have never been given a chance. It is as though someone had insisted that automobiles be designed to fit the existing terrain rather than build roads to adapt to automobiles.

## ARE GROUPS WORTH CONSIDERING AS FUNDAMENTAL BUILDING BLOCKS?

Why would groups be more interesting than individuals as basic design units around which to build organizations? What are the prominent characteristics of small groups? Why are they interesting? Here are several answers:

First, small groups seem to be good for people. They can satisfy important membership needs. They can provide a moderately wide range of activities for individual members. They can provide support in times of stress and crisis. They are settings in which people can learn not only cognitively but empirically to be reasonably trusting and helpful to one another. Second, groups seem to be good problem finding tools. They seem to be useful in promoting innovation and creativity. Third, in a wide variety of decision situations, they make better decisions than individuals do. Fourth, they are great tools for implementation. They gain commitment from their members so that group decisions are likely to be

willingly carried out. Fifth, they can control and discipline individual members in ways that are often extremely difficult through more impersonal quasi-legal disciplinary systems. Sixth, as organizations grow large, small groups appear to be useful mechanisms for fending off many of the negative effects of large size. They help to prevent communication lines from growing too long, the hierarchy from growing too steep, and the individual from getting lost in the crowd.

There is a seventh, but altogether different kind of argument for taking groups seriously. Thus far the designer of organizations seemed to have a choice. He could build an individualized *or* a groupy organization. A groupy organization will, de facto, have to deal with individuals; but what was learned here so long ago is that individual organizations, must, de facto, deal with groups. Groups are natural phenomena, and facts of organizational life. They can be created but their spontaneous development cannot be prevented. The problem is not shall groups exist or not, but shall groups be planned or not? If not, the individualized organizational garden will sprout groupy weeds all over the place. By defining them as weeds instead of flowers, they shall continue, as in earlier days, to be treated as pests, forever fouling up the beauty of rationally designed individualized organizations, forever forming informally (and irrationally) to harass and outgame the planners.

It is likely that the reverse could also be true, that if groups are defined as the flowers and individuals as the weeds, new problems will crop up. Surely they will, but that discussion can be delayed for at least a little while.

## WHO USES GROUPS BEST?

So groups look like interesting organizational building blocks. But before going on to consider the implications of designing organizations around groups, one useful heuristic might be to look around the existing world at those places in which groups seem to have been treated somewhat more seriously.

One place groups have become big is in Japanese organizations (Johnson & Ouchi, 1974). The Japanese seem to be very groupy, and much less concerned than Americans about issues like individual accountability. Japanese organizations, of course, are thus consonant with Japanese culture, where notions of individual aggressiveness and competitiveness are deemphasized in favor of self-effacement and group loyalty. But Japanese organizations seem to get a lot done, despite the relative suppression of the individual in favor of the group. It also appears that the advantages of the groupy Japanese style have really come to the fore in large technologically complex organizations.

Another place to look is at American conglomerates. They go to the opposite extreme, dealing with very large units. They buy large organizational units and sell units. They evaluate units. In effect they promote units by offering them extra resources as rewards for good performance. In that sense conglomerates, one might argue, are designed around groups, but the groups in question are often themselves large organizational chunks.

## GROUPS IN AN INDIVIDUALISTIC CULTURE

An architect can design a beautiful building which either blends smoothly with its environment or contrasts starkly with it. But organization designers may not have the same choice. If we design an organization which is structurally dissonant with its environment, it is conceivable that the environment will change to adjust to the organization. It seems much more likely, however, that the environment will reject the organization. If designing organizations around groups represents a sharp counterpoint to environmental trends, maybe we should abort the idea.

Our environment, one can argue, is certainly highly individualized. But one can also make a less solid argument in the other direction; an argument that American society is going groupy rather than individual this year. Or at least that

it is going groupy as well as individual. The evidence is sloppy at best. One can reinterpret the student revolution and the growth of anti-establishment feelings at least in part as a reaction to the decline of those institutions that most satisfied social membership needs. One can argue that the decline of the Church, of the village and of the extended family is leaving behind a vacuum of unsatisfied membership and belongingness motives. Certainly popular critics of American society have laid a great deal of emphasis on the loneliness and anomie that seem to have resulted not only from materialism but from the emphasis on individualism. It seems possible to argue that, insofar as there has been any significant change in the work ethic in America, the change has been toward a desire for work which is socially as well as egoistically fulfilling, and which satisfies human needs for belongingness and affiliation as well as needs for achievement.

In effect, the usual interpretation of Abraham Maslow's need hierarchy may be wrong. Usually the esteem and self-actualization levels of motivation are emphasized. Perhaps the level that is becoming operant most rapidly is neither of those, but the social-love-membership level.

The rising role of women in American society also has implications for the groupiness of organizations. There is a moderate amount of evidence that American women have been socialized more strongly into affiliative and relational sorts of attitudes than men. They probably can, in general, more comfortably work in direct achievement roles in group settings, where there are strong relational bonds among members, than in competitive, individualistic settings. Moreover it is reasonable to assume that as women take a more important place in American society, some of their values and attitudes will spill over to the male side.

Although the notion of designing organizations around groups in America in 1974 may be a little premature, it is consonant with cultural trends that may make the idea much more appropriate ten years from now.

But groups are becoming more relevant for organizational as well as cultural reasons. Groups seem to be particularly useful as coordinating and integrating mechanisms for dealing with complex tasks that require the inputs of many kinds of specialized knowledge. In fact the development of matrix-type organizations is high technology industry is perhaps one effort to modify individually designed organizations toward a more groupy direction; not for humanistic reasons but as a consequence of tremendous increase in the informational complexity of the jobs that need to be done.

## WHAT MIGHT A SERIOUSLY GROUPY ORGANIZATION LOOK LIKE?

Just what does it mean to design organizations around groups? Operationally how is that different from designing organizations around individuals? One approach to an answer is simply to take the things organizations do with individuals and try them out with groups. The idea is to raise the level from the atom to the molecule, and *select* groups rather than individuals; *train* groups rather than individuals, *pay* groups rather than individuals, *promote* groups rather than individuals, *design jobs* for groups rather than for individuals, *fire* groups rather than individuals, and so on down the list of activities which organizations have traditionally carried on in order to use human beings in their organizations.

Some of the items on that list seem easy to handle at the group level. For example, it doesn't seem terribly hard to design jobs for groups. In effect that is what top management already does for itself to a great extent. It gives specific jobs to committees, and often runs itself as a group. The problem seems to be a manageable one: designing job sets which are both big enough to require a small number of persons and also small enough to require only a small number of persons. Big enough in this context means not only jobs that would occupy the hands of group members but that would provide opportunities for learning and expansion.

Ideas like evaluating, promoting, and paying groups raise many more difficult but interest-

ing problems. Maybe the best that can be said for such ideas is that they provide opportunities for thinking creatively about pay and evaluation. Suppose, for example, that as a reward for good work the group gets a larger salary budget than it got last year. Suppose the allocation for increases within the group is left to the group members. Certainly one can think up all sorts of difficulties that might arise. But are the potential problems necessarily any more difficult than those now generated by individual merit raises? Is there any company in America that is satisfied with its existing individual performance appraisal and salary allocation schemes? At least the issues of distributive justice within small groups would presumably be open to internal discussion and debate. One might even permit the group to allocate payments to individuals differentially at different times, in accordance with some criteria of current contribution that they might establish.

As far as performance evaluation is concerned, it is probably easier for people up the hierarchy to assess the performance of total groups than it is to assess the performance of individual members well down the hierarchy. Top managers of decentralized organizations do it all the time, except that they usually reward the formal leader of the decentralized unit rather than the whole unit.

The notion of promoting groups raises another variety of difficulties. One thinks of physically transferring a whole group, for example, and of the costs associated with training a whole group to do a new job, especially if there are no bridging individuals. But there may be large advantages too. If a group moves, its members already know how to work with one another. Families may be less disrupted by movement if several move at the same time.

There is the problem of selection. Does it make sense to select groups? Initially, why not? Can't means be found for selecting not only for appropriate knowledge and skill but also for potential ability to work together? There is plenty of groundwork in the literature already.

After the initial phase, there will of course be problems of adding or subtracting individuals from existing groups. We already know a good deal about how to help new members get integrated into old groups. Incidentally, I was told recently by a plant manager in the midwest about an oddity he had encountered: the phenomenon of groups applying for work. Groups of three or four people have been coming to his plant seeking employment together. They wanted to work together and stay together.

## COSTS AND DANGER POINTS

To play this game of designing organizations around groups, what might be some important danger points? In general, a group-type organization is somewhat more like a free market than present organizations. More decisions would have to be worked out ad hoc, in a continually changing way. So one would need to schedule more negotiation time both within and between groups.

One would encounter more issues of justice, for the individual vis-à-vis the group and for groups vis-à-vis one another. More and better arbitration mechanisms would probably be needed along with highly flexible and rapidly adaptive record keeping. But modern record-keeping technology is, potentially, both highly flexible and rapidly adaptive.

Another specific issue is the provision of escape hatches for individuals. Groups have been know to be cruel and unjust to their deviant members. One existing escape route for the individual would of course continue to exist: departure from the organization. Another might be easy means of transfer to another group.

Another related danger of a strong group emphasis might be a tendency to drive away highly individualistic, nongroup people. But the tight organizational constraints now imposed do the same thing. Indeed might not groups protect their individualists better than the impersonal rules of present-day large organizations?

Another obvious problem: If groups are emphasized by rewarding them, paying them, promoting them, and so on, groups may begin to perceive themselves as power centers, in competitive conflict with other groups. Intergroup hostilities are likely to be exacerbated unless we can design some new coping mechanisms into the organization. Likert's proposal for solving that sort of problem (and others) is the linking pin concept. The notion is that individuals serve as members of more than one group, both up and down the hierarchy and horizontally. But Likert's scheme seems to me to assume fundamentally individualized organizations in the sense that it is still individuals who get paid, promoted and so on. In a more groupy organization, the linking pin concept has to be modified so that an individual might be a part-time member of more than one group, but still a real member. That is, for example, a portion of an individual's pay might come from each group in accordance with that group's perception of his contribution.

Certainly much more talk, both within and between groups, would be a necessary accompaniment of group emphasis; though we might argue about whether more talk should be classified as a cost or a benefit. In any case careful design of escape hatches for individuals and connections among groups would be as important in this kind of organization as would stairways between floors in the design of a private home.

There is also a danger of overdesigning groups. All groups in the organization need not look alike. Quite to the contrary. Task and technology should have significant effects on the shapes and sizes of different subgroups within the large organization. Just as individuals end up adjusting the edges of their jobs to themselves and themselves to their jobs, we should expect flexibility within groups, allowing them to adapt and modify themselves to whatever the task and technology demand.

Another initially scary problem associated with groups is the potential loss of clear formal individual leadership. Without formal leaders how will we motivate people? Without leaders how will we control and discipline people? Without leaders how will we pinpoint responsibility? Even as I write those questions I cannot help but feel that they are archaic. They are questions which are themselves a product of the basic individual building block design of old organizations. The problem is not leaders so much as the performance of leadership functions. Surely groups will find leaders, but they will emerge from the bottom up. Given a fairly clear job description, some groups, in some settings, will set up more or less permanent leadership roles. Others may let leadership vary as the situation demands, or as a function of the power that individuals within any group may possess relative to the group's needs at that time. A reasonable amount of process time can be built in to enable groups to work on the leadership problem, but the problem will have to be resolved within each group. On the advantage side of the ledger, this may even get rid of a few hierarchical levels. There should be far less need for individuals who are chiefly supervisors of other individuals' work. Groups can serve as hierarchical leaders of other groups.

Two other potential costs: With an organization of groups, there may be a great deal of infighting, and power and conflict issues will come even more to the fore than they do now. Organizations of groups may become highly political, with coalitions lining up against one another on various issues. If so, the rest of the organizational system will have to take those political problems into account, both by setting up sensible systems of intercommunications among groups, and by allocating larger amounts of time and expertise to problems of conflict resolution.

But this is not a new problem unique to groupy organizations. Conflict among groups is prevalent in large organizations which are political systems now. But because these issues have not often been foreseen and planned for, the mechanisms for dealing with them are largely ad hoc. As a result, conflict is often dealt with in extremely irrational ways.

But there is another kind of intergroup power problem that may become extremely important and difficult in groupy organizations. There is a real danger that relatively autonomous and cohesive groups may be closed, not only to other groups but more importantly to staff advice or to new technological inputs.

These problems exist at present, of course, but they may be exacerbated by group structure. I cannot see any perfect way to handle those problems. One possibility may be to make individual members of staff groups part-time members of line groups. Another is to work harder to educate line groups to potential staff contributions. Of course the reward system, the old market system, will probably be the strongest force for keeping groups from staying old-fashioned in a world of new technologies and ideas.

But the nature and degree of many of the second order spinoff effects are not fully knowable at the design stage. We need to build more complete working models and pilot plants. In any case it does not seem obvious that slowdowns, either at the work place or in decision-making processes, would necessarily accompany group based organizational designs.

## SOME POSSIBLE ADVANTAGES TO THE ORGANIZATION

Finally, from an organizational perspective, what are the potential advantages to be gained from a group-based organization? The first might be a sharp reduction in the number of units that need to be controlled. Control would not have to be carried all the way down to the individual level. If the average group size is five, the number of blocks that management has to worry about is cut to 20 percent of what it was. Such a design would also probably cut the number of operational levels in the organization. In effect, levels which are now primarily supervisory would be incorporated into the groups that they supervise.

By this means many of the advantages of the small individualized organization could be brought back. These advantages would occur within groups simply because there would be a small number of blocks, albeit larger blocks, with which to build and rebuild the organization.

But most of all, and this is still uncertain, despite the extent to which we behavioral scientists have been enamoured of groups, there would be increased human advantages of cohesiveness, motivation, and commitment, and via that route, both increased productivity, stronger social glue within the organization, and a wider interaction between organization and environment.

## SUMMARY

Far and away the most powerful and beloved tool of applied behavioral scientists is the small face-to-face group. Since the Western Electric researches, behavioral scientists have been learning to understand, exploit and love groups. Groups attracted interest initially as devices for improving the implementation of decisions and to increase human commitment and motivation. They are not loved because they are also creative and innovative, they often make better quality decisions than individuals, and because they make organizational life more livable for people. One can't hire an applied behavioral scientist into an organization who within ten minutes will not want to call a group meeting and talk things over. The group meeting is his primary technology, his primary tool.

But groups in organizations are not an invention of behavioral types. They are a natural phenomenon of organizations. Organizations develop informal groups, like it or not. It is both possible and sensible to describe most large organizations as collections of groups in interaction with one another; bargaining with one another, forming coalitions with one another, cooperating and competing with one another. It is possible and sensible, too, to treat the decisions that emerge from large organizations as a resultant of the interplay of forces among groups within the organization, and not just the resultant of rational analysis.

On the down side, small face-to-face groups are great tools for disciplining and controlling their members. Contemporary China, for example, has just a fraction of the number of lawyers in the United States. Partially this is a result of the lesser complexity of Chinese society and lower levels of education. But a large part of it, surprisingly enough, seems to derive from the fact that modern China is designed around small groups. Since small groups take responsibility for the discipline and control of their members, many deviant acts which would be considered illegal in the United States never enter the formal legal system in China. The law controls individual deviation less, the group controls it more (Li, 1971).

Control of individual behavior is also a major problem of large complex western organizations. This problem has driven many organizations into elaborate bureaucratic quasi-legal sets of rules, ranging from job evaluation schemes to performance evaluations to incentive systems; all individually based, all terribly complex, all creating problems of distributive justice. Any organizational design that might eliminate much of the legalistic superstructure therefore begins to look highly desirable.

Management should consider building organizations using a material now understood very well and with properties that look very promising, the small group. Until recently, at least, the human group has primarily been used for patching and mending organizations that were originally built of other materials.

The major unanswered questions in my mind are not in the understanding of groups, not in the potential utility of the group as a building block. The more difficult answered question is whether or not the approaching era is one in which Americans would willingly work in such apparently contra-individualistic units. I think we are.

## REFERENCES

Johnson, Richard T., and Ouchi, William G. "Made in America (under Japanese Management)." *Harvard Business Review,* September–October 1974.

Li, Victor. "The Development of the Chinese Legal System" *China: The Management of a Revolutionary Society,* edited by John Lindbeck. Seattle: University of Washington Press, 1971.

Likert, Rensis. *New Patterns of Management,* New York: McGraw-Hill, 1961.

*The U.S. road to disaster—in Vietnam, the Bay of Pigs, Korea, and Pearl Harbor—is paved with*

## 38. GROUPTHINK

Irving L. Janis

*—the desperate drive for consensus at any cost that suppresses dissent among the mighty in the corridors of power.*

"How could we have been so stupid?" President John F. Kennedy asked after he and a close group of advisers had blundered into the Bay of Pigs invasion. For the last two years I have been studying that question, as it applies not only to the Bay of Pigs decision makers but also to those who led the United States into such other major fiascos as the failure to be prepared for the attack on Pearl Harbor, the Korean War stalemate, and the escalation of The Vietnam War.

Stupidity certainly is not the explanation. The men who participated in making the Bay of Pigs decision, for instance, comprised one of the greatest arrays of intellectual talent in the history of American Government—Dean Rusk, Robert McNamara, Douglas Dillon, Robert Kennedy, McGeorge Bundy, Arthur Schlesinger Jr., Allen Dulles, and others.

It also seemed to me that explanations were incomplete if they concentrated only on disturbances in the behavior of each individual within a decision-making body: temporary emotional states of elation, fear, or anger that reduce a man's mental efficiency, for example, or chronic blind spots arising from a man's social prejudices or idiosyncratic biases.

I preferred to broaden the picture by looking at the fiascos from the standpoint of group dynamics as it has been explored over the past three decades, first by the great social psychologist Kurt Lewin and later in many experimental situations by myself and other behavioral scientists. My conclusion after poring over hundreds of relevant documents—historical reports about formal group meetings and informal conversations among the members—is that the groups that committed the fiascos were victims of what I call "groupthink."

## "GROUPY"

In each case study, I was surprised to discover the extent to which each group displayed the typical phenomena of social conformity that are regularly encountered in studies of group dynamics among ordinary citizens. For example, some of the phenomena appear to be completely in line with findings from social-psychological experiments showing that powerful social pressures are brought to bear by the members of a cohesive group whenever a dissident begins to voice his objections to a group consensus. Other phenomena are reminiscent of the shared illusions observed in encounter groups and friendship cliques when the members simultaneously reach a peak of "groupy" feelings.

Above all, there are numerous indications pointing to the development of group norms that bolster morale at the expense of critical thinking. One of the most common norms appears to be that of remaining loyal to the group by sticking with the policies to which the group has already committed itself, even when those policies are obviously working out badly and have unintended consequences that disturb the conscience of each member. This is one of the key characteristics of groupthink.

## 1984

I use the term *groupthink* as a quick and easy way to refer to the mode of thinking that per-

sons engage in when *concurrence seeking* becomes so dominant in a cohesive ingroup that it tends to override realistic appraisal of alternative course of action. Groupthink is a term of the same order as the words in the newspeak vocabulary George Orwell used in his dismaying world of *1984*. In that context, groupthink takes on an invidious connotation. Exactly such a connotation is intended, since the term refers to a deterioration in mental efficiency, reality testing, and moral judgments as a result of group pressures.

The symptoms of groupthink arise when the members of decision-making groups become motivated to avoid being too harsh in their judgments of their leaders' or their colleagues' ideas. They adopt a soft line of criticism, even in their own thinking. At their meetings, all the members are amiable and seek complete concurrence on every important issue, with no bickering or conflict to spoil the cozy. "we-feeling" atmosphere.

## KILL

Paradoxically, soft-headed groups are often hard-hearted when it comes to dealing with outgroups or enemies. They find it relatively easy to resort to dehumanizing solutions—they will readily authorize bombing attacks that kill large numbers of civilians in the name of the noble cause of persuading an unfriendly government to negotiate at the peace table. They are unlikely to pursue the more difficult and controversial issues that arise when alternatives to a harsh military solution come up for discussion. Nor are they inclined to raise ethical issues that carry the implication that *this fine group of ours, with its humanitarianism and its high-minded principles, might be capable of adopting a course of action that is inhumane and immoral.*

## NORMS

There is evidence from a number of social-phychological studies that as the members of a group feel more accepted by the others, which is a central feature of increased group cohesiveness, they display less overt conformity to group norms. Thus we would expect that the more cohesive a group becomes, the less the members will feel constrained to censor what they say out of fear of being socially punished for antagonizing the leader or any of their fellow members.

In contrast, the groupthink type of conformity tends to increase as group cohesiveness increases. Groupthink involves nondeliberate suppression of critical thoughts as a result of internalization of the group's norms, which is quite different from deliberate suppression on the basis of external threats of social punishment. The more cohesive the group, the greater the inner compulsion on the part of each member to avoid creating disunity, which inclines him to believe in the soundness of whatever proposals are promoted by the leader or by a majority of the group's members.

In a cohesive group, the danger is not so much that each individual will fail to reveal his objections to what the others propose but that he will think the proposal is a good one, without attempting to carry out a careful, critical scrutiny of the pros and cons of the alternatives. When groupthink becomes dominant, there also is considerable suppression of deviant thoughts, but it takes the form of each person's deciding that his misgivings are not relevant and should be set aside, that the benefit of the doubt regarding any lingering uncertainties should be given to the group consensus.

## STRESS

I do not mean to imply that all cohesive groups necessarily suffer from groupthink. All ingroups may have a mild tendency toward groupthink, displaying one or another of the symptoms from time to time, but it need not be so dominant as to influence the quality of the group's final decision. Neither do I mean to imply that there is anything necessarily inefficient or harmful about group decisions in general. On the contrary, a group whose members have properly defined roles, with traditions concerning the procedures to follow in pursuing a critical inquiry, probably is capable of making better decisions than any individual group member working alone.

The problem is that the advantages of having decisions made by groups are often lost because of powerful psychological pressures that arise when the members work closely together, share the same set of values, and, above all, face a crisis situation that puts everyone under intense stress.

The main principle of groupthink, which I offer in the spirit of Parkinson's Law, is this: *The more amiability and esprit de corps there is among the members of a policy-making ingroup, the greater the danger that independent critical thinking well be replaced by groupthink, which is likely to result in irrational and dehumanizing actions directed against outgroups.*

## SYMPTOMS

In my studies of high-level governmental decision makers, both civilian and military, I have found eight main symptoms of groupthink.

### 1. Invulnerabilty

Most or all of the members of the ingroup share an *illusion* of invulnerability that provides for them some degree of reassurance about obvious dangers and leads them to become overoptimistic and willing to take extraordinary risks. It also causes them to fail to respond to clear warnings of danger.

The Kennedy ingroup, which uncritically accepted the Central Intelligence Agency's disastrous Bay of Pigs plan, operated on the false assumption at they could keep secret the fact that the United States was responsible for the invasion of Cuba. Even after news of the plan began to leak out, their belief remained unshaken. They failed even to consider the danger that awaited them: a worldwide revulsion against the U.S.

A similar attitude appeared among the members of President Lyndon B. Johnson's ingroup, the "Tuesday Cabinet," which kept escalating the

Vietnam War despite repeated setbacks and failures. "There was a belief," Bill Moyers commented after he resigned, "that if we indicated a willingness to use our power, they [the North Vietnamese] would get the message and back away from an all-out confrontation.... There was a confidence—it was never bragged about, it was just there—that when the chips were really down, the other people would fold."

A most poignant example of an illusion of invulnerability involves the ingroup around Admiral H. E. Kimmel, which failed to prepare for the possibility of a Japanese attack on Pearl Harbor despite repeated warnings. Informed by his intelligence chief that radio contact with Japanese aircraft carriers had been lost, Kimmel joked about it: "What, you don't know where the carriers are? Do you mean to say that they could be rounding Diamond Head (at Honolulu) and you wouldn't know it?" The carriers were in fact moving full-steam toward Kimmel's command post at the time. Laughing together about a danger signal, which labels it as a purely laughing matter, is a characteristic manifestation of groupthink.

## 2. Rationale

As we see, victims of groupthink ignore warnings; they also collectively construct rationalizations in order to discount warnings and other forms of negative feedback that, taken seriously, might lead the group members to reconsider their assumptions each time they recommit themselves to past decisions. Why did the Johnson ingroup avoid reconsidering its escalation policy when time and again the expectations on which they based their decisions turned out to be wrong? James C. Thompson Jr., a Harvard historian who spent five years as an observing participant in both the State Department and the White House, tells us that the policymakers avoided critical discussion of their prior decisions and continually invented new rationalizations so that they could sincerely recommit themselves to defeating the North Vietnamese.

In the fall of 1964, before the bombing of North Vietnam began, some of the policymak-

ers predicted that six weeks of air strikes would induce the North Vietnamese to seek peace talks. When someone asked, "What if they don't?" the answer was that another four weeks certainly would do the trick.

Later, after each setback, the ingroup agreed that by investing just a bit more effort (by stepping up the bomb tonnage a bit, for instance), their course of action would prove to be right. *The Pentagon Papers* bear out these observations.

In *The Limits of Intervention*, Townsend Hoopes, who was acting Secretary of the Air Force under Johnson, says that Walt W. Rostow in particular showed a remarkable capacity for what has been called "instant rationalization." According to Hoopes, Rostow buttressed the group's optimism about being on the road to victory by culling selected scraps of evidence from news reports or, if necessary, by inventing "plausible" forecasts that had no basis in evidence at all.

Admiral Kimmel's group rationalized away their warnings, too. Right up to December 7, 1941, they convinced themselves that the Japanese would never dare attempt a full-scale surprise assault against Hawaii because Japan's leaders would realize that it would precipitate an all-out war which the United States would surely win. They made no attempt to look at the situation through the eyes of the Japanese leaders—another manifestation of groupthink.

## 3. Morality

Victims of groupthink believe unquestioningly in the inherent morality of their ingroup; this belief inclines the members to ignore the ethical or moral consequences of their decisions.

Evidence that this symptom is at work usually is of a negative kind—the things that are left unsaid in group meetings. At least two influential persons had doubts about the morality of the Bay of Pigs adventure. One of them, Arthur Schlesinger, Jr., presented his strong objections in a memorandum to President Kennedy and Secretary of State Rusk but suppressed them when he attended meetings of the Kennedy team. The other, Senator J. William Fulbright, was not a member of the group, but the President invited him to express his misgivings in a speech to the policymakers. However, when Fulbright finished speaking the President moved on to other agenda items without asking for reactions of the group.

David Kraslow and Stuart H. Loory, in the *The Secret Search for Peace in Vietnam,* report that during 1966 President Johnson's ingroup was concerned primarily with selecting bomb targets in North Vietnam. They based their selections on four factors—the military advantage, the risk to American aircraft and pilots, the danger of forcing other countries into the fighting, and the danger of heavy civilian casualties. At their regular Tuesday luncheons, they weighed these factors the way school teachers grade examination papers, averaging them out. Though evidence on this point is scant, I suspect that the group's ritualistic adherence to a standardized procedure induced the members to feel morally justified in their destructive way of dealing with the Vietnamese people—after all, the danger of heavy civilian casualties from U. S. air strikes was taken into account on their checklists.

## 4. Stereotypes

Victims of groupthink hold stereotyped views of the leaders of enemy groups; they are so evil that genuine attempts at negotiating differences with them are unwarranted, or they are too weak or too stupid to deal effectively with whatever attempts the ingroup makes to defeat their purposes, no matter how risky the attempts are.

Kennedy's groupthinkers believed that Premier Fidel Castro's air force was so ineffectual that obsolete B-26s could knock it out completely in a surprise attack before the invasion began. They also believed that Castro's army was so weak that a small Cuban-exile brigade could establish a well-protected beachhead at the Bay of Pigs. In addition, they believed that Castro was not smart enough to put down any possible internal uprisings in support of the exiles. They were wrong on all three assumptions. Though much of the blame was attributable to faulty intelligence, the point is that none of Kennedy's advisers even

questioned the CIA planners about these assumptions.

The Johnson advisers' sloganistic thinking about "the Communist apparatus" that was "working all around the world" (as Dean Rusk put it) led them to overlook the powerful nationalistic strivings of the North Vietnamese government and its efforts to ward off Chinese domination. The crudest of all stereotypes used by Johnson's inner circle to justify their policies was the domino theory ("If we don't stop the Reds in South Vietnam, tomorrow they will be in Hawaii and next week they will be in San Francisco," Johnson once said). The group so firmly accepted this stereotype that it became almost impossible for any adviser to introduce a more sophisticated viewpoint.

In the documents on Pearl Harbor, it is clear to see that the Navy commanders stationed in Hawaii had a naive image of Japan as a midget that would not dare to strike a blow against a powerful giant.

## 5. Pressure

Victims of groupthink apply direct pressure to any individual who momentarily expresses doubts about any of the group's shared illusions or who questions the validity of the arguments supporting a policy alternative favored by the majority. This gambit reinforces the concurrence-seeking norm that loyal members are expected to maintain.

President Kennedy probably was more active than anyone else in raising skeptical questions during the Bay of Pigs meetings, and yet he seems to have encouraged the group's docile, uncritical acceptance of defective arguments in favor of the CIA's plan. At every meeting, he allowed the CIA representatives to dominate the discussion. He permitted them to give their immediate refutations in response to each tentative doubt that one of the others expressed, instead of asking whether anyone shared the doubt or wanted to pursue the implications of the new worrisome issue that had just been raised. And at the most crucial meeting, when he was calling on each member to give his vote for or against the plan, he did not call on Arthur Schlesinger, the one man there who was known by the President to have serious misgivings.

Historian Thompson informs us that whenever a member of Johnson's ingroup began to express doubts, the group used subtle social pressures to "domesticate" him. To start with, the dissenter was made to feel at home, provided that he lived up to two restrictions: (1) that he did not voice his doubts to outsiders, which would play into the hands of the opposition; and (2) that he kept his criticisms within the bounds of acceptable deviation, which meant not challenging any of the fundamental assumptions that went into the group's prior commitments. One such "domesticated dissenter" was Bill Moyers. When Moyers arrived at a meeting, Thompson tells us, the President greeted him with, "Well, here comes Mr. Stop-the-Bombing."

## 6. Self-Censorship

Victims of groupthink avoid deviating from what appears to be group consensus; they keep silent about their misgivings and even minimize to themselves the importance of their doubts.

As we have seen, Schlesinger was not at all hesitant about presenting his strong objections to the Bay of Pigs plan in a memorandum to the President and the Secretary of State. But he became keenly aware of his tendency to suppress objections at the White House meetings. "In the months after the Bay of Pigs I bitterly reproached myself for having kept so silent during those crucial discussions in the cabinet room," Schlesinger writes in *A Thousand Days*. "I can only explain my failure to do more than raise a few timid questions by reporting that one's impulse to blow the whistle on this nonsense was simply undone by the circumstances of the discussion."

## 7. Unanimity

Victims of groupthink share an *illusion* of unanimity within the group concerning almost all judgments expressed by members who speak in favor of the majority view. This symptom results partly from the preceding one, whose effects are augmented by the false assumption that any individual who remains silent during any part of the discussion is in full accord with what the others are saying.

When a group of persons who respect each other's opinions arrives at a unanimous view, each member is likely to feel that the belief must be true. This reliance on consensual validation within the group tends to replace individual critical thinking and reality testing, unless there are clear-cut disagreements among the members. In contemplating a course of action such as the invasion of Cuba, it is painful for the members to confront disagreements within their group, particularly it it becomes apparent that there are widely divergent views about whether the preferred course of action is too risky to undertake at all. Such disagreements are likely to arouse anxieties about making a serious error. Once the sense of unanimity is shattered, the members no longer can feel complacently confident about the decision they are inclined to make. Each man must then face the annoying realization that there are troublesome uncertainties and he must diligently seek out the best information he can get in order to decide for himself exactly how serious the risks might be. This is one of the unpleasant consequences of being in a group of hardheaded, critical thinkers.

To avoid such an unpleasant state, the members often become inclined, without quite realizing it, to prevent latent disagreements from surfacing when they are about to initiate a risky course of action. The group leader and the members support each other in playing up the areas of convergence in their thinking, at the expense of fully exploring divergencies that might reveal unsettled issues.

"Our meetings took place in a curious atmosphere of assumed consensus," Schlesinger writes. His additional comments clearly show that, curiously, the consensus was an illusion—an illusion that could be maintained only because the major participants did not reveal their own reasoning or discuss their idiosyncratic assumptions and vague reservations. Evidence from several sources makes it clear that even the three principals—President Kennedy, Rusk and McNamara—had widely differing assumptions about the invasion plan.

## 8. Mindguards

Victims of groupthink sometimes appoint themselves as mindguards to protect the leader and fellow members from adverse information that might break the complacency they shared about the effectiveness and morality of past decisions. At a large birthday party for his wife, Attorney General Robert F. Kennedy, who had been constantly informed about the Cuban invasion plan, took Schlesinger aside and asked him why he was opposed. Kennedy listened coldly and said, "You may be right or you may be wrong, but the President has made his mind up. Don't push it any further. Now is the time for everyone to help him all they can."

Rusk also functioned as a highly effective mindguard by failing to transmit to the group the strong objections of three "outsiders" who had learned of the invasion plan—Undersecretary of State Chester Bowles, USIA Director Edward R. Murrow, and Rusk's intelligence chief, Roger Hilsman. Had Rusk done so, their warnings might have reinforced Schlesinger's memorandum and jolted some of Kennedy's ingroup, if not the President himself, into reconsidering the decision.

## PRODUCTS

When a group of executives frequently displays most or all of these interrelated symptoms, a detailed study of their deliberations is likely to reveal a number of immediate consequences. These consequences are, in effect, products of poor decision-making practices because they lead to inadequate solutions to the problems under discussion.

First, the group limits its discussions to a few alternative courses of action (often only two) without an initial survey of all the alternatives that might be worthy of consideration.

Second, the group fails to reexamine the course of action initially preferred by the majority after they learn of risks and drawbacks they had not considered originally.

Third, the members spend little or no time discussing whether there are nonobvious gains they may have overlooked or ways of reducing the seemingly prohibitive costs that made rejected alternatives appear undesirable to them.

Fourth, members make little or no attempt to obtain information from experts within their own organizations who might be able to supply more precise estimates of potential losses and gains.

Fifth, members show positive interest in facts and opinions that support their preferred policy; they tend to ignore facts and opinions that do not.

Sixth, members spend little time deliberating about how the chosen policy might be hindered by bureaucratic inertia, sabotaged by political opponents, or temporarily derailed by common accidents. Consequently, they fail to work out contingency plans to cope with foreseeable setbacks that could endanger the overall success of their chosen course.

## SUPPORT

The search for an explanation of why groupthink occurs had led me through a quagmire of complicated theoretical issues in the murky area of human motivation. My belief, based on recent social psychological research, is that we can best understand the various symptoms of groupthink as a mutual effort among the group members to maintain self-esteem and emotional equanimity by providing social support to each other, especially at times when they share responsibility for making vital decisions.

Even when no important decision is pending, the typical administrator will begin to doubt the wisdom and morality of his past decisions each time he receives information about setbacks, particularly if the information is accompanied by negative feedback from prominent men who originally had been his supporters. It should not be surprising, therefore, to find that individual members strive to develop unanimity and esprit de corps that will help bolster each other's morale, to create an optimistic outlook about the success of pending decisions, and to reaffirm the positive value of past policies to which all of them are committed.

## PRIDE

Shared illusions of invulnerability, for example, can reduce anxiety about taking risks. Rationalizations help members believe that the risks are really not so bad after all. The assumption of inherent morality helps the members to avoid feelings of shame or guilt. Negative stereotypes function as stress-reducing devices to enhance a sense of moral righteousness as well as pride in a lofty mission.

The mutual enhancement of self-esteem and morale may have functional value in enabling the members to maintain their capacity to take action, but it has maladaptive consequences insofar as concurrence-seeking tendencies interfere with critical, rational capacities and lead to serious errors of judgment.

While I have limited my study to decision-making bodies in government, groupthink symptoms appear in business, industry and any other field where small, cohesive groups make the decisions. It is vital, then, for all sorts of people—and especially group leaders—to know what steps they can take to prevent groupthink.

## REMEDIES

To counterpoint my case studies of the major fiascos, I have also investigated two highly successful group enterprises, the formulation of the Marshall Plan in the Truman Administration and the handling of the Cuban missile crisis by President Kennedy and his advisers. I have found it instructive to examine the steps Kennedy took to change his group's decision-making processes. These changes ensured that the mistakes made by his Bay of Pigs ingroup were not repeated by the missile-crisis ingroup, even though the membership of both groups was essentially the same.

The following recommendations for preventing groupthink incorporate many of the good practices I discovered to be characteristic of the Marshall Plan and missile-crisis groups:

1. The leader of a policy-forming group should assign the role of critical evaluation to each member, encouraging the group to give high priority to open airing of objections and doubts. This practice needs to be reinformed by the leader's acceptance of criticism of his own judgments in order to discourage members from soft-pedaling their disagreements and from allowing their striving for concurrence to inhibit critical thinking.

2. When the key members of a hierarchy assign a policy-planning mission to any group within their organization, they should adopt an impartial stance instead of stating preferences and expectations at the beginning. This will encourage open inquiry and impartial probing of a wide range of policy alternatives.

3. The organization routinely should set up several outside policy-planning and evaluation groups to work on the same policy question, each deliberating under a different leader. This can prevent the insulation of an ingroup.

4. At intervals before the group reaches a final consensus, the leader should require each member to discuss the group's deliberations with associates in his own unit of the organization—assuming that those associates can be trusted to adhere to the same security regulations that govern the policy-makers—and then to report back their reactions to the group.

5. The group should invite one or more outside experts to each meeting on a staggered basis and encourage the experts to challenge the views of the core members.

6. At every general meeting of the group, whenever the agenda calls for an evaluation of policy alternatives, at least one member should play devil's advocate, functioning as a good lawyer in challenging the testimony of those who advocate the majority position.

7. Whenever the policy issue involves relations with a rival nation or organization, the group should devote a sizable block of time, perhaps an entire session, to a survey of all warning signals from the rivals and should write alternative scenarios on the rivals' intentions.

8. When the group is surveying policy alternatives for feasibility and effectiveness, it should from time to time divide into two or more subgroups to meet separately, under different chairmen, and then come back together to hammer out differences.

9. After reaching a preliminary consensus about what seems to be the best policy, the group should hold a "second-chance" meeting at which every member expresses as vividly as he can all his residual doubts, and rethinks the entire issue before making a definitive choice.

## HOW

These recommendations have their disadvantages. To encourage the open airing of objections, for instance, might lead to prolonged and costly debates when a rapidly growing crisis requires immediate solution. It also could cause rejection, depression and anger. A leader's failure to set a norm might create cleavage between leader and members that could develop into a disruptive power struggle if the leader looks on the emerging consensus as anathema. Setting up outside evaluation groups might increase the risk of security leakage. Still, inventive executives who know their way around the organizational maze probably can figure out how to apply one or another of the prescriptions successfully, without harmful side effects.

They also could benefit from the advice of outside experts in the administrative and behavioral sciences. Though these experts have much to offer, they have had few chances to work on policy-making machinery within large organizations. As matters now stand, executives innovate only when they need new procedures to avoid repeating serious errors that have deflated their self-images.

In this era of atomic warheads, urban disorganization and ecocatastrophes, it seems to me that policymakers should collaborate with behavioral scientists and give top priority to preventing groupthink and its attendant fiascos.

# 39.  QUALITY CIRCLES: AFTER THE HONEYMOON

Edward E. Lawler III and Susan A. Mohrman

The strengths and weaknesses of quality circles, a widely practiced approach to improving organizational performance, have appeared in numerous articles. Both critics and proponents agree that quality circles are typically characterized by a successful start-up or honeymoon period; the initial circles are characterized by high levels of enthusiasm and tend to produce a number of good suggestions. Problems with quality circles typically develop after they become an organization-wide activity, when an effort is made to sustain them over several years. We're going to review several reasons why quality circles typically are difficult to sustain and then look at approaches that deal with the institutionalization and maintenance problems associated with quality circles.

## THE STRUCTURE OF CIRCLES

Quality circles are a parallel-structure approach to getting employees involved in problem solving. A parallel structure is a structure separate and distinct from an organization's regular ongoing activities; so it operates in a special way. In quality circle programs, groups are composed of volunteers from a work area that meet for a few hours every week or two with a special type of leader or facilitator to look at productivity and quality problems. In order to produce change, these groups must sell their ideas to the regular work organization. Because they are a form of parallel organization, they have certain inherent strengths and weaknesses characteristic of all such organizations.

One strength of quality circles is that they allow organizations to deal with issues that are not dealt with in the regular organization, either because of insufficient time, inappropriate definition of responsibilities and goals, or lack of interest on the part of management or staff personnel. In addition, parallel structures can often start quickly and cause only minimal disruption to the organization's performance. The creation of quality circles requires no obvious changes in the regular organization's structure, activities, or responsibilities; nevertheless, circles permit problem solving by individuals who might otherwise not have the opportunity to become involved in this activity. In many organizations quality circles are the only participative management device that managers are willing to accept. They feel this sense of acceptance because quality circles disrupt the status quo only minimally and therefore help keep managerial authority firmly in place.

The problems associated with parallel structures are also significant. Since they are generally viewed as an auxiliary program, they are subject to cancellation. In addition, their kinds of power and problem-solving activities are limited. For example, quality circles typically have the power only to recommend innovations; the decision-making domain remains with the regular organization. Quality circles are authorized to deal only with changes in work methods and procedures or with organizational systems likely to improve quality and productivity. Because they involve only a portion of the employees, parallel organizations can lead to an "in" and "out" group situation and a negative backlash by nonparticipants. Finally, the norms and behaviors in parallel-structure activities may differ dramatically from those that govern the regular organization. Thus participants who are treated as responsible, thinking contributors in the quality circle meeting may receive very different treatment in their daily experiences in the organization. This can lead to internal tension.

Research on quality circles has shown that they go through a series of predictable phases. The first phase, or honeymoon period, is typically very positive. During this phase a small number of groups is formed; these groups are strongly motivated to produce good ideas and improvements, and as a result the organization often realizes significant gains. This period of success is usually followed by the widespread dissemination of quality circles. The organization then counts the number of quality circles and assumes that the more circles there are, the more things are improving.

After the expansion program has triggered the spread of circles throughout the organization, the first significant disillusionment with circles usually sets in. The reasons for this backlash are numerous: the resistance of middle managers, failure to implement some of the ideas generated, nonproductive groups, the extra cost of operating the extensive support systems that groups require, and the failure of some early ideas to produce the level of savings projected. While the initial groups received much high-level attention from sponsors or champions of the process, later groups were usually started more mechanically. Later circles have to complete for management attention; in addition, they are started in an environment in which political or personal dissension has polarized reactions to the quality circle process. At this point, some organizations decide that quality circles were a mistake and abandon them. Other organizations recognize that quality circles have had a positive impact and ask what can be done either to sustain them or to move beyond them to a different form of employee involvement. These questions show a desire to build upon the good features of quality circles and to carry them forward to other kinds of organizational performance improvement approaches.

In our view, quality circles can be an important first step toward organizational effectiveness through employee involvement. Indeed, there are a number of other participative approaches that can build upon the work done in quality circles; there are also some things that can be done to sustain quality circles as an effective parallel structure. The remainder of this article considers various options for companies that have or are considering a quality circle program, such as ways to extend and strengthen the quality circle process and the parallel-structure approach in general. We will also discuss an alternative approach in which teams that are part of the regular organizational structure are responsible for decision making and problem solving. We begin by examining the contributions of quality circles in establishing employee involvement in an organization.

## EMPLOYEE INVOLVEMENT: WHERE DO QUALITY CIRCLES FIT IN?

In thinking about what kind of participative structures are appropriate, an organization must address two important issues: (1) what concerns must be dealt with in a participative manner and (2) how much decision-making authority will be delegated.

Figure 39.1 illustrates the range of choices in these two areas. It differentiates decision styles according to the relative influence of the actual performers of the work and the management structure. It also considers different kinds of decisions ranging from those involving corporate strategy to those related to particular work methods and procedures. As it notes, managers traditionally make all the important strategy, structure, and work-design decisions, as well as most of the ongoing decisions about work procedures.

Quality circles change organizational decision making by providing a vehicle through which the performers can influence their work. Employees can suggest better work methods, procedures, and occasionally organization design alternatives. On the other hand, quality circles are generally discouraged from considering broader policies, strategies, personnel matters, and structures. Quality circles ideas usually must be approved by the regular management and staff structure, mak-

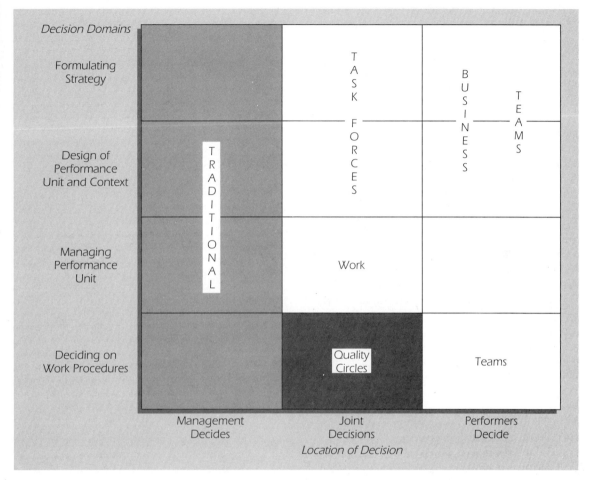

**FIGURE 39.1** Impact of Various Participative Structures in Organizational Decision Making

ing them the result of joint rather than delegated decision making; the upshot of this is that circles are frequently seen as an organizational burden. Instead of transferring responsibility to those who perform the work, they increase the demands on management and staff.

Nevertheless, the use of quality circles does make the organization more participative, and this use can prepare it for other types of participative activities. First, the training programs that are part of most quality circle efforts provide a number of employees with important problem-solving and group-process skills; they also pro-

vide some managers and supervisors with experience as participative leaders. These skills are necessary in virtually every form of participative management.

In addition, quality circles typically establish employee involvement as a credible strategy. Their usually positive results demonstrate conclusively that people at all levels have useful ideas and can contribute meaningful suggestions when given the opportunity. Furthermore, the high volunteer rate usually associated with quality circles convinces managers that people wish to participate.

Finally, quality circles often produce important ideas and ways to improve productivity and quality. The successful implementation of such ideas gives circle members a real sense of accomplishment; it also may lead to greater awareness of how employees can take more responsibility for organizational performance.

Organizations can move beyond quality circles in one of three ways. They can expand the kinds of decisions made by participative groups into the realms of strategy, design, and operations; this is generally accomplished by another parallel structure—the task force or task team. In an alternative approach, organizations can move from a joint decision-making model to one in which work teams are set up, thereby delegating authority downward into the group performing the work. Finally, they can treat the quality circle as the basic building block of participation, altering various aspects of the organizational context to support successful quality circle functioning. These three approaches will be discussed below.

## TASK FORCES

In many respects, creating task forces or task teams is a small, natural step beyond quality circles because they expand the parallel structure approach. Task teams, which involve a cross section of the workforce, usually are assigned specific critical problems. Quality circles training is very appropriate to the problem solving that task forces must do, and task forces often allow the organization to get broad input on problems that quality circles do not normally deal with. For example, they can deal with issues of policy, organization design, and occasionally even corporate strategy. Depending on the kind of participation that the organization wants to give these task teams, they can either decide on policy, strategy, and other organizational issues, or they can simply make recommendations on what should be done.

Like quality circles, task teams are easy to establish and, in many cases, quite productive. Furthermore, like quality circles, they are not ex-

pected to last forever. The task teams themselves have specific life expectancies based on the type of problem they address. New task teams have to be constantly formed if an organization wants to maintain this form of participation. Forming new task teams makes sense if there are always issues to be addressed by the organization, particularly in a dynamic environment requiring constant change and adaptation.

The advantage of task teams is that they can include both the production employees who are a part of quality circles and management people as well. Although some managers who don't like the idea of sharing decision making with lower-level employees may resist task teams, the teams themselves partially eliminate management resistance because managers are included on the task force.

However, task forces share an important problem with quality circles: Only a limited number of people can participate at any one time. As a result, task forces are not a broad participation vehicle. However, because of the limited life expectancy of any particular task team, a number of employees may eventually have the opportunity to serve on one. Because of the increased scope of decisions and the opportunity to involve more people at more organizational levels, task teams can be an important, useful structure for any organization that wishes to broaden the influence that performers have. Companies such as Honeywell and Xerox have successfully expanded their original quality circle program in some of their facilities to include wide usage of task teams.

## WORK TEAMS

Work teams are groups of employees who have the responsibility for producing a product or service. They make most decisions associated with their production activities: They schedule and assign work, decide on methods, and in some cases select their members, decide on their pay, and pick their managers or leaders. Unlike quality circles, work teams are not parallel structures; they are a means of performing the regular production work of an organization. They are sometimes called autonomous work groups, self-managing teams, or semiautonomous groups. As is shown in Figure 39.1, they typically allow employees to make decisions about work methods and procedures and to influence decisions about the day-to-day management of the work area.

Historically, the work team concept grew up quite independently of quality circles. Teams have been strongly recommended as a participative organization design feature for decades, particularly for organizations designed by sociotechnical systems approaches. Many new plants in the United States that have been designed to maximize employee involvement have utilized the work-team model: TRW, Digital Equipment, Procter and Gamble, and Johnson and Johnson have all built plants with teams. Teams are used because they lead to ongoing employee involvement in managing their own work activities. This can be contrasted with the common principle that underlies the implementation of quality circles: The workforce should be involved in productivity and quality enhancement efforts. The former is a commitment to a philosophy on which all aspects of an organization are based; the latter is a limited commitment that may or may not fit the underlying management philosophy.

Going to teams is obviously a dramatic step beyond quality circles; in some respects, however, the former are a logical follow-up to the latter. In effect, circles introduce the organization to participative processes by providing both training for organizational members and real-life examples of how such processes work. In addition, circles may well raise issues that make individuals more aware of barriers to effective performance in the organization, thus making many people eager for new approaches. They may also clarify the ways in which a participative approach conflicts with the traditional management model. Teams may reduce functional divisions by combining responsibility into a team, motivate employees to achieve improvements in performance, and reduce the need for supervision and staff. In light of what we have seen, such teams may seem to be a natural next step.

Despite the potential advantages of teams, we rarely see them occur as a follow-up to quality circles. There are a number of reasons for this. First, they represent a much more dramatic step toward participative management than most organizations are willing to take. As was pointed out, they do in fact require a shift in management philosophy. In addition, they do not naturally evolve from the quality circle programs of most organizations. As will be considered next, they could evolve more directly if certain features of quality circles were designed to facilitate that evolution.

First, we must consider the design of the circles themselves. Quality circles typically take only volunteers from a particular work area and put them into a circle; this means that many people in a work area may not have experience with circles. The team concept does not allow for volunteers; for a team to be effective, everyone in the work area must be a member. In addition, supervisors are critical to the success of a team. In many cases quality circles do not affect the supervisor, and indeed the supervisor's behavior may not be altered as a result of a quality circle program.

If the intention is to move toward teams, these points lead to specific recommendations on quality circle design. First, everyone in the work area should participate in the quality circle program. Secondly, supervisors should be trained as facilitators and should learn the types of leadership skills associated with group decision making. Such training is necessary to prepare them for being team leaders.

If everyone (including the supervisor) is trained, teams may naturally evolve from a quality circle program. This can occur because experience in the parallel organization can be directly transferred to the day-to-day work issues facing a group. We know of one FMC plant where this transition was indeed accomplished. What began as intact work groups that had special "quality circle" meetings to solve problems grew into work teams. Team members were gradually trained in and given responsibility for more aspects of their own management and operations. The FMC plant was fortunately structured so that their work groups fit easily into the work team model. This experience differed from that of a Honeywell plant, which made the transition to self-managing teams only after its plant was gutted and its technical system was redesigned to support them.

An effective team must have responsibility for producing a whole product or service. In many cases, organizations are structured on a functional basis and thus do not contain natural work teams. For example, in a traditionally structured organization machine operators who use the same kinds of equipment usually report to the same supervisor and work together. However, they typically are not a good team because they are responsible for running a machine rather than for producing a product or service. Because members of the work group are not interdependent, many of the gains that teams produce by doing their own coordination and by their problem solving of work quality issues are not available. Thus, even though everyone in a work group or everyone reporting to a particular supervisor is in the same quality circle, a team need not necessarily emerge. It is likely to emerge only, if organization design issues are taken into account and circles are created that have appropriate areas of responsibility.

Some contextual issues must be resolved to enable the transition to work teams. For example, personnel practices are a major issue. One of the reasons why teams are productive is the cross training and consequent flexibility and knowledge of the team members. Pay systems based on inflexible job grades and job descriptions that do not provide increased pay for improved knowledge and skills discourage flexible contributions from team members. In addition, approaches that limit training to specific job-related skills do not develop a broad understanding of business issues in lower-level employees; they need some version of knowledge-based pay and emphasis on cross training and peer training. A work team environment's logic and philosophy differ in such fundamental ways that organizations making the transition to this environment will probably have to modify nearly all their existing personnel systems.

In summary, quality circles can lead to teams, but a number of design features must be built into quality circles if this is to happen. In addition to assuring that supervisors and other employees in the work area are trained, the organizational structure may need to be altered. The best way to form teams is not necessarily on the basis of existing work groups and relationships; new reporting relationships and structures typically are needed. In like manner, changes may be required in many of the major organizational systems, such as personnel practices, that must create a context conducive to work teams.

One implication of this is that although circles may initially operate without major changes in organization design and important relationships, significant organization design changes may have to occur if there is to be movement from a parallel structure approach to one that incorporates work teams. Figure 39.2 summarizes some of the changes that may be required in such a transition.

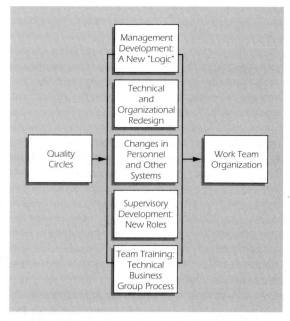

**FIGURE 39.2** Possible Organization Design Changes in the Transition From Quality Circles to Work Teams

## CREATING A SUPPORTIVE WORK ORGANIZATION FOR QUALITY CIRCLES

As has been stressed, one of the reasons quality circles often lose their momentum is that the existing organization is not designed to support the parallel structure created by the quality circle program. People begin to perceive circles as a burden on the organization as they lose their initial enthusiasm and accomplishments are harder to come by. So far we have been emphasizing the development of task for work teams designed to replace or complement quality circles. These approaches in effect open up new participative avenues in the organization. Some characteristics of the existing organization can also be changed to make it more supportive of quality circles and to enhance those circles' effectiveness.

A major candidate for change is the reward system. There is a long history of very successful experience with gainsharing plans, like the Scanlon Plan, that involve the use of parallel organization structures. In these plans, a financial formula is developed for paying out to employees a portion of productivity and/or cost improvements. Experience with these plans shows that a combination of problem-solving groups and performance-improvement bonuses can be a viable long-term strategy for performance improvement.

There are Scanlon Plans in use today that have been in operation for over three decades, and they continue to be effective. A major reason for their long-term effectiveness is that, unlike quality circles, they affect everybody in the organization and reward performance improvement with an important incentive. The effect is to encourage everyone to think of ideas, participate in problem solving, and implement the ideas and suggestions that come out of the problem-solving process. In essence, because everyone in the organization shares in the success of the parallel structure, everyone tries to ensure that the structure works well.

As in the case of the movement to teams, we must point out that the transition to gainsharing may involve fundamental changes in philosophy. Gainsharing is based on the belief that all workers ought to share in financial performance improvements. Many quality circle proponents are quite clear that the benefit to the employee should be intrinsic (outcomes such as satisfaction and pride) rather than financial. The premise of gainsharing is that financial results improve because of everyone's combined efforts; this may conflict with organizational assumptions that such results are the responsibility of management, and that incentives should properly reward managers alone for these results. Gainsharing calls for a broad sharing of information and training about the organization's financial performance, while traditional management thinking argues for keeping this information in the hands of senior management.

In most gainsharing installations, the parallel problem-solving approach is put in simultaneously with the bonus for organizational improvement. However, one need not necessarily follow this particular sequence; indeed, one could very readily follow the installation of quality circles with a gainsharing plan. One problem in the start-up of the typical gainsharing plan is that because there is so much to do, important activities get overlooked. The participative structures frequently do not receive adequate attention because of a tendency to focus solely on the financial part of the plan. In a typical gainsharing plan, for example, people must be trained in the workings of the bonus formula, as well as educated about cost and the organization's financial situation. In addition, problem solving and the suggestion process must be introduced. An alternative to an "all-at-one-time" implementation is to start with the problem-solving process and then move to gainsharing once there are structures and skills in place to generate gain.

Another factor may argue for the use of quality circles before putting a financial bonus in place. Gainsharing uses a fixed historical base to calculate improvements. If the organization has a lot of easily solved problems and is having financial difficulties, it may not make sense to share gains that are gathered from simply putting the house in order. If gainsharing is put in right away, these improvements will result in continual employee bonuses. In the case of an already effectively functioning organization, this usually is not a problem, although it may be in an organization that is performing poorly and needs gains simply to be competitive.

There are other features of the reward system that can be changed to reinforce quality circle activity. For example, some companies in the United States that are committed to sustaining their quality circles have strongly emphasized nonfinancial recognition programs, including convention attendance, circles competitions for best improvement, and meetings with top management to acknowledge superior work. All these programs are potentially effective ways of reinforcing the importance of and sustaining interest in quality circles. Unfortunately, they do not deal with the issue of the nonparticipants; that is, they create neither a participation opportunity nor a reward for individuals who are not in groups.

One way to reduce the discrepancy between people's participative experiences in quality circles and their day-to-day work experiences is to use the human resources systems to develop and reward participative supervisory practices. Supervisors and managers at all levels can be trained in participative techniques, and appraisal, reward, and promotion can be linked to managerial style. Employees who experience a daily environment in which their supervisors solicit input, share information, and are open to suggestions are less likely to resent the time their coworkers spend in circle meetings. "Informal" problem solving is likely to become a regular part of the work setting, and the tension between the participative model of the quality circle and the daily management philosophy will be reduced.

Finally, changes in the information and education systems can help quality circles function more effectively. Most fundamentally, the information system can be designed to enable the regular sharing of key performance measures with all employees in a work unit. When employees in general and quality circle members in particu-

lar are informed of important trends in work-area performance, they can set goals, initiate changes designed to improve performance, and experience satisfaction when performance improves. In addition, the widespread availability of such information, especially if measures are improving, can dispel both managers' and employees' misconceptions that circle meeting is nonproductive and actually impairs unit productivity. Such a clarification is important because the changes caused by quality circles more often have an indirect, cumulative impact on performance rates than a direct, immediately measurable one. Thus the trends can provide "hard" evidence that is often needed to persuade skeptics.

One problem in some quality circles is that the members often lack the economic and business education needed to make good suggestions and decisions. This problem can be partially solved by offering education in economics and organizational performance. Circles often stall after they have addressed the more obvious and easy-to-solve problems in a work area; the circle members do not have enough technical knowledge to go any further. This lack of knowledge may be overcome if technical staff groups provide technical assistance and training to the circles. In addition, the organization's information system can be opened up so that people throughout the organization have a better idea of costs, business performance, and even organizational strategy. Circles often come up with good ideas that are not practical because of strategy changes or business decisions they don't know about. Letting them in on more information can reduce their chances of going down blind alleys and coming up with suggestions for change that are impractical or that can't be implemented.

In summary, changes can be made to an existing organization to help sustain quality circles; Figure 39.3 illustrates these new approaches. The most important of the changes is probably the development of a gainsharing formula that will let everyone participate in the benefits of performance improvement. Other possible approaches include improved information and education for

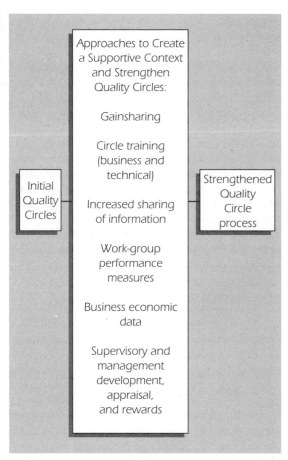

Approaches to Create a Supportive Context and Strengthen Quality Circles:

Gainsharing

Circle training (business and technical)

Increased sharing of information

Work-group performance measures

Business economic data

Supervisory and management development, appraisal, and rewards

Initial Quality Circles

Strengthened Quality Circle process

**FIGURE 39.3** Strengthening the Quality Circle Approach

circle members and the use of training, appraisal, and rewards to develop participative supervision. The suggested reward, information, and education system changes involve changing the work organization in some important ways. In essence, they call for making it a more active organization for lower-level participants by giving them new kinds of knowledge, information, supervision, and rewards. This reinforces the fact that an organization that wants to sustain a participative parallel structure must become more participative in its day-to-day business.

## A STRATEGY FOR INCREASING EMPLOYEE INVOLVEMENT

As the discussion has emphasized so far, things can be done in the organization to support the continued effectiveness of quality circles. On the other hand, quality circles can also be used as a starting point for an organization that wishes to move toward a more participative management approach. Which approach is best? The answer may be somewhat different for organizations that have never had quality circles than it is for organizations that have already engaged in quality circle activity. Let us look first at the issues that confront the former type of organization.

Although quality circles can be a starting point in a move toward participative management, they are not necessarily the best place to start, nor are they guaranteed to lead to other forms of involvement. The argument so far clearly suggests that if they are to lead to more extensive forms of involvement, considerable planning, support, and transition help is needed. Indeed, one clear alternative is to skip quality circles entirely and go directly to teams and other participative structures; this approach has been used in the start-up of many new plants, and in such new organizations as People Express Airlines and American Transtech. In most cases, this is the preferred strategy in a start-up situation; it causes the organization to move more quickly toward creating a participative culture and avoids implementing systems and processes that are out of keeping with a high involvement approach.

The situation may be different, however, in existing organizations. An existing organization may not be ready to move toward a team environment or an environment in which task forces make a number of important organizational decisions. In this case, quality circles can provide a possible first step toward other forms of employee involvement. One must decide at the beginning, however, whether quality circles are an end in themselves or a transition vehicle that will lead to other forms of involvement. As had been noted already, if an organization intends to move to teams and task forces, it must structure circles and train people differently. Finally, an organization with no experience in participation may want to start with a program like gainsharing that introduces a parallel organization structure and simultaneously changes the reward system. When this is successfully done, it can lead to relatively rapid improvement in organizational performance.

In conclusion, an organization without quality circles must plan on a sequence of change interventions that will lead to the type of participative organization desired. The right sequence depends on a number of things, including the technology and the current attitudes and values of the managers and employees. For example, the more traditional the existing organization, the more likely it is that quality circles are a good starting point. If the organization is ready for a more participative approach, then quality circles may be skipped as a first step.

The decisions confronting an organization that already has a quality circle program are much different from those facing an organization with no program. In brief, organizations with quality circles typically face a choice between transitioning them or institutionalizing them. Institutionalizing them can be accomplished by performing the kind of support activities discussed earlier. Transforming them involves the formation of other kinds of parallel structures and/or the development of work teams as the primary focus of idea generation, problem solving, and employee involvement.

The choice between transformation and institutionalization is not an easy one. Our reading of the evidence is that transformation is likely to lead to the greatest long-term organizational effectiveness; however, it is clearly a difficult step

to accomplish, as it involves the development of a new philosophy about managing. In addition, it requires significant changes in managerial behavior and the development of a long-term perspective on organizational performance. A major transition effort in an organization may not be practical or desirable for a number of reasons. For example, the resources may not be available to support it, or instability may be so great that no long-term commitments can be made. Finally, the power structure in the organization may not be receptive to more intensive forms of employee involvement. In this case, the best strategy may be either to allow quality circles to disappear entirely or to make the contextual and structural changes to assure that they continue to operate.

## CONCLUSION

Quality circles are potentially useful in helping move an organization toward greater effectiveness. Their orientation and structures are consistent with a participative approach to management; as such, they pose the following challenge to traditional management approaches: How well can traditional approaches coexist with quality circles? Our view is that, in the long term, quality circles have trouble existing with traditional management approaches; under such conditions, they either fade or require changes in major features of the organization. There is no road map for the use of quality circles. However, some of their strengths and weaknesses suggest that organizations should think carefully before choosing them as an approach to participative management. In most cases, it may be best to transition them to another form of cooperative program.

## SELECTED BIBLIOGRAPHY

This article is a follow-up to an earlier article by Edward E. Lawler III and Susan Mohrman entitled "Quality Circles After the Fad" (*Harvard Business Review,* January–February 1985). Further information on some of the ideas suggested here can be found in Edward E. Lawler III, *High Involvement Management* (Jossey-Bass, 1986). For readers interested in finding out more about work-design and teams, a good basic reference is J. Richard Hackman and Greg R. Oldham, *Work Redesign* (Addison-Wesley, 1980). Further information on reward systems can be found in Edward E. Lawler III, *Pay and Organization Development* (Addison-Wesley, 1981).

Other related publications include Susan A. Mohrman, Gerald E. Ledford, Jr., Edward E. Lawler III, and Alan M. Mohrman, Jr., "Quality of Worklife and Employee Involvement" in C. L. Cooper and I. Robertson (Eds.), *International Review of Industrial and Organizational Psychology 1986* (John Wiley, 1986); Richard E. Walton, "From Control to Commitment in the Workplace" (*Harvard Business Review,* March–April 1985); and Richard E. Walton, "A Vision–Led Approach to Management Restructuring" (*Organizational Dynamics,* Spring 1986).

# CREATIVITY AND INNOVATION IN ORGANIZATIONS

In this section you will learn about both individual and organizational creativity. First you will read about the social conditions that either stimulate or inhibit people's creativity. Then, parallels between the individual and the organization will be drawn. You will learn about the types of people who become independent entrepreneurs or intrapreneurs within corporations. The way organizations should be structured to promote innovation almost directly follows from the characteristics of creative people and the conditions needed to make them bloom. Finally, how organizations as social entities can respond creatively to changes is considered. On the one hand, organizations need to be flexible and unlearn prior behavior to avoid crises. However, organizations also need to set-up measurement systems so that they can recognize when they are making mistakes. Too often changes are introduced without any assessment of whether a new program or idea is truly effective or not.

As you read these selections on creativity try to envision an everyday funnel as a conceptual aid or theoretical metaphor. The mouth of this hypothetical funnel can represent the input of ideas that is then narrowed down to a few selected strategies or projects. Research has shown that the most creative individuals and organizations try to keep a diversity of input, remaining open to ideas that may at first glance seem not to be particularly useful or efficient. However, both creative individuals and organizations also possess mechanisms to sort the novel from the simply bizarre. Individuals use expert knowledge and prior experiences to do the sorting, while organizations use evaluation and budgeting mechanisms to narrow the alternatives. Of course, it is not easy to manage both a wide input of ideas and an efficient sorting mechanism. Yet, individuals and organizations that can effectively funnel original and divergent ideas into a smaller number of viable projects are usually those with the creative advantage.

# Foundations of Individual Creativity

## 40. WITHIN YOU, WITHOUT YOU: THE SOCIAL PSYCHOLOGY OF CREATIVITY, AND BEYOND

Teresa M. Amabile

I study creativity because I'm still trying to figure out something that happened in kindergarten. That's when I first heard the word *creativity*. My teacher had come to our home for the end-of-the-year conference with my mother. While eavesdropping, I heard Mrs. Bollier say, "I think Teresa shows a lot of potential for artistic creativity, and I hope that's something she really develops over the years." I remember feeling thrilled but, sadly, my pride was premature. I haven't done anything even vaguely artistic in the years since; I still draw the way I did in kindergarten. I'd really like to know why.

There are at least two obvious explanations. Mrs. Bollier might have been wrong; maybe I had no particular talent for artwork. I, however, prefer the alternative explanation: I *did* have the beginnings of artistic talent, but my later experiences with art squelched its development. In kindergarten, we had plenty of free access to art materials—easels, paper, lots of paint, clay, and crayons—and plenty of encouragement to experiment with them. The following year, I entered a strict, traditional parochial school where experience with art was limited to an hour every Friday afternoon when, I think, the nuns were too tired to do anything else with us.

Week after week, we were given the same task. Each child would receive a small index-card-sized copy of one of the great masterworks in painting. In second grade, one week, we had Da Vinci's *Adoration of the Magi*. From third grade I remember Chagall's *I and the Village*. Rather than discussing these paintings and artists with us, our teachers instead told us to *copy* them. Given our limited skill development, and our limited materials (loose-leaf paper and a few broken crayons), "art" became an experience in frustration. I couldn't even get all those horses and angels to fit on the page! But, worse than that, we were strictly graded on our monstrosities. I felt my interest in artwork waning, and I no longer pestered my mother to let me draw and color when I was at home.

Only once in those school years did I hear the word *creative*. Inexplicably one day, our teacher told us to take out our art materials and do whatever we wanted. Eager as a prisoner set free, I began drawing a brightly colored abstract mosaic. Sister Carmelita, pacing the aisles, stopped by my desk, lowered her head, and said, "I think maybe we're being a little *too* creative!"

I wondered often what happened to my promised artistic creativity, but my interest in the problem stayed underground for many years. Meanwhile, I was experiencing frustration of a different sort. I had been interested in science throughout high school, but had no idea *which* science to major in once I entered college. I chose chemistry because it looked the hardest. Although I did well, earning A's in my chemistry, physics, and calculus courses, it all left me cold. I worked as a research assistant during the summers, which gave me ample opportunity to observe what I lacked. Each day, our small band of professors and research assistants would troop off to lunch in the cafeteria and seat ourselves around a large table. Each day, the professors could talk of little else but their work—what was going nicely, what had taken a bad turn, what new ideas they had. They spoke with passion and excitement, and by the time we left the table each day, it was strewn with napkins showing hastily sketched equations and models. That passion was what I lacked, and I knew I'd never have it for chemistry; I never found myself wanting to think about my research outside of the laboratory.

I did discover that passion when I took my first psychology course as an elective in college. *Here* was a science I could care about—an exciting science of people, not a boring science of molecules. I had found my true interest, and everything else began to fall into place.

One important piece fell into place when I started the graduate program in psychology at Stanford and learned about Mark Lepper's work on intrinsic motivation. Lepper defined *intrinsic motivation* as the motivation to do an activity for its own sake, because it was intrinsically interesting, enjoyable or satisfying. In contrast, extrinsic motivation was defined as the motivation to do an activity primarily in order to achieve some extrinsic goal, such as a reward. Lepper and his colleagues had investigated the phenomenon they called the "overjustification effect": If an individual who is initially intrinsically interested in an activity engages in that activity in order to meet some extrinsic goal, that individual's intrinsic motivation to engage in that activity in the future will be undermined (e.g., Deci, 1971; Lepper, Greene, & Nisbett, 1973). That certainly sounded like what had happened to me and my artistic potential. Could it be that intrinsic motivation is necessary for creativity?

The overjustification research, however, had not examined creativity or other aspects of performance. It had focused on subsequent interest to engage in an activity. To clarify my hypotheses about the impact of intrinsic/extrinsic motivation on creativity, and to renew my old curiosity about creativity, I began to read the creativity literature—both psychological theory and research, and the self-report writings of individuals recognized for their creativity.

In the psychological literature, I found that little attention had been paid to motivation. Instead, research (most of it done after 1950) had focused on personality characteristics of outstanding creative individuals (e.g., Baron, 1955; Helson, 1965; MacKinnon, 1962), cognitive abilities involved in creative achievement (e.g., Guilford, 1956), the development of creativity tests (e.g., Torrance, 1966), or methods for training creativity skills (e.g., Gordon, 1961; Parnes, 1967; Stein, 1974).

However, there was some psychological literature outside of the "creativity camp" that provided strong suggestive evidence of a link between intrinsic motivation and creativity. Crutchfield's (1955, 1959, 1962) work on conformity found that individuals who had been identified as highly creative were much less likely to conform in the Asch situation than were those identified as less creative. According to Crutchfield, conformity pressures can lead to extrinsic, "ego-involved" motivation, in which finding a solution is simply a means to an ulterior end. This contrasts sharply with intrinsic, "task-involved" motivation, in which the creative act is an end in itself.

McGraw (1978) reviewed a vast literature on problem solving and concluded that reward (an extrinsic motivator) has very different effects on performance, depending on the type of task. *Algorithmic* tasks are those having a clear, straightforward path to solution. *Heuristic* tasks are those with no such clear, straightforward path; some exploration is required. McGraw concluded that performance on algorithmic tasks should be enhanced by increases in extrinsic motivation, but performance on heuristic tasks should be adversely affected. McGraw's descriptions of heuristic tasks clearly included tasks that require creativity.

In his pioneering work on enjoyment, Csikszentmihályi (1975) studied people who were deeply intrinsically involved in activities ranging from chess to musical composition to rock climbing to dancing to surgery. He described the *flow experience* in such individuals, the experience of being totally involved in the activity, where one action flows smoothly into the next and extrinsic concerns disappear.

Csikszentmihályi's description of the flow experience, along with McGraw's assertions about the effect of extrinsic motivation on heuristic tasks, and Crutchfield's discussion of ego-involved and task-involved motivation all fit remarkably well with first-person descriptions of the creative process by widely recognized creative individuals. In reading the autobiographies, letters, and journals of people such as Albert Einstein and Sylvia Plath, I discovered a recurring theme: They felt most inhibited in their creative work when focusing on extrinsic concerns such as expected evaluation, surveillance, or promised reward. They did their most creative work when they experienced the "flow" of deep intrinsic motivation. Using this support from the psycholog-

ical literature, the phenomenological literature, and my own (limited) experience, I formulated what I then called the intrinsic motivation hypothesis of creativity: intrinsic motivation is conducive to creativity, and extrinsic motivation is detrimental. I planned to test this hypothesis by having subjects do creativity tasks in the presence or absence of extrinsic constraints—clearly, a social-psychological paradigm.

When I told my graduate advisers that I wanted to do research in the social psychology of creativity, they informed me that there was no such thing. But, just weeks after that conversation, I opened the new *Journal of Personality and Social Psychology* to find an article by Dean Simonton (1975) with the phrase "social psychology of creativity" splashed boldly about. That was all the encouragement I needed.

## ASSUMPTIONS, DEFINITIONS, AND ASSESSMENTS

Before beginning any creativity experiments, of course, I had to figure out what I was studying and how I was going to measure it. I venture to say that this is the single most difficult problem shared by all creativity researchers. A perusal of previous research revealed that the majority of creativity studies relied on some sort of standardized tests, such as the Torrance Tests of Creative Thinking. Apart from reservations I had about calling performance on these tests "creativity," I was concerned that these tests had all been formulated to pinpoint individual differences in creative ability. To the extent that they were indeed sensitive to such individual differences, these tests were quite appropriate for personality studies of creativity, but quite inappropriate for social-psychological studies of creativity. In my planned studies, I intended to identify social factors that could undermine *any* person's creativity, no matter what that person's baseline level of skill in creative activity. In such studies, individual differences would be error variance, and measures sensitive to such differences would contribute to error.

I decided, instead of using creativity tests for my studies, to simply have subjects make products in response to clearly defined tasks; the tasks would be designed so as not to depend heavily on special skills in drawing, verbal fluency, mathematical ability, or the like. Some such tasks that my students and I have used include making paper collages and writing haiku poems. Once these products have been made in the context of our studies, we have them rated on creativity and other dimensions by experts—people who are familiar with the domain; for example, we ask studio artists to rate the paper collages. This approach to creativity assessment was used by a few previous researchers (e.g., Getzels & Csikszentmihályi, 1976; Kruglanski, Friedman, & Zeevi, 1971), with apparent success. We call it the consensual assessment technique.

The consensual assessment technique for creativity is based on this operational definition: *A product or response is creative to the extent that appropriate observers independently agree it is creative. Appropriate observers are those familiar with the domain in which the product was created or the response articulated* (Amabile, 1982b). Interjudge agreement, clearly, is the most important requirement of this technique. But mere statistical agreement would be suspect without certain precautions: We do not train the judges in any way; we ask them to use their own subjective definitions of creativity; and we ensure that they work independently. Repeatedly, in dozens of studies with small groups of judges, we have found interjudge reliabilities ranging above .70, and often above .80. Moreover, we have found that creativity ratings are statistically separable from other rated product dimensions, such as technical quality or aesthetic appeal.

Although it may be necessary to specify an operational definition of creativity that relies solely on subjective criteria, such a definition is not, by itself, sufficient for a comprehensive theory of creativity—or even for a social psychology of creativity. Any theoretical formulation must make guesses about what judges are responding to when they rate products as more or less cre-

ative. For this reason, we have been guided by a conceptual definition of creativity that is closely aligned with many previous definitions (e.g., Barron, 1955; MacKinnon, 1975; Stein, 1974): A product or response will be judged as creative to the extent that (a) it is both a novel and appropriate, useful, correct, or valuable response to the task at hand, and (b) the task is heuristic rather than algorithmic (Amabile, 1983b).

Our approach to creativity definition and measurement rests on several assumptions about key creativity issues. Indeed, either implicitly or explicitly, all creativity researchers must make assumptions about these issues. I defend mine only by saying that I have not seen persuasive evidence to the contrary. These are the issues: Can creativity be recognized as a quality of products? I believe that the assessment of creativity is much like the judgment of attitude statements on degrees of favorability (Thurstone & Chave, 1929) or the identification of individuals as physically attractive (Walster, Aronson, Abrahams, & Rottman, 1966). Although creativity may be very difficult for judges to define (I have asked them!), it is something they can recognize when they see it. Moreover, experts can agree on the extent to which a given product is creative. And not only can judges recognize creativity in products; I believe they can also recognize it in persons and processes. However, a focus on the *product* seems to me the most straightforward and scientifically conservative; products are the most easily observed discrete units and probably the least subject to disagreement.

Certainly, this approach cannot be used for assessing creativity in products that may be at the frontiers of a domain, where there is bound to be great disagreement as to whether a new idea is highly creative or simply bizarre. But then, *no* approach to creativity assessment will work at those levels. Only the passage of time, and an eventual social consensus, can yield a proper assessment.

Is creativity a continuous or discontinuous quality? I believe that the highest levels of creativity that we see in the world—the greatest scientific advances, the most startling artistic achievements—lie on the high end of the same continuum on which we see everyday "garden variety" creativity—ideas and responses that are more modestly novel and less earth-shattering. I do not believe that there is a discontinuous break in the abilities or thought processes behind differing levels of creativity. The difference seems to lie instead in vastly differing abilities, cognitive styles, motivational levels, and circumstances. The difference is vast—but I do not believe it is a difference in *kind*. Thus I believe it is appropriate to ask expert judges to rate degrees of creativity in products. And I also believe it is justifiable to say that experiments using "ordinary" subjects doing relatively low-level tasks are informative even about Einstein's creativity.

Is the creative process different in different domains? I believe that it is basically the same—that a scientist attempting to develop a new process in her laboratory is going through essentially the same process as an artist in his studio or a poet at her desk. Certainly, different cognitive processes will be differentially important in the various domains. However, in general, the creative process will depend on the same components and be affected by the same social factors. Thus it is appropriate to use tasks from a variety of domains in establishing a social psychology of creativity, or any psychology of creativity.

## EVIDENCE ON THE INTRINSIC MOTIVATION PRINCIPLE OF CREATIVITY

Using the consensual technique for creativity assessment, my students and I have conducted dozens of studies over the past 12 years to test the intrinsic motivation hypothesis of creativity. We find our results sufficiently compelling that we now refer to the intrinsic motivation *principle* of creativity: Intrinsic motivation is conducive to creativity, but extrinsic motivation is detrimental. In other words, people will be most creative when they feel motivated primarily by the interest, enjoyment, satisfaction, and challenge of the work itself—and not by external pressures.

## The Phenomenology of Creativity

The first source of evidence on the intrinsic motivation principle is rather a source of hypotheses about specific social factors that may lead to decrements in intrinsic motivation and creativity: the first-person account. We have studied a great many autobiographies, personal journals, letters, biographies, and interviews of widely recognized creative individuals in a variety of fields. These include writers T. S. Eliot, Anne Sexton, Sylvia Plath, Thomas Wolfe, Fyodor Dostoyevski, D. H. Lawrence, Joyce Carol Oates, Charles Dickens, Gertrude Stein, George Eliot, Isaac Asimov, and John Irving; scientists Albert Einstein, Marie Curie, and James Watson; musician/composers W. A. Mozart and Pablo Casals; artists Pablo Picasso and Ansel Adams; social scientist Margaret Mead; and filmmaker Woody Allen.

Richly complex as they are, these sources strongly suggest the validity of the intrinsic motivation principle in two ways. First, repeatedly, these individuals express high levels of intrinsic motivation for doing their work, The novelist John Irving (*The World According to Garp*) is just one of many examples:

*The unspoken factor here is love. The reason I can work so hard at my writing is that it's not work to me. Or, as I said before, my work is pleasure to me. (Amabile, in press)*

In addition, these creative individuals report numerous incidents in which their intrinsic motivation and creativity were undermined by salient extrinsic constraints. The constraints cited include expected evaluation, strictly regimented educational methods, surveillance, competition, reward, restricted choice, and deadlines. The poet Sylvia Plath provides perhaps the clearest layperson's statement of the intrinsic motivation principle of creativity in action:

*Editors and publishers and critics and the world . . . I want acceptance there, to feel my work good and well-taken. Which ironically freezes me at my work, corrupts my nunnish labor of work-for-itself-as-its-own-reward. (Hughes & McCullough, 1982, p. 305)*

## Experimental Evidence

The second and most important source of evidence on the intrinsic motivation principle is the laboratory experiment. My students and I have used the basic overjustification paradigm in our research: subjects work on an interesting creativity task either in the presence or in the absence of a specific extrinsic constraint. Subsequently, their products are rated on creativity by several independent experts. We have carried out such experiments with a wide range of independent variables (extrinsic constraints), subject groups ranging in age from preschool children to working adults, and a variety of artistic, verbal and problem-solving creativity tasks. Though they are not without their complexities, our results reveal consistent patterns in strong support of the intrinsic motivation hypothesis:

*Evaluation.* Expected evaluation has a detrimental effect on creativity (Amabile, 1979; Amabile, Goldfarb, & Brackfield, in press; Hennessey, 1989). Actual prior positive evaluation has a detrimental effect on subsequent creativity (Berglas, Amabile, & Handel, 1979).

*Surveillance.* Being watched while working has a detrimental effect on creativity (Amabile, Goldfarb, & Brackfield, in press).

*Reward.* Contracted-for reward has a detrimental effect on creativity (Amabile, Hennessey, & Grossman, 1986; Hennessey, 1989). "Bonus" reward (not contracted for) has a positive effect on creativity (Amabile, Hennessey, & Grossman, 1986).

*Competition.* Competing for prizes has a detrimental effect on creativity (Amabile, 1982a, 1987).

*Restricted choice.* Restricted choice in how to do an activity has a detrimental effect on creativity (Amabile & Gitomer, 1984; Hennessey, 1989).

Each of the social-environmental factors shown in our research to negatively affect creativity has also been shown, in overjustification research, to negatively affect intrinsic motivation. In an effort to provide a more direct link between intrinsic motivation and creativity within the same study, we attempted a motivational induction with creative writers. I will describe the study in some detail as a way of illustrating our basic paradigm.

This study (Amabile, 1985) was designed to directly create an extrinsic motivational state in some subjects without going through the intermediate step of first imposing an extrinsic constraint. And the same method was used to directly create an intrinsically motivated state in other subjects. For this purpose, we borrowed a technique from Salancik (1975). We asked subjects to complete a questionnaire about their attitudes toward the target creativity task (writing). Some were given an intrinsic questionnaire, on which all of the items dealt with the intrinsically interesting aspects of the activity. Other subjects completed an extrinsic questionnaire, which dealt with only extrinsic reasons for doing the activity. The purpose of the questionnaire was simply to lead subjects to think about the activity in intrinsic terms or in extrinsic terms. Then, immediate effects of this intrinsic or extrinsic orientation could be directly observed.

It was important in this study to find subjects who were already involved in this type of creative activity on a regular basis so that we might temporarily influence their orientation toward that activity. To this end, we recruited creative writers, using advertisements such as this: "Writers: If you are involved in writing, especially poetry, fiction, or drama, you can make three dollars for about an hour of your time. We are studying people's reasons for writing."

Most of those who responded to the advertisements were undergraduates or graduate students in English or creative writing at Brandeis University or Boston University, although a few were not affiliated with any university. The most important characteristic of these participants, for our purposes, is that they identified themselves as *writers*—they came to us with a high level of involvement in writing. On a prescreening questionnaire, we discovered that they spent an average of 6.3 hours of their own time per week writing poetry, fiction, or drama; the range was 3 to 18 hours.

Upon arrival at our laboratory, each writer completed a questionnaire on "reasons for writing"—reasons for being involved in writing. (Some subjects, in a control condition, did not complete any questionnaire.) On the intrinsic questionnaire, subjects were asked to rank-order (in terms of importance to them personally) seven reasons for writing; all of these reasons had been consistently rated as intrinsic on a pretest. Two of the intrinsic items were these: "You get a lot of pleasure out of reading something good that you have written"; and "You like to play with words." By contrast, the extrinsic questionnaire asked subjects to rank-order seven reasons that had pretested as strongly extrinsic, such as "You have heard of cases where one bestselling novel or collection of poems has made the author financially secure"; and "You enjoy public recognition of your work." After completing the questionnaire, the writers were asked to write a short haiku-style poem. (Those in the control group were simply asked to write the poem.)

After the study was completed, we asked several poets to judge the poems, using the consensual assessment technique. The results were quite dramatic. As might be expected, the writers in the control group wrote poems that were judged fairly high on creativity; these were, after all, creative writers. The writers in the intrinsic group wrote poems that were judged as somewhat higher in creativity than those in the control group, but the difference was not large. The most important result comes from the extrinsic group. Those writers produced poems that were judged as significantly lower in creativity than the poems produced by either of the other groups.

Consider the implications of this study for "real-world" work environments. These writers entered our laboratory with an intrinsic motivational orientation toward writing. Apparently, we were not able to increase that intrinsic orientation much; the creativity of the intrinsic group isn't notably higher than the creativity of the control group. On the other hand, with a ter-

ribly brief and simple manipulation, we significantly reduced the creativity of writers in the extrinsic group. People who had been writing creatively for years, who had long-standing interests in creative writing, suddenly found their creativity blocked after spending barely five minutes thinking about the extrinsic reasons for doing what they do. (A note about the ethics of this experiment: We fully debriefed all of our participants before they left the lab, and we had all of the extrinsic subjects fill out the intrinsic questionnaire at the end of their experimental sessions.)

In this study, a brief and subtle written manipulation had a significant impact on the creativity of highly motivated individuals. Consider, then, the potential effects of extrinsic constraints in everyday work environments on the creativity of people who work in those environments every day.

## Observational Data

It is one thing to assume that the social-environmental factors we manipulate in the laboratory play an important role in real-world creativity. It is another thing to actually find out. In an attempt to do so, I worked with colleagues at the Center for Creative Leadership to interview a large number of research and development scientists about creative and noncreative events in their work experience (Amabile & Gryskiewicz, 1988). We asked the participants, who were 120 R&D scientists from over 20 corporations, to tell us about an example of high creativity and an example of low creativity from their work experience (defining *creativity* as they saw fit). We told them that we were particularly interested in anything about the events that stood out in their minds—anything about the person or persons involved and anything about the work environment. We felt that, by using this critical incident technique, we would be more likely to avoid the interjection of personal beliefs about creativity than if we simply asked interviewees what they thought was important for supporting or undermining creativity in organizations.

In our search for information about the major influences on creativity and innovation, we did a detailed content analysis of verbatim transcripts of these tape-recorded interviews. The types of things our interviewees talked about fell into four major categories. Rank-ordered by frequency, they are as follows: (a) qualities of environments that promote creativity, (b) qualities of environments that inhibit creativity, (c) qualities of problem-solvers that promote creativity, and (d) qualities of problem-solvers that inhibit creativity. In our system, "qualities of environments" are any factors outside of the problem-solvers themselves (including other people) that appeared to consistently influence creativity positively, as in the high-creativity stories, or negatively, as in the low-creativity stories. "Qualities of problem-solvers" are any factors of ability, personality, or mood within the problem-solvers themselves that seemed to consistently influence creativity either positively or negatively. We found that environmental factors were mentioned much more frequently than personal qualities. Because this finding appeared in both the high- and low-creativity stories, and because a large percentage of the stories did not involve the interviewee as a central character (problem-solver), we feel that this preponderance of environmental factors cannot be dismissed as a simple attributional bias.

The prominence of the environment in these interviews is an important finding for the social psychology of creativity. It suggests that our laboratory research on the effects of social constraints has produced not only statistically significant findings but ecologically significant ones as well. The *environment* was a much more salient factor than the *individual* for these R&D scientists in their experience of specific creative and uncreative events. Does this mean that, in an absolute sense, environmental factors account for more of the variance in creative output than individual difference factors? Does this mean that the forces *within you* are less significant than the forces *without you* in determining the creativity of your behavior? Not necessarily, and not even probably. Certainly, at a macroscopic level, personal factors such as general intelligence, experience in the field, and ability to think creatively are the major influences on output of creative ideas by R&D scientists. But, assuming that hiring practices at major corporations select individuals who exhibit relatively high levels of these personal qualities, the variance above this baseline may well be accounted for primarily by factors in the work environment.

Social factors may be responsible for only a small part of the total variance in creative behavior, but they may account for the lion's share of the variance that anyone can do anything about! It is almost always easier to change the social environment (or one's perception of it) than to change traits and abilities.

Our detailed content analysis of the interviews, done by independent coders, revealed several environmental factors that inhibit creativity. Among these are many that we had already studied in experimental paradigms: constrained choice, an overemphasis on tangible reward, evaluation expectation, and competition. There were other inhibiting factors, however, that remain for future experimental investigation: perceived apathy toward the target project, unclear goals, distraction, insufficient resources, overemphasis on the status quo, and time pressure.

## BEYOND THE INTRINSIC MOTIVATION PRINCIPLE

Clearly, there's much more to the social psychology of creativity than just the intrinsic motivation principle. While I have worked within mainstream social-psychological paradigms to study the effects of specific social constraints on the immediate creative performance of ordinary individuals, Dean Simonton has used pioneering historiometric techniques to study the effects of complex social phenomena (such as cultural diversity, warfare, and zeitgeist) on historically recognized creative achievements (see Simonton, 1984, in press). A comprehensive social psychology of creativity must include this work, as well as the work of others who have studied social influences at the macroscopic level (e.g., Albert, 1980; Andrews, 1975).

The data from the R&D interview study suggest a number of environmental variables that may *enhance* creativity. In our previous devotion to the overjustification paradigm and the intrinsic motivation hypothesis, we *de facto* eliminated an investigation of such variables. It may, in fact, be true that undermining creativity is much easier than stimulating it. But that's no reason not to try.

Recently, our own experimental research has begun moving beyond the simplicity of the intrinsic motivation principle. Nearly all of our previous experiments assumed *a hydraulic* relationship between intrinsic and extrinsic motivation: As extrinsic motivation increases, intrinsic motivation (and creativity) must decrease. However, it seems clear from anecdotal evidence that extrinsic motivators such as reward and competition need not undermine creativity. In fact, for some people, there seems to be an *additive* relationship: not only does their intrinsic motivation remain high, but their creativity may actually be enhanced in the face of extrinsic motivators.

For example, the filmmaker Woody Allen seems to have managed to maintain both a high level of intrinsic motivation and a high level of creativity in an extremely extrinsically oriented profession. He more or less ignores both the awards and the critics, continuing to innovate with new styles and themes. As another example, the scientists Watson and Crick clearly felt strong competitive pressure in their race to discover the structure of DNA (Watson, 1968). Yet, at the moments that they made their greatest breakthroughs, they were so single-mindedly focused on the puzzle before them that they temporarily forgot not only about their competitors and the prizes awaiting the victors but also about the time of day and their own need for food. In another feat of cognitive distancing, the poet Anne Sexton told her agent that, although she would love to make a great deal of money from her books, she knew that she had to forget all about that while actually writing her poems.

Two of our recent studies provide some exciting evidence suggestive of an additive effect of intrinsic and extrinsic motivators. In one study (Hennessey, Amabile, & Martinage, in press), we set out to determine if it would be possible to immunize people against the negative effects of constraint on intrinsic motivation and creativity by training them to think of intrinsic and extrinsic motivation in the way that Allen, Watson, Crick, and Sexton seemed to: I am well aware of my strong intrinsic interest in my work, and that can't be easily shaken; I certainly enjoy the benefits of wealth, fame, and critical acclaim, but I place all that secondary to my own passion for what I do.

Planning to do this training study with children, we made a set of videotapes in which two attractive children answered an adult's questions about their work. The script was written so as to portray these children as models of intrinsic motivation. They spoke excitedly about different aspects of their schoolwork that interested them, and, while acknowledging the importance of good grades and praise from parents, they firmly stated that "those are not what's really important." After the children watched these videotapes, the experimenter led the children to discuss what had been said, and to describe their own intrinsic interests or ways of dealing with constraint. In later testing sessions with a different experimenter, we found that children who had watched the intrinsic motivation training tapes scored higher on a measure of intrinsic motivation (Harter, 1981) than children who had watched tapes on other topics. In addition, although the control-group children exhibited lower creativity when offered a reward, the trained children showed no such decrement. This was what we had predicted. But we got more than we'd bargained for. The trained children produced *higher* levels of creativity under contracted-for reward—a clearly additive effect.

Another, earlier study of ours may provide a clue about the mechanism at work in this surprising additive effect (surprising, at least, to those of us who expected only hydraulic effects). With both adults and children, we found (as expected) that contracted-for reward leads to lower levels of creativity (Amabile, Hennessey, & Grossman, 1986). The design was a basic $2 \times 2$ factorial, where reward was crossed with choice. Thus, subjects in the choice-reward condition had previously chosen to do the activity in order to obtain a reward. Subjects in the no-choice/reward condition, however, were simply given the reward as something that went along with the activity. They were given no choice in the matter; they made no contract with the experimenter. We expected that subjects in this condition would show no decrement in creativity, because they should not have had the self-perception of working on the activity in order to gain the reward (extrinsic motivation). Not only did we find no decrement, we found an *increment*: Subjects in this "bonus" reward condition showed higher levels of creativity than in any of the other three conditions.

We speculate that perhaps the bonus reward enhances *positive affect*, which may simply add on to the conducive effect of intrinsic motivation on creativity. Not only did subjects in this condition *not* have their intrinsic motivation undermined, they were led to feel even better about what they were doing because of the unexpected bonus. Indeed, a postexperimental questionnaire assessing affect lends some support to this speculation.

So it may be that the children in the training study's intrinsic motivation condition learned to interpret extrinsic constraints such as reward in a way that did not detract from intrinsic motivation but instead added to positive affect about task engagement. This possibility seems likely when we consider the kind of statements that appeared in the intrinsic motivation training videotape:

Adult: *It sounds like both of you do the work in school because you like it, but what about getting good grades from your teacher or presents from your parents for doing well? Do you think about those things?*

Tommy: *Well, I like to get good grades, and when I bring home a good report card, my parents always give me money. But that's not what's really important. I like to learn a lot. There are a lot of things that interest me, and I want to learn about them, so I work hard because I enjoy it.*

It appears, then, that the intrinsic motivation principle of creativity, in its simple form, is incomplete. It implies that extrinsic constraints will always undermine creativity. But both observational evidence and experimental evidence suggest that this isn't so. Individual differences in people's *interpretation* of the constraints can significantly affect the outcomes on creativity, whether those individual differences arise through explicit training (as in our study) or occur naturally as personality characteristics.

## BEYOND THE SOCIAL PSYCHOLOGY OF CREATIVITY: WITHIN YOU AND WITHOUT YOU

The intense study of social-environental influences on creativity, which has flourished over the past dozen years, was a necessary correction to the almost exclusive focus on creative *persons* in preceding decades. Clearly, however, in any comprehensive psychology of creativity, both person influences and environment influences must appear prominently. Even in our own research on the social psychology of creativity, we have repeatedly been led to consider the influence of personality, ability, and experience. The R&D scientists we interviewed (Amabile & Gryskiewicz, 1988) may have mentioned work environment factors more frequently than person factors in their stories of high and low creativity, but person factors certainly did appear prominently. Positive personal factors mentioned frequently in the high-creativity stories included personality traits such as persistence, curiosity, energy, and intellectual honesty; self-motivation, the intrinsic motivation of being excited by the work itself; special cognitive abilities; risk orientation; expertise in the area; diverse experience; social skill; and brilliance. Negative personal factors mentioned frequently in the low-creativity stories included being unmotivated, unskilled, inflexible, externally motivated, or socially unskilled.

Earlier, I argued: "Social factors may be responsible for only a small part of the total variance in creative behavior, but they may account for the lion's share of the variance that anyone can do anything about!" I believe this is true and vitally important for anyone wishing to enhance creativity in practice. However, for purposes of theory building, we must pay heed to all factors contributing significantly to the *total variance* in creative behavior.

The componential model of creativity, which we have been using as a theoretical guide in our research, attempts to include all such factors. The model is described in more detail elsewhere (Amabile, 1983a, 1983b, 1988a, 1988b). Figure 40.1 outlines the three major components of creativity included in the model. It is not surprising that intrinsic task motivation is featured as one prominent component, but the factors of talent, personality, and cognitive style that have been so extensively investigated by other researchers are also included. As a way of illustrating the components and their role in the creative process, let me describe the hypothetical (and highly simplified) case of an artist creating a sculpture.

## Domain-Relevant Skills

Domain-relevant skills are the basis from which any performance must proceed. They include memory for factual knowledge, technical profi-ciency, and special talents in the domain in question. A sculptor's domain-relevant skills include her innate talent for visual imagery and realistic rendering of that imagery, her factual knowledge of art history and the properties of the clay she has chosen, her familiarity with the subject she wishes to depict, and the technical skill she has acquired in her craft.

This component can be viewed as the set of cognitive pathways that may be followed to solve a given problem or do a given task. As Newell and Simon (1972, p. 82) poetically describe it, this component can be considered the problem-solver's "network of possible wanderings."

## Creativity-Relevant Skills

Herein lies the "something extra" of creative performance. Assuming that an individual has some incentive to perform an activity, performance will be "technically good" or "adequate" or "acceptable" if the requisite domain-relevant skills are there. However, even with these skills at an extraordinarily high level, an individual will not produce creative work if creativity-relevant skills are lacking. Creativity-relevant skills include a cognitive style favorable to taking new perspectives on problems, an application of heuristics for

| 1<br>Domain-relevant Skills | 2<br>Creativity-relevant Skills | 3<br>Task Motivation |
|---|---|---|
| Includes:<br>– Knowledge about the domain<br>– Technical skills required<br>– Special domain-relevant "talent"<br><br>Depends on:<br>– Innate cognitive abilities<br>– Innate perceptual and motor skills<br>– Formal and informal education | Includes:<br>– Appropriate cognitive style<br>– Implicit or explicit knowledge of heuristics for generating novel ideas<br>– Conducive work style<br><br>Depends on:<br>– Training<br>– Experience in idea generation<br>– Personality characteristics | Includes:<br>– Attitudes toward the task<br>– Perceptions of own motivation for undertaking the task<br><br>Depends on:<br>– Initial level of intrinsic motivation toward the task<br>– Presence or absence of salient extrinsic constraints in the social environment<br>– Individual ability to cognitively minimize extrinsic constraints |

**FIGURE 40.1 Components of Creative Performance**

Source: From Amabile (1983b)

the exploration of new cognitive pathways, and a working style conducive to persistent, energetic pursuit of one's work.

Creativity-relevant skills depend to some extent on personality characteristics related to independence, self-discipline, orientation toward risk taking, tolerance for ambiguity, perseverance in the face of frustration, and a relative unconcern for social approval (Barron, 1955; Feldman, 1980; Golann, 1963; Hogarth, 1980; MacKinnon, 1962; Stein, 1974).

Our sculptor's arsenal of creativity skills might include her ability to break perceptual set when observing physical objects, her tolerance for ambiguity in the process of deciding on a theme and how to render it, her ability to suspend judgment as she plays around with different approaches, and her ability to break out of strict algorithms for sculpting. She might also have learned to employ some of the creativity heuristics described by theorists: "When all else fails, try something counterintuitive" (Newell, Shaw, & Simon, 1962); or "Make the familiar strange" (Gordon, 1961). Finally, if she is productively creative, her work style is probably marked by an ability to concentrate effort for long periods of time (Campbell, 1960; Hogarth, 1980) and an ability to abandon unproductive strategies, temporarily putting aside stubborn problems (Simon, 1966).

## Intrinsic Task Motivation

A person can have no motivation for doing a task, a primarily intrinsic motivation, or a primarily extrinsic motivation; obviously, intrinsic and extrinsic motivation for the same task may coexist. However, one is likely to be primary. As I have argued on the basis of our empirical results, a primarily intrinsic motivation will be more conducive to creativity than a primarily extrinsic motivation. For practical purposes, there are two ways in which motivation can be considered the most important of the three creativity components. First, as I've noted, it may be the easiest to affect in a straightforward way because intrinsic/extrinsic motivation is strongly subject to even subtle social influences. Second,

no amount of skill in the domain or in methods of creative thinking can compensate for a lack of intrinsic motivation to perform an activity. Without intrinsic motivation, an individual either will not perform the activity at all or will do it in a way that simply satisfies the extrinsic goals. But, to some extent, a high degree of intrinsic motivation *can* make up for a deficiency of domain-relevant skills or creativity-relevant skills. A highly intrinsically motivated individual is likely to draw skills from other domains or apply great effort to acquire necessary skills in the target domain.

Task motivation makes the difference between what our sculptor *can* do and what she *will* do. The former depends on her levels of domain-relevant skills and creativity-relevant skills. But it is her task motivation that determines the extent to which she will fully engage her domain-relevant skills and creativity-relevant skills in the service of creative performance.

Within the componential model, task motivation includes two elements: the individual's baseline attitude toward the task and the individual's perceptions of his or her reasons for undertaking the task in a given instance. For example, the sculptor approaches each task with a baseline level of interest—probably quite high for most sculpture tasks but perhaps quite low for printmaking. For any given sculpture task, however, her interest will vary from the baseline as a function of any extrinsic constraints imposed on her (such as competition) *and* her own strategies for dealing with those constraints.

## Stages of the Creative Process

The three components of domain-relevant skills, creativity-relevant skills, and task motivation are the building blocks for the componential model of creativity. The model is, conceptually, a multiplicative one: Each of the components is necessary for some level of creativity to be produced; the higher the level of each of the three components, the higher the overall level of creativity should be.

The three components appear to operate at different levels of specificity. Creativity-relevant skills operate at the most general level; they may influence responses in any content domain. Thus, if the sculptor has a rich store of creativity-relevant skills, she may indeed appear to be a creative "type," in the sense that she produces unusual responses in many domains of behavior. Domain-relevant skills operate at an intermediate level of specificity. This component includes all skills relevant to a general domain, such as sculpture, rather than skills relevant to only a specific task within a domain, such as sculpting a clay bust of Beethoven. Obviously, within a particular domain, skills relevant to any given specific task will overlap with skills relevant to any other task. Finally, task motivation operates at the most specific level. In terms of impact on creativity, motivation may be very specific to particular tasks

within domains, and may even vary over time for a particular task. Our artist may be highly intrinsically motivated to sculpt a friend's head, but she may be singularly uninterested in a commissioned job to sculpt the head of the city's mayor.

How do these building blocks figure into the overall process of individual creativity? Figure 40.2 presents a schematic representation of the componential model of the creative process (Amabile, 1983a, 1983b). This model describes the way in which an individual (such as the sculptor) might assemble and use information in attempting to arrive at a solution, response, or product. In information-processing terms, task motivation is responsible for initiating and sustaining the process; it determines whether the artist even undertakes the task, and it also de-

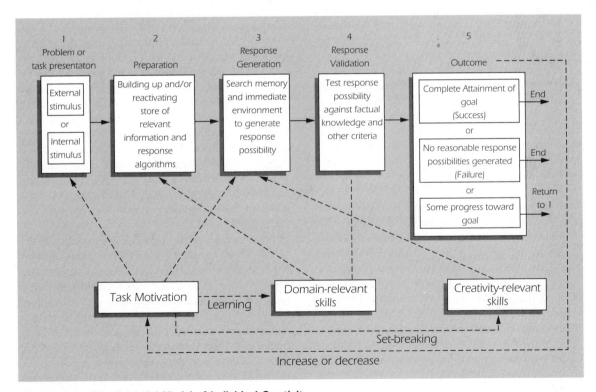

**FIGURE 40.2 Componential Model of Individual Creativity**

Source: From Amabile (1983b)

Note: Broken lines indicate the typical sequence of steps in the process. Only direct and primary influences are depicted here.

termines some aspects of her response generation. Domain-relevant skills are the raw materials that feed the process. They determine what approaches the sculptor will take initially and what criteria she will use to assess the response possibilities that are generated. Creativity-relevant skills act as an executive controller; they can influence the way in which the artist searches for possibilities.

The process outlined in Figure 40.2 applies to both high and low levels of creativity; the level of creativity of a product or response varies as a function of the levels of each of the three components. This model resembles previous theories of creativity in the specification of the stages of problem presentation, preparation, response generation, and response validation (e.g., Hogarth, 1980; Nystrom, 1979; Wallas, 1926)— although there are a number of variations in the exact number and naming of stages in the sequence. This model is more detailed than previous ones, however, in its inclusion of the impact of each of the three components of creativity at each stage in the process. (Note that only direct and primary influences are depicted in the figure.)

The initial step in this sequence is the presentation of the task or the problem. Task motivation has an important influence at this stage. If the sculptor has a high level of intrinsic interest in the task, this interest will often be sufficient to begin the creative process. Under these circumstances, in essence, she poses the problem to herself. For example, she may decide that she wishes to sculpt the head of a friend. In other situations, however, the problem is presented by someone else. The problem might, of course, be intrinsically interesting under these circumstances as well. If that friend came up with the idea and asked the artist to sculpt his head, she might still be intrinsically interested in the task. However, in general, an externally posed problem is less likely to be intrinsically interesting than an internally generated one.

The second stage is preparatory to the actual generation of responses or solutions. At this point, the sculptor builds up or reactivates her store of information about the task, including her knowledge of response algorithms for doing tasks like this. If her domain-relevant skills are rather impoverished at the outset, this stage may be quite a long one during which a great deal of learning takes place. On the other hand, if her domain-relevant skills are already sufficiently rich to afford an ample set of possibilities to explore, the reactivation of this already stored set of information and algorithms may be almost instantaneous.

Note one important implication of this model: Contrary to popular belief, it is not possible to have *too much* knowledge about a task domain. According to this belief, people who have the smallest knowledge base in a domain are able to produce the most creative ideas. Certainly, people who are new to a field often do exhibit a higher level of creativity than those who have a longer work history. But it is clear from empirical research (e.g., Findlay & Lumsden, 1988) that the important distinction is not the *amount* of knowledge but the way in which that knowledge is stored and the ease with which it can be accessed. If the artist stores her information and techniques according to rigid algorithms (which may be more likely for an old-timer than a new arrival), creativity is less probable. But if she stores information in wide categories with easy access of association, increased information should only lead to increased creativity. It is not possible to have too much knowledge; it *is* possible to have algorithms that are applied too inflexibly.

The novelty of the product or response is determined in the third stage. Here, the individual generates response possibilities by searching through the available pathways and exploring features of the environment that are relevant to the task at hand. Both creativity-relevant skills and task motivation play an important role at this stage. The sculptor's existing repertoire of creativity-relevant skills determines her flexibility in exploring cognitive pathways, the attention she gives to particular aspects of the task, and the extent to which she follows a particular pathway in pursuit of a product. In addition, creativity-relevant skills can influence the subgoals of the response-generation stage by determining whether she will generate a large number of response possibilities through a temporary suspension of judgment. Finally, and most important, if the artist's task motivation is intrinsic rather than extrinsic, it can add to her existing repertoire of creativity-relevant skills a willingness to take risks with this particular task and to notice aspects of the task that might not be obviously relevant to creating the final product.

Domain-relevant skills again figure prominently in the fourth stage–the validation of the response possibility that has been chosen on a particular trial. Using her knowledge of the domain, the artist tests the response possibility for correctness or appropriateness, given her particular set of goals. Thus it is this stage that determines whether the product or response will be appropriate, useful, correct, or valuable—the second response characteristic that, together with novelty, is essential for the product to be considered creative according to the conceptual definition of creativity.

The fifth stage represents the decision making that must be carried out on the basis of the test performed in stage four. If the artist feels that this test has been passed—if she believes she has attained her goal—the process terminates. If she sees complete failure—if no reasonable response possibility has been generated—the process will also terminate. If she senses some progress toward the goal—if at least a reasonable response possibility has been generated (or if, in Simon's 1978, terms, there is some evidence of "getting warmer")—the process returns to the first stage, where the problem is once again posed. In any case, information gained from the trial is added to the artist's existing repertoire of domain-relevant skills. If her intrinsic task motivation remains sufficiently high, she will try again, perhaps with information gained from the previous trial being used to pose the problem in a somewhat different form. If, however, her task motivation drops below some critical minimum, she will give up.

For complex tasks, the application of this model to the production of creative responses also becomes complex. Work on any given task or problem may involve a long series of loops through the process until success in a final product is achieved. Indeed, work on what seems to be one task may actually involve a series of rather different subtasks, each with its own separate solution. And, of course, the sequence represented in Figure 40.2 is an idealized one. In actuality, for example, the sculptor may attempt to generate ideas on how to render her subject, have difficulty, go immediately back to the preparation stage to gather more information or learn new techniques, and then continue on with idea generation.

## The Feedback Cycle

The outcome of one cycle of the creative process can directly influence task motivation, thereby setting up a feedback cycle through which future engagement in the same or similar tasks can be affected. If the sculptor has been completely successful, in her view, she will have no motivation to undertake exactly the same task again, because that task has truly been completed. However, with success, her intrinsic motivation for similar sculpting tasks should increase. If complete failure has occurred—if no reasonable response were generated—her intrinsic motivation for the task should decrease. If partial success has been met, intrinsic motivation will increase if she has the sense of getting warmer in approaching her goal. However, it will decrease when she finds herself essentially no closer to the goal than at the outset.

Harter's theory of "effectance motivation" (1978) suggests this influence of process outcome on task motivation. Harter built on White's (1959) definition of the "urge toward competence," a definition proposing a motivational construct that "impels the organism toward competence and is satisfied by a feeling of efficacy" (Harter, 1978, p. 34). According to Harter's theory, failure at mastery attempts eventually leads to decreases in intrinsic motivation striving for competence. However, success (which will be more probable the higher the level of skills) leads to intrinsic gratification, feelings of efficacy, and increases in intrinsic motivation, which, in turn, lead to more mastery attempts. In essential agreement with Harter, a number of social-psychological theorists (e.g., Deci & Ryan, 1985) have proposed that success (confirmation of competence) leads to increased intrinsic motivation.

Through its influence on task motivation, outcome assessment can also indirectly affect domain-relevant and creativity-relevant skills. If the sculptor ends up with a higher level of intrinsic task motivation, set-breaking and cognitive risk taking may become more habitual with her, thereby increasing her permanent repertoire of creativity skills. Also, a higher level of motivation may motivate learning about the task and related subjects, thereby increasing her domain-relevant skills.

## A MAP FOR THE FUTURE

In nearly all of my previous research, I have focused on establishing one link in the model depicted in Figure 40.2: the influence of intrinsic/extrinsic task motivation on response generation. Now, with a bit more information and a great deal less hubris, my students, colleagues, and I are moving beyond the simple establishment of the intrinsic motivation principle of creativity to a broader examination of the social psychology of creativity. At the same time, we are moving beyond the social psychology of creativity toward a more integrated social-personality-cognitive psychology of creativity.

### A More Inclusive
### Social Psychology of Creativity

Within the social psychology of creativity, we are attempting a more macroscopic look at social influences—both negative *and* positive. For example, we are beginning to think of ways in which intrinsic motivation training may be incorporated into school curricula (Hennessey & Amabile, 1987).

In addition, building on the results of the R&D interview study, we have developed an instrument called the Work Environment Inventory (WEI). Designed to assess the presence of factors in the work environment that inhibit or stimulate individual creativity, the WEI is being tested with data collected in dozens of different organizations. As a guide in this work, I have articulated a preliminary model of organizational innovation that incorporates and builds on the componential model of individual creativity depicted in Figure 40.2 (Amabile, 1988a, 1988b). The ultimate goal is to develop and test a comprehensive model of organizational innovation that meets four criteria. First, the entire process of individual creativity must be considered as a crucial element in the process of organizational innovation. Second, the model must attempt to incorporate all aspects of organizations that influence innovation, with innovation being defined as *the successful implementation of creative ideas within an organization*, Third, the model must show the major stages of the organizational innovation process. Fourth, it must describe the influence of organizational factors on individual creativity.

While we are expanding our social-psychological perspective at macroscopic levels above the intrinsic motivation phenomenon, we are also beginning to take a more microscopic look within that phenomenon to discover mechanisms by which it occurs. Specifically, we are addressing three questions: How does motivational state (intrinsic versus extrinsic) influence creative thinking? What is the role of affect? What is the role of individual differences?

### How Motivation Influences
### Creative Thinking

In his classic paper on creative thinking, Campbell (1960) describes the process as involving a consideration of widely varying, blindly generated ideas, followed by a selective retention of those ideas that best fit some criteria. Simonton (1988) suggests much the same process in his "chance-configuration" theory of creativity. And, in his analysis of motivation and cognition, Simon (1967) asserts that the most important function of motivation is the control of attention.

We have used these theories to suggest a model of the way in which motivational orientation might influence creativity. The metaphor for this model is a maze with several exits; performing a task is represented as attempting to find a way out of the maze. The task can be done by rote, using familiar algorithms, and resulting in an uncreative solution; in the maze metaphor, the individual can take the straight, well-worn, familiar pathway out of the maze. This is the route most likely to be taken by extrinsically motivated individuals (those motivated primarily by factors outside of the task itself, outside of the maze). Because they view the task as merely a means to an end, their attention has been narrowed to doing the minimum necessary to meet the extrinsic constraint (see Kruglanski, Stein, & Riter, 1977). However, finding a creative solution requires exploration through the maze, a more heuristic approach to the task. Individuals will only be likely to take this more creative approach if they are initially intrinsically interested in the activity itself *and* if their social environment does not demand a narrowing of behavior into the familiar algorithm.

This model leads to several specific predictions about differences in the ways intrinsically and extrinsically motivated individuals will process tasks, leading ultimately to the more creative outcomes under intrinsic motivation. (Notice, however, that the model would predict no decrements in the more algorithmic *technical quality* of work under extrinsic motivation.) Compared with extrinsically motivated individuals, intrinsically motivated persons should generate and examine a larger number of ideas and possibilities while engaged in the task; make associations and juxtapositions that are more unusual; spend a longer period of time on the activity; become more deeply involved cognitively in the activity, as evidenced by several attention measures; experience more positive affect when *anticipating* working on the task, as well as when

actually working on it; depart more frequently from familiar algorithms for task engagement; spend more time thinking about the task after they have finished it; and produce more creative end products. Some previous studies with various cognitive tasks offer suggestive evidence (e.g., Kruglanski, Stein & Riter, 1977; McGraw & Fiala, 1982; Pittman, Emery, & Boggiano, 1982). We have planned a series of studies to examine these predictions directly.

## The Role of Affect

We will also be investigating the role of affect in the motivation-creativity link. Several theorists (e.g., Csikszentmihályi, 1975; Deci & Ryan, 1985; Izard, 1977) have suggested that intrinsic motivation involves positive affective experience, and extrinsic motivation involves negative affect. There is considerable empirical support for this suggestion (e.g., Pretty & Seligman, 1983; Reeve, Cole, & Olsen, 1986; Ryan, 1982). As I described earlier, we have suggested affect as a possible explanation for the unexpectedly high creativity of subjects in the "bonus" reward condition of our choice-reward study (Amabile, Hennessey, & Grossman, 1986).

Isen and her colleagues have demonstrated that induced positive affect increases the probability of unusual associations, set-breaking responses, heuristic problem-solving strategies, and inclusive categorization of stimuli (e.g., Isen, Daubman, & Nowicki, 1987; Isen, Johnson, Mertz, & Robinson, 1985; Isen, Means, Patrick, & Nowicki, 1982). We have planned a series of studies to examine affect as a possible mediator of the effects of motivational orientation on creativity. Do differences in motivational orientation correspond to differences in affect? Are motivational orientation differences causally prior to affective differences? Are the affective differences necessary to produce differences in creativity? Is there a difference between trait (chronic) and state (temporary) motivation, and between chronic and situation-specific affective states in these effects?

We predict a link between intrinsic motivation, positive affect, and high creativity, but we will attempt to determine the causal direction of this link and whether this link might be found only for state intrinsic motivation. It may be that the more enduring trait intrinsic motivation of individuals actively committed to a creative pursuit in their daily lives is not marked by the kind of positive affect studied by Isen but by a more "sober" positive affect—a sense of intimate involvement with and dedication to the work.

## Toward a Comprehensive Psychology of Creativity

In beginning to examine specific mechanisms and subtle interactions within the intrinsic motivation phenomenon, we have, of necessity, moved beyond the social psychology of creativity toward a broader view of the creative process. We will be looking at reaction times, attentional measures, memory tests, and the use of algorithms, all taken from cognitive psychology. We are beginning to inform our work with concepts from personality psychology as well. We

recognize the significant roles of both situation-induced *and* chronic affective states. We realize that intrinsic/extrinsic motivational orientation is not only a state that can be influenced by the presence or absence of extrinsic social constraints. It is also a *trait*, an enduring attitude that an individual has toward tasks within a domain. We have even developed a questionnaire (the Work Preference Inventory, or WPI) designed to assess individual differences in adults' motivational orientation. Our preliminary results are most encouraging.

This, I believe, is what all of us creativity researchers must do in mapping our future courses. In delving more deeply into the details of the phenomena that interest us, we must constantly attempt to integrate our own perspectives with those offered by others. A comprehensive psychology of creativity *is* within our grasp.

In moving toward that comprehensive understanding, I would still like, somehow, someday, to study the impact of telling subjects that they are "maybe being a little too creative." Then I would like to track down Sister Carmelita and thank her for getting me involved in all of this.

## REFERENCES

Albert, R. S. (1980). Family positions and the attainment of eminence: A study of special family experiences. *Gifted Child Quarterly, 24,* 87–95.

Amabile, T. M. (1979). Effects of external evaluation on artistic creativity. *Journal of Personality and Social Psychology, 37,* 221–223.

Amabile, T. M. (1982a). Children's artistic creativity: Detrimental effects of competition in a field setting. *Personality and Social Psychology Bulletin, 8,* 573–578.

Amabile, T. M. (1982b). Social psychology of creativity: A consensual assessment technique. *Journal of Personality and Social Psychology, 43,* 997–1013.

Amabile, T. M. (1983a). *The social psychology of creativity.* New York: Springer-Verlag.

Amabile, T. M. (1983b). Social psychology of creativity: A componential conceptualization. *Journal of Personality and Social Psychology, 45,* 357–377.

Amabile, T. M. (1985). Motivation and creativity: Effects of motivational orientation on creative writers. *Journal of Personality and Social Psychology, 48,* 393–399.

Amabile, T. M. (1987). The motivation to be creative. In S. Isaksen (Ed.), *Frontiers in creativity: Beyond the basics,* Buffalo, NY: Bearly Limited.

Amabile, T. M. (1988a). From individual creativity to organizational innovation. In K. Gronhaug & G. Kaufman (Eds.), *Achievement and motivation: A social-developmental perspective.* New York: Cambridge University Press.

Amabile, T. M. (1988b). A model of organizational innovation. In B. M. Staw & L. L. Cummings (Eds.), *Research in organizational behavior* (Vol. 10). Greenwich, CT: JAI.

Amabile, T. M. (in press). *Growing up creative.* New York: Crown.

Amabile, T. M., & Gitomer, J. (1984). Children's artistic creativity: Effects of choice in task materials. *Personality and Social Psychology Bulletin, 10,* 209–215.

Amabile, T. M., Goldfarb, P., & Brackfield, S. (in press). Social influences on creativity: Evaluation, coaction, and surveillance. *Creativity Research Journal.*

Amabile, T. M., & Gryskiewicz, S. S. (1988). Creative human resources in the R&D laboratory: How environment and personality impact innovation. In R. L. Kuhn (Ed.), *Handbook for creative and innovative managers.* New York: McGraw-Hill.

Amabile, T. M., Hennessey, B. A., & Grossman, B. S. (1986). Social influences on creativity: The effects of contracted-for reward. *Journal of Personality and Social Psychology, 50,* 14–23.

Andrews, F. M. (1975). Social and psychological factors which influence the creative process. In I. A. Taylor & J. W. Getzels (Eds.), *Perspectives in creativity.* Chicago: Aldine.

Barron, F. (1955). The disposition toward originality. *Journal of Abnormal and Social Psychology, 51,* 478–485.

Berglas, S., Amabile, T. M., & Handel, M. (1979). *An examination of the effects of verbal reinforcement on creativity.* Paper presented at the meeting of the American Psychological Association, New York.

Campbell, D. (1960). Blind variation and selective retention in creative thought as in other knowledge processes. *Psychological Review, 67,* 380–400.

Crutchfield, R. S. (1955). Conformity and character. *American Psychologist, 10,* 191–198.

Crutchfield, R. S. (1959). Personal and situational factors in conformity to group pressure. *Acta Psychologica, 15,* 386–388.

Crutchfield, R. S. (1962). Conformity and creative thinking. In H. Gruber, G. Terrell, & M. Wertheimer (Eds.), *Contemporary approaches to creative thinking.* New York: Atherton.

Csikszentmihályi, M. (1975). *Beyond boredom and anxiety.* San Francisco: Jossey-Bass.

Deci, E. L. (1971). Effects of externally mediated rewards on intrinsic motivation. *Journal of Personality and Social Psychology, 18,* 105–115.

Deci, E. L., & Ryan, R. M. (1985). *Intrinsic motivation and self-determination in human behavior.* New York: Plenum.

Feldman, D. (1980). *Beyond universals in cognitive development.* Norwood NJ: Ablex.

Findlay, C. S., & Lumsden, C. J. (1988). The creative mind: Toward an evolutionary theory of discovery and innovation. *Journal of Social and Biological Structures.*

Getzels, J., & Csikszentmihályi, M. (1976). *The creative vision: A longitudinal study of problem-finding in art.* New York: Wiley Interscience.

Golann, S. E. (1963). Psychological study of creativity. *Psychological Bulletin, 60,* 548–565.

Gordon, W. W. (1961). *Synectics: The development of creative capacity.* New York: Harper & Row.

Guilford, J. P. (1956). The structure of intellect. *Psychological Bulletin, 53,* 267–293.

Harter, S. (1978). Effectance motivation reconsidered: Toward a developmental model. *Human Development, 21,* 34–64.

Harter, S. (1981). A new self-report scale of intrinsic versus extrinsic orientation in the classroom. *Developmental Psychology, 17,* 300–312.

Helson, R. (1965). Childhood interest clusters related to creativity in women. *Journal of Consulting Psychology, 29,* 352–361.

Hennessey, B. A. (1989). The effect of extrinsic constraints on children's creativity while using a computer. *Creativity Research Journal, 2,* 151–168.

Hennessey, B. A., & Amabile, T. M. (1987). *Creativity and learning.* Washington, DC: National Education Association.

Hennessey, B., A., Amabile, T. M., & Martinage, M. (in press). Immunizing children against the negative effects of reward. *Contemporary Educational Psychology.*

Hogarth, R. (1980). *Judgement and choice.* Chichester: John Wiley.

Hughes, T., & McCullough, F. (Eds.). (1982). *The journals of Sylvia Plath.* New York: Dial.

Isen, A. M., Daubman, K. A., & Nowicki, G. P. (1987). Positive affect facilitates creative problem solving. *Journal of Personality and Social Psychology, 52,* 1122–1131.

Isen, A. M., Johnson, M. M. S., Mertz, E., & Robinson, G. F. (1985). The influence of positive affect on the unusualness of word associations. *Journal of Personality and Social Psychology, 48,* 1–14.

Isen, A. M., Means, B., Patrick, R., & Nowicki, G. P. (1982). Some factors influencing decision-making strategy and risk-taking. In M. S. Clark & S. T. Fiske (Eds.), *Affect and cognition: The 17th Annual Carnegie Symposium on Cognition.* Hillsdale, NJ: Lawrence Erlbaum.

Izard, C. (1977). *Human emotions.* New York: Plenum.

Kruglanski, A. W., Friedman, I., & Zeevi, G. (1971). The effects of extrinsic incentive on some qualitative aspects of task performance. *Journal of Personality, 39,* 606–617.

Kruglanski, A. W., Stein, C., & Riter, A. (1977). Contingencies of exogenous reward and task performance: On the "minimax" principle in instrumental behavior. *Journal of Applied Social Psychology, 7,* 141–148.

Lepper, M. R., & Greene, D. (1978). *The hidden costs of reward.* Hillsdale, NJ: Lawrence Erlbaum.

Lepper, M. R., Greene, D., & Nisbett, R. (1973). Undermining children's intrinsic interest with extrinsic rewards: A test of the "overjustification" hypothesis. *Journal of Personality and Social Psychology, 28,* 129–137.

MacKinnon, D. W. (1962). The nature and nurture of creative talent. *American Psychologist, 17,* 484–495.

McKinnon, D. W. (1975). IPAR's contribution to the conceptualization and study of creativity. In I. Taylor & J. Getzels (Eds.), *Perspectives in creativity.* Chicago: Aldine.

McGraw, K. O. (1978). The detrimental effects of reward on performance: A literature review and a prediction model. In M. R. Lepper & D. Greene (Eds.), *The hidden costs of reward*. Hillsdale, NJ: Lawrence Erlbaum.

McGraw, K. O., & Fiala, J. (1982). Undermining the Zeigamik effect: Another hidden cost of reward. *Journal of Personality, 50*, 58–66.

McGuire, W. (1973). The yin and yang of progress in social psychology. *Journal of Personality and Social Psychology, 26*, 446–456.

Newell, A., Shaw, J., & Simon, H. (1962). The processes of creative thinking. In H. Gruber, G. Terrell, & M. Wertheimer (Eds.), *Contemporary approaches to creative thinking*. New York: Atherton.

Newell, A. & Simon, H. (1972). *Human problem solving*. Englewood Cliffs, NJ: Prentice-Hall.

Nystrom, H. (1979). *Creativity and innovation*. London: John Wiley.

Osborn, A. (1963). *Applied imagination: Principles and procedures of creative thinking*. New York: Scribner.

Pames, S. (1967). *Creative behavior guidebook*. New York: Scribner.

Pittman, T. S., Emery, J., & Boggiano, A. K. (1982). Intrinsic and extrinsic motivational orientations: Reward-induced changes in preference for complexity. *Journal of Personality and Social Psychology, 42*, 789–797.

Pretty, G. H., & Seligman, C. (1983). Affect and the overjustification effect. *Journal of Personality and Social Psychology, 46*, 1241–1253.

Reeve, J., Cole, S. G., & Olsen, B. C. (1986). Adding excitement to intrinsic motivation research. *Journal of Social Behavior and Personality, 1*, 349–363.

Ryan, R. M. (1982). Control and information in the intrapersonal sphere: An extension of cognitive evaluation theory. *Journal of Personality and Social Psychology, 43*, 450–461.

Salancik, G. (1975). *Retrospective attribution of past behavior and commitment to future behavior*. Unpublished manuscript, University of Illinois.

Simon, H. (1966). Scientific discovery and the psychology of problem solving. In *Mind and cosmos: Essays in contemporary science and philosophy*. Pittsburgh: University of Pittsburgh Press.

Simon, H. (1967). Understanding creativity. In C. Gowan, G. D. Demos, & E. P. Torrance (Eds.), *Creativity: Its educational implications*. New York: John Wiley.

Simon, H. (1978). Information-processing theory of human problem-solving. In W. K. Estes (Ed.), *Handbook of learning and cognitive processes: Vol. 5. Human information processing*. Hillsdale, NJ: Lawrence Erlbaum.

Simonton, D. K. (1975). Sociocultural context of individual creativity: A transhistorical time-series analysis. *Journal of Personality and Social Psychology, 32*, 1119–1133.

Simonton, D. K. (1984). *Genius, creativity, and leadership: Historiometric inquiries*. Cambridge, MA: Harvard University Press.

Simonton, D. K. (1988). Creativity, leadership, and chance. In R. J. Sternberg (Ed.), *The nature of creativity*. New York: Cambridge University Press.

Simonton, D. K. (in press). *Scientific genius: A psychology of science.* Cambridge: Cambridge University Press.

Stein, M. I. (1974). *Stimulating creativity* (Vol 1). New York: Academic Press.

Thurstone, L., & Chave, E. (1929). *The measurement of attitude.* Chicago: University of Illinois Press.

Torrance, E. P. (1966). *Torrance Tests of Creative Thinking: Norms-technical manual.* Princeton, NJ: Personnel.

Wallas, G. (1926). *The art of thought.* New York: Harcourt, Brace.

Walster, E., Aronson, V., Abrahams, D., & Rottman, L. (1966). Importance of physical attractiveness in dating behavior. *Journal of Personality and Social Psychology, 4,* 508–516.

Watson, J. D. (1968). *The double helix.* New York: Atheneum.

White, R. (1959). Motivation reconsidered: The concept of competence. *Psychological Review, 66,* 297–323.

# Organizational Innovation

## 41.  THE CREATIVE ORGANIZATION

Gary Steiner

## DEFINITIONS

First, a few words about what the key terms in this summary mean: "Creativity" has been defined in a number of ways in the psychological literature, in business discussion, in the arts and sciences generally. Within the transcript of this seminar there appear many explicit, and many more implicit, definitions of varying degrees of generality. We make no attempt to frame a master definition at this point. But for purposes of this overview, it is necessary and hopefully sufficient to make this general distinction: *Creativity* has to do with the development, proposal, and implementation of *new* and *better* solutions; *productivity*, with the efficient application of *current* "solutions."

What "better" means, and who is to say, is one of the sticky methodological issues in the field. What it most often means in these pages is better according to professional colleagues or superiors. The meaning of "solution" obviously varies by field; in the following, solutions range from practical answers to specific problems through new concepts in art, music, or architecture to the most general and abstract conceptualizations that characterize a breakthrough in, say, theoretical physics.

Many of the studies we will cite distinguish "high-creative" from "low-" or "average-creative" groups. It should be clear that "high" and "low" are relative, and not absolute, designations. In most of the samples under investigation, both "high" and "low" groups would qualify as highly creative within the population at large and often even within the profession. It would therefore not have been euphemistic—just too clumsy—to use the designations "more highly" and "less highly" creative. Bear in mind, though, that this is what the shorthand distinction between "high" and "low" means.

## I. THE RAW MATERIAL: INDIVIDUAL CREATIVITY

*Do individual differences in creativity exist? Does it make sense to speak of more and less creative people in some such way as we speak of more and less intelligent, more or less coordinated, or more or less musical people? Or is personal creativity, like fathering twins, mostly a matter of being in the right place at the right time?*

As important as circumstances are in determining who will create what and when, it seems that there are consistent and persistent differences in individual creativity. Holding conditions constant, some people are likely to be more creative than others; and these differences are likely to show up in other situations and at other times. In fact, in most fields, the distribution of creative contributions is something like the distribution of personal income in the United States: a small percentage of people accounts for a large share of the total.

*Are these differences in personal creativity specific to particular areas of endeavor, or is there such a thing as general creativity?*

That issue involves the distinction between *capacity* and *performance*. Except for a few outstanding historical examples, the most creative people in one field are not likely at the same time to be the most creative in another. But this may be largely a matter of specialization in training and effort. Is an unusually creative architect likely to be highly creative in chemistry also, assuming equal training and opportunity? And are highly creative architects, or chemists, distinguished only by greater creativity in their respective professions, or can they be distinguished from their less creative colleagues in personal capacities and characteristics beyond differential performance on the job?

The results of various testing programs suggest that the qualities and capacities that distinguish more from less creative practitioners of given fields *do* extend beyond the specific area of professional competence. Creative architects, for instance, differ not only in the way they approach architecture but also in the way they approach any number of situations and tasks, some far removed and apparently unrelated to the specific demands of their profession.

What is more, there seem to be at least some differences that hold across diverse fields; for ex-ample, some of the same personality characteristics that distinguish between architects of high and average creativity have been observed in studies of creativity not only in industrial research chemists, but even among high school children differing in general creativity.

*Granted that people differ in "creativity," are we really talking about anything more than general intelligence?*

Yes. General intelligence seems to bear about the same relationship to on-the-job creativity at the professional level as weight does to ability in football. You have to have a lot of it to be in the game at all; but among those on the team—all of whom have a great deal of weight to begin with—differences in performance are only slightly, if at all, related to weight. In short, in the total population, creativity in most fields is associated with high intelligence, probably more so in some (e.g., physics) than in others (art). But within a given group of practitioners, operating at roughly the same professional level, differences in general intelligence provide no significant prediction of differences in creative performance.

*What, then, are the characteristics of the creative individual, especially those that might be subject to measurement before the fact so as to make prediction possible?*

Although many characteristics of the creative individual, perhaps some of the most important, undoubtedly vary according to the area of creativity, studies of "highs" and "lows" in various fields are beginning to yield some common denominators. The following list concentrates on those differences that are probably more general. In some cases, this assumption of generality stems only from the fact that it seems reasonable on analysis of the characteristics involved vis-á-vis the general demands of the creative process. In others, the generality of the finding is actually supported by research from independent studies in diverse areas.

## Intellectual Characteristics

Although measures of general intelligence fail to predict creativity, highs, as a group, typically outscore lows in tests of the following mental abilities:

*Conceptual Fluency.* The ability to generate a large number of ideas rapidly: List tools beginning with the letter *t*; novel uses for a brick; possible consequences of a situation; categories into which the names of a thousand great men can be sorted—to name just a few of the tasks that have actually been used.

*Conceptual Flexibility.* The ability to shift gears, to discard one frame of reference for another; the tendency to change approaches spontaneously.

*Originality.* The ability and/or tendency to give unusual, atypical (therefore more probably new) answers to questions, responses to situations, interpretations of events.

Highs, for instance, are more apt to give rare—as well as more—uses of bricks; they give fewer "popular" interpretations of what an inkblot looks like; in high school, uncommon vs. common career aspirations (e.g., explorer rather than lawyer).

*Preference for Complexity.* Highs often exhibit a preference for the complex, and to them intriguing, as against the simple and easily understood.

When confronted with complex inkblots, for instance, they tend to seek a more difficult "whole" interpretation that takes the entire blot into account, rather than to identify detailed aspects that clearly resemble certain things.

The usual interpretation is that highs take complexity as a challenge; that they enjoy the attempt to integrate and resolve it.

## Personality

Several closely related personality characteristics distinguish highs and lows in a number of studies:

*Independence of Judgment.* Highs are more apt to stick to their guns when they find themselves in disagreement with others.

In a situation where an artificially induced group consensus contradicts the evidence of their own senses, lows more often yield in their expressed judgment. The same is true when the issue at stake is not a factual one but involves voicing an opinion on an aesthetic, social, or political matter.

*Deviance.* Highs see themselves as more different from their peers and, in fact, they appear to *be* more different in any number of significant as well as trivial characteristics.

At the extreme, highs sometimes feel lonely and apart, with a sense of mission that isolates them, in their own minds, from average men with average concerns.

*Attitudes toward Authority.* A related distinction with far-reaching implications for organizations has to do with the way authority is viewed. The difference between highs and lows is a matter of degree, but to make the point we describe the extremes.

Lows are more apt to view authority as final and absolute; to offer unquestioning obedience, allegiance, or belief (as the case may be), with respect approaching deference; to accept present authority as "given" and more or less permanent. Highs are more likely to think of authority as conventional or arbitrary, contingent on continued and demonstrable superiority; to accept dependence on authority as a matter of expedience rather than personal allegiance or moral obligation; to view present authority as temporary.

Attitudes toward subordinates are related in the appropriate direction; those who pay unquestioned allegiance tend to expect it, and vice versa.

Similarly, and in general, highs are more apt to separate source from content in their evaluation of communications; to judge and reach conclusions on the basis of the information itself. Lows are more prone to accept or reject, believe or disbelieve messages on the basis of their attitudes toward the sender.

*"Impulse Acceptance."* Highs are more willing to entertain and express personal whims and impulses; lows stick closer to "realistic," expected behavior. Highs pay more heed to inner voices, while lows suppress them in favor of external demands.

So, for example, highs may introduce humor into situations where it is not called for and bring a better sense of humor to situations where it is. And, in general, highs exhibit a richer and more diverse "fantasy life" on any number of clinical tests.

Does the more creative man have more inner impulses or fewer inhibitions, or both, and to what degree? The answer is unknown, but there is at least one intriguing finding that suggests a strange combination of two normally opposing traits:

In the genius and near-genius, a widely used personality test shows "schizoid" tendencies (bizarre, unusual, unrealistic thoughts and urges) *coupled* with great "ego strength" (ability to control, channel, and manipulate reality effectively). This line of inquiry begins to speak the cliché that the dividing line between madman and genius is a fine one. According to this finding, the line is fine, but firm.

In sum, highly creative people are more likely than others to view authority as conventional rather than absolute; to make fewer black-and-white distinctions; to have a less dogmatic and more relativistic view of life; to show more independence of judgment and less conventionality and conformity, both intellectual and social; to be more willing to entertain, and sometimes express, their own "irrational" impulses; to place a greater value on humor and in fact to have a better sense of humor; in short to be somewhat freer and less rigidly—but not less effectively—controlled.

## Approach to Problems

The more detailed aspects of the creative process are taken up in the next section, where we see highs at work. We briefly note three distinctions as personal characteristics of creative problem solvers; all are especially significant in the management of creativity and are elaborated upon later.

*Motivation.* Highs are more perceptive to, and more motivated by, the interest inherent in the problem and its solution. Accordingly, they get more involved in the task, work harder and longer in the absence of external pressures or incentive, and generally place *relatively* greater value on "job interest" versus such extrinsic rewards as salary or status. (See Barron, p. 126, and Steiner, p. 257.) There is no evidence, however, that the *absolute* importance of external incentives is any less for highs than for lows.

*Orientation.* Along somewhat the same lines:

Lows are more likely to see their future largely within the boundaries of one organization, to be concerned chiefly with its problems and with their own rise within it, and to develop extensive ties and associations within the community; in short, to be "local" in their loyalties and aspirations.

Highs are more apt to think in terms of a larger community, both residential and professional; to view themselves more as members of the profession (whether management, chemistry, or teaching) than as members of Company X; to take their cues from the larger professional community and attempt to rise within it; to be more mobile, hence less "loyal" to any specific organization; in short, to be cosmopolitan in orientation and aspiration.

Hence, the local is more willing to change assignments, even professions (for example, from chemistry or engineering to administration), in the interests of the organization and his own career within it. The cosmopolitan is more likely to change organizations to pursue *his* interests and career within the larger profession. In short, highs change jobs to pursue their interests, not their interests to pursue their jobs.

*Pace.* Highs often spend more time in the initial stages of problem formulation, in broad scanning of alternatives. Lows are more apt to "get on with it."

For example, in problems divisible into analytic and synthetic stages, highs spend more time on the former, in absolute as well as relative terms. As a result, they often leave lows behind in the later stages of the solution process, having disposed of more blind alleys and being able to make more comprehensive integrations as a result of more thorough analysis.

One interpretation is that highs have less anxiety to produce, that they are confident enough of their eventual success to be able to step back and take a broad look before making commitments.

*Can such differences be measured reliably enough to be of use in selection programs?*

Many of these qualities can be measured, at least in part, by simple paper-and-pencil tests or other controlled observations. But the instruments are far from perfect and, perhaps more seriously, the correlation between each of these distinguishing characteristics and on-the-job creativity is limited. The characteristics "distinguish" highs from lows only in the sense that highs, on the average, have more of, or more often exhibit, the particular quality. And that is far from saying that all highs have more of each than all lows.[1]

As a result, as with all actuarial predictions of this sort, the procedure becomes more useful as the number of cases to be predicted increases. If many people are to be selected and it is important that some of them will turn out to be highs, a testing program can improve the odds. This would apply, for instance, in the selection of college or graduate students, Air Force Research and Development Officers, or chemists in a major industrial laboratory.

But if few people are being selected and it is important that almost all of them turn out to be highly creative (the chiefs of staff; the top management team; or the scientists to head a project), it is doubtful that, at present, a testing program will improve the odds beyond those of careful personal appraisal and judgment.

In this connection, there is the interesting suggestion (not documented) that highs may themselves be better judges of creativity in others; that it "takes one to tell one."

As the examples suggest, testing to predict creativity is perhaps least effective where needed most: where the importance of the individual cases is the greatest.

*What are the observable characteristics of the creative process; how does it look to an outsider while it is going on?*

The appearance of the creative process, especially in its early stages, poses a problem to administrators. Up to a point, it may be hard to distinguish from totally non-productive behavior: undisciplined disorder, aimless rambling, even total inactivity.

*Irregular Progress.* Creativity is rarely a matter of gradual, step-by-step progress; it is more often a pattern of large and largely unpredictable leaps after relatively long periods of no apparent progress.

The extreme example is the sudden insight that occurs after a difficult problem is put aside, and at a time of no conscious concern with the matter. Many anecdotes support the film cliché where the great man cries "Eureka!" in the middle of the night or while shaving—or, as in this famous case, while getting on a bus:

*Just at this time I left Caen, where I was then living, to go on a geological excursion under the auspices of the school of mines. The changes of travel made me forget my mathematical work. Having reached Coutances, we entered an omnibus to some place or other. At the moment when I put my foot on the step the idea came to me, without anything in my former thoughts seeming to have paved the way for it, that the transformations I had used to define the Fuchsian functions were identical with those of non-Euclidean geometry. I did not verify the idea; I should not have had time, as, upon taking my seat in the omnibus, I went on with a conversation already commenced, but I felt a perfect certainty. On my return to Caen, for conscience' sake I verified the result at my leisure.—Poincaré*

At a level of more immediate concern to most administrators, since few have the problem or the prowess of a Poincaré, the same sort of progress pattern distinguishes creative from merely productive work, and more from less creative activity, in the kind of problem-solving that characterizes the day-to-day activities of the organization.

*Suspended Judgment.* The creative process often requires and exhibits suspended judgment. The dangers of early commitment—sometimes to "incorrigible strategies"—are apparent at various levels. In the perceptual laboratory, for example, people who make an early, incorrect interpretation of a picture in an "ambiguitor" (a device that gradually brings a blurred picture into focus), will tend to retain the wrong perception—actually fail to "see"—even when the picture has been fully and clearly exposed.

Similarly, in the type of small-group problem-solving or decison-making so typical of the modern organization, people will "stick to their guns" to support a position they have taken publicly, beyond its apparent validity and usefulness.

Finally, at the level of the organization itself, financial, technical, or corporate commitments to products, techniques, physical facilities, affiliations, and the like, often stand in the way of change even when it is recognized as necessary and inevitable.

*"Undisciplined" Exploration.* Again, many creators stress the importance of undisciplined thinking, especially in the initial stages, probably because it serves to expand the range of consideration and raw material from which the new solution will emerge.

In this connection, we hear of the use of artificial disorganizers and "boundary expanders," such as alcohol, brain-storming sessions, sometimes even narcotics; and, frequently, the observation that inspiration cannot be willed or worked on, that pressure and preoccupation with the problem are least likely to produce insight—though they may indeed sustain effort in other phases of the process.

The administrative enigma, then, is to distinguish, before the fact, incubation from laziness; suspended judgment from indecision, "boundary expansion" from simple drinking; undisciplined thinking as a deliberate exploratory step from undisciplined thinking as a permanent characteristic; brain-storming from gibberish by committee. In short, how can one tell the temporarily fallow mind—open and receptive, working subconsciously, and just on the threshold of the brilliant flash—from the permanently idle one? There may, of course, not be an answer. In time, outward predictors and distinguishing characteristics (beyond the individual's past history) may

emerge. But for the moment, tolerance for high-risk gambles on creativity is probably one of the prerequisites or costs of playing for the higher stakes creativity provides when it does pay off.

*What are the characteristics of the psychological state optimal for creative production?*

*Motivation.* How much should be at stake; how hard should a man be trying, in order to maximize his chances of being creative? There is an apparent paradox:

First, we often hear that the creative process is characterized by a tremendous sense of commitment, a feeling of urgency, even of mission, that results in enormous preoccupation with the problem and perseverance.

On the other hand, there is evidence that extremely high motivation narrows the focus and produces rigidity, perseveration rather than perseverance, which not only precludes creativity but reduces productivity (freezing up in the clutch). Some go so far as to say that the absence of pressure is a common denominator in situations conducive to creativity.

There are two suggested resolutions: One is that the relationship is curvilinear; that creativity first rises, then falls, with motivation—you need enough to maintain effort at high levels but not so much as to produce panic attempts at immediate solution (jumping out of the window instead of looking for the fire escape). And there is, in fact, good evidence of such a relationship in laboratory studies of human and even animal problem-solving.

The other possible resolution involves a distinction in quality of motivation—between "inner" and "outer," "involvement" and "pressure," "drive" and "stress"—related to the earlier observation that highs are more driven by interest and involvement in the task itself than by external incentives. Perhaps external pressure impedes creativity, while inner drive and task-involvement are prerequisites.

In short, it may very well be that "Genius is 90 percent hard work" but that inducing hard work is unlikely to produce genius.

The two resolutions are not mutually exclusive. Motivation of both kinds may have a breaking point, a level where they do more harm than good; although it seems reasonable to suppose that higher levels of "intrinsic" than of "extrinsic" motivation are compatible with creativity.

At any rate, other things being equal, interest in, and commitment to the problem for its own sake should point to a creative outcome more often than sustained effort purchased by some externally attached reward, simply because the former is more apt to channel energy in the relevant directions.

*Open-Mindedness versus Conviction.* What intellectual attitude toward one's ideas and suggestions is optimal: how much conviction versus continual reappraisal; self-involvement versus objective detachment? Again, both tendencies appear, and in the extreme.

On the one hand, creativity is characterized by a willingness to seek and accept relevant information from any and all sources, to suspend judgment, defer commitment, remain aloof in the face of pressures to take a stand. On the other hand, creators in the process of creating are often described as having conviction approaching zeal.

There may in fact be a sort of simultaneous "antimony" or interaction between "passion and decorum," "commitment and detachment," domination *by* a problem and yet a view of it as objective and external. The process may involve the continual and conflicting presence of both components. Or it may be a matter of stages. Perhaps the creative process is characterized by open-mindedness in the early, idea-getting phases; then by a bull-headed conviction at the point of dissemination and execution.

There could be at least two reasons. A more open mind, that initially examines more alternatives, is more likely to be convinced of the one it finally selects. An early commitment to a less carefully analyzed approach may be more vulnerable in the face of attack; beliefs developed through more painful and agonizing appraisal are more apt to stand the test of time.

In addition, creators almost always find themselves on the defensive in the period after the idea has been developed but before it has been "sold." There is an inevitable stepping on toes, effrontery to the status quo and those responsible for it, that usually leads to some rejection of the maverick, especially if the innovation is not immediately, demonstrably superior. And people on the defensive are apt to overstate their case. In short, open-minded probers may become fervent proselytizers.

As a working summary hypothesis:

In the exploratory, idea-getting stages, there is great interest in the problem; perhaps commitment to its eventual solution but certainly not to any particular approach; an open-minded willingness to pursue leads in any direction; a relaxed and perhaps playful attitude that allows a disorganized, undisciplined approach, to the point of putting the problem aside entirely. But at the point of development and execution, where the selected alternative is pursued, tested, and applied, there is great conviction, dogged perseverance, perhaps strong personal involvement, and dogmatic support of the new way.

## II. THE ORGANIZATION ITSELF

*What does all this have to do with organization? What are the characteristics of the creative organization; and what are the implications of individual creativity, if any?*

There are various ways to approach this question.

One is to reason, deductively, *from* the characteristics of creators and the creative process *to* the kind of environment that ought to be congenial to them and conducive to creative activity. What does the nature of individual creativity imply about the environmental factors that foster or impede it? For the most part, this is the way we proceed in what follows.

Another approach is to treat the organization, as a whole, as the creative unit. Perhaps some of the characteristics that distinguish "high" and "low" individuals also apply to high and low organizations as such.

The characteristics of creative individuals suggest a number of rather direct translations or counterparts at the organizational level; and many of the characteristics independently attributed to creative organizations seem to match items in our description of individual highs.

A brief summary follows. Although this analogizing has serious limitations and may be misleading, the table does serve as an organized index to some of the major characteristics attributed to creative organizations; and it is interesting that so many of them sound like the distinguishing characteristics of individual highs.

Finally, there is direct, empirical study of actual creative organizations. This may well turn out to be the most fruitful approach, but it was not the major focus of the seminar. In part, this reflects the state of knowledge; systematic studies of creative organizations, as such, simply do not exist as yet. In part, the composition of the symposium is responsible. A meeting with six psychologists and one psychoanalyst, against three sociologists, inevitably speaks mostly in psychological terms.

At any rate, we make no attempt to represent, let alone do justice to, the sociological investigation and analysis of organizational factors that relate to creativity. In what follows, we reason and abstract mostly from the nature of individual creativity, partly from rather informal observations of actual organizations.

*What, specifically, can management do—beyond selecting creative participants—to foster creativity within and on the part of the organization?*

*Values and Rewards.* What explicit and implicit goals and values characterize the creative organization? What system of rewards and incentives maximizes creativity?

First the creative organization in fact prizes and rewards creativity. A management philosophy that stresses creativity as an organizational goal, that encourages and expects it at all levels, will increase the chances of its occurrence.

But it is one thing to call for creativity, another to mean it, and still another to reward it adequately and consistently when it occurs. More

specifically, creativity as a value should find expression in the following:

*Compensation.* In most areas of day-to-day functioning, productivity rather than creativity is and should be the principal objective; thus, general reward policies tend to measure and stress regular output. But even where creativity is truly desired and encouraged in good faith, activities that are potentially more creative may be subordinated to those more visibly and closely tied to reward policies. (A familiar academic illustration is the "pressure to publish," which may lead to a plethora of relatively insignificant formula-projects that minimize chances of failure, i.e., nonpublication, but also of creativity.)

In the business enterprise, a similar grievance centers on discrepancies in reward between the sowing and reaping aspects of the operation; with the greater rewards for work that shows immediate, measurable results (e.g., sales) as against that which may pay off in the longer run (such as basic research).

It may be inevitable that work closer to the balance sheet will be more swiftly and fully compensated than efforts that have tenuous, uncertain, and in any case long-range effects on corporate profits. But creativity and guaranteed, immediate results do not go together; not between, nor within, assignments. If creativity is to be fostered, not impeded, by material incentives, they will have to be applied by a different yardstick.

It is probably this simple: Where creativity and not productivity is in fact the goal, then creativity and not productivity should in fact be measured and rewarded. And if creativity is harder to measure and takes longer periods to assess, then this probably requires some speculative investment on the part of the firm that wants to keep and nurture the few men and the few activities that will eventually be worth it.[2]

*Channels for Advancement.* Where concern is with creativity in a professional unit or other specialized function operating within the larger organization, there is this related implication: To the extent possible, there should be formal channels

| The Creative Individual | The Creative Organization |
| --- | --- |
| Conceptual fluency...is able to produce a large number of ideas quickly | Has idea men<br>Open channels of communication<br>*Ad hoc* devices:<br>    Suggestion systems<br>    Brain-storming<br>    Idea units absolved of other resonsibilities<br>Encourages contact with outside sources |
| Originality...generates unusual ideas | Heterogenous personnel policy<br>Includes marginal, unusual types<br>Assigns non-specialists to problems<br>Allows eccentricity |
| Separates source from content in evaluating information...is motivated by interest in problem...follows wherever it leads | Has an objective, fact-founded approach<br>Ideas evaluated on their merits, not status of originator<br>*Ad hoc* approaches:<br>    Anonymous communications<br>    Blind votes<br>Selects and promotes on merit only |
| Suspends judgment...avoids early commitment...spends more time in analysis, exploration | Lack of financial, material commitment to products, policies<br>Invests in basic research; flexible, long-range planning<br>Experiments with new ideas rather than prejudging on "rational" grounds; everything gets a chance |
| Less authoritarian...has relativistic view of life | More decentralized; diversified<br>Administrative slack; time and resources to absorb errors<br>Risk-taking ethos...tolerates and expects taking chances |
| Accepts own impulses...playful, undisciplined exploration | Not run as "tight ship"<br>Employees have fun<br>Allows freedom to choose and pursue problems<br>Freedom to discuss ideas |
| Independence of judgment, less conformity | Organizationally autonomous |
| Deviant, sees self as different | Original and different objectives, not trying to be another "X" |
| Rich, "bizarre" fantasy life *and* superior reality orientation; controls | Security of routine...*allows* innovation<br>"Philistines" provide stable, secure environment that allows "creators" to roam<br>Has separate units or occasions for generating vs. evaluating ideas...separates creative from productive functions |

for advancement and status within the area of creativity.

Where it is impossible to promote a creative chemist without taking him out of chemistry, he faces a choice between money and position on the one hand, and chemistry on the other. The company is likely to lose his services as chemist in either case: to administration within its own walls or to another organization where a chemist as such can get ahead. (This is one of the chief organizational advantages and attractions of the major university for the research scientist or scholar: parallel channels for advancement, of at least equal status, exist outside of administration.)

To some extent this is a matter of size; it is hard to provide for advancement within a department of one or two persons. But size alone is not enough. The nature and number of status levels established, their labels, and especially their actual value within the firm and the larger community, will determine their worth to individuals who hold them.

*"Freedom."* Within rather broad limits, creativity is increased by giving creators freedom in choice of problem and method of pursuit. In line with the high's greater interest and involvement in his work, greater freedom is necessary, to maximize those satisfactions that are important to him and that channel his efforts into avenues most likely to prove creative. (See Alexander, p. 239.) Whether and where there is an upper limit is a point of much contention and no evidence.

But such freedom often puts the appropriate objectives of the organization at odds with the demands of maximum creativity. The symposium itself produced two striking examples.

In one instance, a participant "distracted" himself and the group by working out and presenting an elegant solution to a mathematical problem that had been mentioned only in passing, as a task assigned to subjects in a creativity experiment. From the point of view of the seminar, he was out of bounds. By following his own interests, he was creative. (Would he have arrived at an equally elegant *psychological* insight had he been constrained to the issue as externally defined?)

More dramatically, after the first few hours of the meeting had been spent in rather academic and abstract discussion, one participant reminded us that the purpose of the meeting was to develop useful and understandable guidelines for management and that we had better get on with it. This precipitated a short but heartfelt donnybrook between the advocates of "No nonsense! Keep your eye on the target," and "Take it easy; it's interesting; let's see where it leads"; between "What good is it if you can't tell us what it means for management?" and "Our job is to create, yours to apply."

Both approaches are valid but as means to different ends. Those responsible for a meeting are rightfully concerned with maximizing its output. By the same token, creative individuals who attend it are not so concerned with the product of the particular conference as with the pursuit of interesting lines of inquiry, whether or not they happen to reach fruition during the session. And curtailing and channeling discussion into areas known to be productive obviously limits the chances of coming up with something outside the range of the ordinary.

This, then, is probably one of the principal costs in the nurture of creativity: Except in the rare and fortunate case where a creative individual's interests exactly match the day-to-day operating objectives of his organization, and continue to do so over time, the organization pays a price, at least in the short run, for giving him his head. What he returns to the organization may or may not compensate it many-fold.

*Communication.* Many observations point to the importance of free and open channels of communication, both vertical and horizontal.

On the one hand, potential creators need and seek relevant information whatever its source, within or without the organization; on the other hand, they are stimulated by diverse and complex input.

Equally important, ideas wither for lack of a grapevine. A possible approach, a feasible but half-baked notion, or even a well worked-out solution must be communicated to those with the power to evaluate, authorize, and implement.

The presence of formal channels is not

enough. People must feel free to use them, and channels must not be clogged by routine paperflow that ties up time with "programmed trivia," and creates an air of apathy and neglect toward incoming messages because it is so unlikely that they will contain anything of value.

Since highs tend toward cosmopolitan, professional orientation, the organization must at least provide for and perhaps encourage contact and communication with colleagues and associations on the outside.

As a special case, there is the matter of scientific and professional publication in the appropriate journals, which is often of great personal importance to creators.

There may be problems of security and the natural jealousy of corporate secrets and employee loyalties. But in many cases, these are unrealistic or exaggerated, given the high rate of horizontal mobility, the discretion of the professional, and the fact that most "secrets" are not. At any rate, there may be no reason to think that the balance of payments will be "out"; there should be at least as much information gained as given away in most external contacts. And in many cases, and within broad limits, the net gain in satisfaction, creativity, and perhaps tenure of highs will probably offset the time and trade secrets lost to the outside.

*What, specifically, are the costs of creativity? What must an organization be prepared to give up or tolerate if it wants to increase its creativity?*

Answers were scattered throughout the preceding, but it may help to pull them together.

First, creativity, by definition, is a high-risk enterprise, not for society or industry, at large, but for any given unit that attempts it. The greater the departure from present practice, the less likelihood that the innovation will work; the greater the potential payoff, the less the odds of its occurring. Conversely, the larger the number of workers or units independently pursuing any problem, the better the chances that one or more of them will succeed.

In the abstract, then, decisions as to whether and where to attempt creativity, and how much to try for, are much like decisions concerning what

to insure, and for how much—although the hopes and fears are reversed.

Second, within the unit under consideration, fostering creativity assesses costs in assured productivity. To the extent that energy is consumed in investigation and exploration, it does not go into work known to be productive.

Finally, depending on the personal tastes and preferences of management, there may or may not be costs in "security," "comfort," and "congeniality" of the environment: (*a*) Highs are not as deferent, obedient, flattering, easy to control, flexible to *external* demands and changes, conventional, predictable, and so on, through a long list of disiderata in "good" employees. (*b*) In addition, highs are more mobile, less "loyal"—harder to hold by ordinary extrinsic rewards—but easier to acquire by the offer of interesting opportunities. At any rate, they make for a less stable and secure, more challenging but perhaps more disturbing environment. (*c*) A creative organization itself is more committed to change; operates on a faster track; has a less certain or predictable future than the efficient, me-too operation.

In short, maximizing creativity is not the principal objective of any organization at all times, or even of all organizations at some times. When it is, there are some rough guidelines to how it may be fostered—but not, it is suggested, at no cost.

*Consider the organization as a whole, operating within a larger social and economic environment. What type of situation is most likely to produce a creative organization?*

The seminar produced little agreement, let alone evidence, on this matter. There was some discussion about the effects of competitive position, size, age, and general success of an organization as they affect its need and chances for creativity. But nothing approaching a conclusion is visible.

One of the more interesting recurrent debates centered on the relative merits of firmly led, "one-man" organizations versus decentralized corporate entities; on charismatic, inspired leadership by a "great man" versus the greater democracy of the professionally managed organization. This debate was not resolved, but it does call attention to some distinctions that may be important.

*Some Final Distinctions.* Last, we take note of some distinctions that may be helpful, suggested simply by the experience of trying to discuss "the creative organization." For instance, the preceding debate may reflect a failure to distinguish between a creative organization and one that produces for a creator.

An organization can be an efficient instrument for the execution of externally created ideas and yet not be in itself creative: for instance, a smooth military unit under a great strategist, a top-notch symphony orchestra, or, in the same terms, a business that hums to the tune of a creative president. These may all implement creativity and yield a product appropriately called creative, but they are not, *ipso facto*, creative organizations. And the characteristics that make for creativity within and on the part of an organization as a whole may

in fact be quite different from those that make it the efficient tool of a creative master.

Along the same lines, it may be helpful to distinguish between getting people to be more creative and getting creative people to be more productive. The conditions that induce a Frank Lloyd Wright, an Ogilvy, or a Shockley to turn out more of the same—to repeat or elaborate earlier innovations—may be quite different from those that produce the original and subsequent departures.

In short, organizations, like people, may increase their net yield of creative *products* either by the terms that go into their conception or those that enter into their output. And while the net effects may often be the same, the means are probably not.

For the eventual understanding of "the creative organization," it may be important to learn the difference between creating productivity and producing creativity.

## NOTES

1. In general, validity coefficients for specific tests at best attain values around .60, which means that they predict about 36 per cent of the variation in observed creativity.

2. High potential pay-off and low risk are, unfortunately, incompatible—just as they are in the stock market and at the gambling tables.

## 42. ENTREPRENEURSHIP/INTRAPRENEURSHIP

*Robert D. Hisrich*

The importance of innovation in the development of new products, processes, and services for the market is widely recognized. As early as the

1930s, Schumpeter (1934) linked innovation and the innovation process to the entrepreneur. According to Schumpeter, when the economy is in a stationary state, profit-motivated entrepreneurs will innovate to raise marginal productivity and increase profits. Who are these entrepreneurs? What is their motivation? Can they be a part of an existing organization?

In spite of the increased interest in entrepreneurship, a concise, universally accepted definition has not yet emerged. The term has taken on different meanings since its inception in French in the middle ages when it was literally translated as *between-taker* or *go between*. Most of the definitions of entrepreneurship note that the term refers to behaviors that include demonstrating initiative and creative thinking, organizing social and economic mechanisms to turn resources and situations to practical account, and accepting risk and failure.

*To an economist, an entrepreneur is one who brings resources, labor, materials, and other assets into combinations that make their value greater than before, and also one who introduces changes, innovations, and a new order. To a psychologist, such a person is typically driven by certain forces—need to obtain or attain something, to experiment, to accomplish, or perhaps to escape authority of others.... To one businessman an entrepreneur appears as a threat, an aggressive competitor, whereas to another businessman the same entrepreneur may be an ally, a source of supply, a customer, or someone good to invest in.... The same person is seen by a capitalist philosopher as one who creates wealth for others as well, who finds better ways to utilize resources, and reduce waste, and who produces jobs others are glad to get. (Vesper, 1980, p. 2)*

Each of these views entrepreneurs from a slightly different perspective, and each definition is somewhat restrictive. Entrepreneurs are found in all professions—education, medicine, research, law, architecture, engineering, social work, manufacturing, and distribution. To include all types of entrepreneurial behavior, there is a much broader definition: "Entrepreneurship is the process of creating something different with value by devoting the necessary time and effort, assuming the accompanying financial, psychic, and social risks, and receiving the resulting rewards of monetary and personal satisfaction" (Hisrich & Peters, 1989, p. 6). For persons who actually start their

own business, the experience is filled with enthusiasm, frustration, anxiety, and hard work. There is a high failure rate due to poor sales, intense competition, or lack of capital. The Small Business Administration (SBA) reports, for example, that four out of five new businesses fail within their first five years. The financial and emotional risks indeed are very high.

Due in part to the high risks and cost involved, a hybrid form of entrepreneurship has emerged that is called *intrapreneurship* (Pinchot, 1985). An intrapreneur is a corporate entrepreneur; this allows entrepreneurship to occur in an existing organization. Intrapreneurs, like entrepreneurs, take new ideas and develop solid, functioning, and, it is hoped, profitable businesses. Intrapreneurs possess the same entrepreneurial spirit as entrepreneurs.

The vigor of this entrepreneurial spirit in the United States has posed some questions for psychologists who are frequently asked to deal with entrepreneurship and intrapreneurship. Business organizations, city and state governments, and universities all want to foster this entrepreneurial spirit. What is it? Who has it? How can it be enhanced?

## CHARACTERISTICS OF ENTREPRENEURS

As may be expected, entrepreneurs and intrapreneurs are similar in many respects. They are leaders who have an impact on their cultures, particularly those around them who share in their vision of the creation of something new of value and wealth with potential for new employment. In 1987, almost 850,000 new companies were formed compared to 200,000 in 1965 and only 90,000 in 1950 (Birch, 1987). In addition to these in that year, there were about 400,000 new partnerships and 300,000 newly self-employed people. These 1.5 million new entities correspond to the average annual 1.5 million new private sector jobs created each year in the economy.

Entrepreneurship has resulted in several million new businesses being formed throughout the world, even in controlled economies such as China, Hungary, and Poland. Indeed, millions of company formations occur despite recession, inflation, high interest rates, lack of infrastructure, economic uncertainty, and the fear of failure (Hisrich, 1986). These company formations are very personal human processes that, although unique, have some common characteristics. Like all processes these entail a movement from something to something—a movement from a present life-style to forming a new enterprise.

## Change From Present Life-Style

The decision to leave a present career and life-style is not an easy one. It takes a great deal of energy to change and create something new. Although persons tend to start businesses in familiar areas, two work environments tend to be particularly good in spawning new enterprises: research and development and marketing. Persons develop new product ideas or processes and often leave to form a new company when the new idea is not accepted by the present employer; similarly, some employees in marketing become familiar with the market and unfilled customers' wants and needs and often start new enterprises to fill these needs.

Disruption also causes a person to leave a present life-style. A significant number of companies are formed by people who have retired, who are relocated due to a move by the other member in a dual-career family, or who have been fired. There is probably no greater force than personal dislocation to galvanize a person into action. A study in one major city in the United States indicated that the number of new business listings in the Yellow Pages increased by 12% during a lay-off period (Hisrich, 1984). Another cause of disruption and resulting company formation is the completion of an educational degree. For example, a student who does not receive a promotion after completing a master's degree in business administration may decide to start a new company.

What causes this change due to personal disruption to result in a new company's being formed instead of something else? The decision to start a new company occurs when a person perceives that it is both desirable and possible.

*Desirable.* It is hypothesized that the perception that starting a new company is desirable results in part, from a person's culture, subculture, family, teachers, and peers (Hisrich, 1986). A culture that values the successful creation of a new business will spawn more company formations than one that does not; this is evident in the company formation rate for the United States versus for the Soviet Union. For example, the American culture places a high value on being your own boss, having individual opportunity, being a success, and making money—all aspects of entrepreneurship. Therefore, it is not surprising to find a high rate of company formation in the United States. On the other hand, successfully establishing a new business and making money is not as highly valued, and failure may be a disgrace in the cultures of some countries, such as Ireland and Norway.

However, even an entire culture is not totally for or against entrepreneurship. Many different subcultures that shape value systems are operant within a cultural framework. There are pockets of entrepreneurial subcultures in the United States, of which the more widely recognized ones are: Route 128, Silicon Valley, Dallas–Fort Worth, and the North Carolina Triangle. These subcultures support and even promote entrepreneurship—forming a new company—as one of the best occupations. No wonder more people actively plan to form new enterprises in these supportive environments.

There are of course variations within these subcultures (such as the one in Silicon Valley) caused by family traits and the overall parental relationship. Parents who are supportive and encourage independence, achievement, and responsibility have an influence on the child's desire for entrepreneurial activity (Bowen & Hisrich, 1986).

It is hypothesized that the encouragement to form a company is further influenced by teachers. Teachers can significantly influence persons with regard not only to business careers but to entrepreneurship as one possible career path. Schools with exciting courses in entrepreneurship and innovation tend to spawn entrepreneurs and can actually drive the entrepreneurial environment in an economic area. For example, the number of entrepreneurship courses taken increases the interest in starting a new venture. The Massachusetts Institute of Technology and Harvard are located near Route 128; Stanford is in the Silicon Valley; the University of North Carolina, North Carolina State, and Duke are the points of the North Carolina Triangle; and University of Texas facilitates the activity in the Dallas–Fort Worth area. A strong education base is almost a prerequisite for entrepreneurial activity and company formation in an area.

Finally, it is felt that peers are very important in the decision to form a company. An area with an entrepreneurial pool and meeting places where entrepreneurs and potential entrepreneurs meet and discuss ideas, problems, and solutions spawns more new companies than an area without these features. For example, technology-oriented persons get together regularly at Tulsa Tech Talk to discuss technical problems as well as commercial feasibility and company formation. This has resulted in several new ventures.

*Possible.* Although the desire generated from the culture, subculture, family, teachers, and peers needs to be present before any action is taken, the second part of the equation centers around the question: What makes it possible to form a new company? Several factors—government, background, marketing, role models, and finances—contribute to creating a new venture. The government contributes by providing the infrastructure to support a new venture. It is no wonder that more companies are formed in the United States, given its roads, communication and transportation systems, utilities, and economic stability, than in other countries with what may be available there. Even the tax rate for companies and individuals in the United States is better than countries such as Ireland or England. Countries that have a repressive tax rate, particularly for individuals, can suppress company formation because a significant monetary gain cannot be achieved even though the social, psychological, and financial risks are still present.

The entrepreneur also must have the background needed to make the company formation possible. Knowledge acquired from formal education and previous business experience makes a potential entrepreneur feel capable of forming and managing a new enterprise. Although educational systems are important because they provide the needed knowledge of business, people still tend to start successful businesses infields in which they have worked. In fact, in many cases the idea for the new company occurs while the person is working in a particular business position. Indeed, entrepreneurs are not born; they develop.

Marketing also plays a critical role in forming a new company. Not only must a market of sufficient size be present, but also the marketing know-how of putting together the best total package of product, price, distribution, and promotion to ensure successful product launching. A company is more easily formed in an area where there is market demand and not just new technology aiming at the same market. Some companies that are based on new technology often find that there is no market for this technology and may in time cease to exist.

Perhaps one of the most powerful influences that make company formation seem possible are role models. To see someone else do something and succeed makes it easier to picture oneself doing a similar, and of course, better, activity. A frequent comment of entrepreneurs when informally queried about their motivation for starting their new venture is, "If that person could do it, so can I!"

Finally, financial resources needed to form a new company must be readily available. Although the majority of the start-up money for any new company comes from personal savings, credit, friends, and relatives, there is still often a need for seed (start-up) capital or other types of risk capital (Wetzel, 1986). Risk-capital investors play an essential role in the development and growth of entrepreneurial activity. When seed capital is readily available, more new companies form; this is evident in the increased number of company formations in the United States when there is abundant risk (seed) capital (Wetzel, 1986).

This entrepreneurial decision process occurs in a diverse group of persons with a wide variety of characteristics and backgrounds. Before I consider the various characteristics and backgrounds of the typical entrepreneur, understand that there is really no such thing as a typical entrepreneurial profile. Entrepreneurs come from a variety of educational backgrounds, family situations, and work experiences. An entrepreneur may have previously been a nurse, secretary, assembly line worker, salesperson, mechanic, homemaker, manager, or engineer. An entrepreneur can be a man or a woman, Black or White, college educated or not college educated.

Although many of the various aspects of an entrepreneur's background have been explored, only a few have differentiated the entrepreneur from the general populace or managers. The background areas explored include childhood family environment, education, personal values, age, and work history.

## Childhood Family Environment

Specific topics in the family environment of the entrepreneur while growing up include birth order, parent's occupation and social status, and relationship with the parents. The impact of birth order has had conflicting research results since Hennig and Jardim (1977) found that female executives tend to be first born. Being first born or an only child is postulated to result in the child's receiving special attention and, thereby, developing more self-confidence. In a national sample of 468 female entrepreneurs, Hisrich and Brush (1984) found 50% to be first born. However, in many studies of male and female entrepreneurs the first-born effect has not been present (Bowen & Hisrich, 1986). Because the relation to entrepreneurship has been only weakly demonstrated, further research on the first-born syndrome is needed to determine if it really

does have an effect on a person's becoming an entrepreneur (Auster & Auster, 1981; Chusmin, 1983; Sexton & Kent, 1981).

In terms of the occupation of the entrepreneurs' parents, there is strong evidence that entrepreneurs tend to have self-employed or entrepreneurial fathers. Female entrepreneurs are as likely to report self-employed or entrepreneurial fathers as male entrepreneurs. The independent nature and flexibility of self-employment exemplified by the father or mother is ingrained at an early age. As one entrepreneur stated, "My father was so consumed by the venture he started and provided such a strong example, it never occurred to me to go to work for anyone else." This feeling of independence is often further enforced by the presence of an entrepreneurial mother. Although the results are much less consistent, female entrepreneurs, at least, appear to have more than their share of entrepreneurial mothers (see Table 42.1). Although there are no comparative studies of nonentrepreneurs, the overall parental relationship appears to be a very important aspect of the childhood family environment in establishing a person's desire for entrepreneurial activity. Parents who are supportive and encourage independence, achievement, and responsibility appear to be very important for female entrepreneurs (Hisrich & Brush, 1986). A national study of female entrepreneurs indicated that they tend to grow up in middle- to upper-class environments in which families are likely to be relatively child-centered and be similar to their fathers in personality (Hisrich & Brush, 1984).

## Education

The education of the entrepreneur has received significant research attention (see Table 42.2). Education was important in the upbringing of most entrepreneurs. Its importance is reflected not only in the level of education obtained but also in the fact that it continues to play a major role as entrepreneurs try to cope with problems and to correct deficiencies in business training. Although a formal education is, of course, not necessary for starting a new business, as reflected

**TABLE 42.1**
Occupations of Entrepreneurs' Parents

| Studies of Entrepreneurs in General or Male Entrepreneurs Only | Studies of Female Entrepreneurs |
|---|---|
| Brockhaus (1982) cited four studies suggesting that entrepreneurs tend to have entrepreneurial fathers. | Hisrich and Brush (1983) reported a nationwide sample of 468 female entrepreneurs; 36% had entrepreneurial fathers; 11% had entrepreneurial mothers. |
| Brockhaus and Nord (1979) found that 31 St. Louis male entrepreneurs were no more likely than male managers to have entrepreneurial fathers. | Mescon and Stevens (1982) found that 53% of 108 Arizona real estate brokers had fathers who were entrepreneurs. No mothers were entrepreneurs. |
| Cooper and Dunkelberg (1984) reported that 47.5% of 1,394 entrepreneurs had parents who owned a business. | Sexton and Kent (1981) found that 40% of 48 Texas female entrepreneurs had entrepreneurial fathers and 13% entrepreneurial mothers (vs. 13% and 11% for 45 female executives). |
| Jacobowitz and Vidler (1983) found that 72% of mid-Atlantic state entrepreneurs had parents or close relatives who were self-employed. | Waddell (1983) found that 63.8% of 47 female entrepreneurs reported entrepreneurial fathers, and 31.9% reported entrepreneurial mothers (vs. 42.5% and 8.5% for female managers and 36.2% and 8.5% for secretaries). |
| Shapero and Sokol (1982) reported that 50% to 58% of company founders in the United States had self-employed fathers (at a time when a self-employed persons were only 12% of the work force). They cited data on the same pattern in nine other cultures. | Watkins and Watkins (1983) found that 37% of 58 British female entrepreneurs had self-employed fathers (self-employment in the male United Kingdom labor force is 9%). Sixteen percent of mothers were whole or part owners of businesses (female self-employment was 4%). |

Note. Data are from "The Female Entrepreneur: A Career Development Perspective" by Donald D. Bowen and Robert D. Hisrich, 1986, *Academy of Management Review, 11,* p. 399.

in the success of such high school dropouts as Andrew Carnegie, William Durant, Henry Ford, and William Lear, it does provide a good background, particularly when it is related to the field of the venture. In terms of type and quality of education, female entrepreneurs appear to experience some disadvantage. Although nearly 70% of all female entrepreneurs have a college degree, many with graduate degrees, the most popular college majors are English, psychology, education, and sociology, and a few have degrees in engineering, science, or math (Hisrich & Brush, 1986). Both male and female entrepreneurs have cited educational needs in the areas of finance, strategic planning, marketing (particularly distribution), and management. Entrepreneurs informally have indicated the importance of being able to deal with people and communicate clearly.

## Personal Values

Although there have been many studies to indicate that personal values are important for entrepreneurs, frequently these studies fail to indicate that entrepreneurs can be differentiated on these values from managers, unsuccessful entrepreneurs, or even the general population. For example, whereas entrepreneurs appear to be effective leaders in that they are able to communicate their vision for the company in such a way that others cooperate, the degree of this leadership has not been thoroughly researched nor does the amount distinguish them from successful managers. Although personal value scales for leadership as well as support, aggression, benevolence, conformity, creativity, veracity, and resource-seeking are important for identifying entrepreneurs, they frequently

**TABLE 42.2**
Amount of Education of Entrepreneurs

| Studies | Findings | Comments |
|---|---|---|
| | Entrepreneurs in General | |
| Brockhaus (1982) | Reviewed four studies concluding that entrepreneurs tend to be better educated than the general population, but less so than managers. | All samples were small and limited to one geographical area or industry. |
| Cooper & Dunkelberg (1984) | This was a national survey of 1,805 small business owners that showed that a larger proportion of business starters or purchasers (approximately 64%) have less than a college degree compared to those who inherit or are brought in to run the business (57%). | |
| Gasse (1982) | Reported four studies in which entrepreneurs were better educated than the general public. | Education level varied with industry (e.g., high tech). |
| Jacobowitz & Vidler (1982) | Results of interviews with 430 entrepreneurs showed that they did not prosper in schools; 30% were high school dropouts. Only 11% graduated from a four-year college. | The sample was composed of Pennsylvania and New Jersey entrepreneurs; 11% were female. |

Note. Data are from "The Female Entrepreneur: A Career Development Perspective" by Donald D. Bowen and Robert D. Hisrich, 1986, *Academy of Management Review, 11*, p. 397.

identify successful persons as well (Brockhaus & Horwitz, 1986). However, studies have shown that the entrepreneur has a different set of attitudes about the nature of the management process and business in general (Gasse, 1977). Indeed, the nature of the enterprise and the opportunism, intuition, and individuality of the entrepreneur diverge significantly from the bureaucratic organization and the planning, rationality, and predictability of its managers. Perhaps all these traits are encompassed in a winning image that allows the entrepreneur to create and nurture the new venture. In one study, *winning* emerged as the best term to describe companies that have an excellent overall reputation ("To the Winners," 1986). Five consensus characteristics of these companies were: superior quality in products; quality service to customers; flexibility, or the ability to adapt to changes in the marketplace; high-caliber management; and honesty and ethics in business practices. A successful entrepreneur is almost always characterized as a winner; it is almost a prerequisite for them actually to become one ("To the Winners," 1986).

**TABLE 42.2** *(Continued)*
Amount of Education of Entrepreneurs

| Studies | Findings | Comments |
|---|---|---|
| | Male versus Female Entrepreneurs | |
| Humphreys & McClung (1981) | Of the female entrepreneurs, 54.8% were college graduates. This surpasses the rate for men and women in general, and for male managers and administrators. | Oklahoma sample of 86 female entrepreneurs from all areas of the state. |
| Charboneau (1981) | Quoted 1977 Census Bureau study showing that the averale female entrepreneur is a college graduate. | Also quotes SBA study with similar finding. |
| DeCarlo & Lyons (1979) | Female entrepreneurs have more education than the average adult female. Nonminority female entrepreneurs have more education than minority female entrepreneurs. | 122 female entrepreneurs drawn at random in mid-Atlantic states. |
| Hisrich & Brush (1983) | This nationwide survey showed that 68% of 468 female entrepreneurs were at least college graduates. | |
| Mescon & Stevins (1982) | Two thirds had attended college; 15% had pursued graduate degrees. | Sample of 108 female real estate brokerage owners in Arizona. |
| Sexton & Kent (1981) | Female entrepreneurs were slightly less educated than female executives (44% and 51% college graduates, respectively). Younger female entrepreneurs were better educated than female executives of companies. | Interviewed 93 women (48 female entrepreneurs) from Texas. |

## Age

The relation of age in the entrepreneurial career process has also been carefully researched (Ronstadt, 1982, 1983). In evaluating these results, however, it is important to differentiate between entrepreneurial age (the age of the entrepreneur reflected in the experience in the field of the feature or being self-employed) and chronological age. As is discussed in the next section, entrepreneurial experience is one of the best predictors of success particularly when the new venture is in the same field as previous business experience.

In terms of chronological age, entrepreneurs initiate their entrepreneurial careers at a wide variety of ages. Although an average age has little meaning, generally when appropriate training and preparation are present, earlier starts in an entrepreneurial career are better than later ones.

Also there are milestone years that occur in approximate five-year intervals between 25 and 50 when a person is more inclined to start an entrepreneurial career (Ronstadt, 1984). As one entrepreneur succinctly stated in one survey, "I felt it was now or never in terms of starting a new venture when I approached 30." Generally male entrepreneurs tend to start their first significant venture in their early 30s, whereas female entrepreneurs tend to do this in their middle 30s.

## Work History

Work history is not only a negative displacement (through lack of employment) in the decision to launch a new entrepreneurial venture but is also important in the growth and eventual success of the new venture launched. Although dissatisfaction with various aspects of one's job—challenge, promotional opportunities, frustration, and boredom—often motivates the launching of a new venture, previous technical and industry experience is important once the decision to launch has been made. Particularly important experience areas are: obtaining financing, such as bank financing and venture capital; developing the best product or service for the market; establishing manufacturing facilities; developing channels of distribution; and preparing the marketing plan for market introduction.

As the venture becomes established and starts growing, managerial experience and skills become increasingly important. Although most ventures start with managing one's own activities and those of a few part- or full-time employees, as the number of employees increases along with the size, complexity, and geographical diversity of the business, managerial skills come more and more into play. This is particularly true when the new venture requires the presence of other managers.

In addition to managerial experience, entrepreneurial experience is important. It is generally easier to start a second, third, or fourth venture than it is to start the first one. The need for entrepreneurial experience increases as the complexity of the venture increases. Most en-

trepreneurs indicate that their most significant venture is not their first one (Hisrich & Brush, 1986). Throughout their entrepreneurial careers entrepreneurs are exposed to more corridors of new venture opportunities than workers in other career paths.

## Motivation

What motivates an entrepreneur to take all the risks in launching a new venture and to pursue an entrepreneurial career despite the overwhelming odds against success when the SBA indicates that 75% of all businesses fail within the first five years? Although many people are interested in starting a new venture and even have the background and financial resources to do so, few decide to actually start their own business. Persons who are comfortable and secure in a job situation, have a family to support, and like their present life-style and reasonably predictable leisure time often do not want to take the risks associated with venturing out alone.

Although the motivations for venturing out alone vary greatly, the reason cited most frequently in a national survey of 468 female entrepreneurs for becoming an entrepreneur is independence; that is, they do not want to work for anyone else (Hisrich & Brush, 1984). This desire to be one's own boss is what drives both male and female entrepreneurs to accept all the social, psychological, and financial risks and work the numerous hours needed to create and nurture a successful new venture. Nothing less than this motivation would be strong enough to successfully launch a new venture. Other motivating factors differ between male and female entrepreneurs (Hisrich & Peters, 1989). Money is the second reason for starting a new venture for men, whereas job satisfaction, achievement, opportunity, and money are the reasons in rank order for women.

## Role Models and Support Systems

Several entrepreneurs have informally mentioned that one of the most important facts to influence them in their career choice are role models. Role models can be parents, brothers or sisters, other relatives, successful entrepreneurs in the surrounding community, or nationally touted entrepreneurs. Frequently successful entrepreneurs provide a catalyst for potential entrepreneurs who scrutinize them to launch a venture. As one entrepreneur indicated to me in a personal interview, "After evaluating Ted and his success as an entrepreneur, I knew I was much smarter and could do a better job. So, I started my own business."

Role models also can serve in a supportive capacity as mentors during and after the launch of, the new venture. Indeed, an entrepreneur needs a strong support and advisory system in every phase of the new venture. This support system is perhaps most crucial during the start-up phase in providing information, advice, and guidance on such matters as organizational structure, needed financial resources, marketing, and market segments. Because entrepreneurship is a social role embedded in a social context, it is important for an entrepreneur early on to establish connections to these support resources.

As initial contacts and connections expand, they form a network with similar properties prevalent in a social network-density (extensiveness of ties between two persons) and centrality (the total number of persons in the network). The strength of the tie between the entrepreneur and any individual in the network is, of course, dependent on the frequency, level, and reciprocity of the relationship. The more frequent, the more in-depth, and the more mutually beneficial a relationship is, the stronger and more durable is the network between the entrepreneur and the individual (Aldrich, Rosen, & Woodward, 1987; Carsrud, Gaglio, & Olm, 1986).

## Moral Support Network

It is important for every entrepreneur to establish a moral support system of family and friends—a cheering squad. This cheering squad is particularly important during the many difficult times and the loneliness that occur through-

out the entrepreneurial process. The majority of entrepreneurs in a sample of 468 indicated that their spouse was their biggest supporter (Hisrich & Brush, 1984). This support provides more understanding during the excessive amount of time that needs to be devoted to the new venture.

Friends also play key roles in a moral support network. Not only can friends provide advice that is often more honest than that received from other sources, but they also provide encouragement, understanding, and even assistance. Entrepreneurs can confide in friends without fear of criticism.

Finally, relatives (children, parents, grandparents, aunts and uncles) can also be strong sources of moral support, particularly if any are also entrepreneurs. As one entrepreneur stated, "The total family support I received was the key of my success. Having an understanding cheering squad giving me encouragement allowed me to persist through the many difficulties and problems" (Hisrich & Brush, 1986).

## Professional Support Network

In addition to moral encouragement, the entrepreneur needs advice, information, and resources throughout the establishment and growth of the new venture. These can be obtained through networking.

Although a large number of business formations occur without any major planning, conceptually a strong situational determinant in developing a new venture is the density of the entrepreneur's business contacts or linkages. The process of sharing contacts and obtaining resources has been found to have a significant relationship with business foundings and profitability (Aldrich et al., 1987). Although developing contacts was significant for business foundings, maintaining contacts was a significant predictor for early profit.

What should be the composition of these contacts and of the networks itself? One network group should be business associates who are themselves self-employed, because they have experienced the process of starting and developing a business. Besides these, there are other categories of persons who would be valuable: clients or buyers of the entrepreneur's product or service; suppliers; experts in various business matters (lawyers, financiers, bankers, marketing experts, and accountants); and colleagues or associates from trade associations of professional groups.

The client group is a particularly important group to cultivate. This group not only represents the sources of revenue to the venture but can also be the best source of advertising—word of mouth. There is nothing better than word-of-mouth advertising from satisfied customers to help establish a winning business reputation and promote goodwill. Customers, excited about the entrepreneur's concern about the product or service to fulfill their need, happily provide valuable feedback on the product or service that is offered as well as on new products or services that are being developed.

Suppliers are another important ingredient in the professional support network because they help establish credibility with creditors and customers as well. A new venture needs to establish a solid track record with suppliers in order to build a good relationship and ensure adequate availability of raw materials and other resources. Suppliers can also provide good information on the nature and trends in the industry as well as the nature and direction of competition.

Besides mentors and business associates, trade associations can provide an excellent mechanism for a professional support network. Trade association members can be developed into a regional or national network and should be carefully cultivated to keep the new venture competitive. Trade associations are familiar with any new developments and can provide overall industry data.

Finally, personal affiliations of the entrepreneur can also form a valuable professional support network. Affiliations developed with people through hobbies, sporting events, clubs, civic involvements, and school alumni groups are excellent potential sources of referrals, advice, and information.

Regardless of the actual nature, each en-trepreneur needs to establish both a moral and a professional support network. These contacts provide confidence, support, advice, and information. As one entrepreneur indicated, "In your own business, you are all alone. There is a definite need to establish support groups to share problems with and gain overall support for the new venture" (Hisrich & Brush, 1984).

## MALE VERSUS FEMALE ENTREPRENEURS

Even though there has been significant growth in female self-employment, much of what is known about the characteristics of entrepreneurs, their motivations, backgrounds, families, educational background, occupational experience, and problems is based on studies of male entrepreneurs (Carsrud & Olm, 1986). This is not surprising because, according to the Small Business Administration, men make up the majority of those who start and own their own businesses.

Although, overall, men and women entrepreneurs are very similar, in some respects women entrepreneurs possess different motivations, business skill levels, and occupational backgrounds than their male counterparts (Hisrich & Brush, 1986). Factors in the start-up process of a business for male entrepreneurs are also dissimilar to those for women, especially in such areas as support systems, sources of funds, and problems encountered. Although there are more similarities than differences, male and female entrepreneurs do differ in several ways. For instance, in terms of motivation, men are often motivated by the drive to control their own destiny, to make things happen. This drive often stems from disagreements with their bosses or a feeling that they can run things better. In contrast, women tend to be more motivated by independence and achievement that arise from frustration with a job in which they have not been allowed to perform at the level of which they are capable.

Departure points and reasons for starting the business are similar for both men and women. Both generally have a strong interest and experience in the area of their venture. However, for men the transition from a past occupation to the new venture is often facilitated when the new venture is an outgrowth of a present job, sideline, or hobby. Women, on the other hand, often leave a previous occupation with only a high level of job frustration and enthusiasm for the new venture rather than extensive managerial experience, which makes the transition more difficult.

Start-up financing is another area where male and female entrepreneurs differ. Whereas men often list investors, bank loans, or personal loans, in addition to personal funds, as sources of start-up capital, women usually rely solely on personal assets or savings—reflecting the fact that the service companies typically formed generally need little, if any, start-up capital.

Occupationally, there are also differences between men and women entrepreneurs. Although both groups tend to have at least some experience in the field of their ventures, men more often are recognized specialists in their field or have attained competence in a variety of business skills. In addition, the nature of their experience is often in manufacturing, finance, or technical areas. Most women, in contrast, usually have administrative experience, which is limited to the middle management level, usually in more service-related areas such as education, secretarial, or retail sales.

In terms of personality, there are strong similarities between male and female entrepreneurs. Both tend to be energetic, goal oriented, and independent. However, men are often more confident and less flexible and tolerant than women, which can result in different management styles for the new venture.

The backgrounds of male and female entrepreneurs tend to be similar except that most women are a little older when they embark on their venture (35–45 vs. 25–35) and their educational backgrounds are different. Men often have studied in technical or business-related areas, whereas most women have a liberal arts education.

Support groups also provide a point of contrast between the two. Men usually list outside advisors (e.g., lawyers and accountants) as most important supporters with the spouse second. Women list their spouses first, close friends second, and business associates third. Moreover, women usually rely extensively on a variety of sources for support and information such as trade associations and women's groups, whereas men are not as likely to have as many outside supporters.

Finally, businesses started by men and women entrepreneurs differ in terms of the nature of the venture. Women are more likely to start a business in a service related area—retail, public relations, or educational services—whereas men are more likely to enter manufacturing, construction, or high-tech fields. The result is often smaller women-owned businesses with lower net earnings. However, opportunities for women are greater than ever; women are starting businesses at a faster rate than men—almost three times the rate—according to the SBA.

## CORPORATE VERSUS INTRAPRENEURIAL CULTURE

The various business and sociological conditions have indeed given rise to a new era in American business, the era of the entrepreneur. There are probably no better known entrepreneurs than Sam Walton and Steve Jobs. Walton, the entrepreneur who founded the Wal-Mart empire, has been frequently identified as the richest man in America. After successful retail careers with J. C. Penney and Ben Franklin stores, Sam Walton opened his first Wal-Mart store in Rogers, Arkansas in 1952, a first step in his plan to operate discount stores in smaller cities and towns that are largely ignored by discount chains. The plan developed into one of the most profitable retail empires in the country today. Steve Jobs became a successful entrepreneur through his obsession with electronics. He joined with Steve Wozniak to design and build the first easy-to-use personal computer. The first 200 of these primitive computers were produced in 1976 in Steve Job's parents' garage by using parts purchased on credit.

This primitive computer was the basis of the highly successful Apple II, first sold in 1977. Jobs's obsession with his own vision, through which he had started Apple Computer, also created problems and almost the demise of the company. He refused to allow the Apple II to be marketed as a business computer and insulated managers in different divisions of the company from each other. After a bitter struggle in 1985, Steve Jobs was asked to resign from the company he founded. However, his obsession continues to be at work as Steve Jobs has announced a new computer—the first product of his new company NEXT.

The current media exposure and success of these and other entrepreneurs are threatening to established corporations. In some cases, small, aggressive, entrepreneurially driven firms have developed new products and become dominant in their markets. Recognizing the problem, some companies are attempting to create the same entrepreneurial spirit, the challenges and rewards of entrepreneurship, within their own organizations. But what are the differences between corporate and entrepreneurial cultures? Between managers, entrepreneurs, and intrapreneurs?

The typical corporate culture has a climate and reward system that favors conservative decision making. Emphasis is on gathering a large amount of data on which to base a rational decision, and risky decisions often are postponed until enough hard facts can be gathered or a consultant is hired to illuminate the unknown. This was just one of the many problems encountered by Art Fry in his attempt to launch Post-It Notes within the traditional organizational structure of 3M. The results of the surveys conducted by the marketing department of potential customers about the concept of a paper with a weak adhesive on it were terrible. Of course, because there had never before been a piece of paper capable of attaching and detaching easily, people really could not imagine how to use it. To overcome this difficulty, Fry distributed samples in several different formats (including the little yellow note pads that are presently marketed) to employees as well as executives throughout 3M. By monitoring the usage over time and comparing the usage rates with

Magic Tape, 3M's biggest office supply seller, Fry discovered that people used the note pads more, and he convinced top management that there was indeed a market. In many companies there are frequently so many sign offs and approvals required for a large scale project such as Post-It Notes that no individual feels personally responsible (Fast, 1979).

Although traditional corporate cultures do vary greatly from a more bureaucratic inflexible system to a more entrepreneurial flexible one, in the extreme cases the usually guiding principles are: Follow the instructions given; do not make any mistakes; do no fail; do not take initiative but wait for instructions; stay within your turf; and protect your backside. This restrictive environment is not conducive to creativity, flexibility, independence, and risk taking—the characteristics of entrepreneurs and intrapreneurs. The guiding principles of a good entrepreneurial-intrapreneurial climate are quite different: Develop visions, goals, and action plans; take action and be rewarded; suggest, try, and experiment; create and develop regardless of the area; and take responsibility and ownership. This environment, of course, supports individuals in their effort to create something new.

In addition to the corporate climate, there are differences in the shared values and norms of the two cultures. The extreme traditional corporation is hierarchical in nature with established procedures, reporting systems, lines of authority and responsibility, instructions, mandates, standardized hours, and control mechanisms. These cultural aspects support the corporate climate in prohibiting new venture creation. The culture of a strong intrapreneurial firm is in stark contrast. Instead of an hierarchical structure with all the accompanying problems, an intrapreneurial climate has a flat organizational structure with networking, teamwork, sponsors, and mentors abounding. Close working relationships are established that allow vision and objectives to be accomplished through an atmosphere of trust and counsel. Tasks are viewed as fun activities (not chores) with participants gladly putting in the amount of hours necessary to get the job

**TABLE 42.3**
Comparison of Entrepreneurs, Intrapreneurs, and Traditional Managers

| Trait | Traditional managers | Entrepreneurs | Intrapreneurs |
|---|---|---|---|
| Primary motives | Promotion and other traditional corporate rewards, such as office, staff, and power. | Independence, opportunity to create, and money. | Independence and ability to advance in the corporate setting receiving the corporate rewards. |
| Time orientation | Short run—meeting quotas and budgets, weekly, monthly, quarterly, and the annual planning horizons. | Survival and achieving 5 to 10-year growth of business. | Between entrepreneurial and traditional managers, depending on urgency to meet self-imposed and corporate timetables. |
| Activity | Delegates and supervises more than direct involvement. | Direct involvement. | Direct involvement more than delegation. |
| Risk | Careful. | Moderate risk taker. | Moderate risk taker. |
| Status | Concerned about status symbols. | No concern about status symbols. | Not concerned about traditional corporate status symbols—desires independence. |
| Failure and mistakes | Tries to avoid mistakes and suprises. | Deals with mistakes and failures. | Attempts to hide risky projects from view until ready. |
| Decisions | Usually agrees with those in upper management positions. | Follows dream with decisions. | Able to get others to agree to help achieve dream. |
| Who serves | Others. | Self and customers. | Self, customers, and sponsors. |
| Family history | Family members worked for large organizations. | Entrepreneurial small-business, professional, or farm background. | Entrepreneurial small-business, professional, or farm background. |
| Relationship with others | Hierarchy as basic relationship. | Transactions and deal making as basic relationship. | Transactions within hierarchy. |

Note. Table adapted from *Intrapreneuring* by Gifford Pinchot III. Reprinted by permission of Harper Collins Publishers. Copyright 1985 by Gifford Pinchot III.

done. Instead of building barriers to protect turfs, advice and cross-fertilization freely occur within and across functional areas and even divisions.

As may be expected, these two different cultures reflect different types of individuals and management styles. A comparison of traditional managers, entrepreneurs, and intrapreneurs indicates these differences (see Table 42.3). Although traditional managers are motivated primarily by promotion and typical corporate rewards, entrepreneurs and intrapreneurs thrive on independence and the ability to create. Intrapreneurs expect their performance to be suitably rewarded, as do entrepreneurs, except the source and form of the reward may differ.

The difference between the three groups is also reflected in their time orientation. Managers emphasize the short run—return on investment, sales, price of stock, and profits; entrepreneurs are concerned with the long run—that the enterprise last, that it exist instead of go bankrupt, and that sales and profit enable it to survive and grow; and intrapreneurs, a product of both the large and the small, are somewhere in between. Similarly the primary mode of activity of intrapreneurs falls between the delegation employed by managers and the direct involvement of entrepreneurs. Whereas intrapreneurs and entrepreneurs are both moderate risk takers, managers are much more cautious about taking any risks at all. "Protecting one's backside" is a way of life of many traditional managers. These managers attempt to avoid mistakes and failures at almost any cost. On the other hand, entrepreneurs usually fail at least once, and intrapreneurs learn to conceal risky projects until the last possible moment.

Although the traditional manager reports to those in the corporation at a higher level in the organization, entrepreneurs serve themselves and of course their customers, and intrapreneurs add sponsors to these two categories. Instead of building strong relationships with those around them as is the case with entrepreneurs and intrapreneurs, managers tend to follow the relationships indicated in the formal organizational chart.

## CLIMATE FOR INTRAPRENEURSHIP

How can the climate for intrapreneurship be established in an organization? In establishing an intrapreneurial environment, certain factors and leadership characteristics need to be operant (Hisrich & Peters, 1989; Kanter, 1983; Pinchot, 1985). The first characteristic is that the organization operates on the frontiers of technology and new ideas are encouraged and supported, not discouraged, as frequently occurs in firms where rapid return on investment and high

sales volume requirements exist. It is particularly important that research and development operate on the cutting edge of the technology of the industry in order for new ideas to be continually generated.

Second, experimentation must be encouraged. New products or services do not instantaneously appear but rather are often a result of a series of trials and errors. It took time and some product failures before the first marketable computer appeared. A company that wants to establish an intrapreneurial spirit has to first establish an environment that allows mistakes and failures. Even though this is in direct opposition to the established corporate career and promotion system, without the opportunity to fail, few if any corporate intrapreneurial ventures will be undertaken. Almost every entrepreneurial career has at least one failure.

Third, an organization should ensure there are no initial opportunity parameters to inhibit free creative problem solving. Frequently, various turfs in an organization are protected, which frustrates attempts by potential intrapreneurs to establish new ventures. In one consulting experience with a Fortune 500 company, the attempt at establishing an intrapreneurial environment ran into problems and eventually failed when the potential intrapreneurs were informed that a proposed product was not possible because it was in the domain of another division.

Fourth, the resources of the firm must be available and easily accessible. As one intrapreneur stated, "If my company really wants me to take the time, effort, and career risks to establish a new venture then it needs to have money and people resources on the line." Very often funds are not allocated to the task of creating something new but rather are committed to solving problems that have more immediate impact on the bottom line. When these funds are available, all too often the established reporting requirements make them so difficult to obtain that frustration and dissatisfaction occur.

Fifth, a multidiscipline, team-work approach needs to be encouraged. This open approach with participation by individuals regardless of area is the antithesis of corporate organizational structure and theory. Take for example the formation of Wil Tel, an intrapreneurial division of The Williams Company, a typically structured oil and gas company with the traditional lines of authority and responsibility. The company was hard hit by the recessions in the energy and agricultural industries, which resulted in a 69% decrease in profits in a short period of time. Roy Wilkins, an executive in one division of the company, championed the expenditure of $200 million to run fiber optic cable through a network of unused pipeline, which allowed the company to enter the telecommunication industry just as AT&T was breaking up. The success of this intrapreneurial venture is attributed in part to the availability of Joe Williams, president of The Williams Company, to any member of the Wil Tel team and to his commitment of resources to an extremely risky venture in a field totally foreign to the company. In successful cases of intrapreneurship, one key ingredient is *skunkworks* that involve key people before the venture is formally recognized and announced. These skunkworks are frequently the unnoticed version of the intrapreneurial venture. Take, for example, the case of Michael Phillips. He was able to launch a string of major banking innovations including consumer certificates of deposit, simplified checking accounts, and Master Charge in the Bank of California before management was fully aware of his activities. When they did become aware, Michael Phillips was able to show success rather than just ideas, which made it difficult for any valid objections. A company understanding this tendency can actually facilitate internal venturing by legitimizing and formalizing the skunkworks that are already occurring. Developing the needed team work for intrapreneurship is further complicated by the fact that team members' promotion and overall career within the corporation is related to performance in their current position, not their contribution to the new intrapreneurial venture. Organizations interested in establishing a strong intrapreneurial environment need to recognize and credit team members' contribution to the intrapreneurial effort.

Besides encouraging team work, the corporate environment must establish a long time horizon for evaluating the success of the overall program as well as that of each individual venture. If a company is not willing to invest money with no expectation of return for five to ten years, then it should not attempt to create an internal venturing program (Siegel, Siegel, & MacMillan, 1988). This patient money in the corporate setting is no different than the investment-return time horizon used by venture capitalists who invest in a start-up entrepreneurial effort.

Sixth, the spirit of intrapreneurship cannot be forced on persons: it must be on a volunteer basis. There is a difference between corporate thinking and intrapreneurial thinking, and individuals perform much better on one side or the other of the continuum. The majority of managers in a corporation are not capable of being successful intrapreneurs. This self-selection of participants must be accompanied by a policy to allow each participant to carry a project through to completion. This is in opposition to most corporate procedures for new product development and introduction, in which different departments and persons are involved in each stage of the development process. An intrapreneur, willing to spend the excess hours and effort to create a new venture, falls in love with the venture and will do almost anything to help ensure its success.

Seventh, the intrapreneur needs to be appropriately rewarded for all the energy and effort expended in the creation of the new venture. Broad performance objectives should be established, and the intrapreneur should receive rewards on their attainment. Of course, an equity or ownership position in the new venture is the best motivational reward for the amount of activity and effort needed for success (Block & Ornati, 1987).

Eighth, a corporate environment favorable for intrapreneurship has sponsors and champions throughout who not only support the creative activity and any resulting failures but who have the planning flexibility to establish new objectives and directions as needed. As one manager indicated in a personal interview, "For a new business venture to succeed the intrapreneur needs to be able to alter plans when needed and not be concerned about how close they come to achieving the previously stated objectives." Corporate structures frequently measure managers on their ability to come in close to plan regardless of the quality of performance reflected in this accomplishment (MacMillan, Block, & Narashima, 1986).

Finally, and perhaps most important, the intrapreneurial activity must be wholeheartedly supported and embraced by top management (George & MacMillan, 1985). Top management must support the effort by physical presence as well as making sure the personnel and financial resources are easily available. Without top management support a successful intrapreneurial environment cannot be created.

## CHARACTERISTICS OF INTRAPRENEURS

Within this overall corporate environment, there are certain characteristics that appear to be needed to at least some extent for a person to be a successful intrapreneur. These include understanding the environment, being visionary and flexible, creating management options, encouraging team work, encouraging open discussion, building a coalition of supporters, and persisting.

In order to establish a successful intrapreneurial venture, creativity and a broad understanding of the internal and external environments must be present. Creativity, perhaps at its lowest level in large organizations, generally tends to decrease with age and education.

The person who is going to establish a successful new intrapreneurial venture must also be a visionary leader—a person who dreams great dreams. Although there are many definitions of leadership, the one that best describes the needed intrapreneurial leadership is "a leader is like a gardener. When you want a tomato, you take a seed, put it in fertile soil, and carefully water under tender care. You don't manufacture tomatoes you grow them." Martin Luther King, Jr., said, "I have a dream," and thousands followed in spite

of overwhelming obstacles. In order to establish a successful new venture, the intrapreneurial leader must have a dream and work against all the obstacles and inertia to achieve it by selling the dream to others. Chuck House did this on the moon monitor project (an intrapreneurial venture at Hewlett Packard) by allowing others to help develop the final vision through exploring markets particularly meaningful to them (Pinchot, 1985).

The third characteristic is that the intrapreneur must be flexible and an experienced venture champion (DeSarbo, MacMillan, & Day, 1987). An intrapreneur does not mind the store but is playful and irreverent. By challenging the beliefs and assumptions of the corporation, an intrapreneur has the opportunity of creating something new. Of course, this is not the standard of operation taught in most graduate and undergraduate business schools.

The intrapreneur must encourage team work and use a multidisciplined approach. Again, this violates the organizational practices taught in most business schools that are embodied in the established corporate structure. In every new company formation, a broad range of business skills, such as engineering, production, marketing, and finance, are needed. Obtaining these skills in forming a new venture usually requires crossing the established departmental lines, structure, and reporting system. This crossing can of course cause some significant disruption, particularly when unconfident turf-protecting managers are involved. To minimize the negative impact of any disruption caused, the intrapreneur must also be a good diplomat.

In developing the team needed for creating something new, open discussion must always be encouraged. Many corporate managers have forgotten the frank, open discussions and disagreements that were a part of their educational process and instead spend time building protective barriers in their "corporate empire." A successful new intrapreneurial venture can only be formed when the team involved feels the freedom to disagree and break down an idea until the best solution is reached. The degree of openness obtained in the team is dependent on the degree of openness of the intrapreneur. One of the keys to success in building a strong open team is to avoid hostile conflicts. This comes naturally to many intrapreneurs like Hulki Aldikacti. In developing the intrapreneurial venture—the Fiero—in the Pontiac division of General Motors, Hulki kept the focus of all the team discussions on the product and its effect on the customers, not on personalities of the team. Through his own behavior and comments, the focus was kept on what was best for the new car that the team was struggling to build instead of individuals and their respective turfs (Pinchot, 1985).

Openness assists in developing a strong coalition of supporters and encouragers. The intrapreneur must encourage and affirm each team member, particularly during problem times. This encouragement is one of the replacements of the usual motivators of career path and job security, which are not operational in establishing a new intrapreneurial venture. A good intrapreneur makes everyone a hero.

Finally, but not of least importance, is persistence. Throughout the establishment of any new intrapreneurial venture, frustration and obstacles will occur. Only by persistence on the part of the intrapreneur will these be overcome and a new venture be created and successful commercialization result.

## ESTABLISHING INTRAPRENEURSHIP OR ENTREPRENEURIAL SPIRIT IN THE ORGANIZATION

An organization needs to implement a procedure to establish an intrapreneurial environment. Although this can be done by employees of the organization, it is frequently easier to use an outsider to facilitate the process. This is particularly advantageous when the environment of the organization is very traditional in nature and has a history of very little change.

The first step in this process is to secure commitment by top management to establishing intrapreneurship in the organization. Without this commitment the organization will never go through all the corporate cultural changes necessary for implementation. Once the top management of the organization has committed to the concept, it should be introduced throughout the organization through seminars in which the aspects of intrapreneurship are presented and strategies are developed to transform the organizational culture into an intrapreneurial one. During this process general guidelines need to be established for developing intrapreneurial ventures. After the initial framework is established and the concept embraced, intrapreneurial leaders need to be identified, selected, and trained. The training should focus on obtaining resources within the organization, identifying viable opportunities and their markets, and developing the appropriate business plan.

Ideas and general areas that top management are willing to support should be delineated along with the amount of risk money that is available for initial seed funding to further develop the concept. Also, overall program expectations and the target results of each intrapreneurial venture should be established. These should be as specific as possible in terms of the time frame, volume, profitability, and impact on the organization. Along with the intrapreneurial training, a mentor-sponsor system should also be established. Without sponsors or champions abounding, there is not much possibility that the culture of the organization can be transformed into an intrapreneurial one.

After the initial commitment and training, a group of managers interested in the program should train and share experiences with other members. My experience has indicated that these training sessions should be conducted about one day per month over an eight-month period. Informational items about intrapreneurship in general and the specifics of the company's activities should be disseminated through the company's newsletter or some other vehicle.

It is essential that concrete activities occur within the eight-month period that develop ideas into marketable products or services, the basis of the new business venture units. The intrapreneurial team will need to develop a business plan, obtain customer reaction and some initial intentions to buy, and learn how to coexist within the organizational structure during this process.

A strong organizational support structure for intrapreneurship should slowly emerge. This is particularly important because intrapreneurship is a secondary activity in the organization, not the primary one. Because intrapreneurial ventures do not immediately impact the bottom line, they can be easily overlooked and not receive the attention and funding needed. Providing the investment funds necessary for an intrapreneurial venture to develop and compete in external markets is essential for the success of the program. To be successful a venture needs flexible, innovative behavior, and the intrapreneurs must have complete authority over expenditures. When the intrapreneur has to justify expenses on a daily basis, it is really not a new venture but merely an operational extension of the funding source (Miller & Friesen, 1982; Peterson & Berger, 1971).

Rewards need to be tied to the performance of the intrapreneurial unit. This encourages the team members to work harder and compete more effectively while they directly benefit from their efforts. Because the intrapreneurial venture is a part of the larger organization, most of the compensation will probably need to be in the form of salary. However, incentives should be established to reward such things as performance and cooperation with other areas of the company as well as to reward other areas of the company that cooperate and support the intrapreneurial venture.

Finally, an evaluation system needs to be established that allows successful intrapreneurial units to expand and unsuccessful ones to be eliminated. An intrapreneurial unit should expand as the market demand warrants. Constraints can be established to ensure that the expansion is not in juxtaposition to the mission statement of the overall organization. Similarly, intrapreneurial venture units that do not perform should not be allowed to exist just because of vested interests. In order to have a successful in-

trapreneurial environment, it is just as important to allow some ventures to fail as to allow efficient ones to expand. Some ventures of course may be continued even if unprofitable if the venture is positively impacting some other part of the larger organization, blocking some competitive entrance, or laying the groundwork for entering some new strategic business area.

Through these efforts and by developing intrapreneurial leaders and effectively managing creativity and leadership in the organization, a corporate culture can slowly be changed to an intrapreneurial one. In this new intrapreneurial culture, self-actualization can occur when people do indeed create something new of value and are not worried about protecting their backside and minding the store. The guiding principle of management then becomes that it is easier to beg forgiveness than to ask permission.

## THE FUTURE

But what about the future? Will there be more managerial and less entrepreneurial-intrapreneurial emphasis? Part of the answer to this question lies in the viability, acceptance, and interest in the field by persons in other disciplines, such as industrial/organizational psychologists. There are many roles industrial/organizational psychologists can perform in relation to entrepreneurs and intrapreneurs. For example, they can help develop university curricula for entrepreneurs and intrapreneurs, contribute to the development of the theory of entrepreneurship-intrapreneurship that needs to emerge, or help identify potential sources for intrapreneurs in an organization. By evaluating and researching the constructs and theories in their field as they apply to entrepreneurship and intrapreneurship, industrial/organizational psychologists can significantly contribute to the understanding of the overall process as well as the development of an integrated theory. Through this effort they not only will contribute to the understanding of the field but will help organizations successfully apply the knowledge gained.

# REFERENCES

Aldrich, H., Rosen, B., & Woodard, W. (1987). The impact of social networks on business foundings and profit: A longitudinal study. *Proceedings of the Entrepreneurship Research Conference.* 154–168.

Auster, C. J., & Auster, D. (1981). Factors influencing women's choices of nontraditional careers. *Vocational Guidance Quarterly, 29,* 253–263.

Birch, D. L. (1987, March). The atomization of America. *INC.*, pp. 21–22.

Block, B., & Ornati, O. A. (1987). Compensating corporate venture managers. *Journal of Business Venturing, 2,* 41–51.

Bowen, D. D., & Hisrich, R. D. (1986). The female entrepreneur: A career development perspective. *Academy of Management Review, 11,* 393–407.

Brockhaus, R. H. (1982). The psychology of the entrepreneur. In C. A. Kent, D. L. Sexton, & K. H. Vespers (Eds.), *Encyclopedia of entrepreneurship* (pp. 39–71). Englewood Cliffs, NJ: Prentice-Hall.

Brockhaus, R. H., & Horwitz, P. S. (1986). The psychology of the entrepreneur. In D. L. Sexton & R. W. Smilar (Eds.), *The art and science of entrepreneurship* (pp. 25–48). Cambridge, MA: Ballinger.

Brockhaus, R. H., & Nord, W. R. (1979). An exploration of factors affecting the entrepreneurial decision: Personal characteristics vs. environmental conditions. *Proceedings of the 39th Annual Meeting of the Academy of Management,* 368–372.

Carsrud, A. L., Gaglio, C. M., & Olm, K. W. (1986). Entrepreneurs—Mentors, networks, and successful new venture development: An exploratory study. *Proceedings of the Entrepreneurship Research Conference,* 229-235.

Carsrud, A. L., & Olm, K. W. (1986). The success of male and female entrepreneurs: A comparative analysis. In R. W. Smilar & R. L. Kuhn (Eds.), *Managing take-off in fast growth firms* (pp. 147–162). New York: Praeger Press.

Charboneau, P. I. (1981, June). The woman entrepreneur. *American Demographics*, pp. 21–23.

Chusmin, J. J. (1983). Characteristics and predictive dimensions of women who make nontraditional vocational choices. *Personal and Guidance Journal, 62,* 43–47.

Cooper, A. C., & Dunkelberg, W. C. (1984). *Entrepreneurship and paths to business ownership* (Paper No. 846). West Lafayette, IN: Purdue University, Krannert Graduate School of Management.

De Carlo, I. F., & Lyons, P. R. (1979). A comparison of selected personal characteristics of minority and non-minority female entrepreneurs. *Proceedings of the 39th Annual Meeting of the Academy of Management,* 369–373.

De Sarbo, W., MacMillan, I. C., & Day, D. L. (1987). Criteria for corporate venturing: Importance assigned by managers. *Journal of Business Venturing, 2,* 329–350.

Fast, N. (1979). A visit to the new venture graveyard. *Research Management, 22,* 18–22.

Gasse, Y. (1977). *Entrepreneurial characteristics and practices.* Sherbrooke, Quebec, Canada: Rene Prumer Imprimeur.

Gasse, Y. (1982). Elaborations on the psychology of the entrepreneur. In C. A. Kent, D. L. Sexton, & K. H. Vespers (Eds.), *Encyclopedia of entrepreneurship* (pp. 57–71). Englewood Cliffs, NJ: Prentice-Hall.

George, R., & MacMillan, I. C. (1985). New venture planning: Venture management challenges. *Journal of Business Strategy, 6*, 85–91.

Hennig, M., & Jardim, A. (1977). *The managerial woman.* Garden City, NY: Anchor Press/Doubleday.

Hisrich, R. D. (1984). *Entrepreneurship and the economic climate: A preliminary investigation.* Boston: Boston College Press.

Hisrich, R. D. (Ed.). (1986). *Entrepreneurship, intrapreneurship, and venture capital: The foundation of economic renaissance.* Lexington, MA: Lexington Books.

Hisrich, R. D., & Brush, C. G. (1983). The woman entrepreneur: Implications of family, educational, and occupational experience. In J. A. Hornaday, J. A. Thomas, & K. H. Vespers (Eds.), *Frontiers of entrepreneurship research* (pp. 255–278). Wellesley, MA: Boston College, Center for Entrepreneurial Studies.

Hisrich, R. D., & Brush, C. G. (1984). The woman entrepreneur: Management skills and business problems. *Journal of Small Business Management, 22*, 30–37.

Hisrich, R. D., & Brush, C. G. (1986). *The woman entrepreneur: Starting, financing, and managing a successful new business.* Lexington, MA: Lexington Books.

Hisrich, R. D., & Peters, M. P. (1989). *Entrepreneurship: Starting, developing, and managing a new enterprise.* Homewood, IL: BPI/Irwin.

Humphreys, M. A., & McClung, J. (1981). Women entrepreneurs in Oklahoma. *Review of Regional Economics and Business, 6*(2), 13–21.

Jacobowitz, A., & Vidler, D. C. (1982). Characteristics of entrepreneurs: Implications for vocational guidance. *Vocational Guidance Quarterly: 30*, 252–257.

Kanter, R. M. (1983). *The change masters.* New York: Simon & Schuster.

MacMillan, I. C., Block, Z., & Narashima, P. N. (1986). Corporate venturing: Alternatives, obstacles encountered, and experience effects. *Journal of Business Venturing, 1*, 177–191.

Mescon, T., & Stevens, G. E. (1982). Women as entrepreneurs: A preliminary study of female realtors in Arizona. *Arizona Business, 29* (7), 9–13.

Miller, D., & Friesen, P. (1982). Innovation in conservative and entrepreneurial firms: Two models of strategic momentum. *Strategic Management Journal, 3*, 1–25.

Peterson, R., & Berger, D. (1971). Entrepreneurship in organizations. *Administrative Science Quarterly, 16*, 97–106.

Pinchot, G., III. (1985). *Intrapreneurship.* New York: Harper & Row.

Ronstadt, R. C. (1982). Does entrepreneurial career path really matter? *Proceedings of the Entrepreneurship Research Conference*, 540–567.

Ronstadt, R. C. (1983). The decision not to become an entrepreneur. *Proceedings of the Entrepreneurship Research Conference*, 192–212.

Ronstadt, R. C. (1984). *Entrepreneurship: Text, cases, and notes.* Dover, MA: Lord.

Schumpeter, J. A. (1934). *Theory of economic development: An inquiry into profits, capital, credit, interest, and the business cycle.* New York: Oxford University Press.

Sexton, D. L., & Kent, C. A. (1981). Female executives and entrepreneurs: A preliminary comparison. *Proceedings of the Entrepreneurship Research Conference*, 40–55.

Shapero, A., & Sokol, L. (1982). The social dimensions of entrepreneurship. In C. A. Kent, D. L. Sexton, & K. H. Vespers (Eds.), *Encyclopedia of entrepreneurship* (pp. 72–90). Englewood Cliffs, NJ: Prentice-Hall.

Siegel, R., Siegel, E., & MacMillan, J. C. (1988). Corporate venture capitalists: Autonomy, obstacles, and performance. *Journal of Business Venturing, 3*, 233–248.

To the winners belong the spoils. (1986, September 25). *Marketing News*, pp. 1, 13.

Vesper, K. (1980). *New venture strategies.* Englewood Cliffs, NJ: Prentice-Hall.

Waddell, F. T. (1983). Factors affecting choice, satisfaction, and success in the female self-employed. *Journal of Vocational Behavior, 23*, 294–301.

Watkins, J. M., & Watkins, D. S. (1983). The female entrepreneur: Her background and determinants of business choice—some British data. In J. A. Hornaday, J. A. Thomas, & K. H. Vespers (Eds.), *Frontiers of entrepreneurship research* (pp. 271–288). Wellesley, MA: Boston College, Center for Entrepreneurial Studies.

Wetzel, W. E. (1986). Entrepreneurs, angels, and economic renaissance. In R. D. Hisrich (Ed.), *Entrepreneurship, intrapreneurship, and venture capital: The foundation of economic renaissance* (pp. 119–140). Lexington, MA: Lexington Books.

# 43. TO AVOID ORGANIZATIONAL CRISES, UNLEARN

Paul C. Nystrom and William H. Starbuck

Organizations learn. Then they encase their learning in programs and standard operating procedures that members execute routinely. These programs and procedures generate inertia, and the inertia increases when organizations socialize new members and reward conformity to prescribed roles. As their successes accumulate, organizations emphasize efficiency, grow complacent, and learn too little. To survive, organizations must also unlearn.

Top managers' ideas dominate organizational learning, but they also prevent unlearning. Encased learning produces blindness and rigidity that may breed full-blown crises. Our studies of organizations facing crises show that past learning inhibits new learning: Before organizations

*Organizational Dynamics*, Spring 1984. ©1984, Periodicals Division, American Management Associations. All rights reserved. Reprinted with permission.

will try new ideas, they must unlearn old ones by discovering their inadequacies and then discarding them. Organizations in serious crises often remove their top managers as a way to erase the dominating ideas, to disconfirm past programs, to become receptive to new ideas, and to symbolize change.

This article begins by describing some organizational crises and the ways in which top managers' past learning only made the crises worse. The following section shows how clever managers have executed remarkable turnarounds by changing their organizations' beliefs and values. After considering why organizations unlearn by the drastic step of replacing top managers en masse, the article urges top managers to accept dissents, to interpret events as learning opportunities, and to characterize actions as experiments.

## LEARNING FROM CRISES

Many managers and scholars think that organizational survival indicates effectiveness. Survival is an insufficient measure of effectiveness, but the organizational survival rates are so low that there is clearly much room for improvement. Table 43.1 gives some approximate statistics for American corporations: Only 10 percent survive 20 years. Moreover, of those that do survive 20 years, more than a fourth disappear during the ensuing five years. The statistics for U.S. federal agencies look much like those for corporations.

A crisis is a situation that seriously threatens an organizations's survival. We have spent several years studying organizations in crises—why crises arise, and how organizations react. Our studies suggest that most organizational failures are quite unnecessary. The following two cases illustrate typical patterns.

Company H successfully published a prestigious daily newspaper for more than 100 years. Circulation reached a new peak in 1966, and the managers invested in modern printing equipment. The following year, circulation leveled off and advertising income dropped, while costs increased. Despite altered accounting procedures, the next year brought losses and a severe cash shortage. The board reacted by focusing even more intensely on cost control; a proposal to change the product a bit was rejected with laughter. Another bad year led the managers to raise prices radically and to form a task force to study corrective actions. Of five alternatives proposed by the task force, the board chose the only one that avoided all strategic reorientation. That is, the board decided to concentrate on those things the organization had always done best and to cut peripheral activities. Many key staff departed. Financial losses escalated. In 1972, the managers sold the printing equipment to pay operating costs, and Company H disappeared altogether a year later.

**TABLE 43.1**
Survivals by U.S. Corporations

| Ages in Years | Percentages Surviving to Various Ages | Percentages Surviving at Least Five Years After Various Ages |
|---|---|---|
| 5 | 38 | 55 |
| 10 | 21 | 65 |
| 15 | 14 | 70 |
| 20 | 10 | 73 |
| 25 | 7 | 76 |
| 50 | 2 | 83 |
| 75 | 1 | 86 |
| 100 | 0.5 | 88 |

In the late 1960s, Company F made and sold mechanical calculators as well as typewriters and office furnishings. The company had succeeded consistency for nearly 50 years, and its top managers believed that no other company in the world could produce such good mechanical calculators at such low costs. These beliefs may have been accurate, but they soon proved irrelevant, for an electronic revolution had begun. Although some of the company's engineers had designed electronic calculators and computers, the board decided against their production and sale. The board understood how to succeed with mechanical calculators, the company had invested heavily in new plants designed specifically to manufacture mechanical calculators, this industry had always evolved slowly, and the board believed that customers would switch to electronic calculators only gradually. However, sales began a dramatic decline in 1970, and profits turned into losses. The board retrenched by closing the factories that manufactured typewriters and office furnishings in order to concentrate on the company's key product line: mechanical calculators. After three years of losses, bankruptcy loomed and the board sold Company F to a larger company. What happened next is reported later in this article.

These cases illustrate that top managers may fail to perceive that crises are developing. Other people see the looming problems, but either their warnings do not reach the top, or the top managers discount the warnings as erroneous. When top managers eventually do notice trouble, they initially attribute the problems to temporary environmental disturbances, and they adopt weathering-the-storm strategies: Postpone investments, reduce maintenance, halt training, centralize decision making, liquidate assets, deny credit to customers, raise prices, leave positions vacant, and so forth. During this initial phase of crises, top managers rely on and respond to routine formal reports, particularly accounting statements, that present only superficial symptoms of the real problems. A major activity becomes changing the accounting procedures in order to conceal the symptoms.

In real crises, weathering-the-storm strategies

work only briefly. Then the symptoms of trouble reappear; only this time, the organizations start with fewer resources and less time in which to act. The second phase in organizations' reactions to crises involves unlearning yesterday's ideas. People in organizations rarely abandon their current beliefs and procedures merely because alternatives might offer better results: They know that their current beliefs and procedures have arisen from rational analyses and successful experiences, so they have to see evidence that these beliefs and procedures are seriously deficient before they will even think about major changes. Continuing crises provide this evidence. People start to question the conceptual foundations of their organizations, and they lose confidence in the leaders who advocated and perpetuated these concepts. Conflicts escalate as dissenters, voicing new ideas, challenge the ideas of top managers.

## REORIENTING BY CHANGING COGNITIVE STRUCTURES

Some people see potential crises arising and others do not; some understand technological and social changes and others do not. What people can see, predict, and understand depends on their cognitive structures—by which we mean logically integrated and mutually reinforcing systems of beliefs and values. Cognitive structures manifest themselves in perceptual frameworks, expectations, world views, plans, goals, sagas, stories, myths, rituals, symbols, jokes, and jargon.

Not only do top managers' cognitive structures shape their own actions, they strongly influence their organizations' actions. Albert King conducted a field experiment that reveals the power of a top manager's expectations. A top manager of Company J told the managers of plants 1 and 2 that he expected job redesigns would raise productivity, and he told the managers of plants 3 and 4 that he expected job redesigns would improve industrial relations but would not change productivity. What actually happened matched the top manager's initial statements. In plants 3 and 4, productivity remained about the same, and absenteeism declined. In plants 1 and 2, productivity increased significantly, while absenteeism remained the same. What makes the experiment even more interesting is that different types of job redesign were used in plants 1 and 3 than in plants 2 and 4. Plants 1 and 3 implemented job enlargement whereas plants 2 and 4 implemented job rotation, yet both types of job redesign produced the same levels of productivity and absenteeism. Thus, differences in actual job activities produced no differences in productivity and absenteeism, whereas different expectations did produce different outcomes.

Expectations and other manifestations of cognitive structures play powerful roles in organizational crises, both as causes and as possible cures. The Chinese exhibited great wisdom when they formed the symbol for crisis by combining the symbols for danger and opportunity: Top managers' ideas strongly influence whether they and their organizations see opportunities as well as dangers. For example, Company F, one of the companies described earlier in this article, surmounted its crisis primarily because a change in its top managers introduced different beliefs and perceptions.

Its top managers and board saw Company F as being designed to adapt to slow, predictable changes in technologies and markets. They initially predicted that electronic calculators would have slow, predictable effects, and the sudden electronic revolution both bewildered and terrified them. They decided that, for their company, the electronic revolution posed an insurmountable challenge. As it floundered at the brink of disaster, Company F was acquired by Company E, which promptly fired all of F's former top managers.

The top managers of Company E soon discovered opportunities that seemed obvious to them: Demands for typewriters and office furnishings were two to three times production capacities; sales staff had been turning down orders because the plants could not fill them! Also, the company's engineers had designed good electronic calculators and computers that the previous board had refused to put into produc-

tion. The new top managers talked optimistically about opportunities rather than dangers, challenges rather than threats. They borrowed a small amount of money from the parent company with which to experiment, they converted plants producing mechanical calculators into ones making typewriters and office furnishings, and they authorized production and energetic marketing of electronic products. Within a year of acquisition, losses converted into profits, production and employment began rising, and optimism prevailed again.

Top managers' cognitive structures also block recoveries from crises. In Company H, the newspaper described earlier, the top managers' beliefs intensified their commitment to a faulty strategy, generating actions and inactions that sealed the company's fate.

Top managers who clung steadfastly to incorrect ideas also undermined the success of Company T, which made and sold consumer electronics equipment such as television receivers, tape recorders, loudspeakers, and radios. Sales had doubled about every three years over its 40 years' existence. The top managers invested in two new plants in order to replace labor with capital because they thought that labor costs were rising too rapidly relative to sales revenues. Sales growth slowed substantially while these new plants were being constructed. The top managers attributed this deceleration to various environmental factors even though available evidence contradicted each of their attributions. The top managers asserted that these problems would be solved by the new plants with low labor costs that would enable lower prices. In the fourth year of this crisis, the national government lent Company T many millions of dollars to save it from collapse. But the loan only postponed the collapse for two years . . . and increased its cost.

## A Harsh Way to Unlearn

Organizations succumb to crises largely because their top managers, bolstered by recollections of past successes, live in worlds circumscribed by their cognitive structures. Top managers misperceive events and rationalize their organizations' failures. Some top managers, like those in Company F, admit privately that they do not understand what is happening and do not know what to do, while publicly they maintain facades of self-assurance and conviction. Other top managers, like those in Company T, never doubt that their beliefs and perceptions have more validity than anyone else's.

Because top managers adamantly cling to their beliefs and perceptions, few turnaround options exist. And because organizations first respond to crises with superficial remedies and delays, they later must take severe actions to escape demise. They must replace constricting, hopeless cognitive structures. But if only one or a few new managers join an ongoing group, either they adopt the prevailing cognitive structure or the other managers regard them as deviants with foolish ideas. Crises intensify these social processes by creating a wagon-train-surrounded-by-Indians atmosphere. So the top managers must be removed as a group, except for the rare individuals who dissented from the prevailing beliefs and perceptions. Moreover, revitalizing a crisis-ridden organization requires enthusiasm and energy... these from people who have grown cynical after hearing their top managers make failed promises and hollow excuses for several years. Before they will replace their cynicism with effort and vision, the people have to be convinced that this time, at last, someone is serious about making real changes. One way to do this, usually the only way, is to turn the former top managers into scapegoats.

Cognitive reorientations spark corporate turnarounds. Some enterprising people take over ailing corporations and successfully convert losses into profits by seeing opportunities that the former managers overlooked. Conversely, William Hall reported that turnaround efforts generally fail when firms in stagnating industries get subsidies from their parent corporations or from governments. The difference in outcomes seems to spring from infusions of new ideas, not solely infusions of financial resources. Indeed, the financial infusions are usually small in successful turnarounds. Strategic reorientations are rooted in cognitive shifts, and turnarounds almost always involve both significant changes in top management and changes in overall strategies.

Company S, which made ferrous screws, lapsed into persistent losses caused by aging machinery and brisk competition. A new president and vice-president for marketing embarked on a strategic reorientation: shifting from large orders of ferrous screws to small orders of nonferrous screws. But two years of persuasion failed to loosen the other top managers' adherence to old modes of acting and thinking. Because the two new managers could not afford to waste more time, they replaced their colleagues. Company S subsequently achieved substantial success.

Removing people is a quick, effective way of erasing memories. Our colleague, Bo Hedberg, reviewed the psychological literature and concluded that unlearning must precede the learning of new behaviors. But top managers show a quite understandable lack of enthusiasm for the idea that organizations have to replace their top managers en masse in order to escape from serious crises. This reluctance partially explains why so few organizations survive crises.

## UNLEARNING CONTINUOUSLY

Top managers might try to keep emerging crises from becoming serious, by reacting promptly to early symptoms of trouble and by avoiding weathering-the-storm strategies and superficial cover-ups. But not all symptoms warrant prompt reactions, and weathering-the-storm strategies can be useful. The top managers we studied all believed that they were acting wisely (at least when they took the actions), but they were misled by their faulty beliefs and perceptions. Faulty cognitive structures do not always plunge organizations into crises, but they do always keep managers from controlling their organizations' destinies.

To stay in control of their futures, top managers have to combat the inevitable errors in their own beliefs and perceptions. This is, of course, very difficult. It demands exceptional objectivity and humility as well as enough self-confidence to face errors within oneself. But it is easier to keep managers' cognitive structures continuously realistic and up-to-date than to try abruptly to correct errors that have added up and reinforced each other. And it is easier to correct cognitive structures while things are going well than to do so after troubles develop.

Top managers can stimulate their own unlearning and new learning in at least three ways: They can listen to dissents, convert events into learning opportunities, and adopt experimental frames of reference. The next three sections give examples of ways in which top managers can use these methods to benefit themselves and their organizations. However, we intentionally stop short of offering how-to-do-it prescriptions. Managers often get into trouble by trying to follow prescriptions that have been formulated by someone else in a different situation. For one thing, obeying someone else's prescriptions requires a partial substitution for one's best judgment. The simpler and more practical prescriptions sound, the more trust one puts in them, and so the more danger they pose. For another thing, effective methods of getting things done respect the constraints and exploit the opportunities that distinguish specific situations. We also question the view that "If managers knew how to do it, they would already be doing it." Many managers exhibit great skill at creating pragmatic techniques and procedures to achieve the goals they are pursuing. Top managers who want to unlearn will likely find ways to do it, ways that mesh with the other aspects of their jobs. But the top managers we studied never looked upon their past learning as impediments and they never tried to unlearn.

## Listening to Dissents

Complaints, warnings, and policy disagreements should cause reflection that sometimes leads to unlearning. Because such messages assert that something is wrong, top managers ought to respond by reconsidering their beliefs and practices. However, well-meaning colleagues and subordinates normally distort or silence warnings and dissents. So top managers receive only some of the messages sent, and even these messages arrive in watered-down forms, often accompanied by defensive rationalizations.

Moreover, research shows that people (including top managers) tend to ignore warnings of trouble and interpret nearly all messages as confirming the rightness of their beliefs. They blame dissents on ignorance or bad intentions—the dissenting subordinates or outsiders lack a top manager's perspective, or they're just promoting their self-interests, or they're the kind of people who would bellyache about almost anything. Quite often, dissenters and bearers of ill tidings are forced to leave organizations or they quit in disgust, thus ending the dissonance. For example, after Company F had struggled with its crisis for two years, the head of the typewriter division quit in protest over his colleagues' decisions to sell typewriter plants in order to get funds to subsidize the production of mechanical calculators. His division was the only division earning a profit.

Lyman Porter and Karlene Roberts reviewed research showing that top managers do not listen carefully to their subordinates. People in hierarchies talk upward and listen upward: They send more messages upward than downward, they pay more attention to messages from their superiors than to ones from their subordinates, and they try harder to establish rapport with superiors than with subordinates. People also bias their upward messages to enhance good news and to suppress bad news, yet they overestimate how much real information they transmit upward. Although these communication patterns are understandable, they are also harmful. In every crisis we studied, the top managers received accurate warnings and diagnoses from some of their subordinates, but they paid no attention to them. Indeed, they sometimes laughed at them.

After studying 20 corporations enmeshed in crises, Roger Dunbar and Walter Goldberg concluded that the chief executives generally surrounded themselves with yes-sayers who voiced no criticisms. Worse yet, the yes-sayers deliberately filtered out warnings from middle managers who saw correctly that their corporations were out of touch with market realities. Many of these middle managers resigned and others were fired for disloyalty.

Top managers might maintain more realistic cognitive structures if they would personally interview some of the people leaving their organizations. But why wait until people exhaust their loyalty and decide to leave? Top managers should listen to and learn from dissenters, doubters, and bearers of warnings. Not all dissents are valid, and warnings are often wrong, but dissents and warnings should remind one that diverse world views exist, that one's own beliefs and perceptions may well be wrong. Indeed, top managers should worry if they hear no such messages: Long silences signal distortion, not consensus. Although consensus sometimes occurs within top-management groups, we have found no organizations in which strong consensus pervaded the managerial ranks. Furthermore, Peter Grinyer and David Norburn conducted careful research that found no benefits from strategic consensus: Firms in which managers disagree about goals, policies, and strategies earn just as much profit as firms in which managers agree.

How are top managers to know which dissents and warnings to consider seriously? They certainly dare not rely on their own judgments about ideas' validity because everyone's beliefs and perceptions contain errors. Messages that sound obviously correct add little to knowledge. On the other hand, messages that sound fanciful can highlight defects in one's knowledge, because they arise from premises quite different from one's own.

We recommend this screening procedure: First, assume that all dissents and warnings are at least partially valid. Second, evaluate the costs or benefits that would accrue if messages turn out to be correct: Fanciful messages typically entail high costs or benefits; realistic messages likely entail low costs or benefits. Third, try to find some evidence, other than the messages' content, about the probabilities that messages might prove to be correct. For instance, have the messages' sources acted as if they truly believe what they are say-

ing? Are the sources speaking about their areas of special expertise? Fourth, find ways to test in practice those dissents and warnings that might yield significant costs or benefits. Launch experimental probes that will confirm, disconfirm, or modify the ideas.

## Exploiting Opportunities

Changes induce people to question their world views. One very successful organization, Company G, actually appointed a vice-president for revolutions, who stepped in approximately every four years and shook up operations by transferring managers and reorganizing responsibilities. When asked how he decided what changes to make, he answered that it make little difference so long as the changes were large enough to introduce new perceptions. Statistics show that productivity rose for about two years after each shakeup, then declined for the next two years, until another shakeup initiated another productivity increase.

Company G's practice should be imitated widely. The vice-president for revolutions injected unexpected and somewhat random question marks into operations that, otherwise, would have grown smug and complacent through success and would have lost opportunities and alertness through planning. Indeed, Company G itself might have benefited from more frequent doses of its own medicine: Shouldn't the shakeups have happened every two years, when productivity had peaked and before it began to decline?

However, managers would not have to generate so many question marks if they turned spontaneous events into question marks. Managers can create unlearning opportunities by analyzing the consequences of such events as new laws, technological innovations, natural disasters, disrupted supplies, fluctuating demands for outputs, and recessions. Our colleague, Alan Meyer, learned a lot about the dynamics of hospital organizations because he happened to be studying some hospitals when they were jolted by a doctors' strike. To his surprise, he found that ideologies were more powerful than structures as forces guiding organizational responses. The hospitals that took best advantage of the strike were ones with ideologies that cherish dispersed influence in decision making, frequent strategic reorientations, and responsiveness to environmental events. Such hospitals both anticipated the effects of the strike and used the strike as a stimulus for long-run improvements.

One of the most successful adaptations to the doctor's strike was made by Hospital C. This hospital's culture values innovation, professional autonomy, and pluralism; its administrator urges the subunits to act entrepreneurially and to maintain bonds with the community. The administrator himself devotes 70 percent of his time to outside relationships, and he predicted the strike two months before it began—well before other hospitals anticipated it. Because he purposely avoids codifying procedures and formalizing relationships, he subtly encouraged the (overtly spontaneous) coalescing of an informal group to consider the strike's impacts. This group sent all supervisors a scenario of what might happen and asked them to write up plans for response. When the strike occurred, Hospital C cut costs and reallocated resources so quickly that it continued to earn a profit; and after the strike ended, the hospital easily adapted back. The administrator said, "We learned that we could adapt to almost anything—including a drastic drop in our patient load—and, in the process, we discovered some new techniques for cutting our operating costs."

## Experimenting

Experimentation offers many benefits as a central frame of reference for top managers. People who see themselves as experimenting are willing to deviate temporarily from practices they consider optimal in order to test the validity of their assumptions. When they try out other people's ideas that they themselves expect to be suboptimal or foolish, they create opportunities to surprise themselves. They also manage experiments in ways that cut down the losses that failures would produce; for instance, they attend carefully to feedback. Because they place fewer personal stakes on outcomes looking successful, they evaluate outcomes more objectively. They find it easier to modify their beliefs to accommodate new observations. And they keep on trying for improvements because they know experiments never turn out perfectly.

A team from McKinsey & Company studied ten companies that executives think are unusually well run. Experimenting tops the list of characteristics they have in common. To quote Thomas Peters' conclusion from *Business Week* (July 21, 1980):

*Controlled experiments abound in these companies. The attitude of management is to "get some data, do it, then adjust it," rather than wait for a perfect overall plan.*

Managers can program some searches for better ideas. For example, evolutionary operation (EVOP) is a well thought-out method for continual experimentation. The basic idea is to run experiments that entail little risk because they deviate only incrementally from what the experimenters believe to be optimal operation. The experiments should be planned and interpreted by committees that are carefully designed to meld technical expertise and political clout. Although George Box and Norman Draper created EVOP as a way to improve manufacturing processes, the basic ideas generalize to repetitive activities in finance, marketing, personnel management, and office procedures.

Experiments need not be carefully designed in order to be revealing, and they need not be revealing in order to stimulate unlearning, but it is better to use experiments fruitfully. Company K's experience suggests some of the differences between fruitful and unfruitful experiments.

Company K had successfully made and repaired railroad rolling stock for almost 90 years; then, in 1963, the nation's major railroad announced that it would buy no more new rolling stock from anyone for the foreseeable future. Company K's managers saw the railroad industry collapsing about them, so they studied several possibilities and chose three new product lines for development. After two years, however, the company had achieved no sales whatever in two of these lines. The managers launched two more experimental product lines, but they concentrated their efforts on the one new product line that looked most promising: a small automobile. Sales multiplied two and a half times over the next five years, but profits were only 0.8 percent of sales! Despite frequently repeated dire predictions, railroad rolling stock was accounting for 95 percent of sales; and despite frequent hopeful predictions, the automobile had not yet gotten into production and was generating high costs. When the automobile finally did come into production in 1970 the result was horrendous losses in both 1970 and 1971—so horrendous that the directors decided to close the company.

Why did Company K's experiments turn out so badly? One reason was too many eggs in one basket. The managers poured all their energies and most of their company's money into the automobile; their experiments with other new product lines were half-hearted and ritualistic. A second reason was an absence of feedback. The managers ignored evidence that the automobile project was developing badly and evidence that the rolling-stock business was doing well. Nor did they learn from their failures. Recall that two of their experimental product lines yielded zero sales: Might this have occurred because Company K had no sales personnel, not even a sales manager? Might it have forewarned what would happen when the automobile came into production? Company K did add a sales department to promote the automobile: a sales manager and one salesman!

Shortly after the directors decided to close Company K, five of the six top managers and half of the lower-level employees departed voluntarily. The board appointed the remaining senior manager president, with orders to continue shutting the company down. Instead, the new president (who had nothing to lose) launched some new experiments. These disclosed substantial foreign demand for railroad rolling stock—the pre-

vious managers had ignored foreign markets. The experiments also showed that the blue-collar workers could run the factory themselves with very little assistance from managers—the previous managers had created a competitive game in which managers and workers were trying to outsmart each other. In fact, after they took charge, the blue-collar workers doubled productivity: By 1974, production was 36 percent higher than in 1963 even though employment was only 69 percent of the earlier figure. Two new product lines were tried, and one of these became as important as rolling stock. By then, the directors had decided to keep the company in business. Profits in 1975 were six times the highest profits the company had ever earned previously, and they have continued upward since.

Why did the second wave of experiments turn out so differently? The directors' decision to close Company K initiated unlearning: The people who departed took with them their convictions about how the company should operate and what opportunities the environment offered; the people who remained became ready to abandon their past beliefs. No longer sure they knew what to do, people tried some experiments that they would previously have rejected as outrageous or silly. The company had no resources to squander on experiments that were turning out badly, so everyone paid close attention to how the experiments were turning out: Feedback quickly had real effects. Not least, the new president was an unusually wise man who knew how to engender enthusiasm, entrepreneurship, and a team spirit.

## CONCLUSION

Our studies underline top managers' dominance of their organizations' survival and success. Top managers are the villains who get blamed for steering organizations into crises, and they are the heroes who get the credit for rescuing organizations from crises. Such blaming and crediting are partly ritualistic, but also partly earned. Top managers do in fact guide organizations into crises and intensify crises; they also halt crises by disclosing opportunities, arousing courage, and stirring up enthusiasm.

The top managers who instigate dramatic turnarounds deserve admiration, for they have accomplished very difficult tasks of emotional and conceptual leadership. Even greater heroes, however, are the top managers who keep their organizations from blundering into trouble in the first place. To do this, they have had to meet the still more difficult challenge of conquering the errors in their own beliefs and perceptions.

## SELECTED BIBLIOGRAPHY

For more detailed descriptions of our studies about organizational crises, see Paul Nystrom, Bo Hedberg, and William Starbuck's "Interacting Processes as Organization Designs" in Ralph Kilmann, Louis Pondy, and Dennis Slevin's (eds.) *The Management of Organization Design*, Vol. 1 (Elsevier North-Holland, 1976); William Starbuck and Bo Hedberg's "Saving an Organization from a Stagnating Environment" in Hans Thorelli's (ed.) *Strategy + Structure = Performance* (Indiana University Press, 1977); William Starbuck, Arent Greve, and Bo Hedberg's "Responding to Crises" (*Journal of Business Administration*, Spring 1978); William Starbuck and Paul Nystrom's "Designing and Understanding Organizations" in Paul Nystrom and William Starbuck's (eds.) *Handbook of Organizational Design*, Vol. 1 (Oxford University Press, 1981); and in Bo Hedberg's "How Organizations Learn and Unlearn" in Paul Nystrom and William Starbuck's (eds.) *Handbook of Organizational Design*, Vol. 1 (Oxford University Press, 1981).

Related studies of organizational crises appear in Roger Dunbar and Walter Goldberg's "Crisis Development and Strategic Response in European Corporations" in Carolyne Smart and William Stanbury's (eds.) *Studies on Crisis Management* (Toronto's Institute for Research on Public Policy, 1978); also see William Hall's "Survival Strategies in a Hostile Environment" (*Harvard Business Review*, September–October 1980).

More information on Albert King's study of job redesigns appears in "Expectation Effects in Organizational Change" (*Administrative Science Quarterly*, June 1974).

Research concerning communications between people in superior and subordinate roles is reviewed in Lyman Porter and Karlene Roberts' "Communication in Organizations" in Marvin Dunnette's (ed.) *Handbook of Industrial and Organizational Psychology* (Rand McNally, 1976).

Alan Meyer's study of hospitals' reactions to the physicians' strike are reported in his article, "How Ideologies Supplant Formal Structures and Shape Responses to Environments" (*Journal of Management Studies*, January 1982).

A detailed study of 21 companies' planning systems appears in Peter Grinyer and David Norburn's "Planning for Existing Markets: Perceptions of Executives and Financial Performance" (*Journal of the Royal Statistical Society*, Series A, Vol. 138, Part 1, 1975).

Readers interested in EVOP philosophy and procedures should refer to George Box and Norman Draper's *Evolutionary Operation* (Wiley, 1969).

# 44.   THE EXPERIMENTING ORGANIZATION

Barry M. Staw

The last decade has witnessed a burgeoning of interest in the evaluation of social programs. As a result, we might conclude that there has been substantial progress toward achieving what Donald T. Campbell has labeled the "experimenting society." At the same time, however, it is important to recognize that most of this activity has been centered on the evaluation of externally visible health, education, and welfare reforms. So far, few evaluation studies have been conducted *within* private or public organizations to test whether internal innovations are effective or not. Instead of being assigned to internal evaluation tasks, staff trained in behavioral research generally find themselves confined to more established functions such as personnel selection, testing, and market research. Even the academic discipline of organizational behavior, whose province is the study of the internal workings of organizations, has largely ignored evaluation research as an important input to administrative decision making. The purpose of this article is to explore some of the implications of evaluation research for organizational decisions and to discuss the problems as well as the prospects of an "experimenting organization."

## THE CURRENT STATE OF ADMINISTRATIVE DECISION MAKING

Most organizational decisions are, by necessity, formulated within a context of uncertainty. For example, when deciding to start a new employee compensation scheme, a new training procedure, or a job enrichment program, an administrator is often quite uncertain whether the new program will prove effective. In facing these kinds of decisions, the manager usually comes equipped only with what we may call a "lay psychology of organizational effectiveness." That is, through his or her own personal experiences in organizational settings, and through observing the experiences of others, an administrator may have constructed a theory to explain what contributes to making an organization effective. There is one key problem with this lay theory of effectiveness. It may be wrong!

The major shortcoming of lay theories is the weakness of their supporting data. An administrator may have constructed a theory of effectiveness merely by observing two work groups that differ in performance and in some other characteristic, such as group cohesiveness. If the differences between the two groups on both performance and cohesiveness are substantial, he or she may conclude that cohesiveness is the prime cause of performance. Moreover, if several groups exhibit the same pattern, the individual's confidence in this causal inference is likely to increase. Unfortunately, neither of these sources of data provides a highly valid basis for causal inference.

In the case of the two-group comparison, random error may have accounted for the result; comparing the performance of many such groups can lessen the threat of statistical instability, but the accuracy of causal inference is not greatly increased. The chief problem with drawing causal inferences from a cross-sectional comparison such as this is that any other factor may have caused cohesiveness and performance to vary together. In addition, the direction of causation may be reversed; that is, good performance may have led to group cohesiveness.

In constructing a theory of organizational effectiveness, a manager also may have utilized longitudinal data. Rather than relying solely upon current differences between individuals or groups, a person may look for covariation in their relationship over a period of time. For example, the manager may have noticed that the cohesiveness of a group has increased over some extended time period and that concurrently production has gone up. Research on the psychology of perception has shown that people are likely to draw causal inferences when two things vary together or when a change in one variable closely follows a change in another. Unfortunately, however, the casual observation of covariation over time constitutes one of the weakest of research designs. There are no controls for extraneous influences that may account for the changes and no truly comparable groups to serve as a basis of comparison. Thus even longitudinal data may provide a poor base for drawing causal inferences if the situation is uncontrolled. Given this state of affairs, what is the beleaguered administrator to do?

## CONSULTING THE EXPERTS

The administrator may sometimes turn to the behavioral scientist for help. Behavioral scientists lay claim to a relatively objective view of persons and things—for example, behavior, technology, and structure—within organizational settings and have amassed an impressive body of research findings. Moreover, researchers in organizational behavior frequently view their role as one of providing practicing administrators with theories that are ostensibly an improvement over the commonly held lay theories of practitioners. Many of these "expert" theories, however, are based on research designs that are not much further advanced than those used by the lay observer of behavior.

One problem with data in the field of organizational behavior is that it may merely feed back to administrators their own lay theories of effectiveness. Research data, for example, show that questionnaire responses to items on influence, openness to change, cohesiveness, and satisfaction correlate significantly with organizational performance. Recent research, however, has shown that beliefs about performance *also* influence our beliefs about other processes that occur in social situations. Once we know that an individual, group, or organization is a high or low performer, we are prone to make attributions consistent with this evaluation along many other dimensions. For example, regardless of the actual level of functioning of various processes in a group, research has demonstrated that knowledge that the group performed effectively will lead to the conclusion that it was also cohesive, high in communication, high in mutual influence, and highly satisfied. Thus when the organizational researcher attempts to show that various self-report measures are the causes of performance, he may merely be tapping a preexisting lay theory of effectiveness. In essence, self-reports taken from people in organizations reflect only their attributions and not true causal relationships.

In addition to the attribution problem in interpreting cross-sectional data, there are difficulties of reversed or reciprocal causation. As an example of high-quality cross-sectional research, let us examine the recent work of Richard Hackman and Greg Oldham. They measured job characteristics using both observer and self-rating forms and correlated these data with measures of work performance.

Several characteristics of job enrichment, such as task variety, significance, and identity, correlated significantly with high performance and would seem to be determinants of task behavior in organizations. However, we must exercise caution in drawing such causal inferences because the best performers in an organization are likely to be awarded the most enriched and responsible jobs. And, although the Hackman and Oldham data indicate that the relationship between task characteristics and performance is strongest for persons with potent higher-order needs, this relationship could also be causally reversed. High performance may not only generally lead supervisors to assign enriched jobs to subordinates, but this effect may be especially strong for those with high needs for autonomy and self-actualization. These persons may not merely wait to be assigned to challenging jobs; they may *actively lobby* for them.

Because of the difficulties of interpreting cross-sectional survey data, many researchers have resorted to laboratory experimentation. This provides much greater confidence in internal validity, since changes in one variable are introduced, effects are observed in a second variable, and extraneous factors are controlled. The problem is that with each additional experimental control, the laboratory situation becomes more and more divorced from everyday life. Hence we cannot with confidence often generalize their results to the real world of the organization. The more the research participants, experimental treatments, and settings differ from the real world, the lower the external validity.

The organizational researchers often face a dilemma in attempting to increase both internal and external validity. Those techniques that help them to interpret cause-effect relationships with increased validity may at the same time decrease *external* validity; and, conversely, efforts to make effects more generalizable to nonlaboratory settings may reduce *internal* validity. Coordinated efforts are therefore needed to tie laboratory and field research together, and also we desperately need more field studies that use methods with greater internal validity. To date, relatively few findings have been validated in both laboratory and field settings or through controlled field experiments. Research on goal-setting and reinforcement techniques provide some notable exceptions, however.

## FURTHER LIMITS OF APPLICATION

Several additional factors limit the applicability of research findings. First, the behavioral sciences as a whole reflect a serious reluctance to report negative results. Data that are statistically significant and that reinforce a preexisting hypothesis are much more likely to be published than negative or inconsistent data. A second limitation is the widespread use of reconstructed logic in the presentation of research studies. As noted by William Notz, Paul Salipante, and James Waters, a theory is often fitted to data after the fact or is amplified in aspects that are consistent with the reported findings. Hypotheses and research designs are seldom as explicitly *a priori* as is suggested when they are presented in published form. In large part, this bias is traceable to the fact that the author is judged professionally in the role of *advocate*— that is, on the consistency of his argument as well as on the strength of his data. The use of reconstructed logic can attach undue credibility to a particularly theory, especially if its author is an articulate advocate.

A third problem, and perhaps the most serious one in applying organizational research findings, stems from a common misunderstanding of normative as against descriptive research. Most descriptive studies report on cause-effect relationships found in the behavior of groups, individuals, or organizations. Ideally, the documentation of such findings can constitute a science of behavior and lead to a more accurate description of the social world. However, from a normative perspective some authors have used these descriptive data to prescribe what *should* be done in a given situation. For example, Victor Vroom and Phillip Yetton prescribe conditions under which leaders should be participative or authoritarian in order to achieve maximum results. Their theoretical model is based on a substantial amount of descriptive research in small group behavior and is likely to be accurate. But, as Chris Argyris has cogently noted, Vroom and Yetton have implicitly accepted the status quo and made it the desired state by building it into their normative model. Argyris argues that knowing how individuals react to participative or authoritarian management under existing conditions does not mean these reactions cannot be changed in the future. Thus, in deriving prescriptive statements from descriptive data, the researcher should be aware of his tacit role either as defender of tradition or as change agent.

## HOW THE BEHAVIORAL SCIENCES CAN CONTRIBUTE TO MANAGEMENT

It may seem that we are pessimistic about what behavioral science can contribute to practicing administrators. We have noted that research findings may be questionable in terms of internal or external validity and are seldom high on both dimensions. Furthermore, we have noted that there is bias in the selection of published research to favor both statistically significant results and reconstructed logic. Last, we have noted that what should exist need not be the same as what does exist, and prescriptive statements need not be totally consistent with previous descriptive research. What is the purpose of these caveats? Where do they leave the practicing manager?

At present, the behavioral sciences utilize what Donald Schon has labeled a center-periphery model of dissemination. This model rests on the assumption that internally valid and generalizable findings are held by behavioral researchers (at the center of knowledge) and that the primary job is to disseminate this expertise to users at the periphery. Obviously, as we have seen, this is an erroneous view of the applicability of behavioral research. Because there are few behavioral principles that can be readily applied in a formulalike fashion, potential users might well be cautious of the zealous purveyor of such research findings.

A more realistic view is to acknowledge the uncertainty present in the social sciences and to accept the source of innovation at a more local level. From the manager's point of view, behavioral findings should be appraised in terms of best guesses: what is most likely, second most likely, and least likely to work. Once the existing research literature is assessed in terms of its internal and external validity, the manager should *experimentally* undertake the seemingly best course of action. According to this model, the manager should be the focus of innovation, utilizing the social science community as a peripheral resource. As proposed by Notz, Salipante, and Waters, the practitioner should be the one who ultimately tests the usefulness of any given theory or set of research findings.

When the role of behavioral science shifts from center to periphery, its educational task also shifts. Instead of persuading practitioners to adopt one particular theory and reject another, it may expend more energy on training practitioners in evaluation skills, skills needed to ascertain whether a particular program is working or not. These evaluation skills can be viewed as tools that improve upon those normally available to the lay administrator in assessing cause-effect relationships. Since there are already entire volumes devoted to the development of appropriate evaluation techniques, we will mention only a few methods that are especially applicable to organizational administrators.

### Methods of Evaluating Change in Large Organizations

When an organization is large, it is often possible to introduce a change (for example, a job redesign, a participation system, or an incentive scheme) on a truly experimental basis. That is, individuals, intact work groups, or even entire plants may be assigned randomly to experimental and control conditions and measures taken both before and after the experimental treatment or change.

Random assignment is what equates an experimental and control group so that true comparisons can be made. Moreover, when a change is experimentally introduced by a manager, the order of cause-effect relationships can be inferred with relative confidence. In the case of job enrichment, for example, we would know that work quality is *not* what has caused an increase in task responsibility if the administrator first increased responsibility and then quality increased. Correlational studies showing a strong relationship between work quality and responsibility cannot tell us the direction of causation because they tap into a system following changes that have already taken place.

As Cook and Campbell have noted, there

are conditions especially conducive to true experimentation within organizations. Most commonly, an innovation cannot be implemented with all individuals or units at once. In such situations, the most equitable way of distributing an improvement—for example, a job change—is through random assignment. In addition, even when priorities can be clearly established, experimentation may still be possible. If the population is large enough, individuals or groups can be ranked in the order of their need. Those who clearly will benefit most from the change can get it immediately, while those who clearly won't benefit can be denied the opportunity. However, within a range of need ambiguity, individuals or groups can be randomly assigned to experimental and control groups. If this subgroup is large enough, a true experiment may result.

A second and perhaps most important factor conducive to true experimentation is uncertainty over the results of an innovation. If a manager is uncertain about the utility of a change, he or she should want to gather the most unambiguous data on its effects. Random assignment of individuals or subunits into experimental and control groups greatly increases the interpretability of results. Moreover, if there is some possibility that a change may produce negative instead of positive results, random assignment of the intervention is the most equitable way to assign the risk. Unfortunately, few innovations are so realistically assessed at the outset, and overly optimistic administrators often see little reason to deny individuals or work groups the opportunity to participate in a "sure winner."

Although true experimentation with random assignment to experimental and control groups is best for causal inference, it is not always the most practical course of action. Often individuals cannot be randomly assigned to experimental and control groups because such a procedure might disrupt normal production systems (as in the case of job enlargement) or produce inequities between experimental and control groups (for example, in the case of changes in incentives or rewards). In addition, there may be too few work groups for randomization to work effectively in equating the experimental and control groups.

In such cases, the best procedure is to employ a time-series design. A time-series design basically utilizes a large number of observations before and after an experimental change and may or may not involve a comparison group. By taking numerous measurements before and after a change, we can rule out many of the most common threats to internal validity.

However, one possible threat to validity that is not controlled and that may be problematical is called a "history" artifact. The manager must ask whether any other *external* event could have accounted for the change. For example, has production increased because of new job standards, plant modernization, leadership changes, or any other factor in addition to the introduction of job enrichment? Having a control group that is measured before and after the change will help in this inference process if both groups were subject to similar external forces.

Time-series designs are easily implemented within organizational settings, because they involve little or no disruption of ongoing operations. What they demand, however, is extensive use of archival data. Because it is nearly impossible to gather enough questionnaire data to construct a time series of before and after measures, it is necessary to rely almost exclusively upon behavioral indicators or archives to show an intervention's effect. If a company implements a program of job enlargement, for example, we cannot repeatedly ask employees their level of satisfaction with the job. Instead, to form a time series, we must utilize routinely collected behavioral observations in areas such as absenteeism, turnover, and work quantity and quality.

It is usually necessary to show a rather large "discontinuity" or change in a time series in order to demonstrate a statistically significant effect. There are a number of techniques to analyze time-series data and the reader is encouraged to consult the recent book by Thomas D. Cook and Donald T. Campbell for a detailed discussion of this matter. Yet, it is important to note that in "selling" a new program to top management, effects must often be more than just statistically significant. To convince people in an organization that they should change an established mode of operation, effects must generally be visible to the eye as well as to the computer. Thus calculation of simple $t$-tests between several before and after observations as well as some careful eyeballing of the data can often be practically sufficient—although technically insufficient—to discern a large effect. The manager should be careful to ascertain, however, that the discontinuity in a series of data is real and not merely a repetition of a weekly, monthly, or some other cycle or a continuation of a long-term linear trend.

We should also emphasize that in constructing a time series the manager can use data not collected routinely in organizational records. If creative, the manager can collect new data on many substitutes for attitudinal variables. For example, how early in the day a worker starts cleaning up may indicate his overall attitude toward the job; the number of cigarette buttes found in the ashtrays during departmental meetings may reflect the degree of intradepartmental conflict or tension; the number of employees using the company's product (for example, in an automobile plant) may reflect organizational loyalty or identification.

Although the time-series design explicitly demands nothing more than careful documentation and observation, its power can also be improved by an administrative attitude of tentativeness. If an innovation is first implemented on an experimental basis in a small part of an organization, it may be subsequently implemented on an increasingly broad scale. Such a replicated time-series design offers both a powerful basis from which to infer cause-effect relations and a high degree of generalizability. By planning the introduction of a change at several points in time, we can rule out history as an alternative explanation of the change. Moreover, we can be relatively more certain that the observed change was not due to the mere instability of the measures and can be more confident that the change will apply to other units in the organization.

The major requirement of a replicated time-series design is separation of the various experimental groups. If the groups can communicate and/or observe each other, the change in one group may spill over or diffuse to the others. This could result in either interunit jealousy and a deterioration in attitudes or the development of rivalry that could actually improve morale and/or performance. In either case we don't have a true replication. A second and more serious problem for interpreting time series is the requirement of a relatively quick, high-impact intervention. If a change is slow and incremental, as most OD interventions are, it is often difficult to separate treatment-induced change from statistical error and other influences, both internal and external. Still, regardless of these limitations, time-series techniques are a powerful tool in the evaluation of large-scale administrative changes, and they ought to be used much more extensively.

## Methods of Evaluating Change in Small Managerial Units

We have seen how a manager can make large-scale changes and use these changes to infer cause-effect relationships. Now let's imagine one is supervising four people face to face. Does the manager of a small unit also have the capacity to make valid causal inferences?

An immediate response is no. The manager of a small unit cannot readily change two people's jobs, for example, while leaving the jobs of two others alone. Moreover, random assignment with such small samples, combined with the high degree of interaction among all the individuals involved, would provide little internal validity. A time-series analysis is possible with a few subjects although the significance of the changes will obviously be more difficult to infer because of the statistical unreliability of such a small sample.

Must we then conclude that our only real leverage in improving decision-making skills of small unit managers is by making newer and better theory available to them? Certainly, in the role of training future managers the organizational behaviorist is chiefly concerned with transmitting expert theories of leadership, motivation, and group process and dispelling lay theories. Yet there is room for improvement in methodological skills at this level too. When sample size is small and statistical power is correspondingly weakened, we should resort to more qualitative research techniques.

Training for the evaluation of small unit changes should concentrate on interviewing and observational techniques. We can train managers to recognize facial expression, physical distance, and other nonverbal cues in evaluating attitudes and beliefs. Furthermore, managers can be trained to conduct clinically oriented interviews to discover the source of problems, as well as possible remedies.

Related techniques of interaction analysis and sensitivity training are already available and are used in professional programs. What we need is to recognize these tools as data-gathering devices and couple them with other less obtrusive forms of measurement. For example, if the manager changes the jobs of several employees, he or she should look for behavioral indicators of changes in attitude and performance, in addition to those that can be ascertained by questionnaires and traditional interviews.

Unfortunately, advocates of qualitative and quantitative research techniques have not recognized the special role of each other's methodology. Proponents of qualitative techniques may be interested in promoting new forms of human interaction rather than in using their techniques to gather research data. Meanwhile, proponents of quantitative analysis have tended to restrict their attention to the testing of theory rather than to how practitioners can measure and evaluate their own changes. Needless to say, the operating manager has much to gain by synthesizing both forms of analysis.

## FORMATIVE VERSUS SUMMATIVE EVALUATION

To this point our discussion has centered on how the behavioral sciences might improve causal inference in organizational settings. However, the evaluation techniques elaborated so far attack only part of the problem. Although tools such as experimental and quasi-experimental design help us in gathering internally valid data, they presume a clearly formulated or at least explicitly chosen program of action. It is assumed, for example, that in evaluating the results of job enrichment, administrators know what job enrichment is and have chosen a particular aspect of it—for example, increased task variety—to implement.

The process of inferring whether an intervention "worked" or has had a positive effect is referred to as *summative evaluation*. By contrast, *formative evaluation* is the process of selecting program goals and constructing an intervention. Formative evaluation is comparable to the pilot study of a research project in which the researchers gather information about how they should proceed with a full-scale test of a hypothesis. As Paul Wortman notes, the procedures in formative evaluation remain more an art than a science.

There is no convenient list of techniques and methods for conducting a formative evaluation and no list of threats to its validity. Presumably, however, the successful builders of interventions must search for the correct blend of expert and lay theories of organizational effectiveness, must be able to evaluate the prospects of success in their own situation, and must conduct some inquiry—for example, through interviews with other administrators or subordinates or a search of prior records—into the likely consequences of any changes.

Wortman has described how formative and summative evaluation can be effectively combined in program evaluation. His basic point is that the qualitative and quantitative techniques used in formative and summative evaluations form complementary rather than competing forms of evaluation. Thus we can imagine a manager first making small-scale changes, as in a pilot study, and using primarily qualitative analysis techniques. Then, when the administrator has a greater fund of knowledge and has built what seems to be a successful intervention, the change can be implemented on a larger scale. This large-scale change can then be evaluated using experimental and/or time-series research designs.

## Problems in Moving from Formative to Summative Evaluation

Though the sequential use of formative and summative evaluation makes intuitive sense, is it realistic in most administrative settings? At what stage is the administrator willing to regard his innovation as in place and ready for testing? As Charles Lindblom has noted, the answer may be *never*!

The administrative process, as Lindblom defines it, may be a perpetual sequence of making incremental changes or "tinkering with the treatment." Lindblom describes the public administrator, for example, as one who makes a number of successive comparisons that are limited in scope, rather than as someone who attempts to comprehensively analyze problems, set specific goals, and implement solutions. In Lindblom's view, incrementalism is the most rational way to address any complex social problem, and he labels this process the "science of muddling through."

The incrementalism explicit in Lindblom's science of muddling through is not inconsistent with the concept of the experimenting organization. A manager's willingness to change a policy or a course of action on the basis of fresh data is the *essence* of social experimentation. However, there may still be important differences between the manager's and the organization's preferred form of incrementalism.

From the organization's point of view, it would seem generally preferable to construct an intervention on the basis of formative evaluation and then subject it to a rigorous test through summative evaluation. But from the individual manager's point of view it may seem preferable to forge an acceptable intervention through a succession of limited comparisons without ever subjecting the intervention to a summative evaluation. By remaining at the formative evaluation stage, managers may continually revise a program, or even its goals, to meet the demands of clients and other managers. Lindblom would argue that this process of revision never ends for managers, especially in the public sector. Of necessity, the administrator may have to go on shaping and reshaping a program to retain the support of shifting coalitions of power within organizations and their environments. Obviously, such political considerations will often determine the nature and scope of any evaluation effort and must be seriously examined in the initial design of a program evaluation.

## THE TRAPPED ADMINISTRATOR

Although managers may be willing to make incremental changes in an intervention, they may hesitate to backtrack or make changes that can be construed as an admission of previous error. In fact, there are evidences, such as the U.S. intervention in the Indochina war, that decision makers will even escalate their commitment following negative results rather than undertake any major shifts in policy. The Indochina war effort is comparable to an investment decision context in which it is deemed possible to recoup an initial loss by increasing the investment. An analogy may also be drawn with an organization's decision on the amount of advertising needed to launch a new product or the amount of R&D expenditure needed to develop a new or improved product. Each of these situations poses a difficulty when negative results occur. Should losses be accepted and the program scuttled? Or should investment be escalated in an effort to turn the situation around?

Using a simulated business decision case, Staw experimentally tested for the tendency to escalate following the receipt of negative consequences. In this study, business school students were asked to allocate research and development funds to one of two operating divisions of a company. They were then given the results of their initial decisions and asked to make a second allocation of R&D funds. Other students also were assigned to a situation in which they did not make the initial allocation decision *themselves* but were told that it was made earlier by another financial officer of the firm.

The results of the experiment were as follows: (1) The main effect of responsibility was that subjects allocated more money when *they* rather than another financial officer had made the initial decision; (2) the main effect of consequences was that subjects allocated more money to the declining than to the improving division; and (3) there was a significant interaction of responsibility and consequences—since subjects allocated even more money when they were responsible for negative consequences than would be expected by the two main effects acting alone. Personal responsibility for negative consequences may therefore be a great cause of escalation.

From the experimental results described above and from descriptive analyses of real-world escalations (see, for example, *The Pentagon Papers*), it is possible to conclude that administrators can become trapped by their own previous mistakes. A key problem the administrator faces is knowing when it is appropriate to accept his or her losses and when one should enlarge the stakes.

Examples are legion of leaders who are perceived as strong and courageous after they followed either of these strategies. For example, Lyndon Johnson's leadership ability was assailed for following the escalation route. However, if Johnson's strategy had succeeded in Indochina, no doubt he would have been hailed as a wise and bold leader. Unfortunately, from the administrator's perspective there are no statistical techniques that will substitute for good judgment on this classic investment problem.

Staw and Fox recently found that many decision makers attempt to test the system by allocating a substantial amount of resources to the problem; then, if there is no effect, they reduce their commitment *substantially*. This strategy seems appropriate for actions that require a large, immediate expenditure for resources to create an impact—for example, advertising a new product—but quite inappropriate for actions that require a slow-developing commitment—such as many OD interventions. As mentioned earlier, OD interventions not only pose difficulties in judgment but also are especially troublesome for detecting changes using statistical techniques, such as time-series analysis.

In addition to the problem of knowing how much investment is enough to create a change, there is likely to be a second and even more important cause of trapped administrators. From the manager's point of view, a program sometimes must be *made to work at almost any cost*. A program that fails is commonly treated as an administrative failure and can be cause for demotion or dismissal. Few organizations have embraced an experimental philosophy of replacing ineffective programs with more promising candidates. Instead, programs are advocated and implemented by ambitious managers who, in case of failure, are replaced by other and more promising managers.

Thus evaluation apprehension is a likely cause of administrative defense and advocacy of programs that appear to others as obvious failures. Moreover, because evaluation in organizations is generally centered on individual rather than program performance, there may also be pressure throughout the system to bias the data on which evaluation is based. Close associates of administrative heads may hesitate to relay negative information, and lower-level officials may be selective in the information they pass upward.

As a number of research studies have shown, there may be pressure at the individual, group, and organizational levels to report successes and deemphasize any information that could be construed as a failure. Thus a great deal of work needs to be done in designing an organizational system that can effectively monitor, feed back, and utilize negative as well as positive data.

## Organizational Solutions to Evaluation Apprehension

The most obvious way to relieve the apprehension that so frequently accompanies evaluation research is to take specific measures to ensure that the evaluations are of *programs*, not *people*. As Donald Campbell has noted, decisions about the salary, grade, or promotion of program administrators should be divorced from program evaluation and reporting procedures. Campbell goes so far as to recommend the separation of program funding decisions from evaluation research activities.

Taken literally, this solution is similar to one that is frequently advocated for other kinds of performance evaluation systems within organizations. For example, in the context of personnel evaluation it is not in the employee's best interest to present any negative information to his superior. However, it is precisely such weaknesses that need to be communicated in order for the supervisor to provide proper counsel and guidance. Hence it is sometimes suggested that performance evaluation be temporally and even functionally separated for salary review and employee development sessions. The only hitch is that, even with spacing in time or some other form of separation, any perceived relationship between the communication of negative information and salary decisions is likely to lead to future defensiveness and the filtering out of negative data.

In the contexts of both program evaluation and personnel evaluation, the conflict is very real between the organizational functions of feedback and resource allocation. The desire to know what programs are working well and to allocate money to the most effective is similar to the need to know who are the best-performing workers so as to distribute rewards as a result of performance. From the organization's point of view, rewards that are not contingent upon behavior will decrease task motivation; likewise, resources that are not allocated to the most effective program, or perhaps to the most effective program administrator, may be misspent or wasted. However, from the individual employee's or program administrator's point of view, efforts will be taken to ensure that reports are positive, show improvement, and will closely monitor *whatever criteria* are utilized in resource allocation decisions.

Given the inherent conflict between resource allocation and feedback processes, program evaluation will no doubt always retain some aspects of a police function. Teams of evaluators will be viewed warily, and data will continue to be made available only selectively. At the same time, evaluators will attempt to find unobtrusive and seemingly incorruptible measures of program effectiveness.

If organizations opt to recognize such conflict as intractable, they may concentrate on developing structures to manage the conflict. One possibility is that of building a quasi-legal system within organizations in which both pro and con arguments are voiced, evidence presented, and resource allocation decisions made by a single authority or unbiased panel. Some top-level administrators may already use an informal variety of this kind of advocacy system.

The astute administrator may make certain that some individuals within policymaking groups serve as a devil's advocate and that varying viewpoints are sufficiently aired. Irving Janis noted, for example, that John Kennedy used such a procedure during the Cuban missile crisis but failed to do so during the Bay of Pigs fiasco. Our proposal is to formally build into the organization the roles of protagonist and antagonist in the allocation of resources, at least for resources of any magnitude.

A second way of dealing with the conflict between resource allocation and feedback is to reduce it by decoupling these organizational processes. Summative or outcome evaluation can be deemphasized; instead, efforts can be made to concentrate on formative evaluation, in which programs are revised rather than scrapped in their entirety. Formative evaluation is less likely to be threatening than summative evaluation since it focuses on improving the program rather than evaluating its impact in comparison to the alternative deployment of resources. Unfortunately, the deemphasis of summative evaluation may also drastically reduce organizational efficiency or cost-effectiveness.

A better strategy for decoupling feedback and allocation processes is for the organization to guarantee continued funding of a particular organizational unit and to encourage that unit to experiment with various programs. Carried to its extreme, the organization could reward organizational units and administrators, not on their overall results, but on the quality of their experimentation and program evaluation techniques.

A third solution to evaluation apprehension is to design organizational reward systems so that resources are highly contingent upon performance. However, at the same time, an evaluation research group might be established that would function as an in-house consulting unit. The idea here is not only to *increase* pressure on individuals and work units to perform but also to offer free consulting on evaluation as an aid in improving unit performance. Obviously, for this solution to work, managers must perceive the in-house consulting group to be politically neutral and the data offered to program evaluators must be held confidential. If such a system functioned successfully, organizational units might feel encouraged to experiment in order to increase their own monitored effectiveness. They might simultaneously utilize two methods and then choose the best, or sequentially explore new program tools and procedures. This solution has not yet been implemented in any organization known to the author, but it seems to be a promising alternative.

## OPERATIONALISM VERSUS GOAL ACCOMPLISHMENT

In addition to data biasing, one other key difficulty with program evaluation merits attention. Within organizations, program evaluation may often be subject to a confusion between measured improvement and goal accomplishment. There may tend to be undue emphasis on a particular indicator of effectiveness at the expense of the overall construct of effectiveness itself.

The problem is best illustrated in the context of performance contracting in education. When private contractors are paid on the basis of improvement in students' reading or math scores, they tend to "teach for the test," giving examples of test materials and devoting most of the class time to tested skills. Although test scores may improve, the educational effectiveness of the program may be low. Similarly, organizational

units may focus unduly on those behaviors that are measured and weighed heavily within a program evaluation. To keep a mental health program's hospital recidivism rate low, patients may not be referred to hospitals; and to keep employee turnover down, poor workers may be permitted to stay on the job.

One solution to this problem is to use multiple indicators of effectiveness. For example, in addition to measuring the number of absences before and after a program of applied reinforcement for work attendance, we should also measure work quality, quantity, and satisfaction. As shown recently by Staw and Oldham, there may be some positive consequences of absenteeism. When an individual is highly dissatisfied with a work role, absenteeism may serve as a maintenance function or safety valve, thus attempts to increase attendance without also improving the job itself may produce negative side effects. Individuals may increase their attendance if a reward or the avoidance of punishment depends on it, but they may show up only to produce shoddy work. The crucial point is that program evaluators should try to avoid concentrating upon single indicators of success.

Of course, even with multiple criteria of effectiveness, there may still be some focusing of local effort on a presumed hierarchy of results. No matter how many formal indicators of success, program administrators still may attempt to discern which, in the final judgment, are *the* most important indicators affecting resource allocation. The weighting of effectiveness indicators should thus be made an *explicit and publicly designated aspect* of the evaluation process so that local organizational units can legitimately focus their attention on the most important criteria.

No doubt an evaluation team will often have to get higher-level management to specify clearly what the criteria for effectiveness are. This process, like the setting of organizational objectives, may even prove to be one of the most valuable aspects of program evaluation. For example, when managers and participants in the program disagree among themselves on what criteria should be used in evaluating a program, such disagreement can result in a positive program of participative goal setting. Joint participation of program administrators, program participants, and higher-level managers in criteria selection may turn out to be a crucial precondition of successful evaluation within organizations.

## CONCLUSIONS

In this article we have discussed several of the difficulties that confront evaluation research within organizations. We have offered some suggestions on how to minimize problems, such as evaluation apprehension, biasing of data, and overfocusing on concrete measures of effectiveness. This is not to suggest that program evaluation is easy, fool-proof, or even necessarily accurate. Some problems may be inherent in any attempt to assess the effectiveness of an organizational program.

Our main purpose has been to promote a measure of cautious optimism about evaluation activities within organizations. Administrators are viewed here as having the innate capacity to make relatively rational causal inferences and of being able to evaluate both large and small unit changes. In fact, the chief difficulty confronting organizational administrators, in our view, is the lack of appropriate data and research design capability *within* organizations.

Instead of merely offering new or revised theories for administrators to use across the board, behavioral scientists should concentrate more on transferring methodological skills to practicing administrators so that they themselves can experimentally test the usefulness of various theories, including the ones they have developed on their own. In this way, organizational researchers may make their greatest contribution to the organizations they study—and to the behavioral sciences.

## SELECTED BIBLIOGRAPHY

For a more complete discussion of methodology relating to experimentation, the reader should consult Donald T. Campbell and Julian C. Stanley's *Experimental and Quasi-Experimental Designs for Research* (Rand McNally, 1966) and Thomas D. Cook and Donald T. Campbell's *The Design and Conduct of Quasi-Experiments and True Experiments in Field Settings* (Rand McNally, 1977).

For an excellent critique of the current role of applied behavioral science and some possible changes in that role, the reader should also look at William Notz, Paul Salipante, and James Water's "Innovation in Sit: A Contingency Approach to Human Resource Development," a faculty working paper available from the Faculty of Administrative Studies, University of Manitoba, Winnipeg, Canada.

For a more detailed analysis of the problem of administrators becoming trapped in policy decisions, see Barry Staw's "Knee-Deep in the Big Muddy: A Study of Escalating Commitment to a Chosen Course of Action" (*Organizational Behavior and Human Performance*, 1976, No. 16, pp. 27–44); also Barry Staw and Frederick Fox's, "Escalation: The Determinants of Commitment to a Chosen Course of Action" (*Human Relations*, May 1977, pp. 431–450).

# ORGANIZATIONAL EFFECTIVENESS

This last section of the book addresses the most difficult but important issue — organizational effectiveness. Exactly what constitutes an effective organization is not a simple question, since it depends on whose definition of effectiveness one uses and the perspective one takes in making the judgment. However, organizations must all face this issue in deciding upon a direction to pursue and where to place their energies and resources.

In this section you will first read an introductory piece on the nature of organizational effectiveness. Then the issue of how to maintain an adaptive organization, one that fits with the environment and one that can change as the environment changes, is considered. You will read a selection describing historical instances of positive adaption as well as failure to meet demands of the market environment. Another reading describes how organizations tend to go through long periods of constancy, punctuated by shorter, more intense periods of discontinuity. Then you will see how organizations can negotiate their environments through lobbying, mergers, and strategic alliances, in efforts to control rather than be controlled by their economic situation. Finally, the challenges facing organizations of the future are addressed. You will learn that if organizations are to be competitive in the world economy they must use new organizational designs and management procedures — in short, to understand and change both individual and organizational behavior.

After completing the readings of this final section, do not expect to be an expert on organizational design and effectiveness. These questions require much further study and broad experience in managing organizations. What these readings will provide however is sound consciousness raising; that is, an awareness of the complex issues involved in maintaining an effective and adaptive organization. Armed with this kind of knowledge you will have begun building your qualifications for becoming a thoughtful and responsive manager.

# Foundations of Effectiveness

## 45.   GOALS AND EFFECTIVENESS

Richard H. Hall

The plan of this reading is to examine the nature of organizational goals, as abstractions and as practical and research issues, and then to consider varying approaches to effectiveness. Since effectiveness can be approached from more perspectives than just that of the organization itself, the discussion here will examine the other parties concerned with respect to how an organization accomplishes what it sets out to do and how it affects them.

## ORGANIZATIONAL GOALS

"An organizational goal is a desired state of affairs which the organization attempts to realize."[1] This desired state of affairs is by definition many things to many people. In a large organization, top executives may see the organization seeking one kind of state while those in the middle and lower echelons may have drastically different goals for the organization and for themselves personally. Even in an organization in which there is high participation in decision making and strong membership commitment, it is unlikely that there will be totally unanimous consensus on what the organization should attempt to do, let alone on the means of achieving these ends.

The goal idea at first glance seems most simple in the case of profit-making organizations. Indeed, much of the research on effectiveness has used this type of organization because of goal clarity. The readily quantifiable profit goal is not such a simple matter, however. It is confounded by such issues as the time perspective (long-run or short-run profits); the rate of profit (in terms of return to investors); the important issue of survival and growth in a turbulent and unpredictable environment that might in the short run preclude profit making; the intrusion of other values, such as providing quality products or services, or benefiting mankind; and the firm's comparative position vis-à-vis others in the same industry. Leaving aside for the moment the question of *whose* goals these alternative values might represent, the difficulties apparent in the straightforward profit-making firm are indicative of the difficulties inherent in determining what the goals of an organization really are. When the situation is shifted to a consideration of the goals of a government agency, university, or church, the determination of the organization's goals becomes almost impossible.

Take, for example, the case of a governmental regulative agency charged with administering the public utilities laws and regulations of a state. A casual view suggests that this is a unitary goal, assuming that the laws and regulations are clearly stated. However, this assumption is seldom met, given the large number of lawyers and other technical experts employed by the agency for the purpose of developing and defending interpretations of the existing laws. Administration in such a case is not a simple matter either, since the choice between active and passive administration is a political and organizational football. The well-known distinction between the letter and the intent of the law becomes an issue for such agencies as they develop their operating procedures. What is the goal for the agency? If it is staffed by personnel who have values above and beyond simply administering the existing laws (every organization contains personnel with differing values), their own values toward social action or inaction can clearly modify the stated goals of the organization. In the case of the public utilities agency, beliefs in such diverse areas as air and water pollution, the nature of the publics served by the agency (the public, segments of the public, or the organizations involved), the desirability of maintaining certain public services despite their unprofitability (as in the case of railroad passenger service), and competition versus monopoly in public services—these merely exemplify the range of alternatives available as goals for this organization aside from those found in its formal charter.

The three commonly stated goals of colleges and universities—teaching, research, and public service—are almost by definition too vague to serve as much of a guide for organizational analysis or practice. In the light of contemporary reality, it can also be seen that they have become essentially incompatible in practice. Universities and colleges tend to concentrate on one of the three goals to the exclusion of the others. While emphases change, the basic issue of deciding among these goals remains. And also, since each contains vast uncertainties—exactly what is meant by good teaching, research, or service?—the use of the goal concept in this setting becomes excruciatingly difficult.

With an understanding of some of the difficulties in the utilization of the goal concept, let us examine the concept more systematically.

## The Meaning of Organizational Goals

Organizational goals can be approached from a variety of perspectives. Parsons has cogently pointed out that organizational goals are intimately intertwined with important and basic societal functions, such as integration, pattern maintenance, and so on.[2] From this point of view, organizational goals are really an extension of what the society needs for its own survival. At the other extreme is the position that organizational goals are nothing more than the goals of the individual members of the organization. Both positions disguise more than they illuminate. If the level of analysis is kept in the broad societal-function framework, the variations in goals and activities among organizations performing the same basic functions are ignored. If the level of analysis focuses on just the variety of individual goals, the whole point of organizations is missed—if there were only individual goals, there would be no point in organizing. Clearly, many individuals may have the same goal, such as making a profit, furthering a cause, or destroying an enemy. Clearly also, however, when these people come together in the form of an organization, the profit, cause, or destruction becomes an abstraction toward which they work together.

Organizational goals by definition are creations of individuals, singly or collectively. At the same time, the determination of a goal for collective action becomes a standard by which the collective action is judged. As we will see, the collectively determined, commonly based goal seldom remains constant over time. New considerations imposed from without or within deflect the organization from its original goal, not only changing the activities of the organization, but also becoming part of the overall goal structure. The important point is that the goal of any organization is an abstraction distilled from the desires of members and pressures from the environment and internal system. While there is never 100 percent agreement among members as to what organizational goals are or should be, members can articulate a goal that is a desired state for the organization at some future point in time.

This approach is in some ways similar to that of Herbert Simon. Simon's major focus is on decision making within the organization. He notes that:

*When we are interested in the internal structure of an organization, however, the problem cannot be avoided . . . Either we must explain organizational behavior in terms of the goals of the individual members of the organization, or we must postulate the existence of one or more organizational goals, over and above the goals of the individuals.*[3]

Simon then goes on to differentiate between the goals or value premises that serve as inputs to decisions and motives, and the causes that lead individuals to select some goals over others as the basis for their decision making. He keeps the goal idea at the individual level, but offers the important notion that the goals of an organization at any point in time are the result of the interaction among the members of the organization.

To this we would add that external conditions also affect the nature of an organization's goals. An example is the case of many current military organizations. The official goal is typically to protect the state and its people from external threats. The leaders of the military organization may come to believe, for any number of reasons, that the goal is to be victorious over a wide variety of enemies (this is not necessarily the same as protecting the state). This then becomes the goal until it is modified by interactions or conflicts with lower-level personnel, or with

external forces in the form of some type of civilian control, with the goal again becoming altered to engagement in limited wars without winning or protecting the state. In this hypothetical and oversimplified example, the goals of individual organization members, particularly those in high positions, are crucial in goal setting. These goals are modified in the course of internal and external interactions.

In Simon's approach, goals become constraints on the decision-making process. The constraints are based on abstract values around which the organization operates. Decisions are made within the framework of a set of constraints (goals), and organizations attempt to make decisions that are optimal in terms of the sets of constraints they face. While the approach taken here is not based solely on the decision-making framework, the perspective is the same. Organizational actions are constrained not only by goals, but also by the external and internal factors that have been discussed. In probably the great majority of cases, goals are one, if not the only, relevant constraint.

## Operative Goals

Treating goals as abstract values has the merit of showing that organizational actions are guided by more than the day-to-day whims of individual members. At the same time, abstract values are just that—abstract. They must be converted to specific guides for the actual operations of an organization. Perrow takes this position when he distinguishes between "official" and "operative" organizational goals.[4] Official goals are "the general purposes of the organization as put forth in the charter, annual reports, public statements by key executives and other authoritative pronouncements." Operative goals, on the other hand, "designate the ends sought through the actual operating policies of the organization; they tell us what the organization actually is trying to do, regardless of what the official goals say are the aims."

This distinction is grounded in reality. Two organizations, both with the official goal of profit making, may differ drastically in the amount of emphasis they place on making profits. Blau's examination of two employment agencies with the same goals shows wide variations between the agencies in what they were actually trying to accomplish.[5] In his discussion of this point, Perrow states:

*Where operative goals provide the specific content of official goals, they reflect choices among competing values. They may be justified on the basis of an official goal, even though they may subvert another official goal. In one sense they are means to official goals, but since the latter are vague or of high abstraction, the "means" become ends in themselves when the organization is the object of analysis. For example, where profit making is the announced goal, operative goals will specify whether quality or quantity is to be emphasized, whether profits are to be short run and risky or long run and stable, and will indicate the relative priority of diverse and somewhat conflicting ends of customer service, employee morale, competitive pricing, diversification, or liquidity. Decisions on all these factors influence the nature of the organization, and distinguish it from another with an identical official goal.[6]*

From this perspective, operative goals become the standards by which the organization's actions are judged and around which decisions are made. In many cases these operative goals reflect the official goals, in that they are abstractions made more concrete. However, operative goals can evolve that are basically unrelated to the official goals. In this regard, Perrow notes:

*Unofficial operative goals, on the other hand, are tied more directly to group interests, and while they may support, be irrelevant to, or subvert official goals, they bear no necessary connection with them. An interest in a major supplier may dictate the policies of a corporation executive. The prestige that attaches to utilizing elaborate high-speed computers may dictate the reorganization of inventory and accounting departments. Racial prejudice may influence the selection procedures of an employment agency. The personal ambitions of a hospital administrator may lead to community alliances and activities which bind the organization without enhancing its goal achievement. On the other hand, while*

*the use of interns and residents as "cheap labor" may subvert the official goal of medical education, it may substantially further the official goal of providing a high quality of patient care.[7]*

Operative goals thus reflect the derivation and distillation of a set of goals from both official and unofficial sources. These operative goals are developed through interaction patterns within the organization, but persist after the interactions are completed. They reflect the "desired state of affairs," or abstract official goals, the modifications and subversions of these by personnel in decision-making positions, and the force of pressures from the external environment. It is the combination of official goals with internal and external factors that leads to an existing set of operative goals.

If the use of unofficial goals is carried too far, of course, every organization could be viewed as having a huge, perhaps infinite, number of such goals. The distinction must be made, therefore, between goals and operating policies and procedures. The latter are the exact specifications, formally or informally stated, of what individual actors at all levels are to do in their daily activities. Goals, on the other hand, remain at the abstract level, serving as constraining or guiding principles from which policies and procedures can be derived. Operative goals are abstractions in the same way as official goals. They are a set of ideas about where the organization should be going, which are operationalized into specific plans and procedures.

## The Determination of Organizational Goals

How does one find out exactly what the goals of an organization are? From the research point of view, this is a vital step if there is to be any concern with issues such as effectiveness, personnel and resource allocation, or optimal structuring. In a very real sense, organizational research must be concerned with goals if it is to be anything more than simply descriptive. For the member of the organization at any level, goal determination is similarly vital. If he misses what the goals really are, his own actions may not only not contribute to the organization, they may contribute to his own organizational demise. Members of organizations must know the "system" if they are to operate within it or to change it. From the discussion above, it should be clear that the "system" is much more than official statements.

The vital importance of understanding operative goals can perhaps best be exemplified by an actual case.[8] The case in point is the familiar one of the goals of a university. The University of Minnesota *Faculty Information* booklet contains the following statements:

## TEACHING
*The University emphasizes excellence in teaching. The first duty of every faculty member engaged in instruction is the communication of knowledge and values to students, and the stimulation of their intellectual ability, curiosity, and imagination.*

## RESEARCH
*Research is the second strong arm of the University. The faculty member is aided in obtaining funds and facilities for research, and is encouraged to contribute to the ever-expanding realms of human knowledge.*

## PUBLIC SERVICE AND PROFESSIONAL COMMITMENTS
. . . . . . . . . . .

## UNIVERSITY SERVICE
. . . . . . . . . .

## COMMUNITY SERVICE
. . . . . . . . . .[9]

As everyone must know, these goals are not equally stressed, even though the official pronouncement would lead one to believe otherwise. If a new (or old) faculty member actually believed what he read, he would probably soon find himself at a distinct disadvantage. One of the questions asked of the faculty, in at least one department, when salary increases for the coming year were being considered was the number of offers from other universities that each had received. The larger the number of offers, apparently, the greater the likelihood of receiving a substantial

raise, and vice versa. But the vast majority of such offers are forthcoming to those who are active in the research side of the goal equation, since the other factors cannot be readily visible to other institutions. This is not an unusual case, nor is the meaning of it limited to colleges and universities. Knowledge of operative goals is imperative for effective functioning and for the effective implementation of one's own ideas. At the extreme, such knowledge is necessary for individual survival in organizations.

Operative-goal determination for the individual is obviously important. It is plainly part of the ongoing organizational system, also, and thus central to organizational functioning. It is equally important for the organizational analyst. The significance of operative goals forces the analyst to go beyond the more easily determined official goals. The key to finding out what the operative goals are lies in the actual decisions of the top decision makers in the organization. The kinds of decisions they make about allocation of resources (money, personnel, equipment, etc.) are a major indicator. In a study of juvenile correctional organizations, Mayer Zald found that resources were consistently allocated to the custodial and traditional aspects of the institutions rather than to professional treatment personnel, despite official pronouncements that rehabilitation was the goal.[10] Although lower-level personnel influence the decisions made in the organization, it is the people near or at the top who have the major and sometimes final say in organizational matters.

The determination of these operative goals is more easily said than done. Organizations may be reluctant to allow the researcher or member access to the kinds of records that show the nature of resource allocation. In interviews they may tend to repeat the official goal as a form of rhetoric. However, the analyst or member can determine operative goals through the use of multiple methods of data collection from a variety of goal indicators, such as the deployment of personnel, growth patterns among departments, examination of available records and so on.

Since operative goals reflect what the major decision makers believe to be the critical areas and issues for the organization, it follows that the operative goals will shift as internal and external conditions impinge upon the organization. ... these conditions can deflect the organization from a pursuit of its goals. In a real sense, the operative goals are deflected by these threats or conditions during periods of severe stress. At the same time, *the operative goals will usually reflect some variation on the theme of the official goal.* That is, operative goals are generally based on the official goals, even though there is not perfect correspondence. Profit-making organizations vary in their emphases; colleges and universities pay more or less attention to teaching, research, and so on; and hospitals are concerned to varying degrees with teaching, patient care, and research. If the official goals remain the same when pressures, conditions, and priorities change, the shift in operative goals will be mainly in emphasis.

## Changes in Organizational Goals

Organizational goals change for three major reasons. The first is direct pressure from external forces, which leads to a deflection from the original goals. Second is pressure from internal sources. This may lead the organization to emphasize quite different activities than those originally intended. The third factor is changed environmental and technological demands that lead the organization to redefine its goal. While this is similar to the first reason, the factors here occur in *indirect* interaction with the organization, whereas in the first case the organization is in *direct* interaction with the relevant environmental factors.

The impact of external relationships on goals is best seen in Thompson and McEwen's analysis of organization-environmental interactions.[11] They note that organizational goal setting is affected by competitive, bargaining, cooptative, and coalitional relationships with the environment. In the competitive situation—"that form of rivalry between two or more organizations which is mediated by a third party"—organizations must devote their efforts toward gaining support for their continued existence. Competition is most

easily seen among business firms that compete for the customer's dollar, but it is also very evident among government agencies as they compete for a share of the tax dollar or among religious organizations as they compete for members and their support. (Religious and other voluntary organizations must also compete with alternative organizations for members and money.) Competition partially controls the organization's "choice of goals" that its energies must be turned to the competitive activity. Continuous support is vital for continued survival as an organization.

Bargaining also involves resources, but in this case the organization is in direct interaction with supplier, consumer, and other organizations. In the bargaining situation, the organization must "give" a little to get what it desires. Bargaining takes place in standard relationships between two organizations, as in the case where a routine supplier is asked to alter its goods for the organization. This "custom" order will cost the supplier more money and hence he bargains for a better price, with the organization bargaining to get its custom equipment at the old price. Thompson and McEwen note that universities will often bargain away the name of a building for a substantial gift. Government agencies may bargain by not enforcing certain regulations in order to maintain support for the seeking of other goals. The impact of bargaining is more subtle than that of competition, but it has a similar impact on goal setting.

Cooptation is "the process of absorbing new elements into the leadership or policy-determining structure of an organization as a means of averting threats to its stability or existence."[12] The classic study of cooptation is Selznick's *TVA and the Grass Roots,* in which he documents the impact of bringing new societal elements into the governing structure of the TVA.[13] The organization shifted its emphases partially as a result of new pressures brought to bear in the decision-making system. It is no accident that boards of directors or trustees contain members from pressure groups important to the organizations involved. If a member of a group that is antipathetic to the organization can be brought into the organization, the antipathy can be minimized. At the same time, the presence of that person on a controlling board has an influence on decisions made, even though the hostility rate may be down. The recent movement toward "student power" among high school and college students is interesting to observe in this regard. It is predicted that student members of college and university governing bodies and boards of trustees will be coopted—that is, the students will become part of the power structure and take its view—but also that the organizations involved will find their goal setting at least minimally influenced by the presence of the students. Cooptation is thus a two-way street. Both those coopted and those doing the coopting are influenced.

The final type of external relationship is coalition, or the "combination of two or more organizations for a common purpose. Coalition appears to be the ultimate or extreme form of environmental conditioning of organizational goals."[14] While seeking common purposes, coalitions place strong constraints on the organizations involved, since they cannot set goals in a unilateral fashion.

Although it is clear that other environmental factors also affect the nature of organizational goals, Thompson and McEwen's analysis centers around transactions with other organizations. They suggest a very important consideration in the determination of the operative goals of an organization: Organizations operate in a "field" of other organizations,[15] and these affect what the focal organization does. While this has been amply demonstrated in economic analysis of market competition, the impact goes beyond this type of relationship. The interactions we have described are direct evidence that the use of official-goal statements would be misleading, since the transactions with other organizations by definition would deflect an organization from its official goal.

Operative goals are also affected by what goes on inside an organization. A given set of goals may be altered drastically by changes in the power system of the organization; new types of person-

nel, as in the case of a sudden influx of professionals; and the development of new standards that supersede those of the past. Etzioni has called this phenomenon "goal displacement."[16]

Goal displacement is clearly evident in Robert Michels' analysis of Socialist parties and labor unions in Europe in the early twentieth century.[17] In this study he developed the idea of the "iron law of oligarchy." Michels pointed out that these revolutionary groups began as democratic organizations. The need for organization to accomplish the revolutionary purposes (operative goals) led to the establishment of leaders of the organizations. The leaders, tasting power, did not want to relinquish it, and therefore devoted much of their energies to maintain their positions. Since members of most voluntary organizations, even revolutionary parties, are politically indifferent, and since the skills necessary for leading the parties are not universally distributed, the leaders could rather easily perpetuate themselves in power—in part by coopting or purging the young potential leaders. The emphasis in the parties shifted to organizational maintenance, at the expense of militancy and revolutionary zeal. Close parallels to this situation exist in contemporary revolutionary and militant movements of every political and social persuasion.

A different form of goal displacement can be seen in Robert Scott's analysis of the "sheltered workshop for the blind."[18] When these workshops were formed in the early twentieth century, the overall goal was to integrate the blind into the industrial community. However, it was recognized that many blind people could not work in regular factories, and so the sheltered workshops were developed to provide the blind with work (making brooms and mops, weaving, chair caning, etc.) as a social service. Owing to a series of events, the workshops began to define themselves as factories in competition with non-blind producers of goods. The emphasis shifted from helping the blind to employing competent workers (not necessarily mutually exclusive categories), and the social-service function largely fell by the wayside. Part of the reason for the shift in emphasis lay in changed environmental conditions, with an increased demand for the workshops' products. But it appears that these demands could have been resisted and the original intent of the workshops maintained intact. The internal decision-making process led to the development of clearly different goals from those professed at the outset.

Still another type of displacement can be seen in what Etzioni calls "overmeasurement" and Bertram Gross labels "number magic."[19] Both refer to the tendency for organizations of all types to organize their energies (goals) around activities that are easily quantified. Easy quantification leads to counting publications of university faculty rather than evaluating classroom performance, looking at output per worker rather than "diligence, cooperation, punctuality, loyalty, and responsibility,"[20] and counting parishioners in a church rather than assessing the spiritual guidance of the parishioners.[21] These examples could be multiplied many times for many organizations. The obvious solution to this problem is to use multiple indicators for determining the extent to which organizations are achieving their goals. When this is not done and the easily quantifiable measure is stressed, organizational goals become deflected toward the achievement of the easily measured aspect.[22] This may in turn actually defeat the purpose for which the organization was designed. These internal sources of goal change can be found in any organization and are a basic part of the determination of the operative goals. In the extreme cases discussed here, the changes are rather clearly dysfunctional in terms of the official and original operative goals; but the processes inherent in these changes are a normal part of the goal-setting process.

The final source of goal change is a more generalized environmental pressure—generalized, that is, in terms of falling within abstract categories such as technological development, cultural changes, and economic conditions; however, the impact on the organization is direct. Several studies are available that provide direct evidence for this basis of goal change. Perhaps the most dramatic evidence comes from David L. Sills' analysis of the national Foundation for In-

fantile Paralysis.[23] Although the study was completed before the transition to be discussed was accomplished, the change in operative goals is very evident. The foundation was formed to assist in the prevention and treatment of polio through research, coordinating, and fund-raising activities. At the time the foundation was organized, polio was a major health problem, highlighted by Franklin D. Roosevelt's crippled condition as a result of the disease. Roosevelt himself founded the organization in 1938 at the height of his own popularity and the seriousness of the polio problem. The organization grew rapidly, and its March of Dimes became a very successful volunteer fund-raising effort.

In less than two decades, the organization accomplished its primary goal. Through the development of the Salk and Sabine vaccines, polio has largely been eliminated as a serious health hazard. Rehabilitation facilities have been consistently improved to assist those who suffer from the effects of polio contracted in the past (the number of new cases at present is insignificant). For the organization, these events presented a clear dilemma. The choice was between going out of business and developing a new goal. The latter alternative was chosen, as the organization decided to concentrate on "other crippling diseases," with particular emphasis on birth defects. Sills suggests that the presence of a strong national headquarters together with committed volunteers should maintain the organization over time. The historical evidence seems to confirm this, although the organization does not appear to be as strong as it was during the polio epidemics.

The volunteer and nonvolunteer members of this organization had a vested interest in its maintenance. At the same time, technological developments outside the organization made its continuation questionable because of its operative goals at that time. The focus of the organization shifted to adapt to the changed technology. While some of the operative goals remained the same, others shifted to meet the new concerns.

The impact of technological shifts can also be seen in Lawrence and Lorsch's analysis of firms in the plastics industry. In this case, technological change, in the form of a rapidly changing "state of the art," is an ever-present and pressing factor of the environment. In discussing the performance of organizations in this industry, Lawrence and Lorsch comment:

*The low-performing organizations were both characterized by their top administrators as having serious difficulty in dealing with this environment. They had not been successful in introducing and marketing new products. In fact, their attempts to do so had met with repeated failures. This record, plus other measures of performance available to top management, left them with a feeling of disquiet and a sense of urgency to find ways of improving their performance.*[24]

This sense of urgency would be translated into altered operative goals for the organization as it seeks to cope more effectively with the rapidly changing technological system.

Technology is not the only environmental factor impinging upon the organization, despite its apparent centrality. The general values in the environment surrounding an organization also affect its operation. Burton Clark's analysis of the adult education system in California indicates clearly that an organization is vitally affected by the values of those whom it serves and whose support it seeks.[25]

The adult education system's official goals are concerned with relatively lofty matters, such as awareness of civic responsibilities, economic uplift, personal adjustment in the family, health and physical fitness, cultural development, broadened educational background, and the development of avocational interests. This educational system suffers from a number of handicaps. It is part of the public educational system but not part of the normal sequence. It is a "peripheral, nonmandatory" part; and this marginality is heightened by the fact that the system operates on an "enrollment economy." That is, school income is determined largely by attendance (paid) in classes. If attendance declines, support for the program from tax revenues is likely also to decline. Course enrollments become "*the* criterion by which courses are initiated and continued."[26]

Courses are offered only if they are popular. It is not surprising, therefore, to find classes in cake decorating, rug making, and square dancing. While these are legitimate avocational activities, the pressure for courses such as these precludes much attention being paid to the other official goals and increases the criticisms of the adult education program from other segments of the educational enterprise. The adult education administrators are thus caught in the bind of trying to maintain attendance in the face of competing demands for the potential student's time and trying to satisfy the pertinent criticism of other educators and members of the legislature. The values of the clientele are inconsistent with those of the system itself. The organization adapts to their demands, but then finds itself out of phase with another part of its relevant environment.

Organizations in the service area are constantly confronted with changed values that make their services in greater or lesser demands. Colleges and universities were unprepared for the rise in enrollments caused by the increased valuation placed on education during most of the 1960s. While demographic conditions would have led to a prediction of some increase, more than the expected proportions of high school graduates opted for college as opposed to other endeavors (for whatever reason). These changed values have obviously affected the goals of the organizations as they are forced to "process" students at the expense of some of the traditional goals.[27]

Shifts in cultural values and their impact on the goals of organizations are obvious in the profit-making sector also. While the goals of profit may remain, the operative goals shift as more energies are put into market research and as organizations redefine themselves as "young" organizations for the "now" generation. These are often more than advertising slogans, in that internal transformations have occurred to refocus the organizations' activities.

Shifts in the economic and political systems surrounding an organization would have similar influences on the goals of the organization involved. While much more than goals are affected by these interactions with the environment, it should be clear that organizational goals, like the organizations for which they serve as constraints and guides for action, are not static. Internal and external factors affect them. The relative strength of the various factors affecting goals, which would include the decision-making and power processes within the organization, have not been determined. We do know that these factors are operative, but we cannot specify the conditions under which the importance of these factors varies.

## The Utility of the Goal Concept

The factors that affect goals, and the fact that the meaningful goals for an organization are not those officially pronounced, might lead us to reject the goal concept altogether. But there is still the simple but basic fact that the organization would not exist if it were not for some common purpose. Except in the case of conscription, as in the military system or the public schools, members come to the organization willingly, if not enthusiastically. In all cases, the organization engages in some activity. This activity is not simply random behavior; it is based on some notion of what the purpose of the action is.

This purpose or goal is the basis for organizational activities. It is true that means can come to be emphasized more heavily than the goal itself, that members of the organization may have no idea of why they are doing what they are doing, and that ritualistic adherence to outmoded norms may become the norm; but these behaviors would be impossible without the presence of a goal. Even when forgotten or ignored, the goal is still the basis for the organization, since the means would not have developed without it in the first place.

From the discussion above, it is clear that most organizations have more than one goal. These multiple goals may be in conflict with one another; even then, they are still a basis for action. The action itself may or may not conflict with conflicting goals. The relative importance of the goals can be determined by the way the organization allocates its resources to them. Since

both external and internal pressures affect goals, along with the more rational process of goal setting, goals cannot be viewed as static. They change, sometimes dramatically, over time. These changes, it should be stressed, can occur because of decision making within the organization. This decision making is almost by definition a consequence of internal or external forces. Goal alterations decided within the organization are a consequence of the interactions of members who participate in the goal-setting process. This can be done by an oligarchic elite or through democratic processes (in very few organizations would a total democracy prevail).

Shifts in goals can also occur without a conscious decision on the part of organization members—that is, as a reaction to the external or internal pressures without a conscious reference to an abstract model of where the organization is going. While this is not goal-related behavior, the persistence of such activities leads to their becoming operative goals for the organization, as where the organization focuses its efforts on achieving easily measured objectives at the expense of more central but less easily measured goals.

It is at this point, of course, that the goal concept is most fuzzy. If an organization is oriented toward some easily quantifiable objective for the sake of measuring its achievements, the analyst can stand back and say, "Aha, this organization isn't doing what it is supposed to do!" At the same time, the easily quantified goal is an abstraction despite its easy quantification, just as is the possibly more lofty objective that serves as the analyst's point of departure. The analyst can also point out the deflections that occur as a result of the external and internal pressures discussed. Concentration upon deflections from official goals, whether they are due to quantification or external and internal pressures, can lead to the decision that goals are really not relevant for organizational analysis. It is at this point that the work of Perrow and Simon is most pertinent. Perrow's emphasis on the operative goals, however they are developed, and Simon's notion that goals place constraints on decision making both suggest that goals are relevant, even central, for organizational analysis. It does not matter what the source of operative goals might be; what does matter is that they come into the decision-making and action processes of the organization. They are still abstractions around which the organization and its members behave.

The goal concept, with the modifications we have discussed, is vital in organizational analysis. The dynamics of goal setting and goal change do not alter the fact that goals still serve as guides for what happens in an organization. If the concept of goals is not used, organizational behavior becomes a random occurrence, subject to whatever pressures and forces exist at any point in time. Since organizations have continuity and do accomplish things, the notion of goals as abstractions around which behavior is organized remains viable.

The analysis of goals is a rather empty exercise until the second part of the equation is added. Since a goal is something that is sought, the seeking leads to the issue of goal accomplishment, or effectiveness. Since goals are seldom accomplished, except in rare cases such as that of the National Foundation for Infantile Paralysis, *effectiveness* is a more usable term than *accomplishment*. The discussion of effectiveness that follows is based on the goal notion that has been developed...that organizations attempt to be rational and goal-seeking, but are deflected by the kinds of pressures and forces that have been described.

## EFFECTIVENESS

Effectiveness has been defined as the "degree to which [an organization] realizes its goals."[28] From the discussion of goals, it should be clear that effectiveness is not a simple issue. The basic difficulty in analyzing it is the fact of multiple and often conflicting goals in many organizations. Effectiveness in one set of endeavors may lead to noneffectiveness in another, particularly in the case of multipurpose organizations.

Effectiveness is a difficult issue from another standpoint. *Efficiency* is often confused with effectiveness. Etzioni defines efficiency as the "amount of resources used to produce a unit of output."[29] Clearly, an organization can be efficient without being effective, and vice versa. Recent controversies regarding certain poverty programs illustrate this point. The costs (efficiency) of producing a well-trained and well-adjusted person who came from a disadvantaged background were higher than those of producing a college graduate at some elite universities. The programs may have been effective—although this was never directly confirmed—but they were not efficient, at least from the point of view of many legislators. Efficiency and effectiveness are often closely related, but it is dangerous to assume without careful investigation that they are identical.

Despite the difficulties with the concept of effectiveness, it is one that captures the attention of almost everyone concerned with organizations. For the organization member, the effectiveness issue really boils down to the question, "Is is worth it?" While not every member is concerned with the issue, certainly those in decision-making positions are. For the organizational analyst, the same question applies, since he also wants to know whether the relationships he is examining mean anything.

## The Goal Approach

The interest in effectiveness has not led to a definitive set of studies or conceptual approaches to the issue. A good part of the difficulty in assessing effectiveness lies in the problems surrounding goals. Most analyses of effectiveness are built around some version of a goal model of organization. In a relatively early study of effectiveness, Basil Georgopoulos and Arnold Tannenbaum argued that measures of effectiveness must be based on organizational means and ends, rather than relying on externally derived criteria.[30] They found that productivity, flexibility, and absence of strain and conflict were both interrelated and associated with independent assessments of effectiveness. These indicators of effectiveness were closely related to the goals of the organizations studied.

In a major effort to make some sense of the effectiveness issue, James Price has recently compiled a set of propositions dealing with effectiveness.[31] The propositions are drawn from some fifty research monographs (not all concerned specifically with effectiveness) and deal with a variety of qualities assumed by Price to be indicators of effectiveness—including productivity, morale, conformity, adaptiveness, and institutionalization. Productivity is taken as the indicator most closely related to effectiveness. Unfortunately, as Price notes, the indicators themselves do not vary together in actual practice, and what might by related to morale might be unrelated to productivity. This problem illustrates a major issue in the analysis of organizational effectiveness: Since organizations generally pursue more than one goal, the degree of effectiveness in the attainment of one goal may be inversely related to the degree in the attainment of other goals. This sort of thing does occur quite often, apparently, and so organizations must choose between the goals they seek to attain, thus reinforcing the idea that the operative goals of the organization are the result of internal choice processes and external pressures. This point also raises the strong possibility that *organizations cannot be effective*, if the idea is accepted that almost every organization has multiple goals.

Despite these problems, which Price acknowledges in part, he then links organizational characteristics to effectiveness. He suggests, for example, that organizations are likely to be more effective when they have a high degree of division of labor, specialized departmentalization, and continuous systems of assembling output... Also related to effectiveness are such things as the acceptance of the legitimacy of the decision-making system, a high degree of organizational autonomy, and high rates of communication within the organization.[32] Although the propositions may be oversimplified, as William Starbuck has suggested,[33] they provide a starting point from which systematic examinations of effectiveness may begin. Rather than propositions, Price's work actually presents a series of hypotheses about effectiveness that are subject to empirical verification.

An additional problem with the Price inventory, and one that characterizes most effectiveness studies, is the use of productivity as the major indicator. This is misleading and/or inapplicable in service organizations and less than perfect in many production organizations. The positive role of conflict in certain circumstances is also typically ignored.

The Price analysis is based on the assumption that organizations are goal-seeking entities. It also recognizes that the attainment of one goal may operate against (be dysfunctional for) the attainment of another. The more complex the organization in terms of the operative goals on which it is based, the more difficult the effectiveness issue becomes. The problem becomes further compounded, of course, when an organization stresses the easily quantifiable measures of effectiveness when these are not true indicators of its total purposes.

## The System-Resources Approach

Stanley Seashore and Ephraim Yuchtman[34] have attempted to avoid some of the pitfalls of the goal approach by essentially ignoring organizational goals in their analyses of effectiveness. They criticize those who use the goal approach on the ground that the determination of goals is extremely difficult, if not impossible. Their criticism is largely of those who advocate the use of the official, rather than operative goals. Where they do consider the operative goals, they note that there are often conflicting goals for the same organization. Instead of the goal model, Seashore and Yuchtman suggest the use of a "system-resources" model for the analysis of organizational effectiveness.

The system-resources approach is based on the idea of the organization as an open system. As such, it engages in exchange and competitive relationships with the environment. Effectiveness becomes the "ability of the organization, in either relative or absolute terms, to exploit its environment in the acquisition of scarce and valued resources."[35] These resources are acquired in the competitive and exchange relationships. An organization is most effective when it "maximizes its bargaining position and optimizes its resource procurement." This approach links the organization back into the society by noting that it is in interaction with the environment and thus must gain resources from that source.

In an empirical examination of this approach, Seashore and Yuchtman used data from 75 insurance sales agencies located in different communities throughout the United States. Data from these agencies were factor-analyzed. The analysis yielded ten factors that were stable over time. These were:

1. Business volume
2. Production cost
3. New member productivity
4. Youthfulness of members
5. Business mix
6. Manpower growth
7. Management emphasis
8. Maintenance cost
9. Member productivity
10. Market penetration[36]

These factors are not taken as indicators for all organizations. The factors of youthfulness of members, for example, while related to performance in this case, may be part of a phase or cycle in the life of these organizations. In interpreting the results of this analysis, Seashore and Yuchtman note that factors such as business volume and penetration of the market could be considered goals, but member productivity and youthfulness certainly cannot. They conclude that while not all the factors associated with performance can be considered as goals, they can be regarded as important resources gleaned from the environment.

This approach would essentially do away with goals as a component of the analysis of effectiveness. It also suggests that there is no universal standard by which effectiveness can be judged, making the effectiveness issue one that would have to be handled organization by organization, or at least type of organization by type of organization.

Viewed from another perspective, the Seashore-Yuchtman approach does not differ markedly from the one that has already been discussed. The acquisition of resources from the environment is based upon the official goal of the organization (Seashore and Yuchtman use the term *ultimate criterion*[37]). Movement toward this goal or ultimate criterion is difficult if not impossible to measure. The next step is to specify the operative goals (*penultimate criteria* in the Seashore-Yuchtman approach) and other activities in which the organization engages. Performance or effectiveness according to these criteria is more easily assessed. Growth in business volume is an operative goal in this sense, while youthfulness in members is merely a cyclical factor associated with performance on the other factors. The issue of goals versus resource allocation is therefore in many ways an argument over semantics. The acquisition of resources does not just happen.[38] It is based on what the organization is trying to achieve—its goal—but is accomplished through the operative goals. The Seashore-Yuchtman perspective is very useful in its attention to environmental transactions and its use of organizationally based data. Although they argue against the goal model, their own work is not that much different from the perspective taken here. Their approach is an empirical verification of the importance of the operative-goal concept.

This discussion of organizational effectiveness leads to the conclusion that there is no single indicator of effectiveness, even a group of common indicators, that can be used across organizations. Instead, the approach must be that operative goals serve as the bases for assessments of effectiveness. These operative goals are built around acquiring and maintaining environmental support. To these external considerations must be added the internal factors that Price suggests—morale, adaptiveness, and so on.

## The Multiple Criteria of Effectiveness

The relevance of the multiple-criteria approach to effectiveness is seen in practice when data from business managers is considered. Thomas Mahoney and William Weitzel examined the criteria that managers used in assessing the performance of subunits under their direction.[39]

*General business managers tend to use productivity and efficient performance. These high-order criteria refer to measures of output, whereas lower-order criteria tend to refer to characteristics of the organization climate, supervisory style, and organizational capacity for performance. The research and development managers, on the other hand, use cooperative behavior, staff development, and reliable performance as high-order criteria; and efficiency, productivity, and output behavior as lower-order criteria.[40]*

These differences can be found within the same organization.

This research demonstrates the fact that effectiveness criteria as developed by the organization itself do not vary together. In a very real sense, the complex organization thus cannot be effective, if effectiveness is taken in a global or ultimate sense. It can be effective on one or several criteria, but must be less effective or ineffective on others. In fact, efforts to increase effectiveness on one criterion can provide an oppositional force to achieving effectiveness on another. The fact that choices among criteria must be made reinforces the utility of the goal concept, since these choices will be based at least partially on the operative goals of the moment.

Implicit in the discussions of effectiveness, regardless of perspective, is the assumption that the organization operates in a relatively free market and the customer or client is free to select an alternative organization if his needs are not being met. When he shifts to another organization, resources are not allocated to the original organization and effectiveness diminishes. In the goals perspective, profits or community support would decrease as this occurs. The free-market assumption is an important one and makes sense for many organizations. There are, however, many organizations that have an essentially captive market. This can be most easily seen in the case of some service organizations, such as schools or public welfare agencies, but it is also the case for the military and for many business organizations that enjoy a near monopoly in an area. In these cases, an important consideration in the effectiveness equation is typically ignored—the response of the customer or client to the organization.

If the client is not receiving the services he feels are important to him, the organization cannot be judged as being totally effective, regardless of what the organization members themselves think. For example, if a particular form of public welfare makes the recipients feel degraded and does not help them move into a more meaningful life style, the welfare system in question is not as effective as it might be. In fact, it could be posited that the conditions under which the organization might judge itself to be effective, such as the number of cases handled or the amount of money disbursed, might be counter to the client perception of what the organization should be doing.

This consideration raises again the point that it is difficult for organizations to be effective. In this case the organization might be achieving its multiple goals as it sees it, but be ineffective in accomplishing what its clients see as being of primary importance. In issues like this, of course, it is difficult, if not impossible, to determine the extent to which the "experts" in the organization should be listened to as opposed to a concern with lay opinion. The potential for conflict must be recognized, however, and the organization should be aware of the values of its constituents.

Recent client and consumer movements should bring this issue into the open more clearly. At the present time, it is difficult to determine how the organizations involved will react, other than with resistance.

## SUMMARY AND CONCLUSIONS

This reading has been concerned with two central but controversial issues in organizational analysis. Perspectives on goals have ranged from seeing them as the key to understanding organizations to considering them of no use whatsoever. The approach taken here has been to acknowledge the fact that official goals do not tell us very much about the organization, and to adopt instead the operative-goal concept, as a means of focusing on what organizations actually do. The operative goals serve as abstract ideas around which behavior is organized. These ideas take the form of constraints on decision making in determining where the organization's resources will be placed. The operative goals can and usually do change as a result of internal and external factors. These changes can deflect the organization quite dramatically from its original (official) purposes, reflecting a response to reality in most cases. Changes in goals can also lead to the disintegration of an organization, if the new

operative goals do not allow the organization to have sufficient resources brought in to ensure survival. Operative goals are translated into policies that guide the day-to-day activities of the organization. Changes in policy reflect alterations in the pattern of the organization's goals.

Effectiveness was treated within the operative-goals framework. Since the very concept of operative goals suggests a complex goals structure, effectiveness cannot be viewed from an all-or-none perspective. Effectiveness is a relative phenomenon, with an absence of covariation among many of the criteria and possibly inverse relationships among others. The complexity of organizations, almost by definition, precludes effectiveness on all criteria. The specific type of effectiveness sought reflects the operative goals as they have evolved over time.

## NOTES

1. Amitai Etzioni, *Modern Organizations* (Englewood Cliffs, N.J.: Prentice-Hall, Inc., 1964), p.6.

2. Talcott Parsons, *Structure and Process in Modern Societies* (New York: The Free Press, 1960), pp. 17–22 and 44–47.

3. Herbert A. Simon, "On the Concept of Organizational Goal," *Administrative Science Quarterly* 9, no. 1 (June 1964): 2.

4. Charles Perrow, "The Analysis of Goals in Complex Organizations," *American Sociological Review* 26, no. 6 (December 1961): 855.

5. Peter M. Blau, *The Dynamics of Bureaucracy* (Chicago: University of Chicago Press, 1955).

6. Perrow, "Analysis of Goals," pp. 855–56.

7. Ibid., p. 856.

8. Cases and case studies are useful as examples, but they cannot be used as bases for generalizations concerning other organizations, even of a very similar type.

9. *Faculty Information* (Minneapolis: University of Minnesota, 1966), pp. 7–8.

10. Mayer N. Zald, "Comparative Analysis and Measurement of Organizational Goals: The Case of Correctional Institutions for Delinquents," *The Sociological Quarterly* 4, no. 2 (Spring 1963): 206–30.

11. James D. Thompson and William J. McEwen, "Organizational Goals and Environment: Goal Setting as an Interaction Process," *Administrative Science Quarterly* 23, no. 1 (February 1958).

12. Ibid., p. 27.

13. Philip Selznick, *TVA and the Grass Roots* (New York: Harper Torchbook Edition, 1966).

14. Thompson and McEwen, "Organizational Goals and Environment," p. 28.

15. For a further discussion of this point, see Roland L. Warren, "The Interorganizational Field as a Focus for Investigation," *Administrative Science Quarterly* 12, no. 3 (December 1967): 396–419.

16. Etzioni, *Modern Organizations*, p. 10.

17. Robert Michels, *Political Parties* (New York: The Free Press, 1949).

18. Robert A. Scott, "The Factory as a Social Service Organization: Goal Displacement in Workshops for the Blind," *Social Problems* 15, no. 2 (Fall 1967): 160–75.

19. Etzioni, *Modern Organizations*, pp. 8–10; and Bertram M. Gross, *Organizations and Their Managing* (New York: The Free Press, 1968), p. 293.

20. Gross, *Organizations and Their Managing*, p. 295.

21. Etzioni, *Modern Organizations*, p. 10.

22. For an extended discussion of this point, see W. Keith Warner and A. Eugene Havens, "Goal Displacement and the Intangibility of Organizational Goals," *Administrative Science Quarterly* 12, no. 4 (March 1968): 539–55.

23. David L. Sills, *The Volunteers* (New York: The Free Press, 1957).

24. Paul R. Lawrence and Jay W. Lorsch, *Organization and Environment: Managing Differentiation and Integration* (Cambridge: Harvard Graduate School of Business Administration, 1967), p. 42.

25. Burton R. Clark, "Organizational Adaptation and Precarious Values," *American Sociological Review* 21, no. 3 (June 1956): 327–36.

26. Ibid., p. 333.

27. The case of the WCTU, discussed earlier, illustrates what happens when an organization *does not* adapt to changed values. The current shifts in college enrollment illustrate still another shift of values.

28. Etzioni, *Modern Organization*, p. 8.

29. Ibid.

30. Basil S. Georgopoulos and Arnold S. Tannenbaum, "A Study of Organizational Effectiveness," *American Sociological Review* 22, no. 5 (October 1957): 534–40.

31. James L. Price, *Organizational Effectiveness: An Inventory of Propositions* (Homewood, Ill.: Richard D. Irwin, Inc., 1968).

32. Ibid., pp. 203–4.

33. William H. Starbuck, "Some Comments, Observations and Objections Stimulated by 'Design of Proof in Organizational Research,'" *Administrative Science Quarterly* 13, no. 1 (June 1968): 135–61.

34. Stanley E. Seashore and Ephraim Yuchtman, "Factorial Analysis of Organizational Performance," *Administrative Science Quarterly* 12, no. 3 (December 1967): 377–95; and Yuchtman and Seashore, "A System Resource Approach to Organizational Effectiveness," *American Sociological Review* 32, no. 6 (December 1967): 891–903.

35. Yuchtman and Seashore, "A System Resource Approach," p. 898.

36. Seashore and Yuchtman, "Factorial Analysis," p. 383.

37. Ibid., p. 378.

38. Mayer N. Zald, in "Urban Differentiation, Characteristics of Boards of Directors, and Organizational Effectiveness," *American Journal of Sociology* 73, no 3 (November 1967), uses the acquisition of resources as the criterion for effectiveness. In this case, the presence of high-status members on the boards of directors of YMCA branches is related to effectiveness because of their success in bringing in resources.

39. Thomas A. Mahoney and William Weitzel, "Managerial Models of Organizational Effectiveness," *Administrative Science Quarterly* 14, no. 3 (September 1969): 357–65.

40. Ibid., p. 362.

# Adapting the Organization to a Changing Environment

## 46. FIT, FAILURE, AND THE HALL OF FAME

Raymond E. Miles and Charles C. Snow

There is currently a convergence of attention and concern among managers and management scholars across basic issues of organizational success and failure. Whether attention is focused on the very survival of organizations in aging industries, the pursuit of excellence in mature industries, or the preparation of organizations for the rapidly approaching challenges of the 21st century, the concern is real and highly motivated. U.S. managers and organizations have been indicted for low productivity, and management scholars have recognized the fragmentation of their literature and called for a new synthesis.

Clearly, neither organizational success or failure has an easy explanation. Nevertheless, it is becoming increasingly evident that a simple though profound core concept is at the heart of many organization and management research findings as well as many of the proposed remedies for indus-

trial and organizational renewal. The concept is that of *fit* among an organization's strategy, structure, and management processes.

Successful organizations achieve strategic fit with their market environment and support their strategies with appropriately designed structures and management processes. Less successful organizations typically exhibit poor fit externally and/or internally. A conceptual framework can be built upon the process of fit that will prove valuable to both managers and management scholars as they sift through current theories, perspectives, and prescriptions in search of an operational consensus. The main features of such a framework are structured around four main points:

- *Minimal* fit among strategy, structure, and process is essential to all organizations operating in competitive environments. If a misfit occurs for a prolonged period, the result usually is failure.

- *Tight* fit, both internally and externally, is associated with excellence. Tight fit is the underlying causal dynamic producing sustained, excellent performance and a strong corporate culture.

- *Early* fit, the discovery and articulation of a new pattern of strategy, structure, and process, frequently results in performance records which in sporting circles would merit Hall of Fame status. The invention or early application of a new organization form may provide a more powerful competitive advantage than a market or technological breakthrough.

- *Fragile* fit involves vulnerability to both shifting external conditions and to inadvertent internal unraveling. Even Hall of Fame organizations may become victims of deteriorating fit.

## MINIMAL FIT, MISFIT, AND FAILURE

The concept of fit plays an undeniably important role in managerial behavior and organizational analysis. Fit is a process as well as a state—a dynamic search that seeks to *align* the organization with its environment and to *arrange* resources internally in support of that alignment. In practical terms, the basic alignment mechanism is *strategy*, and the internal arrangements are *organization structure and management processes*. Because in a changing environment it is very difficult to keep these major organizational components tightly integrated, perfect fit is most often a condition to be strived for rather than accomplished.

Although fit is seldom referred to explicitly, it has appeared as the hallmark of successful organizations in a variety of settings and circumstances. For example, in our own studies of organizational behavior in many widely different industries, we have regularly found that organizations of different types can be successful provided that their particular configuration of strategy, structure, and process is internally and externally consistent.[1] In his landmark historical analysis, Alfred Chandler found that the companies now recognized as the pioneers of the divisional organization structure were among the first to identify emerging markets, develop diversification strategies to meet these market needs, and to revamp their organization structures to fit the new strategies.[2] In their study of management of innovation in electronics firms, Tom Burns and G. M. Stalker found that organizations pursuing innovation strategies had to use flexible, organic structures and management processes; rigid, mechanistic approaches did not fit with such strategies.[3] Finally, in another highly acclaimed study, Paul Lawrence and Jay Lorsch found that successful organizations in three quite different industries were those that were sufficiently differentiated to deal with the complexities of their industrial environments while simultaneously being tightly integrated internally.[4]

These and other studies conducted by organization theorists have essentially if not directly reaffirmed the importance of fit. In addition, recent research in sociology and economics has supported the idea that achieving at least minimal fit is closely associated with organizational success. Industrial economists have identified a set of generic strategies that generally fit most industries, as well as some of the organizational and managerial characteristics associated with these strategies.[5] Sociologists, borrowing concepts and theories from biology, have examined, within different populations of organizations, certain features that fit (or do not fit) particular environments.[6] In sum, the concept of fit may at first glance appear to be obvious, but many studies from several disciplines indicate that while fit is fundamental to organizational success, it is enormously difficult to achieve and/or maintain.

### Fit and Survival

It is appropriate to distinguish between degree of fit as well as the nature of fit, specifically that *minimal fit is required for organizational survival*. Under some circumstances, organizations that are "misfits" in their industries may survive, but sooner or later they must adjust their behavior or fail. For example, in one of our studies, the objective was to determine if certain strategies were both feasible and effective in different industries.[7] The industries selected for study were air transportation, autos, plastics, and semiconductors. We found that in general some strategies were effective and others were not. Organizations that we called "Defenders," "Prospectors," and the "Analyzers" were all effective; i.e., they met the test of minimal fit in each industry. On the other hand, organizations identified as "Reactors" were generally ineffective, except in the air transportation industry which was highly regulated at the time (1975). Reactors are organizations that have either a poorly articulated strategy, a strategy inappropriate for the industrial environment, or an organization structure and management system that does not fit the strategy. The findings from this study suggest that in competitive industries, there is a set of feasible strategies (e.g., Defender, Prospector, Analyzer) each of which can be effective. Moreover, misfits—organizations whose behavior lies outside of the feasible set—tend to perform poorly unless they are in a "protected" environment such as that provided by government regulation.

## Fit and Misfit

The line of demarcation between minimal fit and misfit, however, is not obvious. No whistles blow warning an organization that its internal or external fit is coming undone. The process is more likely to be marked by a general deterioration whose speed is affected by competitive circumstances. For example, an in-depth study of the major firms in the tobacco industry during the years 1950–1975 illustrates the point.[8] Few American industries have experienced the degree of negative pressure that was exerted on the tobacco industry during these years, and the experiences of four companies (Philip Morris, R. J. Reynolds, American Brands, Liggett & Meyers) pointedly show how organizations struggle to maintain an alignment with their shifting environments over time.

Each of the companies responded differently to severe, uncontrollable jolts such as the Sloan-Kettering Report linking smoking to cancer (1953), the Surgeon General's Report reaffirming this conclusion (1964), and events leading to and concluding with a ban on broadcast advertising of cigarettes (1970). Philip Morris, relying on a Prospector strategy, engaged in a series of product and market innovations that propelled the company from last among the major firms in 1950 market share to first today. R. J. Reynolds largely pursued an Analyzer strategy—rarely the first-mover in product-market innovations but always an early adopter of the successful innovations of its competitors—and today it ranks a close second to Philip Morris. Both of these companies currently exhibit a minimal if not strong fit with environmental conditions in the tobacco industry.

American Brands followed a Defender strategy in which it tried to maintain its traditional approach in the face of these environmental changes. This strategy essentially amounted to continued reliance on nonfiltered cigarettes even though the filtered cigarette market segment was growing steadily. American Brands, probably not wanting to cannibalize its sales of nonfiltered cigarettes, was at least ten years behind Philip Morris and R. J. Reynolds in entering the filtered cigarette market, and, during this period, the company fell from first to fourth place in overall market share. The company's internal fit among strategy, structure, and process was a good one throughout the mid-1950s to mid-1960s, but its strategic fit with the market underwent a gradual decline. Certainly, in retrospect, one could argue that American Brands was a misfit during this time, and the firm paid for it in declining performance.

Lastly, Liggett & Meyers behaved almost as a classic Reactor throughout this quarter-century period. It demonstrated substantially less internal consistency than its competitors, fared poorly in its product-market strategy, and doggedly hung on to its approach despite unfavorable performance. Described by one source as "always too late with too little," Liggett & Meyers in the late

1970s was searching for someone to purchase its tobacco business. Here was a misfit bordering on failure.

In the case of the tobacco industry, major environmental changes resulted in declining fit and performance for one company and near-failure for another. Organizational misfit does not, however, have to come from external changes; it can result from internal shifts generated by the organization itself. To illustrate internally generated misfit, consider the well-known case of organizational disintegration and resurrection, the Chrysler Corporation.[9]

From a strong position as the country's second largest automobile manufacturer in the 1930s, Chrysler arguably began to decline in the post-World War II period when it changed its strategy without significantly altering its organization structure or management processes. Prior to the 1950s, Chrysler kept its capital base as small as possible, subcontracted out a substantial part of its production, and rode its suppliers hard to keep costs down. But then Chrysler decided to emulate both General Motors and Ford, even to the point of matching their product lines model for model. From the early 1960s until its Federal bailout in the 1970s, Chrysler seemed determined to be a full-line, worldwide, direct competitor of Ford and GM.

To support this product-market strategy, however, Chrysler was late in forming a subsidiary to monitor its distributors, late in making the necessary foreign acquisitions, and often late in designing its greatly broadened product line which was done mostly by a single, centralized engineering group. In fact, Chrysler largely remained a functionally departmentalized and centralized organization long after it adopted a strategy of diversification. Managerial problems in the areas of cost control, inventory, and production merely added to the misfit between Chrysler's strategy and its structure and management system. Despite its recent public attention and economic rebound, the company has not yet achieved stable performance.

In sum, the consequence of misfit is declining performance if not complete failure. Organizational misfits can be protected by a benign environment, sometimes for lengthy periods of time, but minimal fit is required for survival in competitive environments. However, minimal fit, as the term implies, does not guarantee excellent performance.

## TIGHT FIT: THE FOUNDATION FOR EXCELLENCE

Corporate excellence requires more than minimal fit. Truly outstanding performance, achieved by many companies, is associated with tight fit—both externally with the environment and internally among strategy, structure, and management process. In fact, *tight fit is the causal force* at work when organizational excellence is said to be caused by various managerial and organizational characteristics.

In the late 1940s and early 1950s, Peter Drucker studied a number of top U.S. corporations, including General Motors, General Electric, IBM, and Sears, Roebuck.[10] Based on his observations, Drucker associated the widely acclaimed achievements of these organizations with such managerial characteristics as delegation and joint goal setting (MBO) and with organizational characteristics emphasizing the decentralization of operating decisions. He saw overstaffing as a threat to corporate responsiveness and argued that the best performance comes when jobs are enriched rather than narrowed. Finally, he felt that the overall key to the success of these companies was that they knew what business they were in, what their competencies were, and how to keep their efforts focused on their goals.

Some thirty years later, Thomas Peters and Robert Waterman studied 62 U.S. companies and produced their own checklist of characteristics associated with corporate excellence.[11] As had Drucker before them, they noted that organizations with records of sustained high performance tended to have a clear business focus, a bias for action, and lean structures and staffs that facilitated the pursuit of strategy.

Drucker clearly acknowledged the importance of organization structure and was convinced at the time that the federally decentralized (i.e., multidivisional) organization structure was the design of the future. He did not, however, probe the relationship between alternative strategies and their appropriate structures and management processes. Similarly, while Peters and Waterman stressed structural leanness and responsiveness as universally valuable characteristics, they also noted the requirement of achieving a close fit among the seven "S's" of strategy, structure, skills, systems, style, shared values, and staff (people). Again, however, Peters and Waterman did not discuss the possible alternative organization forms appropriate for different strategies. In our view, the observations of Drucker, Peters, and Waterman are accurate and extremely valuable. The discovery thirty years apart of the association of similar characteristics with organizational excellence is a powerful argument for the validity of that association—but it is not an explanation of why that association exists nor of the causal force that may be involved.

Both the managerial and organizational characteristics described by these observers, and the outstanding performance achieved by the organizations that they have examined, are the result of the achievement—by discovery or by design—of tight fit. That is, such characteristics as convergence on a set of core business values—doing what one does best, a lean action-oriented structure that provides opportunities for the full use of people's capabilities at all levels, etc.—essentially flow from the achievement of tight fit with the environment and among strategy, structure, and process. In short, the causal dynamic of tight fit tends to operate in four stages:

- First, the discovery of the basic structure and management processes necessary to support a chosen strategy create a *gestalt* that becomes so obvious and compelling that complex organizational and managerial demands appear to be simple.

- Second, *simplicity* leads to widespread understanding which reinforces and sustains fit. Or-

ganization structure and key management processes such as reward and control systems "teach" managers and employees the appropriate attitudes and behaviors for maintaining focus on strategic requirements.

- Third, simplicity *reduces the need for elaborate coordinating mechanisms*, thereby creating slack resources that can be reallocated elsewhere in the system.

- Fourth, as outstanding performance is achieved and sustained, its *association* with the process by which it is attained is reinforced, and this serves to further simplify the basic fit among strategy, structure, and process.

It should be emphasized that we do not specify "finding the right strategy" as an important element of this causal linkage. In fact, finding strategy-structure-process fit is usually far more important and problematic. It may be that there is less to strategy than meets the eye. At any moment, in any given industry, it is likely that several organizations are considering the same strategic moves; to diversify, retrench, acquire other firms, etc. For example, in the 1920s, the top executives of Sears, Roebuck did not have a secret crystal ball that forecast the effects of the automobile on retail trade. Indeed most organizations—including Sears' major competitor, Montgomery Ward—saw similar trends. It was the case, however, that well ahead of competitors Sears developed a structure that would allow it to operate as a high-quality, low-cost nationwide retailing organization.

It is valuable, of course, that the chosen strategy be articulated—for example, Sears pursued the image of "a hometown store with nationwide purchasing power." Nevertheless, it is when the blueprint of how to achieve such strategic goals is drawn that real understanding begins to emerge throughout the system. As clarity involving means emerges, that which was enormously complex and apparently beyond accomplishment, now seems straightforward and easy to achieve.

The process of searching for, discovering, and achieving tight fit is pervasive. At the individual level, for instance, learning to drive a car, fly an airplane, or serve a tennis ball are all activities that at first appear complex and difficult to learn but once mastered seem to be relatively simple. Mastery occurs, however, only when the gestalt is apprehended, felt, and understood. The same learning process occurs within organizations. The Baltimore Orioles, for example, believe they know how and why they won the recent World Series and have enjoyed success over the years. Strategy, structure, and process fit and are well understood by members at all levels of the organization. From the front office to the manager, coaches, and players (including those in the farm system), it seems clear how one goes about building a world-champion team. Much of the same could be said for Procter & Gamble, Johnson & Johnson, Minnesota Mining & Manufacturing, McDonald's, Schlumberger, and other excellent companies.

In sum, what we are suggesting is that focus, leanness, action, involvement, identification, etc., are likely *products* of tight fit. Fit simplifies complex organizational and managerial arrangements, and simple systems facilitate leanness, action, and many other observed manifestations of excellence. As one understands the system, one feels more a part of it, and as one's role becomes clear to self and others, participation is facilitated, almost demanded. Closeness and understanding provide a common culture, and stories and myths emerge that perpetuate key aspects of culture.

## EARLY FIT: A KEY TO THE HALL OF FAME?

To this point we have argued that minimal fit is necessary for an organization's survival and that tight fit is associated with excellent performance. We now suggest that *early fit—the discovery and articulation of a new organization form—can lead to sustained excellence* over considerable periods of time and thus a place in some mythical Hall of Fame.

Picking a Hall of Fame company is difficult. In sports, Hall of Fame performers are individuals who have been selected only after their careers are over, and sometimes selection is preceded by

an interval of several years so that the decision is relatively objective, based on complete information, and final. Organizations, on the other hand, are ongoing systems; therefore, any given Hall of Fame nominee might immediately have one or more "off" years. Nevertheless, some organizations would be likely to appear on every pundit's Hall of Fame list, and we believe that most of these organizations would share the characteristic of an early organizational breakthrough that was not quickly or easily matched by their competitors at the time.

There are, of course, many ways that companies can achieve a competitive advantage. For example, obtaining a patent on a particular product or technology gives a firm an edge on its competitors. Cornering the supply of a key raw material through location or judicious buying may permit a company to dominate a particular business. An innovative product design or the development of a new distribution channel can provide an organization with a competitive lead that is difficult to overcome. Yet all of these competitive advantages are more or less temporary—sooner or later competitors will imitate and improve upon the innovation and the advantage will disappear. Such abilities, therefore, do not guarantee induction into the Hall of Fame.

Sustained corporate excellence seems to have at least one necessary condition: the innovating or early application of—and rapid tight fit around—a new organization form. Achieving early fit succeeds over the proprietary advantages mentioned above because a new organization form cannot be completely copied in the short or even intermediate run. In this century, certain firms would appear to merit Hall of Fame nomination based on broad criteria such as product excellence, management performance, market share and responsiveness, and the like. We will discuss five of our own nominees all of which meet these criteria but also share the characteristic of early fit through invention or application of a new organization form: Carnegie Steel, General Motors, Sears, Roebuck, Hewlett-Packard, and IBM.

## Carnegie Steel

Carnegie Steel was one of the first companies to employ the fully-integrated functional organization form complete with centralized management and technical specialization.[12] In his early thirties, Andrew Carnegie left a position with the railroad to concentrate on manufacturing steel rails. Convinced that the management methods he and others had pioneered on the railroad could also be applied to the manufacturing sector, Carnegie essentially started the modern steel business in the U.S. and he played a major role in forging the world's first billion-dollar corporation, U.S. Steel.

At the heart of Carnegie Steel's success was its reliance on centralized management (particularly cost accounting and control) and full vertical integration. Carnegie recognized early the benefits of vertical integration in the fragmented, geographically dispersed steel industry in the latter half of the 19th century, and his company integrated backward into the purchase of ore deposits and the production of coke as well as forward into manufacture of finished steel products. Vertical integration permitted a new external alignment in the steel industry: substantially larger market areas could now be served much more quickly, efficiently, and profitably. Carnegie Steel supplemented its functional organization structure with careful plant design and transportation logistics, continuous technological improvements, successful (though limited) product diversification, and innovative human resources management practices and labor relations. Thus, internally, there was rapid development of a tight fit between management processes and the company's pioneering strategy and structure.

Carnegie Steel, of course, did not invent the vertically integrated, functional organization form; elements of the model were already available. However, the company's early and complete use of this form dramatically altered the steel business in a way that was not matched by competitors for decades. (See Table 46.1 for the evolution of major organization forms and our prediction of the next new form.)

## General Motors

General Motors has the strongest claim as the inventor of the "federally decentralized" or divisional organization structure. Among the early automobile makers, William C. Durant was one of the strongest believers in the enormous potential market for the moderate-priced car.[13] Acting on his beliefs, Durant put together a group of companies engaged in the making and selling of automobiles, parts, and accessories. In 1919, the total combined assets of Durant's General Motors made it the fifth largest company in the U.S. But although Durant had spotted a potentially large opportunity, and had moved rapidly to create an industrial empire to take advantage of it, he had little interest in developing an organization structure and management system for the enterprise he had created.

Indeed, in combining individual firms into General Motors, Durant relied on the same organizational approach of volume production and vertical integration that he had used in his previous managerial positions and that was popular at the time. However, this approach led to little more than an expanding agglomeration of different companies making automobiles, parts, accessories, trucks, tractors, and even refrigerators. An unforeseen collapse in the demand for automobiles in 1920 precipitated a financial crisis at General Motors, which was quickly followed by Durant's retirement as President. Pierre du Pont, who had been in semi-retirement from the chemical company, agreed to take the presidency of GM. One of du Pont's first actions was to approve a plan devised by Alfred P. Sloan, a high-level GM executive whose family firm had been purchased by Durant, that defined an organization structure for General Motors.

Sloan's plan, which went into effect in early 1921, called for a general office to coordinate, appraise, and set broad goals and policies for the numerous, loosely controlled operating divisions of GM. The general officers individually were to supervise and coordinate different groups of divisions and collectively were to help make policy for the corporation as a whole. Staff specialists

**TABLE 46.1**
Evolution of Organization Forms

|  | Product-Market Strategy | Organization Structure | Inventor or Early User | Core Activating and Control Mechanisms |
|---|---|---|---|---|
| 1800 | Single product or service. Local/regional markets | Agency | Numerous small owner-managed firms | Personal direction and control |
| 1850 | Limited, standardized product or service line. Regional/national markets | Functional | Carnegie Steel | Central plan and budgets |
| 1900 | Diversified, changing product or service line. National/international markets | Divisional | General Motors Sears Roebuck Hewlett-Packard | Corporate policies and division profit centers |
| 1950 | Standard and innovative products or services. Stable and changing markets | Matrix | Several aerospace and electronics firms (e.g., NASA, TRW, IBM, Texas Instruments) | Temporary teams and lateral resource allocation devices such as internal markets, joint planning systems, etc. |
| 2000 | Product or service design. Global changing markets | Dynamic network | International construction firms; Global consumer goods companies: Selected electronics and computer firms (e.g., IBM) | Broker-assembled temporary structures with shared information systems as basis for trust and coordination. |

were to advise and serve both the division managers and the general officers and to provide business and financial information necessary for appraising the performance of the individual units and for formulating overall policy. Although most of Sloan's proposals had been carried out by the end of 1921, it was not until 1925 that the original plan resulted in a smooth-running organization. The multidivisional decentralized structure allowed GM to diversify a standard product, the automobile, to meet a variety of consumer needs and tastes while maintaining overall corporate financial synergy.

From 1924 to 1927, General Motors' market share rose from 19 to 43 percent. Unlike its major competitor, Ford, which was devastated by the Depression, GM's profits grew steadily throughout the Depression and World War II. It has been the leading automobile manufacturer in the world since its implementation of the divisional structure and for years was the corporate model for similar structural changes in other large American industrial enterprises.

## Sears, Roebuck

Just as General Motors can make a strong claim to the invention of the divisional structure for product diversification, Sears, Roebuck can claim to have been one of the earliest users of this structure outside of manufacturing. Sears has long enjoyed its reputation as the world's most successful retailer.[14] Since its inception in 1895, Sears has undergone two periods where it achieved an "early fit" among its competitors. The first phase of the Sears story began in 1895 when Julius Rosenwald, a consummate administrator, joined Richard Sears, a brilliant merchandiser, and together they built a company catering to the American farmer. Sears, Roebuck's Chicago mail-order plant was a major innovation in the retailing business. Designed by Otto Doering in 1903, this modern mass-production plant preceded by five years Henry Ford's acclaimed automobile assembly line, and it ushered in the "distribution revolution" that was so vital a factor in early 20th century America's economic growth.

The second phase of the Sears story began in 1924 when Robert E. Wood left Montgomery Ward to join the company. Since farmers could now travel to cities in their automobiles and the urban population was more affluent, retail selling through local stores appeared to be more promising than mail-order sales. Promoted to President in 1928, Wood, with his new hand-picked management team, moved ahead rapidly to create a nationwide retail organization. Montgomery Ward and other retail chains of the period (e.g., J. C. Penney, Eaton's, Woolworth's, Grant's, Kresge's) have not been able to this day to match Sears' performance.

The organization form developed at Sears bore many similarities to GM's multidivisional structure, but it was geared toward retailing rather than manufacturing. Whereas GM diversified by product, Sears diversified by geographic territory. Each of the territorial units became full-fledged autonomous divisions with their managers responsible for overall operating results, and the Chicago headquarters remained a central office with staff specialists and general executives. Sears' ultimate tight internal and external fit was not accomplished nearly as rapidly as those of Carnegie Steel or General Motors, but it was achieved first among Sears' competitors and gave the company a competitive advantage that has not, until recently, been seriously threatened.

## Hewlett-Packard

The decentralized, divisional structure developed by General Motors and Sears (along with a few other outstanding companies such as Du Pont and Standard Oil of New Jersey) flourished in the 1950s under the spotlight of publicity from management consulting firms and from academics like Peter Drucker. For most companies, however, the divisional structure did not serve as a proprietary advantage but merely as a necessary means of maintaining alignment with a market demanding diversity. Nevertheless, one outstanding company, a Hall of Fame nominee on many early ballots, has taken this organization structure to new heights in its pursuit of leading-edge technological developments in an emerging industry. The company is Hewlett-Packard and the industry, of course, is electronics. Founded in 1939 by William Hewlett and David Packard, this company is the world's largest manufacturer of test and measurement instruments as well as a major producer of small computers. The company is noted for its strong corporate culture and nearly continuous high performance in a very demanding industrial environment.

From the beginning, Hewlett-Packard has pursued a strategy that brings the products of scientific research into industrial application while maintaining the collegial atmosphere of a university laboratory. This means that the firm concentrates on advanced technology and offers mostly state-of-the-art products to a variety of industrial and consumer markets. A given product line and market are actively pursued as long as the company has a distinctive technological or design advantage. When products reach the stage where successful competition depends primarily on low costs and prices, Hewlett-Packard often moves out of the arena and turns its attention to a new design or an entirely new product. As a company that achieved early fit, its technological diversification rivals General Motors' product diversification and Sears' territorial diversification.

Hewlett-Packard's strategy of technological innovation is supported by an organization structure and management system that may be unparalleled in flexibility. The fundamental business unit is the product division, an integrated, self-sustaining organization with a great deal of independence. New divisions arise when a particular product line becomes large enough to support its continued growth out of the profit it generates. Also, new divisions tend to emerge when a single division gets so large that the people involved start to lose their identification with the product line. Most human resources management practices—especially those concerning hiring, placement, and rewards—are appropriately matched with the company's structural and strategic decentralization.

## International Business Machines

Any Hall of Fame list must include IBM.[15] One of the largest producers of calculating, computing, and office machinery, IBM is arguably the best managed company in the United States, perhaps the world. Paradoxically, IBM's nomination to the Hall of Fame cannot be based on the invention of a particular organization form—nor, for that matter, a management innovation or technological break-through. The company is simply good at everything it does; it is a polydextrous organization that is consistently quick to adopt and refine any approach that it can use to its advantage.

The company was born when Thomas Watson, Sr., joined the Computing-Recording Corporation in 1914 and renamed it International Business Machines in 1924. However, the modern IBM dates to the stewardship of Thomas Watson, Jr., who was chief executive officer from 1956 to 1971. Today IBM is the most profitable U.S. industrial company, and its form of organization is a combination of time-honored and advanced approaches.

IBM takes advantage of two key characteristics of the functional organization, vertical integration and production efficiency. For example, IBM is the world's largest manufacturer of memory chips and installs its entire output in its own machines. And beginning in the late 1970s, a series of huge capital improvements has made IBM one of the most automated and lowest-cost producers in the industry.

IBM has also relied to a limited extent on acquisitions, a characteristic most often associated with the divisional organization. Unlike many large conglomerates, the company is very selective about its acquisitions, the most recent of which is intended to help IBM create the futuristic electronic office.

Finally, IBM uses a variety of the most advanced approaches to organization and management. First, the company has created at least 15 internal new ventures groups in the last few years to explore new business opportunities. The new units are independently run, but they can draw on IBM resources. Second, the company has increased its use of subcontracting. In its most recent product venture, the personal computer, IBM relied largely on parts obtained from outside suppliers and is selling the machine through retail outlets like Sears and ComputerLand as well as its own sales network. Software for the machine was developed by inviting numerous software firms to supply ideas and materials. Third, besides being a vigorous competitor, IBM has formed many successful cooperative agreements with other companies, especially in Japan and Europe. It is generally acknowledged that substantially more cooperative arrangements involving business firms, as well as governments and universities, will be needed in coming years to supplement traditional competitive practices. And, lastly, IBM is international in scope. It is the leading computer firm in virtually every one of the approximately 130 countries where it does business.

In sum, a close, current look at the Hall of Fame companies just described would probably not uncover the maintenance of perfect fit. As suggested earlier, even these organizations are vulnerable to external and internal slippage, perhaps even distortion. Therefore, it is important to explore the processes by which tight fit may be eroded.

## THE FRAGILITY OF FIT

As noted earlier, fit is a process as well as a state. Environmental factors outside an organization's control are constantly changing and may require incremental or major strategic adjustment. Strategic change, in turn, is likely to require changes in organization structure and/or management processes. When environmental jolts are extreme, some organizations may be unwilling or unable to adjust—recall the earlier examples from the tobacco industry and witness the recent plight of several airline companies under deregulation.

However, environmental change is not the only cause of alignment deterioration. For example, misfit may occur when organizations voluntarily change their strategies but fail to follow through with appropriate structural and managerial adjustments, as illustrated by the case of Chrysler. An even more intriguing alignment-threatening process is also demonstrable, one which may well account for more deterioration of fit than either environmental jolts or unsupported strategic changes. This process involves voluntary internal structure and process changes that are made without concern for their longer-run consequences for strategy and market responsiveness. Although usually subtle and long-term in its development, this process of internal unraveling underscores the point that an organization's fit at any given time may be quite fragile.

Recall the earlier description of how the discovery of tight fit results in system simplicity: When strategy, structure, and process are completely aligned, both goals and means are visible, and task requirements are obvious and compelling. Resources previously required for coordination or troubleshooting can be redeployed in the primary system, and even tighter fit may result. However, as the spotlight of tight fit illuminates the overall system for everyone to see and understand, its bright glare may also begin to highlight the organization's inherent deficiencies. That is, each pattern of fit has its own distinct contribution to make. For example, the functional organization form is ideal for efficient production of standard goods or services and the divisional form is most appropriate for diversification. Each form not only has its own strengths but also its own built-in limitations. The form best suited for efficiency is vulnerable to market change, and the form suited to diversification is sometimes clearly redundant.

As the pattern of fit becomes increasingly clear to managers and employees of excellent (tight fit) companies, they can easily describe why the organization prospers. But at least some members of these same companies can also point to the system's shortcomings. For example, in a vertically integrated, centralized, functional organization, perceptive managers will advocate the creation of task forces, project groups, or even separate divisions to facilitate quick development of new products or services. Conversely, one can anticipate in a decentralized, divisional structure that cost-conscious managers will suggest standardizing certain components or services across divisions in order to reduce redundancy and achieve scale economies. Most organizations regularly make minor adjustments in their structures and processes to accommodate demands for which their systems were not designed. In some organizations, however, what begins as a limited adjustment may over time grow into a crippling, step-by-step unraveling of the entire system. Moreover, this may occur without conscious long-term planning or even awareness. Two brief examples, both associated with companies on our Hall of Fame list, serve as illustrations.

At General Motors, once Sloan's federally decentralized structure was fully in place, managers began to recommend standardization of various product components and production processes. Some aspects of engineering and production had been coordinated across divisions from the beginning, but the advocates of full-scale standardization finally began to override the divisional structure in the 1950s. Many readers may recall the "scandal" that occurred when buyers discovered that the General Motors' engine in their cars had not been made by that division and, in some cases, even by a division of lower status. In fact, those engines had been manufactured according to policies that reflected increasing interdivisional coordination and centralization of decision making. During the 1950s and 1960s when General Motors appeared invulnerable to competition—foreign or domestic—the cost of increased centralization and coordination was probably not visible. It almost appeared that the company could have its diversity and its cost savings, too. One wonders how much more rapidly General Motors might have responded to the challenge of foreign competition if it had been able to do so by simply aiming the operations of one autonomous division toward Japan and another toward Europe. In general, the more attention that is devoted to the known shortcomings of a particular organization form, the more likely is the possibility of unraveling a successful fit.

Could a similar process occur at Hewlett-Packard? In recent months, the company has been beset with problems caused by its decentralized management system and entrepreneurial culture, including overlapping products, lagging development of new technology, and a piecemeal approach to key markets.[16] The response to these problems was the launching of several programs to improve planning, coordinate marketing, and strengthen the firm's computer-related research and development efforts.

Hewlett-Packard's current CEO, John Young, recognizes that these organizational changes involve trade-offs; the benefits obtained from cross-divisional coordination have to be weighed against the threats to the entrepreneurial spirit of the various divisions. That is, the use of program managers and strategic coordinators to align product designs, to force the divisions to share components, and to coordinate pricing and marketing strategies has generated a number of successful cross-divisional development projects. However, these successes have been offset by a wave of manager and engineer defections to other companies. Thus, only time will tell if this reorganization improves the company's internal fit or begins to unravel the core threads among strategy, structure, and process that have produced Hewlett-Packard's success.

The moral of these examples is not that managers of excellent companies should not try to improve performance. Rather, it is that rearranging organization structure and management systems may in some cases preclude an organization from pursuing its desired strategy. Managers of truly outstanding companies recognize the strengths and limitations of alternate organization forms, and they will not undo a crucial link among strategy, structure, or process in order to "solve" predictable problems.

# FUTURE FIT:
# A NEW ORGANIZATION FORM

Our argument concerning the effects of minimal, tight, and early fit on organizational performance is based on the belief that the search for fit has been visible in organizations for at least the past 100 years. But will this search continue in the future? We believe it will. In fact, many managers are now considering a new organization form and are experimenting with its major components and processes in their organizations. The reality of this new form, therefore, simply awaits articulation and understanding.

In this century, there have been three major breakthroughs in the way organizations have been designed and managed (see again Table 46.1). The first breakthrough occurred at the turn of the century in the form of the functional organization. Prior to that time, small firms had relied on an informal structure in which the owner-manager's immediate subordinates acted as all-purpose "agents" of the chief executive, solving whatever problems arose. There was very little of the technical specialization found in today's organizations. The functional form allowed those companies that adopted it to become very large and to specialize in a limited set of products and markets. Next came the divisional form, which facilitated even more organizational growth, but, more importantly, it facilitated diversification in both products and markets. The third breakthrough was the matrix structure in which elements of the functional and divisional forms were combined into a single system able to accommodate both standard and innovative products or projects.

Now a promising new organization form is emerging, one that appears to fit the fast-approaching conditions of the 21st century. As was true of previous forms, elements of this new form are sprouting in several companies and industries simultaneously.

■ *Large construction firms.* The construction industry has long been known for its use of subcontracting to accomplish large, complex tasks.

Today, the size and complexity of a construction project can be immense, as evidenced by the multinational consortium of companies now building an entire city in Saudi Arabia. Under such circumstances, companies must be able to form a network of reliable subcontractors, many of them large firms which have not worked together before. Some companies, therefore, have found it advantageous to focus only on the overall design and management of a project, leaving the actual construction to their affiliates.

■ *Global consumer goods companies.* Standardized products such as clothes, cameras, and watches can be designed, manufactured, and marketed throughout the world. Companies engaged in this type of business are prime examples of the "world enterprise": buying raw materials wherever they are cheapest, manufacturing wherever costs are lowest, and selling wherever the products will bring the highest price. To do so, however, requires many different brokers—individuals and groups who bring together complementary resources. All of the participants in the process—designers, suppliers, manufacturers, distributors, etc.—must be coupled into a smooth-running operation even though they are continents apart.

■ *Electronics and computer firms.* Certain firms in these industries already are dealing with conditions that in the future will be widespread: rapid change, demassification, high technology, information abundance, and so on.[17] In these companies, product life cycles are often short and all firms live under the constant threat of technological innovations that can change the structure of the industry. Individual firms must constantly redesign their processes around new products. Across the industry, spinoff firms are continually emerging. Thus, a common development model includes venture capitalists working with high-technology entrepreneurs in the development, manufacture, and distribution of innovative products or services.

Across these three examples, some key characteristics of the new organization form are clearly visible. Organizations of the future are likely to be *vertically disaggregated*: functions typically encompassed within a single organization will instead be performed in independent organizations. That is, the functions of product design and development, manufacturing, and distribution, ordinarily integrated by a plan and controlled directly by managers, will instead be brought together by *brokers* and held in temporary alignment by a variety of *market mechanisms*.

For example, one form of a vertically disaggregated organization held together by a market mechanism is the franchise system, symbolized by McDonald's or H&R Block. In a franchise system, both the product or service and its basic recipe are provided by the parent corporation to a local management group. Such a model, however, seems appropriate only for a limited set of standard goods or services. In our view, a more flexible and comprehensive approach—and hence a better analog of the organization of the future—is the "designer" system associated with companies such as Yves St. Laurent or Gucci. In these companies, design skills can be applied in a variety of arenas, from electronics to household goods to personal products or services. Similarly, production expertise can be contracted for and applied to a wide array of products or services, as can skills in marketing and distribution. Thus, we expect the 21st century firm to be a temporary organization, brought together by an entrepreneur with the aid of brokers and maintained by a network of contractual ties. In some instances, a single entrepreneur will play a lead role and subcontract for various services. This same individual may also serve as a consultant to others attempting to form their own organizational networks. In other cases, linkages among equals may be created by request through various brokers specializing in a particular service.

Given these characteristics, we have found it useful to refer to this emerging form as the *dynamic network* organization. However, the full realization of this new type of organization awaits the development of a core activating and control mechanism comparable to those that energized the previous organization forms (e.g., the profit center in the divisional form). Our prediction is that this mechanism essentially will be a broad-access computerized information system. Note that most of today's temporary organizations (e.g., a general contractor) have been put together on the basis of lengthy experience among the key participants. Under future conditions of high complexity and rapid change, however, participants in the network organization will first have to be identified, trust between the parties will be a major issue, and fixed-fee contracts specified in advance will usually not be feasible. Therefore, as a substitute for lengthy trust-building processes, participants will have to agree on a general structure of payment for value added and then hook themselves together in a full-disclosure information system so that contributions can be mutually and instantaneously verified. Properly constructed, the dynamic network organization will display the technical expertise of the functional form, the market focus of the divisional form, and the efficient use of resources characteristic of the matrix. And, especially important, it will be able to quickly reshape itself whenever necessary.

## CONCLUSION

The United States is in a period of economic challenge and organizational upheaval. There are myriad prescriptions for industrial and organizational renewal, and many of the factors linked to organizational success are being rediscovered today after a thirty-year hiatus. Our own analysis, however, indicates that these characteristics, while important, are merely manifestations of a more fundamental, dynamic process called fit—the search for an organization form that is both internally and externally consistent. We have argued that minimal fit is necessary for survival, tight fit is associated with corporate excellence, and early fit provides a competitive advantage that can lead to the organization Hall of Fame. Tomorrow's Hall of Fame companies are working on new organization forms today.

## REFERENCES

1. Raymond E. Miles and Charles C. Snow, *Organizational Strategy, Structure, and Process* (New York: McGraw-Hill, 1978).

2. Alfred D. Chandler, Jr., *Strategy and Structure* (New York: Doubleday, 1962).

3. Tom Burns and G. M. Stalker, *The Management of Innovation* (London: Tavistock, 1961).

4. Paul R. Lawrence and Jay W. Lorsch, *Organization and Environment* (Boston: Harvard Graduate School of Business Administration, 1967).

5. Michael E. Porter, *Competitive Strategy* (New York: Free Press, 1980).

6. Michael T. Hannan and John H. Freeman, "The Population Ecology of Organizations," *American Journal of Sociology*, vol. 82 (March 1977): 929–964; and Howard E. Aldrich, *Organizations and Environments* (Englewood Cliffs, NJ: Prentice-Hall, 1979).

7. Charles C. Snow and Lawrence G. Hrebiniak, "Strategy, Distinctive Competence, and Organizational Performance," *Administrative Science Quarterly*, vol. 25 (June 1980): 317–336.

8. Robert H. Miles, *Coffin Nails and Corporate Strategies* (Englewood Cliffs, NJ: Prentice-Hall, 1980).

9. The description of Chrysler Corporation was adapted from James Brian Quinn, *Chrysler Corporation*, copyrighted case, The Amos Tuck School of Business Administration, Dartmouth College, 1977.

10. Peter F. Drucker, *The Practice of Management* (New York: Harper & Row, 1954).

11. Thomas J. Peters and Robert H. Waterman, *In Search of Excellence: Lessons from America's Best Run Companies* (New York: Free Press, 1983), Chapter 3.

12. The description of Carnegie Steel was adapted from Paul R. Lawrence and Davis Dyer, *Renewing American Industry* (New York: Free Press, 1983), Chapter 3.

13. The description of General Motors was adapted from Chandler, op. cit., Chapter 3.

14. The description of Sears, Roebuck was adapted from Chandler, op. cit., Chapter 5; and from Drucker, op. cit. Chapter 4.

15. The description of IBM was adapted from "The Colossus That Works," *Time*, July 11, 1983, pp. 44–54.

16. "Can John Young Redesign Hewlett-Packard?" *Business Week*, December 6, 1982, pp. 72–78.

17. For a complete discussion of these conditions, see Alvin Toffler, *The Third Wave* (New York: Bantam Books, 1981); and John Naisbitt, *Megatrends* (New York: Warner Books, 1982).

# 47.  CONVERGENCE AND UPHEAVAL: MANAGING THE UNSTEADY PACE OF ORGANIZATION EVOLUTION

Michael Tushman, William Newman, and Elaine Romanelli

A snug fit of external opportunity, company strategy, and internal structure is a hallmark of successful companies. The real test of executive leadership, however, is in maintaining this alignment in the face of changing competitive conditions.

Consider the Polaroid or Caterpillar corporations. Both firms virtually dominated their respective industries for decades, only to be caught off guard by major environmental changes. The same strategic and organizational factors which were so effective for decades became the seeds of complacency and organization decline.

Recent studies of companies over long periods show that the most successful firms maintain a workable equilibrium for several years (or decades), but are also able to initiate and carry out sharp, widespread changes (referred to here as reorientations) when their environments shift. Such upheaval may bring renewed vigor to the enterprise. Less successful firms, on the other hand, get stuck in a particular pattern. The leaders of these firms either do not see the need for reorientation or they are unable to carry through the necessary frame-breaking changes. While not all reorientations succeed, those organizations which do not initiate reorientations as environments shift underperform.

This article focuses on reasons why for long periods most companies make only incremental changes, and why they then need to make painful, discontinuous, system-wide shifts. We are particularly concerned with the role of executive leadership in managing this pattern of convergence punctuated by upheaval. Here are four examples of the convergence/upheaval pattern:

■ Founded in 1915 by a set of engineers from MIT, the General Radio Company was established to produce highly innovative and high-quality (but expensive) electronic test equipment. Over the years, General Radio developed a consistent organization to accomplish its mission. It hired only the brightest young engineers, built a loose functional organization dominated by the engineering department, and developed a "General Radio culture" (for example, no conflict, management by consensus, slow growth). General Radio's strategy and associated structures, systems, and people were very successful. By World War II, General Radio was the largest test-equipment firm in the United States.

After World War II, however, increasing technology and cost-based competition began to erode General Radio's market share. While management made numerous incremental changes, General Radio remained fundamentally the same organization. In the late 1960s, when CEO Don Sinclair initiated strategic changes, he left the firm's structure and systems intact. This effort at doing new things with established systems and procedures was less than successful. By 1972, the firm incurred its first loss.

In the face of this sustained performance decline, Bill Thurston (a long-time General Radio executive) was made President. Thurston initiated system-wide changes. General Radio adopted a more marketing-oriented strategy. Its product line was cut from 20 different lines to 3; much more emphasis was given to product-line management, sales, and marketing. Resources were diverted from engineering to revitalize sales, marketing, and production. During 1973, the firm moved to a matrix structure, increased its emphasis on controls and systems, and went outside for a set of executives to help Thurston run this revised General Radio. To perhaps more formally symbolize these changes and the sharp move away from the "old" General Radio, the firm's name was changed to GenRad. By 1984, GenRad's sales exploded to over $200 million (vs. $44 million in 1972).

After 60 years of convergent change around a constant strategy, Thurston and his colleagues (many new to the firm) made discontinuous system-wide changes in strategy, structure, people, and processes. While traumatic, these changes were implemented over a two-year period and led to a dramatic turnaround in GenRad's performance.

■ Prime Computer was founded in 1971 by a group of individuals who left Honeywell. Prime's initial strategy was to produce a high-quality/high-price minicomputer based on semiconductor memory. These founders built an engineering-dominated, loosely structured firm which sold to OEMs and through distributors. This configuration of strategy, structure, people, and processes was very successful. By 1974, Prime turned its first profit; by 1975, its sales were more than $11 million.

In the midst of this success, Prime's board of directors brought in Ken Fisher to reorient the organization. Fisher and a whole new group of executives hired from Honeywell initiated a set of discontinuous changes throughout Prime during 1975–1976. Prime now sold a full range of minicomputers and computer systems to OEMs and end-users. To accomplish this shift in strategy, Prime adopted a more complex functional structure, with a marked increase in resources to sales and marketing. The shift in resources away from engineering was so great that Bill Poduska, Prime's head of engineering, left to form Apollo Computer. Between 1975–1981, Fisher and his colleagues consolidated and incrementally adapted structure, systems, and processes to better accomplish the new strategy. During this convergent period, Prime grew dramatically to over $260 million by 1981.

In 1981, again in the midst of this continuing sequence of increased volume and profits, Prime's board again initiated an upheaval. Fisher and his direct reports left Prime (some of whom founded Encore Computer), while Joe Henson and a set of executives from IBM initiated wholesale changes throughout the organization. The firm diversified into robotics, CAD/CAM, and office systems; adopted a divisional structure; developed a more market-driven orientation; and increased controls and systems. It remains to be seen how this "new" Prime will fare. Prime must be seen, then, not as a 14-year-old firm, but as three very different organizations, each of which was managed by a different set of executives. Unlike General Radio, Prime initiated these discontinuities during periods of great success.

■ The Operating Group at Citibank prior to 1970 had been a service-oriented function for the end-user areas of the bank. The Operating Group hired high school graduates who remained in the "back-office" for their entire careers. Structure, controls, and systems were loose, while the informal organization valued service, responsiveness to client needs, and slow, steady work habits. While these patterns were successful enough, increased demand and heightened customer expectations led to ever decreasing performance during the late 1960s.

In the face of severe performance decline, John Reed was promoted to head the Operating Group. Reed recruited several executives with production backgrounds, and with this new top team he initiated system-wide changes. Reed's vision was to transform the Operating Group from a *service*-oriented back office to a *factory* producing high-quality products. Consistent with this new mission, Reed and his colleagues initiated sweeping changes in strategy, structure, work flows, controls, and culture. These changes were initiated concurrently throughout the back office, with very little participation, over the course of a few months. While all the empirical performance measures improved substantially, these changes also generated substantial stress and anxiety within Reed's group.

■ For 20 years, Alpha Corporation was among the leaders in the industrial fastener industry. Its reliability, low cost, and good technical service were important strengths. However, as Alpha's segment of the industry matured, its profits declined. Belt-tightening helped but was not enough. Finally, a new CEO presided over a sweeping restructuring: cutting the product line, closing a plant, trimming overhead; then focusing on computer parts which call for very close tolerances, CAD/CAM tooling, and cooperation with customers on design efforts. After four rough years, Alpha appears to have found a new niche where convergence will again be warranted.

These four short examples illustrate periods of incremental change, or convergence, punctuated by discontinuous changes throughout the organization. Discontinuous or "frame-breaking" change involves simultaneous and sharp shifts in strategy, power, structure, and controls. Each example illustrates the role of executive leadership in initiating and implementing discontinuous change. Where General Radio, Citibank's Operating Group, and Alpha initiated system-wide changes only after sustained performance decline, Prime proactively initiated system-wide changes to take advantage of competitive/technological conditions. These patterns in organization evolution are not unique. Upheaval, sooner or later, follows convergence if a company is to survive; only a farsighted minority of firms initiate upheaval prior to incurring performance declines.

The task of managing incremental change, or convergence, differs sharply from managing frame-breaking change. Incremental change is compatible with the existing structure of a company and is reinforced over a period of years. In contrast, frame-breaking change is abrupt, painful to participants, and often resisted by the old guard. Forging these new strategy-structure-people-process consistencies and laying the basis for the next period of incremental change calls for distinctive skills.

Because the future health, and even survival, of a company or business unit is at stake, we need to take a closer look at the nature and consequences of convergent change and of differences imposed by frame-breaking change. We need to explore when and why these painful and risky revolutions interrupt previously successful patterns, and whether these discontinuities can be avoided and/or initiated prior to crisis. Finally, we need to examine what managers can and should do to guide their organizations through periods of convergence and upheaval over time.

## THE RESEARCH BASE

The research which sparks this article is based on the abundant company histories and case studies. The more complete case studies have tracked individual firms' evolution and various crises in great detail (e.g., Chandler's seminal study of strategy and structure at Du Pont, General Motors, Standard Oil, and Sears[1]). More recent studies have dealt systematically with whole sets of

companies and trace their experience over long periods of time.

A series of studies by researchers at McGill University covered over 40 well-known firms in diverse industries for at least 20 years per firm (e.g., Miller & Friesen[2]). Another research program conducted by researchers at Columbia, Duke, and Cornell Universities is tracking the history of large samples of companies in the minicomputer, cement, airlines, and glass industries. This research program builds on earlier work (e.g., Greiner[3]) and finds that most successful firms evolve through long periods of convergence punctuated by frame-breaking change.

The following discussion is based on the history of companies in many different industries, different countries, both large and small organizations, and organizations in various stages of their product class's life-cycle. We are dealing with a widespread phenomenon—not just a few dramatic sequences. Our research strongly suggests that the convergence/upheaval pattern occurs within departments (e.g., Citibank's Operating Group), at the business-unit level (e.g., Prime or General Radio), and at the corporate level of analysis (e.g., the Singer, Chrysler, or Harris Corporations). The problem of managing both convergent periods and upheaval is not just for the CEO, but necessarily involves general managers as well as functional managers.

## PATTERNS IN ORGANIZATIONAL EVOLUTION: CONVERGENCE AND UPHEAVAL

### Building on Strength: Periods of Convergence

Successful companies wisely stick to what works well. At General Radio between 1915 and 1950, the loose functional structure, committee management system, internal promotion practices, control with engineering, and the high-quality, premium-price, engineering mentality all worked together to provide a highly congruent system. These internally consistent patterns in strategy, structure, people, and processes served General Radio for over 35 years.

Similarly, the Alpha Corporation's customer driven, low-cost strategy was accomplished by strength in engineering and production and ever more detailed structures and systems which evaluated cost, quality, and new product development. These strengths were epitomized in Alpha's chief engineer and president. The chief engineer had a remarkable talent for helping customers find new uses for industrial fasteners. He relished solving such problems, while at the same time designing fasteners that could be easily manufactured. The president excelled at production—producing dependable, low-cost fasteners. The pair were role models which set a pattern which served Alpha well for 15 years.

As the company grew, the chief engineer hired kindred customer-oriented application engineers. With the help of innovative users, they developed new products, leaving more routine problem-solving and incremental change to the sales and production departments. The president relied on a hands-on manufacturing manager and delegated financial matters to a competent treasurer-controller. Note how well the organization reinforced Alpha's strategy and how the key people fit the organization. There was an excellent fit between strategy and structure. The informal structure also fit well—communications were open, the simple mission of the company was widely endorsed, and routines were well understood.

As the General Radio and Alpha examples suggest, convergence starts out with an effective dovetailing of strategy, structure, people, and processes. For other strategies or in other industries, the particular formal and informal systems might be very different, but still a winning combination. The formal system includes decisions about grouping and linking resources as well as planning and control systems, rewards and evaluation procedures, and human resource management systems. The informal system includes core values, beliefs, norms, communication patterns, and actual decision-making and conflict resolution patterns. It is the whole fabric of structure,

systems, people, and processes which must be suited to company strategy.[4]

As the fit between strategy, structure, people, and processes is never perfect, convergence is an ongoing process characterized by incremental change. Over time, in all companies studied, two types of converging changes were common: fine-tuning and incremental adaptations.

- *Converging Change: Fine-Tuning*—Even with good strategy-structure-process fits, well-run companies seek even better ways of exploiting (and defending) their missions. Such effort typically deals with one or more of the following:

  - *Refining* policies, methods, and procedures.
  - Creating *specialized units and linking mechanisms* to permit increased volume and increased attention to unit quality and cost.
  - *Developing* personnel especially suited to the present strategy—through improved selection and training, and tailoring reward systems to match strategic thrusts.
  - Fostering individual and group *commitments* to the company mission and to the excellence of one's own department.
  - Promoting *confidence* in the accepted norms, beliefs, and myths.
  - *Clarifying* established roles, power, status, dependencies, and allocation mechanism.

The fine-tuning fills out and elaborates the consistencies between strategy, structure, people, and processes. These incremental changes lead to an ever more interconnected (and therefore more stable) social system. Convergent periods fit the happy, stick-with-a-winner situations romanticized by Peters and Waterman.[5]

- *Converging Change: Incremental Adjustments to Environmental Shifts*—In addition to fine-tuning changes, minor shifts in the environment will call for some organizational response. Even the most conservative of organizations expect, even welcome, small changes which do not make too many waves.

A popular expression is that almost any organization can tolerate a "ten-percent change." At any one time, only a few changes are being made; but these changes are still compatible with the prevailing structures, systems, and processes. Examples of such adjustments are an expansion in sales territory, a shift in emphasis among products in the product line, or improved processing technology in production.

The usual process of making changes of this sort is well known: wide acceptance of the need for change, openness to possible alternatives, objective examination of the pros and cons of each plausible alternative, participation of those directly affected in the preceding analysis, a market test or pilot operation where feasible, time to learn the new activities, established role models, known rewards for positive success, evaluation, and refinement

The role of executive leadership during convergent periods is to reemphasize mission and core values and to delegate incremental decisions to middle-level managers. Note that the uncertainty created for people affected by such changes is well within tolerable limits. Opportunity is provided to anticipate and learn what is new, while most features of the structure remain unchanged.

The overall system adapts, but it is not transformed.

*Converging Change: Some Consequences.* For those companies whose strategies fit environmental conditions, convergence brings about better and better effectiveness. Incremental change is relatively easy to implement and ever more optimizes the consistencies between strategy, structure, people, and processes. At AT&T, for example, the period between 1913 and 1980 was one of ever more incremental change to further bolster the "Ma Bell" culture, systems, and structure all in service of developing the telephone network.

Convergent periods are, however, a double-edged sword. As organizations grow and become more successful, they develop internal forces for stability. Organization structures and systems become so interlinked that they only allow compatible changes. Further, over time, employees develop habits, patterned behaviors begin to take on values (e.g., "service is good"), and employees develop a sense of competence in knowing how to get work done within the system. These self-reinforcing patterns of behavior, norms, and values contribute to increased organizational momentum and complacency and, over time, to a sense of organizational history. This organizational history—epitomized by common stories, heroes, and standards—specifies "how we work here" and "what we hold important here."

This organizational momentum is profoundly functional as long as the organization's strategy is appropriate. The Ma Bell and General Radio culture, structure, and systems—and associated internal momentum—were critical to each organization's success. However, if (and when) strategy must change, this momentum cuts the other way. Organizational history is a source of tradition, precedent, and pride which are, in turn, anchors to the past. A proud history often restricts vigilant problem solving and may be a source of resistance to change.

When faced with environmental threat, organizations with strong momentum

- may not register the threat due to organization complacency and/or stunted external vigilance (e.g., the automobile or steel industries), or
- if the threat is recognized, the response is frequently heightened conformity to the status quo and/or increased commitment to "what we do best."

For example, the response of dominant firms to technological threat is frequently increased commitment to the obsolete technology (e.g., telegraph/telephone; vacuum tube/transistor; core/semiconductor memory). A paradoxical result of long periods of success may be heightened organizational complacency, decreased organizational flexibility, and a stunted ability to learn.

Converging change is a double-edged sword. Those very social and technical consistencies which are key sources of success may also be the seeds of failure if environments change.

The longer the convergent period, the greater these internal forces for stability. This momentum seems to be particularly accentuated in those most successful firms in a product class (for example, Polaroid, Caterpillar, or U.S. Steel), in historically regulated organizations (for example, AT&T, GTE, or financial service firms), or in organizations that have been traditionally shielded from competition (for example, universities, not-for-profit organizations, government agencies and/or services).

## On Frame-Breaking Change

*Forces Leading to Frame-Breaking Change.* What, then, leads to frame-breaking change? Why defy tradition? Simply stated, frame-breaking change occurs in response to or, better yet, in anticipation of major environmental changes—changes which require more than incremental adjustments. The need for discontinuous change springs from one or a combination of the following:

- *Industry Discontinuities*—Sharp changes in legal, political, or technological conditions shift the basis of competition within industries. *Deregulation* has dramatically transformed the financial services and airlines industries. *Substitute product technologies* (such as jet engines, electronic typing, microprocessors) or *substitute process technologies* (such as the planar process in semiconductors or float-glass in glass manufacture) may transform the bases of competition within industries. Similarly, the emergence of industry standards, or *dominant designs* (such as the DC-3, IBM 360, or PDP-8) signal a shift in competition away from product innovation and towards increased process innovation. Finally, *major economic changes* (e.g., oil crises) and *legal shifts* (e.g., patent protection in biotechnology or trade/regulator barriers in pharmaceuticals or cigarettes) also directly affect bases of competition.

- *Product-Life-Cycle Shifts*—Over the course of a product class lifecycle, different strategies are appropriate. In the emergence phase of a product class, competition is based on product innovation and performance, where in the maturity stage, competition centers on cost, volume, and efficiency. Shifts in patterns of demand alter key factors for success. For example, the demand and nature of competition for minicomputers, cellular telephones, wide-body aircraft, and bowling alley equipment was transformed as these products gained acceptance and their product classes evolved. Powerful international competition may compound these forces.

- *Internal Company Dynamics*—Entwined with these external forces are breaking points within the firm. Sheer size may require a basically new management design. For example, few inventor-entrepreneurs can tolerate the formality that is linked with large volume; even Digital Equipment Company apparently has outgrown the informality so cherished by Kenneth Olsen. Key people die. Family investors may become more concerned with their inheritance taxes than with company development. Revised corporate portfolio strategy may sharply alter the role and resources assigned to business units or functional areas. Such pressures, especially when coupled with external changes, may trigger frame-breaking change.

*Scope of Frame-Breaking Change.* Frame-breaking change is driven by shifts in business strategy. As strategy shifts so too must structure, people, and organizational processes. Quite unlike convergent change, frame-breaking reforms involve discontinuous changes throughout the organization. These bursts of change do not reinforce the existing system and are implemented rapidly. For example, the system-wide changes at Prime and General Radio were implemented over 18–24-month periods, whereas changes in Citibank's Operating Group were implemented in less than five months. Frame-breaking changes are revolutionary changes *of* the system as opposed to incremental changes *in* the system.

The following features are usually involved in frame-breaking change:

- *Reformed Mission and Core Values*—A strategy shift involves a new definition of company mission. Entering or withdrawing from an industry may be involved; at least the way the company expects to be outstanding is altered. The revamped AT&T is a conspicuous example. Success on its new course calls for a strategy based on competition, aggressiveness, and responsiveness, as well as a revised set of core values about how the firm competes and what it holds as important. Similarly, the initial shift at Prime reflected a strategic shift away from technology and towards sales and marketing. Core values also were aggressively reshaped by Ken Fisher to complement Prime's new strategy.

- *Altered Power and Status*—Frame-breaking change always alters the distribution of power. Some groups lose in the shift while others gain. For example, at Prime and General Radio, the engineering functions lost power, resources, and prestige as the marketing and sales functions gained. These dramatically altered power distributions reflect shifts in bases of competition and resource allocation. A new strategy must be backed up with a shift in the balance of power and status.

- *Reorganization*—A new strategy requires a modification in structure, systems, and procedures. As strategic requirements shift, so too must the choice of organization form. A new direction calls for added activity in some areas and less in others. Changes in structure and systems are means to ensure that this reallocation of effort takes place. New structures and revised roles deliberately break business-as-usual behavior.

- *Revised Interaction Patterns*—The way people in the organization work together has to adapt during frame-breaking change. As strategy is different, new procedures, work flows, communication networks, and decision-making patterns must be established. With these changes in work flows and procedures must also come revised norms, informal decision-making/conflict-resolution procedures, and informal roles.

- *New Executives*—Frame-breaking change also involves new executives, usually brought in from outside the organization (or business unit) and placed in key managerial positions. Commitment to the new mission, energy to overcome prevailing inertia, and freedom from prior obligations are all needed to refocus the organization. A few exceptional members of the old guard may attempt to make this shift, but habits and expectations of their associations are difficult to break. New executives are most likely to provide both the necessary drive and an enhanced set of skills more appropriate for the new strategy. While the overall number of executive changes is usually relatively small, these new executives have substantial symbolic and substantive effects on the organization. For example, frame-breaking changes at Prime, General Radio, Citibank, and Alpha Corporation were all spearheaded by a relatively small set of new executives from outside the company or group.

*Why All at Once?* Frame-breaking change is revolutionary in that the shifts reshape the entire nature of the organization. Those more effective examples of frame-breaking change were implemented rapidly (e.g., Citibank, Prime, Alpha). It appears that a piecemeal approach to frame-breaking changes gets bogged down in politics, individual resistance to change, and organizational inertia (e.g., Sinclair's attempts to reshape General Radio). Frame-breaking change requires discontinuous shifts in strategy, structure, people, and processes concurrently—or at least in a short period of time. Reasons for rapid, simultaneous implementation include:

- *Synergy* within the new structure can be a powerful aid. New executives with a fresh mission, working in a redesigned organization with revised norms and values, backed up with power and status, provide strong reinforcement. The pieces of the revitalized organization pull together, as opposed to piecemeal change where one part of the new organization is out of synch with the old organization.

- *Pockets of resistance* have a chance to grow and develop when frame-breaking change is implemented slowly. The new mission, shifts in organization, and other frame-breaking changes upset the comfortable routines and precedent. Resistance to such fundamental change is natural. If frame-breaking change is implemented slowly, then individuals have a greater opportunity to undermine the changes and organizational inertia works to further stifle fundamental change.

■ Typically, there is a *pent-up need for change*. During convergent periods, basic adjustments are postponed. Boat-rocking is discouraged. Once constraints are relaxed, a variety of desirable improvements press for attention, the exhilaration and momentum of a fresh effort (and new team) make difficult moves more acceptable. Change is in fashion.

■ Frame-breaking change is an inherently *risky and uncertain venture*. The longer the implementation period, the greater the period of uncertainty and instability. The most effective frame-breaking changes initiate the new strategy, structure, processes, and systems rapidly and begin the next period of stability and convergent change. The sooner fundamental uncertainty is removed, the better the chances of organizational survival and growth. While the pacing of change is important, the overall time to implement frame-breaking change will be contingent on the size and age of the organization.

*Patterns in Organization Evolution.* This historical approach to organization evolution focuses on convergent periods punctuated by reorientation—discontinuous, organization-wide upheavals. The most effective firms take advantage of relatively long convergent periods. These periods of incremental change build on and take advantage of organization inertia. Frame-breaking change is quite dysfunctional if the organization is successful and the environment is stable. If, however, the organization is performing poorly and/or if the environment changes substantially, framebreaking change is the only way to realign the organization with its competitive environment. Not all reorientations will be successful (e.g., People Express' expansion and upscale moves in 1985–86). However, inaction in the face of performance crisis and/or environmental shifts is a certain recipe for failure.

Because reorientations are so disruptive and fraught with uncertainty, the more rapidly they are implemented, the more quickly the organization can reap the benefits of the following convergent period. High-performing firms initiate reorientations when environmental conditions shift and implement these reorientations rapidly (e.g., Prime and Citibank). Low-performing organizations either do not reorient or reorient all the time as they root around to find an effective alignment with environmental conditions.

This metamorphic approach to organization evolution underscores the role of history and precedent as future convergent periods are all constrained and shaped by prior convergent periods. Further, this approach to organization evolution highlights the role of executive leadership in managing convergent periods *and* in initiating and implementing frame-breaking change.

## EXECUTIVE LEADERSHIP AND ORGANIZATION EVOLUTION

Executive leadership plays a key role in reinforcing system-wide momentum during convergent periods and in initiating and implementing bursts of change that characterize strategic reorientations. The nature of the leadership task differs sharply during these contrasting periods of organization evolution.

During convergent periods, the executive team focuses on *maintaining* congruence and fit within the organization. Because strategy, structure, processes, and systems are fundamentally sound, the myriad of incremental substantive decisions can be delegated to middle-level management, where direct expertise and information resides. The key role for executive leadership during convergent periods is to reemphasize strategy, mission, and core values and to keep a vigilant eye on external opportunities and/or threats.

Frame-breaking change, however, requires direct executive involvement in all aspects of the change. Given the enormity of the change and inherent internal forces for stability, executive leadership must be involved in the specification of strategy, structure, people, and organizational processes *and* in the development of implementation plans. During frame-breaking change, executive leadership is directly involved in *reorienting* their organizations. Direct personal involvement of senior management seems to be critical to implement these system-wide changes (e.g., Reed at Citibank or Iacocca at Chrysler). Tentative change does not seem to be effective (e.g., Don Sinclair at General Radio).

Frame-breaking change triggers resistance to change from multiple sources change must overcome several generic hurdles, including:

- Individual opposition, rooted in either anxiety or personal commitment to the status quo, is likely to generate substantial individual resistance to change.

- Political coalitions opposing the upheaval may be quickly formed within the organization. During converging periods a political equilibrium is reached. Frame-breaking upsets this equilibrium; powerful individuals and/or groups who see their status threatened will join in resistance.

- Control is difficult during the transition. The systems, roles, and responsibilities of the former organization are in suspension; the new rules of the game—and the rewards—have not yet been clarified.

- External constituents—suppliers, customers, regulatory agencies, local communities, and the like—often prefer continuation of existing relationships rather than uncertain moves in the future.

Whereas convergent change can be delegated, frame-breaking change requires strong, direct leadership from the top as to where the organization is going and how it is to get there. Executive leadership must be directly involved in: motivating constructive behavior, shaping political dynamics, managing control during the transition period, and managing external constituencies. The executive team must direct the content of frame-breaking change *and* provide the energy, vision, and resources to support, and be role models for, the new order. Brilliant ideas for new strategies, structures, and processes will not be effective unless they are coupled with thorough implementation plans actively managed by the executive team.[6]

## When to Launch an Upheaval

The most effective executives in our studies foresaw the need for major change. They recognized the external threats and opportunities, and took bold steps to deal with them. For example, a set of minicomputer companies (Prime, Rolm, Datapoint, Data General, among others) risked short-run success to take advantage of new opportunities created by technological and market changes. Indeed, by acting before being forced to do so, they had more time to plan their transitions.[7]

Such visionary executive teams are the exceptions. Most frame-breaking change is postponed until a financial crisis forces drastic action. The momentum, and frequently the success, of convergent periods breeds reluctance to change. This commitment to the status quo, and insensitivity to environmental shocks, is evident in both the Columbia and the McGill studies. It is not until financial crisis shouts its warning that most companies begin their transformation.

The difference in timing between pioneers and reluctant reactors is largely determined by executive leadership. The pioneering moves, in advance of crisis, are usually initiated by executives within the company. They are the exceptional persons who combine the vision, courage, and power to transform an organization. In contrast, the impetus for a tardy break usually comes from outside stakeholders; they eventually put strong pressure on existing executives—or bring in new executives—to make fundamental shifts.

## Who Manages the Transformation

Directing a frame-breaking upheaval success-fully calls for unusual talent and energy. The new mission must be defined, technology se-lected, resources acquired, policies revised, values changed, organization restructured, people reas-sured, inspiration provided, and an array of in-formal relationships shaped. Executives already on the spot will probably know most about the specific situation, but they may lack the talent, energy, and commitment to carry through an in-ternal revolution.

As seen in the Citibank, Prime, and Alpha ex-amples, most frame-breaking upheavals are man-aged by executives brought in from outside the company. The Columbia research program finds that externally recruited executives are more than three times more likely to initiate frame-breaking change than existing executive teams. Frame-breaking change was coupled with CEO succes-sion in more than 80 percent of the cases. Fur-ther, when frame-breaking change was combined with executive succession, company performance was significantly higher than when former exec-utives stayed in place. In only 6 of 40 cases we studied did a current CEO initiate and imple-ment multiple frame-breaking changes. In each of these six cases, the existing CEO made ma-jor changes in his/her direct reports, and this revitalized top team initiated and implemented frame-breaking changes (e.g., Thurston's actions at General Radio).[8]

Executive succession seems to be a powerful tool in managing frame-breaking change. There are several reasons why a fresh set of executives are typically used in company transformations. The new executive team brings different skills and a fresh perspective. Often they arrive with a strong belief in the new mission. Moreover, they are unfettered by prior commitments linked to the status quo; instead, this new top team sym-bolizes the need for change. Excitement of a new challenge adds to the energy devoted to it.

We should note that many of the executives who could not, or would not, implement frame-breaking change went on to be quite successful in other organizations—for example, Ken Fisher at Encore Computer and Bill Podusk at Apollo Computer. The stimulation of a fresh start and of jobs matched to personal competence applies to individuals as well as to organizations.

Although typical patterns for the when and who of frame-breaking change are clear—wait for a financial crisis and then bring in an outsider, along with a revised executive team, to revamp the company—this is clearly less than satisfactory for a particular organization. Clearly, some com-panies benefit from transforming themselves be-fore a crisis forces them to do so, and a few ex-ceptional executives have the vision and drive to reorient a business which they nurtured during its preceding period of convergence. The vital tasks are to manage incremental change during con-vergent periods; to have the vision to initiate and implement frame-breaking change prior to the competition; and to mobilize an executive team which can initiate and implement both kinds of change.

## CONCLUSION

Our analysis of the way companies evolve over long periods of time indicates that the most effec-tive firms have relatively long periods of conver-gence giving support to a basic strategy, but such periods are punctuated by upheavals—concurrent and discontinuous changes which reshape the en-tire organization. Managers should anticipate that when environments change sharply:

- Frame-breaking change cannot be avoided. These discontinuous organizational changes will either be made proactively or initiated un-der crisis/turnaround condition.

- Discontinuous changes need to be made in strategy, structure, people, and processes con-currently. Tentative change runs the risk of be-ing smothered by individual, group, and orga-nizational inertia.

- Frame-breaking change requires direct execu-tive involvement in all aspects of the change, usually bolstered with new executives from outside the organization.

- There are no patterns in the sequence of frame-breaking changes, and not all strategies will be effective. Strategy and, in turn, structure, systems, and processes must meet industry-specific competitive issues.

Finally, our historical analysis of organizations highlights the following issues for executive leadership:

- Need to manage for balance, consistency, or fit during convergent period.
- Need to be vigilant for environmental shifts in order to anticipate the need for frame-breaking change.
- Need to effectively manage incremental as well as frame-breaking change.
- Need to build (or rebuild) a top team to help initiate and implement frame-breaking change.
- Need to develop core values which can be used

as an anchor as organizations evolve through frame-breaking changes (e.g., IBM, Hewlett-Packard).

- Need to develop and use organizational history as a way to infuse pride in an organization's past and for its future.
- Need to bolster technical, social, and conceptual skills with visionary skills. Visionary skills add energy, directions, and excitement so critical during frame-breaking change.

Effectiveness over changing competitive conditions requires that executives manage fundamentally different kinds of organizations and different kinds of change. The data are consistent across diverse industries and countries, an executive team's ability to proactively initiate and implement frame-breaking change *and* to manage convergent change seem to be important factors which discriminate between organizational renewal and greatness versus complacency and eventual decline.

# REFERENCES

1. A. Chandler, *Strategy and Structure* (Cambridge, MA: MIT Press, 1962).

2. D. Miller and P. Friesen, *Organizations: A Quantum View* (Englewood Cliffs, NJ: Prentice-Hall, 1984).

3. L. Greiner, "Evolution and Revolution as Organizations Grow," *Harvard Business Review* (July/August 1972), pp. 37–46.

4. D. Nadler and M. Tushman, *Strategic Organization Design* (Homewood, IL: Scott Foresman, 1986).

5. T. Peters and R. Waterman, *In Search of Excellence* (New York, NY: Harper and Row, 1982).

6. Nadler and Tushman, op. cit.

7. For a discussion of preemptive strategies, see I. MacMillan, "Delays in Competitors' Responses to New Banking Products," *Journal of Business Strategy*, 4 (1984): 58–65.

8. M. Tushman and B. Virany, "Changing Characteristics of Executive Teams in an Emerging Industry," *Journal of Business Venturing* (1986).

## 48. BEYOND MANAGEMENT AND THE WORKER: THE INSTITUTIONAL FUNCTION OF MANAGEMENT

Jeffrey Pfeffer

Theory, research, and education in the field of organizational behavior and management have been dominated by a concern for the management of people *within* organizations. The question of how to make workers more productive has stood as the foundation for management theory and practice since the time of Frederick Taylor. Such an emphasis neglects the institutional function of management. While managing people within organizations is critical, managing the organization's relationships with other organizations such as competitors, creditors, suppliers, and governmental agencies is frequently as critical to the firm's success.

Parsons (1960) noted that there were three levels in organizations: (a) the technical level, where the technology of the organization was used to produce some product or service; (b) the administrative level, which coordinated and supervised the technical level; and (c) the institutional level, which was concerned with the organization's legitimacy and with organization-environment relations. Organization and management theory has primarily concentrated on administrative level problems, frequently at very low hierarchical levels in organizations.

Practicing managers and some researchers do recognize the importance of the institutional context in which the firm operates. There is increasing use of institutional advertising, and executives from the oil industry, among others, have been active in projecting their organizations' views in a variety of contexts. Mintzberg (1973) has identified the liaison role as one of ten roles managers fill. Other authors explicitly have

noted the importance of relating the organization to other organizations (Pfeffer & Nowak, unpub. ms.; Whyte, 1955).

Saying that the institutional function is important is different from developing a theory of the organization's relationships with other organizations, a theory which can potentially guide the manager's strategic actions in performing the function of institutional management. Such a theory is needed, and data are accumulating to construct such a theory.

The purposes of this article are: (a) to present evidence of the importance of the institutional function of management; and (b) to review data consistent with a model of institutional management. This model argues that managers behave as if they were seeking to manage and reduce uncertainty and interdependence arising from the firm's relationships with other organizations. Several strategic responses to interorganizational exchange, including their advantages and disadvantages, are considered.

### INSTITUTIONAL PROBLEMS OF ORGANIZATIONS

Organizations are open social systems, engaged in constant and important transactions with other organizations in their environments. Business firms transact with customer and supplier organizations, and with sources of credit; they interact on the federal and local level with regulatory and legal authorities which are concerned with pollution, taxes, antitrust, equal employment, and

Jeffrey Pfeffer, "Beyond Management and the Worker: the Institutional Function of Management," from *Academy of Management Review* 1, 1976, pp. 36–46. Reprinted by permission of the author and publisher.

myriad other issues. Because firms do interact with these other organizations, two consequences follow. First, organizations face uncertainty. If an organization were a closed system so that it could completely control and predict all the variables that affected its operation, the organization could make technically rational, maximizing decisions and anticipate the consequences of its actions. As an open system, transacting with important external organizations, the firm does not have control over many of the important factors that affect its operations. Because organizations are open, they are affected by events outside their boundaries.

Second, organizations are interdependent with other organizations with which they exchange resources, information or personnel, and thus open to influence by them. The extent of this influence is likely to be a function of the importance of the resource obtained, and inversely related to the ease with which the resource can be procured from alternative sources (Jacobs, 1974; Thompson, 1967). Interdependence is problematic and troublesome. Managers do not like to be dependent on factors outside their control. Interdependence is especially troublesome if there are few alternative sources, so the external organization is particularly important to the firm.

Interdependence and uncertainty interact in their effects on organizations. One of the principal functions of the institutional level of the firm is the management of this interdependence and uncertainty.

## THE IMPORTANCE OF INSTITUTIONAL MANAGEMENT

Katz and Kahn (1966) noted that organizations may pursue two complementary paths to effectiveness. The first is to be as efficient as possible, and thereby obtain a competitive advantage with respect to other firms. Under this strategy, the firm succeeds because it operates so efficiently that it achieves a competitive advantage in the market. The second strategy, termed "political," involves the establishment of favorable

exchange relationships based on considerations that do not relate strictly to price, quality, service, or efficiency. Winning an order because of the firm's product and cost characteristics would be an example of the strategy of efficiency; winning the order because of interlocks in the directorates of the organizations involved, or because of family connections between executives in the two organizations, would illustrate political strategies.

The uses and consequences of political strategies for achieving organizational success have infrequently been empirically examined. Hirsch (1975) has recently compared the ethical drug and record industries, noting great similarities between them. Both sell their products through gatekeepers or intermediaries—in the case of pharmaceuticals, through doctors who must write the prescription, and in the case of records, through disc jockeys who determine air time and, consequently, exposure. Both sell products with relatively short life cycles, and both industries place great emphasis on new products and product innovation. Both depend on the legal environment of patents, copyrights, and trademarks for market protection.

Hirsch noted that the rate of return for the average pharmaceutical firm during the period 1956–66 was more than double the rate of return for the average firm in the record industry. Finding no evidence that would enable him to attribute the striking differences in profitability to factors associated with internal structural arrangements, Hirsch concluded that at least one factor affecting the relative profitability of the two industries is the ability to manage their institutional environments, and more specifically, the control over distribution, patent and copyright protection, and the prediction of adoption by the independent gatekeepers.

In a review of the history of both industries, Hirsch indicated that in pharmaceuticals, control over entry was achieved by (a) amending the patent laws to permit the patenting of naturally occurring substances, antibiotics; and (b) instituting a long and expensive licensing procedure required before drugs could be manufactured and marketed, administered by the Food and Drug Administration (FDA). In contrast, record firms have much less protection under the copyright laws; as a consequence, entry is less controlled, leading to more competition and lower profits. While there are other differences between the industries, including size and expenditures on research and development, Hirsch argued that at least some of the success of drug firms derives from their ability to control entry and their ability to control information channels relating to their product through the use of detail personnel and advertising in the American Medical Association Journals. Retail price maintenance, tariff protection, and licensing to restrict entry are other examples of practices that are part of the organization's institutional environment and may profoundly affect its success.

## MANAGING UNCERTAINTY AND INTERDEPENDENCE

The organization, requiring transactions with other organizations and uncertain about their future performance, has available a variety of strategies that can be used to manage uncertainty and interdependence. Firms face two problems in their institutional relationships: (a) managing the uncertainty caused by the unpredictable actions of competitors; and (b) managing the uncertainty resulting from noncompetitive interdependence with suppliers, creditors, government agencies, and customers. In both instances, the same set of strategic responses is available: merger, to completely absorb the interdependence and resulting uncertainty; joint ventures; interlocking directorates, to partially absorb the interdependence; the movement and selective recruiting of executives and other personnel, to develop interorganizational linkages; regulation, to provide government enforced stability; and other political activity to reduce competition, protect markets and sources of supply, and otherwise manage the organization's environment.

Because organizations are open systems, each strategy is limited in its effect. While merger or some other interorganizational linkage may manage one source of organizational dependence, it probably at the same time makes the organizations dependent on yet other organizations. For example, while regulation may eliminate effective price competition and restrict entry into the industry (Jordan, 1972; Pfeffer, 1974a; Posner, 1974), the regulated organizations then face the uncertainties involved in dealing with the regulatory agency. Moreover, in reducing uncertainty for itself, the organization must bargain away some of its own discretion (Thompson, 1967). One can view institutional management as an exchange process—the organization assures itself of needed resources, but at the same time, must promise certain predictable behaviors in return. Keeping these qualifications in mind, evidence on use of the various strategies of institutional management is reviewed.

### Merger

There are three reasons an organization may seek to merge—first, to reduce competition by absorbing an important competitor organization; second, to manage interdependence with either sources of input or purchasers of output by absorbing them; and third, to diversify operations and thereby lessen dependence on the present organizations with which it exchanges (Pfeffer, 1972a). While merger among competing organizations is presumably proscribed by the antitrust laws, enforcement resources are limited, and major consolidations do take place.

In analyzing patterns of interorganizational behavior, one can either ask executives in the organizations involved the reasons for the action, or alternatively, one can develop a hypothetical model of behavior which is then tested with the available data. Talking with organizational executives may not provide the real reasons behind interorganizational activity since (a) different persons may see and interpret the same action in different ways; (b) persons may infer after the fact the motives for the action or decision; and (c) persons may not be motivated to tell the complete truth about the reasons for the behavior.

Much of the existing literature on interorganizational linkage activity, therefore, uses the method of empirically testing the deductions from a hypothetical model of interorganizational behavior.

The classic expressed rationale for merger has been to increase the profits or the value of the shares of the firm. In a series of studies beginning as early as 1921, researchers have been unable to demonstrate that merger active firms are more profitable or have higher stock prices following the merger activity. This literature has been summarized by Reid (1968), who asserts that mergers are made for growth and that growth is sought because of the relationship between firm size and managerial salaries.

Growth, however, does not provide information concerning the desired characteristics of the acquired firm. Under a growth objective, any merger is equivalent to any other of the same size. Pfeffer (1972a) has argued that mergers are undertaken to manage organizational interdependence. Examining the proportion of merger activity occurring within the same two-digit SIC industry category, he found that the highest proportion of within-industry mergers occurred in industries of intermediate concentration. The theoretical argument was that in industries with many competitors, the absorption of a single one did little to reduce competitive uncertainty. At the other extreme, with only a few competitors, merger would more likely be scrutinized by the antitrust authorities and coordination could instead be achieved through more informal arrangements, such as price leadership.

The same study investigated the second reason to merge: to absorb the uncertainty among organizations vertically related to each other, as in a buyer-seller relationship. He found that it was possible to explain 40 percent of the variation in the distribution of merger activity over industries on the basis of resource interdependence, measured by estimates of the transactions flows between sectors of the economy. On an individual industry basis, in two-thirds of the cases a measure of transactions interdependence accounted for 65 percent or more of the variation in the pattern of merger activity. The study indicated that it was possible to account for the industry of the likely merger partner firm by considering the extent to which firms in the two industries exchanged resources.

While absorption of suppliers or customers will reduce the firm's uncertainty by bringing critical contingencies within the boundaries of the organization, this strategy has some distinct costs. One danger is that the process of vertical integration creates a larger organization which is increasingly tied to a single industry.

The third reason for merger is diversification. Occasionally, the organization is confronted by interdependence it cannot absorb, either because of resource or legal limitations. Through diversifying its activities, the organization does not reduce the uncertainty, but makes the particular contingency less critical for its success and well-being. Diversification provides the organization with a way of avoiding, rather than absorbing, problematic interdependence.

Merger represents the most complete solution to situations of organizational interdependence, as it involves the total absorption of either a competitor or a vertically related organization, or the acquisition of an organization operating in another area. Because it does involve total absorption, merger requires more resources and is a more visible and substantial form of interorganizational linkage.

## Joint Ventures

Closely related to merger is the joint venture: the creation of a jointly owned, but independent organization by two or more separate parent firms. Merger involves the total pooling of assets by two or more organizations. In a joint venture, some assets of each of several parent organizations are used, and thus only a partial pooling of resources is involved (Bernstein, 1965). For a variety of reasons, joint ventures have been prosecuted less frequently and less successfully than mergers, making joint ventures particularly appropriate as a way of coping with competitive interdependence.

The joint subsidiary can have several effects on competitive interdependence and uncertainty.

First, it can reduce the extent of new competition. Instead of both firms entering a market, they can combine some of their assets and create a joint subsidiary to enter the market. Second, since joint subsidiaries are typically staffed, particularly at the higher executive levels, with personnel drawn from the parent firms, the joint subsidiary becomes another location for the management of competing firms to meet. Most importantly, the joint subsidiary must set price and output levels, make new product development and marketing decisions and decisions about its advertising policies. Consequently, the parent organizations are brought into association in a setting in which exactly those aspects of the competitive relationship must be jointly determined.

In a study of joint ventures among manufacturing and oil and gas companies during the period 1960–71, Pfeffer and Nowak (in press, a, b) found that 56 percent involved parent firms operating in the same two-digit industry. Further, in 36 percent of the 166 joint ventures studied, the joint subsidiary operated in the same industry as *both* parent organizations. As in the case of mergers, the proportion of joint venture activities undertaken with other firms in the same industry was related to the concentration of the firm's industry being intermediate. The relationship between concentration and the proportion of joint ventures undertaken within the same industry accounted for some 25 percent of the variation in the pattern of joint venture activities.

In addition to considering the use of joint ventures in coping with competitive interdependence, the Pfeffer and Nowak study of joint ventures examined the extent to which the creation of joint subsidiaries was related to patterns of transaction interdependence across industries. While the correlations between the proportion of transactions and the proportion of joint ventures undertaken between industry pairs were lower than in the case of mergers, statistically significant relationships between this form of interorganizational linkage activity and patterns of resource exchange were observed. The difference between mergers and joint ventures appears to be that mergers are used relatively more to cope with buyer-seller interdependence, and joint ventures are more highly related to considerations of coping with competitive uncertainty.

## Cooptation and Interlocking Directorates

Cooptation is a venerable strategy for managing interdependence between organizations. Cooptation involves the partial absorption of another organization through the placing of a representative of that organization on the board of the focal organization. Corporations frequently place bankers on their boards; hospitals and universities offer trustee positions to prominent business leaders; and community action agencies develop advisory boards populated with active and strong community political figures.

As a strategy for coping with interdependence, cooptation involves some particular problems and considerations. For example, a representative of the external organization is brought into the focal organization, while still retaining his or her original organizational membership. Cooptation is based on creating a conflict of interest within the coopted person. To what extent should one pursue the goals and interests of one's organization or principal affiliation, and to what extent should one favor the interests of the coopting organization? From the point of view of the coopting organization, the individual should favor its interests, but not to the point where he or she loses credibility in the parent organization, because at that point, the individual ceases to be useful in ensuring that organization's support. Thus, cooptation requires striking a balance between the pressures to identify with either the parent or coopting institution.

Furthermore, since cooptation involves less than total absorption of the other organization, there is the risk that the coopted representative will not have enough influence or control in the principal organization to ensure the desired decisions. Of course, it is possible to coopt more than a single representative. This is frequently done when relationships with the coopted organization are particularly uncertain and critical. Cooptation may be the most feasible strategy when total absorption is impossible due to financial or legal constraints.

Interlocks in the boards of directors of competing organizations provide a possible strategy for coping with competitive interdependence and the resulting uncertainty. The underlying argument is that in order to manage interorganizational relationships, information must be exchanged, usually through a joint subsidiary or interlocking directorate. While interlocks among competitors are ostensibly illegal, until very recently there was practically no prosecution of this practice. In a 1965 study, a subcommittee of the House Judiciary Committee found more than 300 cases in which direct competitors had interlocking boards of directors. In a study of the extent of interlocking among competing organizations in a sample of 109 manufacturing organizations, Pfeffer and Nowak (unpub. ms.) found that the proportion of directors on the board from direct competitors was higher for firms operating in industries in which concentration was intermediate. This result is consistent with the result found for joint ventures and mergers as well. In all three instances, linkages among competing organizations occurred more frequently when concentration was in an intermediate range.

Analyses of cooptation through the use of boards of directors have not been confined to business firms. Price (1963) argued that the principal function of the boards of the Oregon Fish and Game Commissions was to link the organizations to their environments. Zald (1967) found that the composition of YMCA boards in Chicago matched the demography of their operating areas, and affected the organizations' effectiveness, particularly in raising money. Pfeffer (1973) examined the size, composition, and function of hospital boards of directors, finding that variables of organizational context, such as ownership, source of funds, and location, were important explanatory factors. He also found a relationship between cooptation and organizational effectiveness. In 1972, (1972b) he found that regulated firms, firms with a higher proportion of debt in their capital structures, and larger firms tended to have more outside directors. Allen (1974) also

found that size of the board and the use of cooptation was predicted by the size of the firm, but did not replicate Pfeffer's earlier finding of a relationship between the organization's capital structure and the proportion of directors from financial institutions. In a study of utility boards, Pfeffer(1974b) noted that the composition of the board tended to correlate with the demographics of the area in which the utility was regulated.

The evidence is consistent with the strategy of organizations using their boards of directors to coopt external organizations and manage problematic interdependence. The role of the board of directors is seen not as the provision of management expertise or control, but more generally as a means of managing problematic aspects of an organization's institutional environment.

## Executive Recruitment

Information also is transferred among organizations through the movement of personnel. The difference between movement of executives between organizations and cooptation is that in the latter case, the person linking the two organizations retains membership in both organizations. In the case of personnel movement, dual organizational membership is not maintained. When people change jobs, they take with themselves information about the operations, policies, and values of their previous employers, as well as contacts in the organization. In a study of the movement of faculty among schools of business, Baty et al. (1971) found that similar orientations and curricula developed among schools exchanging personnel. The movement of personnel is one method by which new techniques of management and new marketing and product ideas are diffused through a set of organizations.

Occasionally, the movement of executives between organizations has been viewed as intensifying, rather than reducing, competition. Companies have been distressed by the raiding of trade secrets and managerial expertise by other organizations. While this perspective must be recognized, the exchange of personnel among organizations is a revered method of conflict *reduction* between organizations (Stern et al., 1973). Personnel motivation inevitably involves sharing information among a set of organizations.

If executive movement is a form of interfirm linkage designed to manage competitive relationships, the proportion of executives recruited from within the same industry should be highest at intermediate levels of industrial concentration. Examining the three top executive positions in twenty different manufacturing industries, the evidence on executive backgrounds was found to be consistent with this argument (Pfeffer & Leblebici, 1973). The proportion of high level executives with previous jobs in the same industry but in a different company was found to be negatively related to the number of firms in the industry. The larger the number of firms, the less likely that a single link among competitors will substantially reduce uncertainty, but the larger the available supply of external executive talent. The data indicated no support for a supply argument, but supported the premise that interorganizational linkages are used to manage interdependence and uncertainty.

The use of executive movement to manage noncompetitive interorganizational relationships is quite prevalent. The often-cited movement of personnel between the Defense Department and major defense contractors is only one example, because there is extensive movement of personnel between many government departments and industries interested in the agencies' decisions. The explanation is frequently proposed that organizations are acquiring these personnel because of their expertise. The expertise explanation is frequently difficult to separate from the alternative that personnel are being exchanged to enhance interorganizational relationships. Regardless of the motivation, exchanging personnel inevitably involves the transfer of information and access to the other organization. It is conceptually possible to control for the effect of expertise—in other words, taking expertise into account, is there evidence that recruiting patterns reflect the influence of factors related to institutional management?

## Regulation

Occasionally, institutional relationships are managed through recourse to political intervention. The reduction of competition and its associated uncertainty may be accomplished through regulation. Regulation, however, is a risky strategy for organizations to pursue. While regulation most frequently benefits the regulated industry (Jordan, 1972; Pfeffer 1974a) the industry and firms have no assurance that regulatory authority will not be used against their interest. Regulation is very hard to repeal. Successful use of regulation requires that the firm and industry face little or no powerful political opposition, and that the political future can be accurately forecast.

The benefits of regulation to those being regulated have been extensively reviewed (Posner, 1974; Stigler, 1971). Regulation frequently has been sought by the regulated industry. Currently, trucking firms are among the biggest supporters of continued regulation of trucking. Since the Civil Aeronautics Board was created in 1938, no new trunk carriers have been started. Jordan (1970) found that air rates on intrastate (hence not regulated by the CAB) airlines within California are frequently 25 percent or more lower than fares on comparable routes of regulated carriers. Estimates of the effects of regulation on prices in electric utilities, airlines, trucking, and natural gas have indicated that regulation either increases price or has no effect.

The theory behind these outcomes is still unclear. One approach suggests that regulation is created for the public benefit, but after the initial legislative attention, the regulatory process is captured by the firms subject to regulation. Another approach proposes that regulation, like other goods, is acquired subject to supply and demand considerations (Posner, 1974). Political scientists, focusing on the operation of interest groups, argue that regulatory agencies are "captured" by organized and well-financed interests. Government intervention in the market can solve many of the interdependence problems faced by firms. Regulation is most often accompanied by restriction of entry and the fixing of prices, which tend to reduce market uncertainties. Markets may be actually allocated to firms, and with the reduction of risk, regulation may make access to capital easier. Regulation may alter the organization's relationships with suppliers and customers. One theory of why the railroads were interested in the creation of the Interstate Commerce Commission (ICC) in 1887 was that large users were continually demanding and winning discriminatory rate reductions, disturbing the price stability of railroad price fixing cartels. By forbidding price discrimination and enforcing this regulation, the ICC strengthened the railroads' position with respect to large customers (MacAvoy, 1965).

## Political Activity

Regulation is only one specific form of organizational activity in governmental processes. Business attempts to affect competition through the operation of the tariff laws date back to the 1700s (Bauer et al., 1968). Epstein (1969) provided one of the more complete summaries of the history of corporate involvement in politics and the inevitability of such action. The government has the power of coercion, possessed legally by no other social institution. Furthermore, legislation and regulation affect most of our economic institutions and markets, either indirectly through taxation, or more directly through purchasing, market protection or market creation. For example, taxes on margarine only recently came to an end. Federal taxes, imposed in 1886 as a protectionist measure for dairy interests, were removed in 1950, but a law outlawing the sale of oleo in its colored form lasted until 1967 in Wisconsin.

As with regulation, political activities carry both benefits and risks. The risk arises because once government intervention in an issue on behalf of a firm or industry is sought, then political intervention becomes legitimated, regardless of whose interests are helped or hurt. The firm that seeks favorable tax legislation runs the risk of creating a setting in which it is equally legitimate to be exposed to very unfavorable legislation. After

an issue is opened to government intervention, neither side will find it easy to claim that further government action is illegitimate.

In learning to cope with a particular institutional environment, the firm may be unprepared for new uncertainties caused by the change of fundamental institutional relationships, including the opening of price competition, new entry and the lack of protection from overseas competition.

## CONCLUSION

The institutional function of management involves managing the organization's relationships with other organizations. Table 48.1 presents strategies of institutional management with their principal advantages and disadvantages. From observation of organization activities, the most common response to interdependence with external organizations seems to be the attempt to develop some form of interorganizational linkage to ensure the continuation of favorable relationships with important organizations in the environment.

All such interfirm linkages have costs, with the most fundamental being the loss of the organization's autonomy. In return for the certainty that one's competitors will not engage in predatory price cutting, one must provide assurances about one's own behavior. For example, cooptation involves the possibility of acquiring the support of an external organization, but at the same time the firm gives up some degree of privacy over its internal information and some control over its operations and decisions.

Variables affecting responses to the organization's environment can be specified. Actions taken to manage interdependencies are related to the extent of the interdependence and its importance to the organization. The response to competitive interdependence is related to measures of industry structure, and particularly to the necessity and feasibility of developing informal, interorganizational structures. Two important issues remain. First, is effective institutional man-

**TABLE 48.1**

Advantages and Disadvantages of Strategies of Institutional Management

| Strategy | Advantages | Disadvantages |
|---|---|---|
| Merger | Completely absorbs interdependence | Requires resources sufficient to acquire another organization<br>May be proscribed by antitrust laws, or infeasible for other reasons (e.g., a governmental unit cannot be absorbed by a firm) |
| Joint ventures | Can be used for sharing risks and costs associated with large or technologically advanced activities<br>Can be used to partially pool resources and coordinate activities. | Is available only for certain types of organizations, though less restricted than merger (COMSAT, for instance, brings together government and business) |
| Cooptation | Relatively inexpensive | May not provide enough coordination of linkage between organizations to ensure performance<br>Coopted person may lose credibility in original organization |
| Personnel movement | Relatively inexpensive<br>Almost universally possible | Person loses identification with original organization, lessening influence there<br>Linkage is based on knowledge and familiarity, and on a few persons at most, not on basic structural relationships |
| Regulation | Enables organization to benefit from the coercive power of the government | Regulation may be used to harm the organization's interests |
| Political activity | Enables organization to use government to modify and enhance environment | Government intervention, once legitimated, may be used against the organization as well as for its benefit |

agement associated with favorable outcomes to the organization? Second, given the importance of institutional management, why are some organizations more successful than others at this task?

The effect of institutional management on firm performance is difficult to measure, and seldom has been examined. To examine the effect of successful institutional management, an outcome measure is needed. Profit is only one possibility, because there is evidence that the reduction of uncertainty may be sought regardless of its effect on profit (Caves, 1970). Whatever criterion is chosen is affected by many factors. To attribute a result to institutional management, other causes must be controlled. Nevertheless, institutional management receives a great deal of management attention in some firms and a firm's interorganizational relationships may be important to its success and survival.

Of even more fundamental interest is the question of why some firms are able to develop more effective strategic responses to their institutional environments. It is possible that effective institutional management requires fundamentally different structures of top management, of the development of excess managerial capacity, or the development of particular types of information systems. It is easier to find successful institutional management than to identify critical variables enabling it to develop in the first place. For example, some universities have better relationships with their state legislatures than do others. It is possible to retrospectively infer explanations as to why this is so. What remains to be done is to explain those factors that could be designed into an organization initially to ensure effective institutional management in the future.

Considering its probable importance to the firm, the institutional function of management has received much less concern than it warrants. It is time that this aspect of management receives the systematic attention long reserved for motivational and productivity problems associated with relationships between management and workers.

## REFERENCES

Allen, Michael Patrick. "The Structure of Interorganizational Elite Cooptation: Interlocking Corporate Directorates." *American Sociological Review* 39 (1974): 393–406.

Baty, Gordon B.; Evan, William M.; and Rothermel, Terry W. "Personnel Flows as Interorganizational Relations." *Administrative Science Quarterly* 16 (1971): 430–43.

Bauer, Raymond A.; de Sola Pool, Ithiel; and Dexter, Lewis Anthony. *American Business and Public Policy*. New York: Atherton Press, 1968.

Bernstein, Lewis. "Joint Ventures in the Light of Recent Antitrust Developments." *The Antitrust Bulletin* 10 (1965): 25–29.

Caves, Richard E. "Uncertainty, Market Structure, and Performance: Galbraith as Conventional Wisdom." In *Industrial Organization and Economic Development*, edited by J. W. Markham and G. F. Papanek, pp. 283–302. Boston: Houghton Mifflin, 1970.

Epstein, Edwin M. *The Corporation in American Politics*. Englewood Cliffs, New Jersey: Prentice-Hall, 1969.

Hirsch, Paul M. "Organizational Effectiveness and the Institutional Environment." *Administrative Science Quarterly* 20 (1975): 327–44.

House of Representatives, Staff Report to the Antitrust Subcommittee of the Committee on the Judiciary. *Interlocks in Corporate Management*. Washington, D.C.: U.S. Government Printing Office, 1965.

Jacobs, David. "Dependency and Vulnerability: An Exchange Approach to the Control of Organizations." *Administrative Science Quarterly* 19 (1974): 45–59.

Jordan, William A. *Airline Regulation in America: Effects and Imperfections*. Baltimore: Johns Hopkins University Press, 1970.

————."Producer Protection, Prior Market Structure and the Effects of Government Regulation." *Journal of Law and Economics* 15 (1972): 151–76.

Katz, Daniel, and Kahn, Robert L. *The Social Psychology of Organizations*. New York: John Wiley, 1966.

MacAvoy, Paul W. *The Economic Effects of Regulation*. Cambridge, Mass.: MIT Press, 1965.

Mintzberg, Henry. *The Nature of Managerial Work*. New York: Harper and Row, 1973.

Parsons, Talcott. *Structure and Process in Modern Societies*. Glencoe, Illinois: Free Press, 1960.

Pfeffer, Jeffrey. "Merger as a Response to Organizational Interdependence." *Administrative Science Quarterly* 17 (1972): 382–94. (a)

————."Size and Composition of Corporate Boards of Directors: The Organization and its Environment." *Administrative Science Quarterly* 17 (1972): 218–28. (b)

————."Size, Composition and Function of Hospital Boards of Directors: A Study of Organization-Environment Linkage." *Administrative Science Quarterly* 18 (1973): 349–64.

————."Administrative Regulation and Licensing: Social Problem or Solution?" *Social Problems* 21 (1974): 468–79. (a)

————."Cooptation and the Composition of Electric Utility Boards of Directors." *Pacific Sociological Review* 17 (1974): 333–63. (b)

————.and Leblebici, Huseyin. "Executive Recruitment and the Development of Interfirm Organizations." *Administrative Science Quarterly* 18 (1973): 449–61.

————.and Nowak, Phillip. "Joint Ventures and Interorganizational Interdependence." *Administrative Science Quarterly*. in press. (a)

————."Organizational Context and Interorganizational Linkages Among Corporations." Unpublished manuscript, Berkeley: University of California.

————."Patterns of Joint Venture Activity: Implications for Antitrust Policy." *The Antitrust Bulletin*, in press. (b)

Posner, Richard A. "Theories of Economic Regulation." *Bell Journal of Economics and Management Science* 5 (1974): 335–58.

Price, James L. "The Impact of Governing Boards on Organizational Effectiveness and Morale." *Administrative Science Quarterly* 8 (1963): 361–78.

Reid, Samuel R. *Mergers, Managers, and the Economy*. New York: McGraw-Hill, 1968.

Sayles, Leonard R. *Managerial Behavior: Administration in Complex Organization*. New York: McGraw-Hill, 1964.

Stern, Louis W.; Sternthal, Brian; and Craig, C. Samuel. "Managing Conflict in Distribution Channels: A Laboratory Study." *Journal of Marketing Research* 10 (1973): 169–79.

Stigler, George J. "The Theory of Economic Regulation." *Bell Journal of Economics and Management Science* 2 (1971): 3–21.

Thompson, James D. *Organizations in Action*. New York: McGraw-Hill, 1967.

Whyte, William F. *Street Corner Society*. Chicago: University of Chicago Press, 1955.

Zald, Mayer N. "Urban Differentiation, Characteristics of Boards of Directors and Organizational Effectiveness." *American Journal of Sociology* 73 (1967): 261–72.

# 49.   BEYOND THE COWBOY AND THE CORPOCRAT: A CALL TO ACTION

Rosabeth Moss Kanter

Slowly but surely, America is waking up to the emerging economic realities. Across the business landscape, companies in many different industries, of many different ages and sizes, are reshaping themselves into contenders in the global corporate Olympics. The motivation for adopting the new forms is mixed. Companies are as much pushed by their need to reduce costs and manage constrained resources as they are pulled by the lure of entrepreneurial opportunities as barriers to worldwide business activity fall away. The changes are implemented poorly in some cases and well in others. For people, the new business forms are accompanied by insecurity and overload at the same time that they generate more exciting and involving workplaces and give more people more chances to operate like entrepreneurs, even from within the corporate fold.

But despite the unsolved problems, slowly but surely, America is learning how to compete in the corporate Olympics.

Rapid change in the business environment makes the Olympic contest sometimes resemble the croquet game in *Alice in Wonderland* .... In that kind of game, every element is in motion—technology, suppliers, customers, employees, corporate structure, industry structure, government regulation—and none can be counted on to remain stable for very long. It is impossible to win a game like that by using the old corporate forms: elaborate hierarchies and slow decision-making processes; in-house rivalries and adversarial relationships with stakeholders; risk-averse systems that crush new ideas not directly related to the mainstream business; and

rewards geared to climbing the ladder from position to position rather than to accomplishment or contribution.

But even though that game is fraught with uncertainty and lack of control, there is a way to win it. A contest that puts a premium on responsiveness and teamwork can be won by employing four F's: being Focused, Fast, Friendly, and Flexible.

For corporations to get in shape for Olympic competition, then, they must evolve flatter, more focused organizations stressing synergies; entrepreneurial enclaves pushing newstream businesses for the future; and strategic alliances or stakeholder partnerships stretching capacity by combining the strength of several organizations. Together, these strategies constitute the strategic, business action agenda.

## SYNERGIES

The first major component of post-entrepreneurial strategy is to seek that combination of businesses, array of internal services, and structure for organizing them that promotes synergies—a whole that multiplies the value of the parts. Olympic contenders need leaner, more cooperative, more integrated organizations. Compared to the traditional corporation, post-entrepreneurial companies have fewer layers of management and smaller corporate staffs; they minimize the interveners that delay action. A key concept guiding the post-entrepreneurial corporation is focus: ensuring that people at all levels are able to concentrate on contributing what they do best, in a company itself fully focused on maximizing its core business competence.

Driven by an imperative to make sure that all activities "add value," post-entrepreneurial companies decentralize some functions, putting them close to the business unit those functions support; they contract out for some services, turning to suppliers that are specialists in that area and reducing the need for the company to manage activities largely unrelated to their core business competence; and they convert some service departments into "businesses" that compete with external suppliers to sell their wares both inside and outside the company. Such organizational changes allow post-entrepreneurial companies to do more with less, because their staffs are smaller, their fixed costs are lower, resources are available closer to the site of the business action, and all departments are more clearly focused on their contributions to the business.

To move from simply adding value to multiplying it, the post-entrepreneurial company also builds the connections between its various products or businesses, encouraging such cooperative efforts as cross-selling, product links in the marketplace, exchange of technological or market information, resource sharing to apply one unit's competence to another's problem, or letting each division serve as the "lead" for particular innovations. This means that the typical post-entrepreneurial company is less diversified than the traditional corporation, tending to add only those businesses that build on existing competence or can extend it.

But the search for synergies is sometimes forgotten in a corporation's rush to restructure. Many cut costs without considering the consequences. They work on the "use less" side of the equation but not the "achieve more" side. Or they acquire new businesses because theoretically there is a "fit," but then foster rivalries that interfere with getting benefits from that strategic fit. Reshaping an organization to create more value runs the risk of subtracting value rather than adding it. The issue is how to restructure thoughtfully instead of downsizing mindlessly. There are two principal problems: poor

management of the transition itself and setting up contests that produce "winners" and "losers."

First, top management typically overestimates the degree of cooperation it will get and underestimates the transition costs. Among the byproducts of significant restructuring are discontinuity, disorder, and distraction—all of which tend to reduce productivity. People can lose energy, projects can lose key resources, and initiative can grind to a halt. Faith in leaders can be diminished, and power differences are made uncomfortably visible, showing many people that they lack control over their own fates. But even if some of these transition problems are temporary, a more permanent residue can be left: an undermining of commitment to the future. "Shall I write the list of our locations in pencil?" one manager asked.

The second danger is inducing the "mean" along with the "lean"—a cowboy style of management that encourages groups to shoot it out with one another in internal competitions. Such in-house rivalries can stem from any situation that promotes battles over scarce resources among groups with a reason to be antagonistic to one another—for example, the conquerors and the vanquished after an acquisition, parallel start-ups with the goal of only one survivor, or creeping market boundaries that cause divisions of the same company to seek one another's customers. But in-house competition undermines goal achievement, leading groups to emphasize defeating their rivals instead of strong task performance. It can drive out innovation and lower standards.

The management challenge is to retain value and increase it by handling transitions so that they reinforce commitment and build the cooperation that brings synergies. This means, first of all, managing with an eye on the past and the future as well as the present: in any major change, minimizing the losses people have to face while allowing grieving about the past; providing positive visions of the future; and reducing the uncertainty of the present by active communication. After a transition, it means actively organizing to motivate the search for synergies: championing the cause from the top, providing forums to help managers identify opportunities outside their own areas, offering incentives and rewards for teamwork, making resources available for joint projects, and promoting relationships and communication to help people know one another and share information across diverse areas—to perceive that their fate is shared and they can help one another.

The post-entrepreneurial emphasis on synergies decreases the "vertical" dimension of organization, with its elaborate corporate hierarchies and large central staffs, and increases the "horizontal" dimension—the direct cooperation between peers across divisions and departments.

# ALLIANCES

The second major component of post-entrepreneurial strategy involves developing close working relationships with other organizations, extending the company's reach without increasing its size. Strategic alliances and partnerships are a potent way to do more with less. They permit the company to remain lean, controlling costs, while gaining access to more capacity than what is owned or employed directly. The traditional corporation was stuck with the limitations of do-it-oneself-or-don't-do-it-at-all mentalities. Partnerships are a flexible alternative to acquisition, with a more modest investment and the ability to remain independent. The leaner organization that contracts out for services depends on the suppliers of those services and therefore benefits from close cooperation with them. Furthermore, in a rapidly changing business environment, alliances with other organizations on whom one company depends are a powerful way to ensure that all change in the same direction, thereby reducing uncertainty. The traditional corporation's mistrust of outsiders and desire for control made it impossible to plan jointly with customers or suppliers.

Post-entrepreneurial companies find a number of benefits in coalitions with other companies: information access, windows on technology, speed of action, and mutual accommodation to innovation that creates faster payback.

Post-entrepreneurial companies pool resources or link their systems to create even greater joint capacity in a variety of ways. There are groups of companies contributing to consortia that provide a special service for all of them, joint ventures to pursue particular business opportunities, and partnerships between a company and its suppliers, customers, or even unions.

Strategic alliances and partnerships blur the boundaries between organizations, permitting them to take advantage of one another's capacities and to coordinate their activities for mutual benefit. This coordination requires degrees of information-sharing unprecedented in the traditional corporation. And it is not only the external ally who gets more information; it is also the managers inside who have to know more in order to be intelligent representatives to the partnership. In general, effective alliances create multiple links between the allies: joint planning at the strategic level, technical data exchange at the professional level, and direct data links at the production level. The connections multiply. One partner company may make investments in the other that resemble the investments a corporation might make in one of its divisions: management conferences to review business plans, staff training programs, performance appraisal programs, and recognition events. The relationships may get even more intertwined when companies are both suppliers and customers to one another.

Becoming "PALs" with other organizations makes the post-entrepreneurial corporation different from the traditional corpocracy in a number of ways; it changes what and how managers manage. Alliances can rapidly move a company to a participative standard; instead of commanding subordinates in a hierarchy, alliance managers engage in discussions with partners of similar standing over whom they have no formal authority and whose careers they do not control. Thus the skills they must exercise are different. They must understand how to balance the interests of multiple constituencies (for example, their company's desires and those of the partner), how to establish egalitarian relationships, how to identify shared goals and search for consensus, how to earn respect when it is not automatically coupled to rank, and how to be sensitive to symbols and signals that affect the level of trust in the relationship.

Alliances and partnerships are thus vulnerable to a number of management failures. Sometimes they fall apart because of shifts in the strategy or circumstances of one of the partners, which means that the alliance is no longer valuable or desirable. But more often they suffer because the companies entering into them simply do not do what it takes to achieve the benefits of alliance. Successful partnerships imply a degree of equality to which some companies and some managers are unwilling to move; they would rather try to duplicate traditional command conditions by manifesting less commitment than the partner, maintaining an imbalance of resources or information or starving the partnership by not supplying enough of these, and monopolizing the benefits. The partner, in turn, may have prematurely placed trust in the relationship, arousing so much resentment when the trust is violated that cooperation ceases. Or the domain for the alliance may be so circumscribed that effective action to derive benefits for all parties is impossible; the organizations fail to link their systems or plan together or find a framework for resolving differences, and meanwhile, each has other loyalties that conflict with the partnership, including the pull of internal corporate politics.

Clearly, partnerships are not a casual matter, and they should not be entered into casually, or they will absorb time and energy without bringing benefits and raise expectations only to frustrate them, which is more disappointing than never to have been promised anything. For all the fanfare surrounding industry research consortia like Bellcore for the regional telephone operating companies or the Microelectronics and Computer Corporation, experience suggests that the companies entering into such alliances are only weakly committed, and, in turn, the consortia produce little that they define as benefits—reinforcing their lack of commitment in a vicious

circle. Being only casually a partner is like being only somewhat married.

The management challenge, then, is to select only those relationships that are sufficiently important that they will be entered into with full commitment and with a willingness to invest the resources and make the internal changes that successful external partnerships entail—the sharing of information, the linking of systems, and the establishment of agreements for governing the partnership. The "six *I*'s" of successful alliances— Importance, Investment, Interdependence, Integration, Information, Institutionalization—make it possible for the post-entrepreneurial corporation to use partnerships to do more with less. But they also require major shifts away from bureaucracy and hierarchy.

## NEWSTREAMS

The third major post-entrepreneurial strategy is to actively promote newstreams—a flow of new business possibilities within the firm. To do more with less in the demanding context of the global Olympics means being able to capture and develop opportunities as they arise, to ensure that good ideas don't slip away and that new ventures are ready to join the mainstream business or lead the company in new directions. Thus, post-entrepreneurial companies extend the domain for invention well beyond the R&D department, and the domain for new venture formation well beyond the acquisition department. They are unlike traditional corporations in giving more people, at more levels, the chance to develop and lead newstream projects.

While post-entrepreneurial companies want a climate for innovation in which every employee feels that innovation is part of his or her job, they do not just depend on the lucky break of an innovation's spontaneously arising in some corner of the company and making its way to a leader's attention. Instead, they create official channels to speed the flow of new ideas: for example, special funds to support new ideas without eating into mainstream business budgets; centers for creativity to speed the application of new ideas; incentives to find and nurture employee-led projects; incubators to grow new ventures; or investments in new technology ventures outside that can be linked to established businesses inside. The managers who preside over newstream channels may simply act as scouts to find ideas already under development, or they may more actively coach potential project developers and inspire them to come forward.

But simply establishing newstream channels does not automatically assure that newstream projects will be successful. Just as with the other two post-entrepreneurial strategies, success depends on the effectiveness and appropriateness with which the strategy is implemented; it requires a management sensibility not part of the traditional repertoire. The very existence of newstreams generates tensions and dilemmas because the requirements for nurturing a new venture conflict with management systems geared for running mainstream businesses—or at least better tolerated by the mainstream.

For one thing, "planning" for a newstream means placing bets rather than being able to predict a relatively assured set of results from a known line of business. Newstreams are not yet routinized; they are characterized instead by unexpected events, which makes scheduling difficult. Newstreams are uncertain in a number of respects; their course is bumpy, and they rock boats because they are controversial. Newstream projects are intense; they absorb more mental and emotional energy than established activities, generate new knowledge at a rapid rate, require excellent communication among those with fragments of knowledge, and are thus more dependent on teamwork and more vulnerable to turnover. Finally, newstreams benefit from autonomy—perhaps places of their own for the projects, removed from the mainstream and allowing experimentation, but certainly newstreams need a separation of style and procedures so that development projects can move quickly without the constraints deemed necessary to control the established mainstream business.

When newstreams dry up without producing benefits for the company, it is often because of a failure to understand the requirements for newstreams. Sometimes companies expect quicker and greater financial returns than the newstream can support; sometimes they choose newstreams only for their financial promise and not for the ways they might be useful to the mainstream business; sometimes they place a few big bets rather than nurturing a flow of many more modest newstream ideas. When a company counts on newstreams for more than they can handle, it often kills them with management attention, imposing mainstream systems that hinder rather than help.

There is also a tension between the streams that makes traditional mainstream managers uneasy; the newstream quest for autonomy conflicts with the mainstream push for control. Mainstream people may resent the "privileges" newstream people have in being freed from traditional constraints; newstream people may argue, in turn, that they are more vulnerable, taking greater career risks. In many ways, the existence of newstreams flowing alongside the mainstream business loosens traditional hierarchical authority, undermines respect for bureaucracy, weakens corporate identification in favor of project identification, and teaches people they can rely on themselves, thereby reducing their dependency on the corporation to give them a career. The corporate "haves" become the people with the freedom to pursue their ideas; the "have-nots" are those still encumbered with the shackles of bureaucracy.

## THE COMING DEMISE OF BUREAUCRACY AND HIERARCHY

The three post-entrepreneurial strategies can change sluggish organizations into agile, athletic champions in the global corporate Olympics. They can show bloated, elephantine corpocracies how to dance. But they are not quick fixes; they are fundamentally different ways of organizing to get the work done, with revolutionary consequences for management. They simply do not work when companies try to employ them mindlessly or casually: for example, using a slash-and-burn approach to restructuring, cutting staff to the bone without rethinking how the work gets done; spending large sums to acquire promising businesses without dedicating resources to integrating them well; heralding "alliances" without making the underlying commitment to behave more cooperatively; or throwing money into new ventures without giving them the ability to produce results. Instead of being able to do more with less, companies that do not move in more people-sensitive and less bureaucratic directions, more cooperative and less hierarchical directions, will find themselves doing less with more.

The corporation itself is being turned inside-out, like a reversible garment worn out on one side. Some executives I know are beginning to draw their organization charts upside-down, with managers at the bottom supporting the line employees at the top. But inside-out is an even more accurate image for the new organization. There is more "detachment" of what was once "inside" the corporation's protective shell (for example, employees being replaced by contingent workers and staff departments being spun off as independent contractors) and more "attachment" to what was once "outside" (for example, closer, more committed relationships with suppliers, customers, and even competitors). We are watching a simultaneous loosening of formerly strong relationships and strengthening of formerly loose relationships. Those groups brought closer clearly benefit, but those cast out are often cast adrift.

The new corporate ideal involves a smaller fixed core, but a larger set of partnerlike ties. There is less "inside" that is sacred—permanent, untouchable, unchangeable people, departments, business units, or practices—but more "outside" that is respected, representing opportunities for deal-making or leverage via alliances. This ideal represents a reversal of the old corporate imperative to get as big as possible, in order to have power and control over the business environment. In an environment of turbulence and high

uncertainty, vast size can instead produce rigidity and sluggishness—like the overage, overweight former athletes many large American corporations have become. Increasingly today the corporate ideal lies in how *small* an organization can be and still get the job done.

Other analysts have noted this reversal in a number of different ways. TRW economist Pat Choate has heralded the coming of a "high flex society," pointing to the new social policies required to increase business flexibility by helping individuals be more flexible in their job choices over their lifetimes. Michael Piore and Charles Sabel, writing on *The New Industrial Divide*, point to the competitive virtues of the small, focused company involved in a network of other companies providing complementary skills—a virtue they label "flexible specialization." Raymond Miles has argued that the new corporation will resemble a "switchboard"—a small communications center managing a network of relationships.[1]

This post-entrepreneurial style of management is not simply another fad, another one-shot program to be added to all the other things corporations are attempting to do. It represents a fundamentally different set of organizing principles from bureaucracy, a different way of conducting corporate life. These values and practices are often present as a matter of course in new ventures, but now they are increasingly finding their place in established corporations as well. Whereas bureaucratic management is inherently preservation-seeking, entrepreneurial management is inherently opportunity-seeking. The major concern of bureaucracy is to administer a known routine uniformly, guided by past experiences, whereas the major concern of an entrepreneurial organization is to exploit opportunity wherever it occurs and however it can be done, regardless of what the organization has done in the past. The post-entrepreneurial organization brings entrepreneurial principles to the established corporation.

All of these developments represent a dramatic new corporate ideal, one very different from the old-style corpocracy:

- Bureaucracy tends to be position-centered, in that authority derives from position, and status or rank is critical. Post-entrepreneurial organizations tend to be more person-centered, with authority deriving from expertise or from relationships.

- Bureaucratic management is repetition-oriented, seeking efficiency through doing the same thing over and over again. Post-entrepreneurial management is creation-oriented, seeking innovation as well as efficiency.

- Bureaucratic management is rules-oriented, defining procedures and rewarding adherence to them. Post-entrepreneurial management is results-oriented, rewarding outcomes.

- Bureaucracies tend to pay for status, in the sense that pay is position-based, positions are arrayed in a hierarchy, and greater rewards come from attaining higher positions. Post-entrepreneurial organizations tend to pay for contribution, for the value the person or team has added, regardless of formal position.

- Bureaucracies operate through formal structures designed to channel and restrict the flow of information. Post-entrepreneurial organizations find opportunities through the expansion of information, through the ability to maximize all possible communication links—with coalition partners inside and outside the organization.

- Bureaucracies assign specific mandates and territories, to circumscribe the action arena. In post-entrepreneurial organizations, charters and home territories are only the starting point for the creation of new modes of action; furthermore, opportunities come from the ability to make relationships across territories.

- Bureaucracies seek ownership and control. Post entrepreneurial organizations seek leverage and experimentation.

Thus, to use an overworked expression, the dominant business paradigm is changing.

Three principles emerge from observing the new organizational strategies in practice, intertwined post-entrepreneurial principles that create the flexibility required to meet the strategic challenge of doing more with less:

- Minimize obligations and maximize options. Keep fixed costs low and as often as possible use "variable" or "contingent" means to achieve corporate goals.

- Find leverage through influence and combination. Derive power from access and involvement, rather than from full control or total ownership.

- Encourage "churn." Keep things moving. Encourage continuous regrouping of people and functions and products to produce unexpected, creative new combinations. Redefine turnover as positive (a source of renewal) rather than negative.

In this context, each of the popular management buzzwords and fads of the last decade seems a way station on the road to a more comprehensive rethinking of corporate strategy and organizational form. For example, participative management and employee involvement, "intrapreneurship" and "quality circles" have each found their niche and reached their logical limits in many companies. Advocates have rightly praised these corporate innovations for their benefits—usually local increases in productivity, quality, or innovation. Skeptics have rightly condemned them for being faddish, superficial, quick fixes with fragmented implementation. Still, in retrospect, each has been important in moving corporations toward challenging the old managerial assumptions, loosening their structures, and experimenting with new practices. One offshoot of many of these programs is the weakening of hierarchy and the reduction of levels of organizations as employees are given more opportunities to influence decisions and exercise control.

Alongside the *propeople* corporate policies popular in the last decade, however, are a number of other business maneuvers often characterized as *antipeople*: financial manipulation and a takeover binge leading to involuntary restructuring and job displacement. Ironically, these manipulations also tend to create leaner, less hierarchical organizations, as acquirers seek to reduce costs by eliminating corporate staffs and unnecessary layers of management or divesting business units that can function alone, thereby, giving them entrepreneurial independence. But when done for financial speculation rather than to enhance long-term capacity, this strategy can subtract value rather than add it.

The post-entrepreneurial principles I have identified clearly have both an upside and a downside. At their best, they increase opportunity, giving people the chance to develop their ideas, pursue exciting projects, and be compensated directly for their contributions. At their best, they encourage collaboration across functions, across business units, and even across corporations. The business benefits from the use of these principles are lower fixed costs and increased entrepreneurial reach.

But at their worst, the same strategies can lead to displacement instead of empowerment, rivalries instead of teamwork, and short-term asset-shuffling and one-night stands with the latest attractive deal instead of long-term commitments to build capacity. The same strategies executed unwisely and without concern for the organizational and human consequences will not produce continuing business benefits — especially if people with-hold effort and commitment for fear of being displaced or to hedge their own bets against change.

It is not the strategies themselves but their execution that make the difference in whether the consequences for people are expanded entrepreneurial opportunity or anxiety, insecurity, and loss of motivation to produce....

## NOTE

1. Pat Choate and J. K. Linger, *The High-Flex Society: Shaping America's Economic Future* (New York: Knopf, 1987); Michael J. Piore and Charles F. Sabel, *The Second Industrial Divide: Possibilities for Prosperity* (New York: Basic Books, 1984), Raymond E. Miles and Charles C. Snow, "Organizations: A New Concept for New Forms," *California Management Review*, vol. 28, no. 3 (Spring 1986), pp. 62–73.